DICTIONARY OF SAINTS

DICTIONARY
of SAINTS

SECOND EDITION

JOHN J. DELANEY

IMAGE

DOUBLEDAY

NEW YORK   LONDON

TORONTO   SYDNEY   AUCKLAND

IMAGE

AN IMAGE BOOK
PUBLISHED BY DOUBLEDAY
a division of Random House, Inc.

IMAGE, DOUBLEDAY, and the portrayal of a deer drinking from a stream are
registered trademarks of Random House, Inc.

Book design by Ellen Cipriano

Library of Congress Catalog Card Number
79-7783

ISBN 0-385-51520-0

April 2005

First Image Books Edition

3   5   7   9   10   8   6   4

To
The two wonderful women in my life
My mother
and
My beloved Ann

CONTENTS

INTRODUCTION

At the outset, it should be made clear that the purpose of this work is to make available in a single volume an up-to-date, easy-to-use compendium of factual information about the some five thousand saints included herein. Further, it is designed to provide relatively short entries on those saints and *beati* about whom I believe the modern reader would be most likely to seek information.

The information provided covers the events and activities in the lives of these saints insofar as we have information about them so that entries will vary in length and scope depending on our present knowledge of them. Consequently, the entries will vary in length from a few lines to a page or more as the case may be but in all cases I have attempted to provide concise, comprehensive, and accurate information. It should be emphasized there are no new or startling discoveries or information contained in the entries since no original or newly discovered manuscripts or material of a similar nature were used in compiling the material. The book is not designed primarily for the scholar, though hopefully the scholar will find it useful for ready reference, but rather for the general reader seeking a concise résumé of the pertinent facts in particular saints' lives, supplying all the information such a reader might reasonably expect in brief but comprehensive compass.

The saints are a fascinating company of men, women, and children who devoted their lives to Christ and his teachings in widely varied ways. They came from every walk of life—from poor peasant tilling his soil to eke out a living and poverty-stricken slum dweller of a large city to emperor and king. Murderers, cutthroats, and robbers who repented of their evil lives are listed next to holy men and women who lived lives of holiness and austerity from early childhood. Men, women, and children, black, white, red, yellow, brown, clergy and laity, powerful and helpless, eloquent and tongue-tied—all are represented in this glorious company.

The forms of their sanctity are as varied as all mankind—men and women living lives of great austerity alone on barren islands or in deserts performing the most astonishing mortifications and penances; others living in crowded cities ministering to the needy and stricken; and still others living in castles and at royal courts. Some of the saints performed the most menial tasks in almost total obscurity; others worked in the full glare of the prominence accorded men and women in prominent positions. For the Church, like her Master, ignores the arbitrary distinctions humans make—class, race, color, position—in choosing her saints but rather selects those who in some outstanding way have devoted themselves to following the path laid out for all men and women by God-become-man, Jesus Christ. Given the dazzling diversity and varied appeal of the saints, it is a pity that in recent years the appeal of the saints has sunk to an all-time low. In part this is due to the skepticism that became so prevalent in the 1960s and its consequent demythologizing of heroes with no distinction. In part it is due to the "now generation" attitude—that all past history is irrelevant and all knowledge is strictly the province of the present generation. As if that generation had sprung up full-blown, all-knowing, all-wise, and with no ties to or acknowledgment of the accomplishments of the past that led to the incredible store of knowledge we have accumulated in the twentieth century! Fortunately there has been a change in this attitude, as even its most ardent practitioners came to realize that this generation is no more adept at solving the problems that have plagued mankind for millennia than those that have preceded us.

But also to be faced and accepted is the fact that often many of the saints do not have meaning for us today, that many of the so-called miracles attributed to them are fantastic and bizarre and meaningless, and that many of the practices of some of the saints not only have no place in the modern world but are actually repugnant to our modern sensibilities. What can a Simeon Stylites sitting on a pillar for thirty-six years offer us who live in the last quarter of the twentieth century? What would happen to a preacher today who beat himself with whips and chains before his sermon and then stumbled to the pulpit with blood streaming down his face and body to begin his sermon, as did many of the most eloquent preachers of the Middle Ages? Who today can understand and appreciate the drastic bodily mortifications and penances many saints imposed on themselves for decades of their lives? Who today can believe that at a word a mere mortal could divert a river or dry up a lake? Or fantastic miracles performed seemingly at a whim? None of these make much sense to people today and often rightly so.

One can merely point out that to judge the actions of people hundreds and thousands of years ago by today's standards is to take them out of their historical context and thus render them and their actions devoid of any meaning. Men and women's actions must be judged with a knowledge of their historical background if we are to have any intelligent appreciation of what they were doing and why. And lest any twentieth-century inhabitant wax smug over his or her mores, consider what a generation five hundred years hence will have to say of a generation that has been embroiled in a series of wars that cost millions of lives, caused untold suffering, and now faces the possibility of nuclear holocausts? Of a generation that had the wherewithal to end poverty and famine and fails to do so? Of a generation that spends hundreds of billions of dollars on armaments to destroy, and piddling amounts on research to wipe out cancer and cure? Let us be wary of judging too harshly another generation.

Also to be remembered is the fact that early and medieval Christians were very much aware that they strove for the perfection so dazzlingly lived by Jesus Christ. Consequently, they were prone to attribute to their saints the holiness, love, and supernatural gifts possessed and so freely dispensed by him during his time on earth. Time and again miracles are attributed to the saints that are carbon copies of those performed by Jesus. What their biographers and followers were doing in legendary form was to symbolize that Christ lives in all of us and to show this through a reproduction in some measure in the lives of the saints the qualities that made the Savior their Lord.

But let us concede that many saints acted in ways that are strange and stretch the bounds of our credulity today. The fact still remains that the pages of history are filled with tales of men and women who suffered cruelly and gave their lives for their faith, of men and women who made incredible sacrifices to help their fellow creatures, who gave up lives of wealth and luxury to follow the way of the Lord, who went to the remote corners of the earth to help their fellow men and women. Who would dare say Francis of Assisi is not relevant today? Who could deny the courage and appeal of Thomas More resisting tyranny that still persists in the modern world—the dictator who tramples on basic human rights? Who can fail to thrill at the exploits of Paul or Francis Xavier? And there are thousands of men and women saints whose actions and lives are as real and meaningful today as in the eras in which they lived. Furthermore, there are men and women living and working in this very tumultuous and chaotic twentieth century who are living lives of holiness and charity and sacrifice who someday in the future will be recognized as the saints they are for the qualities that made the saints of the past.

In short, what I plead for when one considers the saints is that they be recognized for what they are: real men and women who struggled desperately, sometimes against incredible odds, sometimes against a most mundane background, as they strove to live lives of perfection to the best of their abilities in the service of the Master; imperfect human beings molded in large measure by the times in which they lived. Knowledge of their historical background often offers whole new insights into the activities of the saints that might otherwise seem inexplicable.

A word about the saints included: All the saints of the Roman Calendar are to be found in these pages, but there are also thousands of others, including many who some may have felt had been disowned by the Church a few years ago, such as St. Ursula, St. Philomena, St. Barbara, and St. Catherine of Alexandria, when they were dropped from the liturgical calendar. But such is not the case. The Vatican weekly *L'Osservatore Della Domenica* explained it this way: "Generally the removal of a name from the calendar does not mean passing judgment on the nonexistence of a saint or lack of holiness. Many have been removed because all that remains certain about them is their names, and this would say too little to the faithful in comparison with many others. Other feasts were removed because they lacked universal significance." In short, the Church did not rule out the legitimacy of any saint's claim to sainthood in the reorganization of the liturgical year and calendar for the Roman Rite as approved by Pope Paul VI in his 1969 *motu proprio Paschalis mysterii*. It merely relegated to another category (not included in the revised calendar) saints who had formerly been included. The key words of *L'Osservatore*'s remark above is that some saints have been removed "because all that remains *certain* about them is their names . . ." (italics mine).

But much of our knowledge of many saints is not known with any degree of certainty. It is based on legend, myth, tradition, distorted biographies, hearsay—what have you. But as modern scholars know, much that is legendary and mythical is a method—often very practical—of passing to future generation a fact or a truth. Often the core of truth is so embellished and exaggerated over the centuries that it is obscured. But the basic fact or truth is there, often requiring decades of scholarly research to sift aside the accretions of centuries to reveal the truth. And so it is with saints' lives and activities. The human tendency to exaggerate, especially about our greats, is applied to the saints as well as to other people and aspects of history; so one must be careful not to dismiss accounts that seem incredible, for buried therein may be a rich and rewarding lode of truth.

Just two examples, one from the secular world and one from the world of religious, will serve to underline this point. For centuries, the most distinguished scholars treated the *Iliad* and *Odyssey* as mythical—magnificent literature but strictly imaginative with no basis in fact. Then, in the nineteenth century, the self-made expert on Homer, the German Heinrich Schliemann, in the face of universal scholarly derision, basing his research and excavations entirely on information he gleaned from Homer's works, unearthed the so-called mythical city of Troy, proving the great classic was indeed grounded in fact. On a smaller scale and in more recent times, an intrepid voyager named Tim Severin, after studying the account of sixth-century St. Brendan's account of his seven-year voyages in a skin-covered *curragh* in *Navigatio Sancti Brendani Abbatis*, which scholars had long since dismissed as a mythical account of a journey to North America, constructed a skin-covered boat according to Brendan's instructions and following his directions sailed to Newfoundland via Iceland and Greenland in 1976–77. Again myth, though subject to great exaggeration, was proved to be truth once the exaggerated language and claims had been discounted and interpreted.

And so much of the information about the lives and activities of the saints included in this volume is based on sources that can by no stretch of the imagination be considered "certain." But in many cases these legends, myths, traditions, and untrustworthy sources are the only sources of information.

Consequently I have not hesitated to use such material, but where I have done so I have been careful to point out that the sources are unreliable and the material is often legendary. But I emphasize the core of truth and fact in practically any myth or legend, so much material cannot be arbitrarily discarded in a book of this nature. That myth and legend are often fact in different garb is not sufficiently appreciated though legend, myth, and rumor are frequently integral parts of portraits of even modern and contemporary great figures, despite the modern insistence on factual approaches. The answer, of course, is that though we accept and understand our own myths, we tend to discount those of other eras because the forms they take are often unfamiliar to us. Information from such sources is valid material for reconstructing the lives of long-gone people but must be used with care and understanding.

Which brings us to a consideration of the nature of sainthood and how it is achieved. We are all familiar with the modern process of beatification and canonization. Intensive investigation is conducted of the life, holiness, activities, writings, and miracles of the person proposed for canonization, extending over years, decades, even centuries before the infallible papal declaration is made during the elaborate canonization ritual in St. Peter's in Rome, when the Pope declares that a person who died a martyr and/or practiced Christian virtue to a heroic degree is now in heaven and worthy of honor and imitation by the faithful. But this process is a comparatively recent development in the history of the Church. The first official canonization by a Pope was of St. Ulrich by Pope John XV in 993; the process of canonization was not reserved to the Holy See until 1171 by Pope Alexander III; and the present process dates back to 1588, when Pope Sixtus V established the Sacred Congregation of Rites principally to handle cases for beatification and canonization, now handled by the Congregation for the Causes of Saints.

In the early days of Christianity, cults developed around certain holy individuals, which grew until the person was acclaimed a saint. Practically all martyrs in early Christianity were considered saints, though public official honor required the authorization of the local bishop. Many of the claims of these early saints have been investigated officially by the Church in modern times and their cults have been approved or sanctioned; in other such cases the claim has been disallowed. But many of these early saints' claims to sainthood rest on veneration accorded them from earliest times with no records or documents to substantiate their claims surviving. These are accepted by the Church for the recognition given them by their early bishops and contemporaries, but their cults are restricted to local areas. In all probability many of these saints would be unable to withstand the scrutiny given candidates for canonization today, but as I have earlier pointed out, different eras have different methods, and though the methods of making a saint in the past differed from our own criteria it would be eminently unfair to arbitrarily dismiss these earlier saints from veneration by the faithful who desire to pay tribute to them.

All persons recognized as saints by these various means are enrolled in the Canon of the Saints and his or her name is inserted in the Roman Martyrology or official catalogue proposed for the veneration of the Universal Church.

And so included in the present work is a wide variety of saints and *beati*, some canonized or beatified by our modern method but far more by the less demanding criteria of the past. All are worthy of inclusion.

Now for a word on how to use this volume. All entries are saints unless it is indicated that they are Blessed (Bl.) or Venerable (Ven.), titles given to those persons along the way to canonization who do not necessarily become saints but are worthy of veneration. The names are arranged alphabetically; when there are more than one saint with the same name they are arranged chronologically under that name. Saints with surnames and/or descriptive appellations attached to their names are arranged alphabetically under the saints' names, with the names with no surname or descriptive appellation listed first (and arranged chronologically) followed by the saints' names with surnames and descriptive appellations following arranged alphabetically according to surname. For example:

John (d. c. 362)
John I (d. 526)
John III (d. 577)
John (d. c. 800)
John I, Bl. (d. 1146)
John the Almsgiver (c. 550–c. 619)
John of Alvernia (1259–1322)
John the Baptist (1st century)

Note that the numerals after a saint's name are ignored in arranging the order of listing. Also a surname, identifying appellation, and identifying place name are treated alike and arranged in alphabetical order so that John of Avila precedes John the Baptist—the "of" and the "the" being ignored in the alphabetical arrangement.

The dates after each entry are the birth and death dates of the saint. Where there is only one date, preceded by d., it is the date of death. Where c. precedes a date, it indicates there is an uncertainty about that date and that this is the most plausible date without absolute certainty.

There are numerous cross references throughout and they all fall into one of two categories: 1. The cross reference is the name of a person described in another person's entry. In this case the name of the saint will be followed by the date of birth. For example:

Mareas (d. c. 342). *See* Abdiesus.

2. The cross reference is merely another name of the saint referred to. For example:

Leufroy. *See* Leutfridus.

In some cases there will be several identical names of persons to whom the reference is made. In such cases the name referred to will have the date of death after it to facilitate tracking it down. For example:

Leu. *See* Lupus (d. 623).

For saints in modern times the entry will be found under the surname. For example, Elizabeth Ann Seton will be listed under Seton, Elizabeth Ann; Thomas More will be listed under More, Thomas. Since the time when alphabetizing under surnames became common practice varies, some latitude is taken with names from the thirteenth and fourteenth centuries. In such case the name will be found listed under its most common usages; in some cases, to facilitate finding the name, there will be a dual listing. For example, most people know Bernadette of Lourdes but are not aware that her family name was Soubirous. The main entry is under Soubirous, but there is also a cross reference to Bernadette of Lourdes.

And finally, the date after an entry is the feast date of the saint, which usually, though not always, is the date of his or her death. Where there is no feast date at the end of the entry, there will be a death date in the body of the entry, and this is the feast day.

All saints in the revised Roman Calendar are included, and with the other saints in the volume will hopefully provide information about practically any saint that the general readership envisioned for this volume may want information about.

Though designed to be used for readily accessible and easy-to-use reference, it is the fervent hope of the author that it will be used for more than mere reference and will lead the peruser to further study and a deeper understanding of the saints and an awareness of the riches God has bestowed on mankind in his saints.

"The Church has always believed that the apostles and Christ's martyrs, who gave the supreme witness of faith and charity by the shedding of their blood, are closely united with us in Christ; she has always venerated them with the Blessed Virgin Mary and the holy angels, with a special love, and has asked piously for the help of their intercession. Soon there were added to these others who had chosen to imitate more closely the virginity and poverty of Christ, and still others whom the outstanding practice of the Christian virtues and the wonderful graces of God recommended to the pious devotion and imitation of the faithful.

"Exactly as Christian communion between men on their earthly pilgrimage brings us closer to Christ, so our community with the saints joins us to Christ, from whom as from its fountain and head issues all graces and the life of the People of God itself. It is most fitting, therefore, that we love those friends and co-heirs of Jesus Christ who are also our brothers and outstanding benefactors, and that we give due thanks to God for them, humbly invoking them, and having recourse to their prayers, their aid and help in obtaining from God through his son, Jesus Christ, Our Lord, our only Redeemer and Savior, the benefits we need. Every authentic witness of love, indeed, offered by us to those who are in heaven tends to and terminates in Christ, "the crown of all the saints," and through him in God who is wonderful in his saints, and is glorified in them."

Dogmatic Constitution on the Church, No. 50

AARON (d. c. 304). *See* Julius.

AARON (6th century). A native of Britain, he went to Brittany, where he became a hermit on Cesabre (St. Malo) island, attracted numerous disciples, among them St. Malo of Wales, and became their abbot. June 22.

AARON, BL. (d. 1059). Probably a monk under St. Odilo at Cluny, he went to Poland, became the first abbot of the Benedictine abbey at Tyniec, and in 1046 was named first archbishop of Cracow. October 9.

ABACHUM (d. c. 260). *See* Marius.

ABBAN (5th–6th centuries). The lives of several Irish saints of this name have become inextricably confused. Among them are: the nephew of St. Ibar who founded Kill-Abban Abbey in Leinster, Ireland (March 16); the hermit who lived at Abingdon, England, and was also known as Ewen (May 13); the nephew of St. Kevin who founded several monasteries in southern Ireland, notably Magh-Armuidhe (Adamstown) in Wexford (October 27); and the founder of Ros-mic-treoin (New Ross) who worked and died in Wexford (December 22).

ABBO (d. c. 860). A monk of St. Germain Monastery at Auxerre, France, he was elected abbot there and in 857 was named bishop of Auxerre but resigned two years later. December 3.

ABBO. *See* Goericus.

ABBO OF FLEURY (c. 945–1004). Born near Orléans, France, he studied at Paris, Rheims, and Orléans, and settled at the monastery of Fleury-sur-Loire. In about 986 he became director of the monastery school in Ramsey, Huntingdonshire, England, but returned to Fleury two years later to resume his studies. He was elected abbot in a disputed election, which was not finally accepted until quite some time later through the help of Gerbert, who later became Pope Sylvester II in 999. Abbo fought for monastic independence of bishops, was mediator between the Pope and the King of France, was active in settling disputes in various monasteries, and was murdered while attempting to settle a dispute among the monks at La Réole in Gascony. He was widely known as a scholar in astronomy, mathematics, and philosophy, wrote a life of St. Edmund, and edited a collection of canons. November 13.

ABBOT, BL. HENRY (d. 1597). A resident of Howden, East Riding, Yorkshire, England, he was betrayed by a Protestant minister pretending to seek a priest so he could be reconciled to the Church, and was hanged, drawn, and quartered at York on July 4. He was beatified in 1929.

ABDECHALAS (d. 341). *See* Simeon Barsabae.

ABDIESUS (d. c. 342). With hundreds of others, Abdiesus, a deacon, suffered martyrdom during the persecution of Christians in Persia in 341–80 during the reign of King Sapor II. Some of the others martyred were: Azades, a eunuch who had been a favorite of the King, Acepsimas, Bicor, Mareas, and Milles, bishops; Abrosimus, a priest; Azadanes, another deacon; and Tarbula, sister of St. Simeon, who was accused of witchcraft and sawed to death on May 5. April 22.

ABDON (d. c. 303). He and his fellow Persian nobleman, Sennen, were arrested during Diocletian's persecution of the Christians, brought to Rome in chains, and when they refused to sacrifice to pagan gods, were exposed to wild beasts. When they were unharmed by the beasts, they were hacked to pieces by gladiators. July 30.

ABEL, BL. THOMAS (c. 1497–1540). After receiving his doctorate in divinity from Oxford, he was ordained, and became chaplain to Catherine of Aragon, wife of Henry VIII. Sent with a letter from Catherine to Emperor Charles V to secure the brief of Pope Julius II permitting Henry to marry Catherine, he told the Emperor the Queen had been coerced into writing the letter and returned to England without the brief. Henry evidently suspected what he had done and harassed him and when he published *Invicta Veritas,* opposing university support of Henry's efforts to end his marriage to Catherine, he was imprisoned in the Tower of London in 1532. Released, he was again arrested, supposedly for his implication in the Holy Maid of Kent affair in 1533, and after six years' imprisonment he was briefly released on parole by the warden. He was again brought back to prison, and the warden was sent to the Tower. Abel was attainted of high treason in 1540 for denying the ecclesiastical supremacy of the King and hanged, drawn, and quartered at Smithfield on July 30

with B. B. Edward Powell and Richard Fetherston. He was one of the fifty-four English martyrs beatified in 1886 by Pope Leo XIII. July 30.

ABELLON, BL. ANDREW (1375–1450). Born in St. Maximin, Provence, France, he became a Dominican and then prior of St. Mary Magdalen monastery there; are the monastery's reputed relics of Mary Magadalen made it a great pilgrimage center. He was active in missionary activities and had some reputation as an artist. His cult was confirmed in 1902. May 17.

ABENNER. *See* Josaphat.

ABERCIUS (d. c. 200). A resident of Phrygia Salutaris, Abercius Marcellus is now believed to have been bishop of Hierapolis, though an inscription on his tomb led many scholars to believe he was a priest of Cybele or some syncretistic cult. According to the inscription, when he was seventy-two he was summoned to Rome by Emperor Marcus Aurelius to rid his daughter Lucilla of a devil and did so successfully. A Greek hagiographer used this epitaph to write an exaggerated life of Abercius rife with legends from other saints' lives, adding the inscription to it. This life cast suspicion on the whole story but scholars now believe the inscription was authentic and Abercius was a real person active in conversion work. He has been venerated by the Greeks since the tenth century. October 22.

ABIBAS (1st century). The second son of Gamaliel (who was St. Paul's teacher and an important member of the Sanhedrin), he later became a Christian as had his father. August 3.

ABIBUS (d. 297). *See* Hipparchus.

ABIBUS (4th century). *See* Gurias.

ABRA (d. c. 342–c. 360). The daughter of St. Hilary of Poitiers, she was born before he became bishop. She consecrated herself to God on Hilary's advice but died when she was only eighteen. December 12.

ABRAHAM (d. 339). *See* Sapor.

ABRAHAM (d. c. 345). The bishop of Arbela, Assyria, he suffered martyrdom at Telman during the persecution of King Sapor II of Persia. February 12.

ABRAHAM (d. 367). Born at Menuf, Egypt, he became a disciple of St. Pachomius and then spent seventeen years living as a hermit in a cave. He is often surnamed "the Poor" or "the Child." October 27.

ABRAHAM (d. c. 480). Born in Asia Minor near the Euphrates River, he went to Egypt and was captured by bandits, who held him for five years before he escaped. He went to Gaul, became a hermit near Clermont, was ordained, and became abbot of St. Cyriacus Abbey.

ABRAHAM (6th century). Author of several theological treatises, he built monasteries in Constantinople and Jerusalem for his disciples, who became known as Abrahamites, and later was named archbishop of Ephesus. October 28.

ABRAHAM OF CARRHAE (d. c. 422). Born in Cyrrhus, Syria, he became a hermit in the desert, where he preached the gospel and became known for his attempts to convert the unbelievers in a town on Mount Lebanon. Ostracized and attacked on all sides, he persisted, and when he saved the inhabitants from debtors' jail by arranging to pay their taxes, he won them over. He returned to the desert but soon after was named bishop of Carrhae, Mesopotamia, which he also converted to Christianity. He

died in Constantinople while visiting Emperor Theodosius II. February 14.

ABRAHAM KIDUNAIA (6th century). Born of wealthy parents in Edessa, Mesopotamia, he ran away from a marriage arranged by his parents to lead a celibate and eremitical life in the desert in a sealed cabin with a single opening through which he received food; on the death of his parents, he gave his inheritance to the poor. At the request of the bishop of Edessa he reluctantly left his cell to convert a colony of unbelievers at nearby Beth-Kiduna. He was ordained, went to Beth-Kiduna, preached, and destroyed the idols in the town. Beaten up and driven away by the villagers, he returned and persisted in his mission until in a few years he converted the town to Christianity, then returned to his cell, where he remained until his death at seventy. March 16.

ABRAHAM OF KRATIA (474–c. 558). Born in Emesa, Syria, he became a monk but was forced to flee to Constantinople because of raids on the community to which he belonged. He became procurator of a monastery there, and when he was twenty-six he became abbot of the monastery in Kratia. After a decade as abbot he decided to leave the monastery and went to Palestine, to seek solitude for a life of contemplation. He was forced to return by his bishop, and shortly after his return was made bishop of Kratia. He served in this office for thirteen years when he again fled to Palestine in quest of solitude and spent the rest of his life in a monastery there. December 6.

ABRAHAM OF ROSTOV (12th century). Born of heathen parents near Galich, he is reputed to have been cured of a disease as a young man when he called upon the Christian God, was baptized, and became a monk. He went to

Rostov, Russia, to preach the gospel, founded a monastery of which he became abbot, built two churches there, and was extremely active and effective in conversion work. October 29.

ABRAHAM OF SMOLENSK (d. 1221). Born in Smolensk, Russia, he was early orphaned, gave his inheritance to the poor, became a priest in Bogoroditskaya monastery, and was widely known for his concern for the sick and the poor. A biblical scholar and an effective preacher, he offended the authorities by his emphasis on poverty, the need for leading an austere life, and his preaching on the Last Judgment. When forbidden to preach by his abbot he went to Holy Cross Monastery, also in Smolensk. There his preaching, learning, and popularity aroused further ire and he was charged with heresy, posing as a prophet, and immorality, and though he seems to have been cleared in two trials, he was ordered back to Bogoroditskaya by Bishop Ignatius of Smolensk and deprived of his priestly functions. A prolonged drought in the city led to a popular demand for his reinstatement, and a further examination of the case led to his complete exoneration by the bishop, who begged his forgiveness. He was appointed abbot of the small, run-down Mother of God monastery and spent the rest of his life there revered for his holiness and venerated for the humility and dignity with which he had borne the five years of unjust accusations and vilifications. August 21.

ABREAU, BL. EMMANUELLE D' (d. 1737). See Alvarez, Bl. Bartholomew.

ABROSIMUS (d. c. 342). See Abdiesus.

ABUNDANTIUS (d. c. 304). See Abundius.

ABUNDIUS (d. c. 304). A priest of Rome, he was arrested with Abundantius, a deacon, and when they refused to worship the god Hercules, were imprisoned in the Mammertine prison, tortured, and condemned to death. According to legend, on the way to where they were to be executed, they passed a Senator Marcian, whose son John had just died. Abundius asked Marcian to bring him the body; when Marcian did so Abundius prayed over it and John came to life. Marcian and John at once became Christians and they too were condemned, and all four were beheaded. September 16.

ABUNDIUS (d. 469). Born in Thessalonica, he was ordained, and was named bishop of Como, Italy. A noted theologian, he attended the Council of Constantinople in 450; he was sent on a mission to Emperor Theodosius II by Pope Leo the Great, which led to the Council of Chalcedon in 451 when he was Leo's legate; at the Council of Milan the following year, he refuted Eutychianism. April 2.

ABUNDIUS (d. 854). A priest at Ananelos near Cordova, Spain, he was beheaded at Cordova when he refused to abandon his religion when brought before the Moorish caliph there for preaching against Mohammedanism.

ACACIUS (d. c. 251). Also known as Achatius, the facts of his life are uncertain. He may have been bishop of Antioch or of Militene and may not have been a bishop at all. He was prominent in Christian circles in Antioch and when summoned to appear before the local Roman official, Martian, a dialogue on Christianity and its teachings as compared to other religions ensued, which has come down to us. Acacius refused to sacrifice to pagan gods, and when he would not supply the names of his fellow Christians was sent to prison. Supposedly when Emperor Decius received Martian's report of the trial he was so impressed by both men that he promoted Martian and pardoned Acacius. Though listed as a martyr there is no evidence he died for the faith. March 31.

ACACIUS (d. c. 303). A Cappadocian by birth, also known as Agathus, he was a centurion in the imperial army, was arrested for his faith on charges by Tribune Firmus in Perinthus, Thrace, tortured and then brought to Byzantium (Constantinople), where he was scourged and beheaded. May 8.

ACACIUS (d. c. 305). A priest at Sebaste, Armenia, during Diocletian's persecution, he was arrested and executed under the governor Maximus with seven women and Hirenarchus, who was so impressed with the devotion to their faith he became a Christian and suffered the same fate. November 27.

ACACIUS (d. 425). Bishop of Amida (Diarbekir), Mesopotamia, he sold the sacred vessels of his church to aid victims of the Persian persecution. His action so impressed King Bahram V that he is reported to have ordered an end to the persecution of the Christians. April 9.

ACARIE, BL. MARIE (c. 1566–1618). The daughter of a government official named Nicholas Aurillot and christened Barbara, she was born in Paris on February 1 and was educated at an aunt's convent at Longchamps. She was early attracted to the religious life but instead was married at seventeen to Peter Acarie, an aristocrat who was a French treasury official, and the couple had six children. Peter supported the Catholic League against Henry IV, and when Henry triumphed and became King, Peter's estates were seized, he was banished from Paris, and the family was impoverished. His wife took the matter to court, secured his innocence of

charges of conspiring against the King, and was able to restore some of the family fortune. She became active in charitable affairs, had the favor of Henry and Mary of Medici for her good works, was counseled by St. Francis de Sales, and as a result of visions of Teresa of Avila was responsible for bringing the Discalced Carmelites to France by founding a Paris convent in 1604, followed by four others in the next five years. When Peter died in 1613 she joined the Carmelites at Amiens as a lay sister, taking the name Marie of the Incarnation. Throughout her life she experienced visions, ecstasies, and other supernatural gifts. She died at Pontoise, France, and was beatified in 1791. April 18.

ACCA (c. 660–740). A Northumbrian, he was raised and educated in the household of St. Bosa, became the companion of St. Wilfrid, who made him abbot of St. Andrew's monastery in Hexham, and succeeded Wilfrid to the see of Hexham when Wilfrid died in 709. Acca was a scriptural scholar, founded a library in Hexham, and was active in promoting learning through his patronage of scholars and musicians. For unknown reasons he was obliged to leave Hexham in 732 and is believed to have lived in exile and died in Withern, Galloway. October 20.

ACCURSIO (d. 1220). *See* Berard.

ACEPSIMAS (d. c. 342). *See* Abdiesus.

ACEPSIMAS (d. 376). The bishop of Hnaita, Persia, he was tortured and beaten to death on October 10 during the persecution of King Sapor II, though Acepsimas was in his eighties. April 22.

ACEPSIMAS (5th century). A hermit for sixty years in a cave near Cyrohas, Syria, he died shortly after he was ordained. November 3.

ACESTES (1st century). According to legend, he was one of the three soldiers who escorted St. Paul to his death. Converted by Paul, they too were beheaded for their faith at the same time. July 2.

ACHARD. See Aichardus.

ACHARIUS (d. 640). A monk at Luxeuil under St. Eustace, he was named bishop of Noyon-Tournai in 621. He helped St. Amandus in his missionary work and was instrumental in having St. Omen named bishop of the see of Thérouanne. November 27.

ACHATIUS. See Acacius (d. c. 251).

ACHILLAS (d. 313). Bishop of Alexandria, he ordained Arius, who was to head the heresy named after him, and was attacked by the Meletians for his orthodoxy. November 7.

ACHILLEUS (1st century). See Nereus.

ACHILLEUS (d. c. 212). See Felix.

ACHLER, BL. ELIZABETH (1386–1420). Born in Waldsee, Württemberg, of poor parents, she became a Franciscan tertiary when fourteen at the suggestion of her confessor, Fr. Conrad Kügelin. At seventeen she joined four other tertiaries at Reute, near Waldsee, and spent the rest of her life in this community. She enjoyed ecstasies and visions of heaven and purgatory, went for months without food, was subjected to diabolical visions, and at times displayed the stigmata, which bled on Fridays and during Lent. She died at Reute, and her cult was approved in 1766. November 17.

ACISLUS (d. 4th century). That Acislus lived and was martyred is accepted as fact, but otherwise there is no reliable information about him. According to St.

Eulogius' *Memorial of the Saints,* he and his sister Victoria lived in Cordova, Spain, were beaten and tortured as Christians, and when they refused to denounce their religion, Acislus was beheaded and Victoria was killed by arrows. When they lived is uncertain, though a tradition says they were martyred during Diocletian's reign; and though they have an office in the Mozabic Liturgy, there is doubt among scholars as to whether there ever was a Victoria. Acislus is mentioned with St. Zoilus in a poem by Prudentius. June 27.

ACUTIUS (d. c. 305). See Januarius.

ACYLLINUS (d. 180). See Speratus.

ADA (7th century). The niece of St. Engelbert, she became a nun at Soissons, and then abbess of St. Julien-des-Prés at Le Mans, France. December 4.

ADAUCTUS (d. c. 304). See Felix.

ADALBALD OF OSTREVANT (d. 652). A noble at the court of Dagobert I, he participated in several expeditions to Gascony to put down uprisings by the Gascons. While there he met a nobleman named Ernold, whose daughter Rictrudis he married, to the displeasure of many of Ernold's Gascon relatives. They devoted much of their time to helping the sick and the poor. Sometime later while he was on a trip to Gascony, Adalbald was attacked and killed by some of his wife's relatives near Périgueux. There is no evidence he was martyred for his faith, but he was named a martyr in accordance with the custom of the times of so naming a religious person who was murdered. Also numerous miracles were reported at his tomb. February 2.

ADALBERO, BL. (d. 909). Of a noble family and uncle of St. Ulric, he joined the Benedictines at Dillengen in 850, was later named abbot of Ellswangen, then of Lorsch, which he restored, and sometime after 887 was named bishop of Augsburg. He was an adviser of Emperor Arnulf, whose son Louis he tutored and served as his regent in his youth. April 28.

ADALBERO (d. 1005). Of a noble family, he studied at the Benedictine abbey of Gorze, was named bishop of Verdun in 984, was transferred to Metz later the same year, and founded numerous monasteries, which observed the Cluniac observance about which he was so enthusiastic. December 15.

ADALBERO, BL. (1045–90). Son of count Arnold of Lambach in Austria, he studied at Paris, was named bishop of Würzbury, and was driven from his see in 1085 when he supported Pope Gregory VII against Emperor Henry IV. Adalbero retired to the Benedictine abbey of Lambach, where he died. His cult was approved in 1883. October 6.

ADALBERO, BL. (d. 1128). Brother of Count Godfrey Le Barbu of Louvain, Adalbero became a canon of Metz, and then was named bishop of Liège, where he founded St. Giles monastery. January 1.

ADALBERT OF EGMOND (d. c. 705). A Northumbrian, he accompanied St. Egbert to Ireland and became a deacon at Rathmelsigi Monastery. Adalbert accompanied St. Willibrord and his companions on a mission to Friesland in 690 to convert the area to Christianity, and was most successful around Egmond, where he converted most of the inhabitants by his persuasiveness, personal example, and piety. He may have succeeded Willibrord as abbot of Epternach. Miracles were reported at his tomb, which became a center of pilgrimages. June 25.

ADALBERT OF MAGDEBURG (d. 981). A monk of St. Maximin Benedictine monastery in Trèves, he was sent by Emperor Otto the Great to convert the Russian subjects of Princess Olga at her request after she became a Christian in Constantinople at seventy. When Olga's son Svyatoslav, a pagan, took the crown from her in 961, the missionaries were forced to flee, and some were killed near Kiev. Adalbert escaped, spent four years at the imperial court in Mainz, and then was made abbot of Weissenburg abbey, where he became known for his patronage of learning. He was named first archbishop of Magdeburg, Saxony, at Otto's insistence in 962, with jurisdiction over Slavs. He spent the rest of his life trying to spread Christianity among the Wends and reforming religious groups in his diocese. He died on a visit to Merseburg. June 20.

ADALBERT OF PRAGUE (956–97). Born in Bohemia of a noble family, he studied under St. Adalbert in Magdeburg (who named him Adalbert at confirmation; his baptismal name was Voytiekh), returned to Bohemia on Adalbert's death in 981, and the next year was named bishop of Prague. Discouraged by his inability to convert nonbelievers and to get his fellow Christians to live a Christian life, he went to Rome in 990 (though there may have been political reasons for his move). He became a Benedictine monk at St. Boniface and Alexis Abbey in Rome but was ordered back to Prague by Pope John XV at the request of Duke Boleslaus of Poland. Feelings rose high when Adalbert gave sanctuary to a noblewoman convicted of adultery; when she was dragged from the church and murdered, he excommunicated all involved in her death; whereupon he was again forced to leave Prague. He went back to the monastery in Rome, was again ordered back to Prague by Pope

Gregory V, but when threats of violence and unrest were made by his opponents, he went at Duke Boleslaus' request to Pomerania to convert the pagans. He also went to Hungary and possibly Russia. Regarded as Polish spies, he and two companions, Benedict and Gaudentius, after some success in Danzig, were murdered. April 23.

ADALGIS (d. 686). An Irish monk who was a disciple of St. Fursey, he went to France, worked as a missionary around Arras and Laon, and founded a monastery at Thiérarche, Picardy. June 2.

ADALGOTT (d. 1165). A monk at Clairvaux under St. Bernard, he was named abbot of the Benedictine abbey at Dissentis and bishop of Chur, where he founded a hospital, in 1150. October 3.

ADALHARD (753–827). Grandson of Charles Martel and son of Bernard, King Pipin's brother, and also known as Adelard, he probably studied under Alcuin, and became a monk at Corbie, Picardy, in 773. Though he preferred the life of the monastery, he was brought to the court by his cousin Charlemagne, and became one of his advisers. He was chief minister to Charlemagne's oldest son, Pepin, and when Pepin died in 810 was named tutor of Pepin's son Benard. Adalhard was exiled to an island off the coast of Aquitaine when accused of supporting a revolt against Emperor Louis the Debonair. After five years Louis decided he was innocent and recalled him to the court in 821, but he was soon after again banished, this time to Corbie, where his reputation for holiness, austerity, and concern for the poor and the sick soon spread. He established another monastery, Corvey in Paderborn, and made both monasteries centers of learning and teaching, not only in Latin but also in the vernacular of German and French. He died at Corbie. January 2.

ADALRIC (d. 888). *See* Ageranus.

ADAM (d. c. 1210). A native of Ferno, Italy, he became a hermit on nearby Mount Vissiano, then a Benedictine monk at San Sabine abbey and was later named abbot. May 16.

ADAM OF LOCCUM, BL. (d. c. 1210). A priest and sacristan at the Cistercian abbey of Loccum in Hanover, Germany, he was known for his devotion to Mary and was reputed to have experienced visions of Mary and to have performed numerous miracles. December 22.

ADAMNAN (c. 624–704). Born in Drumhome, Donegal, Ireland, he became a monk at the monastery there and later at Iona, of which he became ninth abbot in 679. He gave sanctuary to Aldfrid when the crown of Northumbria was in dispute after the death of Aldfrid's father, King Oswy. In 686, when Aldfrid had ascended the throne, Adamnan visited him to secure the release of Irish prisoners. Two years later Adamnan visited several English monasteries and was induced by St. Ceolfrid to adopt the Roman calendar for Easter. Adamnan worked ceaselessly thereafter with much success to get Irish monks and monasteries to replace their Celtic practices with those of Rome. His success in convincing the Council of Birr that women should be exempt from wars and that women and children should not be taken prisoners or slaughtered caused the agreement to be called Adamnan's law. A scholar noted for his piety, he wrote a life of St. Columba, one of the most important biographies of the early Middle Ages. He also wrote *De locis sanctis,* a description of the East told to him by a Frank bishop, Arculf, whose ship was driven ashore near Iona on the way back from Jerusalem. Adamnan is thought by some in Ireland to be the same as St. Eunan, though this is uncertain. He died at Iona on September 23.

ADAMNAN OF COLDINGHAM (d. c. 680). An Irish pilgrim, he became a monk under St. Ebba at the monastery of Coldingham off the southeast coast of Scotland and became known for his austerity and the gift of prophecy. His cult was confirmed by Pope Leo XIII in 1898. January 31.

ADAUCTUS (d. c. 304). *See* Felix.

ADAUCTUS (d. c. 312). A native of Ephesus, he was executed there for his faith during the persecution of Maximinus Daza. His daughter Callisthene managed to escape a martyr's death and devoted herself to charitable work until her death at Ephesus. October 4.

ADAUCUS (d. 303). An Italian of noble birth and repeatedly honored by the Emperor, he was a *questor* at the time he and many others were burned to death for their faith when an entire Christian Phrygian town was burned to the ground by order of Emperor Galerian Maximian. February 7.

ADDAI (d. c. 180). According to legend, as a result of correspondence between the Oesrvene King Abgar the Black and Christ in which Abgar asked the Lord to cure him of an incurable disease, and Christ promised to send one of his disciples to Abgar, the apostle Thomas sent Addai, one of the seventy-two disciples, to Abgar's court at Edessa, Mesopotamia. Addai cured Abgar and converted him and his people to Christianity. Among the converts was Aggai, the royal jeweler, whom Addai consecrated bishop and named his successor; Aggai later suffered martyrdom for his missionary activities. Addai also sent his disciple Mari as a missionary to

Nisibis, Nineveh, and along the Tigris. Mari built churches and monasteries, destroyed pagan temples, and made many converts until his death near Seleucia-Ctesiphon. All that is known with any degree of certainty is that Addai was probably a missioner around Edessa toward the end of the second century and that Addai and Mari have been venerated as the holy apostles of Syria and Persia since earliest times. August 5.

ADELA (d. c. 734). Daughter of Dagobert II, King of the Franks, and sister of Irmina, she became a nun on the death of her husband, Alberic, was founding abbess of a monastery at Pfalzel near Trèves, and was a disciple of St. Boniface. December 24.

ADELAIDE. Also *see* Aleydis, another form of the name.

ADELAIDE (931–99). Daughter of Rudolf II of Upper Burgundy, she married Lothair of Italy when sixteen as part of the terms of a treaty between her father and Hugh of Provence, Lothair's father, when she was two. Lothair died in 950, possibly poisoned by his successor, Berengarius, who imprisoned Adelaide when she refused to marry his son. She was freed by the invading German King Otto the Great and married him in Pavia in 951. He was crowned Emperor in Rome the following year and died in 973. His son Otto II succeeded him and because of the enmity of Otto's wife Theophano, Adelaide left the court but the two were reconciled by Abbot Majolus of Cluny. When Otto died in 983, his infant son Otto III succeeded to the throne, with Theophano as regent. She drove Adelaide from the court, but when Theophano died in 991, Adelaide returned as regent. She was active in founding and restoring monasteries and in working for the conversion of the Slavs. She died in a monastery she had founded at Selta, near Cologne, on December 16.

ADELAIDE OF BELLICH (d. c. 1015). The daughter of Megengose, count of Guelder, she was abbess of Bellich convent, near Bonn, and also at St. Mary's in Cologne, both built by her father, where she died, known for her aid to the poor. February 5.

ADELARD. See Adalhard.

ADELELMUS (d. c. 1100). Also known as Aleaume (and Lesmes in Spain), he was born at Laudun, Poitou, and became a French soldier. While on a pilgrimage to Rome, he met St. Robert at Chaise-Dieu monastery, and on his return became a Benedictine monk there. Constance of Burgundy, Queen of Castile, impressed by his holiness and the stories of miracles he performed, invited him to Burgos, Spain, where King Alphonsus VI built him a monastery of which he became abbot. He joined in the war against the Moors and after his death was named patron of Burgos. F.D. January 30.

ADELINA (d. 1125). Granddaughter of William the Conqueror and sister of St. Vitalis, she became abbess of the Benedictine convent of La Blanche at Moriton, Normandy, which Vitalis had founded. October 20.

ADELOGA (d. c. 745). A Frankish princess, she founded the Benedictine convent of Kitzingen in Franconia and was its first abbess. February 2.

ADEODATUS I. See Deusdedit.

ADEODATUS ARIBERT (d. 1391). See Tavelic, Nicholas.

ADILIA. See Odilia.

ADJUSTUS (d. 1220). See Berard.

ADJUTOR (d. 1131). A Norman knight and lord of Vernon-sur-Seine, he went on the First Crusade in 1095, was captured by the Moslems, but escaped from prison, and on his return to France became a monk at the abbey of Tiron. He led the life of a recluse there the last years of his life and died at Tiron on April 30.

ADO, BL. (d. 875). Sent to the abbey of Ferrières, near Sens, for his education, he became a monk there under Lupus Servatus and acquired a reputation for holiness and learning. At the request of Abbot Markward of Prüm he went to Prüm to teach, but dissensions caused him to leave. When he came to Lyons, he was appointed pastor of St. Romanus by St. Remigius, archbishop of Lyons. In 859 Ado became archbishop of Vienne. He put into effect many reforms, opposed the efforts of Lothair II of Lorraine to put aside his lawful wife, and was instrumental in having the proceedings of the synod of Metz authorizing Lothair's marriage to his mistress annulled. He wrote lives of St. Desiderius and St. Theuderis, *A Universal Chronical of the Six Ages of the World,* and was author of an untrustworthy martyrology compiled in 855–60. He died in Vienne on December 16.

ADOLF OF OSNABRÜCK (d. 1224). A member of the family of the Counts of Tecklenburg in Westphalia, he became a canon at Cologne in his youth, left to become a monk at the Cistercian monastery of Camp, and was elected bishop of Osnabrück in 1216. His episcopate was marked by his piety and his charitable works. He died on June 30. February 14.

ADRIAN (d. c. 304). According to legend he was a pagan officer at the imperial court of Nicomedia. Impressed by the courage of a group of Christians who were being tortured, he declared himself a Christian and was imprisoned with them and suffered excruciating tortures before he was put to death. His young wife, Natalia, who was present at his death (she had bribed her way into the prison), comforted him in his agony, recovered one of his severed hands, and took it to Argyropolis near Constantinople, where she fled to escape the importunities of an imperial official of Nicomedia who wanted to marry her. She died there peacefully on December 1. Adrian is the patron of soldiers and butchers. September 8.

ADRIAN (d. 309). With his companion Eubulus, he was tortured and put to death in Caesarea, Palestine, for his faith, during the governorship of Firmilian, while on a visit from Batanea to minister to the local Christians. March 5.

ADRIAN (d. 710). Born in Africa, he became abbot of the monastery at Nerida, near Naples, declined an appointment as archbishop of Canterbury, but accompanied St. Theodore to England when the latter was appointed archbishop. Theodore appointed him abbot of SS. Peter and Paul monastery (later changed to St. Augustine's) in Canterbury, and during his thirty-nine years' abbacy the monastery became renowned as a center of learning. He died on January 9 in Canterbury, and his tomb soon became famous for the miracles wrought there.

ADRIAN (d. c. 875). Possibly of royal descent, he was born in Pannonia, Hungary, where he was bishop, and came to Scotland as a missionary. He retired to a monastery on the Isle of May in the Firth of Forth, where he and all his companions were murdered by marauding Danes. He may also have done mis-

sionary work in Ireland, may have been bishop of St. Andrew, and is believed by some scholars to be the same as St. Odhren of Ireland. March 4.

ADRIAN III (d. 885). Little is known of Adrian or his pontificate and why he is venerated as a saint, though it is known he worked to mitigate the rigors of a famine in Rome. Of Roman descent, he was elected Pope probably on May 17, 884, opposed the aristocratic faction in Rome led by Formosus, bishop of Porto, had George of the Aventine, a member of the Formosan group and notorious for several murders he committed, tried, condemned, and blinded, and had a widow of one of the opposing nobility whipped naked through the streets of Rome. He died either in early September or on July 8 near Modena while on the way to a diet in Worms, Germany, at the invitation of Emperor Charles the Fat, probably to settle the question of Charles' succession. July 8.

ADULF (7th century). See Botulph.

ADVENTOR (d. c. 287). See Maurice.

AEDESIUS (d. 306). Brother of St. Apphian, he was tortured and then drowned when he publicly reproved the judge who had sent consecrated Christian virgins to brothels. April 8.

AEDESIUS (4th century). See Frumentius.

AEDH DUBH (d. 639). King of Leinster, Ireland, he abdicated in 592 to enter the monastery of Kildare and was named its bishop in 630. January 4.

AEDH MAC BRICC (d. 589). The lives of this saint are full of extraordinary tales of miracles of healing, transit through the air, and other marvels. The son of Breece of the Hy Neill, he worked on his father's farm, was dissuaded by Bishop Illathan of Rathlihen, Offay, from kidnaping a girl from his brothers' household when they refused him his inheritance on his father's death, and remained with the bishop. He founded a monastery at Cill-áir in Westmreath and eventually became a bishop. He is reputed to have cured St. Brigid of a headache, so is often called on to cure headaches. November 10.

AEGIDIUS. A variation of Giles.

AELRED (1110–67). Born in Hexham, England, and also known as Ethelred, he became master of the household in the court of King David of Scotland, beloved for his piety, gentleness, and spirituality. Desiring a more austere life than he could lead at the court, he left Scotland when twenty-four and became a Cistercian monk at Rievaulx, Yorkshire, England. He was made abbot of a new Cistercian monastery in Revesby, Lincolnshire, in 1142, and five years later returned to Rievaulx as abbot. Famed for his preaching and asceticism, he traveled widely in England and Scotland and was considered a saint in his own lifetime. He wrote on the spiritual life in *On Spiritual Friendship* and composed numerous sermons and prayers. He died at Rievaulx on January 12. February 3.

AEMILIUS (d. c. 250). *See* Castus.

AENGUS. *See* Oengus.

AENGUS MACNISSE. *See* Macanisius.

AFAN (d. c. 6th century). Nothing is known of him except an inscription in a churchyard in Lanafan Fawr, Brecknock, Wales, that St. Avan the bishop was interred there. November 16.

AFRA (d. 304). According to legend she was a prostitute in Augsburg who during Diocletian's persecution refused to sacrifice to the pagan gods and was burned to death. Her body was rescued and taken to a sepulcher by her mother, Hilaria, and her servants Digna, Eunomia, and Euprepia. Apprehended by the authorities, all four were locked in the sepulcher and burned to death when they too refused to sacrifice to the gods. Another legend says Afra was converted by Bishop Narcissus of Gerona in Spain, but all that is known with any certainty is that an Afra suffered martyrdom in Cologne and has been venerated there for centuries. August 5.

AGABUS (1st century). A Jewish-Christian prophet from Jerusalem, he came to Antioch, and predicted a famine throughout the Roman Empire (Acts 11:28–29), which actually occurred in 49 during the reign of Emperor Claudius. He is probably the same Agabus who predicted Paul's imprisonment in Jerusalem (Acts 21:10 ff.). According to tradition, he died a martyr at Antioch. February 13.

AGAMUND (d. 870). *See* Theodora.

AGAPE (d. 304). Agape and her sisters Chionia and Irene, Christians of Thessalonica, Macedonia, were convicted of possessing texts of the scriptures despite a decree issued in 303 by Emperor Diocletian naming such possessions a crime punishable by death. When they further refused to offer sacrifice to pagan gods the governor, Dulcitius, had Agape and Chionia burned alive. When Irene still refused to recant, Dulcitius ordered her sent to a house of prostitution. There, when she was unmolested after being exposed naked and chained she was put to death either by burning or by an arrow through her throat. April 3.

AGAPE (date unknown). Though listed in early martyrologies, nothing is known of her, though a doubtful tradition has her martyred during a persecution of the Christians at Terni or more probably at Antioch. February 15.

AGAPITUS (d. c. 118). *See* Eustace.

AGAPITUS (date unknown). A martyr buried at Palestrina, dubious tradition has him a fifteen-year-old Christian boy who was tortured and beheaded by order of the governor of Antioch during the reign of Emperor Aurelian when Agapitus refused to recant his Christian faith. April 18.

AGAPITUS (d. 258). *See* Sixtus II.

AGAPITUS (d. 536). A Roman, son of a priest named Gordian who had been murdered, Agapitus was archdeacon of the Roman clergy and an old man when elected Pope on May 13, 535. He died in Constantinople on April 22 after an eleven-month reign while on a mission for Ostrogoth King Theodahad to convince Justinian to call off a threatened invasion of Italy. Agapitus was unsuccessful, but while there he convinced Justinian to remove Patriarch Anthimus, a monophysite, and replace him with Mennas, whom Agapitus consecrated.

AGAPIUS (d. 259). During the persecution of Valerian, he and St. Secundinus, both Spaniards and either priests or bishops, were banished to Africa and with Emilian, a soldier, Tertula and Antonia and an unnamed woman with two children were executed at Citra, Algeria. April 29.

AGAPIUS (d. c. 306). A Christian of Caesarea in Palestine, he was arrested three times and imprisoned for his faith and then released during Diocletian's persecution. When arrested a fourth time he was condemned to death but was offered his freedom if he would give up his faith. When he refused, he was almost killed by a bear, returned to prison, and the next day was drowned. November 20 (also August 19).

AGAPIUS (d. 306). *See* Timothy (d. 304).

AGATHA (date unknown). According to untrustworthy legend she was born either in Palermo or Catania, Sicily, of a wealthy family and early dedicated herself to God and a life of chastity. During one of the Emperor's persecutions, Quintian, a consul who desired her, used the persecutions as a pretext to possess her. When she refused he subjected her to all kinds of indignities and tortures, sending her to a house of prostitution, racking her, cutting off her breasts, and then rolling her over red-hot coals until she died. She is often depicted in art holding a pair of pincers or bearing her breasts on a plate; later these were mistaken by some to be bread and led to the practice of blessing bread on St. Agatha's day. She is the patron of nurses. February 5.

AGATHA (d. 1024). Despite the ill treatment and the jealousy of her husband, Count Paul of Carinthia, her patience and devotion prevailed and she eventually converted him. She was venerated in Carinthia as a model wife. February 5.

AGATHADORUS (d. 170 or 250). *See* Carpus.

AGATHANGELO OF VEDOME. *See* Noury, Bl. Agathangelo.

AGATHANGELUS (d. c. 308). *See* Clement.

AGATHO. *See* Julian (d. 250).

AGATHO (d. 681). A Sicilian, probably from Palermo, he was married for twenty years and successful in financial matters when he became a monk at St. Hernes monastery in Palermo (he may be the Agatho referred to in a letter from Gregory the Great authorizing the abbot to accept him if his wife entered a convent). He succeeded Donus as Pope on June 27, 678. He settled a dispute between Bishop Wilfrid of York and Archbishop Theodore of Canterbury, but the most important event of his pontificate was the Council of Constantinople, November 680–September 681, to which Agatho sent legates and a letter that condemned the monothelite heresy and expounded traditional Catholic belief in two wills in Christ, one divine, one human. Most bishops there, led by Patriarch George of Constantinople, accepted, saying, "Peter has spoken by Agatho." The monothelite heresy was condemned and Constantinople was reunited to Rome in what is now named the Sixth General Council of the Church. By the time its decrees reached Rome, Agatho had died. January 10.

AGATHONICE (d. c. 170 or 250). *See* Carpus.

AGATHOPUS (d. 303). A deacon, he and Theodulus, a lector, were cast into the sea at Thessalonica, with rocks tied around their necks, and drowned for their Christian faith and for possessing copies of Scripture, by order of the governor, Faustinus, during the persecution of Maximian. April 4.

AGATHUS. *See* Acacius (d. c. 303).

AGERANUS (d. 888). A Benedictine monk at Bèze, Côte-d'Or, he remained there with a priest, Ansuinus; four other monks, Berard, Genesius, Rodron, and Sifrard; and a boy named Adalric after all the other monks had fled during the Norman invasion. All seven were murdered by the invaders. May 21.

AGERICUS (c. 521–88). Born near Verdun, France, and also known as Airy, he became a priest at SS. Peter and Paul church there, and about 554 succeeded St. Desiderious as bishop of Verdun. Known for his aid to the poor, he became adviser of King Childebert and was distraught when he was unable to prevent the murder of Bertefroi, leader of a group of rebelling nobles, in his own chapel by the king's troops. He was reputed to have performed several miracles before his death in Verdun. December 1.

AGGAI (d. c. 180). *See* Addai.

AGILBERT (d. c. 685). A Frank who had studied under abbot Ado at Jouarre monastery in Ireland and was a bishop, he was invited by King Coenwalh of the West Saxons to remain in Wessex as bishop. He was active in missionary activities, ordained St. Wilfrid, and with him was a leader in the group seeking to replace the Celtic customs with Roman at the synod of Whitby. He resigned his see when Coenwalh divided his diocese and returned to France, where he became bishop of Paris in 668. Coenwalh later invited him back but he refused and sent his nephew Eleutherius in his place. October 11.

AGILEUS (d. c. 300). A Christian in North Africa, he was martyred at Carthage. St. Augustine preached a sermon on his birthday in his honor. October 15.

AGILULF (d. 751). Educated at the Benedictine monastery of Stavelot-Malmédy, he was educated there under Abbot Angelinus, became abbot, and soon after was named bishop of Cologne in 747. His murder is attributed to

Charles Martel, illegitimate son of King Pepin, when he learned Agilulf had tried to persuade the King on his deathbed not to name Martel his successor. July 9.

AGILUS (c. 580–650). Also known as Ayeul, he was a young Frankish nobleman who became a monk at Luxeuil under St. Columbanus, served as a missionary in Bavaria for a time, and was named abbot of Rebais near Paris on his return. August 30.

AGNELLUS (d. c. 596). A hermit near Naples, he became abbot of nearby San Gaudioso, was credited with numerous miracles, and is one of the patrons of Naples, often successfully invoked against invaders. December 14.

AGNELLUS OF PISA, BL. (c. 1195–1236). Born in Pisa of the noble Agnelli family, he was received into the Franciscans there by St. Francis, became a deacon and *custos* of the friary in Paris, and in 1224 was appointed by Francis to establish the Franciscans in England. With eight associates they founded the province, establishing houses in Canterbury and London and later established a school for friars at Oxford, which rapidly became a great center of learning. He was noted for his holiness and firm adherence to the Franciscan rule of poverty, was a friend of King Henry III, and helped to avert a civil war between Henry and Earl Marshall and died at Oxford on May 7. He was beatified in 1892. March 13 (by the Franciscans May 7).

AGNES (d. c. 304). Of a wealthy Roman family and noted for her beauty, she early resolved to live a life of purity, consecrating her virginity to God. She was denounced as a Christian to the governor during Diocletian's persecution by unsuccessful suitors and though only thirteen refused to be intimidated by the

governor's display of instruments of torture. Infuriated, he sent her to a house of prostitution in Rome, where she successfully retained her purity by her saintly bearing, and in one instance by a miracle. When returned to the governor he ordered her beheaded, which was done. (Some authorities believe she was stabbed in the throat). Although much of her story is unreliable, there is no doubt that Agnes suffered martyrdom and was buried on the Via Nomentana, where a cemetery was named after her. Over the centuries she has become the great Christian symbol of virginal innocence, usually represented in art by a lamb *(agnus-Agnes)*. January 21.

AGNES OF ASSISI (c. 1197–1253). Born in Assisi, the younger sister of St. Clare, she joined Clare when fifteen at the Benedictine convent of Sant' Angelo di Panzo, determined to follow her sister's life of poverty and penance, resisted her relatives' attempts to force her to return home, and was given the habit by St. Francis and sent to San Damiano with Clare, thus founding the Poor Clares. She was made abbess of the Poor Clares convent at Monticelli near Florence by Francis in 1219, established convents at Mantua, Venice, and Padua, and supported her sister's struggle for poverty in their order. Agnes was with Clare at her death and died three months later, on November 16, reportedly as predicted by Clare. Many miracles have been reported at her tomb in Santa Chiara church in Assisi.

AGNES OF BOHEMIA (1205–1282). Daughter of the King and Queen of Bohemia, sister of King Wenceslaus, and related to St. Elizabeth of Hungary, Agnes was educated by Cistercian nuns. Despite her call to religious life she was, as a princess, three times promised in marriage to further political consolidations. One suitor prince died, a second chose another bride and the third, Emperor Frederick, yielded when Agnes persuaded Pope Gregory IX to intervene. Wealthy, she built a Franciscan hospital, established clinics, and a Franciscan friary as well as a Poor Clare convent for five nuns sent by Clare herself. She became a Poor Clare at age twenty-nine and spent fifty years in the cloister. She was canonized in 1989. March 6.

AGNES OF MONTEPULCIANO (c. 1268–1317). Born in Gracchiano-Vecchio, Tuscany, she entered the convent at nearby Montepulciano when only nine. When a new convent was opened at Procena she was transferred there and soon became abbess although only fifteen, attracting many postulants by the sanctity and austerity of her life. About 1300 the inhabitants lured her back to Montepulciano by building a new convent of which she became prioress, and which she put under the Dominican rule. She was famous for her visions (she was reported to have received Communion from an angel and held the infant Christ in her arms), experienced levitation, and performed many miracles. She died in the convent at Montepulciano, and was canonized in 1726. April 20.

AGNES OF POITIERS (d. 586). A friend of the poet Venantius Fortunatus, she was named abbess of Holy Cross convent at Poitiers, France, by St. Radegund and introduced in the convent a rule given her by St. Caesarius. May 13.

AGOBARD (d. c. 769–840). Born in Spain, he fled to France in his youth to escape a Moorish invasion and became a priest at Lyons. He was named archbishop there in 813, was deeply involved in secular as well as ecclesiastical affairs, and wrote on theology and the liturgy. June 6.

AGRARIUS (d. 413). *See* Marcellinus.

AGRECIUS (d. c. 329). The only thing of certainty known of him is that he was bishop of Trèves and attended the Council of Arles in 314. According to untrustworthy legend, he was patriarch of Antioch when appointed bishop of Trèves at the request of Empress Helena and devoted himself to reconverting the area around Trèves. In the same legend Helena sent him some of the relics she had discovered when she found the True Cross, including one of the nails, the knife used at the Last Supper, Christ's robe, and the bodies of Martha and Lazarus. Scholars agree the whole account is sheer fiction. January 13.

AGRICOLA (d. c. 304). In 393 Bishop Eusebius of Bologna found out that the bodies of two Christian martyrs were buried in the Jewish cemetery there. They were exhumed in the presence of St. Ambrose of Milan, who referred to them in a sermon as martyrs—the only fact we know about them. Later legend has Agricola a Bolognese and Vitalis his slave; according to the legend, Vitalis was slain first in the amphitheater for his religion, and when Agricola still refused to recant after his slave's execution, he was crucified, probably during Diocletian's persecution. November 4.

AGRICOLA (c. 497–580). Son of a Gallo-Roman senator and also known as Arègle, he was made bishop of Chalon-sur-Saône, France, in 532. He was a friend of St. Gregory of Tours, lived a simple, austere life devoted to the spirituality of his people, and in the forty-eight years of his bishopric attended several Church councils and enlarged and beautified many of the churches of his diocese. He died in his see city. March 17.

AGRICOLUS (c. 630–c. 700). Unreliable tradition has him born in 630, the son of Magnus, a Gallo-Roman senator who became a monk at Lérins on the death of his wife, and bishop of Avignon in 656. Agricolus went to Lérins when fourteen, was later ordained, and sixteen years later was brought to Avignon by his father, consecrated coadjutor bishop in 660, and succeeded to the see on the death of Magnus in 670. He was famed for his prowess as a preacher and his aid to the sick and the poor. He was named patron of Avignon in 1647. September 2.

AGRIPPINA (d. c. 262). Believed to have been from a good family, she was beheaded or scourged to death in Rome during the persecution of Valerian or Diocletian. Supposedly her body was brought to Mineo, Sicily (the Greeks claim to Constantinople), by three women and is there venerated as a martyr, reputed to have performed many miracles. June 23.

AGUIRRE, MARTIN DE (d. 1597). Born at Vergara, near Pamplona, Navarre, Spain, he studied at Alcalá, and in 1586 he joined the Franciscans. After his ordination he served as a missionary in Mexico and at Manila in the Philippines and was then sent to Japan, where with twenty-five other Catholics he was crucified on February 5 near Nagasaki for his faith during the persecution of Christians by the *taikō*, Toyotomi Hideyoshi. They were all canonized as the Martyrs of Japan in 1862. February 6.

AICHARDUS (d. 687). Also known as Achard, he was sent to a monastery in Poitiers as a child to be educated, was destined for the military by his father, one of Clotaire II's officers, but at his mother's intercession was allowed to make his own choice of vocation and opted for the clerical life. He became a monk at St. Jouin abbey in Ansion,

Poitou, where he spent the next thirty-nine years of his life. He was then made prior of the new St. Benedict priory, founded by St. Philibert, at Quinçay. He succeeded St. Philibert as abbot of the nine-hundred-member monastery at Jumièges, where Aichardus' example brought the monks to a strict observance of their rule. He died at Jumièges. September 15.

AIDAN (d. 626). Information about the life of Aidan is entirely from legendary sources. Also known as Maedoc, he was born in Connaught, Ireland, had portents attached to his birth and childhood, and after a stay at Leinster, went to St. David monastery in Wales to study Scripture. He remained there for several years, reputedly repelling several Saxon raids by miracles, and then returned to Ireland, built a monastery at Ferns, Wexford, and eventually was consecrated bishop there. His miracles are legendary and reveal him as a man of great kindness to animals and to his fellow man. He is represented in art by a stag, reputedly because he once made a stag invisible to save it from hounds. January 31.

AIDAN OF LINDISFARNE (d. 651). Born in Ireland, he may have studied under St. Senan before becoming a monk at Iona. At the request of King Oswald of Northumbria, Aidan went to Lindisfarne as bishop and was known throughout the kingdom for his knowledge of the Bible, his learning, his eloquent preaching, his holiness, his distaste for pomp, his kindness to the poor, and the miracles attributed to him. He founded a monastery at Lindisfarne that became known as the English Iona and was a center of learning and missionary activity for all of northern England. He died at the royal castle at Bamburgh. August 31.

AIGNAN. *See* Anianus.

AIGULF (c. 630–c. 676). Born at Blois, France, he became a Benedictine monk at Fleury and about 670 became abbot at Lérins. His efforts to reform the abbey brought resistance from some of the monks, two of whom persuaded the soldiers sent by the local governor to restore order to kidnap Aigulf and four of his followers. The soldiers took them to the island of Capria near Corsica, blinded and tortured them, and then put Aigulf and three of his monks to death, though there is a possibility they may have been killed by Moors. In a biography written by a monk of Fleury about 850, he headed a party of monks sent to Italy to rescue the relics of St. Benedict from the Lombards. September 13.

AIGULF (d. 836). Born at Bourges, France, he became a hermit there on the death of his parents, acquired a great reputation for sanctity, and was chosen bishop of Bourges about 811. He attended the Council of Toulouse in 829 and was one of those chosen to decide the fate of Archbishop Ebbo of Rheims and two other bishops who had participated in a revolt against Louis the Debonair led by Louis' sons. He is also known as Ayoul. May 22.

AILBHE (d. c. 526). That he was a preacher in Ireland is probably true, but all else about him is known only through legend and myth. Among them is the legend that he was abandoned as an infant, suckled and raised by a wolf, and that years later, while he and some companions were hunting, an aged female wolf ran to him for protection. One story says he was baptized by a priest while a boy in northern Ireland; another that he was baptized and raised in a British settlement in Ireland, and then went to Rome, where he was consecrated a bishop. He undoubtedly was a most effective missionary and may have received a grant from King Aengus of Munster of the Aran Islands for St. Enda, who founded a monastery at Killeaney Inishmore. He is also reputed to have been the first bishop of Emly and the author of a monastic rule. Also known as Ailbe and Albeus, he may have died in 526, 531, or 541. September 12.

AILERAN (d. 664). A monk at the monastery of Clonard, Ireland, he became rector in 650 and wrote lives of SS. Brigid, Fechin, and Patrick, and also several treatises. December 29.

AIMO (d. 1173). Born near Rennes, France, he joined the Benedictines at Savigny in Normandy. He was thought to have leprosy, took care of two monks of the community who were afflicted with the dread disease, and was later ordained when it was found out he was not a leper. He was gifted with several mystical experiences. April 30.

AIMO TAPARELLI, BL. (1395–1495). Born of a noble family at Savigliano, Piedmont, Italy, he joined the Dominicans, served as chaplain to Duke Amadeus of Savoy, and was inquisitor general for Lombardy and Liguria. His cult was confirmed in 1856. August 18.

AIRY. *See* Agericus.

ALACOQUE, MARGARET MARY (1647–90). Daughter of Claude Alacoque and Philiberte Lamyn, she was born on July 22, at L'Hautecour, Burgundy, France, was sent to the Poor Clares' school at Charolles on the death of her father, a notary, when she was eight. She was bedridden for five years with rheumatic fever until she was fifteen and early developed a devotion to the Blessed Sacrament. She refused marriage, and in 1671 she entered the Visitation convent at Paray-le-Monial and was professed the next year. From the time she was twenty, she experienced visions of Christ, and on December 27, 1673, she began a series of revelations that were to continue over the next year and a half. In them Christ informed her she was his chosen instrument to spread devotion to his Sacred Heart, instructed her in a devotion that was to become known as the Nine Fridays and the Holy Hour, and asked that the feast of the Sacred Heart be established. Rebuffed by her superior, Mother de Saumaise, in her efforts to follow the instructions she had received in the visions, she eventually won her over but was unable to convince a group of theologians of the validity of her apparitions, nor was she any more successful with many of the members of her community. She received the support of Bl. Claud La Colombière, the community's confessor for a time, who declared that the visions were genuine. In 1683 opposition in the community ended when Mother Melin was elected superior and named Margaret Mary her assistant. She later became novice mistress, saw the convent observe the feast of the Sacred Heart privately beginning in 1686, and two years later a chapel was built at Paray-le-Monial to honor the Sacred Heart; soon observation of the feast of the Sacred Heart spread to other Visitandine convents. Margaret Mary died at Paray-le-Monial on October 17, and was canonized in 1920. She, St. John Eudes, and Bl. Claud La Colombière are called the "saints of the Sacred Heart"; the devotion was officially recognized and approved by Pope Clement XIII in 1765, seventy-five years after her death.

ALARICUS, BL. (d. 975). Son of Duke Burnhard II of Swabia, he was educated at Einsiedeln, Switzerland, became a monk there, and then lived as a hermit on an island in Lake Zurich, near Zurich. September 29.

ALBAN (d. 304). Probably the first martyr of Britain, his life story is based on unverifiable legend. According to it, he was a leading citizen of Verulamium (now St. Albans), Hertfordshire, England, who hid a priest during the persecution of Diocletian. Alban was so impressed by the priest, he was converted to Christianity, changed clothes with the priest, and was mistakenly arrested as the priest because he was wearing his clothes. When he refused to worship the pagan gods, he was tortured, ordered to be executed, reportedly performed several miracles on the way to the execution grounds, and was beheaded. June 22.

ALBAN. See Roe, Bl. Bartholomew.

ALBAN OF MAINZ (5th century). Also known as Albinus, legend has him a Greek or Albanian priest who accompanied St. Ursus from the island of Naxos to Milan to escape Arian persecution. There St. Ambrose welcomed them and encouraged their desire to evangelize in Gaul and Germany. Ursus was killed on the way in the Val d'Aosta, but Alban settled in Mainz, where he fought the Arians and preached to the barbarians. He was killed and then beheaded at Hanum, probably during a Vandal raid sometime before 451. June 21.

ALBERGATI, BL. NICHOLAS (1375–1443). Born at Bologna, Italy, he studied law, but when twenty he joined the Carthusians. He served as prior of several Carthusian houses, and in 1417, against his will, he was named bishop of Bologna. He served on several papal diplomatic missions to France and Lombardy, was made a cardinal in 1426, made a reputation as a peacemaker, participated in the Council of Basel, and was active in the negotiations that led to the reunion of the Greek Church to Rome at Ferrara-Florence. He wrote several theological treatises, encouraged learning, and was appointed chief penitentiary by Pope Eugene IV. Alban died at Siena, and his cult was approved in 1744. May 9.

ALBERIC (d. 784). Nephew of St. Gregory of Utrecht and a friend of Alcuin, he joined the Benedictines, became prior of the Utrecht cathedral, and in 775 was named bishop of Utrecht on the death of Gregory, who had administered the see (though never a bishop) since 755. Noted for his learning, Alberic was also known for his successful missionary work among the Teutons. He died on August 21. November 14.

ALBERIC (d. 1109). A hermit near Châtillon-sur-Seine, France, he and fellow hermits built a monastery at Molesmes with Robert as abbot and Alberic as prior. The monastery flourished, but new monks ignored the strict rule; Robert left and Alberic was imprisoned. He left too, returned, was unsuccessful in reforming the monastery, and in 1098 twenty-one monks left and established a new monastery at Cîteaux with Robert as abbot, Alberic as prior, and Stephen Harding as subprior—thus establishing the Cistercians with the three as cofounders. Robert returned to Molesmes soon after and Alberic was elected abbot. He restored the primitive Benedictine rule and added new austerities to it, thus putting his stamp on the Cistercian observance, though his successor, Stephen Harding, was mainly responsible for the characteristics associated with the Cistercians. Alberic died at Cîteaux on January 26.

ALBERIONE, BL. GIACOMO (1884–1971). Responsible for many religious publications, he is regarded as one of the most outstanding apostles of the twentieth century in proclaiming the love of God through the media. Bl. Giacomo felt the call of God from a very early age and entered seminary at age sixteen. His goal, derived from divine inspiration, was to preach the Gospel to a wider audience using modern communication. He founded the St. Paul Pious Society, the first of ten branches of the Pauline Family, which today heads some of the largest-circulation Catholic media in the world. The publications he directly launched include a periodical devoted to Mary, a magazine for priests, a weekly for Christian families, a monthly in Latin, a monthly dedicated to teaching doctrine, and a weekly children's magazine. Although he struggled with scholiosis, Bl. Giacomo realized his lifelong mission of reaching a multitude of people and spreading his preaching. He was beatified in 2003.

ALBERT (Adam Chmielowski) (1845–1916). A Krakow, Poland, aristocrat and artist, he lost a leg fighting in an insurrection. Compassionate toward the poor, Albert became a Franciscan tertiary. In 1887 he founded the Brothers of the Third Order of Saint Francis and the Servants of the Poor (Albertines, or Gray Brothers). In 1891 he established the Gray Sisters to work with the hungry and homeless. He was canonized in 1989. June 17.

ALBERT OF BERGAMO, BL. (d. 1279). A farmer at Ogna near Bergamo, Italy, where he was born, he married and became a Dominican tertiary, noted for his help to the poor and destitute. He made a pilgrimage to Rome, Jerusalem, and Compostela and then settled in Cremona, where he became famous for the miracles attributed to him. His cult was approved in 1748. May 11.

ALBERT THE GREAT (c. 1206–80). Eldest son of the count of Bollstädt, he was born in the family castle at Lauingen, Swabia, Germany, studied at the University of Padua, and in 1223 became a Dominican there despite family opposition. He was teaching at Cologne in 1228 and later taught at Hildesheim, Freiburg-im-Breisgau, Regensburg, and Strasbourg. By the time of his return to Cologne, he had a widespread reputation for his learning and intellect. He went to teach and study at the university of Paris, where he received his doctorate in 1245, and he was named regent of the newly established *studia generalia* at Cologne in 1248. Among his students at Paris and Cologne was Thomas Aquinas, whose genius he early perceived and proclaimed; Aquinas was to be his close friend and comrade in intellect until his death in 1274. Albert was named provincial of his order in 1254, went to Rome in 1256 to defend the mendicant orders against attacks by William of St. Armour (who was condemned later in the year by Pope Alexander IV), and while there served as personal theologian to the Pope. Albert resigned his provincialate in 1257 to devote himself to study, and in 1259 with Peter of Tarentasia and Thomas Aquinas drew up a new study curriculum for the Dominicans. Against his wishes, he was appointed bishop of Regensburg in 1260 but resigned two years later to resume teaching at Cologne. He was active in the Council of Lyons in 1274, working for the reunion of the Greek Church with Rome. He fiercely and brilliantly defended Aquinas and his position against Bishop Stephen Tempier of Paris and a group of theologians at the university there in 1277. In 1278 a memory lapse progressed into two years of ailing health and mind, which led to his death in Cologne on November 15. He was canonized and declared a Doctor of the Church by Pope Pius XI in 1931. Albert was one of the great intellects of the medieval Church. He was one of the first and among the greatest of natural scientists. His knowledge of biology, chemistry, physics, astronomy, and geography (one of his treatises proved the earth to be round) was so encyclopedic, he was often accused of magic. He wrote profusely on logic, metaphysics, mathematics, the Bible, and theology. He pioneered the Scholastic method, so brilliantly developed by his pupil and disciple, Thomas Aquinas, by applying Aristotelian methods to revealed doctrine. A keen student of Arabic learning and culture, his and Aquinas' adaptation of Aristotelian principles to systematic theology and their attempts to reconcile Aristotelianism to Christianity caused bitter opposition among many of their fellow theologians. His brilliance and erudition caused him to be called "the Universal Doctor" by his contemporaries. Among his many works are *Summa theologiae, De unitate intellectus contra Averrem, De vegetabilibus,* and *Summa de creaturis.*

ALBERT OF JERUSALEM (c. 1149–1214). Of a well-known family in Parma, Italy, he studied theology and law, became a canon at Holy Cross abbey in Mortara, and in 1184 became bishop of Bobbio. He was shortly after translated to Vercelli, mediated a dispute between Frederick Barbarossa and Pope Clement III, was Pope Innocent III's legate to northern Italy, and in 1199 negotiated a peace between Parma and Piacenza. In 1205, he was appointed patriarch of Jerusalem, which had been established as a Latin kingdom by the crusaders in 1099. Since the Saracens had recaptured Jerusalem in 1187, he was obliged to establish his see at Akka. He took a prominent role in the civil and ecclesiastical affairs of the kingdom, often mediating disputes between the different Frankish factions. He is especially known for a rule he composed for St. Brocard, prior of the hermits living on Mount Carmel, which became the first rule of the Carmelites. He was stabbed to death in Akka by a man he had discharged as head of Holy Ghost Hospital there. September 25.

ALBERT OF LOUVAIN (c. 1166–1202). Son of Duke Godfrey III of Brabant, he was made a canon of Liège when twelve but gave up the benefice when twenty-one and became a knight of Count Baldwin V of Hainault, the bitter enemy of Brabant. Though he proposed going on crusade he never did and at that time resumed his clerical life and received back his canonry. He became an archdeacon of Brabant and provost, and in 1191 was elected bishop of Liège over Albert of Rethel, Baldwin's cousin and uncle of Henry VI's wife, Constance. When the loser appealed to Henry, the Emperor deposed Albert of Louvain and appointed Lothaire, provost of Bonn, bishop. Albert appealed to Rome in person, and Pope Celestine III declared his election valid. Albert was ordained priest and consecrated bishop in Rheims by Archbishop William when Archbishop Bruno of Cologne, for fear of the Emperor, refused to do so. Lothaire, supported by Henry, refused to surrender the see, and Henry forced the clergy of the diocese to submit to him. On November 24, Albert was murdered by a group of Henry's knights while on his way to Saint-Remi abbey just outside of Rheims. Lothaire was excommunicated and exiled, and Henry was forced to do penance. November 21.

ALBERT OF MONTECORVINO (d. 1127). Brought to Montecorvino, Apulia, Italy, by his Norman father as a child, Albert became bishop there, and though he became blind, ruled successfully, famed for his visions and miracles. April 5.

ALBERT OF TRAPANI (d. c. 1307). Born at Trapani, Sicily, he joined the Carmelites there, was ordained, and then sent to Messina, where he became famous for his miracles and preaching. He spent his last years living as a hermit near Messina. His cult was approved in 1476. August 7.

ALBERTA (3rd century). *See* Faith.

ALBERTINUS (d. 1294). A monk at Holy Cross monastery at Fonte Avellana, Italy, he was elected prior general of his congregation when the Benedictine group, of which he was a member, was merged with the Camaldoles in 1270, and acted as peacemaker between the bishop of Gubbio and his flock. His cult was confirmed by Pope Pius VI. August 31.

ALBERTONI, BL. LOUISA (1473–1533). Born of a leading family in Rome, she married wealthy James de Cithara, and when he died in 1506 became a Franciscan tertiary. She spent her wealth ministering to the poor and the sick; the later years of her life were poverty-ridden after she had exhausted her funds in her charitable works. She experienced ecstasies, was gifted with levitation, and was credited with numerous miracles after her death on January 31. Her cult was confirmed in 1671. February 28.

ALBERTUS MAGNUS. *See* Albert the Great.

ALBEUS. *See* Ailbhe.

ALBINA (d. 250). A young Christian girl, she suffered martyrdom for her faith during Decius' persecution at Caesarea or according to the Roman Martyrology at Formiae (Gata, Campagna, Italy), near Naples. December 16.

ALBINIANI, BL. INES (1625–96). Born near Valencia, Spain, of poor parents, she joined the Augustinian hermitesses at Beniganim, taking the name Sister

Josepha Maria of St. Agnes. She practiced severe austerities, was known for her prophecies, and was consulted by people from all walks of life for her spiritual insights. She died on January 21, and was beatified in 1888.

ALBINUS (d. c. 550). Born at Vannes, Brittany, and also known as Aubin, he entered the monastery of Tincillac when a youth, was elected abbot when he was thirty-five, and was named bishop of Angers in 529. He was known for his generosity to the sick and the indigent, widows, and orphans, for his work in ransoming slaves, and for his holiness and the many miracles he is reputed to have performed both during his lifetime and after his death. March 1.

ALBINUS (d. c. 760). An Anglo-Saxon named Witta, he became a Benedictine monk and accompanied St. Boniface to Germany and worked with him on his missionary labors. Albinus was named bishop of Buraburg, Hesse, in 741, and died sometime after 760. October 26.

ALBINUS. See Alban of Mainz.

ALBRIZZI, BL. MAGDALEN (d. 1465). Of a noble family, she was born at Como, Italy, and when her parents died became a nun at nearby Brunate, and in time was named abbess. She affiliated the convent with the Hermits of St. Augustine, built a hospice in Como for her nuns and for young women, encouraged frequent Communion, and became known for her miracles of healing and her gift of prophecy. Her cult was approved in 1907. May 15.

ALBURGA (d. c. 800). The sister of King Egbert of Wessex, she married Wulfstan of Wiltshire, founded Wilton abbey near Salisbury, and on the death of Wulfstan, became a nun there. December 25.

ALCMUND (d. 781). Only that he became seventh bishop of Hexham, England, in 767 is all that is known about him. Tradition says he appeared in a vision to a resident of Hexham about 1032 and told him to have his body, which had been buried in the cemetery outside the cathedral and whose whereabouts had been lost during Danish raids, moved to a more fitting burial place in the cathedral, which was done. September 7.

ALCMUND (d. c. 800). The son or nephew of St. Alhred of Northumbria, untrustworthy sources have him slain in Shropshire while attempting to regain his father's throne after his brother Osred had been killed in a similar attempt in 792. Miracles were reported at his tomb at Lilleshall after his death. March 19.

ALCOBER, BL. JOHN (1694–1748). Born in Gerona, Spain, he joined the Dominicans and was sent to China in 1728. He was captured in 1746 when a persecution of Christians broke out and was imprisoned for a year in Foochow with a group of fellow Dominicans, among them Peter Sanz, vicar apostolic of Fu-kien. They were all executed by being strangled in prison on December 30, and the whole group was beatified in 1893. May 26.

ALCUIN (c. 735–804). Probably born in York, England, he studied under St. Egbert, was a disciple of Bede at the York cathedral school, and in 767 became its head. Under his direction it became a well-known center of learning. He was invited by Charlemagne to set up a school at his court in Aachen in 781 and became Charlemagne's adviser. He was appointed abbot of St. Martin's abbey at Tours in 796 by Charlemagne and later of abbeys at Ferrières, Troyes, and Cormery; it is not certain if Alcuin was ever ordained beyond the diaconate, though some scholars believed he did become a priest in his later years. Under his direction the school at Aachen became one of the greatest centers of learning in Europe. He was the moving force and spirit in the Carolingian renaissance and made the Frankish court the center of European culture and scholarship. He fought illiteracy throughout the kingdom, instituted a system of elementary education, and established a higher educational system based on the study of the seven liberal arts, the trivium and the quadrivium, which was the basis of the curriculum for medieval Europe. He encouraged the use of ancient texts, was an outstanding theologian, and fought the heresy of Adoptionism, which was condemned at the Synod of Frankfurt in 794, and exerted an influence on the Roman liturgy that endured for centuries. He wrote biblical commentaries and verse and was the author of hundreds of letters, many still extant, and a widely used rhetoric text, *Compendia*. He died at St. Martin's in Tours, where he had developed one of his most famous schools, on May 19. Though his cult has never been formally confirmed, he is often referred to as Blessed; he may also have been a Benedictine.

ALDA, BL. (1249–1309). A native of Siena, and also known as Aude and Aldobrandesca, she gave away all her possessions on the death of her husband and devoted herself to aiding the poor. She spent the last part of her life ministering to the sick in the hospital at Siena, subjecting herself to great mortifications. She experienced visions and ecstasies during her lifetime. April 26.

ALDATE (5th century). A Briton who according to unreliable sources was bishop of Gloucester and roused the countryside to resist the pagan invasions of western Britain. February 4.

ALDEGUNDIS (630–84). Born in Hainult, Belgium, she joined her sister St. Waldeturdis, who had founded a convent at Mons and then lived as a hermitess; her cell developed into the Benedictine monastery of Mauberge. She died of cancer on January 30.

ALDEMAR (d. c. 1080). Born at Capua, Italy, he became a monk at Monte Cassino and then was made director of a convent built at Capua by Princess Aloara, where he is reputed to have performed miracles and became known as "the Wise." When a dispute developed between Aloara and the abbot over his return to Monte Cassino, he settled at Boiana, fled when one of his companions there tried to kill him, and built a monastery at Bocchignano, in the Abruzzi, and several other houses that he directed until his death. March 24.

ALDERICUS (780–841). Also known as Audry, he was born in the Gatinais, joined the Benedictines at Ferrières, France, became a priest at Sens and later chancellor, and in 828 was named bishop of Sens, known for his encouragement of ecclesiastical studies. October 10.

ALDHELM (c. 639–709). Related to King Ine of the West Saxons, he was born in Wessex, England, studied at Malmesbury, probably became a Benedictine monk at Canterbury (though this may have been earlier), and studied there under St. Adrian. He then returned to Malmesbury as director of the school there and about 683 became abbot. He was adviser to Ine, was known for his scholarship and spirituality, advanced education in all of Wessex, founded several monasteries, and was active in supplanting the Celtic liturgical customs with those of Rome. He was appointed bishop of Sherborne in 705 and died on a visitation to Doulting. He wrote

Latin poems and a treatise on virginity, composed ballads and songs in English and Latin, and is considered the first English scholar of distinction. May 25.

ALDOBRANDESCA. *See* Alda.

ALDRIC (c. 800–56). Born of a noble family, he was sent, when a child, to Charlemagne's court by his father, entered the bishop's school at Metz about 821, and became a monk there. After his ordination he became the chaplain and confessor of Emperor Louis the Pious and in 832 was named bishop of Le Mans. He built several churches and monasteries, was devoted to the care and aid of the poor, and supported Louis and his successor, Charles the Bold, in the disputes over the division of the Frankish empire among Louis' sons. He was expelled from his see in a dispute with the monks of Saint-Calais because of his claim they were under his rule, but returned a year later. Paralyzed the last two years of his life, he died on January 7.

ALEAUME. *See* Adelelmus.

ALED. *See* Almedha.

ALEXANDER (d. c. 113). Tradition has him tortured and executed on the Via Nomentana near Rome with two priests, Eventius and Theodulus, who after a lengthy imprisonment were burned and then beheaded during Hadrian's persecution. Although called Pope Alexander in the Roman Martyrology, it is believed this is an erroneous listing. May 3.

ALEXANDER (d. c. 165). *See* Felicity.

ALEXANDER (d. c. 172). He and St. Caius were active in combating the Montanists until they suffered martyrdom at Apamea, Phrygia, during the reign of Marcus Aurelius. March 10.

ALEXANDER (d. 177). *See* Pothinus.

ALEXANDER (d. 178). A resident of Lyons in Gaul, he and his friend Epipodius fled the city to escape the persecution of Marcus Aurelius but were captured and tortured. Epipodius was beheaded and two days later Alexander died of the tortures he had endured as he was fastened to a cross for his crucifixion. April 22.

ALEXANDER (2nd century). A bishop near Rome, he became famous for his miracles, was arrested and tortured and then executed for his faith on the Claudian Way twenty miles from Rome during the reign of Emperor Antoninus. September 21.

ALEXANDER (d. c. 250). Born at Fermo, Italy, he became bishop there and suffered martyrdom during Decius' persecution of the Christians. January 11.

ALEXANDER (d. 250). *See* Epimachus.

ALEXANDER (d. 260). He and SS. Malchus and Priscus were martyred for their religion during Valerian's reign by being killed by wild beasts in the arena at Caesarea, Palestine. March 28.

ALEXANDER (d. c. 284). *See* Thalelaeus.

ALEXANDER (d. c. 287). *See* Maurice.

ALEXANDER (d. c. 290). *See* Victor of Marseilles.

ALEXANDER (d. 313). A soldier, he tried to save St. Antonina, who had been condemned to death for her Christianity, by changing clothes with him during the persecution of Maximian in Constantinople. When the ruse was discovered, both were tortured and then burned to death. May 3.

ALEXANDER (c. 250–328). Named bishop of Alexandria in 313, he was an implacable opponent of Arianism. When his mild censures failed to bring Arius back to orthodoxy, Alexander excommunicated him at a meeting of his clergy about 321; the excommunication was confirmed by a bishops' council at Alexandria. Alexander is reputed to have drawn up the Acts of the first General Council of Nicaea in 325, where Arianism was formally condemned. He died at Alexandria. February 26.

ALEXANDER (c. 244–340). Elected patriarch of Constantinople in 317, when he was seventy-three, he was known for his wisdom and his holiness. He attended the Council of Nicaea in 325 and was active in his opposition to Arius and Arianism. In 336, Arius came to Constantinople with an order from the Emperor that he be received into the Church there. Reportedly Alexander prayed that either he or Arius be removed; the day before the scheduled reception, Arius died. August 28.

ALEXANDER (d. 397). *See* Sisinius.

ALEXANDER (d. 590). The bishop of Fiesole, Italy, he incurred the enmity of the rulers of Lombardy for his defense of ecclesiastical rights and was ambushed and drowned near Bologna. June 6.

ALEXANDER AKIMETES (d. c. 430). A native of Asia Minor, he studied at Constantinople, where he was converted to Christianity, was a hermit in Syria for eleven years, and then went as a missionary to Mesopotamia. He founded a monastery, went to Antioch, where he encountered resistance, and then established a monastery at Constantinople. He was again forced to leave and then built a monastery at Gomon, where he died. He is reputed to have converted Rabulas, who later

became bishop of Edessa and is known as the founder of a service in which relays of his four hundred monks sang the divine office continuously day and night. February 23.

ALEXANDER THE CHARCOAL-BURNER. *See* Alexander of Comana.

ALEXANDER OF COMANA (d. c. 275). Surnamed "the charcoal-burner," since that was his profession, he was appointed bishop of Comana, Pontus, by St. Gregory Thaumaturgus, bishop of Neocaesarea, who, unable to find a suitable candidate for the see, interviewed him when his name was derisively suggested and found him a wise and holy man worthy of being a bishop. He was burned to death in Comana for his faith during Decius' persecution of Christians. August 11.

ALEXANDER OF JERUSALEM (d. 251). A native of Cappadocia, he studied at Alexandria, where Origen was a fellow student, and was named bishop of his native city. He was imprisoned for his faith during Severus' persecution but was released and then went on pilgrimage to Jerusalem, where he was made coadjutor in 212—the first known instance of a coadjutor and of a bishop translated from one see to another. He gave refuge to the exiled Origen and participated in Origen's ordination, for which he was censured by Bishop Demetrius of Alexandria. He founded a library and school at Jerusalem, was imprisoned at Caesarea during Decius' persecution, and died in prison there. March 18.

ALEXIS (5th century). An unknown biographer who refers to him only as the "Man of God" states he was the son of a wealthy Roman senator, was known for his charity even as a child, and to please his parents married a wealthy Roman girl. They parted by mutual consent on their wedding day and he went to Syria, where he spent seventeen years in abject poverty and great holiness in a shack adjoining a church dedicated to Mary in Edessa. When a statue of Mary spoke revealing him to the people of Edessa as the "Man of God," he returned to Rome where his father, not recognizing the bedraggled beggar as his son, gave him a job and a place to live under a staircase in his home. Unrecognized by all, he lived there for seventeen years, humbly, uncomplainingly, and patiently; his identity was revealed only at his death, when his autobiography was found. His story spread to the West in the ninth and tenth centuries but was undoubtedly a pious myth. At best, scholars believe he may have lived, died, and was buried in Edessa and was not the man whose bones were found in St. Boniface church in Rome in 1217 and was believed to be those of Alexis, as the "Man of God" came to be called. July 17.

ALEYDIS (d. 1250). Born at Schaerbeek, near Brussels, she was sent to the nearby Cistercian convent of La Cambre when seven and spent the rest of her life there, impressing all with her humility. Isolated because of the leprosy she contracted, she suffered greatly, became blind and was paralyzed, and died at the convent on June 11. Devoted to the Eucharist, she was credited with numerous miracles and experienced visions and ecstasies. Her cult was authorized in 1907. June 15.

ALFERIUS (930–1050). Born in Salerno, Italy, of the princely Pappacarboni family, he vowed to enter the religious life if cured of an illness he contracted on a mission to the French court for Duke Gisulf of Salerno. He was cured and became a monk at Cluny, and was brought back by Gisulf to reform the monasteries in his dukedom. When unsuccessful he became a hermit about 1011 outside of Salerno, attracted numerous disciples, and selected twelve around whom grew the Benedictine abbey of La Cava. He is reputed to have lived to 120. His cult was approved in 1893. April 12.

ALFIELD, BL. THOMAS (d. 1585). Born in Gloucester, England, he was raised a Protestant and educated at Eton and Cambridge. He was converted to Catholicism in 1576, went to Douai, and was ordained in Rheims in 1581. He was sent on the English mission, worked with Edmund Campion, was arrested in 1582, and when subjected to torture in the Tower, apostatized. On his release, he returned to Rheims, recanted his apostasy, returned to the Church, and was returned to the English mission. Late in 1584, he was arrested with Thomas Webley, a dyer of Gloucester, and imprisoned in the Tower for distributing copies of Cardinal Allen's *True and Modest Defence,* proving Catholics in England were being persecuted not for treason but for their religion. Both were tortured and then hanged at Tyburn on July 6 after refusing an offer of freedom if they would acknowledge the ecclesiastical supremacy of the Queen. Alfield was beatified in 1929.

ALFRICK (d. 1005). A monk at the Benedictine abbey of Abingdon, England, he became abbot, was named bishop of Wilton in 990, and five years later was named archbishop of Canterbury. He ruled during the Danish invasion of England. November 16.

ALFWOLD (d. c. 1058). A Benedictine monk at Winchester, England, he was named bishop of Sherborne in the reign of Edward the Confessor and was known for the asceticism of his life. March 25.

ALICE. *See* Aleydis.

ALIPIUS. See Alypius.

ALLEMAND, BL. LOUIS (c. 1380–1450). Born at Arbent, France, he studied law at the University of Avignon, received his law degree, and was the beneficiary of several ecclesiastical benefices through the influence of his uncle. He attended the synod of Pisa, which attempted unsuccessfully to end the Great Schism in 1409 and the General Council of Constance in 1414, and was vice chamberlain at the conclave of 1416, which elected Pope Martin V, finally ending the Great Schism. He was named bishop of Manguelonne by Martin in 1418, was advanced to the archbishopric of Arles, was made governor of Romagna, Bologna, and Ravenna in 1423, and was created a cardinal in 1426. An uprising in Bologna drove him from the city, and he retired to Rome. When a longtime opponent, Gabriello Cardinal Condulmerio, was elected Pope as Eugene IV in 1431 and dissolved the Council of Basel called by Pope Martin V, Allemand was forbidden to leave Rome by Eugene but escaped to Arles and became a leader of the conciliar party opposed to papal supremacy, which refused to obey the papal order for the council's dissolution. When his followers at the council ordered Eugene to appear before it, the Pope ordered the council reconvened at Ferrara. Allemand and his followers refused and continued a rump council at Basel, declared Eugene deposed, and elected Amadeus of Savoy to replace Eugene as Felix V in 1439; whereupon Eugene excommunicated Allemand in 1440. When Eugene died in 1447, Felix resigned in favor of the new Pope, Nicholas V, and Nicholas revoked all excommunications and penalties imposed on the conciliar party and restored Allemand as cardinal. He returned to his see at Arles, where he spent the rest of his life in prayer and penances. After his death, miracles were reported at his tomb and a cult developed that was approved by Pope Clement VII in 1527. September 17.

ALLOWIN. See Bavo.

ALLUCIO (d. 1134). A shepherd in Pescia, Tuscany, he became director of the almshouse in Valdi Nievole and built shelters at river crossings and mountain passes that were run by young men who became known as the Brothers of St. Allucio. He ended the war between Ravenna and Faenza and is reported to have performed numerous miracles. His cult was approved by Pope Pius IV. October 23.

ALMACHIUS (d. c. 400). An Eastern ascetic who was stoned to death in Rome when he tried to stop a contest between gladiators in the arena, his death, according to Theodoret, caused Emperor Honorius to abolish gladiatorial contests. He is also known as Telemachus. January 1.

ALMATO, BL. PETER (1830–61). Born at Sassera, Spain, he joined the Dominicans, was sent to the Philippines as a missionary, and in 1855 was sent to Tonkin in Indochina. He was captured and beheaded on November 1 with Bl. Jerome Hermosilla, vicar apostolic of East Tonkin, and Bl. Valentine Berrio-Ochoa, vicar apostolic of Central Tonkin. They were beatified in 1906. November 6.

ALMEDHA (6th century). According to Welsh legend she was the daughter of King Brychan and early dedicated herself to God. She fled to Llanddew to escape marriage to a young prince, then to Llanfillo and later to Llechfaen, in all of which places she was ignored and refused help. She finally settled in a cell near Brecon provided by the lord there. Supposedly her suitor caught up with her there and when she resisted him he cut off her head with his sword; reputedly a spring of water appeared where her head had fallen. She had prophesied dire things for the villages that had rejected her, and these predictions are said to have materialized after her death. She is also known as Aled and Eiluned, and some scholars believe her story is the same as that told of St. Winifred. August 1.

ALMOND, JOHN (1577–1612). Born at Allerton, near Liverpool, England, he spent his boyhood in Ireland, and then studied at the English college in Rheims, where he was ordained in 1598, and in Rome. He was sent on the English mission in 1602 and ministered to the Catholics of England for a decade until he was arrested and imprisoned for a time in 1608. He was again arrested in 1612, and when he refused to take the Oath of Supremacy, he was convicted of treason for being a priest and hanged, drawn, and quartered at Tyburn on December 5. He was canonized by Pope Paul VI in 1970.

ALNOTH (d. c. 700). A cowherder who lived on the estate of St. Werburga's monastery at Weedon, Northamptonshire, England, he was venerated for his holiness. He later became a hermit near Stowe and was murdered there by bandits. February 27.

ALODIA (d. 851). The daughter of a Mohammedan father and a Christian mother, she and her sister Nunilo lived at Huesca, Spain, and were raised as Christians. Despite the opposition of a Mohammedan stepfather, they decided to live lives of chastity devoted to God and refused numerous offers of marriage. During the persecution of Moorish Abdur Rahman II, they were arrested, and when they refused to abjure their religion even when sent

among prostitutes, they were beheaded. October 22.

ALOYSIUS GONZAGA. See Gonzaga, Aloysius.

ALPAIS, BL. (c. 1150–1211). A peasant, she was born in Cudot, France, and worked in the fields until stricken by a disease, possibly leprosy. Reportedly cured by a vision of Mary, she was again stricken and confined to bed. A contemporary biographer reported that for years at a time she neither drank nor ate anything except the Eucharist, a fact confirmed by a commission appointed by Archbishop William of Sens—the first instance of a person deriving sustenance solely from the Eucharist. Her visions, ecstatic state, the extraordinary endurance of her sufferings, and her miracles drew thousands to Cudot. Her cult was confirmed in 1874. November 3.

ALPHAEUS (d. 303). A native of Eleutheropolis and a lector at the church in Caesarea, Palestine, he was arrested and tortured during Diocletian's persecution of Christians. Also arrested was Zacheus, a deacon at Gadara. They were both beheaded for their faith. November 17.

ALPHEGE (d. 951). Surnamed "the Elder" or "the Bald" and also known as Elphege, he was bishop of Winchester, England, and ordained St. Dunstan, who was responsible for the restoration of monasticism to England. Alphege was noted for his holiness and the gift of prophecy. March 12.

ALPHEGE (c. 954–1012). Also known as Elphege, he became a Benedictine monk at Deerhurst monastery, Gloucestershire, England, when a young man but left to become a hermit at Bath. He was appointed abbot of the monastery there and enforced a strict rule. Over his objections he was appointed bishop of Winchester in 984, eliminated poverty in his diocese through his aid to the poor, and continued to live a life of great austerity. In 1006 he was appointed archbishop of Canterbury, receiving the pallium from Pope John XVIII in Rome. When the Danes and Earl Edric besieged Canterbury, he refused to leave. When the city fell he was imprisoned for exhorting the pillaging Danes to desist from their murdering and looting. When an epidemic broke out he was released to minister to the ill, but when he refused to pay a ransom of three thousand gold crowns for his permanent release, he was taken to Greenwich and put to death. Danish King Canute brought his body to Canterbury in 1023 from London, where it had been buried. April 19.

ALPHIUS (d. 251). Unreliable legends have Alphius, Philadelphus, and Cyrinus brothers, probably born in Vaste, Italy, who with their sister Benedicta and several companions were arrested during Decius' persecution of Christians, taken to Rome, and tortured. They were then taken to Pozzuoli, near Naples, where one of the group, Onesimus, was executed, and then to Sicily, where all were put to death at Lentini for their faith. Alphius, twenty-two, had his tongue torn from his mouth; Philadelphus, twenty-one, was burned to death; and Cyrinus, nineteen, was boiled to death. May 10.

ALPHONSUS MARY LIGUORI. See Liguori, Alphonsus Mary.

ALPHONSUS RODRIGUEZ, BL. See Rodriguez, Bl. Alphonsus.

ALTMAN (c. 1020–91). Born at Paderborn, Westphalia, he studied at Paris, was ordained, became canon head of the cathedral school at Paderborn, then

provost of the chapter at Aachen and chaplain to Emperor Henry III. Altman went on a pilgrimage to the Holy Land in 1064, was captured with thousands of his fellow pilgrims by the Saracens in Palestine, but eventually reached Jerusalem when they were released through the intercession of a friendly emir. By the time the pilgrimage reached home half the party had died of sickness, hardships, and attacks by the Saracens. He was named bishop of Passau on his return in 1065 through the good offices of dowager Empress Agnes. He put into effect plans to reform the diocese, improve education, and help the poor; he founded an Augustinian abbey at Göttweig, and he reformed several others. When he attempted to enforce Pope Gregory VII's renewal of the decrees forbidding simony and married clergy, most of his clergy refused to obey. The next year his support of Gregory's decree forbidding lay investiture added Emperor Henry to the list of his enemies, and he was driven from his see. He went to Rome, was appointed apostolic delegate to Germany by Gregory, and was again driven from his see when he returned there in 1081. He spent the rest of his life in the abbey of Göttweig, Austria, still working to reform his see. His cult was confirmed by Pope Leo XIII. August 8.

ALTO (d. c. 760). Probably an Irishman, he became a hermit near Augsburg, Germany, about 743. He so impressed King Pepin by his holiness and missionary activities that Pepin gave Alto a parcel of land near Altomünster, Bavaria, on which Alto built a monastery. February 7.

ALVAREZ OF CORDOVA, BL. (d. c. 1430). Born either in Lisbon, Portugal, or Cordova, Spain, he entered the Dominican convent at Cordova in 1368.

He became known for his preaching prowess in Spain and Italy, was confessor and adviser of Queen Catherine, John of Gaunt's daughter, and tutor of King John II in his youth, reformed the court, and then left the court to found a monastery near Cordova. There the Escalaceli (Ladder of Heaven) that he built became a center of religious devotion. He successfully led the opposition to antipope Benedict XII (Peter de Luna), and by the time of his death was famous all over Spain for his teaching, preaching, asceticism, and holiness. His cult was confirmed in 1741. February 19.

ALVAREZ, BL. BARTHOLOMEW (d. 1737). Born near Braganza, Portugal, he joined the Jesuits in 1723, was sent as a missionary to Tonkin, Indochina, labored there until 1736, when he was arrested, and was beheaded in 1737 with Bl. Emmanuele d'Abreau, Jon Gaspard Cratz, and Vincent da Cunha for his faith. January 12.

ALYPIUS (c. 360–430). Born at Tagaste, North Africa, he was a close friend of St. Augustine from their childhoods, and studied under him at Carthage, becoming a Manichaean with him until his father forbade him to associate with Augustine. Alypius went to Rome to study law, rejoined Augustine when he came to Rome, accompanied him to Milan, and was baptized with Augustine there in 387. Alypius was with Augustine at Cassiciacum and returned to Africa with him in 388. They lived in a community established by Augustine dedicated to prayer and penance at Tagaste for three years, and then they went to Hippo, where they were both ordained. After a pilgrimage to Palestine, Alypius became bishop of Tagaste about 393, served for more than three decades, and was the confidant and aide of Augustine

for the rest of his life. He is prominently featured in the dialogues Augustine wrote at Cassiciacum. His name is also spelled Alipius. August 18.

AMADEUS OF LAUSANNE, BL. (1110–59). Of the royal house of Franconia, he was born in the family castle at Chatte, Dauphiné, was educated at Bonnevaux, and then went to Cluny with his father, who had become a Cistercian monk in 1118. Amadeus then spent some time in the household of Henry V but soon left in 1124 to become a Cistercian at Clairvaux. In 1139, he was appointed abbot of Hautecombe, Savoy, and consolidated the Reform that had been instituted there a few years earlier. In 1144 he was appointed bishop of Lausanne. He acted as coregent for Humbert when the latter's father, Duke Amadeus III of Savoy, went on the Second Crusade, and in 1155 he was appointed chancellor of Burgundy by Frederick Barbarossa. His cult was approved in 1910. January 28.

AMADEUS OF PORTUGAL, BL. (1420–82). João Mendes da Silva was born in Portugal, the son of the count of Viana and brother of Bl. Beatrice da Silva. He married but soon after entered a Hieronymite monastery in Spain, and then about 1452 joined the Franciscans as a lay brother at Ubeda, Lombardy. He was ordained in 1459 and soon was widely known for his holiness and miracles. He set about reforming the Franciscans, and in 1469 he founded Notre Dame de la Paix convent in Milan, which became the center of his reform, which spread all over Italy. He was confessor for the Pope for a time but then returned to Milan, where he died. His followers were called Amadeans or Amadists. August 10.

AMADEUS IX OF SAXONY, BL. (1435–72). Son of Duke Louis I of Savoy and grandson of Amadeus VIII of Savoy (antipope Felix V), he was born at Thonon, Savoy, and was betrothed when an infant, as a peace gesture, to Yolanda, daughter of Charles VII of France; the couple were married in 1451. He succeeded his father as duke of Savoy, was known for his private austerities, almsgiving, and concern for the poor, and administered the dukedom well, though some historians believe his vacillating policies caused great dissension in Savoy. A victim of epilepsy from childhood, he resigned his dukedom to his wife, which set off a revolt and caused his imprisonment. He was freed by his brother-in-law, King Louis XI of France, but died soon after, on March 30. He was beatified in 1677.

AMADOUR (no date). Also known as Amator, fanciful legend has him a servant in the household of the Holy Family. He married St. Veronica, was driven from Palestine by a persecution of Christians, and went to Gaul, where he evangelized the area around Bordeaux. He went to Rome, where he witnessed the deaths of Peter and Paul, and then returned to Gaul, where he continued his missionary activities and founded several monasteries. When Veronica died he became a hermit at Quercy, where he built a shrine to our Lady. A shrine at Quercy called Rocamadour did in fact become a great sanctuary. August 20.

AMALBURGA (d. c. 690). Born in Brabant, a relative of Pepin of Landen, she married Count Witger and the couple had three children. After her husband became a Benedictine monk at Lobbes, she became a Benedictine nun at Mauberg, Flanders, where she died. Her story is often confused with that of another Amalburga (d. 770), a nun in Munsterbilzen, Belgium, whom a spurious legend has a woman of great beauty who was harassed by King Pepin when

she refused to marry his son Charles. July 10.

AMAND (c. 584–c. 679). Born at Nantes, Lower Poitou, France, he became a monk about 604 at a monastery on the island of Yeu, was ordained at Tours, and then lived as a hermit for fifteen years at Bourges. On his return from a pilgrimage to Rome, he was consecrated a missionary bishop in 629, with no see, and devoted himself to missionary activities in Flanders, Carinthia, and probably Germany. He was banished for censuring King Dagobert I, was recalled, and then despite initial difficulties, was highly successful in evangelizing the area around Ghent. He founded numerous monasteries in Belgium, may have been chosen bishop of Maestricht, but after three years resigned to return to missionary work. He spent the last years of his life as abbot of Elnon, where he died. February 6.

AMANDUS (d. c. 431). Ordained a priest by Bishop Delphinus of Bordeaux, Amandus instructed St. Paulinus of Nola in the faith, had a lifelong correspondence with him, and succeeded Delphinus as bishop of Bordeaux about 400. Amandus resigned the see to St. Severinus but resumed it on Severinus' death about 405 and was noted for his holiness and episcopal ability. June 18.

AMANNI, BL. MARCOLINO (1317–97). Born at Forlì, Italy, he joined the Dominicans when only ten, lived a life of great holiness and austerity, and died on January 2 at Forlì. His cult was confirmed in 1750. January 24.

AMANTIUS (date unknown). Said to have been bishop of Noyon, France, he evangelized the area around Cannes, where he and five other priests, three of whom were his brothers, were martyred for their faith. June 6.

AMANTIUS (d. 120). *See* Getulius.

AMARIN (d. 676). *See* Praejectus.

AMASIUS (d. 356). A Greek who was forced to leave his native land because of an Arian persecution, he immigrated to Italy and became bishop of Teano there in 346. January 23.

AMATA, BL. (13th century). *See* Diana, Bl.

AMATOR. *See* Amadour.

AMATOR (d. 418). The son of influential parents in Auxerre, France, and also known as Amatre, his story is told in a fictional and unreliable biography written a century and a half after his death. According to it, he was affianced against his will, had the unusual experience of having Bishop Valerian read the rites for the ordination of a deacon at his wedding instead of the wedding rite, and convinced his fiancée to live a life of virginity. She entered a convent and he became a priest, was later made bishop of Auxerre, was successful in conversion work, built churches, and was credited with performing miracles. He was forced to leave his see when he was threatened with death by Germanus, the governor of Auxerre, for interfering with an old pagan rite performed by the governor. On his return, he tricked Germanus into the cathedral and made him bishop-designate of Auxerre. There is a strong possibility that Amator was the bishop who ordained St. Patrick. Amator died at Auxerre. May 1.

AMATRE. *See* Amator.

AMATUS (d. c. 630). Born in Grenoble, France, of a Gallo-Roman family, and also known as Amé, he was taken as a child to St. Maurice abbey at Agaunum, where he spent the next thirty years. He became a Benedictine monk there and during his last few years at the abbey, he lived as a hermit. In 614, at the instigation of St. Eustace, he became a monk at the monastery of Luxeuil. He was responsible for the conversion of Romaric, a Merovingian nobleman, who gave his belongings to the poor, became a monk at Luxeuil, and in about 620 founded a double monastery at Habendum (later renamed Remiremont) with Amatus its first abbot. Amatus spent the last years of his life there and died there. September 13.

AMBOISE, BL. FRANCES D' (1427–85). Daughter of Louis d'Amboise, she was betrothed at four to the son of Duke John V of Brittany, raised at John's court, and when fifteen was married to John's son Peter. Peter became duke in 1450, and Frances devoted herself to charitable works. When Peter died in 1457, she resisted the efforts of King Louis XI to have her marry, founded a Poor Clare convent at Nantes and a Carmelite convent at Vannes in 1463, and became a nun at Vannes in 1468. She was elected prioress in 1472, founded another Carmelite convent at Couets, and died there. Her cult was approved in 1863. November 5.

AMBROSE (d. c. 250). A wealthy nobleman at Alexandria, Egypt, he became a friend of Origen and aided him financially. Ambrose was imprisoned during Maximinus' persecution but was later released. March 17.

AMBROSE (c. 340–97). Born in Trier, Germany, son of Ambrose, the practorian prefect of Gaul, he was taken back to Rome when a child on the death of his father. He became a lawyer there noted for his oratory and learning. His success led Ancius Probus, praetorian prefect of Italy, to name him his assessor, and Emperor Valentinian appointed him governor of Liguria and Aemilia with his capital at Milan about 372, a position he filled with great ability and justice. In 374 the death of Auxentius, bishop of Milan and an Arian, threw the city into turmoil as Arians and Catholics fought to have their candidate made bishop. When Ambrose, nominally a Christian but not yet baptized, went to the cathedral to attempt to quiet the seething passions, he was unanimously elected bishop by all parties. Despite his refusal to accept the office, he was forced to do so when the Emperor confirmed the election. He was baptized and on December 7, 374, was consecrated bishop. He gave away all his possessions, began a study of theology, the Bible, and the great Christian writers under his former tutor, Simplician, and began to live a life of great austerity. He soon became the most eloquent preacher of his day and the most formidable Catholic opponent of Arianism in the West. He became an adviser to Emperor Gratian and in 379 persuaded him to outlaw Arianism in the West. In 383, when Emperor Gratian was killed in battle by Maximus, Ambrose persuaded Maximus not to attempt to extend his domain into Italy against the new young Emperor Valentinian II. Ambrose was successful in defeating an attempt by Quintus Aurelius Symmachus to restore the cult of the goddess of victory in Rome, and in 385 successfully resisted Valentinian's order to turn over several churches in Milan to a group headed by Valentinian's mother, Empress Justina, a secret Arian. In 386, Ambrose flatly refused to obey an imperial edict that practically proscribed Catholic gatherings and forbade any opposition to turning churches over to Arians. When the conflict between Catholics and Arians deepened, Maximus invaded Italy despite Ambrose's pleas. Valentinian and Justina fled and sought the aid of Eastern Emperor Theodosius I, who defeated Maximus

and had him executed in Pannonia and restored Valentinian to the throne; Theodosius now controlled both Eastern and Western empires. At Milan Theodosius convinced Valentinian to denounce Arianism and recognize Ambrose, but himself soon came into conflict with Ambrose when Ambrose denounced his order to the bishop of Kallinikum, Mesopotamia, to rebuild a Jewish synagogue destroyed by the Christians there, an order he rescinded. In 390, the two clashed again when Theodosius' troops massacred some seven thousand people in Thessalonica in reprisal for the murder of the governor, Butheric, and several of his officers. Ambrose denounced the Emperor for his action and refused him the sacraments until he performed a severe public penance—which Theodosius did. In 393, Valentinian II was murdered in Gaul by Arbogastes, whose envoy, Eugenius, had attempted to restore paganism. Ambrose denounced the murder, and the defeat and execution of Arbogastes at Aquileia by Theodosius finally ended paganism in the Empire. When Theodosius died a few months after his victory, it was in the arms of Ambrose, who preached his funeral oration. Ambrose died two years later, in Milan, on April 4. Ambrose was one of the great figures of early Christianity, and more than any other man he was responsible for the rise of Christianity in the West as the Roman Empire was dying. A fierce defender of the independence of the Church against the secular authority, he wrote profusely on the Bible, theology, asceticism, mainly based on his sermons, and numerous homilies, psalms, and hymns written in iambic dimeter that became the standard for Western hymnody. He brought St. Augustine, who revered him, back to his Catholic faith, baptizing him in 387, and was considered by his contemporaries as the exemplar par excellence of what a bishop should be—holy, learned, courageous, patient, and immovable when necessary for the faith—a worthy Doctor of the Church. His best-known works are *De officiis ministrorum*, a treatise on Christian ethics especially directed to the clergy, *De virginibus*, written for his sister St. Marcellina, and *De fide*, written against the Arians for Gratian. December 7.

AMBROSE AUTPERT (d. c. 778). An official at the court of King Pepin the Short, Ambrose Autpert was so impressed by the monks of St. Vincent monastery at Benevento, Italy, while visiting there while on the King's business in Italy that he became a Benedictine monk there, and was ordained. A tutor and friend of Charlemagne, he became known for his holiness and learning, for the lives of the saints, theological treatises, and for a commentary on Revelation that he wrote. He was elected abbot of St. Vincent's in a disputed election and died on the way to Rome, where Pope Adrian I had summoned both candidates to settle the matter. July 19.

AMBROSE OF SIENA, BL. *See* Sansedoni, Bl. Ambrose.

AMÉ. *See* Amatus.

AMIAS, BL. JOHN (d. 1589). Born near Wakefield, England, he became a cloth dealer there, married, and when widowed went to study at Douai College in Rheims, where he was ordained in 1581. He was sent on the English mission, worked among the Catholics there for seven or eight years, and then was arrested. Convicted of treason because of his priesthood, he was hanged, drawn, and quartered at York with Bl. Robert Dalby on March 16. Amias was beatified in 1929.

AMICI, BL. BERNARDINO (1420–1503). Born at Fossa, Italy, he studied at

nearby Aquila and law at Perugia, and joined the Franciscans there in 1445. He was ordained, began preaching, and soon had a reputation for his effective preaching. In 1464, he resolved the quarrels of the monks of different nationalities of Dalmatia and Bosnia by uniting them into one province, refused the see of Aquila when it was offered to him, and died at St. Julian friary near Aquila. He wrote a biography of St. Bernardino of Siena and *Chronicle of the Friars Minor of the Observance*. His cult was approved in 1828. November 27.

AMICUS (c. 925–c. 1045). A priest at Camerino, Italy, he became a hermit, then a Benedictine monk, and later resumed his eremitical life in the Abruzzi, where he attracted a following. He spent the last years of his life at St. Stephen's monastery in Fonteavellana, where he died reputedly at the age of 120. November 3.

AMIDEI, BARTHOLOMEW (d. 1276). *See* Monaldo, Buonfiglio.

AMMIANUS (d. c. 251). *See* Myrope.

AMMON (d. 250). During the trial of a group of Egyptian Christians during Decius' persecution, five of the soldiers guarding the prisoners, Ammon, Zeno, Ptolemy, Ingenes, and Theophilus, exhorted a Christian wavering under torture to stand fast in his faith. When the judge saw what they were doing he had them added to the prisoners and then had them all beheaded. December 20.

AMMON (c. 288–c. 350). When his wealthy parents died, he allowed himself to be married against his will when he was twenty-two but persuaded his wife to live with him as sister and brother. After eighteen years of this marriage, he retired to the desolate swampland of

Nitria, seventy miles from Alexandria, to live as a hermit. He soon attracted disciples with his holiness, austerities, mortifications, and miracles, and on the advice of St. Antony established a loosely organized monastery for them—probably the first monastery in Nitria; in time it attracted thousands to an eremitical way of life. October 4.

AMMONARIA (d. 250). *See* Epimachus.

AMMONIUS (d. 250). He and Moseus, a fellow soldier, were sentenced to life imprisonment in the mines of Bithynia but were later burned to death at Astas for their faith. January 18.

AMPHILOCHIUS (d. 400). Born in Cappadocia and a close friend of his cousin St. Gregory Nazianzen and of St. Basil, with whom he studied at Constantinople, he became a rhetor at Constantinople, and when beset with financial troubles, retired to his father's home near Nazianzen to care for his aged parent. He was appointed bishop of Iconium in 374, probably at Basil's instigation, against his wishes. He was a vigorous opponent of the Arian heresy, was active in the same cause at the Council of Constantinople in 381, and was responsible for the decrees of Emperor Theodosius I forbidding Arians to hold meetings. Amphilocius also fought the Messalians and their belief that prayer alone was necessary for salvation. Some of his correspondence with Gregory and Basil is still extant. November 23.

AMPHION (4th century). Bishop of Epiphania, Cilicia, he was elected bishop of Nicomedia by the Catholics at the outbreak of the Arian heresy. He attended the Council of Nicaea in 325, and was highly praised by St. Athanasius. June 12.

AMPLIATUS (1st century). He is mentioned by St. Paul (Rom. 16:8–9) with

SS. Narcissus and Urban and others. According to tradition, he was made a bishop and with Narcissus and Urban preached in the Balkans with St. Andrew, where the three suffered martyrdom. October 31.

ANACLETUS. *See* Cletus.

ANANIAS (1st century). The disciple who was commanded by the Lord to seek out Saul, he brought Saul's eyesight back by laying hands on him and then baptized him (Acts 9:10–19), bringing to Christianity one of its greatest missionaries, Paul. According to tradition, Ananias worked as a missionary in Damascus and Eleutheropolis, and suffered martyrdom. January 25.

ANANIAS (d. 341). *See* Simeon Barsabae.

ANASTASIA (d. c. 65). *See* Basilissa.

ANASTASIA (d. c. 257). Eastern tradition has her a woman of twenty living in Rome in a community of virgins consecrated to God who was subjected to horrible tortures by order of the prefect, Probus, during Valerian's persecution and then beheaded. When she asked for water, Cyril brought her some; whereupon he too was executed. The whole story is probably a pious fiction. October 28.

ANASTASIA (d. c. 304). Possibly a native of Sirmium, Pannonia, she was martyred during Diocletian's persecution of Christians there. According to legendary sources she was the daughter of Praetextatus, a noble Roman, and married Publius, a pagan. On the death of Publius while he was on a mission to Persia, she went to Aquileia to minister to the Christians suffering persecution during Diocletian's persecution, was herself arrested as a Christian, and was burned to death on the island of Palmaria after a ship she was on with a group of pagan prisoners was miraculously rescued by St. Theodota. She has been venerated in Rome since the fifth century, but aside from that fact all else about her is probably pious fiction. December 25.

ANASTASIA PATRICIA (6th century). A fanciful and romantic legend according to which she was the beautiful daughter of an Egyptian nobleman and a lady-in-waiting at the court of Emperor Justinian in Constantinople. To escape the attentions of the Emperor, she left the court and entered a convent in Alexandria. On the death of Justinian's wife, Theodora, the Emperor again sought her, whereupon she fled to the desert and met Abbot Daniel, who allowed her to dress as a monk and live as a hermit in his community, where she lived a solitary life of constant prayer and austerity until her death twenty-eight years later. March 10.

ANASTASIUS (d. 251). A tribune in Emperor Decius' army, he was converted to Christianity by the constancy and courage of the Christian martyrs he was torturing in his official capacity. He, his family, and his servants were all beheaded when it was discovered he was Christian a few days later. May 11.

ANASTASIUS (d. c. 304). Born at Aquileia, near Venice, he was a fuller who moved to Split, Dalmatia, where he was executed by being cast into the sea with a rock around his neck during Diocletian's persecution when he refused to renounce his faith. September 7.

ANASTASIUS (d. 583). A deacon at Cordova, Spain, he became a Benedictine monk at the double monastery at Tábanos near Cordova. He was beheaded with St. Felix, a native of Alcala who had been a monk at Asturias before coming to Tábanos, and St. Digna, a nun

in the convent of the double monastery, by order of the Moorish caliph, for their faith. June 14.

ANASTASIUS I (d. 404). Born in Rome, the son of Maximus, he was elected Pope on November 27, 399. His pontificate was marked by his condemnation of Origen, his urging the African bishops to continue their opposition to Donatism, and his personal holiness and poverty. He died in Rome. December 19.

ANASTASIUS I (d. 599). Patriarch of Antioch, he was a taciturn man of great learning and holiness who was banished from his see by Emperor Justin II for his opposition to several imperial decrees about the body of Christ and was not restored to his see until twenty-three years later, in 573, by Pope St. Gregory the Great and Emperor Maurice. April 21.

ANASTASIUS II (d. 609). The successor of Anastasius I as patriarch of Antioch in 599, he was urged by Pope St. Gregory the Great to rid his see of simony when the Pope approved his orthodoxy and his election. He was murdered by an uprising of Syrian Jews rebelling against their forced conversion to Christianity by Emperor Phocas. December 21.

ANASTASIUS (d. c. 1040). The first archbishop of Hungary, he was probably a Croat or a Czech from Bohemia named Radla who became a monk at Brevno taking the name Anastasius (or Astrik or Astericus). He engaged in missionary work among the Magyars, was in the service of the wife of Duke Géza in 997, and was named first abbot of St. Martin's in Pannonhalma, the first monastery in Hungary, which Géza founded. When St. Stephen succeeded his father Géza as duke, Anastasius set up a hierarchy, renewed his evangelization work among the Magyars, to which he devoted the rest of his life, and was appointed archbishop of the Hungarian Church with his see probably at Kalocsa. A visit to Pope Sylvester II in Rome probably was responsible for Stephen receiving papal recognition as King of the Hungarians and his crowning by Emperor Otto III in 1001 with a crown sent by the Pope to him through Anastasius. He worked closely with Stephen the rest of his life and died two years after him. November 12.

ANASTASIUS (c. 1020–85). Born in Venice, he became a monk at Mont St. Michel but left to live as a hermit on the island of Tombelaine off the coast of Normandy. About 1066 St. Hugh convinced him to become a monk at Cluny; seven years later he went on a mission to Spain for Pope St. Gregory VII, and on his return in about 1080 spent another seven years at Cluny before resuming his eremitical life near Toulouse. He died on the way back to Cluny. October 16.

ANASTASIUS THE PERSIAN (d. 628). A soldier named Magundat in the Persian army, he was attracted to Christianity when he saw the relics of the True Cross brought back by Chosroës from the sack of Jerusalem to Persia in 614, left the army, and was baptized in Jerusalem by Bishop Modestus, taking the name Anastasius. He became a monk at Jerusalem in 621, went to Caesarea, Palestine, and was arrested there for preaching against pagan worship. He was tortured, and when he would not recant and worship the sun, he was sent to King Chosroës in Bethsaloe, Assyria. When further torture did not shake him, he was strangled and then beheaded after sixty-eight other Christians had met a similar fate in his presence. January 22.

ANASTASIUS THE SINAITE (d. c. 700). Born in Alexandria, he became a hermit on Mount Sinai and abbot of the community there. He was so active in his opposition to monophysites, Monothelites, and Jews, he was called "the new Moses." He was an active and influential participant in the Christological controversies of his times and wrote several ascetical and theological treatises, some of which are still extant. April 21.

ANATOLIA (d. c. 250). With her sister Victoria, she refused importunate suitors; both were imprisoned and starved by their suitors but persisted in refusing marriage. Anatolia was converted to Christianity and converted many in Picenum before being denounced for her faith, for which she was tortured and executed at Thora on Lake Velino in Italy. When Victoria refused to sacrifice to pagan gods, she too was executed, perhaps at Tribulano. The guard was converted by their example and was also martyred. Their whole story is probably a pious myth, though they did actually live. December 23.

ANATOLIUS (d. c. 283). A native of Alexandria, he was renowned as a philosopher, scientist, and mathematician, and was head of the Aristotelian school in Alexandria. During a Roman attack on Brychion, a suburb of Alexandria, during Prefect Aemilian's revolt in 262, he was able to secure safe passage for noncombatants. He later went to Palestine, where he was an assistant to the bishop of Caesarea, and in 269 he was chosen bishop of Laodicea, Syria, succeeding an old friend, Eusebius, on his death. July 3.

ANATOLIUS (d. 458). A native of Alexandria, he had opposed Nestorianism at the Council of Ephesus, and was appointed patriarch of Constantinople, succeeding St. Flavian. Because he was consecrated by Dioscorus, a monophysite, he was suspect by Pope St. Leo but was accepted as patriarch when he required his metropolitans to accept Leo's *Tome* to Flavian condemning Nestorius and Eutyches. Anatolius was active in the Council of Chalcedon unequivocally accepting papal authority, though Leo refused to accept the decree that Constantinople outranked the sees of Alexandria and Antioch. There has been much controversy over some of Anatolius' actions, and Baronius condemned him for his ambivalent attitude to heresy, his personal ambition, and the methods employed to have him made patriarch. He died on July 3.

ANCINA, BL. JUVENAL (1545–1604). Born at Fossano, Piedmont, Italy, of a distinguished family, and baptized John Juvenal, he studied at Montpellier, Savoy, Padua, and Turin, and received his doctorates in medicine and philosophy. He was appointed professor of medicine at Turin in 1569 and built up a lucrative practice, devoting much of his time to treating the sick poor *gratis*. In 1575, he went to Rome as private physician to the Duke of Savoy's ambassador to the Holy See, Frederick Madrucci, studied theology under Robert Bellarmine, and met Baronius and Philip Neri. In 1578, with his brother John Matthew, he was admitted to the Congregation of the Oratory by Philip Neri. Ancina was ordained in 1582 and four years later was sent to the Naples Oratory. He became noted for his preaching (he was called "the Son of Thunder"), conversions, and care of the sick and the poor. He organized a group of women into a confraternity to help at the Hospital for the Incurables and became interested in church music. He was recalled to the Rome Oratory in 1596 to take the place of Baronius, who had been made a cardinal, worked in the Piedmont area, met St. Francis de Sales, and in 1602 was appointed bishop of Saluzzo. While on a visitation of his diocese, he was poisoned by a friar he had reprimanded for having an affair with a nun and died a few days later at Saluzzo, on August 31. Throughout his life, he was credited with miracles and the gift of prophecy. He was beatified in 1869.

ANDEOL. *See* Antiochus (4th–5th centuries).

ANDETON, BL. ROBERT (d. 1586). Born at Chorley, Lancashire, England, he was educated at Oxford and ordained in 1585 at Rheims with Bl. William Marsden, a fellow Lancashireman who had also been educated at Oxford. Both were sent on the English mission but never reached England. They were forced to land on the Isle of Wight when their ship was driven off course, arrested when it was found they were priests, and then sentenced to death for their priesthood. After a legal pretense of consultation with London by the authorities on Wight, their sentence was upheld and they were hanged on Wight on April 25. They were beatified in 1929.

ANDLAYER, BL. MODESTE (1847–1900). *See* Mangin, Bl. Leon.

ANDLEBY, BL. WILLIAM (d. 1597). Born at Etton, Yorkshire, England, he was raised a Protestant, educated at Cambridge, and while on the way to join the Dutch to fight the Spaniards was converted to Catholicism by Dr. Allen at Douai. Andleby was ordained in 1577, sent on the English mission, and worked among the Catholics in Yorkshire and Lincolnshire for the next twenty years. He was finally caught and hanged, drawn, and quartered at York on July 4 for his Catholic priesthood. Also hanged with him was Thomas Warcop for giving him shelter. They were beatified in 1929.

ANDOCHIUS (2nd century). A priest sent with Thyrsus, a deacon, to Gaul by St. Polycarp, bishop of Smyrna, as a missionary, he settled at Autun, converted the merchant, Felix, at whose home he was staying, and then the three of them were tortured and put to death for their faith. September 24.

ANDREASI, BL. OSANNA (1449–1505). Born on January 17 at Mantua, Italy, of noble parents, she is said to have received her first supernatural experience, a vision of Paradise, when only five. She resisted her father's desire for her to marry, and when seventeen she became a Dominican tertiary novice, though she was not to be professed until thirty-seven years later. She practiced great austerities, spent a fortune aiding the poor, and experienced numerous visions of Christ, in which she participated in the Passion, and of our Lady. In 1478, Duke Frederick of Mantua placed her in charge of his household when he went off to war. She was greatly influenced by Savanorola, deploring as he did the low moral tone of Italian life, and in turn influenced Girolamo da Monte Oliveto, who published *Spiritual Colloquies,* a record of their conversations on spiritual matters, after her death on June 20. Her cult was approved by Popes Leo X and Innocent XIV.

ANDREW (1st century). The son of John, a fisherman, and brother of Simon Peter, he was a native of Bethsaida, Galilee, and a fisherman. He became a disciple of John the Baptist, and when he met Jesus at Jesus' baptism by the Baptist, Andrew was called to be Christ's first disciple and then brought Peter to Jesus. For a time, they followed him intermittently, but when the Savior returned to Galilee, he called them from their fishing, saying he would make them fishers of men. After Jesus' death, he is reputed to have preached in Scythia and Greece, and later a dubious tradition has him going to Byzantium, where he appointed Stachys bishop. Where and how he died are uncertain, but a very old tradition has him crucified at Patras, Acaia, on an X-shaped cross. He is the patron saint of Russia, though the tradition he preached there is unfounded, and of Scotland, where another tradition says some of his relics were brought in the fourth century in consequence of a dream to St. Rule, who was custodian of Andrew's relics. Reportedly an angel guided Rule to a place called St. Andrew's, and he became its first bishop and evangelized the Scots in the area for three decades. November 30.

ANDREW (1st century). He and St. Aponius suffered martyrdom for their faith during the persecution launched by King Herod in which St. James the Greater was beheaded (Acts 12). February 10.

ANDREW (d. 251). *See* Peter of Lampsacus.

ANDREW (d. c. 880). A young Irishman, he accompanied his teacher, St. Donatus, to Rome on a pilgrimage. On their return, they stopped at Fiesole, where Donatus supposedly was miraculously made bishop and ordained Andrew deacon. Andrew founded a monastery, rebuilt a church, and was known for his holiness. The whole story is based on a suspect legend. August 22.

ANDREW OF ANAGNI, BL. (d. 1302). A nephew of Pope Alexander IV, Andrew Conti was born at Anagni, Italy, and became a Franciscan lay brother. He refused a cardinalate from Pope Boniface VIII to continue his humble way of life. Andrew died on February 1, and was beatified in 1724. February 17.

ANDREW OF ANTIOCH, BL. (c. 1268– c. 1348). Born in Antioch of Norman stock, he became an Augustinian canon at the Holy Sepulcher basilica in Jerusalem and was appointed to the honorary but meaningless position of keybearer—meaningless since the Mohammedans possessed the actual keys and ruled the city at that time. He was sent to tour Augustinian houses in Europe to raise funds for the canons but died while on the trip at Annecy, Savoy, on March 27, greatly revered for his holiness. November 30.

ANDREW AVELLINO. *See* Avellino, Andrew.

ANDREW CACCIOLI, BL. (d. 1254). Born at Spello, Italy, he became a diocesan priest at Spoleto, and when twenty-nine he gave all his considerable wealth to the poor and was received into the Franciscans by St. Francis. Andrew engaged in missionary work in Lombardy, favored a strict interpretation of Francis' rule against Brother Elias' proposed new relaxed rule, and was imprisoned for his stand during the strife that rent the Franciscans over the interpretation of Francis' rule after his death. He directed the Poor Clares in Spello and died there in a house he had founded, venerated for the visions he experienced and his reported miracles. His cult was confirmed by Pope Clement XII. June 3.

ANDREW THE CALYBITE (d. 766). Also called Andrew of Crete, where he was born, he was imprisoned when he protested the torture of several Christians to Emperor Constantine V in Constantinople and accused him of heresy for his campaign against images. For his action, he was scourged, and while being dragged through the streets was stabbed by an iconoclast and died from the wound. October 20.

ANDREW OF CRETE (c. 660–c. 740). Born in Damascus, he became a monk at St. Sabas in Jerusalem when fifteen, was sent to Constantinople by Patriarch Theodore of Jerusalem to accept the decrees of the Council of Constantinople in 685, and stayed on there as head of an orphanage and of an old men's home. He was named archbishop of Gortyna, Crete, and in 712 attended a synod invoked by Phillipicus Bardanes, a monothelite, who had seized the imperial crown and denounced the decisions of the Council of Constantinople. When Anastasius II defeated Bardanes, Pope Constantine accepted the explanation of Andrew's patriarch that he had attended under duress. Also surnamed "of Jerusalem," Andrew was known as a forceful preacher, wrote many hymns, and is believed to have inaugurated a form of hymnody known as *kanon* in the Byzantine liturgy. July 4.

ANDREW OF CRETE. *See* Andrew the Calybite.

ANDREW FRANCHI BOCCAGNI, BL. (1335–1401). Born in Pistoia of a noble family, he joined the Dominicans, became a renowned preacher, and after serving as prior at three convents in Italy, was appointed bishop of Pistoia in 1378. He lived simply, ruled well, and helped the poor but resigned in 1401 and retired to his former convent at Pistoia, where he died on May 26. His cult was confirmed for Pistoia and the Dominicans in 1921. May 30.

ANDREW DE' GALLERANI, BL. (d. 1251). A Sienese soldier who had fought against the Orvietans, he devoted himself to works of mercy after he had killed a man. He founded a hospital and the Society of Mercy to minister to the sick in Siena and had many miracles attributed to him. His Society was merged with the Dominicans in 1308. He is also known as Andrew of Siena. March 19.

ANDREW OF JERUSALEM. *See* Andrew of Crete.

ANDREW OF MONTEREALE, BL. (1397–1480). Born in Mascioni, Italy, he joined the Augustinian Hermits when only fourteen, was ordained, and preached throughout Italy and France the next half century. Renowned for his holiness, austerity, and learning, he was for a time provincial of Umbria. His cult was confirmed in 1764. April 12.

ANDREW GREGHO OF PESCHIERA, BL. (d. 1485). Of Greek ancestry, he was born at Peschiera, near Verona, Italy, joined the Dominicans in Brescia when a youth, studied at San Marco friary in Florence, and was ordained. He worked as a missionary in the Valtelline district along the Swiss-Italian border for forty-five years in the face of great opposition from the irreligious people of the area and helped found a Dominican house at Morbegno, where he died on January 18 in the same austerity, humility, and poverty he had lived all his religious life. January 19.

ANDREW OEXNER OF RINN, BL. (1459–62). Born in Rinn, near Innsbruck, he was put in the care of his Uncle Mayer, an innkeeper, when he was two years old. When the child's body was found slashed with knives and hanging from a tree, Mayer said he had sold him to Jewish peddlers, as he had not wanted to be bothered with his upbringing. He was judged insane and it is believed he killed the boy. However, years later in 1475, when Jews in Trent, under torture, admitted they had killed a boy in Trent, the residents of Rinn decided they had also killed Andrew. The place of his death became a shrine, miracles were reported, and Andrew was considered a martyr. Although Pope Benedict XV allowed a local cult in 1750, he turned down a request in 1755 that Andrew be canonized. July 12.

ANDREW OF SIENA, BL. See Andrew De' Gallerani, Bl.

ANDREW OF STRUMI, BL. (d. 1097). Born at Parma, Italy, and known as "the Ligurian," he was a follower of Arialdo, a deacon who was the leader in the Pataria reform movement in Milan. When Arialdo was murdered, Andrew became a Vallombrosan, and later was made abbot of San Fedele in Strumi. He negotiated a peace between Florence and Arezzo, was instrumental in having several churches and priories in the two cities become associated with the Vallombrosans, and wrote several lives of religious. March 10.

ANDREW THE TRIBUNE (d. c. 300). A tribune in the army of Galerius sent by Emperor Diocletian against the Persians, he called upon Christ in a battle, and when the army was victorious, he and some of his men decided to become Christians. Discharged by their superior, Antiochus, on Galerius' orders, they were baptized by Bishop Peter of Caesarea, and then arrested by Seleucus, military governor of Cilicia. He had them executed in the Taurus Mountains in Cilicia for their faith. The story is untrustworthy, but Andrew is known in the East as "the Great Martyr." August 19.

ANDRONICUS (d. 304). See Tarachus.

ANDRONICUS (5th century). A silversmith born in Alexandria, he migrated to Antioch with his wife, Athanasia, and two children. On the death of the children, the bereaved Athanasia had a vision assuring her the children were in heaven. They decided to renounce the world, went to Egypt, and joined St. Daniels' solitaries at Skete. Daniel sent Andronicus and Athanasia to separate cells in the monastic settlement of Tabenna, with Athanasia dressed as a man. After twelve years, Andronicus met an old monk named Athanasius and the two went on pilgrimage to Jerusalem; on their return they decided to join a monastery named Eighteen near Alexandria. When the old monk died he left a note in which it was revealed that "he" was Athanasia. A week later, Andronicus died, and the two were buried together. October 9.

ANGADRISMA (c. 615–95). According to legend she was educated at Thérouanne by St. Omer and by her cousin St. Lambert. She wanted to become a nun but was promised in marriage to St. Ansbert of Chaussy. In answer to her prayers to be spared the marriage, she contracted leprosy. Ansbert married someone else, and the disease disappeared when she received the veil from St. Ouen. She later became abbess of Aroël, a Benedictine monastery near Beauvais, and was known for her holiness and the miracles she is said to have performed. October 14.

ANGELA OF FOLIGNO, BL. (c. 1248–1309). Born in Foligno, Italy, she was married to a wealthy man, and the couple had several children. She followed a frivolous style of living until a vision she experienced in 1285 changed her life. She became a Franciscan tertiary, gave away all her possessions on the death of her husband, devoted herself to a spiritual life, and gathered around her a group of tertiaries devoted to helping the poor and the sick. She experienced vivid visions, particularly of the Passion and death of Christ, accounts of which she dictated to her confessor, Friar Arnold of Foligno, at his request, and which reveal her to be one of the great Christian mystics. She died on January 4, and her cult was confirmed in 1693. She is sometimes called St. Angela. Editions of her revelations have been published in several languages, and in English as *The Book of the Divine Consolation of Bl. Angela of Foligno.* January 7.

ANGELINA ANGIOBALLI OF MARSCIANO, BL. (1377–1435). Born at Montegiove, Italy, of a noble family, she married John of Terni, count of Civitella, when fifteen, and when he died two years later, she became a Franciscan tertiary and made her home into a house for secular tertiaries living in community. Her preaching about the desirability of virginity caused great controversy, and she was accused of sorcery and Manichaeanism. King Ladislaus of Naples dismissed the charge but soon after exiled her and her companions. After a visit to Assisi in 1397, she decided to found an enclosed monastery of the third order regular of St. Francis (the first with vows and enclosure) at Foligno and secured the bishop's approval. It was so successful she established another fifteen during the rest of her life. Her cult was approved in 1825. July 13.

ANGELIS, BL. JEROME DE (d. 1623). Born at Castrogiovanni, Sicily, he abandoned his study of law to join the Jesuits at Messina, and was ordained at Lisbon. He was sent as a missionary to Japan in 1601 and served there for twenty-two years, mainly on Hondo. He was betrayed to the Japanese officials and burned to death for his Catholicism on December 4 at Yedo (Tokyo) with BB. Simon Yempo and Peter Galvez. They were beatified in 1867. December 5.

ANGELO (d. 1220). From unreliable sources, he was the son of converted Jews in Jerusalem and joined the Carmelites with his twin brother when he was eighteen. He became a hermit but after five years of the eremitical life, he went to Sicily, reputedly at the command of the Lord. He was highly successful in convert work, especially with Jews, at Palermo and Leocata, where he was stabbed to death by one Berengarius, who was enraged at his success. May 5.

ANGELO (d. 1227). *See* Daniel.

ANGELO, BL. (1226–1312). The son of Count Bernard of Torre and Vignole, he was born at Foligno, Italy, became an Augustinian at Botriolo when twenty, and founded Augustinian houses at Foligno, Gualdo Cattaneo, and in 1275 at Montefalco, where he served as prior for the next seventeen years. He spent the last twenty years of his life at Foligno, venerated for his holiness, and died there on August 27. His cult was approved in 1891.

ANGELO, BL. (1669–1739). Born at Acri, Italy, he was refused admission to the Capuchins twice but was accepted on his third attempt in 1690, and was ordained. Unsuccessful in his first sermons, he eventually became a famous preacher after a tremendous success when he preached in Naples during Lent in 1711. For the rest of his life, he preached missions in Calabria and Naples, converting thousands and performing many miracles of healing. He was reputed to have had the gifts of prophecy and bilocation, experienced visions and ecstasies, and was a sought-after confessor with the ability to see into men's souls. He died in the friary at Acri on October 30, and was beatified in 1825.

ANGELO OF FURCIO, BL. (d. 1327). Born at Furcio, Italy, he was early dedicated to the priesthood as a result of a vision his parents experienced. He was educated at his uncle's abbey in Cornaclano, and on his father's death he joined the Augustinians at Vasto d'Aimone. He spent two years studying at Paris, received his licentiate, and then became a professor of theology at the Augustinian college in Naples, where he died. His cult was confirmed in 1888. February 6.

ANGELO OF GUALDO, BL. (c. 1265–1325). Born at Gualdo, Italy, he made several pilgrimages in his youth and then became a Camaldolese lay brother. He lived as a hermit for forty years and died on January 25. His cult was approved in 1825. February 14.

ANGELO SCARPETTI OF BORGO, BL. (d. 1306). Born of a noble family at Borgo San Sepolchro, Italy, he became an Augustinian and was a fellow student of St. Nicholas of Tolentine. Angelo founded several Augustinian houses in England, lived as a hermit, and was venerated as a holy man. His cult was confirmed in 1921. February 15.

ANGILBERT (c. 740–814). Nicknamed "Homer" because of his Latin verses, he was raised at the court of Charlemagne and studied under Alcuin. He married Charlemagne's daughter, Bertha (some scholars believe it was an affair rather than a marriage), but turned to the religious life when his prayers for a successful resistance to a Danish invasion were answered when a storm scattered the Danish fleet. Bertha entered a convent and he became a monk, spending the last years of his life at Centula, of which he was abbot and where he established a library. He also introduced continuous chanting in the abbey, using his three hundred monks in relays to do so. He was a close friend and confidant of Charlemagne, was his court chaplain and privy councilor, undertook several diplomatic missions for the Emperor, and was one of the executors of the Emperor's will. February 18.

ANIANUS (1st century). The apochryphal Acts of Mark have him a shoemaker in Alexandria who became second bishop of the city. Other sources have him a noble who was named bishop by Mark, whom he succeeded. April 25.

ANIANUS (d. c. 453). Born at Vienne, France, he became a hermit there and then went to Orleans, where he was ordained by Bishop Evurtius, whom he succeeded as bishop of Vienne when Evurtius died. Anianus helped defend Orleans against Attila and was responsible for securing the help of the Roman general Aetius who drove Attila from the city. Anianus is also known as Aignan. November 17.

ANICETUS (d. c. 166). A Syrian from Emesa, he became Pope about 155 and actively opposed Marcionism and Gnosticism. His pontificate saw the appearance of the controversy between East and West over the date of Easter. St. Polycarp, a disciple of John, is reported to have visited him in Rome about the dispute, which was to accelerate and grow more heated over the following centuries. April 17.

ANNA (1st century). Daughter of Phanuel and a prophetess, she was a widow of eighty-nine, living in the Temple, when the child was presented at the Temple, whereupon she prophesied he was the redeemer of Israel (Luke 2:36–38). September 1.

ANNE (1st century B.C.). According to the apochryphal *Protevangelium of James,* she was the wife of Joachim, both of whom were desolate because of their childlessness. One day while Anne was praying, an angel appeared to her and told her she would have a child, and Anne promised to dedicate the child to God. The child was Mary, mother of Jesus. Other unreliable legends have her born in Nazareth, the daughter of Akar, a nomad. She married Joachim when about twenty and gave birth to Mary when she was forty. Joachim died just after the birth of Christ. All of the above is from untrustworthy sources, and we

know nothing with certainty about the grandmother of Jesus, not even her name. July 26.

ANNE (c. 840–c. 918). Also known as Susanna, she was born in Constantinople of wealthy parents and was forced to flee when Emperor Basil the Macedonian supported the suit for her hand by one Agarenus. She went to Leucadia, Epirus, about 896 and lived there as a hermit the last twenty-two years of her life. She may be the same as Maura mentioned on November 30 in the Roman Martyrology as having suffered martyrdom in Constantinople, since Leucadia is also known as Maura. July 23.

ANNE OF ST. BARTHOLOMEW. *See* García, Bl. Anne.

ANNEMUND (d. 658). Son of the Gallo-Roman prefect at Lyons, Gaul, he was raised at the court of Dagobert I and became an adviser to Clovis II. He was appointed bishop of Lyons, became a great friend of St. Wilfrid of York, who stayed with him for three years and whom he tonsured. During the strife following the death of Clovis, both were captured by a company of soldiers at Mâcon. Annemund was slain, probably at the instigation of Ebroin, mayor of the palace, on September 28, but Wilfrid was released because he was a foreigner. Bede refers to Annemund as Dalfinus. September 28.

ANNO (1010–75). Son of Count Walter, a poor Swabian nobleman, he studied at the cathedral school of Bamberg and became its master and one of Henry III's chaplains. In 1056, Anno was appointed archbishop of Cologne and Henry's chancellor. When on the death of Henry his young son Henry IV was kidnapped in 1062, Anno acted as regent with

Archbishop Adalbert of Bremen. When Henry came of age, he retained only Adalbert and dismissed Anno. Anno supported Pope Alexander II against antipope Cadulus of Parma but was accused of maintaining relations with Cadulus by Rome; Anno was also accused of simony but was exonerated, though he evidently was guilty of nepotism. A particularly flagrant instance was when he became involved in a dispute with Count Theodoric when he appointed his nephew Conrad bishop of Trier over the vigorous objections of the clergy and laity of the see. When Conrad tried to occupy the see, he was attacked by Count Theodoric, imprisoned, and then murdered. Though very much a man of his times and constantly involved in the murky politics of his era, Anno did establish monasteries, reformed existing ones, and donated large sums of money to the poor. He spent the last years of his life doing penance at the abbey he had founded at Siegburg, and he died there on December 4.

ANSANUS (d. c. 304). Untrustworthy legend has him a Roman boy who was denounced by his father when Ansanus became a Christian at twelve. He escaped and earned the sobriquet "the Baptizer" for his many converts in Bagnorea and Siena. He was later captured and beheaded during Diocletian's persecution of the Christians. He is venerated in Siena as its first apostle. December 1.

ANSBALD (d. 886). Born in Luxembourg, of a noble family, he became a Benedictine monk at Prüm, was named abbot of St. Hubert, and in 860 became abbot of Prüm. With the help of Charles the Fat, he rebuilt Prüm after its destruction by the Normans in 882. July 12.

ANSBERT (d. c. 695). King Clotaire III's chancellor, he later became abbot of

Fontenelle and confessor of King Theodoric III. Ansbert was chosen bishop of Rouen, succeeding St. Ouen, in 684, ruled his see well but was exiled, probably for political reasons, to the monastery of Hautmont by Pepin, mayor of the palace, and died there. February 9.

ANSEGIUS (c. 770–833). Born in the Lyonnais, France, he became a Benedictine monk at Fontenelle when eighteen, and was appointed administrator of St. Sixtus abbey at Rheims and St. Menge near Chalons by Charlemagne, whose adviser he was. He was then appointed abbot of the run-down abbey of St. Germer-de-Fly in Beauvais, which he rejuvenated. He was later appointed abbot of the abbey of Luxeuil by Louis the Debonair and was successful in rehabilitating it both spiritually and physically after it had been all but destroyed by the Vandals. He was made abbot of Fontenelle in 823 and during the next decade revitalized it making its library famous, especially for its collection of capitularies. He died there on July 20.

ANSELM (c. 1033–1109). Born at Aosta, Italy, he was refused entrance to a monastery when he was fifteen because of his father's disapproval, and led a worldly life. He left home in 1056 to study in Burgundy and in 1059 became a disciple and friend of Lanfranc at Bec in Normandy. Anselm became a monk there about 1060 and three years later succeeded Lanfranc as prior when Lanfranc was elected abbot of St. Stephen's in Caen. Anselm was named abbot of Bec in 1078, a position that required him to visit England to inspect abbey property there. In 1092, the English clergy elected Anselm archbishop of Canterbury, which position had been vacant since the death of Lanfranc, who had been archbishop since 1070, three years earlier. Anselm refused to compromise the spiritual independence of the archdiocese in consequence, of which King William II (William Rufus) refused his approval. Anselm did not leave Bec until 1093, and almost on his arrival came into bitter dispute with King William. The King refused to permit the calling of needed synods and demanded an exhorbitant payment from Anselm as the price of his nomination to the see, and Anselm refused to pay it. Though some recalcitrant bishops backed William, the barons upheld Anselm. In 1097, he went to Rome, where Pope Urban I refused William's demand that he depose Anselm, whereupon William threatened to exile Anselm and confiscated diocesan properties. The Pope supported Anselm, refused his offer to resign, and ordered William to permit Anselm to return to England and to return all confiscated property to him. In 1098, at Urban's request, Anselm attended the Council of Bari and ably defended the *Filioque* of the Creed in the East-West controversy on the procession of the Holy Spirit. Anselm returned to England on the death of William in 1100 but again encountered difficulties with William's successor, Henry II, when Anselm refused the demands of the new King for lay investiture. In 1103, Anselm again went to Rome, and Pope Paschal II supported his refusal of lay investiture of bishops to Henry. Once again Anselm was threatened with exile and confiscation of Church revenues, but a reconciliation was effected when Henry renounced his right to the investiture of bishops and abbots, and Anselm in turn agreed they could pay homage to the King for their temporal possessions. The reconciliation endured for the rest of Anselm's life, and in 1108, Henry appointed him regent while he was in Normandy. In 1102, at a council in Westminster, Anselm vigorously denounced the slave trade. Though preoc-

cupied for many years with defending Church rights against English kings, Anselm was a preeminent theologian and has been called "the Father of Scholasticism." He believed revelation and reason could be harmonized and was the first to incorporate successfully the rationalism of Aristotelian dialectics into theology. He was the author of *Monologium,* on the existence of God, and *Proslogium,* which deduces God's existence from man's notion of a perfect being, which influenced the great thinkers of later ages, among them Duns Scotus, Descartes, and Hegel. Anselm's *Cur Deus homo?* was the outstanding theological treatise on the Incarnation in the Middle Ages. Among his other writings are *De fide Trinitatis, De conceptu virginali, De veritate, Liber apologeticus pro insipiente,* letters, prayers, and meditations. He died at Canterbury on April 21, and was named a Doctor of the Church in 1720.

ANSELM (1036–86). Born at Mantua, Italy, he was named bishop of Lucca in 1073 by his uncle Pope Alexander II, who had just vacated the see. Anselm immediately became embroiled in a dispute about imperial investiture and refused to accept the symbols of his office from Emperor Henry IV. Anselm eventually did, but then retired to the Cluniac monastery at Polirone and became a Benedictine monk. Recalled by Pope Gregory VII, he soon became involved with his canons over their lack of observance of an austere life. When they were placed under an interdict by the Pope and excommunicated, they revolted, were supported by the Emperor, and in 1079, drove Anselm from his see. He retired to Canossa, became spiritual director of Countess Matilda, reformed the monks and canons in the territory she controlled, and was a firm supporter of Pope Gregory's struggle to end lay investiture. After Gregory's death Pope Victor III appointed him apostolic visitor to administer several dioceses in Lombardy vacant because of the investiture struggle. He died in Mantua, held in high regard for his holiness, austerity, biblical knowledge, and learning. March 18.

ANSELM OF NONANTOLA (d. 803). Duke of Friuli and aid to Langobard King Aistulf, his brother-in-law, he was a noted and successful soldier. Always interested in religion, he founded monasteries in Fanno and Nonantola and about 753 became a Benedictine monk and abbot of Nonantola. He built hospitals and hospices, had a thousand monks under him, and developed Nonantola into a famous monastery. Aistulf's successor, Desiderius, exiled him to Monte Cassino for seven years but Charlemagne restored him to Nonantola, where he died. March 3.

ANSFRID (d. 1010). Count of Brabant and friend of Emperor Otto III, whom he served, he was named bishop of Utrecht in 994 despite some opposition. He founded a convent at Thorn and an abbey at Heiligenberg. When stricken with blindness, he retired to Heiligenberg and died there. May 11.

ANSGAR (c. 801–65). Born of a noble family near Amiens, he became a monk at Old Corbie monastery in Picardy and later at New Corbie in Westphalia. He accompanied King Harold to Denmark when the exiled King returned to his native land and engaged in missionary work there; Ansgar's success caused King Björn of Sweden to invite him to that country, and he built the first Christian church in Sweden. He became abbot of New Corbie and first archbishop of Hamburg about 831, and Pope Gregory IV appointed him legate to the Scandinavian countries. He labored at his missionary works for the next fourteen years but saw all he had accom-

plished destroyed when invading pagan Northmen in 845 destroyed Hamburg and overran the Scandinavian countries, which lapsed into paganism. He was appointed first archbishop of Bremen about 848, and the see was united with that of Hamburg by Pope Nicholas I. Ansgar again returned to Denmark and Sweden in 854 and resumed his missionary activities, converting Erik, King of Jutland. Ansgar's success was due to his great preaching ability, the austerity and holiness of his life, and the miracles he is reputed to have performed. Though called "the Apostle of the North" and the first Christian missionary in Scandinavia, the whole area lapsed into paganism again after his death at Bremen on February 3. His name is also spelled Anskar.

ANSKAR. *See* Ansgar.

ANSOVINUS (d. 840). Born at Camerino, Italy, he was ordained and then lived as a hermit at Castel-Raimondo, where his sanctity and reputed miracles attracted attention. He became confessor of Louis the Pious, was elected bishop of Camerino, and ruled until his death there. March 13.

ANSTRUDIS (d. c. 700). Also known as Austrude, she was probably the daughter of SS. Salaberga and Blandinus. She succeeded her mother as abbess of the abbey at Laon that Salaberga had founded. She incurred the enmity of Ebroin, mayor of the palace, by opposing him when her brother Baldwin was murdered and was subjected to many harassments until Bl. Pepin of Landen put her under his protection. October 17.

ANSUINUS (d. 888). *See* Ageranus.

ANSURIUS (d. 925). Elected bishop of Orense, Spanish Galicia, in 915, he helped found the Benedictine abbey of

Ribas de Sil, resigned his bishopric in 922, and spent the rest of his life as a monk at Ribas de Sil. He is also called Isauri. January 26.

ANTELLA, BENEDICT DELL' (1203–68). *See* Monaldo, Buonfiglio.

ANTHELM (1107–78). Born in the castle of Chignin near Chambéry, Savoy, he became a secular priest but joined the Carthusians about 1137. He was sent to the Grande Chartreuse, was elected seventh abbot in 1139, rebuilt its physical facilities, and established it as the mother house of the order. He called the first general chapter of the Carthusians, united the charter houses (previously under the jurisdiction of local bishops), and had Bl. John the Spaniard draw up a constitution for women wishing to live under the Carthusian rule. He resigned his abbacy in 1152 to live as a hermit but served as prior of Portes in 1154–56. On his return to Grande Chartreuse, he was active in rallying support for Pope Alexander III against antipope Victor IV, who had the backing of Emperor Frederick Barbarossa. Over his objections, Anthelm was named bishop of Belley in 1163. He instituted widespread reforms in the see, restored a celibate clergy, punished wrongdoers, and excommunicated Count Humbert III of Maurienne when one of his priests was killed on a mission to free a priest imprisoned by Humbert. Anthelm retired to Portes to protest the lifting of the excommunication by Pope Alexander but remained on good terms with the Pope, who later asked him to go as papal legate to England to settle the conflict between Henry II and Thomas Becket; unfortunately, he was unable to go. His last years were spent working with lepers and the poor. He died on June 26, and while he lay dying was visited by Humbert seeking his forgiveness.

ANTHERUS (d. 236). A Greek, the son of one Romulus, he was elected Pope on November 21, 235, but ruled only forty-three days when he died on January 3, probably a martyr. During his short tenure, he ordered copies of the trials of the martyrs to be collected and kept in the episcopal archives.

ANTHIMUS (d. 303). A priest in Rome, he converted a prefect there to Christianity and was ordered drowned for his action. Reportedly miraculously saved, he was recaptured and then beheaded. May 11.

ANTHIMUS (d. 303). Bishop of Nicodemia, Bithynia, he was beheaded for his faith, with eleven followers, during the persecution of Diocletian and Maximian. April 27.

ANTHIMUS (d. c. 303). *See* Cosmas.

ANTHONY. *See* Anthony.

ANTHONY OF PADUA (1195–1231). Born in Lisbon, Portugal, Ferdinand de Bulhoes was the son of a knight at the court of King Alfonso II of Portugal. He studied as a youth under the priests of the Lisbon cathedral, joined the Canons Regular of St. Augustine at their house near the city when fifteen, and in 1212 was transferred to the priory at Coimbra because he found the visits of friends too disturbing, and was ordained in 1219 or 1220. He transferred to the Franciscans in 1221, taking the name Anthony, went to Morocco to preach to the Moors but was forced to return because of illness, and arrived back in time to participate in a general chapter of his order at Assisi in 1221. He was assigned to the hospice of San Paoli near Forli and at an ordination there delivered a sermon that was to launch him on his career as a preacher. He was assigned to preaching all over Italy and was sensationally successful. His sermons, noted for their eloquence, fire, and persuasiveness, attracted huge crowds everywhere he preached. He was appointed the first lector in theology for the Franciscans, became minister provincial of Emilia or Romagna, was envoy from the 1226 general chapter to Pope Gregory IX, and secured the Pope's release from his official duties to devote himself to preaching. His success as a convertmaker and confessor was phenomenal. He settled in Padua after 1226 and his bold and brilliant preaching, attacking corruption and wrongdoing wherever he saw them, and completely reformed the city. He worked to abolish debtors' prisons, helped the poor, and worked ceaselessly and untiringly with heretics. In 1231, exhausted and plagued with dropsy, he went to Camposanpiero for a brief respite but died on the way back to Padua in a Poor Clare convent at Arcella just outside Padua on June 13 at the age of thirty-six. He was canonized the following year and declared a Doctor of the Church by Pope Pius XII in 1946. Stories of the miracles Anthony wrought and of his preaching prowess are legendary, and he was undoubtedly one of the greatest preachers of all times. His contemporaries called him "Hammer of the Heretics" and "Living Ark of the Covenant," and he is known as the "Wonder Worker" for the miracles he wrought. He is the patron of the poor (alms given for his intercession are called St. Anthony's bread) and oppressed and he is widely invoked for the return of lost articles. His depiction in art with the Infant Jesus on his arm is because of an episode in which a visitor reported this happening.

ANTHUSA (8th century). A hermitess, she was named abbess of a convent near Constantinople. Known for her veneration of sacred images, she was tortured by order of Emperor Constantine Copronymus but was released through the intercession of the Empress, whose friend she became. July 27.

ANTIDE THOURET, JOAN (1765–1826). Born on November 27 at Sancey-le-Long, France, daughter of a tanner, she became head of her father's household on the death of her mother when she was sixteen; in 1787, she joined the Sisters of Charity of St. Vincent de Paul in Paris. When religious orders in France were abolished by the revolutionary government in 1793, she had not yet been professed and returned to Sancey. She opened a school for children there, aided the poor and sick, and hid priests from the persecution of the revolutionaries. Denounced for this latter activity, she was forced to flee and went to Switzerland in 1796, accompanied the Sisters of Christian Retreat to Germany, but then returned to Switzerland. She was invited to open a school at Besançon and did so in 1799 with four sisters. The community grew, she was placed in charge of the municipal female asylum at Belleveaux, and in 1807 her rule was approved by Archbishop Le Coz of Besançon. The group spread to Switzerland, Savoy, and Naples, and in 1818, Pope Pius VII gave it his approval with the name Daughters of Charity under the protection of St. Vincent de Paul. When Archbishop de Pressigny of Besançon refused to accept a provision of the Holy See's approbatory brief that future convents of the congregation were to be subject to local bishops and not to the archbishop of Besançon, as had been the situation up to that time, and even forbade members of the community in France to communicate with others outside of France, a schism developed; even Joan was refused admission to the mother house in Besançon. She spent the last years of her life founding convents in Italy, years saddened by her inability to solve the split in her community. She died on August 24, and was canonized in 1934. August 25.

ANTIOCHUS (3rd century). A physician at Sebaste (Sivas, Turkey), he was beheaded for his faith by order of Governor Hadrian. Antiochus' executioner, Cyriacus, was so impressed by him he was converted and was himself martyred. July 15.

ANTIOCHUS (d. 303). *See* Nicostratus.

ANTIOCHUS (4th–5th centuries). A priest at Lyons, Gaul, he was sent to Egypt about 381 to persuade the bishop of Lyons, St. Justus, who had become a hermit there, to return to his see. Unsuccessful, he returned to Lyons and was elected bishop to replace Justus. He is also known as Andeol. October 15.

ANTIPAS (d. c. 90). Called by St. John "my faithful witness" (Acts 2:13), he was bishop of Perganum in Asia Minor and was burned to death for his faith during Diocletian's persecution. April 11.

ANTONIA. *See* Antonina.

ANTONIA (d. 259). *See* Agapius.

ANTONIA OF FLORENCE (1400–72). Born in Florence, Italy, and widowed when still young, she became a Franciscan tertiary regular at Florence under Bl. Angelina of Marsciano, was made superior of St. Anne's convent in Foligno, and then of the convent in Aquila. Desirous of a stricter rule, through the good offices of St. John Capistran, she was appointed superior of the newly built Corpus Christi monastery that followed the rule of St. Clare in 1447, and soon attracted hundreds of nuns by her holiness and her patience in the face of much suffering and illness. She resigned as superior in 1454. She was reputed to have had visions and the gift of levitation. Her cult was approved in 1847. February 28.

ANTONINA (d. c. 304). Tortured and martyred during Diocletian's persecution, she probably suffered martyrdom at Nicaea, Bithynia, during the governorship of Priscillian, although Cea in Bithynia, Cea in the Aegean, and Ceja in Spanish Galicia also claim the honor. She is also known as Antonia and may be the same saint listed in the Roman Martyrology on March 1 and on May 4. June 12.

ANTONINA (d. 313). *See* Alexander.

ANTONINUS (d. 186). A public executioner at Rome during the reign of Emperor Commodus, he was awaiting the result of St. Eusebius' trial when he experienced a vision that caused him to announce that he was a Christian, whereupon he was beheaded for his new faith. August 22.

ANTONINUS (3rd century). A soldier in the Theban Legion, he was executed for his Christianity near Piacenza, Italy. Reputedly, some of his blood, kept in a vial, liquefies and bubbles, much as does that of St. Januarius. September 30.

ANTONINUS (4th century). An Eastern legend has him a stonemason in Aribazus, Syria, who denounced his fellow villagers for worshiping idols. After living as a hermit for two years, he returned to the village and destroyed the idols there. He was driven from the village, went to Apamaea, Syria, where he built a church, which so enraged the inhabitants of the town that they murdered him. Some authorities believe he was martyred at Pamiers, France. September 2.

ANTONINUS (d. 830). Born in Picenum, southern Italy, he became a monk in his youth, migrated to Castellamare, near Sorrento, and with the bishop of Castellamare, St. Catellus, became a hermit on top of nearby Monte Angelo. As the result of a vision of St. Michael the Archangel, they built an oratory to Michael. Catellus was charged with neglecting his diocese and was imprisoned in Rome, but Antoninus remained, and by his holiness and vision made it a place of pilgrimage. He returned to Sorrento at the supplication of the inhabitants, became abbot of St. Agrippinus monastery, and is reputed to have repulsed a Saracen attack on the city by a miracle after his death. February 14.

ANTONINUS OF FLORENCE. See Pierozzi, Antony.

ANTONY (251–356). Born at Koman, near Memphis, Upper Egypt, of well-to-do Christian parents, he distributed their inheritance on their death about 269, placed his sister in a convent, and in 272 became a hermit in a tomb in a cemetery near Koman. He lived a life of prayer, penance, and the strictest austerity, ate only bread and water once a day, and engaged in struggles with the devil and temptations that are legendary. About 285, in quest of greater solitude, he left this hermitage and took up residence in an old fort atop Mount Pispir (now Der el Memun), living in complete solitude and seeing no one, eating only what was thrown to him over the wall of the fort. After twenty years, in 305, he emerged to organize at Fayum the colony of ascetics that had grown around his retreat into a loosely organized monastery with a rule, though each monk lived in solitude except for worship. It was the first Christian monastery. In 311, at the height of Emperor Maximin's persecution, he went to Alexandria to give encouragement to the Christians being persecuted there. He returned when the persecution subsided and organized an-

other monastery at Pispir but again retired, this time to Mount Kolzim near the Red Sea, with a disciple, Macarius. About 355, Antony again went to Alexandria to join those combating Arianism, working with his close friend St. Athanasius, whose *Vita Antonii* is the chief source of information about Antony. On his return, he retired to a cave on Mount Kolzim, where he received visitors and dispensed advice until his death there on January 17. Antony was the founder of Christian monasticism and was famous all over the civilized world for his holiness, asceticism, and wisdom, and was consulted by people from all walks of life, from Emperor Constantine to the humblest monk. January 17.

ANTONY (d. c. 1342). See John.

ANTONY OF AMANDOLA, BL. (c. 1260–1350). Born near Ascoli Piceno, Italy, he joined the Augustinians in 1306 and was noted for his charity and the miracles attributed to him. His cult was confirmed in 1759. January 28.

ANTONY DELLA CHIESA, BL. (1394–1459). Son of the Marquis della Chiesa, he was born at San Germano, Italy. Despite his parents' objections, he joined the Dominicans when twenty, accompanied St. Bernardino of Siena on some of his missions, and became renowned as a preacher and confessor. He served as prior of friaries in Como, Savona, Florence, and Bologna, and was one of the leaders of the opposition to antipope Felix V (Amadeus of Savoy). Antony was captured by pirates while at sea on the way from Savona to Genoa but was released unharmed. He fought usury, was credited with performing miracles, and had the ability to read men's consciences. His cult was approved in 1819. July 28.

ANTONY OF HOORNAER (d. 1572). *See* Pieck, Nicholas.

ANTONY KAULEAS (829–901). Of Phrygian descent, he was born near Constantinople, entered a monastery there on the death of his mother, and in time became abbot. He was chosen patriarch of Constantinople in 893 and was active in reconciling differing theological factions. February 12.

ANTONY OF LÉRINS (c. 468–520). Born at Valeria, Lower Pannonia, he was raised by St. Severinus at Faviana, when his father died when he was eight, and later by his uncle Bishop Constantius, of Lorsch, Bavaria. Antony became a monk and about 488 returned to Italy and joined a priest named Marius and his disciples at Lake Como. Antony lived the eremitical life there but was so besieged by disciples that he left, went to Gaul, and became a monk at Lérins, where he lived the last two years of his life and died, revered for his holiness and miracles. December 28.

ANTONY MANZI THE PILGRIM, BL. (c. 1237–67). Of a wealthy family, he was born in Padua, Italy, gave his inheritance to the poor when his father died, and was castigated for his action by his family. He decided to live as a pilgrim, wandered all over Europe living on alms and in the greatest austerity, made pilgrimages to Rome and Jerusalem, and then returned to Padua. Still considered an outcast there, even by his two nun sisters, he lived in a church outside the city and died there. When miracles occurred at his grave, the citizens of Padua sought to have him canonized—a request that was refused by the Pope, though his cult is still kept in Padua. February 1.

ANTONY PECHERSKY (983–1073). Born at Lubech, Ukraine, he became a hermit but decided he needed to be educated for that life and went to Mount Athos, where he became a hermit attached to the monastery of Esphigmenou. After several years there, he returned to Russia and built a hermitage at Kiev on the Dnieper River. His wisdom and holiness attracted others seeking the eremitical life, and from these beginnings grew the Caves of Kiev (Kiev-Pecherskaya Laura), the first Russian monastery established by Russian monks for Russians, on land granted him by Prince Syaslav. Antony established another monastery at Chernigov but returned to his cave at the Pecherskaya Laura and lived there the rest of his life. With Theodosius Pechersky, he is considered the father of Russian monasticism. July 10.

ANTONY OF ST. BONAVENTURE, BL. (1588–1628). Born at Tuy, Galicia, Spain, he studied at Salamanca, joined the Franciscans, and was sent as a missionary to the Philippines. He was ordained in Manila and was then sent to Japan, where he was extremely successful in conversion work, converting thousands to Christianity. He was burned to death for his Christianity at Nagasaki, and was beatified in 1867. September 8.

ANTONY OF SIENA, BL. (d. 1311). Of the leading Sienese de' Patrizi family, little is known of him beyond the fact that he joined the Hermits of St. Augustine, became superior of their house at Monteciano, and was known for the holiness of his life. His cult was approved in 1804. April 27.

ANTONY OF STRONCONE, BL. *See* Vici, Bl. Antony.

ANTONY OF TUY, BL. (d. 1628). A Franciscan priest, he labored as a missionary in Japan for ten years, converting thousands, until he was imprisoned and then burned to death at Nagasaki on September 8. He was beatified with 205 other martyrs of the persecution of Shōgun Ieyasu and his son Hidetaka by Pope Pius IX in 1867. June 1.

ANTONY OF WEERT (d. 1572). *See* Pieck, Nicholas.

ANYSIA (d. c. 304). A Christian of Thessalonica who used the wealth her parents left her to help the poor, she was sworded to death by a soldier while on the way to a meeting of Christians when she resisted his efforts to drag her to sacrifice to the gods when he found she was a Christian. December 30.

ANYSIUS (d. c. 410). Named bishop of Thessalonica in 383, he was a friend of St. Ambrose, and was appointed vicar apostolic in Illyrium by Pope Damasus. He was one of the sixteen Macedonian bishops who in 404 appealed to Pope Innocent on behalf of St. John Chrysostom, whom he firmly supported. December 30.

APARICIO, BL. SEBASTIAN (1502–1600). Born of poor parents at Gudina, Spanish Galicia, he worked as a servant and as a farmhand in his youth and then went to Mexico. He settled at Puebladelos Angeles, established a freight and postal service, and became wealthy. He lived austerely, was known for his generous charities to the poor, and in 1552 he retired to an estate near Mexico City. He married twice after he was sixty, but both wives died. He survived a serious illness when seventy, gave his wealth to the Poor Clares, became a Franciscan tertiary, and then joined the Franciscans in Mexico City. He was sent to Tecali and then Puebla, where he spent the last quarter century of his life. He died at Tecali, and was beatified in 1787. February 25.

APELLES (1st century). Traditionally considered the first bishop of Smyrna, he is named in the Roman Martyrology with St. Lucius, bishop of Laodicea, as "among the first disciples of Christ." April 22.

APHRAATES (d. c. 345). Of a pagan family, he was born in Syria on the Persian border, was converted to Christianity, and became a hermit at Edessa in Mesopotamia, living in the greatest austerity. He then moved to a hermitage next to a monastery in Antioch and attracted great numbers of visitors drawn by his holiness and reported miracles. He publicly opposed the Arians, who tried to have him exiled, but Emperor Valens refused to do so, reportedly because he thought the death of one of his attendants who had threatened to murder Aphraates was retribution for his threat. Some scholars consider him to be the same as the bishop of the monastery of Mar Mattai near Mosul, Mesopotamia, and the author of *Demonstrations,* twenty-three treatises written between 336 and 345, the oldest extant document of the Church in Syria, which give a survey of the Christian faith, who may have suffered persecution at the hands of King Sapor the Great and was known as "the Persian Sage." April 7.

APODEMUS (d. 304). *See* Optatus.

APOLLINARIS (1st century). According to legend, he was born at Antioch, became one of St. Peter's disciples, and was appointed first bishop of Ravenna, Italy. He reportedly made many converts, preached at Bologna, and was banished when he converted the patrician Rufinus. Apollinaris suffered shipwreck in Dalmatia, was driven from his see three times during his bishopric, and fled into hiding a fourth time when Emperor Vespasian banished all Christians, was discovered and beaten by a mob at Classis, a suburb of Ravenna, but survived. July 23.

APOLLINARIS (d. c. 179). Bishop of Hierapolis, Phrygia, Claudius Apollinaris was famed for his teaching and his writings, none of which have survived. In them he attacked various heretics, particularly the Encratites and the Montanists. He was called "the Apologist" for an apologia of Christianity he directed to Emperor Marcus Aurelius. In it Apollinaris described a miracle that had brought victory to the Emperor in Germany when his army was surrounded by Quadi in Moravia and threatened with annihilation—a miracle ascribed by Apollinaris to the prayers of the 12th Legion, which was mainly Christian. The apologia resulted in an imperial edict forbidding the denunciation of Christians for their religion. He is also known as Apollinaris the Apologist. January 8.

APOLLINARIS (d. c. 290). Public executioner at the Rheims prison, he was so impressed with the courage and constancy of St. Timothy under torture that he became a Christian. Both were beheaded for their faith. August 23.

APOLLINARIS (c. 453–c. 520). The son of St. Hesychius, bishop of Vienne, France, he studied under St. Mamertus, and about 492 was consecrated bishop of Valence by his brother St. Avitus of Vienne. Apollinaris was forced into exile with other prelates when a synod of bishops condemned an official of King Sigismund of Burgundy for an incestuous marriage and the King supported the official. Apollinaris was recalled when his cloak cured the King of a mysterious ailment. Apollinaris died at Valence. October 5.

APOLLINARIS THE APOLOGIST. *See* Apollinaris (d. c. 179).

APOLLINARIS SYNCLETICA (no date). Though listed in the Roman Martyrology, her story is probably a pious fiction. Supposedly the daughter of an Emperor, she left home, donned male attire, and lived as a hermit in the desert with the name Dorotheus. When her sister was possessed she was brought to Dorotheus, who cured her. Later accused of improper conduct, Dorotheus was brought before her father, to whom she revealed her true identity. She then returned to the desert, where her sex was revealed only on her death. January 5.

APOLLO (c. 305–95). A hermit who founded a community of monks at Hermopolis and became their abbot when he was eighty, he was famous for the miracles he is reported to have performed. January 25.

APOLLONIA (d. 249). During the reign of Emperor Philip, mobs at Alexandria ranged the streets torturing and killing Christians. Among their victims was Apollonia, an old deaconess, who was tortured when she would not renounce her Christianity and when given a moment's respite leaped voluntarily into the fire the mob had built and was threatening to throw her into. She is represented in art by a gold tooth or pincer, since her teeth were pulled out during her torture. In the same mob action, Metras, an old man, was tortured and stoned to death; Quinta was scourged and stoned to death when she refused to sacrifice to pagan gods; and Serapion was tortured and thrown from the roof of his home to his death. Apollonia is the patron of dentists. February 9.

APOLLONIUS (d. c. 305). A Christian deacon at Antinoë in the Thebaïd, he converted Philemon, a musician and entertainer, and both were arrested during Diocletian's persecution and then taken to Alexandria, where they were thrown into the sea and drowned. A fanciful legend has Apollonius hire the pagan piper Philemon to disguise himself as Apollonius and sacrifice to the gods in his place. When arraigned, Philemon declared himself a Christian but was regarded as a jester; he persisted in his avowal and was miraculously baptized. Meanwhile, Apollonius also was arrested and declared his Christianity. Despite several remarkable miracles, they were eventually sewed into sacks with an official at the trial whom they had converted, and all were thrown into the sea and drowned. March 8.

APOLLONIUS THE APOLOGIST (d. c. 185). A Roman senator, he became a Christian and was denounced by one of his slaves to Perennis, the praetorian prefect, for his Christianity. Though the slave was put to death as an informer, Perennis demanded that Apollonius renounce his Christianity. When the senator refused, the case was remanded to the Senate, where a remarkable dialogue took place between Perennis and Apollonius in which Apollonius defended his religion. Despite his eloquent defense, Apollonius was sentenced to death and beheaded. April 18.

APONIUS (1st century). *See* Andrew.

APPHIA (1st century). *See* Philemon.

APPHIAN (c. 286–306). Born at Lycia, he studied at the Berytus schools in Phoenicia, was converted to Christianity, and went to Caesarea, Palestine, to live with Eusebius. When a decree from Emperor Maximian ordered public sacrifice to the gods, Apphian denounced the sacrifice to the governor, who had him seized, subjected to horrible torture, and thrown into the sea and drowned. Reportedly an earthquake followed his death and cast up his body onto the shore, though his feet were weighted with stones. April 2.

APRONIAN (d. c. 304). An executioner during Diocletian's persecution of Christians, he was so impressed by St. Sisinnius, whom he was taking to be tried for his Christianity, that he became a convert and was beheaded for his faith at Ancona, Italy. February 2.

APULEIUS (1st century). According to the Roman Martyrology, he and SS. Marcellus, Sergius, and Bacchus were followers of Simon Magus, were converted by St. Peter, and were martyred in Rome after Peter's death there. This is probably an apochryphal tale, as there is no other record of Apuleius, but a Marcellus did suffer martyrdom at Capua. October 7.

AQUAVIVA, BL. RUDOLF (1550–83). Son of the Duke of Atri, he joined the Jesuits when eighteen, was ordained at Lisbon, and was sent as a missionary to Goa, India. In 1579, he was sent to the court of the Great Mogul Akbar near Agra but was unsuccessful in his attempt to convert him to Christianity. In 1583, he was made superior of the Salsette mission north of Bombay. With Fr. Alfonso Pachecho, born in Minayá, Castile, in 1550, who had joined the Jesuits in 1566 and been ordained at Goa, and Fr. Peter Berno, a Swiss, both of whom had participated in two Portuguese military expeditions against the village of Cuncolim north of Bombay, Fr. Antony Francisco, an Italian, and Br. Francis Aranha, a native of Braga, Portugal, and mission architect at Goa who had been in India for twenty-three years, he set out in July 1583 to build a church at Cuncolim, which was to be headquarters for conversion work in the area. They were met by an armed force of Hindu natives near the village and all were killed. They were beatified in 1893. July 27.

AQUILA (1st century). A Jewish tent-maker, he and his wife Prisca (or Priscilla) were forced to leave Rome when Emperor Claudius forbade Jews to live there. They went to Corinth, where St. Paul lived with them during his stay there and may have converted them to Christianity. They accompanied Paul to Ephesus and remained there; Paul stayed with them on his third missionary journey. They then returned to Rome, where their house was also used as a church and then went back to Ephesus. They suffered martyrdom in Asia Minor, according to the Roman Martyrology, but a tradition has them martyred in Rome. July 8.

AQUILINA (c. 3rd century). Born of Christian parents in Biblus, Phoenicia, she was arrested during Diocletian's persecution of Christians, and though only twelve was beaten and decapitated by order of the magistrate, Volusian, when she would not renounce her faith. June 13.

AQUILINUS (d. 180). See Speratus.

AQUILINUS (d. 650). Born in Bavaria, he left his native land to avoid being made a bishop, went to Italy, and settled in Milan. A vigorous opponent of Arianism, he was so effective in his preaching against the heresy that a group of Arians murdered him. January 29.

AQUILINUS (c. 620–c. 695). Born at Bayeux, France, he was a soldier in the forces of Clovis II. He married at Chartres on his return from a campaign against the Visigoths about 660, and he and his wife moved to Evreux, where they devoted themselves to aiding the poor. About 670, he was made bishop of Evreux, spent much of his time as a hermit in a cell near his cathedral, and was blind during the last few years of his life, when he is reputed to have performed miracles. October 19.

AQUINAS. See Thomas Aquinas.

ARAGHT. See Attracta.

ARANHA, BL. FRANCIS (d. 1583). See Aquaviva, Bl. Rudolf.

ARBOGAST (6th century). Born in Aquitaine, he became a hermit in Alsace and was appointed bishop of Strasbourg by King Dagobert, whose son he is reputed to have revived after he was killed by a wild boar. July 21.

ARBUES, PETER (c. 1440–85). Born at Epila, Aragon, Spain, he studied canon law and theology at the Spanish college in Bologna, became an Augustinian at Saragossa in 1478, and in 1484 was appointed provincial inquisitor for Aragon by Torquemada. Reputed cruelties and his activities against usurers, Maranos, and Moriscos (Jews and Moors converted to Christianity but privately practicing their own religion) made him many enemies. He was stabbed to death on September 14 while praying in St. Savior cathedral at Saragossa and died two days later. He was canonized in 1867. September 17.

ARCADIUS (d. c. 304). Probably a resident of Caesarea in Mauritania, he suffered martyrdom by being hacked to pieces for his faith during the persecution of Christians by Valerian or Diocletian. January 12.

ARCADIUS (d. 437). The Roman Martyrology lists Arcadius, a married man with children, Paschasius and Eutychian, brothers, and Probus as Spaniards who when they refused to embrace Arianism during the Vandal persecution were exiled to Africa by Arian King Genseric, tortured, and then put to death. At the same time, the younger brother of Paschasius and Eutychian, Paulillus, was tortured, and then died of exposure. November 13.

ARCHANGELUS OF CALAFATIMI, BL. (d. 1460). Born at Calafatimi, Sicily, he became a hermit but was forced to abandon his eremitical way of life when Pope Martin V ordered the hermitages in Sicily closed. Archangelus then joined the Observant Franciscans and was active in spreading his branch of the Franciscans throughout Sicily. His cult was confirmed in 1836. July 30.

ARCHELAUS (3rd century). Though listed in the Roman Martyrology as bishop of Kashkar, Mesopotamia, and a man famed for his learning and holiness who debated with Manes, he is in all probability a fictitious character. December 26.

ARCHINIMES (d. c. 455). *See* Armogastes.

ARCHIPPUS (1st century). Traditionally considered the first bishop of Colossae, he was admonished by St. Paul, "Remember the service that the Lord wants you to do and try to carry it out." (Col. 4:17). March 20.

ARDALION (d. c. 300). Probably a pious fiction according to which he is reputed to have been an actor during the reign of Emperor Maximinian who, while ridiculing a condemned Christian on the stage, was suddenly converted to Christianity during the applause that followed his burlesque, announced that fact to his audience, was arrested, and then was burned alive for his new faith. April 14.

ARDO (d. 843). A native of Languedoc named Smaragdus, he became a monk at Aniane, taking the name Ardo, under Benedict of Aniane, and was ordained. He became director of the monastery school at Aniane, which became one of the best-known schools in the realm, accompanied Benedict on his journeys, and in 814, when Benedict was leaving Aniane to serve at another monastery at the request of Louis the Pious, he named Ardo superior in his place. Ardo wrote a biography of Benedict. March 7.

AREDIUS (d. 591). Also known as Yrieux, he was born at Limoges, France, served for a time at the royal court, and then left to pursue a religious life. He was founder-abbot of Atane abbey in the Limousin, and the village that grew up around the abbey was named after him. August 25.

ARÉGLE. *See* Agricola (d. 280).

ARETAS (d. 523). Chief of the Beno Harith community of Hadran in southwestern Arabia and also known as Abdullah Ibn Kahn, he and 340 of the townspeople were massacred after they had been offered and accepted amnesty from the band of Jews under Dhu Nowas (Dunaan), a convert to Judaism who had led a revolt against the Aksumite Ethiopians. The massacre horrified the entire civilized world and was denounced by Mohammed in the Koran. October 24.

AREZZO, BL. PAUL BURALI D' (1511–78). Born at Ita, near Gaeta, Italy, he studied law, became a lawyer, and practiced in Naples for a decade. He was appointed royal counselor in 1549 and served until 1558, when he joined the Theatines. He was superior at Theatine houses in Naples and Rome, was appointed bishop of Piacenza, was made a cardinal by Pope Pius V, and later was named archbishop of Naples. He was beatified in 1772. June 17.

ARGEUS (d. 320). He and his brothers, Marcellinus and Narcissus, were soldiers in the Roman army. When it was discovered they were Christians, Marcellinus and Narcissus were beheaded at Tomi in Pontus. Argeus, a mere youth, was imprisoned when he refused military service when inducted into the army, was flogged, and then was drowned. January 2.

ARGYMIRUS (d. 858). Born at Cabra near Cordova, Spain, he became an official in the Mohammedan government there. When it was discovered he was a Christian, he lost his position, whereupon he became a monk. When he later denounced Mohammedanism while preaching, he was arrested and beheaded. June 28.

ARIADNE (d. c. 130). The Christian slave of a Phrygian prince, she was scourged for refusing to participate in a pagan rite on the prince's birthday. She fled and reportedly escaped her pursuers when a rock opened up and enclosed her. September 17.

ARIALDUS (d. 1066). A deacon at Milan, his vigorous opposition to simony there incurred the wrath of his archbishop, who was engaged in simony. He was excommunicated for his activities and then murdered by some of the archbishop's followers. June 27.

ARISTARCHUS (1st century). Born at Thessalonica, Macedonia, he became a follower of St. Paul and accompanied him on several of his trips (Acts 20:4; 27:2). He was imprisoned with Paul at Ephesus and according to tradition was first bishop of Thessalonica and was beheaded with Paul at Rome. August 4.

ARISTIDES (d. c. 123). A philosopher at Athens, he wrote a defense of Christianity that reputedly was given to Emperor Hadrian. St. Jerome praised it highly, and Syrian, Armenian, and Greek versions are still extant. August 31.

ARMAGILLIS. *See* Armel.

ARMEL (d. c. 570). Supposedly a Welshman, he studied under Abbot Carentmael and followed him, with other companions, to Brittany as a missionary. They settled at Plouarzel but were forced to leave by Connor, a local chieftain. They went to Paris, but Armel returned in 555 after Connor had been slain and founded a community near Rennes and another monastery at Ploermel, Brittany, where he died. He is also known as Arzel, Arthmael, and the Latin version of Armel, Armagillis. August 16.

ARMOGASTES (d. c. 455). A member of the household of Theodoric, son of King Genseric of the Vandals, he was tortured by Genseric, who had become an Arian and had launched a persecution of the Catholics. He was banished to the mines of Byzacema, then degraded publicly by being forced to tend cattle at Carthage and died there. Also martyred during Genseric's persecution were Archinimes, a native of Mascula, and Saturus, master of Arian Vandal King Huneric's household, who had been stripped of his possessions and forced to live as a beggar when it was discovered he was a Christian. March 29.

ARNOLD DE' CATTENEI, BL. (1184–1254). Born at Padua, Italy, of a noble family, he joined the Benedictines there and in time became abbot of St. Justina monastery in Padua. He incurred the enmity of Ezzelino da Romano, the Ghibbeline leader and supporter of Emperor Frederick II against the Pope, who held him in prison in chains at Asola for eight years until he died. March 14.

ARNOUL. Another form of Arnulf.

ARNULF (d. c. 643). Of noble parents, he was a member of the court of King Theodebert II of Austrasia, a valiant warrior, and a valued adviser. He married the noble Doda (the marriage of his son Ansegisel to Begga, daughter of Pepin of Landen, produced the Carolingian line of Kings of France), and when Doda became a nun, despite his desire to retire to the monastery of Lérins, he was made bishop of Metz about 610. He played a prominent role in affairs of state, was one of those instrumental in making Clotaire of Neustria king of Austrasia, was chief counselor to Dagobert, son of King Clotaire, when the King appointed him King of Austrasia, and then, about 626, Arnulf resigned his bishopric to retire to a hermitage (later Remiremont monastery), where he died. July 18.

ARNULF (c. 1040–87). Born in Flanders, he served in the armies of Robert and Henry I of France and then became a monk at Saint-Médard monastery at Soissons. For a time he lived as a hermit, then became abbot, and in 1081 was named bishop of Soissons. He resigned his see when forced from it by a usurper and founded a monastery at Oudenbourg, where he lived until his death there. August 15.

ARNULF OF VILLERS, BL. (c. 1180–1228). Born at Brussels, Arnulf Cornebout changed his youthful life of pleasure-seeking to become a lay brother at the Cistercian monastery at Villers, Brabant. His whole life was spent in the greatest austerity, performing penitential exercises and mortifications of the most extreme sort. He was greatly revered for his humility and obedience and his gifts of prophecy and miracles. He died on June 30.

ARONTIUS (d. c. 303). *See* Honoratus.

ARROWSMITH, EDMUND (1585–1628). Son of a farmer, he was born at Haydock, England, baptized Brian, but always used his confirmation name of Edmund. The family was constantly harassed for its adherence to Catholicism, and in 1605 Edmund left England and went to Douai to study for the priesthood. He was ordained in 1612 and sent on the English mission the following year. He ministered to the Catholics of Lancashire without incident until about 1622, when he was arrested and questioned by the Protestant bishop of Chester. He was released when King James ordered all arrested priests be freed, joined the Jesuits in 1624, and in 1628 was arrested when betrayed by a young man he had censured for an incestuous marriage. He was convicted of being a Catholic priest, sentenced to death, and hanged, drawn, and quartered at Lancaster on August 28. He was canonized as one of the Martyrs of England and Wales by Pope Paul VI in 1970.

ARS, CURÉ D'. *See* Vianney, John Bapist.

ARSACIUS (d. 358). A Persian in the Roman army, he was persecuted for his Christianity during the reign of Emperor Licinius but was then released. Arsacius became a hermit on a tower in Nicomedia, was known for his miracles and the gift of prevision, and was killed on August 24 in an earthquake he had predicted. August 16.

ARSENIUS (d. 250). *See* Dioscorus.

ARSENIUS (c. 355–c. 450). At the recommendation of Pope St. Damasus, Emperor Theodosius the Great appointed the Roman deacon Arsenius tutor of his children. He served at the court for a decade, and about 395 he left Constantinople to live with the monks at Alexandria. On the death of Theodosius, he retired to the wilderness of Skete, was tutored in eremitical customs by St. John the Dwarf, and lived in the greatest austerity, refusing the legacy left him by a relative who was a senator, preferring the life of a solitary to the life of luxury he could have enjoyed with the legacy. Forced to leave Skete about 434 because of barbarian raids, he spent the next ten years on the rock of Troë in Memphis, spent some time on the island of Canopus near Alexandria, but then returned to Troë, where he died. He is often surnamed "the Great." July 19.

ARTALDUS (1101–1206). Born in the castle of Sothonod in Savoy, and also known as Arthaud, he spent the two years after his eighteenth birthday at the court of Duke Amadeus III, and then became a Carthusian at Portes, where he was ordained. He founded a Carthusian charterhouse near his home in Avrières, which soon drew great crowds of people attracted by his reputation for holiness and wisdom. He was appointed bishop of Belley when eighty, over his protests, but resigned two years later and spent the last years of his life at Avrières, where he died. His cult was approved for the diocese of Belley in 1834. October 7.

ARTEMAS (date unknown). A doubtful legend has him a teenager stabbed to death by a group of youngsters for his Christianity, but all that is really known of him is that he was probably martyred at Pozzuoli, near Capua, in the fifth century or earlier. January 25.

ARTEMIUS (d. 302). The warden of a Roman prison, he was converted with his wife, Candida, and daughter Paulina by St. Peter the Exorcist and baptized by St. Marcellinus. Artemius was beheaded for his newfound faith, and his wife and daughter suffered martyrdom by being crushed to death beneath a pile of stones. June 6.

ARTEMIUS (d. 363). An officer in the army of Constantine the Great, he was appointed imperial prefect of Egypt, per-

secuted the orthodox Christians, and instituted a search for St. Athanasius, the champion of the Catholics, and also persecuted pagans, destroying their temples and idols. When Julian the Apostate became Emperor, he had him beheaded and confiscated his property for destroying idols. Though an Arian, he is listed in the Roman Martyrology on October 20.

ARTHAUD. See Artaldus.

ARTHELAIS (c. 544–60). Untrustworthy legend has her the daughter of Proconsul Lucius and his wife, Anthusa, living in Constantinople. When Arthelais' beauty attracted the attention of Emperor Justinian, her family decided she should leave Constantinople, and she fled to her Uncle Narses in Benevento, Italy, where she arrived after a series of miraculous happenings. She was greeted by the entire populace and lived a life of prayer and fasting until she died—at the age of sixteen. March 3.

ARTHMAEL. See Armel.

ARZEL. See Armel.

ASAPH (d. c. 600). Little is known of him, but he is reputed to have been a disciple of St. Kentigern and succeeded him as abbot of a monastery at Llanelwy, Wales, and later succeeded him as first Welsh bishop of the see that later took the name St. Asaph. May 11.

ASCLAS (3rd century). His legendary story has him a native of the Thebaid, Egypt, who was denounced for his Christianity, brought before Arrian, the governor, and tortured. When the governor attempted to cross the Nile River, he was prevented from doing so by a miraculous spell that Asclas put on him. When Asclas told him he would be unable to cross the river until he acknowledged the Christian God in writing, Arrian did so. However, as soon as he crossed the river safely, he had Asclas subjected to further torture and then had him thrown into the river at Antinoe with a rock around his neck to drown him. January 23.

ASELLA (d. c. 406). A Roman girl who took the veil at ten, she became a recluse at twelve and attracted followers. She was visited by Palladius, the bishop-historian, and Jerome praised her highly. December 6.

ASHLEY, BL. RALPH (d. 1606). An Englishman who served as a cook at Douai College in France, he went to Valladolid, Spain, in 1590 and became a Jesuit lay brother. He returned to England in 1598, became an aid and servant to Bl. Edward Oldcorne, was arrested with him in 1604, was subjected to great tortures, and two years later was executed for his faith on April 7 at Worcester. He was beatified in 1929.

ASICUS (d. c. 470). Tradition has him an early disciple of St. Patrick, a married coppersmith and the first abbot-bishop of Elphin monastery in Roscommon, Ireland. He fled his see to live as a hermit on the island of Rathlin O'Birne in Donegal Bay because he felt he was unfit to rule. He was found by his monks seven years later and died at Raith Cungilor (or Racoon) on his way back to Elphin with them. He is also known as Tassach. April 27.

ASKEGA (d. 870). *See* Theodore.

ASPREN (1st century). Tradition says he was cured of a sickness by St. Peter, who baptized him and consecrated him first bishop of Naples. August 3.

ASTERICUS. *See* Anastasius (d. c. 1040).

ASTERIUS (d. c. 303). Asterius, Claudius, and Neon were brothers in Aegea at the time of Diocletian's persecution of Christians. They were denounced as Christians by their stepmother to Lysias, proconsul of Cilicia, tortured, and crucified. At the same time, Domnina, a Christian woman, was scourged to death, and another woman, Theonilla, a widow for twenty-three years, died from scourging and hot coals piled on her stomach. August 23.

ASTERIUS (d. c. 410). Born in Pontus, he was educated by a Goth or Scythian who had been educated at Antioch, became a rhetor, was ordained, and was appointed bishop of Amasea. He was an outstanding preacher, and some twenty-one of his homilies are still extant. October 30.

ASTERIUS OF PETRA (d. c. 365). An Arian, he was converted to orthodox Catholicism and made bishop of Petra, Arabia. He was defamed by the Arians at the Council of Sardica in 347 for his denunciation of Arianism and exiled to Upper Libya in Egypt by Emperor Constantius. Asterius returned in 362 when Emperor Julian the Apostate recalled all banished bishops, and in the same year attended the Council of Alexandria, which dealt with the Meletian schism. He was named to bring the decisions of the Council to Lucifer of Cagliari, who ignored them, and then went on to Antioch to report on the Council to the bishops assembled there. He died soon after at Petra. June 10.

ASTRIK. *See* Anastasius.

ASTYRIUS (d. c. 262). *See* Marinus.

ATHANASIA (5th century). *See* Andronicus.

ATHANASIA (d. c. 860). Born on the island of Aegina, she was widowed when her husband of sixteen days was killed fighting marauding Arabs in Greece. She remarried, and when her second husband wanted to become a monk, she consented and became a nun, using her home as a convent. She was named abbess, moved the convent to Timia, served for seven years as adviser to Empress Theodora from the cell in which she was living in Constantinople, and died in Timia soon after returning there. August 14.

ATHANASIUS (c. 297–373). Probably born of Christian parents at Alexandria, he was well educated, especially in Scripture and theology, was ordained a deacon, and became secretary to Bishop Alexander of his native city about 318. Athanasius was present with his bishop at the Council of Nicaea, which condemned Arianism and excommunicated Arius. Athanasius was elected bishop of Alexandria on Alexander's death about 327 and in addition to his rule as bishop of the city became the spiritual head of the desert hermits and of Ethiopia. He was immediately confronted with a revival of Arianism in Egypt and its rapid growth throughout the Mediterranean world and the continued schism of the Meletians who supported the Arians. In 330, Eusebius of Nicomedia, a supporter of Arius, persuaded Emperor Constantine to direct Athanasius to admit Arius to communion. When Athanasius flatly refused, Eusebius incited the Meletians to use every means to discredit Athanasius; they charged him with various crimes, and when he was cleared at a trial before Constantine they accused him of murdering Arsenius, a Meletian bishop everyone knew was alive and in hiding. Aware of this, Athanasius refused the summons of the Meletians to attend a synod to answer the preposterous charge but was obliged to attend a council at Tyre in 335 when summoned by the Emperor. The council was completely dominated by his enemies and presided over by the Arian who had usurped the bishopric of Antioch. Athanasius was found guilty, and though the Emperor, after an interview with Athanasius, repudiated the findings of the Council, he later reversed himself, and Athanasius in 336 was banished to Trier in Germany. When Constantine died in 337 and his Empire was divided among his sons, Constantine II, Coustans, and Constantius, Constantine recalled him to his see in 338. Eusebius then denounced him to Constantius (Alexandria was in Constantius' portion of the Empire) for sedition and succeeded in having Athanasius again deposed at a synod at Antioch and an Arian bishop intruded into his see. A letter from this synod asking Pope St. Julius to confirm its actions was followed by another one from the orthodox bishops of Egypt supporting Athanasius, a copy of which was also sent to the bishops in the West. When Gregory, a Cappadocian, was installed as archbishop supplanting Athanasius, riots broke out in Alexandria. Athanasius then went to Rome to attend a synod suggested to Pope Julian I to hear the case; when none of the Eusebians showed up for the synod, it proceeded with its deliberations and completely vindicated Athanasius, a decision that was confirmed by the Council of Sardinia. It was while he was in Rome that Athanasius established close contact with the bishops of the West who supported him in his struggles. He was unable to return until Gregory died in 345, and Constantius, at the urging of his brother Constans, the Western Emperor, unwillingly restored Athanasius to his see. But when Constans was assassinated in 350, Constantius, now Emperor of both East and West, moved to exterminate orthodoxy and deal with Athanasius once and for all. Constantius caused packed councils at Arles in 353 and at Milan in 355 to condemn Athanasius and exiled Pope Liberius to Thrace, where he forced him to agree to the censures. Arianism was now in control, but Athanasius continued to resist until one night soldiers broke into his church, killing and wounding many in the congregation. He fled to the desert and was protected there by the monks for the next six years while an Arian bishop, George of Cappadocia, occupied his see. It was during these years that he wrote many of his great theological works. When Constantius died in 361, George was murdered soon after, to be briefly succeeded by Pistus. When the new Emperor, Julian the Apostate, revoked all of his predecessor's banishments of bishops, Athanasius returned to Alexandria. Soon, however, he came into conflict with the new Emperor when he opposed his plans to paganize the Empire and was again forced to flee to the desert. When Julian was killed in 363, Athanasius was brought back by Emperor Jovian, but on his death after only an eight-month reign Athanasius was forced into hiding for the fifth time when the new Emperor, Valens, banished all orthodox bishops in 365. He revoked the order four months later, and Athanasius, after seventeen years of on-and-off exile, returned to his see and spent the last seven years of his life in Alexandria helping build the new Nicene party whose support secured the triumph of orthodoxy over Arianism at the General Council of Constantinople in 381. He died in Alexandria on May 2. Athanasius is one of the great figures of Christianity. A Doctor of the Church and called "the champion of orthodoxy," he resolutely opposed one of the greatest threats Christianity ever faced—Arianism—and persevered in the face of trials and difficulties that at times seemed insuperable

in a struggle that was eventually won. A friend of the monks Pacholius and Serapion and St. Antony, whose biography he wrote, he aided the ascetic movement in Egypt and was the first to introduce knowledge of monasticism to the West. Through it all, he guided his flock and found time to write treatises on Catholic doctrine that illuminated the areas in which he wrote. Among his outstanding works are *Contra gentes* and *De incarnatione verbi Dei*, defenses of the Incarnation and redemption written early in his life (318–23), and the major treatises he produced in exile: *Apologia to Constantius, Defense of Flight, Letter to the Monks,* and *History of the Arians.* He did not write the Athanasian Creed, but it was drawn from his writings, probably by some unknown cleric.

ATHANASIUS (c. 830–72). Son of the duke of Naples, he was born in Naples, helped repair the depredations of the Saracens, and was active in ransoming Christian prisoners from the Mohammedans. He was named bishop of Naples about 850 when he was only twenty, attended the Lateran Council in 863, was imprisoned by his nephew, Duke Sergius II of Naples, when he denounced Sergius for immorality and simony, and when released by the demands of the Neapolitans, moved to the island of the Savior near Naples. When he refused Sergius' demand that he resign, only the intervention of Emperor Louis II prevented the bishop's capture and imprisonment. When the duke attacked Athanasius' followers and looted the episcopal treasury in Naples, Pope Adrian II excommunicated the duke. Before Louis could intervene with his troops, Athanasius died at Veroli, near Monte Cassino, on July 15.

ATHANASIUS (d. c. 885). Born at Catania, Sicily, he fled his homeland when the Saracens invaded Sicily, went to Greece, became a Basilian monk at Patras, and later was named bishop of Modon. January 31.

ATHANASIUS THE ATHONITE (c. 920–c. 1000). Son of an Antiochene and baptized Abraham, he was born at Trebizond, studied at Constantinople, and became a monk, taking the name Athanasius, at St. Michael's monastery at Kymina, Bithynia, a *laura* (a group of monasteries where the monks lived individual lives around their church). To avoid being named abbot of St. Michael's he went to Mount Athos in Greece. There an old friend from Constantinople, Nicephorus Phocas, asked his help in preparing an expedition against the Saracens. On its successful completion, Athanasius returned to Mount Athos and with money given him by a grateful Phocas began the first monastery on Athos in 961. When Nicephorus Phocas became Emperor, Athanasius fled to Cyprus to avoid being called to the court, but the Emperor found him, reassured him, and gave him money to continue his work on Athos. Athanasius encountered great opposition from hermits living on Mount Athos long before he had arrived there as he attempted to install the *laura* system there. He escaped two murder attempts, and resistance ended only when Emperor John Tzimisces forbade any opposition to Athanasius. In time he became superior over fifty-eight communities of monks and hermits on the Mount. Thousands of monks still live and pray there today; it is now and has been for centuries the center of Eastern Orthodox monasticism and not in communion with Rome. Athanasius and five of his monks were killed when the arch of a church on which they were working collapsed. July 5.

ATHELM (d. c. 923). Uncle of St. Dunstan, he became a Benedictine monk at Glastonbury and was later abbot there, was named first bishop of Welks in 909, and succeeded to the archbishopric of Canterbury in 914. January 8.

ATHENODORUS (d. c. 269). Of a distinguished pagan family, and brother of St. Gregory Thaumaturgus, he was born at Neocaesarea, Mesopotamia. He accompanied Gregory and his sister, on her way to meet her husband at Caesarea, Palestine, about 223, to continue their law studies at Bairut, but met Origen at Caesarea, were converted by him, and became his disciples. Athenodorus was later made bishop of a see in Pontus and suffered martyrdom during the reign of Aurelian. October 18.

ATHENOGENES (d. c. 305). A bishop and theologian, he was burned to death with ten of his disciples at Sebaste, Armenia, during Diocletian's persecution of the Christians. Athenogenes was the author of a hymn proclaiming the divinity of the Holy Spirit. July 16.

ATTALAS (d. 627). Born in Burgundy, he studied under Bishop Aregius of Gap, became a monk at Lérins, but then went to Luxeuil under St. Columban in search of a stricter rule. Attalas accompanied Columban when the Irish monk missionaries in France were exiled by King Theodoric of Austrasia when Columban denounced him for his concubines. Eventually they founded a monastery at Bobbio, between Milan and Genoa in Italy, on land granted them by King Agilulf of the Lombards. When Columban died a year later in 615, Attalas became abbot. Despite some opposition to the rigor and severity of his rule, Bobbio under his abbacy became one of the great monastic centers of northern Italy. Like Columban, he was a vigorous opponent of Arianism, and was known for the miracles he performed.

He died at Bobbio and was buried there in the tomb with Columban. March 10.

ATTALUS (d. 177). A native of Pergamos and a Roman citizen, he was arrested with forty-seven other Christians at Lyons, tortured, and exposed to the wild beasts in the amphitheater. However, because of his Roman citizenship, he was not executed at once but was roasted to death when the Emperor's permission for his execution arrived. June 2.

ATTICUS (d. 425). Born at Sebaste, Armenia, he was educated there by Macedonian monks, but when a youth, he went to Constantinople, rejected their heretical teaching, and was ordained. He and Arascius accused St. John Chrysostom at the notorious Council of the Oak, which deposed John in 405 as patriarch of Constantinople. Atticus succeeded Arsacius, the usurping patriarch of Constantinople, in 406, secured the recognition of Pope Innocent I as patriarch, and in time became a zealous promoter of orthodoxy. He drove the Messalians from Pamphylia, and was praised by Pope Celestine I as a "true successor of Chrysostom" for his opposition to Pelagianism. He died at Constantinople on October 10. January 8.

ATTILANUS. See Froilan.

ATTO (1070–1166). Born at Badajoz, Spain (some Italians claim at Florence, Italy), he joined the Vallambrosans in Tuscany, became abbot general in 1105, and was named bishop of Pistoia in 1135. He wrote an account of the shrine of Compostela in Spain and biographies of SS. John Gualbert and Bernard of Parma. May 22.

ATTRACTA (6th century). Also known as Araght, legend has her the daughter of a noble Irish family who, when refused permission by her father to become a nun, fled to St. Patrick at Coolavin and received the veil from him. She founded a hospice on Lough Gara, which endured for a thousand years as Killaraght. The legends also attribute spectacular miracles to her. In reality, she probably lived a century after Patrick. August 11.

AUBERT (d. c. 669). Except that he became bishop of Cambrai sometime after 532, little is known of him. He is believed to have helped a group of well-known laypeople to the monastic life and to have performed numerous miracles. December 13.

AUBERT (d. c. 725). The bishop of Avranches, France, he built Mont St. Michel early in the eighth century in response to an order from St. Michael he received in a vision. September 10.

AUBIERGE. See Ethelburga (d. c. 664).

AUBIN. See Albinus.

AUDARD. See Theodard (d. 893).

AUDAX (d. c. 250). See Anatolia.

AUDE. See Alda.

AUDIFAX (d. c. 260). See Marius.

AUDOENUS. See Ouen.

AUDOMARUS. See Omer.

AUDREY. See Etheldreda.

AUDRY. See Aldericus.

AUGEBERT (7th century). See Felix.

AUGURIUS (d. 259). See Fructuosus.

AUGUSTINE (354–430). Born at Tagaste, northern Africa, son of

Patricius, a pagan Roman official, and Monica, a Christian, he received a Christian upbringing and in 370 went to the university at Carthage to study rhetoric with a view to becoming a lawyer. He gave up law to devote himself to literary pursuits and gradually abandoned his Christian faith, taking a mistress with whom he lived fifteen years and who bore him a son, Adeodatus, in 372. He became keenly interested in philosophy and about 373 he embraced Manichaeism. After teaching at Tagaste and Carthage for the next decade, he went to Rome in 383 and opened a school of rhetoric but became discouraged with his students' attitudes, and in 384 he accepted the chair of rhetoric at Milan. There, impressed by the sermons of Ambrose, bishop of Milan, and of his tutor, Simplicianus, he returned to his Christian faith and was baptized on Easter Eve in 387. With his mother, brother, and several others, he lived a community life of prayer and meditation. Later in 387, he started back to Africa, and on the way, Monica died at Ostia. The following year he founded a sort of monastery at Tagaste, and in 389 Adeodatus died. In 391, he was seized by the populace of Hippo and ordained there. He established a religious community and though continuing to live a monastic life, began to preach; he met with phenomenal success. In 395, he was made coadjutor to Bishop Valerius of Hippo and succeeded to the see on Valerius' death the following year. He became the dominant figure in African Church affairs and was the leader in the bitter fights against Manichaeism, Donatism, and Pelagianism. He died at Hippo during Genseric's siege of the city on August 28. Augustine's towering intellect molded the thought of Western Christianity to such an extent that his ideas dominated the thinking of the Western world for a thousand years after his death. He wrote profusely, expositing and defending the faith, and to this day many of his two hundred treatises, some three hundred letters, and nearly four hundred sermons are of major import in theology and philosophy. Among his best-known works are his *Confessions,* one of the great spiritual classics of all times; *City of God,* a magnificent exposition of a Christian philosophy of history; *De Trinitate; De doctrina christiana; Enchiridion;* and his treatises against the Manichaeans and the Pelagians. Called Doctor of Grace, he is one of the greatest of the Fathers and Doctors of the Church, and with the possible exception of Thomas Aquinas, the greatest single intellect the Catholic Church has ever produced. August 28.

AUGUSTINE OF BIELLA. *See* Fangi, Bl. Augustine.

AUGUSTINE OF CANTERBURY (d. 604). A Roman, and prior of St. Andrew's monastery in Rome, he was sent with some forty of his monks by Pope St. Gregory the Great to evangelize the English in 596. Although the group desired to turn back, Gregory refused them permission to do so and they landed on the isle of Thanet in England in 597. They were favorably received by King Ethelbert of Kent, who was baptized the year of their arrival. Augustine then went to France to be consecrated bishop and on his return was highly successful, making thousands of converts. He built a church and Benedictine monastery at Canterbury on land given him by the King but was unsuccessful in his attempts to convince the bishops observing the Celtic rites in Britain to adopt the discipline and practices of Rome; they also refused to recognize him as their metropolitan. He spent the rest of his life working in Kent and established sees at London and Rochester. He died on May 26, the first archbishop of Canterbury and "the Apostle of the English." He was sometimes called Austin.

AUGUSTINE GAZATICH, BL. (c. 1260–1323). Born at Trogir, Dalmatia, he joined the Dominicans about 1280, studied at Paris, and then preached with great success in Dalmatia, where he established several Dominican houses. He gave missions in Italy, Bosnia, and Hungary, and in 1303 was named bishop of Zagreb, Croatia, by Pope Benedict XI, whom he had met while in Hungary. He instituted widespread reforms in his diocese and encouraged learning and the study of the Bible. He attended the Council of Vienne in 1311–12 and clashed with the governor of Dalmatia, Miladin, and denounced his tyrannical rule. In 1317, Augustine was translated to Lucera, Italy, and corrected religious abuses that had crept into the see during the Saracen occupation. He died on August 3, venerated for his charity and the gift of healing. His cult was confirmed in 1702.

AUGUSTINE NOVELLO, BL. (d. 1309). Matthew of Termini (Taormina), Sicily, studied law at Bologna, became a brilliant law teacher there, and then served as King Manfred's chancellor. Wounded and left for dead on the battlefield at Benevento where Manfred was killed, he joined the Hermits of St. Augustine incognito as a lay brother, taking the name Augustine Novello, fulfilling a vow he had made on the battlefield to God. His identity was revealed when a brief he filed on behalf of his order was so brilliant his opponents said it could only be the work of Matthew of Termini. He helped draw up new constitutions for his order, was made penitentiary to the papal court by Pope Nicholas IV, and served as Pope Benedict VIII's papal legate to Siena. Elected prior general of his order in 1298, he resigned two years later and

retired to St. Leonard hermitage, which he had built near Siena, and died there on May 19.

AULAIRE. See Eulalia of Barcelona.

AUNACHARIUS (d. 605). Also known as Aunaire, he was born of a noble family and spent his youth in the court of King Guntram of Burgundy. He left the royal court to serve under bishop Syagrius of Autun, who ordained him, and was elected bishop of Auxerre in 561. He was active in civil as well as ecclesiastical matters, attended synods in Paris and Macon, held two in his own see, and introduced numerous reforms in his diocese. He died on September 25.

AUNAIRE. See Aunacharius.

AUREA (d. 666). A Syrian, she was named superior of St. Martial convent in Paris in 633 by St. Eligius and governed for thirty-three years until she died with 160 of her community of the plague. October 4.

AUREA (d. 856). Born at Cordova, Spain, she became a Christian after her husband died and then a nun at Cuteclara. After twenty years there, her family denounced her as a Christian to the Moorish authorities, and she was beheaded for her faith. July 19.

AUREA (c. 1042–c. 1069). A native of Villavelayo, Spain, during the Moorish occupation of Spain, she became a nun at nearby Benedictine San Millán de la Cogolla abbey and lived as a solitary famed for her visions and miracles. March 11.

AURELIAN (d. 551). Named bishop of Arles in 546, he founded a monastery and a convent there, and was papal vicar for Gaul. He died at Lyons. June 16.

AURELIUS (d. 429). A deacon at Carthage, he was made bishop of that see in 392, vigorously combated Donatism and Pelagianism, and convened several synods to combat these heresies. He was a close friend of St. Augustine, who wrote his treatise *On the Work of Monks* in response to Aurelius' complaint about some lax monks. July 20.

AURELIUS (d. c. 852). According to his biography by St. Eulogius of Toledo, he was the son of a Moor and a Spanish woman, was orphaned as a child, and was secretly raised a Christian by his aunt during the Moorish persecution of Christians. He married a half Moorish woman, Sabigotho, who took the name Natalie when he converted her to Christianity. They were both beheaded for practicing their religion openly together with George, a monk from Jerusalem whom Aurelius had befriended. July 27.

AUREUS (date unknown). The bishop of Mainz, he was driven from his see when the Huns invaded the area. On his return, his sister Justina and several others were murdered while he was saying Mass. June 16.

AUSTIN. *See* Augustine of Canterbury.

AUSTINDUS (d. 1068). Born at Bordeaux, France, he became a Benedictine monk at St. Orens abbey at Auch, and when elected abbot, he put into effect the Cluniac observance at the abbey. He was named archbishop of Auch in 1041, in which position he was a fierce opponent of simony. September 25.

AUSTREBERTA (630–704). The daughter of the Count Palatine Badefrid and St. Framechildis, she was born near Thérouanne, Artois, ran away from home to escape an unwanted marriage,

and received the veil from St. Omer, who convinced her family of the genuineness of her calling. She joined the convent at Port (Abbeville), became abbess there, and was noted for her holiness, humility, visions, and miracles. She later was appointed abbess of a monastery in Pavilly, where despite great opposition, she restored discipline and a proper observance of the rule. February 10.

AUSTREGISILUS (551–624). The son of a poor Bourges nobleman, the death of an opponent just before their ordeal by battle at the court of King Guntramnus caused Austregisilus to turn to the religious life. He was ordained by St. Aetherius, was elected abbot of St. Nazaire abbey at Lyons, and in 612 was named bishop of Bourges, where he remained until his death. He is also known as Outril. May 20.

AUSTREMONIUS (3rd century). According to St. Gregory of Tours, he was one of the seven missionaries sent from Rome in the third or fourth century to evangelize Gaul, and is venerated in Clermont as St. Stremoine, its first bishop. Another legend has him one of Christ's seventy-two disciples killed and decapitated by a Jewish rabbi whose son he had converted. November 1.

AUSTRUDE. *See* Anstrudis.

AUTBERT. *See* Aubert.

AUTONOMOUS (d. c. 300). An Italian bishop, he fled to Bithynia to escape Diocletian's persecution of the Christians, converted many, and then suffered martyrdom for his faith. September 12.

AUXENTIUS (4th century). A soldier in the army of Emperor Licinius, he was persecuted when he refused to worship pagan gods but escaped with his life. He was later ordained, and then became bishop of Mopsuestia, Cilicia. December 18.

AUXENTIUS (d. 304). *See* Eustratius.

AUXENTIUS (d. 473). The son of Addas, a Persian, he was an equestrian guard of Emperor Theodosius who left the guard to become a hermit in the desolate area around Mount Oxia near Constantinople. He later cleared himself of charges of Eutychianism before Emperor Marcion and resumed his eremitical life on Mount Skopa near Chalcedon, where he attracted numerous disciples by his austerity and holiness. He also attracted a group of women who formed a community of nuns at the foot of the mountain. He died in his hermitage on Skopa on February 14.

AUXILIUS (5th century). With SS. Isserninus and Secundinus, he worked with St. Patrick in his missionary activities. They all signed a decree, still extant, telling the clergy that they might appeal to Rome against judgments made by the see of Armagh. December 6.

AVA (d. c. 850). Daughter of King Pepin, she was cured of blindness by St. Rainfredis, became a Benedictine nun at Dinart, Hainault, and later was elected abbess. April 29.

AVELLINO, ANDREW (1521–1608). Born at Castronuovo, Italy, he was baptized Lorenzo, studied civil and canon law in Naples, received his doctorate, and was ordained. After a period as a canon lawyer, he turned to pastoral work and in 1556 was assigned the task of reforming Sant' Arcangelo convent in Baiano, where he was almost killed by those opposing his reforms. He left Baiano and joined the Theatines in Naples, taking the name Andrew. He eventually became superior of the Naples house and was known for his ef-

forts to improve the quality of priests. In 1570, he was sent to Lombardy at the request of St. Charles Borromeo, founded houses at Milan and Piacenza, and was most successful in reforming the area in spite of great resistance. He returned to Naples in 1582 and spent the rest of his life ministering to the spiritual needs of his people, converting many and combating Protestantism. He is credited with many miracles, and blood taken from his body after his death was reported to bubble like that of St. Januarius, also in Naples. An investigation of the matter by Msgr. Pamphili (later Pope Innocent X) gave no credence to the report. Andrew Avellino died in Naples on November 10.

AVERTANUS, BL. (d. 1380). Born in Limoges, even as a child he was drawn to the religious life. He joined the Carmelites at Limoges as a lay brother, went on pilgrimage to the Holy Land with a companion, Romaeus, encountered great difficulties on the way as they fought winter storms crossing the Alps, and died of the plague at St. Peter's hospital in Lucca; Romaeus died a week later. Avertanus was considered remarkable for his holiness by his fellow Carmelites, who attributed to him ecstasies, visions, and the gift of prophecy, and considered him a saint. Romaeus, also a lay brother, had his cult approved by Pope Gregory XVI. February 25.

AVERTINUS (d. c. 1180). Probably a hermit at Tours, France, untrustworthy legend has him a Gilbertine canon who was made deacon by St. Thomas of Canterbury, accompanied Thomas to the Synod of Tours in 1163, and after Thomas was slain, settled in Touraine, where he died. May 5.

AVITUS (d. c. 525). The son of Isychius, bishop of Vienne, he was born at Auvergne and named Alcimus Ecdicius

Avitus. He succeeded his father as bishop of Vienne in 490, became known for his wisdom, learning, and charity, and ransomed many Ligurian captives of the Burgundians. He converted King Sigismund of Burgundy to Christianity in 516, caused Sigismund to rebuild Aganaum monastery in retribution for his murder of his son, Sigeric (a murder he committed on the accusations of Sigeric's stepmother, which were later proved to be false), and presided over the Council at Epaon in 517. He wrote an allegorical epic on the creation of man, *De spiritualis histoiae gestae,* a poem on chastity, *De laude virginitatis,* and homilies and letters, some of which are still extant. February 5.

AVITUS (d. c. 530). According to Gregory of Tours, he was an abbot at Perche, France, and was unsuccessful in an attempt to save St. Sigismund and his wife and sons from being executed by King Clodomir. Unverifiable legend had Avitus a lay brother at Micy abbey who left to become a hermit and was elected abbot against his will. He later fled the monastery and lived as a hermit in Maine; King Clotaire built a church and monastery for him at Châteaudun. June 17.

AYALÁ, BL. FERDINAND (d. 1617). Born at Ballesteros, near Toledo, Spain, he joined the Augustinians in 1603, and was sent to Mexico as a missionary and then to Japan. He became vicar provincial there in 1605 and was arrested with Bl. Alphonsus Navarette at Omura on the outbreak of a persecution of Christians. They were both beheaded for their faith on June 1, and beatified in 1867.

AYBERT (1060–1140). Born at Espain, France, he joined a priest named John at Crespin abbey and lived as a solitary with him. They accompanied the abbot on a trip to Rome, decided on his return to join the abbey, spent the next quarter of

a century as procurator and cellarer of the abbey, and then resumed his life as a hermit. He was ordained a priest and attracted great numbers of visitors by his holiness. His practice of reciting fifty Ave Marias in succession was a precursor of the rosary. April 7.

AYEUL. *See* Agilus.

AYMARD (d. 965). He became third abbot of Cluny, succeeding St. Odo, in 942 and continued Odo's reforms. He resigned in 948 because of blindness and died at Cluny on October 5.

AYOUL. *See* Aigulf (d. 836).

AYRALD, BL. (d. c. 1146). The son of Count William II and brother of Pope Callistus II, King Raymond of Castile, and Count Henry of Portugal, he joined the Carthusians at Portes and in time became prior. He was appointed bishop of Maurienne and probably died there. January 2.

AZADANES (d. c. 342). *See* Abdiesus.

AZADES (d. c. 342). *See* Abdiesus.

AZEVEDO, BL. IGNATIUS (1528–70). Of a wealthy family, he was born at Oporto, Portugal, and joined the Jesuits when twenty. In 1554, he became rector of St. Antony College in Lisbon, served briefly as vice provincial of Portugal, and then was appointed rector of the college at Braga. In 1566, he was appointed inspector of Jesuit missions in Brazil, asked for additional missionaries on his return, and in 1570 set out for Brazil with thirty-nine fellow Jesuits. The ship on which they sailed, the *Santiago,* was attacked and captured near the Canary Islands by a French privateer commanded by Huguenot Jacques Sourie, who had all the missionaries put to death. They were all beatified in 1854. July 15.

B

BABA, BL. LOUIS (d. 1624). *See* Sotelo, Bl. Louis.

BABYLAS (d. c. 250). He became bishop of Antioch about 240, refused to allow Philip the Arabian into his church until he had done penance for the murder of his predecessor, Emperor Gordian, and suffered martyrdom during Decius' persecution. January 24.

BACCHUS (d. 303). *See* Sergius.

BADEMUS (d. 376). Born in Bethlapat, Persia, he founded a monastery near there and was its abbot. With seven of his monks, he was imprisoned and tortured during the persecution of King Sapor II of Persia and then murdered by Nersan, a Christian who had been promised his freedom if he would prove his denial of his Christianity by murdering Bademus. April 10.

BADUARIO, BL. BONAVENTURE (1332–86). Of a leading Paduan family, he was born at Peraga, near Padua, became an Augustinian in his youth, and studied at Paris. He became a professor of theology at Bologna, was elected prior general of his order in 1377, was named cardinal the following year, the first of his order to be so named, and served as papal legate for Pope Urban VI. Baduario clashed with the ruler of Padua, Prince Francis of Carrara, a relative, over Church rights, and was killed by an arrow in Rome, reputedly at the instigation of Francis. Baduario wrote several treatises and was a friend of Petrarch, preaching his funeral oration. June 10.

BAGNES, BL. MARY BARTHOLOMEA (1511–77). Of a noble Florentine family, and born in Florence, she suffered stomach trouble from infancy due to the inadequate feeding she received as an infant from her foster mother. When her father announced she was to be married after she had decided on a religious life, she had a nervous breakdown and became a bedridden invalid the rest of her life. She bore her afflictions with great fortitude, exerted great spiritual influence on many who visited her for advice and consolation, became a Dominican tertiary when thirty-two, and experienced visions. She died after suffering her invalidism for forty-five years. Her cult was approved by Pope Pius VII. May 27.

BAGNUS (d. c. 710). A disciple of St. Wandregisilus and a Benedictine monk at Fontenelle abbey, he was named bishop of Thérouanne about 689. He successfully evangelized the area around Calais, resigned his see after twelve years, and returned to Fontenelle as a monk. He was elected abbot there about 704 and probably also of Fleury, which Pepin had just restored, and died at Fontenelle. He is also known as Bain. June 20.

BAIN. *See* Bagnus.

BAIRRE. *See* Finbar.

BAITHEN (536–c. 599). Said to be a cousin of St. Columba and one of his supporters, he became abbot of Tiree and on the death of Columba in 597 succeeded him as abbot of Iona. He wrote a life of Columba and some poetry. October 6.

BAKHITA, JOSEPHINE (1869–1947). Born in Olgossa, Sudan, the young Josephine was kidnapped. She was sold as a slave more than once, until taken into the household staff of Italian Consul, Callisto Legnani. In 1885 the Legnanis took her to their home in Italy where she went to work for another family, the Michielis, and attended the Venetian catechumenate operated by the Canossian Sisters. When the Michielis wanted her to return with them to Sudan, St. Josephine refused. Since she was over twenty-one years of age, Italian law gave her this freedom of choice and she entered the Canossian community. She lived and worked in Schio, Vicenza, was known as "our Black Mother," and was admired for her virtuous life. She was canonized in 2000. May 17.

BALBINA (2nd century). According to the Roman Martyrology, she was a Roman girl, baptized by Pope Alexander, who was buried on the Appian Way. This seems to be a fictitious story, although there is a Balbina cemetery near the Appian Way on an estate owned by a Christian named Balbina. March 31.

BALDINUCCI, BL. ANTONY (1665–1717). Born in Florence, the son of an author and artist, he was destined for the priesthood by his father from his birth. He joined the Jesuits in 1681, taught at Terni and Rome, and was ordained when thirty. His request to be sent to India as a missionary was denied, but he was assigned to missionary and pastoral work in Viterbo and Frascati, and spent the rest of his life there ministering to the poor and preaching missions. He achieved widespread fame for his eloquent preaching and the unusual methods he employed in the more than five hundred missions he conducted (often he led a procession carrying a cross and scourging himself). He died on November 7, and was beatified in 1893.

BALDOMERUS (d. c. 660). A locksmith in Lyons, France, he was so reputed for his holiness that Viventius, abbot of St. Justus, ordained him subdeacon and installed him in a cell next to the monastery, where he spent the rest of his life in prayer and meditation. He is also known as Galmier. February 27.

BALES, BL. CHRISTOPHER (d. 1590). Born at Coniscliffe, Durham, England, he studied at the English college in Rome and Douai, was ordained at Douai in 1587, and sent on the English mission the following year, using the alias Mr. Rivers. He was arrested two years later, and after being tortured was found guilty of being a Catholic priest exercising his priestly office in England. He was hanged, disemboweled, and quartered in Fleet Street, London, on March 4. His name is also spelled Bayles. He was beatified in 1929.

BALRED. *See* Balther.

BALTHASAR (1st century). It is related (in Matt. 2:1–2) that wise men came from the East to worship the infant Jesus. They were queried by Herod as to the child's whereabouts, found the child, "did him homage," and "offered him gifts of gold and frankincense and myrrh." Warned in a dream, they returned to their own country by a different route so they did not have to report to Herod where Jesus could be found. Ancient tradition calls them "magi" and says there were three of them, named

Balthasar, Caspar, and Melchior. Modern scholars believe they were astrologers from Babylonia or Arabia. July 23.

BALTHASAR OF CHIAVARI, BL. (c. 1420–92). Born in Chiavari, Italy, he joined the Friars Minor of the Observance and was ordained. He accompanied Bl. Bernardino of Feltre on his missions until ill health curtailed his traveling. He then became famous as a confessor. He died at Binasco on October 17, and his cult was confirmed in 1930. October 25.

BALTHER (d. 765). A monk-priest at Lindisfarne, he became a solitary at Tyningham on the Scottish border, and later on the Bass Rock, Northumbria. He lived a life of great austerity and holiness, and died at Aldham. He was also known as Baldred. March 6.

BANDARINUS (d. 566). Appointed bishop of Soissons in 540, he founded Crépin abbey and served as bishop until banished by King Clotaire II. He went to England, where he worked anonymously in an abbey as gardener. His identity was discovered after seven years there, and Clotaire recalled him to his see. August 9.

BANDELLI, STEPHEN (1369–1450). Born in Castelnuova, Italy, he became a Dominican at Pavia, received his doctorate in canon law, and became a professor at the university there. He became a highly successful preacher, attracted huge crowds wherever he preached, converted thousands, and was greatly sought after as a confessor. He died at Saluzzo, near Turin, and his cult was confirmed by Pope Pius IX in 1856. June 13.

BAPTIST OF MANTUA, BL. (1448–1516). Born in Mantua, Italy, and nicknamed Spanuola (the Spaniard) after his Spanish father, though it may have been his surname, he studied philosophy and rhetoric in his youth and became a Carmelite. He was soon recognized as one of the leading scholars of his time, was elected vicar general of the Carmelites at Mantua six times, and against his objections was elected prior general of the Carmelites in 1513. He was consulted by many in high places, gave assistance to the poor and needy, and wrote many verses in Latin. He died at Mantua, and was beatified in 1885. March 20.

BARACHISIUS (d. 327). With a fellow monk, Jonas, at the monastery of Bethasa at Hubaham, Persia, he was arrested during a persecution of King Sapor II when they encouraged a group of Christians facing death to persevere in their faith. They were tortured and questioned, and separately each was told the other had recanted. When they did not break, they were barbarously murdered, Jonas by being pressed to death and his body cut to bits, and Barachisius by having hot brimstone and pitch poured down his throat. March 29.

BARADATES (d. c. 460). A man of great learning, he lived as a hermit in Cyrrhus, Syria, practiced the greatest austerities and penances, and was consulted by Emperor Leo I on the decrees of the Council of Chalcedon. February 22.

BARAT, MADELEINE SOPHIE (1779–1865). Born at Joigny, Burgundy, France, on December 12, the daughter of a cooper, she was educated by her older brother Louis, who later became a priest and who imposed the strictest discipline and penances on her. On his recommendation, Fr. Varin, who planned to form an institute of women to teach girls, a female counterpart of the Jesuits, received her and three companions into the religious life in 1800, thus founding the

Society of the Sacred Heart of Jesus. They founded their first convent and school at Amiens the following year, and in 1802 Madeleine, though the youngest member of the group, now grown to twenty-three, was appointed superior; she was to rule for sixty-three years. The society spread throughout France, absorbed a community of Visitation nuns at Grenoblein in 1804 (among whom was Bl. Philippine Duchesne, who was to bring the Society to the United States in 1818), and received formal approval from Pope Leo XII in 1826. In 1830 the Society's novitiate at Poitiers was closed by the revolution, and Madeleine founded a new novitiate in Switzerland. By the time of her death in Paris on May 21, she had opened more than one hundred houses and schools in twelve countries. She was canonized in 1925. May 25.

BARBARA (4th century). Although one of the most popular saints of the Middle Ages, scholars doubt if there ever really was a virgin martyr named Barbara. An elaborate legend has her the daughter of a pagan *paynim* Dioscorus in the time of Emperor Maximian who resisted her father's demands that she marry. She lived in a tower, and during the absence of her father had three windows built into a bathhouse he was having constructed (she did this to explain the Trinity), but was miraculously spared the wrath of her father when he returned and found what she had done. However, he took her before a judge, who had her tortured. Not satisfied with this punishment, her father took her up a mountain, killed her, and was then destroyed by fire from heaven as he came down from the mountain. The site of her martyrdom was variously described as at Antioch, Heliopolis, Nicomedia, and Rome. She is one of the Fourteen Holy Helpers and is the patroness of architects and builders. December 4.

BARBARIGO, GREGORY (1625–97). Born in Venice on September 16, of a noble family, he was educated there, and in 1648 accompanied the Venetian ambassador to Munster for the signing of the Treaty of Westphalia ending the Thirty Years' War. There he met the apostolic nuncio, Fabio Chigi, who when he became Pope Alexander VII appointed him bishop of Bergamo in 1657, created him a cardinal in 1660, and translated him to Padua in 1664. He was famous for his prodigious charities, encouraged learning, and founded a seminary for priests, endowing it with a printing press and a library. He was also active in laboring to effect a reunion with the Greek Church. He died at Padua on June 18, and was canonized by Pope John XXIII in 1960. June 17.

BARBASYMAS (d. 346). Made metropolitan of Seleucia and Ctesiphon in 342, he was imprisoned and tortured with sixteen priests for eleven months by King Sapor II of Persia. When Barbasymas spurned a golden cup filled with a thousand gold coins if he would worship the sun, all were beheaded at Ledistan in Huzistan. January 14.

BARBATUS (c. 612–82). Probably a native of Benevento, Italy, he was ordained and engaged in pastoral work at Marcona. He was transferred to Benevento, and legend says he was at first unsuccessful in converting the inhabitants, but finally did so when his promise that the siege of the city by Emperor Constans II in 663 would be lifted was fulfilled. He was chosen bishop of the city after the siege was lifted, evangelized the area around Benevento, attended the Council of Constantinople in 680, which condemned the Monothelites, and died in Benevento on February 29. February 19.

BARBEA (d. 101). *See* Sarbelius.

BARBERI, BL. DOMINIC (1792–1849). Born near Viterbo, Italy, on June 22, he joined the Passionists in 1814, taking the name Dominic of the Mother of God, and was ordained in 1818. He taught for ten years, served in several posts of his order, and in time became provincial. He founded the first Passionist retreat in Belgium, in Ere, in 1840, and in 1842 he established the Passionists in England at Aston Hall, Staffordshire. He was known for his asceticism and learning, published sermons, theological, and ascetical works, founded two other Passionist houses in England, and received several members of the Oxford movement into the Church, notably John Henry Newman. Barberi died at Reading, England, on August 27, and was beatified in 1964.

BARBIERI, CLELIA (1847–1870). Founder of the Congregation of Minims of the Sorrowful Mother, Clelia's order ministered to the sick, elderly, lonely, and poor. In the convents she founded, her voice has been mysteriously heard singing along with the nuns. Recognized as the patron of people ridiculed for their piety, she was canonized in 1989.

BARDO (c. 982–1053). Born at Oppershofen in the Welterau, Germany, he was educated at the abbey of Fulda and became a Benedictine monk there. He was made abbot of Kaiserswerth about 1029 and of Horsfeld in 1031; later in the same year he was named archbishop of Mainz. Though for a time chancellor and chief almoner of the Empire, he continued to live most austerely and was noted for his aid to the poor, his enforcement of clerical celibacy, and his active opposition to simony. He died on June 10. June 15.

BARDOLENUS (d. c. 677). A monk at Luxeuil under St. Columban, Bardo-lenus became first abbot of St. Peter's monastery near Paris and with St. Fursey founded several churches and hospitals there. June 26.

BARHADBESABA (d. 355). A deacon at Arbele, Persia, during the persecution of King Sapor II, he was tortured by Sapor Tamsapor, governor of Adiaben, and when he refused to sacrifice to fire and water was ordered to be beheaded by Aggai, a Christian apostate, who bungled the job but finally succeeded in beheading him. July 15.

BARKWORTH, BL. MARK (1572–1601). Born in Lincolnshire, England, he was raised a Protestant, graduated from Oxford, and while on a trip to Europe visited Douai and became a Catholic. He studied for the priesthood and was ordained at Valladolid, Spain, in 1599. Sent on the English mission, he became a Benedictine at Hirache abbey, Navarre, while on the way back to England. He was arrested a few months after he landed in England, where he had labored under the alias of Lambert. He was tried and convicted of being a priest by three apostates who were probably former students of his, and with Fr. Roger Filcock, was hanged, drawn, and quartered on February 27 at Tyburn, the first English Benedictine martyr.

BARLAAM (4th century). Martyred at Antioch, untrustworthy legend has him an illiterate peasant who was imprisoned and tortured for his faith. When his judge could not force him to sacrifice to the gods, he held Barlaam's hand over red-hot coals and sprinkled hot incense over the hand, reasoning the intense heat would cause Barlaam to shake off the hot incense, thus giving the impression he was sacrificing to the gods. But Barlaam held his hand unflinchingly until it was consumed. November 19.

BARLAAM (d. 1193). Of a wealthy Novgorod family and christened Alexis, he gave his inheritance after his parents' death to the poor and became a hermit at Khityn on the Volga River. His holiness attracted numerous disciples, whom he organized into a monastic community, taking the name Barlaam. He died on November 6, and his grave became a pilgrimage site when numerous miracles were reported there.

BARLOW, AMBROSE (1585–1641). The fourth of fourteen children of Sir Alexander Barlow and christened Edward, he was born in Barlow Hall, Manchester, England, and brought up a Protestant. He was converted to Catholicism, went to Douai in 1614, studied there and at Valladolid, Spain, then joined the Benedictines at St. Gregory's in Douai, taking the name Ambrose, in 1615. He was ordained in 1617 and then returned to England, where he engaged in pastoral work in Lancashire. He was arrested four times in the next two and a half decades but each time was released. However, when priests, in 1641, were ordered from England or be labeled traitors and suffer the consequences of that state, he stayed on and was arrested on Easter of that year. When he refused to discontinue his priestly duties if released he was condemned to be executed. He refused to allow his friends to intercede for him and was hanged, disemboweled, and quartered in Lancaster on September 10, a week after he had been named prior of Canterbury. He was canonized by Pope Paul VI in 1970 as one of the Forty Martyrs of England and Wales.

BARNABAS (1st century). All we know of Barnabas is to be found in the New Testament. A Jew, born in Cyprus and named Joseph, he sold his property, gave the proceeds to the apostles, who gave him the name Barnabas, and lived in common with the earliest converts to Christianity in Jerusalem. He persuaded the community there to accept Paul as a disciple, was sent to Antioch, Syria, to look into the community there (Acts 11:22ff.), and brought Paul there from Tarsus. With Paul he brought Antioch's donation to the Jerusalem community during a famine, and returned to Antioch with John Mark, his cousin. The three went on a missionary journey to Cyprus, Perga (whence John Mark returned to Jerusalem), and Antioch in Pisidia, where they were so violently opposed by the Jews that they decided to preach to the pagans. They then went to Iconium and Lystra in Lycaonia, where they were first acclaimed gods and then stoned out of the city, and then returned to Antioch in Syria. When a dispute arose regarding the observance of the Jewish rites, Paul and Barnabas went to Jerusalem, where at a council it was decided pagans did not have to be circumcised to be baptized. On their return to Antioch, Barnabas wanted to take John Mark on another visitation to the cities where they had preached, but Paul objected because of John Mark's desertion of them in Perga. Paul and Barnabas parted, and Barnabas returned to Cyprus with Mark; nothing further is heard of him, though it is believed his rift with Paul was ultimately healed. Tradition has Barnabas preaching in Alexandria and Rome, the founder of the Cypriote Church, the bishop of Milan (which he was not), and has him stoned to death at Salamis about 61. The apochryphal *Epistle of Barnabas* was long attributed to him, but modern scholarship now attributes it to a Christian in Alexandria between 70 and 100; the *Gospel of Barnabas* is probably by an Italian Christian who became a Mohammedan; and the *Acts of Barnabas* once attributed to John Mark are now known to have been written in the fifth century. June 11.

BARNARD (777–841). Born in the Lyonnasie, France, he was raised at Charlemagne's court, restored Ambronay abbey, and became a Benedictine monk there. He was later elected abbot and in 810 was named archbishop of Vienne. He became a most influential prelate, founded Romans abbey about 837, and died there. His cult was approved in 1907. January 23.

BARONTIUS (d. c. 695). Abandoning his pleasure-seeking way of life, he distributed his wealth to the poor (though secretly retaining some of it) and went with his son to the abbey of Lonray in Berry, France, and became a monk there. Stricken by a sudden illness, he had a series of visions of St. Raphael, St. Peter, and hell and purgatory that so impressed him he gave all of his remaining possessions to the poor, made a pilgrimage to Peter's tomb in Rome, and on his return became a hermit with a monk named Desiderius near Pistoia. March 25.

BARR. *See* Finbar (d. 633).

BARRFOIN (6th century). An Irish monk (he may also have been a bishop) in charge of the church founded by St. Columba at Drum Cullen, Offaly, he preached in Offaly and Donegal, where he lived at Killbarron. Supposedly during one of his missionary journeys he voyaged to America and relayed his experiences and discovery to St. Brendan the Navigator. May 21.

BARROTTI, BL. ODDINO (1324–1400). Born at Fossano, Piedmont, Italy, he was appointed curate at St. John the Baptist church there about 1360. He lived so austerely that he was ordered by the bishop of Turin to relax his austerities. In 1374 he was appointed provost of the collegiate chapter at Fossano and rector of the canon church. He resigned four years later, became a Franciscan tertiary, and made his residence into a home for the destitute. After a trip to the Holy Land in 1381, he became head of the Guild of the Cross devoted to caring for the sick and sheltering pilgrims and built a hospital and a hospice for them. He became provost again in 1396 and pastor of the parish at which he had begun his priestly life, and died there four years later of the plague he contracted while ministering to the plague-stricken of Fossano. His local cult was confirmed in 1808. July 21.

BARROW, BL. WILLIAM (1609–79). Born in Lancashire, England, he joined the Jesuits at St. Omer in 1632, when twenty-three, and was sent to minister to the Catholics of England in 1645. He worked in England for more than three decades, mainly in London, until he was arrested and charged with complicity in the "popish plot" fabricated by Titus Oates. Convicted on perjured testimony by Oates and two of his henchmen, he was hanged, drawn, and quartered at Tyburn. He was widely known as William Harcourt and also used the alias Waring. He was beatified in 1929. June 20.

BARSABAS (4th century). A pious fiction with no foundation in fact according to which he was an abbot in Persia and was arrested with twelve of his monks during the persecution of King Sapur II. They were all cruelly tortured and then beheaded. A passing Mazdean, impressed by their fortitude and constancy under torture, joined them and was executed with them. December 11.

BARSANUPHIUS (d. c. 550). An Egyptian, he became a hermit in a cell adjoining the monastery at Gaza, Palestine, was consulted by many for his holiness and spiritual wisdom, communicated only in writing, and supposedly existed without food and water for years. April 11.

BARSIMAEUS (d. c. 250). The Roman Martyrology lists him as bishop of Edessa, Syria; he was a successful convertmaker, and he suffered martyrdom there. The Syrian Acts on which information of Barsimaeus is based have been proven false; he was not martyred, and the whole story may be a fiction. January 30.

BARTHOLOMEW (1st century). All that is known of him with certainty is that he is mentioned in the synoptic gospels and Acts as one of the twelve apostles. His name, a patronymic, means "son of Tolomai," and scholars believe he is the same as Nathanael mentioned in John, who says he is from Cana and that Jesus called him an "Israelite . . . incapable of deceit." The Roman Martyrology says he preached in India and Greater Armenia, where he was flayed and beheaded by King Astyages. Tradition has the place as Abanopolis on the west coast of the Caspian Sea and that he also preached in Mesopotamia, Persia, and Egypt. The Gospel of Bartholomew is apochryphal and was condemned in the decree of Pseudo-Gelasius. August 24.

BARTHOLOMEW (d. 1050). Born at Rossano, Italy, he became a disciple of St. Nitus, founder of the Greek abbey of Grottaferrata in Frascata, near Rome, became abbot, completed the buildings started by his predecessor, and made the monastery a center of learning and manuscript copying. He is reputed to have convinced Pope Benedict IX to resign and do penance at Grottaferrata as a monk, but Benedict was still claiming the papacy when Bartholomew died. He also composed several hymns. November 11.

BARTHOLOMEW (d. 1067). Abbot of the Benedictine abbey of Marmoutier, he was named archbishop of Tours in 1052. His efforts to bring Berengarius back to the Church were fruitless. November 11.

BARTHOLOMEW BREGANZA, BL. (c. 1200–71). Born at Vicenza, Italy, and educated at Padua, he was received into the Dominicans about 1220, and then served as prior of several Dominican houses. In 1233, with Fr. John of Vicenza, he founded the *Fratres Gaudentes,* a military order to keep public order in Bologna, which spread to towns all over Italy. He was made bishop of Nimesia, Cyprus, in 1248, became a friend of St. Louis of France, was papal legate to King Henry II of England, and in 1256 was translated to Vicenza. There he came into conflict with Ezzolina da Romano, leader of the Ghibellines, who caused his exile. On his return he labored to reconstruct his see, and died on July 1. He wrote sermons, scriptural commentaries, and a treatise on the *Hierarchy* of Dionysius the Areopagite. His cult was confirmed in 1793. October 23.

BARTHOLOMEW OF CERVERE, BL. (1420–66). Son of a nobleman, he was born at Savigliano, Italy, entered the Dominican priory there as a youth, and studied at Turin, where he had an outstanding record of scholarship. He was made inquisitor of Piedmont and was murdered by heretics near Cervere. His cult was approved by Pope Pius IX. April 22.

BARTHOLOMEW OF FARNE (d. 1193). A native of Whitby, Northumbria, and named Tostig by his Scandinavian-descended parents, he went to Norway, was ordained there, and on his return to Britain became a monk at Durham, taking the name Bartholomew. He then became a solitary on the desolate island of Farne off the coast of Northumbria, where he spent the next forty-two years, except for a year when he left because of a quarrel with another hermit.

Bartholomew was reputed to have performed miracles. June 24.

BARULA (d. 304). *See* Romanus.

BASIL (d. 362). A priest of Ancrya under Bishop Marcellus, he defended the bishop when he was deposed by the Arians and was tortured and then executed during the reign of Julian the Apostate for refusing to cease his preaching against the pagan gods. March 22.

BASIL (d. 370). He and St. Emmelia were the parents of SS. Basil, Gregory of Nyssa, and Macrina the Younger. They were exiled for their Christianty during the persecution of Galerius Maximinus but were later allowed to return to Caesarea, Cappadocia, where they lived the rest of their lives. May 30.

BASIL (329–79). One of ten children of St. Basil the Elder and St. Emmelia, he was born in Caesarea, Cappadocia, Asia Minor, and was educated by his father and his grandmother, St. Macrina the Elder. He took advanced studies at Constantinople and Athens, where Gregory Nazianzen and the future Emperor Julian the Apostate were classmates. On the completion of his studies, Basil taught rhetoric at Caesarea and then decided to pursue the religious life. He was baptized, visited monasteries in Palestine, Syria, and Egypt, and in 358 settled as a hermit by the Iris River in Pontus. He attracted numerous disciples, whom he organized into the first monastery in Asia Minor. He was ordained in 363 at Caesarea but returned to Pontus because of a disagreement with Archbishop Eusebius. Basil remained there until 365, when his friend Gregory requested his assistance in combating Arianism in Nazianzus. He returned to Caesarea, was reconciled to Eusebius, and in 370, on Eusebius' death, was elected archbishop of Caesarea and con-

sequently metropolitan of some fifty suffragen bishops, despite the opposition of Arian Emperor Valens. When Valens launched his persecution of the orthodox, he demanded that Basil submit to his demands; Basil refused, and in the confrontation of wills that followed, Valens capitulated and left Caesarea. Basil was soon faced with another struggle when Bishop Anthimus of Tyana claimed to be metropolitan of New Cappadocia when Cappadocia was divided, politically, into two provinces; Basil was forced to submit to the partition of his see into two dioceses. He was active in helping the sick and the poor, built a hospice and a huge complex to minister to the ill, and attracted huge throngs with his preaching. He became the leader of the Orthodox in the East in the continuing struggle against Arianism, though not too successful in securing aid from Rome and the West against the heresy that threatened to destroy the Church in the East. He died at Caesarea on January 1 (when his feast is celebrated in the East), a few months after Valens died on the battlefield, and the accession of Gratian to the throne halted the spread of Arianism. Basil was one of the giants of the early Church. He was responsible for the victory of Nicene orthodoxy over Arianism in the Byzantine East, and the denunciation of Arianism at the Council of Constantinople in 381–82 was in large measure due to his efforts. The organization and rule he devised at Pontus became the basis of monastic life in the East (as was so of Benedict in the West) and remains so to the present day. Basil fought simony, aided the victims of drought and famine, strove for a better clergy, insisted on a rigid clerical discipline, fearlessly denounced evil wherever he detected it, and excommunicated those involved in the widespread prostitution traffic in Cappadocia. He was learned, accomplished in statesmanship, a man of great personal holiness, and one of the great orators of Christianity. His doctrinal writings and his four hundred letters (many still extant) had tremendous influence. Among his outstanding treatises are *On the Holy Spirit,* the three *Books* against Eunomius, and with Gregory Nazianzen, he compiled a selection of passages from Origen, *Philocalia.* He is a Doctor of the Church and patriarch of Eastern monks. January 2.

BASIL THE YOUNGER (852–952). A hermit near Constantinople, he was arrested and brought to Constantinople and tortured as a spy. Miraculously saved from death, he was released and became famed for his miracles and holiness. Despite this he was persecuted for his denunciations of the evil lives of the aristocracy, including Princess Anastasia. He died in Constantinople. March 26.

BASILIDE (d. c. 202). *See* Plutarch.

BASILIDES (d. 205). A soldier in the prefect's guard in Egypt, he was assigned the task of escorting St. Potamiana to the place of her execution during the persecution of Septimus Severus. He shielded her from the mob along the way, was converted, and soon after suffered martyrdom himself. June 30.

BASILIDES (3rd century). The Roman Martyrology on June 12 lists four soldiers, Basilides, Cyrinus, Nabor, and Nazarius, who were scourged and then beheaded for their faith at Rome during Decius' persecution. The whole story is suspect, though a Basilides was martyred in Rome and was buried on the Via Aurelia. Basilides is also listed as martyred under Aurelian in the Roman Martyrology on June 10. June 12.

BASILISSA (d. c. 65). Questionable legend has her and Anastasia noble Romans who were converted by and became disciples of St. Peter and St. Paul. When they recovered and buried the bodies of the two saints after their executions, they were imprisoned for doing so, tortured, and then beheaded by order of Emperor Nero when they acknowledged their Christianity. April 15.

BASILISSA. *See* Julian (d. c. 304).

BASILISSA. *See* Basilla.

BASILLA (d. 304). A member of a noble Roman family and also known as Basilissa, she refused to marry Pompeius, a Roman patrician, after her conversion to Christianity. She was beheaded for her faith when she was denounced to Emperor Galienus by Pompeius and remained steadfast in her refusal to marry him. The facts of the story are uncertain. May 20.

BASLE. *See* Basolus.

BASOLUS (c. 555–c. 620). Born at Limoges, France, he was a soldier but left the military to become a monk at the monastery of Verzy. He then became a solitary on a hill overlooking Rheims and remained there the next forty years until his death. Also known as Basle, he is reported to have performed numerous miracles. November 26.

BATHILDIS (d. 680). Born in Britain, she was brought as a slave to the household of the mayor of the palace under King Clovis II in France. Evidently of great ability, she advanced herself and in 649 married Clovis, bearing him three sons, each of whom became King: Clotaire III, Childeric II, and Thierry III. On the death of Clovis in 655, she became regent and ruled capably and wisely. She ransomed many captives, helped promote religion in the realm, and endowed and founded numerous monasteries, including St. Denis, Corbie, and Chelles, where she retired about 665. She died there on January 30, and was canonized by Pope Nicholas I.

BAUDELIUS (d. c. 380). Unreliable sources have him a missionary who came to southern Gaul and was beheaded at Nimes, when he preached on Christianity during a festival in honor of Jupiter. He is a patron of Nimes, but the year of his death is uncertain—187, 297, or 380. May 20.

BAVO (d. c. 655). A nobleman of Hesbaye, Brabant, and also known as Allowin, he gave away his possessions on the death of his wife and became a Benedictine monk at Ghent under St. Amand, whom he accompanied on missionary journeys to France and Flanders. He then became a hermit at Mendonck but later returned to Ghent, where he lived as a hermit until his death there. October 1.

BAYA. See Brigid (5th century).

BAYLES, BL. CHRISTOPHER. See Bales, Bl. Christopher.

BAYLON, PASCHAL (1540–92). Born at Torrehermosa, Aragon, he was a shepherd in his youth, taught himself to read and write. He was refused admission to the Franciscans, but a few years later, in 1564, he became a Franciscan lay brother of the Alcantarine reform. He served most of his life as porter at different friaries in Spain known for his mortifications, charities, and devotion to the sick and the poor. He had an intense devotion to the Eucharist, which he successfully defended against a Calvinist minister in France, and was reputed to have possessed supernatural gifts. He died at the friary at Villareal, was canonized in 1690, and was declared the patron

of Eucharistic confraternities and congresses in 1897. May 17.

BEAN (11th century). He was first bishop of Mortlach, which became Aberdeen, Scotland. October 26.

BEATRICE (d. c. 304). See Simplicius.

BEATRICE D'ESTE I, BL. (1206–26). Daughter of Marquis Azzo of Este, she was orphaned when only six, resisted her family's desire for her to marry, and became a Benedictine nun at Solarola, Italy, when fifteen. She was transferred to Gemmola, where she died, held in great veneration for her holiness. Her cult was approved in 1763. May 10.

BEATRICE D'ESTE II, BL. (d. 1262). Niece of Bl. Beatrice d'Este I, she became a Benedictine nun at St. Antony's convent in Ferrara, Italy, which was founded by her family at her request, after her fiancé was killed in battle, and lived there the rest of her life. Her cult was confirmed in 1774. January 18.

BEATRICE OF ORNACIEU, BL. (d. 1309). Born in the Ornacieu castle at Isère, France, she became a Carthusian at Parménie as a youth, and lived a life of great austerity, gifted with visions of Christ, and performed great penances to resist diabolical tortures inflicted on her. Unsuccessful in an attempt to establish a new foundation at Eymeu, she returned to Parménie and died there on November 25. Her cult was confirmed in 1869. February 13.

BEATUS (d. c. 798). A monk at St. Martin's monastery in Liebana, near Santander, Spain, he denounced the heretical Adoptionist teachings of Archbishop Elipandus of Toledo and with Etherius, later bishop of Osma, reconverted many who had been led astray. To refute the archbishop's censure of

Beatus to his abbot, Fidelis, Beatus, and Etherius in 786 wrote *Liber adversus Elipandum.* Beatus also wrote a commentary on the Apocalypse and probably composed several hymns of the Mozarabic liturgy. February 19.

BEATUS OF LUNGERN (d. c. 112). A hermit who lived and died in a cave on Mount St. Beatenberg, Switzerland, his untrustworthy legendary story has him the apostle of Switzerland, baptized in England by St. Barnabas and ordained in Rome by St. Peter, who sent him to evangelize the Swiss. His cave became a place of pilgrimage and his legend has him fighting and slaying a dragon there. May 9.

BEATUS OF VENDÔME (3rd century). A missionary who evangelized the districts of Garonne, Vendôme, Laon, and Nantes in France, he died at Chevresson, near Laon. May 9.

BECHE, BL. JOHN (d. 1539). Also known as Thomas Marshall, he received his doctorate in divinity from Oxford in 1515 and became abbot of St. Werburgh's in Chester; in 1533, he was elected abbot of St. John's abbey in Colchester. Though he was a friend of Thomas More and Bishop John Fisher, and opposed to the policies of King Henry VIII, he and the members of his community took the Oath of Supremacy in 1534. When he opposed the dissolution of St. John's and spoke against the execution of More and Fisher, he was arrested and imprisoned in the Tower in London. He was tried at Colchester, convicted of treason, and hanged, drawn, and quartered there on December 1. He was beatified in 1895.

BEDE THE VENERABLE (c. 672–735). Born near St. Peter and St. Paul monastery at Wearmouth-Jarrow, England, he was sent there when three and educated by Abbots Benedict Biscop and Ceolfrid. He became a monk at the monastery, was ordained when thirty, and except for a few brief visits elsewhere spent all of his life in the monastery, devoting himself to the study of Scripture and to teaching and writing. He is considered one of the most learned men of his time and a major influence on English literature. His writings are a veritable summary of the learning of his time and include commentaries on the Pentateuch and various other books of the Bible, theological and scientific treatises, historical works, and biographies. His best-known work is *Historia ecclesiastica,* a history of the English Church and people, which he completed in 731. It is an account of Christianity in England up to 729 and is a primary source of early English history. Called "the Venerable" to acknowledge his wisdom and learning, the title was formalized at the Council of Aachen in 853. He was a careful scholar and distinguished stylist, the "father" of English history, the first to date events *anno Domini* (A.D.), and in 1899 was declared the only English Doctor of the Church. He died at Wearmouth-Jarrow on May 25.

BEE. *See* Bega.

BEGA (7th century). According to legend she was the daughter of an Irish King, fled on the day of her marriage to a son of the King of Norway, and was miraculously transported to Cumberland. She lived as a hermitess for a while but on the advice of St. Oswald, she received the veil from St. Aidan and founded St. Bee's (Copeland) monastery. As abbess, she was venerated for her aid to the poor and the oppressed. September 6.

BEGGA (d. 693). Daughter of Pepin of Landen, mayor of the palace, and St. Itta, she married Ansegilius, son of St.

Arnulf of Metz, and their son was Pepin of Herstal, founder of the Carolingian dynasty of rulers of France. On the death of her husband in 691, she built a church and convent at Andenne on the Meuse River and died there. December 17.

BELL, BL. JAMES (c. 1520–84). Born in Warrington, England, he was educated at Oxford and was ordained. He apostasized when Elizabeth became Queen but was later reconciled to the Church and returned to his priestly duties. He was arrested as a Catholic priest and imprisoned at Lancaster. When he acknowledged his priesthood and refused to accept the ecclesiastical supremacy of the Queen, he was convicted of treason and executed with Bl. John Finch at Lancaster on April 20. Both were beatified in 1929.

BELLACI, BL. THOMAS (1370–1447). Born in Florence, he spent his youth in dissipated living but then reformed and became a lay brother with the Observant friars at Fiesole, Italy. He lived a life of great austerity, practicing the most rigid penances and mortifications, and was appointed master of novices. He accompanied Friar John of Stroncone to Naples to spread the reform in that kingdom in 1414, and in 1420, with Bl. Antony of Stroncone, he went to Tuscany to oppose the Fraticelli and established several Franciscan foundations. He accompanied Friar Albert of Sarzana on his papal diplomatic mission to Syria and Persia in 1439, and with three others went to Ethiopia to preach. They were captured there three times by the Turks and sentenced to death for preaching Christianity to the Mohammedans but were ransomed by Pope Eugene IV. Bl. Thomas died at Rieti on October 31 while on the way to Rome to get permission to go to the East again. His cult was approved in 1771. October 25.

BELLARMINE, ROBERT FRANCIS ROMULUS (1542–1621). Born at Montepulciano, Tuscany, Italy, on October 4, he joined the Jesuits, despite his father's opposition, in 1560. He studied at Florence and Mondovi and then at Padua and Louvain and was ordained at Ghent in 1570. He was appointed a professor at Louvain, the first Jesuit to become a professor at Louvain, lectured on Thomas Aquinas' *Summa,* counteracted Baius' teaching, and gained a reputation for his learning and brilliant preaching. He studied Scripture and the Church Fathers and learned Hebrew for his studies. In 1576, he was recalled to Rome, where he occupied the chair of controversial theology at the newly founded Roman College for eleven years. It was during this period that he prepared his monumental *Disputationes de controversiis Christianae Fidei adversus hujus temporis Haereticos,* a study of the Catholic faith to refute the Protestant *Centuries of Magdeburg.* He was sent on an unsuccessful mission to Paris in 1589, enduring the eight-month siege of Paris by Henry of Navarre. In 1592, he was the leader in preparing the Clementine revised version of the Vulgate, for which he wrote an Introduction, was named rector of the Roman College in 1592, and in 1594 became provincial of the Naples province of the Jesuits. He became Pope Clement VIII's theologian in 1597, prepared two catechisms that were still in use in modern times, and in 1599 was created a cardinal by Clement. He was appointed archbishop of Capua in 1602 but was recalled to Rome three years later by the newly elected Pope Paul V. Bellarmine soon became the most effective spokesman and apologist of the Church in the later years of the Counter Reformation, noted, in his opposition to the Protestants, for his reasoning and rational argumentation rather than for rhetoric and dogmatic assertions. He was the great champion of the papacy, brilliantly defending the interdict placed on Venice against Fra Paoli Sarpi. Bellarmine overwhelmed King James I of England, who had written two books defending his theory of supremacy in the controversy that developed when Archpriest Blackwell took an Oath of Allegiance to the King that denied papal jurisdiction in temporal matters. Bellarmine incurred further royal opposition with his *De potestate papae*, denying the divine right of kings, which was publicly burned by the Paris *parlement*. However, he alienated Pope Sixtus V when he declared Popes had only indirect jurisdiction over secular rulers; Sixtus threatened to put the first volume of *Disputationes de controversiis* on the Index but died before doing so. Bellarmine's position became basic Catholic teaching on the subject. He became embroiled in the controversy over his friend Galileo, who accepted his admonition in 1610 that it would be wise to advance his findings as hypotheses rather than as fully proved theories. In the last decade of his life, his writings were on spiritual matters, among them *Art of Dying Well* and a commentary on the Psalms. He retired to St. Andrew's novitiate in Rome the last days of his life and died there on September 17. He was canonized in 1930 and declared a Doctor of the Church in 1931. September 17.

BELLESINI, BL. STEPHEN (1774–1840). Born at Trent, Italy, on November 25, he joined the Hermits of St. Augustine when sixteen. He studied at Rome and Bologna, became an excellent teacher of children and a forceful speaker, returned to Trent when the revolution broke out, and when the Augustinians were dissolved he became inspector of schools for the government in the Trentino. When the Augustinians were reactivated in the Papal States, he rejoined them in Bologna. He served as master of novices in Rome and then at

Città della Pieve, and then became a parish priest at Genazzana. He died there on February 2 of cholera he contracted while ministering to the stricken. He was beatified in 1904. February 3.

BELLUDI, BL. LUKE (1200–c. 1285). Born of a wealthy family near Padua, Italy, he was received into the Franciscans at Padua when twenty by St. Francis of Assisi. Bl. Luke met and became the close associate of St. Anthony of Padua, tending him on his deathbed, became minister provincial of his order, and built the basilica that still houses Anthony's remains. Bl. Luke's cult was confirmed in 1927. February 17.

BELSON, VEN. THOMAS (d. 1589). Born at Brill, Buckinghamshire, England, he studied at Rheims, and on his return to England, he was arrested at Oxford with two priests, George Nichols and Richard Yaxley, and Humphrey Prichard, his Welsh servant. They were all tried in London, tortured in the Tower, and then returned to Oxford, where they were executed for their faith. July 5.

BENEDICT (c. 480–c. 547). Born in Nursia, Italy, he was educated in Rome, was repelled by the vices of the city and in about 500 fled to Enfide, thirty miles away. He decided to live the life of a hermit and settled at mountainous Subiaco, where he lived in a cave for three years, fed by a monk named Romanus. Despite Benedict's desire for solitude, his holiness and austerities became known and he was asked to be their abbot by a community of monks at Vicovaro. He accepted, but when the monks resisted his strict rule and tried to poison him, he returned to Subiaco and soon attracted great numbers of disciples. He organized them into twelve monasteries under individual priors he appointed, made manual work part of the program, and soon

Subiaco became a center of spirituality and learning. He left suddenly, reportedly because of the efforts of a neighboring priest, Florentius, to undermine his work, and in about 525 settled at Monte Cassino. He destroyed a pagan temple to Apollo on its crest, brought the people of the neighboring area back to Christianity, and in about 530 began to build the monastery that was to be the birthplace of Western monasticism. Soon disciples again flocked to him as his reputation for holiness, wisdom, and miracles spread far and wide. He organized the monks into a single monastic community and wrote his famous rule prescribing common sense, a life of moderate asceticism, prayer, study, and work, and community life under one superior. It stressed obedience, stability, zeal, and had the Divine Office as the center of monastic life; it was to affect spiritual and monastic life in the West for centuries to come. While ruling his monks (most of whom, including Benedict, were not ordained), he counseled rulers and Popes, ministered to the poor and destitute about him, and tried to repair the ravages of the Lombard Totila's invasion. He died at Monte Cassino on March 21.

BENEDICT II (d. 685). Born in Rome, and active in Church affairs since his youth, he was an expert in Scripture and sacred music. Elected to succeed St. Leo II as Pope in 683, his consecration was delayed almost a year until June 26, 684, awaiting the Emperor's confirmation. During his pontificate he secured a decree from Emperor Constantine the Bearded permitting the exarch of Ravenna to confirm papal elections, thus eliminating the long delays. Benedict was highly regarded by Constantine, who sent him locks of his sons' hair, thus making them the Pope's spiritual sons. Benedict was successful in bringing back to orthodoxy Macarius, ex-patriarch of

Antioch, from his Monothelitism, and restored several Roman churches. He died on May 8 in Rome, and was named patron of Europe by Pope Paul VI in 1964. July 11.

BENEDICT (d. 997). See Adalbert of Prague.

BENEDICT (d. 1003). A hermit at a monastery under St. Romuald near Ravenna, Italy, he was sent to Poland to evangelize the Slavs with several other monks, at the request of Emperor Otto III. They set up a foundation at Kazimierz, and there Benedict and four fellow monks, Christian, Isaac, John, and Matthew, were murdered by pagan robbers on November 11. The five are venerated in Poland as the Five Polish Brothers, though they were neither Polish nor brothers. November 12.

BENEDICT XI, BL. (1240–1304). Born in Treviso, Italy, Nicholas Boccasini was educated there and at Venice, where he joined the Dominicans when he was fourteen. He became a professor and taught at Venice and Bologna, served as Dominican prior general of Lombardy, and in 1296 was elected master general of the Order. He was made a cardinal in 1298 and bishop of Ostia and served as papal legate to Hungary to try to settle a civil war there. He was one of only two cardinals who supported Pope Boniface VIII against the infamous charges of Philip the Fair of France and was in favor of Boniface's unpromulgated decree excommunicating Philip. It was Benedict who rallied papal forces and rescued Boniface from Anagni, where he had been imprisoned by William Nogaret, Philip's councilor. Benedict was elected Pope on October 22, 1303, made an uneasy peace with Philip, worked to reconcile warring factions in Europe and the Church and to increase spirituality, but died suddenly in Perugia on July 7 only eight months after his election. Some scholars believe he may have been poisoned. He was beatified in 1736.

BENEDICT OF ANIANE (c. 750–821). Son of Aigulf of Maguelone, he was cupbearer to King Pepin and Charlemagne and served in the army in Lombardy. He left the army and became a Benedictine at St. Seine, near Dijon, France, in 773. He refused the abbacy there and in 779 returned to Languedoc, where he had lived as a hermit on his estate, attracted numerous disciples, and built a monastery and a church. Supported by Emperor the Pious, who built a monastery for him at Inde, near Aachen, he became director of all the monasteries in the Empire and instituted widespread reforms, though because of opposition they were not as drastic as he wanted. In 817, his *Capitulare monasticum,* a systemization of the Benedictine rule was approved by the Council of Aachen as the rule for all monks in the Empire. He also compiled the *Codex regularum,* a collection of all monastic regulations, and *Concordia regularum,* showing the resemblance of Benedict's rule to those of other monastic leaders. He is considered the restorer of Western monasticism and is often called the "second Benedict." February 11.

BENEDICT BISCOP (c. 628–90). Of noble parents and a courtier at the court of King Oswy of Northumbria, his real name was Biscop Baducing. He went on pilgrimage to Rome in 653 and on his return decided to devote himself to biblical studies and spiritual matters. On the way back from a second trip to Rome, he became a monk at Lérins in 666 and remained there for two years. On a third trip to Rome, Pope St. Vitalian in 669 assigned him to accompany St. Theodore, the new archbishop of Canterbury, and St. Aidan back to England. Theodore appointed him abbot of SS. Peter and Paul

monastery at Canterbury, and two years later he was back in Rome collecting relics, religious articles, paintings, and manuscripts. In 674 he founded a monastery at the mouth of the Wear River and it became Wearmouth, dedicated to St. Peter and built of stone, with a lead roof and glass windows, all unknown in the buildings in England of that time, by artisans he brought over from France. He built a second monastery six miles away on the Tyne River in 682, dedicated it to St. Paul, and called it Jarrow. He made a fifth trip to Rome and brought back more treasures and Abbot John of St. Martin's there, the archcantor of St. Peter's and a musical expert, to teach the monks of Wearmouth and Jarrow how to sing the Divine Offices and Gregorian Chant. Under his direction the two monasteries became outstanding centers of learning and Roman liturgical practices, and their collection of books, manuscripts, and religious art was unequaled in all of England. Paralyzed and bedridden the last three years of his life, Benedict died on January 12. His life was written by Bede, the famous English historian, who had been entrusted to his care at the age of seven.

BENEDICT THE BLACK. *See* Benedict the Moor.

BENEDICT THE BRIDGE-BUILDER. *See* Bénezet.

BENEDICT CRISPUS (d. 725). Mentioned in the Roman Martyrology on March 11, all that is known of him is that he was archbishop of Milan, was involved in a lawsuit in Rome that he lost, and wrote the epitaph for the tomb of Caedwalla, the English King buried in St. Peter's in Rome.

BENEDICT THE HERMIT (d. c. 550). A solitary in the Campagnia, Italy, he knew St. Benedict and is mentioned in the *Dialogues* of St. Gregory as having miraculously escaped death in an oven at the hands of the invading Goths under Totila. March 23.

BENEDICT THE MOOR (1526–89). Born a slave near Messina, Italy, he was freed by his master and became a solitary, eventually settling with other hermits at Montepellegrino. He was made superior of the community, but when he was about thirty-eight, Pope Pius IV disbanded communities of solitaries and he became a Franciscan lay brother and the cook at St. Mary's convent near Palermo. He was appointed, against his will, superior of the convent when it opted for the reform, though he could neither read nor write. After serving as superior, he became novicemaster but asked to be relieved of this post and returned to his former position of cook. His holiness, reputation for miracles, and his fame as a confessor brought hordes of visitors to see the obscure and humble cook. He died at the convent, was canonized in 1807, and is the patron of blacks in the United States. The surname "the Moor" is a misnomer originating from the Italian *il moro* (the black). April 4.

BENEDICT RICASOLI, BL. (d. 1107). Born at Coltiboni, Italy, he became a monk at the abbey there, built on ground donated to St. John Gualbert, founder of the Benedictine congregation of St. John Gualbert, by Benedict's parents who were friends of John, but left the abbey to live as a solitary nearby, where he died on January 20. His cult was confirmed in 1907.

BENEN (d. 467). Son of Sechnan, a chieftain in Meath, Ireland, who had been converted by St. Patrick, he was very attached to Patrick as a boy. He later became his disciple and companion, and eventually his confidant and right-hand man, and in time succeeded him as chief bishop of Ireland. He is credited with evangelizing Clare, Kerry, and Connaught, and reportedly headed a monastery at Drumlease, built by Patrick, for some twenty years. He is also known as Benignus. November 9.

BÉNEZET (d. 1184). A shepherd in Savoy, he secured the reluctant consent of the bishop of Avignon to build a bridge across the Rhône in response to a vision he had experienced. He began work in 1177 on a stone span that was completed four years after his death. So many miracles were reported at his tomb that a chapel was built on the bridge to house his body. He is also known as Little Benedict the Bridge-builder. April 14.

BENFATTI, BL. JAMES (d. 1338). Born at Mantua, Italy, he became a Dominican and the friend and adviser of Nicholas Boccasini, master general of the Dominicans and later Pope Benedict XI, who appointed him bishop of Mantua about 1303, where he became known as "the Father of the Poor." He died at Mantua on November 19, and when miracles were reported at his tomb, a cult grew up, which was confirmed in 1859. November 26.

BENIGNUS. *See* Benen.

BENIGNUS (3rd century). Though venerated in Dijon, France, nothing is known of him for certain, including the Roman Martyrology's statement that he was a disciple of St. Polycarp in Smyrna (which was not so) and was martyred at Dijon during the reign of Marcus Aurelius. November 1.

BENILDE. *See* Romancon, Benilde.

BENINCASA, BL. (1376–1426). A member of a noble Florentine family, he joined the Servites when quite young and became a hermit at Montagnata. In quest of greater seclusion, he moved to a spot near Siena and became known for his holiness, healing powers, and spiritual advice and wisdom. His cult was confirmed in 1829. May 11.

BENJAMIN (d. c. 421). A deacon, he was imprisoned for preaching Christianity during the persecution of Yezdigerd of Persia and his son Varanes. Benjamin was released at the intercession of the Emperor in Constantinople, who promised he would stop preaching. As soon as he was released he again began preaching, was arrested and tortured, and then was impaled when he refused to agree to stop his preaching if released again. March 31.

BENNO (d. 940). Of a noble Swabian family, he became a canon at Strasbourg and in 906 a hermit on Mount Etzel in the canton of Schwyz, Switzerland. He occupied the hermitage in which St. Meinrad had lived, restored a shrine to Mary, and soon attracted disciples. In 927, he was named bishop of Metz by German King Henry I the Fowler in opposition to a locally elected candidate; two years later he was blinded by the enemies his reforms and the method of his appointment had made. He resigned his see and returned to Mount Etzel, where he was joined in 934 by Eberhard, provost of Strasbourg cathedral, and Benno's hermitage was developed into a monastery that in time became the famous Einsiedeln monastery. He died on August 3 and has long been venerated, though his cult has never been formally recognized.

BENNO OF MEISSEN (1010–c. 1106). Son of Count Frederick of Bultenburg, he was born in Hildesheim, Germany, was educated under Bishop St. Bernward there, and became a canon at the collegiate church of Goslar, Hanover.

Benno served as chaplain of Emperor Henry IV, was appointed bishop of Meissen in 1066, and was imprisoned for a year for supporting the nobles' revolt against Henry. Benno supported Pope Gregory VII against Henry and in 1085 was deposed by the German bishops supporting the Emperor at the synod of Mainz. He was reinstated in 1088 by antipope Guibert, whom he backed, but in 1097 Benno changed his allegiance to Pope Urban II. Benno was heavily involved in politics but spent the last years of his life as a missionary to the Wends. His canonization in 1523 caused Martin Luther to write a denunciatory polemic about it. June 16.

BENNO OF OSNABRÜCK, BL. (d. 1088). Born at Löhengrin, Swabia, he was educated under Bl. Herman the Cripple at Reichenau and became so expert in architecture that he was appointed Emperor Henry III's official architect. Benno saved the cathedral at Speyer from collapsing, was made director of the cathedral school at Hildesheim in 1047, and on his return from Henry's campaign in Hungary, he was appointed provost of the cathedral at Goslar. In 1068, he was appointed bishop of Osnabrück. He was a supporter of Henry, acting as his envoy to Pope Gregory VII several times, and in 1076 signed the Emperor-inspired Synod of Worms deposition of Gregory. When Gregory excommunicated all those participating in the synod, Benno joined the other bishops who went to Canossa in Italy to beg the Pope's pardon. To escape taking sides again, Benno hid when Henry was excommunicated in 1080. Benno died at the Benedictine monastery at Iburg, which he had founded. July 12.

BENTIVOGLIA, BL. (d. 1232). Born of well-to-do parents in Bentivoglia, Marches, Italy, he joined the Franciscans, was known for his fervor and charity, and his piety and a miracle are mentioned in St. Francis' *Fioretti*. Bl. Bentivoglia died on December 25 at his birthplace. December 1.

BENVENUTO, BL. (d. 1232). Born in Gubbio, Umbria, Italy, he became a soldier but in 1222 joined the Franciscans and at his request was put in charge of lepers. He lived a life of holiness, filled with visions and miracles. He died at Corneto, Apulia, and at the request of the bishops of Venice and Amalfi, his cult was approved for those cities in 1236. June 27.

BENVENUTO MARENI, BL. (d. 1289). Born in Recanati, Italy, he became a Franciscan lay brother, noted for his piety, visions, and ecstasies. He died at Recanati on May 5, and his cult was confirmed by Pope Pius VII. May 21.

BEOCA (d. c. 870). Abbot of Chertsey Abbey, Sussex, England, he, a priest named Hethor, and ninety members of his community were murdered by raiding Danes. April 10.

BERARD (d. 888). *See* Ageranus.

BERARD (d. 1220). A native of Carbio, Italy, and of the noble Leopardi family, he was received into the Franciscans by St. Francis in 1213. He and his fellow Franciscan priests Peter and Odo and two lay brothers, Accursio and Adjustus, were sent to preach to the Mohammedans by Francis in 1219. After being banished by the Moors at Seville, they went to Morocco, and when they refused to leave or to stop preaching, Sultan Abu Jacob cut their heads asunder with his scimitar on January 16. They were canonized in 1481.

BERCHARIUS (d. c. 696). A native of Aquitaine, he became a monk at Luxeuil,

was ordained, was the first abbot of the monastery at Hautvillers founded by St. Nivard, and founded a monastery, Montier-en-Der, and a convent for women, Puellemontier. He was stabbed to death by a monk, Daguin, whom he had disciplined, and died two days later, on March 26 in 685 or 696. October 16.

BERCHMANS, JOHN (1599–1621). Eldest son of a shoemaker, he was born at Diest, Brabant, early wanted to be a priest, and when thirteen became a servant in the household of one of the cathedral canons at Malines, John Froymont. In 1615, he entered the newly founded Jesuit college at Malines, and the following year became a Jesuit novice. He was sent to Rome in 1618 to continue his studies, and was known for his diligence and piety, impressing all with his holiness and stress on perfection in little things. He died there on August 13. Many miracles were attributed to him after his death, and he was canonized in 1888. He is the patron of altar servers. November 26.

BERHTWALD (d. 731). Abbot of Reculver, Kent, England, and a noted Scripture scholar, he was elected archbishop of Canterbury on July 1, 692, succeeding Theodore, and reigned for thirty-seven years. January 9.

BERHTWALD (d. 1045). A Benedictine monk at Glastonbury abbey, he became bishop of Ramsbury in 1005, was reputed to have experienced visions and to have made prophecies, and was generous to Glastonbury and Malmesbury abbeys. He is also known as Brithwald. January 22.

BERNADETTE OF LOURDES. *See* Sourbirous, Marie Bernarde.

BERNARD (c. 778–842). Of a distinguished family and a member of

Charlemagne's court, he married and about 800 founded the monastery of Ambronay. He later became a monk there and in time abbot. He was appointed archbishop of Vienne in 810, founded the abbey of Romans about 837, where he was buried after his death on January 23, and was noted for his saintliness and insistence on strict ecclesiastical discipline.

BERNARD (d. 1133). Of the noble Florentine Uberti family, he joined the Vallombrosans, became abbot of San Salvio monastery, and was elected general of the Vallombrosans. He was made a cardinal by Pope Urban II in 1097 and served as papal legate. He was appointed bishop of Parma in 1106, supported the legitimate Pope and the reforms of Pope Gregory VII, and was driven into exile in 1104 by the followers of antipope Maginulf. Bernard's protests against the Hofenstauens' proclamation of Conrad as German King in 1127 over Lothair II (Lothair was to be crowned Emperor in 1133) again caused Bernard to be driven from Parma, but he returned and died there on December 4.

BERNARD (1090–1153). Son of Tescelin Sorrel and Aleth, daughter of the lord of Montbard, he was born at Fontaines les Dijon, the family castle near Dijon, Burgundy, the third son of seven children. He was sent to study at Châtillon and after a frivolous youth decided, on the death of his mother, to pursue a religious life. In 1112, he persuaded thirty-one of his friends and relatives (including four of his brothers) to go with him to Citeaux, which had been founded in 1098, the first Cistercian monastery, which observed a strict interpretation of the Benedictine rule. They were welcomed by the abbot, St. Stephen Harding. In 1115 Bernard was sent with twelve monks to found a Cistercian house at Langres, with Bernard as abbot. Though there were initial difficulties because of Bernard's strict discipline and austerities, his holiness soon attracted scores of disciples. The name was changed from the Vallée d'Absinthe to Clairvaux and was to become the mother house of some sixty-eight Cistercian monasteries established by its monks. Bernard soon became involved in matters outside the monastery as his reputation for learning and wisdom spread, and he soon was one of the most powerful influences in Europe, consulted by rulers and Popes. He supported the legitimacy of Pope Innocent II's election in 1130 against the claims of antipope Anacletus II and successfully led the struggle that led to Innocent's acceptance as Pope. Bernard was the leader in convincing the Lombards to accept Lothaire II as Emperor. In 1140 Bernard began preaching in public and was soon regarded with awe for the miracles attributed to him and for the eloquence of his preaching, for which he was acclaimed as the greatest preacher of his times. He was the leader in the attacks on Abelard questioning his rationalism and extreme exaltation of human reason and opposed it with his own certitude of faith and reliance on traditonal authority. He was instrumental in having Abelard condemned at the Council of Sens and forcing him into retirement. In 1142, Bernard arbitrated the disputed succession to the see of York in England, and in the same year he saw the abbot of the Cistercian Tre Fontane monastery in Rome, whom he had brought to Clairvaux as a postulant, Peter Bernard Paganelli, elected Pope as Eugene III. In 1145 the papal legate asked him to go to Languedoc in southern France to combat the Albigensian heresy, and his preaching was most successful, though not enduring. In 1146 he helped stop a series of *pogroms* in the Rhineland, and in the same year, at Eugene's request, he preached a crusade against the Turks, who had captured Edessa on Christmas in 1144. He roused all of Europe to the Second Crusade, headed by Emperor Conrad III and Louis VII of France, which was to end in disaster—a fate he blamed on the wickedness and lack of dedication of the crusaders. In 1153 Bernard left Clairvaux to effect a peace between the duke of Lorraine and the inhabitants of Metz, which had been attacked by the duke. He was stricken on his return and died at Clairvaux on August 20. Bernard is considered the second founder of the Cistercians, and from the time at twenty-five when he became abbot of Clairvaux he soon became the dominant influence in the religious and political sphere of Western Europe. His influence during the last forty years of his life was enormous and he was prominently involved in practically every major event of those years. His mystical writing, especially *De Diligendo Deo,* one of the outstanding medieval mystical works, formed the mysticism of the Middle Ages, and his other writings, his more than three hundred sermons, his treatise *De consideratione,* written for Pope Eugene's guidance, some five hundred known letters, his reflections on Scripture, and his deep devotion to Mary and the Infant Jesus all had a profound effect on Catholic spirituality. Called the Melliifluous Doctor, he was canonized in 1174, was formally declared a Doctor of the Church in 1830, and is considered the last of the Fathers of the Church. August 20.

BERNARD (d. c. 1180). The son of the Moslem caliph of Lérida in Catalonia, Spain, and named Achmed, he was converted to Christianity and became a Cistercian monk at Poblet near Tarragona, taking the name Bernard. He converted his two sisters, Zaida and Zoraida, who took the names Gracia and Mary, respectively, but when he at-

tempted to convert their brother Almanzor, he denounced them to the Moorish authorities and all three were beheaded for their new faith. June 1.

BERNARD OF BADEN, BL. (c. 1429–58). Son of Margrave James I of Baden and Catherine, daughter of Charles II of Lorraine, he was interested in literature and things military as a young man. He turned over to his brother his right of succession to secure support for his participation in a crusade against the Turks, whose capture of Constantinople in 1453 had aroused the whole Christian world. He died at Moncalieri, Italy, while on his way to see Pope Callistus to interest him in his plan. Many miracles were reported at his tomb and he was beatified in 1479. July 15.

BERNARD OF CAPUA (d. 1109). All that is known of him is that he was born at Capua, Italy, was confessor and adviser of Duke Richard II of Capua; was appointed bishop of Foro-Claudio, Italy, and moved the see to Caleno in 1100. March 12.

BERNARD OF CORLEONE. *See* Latini, Bl. Bernard.

BERNARD OF MENTHON. *See* Bernard of Montjoux.

BERNARD OF MONTJOUX (c. 996–1081). Probably born in Italy, he became a priest, was made vicar general of Aosta, and spent more than four decades doing missionary work in the Alps. He built schools and churches in the diocese but is especially remembered for two Alpine hospices he built to aid lost travelers in the mountain passes named Great and Little Bernard after him. The men who ran them in time became Augustinian canons regular and built a monastery. The order continued into the twentieth century. He was proclaimed the patron saint of Alpinists and mountain climbers by Pope Pius XI in 1923. He is sometimes fallaciously referred to as Bernard of Menthon and the son of Count Richard of Menthon, which he was not. May 28.

BERNARD OF OFFIDA, BL. (1604–94). Born at Apignano, Marches, Italy, he was a shepherd at seven, became a Capuchin lay brother at Offida in 1626, and worked at menial tasks at various houses of his order. When sixty, he was made a *quaestor* (beggar of alms) at the friary of Offida and attracted throngs of people seeking his advice, miracles, and good offices as peacemaker. He died on August 22, and was beatified in 1795. August 26.

BERNARD THE PENITENT (d. 1182). Born at Maguelone, Provence, France, he participated in some kind of uprising against the governor and in 1170 was given a series of penances by the bishop of Maguelone to be performed over a seven-year period. Weighted down with chains, he went on several penitential pilgrimages but in time settled at Saint-Omer near St. Bertin monastery. There he became known for his austerities and saintliness and became a monk at St. Bertin. He is reputed to have performed many miracles and to have had the gift of prophecy. April 19.

BERNARD OF TIRON (d. 1117). Also known as Bernard of Abbeville, he was born near Abbeville, France, became a monk of St. Cyprian's near Poitiers, was named prior of St. Sabinus, which he tried to reform, and then, after some twenty years, left to become a hermit at Craon. He returned to St. Cyprian's and became abbot but resigned in a dispute with Cluny and resumed his eremitical way of life. He engaged in missionary work and in 1109 built a monastery in

the forest of Tiron in Picardy, whose congregation spread throughout France and to England and Scotland. His cult was confirmed in 1861. April 14.

BERNARDINO OF FELTRE. *See* Tomitani, Bl. Bernardino.

BERNARDINO OF FOSSA. *See* Amici, Bl. Bernardino.

BERNARDINO OF SIENA (1380–1444). Son of the governor of Massa Marittima, Italy, where he was born Bernardino degli Albizzeschi, he was orphaned at seven, and was raised by an aunt. He joined a confraternity of our Lady when seventeen, ran the hospital at Siena during a plague in 1400, joined the Franciscans, and was professed in the nearby convent of Colombaio in 1403. He was ordained the following year and then lived as a solitary at Colombaio for the next twelve years. In 1417 he began to preach at Milan, and in a short time his eloquence and fiery sermons attracted attention. He preached missions all over Italy and attracted great crowds as he preached devotion to the Holy Name and denounced the evils of the times. He declined the bishopric of Siena in 1427 after Pope Martin V had cleared him of all charges made against him by his enemies, later declined the sees of Ferrara and Urbino, and was elected vicar general of the Friars of the Strict Observance in 1430. He rejuvenated and reformed the order, increasing its numbers from three hundred to over four thousand, and was really its second founder. He resigned as vicar general in 1442 to return to his preaching and missions and died at Aquila while on a mission trip on May 20. He was canonized in 1450.

BERNO (d. 927). Of a wealthy family, he was born in Burgundy, joined the Benedictines at St. Martin's, Autun, became abbot of Baume-les-Messieurs, and when he finished its reform, he founded Gigny and became its abbot. In 1910, Duke William of Aquitaine made him abbot of a monastery he was founding in central France, and thus Berno became first abbot of Cluny, which in the years to come was to have an enormous impact on monasticism in Europe. January 13.

BERNO, BL. PETER (d. 1583). Born at Ancona, Switzerland, he studied at Rome, joined the Jesuits, was sent to India, and was ordained in Goa. He was murdered with Bl. Rudolf Aquaviva and several others near Cuncolim by a group of Hindus objecting to their preaching Christianity and their plan to build a church in Cuncolim. He was beatified in 1893. July 27.

BERNWARD (d. 1022). Of a Saxon family, he was raised by his uncle Bishop Volkmar of Utrecht when orphaned as a child. He studied at the cathedral school of Heidelberg and at Mainz, where he was ordained. In 987, he became imperial chaplain and tutor to the child Emperor Otto III. He was elected bishop of Hildesheim in 993, built St. Michael's church and monastery there, and administered his see capably. He was interested in architecture, art, and metalwork, and created several metalwork pieces. He was engaged in a dispute for years with Archbishop Willigis of Mainz over episcopal rights to the Gandersheim convent, but eventually Rome ruled in Bernward's favor. He became a Benedictine in later life and died on November 20. He was canonized in 1193.

BERRIO-OCHOA, BL. VALENTINE (1827–61). Born at Ellorio, Spain, of an impoverished noble family, he served as a joiner's apprentice in his youth and then joined the Dominicans. He was

sent as a missionary to the Philippines, went to Indochina in 1856, and two years later was named vicar apostolic of central Tonkin. He was betrayed by an apostate during the persecution of Christians and imprisoned with Bl. Jerome Hermosilla, vicar apostolic of eastern Tonkin, and Bl. Peter Almató. All three were beheaded on November 1, and beatified in 1906. November 6.

BERTHA (d. c. 725). Married to a nobleman at twenty and mother of five daughters, she became a nun, with two of her daughters, on the death of her husband, at a convent she had built at Blangy, France. She later became a hermitess there. July 4.

BERTHA (d. c. 840). Related to the Dukes of Lorraine, she owned extensive properties on the Rhine, married a pagan, and when he was killed in battle, devoted herself to raising her son Rupert as a Christian. She founded several hospices for the poor, and after a visit to Rome, they gave away their possessions and became hermits near Bingen (Rupertsberg), Germany. He died when twenty and she spent the remaining twenty-five years of her life there. May 15.

BERTHELOT, BL. DIONYSIUS (1600–38). Born at Honfleur, France, and baptized Peter, he became a trader in the East Indies after a French ship he was on had been captured and destroyed by Dutch privateers and he escaped to Java. He served on several Portuguese expeditions as pilot and cartographer, and in 1635 he joined the Carmelites at Goa, taking the name Dionysius of the Nativity, and was ordained in 1638. While acting as pilot for a Portuguese diplomatic mission to Sumatra, he and the whole delegation were seized and imprisoned by the Sumatrans at Achin (Koetaraja). When Dionysius refused to renounce his faith, he and a fellow Carmelite, a lay brother named Redemptus of the Cross (Thomas Rodriguez da Cunha), were put to death. They were beatified in 1900. November 29.

BERTHOLD (c. 1090–1142). Born on the shores of Lake Constance, he became a Benedictine monk at Sankt Blasien on the death of his wife in 1120. He became prior of Goettweig in the Black Forest and then abbot at Steyer-Garsten, founded by Margrave Ottokar of Styria. Berthold soon established Steyer-Garsten as a center of spirituality and built a hospice and hospital there. He was known for his holiness, austerity, and concern for the poor, and as a preacher and confessor; several miracles were attributed to him. July 27.

BERTHOLD (d. c. 1195). Born at Limoges, France, he studied at Paris and was ordained there. He went on the Crusades with Aymeric, a relative, and was in Antioch during its siege by the Saracens, during which he had a vision of Christ denouncing the evildoing ways of the Christian soldiers and labored to reform them. He organized and became superior of a group of hermits on Mount Carmel, and is thus considered by some to be the founder of the Carmelites, and ruled for forty-five years. March 29.

BERTHOLD OF RATISBON, BL. (c. 1210–72). Born at Ratisbon, Germany, he joined the Franciscans and preached with great success in Bavaria and Switzerland. He engaged in missionary work in Austria, Bohemia, Moravia, and Silesia, and in 1263 was named by Pope Urban IV to preach a crusade, working with Albertus Magnus. He preached to huge crowds, and his sermons, later written in Latin, are valuable sources of information about the period. He died at Ratisbon. December 14.

BERTILDA OF MAREUIL (8th century). Of noble parents, she married a nobleman, was active in charitable work, and on his death lived as a hermitess at Mareuil, France, building a church adjacent to her cell. January 3.

BERTILLA (d. c. 705). Born near Soissons, France, she became a Benedictine nun at Jouarre monastery, near Meaux, and became first abbess of Chelles when it was refounded by the wife of Clovis II, St. Bathildis. She gave the veil to Bathildis about 665 and also to the widow of King Ethelhere of the East Angles, Hereswitha. She enforced strict discipline at the abbey, practiced great austerities and penances, and was known for her holiness during the forty-six years she was abbess. November 5.

BERTINUS (d. 700). With St. Mommolinus and St. Bertrand, all natives of Coutances, France, he was a monk at Luxeuil when he was sent with them to assist St. Omer, bishop of Therouanne, in evangelizing the Morini around Pasde-Calais. They built a monastery at what is now St. Mommolin with Mommolinus as abbot, and another one at Sithiu, of which Mommolinus also became abbot. When Mommolinus was appointed bishop of Noyon about 661, Bertinus became abbot of Sithiu and built it into one of the great monastic centers of France (it was later renamed St. Bertin's) and evangelized the whole area. A church he built with St. Omer near Sithiu in 663 afterward became the cathedral of the see of St. Omer. September 5.

BERTONI, GASPAR (1777–1853). Founder of the Congregation of the Sacred Stigmata of Our Lord Jesus Christ (Stigmatines) in 1816, Brunora Ravelli Bertoni was the son of a wealthy and pious family and had his first vision at his First Communion. During the twenty-year French occupation of northern Italy, Gaspar worked in hospitals for the sick and wounded. He was ordained chaplain to the Saint Magdalen Canossa sisters in 1800 and canonized in 1989.

BERTONI, BL. JAMES (1444–83). Sent by his father to the Servite priory in Faenza, Italy, when only nine, he became a Servite there, was ordained, and served as procurator of the priory. He was known for his holiness, and miracles were reported at his tomb after his death on May 25. His cult was approved in 1766. May 30.

BERTOUL. *See* Bertulf.

BERTRAN, LOUIS (1526–81). Born at Valencia, Spain, he joined the Dominicans when eighteen, and was ordained in 1547. He served as master of novices for some thirty years of his life, became an outstanding preacher, and in 1557 he met and encouraged St. Teresa of Avila in her proposed reform of the Carmelites. In 1557 he did heroic work in the plague that ravaged Valencia, and in 1562 he went to Colombia as a missionary. He traveled throughout the Caribbean area, converting thousands and trying to secure better treatment for the Indians. He became known for his prophecies, miracles, and gift of tongues. He returned to Valencia in 1569 and spent the rest of his life as prior of several houses and in training preachers. He died on October 9, and was canonized in 1671.

BERTRAND (c. 553–623). Born at Autun, France, he was ordained in Paris by St. Germanicus, served at the cathedral school there and became archdeacon, and was appointed bishop of Le Mans in 587. He supported the Neustrian kings, was driven into exile when their fortunes were in decline sev-

eral times, but was reinstated by King Clotaire II in 605. Bertrand was noted for his aid to the poor, his interest in agriculture, especially grape growing, and he founded a monastery, a hospice, and a church. June 30.

BERTRAND (d. 1123). Son of a high military officer, he decided against a military career and became a canon at Toulouse, and archdeacon. About 1075, he became bishop of Comminges, France, and ruled the see for the next forty-eight years. He reformed the diocese, put the canons under the rule of St. Augustine, persuaded marauding troops to return the cattle they had seized, and had several miracles attributed to him. He was probably canonized by Pope Honorius III sometime before 1309. October 16.

BERTRAND OF GARRIGUES (d. c. 1230). Born at Garrigues, southern France, he became a Cistercian priest and preached in that area, which was rent by civil war and the Albigensian heresy. In 1215, he joined St. Dominic with five other preachers (the beginning of the Dominicans) and was sent to Paris by Dominic in 1217 to found a house near the university. Soon recalled to Rome, he then established the Order in Bologna, accompanied Dominic to Paris in 1219, and became prior provincial of Provence when the Order was organized into eight provinces at the general chapter at Bologna in 1221. He spent the rest of his life preaching in southern France, established the priory of Marseilles, and died at the abbey of Boucher in southern France. His cult was confirmed in 1881. September 6.

BERTULF (d. 640). A pagan, he was converted to Christianity by his relative St. Arnulf of Metz and became a monk at Luxeuil about 620. After several years there, he went to Bobbio in Italy, and in

627 became abbot. He later was involved in a dispute with Bishop Probus of Tortona, who claimed jurisdiction over Bobbio, but Pope Honorius I made the abbey exempt from episcopal control and directly subject to the Holy See, the first such recorded exemption. Bertulf was reputed to have performed miracles and was held in high regard for his holiness and the austerity of his rule. August 19.

BERTULF (d. c. 705). Born of pagan parents in Germany, he went to Flanders, was converted to Christianity, and became steward for Count Wambert. He accompanied the count on pilgrimage to Rome, and on the death of the count and his wife, who willed him their estate, he retired to a monastery he had founded at Renty and remained there until his death. He is also known as Bertoul. February 5.

BESAS (d. 250). *See* Julian.

BESSARION (4th century). A native of Egypt, he became a hermit under St. Antony and then Macarius, subjected himself to great mortifications, and had many miracles attributed to him. June 17.

BETTELIN (8th century). A hermit and a disciple of St. Guthlac in Croyland, England, his fictitious legend has him the son of a Stafford ruler who fell in love with a princess while on a visit to Ireland. On their return to England she died a terrible death, when while he was gone for a midwife when the pangs of childbirth overtook her in a forest, she was torn to pieces by ravenous wolves, whereupon he became a hermit. Later legend has him leaving his hermitage to drive off invaders with an angel's assistance. He then spent the rest of his days in his cell, where he died. September 9.

BEUNO (d. c. 640). His untrustworthy legend has him a monk in Wales who founded his own community and performed numerous miracles, among them restoring St. Winifred's head after she was beheaded. However, he does seem to have been an effective preacher who evangelized much of North Wales and founded a monastery at Clynnog Fawr (Carnavonshire). April 21.

BEUZEC. *See* Budoc.

BIANCHI, FRANCIS XAVIER (1743–1815). Born at Arpino, Italy, he studied at Naples, was tonsured at fourteen, and despite his father's objections, joined the Congregation of Clerks Regular of St. Paul (the Barnabites). He was ordained in 1767, served as president of two colleges, and became famous for his gift of prophecy and the miracles credited to him (he is reported to have stopped the flow of lava from the erupting Vesuvius in 1805). In ill health, he was left alone at his college when his order was expelled from Naples, and he died there on January 31. He was canonized in 1951.

BIANCONI, BL. JAMES (1220–1301). Born at Mevania (Bevagna), Umbria, Italy, he joined the Dominicans at Spoleto when sixteen and sometime later became founding prior of a Dominican house at Mevania. He was active in helping the residents of the town after it was looted and sacked by Emperor Frederick II in 1248, lived a life of extreme poverty, fought antimonianism in Umbria, and was blessed with supernatural gifts. He died at Mevania, and his cult was approved by Pope Boniface IX in 1400 and by Pope Clement X in 1674. August 23.

BIBIANA (4th century). Though the church of St. Bibiana in Rome dates from the fifth century, attesting to the veneration early paid her, her legend is untrustworthy. According to it she was the daughter of the ex-prefect, Flavian, who had been tortured for his faith and banished to Acquapendente during the persecution of Julian the Apostate. After Flavian's death, his wife, Dafrosa, was beheaded and Bibiana and her sister, Demetria, were deprived of all their possessions and then were arrested. Demetria dropped dead on her arrest, and Bibiana was scourged to death. She is also known as Viviana. December 2.

BIBLIA (d. 177). *See* Pothinus.

BICCHIERI, BL. EMILY (1238–1314). Born at Vercelli, she refused her father's plans for her to marry and convinced him to build a convent—the first of Dominican regular tertiaries—of which she became abbess when twenty. She was noted for her frequent communions (uncommon in those days), her ecstasies and visions, and the miracles attributed to her. She died on May 3, and her cult was approved in 1769. August 19.

BICHIER DES ANGES, ELIZABETH (1773–1838). born in the Chateau des Anges at Le Blanc, France, daughter of Antony Bichier, lord of the manor, she was christened Joan Elizabeth Mary Lucy but always used Elizabeth. She was educated in a convent in nearby Poitiers and when her father died fought successfully to save her family's property from confiscation by the National Assembly. She moved to Bethines, a suburb of Poitiers, with her mother in 1796 and devoted herself to keeping religion alive in the village against the atheism and constitutional priests of the revolutionary regime. In 1797, she met and became friends with Abbe Fournet (St. Andrew Fournet), who drew up a rule for her to follow as she dedicated her life to teaching and to the care of the sick and needy. When her mother died

in 1804, she went as a novice to the Carmelite convent in Poitiers and then to the Society of Providence to prepare herself to be a member of a community of nuns Abbe Fournet proposed to establish. When Elizabeth returned she was put in charge of a group of women he had formed into a community to teach children and to care for the sick and aged. The group took vows in 1807 and had its rule approved by the bishop of Poitiers in 1816. The congregation, the Daughters of the Cross, spread despite several jurisdictional disputes and by 1830 had some sixty convents all over France. At Elizabeth's encouragement, Michael Garicoits, the spiritual director of the Basque house at Igon, founded the Priests of the Sacred Heart of Betherran; at Abbe Fournet's death in 1834, he became his replacement. Elizabeth died on August 26, and was canonized in 1947.

BICOT (d. c. 342). *See* Abdiesus.

BILFRID (d. c. 758). A monk hermit at Lindisfarne off the coast of Northumberland in northern England, he was an expert goldsmith and bound with gold, silver, and gems the famous St. Cuthbert's copy of the Gospels of Lindisfarne. March 6.

BILLIART, JULIA (1751–1816). Of a well-to-do farming family, she was born on July 12 at Cuvilly, Picardy, France, and christened Marie Rose Julia, she early evinced an interest in religion and helping the sick and the poor. She was paralyzed by a mysterious illness and was forced into hiding when her opposition to constitutional priests and her aid to fugitive priests became known to the revolutionary authorities. She stayed for a time at Amiens with a friend, Frances Blin Bourdon, viscountess of Gezaincourt, who joined her and accompanied her to Bettencourt, where, with a group of women, they conducted catechetical classes for the villagers. There she met Fr. Joseph Verin, and when she returned to Amiens, she began, under his direction, the Institute of Notre Dame, devoted to the spiritual education of poor children, the training of religious teachers, and the Christian education of girls. They opened an orphanage and in 1804, during the course of a mission in Amiens, Fr. EnFantin, after a novena, ordered Julia to walk and she did—after having been an invalid for twenty-two years. The order flourished but trouble developed when Fr. Verin was transferred and his successor as confessor to the Sisters of Notre Dame became antagonistic to the Sisters, as did the Bishop of Amiens, who forced Julia to leave Amiens in 1809. She moved the mother house to Namur, and though she was later exonerated in the affair, she kept the Institute's mother house there. During the rest of her life she worked to expand her Institute, and at her death at Namur on April 8, fifteen convents had been estalished. She was canonized by Pope Paul VI in 1969.

BIRD, BL. JAMES (1574–93). Born and raised a Protestant in Winchester, England, he became a Catholic and on a trip to the Continent stayed for a time at Douai College in Rheims. On his return to England, he was arrested and convicted of treason for asserting that the Pope was the head of the Church. Offered his freedom if he would take the Oath of Supremacy, he refused, was imprisoned, and then hanged, drawn, and quartered at Winchester. He was beatified in 1929. March 24.

BIRGITTA. *See* Bridget.

BIRINUS (d. c. 650). Of German ancestry, he became a priest in Rome, was consecrated bishop in Genoa, and went to Britain as a missionary. On his arrival in 634, he devoted himself to evangelizing the West Saxons, converted their King Cynegils, who gave him Dorchester for his see, and was so successful in his conversions he is called "the Apostle of Wessex." He died on December 3 and was buried at Dorchester. December 5.

BIRNDORFER, CONRAD (1818–94). Born in Parzham, Bavaria, on December 22, the youngest of nine children and baptized John, he became a Capuchin lay brother in 1849 and served as porter at the shrine to our Lady at Altötting for more than forty years. He was noted for his devotion to Mary, his charity, and was gifted with the ability to prophecy and read people's hearts. He died at Altötting on April 21, and was canonized in 1934.

BISCOSSI, BL. SIBYLLINA (1287–1367). Born in Pavia, Italy, she was orphaned as a child, worked as a servant when ten, and went blind when she was twelve. She was cared for by the Dominican tertiaries in Pavia, became a recluse in the Dominican church there, and lived as a hermit for the next sixty-five years, venerated and widely consulted for her spiritual wisdom. Her cult was confirmed in 1853. March 23.

BIZZOLI, FRANCUCCIA (d. 1319). Born at Arezzo, Italy, she joined the Benedictines, taking the name Justina, at St. Mark's convent in Arezzo when thirteen. She spent several years at All Saints convent in Arezzo and then lived as a recluse with an anchoress named Lucia at Civitella. After Lucia's death, she was brought back to All Saints, where she was reputed to have wrought miracles of healing through her prayers. She died there, and her cult was approved in 1890. March 12.

BLAAN. *See* Blane.

BLAISE (d. c. 316). That he was bishop of Sebastea, Armenia, and was martyred by order of Governor Agricolaus of Cappadocia and Lower Armenia during Licinius' persecution is all we know with certainty of Blaise. According to unreliable legend, he was of wealthy Christian parents and was made a bishop in his youth. He became a hermit when persecutions of the Christians began, was brought to Agricolaus by hunters who observed him curing sick and wounded wild animals, and was imprisoned, then tortured and beheaded by the governor for his faith. The blessing of throats on his feast day is attributed to his healing of a young boy who was choking to death from a fish bone in his throat; the two candles used in the ceremony are derived from the candles brought to Blaise in prison by the boy's mother. His name is also spelled Blase. February 3.

BLANCO, FRANCIS (d. 1597). Born at Monterey, Galicia, Spain, he studied at Villanpando, where he was ordained, and was then sent as a missionary to Mexico. He was ordered to Manila in the Philippines and then in 1594 to Japan, where he was crucified with twenty-five others on February 5 near Nagasaki during the persecution of the *taiko,* Toyotomi Hideyoshi. They were all canonized as the martyrs of Japan in 1862. February 6.

BLANDINA (d. 177). *See* Pothinus.

BLANE (d. c. 590). Born on the island of Bute, Scotland, he studied in Ireland for seven years, became a monk there, and on his return to Scotland was ordained and devoted himself to missionary work. He was consecrated bishop, made a pilgrimage to Rome, is credited with performing miracles, and died at Kingarth on Bute. He is also known as Blaan. August 11.

BLASE. *See* Blaise.

BLESILLA (363–83). Daughter of St. Paula, she determined to live a life of great austerity and holiness after she was cured of a fever she contracted at the death of her husband, who died after they were married seven months. St. Jerome translated Ecclesiastes at her request. She died suddenly at Rome when only twenty. January 22.

BOBOLA, ANDREW (1591–1657). Of an aristocratic Polish family, he was born in Sandomir, Poland, joined the Jesuits in 1611 at Vilna, Lithuania, and was ordained in 1622. He engaged in parish work in Vilna, and in 1630 was made superior of the Jesuit house in Bobrinsk, where he became known for his work during a plague there. Beginning in 1636, he spent the next twenty years in successful missionary work, especially among the Orthodox, a success that gained him much opposition and hatred among those opposed to his religion. Because of Cossack, Russian, and Tartar raids on Poland, the Jesuits were forced into hiding; he accepted a house in Pinsk from Prince Radziwell in 1652 and made it into a center for fugitive Jesuits. Five years later he was captured during a Cossack attack on Pinsk, tortured, and after refusing to disown his faith was subjected to further merciless torture and then beheaded at Janow on May 10. He was canonized in 1938. May 16.

BODEY, BL. JAMES (1549–83). Son of a merchant, he was born in Wells, England, studied at New College, Oxford, and became a fellow there when nineteen. In 1577, he went to Douai to study, married on his return to England, and was arrested in 1580 at Winchester for his Catholicism. He was held in prison until 1583, when he was convicted of treason for denying the royal supremacy in ecclesiastical matters, and was hanged at Andover on November 2. He was beatified in 1929.

BODO (d. c. 670). A native of Toul, France, and brother of St. Salaberga, who persuaded him to become a monk and his wife to join her as a nun at Laon, he later became bishop of Toul and founded three monasteries. September 11.

BOETHIUS. *See* Severinus Boethius.

BOGIMILUS (d. 1182). Of noble parents, he was born near Dobrow, Poland, studied at Paris with his twin Boguphalus, built a church at Dobrow, was ordained, and became its pastor. He was appointed chancellor of Gnesen by Archbishop John, his uncle, and became archbishop on John's death in 1167. He founded and endowed a Cistercian monastery at Coronowa, resigned his see in 1172 when his clergy rebelled at his strict discipline, and joined the Camaldolese at Uniedow, where he remained until his death. His cult was approved in 1925. June 10.

BOISIL (d. 664). Trained under St. Aidan, he became a monk at Melrose, England, was ordained, and became abbot. He was a biblical scholar, and was famed for his preaching, his gift of prophecy, his holiness, and his aid to the poor. He died of a plague that wracked England. He is also known as Boswell. February 23.

BOJANI, BL. BENVENUTA (1254–92). Born at Cividale, Friuli, Italy, she became a Dominican tertiary at an early age, lived a life of extreme austerities and penances, was miraculously cured of bad health, which had kept her in her home for five years, and experienced visions and diabolical assaults. She died on October 30, and her cult was approved in 1765. October 30.

BONAVENTURE (1221–74). Giovanni di Fidanza was born in Bagnorea, Italy, son of Giovanni di Fidanza and Maria la Ritella, and according to an untrustworthy legend, received the name Bonaventure from St. Francis of Assisi, who cured him of a childhood illness. He became a Franciscan in 1238 (or 1243) and studied at Paris under Alexander of Hales, whose disciple he became. He taught theology and Scripture at Paris, 1248–55. His teaching was interrupted because of the opposition of the secular professors to the new mendicants. He was involved in the controversy defending the mendicant orders against the attacks, headed by William of Saint-Armour and his book *The Perils of the Last Times,* and wrote *Concerning the Poverty of Christ* in refutation. In 1256 Pope Alexander IV denounced Saint-Armour and ordered the attackers of the mendicant orders to desist. When the mendicant orders were reestablished at Paris, Bonaventure received his doctorate in theology, with Thomas Aquinas, in 1257. Earlier the same year Bonaventure had been elected minister general of the Friars Minor and labored to reconcile the dissident factions in the Order, pursuing a policy of moderation but condemning the policies of the extremist groups. At a general chapter of the Order at Narbonne in 1260, he promulgated a set of constitutions on the rule, which had a profound and lasting impact on the Order. He refused the archbishopric of York in 1265, and in 1271 he helped secure the election of Pope Gregory X. In 1273, he was appointed cardinal-bishop of Albano, and the following year Gregory appointed him to draw up the agenda for the fourteenth General Council at Lyons to discuss reunion of the Eastern churches with Rome. Bonaventure was a leading figure in the success of the Council that effected reunion, but he died at Lyons on July 15 while the Council was still in session.

Bonaventure was an outstanding philosopher and theologian and one of the great minds of medieval times. Known as "the Seraphic Doctor," he wrote numerous treatises, notably his *Commentary on the Sentences of Peter Lombard*, the theological tracts *Breviloquium, Itinerarium mentis in Deum*, and *De reductione artium ad theologium*, the spiritual works *Perfection of Life, Soliloquy*, and *The Threefold Way*, biblical commentaries, some five hundred sermons, and the official Franciscan biography of St. Francis. Bonaventure was canonized in 1482 and declared a Doctor of the Church in 1588. July 15.

BONAVENTURE, BL. (1651–1711). Born at Potenza, Italy, he joined the Conventual Friars Minor at Nocera, spent eight years at Amalfi, where he was master of novices, and died at Ravella on October 26. It is reported that blood flowed from his arm after his death at the order of his superior. He was beatified in 1775.

BONAVENTURE GRAU, BL. (1620–84). Born at Riudoms, near Barcelona, Spain, he was a shepherd, married at seventeen, and when widowered two years later, became a Franciscan lay brother at Escornalbou. To escape the attention his mystical gifts attracted, he was sent to St. Isidore's friary in Rome, where he was made a doorkeeper. Despite his menial position, he continued to attract attention by his holiness and ecstasies. He established several retreat houses. His cult was approved in 1906. September 11.

BONAVITA, BL. (d. 1375). A native of Lugo, near Ravenna, Italy, he was a blacksmith and became a Franciscan tertiary, noted for his holiness, charity, and miracles, proof of which are suspect. Though venerated in his local area, his cult has never been formally approved. March 1.

BONET. *See* Bonitus.

BONFADINI, BL. ANTONY (1400–82). Born in Ferrara, Italy, he became a Franciscan there when thirty-nine and spent the rest of his life preaching and teaching. He died at Cotignola on the way back from a mission to the Holy Land. Miracles were reported at his tomb, and his cult was approved in 1901.

BONIFACE I (d. 422). A Roman priest, he was elected Pope in 418 when an old man, the day after a group of dissidents had seized the Lateran and elected Eulalius Pope. Emperor Honorius called two councils, decided in favor of Boniface, and ousted Eulalius and his faction. Boniface continued his predecessor's opposition to Pelagianism, persuaded Emperor Theodosius II to return Illyricum to Western jurisdiction, and supported Augustine, who dedicated several treatises against Pelagianism to him. He died on September 4.

BONIFACE (d. 484). *See* Liberatus of Capua.

BONIFACE IV (d. 615). Son of a doctor named John, he was born at Valeria, Italy, may have been a student under Gregory the Great, was possibly a Benedictine monk in Rome, and became a *dispensator* when he entered papal service. He was elected Pope in 608, was responsible for converting the Roman temple of the gods, the Pantheon in Rome, into a Christian church, and had correspondence with Columba, who chided him for some of his theological stances while expressing devotion and loyalty to him. May 8.

BONIFACE (c. 680–754). Probably born at Crediton, Devonshire, England, and baptized Winfrid, he was sent to a monastery school near Exeter when seven, then to the Benedictine Nursling abbey in Winchester when fourteen, where he studied under Winbert and became director of the school. He was ordained about 715, was a successful teacher and preacher, but decided he wanted to be a missionary to Friesland. Unsuccessful in a first attempt in 716, he went to Pope Gregory II in Rome in 718 and was sent by the Pope to evangelize the pagans in Germany. He changed his name to Boniface, was a missionary under St. Willibrord in Friesland for three years, and then preached successfully in Hesse. In 722 he was recalled to Rome and was consecrated regionary bishop for Germany, secured a pledge of protection from Charles Martel, and on his return to Germany, preached in Hesse. He won instant success with a huge gathering of pagans at Geismar by demolishing the Oak of Thor, an object of pagan worship, without harm to himself. He then went to Thuringia, established a monastery at Ohrdruf, and was successful in securing English monks as missionaries to Germany. In 731, he was made metropolitan of Germany beyond the Rhine, authorized to create new sees, went to Bavaria as papal legate, and established a hierarchy and several new sees in the area. He founded several monasteries, Reichenau (724), Murbach (728) and Fritzlar (734), and in 735, he and St. Sturmi founded Fulda, which in the years to come became a great monastic center for northern Europe. He reformed the Frankish church, which Charles Martel had plundered, with five synods called after Charles' death in 741 by his sons, Carloman and Pepin, over which he presided between 741 and 747. In 747 his metropolitan see was established at Mainz and he was named primate of Germany by Pope St. Zachary. He was also appointed apostolic delegate for Germany and Gaul, and crowned Pepin sole ruler of Gaul at Soissons when Pepin's brother Carloman entered a monastery. Boniface resigned his see in

754 to spend the last years of his life reconverting the Frieslanders, who had lapsed into their pagan customs after the death of St. Willibrord. He was preparing for the confirmation of some of his converts at Dokkum, Friesland (northern Netherlands), when he and a group of his followers were attacked by a band of pagans and murdered on June 5. Called "the Apostle of Germany," his feast day was extended to the universal church by Pope Pius IX in 1874. June 5.

BONIFACE (974–1009). Of a noble Saxon family, he was born at Querfurt, Germany, and baptized Bruno. He studied at Magdeburg, joined the court of Otto III, was made court chaplain, and accompanied the Emperor to Rome in 998. There he became a Camaldolese monk with the name Boniface about 1000. The following year he entered a monastery at Pereum founded by Otto. When two of its monks, Benedict and John, and three companions (the Five Martyred Brothers whose story he wrote) were martyred in 1003 at Kazimierz, near Gniezno, he went as a missionary to Germany. He was appointed missionary archbishop, preached to the Magyars with considerable success, and then went to Kiev to preach to the Pechenegs. He eventually worked to evangelize the Prussians, and on February 14, he and eighteen companions were massacred on the Russian border near Braunsberg, Poland. He is also known as Bruno of Querfurt and is often called "the Second Apostle of the Prussians." June 19.

BONIFACE (c. 1205–60). Born in Brussels, he studied at Paris, was a noted lecturer there for seven years, and then went to the cathedral school in Cologne when the Paris students boycotted lectures in a dispute between masters and students. He was elected bishop of Lausanne in 1230 but incurred much opposition for his public criticism of the clergy and then angered Emperor Frederick II. Boniface was attacked and wounded in 1239, probably by agents of Frederick, whereupon Boniface resigned his see. He returned to Brussels and took up residence at a Cistercian convent at La Cambre, though he does not seem to have become a Cistercian, and died there. His cult was approved in 1702. February 19.

BONIFACE OF SAVOY, BL. (d. 1270). Son of Thomas, count of Savoy, he entered the Grande Chartreuse as a youth, became a Carthusian, and was made prior of Mantua. He served seven years as administrator of the diocese of Belley in 1234–41 and then of Valence. He was elected archbishop of Canterbury in 1241 through the influence of his niece, Eleanor, wife of King Henry III of England, but did not go to his see until 1244. His attempts to reform the see and effect economies in the heavily indebted see met with strenuous opposition, particularly from the suffragans of the various sees he attempted to visit. He excommunicated the bishop of London and the clergy of St. Bartholomew's, and while an appeal to Rome upheld his visitation rights he was forced to rescind his excommunications, and his visitations had restrictions placed on them. He acted as regent for Henry while the King was out of the country, accompanied him on a diplomatic mission to France, and successfully negotiated a peaceful solution to difficulties over the succession in his native Savoy. He died on the way to a crusade with Edward I at the castle of Sainte-Hélène des Millières in Savoy. Boniface's cult was confirmed in 1838. July 14.

BONIFACE OF TARSUS (d. c. 306). Chief steward of wealthy, beautiful Aglaë in Rome, with whom he lived a dissolute life, his lifestyle changed when she sent him to the East for martyrs' relics. When he arrived at Tarsus in Cilicia, a persecution of Christians was in progress. Despite this, he proclaimed the Christian message to Simplicius, the governor, who had him tortured and then thrown into a cauldron of boiling pitch; when he was miraculously saved the governor had him beheaded. His remains were brought back to Rome, where his former mistress, Aglaë, built a church to enshrine them and then spent the remaining fifteen years of her life doing penance. Her body was buried beside him in the church she had built. Their story was very popular in the Middle Ages but most of it is probably pious fiction. May 14.

BONITUS (623–706). Also known as Bonet, he was born in Auvergne, France, became chancellor of Sigebert III of Austrasia, was appointed governor of Marseilles by Thierry III in 677, and was named bishop of Clermont in 689. He resigned the see because of doubts about the validity of his election, led a life of holiness as a hermit at the Benedictine abbey of Manglieu at Clermont, and died at Lyons while returning from a pilgrimage to Rome. January 15.

BONNARD, JOHN LOUIS (1824–52). Born at St. Christôt en Jarret, France, he studied at St. Jodard and the seminaries in Lyons and Paris, joined the Paris Society of Foreign Missions, and was ordained in 1850. He was sent as a missionary to western Tonkin, was arrested in 1852 during a persecution of Christians, and was beheaded. He was beatified as one of the Martyrs of Indochina in 1900.

BONO, BL. CASPAR DE (1530–1604). Born in Valencia, Spain, he was unsuccessful as a silk merchant and became a soldier. When wounded during a battle, he determined to become a Minim friar, joined the Order in 1560, and was ordained the next year. He served as corrector provincial of his province twice, was in pain much of his life, but despite this practiced great austerities, and died in Valencia on July 14. He was beatified in 1786.

BONOMO, BL. GIOVANNA MARIA (1606–70). Born at Asiago, near Vicenza, Italy, she became a Benedictine nun at Bassano, where she served as mistress of novices and in time became abbess; she experienced numerous supernatural phenomena, including the stigmata. She died on March 1, and was beatified in 1783.

BONOSUS (d. 363). He and Maximian were Christian officers in the Herculean cohort at Antioch. When they refused the orders of Julian the Apostate to replace the Christian symbol Constantine had placed on army standards with a pagan ensign on their cohort's standards, they were arrested. When they then refused to worship the pagan gods, they were flogged, racked, and then beheaded. August 21.

BORGIA, FRANCIS (1510–72). Son of the Duke of Gandia of the Spanish branch of the Borgia family and Juana of Aragon, daughter of the illegitimate son of King Ferdinand V of Aragon, he was born at Gandia, near Valencia, Spain. He was educated by his uncle, the archbishop of Saragossa, and in 1528 was made a member of the court of Charles V, and marquis of Lombay. He married Eleanor de Castro in 1529, served as Charles' adviser for ten years, and in 1539 was appointed viceroy of Catalonia by the Emperor. He succeeded to the dukedom of Gandia on the death of his father in 1543. He served as master of the household of Prince Philip and then retired from public life to his estate when Philip's engagement to the

princess of Portugal was broken. When his wife died in 1546, leaving him with eight children, he decided to pursue the religious life that had beckoned him all his life, and in 1548 he decided to join the Jesuits. He went to Rome in 1550, returned to Spain the next year to turn over his inheritance to his son Charles, and was ordained later in the year. He preached in Spain and Portugal, attracting huge crowds to his sermons, and in 1554 was appointed commissary general of the Jesuits in Spain by St. Ignatius. In this position Francis founded numerous monasteries, colleges, and foundations, and ministered to the dowager Queen and the abdicated Charles V. In 1561, Francis was summoned to Rome and in 1565 was elected father general of the Jesuits. During the seven years of his generalate, he expanded the Society, was one of the leaders in combating the Reformation, encouraged Jesuit participation in foreign missionary work, was one of those responsible for the founding of Gregorian University, built Sant' Andrea, and began the Gésu, all in Rome, established the Polish province, built colleges in France, and opened American missions. In 1567, he revised the rules of the Society, and in 1571 accompanied Cardinal Bonelli on a tour through Spain that drew huge crowds to see and hear him. He returned to Rome exhausted from the trip and died there two days later, shortly after midnight September 30. So successful was he in revitalizing and reinvigorating the Jesuits that he is often called their second founder. He was canonized in 1671. October 10.

BORIS (d. 1015). Son of Vladimir of Kiev, and baptized Romanus, he learned of the plans of his brother Svyatopolk to defraud him and another brother Gleb (baptized David) of their inheritance on the death of their father while returning from a military expedition. He refused to claim his legacy by force, as urged by his officers, saying that as a Christian he could not raise his sword against his older brother. He retired to a lonely spot with one of his followers to pray. The next morning a group of Svyatopolk's followers found him and sworded him to death while he prayed for them. Gleb, invited to Kiev by Svyatopolk, was stabbed to death, reportedly by his own cook, when his brother's men boarded his boat on the Dnieper River near Smolensk. Five years later another brother, Yaroslav, buried their bodies in St. Basil's church at Vyshgorod; miracles reported at their graves made it a popular pilgrimage place. Boris is the patron of Moscow, and their cult was confirmed in 1724.

BORROMEO, CHARLES (1538–84). Son of Count Gilbert Borromeo and Margaret Medici, sister of Pope Pius IV, he was born at the family castle of Arona on Lake Maggiore, Italy, on October 2. He received the clerical tonsure when twelve and was sent to the Benedictine abbey of SS. Gratian and Felinus at Arona for his education. He continued his studies at Milan, went to Pavia in 1552 to study civil and canon law under Alciati, and received his doctorate in 1559. In the same year his uncle was elected Pope Pius IV and the following year named him his Secretary of State and created him a cardinal and administrator of the see of Milan. He served as Pius' legate on numerous diplomatic missions, and in 1562 was instrumental in having Pius reconvene the Council of Trent, which had been suspended in 1552. Charles played a leading role in guiding it and in fashioning the decrees of the third and last group of sessions. He refused the headship of the Borromeo family on the death of Count Frederick Borromeo, was ordained a priest in 1563, and was consecrated bishop of Milan the same year. Before

being allowed to take possession of his see, he oversaw the catechism, missal, and breviary called for by the Council of Trent. When he finally did arrive at Trent (which had been without a resident bishop for eighty years) in 1566, he instituted radical reforms, despite great opposition, with such effectiveness that it became a model see. He put into effect measures to improve the morals and manners of clergy and laity, raised the effectiveness of the diocesan operation, established seminaries for the education of the clergy, founded a Confraternity of Christian Doctrine for the religious instruction of children, and encouraged the Jesuits in his see. He increased assistance to the poor and the needy, was most generous in his help to the English college at Douai, and during his bishopric held eleven diocesan synods and six provincial councils. He founded a society of secular priests, Oblates of St. Ambrose (now Oblates of St. Charles) in 1578, and was active in preaching, resisting the inroads of Protestantism, and bringing back lapsed Catholics to the Church. He encountered opposition from many sources in his efforts to reform people and institutions. In 1567, he aroused the enmity of the Milan Senate over episcopal jurisdiction when he imprisoned several laypersons for their evil lives; when the episcopal sheriff was driven from the city by civil officials, he excommunicated them and was eventually upheld by King Philip II and the Pope. Again his episcopal rights were challenged by the canons of Santa Maria della Scala, and he was barred from entering the church, but Philip and the Pope again upheld his position, though the Senate supported the canons. He was wounded by an assassin, Jerome Donati Farina, a Humiliati priest, in 1569 in a plot on his life by the Humiliati to end his insistence on the Order's reform. He helped mitigate the famine that struck Milan in 1570 by securing food for the poor and feeding some three thousand people a day for months. Another conflict with the Senate over his ecclesiastical rights led to the removal of the governor, Luis de Requesens, whom Charles had excommunicated, by Philip, who upheld the claims of the archbishop. When plague struck Milan in 1576 Charles mobilized the clergy and religious to aid the stricken after the governor and other officials had fled the city, personally ministered to the afflicted, and ran up huge debts to care for the thousands of sick, dying, and the dead who littered the streets until the plague finally abated early in 1578. He met and aided many of the young priests sent on the English mission at a gathering in Milan in 1580, and in 1583 was apostolic visitor to Switzerland, where he preached against the Protestants and fought an outbreak of alleged witchcraft and sorcery. He died at Milan on the night of November 3–4, and was canonized in 1610. He was one of the towering figures of the Catholic Reformation, a patron of learning and the arts, and though he achieved a position of great power, he used it with humility, personal sanctity, and unselfishness to reform the Church of the evils and abuses so prevalent among the clergy and nobles of the times. November 4.

BOSA (d. 705). A Benedictine monk at Whitby, England, he became bishop of Deira in 678, with his see at York, when St. Wilfrid was driven out by King Egfrid when he refused to accept the division of his see of York. Wilfrid returned in 686, but Bosa took over the diocese in 691 when Wilfrid was again exiled following a quarrel with King Aldfrid; Bosa ruled it with great holiness and ability until his death. March 9.

BOSCARDIN, BERTILLA (1888–1922). Of a poor peasant family, she was born on October 6 at Gioia di Brendola, Italy,

and christened Anne Frances. She worked for a time as a servant and then joined the Sisters of St. Dorothy of Vicenza when sixteen, taking the name Bertilla. She worked in menial positions in the convent but was given nurse's training at the municipal hospital at Treviso, run by the Sisters, and devoted herself to caring for the sick though desperately ill herself the last twelve years of her life. She died of cancer on October 20 at Treviso. Miracles of healing were reported at her tomb, and she was canonized by Pope John XXIII in 1961.

BOSCO, JOHN (1815–88). Born at Becchi, Piedmont, Italy, of poor parents, he lost his father when two, entered the seminary at Chieri when sixteen, continued his studies at Turin, and was ordained. He began his work with neglected boys at Turin at the encouragement of Fr. Joseph Cafasso, was appointed chaplain of St. Philomena's Hospice for girls there in 1844, and housed his boys in an old building on the grounds of the Hospice. When they became too unruly he was ordered to give up his care of the boys or resign as chaplain. He resigned and with his mother opened a refuge for the boys. He began workshops and schools, built a church for the boys, and by 1856 he was housing 150 boys and had another 500 in oratories with 10 priests. He was immensely successful with the boys, using a minimum of restraint and discipline, lots of love, keeping careful watch over their development, and encouraging them personally and through religion. The work expanded and he paid for it by preaching, writing popular books, and from charitable donations. His need for dependable assistants led him to found the Society of St. Francis de Sales (the Salesians), which received general approval from Pope Pius IX in 1859, though formal approval was not obtained until 1884. By the time of his death, some sixty-four Salesian foundations had been made in Europe and the Americas, and there were almost 800 Salesian priests. In 1872, he founded the Daughters of Our Lady, Help of Christians, to care for poor and neglected girls, and followed this with a third order called Salesian co-operators. He died in Turin on January 31, and was canonized in 1934. January 31.

BOSGRAVE, BL. THOMAS (d. 1594). *See* Cornelius, Bl. John.

BOSTE, JOHN (c. 1544–94). Born at Dufton, Westmorland, England, he studied at Queen's College, Oxford, and was a fellow there. He became a Catholic in 1576, went to Rheims in 1580, and was ordained there the following year. He was sent on the English mission, ministered to the Catholics of northern England, and became the object of an intensive manhunt. He was betrayed by a Francis Ecclesfield near Durham, and taken to London, where he was crippled for the rest of his life by the racking he was subjected to. Sent back to Durham, he was condemned to death for his priesthood and hanged, drawn, and quartered at Dryburn, near Durham, on July 24. He was canonized by Pope Paul VI in 1970 as one of the Martyrs of Durham.

BOSWELL. *See* Boisil.

BOTOLPH. *See* Botulf.

BOTTI, BL. VILLANA DE (d. 1332). Daughter of a Florentine merchant, she made an unsuccessful attempt to enter a convent when thirteen and then was married to Rosso di Piero. She led a scandal-ridden and dissolute life until one day, startled by her appearance, she reformed her life and became a Dominican tertiary. She devoted the rest of her life to penance, prayer, and contemplation, experienced ecstasies and visions of Mary and the saints, and lived a life of great holiness until her death. Her cult was confirmed in 1824. February 28.

BOTULF (d. c. 680). Unreliable sources have him and his brother, Adulf, born of a noble Saxon (other sources say Irish) family. They became monks in Germany (or Gaul) and Adulf was made a bishop, probably regionary, at Utrecht (or Maastricht). Botulf returned to England, was granted property by King Ethelmund of the southern Angles (of whom no record exists), and built a monastery, Icanhoh, in 654. He attracted numerous disciples and was widely known for his learning and holiness. His name is also spelled Botolph. June 17.

BOTVID (d. 1100). Born in Sodermannland, Sweden, he was raised a pagan but was converted to Christianity while in England. He preached in Sweden and with a companion was murdered by a Finnish slave he had bought, set free, and was taking home in his boat. July 28.

BOURGEOYS, BL. MARGARET (1620–1700). Born at Troyes, Champagne, France, she was refused admission to the Carmelites and Poor Clares when she was twenty, was active in a small community in Troyes under Abbé Gendret, and in 1652 went to Montreal, Canada, at the invitation of the governor, Paul de Maisonneuve, as a teacher of the children of the colony. In 1657, she opened the first school there, recruited new helpers for the growing number of students, gained the support of King Louis XIV on a trip to France in 1670, and in 1676 received official approval of her Congregation of Notre Dame of Montreal from Bishop Laval of Quebec. She had difficulties with him and his successor over the concept of an unenclosed community of women, and it was not until 1698 that she and her Sisters were allowed to take their first vows. In the meantime, she had expanded the congregation's activities to other towns in Canada and opened a school for the Iroquois Indians in 1676. She resigned because of ill health in 1693, when she was seventy-three and died seven years later, on January 12. She was beatified in 1950.

BRANDO, BL. MARIA CRISTINA (1856–1906). Fleeing from the wealth she was born into, she led a holy life from childhood, repeating at times: "I must become holy; I want to be a saint." Despite her unstable health, she entered the Monastery of the Sacramentine Nuns. In 1876, she was vested in the religious habit and took the name Sister Maria Cristina of the Immaculate Conception. In 1878, she founded the Congregation of the Sisters, Expiatory Victims of Jesus in the Blessed Sacrament, where she diligently cared for the education of children. She was beatified in 2003.

BRAULIO (d. 651). Born of a noble family in Saragossa, Spain, he became a monk at St. Engratia's there, studied at Seville under St. Isidore, was ordained, and in 631 was elected bishop of Saragossa. An outstanding scholar and preacher, he encouraged learning, fought Arianism, helped Isidore in his efforts to reform the Spanish Church, and wrote a defense of the Spanish bishops against Pope Honorius I's charges that they were neglecting their responsibilities. He was known for his devotion to our Lady, his visions and miracles, his austerity, and for his compassion for and aid to the poor and needy. He wrote the Acts of the Martyrs of Saragossa, a life of St. Emilian, and numerous letters of his are still extant. He died at Saragossa and is the patron of Aragon. March 26.

BRÉBEUF, JOHN DE (1593–1649). Born on March 25, at Condé-sur-Vire,

Normandy, France, he attended the university at nearby Caen, was a farmer on his parents' farm, and in 1617 joined the Jesuits at Rouen. Ordained in 1622 after tuberculosis had almost ended his aspirations to the priesthood, he was sent to Canada at his request in 1625 and labored among the Huron Indians there for the next twenty-four years despite great opposition from the Huguenots, trading company officials, and renegade Indians. His stay there was interrupted when the English captured Quebec in 1629 and ousted the Jesuits. He returned to France, was treasurer at the college in Eu, and then returned to the missions in 1633, when the English returned Canada to the French. When smallpox killed thousands of Indians in 1637, the missionaries were blamed by the medicine men of the tribes for the disaster, but Brébeuf stayed with the Indians until 1640, when he went to Quebec. He remained there for four years and then returned to the Indians. He was captured by Iroquois Indians, the bitter enemies of the French and Hurons, on March 16 at Ste. Marie, near Georgian Bay, and was cruelly tortured for hours until he died. Known for his holiness and courage, he was responsible for some seven thousand conversions among the Indians, and composed a dictionary and catechism in Huron. He was canonized in 1930. October 19.

BRENDAN (c. 484–c. 577). Though one of the most popular of the Irish saints and certainly a real person, much of what we know of him is legendary. Son of Findlugh, he was probably born near Tralee, Kerry, Ireland, and was placed as an infant in the care of St. Ita. When six he was sent to St. Jarlath's monastic school in Tuam for his education, and was ordained by Bishop St. Erc in 512. He founded numerous monasteries in Ireland, the most famous of which was Clonfert, which he founded about 559 and which was a center of missionary activity for centuries. Some three thousand monks lived, studied, and prayed there under his direction. He made missionary journeys to England, Ireland, and Scotland, established several sees in Ireland, and became famed for his voyages, particularly a seven-year journey to the Land of Promise, which he described in his epic saga *Navigatio Sancti Brendani Abbatis*. It was tremendously popular in the Middle Ages and was translated into most European languages. Though scholars long doubted the voyage to the Promised Land he described in the *Navigatio* in the middle of the sixth century could have been to North America, as was sometimes claimed, some modern scholars now believe he may have done just that. In 1976–77, Tim Severin, an expert on exploration, following the instructions in the *Navigatio,* built a hide-covered *curragh* and then sailed it from Ireland to Newfoundland via Iceland and Greenland, demonstrating the accuracy of its directions and descriptions of the places Brendan mentioned in his epic. Brendan probably died while visiting his sister Brig, abbess of a community of nuns at Enach Duin (Annaghdown). He is the patron of sailors. May 16.

BRIANT, ALEXANDER (d. 1581). Born in Somerset, England, he studied at Oxford, where he returned to the Church, and then went to France to study at Douai. He was ordained in 1578 and returned to England the following year. He was active in Somerset but came to London in 1581, where he was arrested at the home of Fr. Robert Persons. He was mercilessly tortured for a month in a futile effort to get him to reveal the whereabouts of Persons, and then was tried with other Catholics on the trumped-up charge of plotting in Rome a rebellion in England. He was found guilty and executed at Tyburn on December 1 with SS. Edmund Campion and Ralph Sherwin. They were all canonized as among the Martyrs of England and Wales by Pope Paul VI in 1970.

BRICE (d. 444). Raised by St. Martin of Tours at Marmoutier and also known as Britius, he became a vain, overly ambitious cleric, holding Martin in great contempt. Despite Brice's attitude, Martin was most patient with him, and in time, in great remorse, he asked Martin's forgiveness for his attitude toward him. He succeeded Martin as bishop of Tours in 397 but reverted to his old ways, neglected his duties, was several times accused of laxness and immorality, and though cleared of the latter charge was exiled from his see. He went to Rome and in the seven years of his exile there repented and completely changed his lifestyle. When the administrator of his see in his absence died, he returned and ruled with such humility, holiness, and ability he was venerated as a saint by the time of his death. November 13.

BRIDE. *See* Brigid.

BRIDGET. *See* Brigid.

BRIDGET (1303–73). Daughter of Birger Persson, governor of Upland, Sweden, and a wealthy landowner, and his second wife Ingeborg Bengtsdotter, she was born on June 14, and was raised by her aunt at Aspenas when her mother died when Bridget was twelve. She early experienced visions, was married when only fourteen to Ulf Gudmarsson when he was eighteen, and they had eight children, one of whom was St. Catherine of Sweden. In 1335, Bridget became lady-in-waiting to Blanche of Namur, who had just married King Magnus II of Sweden. After Bridget's eldest daughter made a bad marriage and her youngest son died about 1340, she made a pilgrimage to the shrine of St. Olaf at

Trondhjem, Norway. On her return she left the court and went on pilgrimage to Compostela with her husband. He became ill at Arras but recovered, as she had been assured in a vision of St. Denis. Her husband died in 1344 at the Cistercian monastery of Alvastra, and she spent the next four years there living a life of great austerity and experiencing numerous visions and revelations, which her confessor assured her were authentic and which were all recorded by Prior Peter of Alvastra. As the result of a revelation, she denounced the King and Queen for their frivolous lives, and when Bridget founded a monastery at Vadstena in 1344, Magnus endowed it. It marked the beginning of the Order of the Most Holy Trinity (the Brigettines), and Vadstena became the intellectual center of fifteenth-century Sweden. She refused to support King Magnus' crusade against the pagan Letts and Estonians, terming it a marauding expedition, and then wrote to Pope Clement VI at Avignon, telling him a vision demanded that he return the papacy to Rome and that he mediate peace between England and France. In disfavor with the court for her outspokenness, she went to Rome in 1349 and impressed the whole city with her austerity, holiness, concern for the poor and pilgrims, and her unceasing efforts to get the Pope to return to Rome. She reformed monasteries around Rome and became famous for her prophecies and denunciations of those in high office, including Pope Urban V, who returned to Rome briefly in 1370 when he approved her constitution for the Brigettines in 1370. She continued her efforts to get the Pope back to Rome when Urban's successor, Gregory XI, remained at Avignon. The last years of her life were marred by the unsavory romance that developed between her son Charles and Queen Joanna I of Naples, both married, while he was on the way to the Holy Land on a pilgrimage with his mother and a group of others. It ended abruptly when he died of a fever a few weeks later. On her way back in 1372, she stopped off at Cyprus to denounce the royal family for its evil ways. She died shortly after her arrival in Rome on July 23. She was canonized in 1391, and is the patron saint of Sweden. Throughout her life Bridget experienced remarkable visions and revelations, which she wrote about in her *Revelations*. After her death the Council of Trent ordered a critical examination of the revelations to be made by John Torquemada, who later became a cardinal; he approved them for reading by the faithful. She is also known as Birgitta. July 23.

BRIEUC (d. c. 510). Of noble pagan parents, he was probably born in Cardiganshire, England, and was educated by St. Germanus at Auxerre, Gaul. When ordained, he returned to England, became known for his miracles, converted his parents, and then reportedly gathered 168 disciples about him and went to Brittany to evangelize that area. He converted Conan, a local chieftain, and then founded a monastery near Tréguier, of which he was abbot. He returned to England on receiving news of a pestilence (which his prayers were believed to have ended), returned to Brittany, and with eighty-four followers founded another monastery (now Saint-Brieuc) on land donated by Rigual, another chieftain he had converted. He died soon after, reputedly at the age of 100. He is also known as Briomaglus and Brioc. May 1.

BRIGID (5th century). Also known as Britt, according to legend, she and her sister Maura were Scottish princesses from Northumbria who were murdered by pagan outlaws at Balagny-sur-Thérain, Picardy, while on their way home from a pilgrimage to Rome. They were buried there and a cult grew up around them, abetted by reports of numerous miracles at their grave. They were enshrined at Nogent-les-Vierges in 1185. July 13. They are believed to be the same as Maura and Britt, two solitaries at Ariacum (St. Maure), who also died in the fifth century and whose remains were miraculously revealed to St. Euphronius according to St. Martin of Tours. A chapel was built, and a cult grew up around them in Touraine, where their feast is observed on January 28. Still another legend links Brigid and Maura with St. Baya, a recluse in Scotland, and her pupil Maura, who attracted disciples and became their abbess. Their feast is celebrated on November 2.

BRIGID (c. 450–525). Probably born at Faughart near Dundalk, Louth, Ireland, her parents were baptized by St. Patrick, with whom she developed a close friendship. According to legend, her father was Dubhthach, and Irish chieftain of Leinster, and her mother, Brocca, was a slave at his court. Even as a young girl she evinced an interest for a religious life and took the veil in her youth from St. Macaille at Croghan and probably was professed by St. Mel of Armagh, who is believed to have conferred abbatial authority on her. She settled with seven of her virgins at the foot of Croghan Hill for a time and about 468 followed Mel to Meath. About 470 she founded a double monastery at Cill-Dara (Kildare) and was abbess of the convent, the first in Ireland. The foundation developed into a center of learning and spirituality, and around it grew up the cathedral city of Kildare. She founded a school of art at Kildare and its illuminated manuscripts became famous, notably the Book of Kildare, which was praised as one of the finest of all illuminated Irish manuscripts before its disappearance three centuries ago. Brigid was one of the most remarkable women of her times,

and despite the numerous legendary, extravagant, and even fantastic miracles attributed to her there is no doubt that her extraordinary spirituality, boundless charity, and compassion for those in distress were real. She died at Kildare on February 1. The Mary of the Gael, she is buried at Downpatrick with St. Columba and St. Patrick, with whom she is the patron of Ireland. Her name is sometimes Bridget and Bride.

BRINDHOLME, VEN. EDMUND (d. 1540). An Englishman, he studied for the priesthood, was ordained on the Continent, and became a parish priest at Calais, then occupied by the English. He was accused, with Clement Philpott, Bl. William Horne, and several others, of plotting to turn the city over to the French and was returned to England. Attainted by Parliament, he was executed at Tyburn on August 4.

BRIOC. *See* Brieuc.

BRIOMAGLUS. *See* Brieuc.

BRITES. *See* Silva, Bl. Beatrice da.

BRITHWALD. *See* Berhtwald.

BRITIUS. *See* Brice.

BRITT (5th century). *See* Brigid.

BRITTO, JOHN DE (1647–93). Reputedly dedicated to St. Francis Xavier by his mother when he recovered from a serious illness when a child, he was born of a noble family at Lisbon, Portugal, on March 1 and was a friend of Infante Don Pedro, who was to become King of Portugal. He joined the Jesuits when fifteen, was ordained, and in 1673 was sent, with sixteen other Jesuits, as a missionary to Goa. He spent the rest of his life doing missionary work in India in Malabar, Tanjore, Marava and Madura, and became superior of the Madura mission. He was most successful because of his policy of adapting to local life in food, dress, and customs, even joining the Brahmin caste to reach the nobility. He was fiercely opposed by Indian pagans and in 1686 was attacked and tortured, with some of his catechists, when he refused to honor the god Siva. He returned to Lisbon soon after but despite efforts to get him to remain in Europe, he returned to Madura in 1691. He was arrested and then beheaded at Oriur, India, on February 4 by order of Rajah Raghunatha for teachings opposed to the local gods. He was canonized in 1947.

BROCADELLI, LUCY (1476–1544). Born at Narni, Italy, the oldest of eleven children, she resisted one attempt to have her marry and then agreed to marry a Count Peter in 1491 on the advice of her confessor and a vision of our Lady she is said to have experienced. They lived together as brother and sister for three years when he released her and she became a Dominican regular tertiary at Rome. She later went to Viterbo and during the three years she was there experienced the stigmata and participated in the Passion every Wednesday and Friday. She was subjected to repeated examinations by skeptics who after thorough investigation were convinced her supernatural experiences were real. When twenty-three, Duke Ercole I of Ferrara built a convent for her at Ferrara and selected Lucretia Borgia to staff it with novices, many unsuited to be nuns, with Lucy as superior. Unable to cope with the problems of that position, she was replaced by Sister Mary of Parma and after the death of the duke in 1505 was relegated to obscurity in the convent for the next thirty-nine years. She died there on November 15 almost forgotten, but miracles at her grave began a cult, which was confirmed in 1710. November 16.

BROCARD (d. c. 1231). A French monk on Mount Carmel, he became superior of the Frankish hermits there in 1195 and imposed on them a rule given him by St. Albert, the papal legate to Palestine. The rule was later attacked for not being formally approved by the Holy See but was confirmed by Pope Honorius III, reportedly as the result of a vision of our Lady to the Pontiff. Brocard, also called Burchard, ruled for thirty-five years. September 2.

BRONISLAVA, BL. (d. 1259). A cousin of St. Hyacinth, she became a Premonstratensian nun near Cracow, Poland, when twenty-five. Because of her holiness and intense contemplation she was allowed to live as a solitary in a cave near the monastery the rest of her life. August 30.

BROWN, BL. WILLIAM (d. 1605). *See* Welbourn, Bl. Thomas.

BRUNO (d. 1045). Son of Duke Conrad of Carinthia, and Baroness Matilda, he became a priest, was named bishop of Würzburg in 1033, and built several churches and St. Kilian's cathedral there. A scholar and an author, he was an adviser of Conrad II and was responsible for his lifting of the siege of Milan. In 1045, while with Emperor Henry III on his expedition against the Hungarians, Bruno was killed near Ips in Austria when the building in which Henry's entourage was lodged, collapsed. May 17.

BRUNO (c. 1030–1101). Born in Cologne of the prominent Hartenfaust family, he studied at the cathedral school at Rheims, and on his return to Cologne about 1055 was ordained and became a canon at St. Cunibert's. He returned to Rheims in 1056 as professor of theology, became head of the school the following year, and remained there until 1074, when he was appointed chancellor of

Rheims by its archbishop, Manasses. Bruno was forced to flee Rheims when he and several other priests denounced Manasses in 1076 as unfit for the office of papal legate. Bruno later returned to Cologne but went back to Rheims in 1080 when Manasses was deposed, and though the people of Rheims wanted to make Bruno archbishop, he decided to pursue an eremitical life. He became a hermit under Abbot St. Robert of Molesmes (who later founded Citeaux) but then moved on to Grenoble with six companions in 1084. They were assigned a place for their hermitages in a desolate mountainous Alpine area called La Grande Chartreuse by Bishop St. Hugh of Grenoble, whose confessor Bruno became. They built an oratory and individual cells, roughly followed the rule of St. Benedict, and thus began the Carthusian Order. They embraced a life of poverty, manual work, prayer, and transcribing manuscripts, though as yet they had no written rule. The fame of the group and their founder spread, and in 1090 Bruno was brought to Rome, against his wishes, by Pope Urban II (whom he had taught at Rheims) as papal adviser in the reformation of the clergy. Bruno persuaded Urban to allow him to resume his eremitical state, founded St. Mary's at La Torre in Calabria, declined the Pope's offer of the archbishopric of Reggio, became a close friend of Count Robert of Sicily, and remained there until his death on October 6. He wrote several commentaries on the Psalms and on St. Paul's epistles. He was never formally canonized because of the Carthusians' aversion to public honors, but Pope Leo X granted the Carthusians permission to celebrate his feast in 1514, and his name was placed on the Roman calendar in 1623. October 6.

BRUNO (1049–1123). Born at Solero, Piedmont, of a noble family, he studied at Bologna, and became a canon at Siena in 1079. He defended Church teaching on the Blessed Sacrament against Berengarius at a council in Rome, and in 1080 was appointed bishop of Segni. An outstanding Scripture scholar, he opposed simony and lay investiture, worked with St. Gregory to reform the Church, and incurred the enmity of Count Ainulf, a follower of Emperor Henry IV, who imprisoned him for three months. In 1095, he resigned his see to become a monk at Monte Cassino, but because of the objections of the people of Segni, he was forced to withdraw his resignation, though he remained at Monte Cassino. He was elected abbot in 1107 but was ordered to resign the abbacy and return to his see by Pope Paschal II when he rebuked the Pontiff for concessions in ecclesiastical matters he had made to Emperor-elect Henry V. Bruno was canonized in 1183. July 18.

BRUNO THE GREAT (925–65). Youngest son of Emperor Henry the Fowler and St. Matilda, he was sent to the cathedral school of Utrecht when four, joined the imperial court when fourteen, and in 940 became personal secretary to Emperor Otto I, his brother. He was ordained in 950, became Otto's chancellor, and in 953 was appointed archbishop of Cologne. He founded the abbey of St. Pantaleon there, insisted on high ecclesiastical standards, reformed monasteries, and encouraged learning. He was made duke of Lorraine by Otto when the Emperor deposed Duke Conrad the Red for leading a rebellion, played a leading role in imperial as well as ecclesiastical affairs, and helped settle numerous political disputes. He was coregent of the Empire when Otto went to Rome to be crowned. Bruno died at Rheims on October 11, and his cult was confirmed in 1870.

BRUNO OF QUERFURT. *See* Boniface (974–1009).

BRUSO, BL. CHRISTINA (1242–1312). Born at Stommeln, near Cologne, Germany, of peasant parents, she ran away from home when thirteen and became a *béguine* at Cologne but soon returned home. She early began to exhibit supernatural gifts and throughout her life seems to have been subjected to divine visitations and satanic violence and attacks. She was thrown about, showered with filth, had pieces of flesh gnawed from her skin; she also experienced ecstasies and for a time displayed the stigmata, which bled profusely during Holy Week. The occurrences were recorded by a Father Peter, a Dominican from Dacia, John, the parish priest, and another John, a schoolteacher at Stommeln, and were vigorously debated. Some scholars accepted their authenticity, while others believed they were the products of a deranged mind. Though the recordings by the priests and the schoolteacher ended in 1288 with Peter's death, Christina lived another twenty-four years, venerated for her sanctity. Her six-century cult was confirmed in 1908. November 6.

BUCHE, BL. HENRY MICHAEL (d. 1666). A shoemaker at Arlon, Luxembourg, he founded a religious guild of shoemakers there, and then in 1645 in Paris, where it was known as *Frères Cordonniers,* and which spread to other cities. He died in Paris on June 9. Though called Blessed, he has never been beatified.

BUDEUX. *See* Budoc.

BUDOC (6th–7th centuries). Unreliable legend has him the son of the King of Goëllo (Tréguier), Brittany, and Azenor, daughter of the ruler of Brest. Budoc was supposed to have been born at sea under incredible circumstances (his mother had been exiled and cast into the sea in a cask, where he was born, at-

tended by St. Brigid). He was raised and educated at a monastery near Waterford, Ireland, became its abbot and was elected bishop, and then returned to Brittany, where he became bishop of Dol, succeeding St. Maglorius, and ruled for twenty-six years. Another tradition in England has him an Irish hermit who immigrated to Britain and settled at Budock near Falmouth. His name is also spelled Budeux and Beuzec. December 9.

BUONACCORSI, BL. BONAVENTURE (c. 1240–1315). A native of Pistoia, Italy, of the noble Buonaccorsi family and a notorious leader of the Ghibellines, he was so impressed by the preaching of St. Philip Benizi at Pistoia in 1276 that he completely reformed his ways and became a Studite monk. In time he was ordained and was called *il beato* for his holiness and miracles. He accompanied Philip on the latter's peacemaking missions to different Italian cities, was made prior at Orvieto in 1282 and then preacher apostolic, and he preached all over Italy. He was named prior at Montepulciano in 1303, helped St. Agnes found her community of Dominican nuns there, of which he was spiritual director, and then returned to Pistoia to preach peace to that civil-war-torn city. He died at Orvieto on December 14, and his cult was confirmed in 1822.

BUONAGIUNTA, JOHN (1206–57). *See* Monaldo, Buonfiglio.

BUONI, BL. JOHN (c. 1168–1249). Of the Buonomini family, he was born at Mantua and spent his youth as an entertainer at various courts, living a licentious life. As a result of a serious illness he suffered when about forty, he changed his lifestyle and became a hermit near Cesena. He attracted numerous disciples, built a church, and organized his followers into a community of penitents, the *Boniti*. He became famous for his austerities, miracles, and as a confessor. He died at Mantua, and his cult was approved in 1483. October 23.

BUONPEDONI, BL. BARTHOLOMEW (d. 1300). Born at Mucchio, Italy, he became an attendant in the infirmary of St. Vitus' abbey at Pisa, a Franciscan tertiary later, was ordained when thirty, and engaged in pastoral work at Peccioli. He contracted leprosy in 1280, went to the leper house of Celloli, became director and chaplain, ministered to his fellow lepers for the next twenty years, and died there on December 12, revered for his holiness and miracles. His cult was confirmed in 1910. December 14.

BURCHARD (d. 754). A priest of Wessex, England, he went as a missionary to Germany about 732 and served under St. Boniface, who consecrated him first bishop of Würzburg. He was sent by Pepin the Short to Rome in 749 and secured Pope St. Zachary's approval of Pepin's accession to the Frankish throne. Burchard founded St. Andrew's abbey in Würzburg and about 753 resigned the bishopric. He spent the last years of his life in monastic retirement at Homburg, where he died on February 2. October 14.

BURCHARD. *See* Brocard.

BURGUNDOFARA (d. 657). Daughter of Count Agneric, courtier of King Theodebert II, she refused her father's demands that she marry and became abbess of a convent she convinced him to build, and ruled for thirty-seven years. Named Evoriacum, the convent was renamed for her after her death, and in time became the famous Benedictine abbey of Faremoutiers. She is also known as Fare. April 3.

BURIN, JACQUES (1756–94). A secular priest, he was imprisoned in 1791 for reading in public Pope Pius VI's condemnation of the Civil Constitution of France, though he had accepted it a few months earlier with reservations. Released, he continued his priestly work disguised as a merchant until he was murdered on October 17 at Champgenêteux. He was beatified in 1955 as one of the martyrs of Laval, which was the capital of Mayenne in western France.

BUS, BL. CESAR DE (1544–1607). Born on February 3 at Cavaillon, France, he became a soldier when eighteen and fought against the Huguenots. He dabbled in poetry and painting after the war, spent three years in Paris, living a pleasure-seeking and dissipated life, and then, on his brother's death, obtained his canonry at Salon solely for the benefices involved. He soon changed his lifestyle, resumed his studies, and was ordained in 1582. He became known for his preaching and charities, and in 1592 he founded the seculars of Christian Doctrine, a congregation of priests dedicated to catechetical instruction, which received the approval of Pope Clement VIII in 1597. He died at Avignon on April 15, and was beatified by Pope Paul VI in 1975.

BUXTON, BL. CHRISTOPHER (d. 1588). Born at Tideswell, Derbyshire, England, he studied there under Nicholas Garlick, who was to suffer martyrdom at Derby in 1588, and went to study for the priesthood in Rheims and then in Rome, where he was ordained in 1586. He was sent on the English mission, was captured soon after his arrival, and imprisoned in Marshalsea. Convicted of being a priest, he was hanged, drawn, and quartered on Oaten Hill outside Canterbury. He was beatified in 1929. October 1.

C

CABRINI, FRANCES XAVIER (1850–1917). The youngest of thirteen children of Augustine Cabrini, a farmer, and Stella Oldini, she was born on July 15 at Sant' Angelo Lodigiano, Italy, and christened Maria Francesca. She was destined to be a schoolteacher but when orphaned at eighteen, she decided to follow a religious life. She was refused by two communities, but in 1874 she was invited by Msgr. Serrati to take over a badly managed orphanage, House of Providence, at Codogno. Fierce opposition by its foundress, Antonia Tondini, eventually led to its closing by the bishop of Todi, who then invited Frances to found an institution. With seven followers, she moved into an abandoned Franciscan friary at Codogno and founded the Missionary Sisters of the Sacred Heart, devoted to the education of girls. The institute received the approval of the bishop in 1880 and soon spread to Grumello, Milan, and Rome. In 1889, Frances went to New York at the invitation of Archbishop Corrigan to work with Italian immigrants. During the next twenty-seven years, in the face of great obstacles, she traveled extensively and the congregation spread all over the United States (in 1892, it opened its first hospital, Columbus, in New York), Italy, South and Central America, and England. Its constitutions received final approval from the Holy See in 1907 (first approval had been in 1887), and by the time of her death in Chicago on December 22 there were more than fifty hospitals, schools, or-phanages, convents, and other foundations in existence. She became an American citizen in 1909. She was canonized by Pope Pius XII in 1946, the first American citizen to be so honored, and was named patroness of immigrants by Pius in 1950. November 13.

CADFAN (6th century). A missionary from Letavia (probably in Brittany but possibly in southeastern Wales) to Wales, he founded monasteries at Towyn in Merioneth and Llangadfan in Montgomeryshire, and later a monastic center on the island of Bardsey, where he was first abbot and which developed into a great center of monasticism. He probably died at Bardsey. November 1.

CADOC (d. c. 575). A Welshman and son of St. Gundleus and St. Gwladys, he was educated by St. Tatheus, an Irishman, at Caerwent. He became a monk, founded a monastery at Llancarfan, near Cardiff, which became famous, studied for three years in Ireland and then at Brednock, and founded a church at Llanspyddid. He returned to Llancarfan as abbot, visited Brittany, Cornwall, and Scotland, made pilgrimages to Rome and Jerusalem, and probably died at Llansannor near Llancarfan. Some authorities believe he was killed near Weedon fighting invading Saxons. September 25.

CADROE (d. 976). Son of a Scottish thane, he studied at Armagh, Ireland, where he became noted for his learning.

He returned to Scotland as a teacher of priests and then went on pilgrimage to various English shrines. While in London, he reportedly miraculously caused a huge conflagration to subside. He then went with several companions to France, where he founded St. Michael's monastery at Thiérache, became a Benedictine at Fleury, then abbot of Waulsort, and at the request of the bishop of Metz, reformed St. Clement Abbey there. March 6.

CAECILIA. A variant of Cecilia.

CAECILIAN (d. 304). *See* Optatus.

CAECILIUS (1st century). *See* Torquatus.

CAEDMON (d. c. 680). A laborer, perhaps a herdsman, at Whitby monastery, England, he is said to have received the gift of composing verses in praise of God in a vision. He became a lay brother there and studied Scripture, which he turned into verses, the first Anglo-Saxon writer of religious poetry. Though only one of his hymns, said to have been composed in a dream, survives, he is called "the Father of English Sacred Poetry." February 11.

CAEDWALLA (c. 659–89). He became the King of the West Saxons in 685 or 686, subjugated Sussex, made Surrey and Kent dependencies, and conquered the Isle of Wight, whose pagan inhabitants he annihilated. Under him Wessex became a powerful kingdom, but in 688, he resigned his throne and went to Rome. He was baptized there on Easter Eve, April 10, by Pope Sergius I, taking the name Peter, died a few days later, and was buried in St. Peter's on April 20. Still to be seen on his tomb in St. Peter's is his metrical epitaph, ordered by Sergius, preserved on the original stone. His name is sometimes spelled Cadwallader. November 12.

CAESARIA (d. c. 529). Sister of Bishop St. Caesarius of Arles, Gaul, she became first abbess of a convent he founded about 512 and ruled over several hundred nuns, devoted to the care of the poor, the sick, and children, until her death on January 12.

CAESARIUS (date unknown). Legend has him a deacon from Africa, who while visiting Terracina, Italy, he protested the pagan custom of sacrificing a youth of the city to Apollo. Caesarius was arrested, imprisoned for two years, and then put in a sack and thrown into the sea with a priest named Julian. November 1.

CAESARIUS OF ARLES (470–543). Of a Gallo-Roman family, he was born at Châlons, Burgundy, decided to pursue an ecclesiastical career, entered the monastery at Lérins when eighteen, and as cellarer incurred the enmity of some of the monks. Illness caused him to leave, but while recuperating at Arles he came to the attention of his Uncle Eonus, the bishop there, who had him transferred from Lérins to his see, and ordained him. After three years spent in reforming a nearby monastery, he was elected, against his wishes, to succeed his uncle as bishop of Arles in 503. Caesarius put into effect numerous reforms, fought Arianism, ordered the Divine Office to be sung in Arles' churches every day of the week, and preached frequently and successfully. He founded a convent at Arles, with his sister Caesaria as abbess, wrote a rule for its nuns, and presided over several synods as metropolitan. In 505, he was banished to Bordeaux by King Alaric II of the Visigoths in the mistaken belief he was trying to make Arles part of the Burgundian kingdom where he had been born, but was recalled when Alaric discovered the falsity of the accuser's charge. Caesarius aided the victims of the siege of Arles by the Burgundian King and was again arrested when Theodoric the Ostrogoth seized Arles; again all charges against him were dropped at a meeting with Theodoric at Ravenna in 513. Caesarius then traveled to Rome, was made apostolic delegate in Gaul, and received the pallium from Pope St. Symmachus, reportedly the first instance in which it was granted to any Western European bishop. After the Franks captured Alres in 536, Caesarius spent most of his time at St. John's convent, where he died on August 27. At the time of his death, he had ruled his see for forty years and was the most famous bishop in Gaul, noted for his holiness, charity, and ability. He was largely responsible for the condemnation of semi-Pelagianism at the Council of Orange in 529 and published an adaptation of Roman law, largely based on the Theodosian code, *Breviarium Alarici*, which became the civil code of Gaul. Several of his sermons have survived.

CAESARIUS OF NAZIANZEN (c. 329–69). Son of Gregory the Elder, bishop of Nazianzen and brother of St. Gregory Nazianzen, he studied philosophy and medicine at Alexandria and Constantinople and became a famous physician. He was named physician to Emperor Julian the Apostate, rebuffed the Emperor's efforts to get him to abjure his religion though he was as yet only a catechumen, and resigned his position. He was later physician to Emperor Jovian, treasurer for Emperor Valens, and in 368 was baptized, after he had narrowly escaped death in an earthquake at Nicaea in Bithynia. His fortune was left to the poor on his death. February 25.

CAFASSO, JOSEPH (1811–60). Born at Castelnuovo d'Asti in the Piedmont, Italy, of peasant parents, he studied at the seminary at Turin, and was ordained in 1833. He continued his theological studies at the seminary and university at Turin and then at the Institute of St. Francis, and despite a deformed spine, became a brilliant lecturer in moral theology there. He was a popular teacher, actively opposed Jansenism, and fought state intrusion into Church affairs. He succeeded Luigi Guala as rector of the Institute in 1848 and made a deep impression on his young priest students with his holiness and insistence on discipline and high standards. He was a sought-after confessor and spiritual adviser, and ministered to prisoners, working to improve their terrible conditions. He met Don Bosco in 1827 and the two became close friends. It was through Joseph's encouragement that Bosco decided his vocation was working with boys. Joseph was his adviser, worked closely with him in his foundations, and convinced others to fund and found religious institutes and charitable organizations. Joseph died on June 23 at Turin, and was canonized in 1947.

CAGNOALD. *See* Chainoaldus.

CAGNOLI, BL. GERARD (c. 1270–1345). Born of noble parents in northern Italy, he was orphaned in his early teens. He gave his inheritance to the poor and lived as a pilgrim and then as a hermit in Sicily until about 1310, when he joined the Franciscans as a lay brother. He lived a life of great austerity and severe penances, experienced visions, and had many miracles attributed to him. He died on December 31, and his cult was confirmed in 1908. December 1.

CAGNOU. *See* Chainoaldus.

CAINNECH. *See* Canice.

CAIUS (d. c. 172). *See* Alexander.

CAIUS (d. 296). Nothing is known of him except from unreliable tradition, which has him a Dalmatian and a relative of Emperor Diocletian. He became Pope in 283, decreed bishops must be priests before consecration, and when Diocletian's persecution of Christians began, fled to a cave, where he lived for eight years until his death. How unreliable the tradition about him as a source of factual information may be judged from the fact that Diocletian's persecution did not begin until six or seven years after his death on April 22.

CAIUS (d. 304). *See* Optatus.

CAJETAN (1480–1547). Son of Count Caspar of Thiene and Mary di Porto, he was born in Vicenza, Italy, and was two when his father was killed fighting for the Venetians against King Ferdinand of Naples. He was raised by his mother, studied at the University of Padua, and received his doctorates in civil and in canon law. He became a senator in Vicenza and in 1506, went to Rome, where Pope Julius II made him a protonotary, and he revived the Confraternity of Divine Love, consisting of devout priests. He resigned the position of protonotary on Julius' death in 1513, was ordained in 1516, and returned to Vicenza. He joined the Oratory of St. Jerome there, worked with the poor and the sick, particularly the incurable, founded a similar oratory at Verona, and in 1520 went to Venice, where he continued his work with the needy. In 1523, he went to Rome and with John Peter Caraffa, later to be Pope Paul IV, Paul Consiglieri and Boniface da Colle founded an institute of clergy devoted to reforming the Church, preaching to the people, aiding the sick, and improving the state of the clergy, which was at a very low ebb. The institute was approved by Pope Clement VII, with Caraffa, bishop of Chieti, as provost general in 1524. Called the Theatines (Theate is the Latin for Chiete), the institute was to consist of regular clergy living in community, bound by vows, and engaged in pastoral work. Not too successful at first, it barely survived the destruction of its house in Rome when Charles V sacked the city in 1527. In 1530, Cajetan was elected superior, but Caraffa was reelected in 1533, and Cajetan then went to Verona and later to Naples, where he fought widespread opposition to the reforms of the bishops there and the heretical teachings so prevalent. Later, with Bl. John Marinoni, he founded the *montes pietatis* to help extend loans to the poor and combat usury. He died in Naples on August 7, and was canonized in 1671. Also known as Gaetano, Cajetan was one of the great Catholic reformers; many of the reforms of the Council of Trent were anticipated by Cajetan and put into effect by him long before that council was convened. August 7.

CALAFATO, EUSTOCHIA (Smerelda Colonna) (1434–1491). A member of the religious order of the Poor Clares, she was the daughter of a Sicilian noble family. Legend has her born in a stable as a result of her pious mother's vision. After a vision of Christ crucified, Smeralda entered the Poor Clare convent of Santa Maria di Basico against her family's wishes. When her brothers threatened to burn the convent, Smerelda returned home. Her piety caused the family to relent and she returned to the convent. As a Poor Clare, she was noted for her aid to the poor, her self-imposed penances, and her adherence to the austerities in a community of such severe discipline Franciscan priests refused to say mass there for fear of encouraging excess. She was canonized in 1988. January 2.

CALASANZ, JOSEPH (1556–1648). Youngest son of Pedro Calasanz, he was born at his father's castle near Peralta de la Sal, Aragon, Spain, on September 11. He studied at Estadilla, the University of Lérida (where he received his doctorate in law), Valencia, and Alcalá, and was ordained in 1583, despite his father's wish that he be a soldier. He was appointed vicar general of Trempe by the bishop of Urgel, who then sent him to revive religion and reform the clergy in a desolate section of his see in the Pyrenees. Successful, he was appointed vicar general of the whole diocese on his return but resigned in 1592 and went to Rome. He became attached to the household of Ascanio Cardinal Colonna, distinguished himself with his heroic work in the plague of 1595, and labored to improve the education of needy children. With two priests he opened a free school in 1597 and became supervisor of a community of teachers that developed to take care of the tremendous increase in the number of students at the school. An investigation of complaints about the school was so favorable that Pope Clement VIII took it under his protection, as did Pope Paul V. Other schools were opened, and in 1621 the community was recognized as a religious Order, the Clerks Regular of Religious Schools, with Joseph as superior general. The last years of his life were saddened by internal dissension when a Fr. Mario Sozzi accused him of incapacity and became general; when Sozzi died in 1643, his successor, Fr. Cherubini, followed his direction. The Order was torn apart by their actions, and in 1645 a commission appointed by the Pope restored Joseph to the generalate. But dissension continued, and in 1646 Pope Innocent X in effect dissolved the congregation by making it a society of secular priests subject to local bishops. Fr. Cherubini, assigned the task of drawing up a new constitution, was convicted of maladministering Nazarene College, of which he was rector, and forced to resign; re-pentant, he was reconciled to Joseph in 1648 on his deathbed. Joseph died a few months later in Rome on August 25, and was canonized in 1767. His foundation was reformed in 1656, restored as a religious order in 1669, and is in existence today, popularly known as the Piarists of Scolopi. He is also referred to as Joseph Calasanctius. August 25.

CALIMERIUS (d. c. 190). A Greek, he was educated in Rome by Pope St. Telesphorus and became bishop of Milan. Calimerius was murdered for his faith by being drowned in a well during the reign of Emperor Commodus. July 31.

CALIXTUS. See Callistus.

CALLISTHENE (4th century). See Adauctus.

CALLISTUS I (d. c. 222). A Roman from the Trastevere section of Rome, son of one Domitius, he was a slave of Carpophorus, who put him in charge of a bank. He lost the bank's money, fled, was caught at Porto and sentenced to a punishment reserved for slaves—the dreaded hand mill. Released at the request of the creditors, he was again arrested for fighting in a synagogue, presumably trying to recover some of the money, and sentenced to the mines in Sardinia. He was again released with other prisoners at the request of Emperor Commodus' mistress, Marcia, and about 199 was made a deacon and director of the Christian cemetery on the Via Appia (now St. Callistus cemetery) by Pope Zephyrinus and became the friend and adviser of the Pope. He was elected to succeed Zephyrinus as Pope in 217 and was denounced by his bitter enemy, St. Hippolytus, a candidate for the papal throne, who set himself up as an anti-pope and who wrote the unfriendly account of him that is the source of most of our information about him. Hippolytus condemned him of leniency to the Monarchian heretics, though Callistus had condemned their leader Sabelius, and for such actions as forgiving repentant murderers and adulterers, permitting multimarried men to become priests, recognizing the marriages of free women and slaves, and refusing to depose repentant bishops who had committed mortal sins. It is believed Callistus was killed in an uprising, and is so considered to be a martyr. October 14.

CALMETTE, CHARLES DE LA (d. 1792). See Du Lau, Bl. John.

CALOCERUS (d. c. 121). See Justinus.

CALOCERUS (3rd century). He and his brother Parthenius were eunuchs from Armenia in the household of Emperor Decius' wife, Tryphonia. They were accused of wasting the heritage of Anatolia (or Callista) who had been left in their care on the death of her father, Aemilian, a consul, who had brought them to Rome, and for being Christians. They were condemned to be burned to death but when the flames left them unharmed, they were beaten to death. The whole story is questionable. May 19.

CALOSIRTO, JOHN JOSEPH OF THE CROSS (1654–1734). Born on the island of Ischia, near Naples, and baptized Carlo Gaetano, he was of a religious bent as a child, and when sixteen, became a Franciscan of the Alcantarine reform at Santa Lucia del Monte Convent in Naples, taking the name John Joseph of the Cross. He was ordained in 1677, became an outstanding confessor, and was novice master at the mother house. He served as superior of the monastery at Piedemonte di Alife three times and became known for his holiness, austerities, and miracles. When a dispute broke out between the Spanish and Italian Alcantarines over the papal brief insisting the minister provincial must be Spanish, he was instrumental in settling the dispute by forming the Italians into a separate province, of which he was elected minister provincial. In addition to his reported miracles, other supernatural gifts attributed to him were visions, ecstasies, levitation, and prophecy. He died on March 1 at Naples, and was canonized in 1839. March 5.

CAMBIANI, BL. PETER (d. 1365). Born in Piedmont, Italy, he joined the Dominicans, and in 1351 was named inquisitor of Piedmont, Upper Lombardy, and Liguria. He worked in that area, especially against the Waldensians, for fourteen years, when he was murdered at Susa by the Waldensians. His cult was confirmed in 1856. November 7.

CAMERINUS (d. c. 303). See Luxorius.

CAMILLUS DE LELLIS. See Lellis, Camillus de.

CAMPION, EDMUND (c. 1540–81). Born in London, son of a bookseller, he was raised a Catholic, given a scholarship to St. John's College, Oxford, when fifteen, and became a fellow when only seventeen. His brilliance attacted the attention of such leading personages as the Earl of Leicester, Robert Cecil, and even Queen Elizabeth. He took the Oath of Supremacy acknowledging Elizabeth head of the Church in England and became an Anglican deacon in 1564. Doubts about Protestantism increasingly beset him, and in 1569 he went to Ireland, where further study convinced him he had been in error, and he returned to Catholicism. Forced to flee the persecution unleashed on Catholics by the excommunication of Elizabeth by Pope Pius V, he went to Douai, France, where he studied theology, joined the Jesuits, and then went to Brno,

Bohemia, the following year for his novitiate. He taught at the college at Prague and in 1578 was ordained there. He and Fr. Robert Persons were the first Jesuits chosen for the English mission and were sent to England in 1580. His activities among the Catholics, the distribution of his *Decem rationes* at the university church in Oxford, and the premature publication of his famous *Brag* (which he had written to present his case if he was captured) made him the object of one of the most intensive manhunts in English history. He was betrayed at Lyford, near Oxford, imprisoned in the Tower of London, and when he refused to apostatize when offered rich inducements to do so, was tortured and then hanged, drawn, and quartered at Tyburn on December 1 on the technical charge of treason but in reality because of his priesthood. He was canonized by Pope Paul VI in 1970 as one of the Forty English and Welsh Martyrs.

CANDIDA (no date). Long venerated in Rome, her remains were enshrined in St. Praxedes church there by Pope St. Paschal I in the ninth century. She was one of a group of martyrs executed for their faith on the Ostian Way.

CANDIDA (d. c. 300). The Roman Martyrology lists her as a maiden of Carthage who was beaten with whips and then executed during the persecution of Christians by Emperor Maximian. September 20.

CANDIDA (d. 302). *See* Artemius.

CANDIDA (d. 798). *See* Emerius.

CANDIDA THE ELDER (d. c. 78). An old woman living in Naples, she was reported to have been baptized and miraculously cured of an ailment by St. Peter when he passed through Naples on his way to Rome. She is also reputed to have converted St. Aspren, who became first bishop of Naples. September 4.

CANDIDA THE YOUNGER (d. c. 586). A married woman living in Naples, she was regarded as a model wife and mother and according to the Roman Martyrology "was famed for miracles." September 10.

CANDIDUS (d. c. 287). *See* Maurice.

CANETULI, BL. ARCHANGELO (d. 1513). A native of Bologna, Italy, he became an Augustinian canon regular after his father and brothers were killed in a riot. He was guestmaster at the Augustinian house in Venice, spent time at St. Ambrose monastery in Gubbio, and died at Castiglione, revered for his holiness and the gift of prophecy he is reported to have had. Supposedly he declined the post of archbishop of Florence when it was offered to him. April 16.

CANICE (c. 515–99). All we know about him is from unreliable legend, according to which he was born at Glengiven, Ireland, became a monk under St. Cadoc at Llancarfan, Wales, and was ordained there. After a trip to Rome, he studied under St. Finnian at Clonard, Ireland, accompanied SS. Kieran, Columba, and Comgall to St. Mobhi at Glasnevin, preached for a time in Ireland, and then went to Scotland. A close friend of Columba's whom he accompanied on a visit to King Brude of the Picts, he was a most successful missionary, built a monastery at Aghaboe, Ireland, and probably one at Kilkenny. He is also known as Kenneth and Cainnech. October 11.

CANISIUS, PETER (1521–97). Born at Nijmegen, Netherlands, on May 8, son of the nine-times-elected burgomaster there, he received his master's from Cologne University, studied canon law at Louvain, and then, inspired by a retreat given by Bl. Peter Fabre at Mainz, joined the Jesuits in 1543. Peter gave his inheritance to the poor, was ordained in 1546, and became noted for his preaching. He attended two sessions of the Council of Trent, was sent to teach at the Jesuits' first school at Messina by St. Ignatius, and then was sent in 1549 to Ingolstadt at the request of Duke William IV of Bavaria to combat Protestantism and revive Catholicism there. He served as rector and then as vice chancellor of the university, effected a religious revival among the people, and in 1552 was sent on a similar mission in Vienna at the request of King Ferdinand. He was most successful, administering the diocese for a year, but refused to consider an appointment to head the see. In 1555, he published the first edition of his *Catechism,* which was to be enormously successful, with hundreds of printings in some fifteen languages. He was sent to Prague in 1556 to help found a new college and while there was appointed provincial of a new province, consisting of southern Germany, Bohemia, and Austria. He traveled all over Germany, lecturing, preaching, debating with Protestants, founding colleges, and restoring Catholicism in the cities in which he preached, and was responsible for the spread of Jesuit influence to Poland. He was in Augsburg, 1559–65, was instrumental in having the Reichstag restore public schools, and when his term as provincial expired, he taught at the Jesuit college at Dillengen, Bavaria. He was court chaplain at Innsbruck and helped heal a rift between the Emperor and Pope Pius IV, was selected to promulgate the decrees of the Council of Trent in Germany, and in 1580 founded a college at Fribourg that became the University of Fribourg; his preaching at Fribourg was a major factor in keeping

Fribourg Catholic. He suffered a stroke in 1591 but continued dictating his writing until his death at Fribourg on December 21. He was a prolific writer, edited the works of St. Cyril of Alexandria and St. Leo the Great, an edition of St. Jerome's letters, a martyrology, a revision of the breviary, and a *Manual of Catholics,* among other works. Often called "the Second Apostle of Germany," after St. Boniface, it was due mainly to Peter's efforts that the Counter-Reformation was successful in southern Germany. He was canonized in 1925, when he was declared a Doctor of the Church. December 21.

CANOSSA, BL. MAGDALEN DI (1774–1835). Daughter of Marquis Ottavio of Canossa, she was born at Verona, Italy. When her father died, her mother remarried when Magdalen was eight, and she and her two sisters and brother were raised by her Uncle Jerome. She entered the Carmelite convent at Conegliano, decided she had no vocation, and returned home. When Napoleon visited the family home in Verona in 1804, she asked him for and received the deserted St. Joseph convent at Verona to be used for poor and deserted girls. In 1808, with several companions, she opened the convent for the education and care of poor and neglected girls, the beginnings of the Canossian Daughters of Charity. The work prospered, and as more women joined the community, Magdalen opened other foundations in Venice, Milan, Bergamo, and Trent—high schools, colleges, retreat centers, and in 1831, organized a congregation of men at Venice to do the same work for boys. She experienced ecstasies, levitation, and visions (it was a vision of our Lady in Venice that had turned her to her works of mercy). She died at Verona on April 10, and was beatified in 1941. She was canonized in 1988. May 14.

CANTIANELLA (d. c. 304). She and her brothers, Cantius and Cantianus, of the noble Roman Anicii family, were orphaned as children and raised as Christians by Protus, their guardian. When Diocletian's persecution of Christians began, they freed their slaves, sold their possessions, distributed the money realized to the poor, and fled to Aquileia. They were captured at Aquae Gradatae, and when they refused to sacrifice to the gods, were beheaded, with Protus, by order of Diocletian. May 31.

CANTIANUS (d. c. 304). *See* Cantianella.

CANTIUS (d. c. 304). *See* Cantianella.

CANUTE (c. 1086). Illegitimate son of King Sweyn Estrithson of Denmark, nephew of King Canute who had reigned over England, he was unsuccessful in an attempt to claim that crown in 1075 but became King of Denmark as Canute IV, succeeding his brother Harold in 1081. He married Adela, sister of Count Roberts of Flanders, aided the clergy and missionaries, built many churches, and in 1085 prepared to invade England when he reasserted his claim to that country. His heavy taxes and disputes with the *jarls* (the nobles) led to a rebellion headed by his brother Olaf, which forced him to abandon the invasion and flee to the island of Funen. He was tracked down by the insurgents and he, his brother Benedict, and seventeen followers were slain on July 19 in the church of St. Alban in Odense, where he had taken refuge. Reportedly numerous miracles occurred at his tomb, and together with the fact that he was kneeling at the altar of the church after confession when he was slain caused Pope Paschal II to authorize his cult at the request of King Eric III of Denmark in 1101. January 19.

CANUTE LAVARD (d. 1131). Son of King Eric the Good of Denmark, he spent part of his youth at the Saxon court, and when he came of age he was made duke of southern Jutland. He fought Viking raids, brought peace and order to his territory, and aided the missionary activities of St. Vicelin. In 1129, Emperor Lothair III recognized him as King of the Western Wends, a move strongly opposed by his uncle, King Nils of Denmark, and which two years later, on January 7, led to Canute's murder near Ringsted by Magnus Nielssen and Henry Skadelaar, his cousins. He was canonized in 1169. He is also known as Knud.

CAPILLAS, BL. FRANCIS (1606–48). Born of peasant parents at Vacherim, Valladolid, Spain, he joined the Dominicans when seventeen, was sent to the Philippines, and was ordained in Manila in 1631. After ten years as a missionary in Luzon, he was sent to Fokien Province in China as a companion to Fr. Francis Diaz. Francis Capillas learned the language and made many converts and was successful in his missionary activities until the fall of the Ming Dynasty, when civil war broke out. While attempting to minister to the Christians of the town of Fogan, a Manchu Tatar stronghold under siege by the forces of the Chinese viceroy, he was captured by the Tatars, accused of spying, tortured, and beheaded on January 15. He was beatified in 1909.

CAPITANIO, BL. BARTHOLOMEA (1807–33). Born at Lovere in the Italian Alps, which was then under Austrian rule, she was unable to secure her parents' permission to become a nun, took vows of perpetual chastity, and devoted herself to educational work with the young. She organized a sodality for the education of the young, met Catherine Gerosa (St. Vincentia Gerosa), who was interested in nursing and helping the sick poor, and together they founded an institute, *Suore della Carità* (Sisters of Charity of Lovere), devoted to the education of the young and providing aid to the sick poor. Despite many difficulties, the congregation eventually secured papal approval and spread. Bartholomea carried on a voluminous correspondence during her brief lifetime; her spiritual notes and instructions were published as *Scritti spirituali,* and some three hundred of her letters were collected and published. She died on July 26 at twenty-six, and was canonized in 1950.

CAPPUCI, BL. PETER (1390–1445). Born at Tiferno (Città di Castello), Italy, he became a Dominican when fifteen and was sent to Cortona, where among his fellow monks were Fra Angelico and St. Antonius. He spent most of his life here, known for his prayerful life, preaching (he was called "the Preacher of Death" because he preached with a skull in his hands), and was reputed to have performed several miracles. His cult was confirmed by Pope Pius VII. October 21.

CAPRAIS. *See* Caprasius.

CAPRASIUS (3rd century). Though he doubtlessly was a real person and probably suffered martyrdom, his fictitious legend has him the first bishop of Agen, France. He followed his flock into hiding during Diocletian's persecution of the Christians, but when Caprasius saw St. Faith martyred before Dacian, prefect of the Gauls, Caprasius proclaimed his faith. He was tortured and imprisoned when he refused offers of wealth to renounce his faith, and the next day, when he remained adamant in proclaiming his faith, he was taken to the temple of Diana, and with his mother, Faith's sister, Alberta, and Primus and Felician, two brothers, and numerous bystanders,

was put to death when they all refused to sacrifice. October 20.

CAPRASIUS (d. 430). A hermit in Provence and also known as Caprais, he accompanied Honoratus and his brother Venantius on a trip to Greece to seek a secluded desert area for a hermitage. When Venantius died at Modon in Greece, Honoratus and Caprasius retired to Lérins off the coast of France, soon attracted numerous disciples, and Caprasius helped Honoratus found a monastery that became a great center of spirituality. June 1.

CARACCIOLO, FRANCIS (1563–1608). Of noble parents, he was born on October 13 at Villa Santa Maria, Abruzzi, Italy, and was christened Ascenio. In fulfillment of a vow to devote his life to God if he was cured of a serious ailment thought to be leprosy when he was twenty-two, he studied at Naples and was ordained. He joined the *Bianchi della Giustizia,* a confraternity devoted to caring for prisoners, and in 1588, he, Fr. John Augustine Adorno, and twelve companions founded the Minor Clerks Regular, devoted to missionary work and to ministering to the sick in hospitals and to prisoners. When Pope Sixtus V approved the foundation in 1588, Adorno was named superior, and Ascanio took the name Francis. They established a house in Naples and then went to Spain, where they were refused permission to found a house by the royal court; they were shipwrecked on the way home. The foundation flourished and soon spread all over Italy, and it was asked to take over Santa Maria Maggiore in Naples. On the death of Adorno, Francis was named superior. On visits to Spain he was more successful than on his previous visit and made foundations at Madrid, Valladolid, and Alcala in 1595 and 1598. He was granted leave to resign as superior after seven years, became prior of Santa Maria Maggiore and master of novices. He died on June 1 at Agnone, where he had gone to establish a new foundation. Miracles were attributed to him, and he was reputed to have had the gifts of ecstasies and prophecy. He was canonized in 1807. June 4.

CARADOC (d. 1124). A harpist at the court of Prince Rhysap Tewdwr of South Wales, he became a monk at Llandaff, was a hermit for several years at St. Cenydd Church in Gower, and then on an island off the coast of Pembroke. Driven off the island by Norse marauders, he and his companions moved to St. Ismael's cell at Haroldston, where Caradoc was superior. April 14.

CARANNOG. See Carantoc.

CARANTAC. See Carantoc.

CARANTOC (6th century). A Welshman, also known as Carannog, he founded a church at Llangrannog, Wales, spent some time in Ireland, and on his return founded a monastery at Cernach (it may have been at Carhampton in Somerset, Crantock in Cornwall, or even possibly in Ireland), of which he was abbot. He is known to have visited Brittany but then returned to Cernach, where he died. He is sometimes identified with a Welsh prince, Carantac, who worked with St. Patrick in the evangelization of Ireland. May 16.

CAREY, BL. JOHN (d. 1594). See Cornelius, Bl. John.

CARILEFUS (d. c. 540). Born in Auvergne, France, and also known as Calais, he was raised at Menat Monastery near Riom, France, and became a monk there with his friend St. Avitus. They transferred to Micy abbey, were ordained, and then Carilefus be-

came a hermit in Maine. His holiness and austerity attracted followers, and he organized them into a monastery of which he became abbot at Anisole. July 1.

CARISSIMUS (d. c. 90). See Romulus.

CARLETTI, BL. ANGELO (1411–95). Born at Chivasso, Italy, of a noble Piedmont family, he received his doctorate in civil and canon law at the University of Bologna and was made a senator on his return to Chivasso. On the death of his mother, he gave his inheritance to the poor and became a Franciscan in Genoa, where he was ordained. He ministered to the sick and the poor, established pawnshops to combat usury, was a successful missionary and confessor in the Piedmont, and served as confessor of Duke Charles I of Savoy. Angelo was vicar general of his order three times, and at the request of Pope Sixtus IV preached among the Saracens, and when eighty to the Waldensians at the request of Pope Innocent VIII. Angelo spent the last two years of his life at a convent at Cuneo, Piedmont, where he died. A book of moral theology, *Summa Angelica,* that he wrote was widely used. April 12.

CARPOPHORUS (d. c. 306). Carpophorus, Severian, Severus, and Victorinus are honored in the Roman Martyrology as "the Four Crowned Martyrs." They were brothers who suffered martyrdom on the Via Lavicana in Rome, scourged to death with leaden whips during the reign of Emperor Diocletian. However, there is much confusion between them and the group of martyrs associated with St. Castorius, especially since the Roman Martyrology describes the martyrdom of four other martyrs, Claudius, Nicostratus, Symphoria and Simplicius (the names associated with Castorius), in the same place and in the same way. November 8.

CARPUS (d. 170 or 250). A bishop from Gurdos, Lydia, he was arraigned, with Papylus, a deacon from Thyatira, before the Roman governor of Pergamus for being a Christian. When he refused to sacrifice to the gods, he was tortured and then burned at the stake; Papylus suffered a similar fate. At the same time, the beautiful Agathonice, sister of Papylus and mother of several children, and her servant Agathadorus were burned alive for their faith. It is uncertain whether their martyrdom occurred during the persecution of Marcus Aurelius or Decius. April 13.

CARRERI, BL. MATTHEW (d. 1470). Born at Mantua, Italy, John Francis joined the Dominicans, taking the name Matthew, and was an advocate of strict observance of the rule among the Dominicans. He became a successful preacher, was devoted to the Passion of Christ, and was taken captive by pirates while on a voyage from Genoa to Pisa. He was set free but then offered himself in place of a woman captive and her daughter, whereupon the pirate captain freed them all. Popularly known as Matthew of Mantua, he died at Vigevana on December 5, and his cult was permitted by Pope Sixtus IV in 1482.

CARTHACH (d. 637). Born at Castlemaine, Kerry, Ireland, and probably named Cuda, he was a swineherd who became a disciple of St. Carthach the Elder, taking his name, who ordained him. About 590, he became a hermit at Kiltulagh and then at Bangor under St. Comgall. After visiting several monasteries, Carthach settled for a time at Rahan in Offaly, and then in 595 founded a monastery there and ruled over eight hundred monks, two of whom, Britons, tried to drown him, as

they felt the time had arrived for the monastery to have a new abbot. He wrote a rule in metrical verse, a later version of which is still extant. He also was probably a bishop at Fircall. After forty years, he and his monks were driven from the monastery by Blathmac, a local ruler. He founded a new monastery at Lismore and spent the last years of his life as a hermit in a nearby cave, where he died on May 14. His is also known as Carthage and Mochuda. His cult was confirmed in 1903.

CARTHAGE. *See* Carthach.

CARVALHO, BL. JAMES (1578–1624). Born at Coimbra, Portugal, he joined the Jesuits in 1594, was sent to India in 1600, and was ordained on Macao. He served as a missionary near Kyoto, Japan, from 1609 to 1614, when he was forced to leave because of persecution of the Christians. He worked at Cochin China the next three years, then returned to Japan in 1617 and worked there until 1623, when he and a group of Christians were arrested at Hokkaido. Though it was midwinter, they were stripped of their clothing and marched across the island to Senda (many were beheaded along the way), where they were tied to stakes in freezing water. All died of exposure to the freezing cold; Fr. Carvalho was the last to die, on February 22. He was beatified in 1867.

CARVALHO, BL. MICHAEL (1577–1627). Born at Brago, Portugal, he joined the Jesuits in 1597, and in 1602 he was sent to Goa, India, where he was ordained. He taught there for fifteen years and then was sent to Japan, entering the country by disguising himself as a soldier as Christians were being persecuted. He was caught, imprisoned in irons for a year, and then burned to death at Ximabara on August 25 with Dominican Peter Vasquez and Franciscans Louis

Solelo, Louis Baba, and Louis Sasanda. Michael was beatified in 1867.

CARVALHO, BL. VINCENT (d. 1632). Born at Alfama, near Lisbon, Portugal, he joined the Augustinians at Lisbon and was sent as a missionary to Mexico in 1621; sent to Japan in 1623, he suffered martyrdom there at Nagasaki by being burned to death. He was beatified in 1867 as one of the Martyrs of Japan. September 3.

CASANOVA, LEONARD (1676–1751). Born at Porto Maurizio, Italy, and baptized Paul Jerome, he was sent to the Jesuit Roman College when he was thirteen. His Uncle Augustine, with whom he was living, wanted him to become a physician, and when he refused, disowned him. He joined the Franciscans of the Strict Observance at Ponticelli in 1697, taking the name Leonard, continued his studies at the Observant St. Bonaventure's in Rome, and was ordained there in 1703. He went to St. Francesco del Monte monastery in Florence in 1709 and from there preached all over Tuscany with tremendous effect. He became guardian of San Francesco, founded a retreat for religious at nearby Incontro, and spent six years conducting missions around Rome. He was named guardian at St. Bonaventure's in 1736 but was released from this position the following year to continue his missions, which were now attracting huge crowds. He was an ardent promoter of the Stations of the Cross devotion (reputedly setting up almost six hundred Stations throughout Italy), and devotion to the Blessed Sacrament, the Sacred Heart, and Mary. He served for a time as spiritual director of Clementina Sobieska, wife of the claimant of the English throne, King James III, and in 1744 was sent to Corsica by Pope Benedict XIV to preach and to restore peace there but was un-

successful, since the Corsicans felt he was more a political tool of the Genoese who ruled the island than a missionary. He returned to Rome from a discouraging missionary tour in 1751 completely exhausted and died at St. Bonaventure the night he arrived, November 26; he had been engaged in the most arduous missionary work for forty-three years. Canonized in 1867, he is the patron of parish missions.

CASAS, PHILIP DE LAS (1571–97). Born on May 1 in Mexico City of Spanish parents, he later joined the Franciscans at Puebla but left the order in 1589. He became a merchant and went to the Philippines. While there he regretted his decision and in 1593 rejoined the Franciscans in Manila. He was on his way back to Mexico City in 1596 to be ordained when his ship was driven off course to Japan. He was arrested late in 1596 and crucified the following year with twenty-five other Christians at Nagasaki on February 5 during the persecution of Christians unleashed by the *Taikó*, Toyotomi Hideyoshi. They were all canonized in 1862 as the Martyrs of Japan of 1597. He is also known as Philip of Jesus. February 6.

CASEY, SOLANUS (Bernard) (1870–1957). A Capuchin priest and doorkeeper at Franciscan friaries in New York and Detroit, he was noted for his charity and gifts of prophecy and healing. He was declared Venerable in 1995.

CASIMIR OF POLAND (1458–84). Third of the thirteen children of King Casimir IV of Poland and Elizabeth of Austria, daughter of Emperor II of Germany, he was born at the royal palace in Cracow on October 3, was taught by Fr. John Diugosz, and from childhood was attracted to a life of holiness, austerity, and charity. Convinced the cause was unjust, he refused to lead an army against King Matthias Corvinus of Hungary in 1471 to seize the Hungarian throne, as his father and the Hungarian nobility demanded. Though confined to the castle of Dobzki, Casimir resisted all efforts to make him change his mind. He also resisted his father's efforts to have him marry and devoted himself to study and prayer. He served as viceroy while his father was out of Poland, 1479–83, and died on March 4 at the court of Grodno while on a visit to Lithuania. Many miracles were reported at his tomb at Vilna, and he was canonized by Pope Adrian VI in 1522. He is the patron saint of Poland and Lithuania. March 4.

CASPAR (1st century). *See* Balthasar.

CASSIAN. *See* John Cassian.

CASSIAN OF IMOLA (date unknown). A christian teacher at Imola, near Ravenna, Italy, he was brought before the governor of the province during a persecution of Christians and when he refused to sacrifice to pagan gods was hacked to death by his students by order of the governor. August 13.

CASSIAN OF NANTES, BL. (d. 1638). *See* Noury, Bl. Francis.

CASSIAN OF TANGIERS (d. c. 298). An official recorder (court stenographer) at the trial of St. Marcellus the Centurion before Deputy Prefect Aurelius Agricolan at Tangiers, he denounced the unjust death penalty imposed on Marcellus, became a Christian, and was imprisoned. Shortly after, he was put to death. He is the patron of stenographers. December 3.

CASSIUS (d. 558). From the *Dialogues* of Gregory the Great, we learn that Cassius was an exemplary bishop of Narni from 537 to 558, noted for his charity and devotion to the people of Narni. He died in Rome, as he had foretold, while on a pilgrimage to that city. June 29.

CASTEÑEDA, BL. HYACINTH (d. 1773). Born at Setavo, near Valencia, Spain, he joined the Dominicans, was ordained, and was sent as a missionary to the Far East and worked in China and Indochina, where he was sent from the Philippines. He was arrested in China, tortured to make him apostatize, but when he remained adamant, he was deported. He went to Tonkin and after three years there, was arrested, tortured, and beheaded on November 7 with Bl. Vincent Liem, a member of a noble Tonkin family who joined the Dominicans, was ordained, and worked under Bl. Hyacinth. He was the first Indochinese Dominican to suffer martyrdom. They were both beatified in 1906.

CASTILLO, BL. JUAN DE (d. 1628). *See* Gonzalez, Bl. Roque.

CASTOR (d. c. 425). Possibly the brother of St. Leontius of Fréjus, Castor was born in Nimes, married a wealthy widow from Marseilles and by mutual consent both entered the religious life. Castor founded the Monanque monastery, near Apt, Provence, France, became its first abbot, and then against his will was named bishop of Apt. It was at his request that St. John Cassian wrote his *De institutis coenobiorum,* on the monastic life; Cassian dedicated it to him. September 2.

CASTORIUS (d. c. 306). He, Claudius, Nicostratus, and Symphorian are called "the Four Crowned Martyrs" who were tortured and executed in Pannonia, Hungary, during the reign of Emperor Diocletian. According to legend, they were employed as carvers at the imperial quarries at Sirmium (Mitrovica, Yugoslavia) and impressed Diocletian with their art, as did another carver, Simplicius. Diocletian commissioned them to do several carvings, which they did to his satisfaction, but they then refused to carve a statue of Aesculapius, as they were Christians. The Emperor accepted their beliefs, but when they refused to sacrifice to the gods, they were imprisoned. When Diocletian's officer Lampadius, who was trying to convince them to sacrifice to the gods, suddenly died, his relatives accused the five of his death; to placate the relatives, the Emperor had them executed. Another story has four unnamed *corniculari* beaten to death in Rome with leaden whips when they refused to offer sacrifice to Aesculapius of all his troops by Diocletian. They were buried on the Via Lavicana and were later given their names by Pope Miltiades. Probably they were the four Pannonian martyrs (not counting Simplicius) whose remains were translated Crowned Ones basilica there. A further to Rome and buried in the Four Crowned Ones basilica there. A further complication is the confusion of their story with that of the group of martyrs associated with St. Carpophorus in the Roman Martyrology under November 8.

CASTULUS OF ROME (d. 286). According to legend, he was the Emperor's chamberlain, sheltered Christians in his home, arranged for Christian services in the palace, and made many converts in Rome. Denounced by Torquatus, an apostate Christian, to Fabian, city prefect, Castulus was tortured and then smothered in a pit. March 26.

CASTUS (d. 250). Castus and Aemilius were African Christians who under torture recanted by later retracted their recantation and were burned to death during the persecution of Christians by Decius. May 22.

CATALD. *See* Cathal.

CATHAL (d. c. 685). Born in Munster, Ireland, be became a pupil and later, noted for his great learning, taught at Lismore. He became headmaster but resigned to go on pilgrimage to Jerusalem. On his way home he was elected bishop of Taranto, Italy, and served there with great distinction and holiness. He is also known as Cataldus and Catald. May 10.

CATHERICK, BL. EDMUND (c. 1605–42). A native of Yorkshire, England, he studied at Douai and was ordained. About 1635, he was sent on the English mission using the alias Huddleston. He was arrested, arraigned before a relative, Justice Dodsworth, at York, and condemned to be executed for his priesthood. He was hanged, drawn, and quartered at York, with Bl. John Lockwood, and was beatified in 1929. April 13.

CATHERINE (d. c. 310). Venerated in the East since the tenth century, nothing of any certainty is known of her. Her unreliable legend has her born in Alexandria of a patrician family and converted to Christianity by a vision. She denounced Emperor Maxentius in person for his persecution of the Christians, and when fifty pagan philosophers were converted by her arguments, he had them burned to death. When she refused his bribe of a royal marriage if she would apostatize, he had her imprisoned. On his return home from a camp inspection, he found that his wife, an officer, and two hundred soldiers of her guard had been converted, he had them all put to death. He then condemned Catherine to death on a spiked wheel, and when the wheel miraculously broke, he had her beheaded. Supposedly her body was brought to the monastery of Mount Sinai, where it reputedly still is. Catherine is one of the Fourteen Holy Helpers, was one of the voices heard by

132 CATHERINE OF BOLOGNA

Joan of Arc, and is the patroness of philosophers, maidens, and preachers. November 25.

CATHERINE OF BOLOGNA. *See* Vigri, Catherine de'.

CATHERINE OF GENOA (1447–1510). Daughter of James Fieschi and Francesca di Negro, she was born in Genoa, their fifth and last child. She early evinced an interest in the religious life, but when her father died, she was married when sixteen to Julian Adorno. He was shiftless, unfaithful, and a spendthrift, and after ten years of marriage his extravagance reduced them to poverty. Julian then reformed his life, became a Franciscan tertiary, and they agreed to live a continent life together. Catherine began to live a most unusual and intensive spiritual life while they devoted themselves to working in the Pammetone hospital, and six years later, in 1479, they went to live in the hospital, of which she was made director in 1490. She almost died of a plague that wiped out three quarters of the inhabitants in 1493, recovered, but was obliged to resign her position in 1496 because of ill health, though she and her husband continued to live in the hospital. Julian died the following year, and about 1499, Catherine met Don Cattaneo Marabotto, who became her spiritual director. Catherine experienced many mystical episodes and suffered from bad health the last years of her life before her death in Genoa on September 14. Her *Dialogue Between the Soul and the Body* and *Treatise on Purgatory* are outstanding documents in the field of mysticism. She was canonized in 1737. September 15.

CATHERINE LABOURÉ. *See* Labouré, Catherine.

CATHERINE MATTEI, BL. (1486–1547). Born in Racconiga, Italy, of

poverty-stricken parents, she had visions of the Holy Child and several saints, later suffered the pain of the stigmata with no physical signs, and when twenty-eight became a Dominican tertiary. Throughout her life she experienced many visions, was reputed to have had the gift of traveling to faraway places with incredible speed, and had many miracles attributed to her. She died after a long illness, and her cult was confirmed in 1810. September 4.

CATHERINE OF PALLANZA, BL. (c. 1437–78). Orphaned as a child when her family was wiped out by the plague near Pallanza, Italy, she was raised by a woman in Milan and when fifteen became a hermitess in a mountainous wilderness near Varese. Her holiness, austerity, and her gift of prophecy attracted other women, and in time she organized them under the Augustinian rule into Santa Maria di Monte convent, of which she served as prioress for four years, until her death. Her cult was approved in 1769. April 6.

CATHERINE OF PARC-AUX-DAMES, BL. (13th century). Of Jewish parents in Louvain, Rachel, when only seven, indicated to a priest visiting her father that she wanted to become a Christian. When twelve she fled her home and he placed her with the Cistercian nuns at Parc-aux-Dames abbey near Louvain, where she was baptized and took the name Catherine. Her parents were unsuccessful in having her returned to them, and she stayed at the abbey until her death, venerated for her visions and for the miracles she is reputed to have performed. May 4.

CATHERINE DEI RICCI (1522–90). Born in Florence of a noted family and named Alexandrina, she became a Dominican at Prato when twelve, taking the name Catherine. In time she became novice mistress and when thirty was elected prioress for life. Beginning in 1542, when she was twenty, and for the next twelve years, she experienced an extraordinary series of visions every week of the events leading to the crucifixion of Christ. She met and conversed with St. Philip Neri in Rome in a vision, though she never met him in person. She also received the stigmata and reportedly received a ring from Christ on Easter in 1542, which appeared as a red circle on her finger to others but as a ring to her. She spent many hours in prayer, was a competent administrator, devoted much time to those seeking her counsel, and aided the sick and the poor of Prato. She died after a long illness on February 2 in Prato, and was canonized in 1747. February 13.

CATHERINE OF SIENA (1347–80). Born on March 25 at Siena, Italy, daughter of a dyer and the youngest of twenty-five children, she began to have the mystical experiences she was to have all her life when she was only six. She resisted all efforts of her parents to have her marry and devoted herself to prayer and fasting. She became a Dominican tertiary when she was sixteen and increasingly experienced visions of Christ, Mary, and the saints, interspersed with diabolical visions and periods of spiritual aridity. She ministered to the ill in hospitals, devoting herself to caring for patients with particularly distressing illnesses like leprosy and advanced cancer cases. Her supernatural gifts attracted ardent supporters, but many believed she was a faker and caused her to be brought before a chapter general of the Dominicans in Florence, where the accusations were dismissed. At this time, Bl. Raymond of Capua was appointed her confessor, in time became her disciple, and later was her biographer. On her return to Siena, she devoted herself to caring for those stricken by a plague that

devastated the city, ministered to condemned prisoners, and was acclaimed for her holiness, aid to the spiritually troubled, and abilities as a peacemaker. She whole-heartedly supported Pope Gregory XI's call for a crusade against the Turks, and while on a visit to Pisa in 1375 (a visit that brought on a religious revival in that city) received the stigmata, invisible during her lifetime but clearly apparent at the time of her death. She was unsuccessful in attempting to mediate between Florence and Pope Gregory, but her meeting with the Pontiff in Avignon and her urging led him to return the papacy to Rome in 1376. At his request, she again returned to Florence, and this time she was successful in reconciling Florence and the Holy See. On her return to Siena, she devoted herself to recording her mystical experiences, which were published as the *Dialogue* of St. Catherine. On Gregory's death in 1378, the Great Schism began when Urban VI's election as Pope was contested by a group of dissident cardinals, who elected Robert of Geneva antipope Clement VII at Fondi and set up a papal court at Avignon. Catherine worked unceasingly to secure support for Urban and end the schism, though never hesitating to censure Urban for some of his actions. He welcomed her criticisms and brought her to Rome, where she continued her efforts to gain support for him. She suffered a paralytic stroke on April 21 and died in Rome a few days later, on April 29. Catherine was one of the greatest of Christian mystics. In addition to her *Dialogue*, some four hundred of her letters to people in every class of society are still extant. She was canonized in 1461, made patron of Italy in 1939, and was declared a Doctor of the Church by Pope Paul VI in 1970. April 29.

CATHERINE OF SWEDEN (c. 1331–81). Fourth of eight children of St. Bridget of Sweden, Catherine Ulfsdotter was born at Ulfasa, Sweden, and when about fourteen was married to Eggard von Kürnen but convinced him to join her in a vow of chastity. In 1350, she visited her mother in Rome and was persuaded by her to stay there with her. Catherine was widowed later the same year, as propheised by her mother, repeatedly refused marriage to persistent suitors, and spent the next twenty-five years as her mother's constant companion. When Bridget died, Catherine returned to Sweden to Vadstena, which Bridget had founded, with her body and devoted herself to organizing the Bridgettines her mother had founded. She spent five years, 1375–80, and finally secured a new papal approval of the congregation from Pope Urban VI. She was in failing health when she returned to Vadstena, and she died there on March 24. In 1484, Pope Innocent VIII gave permission to venerate her as a saint.

CATHERINE TOMÀS (1533–74). Born at Valdemuzza, Majorca, she was orphaned at seven and raised by her uncle. She was treated as a menial in his household, but through the intercession of her confessor was allowed to become a servant to a family in Palma when about fifteen. When she was twenty, she joined the Augustinians at Palma and soon displayed supernatural gifts—ecstasies, prophecies, visions, and even satanic assaults. She died as she prophesied at Palma, and was canonized in 1930. April 1.

CAUN, BL. VINCENT (d. 1626). Born at Seoul, Korea, he was captured by the Japanese and taken to Japan as a prisoner of war in 1591. He was converted to Christianity in Japan, joined the Jesuits at Arima seminary, and served as a catechist in China and Japan for thirty years. He was burned to death at Nagasaki for his faith, with Bl. Francis Pachecho and several other Christians, and was beatified in 1867. June 20.

CEADDA. *See* Chad.

CEALLACH. *See* Celsus of Armagh.

CECELIANUS. *See* Cecilius.

CECILIA (date unknown). Of a patrician family and also known as Cecily, she was born in Rome and raised a Christian. She was married against her will to Valerian (or Valerius) and convinced him to respect her virginity and become a Christian. She also converted his brother Tiburtius. Valerian (feast day, April 14) and Tiburtius devoted themselves to charitable works until apprehended burying the bodies of martyred Christians. They were arraigned before the prefect, Almachius, and when they refused to sacrifice to the gods, were scourged and beheaded at Pagus Triopius, near Rome, together with Maximus (April 14), who had been so impressed by their witness to Christ that he became a Christian. Cecilia buried the three and in turn was arrested. She debated with Almachius and when he was unable to shake her faith, he sentenced her to death. When her sentence of death by suffocation was miraculously prevented, a soldier was assigned to behead her. He bungled the job and she lay dying for three days before expiring on September 16. Though veneration of Cecilia has been for centuries one of the most popular cults in the Church, her story has been constructed from legends, many of which are untrustworthy, so that even the date of her death is uncertain and is estimated as having occurred anywhere from 177 to the fourth century (the Roman Martyrology says Tiburtius and the others suffered martyrdom under Emperor Alexander, who ruled 222–35). She is the patroness of music and musicians, since supposedly at her wedding she did not hear the nuptial music and sounds of merriment but sat apart, singing to God in her heart. November 22.

CECILIA, BL. (d. 1290). Of the noble Roman Caesarini family, she became a nun at San Sisto in Rome when seventeen and was perhaps the first Dominican nun when she convinced the abbess and nuns to accept Dominic's rule. In 1222, she became abbess of St. Agnes convent in Bologna. She had lengthy correspondence with Bl. Jordan, her spiritual adviser, and in her old age dictated her remembrances of Dominic. She was beatified in 1891. January 9.

CECILIUS (d. c. 248). A priest in Carthage, he converted St. Cyprian to Christianity and commended to him the care of his wife and children as he was dying. His name may also be Cecilianus. June 3.

CECILY. *See* Cecilia.

CEDD (d. 664). A native of Northumbria, England, and brother of St. Chad, with whom he was raised, he became a monk at Lindisfarne and in 653 was sent with three other priests to evangelize the Middle Angles when their King Peada became a Christian. Cedd left to preach in Essex when King Sigebert of the East Angles was converted, was consecrated bishop of the East Saxons by St. Finan at Lindisfarne in 654, and spent the rest of his life with the Saxons. He founded monasteries at Bradwell, Tilbury, and Lastingham, built several churches, attended the Synod of Whitby in 664, where he accepted the Roman observances, and died of the plague at Lastingham, Yorkshire, on October 26.

CELESTINE I (d. 432). Born in Campania, Italy, he became a deacon in Rome, and was elected Pope on September 20, 422. He was a stanch supporter of St. Germanus of Auxerre in the fight against Pelagianism, and a friend of St. Augustine, with whom he corre-

sponded. An unyielding foe of Nestorianism, he held a council in Rome in 430 that condemned the heresy and threatened Nestorius with excommunication if he did not desist from his heretical teaching and in 431 sent three legates to the General Council of Ephesus, which formally condemned Nestorianism. He wrote a treatise against semi-Pelagianism and sent Palladius to Ireland to evangelize the Irish; some scholars believe Cedd may have sent Patrick. Cedd died on July 27.

CELESTINE V (1210–96). Born at Isernia in the Abruzzi, Italy, the eleventh of twelve children of peasant parents, Peter di Morone became a hermit when twenty, left his cell to study for the priesthood, and was ordained in Rome. He became a Benedictine at Faizola in 1246 and was permitted to return to his eremitical life on Mount Morone near Sulmona, attracting great crowds. After five years he retired with two companions to Monte Majella in quest of greater solitude but was persuaded to return to Monte Morone, where he organized the hermits into a community and eventually a monastery, with a strict rule, and he was elected abbot. In 1274, he received approval of his order of monks, the Celestines. When the papacy, after the death of Pope Nicholas IV, remained vacant for two years because of political bickering, Peter reputedly threatened the cardinals with the wrath of God if they did not elect a new Pope at once, whereupon at Perugia, they elected the eighty-four-year-old Peter as Pope on July 5, 1294. Despite his grievous misgivings, he was installed as Pope Celestine V on August 29 and immediately became a prey of the scheming King Charles of Naples, who took advantage of his otherworldiness, inexperience, and naïveté. Heartbroken at what was taking place and overwhelmed by the burden of the office he had not sought and was incapable of filling, he abdicated on December 13, 1294, and returned to his monastery. Cardinal Gaetani was elected Pope Boniface VIII to succeed him, and fearful that the great popularity of his holy predecessor might lead some plotters to attempt to put him back on the papal throne and cause a further split in Christendom, Boniface imprisoned Celestine in the castle of Fumone, near Anagni, where he died ten months later, on May 19. He was canonized by Pope Clement V.

CELLACH (c. 9th century). According to tradition, he was abbot of Iona, founded the monastery of Kells, and was later named archbishop of Armagh. April 1.

CELSUS. *See* Nazarius.

CELSUS OF ARMAGH (1079–1129). A layman named Ceallach mac Aedha, he succeeded to the bishopric of Armagh (it was a hereditary see) in 1105 when he was twenty-six, was consecrated bishop, put into effect many reforms in his diocese, and ruled well and effectively. He mediated between warring Irish factions, was a friend of St. Malachy, and ended the hereditary succession to his see by naming Malachy as his successor on his deathbed. He died on April 1 at Ardpatrick, Munster. April 7.

CENNINI, BL. AUGUSTINE (d. 1420). *See* Nerucci, Bl. Laurence.

CEOLFRID (642–716). Probably born in Northumbria, England, he became a monk at Gilling monastery when eighteen and then at St. Wilfrid's monastery at Ripon, where he was ordained. He served as master of novices at Ripon and then was appointed prior of St. Peter's at Wearmouth by St. Benedict Biscop. His strictness with the monks caused such hostility that he returned to Ripon. He

accompanied Benedict to Rome in 678, and when Benedict founded St. Paul Monastery at Jarrow, six miles from Wearmouth, in 685, he made Ceolfrid deputy abbot. Shortly after, a plague wiped out all the monks at Jarrow except Ceolfrid and a young student. When Benedict died in 690, Ceolfrid was elected abbot, ruled with great ability the next quarter century, and developed the twin monasteries into great centers of learning, building up the libraries and becoming a noted biblical scholar. In 716, he resigned because of the infirmities of old age and set out for Rome, where he wanted to die, but died on the way at Langres, Champagne, on September 25. One of his pupils was Bede, the great English historian, who wrote of him in his *Historia Abbatum*.

CEOLWULF (d. c. 764). A king in Northumbria, England, he resigned in 738 after reigning eight years and became a monk at Lindisfarne. He was highly venerated and Bede dedicated his *Ecclesiastical History* to "the Most Glorious King Ceolwulf." January 15.

CÉRASE. *See* Ceratius.

CERATIUS (d. c. 455). That he was bishop of Grenoble, and also known as Cérase, in the middle of the fifth century, attended the Council of Orange in 441 and wrote, with two other bishops, to Pope St. Leo the Great in 450 are known. That he was driven from Grenoble by Burgundian Arians and founded the see of Auch in Aquitaine are from unreliable sources. His cult was confirmed in 1903. June 6.

CERBONIUS (d. c. 575). Driven from Africa by the Vandals, he immigrated with St. Regulus to Tuscany and succeeded Regulus as bishop of Populonia (Piombino). Ordered to be killed by wild beasts by King Totila of the

Ostrogoths, during his invasion of Tuscany, for hiding several Roman soldiers, Cerbonius was miraculously saved, but he spent the last thirty years of his life in exile on Elba. October 10.

CEREALIS (d. 120). *See* Getulius.

CERENICUS. *See* Serenicus.

CERIOLI, BL. PAULA (1816–65). Constance Cerioli was born at Soncino, near Bergamo, Italy, the last of sixteen children. She was married when she was nineteen to a wealthy sixty-year-old widower, Gaetano Buzecchi-Tassi, and when he died in 1854, she decided to devote herself to caring for orphans. She started by taking two orphans into her home at her estate, Cormonte, near Seriate, Lombardy, attracted other women to her work, and in 1857 made her religious vows, taking the name Paula Elizabeth, and the Sisters of the Holy Family of Bergamo was founded. In 1862, she founded a brothers' community to care for male orphans at Villa Campagna near Soncino. Both communities were dedicated to educating and preparing children for a rural life, and the boys were given training in agriculture. She died at Cormonte, and was beatified in 1950. December 24.

CERNEUF. *See* Serenus the Gardener.

CESLAUS, BL. (d. 1242). Of a noble Silesian family and possibly St. Hyacinth's brother, he was ordained, became a canon in Cracow, Poland, a provost at St. Mary's in Sandomir, went to Rome, and was received into the Dominicans by St. Dominic. Bl. Ceslaus preached in Poland, Silesia, Pomerania, and Bohemia, was spiritual adviser to St. Hedwig, was elected provincial of the Polish province, and became prior of a priory at Breslau. His prayers were credited for the defeat of Tartans attacking Breslau in Silesia during their invasion of 1240. His cult was confirmed in 1713. July 17.

CHABANEL, NOEL (1613–49). Born on February 2 near Mende, France, he joined the Jesuits in 1630 and in 1643 was sent as a missionary to the Huron Indians in New France. He became assistant to Fr. Charles Garnier at the Indian village of Etarita in 1649 and was murdered on December 8 by an apostate Indian while returning from a visit to neighboring Ste. Marie. He was canonized in 1930 by Pope Pius XI as one of the Martyrs of North America. September 26.

CHAD (d. 672). Born in Northumbria, England, and also known as Ceadda, he and his brother Cedd studied under St. Aidan at Lindisfarne, became monks there, and when Aidan died, Chad spent several years with St. Egbert at Rathmelsigi in Ireland. Chad went back to England as abbot of Lastingham abbey in Yorkshire which Cedd had founded, and the following year, Chad was appointed bishop of York by King Oswy. Meanwhile, Oswy's son King Alcfrid had appointed Wilfrid bishop of York, and when Theodore, the new archbishop of Canterbury, arrived in England in 669 and visited Northumbria, he accused Chad of an improper consecration. Impressed by Chad's humble acceptance of his verdict, Theodore regularized his consecration and had him appointed bishop of Mercia by Oswy. He established his see at Lichfield, founded Bardney abbey, and built a retreat house near the church at Lichfield. He died at Lichfield. March 2.

CHAERMON (d. 250). Bishop of Nilopolis, Egypt, he fled to the mountains of Arabia when an old man during Decius' persecution of the Christians and was never seen again. December 22.

CHAINOALDUS (d. c. 633). Also known as Cagnoald or Cagnou, and the brother of SS. Faro and Burgundofaro, Chainoaldus was so impressed by St. Columban while the saint was staying at his father's house near Meux, France, that Chainoaldus became a monk at Luxeuil. He accompanied Columban on his missionary travels and his exile at Bobbio, became bishop of Laon, and attended the Council of Rheims in 630. September 6.

CHAMPAGNAT, BL. MARCELLIN (1789–1840). Born at Le Rosey, Loire, France, on May 20, the son of a miller, he studied at Lyons seminary, was ordained in 1816, and was sent to La Valla as a curate. As he ministered to a dying sixteen-year-old boy who was ignorant of the faith, Marcellin committed himself to educating the young. He founded the teaching congregation of the Little Brothers of Mary (the Marist Brothers) in 1817, which received formal approval from Rome in 1836. He published *Guide des Écoles,* which became the basis for Marist teaching in 1853, and died at Notre Dame de l'Hermitage June 6. Today, 5,000 Marist brothers in more than seventy countries around the world carry out his work. He was beatified in 1955. He was canonized in 1999.

CHANEL, PETER MARY (1803–41). Born at Cluet, near Belley, France, he was a shepherd in his youth, studied under the parish priest at Cras, and was ordained in 1827. He served as parish priest at Crozet, joined the Marists in 1831, and was a professor at their seminary in Belley for the next five years. In 1836, he was sent as a missionary to the New Hebrides in the Pacific Ocean, worked with some success on the island of Futuna, and was murdered there on April 28 by order of the chief when he found that his son wanted to be baptized. Peter was canonized by Pope Pius XII in 1954—the first Marist martyr and the first martyr of Oceania. April 28.

CHANTAL, JANE FRANCES DE (1572–1641). Daughter of the president of the Burgundy parliament, Benigne Frémyot, she was born on January 28 in Dijon, France. She married Baron Christopher de Chantal when she was twenty, and the couple had seven children by the time he died in a hunting accident in 1601. She was deeply affected by St. Francis de Sales when she heard him preach in 1604, recognized him from a vision she had had, and convinced him to become her spiritual director. She desired to enter the Carmelites but he convinced her not to do so and in 1607 explained to her his concept of a new congregation he wished to found. After making provision for her children and putting her affairs in order, she, Mary Favre, Charlotte de Bréchard, and a servant, Anne Coste, were clothed by Francis in 1610 in a house on the shores of Lake Annecy, and the Congregation of the Visitation was founded for young girls and widows desirous of following a religious life but unable to follow the severe ascetic life that was customary in the religious houses of that time. Despite numerous difficulties, the order spread all over France, and in the following three decades more than sixty houses were founded. During the last years of her life, Jane experienced periods of spiritual aridity and more than once suffered the torments of the dark night of the soul. She died at Moulins on December 13 on her return from a trip to Paris to visit Queen Anne. Jane was buried at Annecy near St. Francis de Sales, and was canonized in 1767. It was for her and her nuns that St. Francis wrote his great spiritual classic *On the Love of God.* December 12.

CHAPDELAINE, BL. AUGUSTUS (1814–56). Born near Coutances, France, the ninth son of a peasant family, he worked on the family farm as a farmhand in his youth, but when the farm was divided, he left to study for the priesthood. He was ordained, engaged in parish work, and in 1851 joined the Society of Foreign Missions. Soon after he was sent to China, where he worked as a missionary in the apostolic vicariate of Kwang-si. He was arrested in 1854 but freed by an understanding mandarin. Bl. Augustus resumed his work, made numerous converts, but was denounced for his religion to a new mandarin, who subjected him to slow torture until he died when he was beheaded at Kwang-si on February 27. He was beatified in 1900.

CHARITY (2nd century). According to an Eastern allegory explaining the cult of Divine Wisdom, Faith, Hope, and Charity were the daughters of Wisdom (known as Sophia in the Roman Martyrology on September 30), a widow in Rome. The daughters suffered martyrdom during Hadrian's persecution of Christians: Faith, twelve, was scourged, and when unharmed when boiling pitch was poured on her, was beheaded; Hope, ten, and Charity, nine, were also beheaded after emerging, unscathed, from a furnace; and Wisdom died three days later while praying at their graves. August 1.

CHARLEMAGNE, BL. (742–814). The famous King of the Franks who was crowned first Holy Roman Emperor in 800 by Pope St. Leo III, Charlemagne has never been formally canonized, though popular devotion to him became widespread during the great quarrel between the Popes and Emperor Frederick Barbarossa in the twelfth century. The devotion was made compulsory in France in 1475 when a feast in his name was instituted in that country (Joan of Arc had earlier in the century associ-

ated him with St. Louis in her prayers). Pope Benedict XIV allowed the title of Blessed, but the reason for Charlemagne's "canonization" was probably political, due in large measure to his defense of the Church and the papacy. January 28.

CHARLES OF BLOIS, BL. (1320–64). Son of Count Guy de Chatillons of Blois and Margaret, sister of King Philip VI of France, he married Joan of Brittany in 1337 and was involved throughout his lifetime in a series of wars with John of Montfort over his claim to the dukedom of Brittany by virtue of his marriage to Joan. Throughout these wars, he showed compassion for the inhabitants of the cities he captured and for his enemies. De Montfort was backed by King Edward III of England, who in 1346 defeated the French forces at Crecy. Charles was defeated in a battle at La Roche-Derrien, captured, and held for ransom in the Tower of London for nine years. When released in 1355, he continued his struggle for another nine years, until he was killed at the Battle of Auray on September 29. He was intensely religious, founded religious houses, and was reported to have preferred to have been a Franciscan than a soldier. He was long venerated in France, and his cult was approved finally in 1904.

CHARLES BORROMEO. See Borromeo, Charles.

CHARLES THE GOOD (1081–1127). Raised at the court of his grandfather, Count Robert of Flanders, when his father, King St. Canute of Denmark, was slain in an insurrection in 1086, when he was five, he accompanied his uncle, Robert II, on the Second Crusade. Charles later fought with him against the English, was named heir of Baldwin, Robert's son, when Robert died, and became his aide and confidant. Charles became Count of Flanders on Baldwin's death despite the objection of several other claimants, and ruled wisely, with benevolence, justice, and charity. He fought the profiteering that developed during times of famine and scarcity and was murdered while praying in St. Damian church in Bruges by a group of profiteers of that city. His cult was confirmed in 1883. March 2.

CHARLES OF SEZZE. *See* Marchioni, John Charles.

CHASTAN, BL. JAMES HONORÉ. *See* Imbert, Bl. Laurence.

CHEF. *See* Theuderius.

CHELIDONIUS (d. 304). *See* Emeterius.

CHEVREUX, AUGUSTINE AMBROISE BL. (d. 1792). *See* Du Lau, Bl. John.

CHIARITO. *See* Claritus.

CHIEN, BL. FRANCIS (d. 1838). *See* Henares, Bl. Dominic.

CHINA, MARTYRS OF (17th–20th centuries). A large (120) and diverse (Chinese and European) group of Christians slain between 1889 and 1956 because of their faith. Sixty Chinese laypeople, including eight under twenty years of age, were slain because of their faith, along with five European bishops, a bishop-elect, four Chinese secular priests, twenty-five European priests, seven nuns, and eight Chinese catechists.

CHIN-TE, BL. PAULLIEU (1821–1900). *See* Mangin, Bl. Leon.

CHIONIA (d. 304). *See* Agape.

CHRISTIAN, BL. (d. 1186). That he was the abbot of the first Cistercian abbey in

Ireland is known for a fact. Legend says he was born at Bangor, Ulster, and named Giolla Chriost O'Conarchy, became a disciple of St. Malachy, whom he accompanied to Rome, received the habit from St. Bernard at Clairvaux, and when Malachy returned to Ireland in 1142, Christian was made abbot of Mellifont Monastery, which Malachy had just founded. Another legend has him bishop of Lismore and papal legate for Ireland. March 18.

CHRISTIANA. *See* Nino.

CHRISTIANA. *See* Oringa.

CHRISTINA OF AQUILA. *See* Christina Ciccarelli.

CHRISTINA THE ASTONISHING (1150–1224). Born at Brusthem, near Liège, Belgium, she was orphaned at three, had an epileptic fit when she was about twenty-one, and seemed to have died when suddenly she soared to the roof of the church where Mass was being said for her. When the priest ordered her to come down, she did so, and said she had been to hell, purgatory, and heaven and then was allowed to return to earth to pray for the suffering souls in purgatory. This is just one of the incredible events that supposedly took place during her lifetime. She could not tolerate the odor of human beings and resorted to such extraordinary means to escape human contact as climbing trees, soaring to the rafters of churches, and hiding in ovens. She lived a life of poverty and was thought to be insane by many but venerated by others. She spent the last years of her life in St. Catherine convent at Saint-Trond, where she died on July 24.

CHRISTINA OF BOLSENA (3rd century). Of the Roman Anicii family, she was converted to Christianity when a young girl, destroyed the gold and silver pagan images in her father's house, and was miraculously saved from drowning when he threw her into Lake Bolsena with a rock around her neck. After having her tongue cut out and surviving five days in a furnace, she was executed on the magistrate's orders by arrows. Though a young girl probably was martyred for her faith at Bolsena during Diocletian's persecution of the Christians, the incidents above are probably all legendary. She is often confused with Christina of Tyre, whose story is very similar. July 24.

CHRISTINA CICCARELLI, BL. (d. 1543). Born at Lucco, the Abruzzi, Italy, and named Matthia, she became an Augustinian hermitess at Aquila, taking the name Christina, and was noted for her holiness and humility and her gifts of prophesy, ecstasy, and miracles. She became prioress at Aquila, where she died on January 18. Her cult was confirmed in 1841.

CHRISTINA OF TYRE (date unknown). Her untrustworthy legends have her a young girl of Tyre who was imprisoned for her Christianity. She repudiated her mother for trying to argue her into sacrificing to the gods to save her life, was subjected to the most terrible tortures, from which she incredibly recovered, and was finally executed by being shot through the heart with an arrow. Some of the tortures: A fire lighted under he got out of control and burned hundreds to death; her breasts were cut off and milk flowed from them; when her tongue was cut out of her mouth she spoke even more clearly than before; when she picked up her tongue and threw it at the judge, he lost the sight of an eye; and when thrown into the sea she was baptized by Christ and returned to land by the Archangel Michael. It is doubtful if she ever ex-

isted, and the story is probably a pious fiction. July 24.

CHRISTOPHER (d. c. 251). According to tradition he died at Lycia, and many legends have grown up around his name. According to one he was an ugly giant who made his living carrying people across a river. He tried to find someone more powerful than himself and decided this could only be Christ, since the devil feared the Savior. One day one of his passengers was a small child who grew so heavy as they crossed the river he feared they would be drowned. The child then revealed that he was Christ, and the heaviness was caused by the weight of the world he was carrying on his shoulders. Christopher means Christ-bearer, and because of this legend he is the patron of travelers and in modern times particularly of motorists. July 25.

CHRISTOPHER, BL. (1172–1272). A parish priest in the diocese of Cesena, Italy, he left there when about forty, became a disciple of St. Francis, and joined the recently founded Franciscans. He devoted himself to caring for lepers, and later preached against the Albigensians in France and established a Franciscan house at Cahors. His cult was approved in 1905. October 25.

CHRISTOPHER OF MILAN (d. 1484). A Dominican priest in Milan, he was an outstanding preacher and was known as the apostle of Liguria for his great success in evangelizing the area. He became prior of a monastery built by the people of Taggia and was famed for his conversions and his gift of prophecy. He died at Taggia, and his cult was confirmed in 1875. March 1.

CHRODEGANG OF METZ (712–66). Born at Hesbaye, Brabant, near Liège, and a relative of Pepin, Chrodegang was probably educated at St. Trond abbey, and became Charles Martel's secretary and referendary. In 742, though a layman, he became bishop of Metz. He served as ambassador to Pope Stephen III for Pepin, mayor of the palace, and was very much involved in the coronation of Pepin as King of the Franks, the first Carolingian King, in 751, and Pepin's defense of the papacy and Rome against the Lombards and his restoration of the exarchate of Ravenna, which he had won from the Lombards, to the Holy See. Chrodegang put into effect many ecclesiastical reforms in his see, and in large measure, through a code of rules he wrote for his canons, he was responsible for the establishment and spreading of the canon regular movement. He was active in founding and restoring churches and monasteries, including the abbey of Gorze, Italy, introduced the Roman liturgy and Gregorian Chant in his see, and established a choir school at Metz, which became famous all over Europe. He died at Metz on March 6.

CHROMATIUS OF AQUILEIA (d. c. 407). A native of Aquileia, he became a priest, participated in 381 in the Synod of Aquileia, which denounced Arianism, and in 388 was elected bishop of Aquileia. He was a friend of St. Jerome, who dedicated several books to him, encouraged Rufinus, whom he had baptized, to translate Eusebius' *Ecclesiastical History,* and helped finance Jerome's translation of the Bible. Chromatius was unsuccessful in attempts to reconcile Jerome and Rufinus, was a supporter of Chrysostom, was widely regarded as an outstanding scholar and prelate, and wrote several scriptural commentaries. December 2.

CHRYSANTHUS (d. 283). Beyond the fact of his existence and martyrdom, all that is known of him is based on un-

trustworthy legend. An Egyptian, son of a patrician, Polemius, he was brought to Rome from Alexandria during the reign of Numerian, and despite the objections of his father, who had brought him to Rome, was baptized by a priest named Carpophorus. Chrysanthus refused his father's attempts to get him married, finally married Daria, a Greek and a priestess of Minerva, converted her, and convinced her to live with him in chastity. When they converted a number of Romans, Chrysanthus was denounced as a Christian to Claudius, the tribune. Chrysanthus' attitude under torture so impressed Claudius that he and his wife, Hilaria, two sons, and seventy of his soldiers became Christians, whereupon the Emperor had them all slain. Daria was sent to a brothel, where she was defended by a lion, brought before Numerian, who ordered her execution, and was stoned and then buried alive. When several followers of Chrysanthus and Daria were found praying at their crypt, among them Diodorus, a priest, and Marianus, a deacon, they were all entombed alive. October 25.

CHRYSOGONUS (d. c. 304). Venerated in Italy, all that is known of him is that he was martyred at Aquileia, Italy. In the apocryphal legend of St. Anastasia, where he is named as her confessor, he is a Roman official who was imprisoned and beheaded at Aquileia during Diocletian's persecution of the Christians. November 24.

CIARAN. *See* Kieran of Saighir.

CISELLUS (d. c. 303). *See* Luxorius.

CITTINUS (d. 180). *See* Speratus.

CLARE (1194–1253). Born at Assisi, Italy, on July 11, the daughter of the noble Faverone Offreduccio and

Ortolanadi Fiumi, she refused to marry when she was twelve and was so impressed by a Lenten sermon of St. Francis in 1212 that she ran away from her home in Assisi on Palm Sunday and received the habit from Francis at the Portiuncula. Since Francis did not yet have a convent for women, he placed her in the Benedictine convent of St. Paul near Bastia. She resisted the forcible efforts by her family to remove her and bring her home and was moved by Francis to Sant' Angelo di Panzo convent, where she was soon joined by her sister, Agnes, fifteen, who also received the habit from Francis. Her father sent twelve armed men to bring Agnes back, but Clare's prayers rendered her so heavy they were unable to budge her and she remained. In 1215, Clare moved to a house adjoining the church of St. Damiano, was made superior by Francis, and ruled the convent for forty years. The Poor Clares were thus founded, and Clare was soon after joined by her mother, another sister, Beatrice, three members of the famous Ubaldini family of Florence, and others. They adopted a rigid rule, practiced great mortifications and austerities, and took a vow of strict poverty—a vow that was to cause future difficulties. Clare obtained from Pope Innocent III a privilege guaranteeing their absolute poverty, and when Pope Gregory IX in 1228 tried to get the order to accept the ownership and income of land and buildings and offered to absolve Clare from her vow of absolute poverty, she was so convincing in a personal meeting with him that he granted the convents of San Damiano, Perugia, and Florence the *privilegium paupertatis*. Other houses did accept the mitigation, which was the beginning of the two observances among the Poor Clares; when a formal modification of the rule was granted by Pope Urban IV in 1263 to these houses, they became known as Urbanists. In 1247, Pope Innocent IV

again sanctioned the holding of property, and Clare's response was to draw up a rule based on that of Francis, enjoining absolute poverty; Innocent approved it two days before her death. The order flourished and spread to other parts of Italy and to France and Germany, and Clare's influence became such that she was consulted by Popes, cardinals, and bishops. She was credited with many miracles, and in 1241 her prayers were credited with saving Assisi from the besieging soldiers of Emperor Frederick II. She, next to St. Francis, was most responsible for the growth and spread of the Franciscans. She died at Assisi on August 11, and was canonized two years later, in 1255. She is the patroness of television. August 11.

CLARE OF MONTEFALCO (c. 1268–1308). Born at Montefalco, Italy, she became a member of a group of Franciscan tertiaries who founded Holy Cross convent there in 1290. She succeeded her sister Joan as abbess and is credited with performing miracles and experiencing ecstasies and receiving other supernatural gifts. After her death, her blood was reported to liquefy, and the image of a cross was found engraved on her heart when it was examined. She was canonized in 1881. August 17.

CLARE OF PISA, BL. (1362–1419). Daughter of Peter Gambacort, she was born at Pisa, Italy, and named Theodora, was betrothed when seven to Simon de Massa, and was married when twelve. She devoted herself to charitable works and ministering to the sick, and was widowed when fifteen. She resisted her family's efforts to have her married again, joined the Poor Clares, taking the name Clare, and was forcibly removed from the convent and imprisoned by her family for five months in an effort to force her to renounce her religious calling. Despite their every effort she persisted, and finally her father allowed her to enter the Dominican Holy Cross priory. He then built a convent for her and her associate, Mary Mancini, in 1382, which was enclosed and dedicated to a life of contemplation and prayer, and became the center of a reform movement for nuns. Clare became prioress and remained there until her death, known for her charity, austerities, and forgiveness (she forgave Giacomo Appiano, who was responsible for the murders of her father and three brothers during a civil war). Her cult was confirmed in 1830. April 18.

CLARE OF RIMINI, BL. (d. 1346). Of a wealthy family, Clare Agolanti was born at Rimini, Italy, was married when young, was exiled after her husband's death, and on her return saw her father and brother hanged by a rival political faction. She remarried, and after having a vision of Mary one day when she was thirty-four, she became a Franciscan tertiary, abandoned her luxurious style of living, and soon after built a convent for a group of women under her direction. She practiced mortifications and penances that were so extreme she was imprisoned for a time as insane. During the last days of her life she experienced ecstasies that left her blind and mute. She died at Rimini on February 10. Soon after her death, a cult developed at Rimini, which was authorized by Pope Pius VI in 1784. February 10.

CLARET, ANTHONY MARY (1807–70). Son of a weaver, he was born on December 23 in Sallent, Spain, and became a weaver himself. He entered the seminary at Vich in 1829 and was ordained in 1835. Ill health caused him to leave a Jesuit novitiate in Rome, and he returned to pastoral work at Sallent in 1837 and spent the next decade preaching missions and retreats in Catalonia. He went to the Canary Islands and after

fifteen months there (1848–49) with Bishop Codina, Anthony returned to Vich and founded the Missionary Sons of the Immaculate Heart of Mary (the Claretians), dedicated to preaching missions. He was appointed archbishop of Santiago, Cuba, in 1850, and incurred bitter enemies in his efforts to reform the see (he was wounded in an assassination attempt against his life at Holguín in 1856). He returned to Spain in 1857, became confessor of Queen Isabella II, and was deeply occupied with the missionary activities of his congregation. He resigned his see in 1858, was appointed Director of the Escorial, and actively encouraged literature, the arts, and the sciences. He followed Isabella to France when a revolution drove her from the throne in 1868, and after attending Vatican Council I (1869–70), he retired to Prades, France, but was forced to flee to a Cistercian monastery near Narbonne when the Spanish ambassador demanded his arrest. He died there on October 24. Anthony Claret was a leading figure in the revival of Catholicism in Spain, preached over 25,000 sermons, and published some 144 books and pamphlets during his lifetime. He was canonized in 1950.

CLARITUS, BL. (d. 1348). A native of Florence, Italy, Claritus Voglia was married to Nicolasia and by mutual agreement she became a nun at the Augustinian convent he founded in Florence in 1342 and he became a servant in the convent, which in time became known as Il Chiarito, as he was called. He died there of the plague that raged through the city in 1348. May 25.

CLARUS (d. c. 660). Born near Vienne, Dauphiné, France, he became a monk at St. Ferreol Abbey and later was spiritual director of St. Blandina Convent, where his mother and sister were nuns. In time he became abbot of St. Marcellus

Monastery at Vienne and lived there until his death on January 1. He is reputed to have performed numerous miracles, and his cult was confirmed in 1903 by Pope Pius X. He is the patron of tailors.

CLARUS (d. c. 875). A priest, probably born at Rochester, England, he went to Normandy, became a Benedictine monk, lived as a hermit, and settled at Naqueville, near Rouen. When he repulsed the advances of a noblewoman, she had him killed and beheaded near Saint-Clair-sur-Eph. November 4.

CLAUD OF BESANÇON (d. c. 699). Probably born in Franche-Comte of a senatorial family, he was destined for a military career but decided to become a priest. He was ordained and spent the next twelve years as a canon at Besançon. He then entered Condat abbey in the Jura Mountains and became abbot, restoring the monastery, and bringing the rule of St. Benedict to it. In 685, he was chosen bishop of Besançon, ruled until 692, and then returned to Condat, where he died. He may possibly have been a secular priest until he was elected bishop. June 6.

CLAUDIA (1st century). Mother of Linus, who became the second Pope, tradition has her the daughter of British King Caractacus, who was sent to Rome with his family in chains when he was defeated by Aulus Plautius. Released by Emperor Claudius, one of his daughters took the name Claudia, remained in Rome, was baptized, and is the Claudia mentioned in St. Paul's second letter to Timothy. Another tradition has her the daughter of Cogidubnus, a British ally of Claudius, who took the Emperor's name. Martial mentions a British lady, Claudia Rufina, and says she was married to his friend Aulus Pudens, a Roman senator. Another tradition has

this senator the Pudens also mentioned in St. Paul's second letter to Timothy. August 7.

CLAUDIAN (d. 284). *See* Victorinus.

CLAUDIUS (d. 273). *See* Lucillian.

CLAUDIUS (d. 283). A Roman tribune, he and his wife Hilaria and two sons, Jason and Marus, were so impressed by the constancy of St. Chrysanthus under torture that they were converted to Christianity together with seventy of his soldiers. He was flung into a river with a stone around his neck by order of Emperor Numerian. The others were all executed, and Hilaria was imprisoned and died in prison. December 3.

CLAUDIUS (d. c. 303). *See* Asterius.

CLAUDIUS (d. c. 306). *See* Castorius.

CLAVER, PETER (1580–1654). Born at Verdu, near Barcelona, Spain, he studied at the University of Barcelona and joined the Jesuits when he was twenty. He studied further at Montesione College at Palma, Majorca, was greatly influenced by St. Alphonsus Rodriguez, whom he met there, and decided he wanted to work in the New World. After further study at Barcelona, he was sent as a missionary to New Granada in 1610 and was ordained at Cartagena in present-day Colombia in 1615. Cartagena was an important center of the slave trade, and Peter joined Fr. Alfonse de Sandovel in trying to alleviate the horrible conditions of the slaves who poured into the city. He worked in the yards where the slaves were penned after being disembarked from the trip from West Africa, ministering to them with food and medicine, instructing them in the faith, and baptizing them, reportedly making some three hundred thousand converts in the forty years he labored among the slaves. He pleaded with the owners to improve their lot and visited plantations around Cartagena, usually lodging in the slaves' quarters to make sure the few laws for the protection of the slaves were enforced. He ministered to the lepers in St. Lazarus Hospital and to condemned prisoners and was always available as a confessor. He preached in the main plaza of the city, practiced great austerities, and became known as one blessed with supernatural gifts—prophecy, the power to perform miracles, and the ability to read men's minds. He was stricken with a plague that beset Cartagena in 1650 and never recovered from it. Despite his illness, he carried on his work on a much-reduced scale, lived in his cell pretty much neglected by all, and died there on September 8. He was canonized in 1888 and named patron of all missionary activities to Negroes by Pope Leo XIII in 1896. September 9.

CLEMENT I (d. c. 99). All that is known with certainty about Clement is that he was a Roman and suffered martyrdom away from Rome. According to tradition he was probably a freed man in the imperial household and was baptized by St. Peter. He succeeded Cletus as Pope in 91, was exiled to the Crimea by Emperor Trajan, and labored so zealously preaching the faith among the prisoners working in the mines there that he was condemned to death and thrown into the sea with an anchor around his neck. It is also agreed by scholars that he was the author of a letter to the Corinthians in which he rebuked them for a schism that had broken out in their church. The letter is of particular historical importance as one of the outstanding documents of the early Church and significant as an instance of the bishop of Rome intervening authoritatively as the preeminent authority in the affairs of another apostolic church to settle a dispute as early as the first century. November 23.

CLEMENT (d. c. 308). Completely unreliable sources say he was bishop of Ancrya, Galatia, at twenty, devoted himself to the education of the young and poverty-stricken, and with Agathangelus, his deacon whom he had converted, was tortured for years for their faith. They were reportedly miraculously saved from death repeatedly until they were finally executed by sword at Ancrya. January 23.

CLEMENT MARY HOFBAUER. *See* Hofbauer, Clement Mary.

CLEMENT OF OKHRIDA (d. 916). Probably of Slavic descent and from southern Macedonia, he became a bishop during the reign of Khan Simeon, the first Slav to become a bishop. Clement founded a monastery at Okhrida near Velitsa, Bulgaria, which became his primatial see and of which he is considered the founder and first bishop. He was so successful in his missionary work with the Bulgars that he is one of the Seven Apostles of Bulgaria. He died at Okhrida on July 17.

CLEMENT OF OSIMO, BL. (d. 1291). Probably born at Sant' Elpidio, Italy, he is generally regarded as the second founder of the Hermits of St. Augustine. He either composed or revised their constitution, was elected prior general in 1270 and in 1284, and was confessor to Cardinal Gaetani, who later became Pope Boniface VIII. Clement died at Orvieto, where he had resided, and is sometimes known as Clement of Sant' Elpidio, after his birthplace. His cult was approved in 1572. April 8.

CLEOPATRA (4th century). A Christian widow from Palestine, she recovered the body of St. Varus, martyred in Egypt, and shipped it to her native town of Adraha, where she built a shrine for it. When her son died at the dedication of the church, she reviled Varus, but he appeared to her in a dream and told her her son was in good hands and that she could not follow him for some time. She buried her son in the church with Varus, and the tombs became a place of pilgrimage. October 19.

CLEOPHAS (1st century). He was one of the two disciples to whom Jesus appeared on the road to Emmaus after he had risen (Luke 24:13–35). Some scholars believe he is the same as Clopas, the father of one of the women named Mary at the foot of the cross, and perhaps the same as Alphaeus, father of St. James the Less. September 25.

CLET, BL. FRANCIS REGIS (1748–1820). Born at Grenoble, France, the son of a merchant, he studied at the diocesan seminary and joined the Lazarists when twenty-one. He was ordained in 1773, taught theology at Annecy, was named novice master at St. Lazare in Paris in 1788, and went to China in place of another priest in 1791. He worked as a missionary under great difficulties for the next three decades in Hou-Kouang Province, beset with illness, persecutions, and often completely out of touch with his superiors and fellow priests. He managed to evade capture at first when a persecution of Christians began in 1818, but eventually was betrayed, tortured over an eight-month period, and then strangled to death at Wuchang Fu, near Hankow, capital of Hupeh Province, on February 17. He was beatified in 1900.

CLETUS (d. c. 91). All that is known about him is that he was a Roman elected Pope in 76 as the second successor of St. Peter and that he suffered mar-

tyrdom probably in Rome during the persecution of the Christians by Emperor Diocletian. He is also known by the Greek version of his name, Anacletus. April 26.

CLITHEROW, MARGARET (c. 1555–86). Daughter of Thomas Middleton, a wealthy candlemaker, she was born at York, England, married John Clitherow, a well-to-do butcher, in 1571, and was converted to Catholicism two or three years later. Her husband was fined repeatedly because Margaret did not attend Protestant services. She was once imprisoned for two years; on her release she set up a Catholic school for children and arranged to have Mass said in her home or in a house she rented. Her home became one of the most important hiding places for fugitive priests in England. In 1584, she was confined to her home for a year and a half, apparently for sending her eldest son to Douai in France to be educated. She was arrested in 1586, and when a search of her house revealed a secret hiding place with a missal and vessels used in saying Mass, she was accused and found guilty of hiding priests, a capital offense. She was executed at York by being pressed to death under an eight-hundred-pound weight on March 25, and was canonized in 1970 by Pope Paul VI as one of the Forty Martyrs of England and Wales.

CLODOALD (524–60). Grandson of King Clovis of the Franks and youngest son of Clodimir, son of Clovis, who had murdered his cousin St. Sigismund of Burgundy and in turn had been killed fighting Sigismund's brother, King Gondomar of Burgundy, he and his brothers were raised by his grandmother, St. Clotilda; his Uncle Childebert, acted as regent for them. His brothers, Theodoald, ten, and Gunther, seven, were murdered by their Uncle Clotaire of Soissons in a plot with Childebert to seize the throne, but Clodoald, eight, was saved by being sent to Provence. He became a hermit and a disciple of St. Severinus, made no attempt to claim the throne when he came of age, and later built a hermitage at Nogent near Paris, which in time became known as St. Cloud and where he died. He is also known as Cloud and Clou. September 7.

CLODULF (c. 605–c. 696). Son of St. Arnoul, bishop of Metz, and his wife, Doda, who became a nun when her husband was ordained, he too became a priest and in 657 was named bishop of Metz, which he ruled wisely for forty years. He is also known as Cloud and Clou. June 8.

CLOTILDA (c. 474–545). Daughter of King Chilperic of Burgundy, she was born at Lyons, France, and married Clovis, King of the Franks, in 492 or 493. She converted him to Christianity on Christmas Day in 496 after he had won a seemingly lost battle by appealing to "Clotilda's God." Clovis died in 511, and the rest of her life was spent mourning the fratricidal feuds of her three sons, Clodimir, Childebert, and Clotaire, over their inheritance. Anguished at the murder of two of Clodimir's children by Clotaire, she left Paris for Tours and spent the rest of her life helping the sick and the poor. June 3.

CLOU. See Clodoald; Clodulf.

CLOUD. See Clodoald; Clodulf.

CODRATUS OF CORINTH (d. c. 258). Of Greek Christian parents, he was orphaned when a child (tradition says his mother died in the wilds near Corinth while trying to escape Decius' persecution of the Christians), and grew up in the wilderness, where he was born. He studied medicine and then led a life of great asceticism with a group of disci-

ples. During Valerian's persecution, he was haled before Jason, prefect of Greece, with four followers, Dionysius, Anectus, Crescens, and Paul, and when Codratus refused to sacrifice to the gods, all were tortured, thrown to the wild beasts, and when unharmed, were beheaded. March 10.

COEMGEN. See Kevin.

COGITOSUS (8th–9th centuries). A monk of Kildare, Ireland, tradition ascribes to him the authorship of a life of St. Brigid, which is an invaluable source of information about her and her times. April 18.

COLEMAN, BL. EDWARD (d. 1678). Born in Suffolk, England, the son of an Anglican clergyman, he was educated at Cambridge and was converted to Catholicism. He became secretary to the Duchess of York and was arrested during the hysteria generated by the alleged "Popish plot" fabricated by the notorious Titus Oates. Accused of conspiring to overthrow King Charles II, Bl. Edward was convicted of conspiring with a foreign power (France) to restore the Catholic Church in England on the basis of a letter he had written to Fr. La Chaise, the French King's chaplain, seeking funds to finance Catholic activities in England. Bl. Edward was hanged, drawn, and quartered at Tyburn on December 3, the first victim of the Titus Oates plot. He was beatified in 1929.

COLETTE (1381–1447). Daughter of a carpenter named De Boilet at Corbie abbey in Picardy, France, she was born on January 13, christened Nicolette, and called Colette. Orphaned at seventeen, she distributed her inheritance to the poor, became a Franciscan tertiary, and lived at Corbie as a solitary. She soon became well known for her holiness and spiritual wisdom, but left her cell in 1406 in response to a dream directing her to reform the Poor Clares. She received the Poor Clares habit from Peter de Luna, whom the French recognized as Pope under the name of Benedict XIII, with orders to reform the Order and appointing her superior of all convents she reformed. Despite great opposition, she persisted in her efforts, founded seventeen convents with the reformed rule, and reformed several older convents. She was renowned for her sanctity, ecstasies, and visions of the Passion, and prophesied her own death in her convent at Ghent. A branch of the Poor Clares is still known as the Colettines. She was canonized in 1807. February 7.

COLM. See Columba.

COLMAN (d. c. 689). See Kilian.

COLMAN OF CLOYNE (530–606). Born in Munster, Ireland, son of Lenin, he became a poet and later royal bard at Cashel. He was baptized by St. Brendan when fifty with the name Colman. He was ordained, was reputed to be St. Columba's teacher, and became the first bishop of Cloyne, of which he is patron, in eastern Cork. November 24.

COLMAN OF DROMORE (6th century). Tradition has him born in Dalriada, Argullshire, Scotland, taught in his youth by St. Coelan at Nendrum or Mahee Island, and a disciple of St. Ailbhe of Emly. He built a monastery at Dromore, County Down, Ireland, about 514 and was first bishop of that see. His cult was approved in 1903. June 7.

COLMAN OF KILMACDUAGH (d. c. 632). Son of a chieftain, he was born in Ireland, was reportedly made a bishop against his wish, and lived as a solitary at Burren, County Clare. He built a monastery at Kilmacduagh on land donated by a relation of King Guaire of Connacht and is considered the first bishop of that see. October 29.

COLMAN OF LANN ELO (c. 555–611). Of a Meath family, he was born at Glenelly, Tyrone, Ireland, was deeply influenced by his uncle, St. Columba, and in about 590 built a monastery at Offaly called Lann Elo (Lynally). He also founded and became first abbot of Muckamore and later was bishop of Connor. He is probably the author of *Aibgitir in Chrabaid (Alphabet of Devotion)* and is also known as Colman Macusailni. He died at Lynally on September 26.

COLMAN OF LINDISFARNE (c. 605–76). Born in Connacht, Ireland, he became a monk at Iona under St. Columba and was appointed third bishop of Lindisfarne. At the Synod of Whitby in 663 or 664, he was the chief defender of the Celtic ecclesiastical practices against St. Wilfrid and St. Agilbert. When King Oswy ruled for Wilfrid and the Roman practices, Colman resigned his bishopric and with a group of Irish and English monks from Lindisfarne founded a monastery on the Isle of Inishbofin off the coast of Connacht, where they continued their practice of the Celtic rites. When dissension broke out between the Irish and the English monks, he founded another monastery at Mayo and was abbot of both monasteries. February 18.

COLMAN OF STOCKERAU (d. 1012). A Scot or Irish pilgrim on the way to the Holy Land, he was seized at Stockerau, near Vienna, as a spy and hanged on July 13. Reportedly his bearing under persecution, the state of preservation of his body after his death, and the miracles reported at his grave convinced many he was a holy man and a martyr. He is venerated as one of the patron saints of Austria. October 13.

COLOMBIÈRE, BL. CLAUD LA (1641–82). Born at Saint-Symphorien d'Ozen, near Lyons, France, he was educated at the Jesuit college at Lyons, joined the Jesuits in 1659, studied at Avignon and Paris, where he was tutor for Colbert's two sons, and was ordained. He soon acquired a reputation as an outstanding preacher, became superior of Paray-le-Monial College in 1675, was confessor of St. Margaret Alacoque, whose devotion to the Sacred Heart he shared, and was then sent to London as preacher to Mary Beatrice d'Este, Duchess of York. He was falsely accused of complicity in the Titus Oates plot to assassinate King Charles II, imprisoned for exercising his priestly functions and converting Protestants and fallen-away Catholics, and banished from England. He returned to France in 1679 seriously ill from his imprisonment and died on February 15 at Paray-le-Monial. He was beatified in 1929.

COLOMBINI, BL. JOHN (1304–67). Born at Siena, Italy, he became a successful businessman and married Biagia Cerretani. He changed his worldly lifestyle after reading a book of saints' lives, donated much of his wealth to the poor, and converted his home into a hospital. Sometime latter, after providing for his wife, he embraced a life of poverty and penance and devoted himself to ministering to the sick poor in hospitals. He was banished from Siena when he began to attract members of wealthy families as followers and then visited other Italian cities, where his disciples gained the name Gesuati (Jesuats) because of their devotion to the name of Jesus. After an investigation into charges that they were perpetuating the errors of the Fraticelli, Pope Urban V approved the Jesuats as a congregation with the name the Apostolic Clerics of St. Jerome, an institute of lay brothers dedicated to a life of great austerity and to

caring for the sick. Soon after, John was taken ill at Lake Bolsena and died on the way back to Siena. He was beatified by Pope Clement IX. July 31.

COLUMBA (c. 521–97). Also known as Colm, Colum, and Colmcille, he was probably born at Gartan, Donegal, Ireland, the son of Fedhlimidh (or Phelim) and Eithne, both of royal descent. He was baptized one of the names listed above and educated at Moville, where he became a deacon. He then studied at Leinster and continued his studies at Clonard, where he was probably ordained, and then went to Glasnevin under St. Mobhi. When plague caused Glasnevin to be disbanded in 543, he returned to Ulster and spent the next decade and a half preaching and founding monasteries all over Ireland, among them Derry, Durrow, and Kells. He became involved in a dispute with St. Finnian when he copied the first copy of St. Jerome's psalter (owned by Finnian) to reach Ireland, and Finnian claimed his copy; King Diarmaid ruled Columba's copy must go to Finnian. Columba again crossed swords with Diarmaid, this time literally, when Curnan of Connaught, a kinsman who had sought sanctuary with Columba, was murdered by Diarmaid's men. In the family feud that ensued between Diarmaid's men and Columba's clan, some three thousand men were killed at the Battle of Cuil Dremne. A synod at Telltown held Columba responsible and censured him. In remorse, Columba decided to leave Ireland and do penance for the deaths by converting a like number of pagans. In 563, with twelve relatives, he went to Iona off the coast of Scotland and built on that island a monastery that grew into the greatest monastery in Christendom. He devoted himself to evangelizing the Picts of Scotland, converted King Brude at Inverness, and in time evangelized all of Pictland. He attended the Synod of

Drumceat in Meath, Ireland, in 575, where he successfully fought to exempt women from military service, visited Ireland again in 585, and is believed responsible for the Battle of Cuil Feda near Clonard in 587. In the meanwhile, Iona had become famous all over Europe, and his holiness, austerity, and reputation for miracles attracted all manner of visitors to the monastery, where he died on June 9. Columba's influence on Western Christianity was enormous. Monks from Iona went all over Europe, and the monastic rule he developed was practiced widely on the Continent until the Rule of St. Benedict became almost universal. Columba's practices dominated the churches of Scotland, Ireland, and Northumbria though, in time, the Celtic practices he introduced came into conflict with the Roman practices, which eventually supplanted them. June 9.

COLUMBA OF CORDOVA (d. 853). Born at Cordova, Spain, her brother was an abbot, and her sister and her husband founded a double monastery at Tabanos; inspired by their example, she became a nun at Tabanos despite her mother's objections. The nuns were forced to leave Tabanos in 852 and went into hiding in Cordova to escape the Moorish persecution of Christians. However, Columba openly proclaimed her faith to the Moorish magistrate and was beheaded. September 17.

COLUMBA OF RIETA, BL. (1467–1501). Born at Rieta, Italy, daughter of weavers, Angiolella Guardagnoli was called Columba when reportedly a dove lighted on her head when she was being baptized Angiolella. She was educated by Dominican nuns, became a Dominican tertiary when nineteen, and attracted great attention by her ecstasies, visions, prophecies, and reported miracles. In response to a vision, she moved to dissension-plagued Perugia in 1490, founded a monastery there, and soon became its most famous resident. She healed the sick, acted as peacemaker, and was consulted by leaders and by the lowly. She incurred the enmity of Pope Alexander VI's daughter, Lucrezia Borgia, was accused of sorcery, and had her confessor removed, supposedly at Lucrezia's instigation. She overcame all such charges, and her influence remained undiminished until her death in Perugia on May 20. Her cult was confirmed in 1627.

COLUMBA OF SENS (d. 273). Tradition has her a Spaniard born of noble parents who left them when she was sixteen, went to Gaul, was secretly baptized at Vienne, and settled at Sens with a group of Spaniards. She and her companions were executed for their faith by being beheaded near Meux during the reign of Emperor Aurelian. December 31.

COLUMBAN (c. 540–615). Born in West Leinster, Ireland, sometime between 540 and 550, he decided, when a youth, to dedicate himself to God despite his mother's opposition. He lived for a time on Cluain Inis, an island in Lough Erne, with a monk named Sinell, and then became a monk at Bangor. With twelve other monks he was sent as a missionary to Gaul about 585. He built his first monastery at Annegray about 590, and it was so successful that he followed with two more, at Luxeuil and Fontes (Fontaines). Soon his followers spread all over Europe, building monasteries in France, Germany, Switzerland, and Italy. He aroused much opposition, especially from the Frankish bishops, by the Celtic usages he installed in his monasteries and for refusing to acknowledge bishops' jurisdiction over them. He defended his practices in letters to the Holy See and refused to attend a Gallican synod at Chalons in 603 when summoned to explain his Celtic usages. In 610 King

Theodoric II of Burgundy, angered by Columban's denunciation of his refusal to marriage and his practice of keeping concubines, ordered all Irish monks banished from his realm. Columban was shipwrecked on the way to Ireland but was offered refuge by King Theodebert II of Neustria at Metz and began to evangelize the Alemanni in the area around Bregenz on Lake Constance. Though successful, he was again banished in 612, when Burgundy warred against and conquered Neustria; Theodoric now ruled over the area in which Columban was working. Columban decided to flee his old adversary and crossed the Alps to Italy, where he was welcomed to Milan by Arian King Agilulf of the Lombards. Columban founded a monastery at Bobbio, between Milan and Genoa, which became one of the great monasteries of its time—a center of culture, learning, and spirituality. He died there on November 23. Columban wrote his Monastic Rule, sermons, poetry, and treatises against Arianism. November 23.

COLUMCILLE. See Columba.

COMGALL (c. 517–603). Born in Ulster, Ireland, he studied under St. Fintan at Cluain Eidnech Monastery, was ordained, and with several companions became a hermit in Lough Erne. The rule he imposed was so severe that seven of them died. He left the island and founded a monastery at Bangor, where he taught St. Columban. In time, it became the most famous monastery in Ireland, and Comgall is reported to have ruled over some eight thousand monks there and in houses founded from Bangor. He also accompanied St. Columba on a missionary trip to Inverness and founded a monastery at Land of Heth. Comgall died at Bangor after years of suffering brought on by his austerities. May 11.

COMGAN (8th century). Son of Prince Kelly of Leinster, Ireland, he succeeded his father, fled to Scotland with his sister and her children when defeated and wounded in battle with neighboring chieftains, and settled in Lochalse near Skye, where he built a monastery and where he died. October 13.

COMPIÈGNE, MARTYRS OF (d. 1794). At the outbreak of the French Revolution in 1789, a group of twenty-one Discalced Carmelite nuns were living in a monastery at Compiègne, France, that had been founded in 1641. In 1790 the revolutionary authorities ordered the monastery closed and the nuns dispersed. In 1794, sixteen of the twenty-one nuns were accused of violating the law by living as a religious community (they dressed in secular attire but continued their religious life). They were arrested on June 22 and imprisoned in the former Visitation convent in Compiègne. Though they had taken the oath of Liberté-Egalité in 1790, they now formally retracted their oaths and resumed the practice of their religious exercises. On July 12, they were sent to Paris and five days later, after a travesty of a trial, they were convicted of being counter-revolutionists living as religious under obedience to their superiors and conspiring against the people. They were all guillotined on July 17, and were beatified in 1906 as the Martyrs of Compiègne. The nuns who suffered martyrdom were: Marie Claude Brard (Sister Euphrasia of the Immaculate Conception); Madeleine Brideau (Sister St. Louis), the subprior; Marie Croissy (Sister Henrietta of Jesus), grandniece of Colbert; Marie Dufour (Sister St. Martha); Marie Hanisset (Sister Thérèse of the Heart of Mary); Marie Meunier (Sister Constance), a novice; Rose de Neufville (Sister Julie of Jesus); Annette Pebras (Sister Mary Henrietta of

Providence); Marie Anne Piedcourt (Sister Jesus Crucified); Madeleine Lidoine (Mother Thérèse of St. Augustine), the prioress; Angélique Roussel (Sister Marie of the Holy Spirit); Catherine Soiron and Thérèse Soiron, both extern sisters, natives of Compiègne and blood sisters; Anne Mary Thouret (Sister Charlotte of the Resurrection); Marie Trezelle (Sister Thérèse of St. Ignatius); and Elizabeth Vérolot (Sister St. Francis).

CONAN (7th century). That he actually lived is probably true; all else is uncertain. He was probably from Scotland or Ireland, may have taught St. Fiacre during Fiacre's childhood, went from Scotland to the Isle of Man, where he finished the evangelization of the people of that island begun by St. Patrick, and was probably consecrated a bishop. January 26.

CONCORDIA (d. c. 235). *See* Hippolytus.

CONCORDIUS (d. c. 178). A subdeacon, he was arraigned before Torquatus, governor of Umbria, during the reign of Emperor Marcus Aurelius, at Spoleto, Italy, and charged with being a Christian. When he refused to sacrifice to the gods, he was beheaded. January 1.

CONDEDUS (d. c. 685). Probably a Briton, he became a hermit at Fontaine Saint Valery, France, and then a Benedictine monk at Fontenelle. After a time there, he resumed his cremitical life on the island of Belcinae in the Seine near Caudebec, and when King Thierry III granted him the island for a hermitage, he built two chapels on it. He is also known as Condé or Condède. October 21.

CONGAR. *See* Cungar.

CONLAED. *See* Conleth.

CONLETH (d. c. 520). Also known as Conlaed, he was a hermit at Old Connell, Ireland, and an expert metal craftsman. A crozier he made for St. Finbar of Termon Barry is in the Royal Irish Academy and is famous for its beauty and craftsmanship. He was a close friend of St. Brigid and became spiritual director of her convent at Kildare. He later became bishop of Kildare, in which position he was probably ecclesiastical superior over the regionary bishops and abbots of that area. May 20.

CONRAD (d. 1066). Of the noble Pfullingen family of Swabia, he was appointed bishop of Trèves by his uncle, St. Anno, archbishop of Cologne. The selection of the bishop of Trèves had been traditionally a perogative of the Trèves chapter, and the appointment of Anno aroused such opposition that Conrad was seized on his way to Trèves and hurled to his death from one of the towers of Uerzig Castle. June 1.

CONRAD OF ASCOLI, BL. (1234–89). Conrad Miliani was of noble birth and born in Ascoli, Italy, and with his close friend Jerome Masci (later to be Pope Nicholas IV), he joined the Franciscans, received his doctorate at Perugia, and was ordained. While preaching in Rome, he felt called to missionary work and was sent to northern Africa, where he converted thousands. He accompanied his old friend Jerome to France when Jerome became papal legate, returned to Rome, and then was sent to Paris to lecture on theology. He was recalled to Rome to receive a cardinal's red hat but died on the way at Ascoli. He was gifted with ecstasies and prophetic powers (he predicted that Jerome would be Pope when both were boys) and is credited with numerous miracles. Conrad's cult was approved by Pope Pius VI. April 19.

CONRAD OF BAVARIA, BL. (c. 1105–54). The son of Duke Henry the Black of Bavaria, he studied at Cologne but left to join the Cistercians at Clairvaux under St. Bernard. Conrad went to Palestine, with Bernard's permission, to live as a hermit, but ill health and the unsettled conditions there caused him to return home. He died on the way back on March 15 near Bari or Molfetta, Italy. His cult was approved in 1832. February 14.

CONRAD OF CONSTANCE (d. 975). Of the famous Guelph family and son of Count Henry of Altdorf, he was educated at the cathedral school of Constance and was ordained. He was made provost of the cathedral and in 934 was elected bishop of Constance. He gave his share of his inheritance to the Church and to the poor and built and renovated many churches in his see. He accompanied Emperor Otto I to Italy in 962, though he concentrated on ecclesiastical matters and avoided secular affairs during the forty-two years he was bishop. He was canonized in 1123. November 26.

CONRAD OF OFFIDA, BL. (1237–1306). Born at Offida, Italy, he joined the Franciscans when fourteen, served at the friary at Forano and the convent at Alvernia as cook and questor, was ordained, and became known for his holiness, dedication to poverty, and as a preacher. He supported the Spirituals in the controversy that wracked the Franciscans and is mentioned in the *Fioretti* for his vision of our Lady, who laid the infant Jesus in his arms. He died at Bastia, near Assisi, while preaching. His cult was confirmed in 1817. December 14.

CONRAD OF PARZHAM. *See* Birndorfer, Conrad.

CONRAD OF PIACENZA (1290–1351). Of a noble Piacenza family, he married and took up residence at Piacenza. While hunting one day, a fire he made got out of control and burned a neighboring corn field. When he was obliged to sell all of his possessions to pay for the damages, he decided to devote himself to the religious life. He donated what was left of his wealth to the poor, his wife became a Poor Clare nun, and he became a hermit living a life of great austerity as a Franciscan tertiary. He moved to Noto in Sicily to avoid the crowds attracted by his holiness and lived the next thirty years in St. Martin's hospital and in a hermitage founded by a fellow nobleman. The last years of Conrad's life were spent at the grotto of Pizzone outside Noto, where he died and was buried. Numerous miracles were reported at his tomb, and his cult was approved by Pope Paul III. February 19.

CONRAD OF SELDENBÜREN, BL. (d. 1126). Of the noble Seldenbüren family, he built a monastery for men and a convent for women at Engelberg and became a lay brother in the monastery. He was murdered at Zürich by a group claiming the property he had deeded to the monastery. May 2.

CONRAD OF ZÄHRINGEN, BL. (d. 1227). Born at Seyne, France, of a noble family, he was a canon of St. Lambert's in Liège, joined the Cistercians at Villiers in Brabany, and served as abbot of Villiers, Clairvaux, and Citeaux, 1209–17. He became cardinal-bishop of Porto and Santa Rufina in 1219 and was papal legate in Languedoc, 1224–26. He died at Bari, Italy. September 30.

CONRAN (6th century). Long listed as a saint and a bishop in the Orkney Islands, there is no proof of his existence, and scholars now believe him to be a Colum or Colm whose name was transcribed through a scribal error as Conran. February 14.

CONSTANTINE (6th century). King of Cornwall, unreliable tradition has him married to the daughter of the King of Brittany who on her death ceded his throne to his son and became a monk at St. Mochuda Monastery at Rahan, Ireland. He performed menial tasks at the monastery, then studied for the priesthood and was ordained. He went as a missionary to Scotland under St. Columba and then St. Kentigern, preached in Galloway, and became abbot of a monastery at Govan. In old age, on his way to Kintyre, he was attacked by pirates who cut off his right arm, and he bled to death. He is regarded as Scotland's first martyr. March 11.

CONSTANTINE (d. 1321). *See* Theodore (d. 1299).

CONSTANTIUS OF BERNOCCHI, BL. (d. 1481). Born at Fabriano, Italy, he joined the Dominicans at Santa Lucia Convent there when he was fifteen and in time became prior of San Marco in Florence, which he reformed. He became noted for his preaching, had the gift of prophecy, was credited with the ability to perform miracles, and often acted as peacemaker between warring factions. He rebuilt the friary at Ascoli when he took up residence there, and lived there until his death on February 24. His cult was confirmed by Pope Pius VIII in 1811. February 25.

CONTARDO (d. 1249). Of the Este family of Ferrara, Italy, and surnamed "the Pilgrim," he set out on a pilgrimage to Compostela with two companions, was taken ill at Broni, and died in a shack

there. Miracles were later reported at his grave. April 16.

CONVOYON (d. 868). Born in Brittany, he became a deacon at Vannes, then was a hermit, and in 831 founded St. Savior Abbey at Redon and was its abbot. He was a member of a delegation to Rome in 848 to defend several bishops of Brittany charged with simony. He was driven from his abbey by Norsemen and died in exile. January 5.

COOK, BL. HUGH. *See* Faringdon, Bl. Hugh.

CORBINGTON, BL. RALPH (1598–1644). Born on March 25 in Maynooth, Ireland, of a Durham, England family living there in exile, he was brought back to England by his parents when he was five. The entire family eventually became religious. Ralph studied at St. Omer, Seville, and Valladolid, and in 1631 joined the Jesuits at Watten, Flanders. He was sent on the English mission in 1632 and ministered to the Catholics of Durham the next twelve years, using the alias Corby. He was arrested near Newcastle while saying Mass and was sent to London with Bl. John Duckett. Ralph declined an offer to be freed in place of Duckett, but when he refused, both were convicted of being Catholic priests and hanged, drawn, and quartered at Tyburn on September 7. They were beatified in 1929.

CORBINIAN (670–725). Born at Châtres, France, and baptized Waldegiso (his mother changed it to Corbinian), he lived as a solitary at Châtres for fourteen years, attracted disciples whom he organized into a religious community, and then went to Rome. Pope Gregory II sent him to evangelize Germany (he may have been a bishop by then), and he settled at Fresing, Upper Bavaria. When he denounced his patron Duke Grimoald for the marriage of the Duke to his brother's widow, Biltrudis, Corbinian incurred her bitter enmity. When he learned she had plans to have him killed, he fled to Meran, where he remained until Grimoald was killed in battle. He spent the rest of his life in missionary work in Bavaria and founded a monastery at Obermais. His emblem of a bear is attributed to a legend that he made a bear who killed his pack horse take over the work of the horse. September 8.

CORBY, BL. RALPH. *See* Corbington, Bl. Ralph.

CORDERO-MUNOZ, BL. MIGUEL FEBRES (1854–1910). Born at Cuenca, Ecuador, of a distinguished family, and christened Francis, he studied as a child at a Christian Brothers school, joined the Christian Brothers, and became a brother, taking the name Miguel, in 1868. For the next thirty-two years he taught at El Cebollar School in Quito and wrote several textbooks adopted by the Ecuadorean government for use in the schools of that country. In 1907, he was transferred to the Christian Brothers' mother house in Belgium, was assigned to their school in Permia de Mar, near Barcelona, Spain, and died there. He was beatified by Pope Paul VI in 1977 and was praised by the Pontiff for treating the profession of teaching as a true religious vocation.

CORENTIN (6th century). Also known as Cury, legend has him a hermit at Cornouaille (Quimper), Brittany, who was chosen bishop by the people there and was consecrated its first bishop by St. Martin. Corentin is reputed to have performed numerous miracles. Also known in western England, he is the eponymous patron of Cury in Cornwall, England. December 12.

CORMAC (d. 908). King of Munster, Ireland, he was probably the first bishop of Cashel and the compiler of the still-extant Psalter of Cashel. He was killed in battle. September 14.

CORNAY, BL. JOHN CHARLES (1809–37). Born at Loudon, France, he joined the Paris Society of Foreign Missions, was ordained in 1834, and was sent to Indochina, where he worked as a missionary in Ban-no, Annam. He was denounced as a Christian by a bandit and his wife, who had been refused refuge by the Christian villagers, as the organizer of an armed revolt and was arrested. He was imprisoned in a small cage for three months and then was beheaded on September 20. He was beatified in 1900.

CORNELIUS (1st century). A centurion of the Italica cohort stationed at Caesarea, Palestine, he had a vision telling him to send for Peter, who came to his home and baptized him and his household (Acts 10). According to tradition, he became the first bishop of Caesarea. February 2.

CORNELIUS (d. 253). A Roman priest, he was elected Pope to succeed Fabian in an election delayed fourteen months by Decius' persecution of the Christians. The main issue of his pontificate was the treatment to be accorded Christians who had apostasized during the persecution. He condemned those confessors who were lax in not demanding penance of these Christians and supported St. Cyprian, bishop of Carthage, against Novatus and his dupe, Felicissimus, whom he had set up as an antibishop to Cyprian, when Novatus came to Rome. On the other hand, he also denounced the Rigorists, headed by Novatian, a Roman priest, who declared that the Church could not pardon the *lapsi* (the lapsed Christians), and declared himself

Pope—the first antipope. The two extremes eventually joined forces, and the Novatian movement had quite a vogue in the East. Meanwhile, Cornelius proclaimed that the Church had the authority and the power to forgive repentant *lapsi* and could readmit them to the sacraments and the Church after they had performed proper penances. A synod of Western bishops in Rome in October 251 upheld Cornelius, condemned the teachings of Novatian, and excommunicated him and his followers. When persecution of the Christians started up again in 253 under Emperor Gallus, Cornelius was exiled to Centum Cellae (Civita Vecchia), where he died a martyr, probably of hardships he was forced to endure. September 16.

CORNELIUS, BL. JOHN (1557–94). Born of Irish parents at Bodmin, England, he studied for a time at Oxford but then went to the English college at Rheims and Rome, where he was ordained in 1583. He was sent on the English mission in 1584, using the alias Mohun, labored among the English Catholics for a decade, joined the Jesuits, and then was arrested at Lady Arundell's Chidcock Castle in Dorset. With him were arrested Thomas Bosgrave, nephew of Sir John Arundell, and two of the servants in the castle, John Carey and Patrick Salmon. Cornelius was taken to London, racked, without avail, to get him to reveal the names of those who had aided him, and was then returned to Dorset. He was found guilty of high treason for being a Catholic priest, and the other three for aiding and abetting a priest. When they refused to apostatize, they were executed. All four were beatified in 1929. July 4.

CORNELIUS MAC CONCHAIL-LEADH (c. 1120–76). Born in Ireland, he joined the Augustinian canons regular at Armagh in 1140, was elected abbot in 1151, and was named archbishop of Armagh in 1174. He went on pilgrimage to Rome in 1176 and died at Cambéry, Savoy, on the way back to Ireland. June 4.

CORNELIUS OF WYK (d. 1572). *See* Pieck, Nicholas.

CORSINI, ANDREW (1302–73). Born in Florence, Italy, on November 30, he spent his youth in riotous living, was converted by his mother, decided to pursue a religious life, joined the Carmelites, and was ordained in 1328. After pastoral work in Florence, he went to Paris and then Avignon for further study, and in 1332 became prior at Florence. He was named bishop of Fiesole in 1349 over his vigorous objections, became known for his gifts of prophecy and miracles, his devotion to the sick and destitute, his austerities, and his abilities as a peacemaker. Pope Urban V sent him to Bologna to settle disputes between the nobles and the populace, a mission he performed successfully. He died on January 6 at Fiesole, and was canonized by Pope Urban VII in 1629. February 4.

CORSINI, BL. THOMAS (d. 1345). Born at Orvieto, Italy, he joined the Servites as a lay brother there in response to a vision of Mary. He led a life of great holiness and humility as a humble beggar for his order and was reputed to have performed many miracles. He was beatified in 1768. June 23.

COSI, BL. OSANNA (1493–1565). Born at Montenegro in southwestern Yugoslavia of Orthodox parents and baptized Catherine, she tended flocks in her youth, became a servant of a Catholic family in Cattaro, and then became a Dominican tertiary, taking the name Osanna. She lived as a hermitess in a cell next to a church and was greatly sought after for her spiritual counseling. She died on April 27, venerated for her holiness and supernatural gifts. Her cult was confirmed in 1928.

COSIMO DI CARBOGNANO, BL. *See* Keumurgian, Bl. Gomidas.

COSMAS (d. 303). According to legend, Cosmas and Damian were twin brothers born in Arabia. They studied medicine in Syria and then lived at Aegeae, Cilicia, and became widely known for their great medical skills, which they offered without charge to all. As outstanding Christians, they were arrested during a persecution of Christians, tried before Lysias, governor of Cilicia, tortured, and then beheaded for their faith. Their three brothers, Anthimus, Euprepius, and Leontius, also died with them. Many miracles were reported after their deaths, and they are the patrons of physicians after Luke. September 26.

COSTANZA, BL. CAMILLO (1572–1622). Born in Calabria, Italy, he joined the Jesuits, was sent to Japan in 1602, and worked there until 1611, when he was exiled for his missionary activities. He went to Macao, wrote several articles in Japanese defending Christianity against pagan attacks, and in 1621 slipped back into Japan disguised as a soldier. He was captured the next year and burned to death at Firando on September 15. He was beatified in 1867. October 12.

COTTAM, BL. THOMAS (1549–82). Born at Dilworth, Lancashire, England, he was raised a Protestant, graduated from Oxford, and became a Catholic. He went to Douai and Rome, studied for the priesthood, joined the Jesuits in Rome, and was ordained at Rheims. He was sent on the English mission in 1580, was arrested on his landing at Dover, and

imprisoned in the Tower of London. He was subjected to extreme torture and then ordered executed for conspiracy against the Queen but in reality for his Catholic priesthood. He was forced to watch the execution of three fellow priests by hanging, drawing, and quartering and was then subjected to the same form of execution. He was beatified in 1886. May 30.

COTTOLENGO, JOSEPH (1786–1842). Born at Bra, near Turin, Italy, he was ordained and engaged in pastoral work. When a woman he attended died from lack of medical facilities for the poor in Turin, he opened a small home for the sick poor. When it began to expand, he organized the volunteers who had been manning it into the Brothers of St. Vincent and the Daughters of St. Vincent (Vincentian Sisters). When cholera broke out in 1831, the hospital was closed, but he moved it just outside the city at Valdocco and continued ministering to the stricken. The hospital grew and he expanded his activities to helping the aged, the deaf, blind, crippled, insane, and wayward girls until his Piccola Casa became a great medical institution. To minister to these unfortunates, he founded the Daughters of Compassion, the Daughters of the Good Shepherd, the Hermits of the Holy Rosary, and the Priests of the Holy Trinity. Weakened by typhoid he had contracted, he died at Chieri, Italy, and was canonized in 1934. April 30.

COTTUS (d. c. 272). *See* Priscus.

COUDERC, TERESA (1805–85). Born on February 1 at Masle, Sablières, France, and christened Mary Victoria, she joined a community devoted to teaching founded by Fr. J. E. P. Terme in his parish at Aps. When he was sent as a missionary to the Vivrais in southeastern France in 1824, he summoned

Teresa and two other sisters to run a hostel for women at the shrine of St. Francis Regis at La Louvesc in 1827 and appointed Teresa superior of the group, the Daughters of St. Regis, in 1829. They also began giving retreats for laywomen. When Fr. Terme died in 1834, the Jesuits took over the shrine and selected twelve Daughters of St. Regis headed by Mother Teresa to concentrate on giving retreats, and the Congregation of Our Lady of the Retreat in the Cenacle was founded. Mother Teresa resigned as superior in 1838 when financial difficulties beset the congregation, was sent to found a new house at Lyons, and spent the rest of her life as a simple sister of the community except for a short period when she was temporary superioress of the Paris convent. She died at Fourvière on September 26, and was canonized by Pope Paul VI in 1970.

COUSIN, GERMAINE (c. 1579–1601). Born at Pibrac, France, daughter of a farmer, she was raised by her father and a stepmother when her mother died when she was an infant. In poor health all her life and afflicted with scrofula and a paralyzed right hand, she was ill treated by her stepmother. A shepherd when she grew older, she attracted the attention of her neighbors by her piety and supernatural experiences and the miracles they reported. She died at Pibrac, and was canonized in 1867. June 15.

COZACHI, MICHAEL. See Kosaki, Michael.

CRATZ, BL. JOHN GASPARD (d. 1737). See Alvarez, Bl. Bartholomew.

CREMENTIUS (d. 304). See Optatus.

CRESCENTIA (d. c. 300). See Vitus.

CRESCENTIA OF HÖSS, BL. (1682–1744). Born at Kaufbeuren, Bavaria, and baptized Anna, she took up her parents' trade of weaving but when twenty-one became a Franciscan nun. At first she was subjected to much abuse from the older nuns because of her poverty, but eventually her holiness and humility overcame all and she was appointed master of novices and in time superior of the convent. She experienced visions and ecstasies, especially of the Passion, and diabolical torments, and was widely consulted for her spiritual wisdom. She was beatified in 1900. April 5.

CRESCENTIUS (d. c. 90). See Romulus.

CRESCITELLI, BL. ALBERIC (1863–1900). Born near Naples, Italy, he joined the Milan Foreign Missionary Society and was sent to China as a missionary in 1888. He worked along the Han River, establishing schools and missions, was seized by a group of Chinese during the Boxer Rebellion, tortured, and then hacked to death on July 21. He was beatified in 1951. July 24.

CRISIN, BL. MARK. See Körösy, Bl. Mark.

CRISPIN (c. 287). Unreliable legend has Crispin and Crispinian noble Roman brothers who with St. Quintinus went to Gaul to preach the gospel and settled at Soissons. They were most successful in convert work during the day and worked as shoemakers at night. By order of Emperor Maximian, who was visiting in Gaul, they were haled before Rictiovarus (whose position is unknown and even his existence is doubted by scholars), a hater of Christians, who subjected them to torture; when unsuccessful in trying to kill them, he committed suicide, whereupon Maximian had the two brothers beheaded. They are the patrons of shoemakers, cobblers, and leatherworkers. October 25.

CRISPIN OF VITERBO, BL. (1668–1750). Born at Viterbo, Italy, on November 13, Peter Fioretti had an early veneration for Mary. He studied at the Jesuit college, became an apprentice shoemaker, and in time a shoemaker. When twenty-five, he became a Capuchin brother at Viterbo and took the name Crispin. He was assigned menial tasks—gardener at Viterbo, cook at Tolfa—and reportedly effected many miraculous cures during epidemics at Tolfa and Bracciano. He was questor at Orvieto, where he became beloved of the populace, venerated for his miracles, prophecies, and wisdom. He died in Rome on May 19, and was beatified in 1806. May 21.

CRISPINA (d. 304). A native of Thagara, Africa, and wealthy, she was married and the mother of several children when she was arrested for her Christianity during Diocletian's persecution. Tried before Proconsul Anulinus at Thebeste, she was ordered to sacrifice to the gods; when she refused, she was beheaded, probably with several other martyrs, on December 5. She is frequently mentioned by St. Augustine, who preached a panegyric in her honor.

CRISPINIAN (c. 287). *See* Crispin.

CRISPUS (1st century). *See* Gaius.

CROCKETT, BL. RALPH (d. 1588). Born at Barton-on-the-Hill, Cheshire, England, he studied at Cambridge and Oxford and became a teacher in Norfolk and Suffolk. He went to Rheims to study for the priesthood, was ordained there in 1586, and was sent on the English mission. He was arrested with Bl. Edward James, was imprisoned for two and a half years in London, and then was tried in Chichester, where he was hanged, drawn, and quartered for his priesthood. He was beatified in 1929. October 1.

CROESE, FRANCIS MARY (1804–66). Born at Camporosso, Liguria, Italy, on December 12, the son of a farmer, he was christened John and worked on his father's farm when he was old enough to do so. He joined the Conventuals when about eighteen, taking the name Antony, but left after two years to seek a more austere life and joined the Capuchins. He was clothed as a lay brother in 1825 with the name Francis Mary, became questor of the Capuchin house in Genoa, and was soon known all over the city for his miracles of healing and knowledge of persons and events far from Italy. He died on September 17 of the cholera that swept Genoa in 1866, and was canonized by Pope John XXIII in 1962. September 20.

CROISSY, BL. FRANCES DE (1745–95). Born in Paris, she became a Carmelite nun at Compiègne in 1764 and served as prioress for eight years from 1779. She was mistress of novices when the convent was attacked by revolutionaries, and was taken to Paris; they were all then guillotined. She was beatified in 1906. July 17.

CRONAN OF ROSCREA (d. c. 626). Tradition has him the son of Odran, born at Ely O'Carroll, Offaly, Ireland, who became a monk and built some fifty monastic settlements, the first at Puay and the most famous at Roscrea, most of which he gave to anchorites. He became a hermit at Seanross and was blind the last four years of his life. April 28.

CRONION (d. 250). *See* Julian.

CRONION EUNUS (d. 250). *See* Julian.

CTESIPHON (1st century). *See* Torquatus.

CUBY. *See* Cybi.

CUCUPHAS (d. 304). Born of noble parents at Scillis, Africa, he went to Spain, where he suffered martyrdom near Barcelona. He was memorialized by Prudentius, the famous Christian Latin poet. July 25.

CUENOT, BL. STEPHEN THEODORE (1802–61). Born at Beaulieu, France, he joined the Society of Foreign Missions, studied at the Society's seminary in Paris, was ordained, and was sent to Annam in Indochina in 1829. He was ordered to Siam when a persecution of Christians broke out in Annam in 1833, was named vicar apostolic of East Cochin China in 1835, and was consecrated bishop in Singapore. He managed to get back into Annam and labored there the next twenty-five years. Though forced to work underground in the face of the continued persecution of Christians, he established three vicariates in Cochin China, strengthened the Christian communities, and built up a native clergy. He was finally captured during a particularly violent outbreak of persecution of Catholics in the province of Binh-Dinn, imprisoned in a small cage, and died in prison, probably of poison, on November 14, four days before he was scheduled to be beheaded. He was beatified in 1909.

CUMIAN (c. 590–c. 665). Son of King Fiachna of West Munster, Ireland, he became a monk in charge of the school at Clonfert and was later abbot of Kilcummin Monastery, which he had founded. He was noted for his learning and ably defended the Roman liturgical practices against the abbot of Iona, who was a stalwart defender of the Celtic practices. Cumian's defense is still extant, the *Paschal Epistle,* and he also wrote a hymn, some of which is still extant. He is often surnamed Fota or Fada, "the tall." November 12.

CUNEGUND (d. 1033). Daughter of Siegfried of Luxembourg and Hedwig, she married Duke Henry of Bavaria, who succeeded Emperor Otto III as King of the Germans as Henry II in 1002 and was crowned Emperor at Rome in 1014. She was responsible for the founding of the monastery and cathedral at Bamberg by Henry, founded a Benedictine convent at Kaufungen, Hesse, and became a nun there after Henry's death in 1024. She died there on March 3 (possibly in 1039), and was canonized in 1200. An unverified legend states that early in her married life the slander of some of those at the court caused Henry to question Cunegund's constancy; she dispelled all the innuendos by taking the ordeal by fire and emerging unscathed. March 3.

CUNEGUND, BL. (1224–92). Daughter of King Bela IV of Hungary, and also known by her Magyar name, Kinga, she was raised at her father's court and when sixteen was married to King Boleslaus V of Poland. She and Boleslaus took a vow of perpetual chastity. She built several churches and hospitals, helped ransom Christians from the Turks, and was active in helping the poor and the sick. When Boleslaus died in 1279, she became a Poor Clare nun at a convent she had founded at Sandek. Except for a brief period in 1287, when Tartars invaded Poland (her prayers were credited with their abandoning the siege of the castle of Pyenin, where the nuns had taken refuge), she spent the rest of her life there and died there on July 24, noted for her miracles and supernatural gifts. Her cult was approved in 1690. July 23.

CUNGAR (6th century). According to conflicting legends, he was a native of Devon, England, who became a monk and founded a monastery near Yatton, Somerset. He fled to South Wales to escape the Saxons, founded a church near Cardiff, and may have accompanied St. Cybi, when an old man, to Ireland, and later to Anglesey, where Cungar founded a church at Llangefni. One tradition has him dying at Saint-Congard, Morbihan, and he may be the same as St. Docco, who built churches and a monastery in Wales and Cornwall. Also known as Congar and Cyngar, there may have been several different persons known by all these names. November 27.

CUNHA, BL. VINCENT DA (d. 1737). *See* Alvarez, Bl. Bartholomew.

CUNIBERT (d. c. 663). Raised at the court of Clotaire II, Cunibert was ordained and became archdeacon of the church at Trier. He was named bishop of Cologne about 625 and became a most influential figure as royal counselor and one of the two guardians appointed by Dagobert I for his four-year-old son Sigebert when he named him King of Austrasia. Cunibert attended several synods, encouraged the evangelization of the Frisians, and left the court in later years to devote himself to ecclesiastical matters. November 12.

CURY. *See* Corentin.

CUTHBERT (d. 687). Thought by some to be Irish and by others a Scot, Bede, the noted historian, says he was a Briton. Orphaned when a young child, he was a shepherd for a time, possibly fought against the Mercians, and became a monk at Melrose Abbey. In 661, he accompanied St. Eata to Ripon Abbey, which the abbot of Melrose had built, but returned to Melrose the following year when King Alcfrid turned the abbey over to St. Wilfrid, and then became prior of Melrose. Cuthbert engaged in missionary work and when St. Colman refused to accept the decision of the Council of Whitby in favor of the Roman liturgical practices and immigrated with most of the monks of Lindisfarne to Ireland, St. Eata was appointed bishop in his place and named Cuthbert prior of Lindisfarne. He resumed his missionary activities and attracted huge crowds until he received his abbot's permission to live as a hermit, at first on a nearby island and then in 676 at one of the Farnes Islands near Bamborough. Against his will, he was elected bishop of Hexham in 685, arranged with St. Eata to swap sees, and became bishop of Lindisfarne but without the monastery. He spent the last two years of his life administering his see, caring for the sick of the plague that decimated his diocese, working numerous miracles of healing, and gifted with the ability to prophesy. He died at Lindisfarne. March 20.

CUTHBURGA (d. c. 725). Sister of King Ine of Wessex, she was married to Alfrid, who became King of Northumbria in 685. He permitted her to become a nun at Barking Monastery in Essex, and early in the ninth century, with her sister St. Quenburga, she founded an enclosed abbey in Dorset at Wimborne, of which she became abbess. September 3.

CUTHMAN (d. c. 900). Born in southern England, he was a shepherd, cared for his aged mother by begging when necessary, and aided by his neighbors, built a church at Steyning, Sussex. He was credited with performing many miracles. February 8.

CYBARD. *See* Eparchius.

CYBI (6th century). According to tradition, he was born in Cornwall, England, and is also known as Cuby. A cousin of St. David of Wales, he refused to allow himself to be made King and went to

Monmouthshire. He then went to Ireland, spent four years with St. Enda on Aranmore, and after a dispute with a priest named Fintan, went to southern Meath. Cybi founded a monastery on the island of Anglesey, near Holyhead, Wales, evangelized the area around it, and died there. Another tradition has him becoming a disciple of St. Hilary, who made him bishop of Poitiers, France, but this tradition is generally discounted as inaccurate by scholars. November 8.

CYNEBURGA (7th century). Daughter of King Penda of Mercia, she was married to Alcfrid, son of King Oswy of Northumbria. Alcfrid rebelled against his father, and what happened to Alcfrid is not known, but Cyneburga returned to her homeland and founded a convent at Cyneburgecester (Castor), of which she was abbess. Her sister Cyneswide joined the convent (in time succeeding Cyneburga as abbess), as did their relative St. Tibba, who lived as a solitary near the convent. Cyneburga and Cyneswide also helped found the abbey of Medeshamstede (Peterborough). March 6.

CYNESWIDE (7th century). *See* Cyneburga.

CYPRIAN (c. 200–58). Probably born at Carthage, Thascius Caecilius Cyprianus was a pagan rhetorician, lawyer, and teacher. He was converted to Christianity by Caecilius, an old priest, about 246, became a profound scholar of the Bible and the great religious authors, especially Tertullian, was ordained, and in 248, was elected bishop of Carthage. Cyprian was forced to flee Decius' persecution of Christians in 249 but continued to rule his see by letter from his hiding place. Greatly criticized for fleeing, he returned in 251 to find

that many of the faithful had apostatized during the persecution and that a priest named Novatus who had opposed his election was in schism and was receiving back into the Church with no penance those who had lapsed from the faith (the *lapsi*). Cyprian denounced Novatus for his undue leniency and convened a council at Carthage in 251, which set forth the terms under which the *lapsi* could be received back into the Church, excommunicated the schismatic leaders, and asserted the supremacy of the Pope; it was at this council that Cyprian read his famous *De unitate ecclesiae*. Novatus then went to Rome and joined the antipope, Novatian, against Pope Cornelius, whom Cyprian actively supported, rallying the African bishops behind Cornelius. In 252–54 Carthage was stricken with a terrible plague. Although Cyprian was a leader in helping alleviate its effects, the Christians were blamed for the plague, and hatred for Cyprian and the Christians intensified. It was at this time that he wrote *De mortalite* to comfort his flock. Soon after, he and other African bishops came into conflict with Pope St. Stephen when they refused to recognize the validity of baptism by heretics and schismatics, which Stephen had proclaimed valid. Three African councils (255–56) demanded rebaptism for those baptized by schismatics, and Cyprian engaged in an acrimonius correspondence with Stephen, which was cut short when an imperial decree forbidding any assemblage of Christians and requiring all bishops, priests, and deacons to participate in the official state religion ushered in Valerian's persecution of the Christians. Cyprian was arrested, and when he refused to participate was exiled by Paternus, the proconsul, to Curubis, a small town fifty miles from Carthage. The following year an imperial decree ordered that all bishops, priests, and deacons were to be put to death. Cyprian was arraigned before a new proconsul, Galerius Maximus, and when Cyprian persisted in his refusal to sacrifice to pagan gods, he was beheaded on September 14. Cyprian wrote numerous theological treatises on the Church, ministry, the Bible, virginity, and the *lapsi,* and is considered a pioneer of Latin Christian literature. September 16.

CYPRIAN (3rd century). According to the fictional morality story that had great popularity though with no basis in fact, Cyprian was a native of Antioch who became a practitioner of sorcery and black magic. He traveled widely in Greece, Egypt, Macedonia, and the Indies to broaden his knowledge of the black arts. When Aglaïdes, a young pagan, fell in love with the beautiful Justina, a Christian of Antioch, he asked Cyprian to help him win her. Cyprian tried all his black magic and diabolical expertise to win her for himself but was repelled by her faith and the aid of Mary. He called on the Devil, who assailed Justina with every weapon in his arsenal, to no avail. When Cyprian realized the overwhelming power of the forces arrayed against him and the Devil, Cyprian threatened to leave the Devil's service; whereupon the Devil turned on Cyprian, only to be repulsed by the sign of the cross made by a repentant Cyprian, who realized the sinfulness of his past life. He then turned to a priest named Eusebius for instruction and was converted to Christianity. He destroyed his magical books, gave his wealth to the poor, and was baptized, as was Aglaïdes. Justina then gave away her possessions and dedicated herself to God. In time Cyprian was ordained and later was elected bishop of Antioch. He was arrested during Diocletian's persecution of the Christians and tortured at Tyre by the governor of Phoenicia, as was Justina. They were then sent to Diocletian, who had them beheaded at Nicomedia. September 26.

CYPRIAN (d. c. 484). A bishop in northern Africa, he and his fellow bishop, the aged Felix of Abbir, were driven into the Libyan desert with almost five thousand fellow Christians during the persecution of Vandal King Huneric, an Arian, subjected to cruel tortures, and executed. October 12.

CYR. *See* Cyriacus; Julitta.

CYRAN (d. c. 655). Of a noble Frankish family and born in Berry, France, he was a cupbearer at the court of Clotaire II, was engaged to the daughter of a nobleman, but broke the engagement to become a monk at St. Martin's in Tours. When Cyran's father, who had been bishop of Tours, died, Cyran distributed his inheritance to the poor with such lavishness that he was imprisoned for a time as insane. After his release, he joined an Irish bishop, Falvius, on a pilgrimage to Rome; on Cyran's return he founded monasteries at Meobecca and Longoretum (Saint-Cyran) and served as abbot of both. He was especially noted for his great concern for and charity to the poor and his assistance to criminals. He is also known as Sigiramnus. December 5.

CYRIACA (d. 249). Also known as Dominica, she was a wealthy Roman who gave shelter to persecuted Christians in her home, which was also used as headquarters by St. Laurence and others for their charitable works. She was scourged to death for her Christianity. August 31.

CYRIACUS (d. c. 133). Bishop of Ancona, of which he is the patron, he is variously and unreliably conjectured to have been the legendary Jew named Judas Quiriacus who revealed where the Cross was hidden to Empress Helena, was baptized, became bishop of Jerusalem, and was martyred during the persecution of Julian the Apostate; or bishop of Ancona who died or was killed on a pilgrimage to Jerusalem; or as Judas, bishop of Jerusalem, who was killed during a riot there in 133. May 4.

CYRIACUS (d. 304). That a Cyriacus suffered martyrdom in Rome is fact, but the rest of his story is based on dubious legend, according to which he was a deacon who was arrested for helping Christian prisoners working on the construction of the baths of Diocletian. When Cyriacus cured the Emperor's daughter, Artemia, of possession, he was presented with a house, which he used as a church. He did the same for the daughter of the King of Persia, but on Cyriacus' return to Rome from this mission, he was arrested with his coworkers, Largus and Smaragdus, by order of Emperor Maximian. They were all tortured and then beheaded. August 8.

CYRICUS. *See* Julitta.

CYRIL (d. c. 251). Son of a pagan father living in Caesarea, Cappadocia, he was put out of his home when he became a Christian, though he was only a young boy. Brought before the governor, he refused to renounce his new religion despite an offer of freedom if he would sacrifice to the gods, and was thereupon beheaded. May 29.

CYRIL (3rd century). *See* Anastasia.

CYRIL (d. c. 365). A deacon at Heliopolis, Lebanon, he destroyed many pagan idols, and when Julian the

Apostate unleashed his persecution, Cyril was put to death. March 29.

CYRIL (c. 825–69) and **METHODIUS** (c. 826–84). Cyril and Methodius were brothers born at Thessalonika, Greece, of a senatorial family. Cyril was christened Constantine and sent at an early age to study at the imperial university at Constantinople under Photius, was ordained, and in time took over Photius' chair at the university, earning the sobriquet "the philosopher." Methodius became governor of one of the Slav colonies in Opsikion Province and then became a monk. Both were living in a monastery on the Bosporus in 861 when Emperor Michael III sent them to convert the Khazars in the Dnieper-Volga regions of Russia; they learned the Khazar language and made many converts. On their return, Methodius became abbot of a monastery in Greece. In 863, at the request of Prince Rostislav of Moravia, Photius, now patriarch of Constantinople, sent the two brothers to convert the Moravians, since German missionaries had been unsuccessful in their attempts to evangelize them. Their knowledge of the Slavonic tongue made them extremely successful. They invented an alphabet called glagolothic, which marked the beginning of Slavonic literature (the Cyrillic alphabet traditionally ascribed to Cyril was probably the work of his followers), and Cyril, with the help of Methodius, translated the liturgical books into Slavonic. Meanwhile, they had incurred the enmity of the German clergy because of their use of Slavonic in Church services and because they were from Constantinople, which was suspect to many in the West because of the heresy rife there. Further, their missionary efforts were hampered by the refusal of the German bishop of Passau to ordain their candidates for the priesthood. They were summoned to Rome by Pope Nicholas I, who died while they were on the way, and they were received by Pope Adrian II, to whom they presented the relics of Pope St. Clement they had brought with them from the Crimea, where he had died. Adrian received them warmly, was convinced of their orthodoxy, approved their use of Slavonic in the liturgy, and announced that they were to be ordained bishops. While they were in Rome, Cyril became a monk, taking the name by which he has since been known, but died in Rome shortly after, on February 14, and was buried in San Clemente church there. It is uncertain whether he was consecrated before his death, but Methodius was and returned to Moravia a bishop. There, at the request of the princes of Moravia and Pannonia, Pope Adrian formed the archdiocese of Moravia and Pannonia, independent of the German hierarchy, a move fiercely opposed by the German hierarchy, and made Methodius archbishop at Velehrad, Czechoslovakia. In 870, King Louis the German and the German bishops deposed Methodius at a synod at Ratisbon and imprisoned him. He was released two years later by order of Pope John VIII, and he returned to his see, though John deemed it politic to forbid his use of Slavonic in the liturgy. He was again summoned to Rome in 878 when his orthodoxy was impugned and for again using Slavonic in the liturgy. John was convinced of his orthodoxy, and impressed by Methodius' arguments, again permitted the use of Slavonic in the liturgy. Methodius also voyaged to Constantinople to finish the translation of Scriptures that he had begun with Cyril. Methodius' struggle with the Germans was to continue all through the rest of his life, until his death on April 6, probably at Stare Mesto (Velehrad). He and Cyril are called "Apostles of the Slavs," and to this day the liturgical language of the Russians, Serbs, Ukrainians, and Bulgars is that designed by them. Their feast day was extended to the universal Church by Pope Leo XIII in 1880. February 14.

CYRIL (d. 1182). A monk who became a hermit and later was bishop of Turov near Kiev, Russia, he was one of the leading biblical scholars of early Russian Christianity. An outstanding preacher, he is known for his sermons, allegorical interpretations of Scripture, and his spiritual writings. April 28.

CYRIL OF ALEXANDRIA (c. 376–444). Born at Alexandria, Egypt, and nephew of the patriarch of that city. Theophilus, Cyril received a classical and theological education at Alexandria and was ordained by his uncle. He accompanied Theophilus to Constantinople in 403 and was present at the Synod of the Oak that deposed John Chrysostom, whom he believed guilty of the charges against him. He succeeded his Uncle Theophilus as patriarch of Alexandria on Theophilus' death in 412, but only after a riot between Cyril's supporters and the followers of his rival Timotheus. Cyril at once began a series of attacks against the Novatians, whose churches he closed; the Jews, whom he drove from the city; and Governor Orestes, with whom he disagreed about some of his actions. In 430 Cyril became embroiled with Nestorius, patriarch of Constantinople, who was preaching that Mary was not the Mother of God since Christ was divine and not human, and consequently she should not have the word *theotokos* (God-bearer) applied to her. He persuaded Pope Celestine I to convoke a synod at Rome, which condemned Nestorius, and then did the same at his own synod in Alexandria. Celestine directed Cyril to depose Nestorius, and in 431 Cyril presided over the third

General Council at Ephesus, attended by some two hundred bishops, which condemned all the tenets of Nestorius and his followers before the arrival of Archbishop John of Antioch and forty-two followers who believed Nestorius was innocent; when they found what had been done, they held a council of their own and deposed Cyril. Emperor Theodosius II arrested both Cyril and Nestorius but released Cyril on the arrival of papal legates who confirmed the council's actions against Nestorius and declared Cyril innocent of all charges. Two years later Archbishop John, representing the moderate Antiochene bishops, and Cyril reached an agreement and joined in the condemnation, and Nestorius was forced into exile. During the rest of his life Cyril wrote treatises that clarified the doctrines of the Trinity and the Incarnation and that helped prevent Nestorianism and Pelagianism from taking long-term deep root in the Christian community. He was the most brilliant theologian of the Alexandrian tradition. His writings are characterized by accurate thinking, precise exposition, and great reasoning skill. Among his writings are commentaries on John, Luke, and the Pentateuch, treatises on dogmatic theology, an Apologia against Julian the Apostate, and letters and sermons. He was declared a Doctor of the Church by Pope Leo XIII in 1882. June 27.

CYRIL OF CONSTANTINOPLE (d. c. 1235). Often confused with other saints named Cyril, all that is really known of him is that he was a Carmelite, became prior general of the order in Palestine in 1232, and served in that capacity until the year of his death. March 6.

CYRIL OF JERUSALEM (c. 315–86). Probably born of Christian parents, he was raised and well educated in

Jerusalem and was ordained by St. Maximus. Cyril taught catechumens for several years and about 349 succeeded Maximus as bishop of Jerusalem. Cyril was expelled from the see in 357 by Acacius, the Arian bishop of Caesarea, who claimed ecclesiastical jurisdiction over Jerusalem and had an Arian synod condemn him for selling Church possessions to aid victims of a famine, but in reality because of his opposition to Arianism. He went to Tarsus but was recalled by the Council of Seleucia in 359. He was again expelled at Acacius' instigation by Emperor Constantius but recalled in 361 by Emperor Julius the Apostate when Constantius died. Again Cyril was exiled, in 367, when Emperor Valens banished all churchmen recalled during Julian's reign; but Cyril returned once again, in 378. The following year the Council of Antioch sent St. Gregory of Nyssa to Palestine to investigate charges against Cyril arising from his questioning the word *homoousios,* the basic term in the Nicene Creed. Gregory reported that the see of Jerusalem was morally corrupt, torn by factionalism and Arianism, but that its faith and that of Cyril were orthodox. Cyril and Gregory attended the General Council of Constantinople in 381, and Cyril completely accepted the amended Nicene Creed and the term *homoousios.* Cyril was a scriptural scholar, a successful preacher, and his "Catecheses" delivered during Lent in about 347 gives a clear picture of the instruction given those preparing for baptism and of the Palestinian liturgy of the fourth century. Though friendly with many semi-Arian leaders and though Church historians Socrates and Sozomen claim that the criticism that caused Gregory to go to Palestine to investigate had some substance to it, Cyril was a firm opponent of Arianism, and his orthodoxy is unquestioned. He was declared a Doctor of the

Church in 1882 by Pope Leo XIII. March 18.

CYRINUS (d. 251). *See* Alphius.

CYRUS (d. c. 303). An Alexandrian doctor who used his calling to convert many of his patients to Christianity, he joined an Arabian physician named John in encouraging Athanasia and her three daughters to remain constant in their faith under torture at Canopus, Egypt. They were both seized and tortured, and then all six were beheaded. January 31.

D

DA CORI, TOMMASO (1655–1729). Born Francesco Antonio Placidi, he was a Franciscan priest of the Orders of Friars Minor. Noted as a preacher, confessor, and spiritual retreats master, he was canonized in 1999.

DAFROSA (4th century). *See* Bibiana.

DAGOBERT II OF AUSTRASIA (d. 679). Son of King Sigebert III, he succeeded his father in 656 when only a child and was forced into exile and taken to Ireland by Bishop Dido of Poitiers when his guardian Grimoald declared his own son Childebert King. Dagobert regained his throne in 675 when Childeric II was murdered. A good friend of St. Wilfrid, whom he wanted to make bishop of Strasbourg (Wilfrid refused the honor), Dagobert was murdered, reputedly at the instigation of Ebroin, mayor of the palace, on December 23 while hunting in Lorraine. Because of the manner of his death, Dagobert was regarded as a martyr and a cult developed, but there is no satisfactory evidence available to justify his being considered a saint.

DAIRCHEALL. *See* Moling.

DALBY, BL. ROBERT (d. 1589). Born at Hemingborough, Yorkshire, England, he became a Protestant minister and was later converted to Catholicism. He studied for the priesthood at Douai and was ordained. Sent on the English mission, he was captured soon after he landed in England, charged with being a Catholic priest, and was hanged, drawn, and quartered on March 16 at York with Bl. John Amias. Robert was beatified in 1929.

DALFINUS. *See* Annemund.

DALLAN FORGAILL (d. 598). Born in Connaught, Ireland, he was known for his learning and reputedly went blind because of his intensive studying. He wrote poetry, notably his *Ambra Choluim Kille* in praise of St. Columba, and died at the hands of pirates at Inis-coel. January 29.

DALMATIUS (d. 304). Born of pagan parents at Monza, Lombardy, he was converted to Christianity and preached in northern Italy and Gaul. He was named bishop of Pavia, Italy, in 303 and suffered martyrdom the following year during the persecution of Christians by Emperor Maximian. December 5.

DALMATIUS MONER, BL. (1291–1341). Born at Santa Columba, Spain, he studied at the University of Montpellier, in France, and when twenty-five, joined the Dominicans at Gerona. He spent his life teaching, was master of novices for a time, and lived as a hermit the last four years of his life on the friary grounds at Gerona, where he died on September 24. His cult was confirmed in 1721. September 26.

DAMASUS I (c. 304–84). Of Spanish descent, he was probably born in Rome, and became deacon in the church of his father, who was a priest. Damasus was elected Pope in 366 in a bitterly contested election and was faced with an antipope, Ursinus, who was elected by an opposing minority faction. The opposition was put down with great cruelty, and Ursinus was exiled by Emperor Valentinian. Damasus' opponents remained actively opposed to him and in 378 charged him with incontinence—a charge of which he was cleared by a Roman synod. He enforced Valentinian's edict of 370 forbidding gifts by widows and orphans to bishops, was a vigorous opponent of Arianism, and sent legates to the General Council of Constantinople in 381, which accepted papal teaching, again condemned Arianism, and denounced the teaching of Macedonius that the Holy Spirit is not divine. During Damasus' pontificate, in 380, Emperor Theodosius the Great in the East and Emperor Gratian in the West decreed Christianity to be the religion of the Empire. A biblical scholar, Damasus published the canon of Holy Scripture, specifying the authentic books of the Bible as decreed by a council in Rome in 374, and was the patron of St. Jerome, who served as his secretary for a time; it was at Damasus' request that Jerome began his biblical commentaries and translation of the Bible, the Vulgate. Damasus enhanced the prestige of the papacy; proclaimed Rome supreme among the churches; and restored the catacombs, shrines, and tombs of the martyrs, and encouraged pilgrimages to them. He died in Rome on December 11.

DAMIAN (c. 303). *See* Cosmas.

DAMIAN DEI FURCHERI, BL. (d. 1484). Born at Perti, near Genoa, Italy, he joined the Dominicans at Savona and became famed for his preaching and miracles. He died at Reggio d'Emilia,

and his cult was confirmed in 1848 by Pope Pius IX. October 26.

DAMIEN THE LEPER. *See* Veuster, Joseph de.

DANIEL (d. 309). *See* Elias.

DANIEL (d. c. 584). A member of the Strathclyde family, he was born in Wales, founded a monastery in 514 at Bangor Fawr, Carnarvonshire, which developed into the diocese of Bangor, and was consecrated first bishop of that see by St. Dyfrig or perhaps St. David. Daniel was one of the bishops sent to persuade David to attend the synod of Brefi. Known in Wales by the Welsh form of Daniel, Deiniol, the date of his death is uncertain; 544, 545, and 554 are some of the dates advanced, but the tenth century *Annales Cambriae* gives it as 584. September 11.

DANIEL (d. 1227). Franciscan provincial of Calabria, Italy, he joined six Franciscan friars, Angelo, Domnus, Hugolino, Leo, Nicholas and Samuel, in Spain as their superior on their mission to evangelize the Mohammedans in Africa. They were arrested near Ceuta, Morocco, and when they refused to renounce their faith, all seven were beheaded. October 11.

DANIEL, ANTHONY (1601–48). Born on March 27 at Dieppe, France, he studied law but abandoned it to join the Jesuits at Rouen in 1621. He taught there for four years, studied theology at Clermont, was ordained in 1630, and was then assigned to the college at Eu. With three other priests he was sent as a missionary to Cape Breton Island, Arcadia, New France (Canada), in 1632, and a year later was sent to Quebec. He was most successful with his missionary work with the Huron Indians, founded a school for Indian boys at Quebec in

1636, and was martyred by a party of Iroquois, the traditional foe of the Hurons, on July 4 at the Indian village of Teanaustaye near Hillsdale, Ontario. He was canonized by Pope Pius XI in 1930 as one of the Martyrs of North America. October 19.

DANIEL THE STYLITE (c. 409–93). Born at Maratha, near Samosata on the Upper Euphrates, he entered a nearby monastery when twelve and became a monk there. He accompanied his abbot on a trip to Antioch, and on the way they stopped to see St. Simeon the Elder on his pillar. Daniel refused the request of the monks at the monastery to become abbot when the abbot died, made a pilgrimage to the Holy Land, and then after nine years as a hermit at Philempora, near Constantinople, he decided to emulate Simeon and live on a pillar. Daniel spent the next thirty-three years on a series of pillars built near Constantinople and was ordained on one of them when he refused to come down for his ordination. He prophesied a disastrous fire in Constantinople in 465 and became famed for his holiness and miracles of healing, attracting huge crowds with the sermons he delivered from the top of his pillar. He was consulted by Emperors Leo and Zeno, foretold the latter's banishment, and came down from his pillar only once, to denounce Basiliscus for usurping Zeno and supporting the Eutychians; Basiliscus' corruption and monophysite tendencies eventually led to the restoration of Zeno to the throne in 476. Daniel died on his pillar and was buried at its foot. December 11.

DARIA (d. 283). See Chrysanthus.

DASIUS (d. c. 303). Probably a Roman soldier at Durostorum (Silistria, Bulgaria), he was chosen by his comrades to be the leader of the saturnalia who after the revelry would be sacrificed to the pagan god Kronos. Dasius refused to participate because of his Christianity and was then beheaded when he refused to sacrifice before the image of the Emperor. November 20.

DATIUS (d. 552). Bishop of Milan, Italy, from probably 530, he was driven from his see by the Goths, who sacked the city when Byzantine General Belisarius failed to come to its aid in time. Datius may have been taken captive and freed by his friend Cassiodorus. Datius went to Constantinople and supported Pope Vigilius against Emperor Justinian in the Three Chapters controversy in 545, and probably died in Constantinople. January 14.

DATIVUS (d. 304). See Saturninus.

D'AVIANO, BL. MARCO (1631–99). Priest of the Order of Friars Minor Capuchins, D'Aviano was known as "the spiritual doctor of Europe." Christian leaders of Europe asked advice of this Venetian religious, a witness of the struggle between the Republic of Venice and the Ottoman Empire. D'Aviano, as an adviser to the Holy Roman Emperor Leopold I, is best known for helping defeat invading Ottoman Turks who held the cities of Vienna, Buda, and Belgrade under siege. There was concern in 2003 that his beatification would be interpreted as an anti-Muslim sign from the Vatican, but supporters regard the beatification as recognition of his many miracles, his charismatic spiritual leadership, and his powerful spirituality. He is often identified as the inventor and patron saint of the coffee drink cappuccino, but coffee historians highly doubt any connection between the man and the drink. He was beatified in 2003.

DAVID (5th–6th centuries). All the information we have about David is based on the unreliable eleventh-century biog-

172 DAVID

raphy written by Rhygyfarch, the son of Bishop Sulien of St. David's. According to it David was the son of King Sant of South Wales and St. Non, became a priest, studied under St. Paulinus on an unidentified island for several years, and then engaged in missionary activities, founding some dozen monasteries, the last of which, at Mynyw (Menevia) in southwestern Wales, was noted for the extreme asceticism of its rule, which was based on that of the Egyptian monks. David attended a synod at Brefi, Cardiganshire, in about 550 where his eloquence is said to have caused him to be elected primate of the Cambrian Church with the understanding that the episcopal see would be moved from Caerleon to Mynyw, now St. David's. He was supposedly consecrated archbishop by the patriarch of Jerusalem while on pilgrimage to the Holy Land, and a council he convened, called the Synod of Victory because it marked the final demise of Pelagianism, ratified the edicts of Brefi, and drew up regulations for the British Church, all are events that seem to be without any factual foundation. He died at his monastery at Mynyw, and his cult was reputedly approved by Pope Callistus II about 1120. Even his birth and death dates are uncertain, ranging from c. 454 to 520 for the former and from 560 to 601 for the latter. He is the patron saint of Wales. March 1.

DAVID. See Gleb under Boris entry.

DAVID (d. 1321). See Theodore (d. 1299).

DAVID OF MUNKTORP (d. c. 1080). An English monk, he went as a missionary to Sweden, was sent to Västmanland by Bishop Sigfrid of Växio, and founded a monastery at Munktorp. He was extremely successful in his missionary activities, was noted for his holiness and

miracles, and is believed to have been the first bishop of Västeras. July 15.

DAVID I OF SCOTLAND (1084–1153). The son of King Malcolm III and St. Margaret, he was sent to the Norman court in England in 1093, and married Matilda, widow of the earl of Northampton in 1113 (thereby becoming an English baron), and became the earl of Cumbria when his brother Alexander I became King. He succeeded his brother as King of Scotland in 1124 and engaged in a long struggle for the English crown on behalf of his niece Matilda against Stephen, who defeated him at Standard in 1138; he made peace with England the following year. He founded numerous sees and monasteries, established Norman law in Scotland, set up the office of chancellor, began the feudal court, and was noted for his justice, charities, and piety. He died at Carlisle, Scotland, on May 24, and though listed in both Catholic and Protestant calendars, he has never been formally canonized.

DAVIES, VEN. WILLIAM (d. 1593). Born probably at Crois in Yris, Denbighshire, Wales, he studied for the priesthood at Rheims, was ordained in 1585, and was then sent to Wales to minister to the persecuted Catholics there. He was arrested at Holyhead and though treated with kindness by the warden, who allowed him to say Mass, he was condemned for being a Catholic priest and hanged, drawn, and quartered at Beaumaris, Wales. July 27.

DE BETANCURT, PEDRO (1626–1667). Born in the Canary Islands of Spain, Pedro determined in 1650 to join those who were bringing the Gospel to the New World. The trip to Guatemala City was difficult and expensive; consequently by the time he arrived there, he was dependent on local Franciscans for food. He eventually secured employment in a textile factory, but was rejected as an applicant to the Jesuits. In 1655 he became a Franciscan brother whose mission was to serve the poor of the city. Brother Pedro founded schools for the poor, a hospital, and housing for the homeless. He founded the Bethlehemite Brothers and Sisters—the first order founded in the Americas. He was canonized in 2002.

DE CORLEONE, BERNARD (1605–1667). Born the son of a Sicilian shoemaker, there is dispute over a central event in Bernard's early life. Did he, as a skilled teenage fighter, kill the man who attacked him, or did he, as some suggest, severely wound the man, later to embrace him as a friend? Whatever the case, Bernard became known as "the finest blade in Sicily." Following the incident, Bernard sought refuge among the Capuchin Friars in Palermo. In 1632 he became a Capuchin brother. Until his death, he took on a series of mostly menial tasks, tending to the brothers' laundry and the kitchen. He was also known for his devotion to the Eucharist, his intense prayer life, his penitential spirit, and his care of the tabernacle. Bernard was canonized in 2001.

DE MAZENOD, EUGENE (1782–1861). Born into a tumultuous family—his father brought the nobility, his mother the money—during a time of great turmoil, Eugene de Mazenod should have lived a life of ease. The French Revolution intervened, however, forcing the family to flee to Italy, where Eugene spent his formative years. The family moved from city to city and grew increasingly impoverished during these difficult years. Eugene's mother and father separated, and he returned to France in 1802. Despite strong family opposition, he decided to become a priest of the embattled Church. He was ordained in 1811. Seeking ways to reach out to or-

dinary Frenchmen, he founded the Congregation of the Oblates of Mary Immaculate—an order that would eventually send missionaries around the globe. Eugene and his fellow priests reached out to the people, preaching, for example, in the Provencal dialect, rather than the more refined French preferred by the upper classes. He was appointed bishop of Marseille in 1836. During his tenure as bishop, the number of priests in the diocese doubled, ambitious church construction was undertaken, and morale was restored to the church. Said Eugene: "I find my happiness in pastoral work. It is for this that I am a bishop, and not to write books, still less to pay court to the great, or to waste my time among the rich. It is true . . . that this is not the way to become a cardinal, but if one could become a saint, would it not be better still?" He was canonized in 1995. May 21.

DE OROZCO, ALONSO (1500–1591). The son of a castle governor in Toledo, Alonso wrote more than twenty books and became known as one of the great Spanish mystics. At the age of twenty-two he entered the Augustinian novitiate, where his rhetorical talents were discovered and developed. He served as prior to a number of monasteries before being named preacher at the royal courts. That position brought Alonso access to luxury, but he rejected those temptations and lived a simple life. In addition to serving the royal court, Alonso wrote, read, and served the needs of the poor. The death of this "saint of the court" in 1591 was noted by all of Madrid, rich and poor. He was canonized in 2002. September 19.

DEAN, BL. WILLIAM (d. 1588). Born at Linton in Craven, Yorkshire, England, he became a minister and was later converted to Catholicism. He went to Rheims, was ordained there in 1581, and was then sent on the English mission. He was arrested, banished on pain of death, but returned and was arrested in London. He was convicted of being a Catholic priest and hanged at Mile End Green in London. Also executed with him was Ven. Henry Webley, a layman who was convicted of aiding him. William was beatified in 1929. August 28.

DECLAN (c. 6th century). Born at Desi (Decies), Waterford, Ireland, he was baptized by a St. Colman, whose disciple he was, may have made two pilgrimages to Rome, and later became bishop of Ardmore. July 24.

DEICOLUS (c. 530–c. 625). Elder brother of St. Gall and born in Leinster, Ireland, Deicolus was one of the twelve disciples of Columban who accompanied him to France in 576. Deicolus worked with Columban in Austrasia and Burgundy, and when Columban was expelled by Thierry in 610, Deicolus was unable to accompany him into exile because of his age, and he settled at Lure, where he founded a monastery. He lived there as a hermit until his death. January 18.

DEINIOL. See Daniel (d. 584).

DEIRDRE. See Ita.

DELANOUE, BL. JOAN (1666–1736). Born at Saumur, Anjou, France, the daughter of a draper and the youngest of twelve children, she took over the family religious-articles business when her mother died in 1691 and developed into a selfish, avaricious woman whose main preoccupation in life was making money. When she was thirty, she experienced a change of heart when she met a Frances Souchet, a widow from Rennes, who seems to have affected her by messages that Joan finally decided were from God. She closed her shop in 1698 and began to help orphans. In 1704, she, her niece, and two followers were clothed with the religious habit, and the group took the name Sisters of St. Anne of the Providence of Saumur. Two years later Joan leased a large house from the Oratorians, made her first vows, taking the name John of the Cross, and encouraged by St. Louis Grignion de Montfort and despite every obstacle she encountered in the next decade, persisted in her vocation. She received canonical approval from the bishop of Angers for her community, practiced the greatest austerities, and suffered from physical ailments all her life. By 1721 the congregation had begun to spread to other towns and cities in France, and Joan had become well known for her miracles of healing. She died on September 17, and was beatified in 1947.

DEL BUFALO, CASPAR (1786–1837). Born in Rome, he was educated at the Collegio Romano and was ordained in 1808. He was exiled to Corsica for five years during the occupation of Rome by Napoleon's army for refusing to swear allegiance to Napoleon. On Caspar's return he engaged in pastoral work. While conducting a mission at Giano, he conceived the idea of founding a congregation for mission work and in 1815 received formal approval for the Missioners of the Most Precious Blood from Pope Pius VII. Caspar founded houses at Giano, Albano, and, despite great difficulties, in the kingdom of Naples; in time the congregation spread all over Italy. He was also active in charitable works and had as his goal for his missioners the evangelization of the world. He died on December 28 at Albano, a victim of cholera, and was canonized by Pope Pius XII in 1954. January 2.

DELGADO, BL. ALEXIUS (1556–70). Born at Elvas, Portugal, he was a fourteen-year-old Jesuit novice when he and a group of Jesuits under Bl. Ignatius d'Azevedo were massacred by French Huguenot pirates near the Canary Islands while on the way to Brazil to engage in missionary work there. They were beatified in 1854. July 15.

DELGADOY Y CEBRIAN, BL. IGNATIUS (1762–1838). A Spaniard, he joined the Dominicans and in 1788 was sent to Indochina, where he worked as a missionary for fifty years in Tonkin. He became bishop and vicar apostolic of eastern Tonkin and in 1838 was arrested during a persecution of Christians that had been unleased by Minh-Mang, the Annamite ruler. He was exhibited in a small cage at Nam-Dinh and then was sentenced to be beheaded. He died of ill treatment on July 12 before the sentence could be carried out. He was beatified by Pope Leo XIII in 1900. July 11.

DELPHINA, BL. (1283–1360). Born at Château Puy Michel, Languedoc, France, she married St. Elzear when both were sixteen and lived a life of personal piety with him that caused them to be considered an ideal married couple. She accompanied Elzear to Naples in 1317 and became a companion to Queen Sanchia, a position she continued after the death of her husband on a diplomatic mission to Paris in 1323. When Queen Sanchia's husband, King Robert, died, the Queen became a nun at a Poor Clare monastery in Naples, and Delphina remained with her until her death, when she returned to Provence. She gave most of her wealth to the poor and lived as a recluse, at first at Carbrières and then at Apt, where she died, probably on November 26. Her cult was approved by Pope Urban VIII. September 26.

DELPHINUS (d. 403). Second bishop of Bordeaux, France, he attended the Synod of Saragossa in 380, which condemned Priscillianism, corresponded with St. Ambrose, and baptized St. Paulinus of Nola. December 24.

DEMETRIA (4th century). *See* Bibiana.

DEMETRIAN (d. c. 912). Born at Sika, Cyprus, son of a priest, he became a monk at St. Antony's monastery there on the death of his wife and was ordained. He was later elected abbot, served for forty years, and then became bishop of Khytri (Kyrka), despite his objections, and ruled for twenty-five years. During a Saracen raid on Cyprus, he was able to persuade the invaders to release the Christian captives they were about to sell into slavery. November 6.

DEMETRIUS (126–231). Made bishop of Alexandria in 188, he served for forty-three years and made the catechetical school at Alexandria famous. He appointed his young follower Origen (then eighteen) director of the school about 203, defended him in his early years, but later condemned him for preaching as a layman in Caesarea. Fifteen years later Demetrius expelled him from his diocese for being ordained without his permission. October 9.

DEMETRIUS (c. 4th century). A deacon martyred at Sirmium (Mitrovic, Yugoslavia), his fictitious story has him a resident of Salonika who was murdered by Emperor Maximian; other accounts have him a soldier and proconsul who was martyred for his faith. He had great popularity during the Middle Ages and with St. George was a patron of the Crusaders as an exemplar of the ideal for Christian fighting men whose patron he is also. October 8.

DEMETRIUS OF TIFLIS (d. 1321). *See* Thomas of Tolentino, Bl.

DENIS (d. c. 258). Born in Italy, he was sent with six other bishops to Gaul in

250 as missionaries and became the first bishop of Paris. He was so effective in converting the inhabitants around Paris that he was arrested with his priest, St. Rusticus, and deacon, St. Eleutherius, and imprisoned. The three of them were beheaded on October 9 near Paris for their faith during Decius' persecution of the Christians. Their bodies were rescued from the Seine River, and a chapel built over their tomb later became the Benedictine abbey of Saint-Denis. He is the apostle and patron saint of France and is also known as Dionysius of Paris.

DENN, BL. PAUL (1847–1900). See Mangin, Bl. Leon.

DEODATUS (d. c. 679). A native of Gaul and known in France as Dié and Didier, he became bishop of Nevers about 655, attended the Synod of Sens in 657, and several years later resigned his see to become a hermit, at first in the Vosges, and when driven out by the inhabitants, on an island near Strasbourg, which later developed into the famous monastery of Ebersheim. He later returned to the Vosges and founded a monastery, Jointures, of which he became abbot, and remained there until his death. June 19.

DEOGRATIAS (d. 457). A priest of Carthage, he was named bishop of that city, which had been without a bishop for fourteen years after the Arian Vandals occupied it in 439. He spent the three years of his episcopate selling everything he had to ransom and provide quarters for the Christians taken captive to Africa by Genseric following his sack of Rome in 455, incurring the bitter enmity of some of the Arians, who unsuccessfully plotted his assassination. March 22.

DERFEL GADARN (c. 5th century). According to legend, he was a great Welsh soldier who fought at Camlan where King Arthur was killed, may have been a monk at Bardsey, and was later a solitary at Llanderfel, Merionethshire, Wales. A wooden statue of him in the church there was greatly venerated until it was used for firewood in the burning of Bl. John Forest at Smithfield in 1538. April 5.

DESIDERATUS (d. c. 550). Also known as Désiré and brother of Desiderius and Deodatus, he became a courtier at the court of King Clotaire, was active in combating heresy and simony, and in 541 was made bishop of Bourgues. He attended several councils that condemned Nestorianism and Eutychianism, was reputed to have performed miracles, and was known for his peacemaking abilities. He died on May 8.

DESIDERIUS (d. c. 305). See Januarius.

DESIDERIUS (d. 607). Born at Autun, Gaul, and also known as Didier, he became bishop of Vienne. His enforcement of strict clerical discipline, his attacks on simony, and his denunciation of the immorality of Queen Brunhildis' court made him many enemies. He was denounced by the Queen for paganism to Pope Gregory the Great, who completely exonerated him, but was banished by a synod controlled by Brunhildis. Desiderius returned four years later but was murdered by three followers of King Theodoric, whom he had publicly censured. May 23.

DESIDERIUS (d. 655). Also known as Didier and Géry, he was the son of a nobleman, was born at Albi, France, became an official at the court of King Clotaire II at Neustria, and was elected bishop of Cahors in 630 while still a layman, replacing his brother Rusticus, who had been murdered. Desiderius encouraged religious foundations, founded and built a monastery, convent, and churches, restored strict clerical discipline, and was a strong supporter of the monastic life. He died near Albi. November 15.

DESIDERIUS, BL. (d. 1194). Also known as Didier, he was a Belgian Cistercian at the abbey of Cambron and became bishop of Therouanne in 1169. He helped found Blandecques Monastery near Saint-Omer, resigned his see about 1191, and died at Cambron Abbey on January 20 (or perhaps September 2).

DÉSIRÉ. *See* Desideratus.

DESLE. *See* Deicolus.

DESMAISIÈRES, MARY MICHAELEA (1809–65). Born at Madrid of a noble family, the Viscountess of Sorbalàn refused offers of marriage, accompanied her brother to Paris and Brussels when he was ambassador to France and Belgium, and was devoted to religious instruction and aiding the sick and the needy. On her return to Spain in 1848, she organized the Handmaids of the Blessed Sacrament and of Charity to help fallen women, was elected mother general in 1859, and died in Valencia of cholera while ministering to the plague-stricken. She was canonized in 1934. August 25.

DEUSDEDIT (6th century). A shoe-maker in Rome, despite his own poverty he gave away what he earned during the week to those poorer than himself. Pope St. Gregory the Great spoke highly of him. August 10.

DEUSDEDIT (d. 618). Son of a sub-deacon, Stephen, he was born in Rome and was consecrated Pope on October 19, 615. Also known as Adeodatus I, he encouraged the secular clergy and devoted much of his time to aiding the needy, especially during the disastrous earthquake that devastated Rome in August 618. According to tradition, he was the first Pope to use lead seals (bullae) on papal documents, which in time came to be called bulls. He may have been a Benedictine. He died in Rome. November 8.

DEUSDEDIT (d. 836). A monk at Monte Cassino, he was selected abbot in 830 and became known for his concern for and aid to the poor. He was imprisoned by Sicard of Benevento who, seeing his generosity to the poor, was pressuring him to divert monastery funds to his personal treasury. Deusdedit died in prison of maltreatment. October 9.

DEUSDEDIT OF CANTERBURY (d. 664). A South Saxon named Frithona, he became the first Anglo-Saxon to be primate when he succeeded Honorius as archbishop of Canterbury in 653. Nothing further of him is known beyond that he died, probably on October 28, during a plague. July 14.

DEWI. *See* David (5th–6th centuries).

DIANA, BL. (c. 1201–36). A member of the d'Andalo family, she was born near Bologna, Italy, and convinced her father to withdraw his opposition to the founding of a Dominican priory on land he owned in Bologna. Dominic received her vow of virginity, but she was forced to remain at home by her family. Later she joined the Augustinians at Roxana but was forcibly removed from the convent by her family. She was injured in the struggle but later escaped and returned to Roxana. Sometime later Bl. Jordan of Saxony convinced the family to found a Dominican convent in 1222 for her staffed with Diana and four companions and four nuns brought from Rome, two of them Cecilia and Amata. Diana died on January 9, and when

Cecilia and Amata died they were buried with her. All three were beatified in 1891. June 9.

DIARMAID (d. c. 851). Born in Ireland, he became famed for his learning and was named bishop of Armagh in 834. The following year he was driven from his see by the usurper Forau and moved to Connacht, where he ruled as primate. His reign was saddened by the destruction of the churches of Armagh by Scandinavian marauders under Turgesius in 841. April 24.

DICHU (5th century). Son of an Ulster chieftain, he succeeded to the kingdom of Lecale in County Down and bitterly opposed St. Patrick when he landed in Ireland in 432. He became Patrick's first Irish convert, gave Patrick a church in Saul, capital of Lecale, the first of Patrick's foundations in Ireland, and the two became close friends. April 29.

DICKENSON, BL. FRANCIS (d. 1590). A native of Yorkshire, England, he studied at Douai and was ordained. He and Bl. Miles Gerard were sent on the English mission in 1589, and when their ship was wrecked on the coast of Kent, both were arrested. They were tried, found guilty of being Catholic priests, and hanged, drawn, and quartered at Rochester on April 30 (or April 13). He was beatified in 1929.

DICKENSON, BL. ROGER (d. 1591). A native of Lincoln, England, he studied at Rheims and was ordained there. Sent on the English mission, he worked for several years in the Winchester region, aided by Bl. Ralph Milner. Dickenson was arrested and imprisoned but managed to escape when he got the guards drunk. He was recaptured, this time with Milner, convicted of being a Catholic priest, and was hanged, drawn,

and quartered, with Milner, at Winchester on July 7. Dickenson was beatified in 1929.

DIDACUS (c. 1400–63). Born at San Nicolas del Puerto, Spain, of poor parents, he lived as a recluse with a priest nearby in his youth and then became a Franciscan lay brother at Arrizafa. He worked as a missionary in the Canary Islands, became guardian of Fuerteventura there in 1445, and then spent the rest of his life in friaries in Seville, Salcedo, and Alcalá, noted for his healing powers and miracles. He died at Alcalá on November 7, and was canonized in 1588. November 13.

DIDACUS, BL. (1743–1801). Born at Cadiz, Spain, on March 29 and christened Joseph Francis, he joined the Capuchins at Seville in 1759, taking the name Didacus or Diego, and was ordained. He became an eloquent preacher, particularly noted for his sermons on the Trinity, drawing huge crowds wherever he preached. He was beloved as a confessor and was devoted to the sick, the poor, and prisoners. He is reported to have had the gift of levitation. He was beatified in 1894. March 24.

DIDIER. See Deodatus.

DIDIER. See Desiderius.

DIDYMUS (d. c. 304). See Theodora.

DIÉ. See Deodatus.

DIEGO. See Didacus.

DIEGO DE AVEZEDO, BL. (1207). A member of the clergy attached to the cathedral at Osma, Spain, he became provost and in 1201 was named bishop of Osma. In 1206, he was sent by King Alfonso IX of Castile to the Marches to escort back to Spain the bride-to-be of Prince Ferdinand. On arrival, Diego found the girl dead. He then went to Rome, taking with him a member of his party, St. Dominic, a visit that ultimately led to the founding of the Dominicans. In the same year Diego joined the Cistercians at Citeaux and became a leader in the crusade against the Albigensians in Languedoc. He returned to Osma late in 1207 and died there on December 30. February 6.

DIEGO, JUAN (1474–1548). Not much is known of Juan Diego. His very existence has been questioned by some skeptics. Nevertheless, the first native-born saint of the Americas was said to be a widower as well as a devout convert of advancing years when, on his way to Mass, the Virgin Mary appeared to him. She praised his humility and faithfulness and urged him to go to the bishop and request that a church be built where she stood. Told by the local bishop that he required a sign to authenticate Juan's claims, Juan was instructed by the Virgin to gather roses, cover them, and deliver them to the bishop. He did so, and as he unveiled the roses, a picture—*Our Lady of Guadalupe*—emerged on his cloak. The bishop was convinced. Juan lived out his years promoting the apparitions to the Mexican people and thousands of converts to Christianity were made as a result. Juan was canonized in 2002.

DIEM, BL. VINCENT (1838). *See* Dumoulin-Borie, Bl. Peter.

DIEMODA, BL. (c. 1060–c. 1130). Also known as Diemut, she was a Bavarian who became a nun at Wessobrunn and later became a hermitess at a neighboring monastery, devoting herself to prayer and copying manuscripts, some fifty of which are still in existence. March 29.

DIEMUT. *See* Diemoda.

DI GIROLAMO, FRANCIS (1642–1716). Born at Grottaglie, Italy, on December 17, the eldest of eleven children, he was educated by a group of secular priests living in community and was tonsured when he was sixteen. After studying canon and civil law at Naples, he was ordained in 1666, taught at the Jesuit college in Naples, and in 1670, when he was twenty-eight, he became a Jesuit. He joined Fr. Agnello Bruno in mission work in Otranto, 1671–74, and spent the last forty years of his life giving missions in and around Naples. He was a successful preacher, a sought-after confessor, and a well-known figure in the hospitals and prisons of Naples, venerated for his holiness and miracles of healing. He died at Naples, and was canonized in 1839. May 11.

DIGNA (d. 853). *See* Anastasius.

DIMAN (d. 658). A monk under St. Columba, he later was named abbot-bishop of Connor, Ireland. He was one of the Irish bishops to whom Pope St. Honorius wrote in 640 concerning the controversy over the dating of Easter and about Pelagianism. January 6.

DIOCLETUS (d. c. 304). *See* Sisinius.

DIODORUS (d. 283). *See* Chrysanthus.

DIONISIA (d. 250). *See* Epimachus.

DIONYSIA (d. 251). *See* Peter of Lampsacus.

DIONYSIA (d. 484). During the persecution of Catholics in Africa by Arian King Huneric, the beautiful Dionysia was arrested and scourged in the Forum for her faith. When her young son Majorcus wept at the sight, she encouraged him. Both, with her sister Dativa, were burned at the stake; a cousin Emilian, a physician, and Tertius were flayed to death. Also martyred at the same time were Leontia, Boniface, Servus, a resident of Thuburbo, and Victoria, who refused the pleas of her apostate husband to renounce her faith for the sake of her children. December 6.

DIONYSIUS (d. 268). Possibly a Greek, he was a priest in Rome when he was elected Pope on July 22, 259, in an election delayed for a year by the violence of Valerian's persecution of the Christians. About 260 Dionysius issued an important doctrinal letter correcting the phraseology in the writings of Dionysius, bishop of Alexandria, regarding the Trinity, insisting on the true doctrine of three Persons in one divine nature, and condemning Sabellianism. He sent large sums of money to the churches of Cappadocia that had been devastated by marauding Goths and to ransom their Christian captives and was most successful in rebuilding the Church when Emperor Gallienus issued his edict of toleration shortly after Dionysius' election. He died in Rome, the first Pope not listed as a martyr. December 26.

DIONYSIUS (d. 273). *See* Lucillian.

DIONYSIUS (d. c. 360). Elected bishop of Milan in 351, he attended the synod summoned there by Arian Emperor Constantine to condemn Athanasius and was banished to Cappadocia with Eusebius of Vercelli and Lucifer of Cagliari when they refused to sign the condemnation. Dionysius died at Cappadocia. May 25.

DIONYSIUS OF ALEXANDRIA (d. 265). A native of Alexandria, Egypt, he was converted to Christianity by a vision, and became a student at the catechetical school in Alexandria under Origen. Dionysius was appointed head of the catechetical school by Bishop Heraclas in 232 and after fifteen years in that position was elected bishop of Alexandria in 247. He was arrested during Decius' persecution of the Christians in 249 but was rescued by a group of Egyptians and sought refuge in the Libyan desert, whence he ruled his see until the persecution died down. He supported Pope St. Cornelius against an antipope, Novatian, and denounced and fought Novatianism. Dionysius was an outstanding theologian and biblical scholar, was reproved by Pope St. Stephen I for his mistaken view in supporting Cyprian that baptism by heretics was invalid and by Pope St. Dionysius for his view on the Trinity, which Dionysius explained in an apologia to the Pope. Dionysius was banished to Kephro in Libya by Emilian, prefect of Egypt, when Valerian's persecution began in 257. Dionysius returned in 260 to a plague-stricken city in the throes of civil war, with mobs roaming the streets, and devoted himself to aiding the persecuted Christians and the victims of the plague. He died in Alexandria. An indefatigable defender of the faith, he is called "the Teacher of the Catholic Church" by St. Athanasius and is surnamed "the Great" by St. Basil. November 17.

DIONYSIUS THE AREOPAGITE (1st century). It is related (Acts 17:23–34) that Dionysius with a woman named Damaris was converted by St. Paul at the time he delivered his famous sermon on the Unknown God on the Hill of Mars (Areopagus) in Athens. St. Dionysius of Corinth says that he became first bishop of Athens, and Basil's Menology says he was burned to death during Domitian's persecution of the Christians about 95. The Roman Martyrology mistakenly identifies him with Dionysius of Paris, and it is now accepted that he was not the author of four treatises and ten letters on mysticism and theology that were so influential in the Middle Ages and were long attributed to him. October 9.

DIONYSIUS OF CORINTH (d. c. 180). Elected bishop of Corinth about 170, he wrote numerous letters, described in Eusebius' *Ecclesiastical History,* to various Christian communities, teaching orthodoxy, combating heresies, and exhorting them to better lives. Of especial importance is his letter to the Romans attesting to the generosity of the Roman Church and the martyrdom of Peter and Paul there and that the letters of the current Pope, Soter, and of Pope Clement were habitually read in the church at Corinth. April 8.

DIONYSIUS OF THE NATIVITY, BL. *See* Berthelot, Bl. Dionysius.

DIONYSIUS OF PARIS. *See* Denis.

DIOSCORUS (d. 250). A fifteen-year-old boy, he was arrested with Arsenius, Heron, and Isidore at Alexandria during Decius' persecution of the Christians. Though tortured, Dioscorus was released by the judge because of his age, but the others were burned to death when they refused to give up their faith. December 14.

DIOSCORUS (d. 284). *See* Victorinus.

DI ROSA, MARY (1813–55). Born at Brescia, Italy, on November 6 and christened Paula Frances Mary, and of a well-to-do family, her mother died when she was eleven and she was educated by the Visitandine nuns. When seventeen she left school to take over the running of her father's household. Early inclined to a religious life, she dissuaded her father from making a marriage for her and became involved in caring for the spiritual welfare of the girls in her father's textile mill at Acquafredda and his estate at Capriano. She worked in the hospital in Brescia, ministering to the victims of a cholera epidemic in 1836, became directress of a home for abandoned girls the following year, founded a home of her own for girls, and then started a school for deaf and mute girls. In 1840, she was appointed superioress of a religious society of women to care for the sick by her spiritual adviser, Msgr. Faustino Pinzoni, and took the name Maria Crocifissa. The society was called the Handmaids of Charity of Brescia. Despite initial difficulties, the institute received the approval of the bishop of Brescia in 1843, and in the wars that shook Europe in 1848 ministered to the wounded on the battlefields of northern Italy and in the hospitals of Brescia. In 1850, Mary received papal approval of her congregation and died five years later at Brescia on December 15. She was canonized in 1954.

DISIBOD (d. c. 674). An Irish bishop, he became discouraged by his lack of success in preaching to his countrymen and immigrated to Germany, where he was most successful and founded a monastery near Bingen, which was called Disibodenberg after him. September 8.

DISMAS (1st century). All that is known of him is that he is the Good Thief crucified with Christ on Calvary; the other thief is known as Gestas (Luke 23:39–43). A completely unsubstantiated myth from the Arabic Gospel of the Infancy that enjoyed great popularity in the West during the Middle Ages had them two thieves who held up the Holy Family on the way to Egypt. Dismas bought off Gestas with forty drachmas to leave them unmolested, whereupon the Infant predicted they would be crucified with him in Jerusalem and that Dismas would accompany him to Paradise. March 25.

DIVINI, PACIFICO (1653–1721). Born at San Severino, Ancona, Italy, on March

1 and baptized Charles Antony, he was raised with great severity by an uncle when he was orphaned at five. When seventeen, he joined the Observant Friars Minor at Forano, taking the name Pacifico. He was ordained in 1678, taught philosophy for two years, and then became a missionary in the area around Forano. When thirty-five, he lost his sight and hearing and became crippled. Transferred to the friary at San Severino in 1705, he spent the rest of his life there in prayer, fasting, and mortifications. He died there on September 24, venerated for his ecstasies, holiness, and gift of prophecy. He was canonized in 1839.

DOCCO. *See* Cungar.

DODO, BL. (d. 1231). Married against his will, he became a Premonstratensian monk when his father died and his mother and wife entered a convent. He lived as a hermit for four years and then moved to Asch (or Hasch), Friesland, where he became known for his healing powers, visions, and the stigmata found on his body after his death. He was killed when a wall collapsed on him. March 30.

DOGMAEL (6th century). Probably a Welshman, he preached in Pembrokeshire and then went to Brittany. Several churches were named after him, but nothing else is known of him except his father's name, Ithel ab Ceredig ab Cunedda Wledig. June 14.

DOMETIUS. *See* Domitius.

DOMINIC (9th century). A Benedictine monk at Comachio, near Venice, legend names him a pilgrim to the Holy Land in 820 who brought the relics of St. Mark back from Alexandria to Venice, where they are interred in St. Mark's Cathedral. June 21.

DOMINIC (1170–1221). Son of Felix Guzman and Bl. Joan of Aza, he was born at Calaruega, Spain, studied at the University at Palencia, 1184–94, was probably ordained there while pursuing his studies, and was appointed canon at Osma in 1199. There he became prior superior of the chapter, which was noted for its strict adherence to the rule of St. Benedict. In 1203, he accompanied Bishop Diego de Avezedo of Osma to Languedoc, where Dominic preached against the Albigensians and helped reform the Cistercians. Dominic founded an institute for women at Prouille in Albigensian territory in 1206 and attached several preaching friars to it. When papal legate Peter of Castelnan was murdered by the Albigensians in 1208, Pope Innocent III launched a crusade against them headed by Count Simon IV of Montfort, which was to continue for the next seven years. Dominic followed the army and preached to the heretics but with no great success. In 1214, Simon gave him a castle at Casseneuil, and Dominic, with six followers, founded an order devoted to the conversion of the Albigensians; the order was canonically approved by the bishop of Toulouse the following year. He failed to gain approval for his order of preachers at the fourth General Council of the Lateran in 1215 but received Pope Honorius III's approval in the following year, and the Order of Preachers (the Dominicans) was founded. Dominic spent the last years of his life organizing the order, traveling all over Italy, Spain, and France preaching and attracting new members and establishing new houses. The new order was phenomenally successful in conversion work as it applied Dominic's concept of harmonizing the intellectual life with popular needs. He convoked the first general council of the order at Bologna in 1220 and died there the following year on August 6, after being forced by illness to return from a preaching tour in Hungary. He was canonized in 1234. August 8.

DOMINIC (d. 1300). A Dominican friar in Castile, he and a fellow friar, Gregory, were preaching in Aragon when they were killed in a landslide near Perarua. The cult that developed around them was confirmed in 1854. April 26.

DOMINIC OF THE CAUSEWAY (d. c. 1109). A Basque born at Villoria, Spain, he lived as a hermit at Rioja after several attempts to join the Benedictines failed, and then became a follower of St. Gregory of Ostia. On the death of Gregory, he became a hermit in a forest near La Calzada on the road to Compostela and built a highway, a bridge, and a hospice to make the path of the pilgrims a bit less difficult. On his death many miracles were reported at his tomb. May 12.

DOMINIC LORICATUS (995–1060). Dominic was born in Umbria, Italy. When he learned he had been ordained because of his father's bribe of a bishop, Dominic spent the rest of his life doing penance and practicing the most severe mortifications. He became a disciple of John of Montefeltro, living the life of a hermit, and about 1040 Dominic became a Benedictine at Fonte Avellana Hermitage under St. Peter Damian. Dominic later was prior of a hermitage Peter had founded near San Severini and died there on October 14. Dominic's surname, Loricatus (the mailed) was given him because of the coat of rough mail he wore next to his skin.

DOMINIC OF THE MOTHER OF GOD, BL. *See* Barberi, Bl. Dominic.

DOMINIC OF SILOS (c. 1000–73). Born at Canas, Navarre, Spain, of peasant parents, he was a shepherd in his youth, became a Benedictine monk at

San Millan de Cogolla Monastery and in time prior. He was driven from the monastery by Garcia III of Navarre when he refused to surrender part of the monastery grounds to the sovereign's claim and went to San Sebastian Monastery at Silos and became its abbot. He reformed the monastery and built it into one of the leading spiritual houses in Spain; its scriptorium produced outstanding Spanish Christian art. He helped rescue Christian slaves from the Moors and was credited with miracles of healing. He died on December 20.

DOMINIC OF SORA (c. 951–1031). Born at Foligno, Etruria, Italy, he became a Benedictine monk and built numerous monasteries in various parts of Italy. He died at Sora, Italy. January 22.

DOMINICA. *See* Cyriaca (d. 249).

DOMINICA (d. c. 303). According to the Roman Martyrology, she was condemned to death by being exposed to wild beasts, but when she emerged unscathed she was beheaded in Campania for destroying idols during the reign of Emperor Diocletian. July 6.

DOMINICA (d. c. 710). *See* Indractus.

DOMINICI, BL. JOHN (1376–1419). Born at Florence, Italy, he became a Dominican when eighteen, studied at Paris, and became a noted theologian and preacher. He taught and preached at Venice for twelve years, was prior of Santa Maria Novella in Florence, and founded Dominican houses at Fiesole and Venice. He was active in the reform movement of his Order and the education of the young, and became an adviser and confessor to Pope Gregory XII. Bl. John was appointed archbishop of Ragusa and cardinal in 1406 and was one of those who convinced Gregory to resign to end the Western

Schism. Gregory's successor, Pope Martin V, appointed him legate to Bohemia and Hungary to combat the Hussites, but he died of fever soon after his arrival at Buda, on June 10. He wrote a number of scriptural commentaries and hymns in the vernacular and two treatises on education and one on charity. His cult was confirmed in 1832.

DOMITIAN (d. c. 560). A native of Gaul, he was elected bishop of Tongres, moved his see to Maestricht, and was a conspicuous figure at the Synod of Orleans in 549. He was successful in his missionary activities in the Meuse Valley and helped alleviate the suffering of the poor during a famine. May 7.

DOMITILLA (1st century). Flavia Domitilla was the wife of Flavius Clemens, a Roman consul, and daughter of Emperor Domitian's sister. She was converted to Christianity and was banished to the island of Pandatania in the Tyrrhenian Sea for her faith after her husband was martyred in 96. A niece by marriage, also called Domitilla, was banished to the island of Ponza for her faith and may have been burned to death when she refused to sacrifice to the gods. May 12.

DOMITIUS (d. c. 362). A Persian, he was converted to Christianity, became a monk at Nisibis, Mesopotamia, and after being ordained deacon, became a hermit. He drew crowds of people to his cave but incurred the enmity of Julian the Apostate when he denounced his impiety and was stoned to death. His name is also spelled Dometius, and he is probably the same as the Domitius mentioned in the Roman Martyrology on March 23 and July 5. The former was a Phrygian who when he attacked paganism at a circus at Caesarea, Palestine, where the people were honoring the gods with festival games, was killed by sword, as were also Aquila, Eparchius, Pelagia, and Theodosia during the reign of Julian the Apostate; the latter was a Persian or Phrygian monk stoned to death under similar circumstances.

DOMNEVA. See Ermenburga.

DOMNINA (d. c. 303). See Asterius.

DOMNOLUS (d. 581). According to untrustworthy sources, he was abbot of a monastery in Paris, refused the bishopric of Avignon from King Clotaire I, but later accepted the see of Le Mans from the King and was bishop there for twenty-one years. He attended the Council of Tours in 566 and built several churches and a hospice. May 16.

DOMNUS (d. 1227). See Daniel.

DONALD (8th century). A resident of Ogilvy in Forfarshire, Scotland, he formed a religious group with his nine daughters on the death of his wife. They later entered a monastery at Abernethy. July 15.

DONATA (d. 180). See Speratus.

DONATI, BL. BARTHOLOMEW (d. 1420). See Nerucci, Bl. Laurence.

DONATIAN (d. 289 or 304). Of a notable Roman-Gallo family living at Nantes, Brittany, he was charged with being a Christian and refusing to worship to the gods and was imprisoned during the persecution of the Christians by Emperor Maximian. Donatian was soon joined by his brother Rogatian, who professed Christianity but had not yet been formally professed because the local bishop was in hiding. Donatian and Rogatian were both tortured and then beheaded. May 24.

DONATIAN (d. c. 484). He, Fusculus, Germanus, Mansuetus, and Praesidius, all bishops of Byzacene, northern Africa, objected to the edict of Arian King Huneric of the Vandals closing all Catholic churches in Africa and ordering that all the possessions of the Catholic clergy be turned over to the Arian clergy. They were tortured and then banished to the desert, where all died of exposure. Laetus, bishop of Leptis Minor, was imprisoned and then burned to death at the stake at the same time. September 6.

DONATUS (d. c. 303). *See* Honoratus.

DONATUS (d. 362). Second bishop of Arezzo, Italy, the Roman Martyrology says he was martyred there during the persecution of Emperor Julian the Apostate, but there is no factual evidence that he suffered martyrdom. August 7.

DONATUS (d. c. 876). Legend has him an Irishman who, on his way back from a pilgrimage to Rome, stopped off in 829 at Fiesole, Italy, where the people were assembled to elect a new bishop. As he entered the cathedral, church bells began to ring and candles blazed alight, whereupon he was elected bishop. He later became a confidant of Lothair I and his son Louis II. October 22.

DONATUS OF BESANÇON (d. c. 660). A monk at Luxeuil, Gaul, he was named bishop of Besançon in 624. He encouraged monasticism in his see and founded St. Paul Abbey at Besançon. August 7.

DONNAN (d. 618). An Irish disciple of St. Columba, he followed the saint to Iona and later, with fifty-two companions, founded a monastery on the island of Eigg, Inner Hebrides. They were all murdered by raiding bandits just after Donnan had finished saying Mass on Easter. April 17.

DOROTHEUS (d. 303). *See* Peter.

DOROTHEUS (d. c. 362). Legend has him a scholar, the author of several treatises, and a priest at Tyre who was driven into exile during Emperor Diocletian's persecution of Christians. Dorotheus later returned, was chosen bishop of Tyre, attended the Council of Nicaea in 325, and was again forced to flee, to Odyssopolis, Thrace (Varna, Bulgaria), when Julian the Apostate's persecution began. There Dorotheus was arrested and died of the beating he received, reportedly 107 years old. June 5.

DOROTHEUS THE YOUNGER (11th century). Born of noble parents at Trebizond on the Black Sea, he left home when twelve to escape an arranged marriage and became a monk at Genna Monastery at Amisos, Pontus, where he was ordained. Ordered to build a monastery by an unknown stranger, he did so at Khiliokomos, near Amison (Samsun, Turkey), and became its abbot. He experienced ecstasies, was gifted with the ability to prophesy, and reportedly performed numerous miracles. January 5.

DOROTHY (d. 303). According to her apocryphal tradition, she was a resident of Caesarea, Cappadocia, who when she refused to sacrifice to the gods during Emperor Diocletian's persecution of the Christians was tortured by the governor and ordered executed. On the way to the place of execution, she met a young lawyer, Theophilus, who mockingly asked her to send him fruits from "the garden" she had joyously announced she would soon be in. When she knelt for her execution, she prayed, and an angel appeared with a basket of three roses and three apples, which she sent to Theophilus, telling him she would meet him in the garden. Theophilus was converted to Christianity and later was martyred. February 6.

DOROTHY OF MONTAU (1347–94). Born at Montau, Prussia, on February 6, she married a wealthy swordsmith, Albrecht of Danzig, when she was seventeen, and the couple had nine children. Her gentleness and humility completely changed the outlook of the surly Albrecht, and he accompanied her on various pilgrimages. He was not able to accompany her to Rome in 1390 because of illness; on her return she found he had died in her absence. She moved to Marienwerder in 1391 and two years later established her hermitage there, where she died on June 25. She was noted for her visions and her devotion to the Blessed Sacrament, and though never canonized, is considered a patroness of Prussia. October 30.

DOSITHEUS (d. c. 530). A pagan who visited Jerusalem, he was so impressed, he became a monk at Gaza, where he cared for the sick. He became desperately ill himself and died there. February 23.

DOTTI, ANDREW (c. 1250–1315). Born at Borgo San Sepolcro, Tuscany, of a well-known family, he was destined for the military but instead opted for the religious life, became a secular Servite when seventeen, and a few years later a Servite friar. He was ordained, became a member of the monastery of St. Gerard Sostegni, one of the seven founders of the Servites, and engaged in missionary activities and worked with St. Philip Benizi on several of his missionary trips. Andrew served as prior of several Servite houses but in 1310 received permission to live as a hermit at Montevecchio, where he died. The rest of his life was spent in prayer and penance, during which he experienced visions. His cult was approved in 1806. September 4.

DRAUSIUS (d. c. 674). Educated under Bishop St. Anseric of Soissons, France, he became an archdeacon there and then a bishop. He built a monastery at Rethondes and a convent at Soissons and two churches. He died on March 5, admired for his austerities, preaching, and wise administration of his see. He is also known as Drausin. March 7.

DREXEL, KATHARINE MARY (1858–1955). The second daughter of a wealthy Philadelphia family, Katharine Drexel's birth in 1858 was immediately followed by tragedy. Her mother, Hannah, died a little more than a month after Katharine was born. As a result, the first two years of Katharine's life were spent in the care of her aunt and uncle. In 1860, her father remarried. His bride was Emma Bovier, a devout Catholic who raised Katharine, known as Kate to the family, her sister Elizabeth and her half sister Louise. Katharine knew great luxury. The children were tutored at home, pampered with material goods, and traveled the world with their parents. Katharine cared for her stepmother during the course of a long illness and spent that time contemplating a vocation. Her stepmother died, as did her father in 1885, leaving Katharine and her sisters with the income generated by the family's vast estate. Touched by the plight of the American Indians, she and her sisters used much of their money to build schools for the Native Americans. Soon thereafter, awakened to the conditions of African Americans, Katharine once again opened her pocketbook. In 1891 she founded the Sisters of the Blessed Sacrament for Indians and Colored People and embarked on a lifetime of service to African Americans and American Indians. Her growing order founded nearly 100 schools, including Xavier University in New Orleans, the only historically African American college with ties to the Church. Katharine was canonized in 2000. March 3.

DRITHELM (d. c. 700). A resident of Northumbria, England, he reportedly died but then arose, saying he had experienced terrifying visions of heaven, hell, and purgatory. He divided his possessions equally among his wife, children, and the poor, and became a monk at Melrose. His vision caused him to live a life of great austerity and holiness. September 1.

DROCTOVEUS (d. c. 580). Also known as Drotté, he was born at Auxerre, studied under St. Germanus at Saint-Symphorien Abbey at Autun, and was appointed abbot of the monastery in Paris built by King Childebert and attached to St. Germanus' church there when Germanus became bishop of Paris. It was renamed Saint-Germain after Germanus' death. March 10.

DROGO (c. 1105–89). Also known as Druon, he was born of noble Flemish parents, was orphaned at birth, and when eighteen became a penitential pilgrim, visiting several shrines. He then was a shepherd for six years at Sebourg, near Valenciennes, revered by his neighbors for his holiness. He then resumed his pilgrimages and finally became a hermit at Sebourg for forty years until his death there. He is the patron of shepherds. April 16.

DROSTAN (d. c. 610). Of the royal Irish Cosgrach family, he became a monk under St. Columba, was first abbot of Deer Monastery in Aberdeenshire, Scotland, and then went to live as a hermit at Glenesk, Angus. July 11.

DROTTÉ. See Droctoveus.

DRUON. See Drogo.

DUBRICIUS (c. 545). According to legend, he probably was born at Madley, Wales, became a monk, and founded monasteries at Henllan and Moccas. He attracted numerous disciples to the two monasteries, and from them were founded many other monasteries and churches. He and St. Deinol were the two prelates who convinced David to attend the synod of Frefi. Dubricius spent the last years of his life at Ynys Enlli (Bardsey) and died there. Among other unreliable legends attached to his name are that he was the first bishop of Llandaff, archbishop of Caerlon-on-Usk, the bishop who crowned King Arthur at Colchester (he is the high saint of *Idylls of a King*), and that David resigned in his favor as metropolitan of Wales. Dubricius died and was buried on Bardsey Island off the coast of Wales. He is also known as Dyfrig. November 14.

DUCHESNE, BL. ROSE PHILIPPINE (1769–1852). Born on August 29 at Grenoble, France, daughter of a wealthy merchant, she was educated by the Visitation nuns of Sainte Marie d'en Haut, near Grenoble, and when seventeen, despite the objections of her parents, who wanted her married, she joined the Visitation nuns. When they were expelled from France during the Reign of Terror in 1791, she returned home, ministered to the sick, taught, and visited priest prisoners of the Revolution. She attempted to rebuild the convent at which she had been educated after the concordat of 1801 between Pope Pius VII and Napoleon had restored peaceful relations between the state and the Church, but was unsuccessful. In 1804, she persuaded Mother Madelaine Sophie Barat to accept it for her recently founded Society of the Sacred Heart, and with four others Bl. Rose became a postulant of the Society and was professed the following year. In 1818, she was sent as superioress with four nuns to the United States and founded the first American Sacred Heart house at St. Charles, near St. Louis, Missouri—a log cabin. They started the first free school west of the Mississippi there but moved to Florissant near St. Louis the following year; their first American postulant was accepted in 1820. Despite numerous difficulties, the community eventually flourished, and by 1828 it had six houses along the Mississippi River. She was allowed to resign as head of the American branch in 1840 and at the age of seventy-one began a school for Indians at Sugar Creek, Kansas, at the request of Jesuit Father De Smet. Ill health caused her to leave her Indian mission after a year, and she retired to St. Charles, where she died on October 18. She was beatified in 1940 and cannonized in 1988. November 17.

DUCKETT, BL. JAMES (d. 1602). Born at Gilfortriggs, Westmorland, England, he was raised a Protestant, became a printer's apprentice in London, and when he refused to attend Protestant religious services because of doubts about Protestantism, he was imprisoned and served two terms in prison. When released, he took instructions from a Catholic priest and became a Catholic. He devoted himself to spreading his faith by the printing and distribution of Catholic books, and after his marriage to a Catholic widow, he spent nine of the next twelve years in various prisons for his activities. He was accused of printing Father Southwell's *Supplications* (which he did not) by one Peter Bullock, who had bound books for him and was under sentence of death for another crime. When Duckett acknowledged he had Catholic books in his possession, he was found guilty of felony and sentenced to death. He was hanged with his betrayer, whom he forgave and exhorted to be constant in his faith on the gallows, at Tyburn. James was beatified in 1929. April 19.

DUCKETT, BL. JOHN (1613–44). Born at Underwinter, Yorkshire, England, and a relative of Bl. James Duckett, he stud-

ied at Douai and was ordained there in 1639. After three years of further study at Paris, he was sent on the English mission. Arrested a year later with two laymen, he was sent with Fr. Ralph Corby to London, where John admitted he was a priest, for which he was sentenced to death. He was hanged, drawn, and quartered at Tyburn, with Fr. Corby, on September 7, and was beatified in 1929.

DUFRESSE, BL. LOUIS GABRIEL TAUTIN (1751–1815). Born at Ville-de-Lezoux, Clermont, France, he joined the Society of Foreign Missions in Paris in 1774 and was sent to China three years later. He worked as a missionary in Szechwan for seven years until 1785, when he was forced into hiding. After several months he surrendered to authorities to spare his colleagues in the missionary work and was imprisoned in Peking. He was then exiled to Manila, but returned to Szechwan four years later. He was consecrated bishop in 1800 and the following year was named vicar apostolic. He administered his vicariate of some forty thousand converts with great success until a new persecution of Christians was launched. He was arrested in 1815 when betrayed by a renegade Christian and beheaded at Chintai on September 14 for being a foreign preacher. He was beatified in 1900.

DUGLIOLI, BL. HELEN (c. 1473–1520). Born at Bologna, Italy, she was married at seventeen to Benedict dall' Oglio and lived a holy and exemplary married life the next thirty years. A cult spontaneously sprang into existence on her death, and it was confirmed in 1828. September 23.

DULAS. *See* Tatian Dulas.

DU LAU, BL. JOHN (d. 1792). The archbishop of Arles, France, he was one of the 150 clerics imprisoned in the

Carmelite church (Les Carmes) on the Rue de Rennes in Paris by the French revolutionists. On the afternoon of September 2 several hundred rioters invaded the church, sworded the archbishop to death, and after a mock trial more than 100 of the clerics were executed when they refused to take the oath upholding the Civil Constitution of the Clergy, which had been denounced by Pope Pius VI and the French hierarchy. They are known as the Martyrs of Les Carmes, part of the Martyrs of September who were beatified in 1926. Some of the others who suffered martyrdom at this time with the archbishop were: Charles de la Calmette, comte de Valfons, the only layman; François Joseph de la Rochefoucauld, bishop of Beauvais, and his brother Pierre Louis, bishop of Saintes; Augustine Ambroise Chevreux, superior of the Benedictine congregation of St. Maur; and François Hébert, confessor of King Louis XIV. September 2.

DULCISSIMUS (d. c. 90). *See* Romulus.

DUMOULIN-BORIE, BL. PETER (1808–38). Born at Cors, France, he joined the Society for Foreign Missions in Paris in 1829, was ordained in 1832, and was sent as a missionary to Tonkin, Indochina. He worked in Quang-Binh Province until he was arrested. He received the appointment as titular bishop of Acanthus and vicar apostolic of West Tonkin while in prison, was tortured in a futile effort to get him to reveal the names of his missionary colleagues, and was decapitated on November 24. Also executed with him were two priests, BB. Peter Koa and Vincent Diem, natives of Tonkin, who were strangled to death. They were beatified in 1900.

DUNSTAN (c. 910–88). Born of a noble family at Baltonsborough, near Glastonbury, England, he was educated there by Irish monks and while still a youth was sent to the court of King Athelstan. He became a Benedictine monk about 934 and was ordained by his uncle, St. Alphege, bishop of Winchester, about 939. After a time as a hermit at Glastonbury, Dunstan was recalled to the royal court by King Edmund, who appointed him abbot of Glastonbury Abbey in 943. He developed the abbey into a great center of learning while revitalizing other monasteries in the area. He became adviser to King Edred on his accession to the throne when Edmund was murdered, and began a far-reaching reform of all the monasteries in Edred's realm. Dunstan also became deeply involved in secular politics and incurred the enmity of the West Saxon nobles for denouncing their immorality and for urging peace with the Danes. When Edwy succeeded his uncle Edred as King in 955, he became Dunstan's bitter enemy for the abbot's strong censure of his scandalous lifestyle. Edwy confiscated his property and banished him from his kingdom. Dunstan went to Ghent in Flanders but soon returned when a rebellion replaced Edwy with his brother Edgar, who appointed Dunstan bishop of Worcester and London in 957. When Edwy died in 959, the civil strife ended and the country was reunited under Edgar, who appointed Dunstan archbishop of Canterbury. The King and archbishop then planned a thorough reform of Church and state. Dunstan was appointed legate by Pope John XII, and with St. Ethelwold and St. Oswald, restored ecclesiastical discipline, rebuilt many of the monasteries destroyed by the Danish invaders, replaced inept secular priests with monks, and enforced the widespread reforms they put into effect. Dunstan served as Edgar's chief adviser for sixteen years and did not hesitate to reprimand him when he thought it deserved. When Edgar died, Dunstan helped elect Edward the

Martyr King and then his half brother Ethelred when Edward died soon after his election. Under Ethelred, Dunstan's influence began to wane and he retired from politics to Canterbury to teach at the cathedral school and died there. Dunstan has been called the reviver of monasticism in England. He was a noted musician, played the harp, composed several hymns, notably *Kyrie Rex splendens*, was a skilled metalworker, and illuminated manuscripts. He is the patron of armorers, goldsmiths, locksmiths, and jewelers. May 19.

DUTHAC (d. c. 1065). A Scotsman, he was educated in Ireland, was ordained, and became bishop of Ross, Scotland. He was highly venerated for his miracles and prophecies (one of which predicted the Danish invasion). March 8.

DUYNE, GODFREY VAN (d. 1572). *See* Vechel, Leonard.

DYFRIG. *See* Dubricius.

D'YOUVILLE, MARIE MARGUERITE (1701–1771). Born in 1701 in Quebec, Marie Marguerite d'Youville knew suffering. She was raised in poverty as the result of her father's death when she was seven. Her 1722 marriage to Francois d'Youville was an unhappy one; she was a battered wife. Four of her six children died as babies, and her husband, before his death in 1730, was known more for his drinking and illegal liquor trading than for his devotion to his family. Despite her many trials, Marie's faith in God grew strong. Her faith was manifested by her devotion to the poor. From the small proceeds of a store she ran in Montreal, she shared the little she and her surviving two sons had with the poor. In 1737 she founded the Sisters of Charity of Montreal, the "Grey Nuns," with three other devout young women. She and her sisters administered Montreal's Charon Brothers Hospital, the first of her institutional charitable works that has expanded today to include the establishment of hospitals and schools throughout Canada. She was canonized in 1990. December 23.

DYMPHNA (d. c. 650). Her popular legend has her the daughter of a pagan Celtic chieftain, whether Irish, Briton, or Armorican is uncertain, though probably Irish, and a Christian. She fled from home on the death of her mother to escape the incestuous interest of her father and went to Antwerp accompanied by her confessor, St. Gerebernus, and two companions. They then built an oratory at Gheel, near Amsterdam, where they lived as hermits. Tracked down by Dymphna's father, the two companions and the priest were murdered by his men, and Dymphna was beheaded by her father when she refused to return with him. When the bodies of Dymphna and Gerebernus were discovered at Gheel in the thirteenth century, many cures were reported at her tomb of epileptics, the insane, and those possessed. She is the patroness of epileptics and those suffering from mental illnesses. May 15.

E

EADBERT. *See* Edbert.

EANSWIDA (d. c. 640). The daughter of King Edbald of Kent, she resisted her father's plans to marry her to a pagan Northumbrian prince, founded a convent with her father's consent near Folkestone, Kent, in 630 and spent the rest of her life in prayer and penance until her death there on August 31. September 12.

EATA (d. 686). One of the twelve English boys brought to Northumbria by St. Aidan, Eata became abbot of Melrose. He accepted the Roman liturgical observances after the Synod of Whitby and replaced St. Colman (reportedly at Colman's request) as abbot of Lindisfarne when Colman refused to abandon the Celtic observations and migrated to the Isle of Inishbofin off the coast of Connacht. Eata was appointed bishop of Lindisfarne in 678 and later exchanged sees with St. Cuthbert and became bishop of Hexham, where he remained until his death. October 26.

EBBA THE ELDER (d. 683). The sister of SS. Oswald and Oswy, Kings of Northumbria, she refused to marry the King of the Scots and was habited by St. Finan at Lindisfarne. She built the monastery of Ebbchester on ground donated by Oswy and then built a double monastery on the coast of Berwick at Coldingham, of which she was first abbess; evidently her enforcement of discipline was notoriously lax. August 25.

EBBA THE YOUNGER (d. c. 870). Abbess of the Benedictine convent at Coldingham on the Scottish border, she mutilated her face during a raid by Danish marauding forces to repel the raiders intent on rape. All those in the convent were killed when the raiders set fire to the convent. April 2.

EBBO (d. 740). Born at Tonnerre, France, he became a Benedictine monk at St. Pierre-le-Vif in Sens and in 709 was named bishop of Sens. He saved the city from destruction by the Moors when they besieged it in 725. August 27.

EBERHARD, BL. (d. 958). Of Swabia's ducal family, he became provost of the Strasbourg cathedral but resigned in 934 to go to St. Benno's hermitage on Mount Etzel in Switzerland. There he built a Benedictine monastery he named Our Lady of the Hermits, which became famous as Einsiedeln, serving as its first abbot. August 14.

EBERHARD, BL. (d. c. 1150). Count of Mons, Flanders, he came to regret the violence of his military life and for penance became a swineherd at Morimond Cistercian abbey. He became a monk when his identity was discovered, continued his penances, and in 1142 founded Einberg and Mont St. George monasteries. March 20.

EBERHARD (c. 1085–1164). Born at Nuremberg, Germany, of a noble family, he was educated by the Benedictines at Hamberg, where he was ordained and became a canon at the cathedral there. He resigned his canonry to enter Mount St. Michael Abbey, received his master's degree at Paris, became a Benedictine at Prüfening in 1125, and was later appointed abbot of a monastery at Biburg, near Regensburg, founded by his brothers and sisters. The community flourished under his direction, and in 1146 he was appointed archbishop of Salzburg. He acted as mediator in several ecclesiastical disputes and put into effect numerous reforms in his see. He supported Pope Alexander III against Frederick Barbarossa's antipope, Victor IV, and died on June 11 at Rein Cistercian abbey while returning from a peacemaking mission. June 22.

EBERHARD, BL. (d. c. 1178). A Premonstratensian monk at Roth, he was appointed abbot of Marchthal, Swabia, in 1166 when that monastery was rebuilt by Count Hugo of Tübingen at the request of his wife, Elizabeth. April 17.

EBRULF (517–96) Born at Bayeux, Normandy, he was raised at the court of King Childebert I, married, but left the court when he and his wife decided to separate—she to become a nun and he to become a monk at Deux Jumeaux Abbey at Bayeux. He left to live as a solitary in Ouche Forest in Normandy. He converted many to his way of life, became abbot-founder of a monastery at Ouche, and founded several others. He is also known as Evroult. December 29.

EDBERT (d. 698). A biblical scholar and a monk at Lindisfarne, he succeeded St. Cuthbert as bishop of Lindisfarne and was known for his generosity to the poor. His name is also spelled Eadbert. May 6.

EDBURGA (d. 751). Of the royal family of Kent, she was a disciple of St. Mildred and succeeded her as abbess of Minster-in-Thanet. While on pilgrimage to Rome, she met St. Boniface, with whom she engaged in a lengthy correspondence. She was a noted calligrapher and built a new church for her convent at Minster. December 12.

EDBURGA OF WINCHESTER (d. 960). Daughter of King Edward the Elder and his third wife, Edgiva, she became a nun at the abbey at Winchester and later was its abbess, known for her charity and miracles. June 15.

EDDOCWY. *See* Oudoceus.

EDITH OF POLESWORTH (d. c. 925). The sister of King Athelstan of England, she married Viking King Sihtric at York in 925, and when he died the next year she became a Benedictine nun at Polesworth, Warwickshire, where she was noted for her holiness and may have become abbess. She may also have been the sister of King Edgar and aunt of St. Edith of Wilton; or possibly these were two different women named Edith of Polesworth. July 15.

EDITH OF WILTON (962–84). Daughter of King Edgar of England and Wulfrida, she was born at Kemsing, England, and was brought as a very young child to Wilton Abbey by her mother, who later became a nun there and abbess. Edith became a nun when fifteen, declined her father's offer of three abbacies, and refused to leave the convent to become Queen when her half brother King Edward the Martyr was murdered, as many of the nobles requested. She built St. Denis Church at Wilton. September 16.

EDMUND OF ABINGDON (c. 1180–1240). Born at Abingdon, Berkshire, England, on November 30, Edmund Rich studied at Oxford and Paris. He taught art and mathematics at Oxford, received his doctorate in theology, and was ordained. He taught theology for eight years and about 1222 became canon and treasurer of Salisbury Cathedral. He was an eloquent and popular preacher, preached a crusade against the Saracens at the request of Pope Gregory IX in 1227, was elected archbishop of Canterbury in 1233, and was consecrated in 1234 against his wishes. He was an adviser to King Henry III, undertook several diplomatic missions for the King, and in 1237 presided at Henry's ratification of the Great Charter. Edmund protested Henry's action in securing the appointment of a papal legate, Cardinal Ott, to England as an infringement of his episcopal rights. A rebellion by the monks of Christ Church at Canterbury, supported by Henry, to eliminate his rights there caused him to go to Rome in 1237, and on his return he excommunicated seventeen of the monks—an action that was opposed by his suffragans, Henry, and Cardinal Otto who lifted the excommunications. Edmund then became involved in a dispute with Otto over the King's practice of leaving benefices unoccupied so the crown could collect their revenues. When Rome withdrew the archbishop's authority to fill benefices left vacant for six months, he left England in 1240 and retired to the Cistercian abbey at Pontigny. He died at Soissons, France, on November 16 and was canonized in 1247 by Pope Innocent IV. The only surviving medieval hall at Oxford, St. Edmund's, is named in his honor, and according to tradition it was built on the site of his tomb.

EDMUND THE MARTYR (841–70). He was elected King of the East Angles in 855 when only fourteen and of Suffolk the following year. He ruled wisely until 870, when a great invasion of England by the Danes begun in 866 reached his domain. He was captured at Hoxne, Suffolk, by the invaders under Ingvar, subjected to torture, and then beheaded. November 20.

EDWARD THE CONFESSOR (1003–66). Son of King Ethelred III and his Norman wife, Emma, daughter of Duke Richard I of Normandy, he was born at Islip, England, and sent to Normandy with his mother in 1013 when the Danes under Sweyn and his son Canute invaded England. Canute remained in England and the year after Ethelred's death in 1016, married Emma, who had returned to England, and became King of England. Edward remained in Normandy, was brought up a Norman, and in 1042, on the death of his half brother Hardicanute, son of Canute and Emma, and largely through the support of the powerful Earl Godwin, he was acclaimed King of England. In 1044, he married Godwin's daughter Edith. His reign was a peaceful one characterized by his good rule and remission of odious taxes but also by the struggle, partly caused by his natural inclination to favor the Normans, between Godwin and his Saxon supporters and the Norman barons, including Robert of Jumièges, whom Edward had brought with him when he returned to England and whom he named archbishop of Canterbury in 1051. In the same year, Edward banished Godwin, who took refuge in Flanders but returned the following year with a fleet ready to lead a rebellion. Armed revolt was avoided when the two men met and settled their differences; among them was the archbishopric of Canterbury, which was resolved when Edward replaced Robert with Stigand, and Robert returned to Normandy. Edward's difficulties continued after

Godwin's death in 1053 with Godwin's two sons: Harold who had his eye on the throne since Edward was childless, and Tostig, earl of Northumbria. Tostig was driven from Northumbria by a revolt in 1065 and banished to Europe by Edward, who named Harold his successor. After this Edward became more interested in religious affairs and built St. Peter's Abbey at Westminster, the site of the present cathedral, where he is buried. His piety gained him the surname "the Confessor." He died in London on January 5, and he was canonized in 1161 by Pope Alexander III. October 13.

EDWARD THE MARTYR (c. 963–78). Eldest son of King Edward the Peaceful of England and his wife, Ethelfleda, he was baptized by St. Dunstan and became King in 975 on his father's death with the support of Dunstan but against the wishes of his stepmother, Queen Elfrida, who wished the throne for her son Ethelred. Edward ruled only three years when he was murdered on March 18 while hunting near Corfe Castle, reportedly by adherents of Ethelred, though William of Malmesbury, the English historian of the twelfth century, said Elfrida was the actual murderer.

EDWIN (c. 585–633). Son of King Aella of Deira (South Northumbria), he was only three when his father died. Edwin was deprived of the throne by King Ethelfrith of Bernicia (North Northumbria), who seized Aella's kingdom. Edwin spent the next thirty years in Mercia and finally was restored to the throne by King Baedwald of East Anglia, who defeated and killed Ethelfrith at the battle of Idle River in 617. Edwin ruled ably and in 625, after the death of his first wife, married Ethelburga, sister of King Eadbald of Kent, and a Christian, who brought with her to Northumbria her confessor, Paulinus. Edwin established

law and order in the kingdom and soon became the most powerful King in England. Through the efforts of Ethelburga and Paulinus, he was converted to Christianity in 627, and appointed Paulinus, who had baptized him, bishop of York. Many in Edwin's court were also converted, and thus began Christianity in Northumbria. His intention to build a stone church at York (an unprecedented event in those days) never materialized when his kingdom was invaded by pagan King Penda of Mercia and Cadwallon of North Wales. Edwin was defeated and killed at the Battle of Heathfield on October 12.

EEM, THEODORE VAN DER (d. 1572). *See* Pieck, Nicholas.

EGBERT (c. 639–729). An English monk at Lindisfarne, he went to the monastery of Rathmelsigi in Ireland for further study and was ordained. He became known for his holiness and his learning and spent the last thirteen years of his life at Iona trying to convince the monks there to abandon the Celtic liturgical practices in favor of the Roman practices, which by this time had been universally adopted throughout the British Isles. He was finally successful and Iona observed the Roman date for Easter for the first time on the day he died, April 24. According to British historian Bede, he was a bishop.

EGINO (d. 1122). Born at Augsburg, Bavaria, he was sent to SS. Ulric and Afra Abbey there when a child and became a monk. He was expelled by his abbot when he supported the Pope in a dispute with the Emperor and went to St. Blaise Abbey. He returned to Augsburg in 1106 and was named abbot in 1109. He was again forced to leave for his condemnation of the simoniacal activities of Bishop Herimann and went to Rome in 1120. He died at the Camaldolese monastery at Pisa. July 15.

EGWIN (d. 717). Descended from the Mercian Kings, he became a religious in his youth and about 692 was named bishop of Worcester, England. He made a penitential pilgrimage to Rome to defend himself against charges of overseverity with his clergy, and on his return, aided by King Ethelred of Mercia, founded Evesham Monastery (purportedly as the result of a vision of Mary), which developed into one of the great Benedictine monasteries of medieval England. About 709, he made another pilgrimage to Rome, accompanied by King Cenred of Mercia and King Offa of the East Saxons. December 30.

EILUNED. *See* Almedha.

ELDRED (d. 870). *See* Theodore.

ELEAZAR (d. 160 B.C.). *See* Maccabees, the Holy.

ELESBAAN (6th century). At the request of Emperor Justin I and the patriarch of Alexandria, Aksumite King Elesbaan led an expedition against Dunaan, a convert to Judaism, who had led a revolt of Jews and Arabs against the rule of Aksumite Ethiopians at Yemen and had slaughtered every Christian man, woman, and child in the town of Najran in southern Arabia who would not apostatize. Elesbaan defeated and killed Dunaan and then permitted atrocities against Dunaan's followers as dreadful as those committed by Dunaan. Elesbaan is said to have turned over his throne to his son, and he became an exemplary anchorite for the rest of his life. Though he is listed in the Roman Martyrology, he may have been a monophysite. October 24.

ELEUCHADIUS (d. 112). Born in Greece, he went to Italy, where he was converted to Christianity by St. Apollinaris, bishop of Ravenna. He helped run the church there when Apollinaris was away. Eleuchadius was named bishop of that diocese in 100. February 14.

ELEUSIPPUS (d. c. 155). A pious fictional legend has Eleusippus, Meleusippus, and Speusippus triplets who were martyred for their Christianity at Langres, France, during the reign of Marcus Aurelius. January 17.

ELEUTHERIUS (d. c. 189). Son of one Habundius, he was a Greek of Nicopolis, Epirus, who became a deacon in Rome and was elected Pope about 174 to succeed St. Soter. He is known only for his decree that any food fit for humans was suitable for Christians—probably issued against the rigorism of the Gnostics and the Montanists. He probably died on May 24 in Rome. May 26.

ELEUTHERIUS (2nd century). A pious but fictional legend has him a Christian Roman who was educated by a Bishop Dynamius and who became a deacon at sixteen and was ordained when eighteen. When twenty, he was consecrated bishop of Illyrium, was arrested, and was brought before Emperor Hadrian for converting a royal official to Christianity, was miraculously saved from several terrible deaths to which he was condemned, and was eventually clubbed to death with eleven companions. His mother, Anthia, was put to death by sword shortly afterward. April 18.

ELEUTHERIUS (d. c. 258). *See* Dionysius.

ELEUTHERIUS (d. c. 303). According to the Roman Martyrology, he was a soldier in Nicomedia when Emperor Diocletian's palace there was burned. Accused of being the ringleader of a group that had set the fire, he was tortured and then burned to death. October 2.

ELEUTHERIUS (d. 532). Born at Tournai, Gaul, of Christian parents, he became bishop of that city in 486. He was so successful in evangelizing the area with his powerful preaching and denunciation of Arianism that he was attacked by a group of Arians while leaving his church and was so severely beaten he died five weeks later. February 20.

ELEUTHERIUS (d. c. 590). According to St. Gregory's *Dialogues,* he was abbot of St. Mark's Monastery near Spoleto, Italy, performed many miracles, and died in Gregory's monastery in Rome, where he had lived many years prior to his death. September 6.

ELFGETE (d. 870). *See* Theodore.

ELFLEDA (d. 714). The daughter of King Oswy of Northumbria, she was taken when a child to Hartlepool convent and later became a nun there. She accompanied her abbess, St. Hilda, to Whitby, where Hilda founded an abbey, and on the death of Hilda, Elfleda became joint abbess with her mother, Eanfleda. Elfleda was very influential in ecclesiastical affairs, acted as peacemaker in a dispute between St. Wilfrid and St. Theodore, and was a close friend of St. Cuthbert. She died at Whitby. February 8.

ELIAS (d. 309). He and four companions, Daniel, Isaias, Jeremy, and Samuel, were Egyptians who visited Christians condemned to work in the mines of Cilicia during Maximus' persecution, to comfort them. Apprehended at the gates of Cilicia, Palestine, they were brought before the governor, Firmilian, and accused of being Christians. They were all tortured and then beheaded. When Porphyry, a servant of St. Pamphilus, demanded that the bodies be buried, he

was tortured and then burned to death when it was found he was a Christian. Seleucus witnessed his death and applauded his constancy in the face of his terrible death; whereupon he was arrested by the soldiers involved in the execution, brought before the governor, and was beheaded at Firmilian's order. February 16.

ELIAS (d. 310). *See* Peleus.

ELIAS (d. 518). An Arab who was educated in an Egyptian monastery, he was driven from Egypt by monophysite Bishop Timothy the Cat of Alexandria for his Catholic orthodoxy. He went to Palestine, where he stayed for a time at St. Euthymius' *laura,* founded a monastery at Jericho, and was ordained. In 494 he was elected patriarch of Jerusalem. Although he had accepted Emperor Zeno's *Henotikon* of 482, which was condemned for its bias in favor of monophysitism, Elias remained loyal to Rome. In 512 the synod of Sidon supported Elias and his colleague, Bishop Flavian of Antioch, and the decrees of the Council of Chalcedon (451), though the synod had been summoned to denounce Chalcedon and to depose the two bishops, who strongly supported Chalcedon. Elias was exiled to Aila on the Red Sea in 513 when he refused to sign Emperor Anastasius I's formula supporting monophysitism and died there. July 20.

ELIAS (d. 856). According to the eyewitness account of St. Eulogius, he was an aged priest at Cordova, Spain, who was executed for his faith, with Isidore and Paul, two young men he was instructing in the faith. April 17.

ELIGIUS (c. 590–c. 660). The son of Roman-Gallo parents and also known as Eloi, he was born at Chaptel, Gaul. His father, Eucherius, was a metalsmith and apprenticed Eligius to Abbo, a gold-smith, who was master of the mint at Limoges. After his apprenticeship, Eligius worked under Bobbo, the royal treasurer, and became master of the mint for King Clotaire I in Paris. Eligius became a leading craftsman noted for his exquisite work and a close friend of Clotaire. Eligius' increased influence and affluence allowed him to be generous to the poor, to ransom numerous slaves, and to build several churches, and in 632 he founded and built a monastery at Solignac and a convent in Paris built on property granted him by Clotaire's son Dagobert I, who had appointed him his chief counselor in 629. Eligius went on a diplomatic mission to the Bretons for Dagobert in 636 and convinced Breton King Judicael to accept the authority of the Frankish King. Eligius was ordained in 640 and made bishop of Noyon and Tournai. He evangelized Flanders and converted many in the area around Antwerp, Ghent, and Courtrai despite great opposition. He founded a convent at Noyon, acted as counselor to Queen-regent St. Bathildis, and died at Noyon on December 1. He is the patron of metalworkers and metalsmiths and was one of the best-known and -loved persons of his time.

ELIZABETH (1st century). *See* Zachary.

ELIZABETH THE GOOD. *See* Achler, Bl. Elizabeth.

ELIZABETH OF HUNGARY (1207–1231). Daughter of Andrew II of Hungary and Gertrude of Andechs-Meran, she was born at Pressburg (Bratislava) or Saros-Patak, Hungary, and when four was brought to the court of Landgrave Herman I of Thuringia at Wartburg Castle, near Eisenach, as the betrothed of his son Ludwig. They were married in 1221 when Ludwig had become landgrave, had four children, and

were an ideal married couple. She became known for her great charity, built a hospital at the foot of their castle, and another one. They were married six years when Ludwig went on crusade with Emperor Frederick II and died of the plague at Otranto. She was heartbroken, and to add to her troubles she was accused of mismanaging his estate because of her great charity; she was forced to leave Wartburg, probably forced out by her brother-in-law. She made provision for her children and in 1228 became a Franciscan tertiary. She lived for a time at Marburg and devoted herself to caring for the sick, the aged, and the poor at a hospice there. During this time her spiritual adviser was Conrad of Marburg, whose harsh methods of guiding her spiritual life have been sharply criticized. She led a life of exceptional poverty and humility and was allowed back to the castle four years before her death by the usurper, who also recognized her son's succession to the title of landgrave. She died at Marburg on November 17, not yet twenty-four, and soon miracles were reported at her tomb. She was canonized by Pope Gregory IX in 1235.

ELIZABETH OF PORTUGAL (1271–1336). Daughter of King Peter III of Aragon, she was named after her grandaunt, Elizabeth of Hungary. Elizabeth of Portugal was married when twelve to King Denis of Portugal, became known for her piety, charity, and concern for the poor, and founded convents, hospitals, foundling homes, and shelters for wayward girls. She was sometimes called "the Peacemaker" for her role in settling disputes between her husband and their son, Alfonso, who twice led rebellions against his father; between Ferdinand IV of Castile and his cousin Alfonso IV of Aragon; and between Ferdinand and her brother James II of Aragon. She was exiled for a time from the court when Denis thought she was favoring Alfonso. After Denis' death in 1325 she was persuaded to give up her idea of becoming a nun and became instead a Franciscan tertiary. She died on July 4 at Estremoz, Portugal, and was canonized in 1626. She is known as Isabella in Portugal.

ELIZABETH OF SCHÖNAU (c. 1129–64). Of humble birth, she entered the Benedictine double monastery of Schönau near Bonn, Germany, when she was twelve, was professed in 1147, and at once began to practice the greatest austerities. About 1152 she had her first vision, and throughout the rest of her life experienced many supernatural manifestations—visions, ecstasies, prophecies, and often diabolical visitations that left her bruised and beaten. She described her visions, especially of the Passion, Resurrection, and Ascension in three books recorded at first by her brother Egbert, who became a monk at Schönau and later was its abbot. Some of the visions described in her books are inaccurate and have been questioned by scholars, and in one of them she supported antipope Victor IV, a friend of her brother, but her sincerity was never questioned, and she was held in the highest esteem. She became abbess in 1157 and died at Schönau seven years later, on June 18. She has never been formally beatified or canonized, although she is referred to as St. Elizabeth in the Roman Martyrology.

ELMO. See Erasmus.

ELOI. See Eligius.

ELPHEGE. See Alphege.

ELZEAR (1285–1323). Of noble parents, he was born at the family castle at Ansouis, Provence, France, was educated at St. Victor's monastery in Marseilles by his uncle, who was abbot and was mar-

ried to Delphina of Giandièves when both were sixteen. He inherited his father's estate, becoming lord of Ansouis and count of Ariano in the Kingdom of Naples when he was twenty-three. He managed his estate with firmness, prudence, and ability and Elzear and Delphina were regarded as an ideal married couple, known for their holiness and piety. In 1317, they joined the court of King Robert of Naples, and Elzear became tutor to the King's son Charles. Elzear was named justiciar of southern Abruzzi by Robert, acted as Robert's envoy to France to arrange the marriage of Mary of Valois and Charles, fell ill on the trip, and died in Paris on September 27. Elzear was canonized in 1369 in a ceremony attended by Delphina. September 26.

EMERENTIANA (d. c. 304). According to the Roman Martyrology, she was a catechumen in Rome who was stoned to death there while praying at the tomb of her foster sister St. Agnes. January 23.

EMERIC (1007–31). The only son of King St. Stephen of Hungary, who planned to have him succeed him as King, Emeric was killed while hunting. Many miracles were reported at his tomb at Szekesfehervar, and he was canonized, with his father, in 1083. November 4.

EMERUS (8th century). A French Benedictine, he was founder-abbot of St. Stephen of Bañoles abbey near Garona, Spain. His mother, St. Candida (January 27), lived as a recluse near the abbey and died there about 798. January 27.

EMETERIUS (d. 303). Tradition has him and his brother Chelidonius soldiers, sons of St. Marcellus. They were both executed by sword for their faith during Diocletian's persecution of the Christians at Calahorra, Old Castile,

Spain. They are the patrons of Santander in northern Spain. March 3.

EMILIAN (d. 259). *See* Agapius.

EMILIAN CUCULLATUS (d. 574). A shepherd at La Rioja, Navarre, Spain, he became a hermit when twenty and then after a brief stay at home spent the next forty years as a hermit in the mountains around Burgos when at the insistence of the bishop of Tarazona, he was ordained. He became a parish priest at Berceo but because of his excessive charity was forced to leave and with several disciples resumed his eremitical life. Tradition says the mountain hermitage he occupied near Burgos became the site of the Benedictine monastery of La Cogolla. He is known in Spain as San Millan de la Cogolla—the cowled St. Emilian. November 12.

EMILIANA (d. c. 550). Aunt of St. Gregory the Great, she and her sister Tharsilla lived a life of prayer and great austerity in Rome at the home of their brother, Gregory's father. Emiliana died on January 5, a few days after Tharsilla (also spelled Tarsilla). December 24.

EMILIANI, JEROME (1481–1537). Born at Venice, Italy, he became a soldier and was commander of the League of Cambrai forces at Castelnuevo near Treviso. When Castelnuevo fell to the Venetians, he was captured and imprisoned. He escaped, reformed his carefree lifestyle, became mayor of Treviso, and then returned to Venice, where he was ordained in 1518. While aiding plague and famine victims, he was especially touched by the plight of orphans and decided to devote himself to aiding orphans and founded orphanages at Brescia, Bergamo, and Como, a hospital at Verona, and a home for repentant prostitutes. About 1532, he and two other priests founded a congregation that became known as the Clerks Regular of Somascha, named after the town in which they established their first house, devoted to caring for orphans and educating children and priests. He died on February 8 at Somascha of an infectious disease he caught while ministering to its victims. His congregation was papally approved in 1540, and he was canonized in 1767. He was named patron saint of orphans and abandoned children in 1928.

EMILY DE RODAT. *See* Rodat, Emily de.

EMMA (d. c. 1045). A relative of Emperor St. Henry II and also known as Hemma, she was raised at Henry's court by St. Cunegund, and according to legend was married to Landgrave William of Friesach. Their two children were murdered during an uprising at mines owned by William. Griefstricken, he made a pilgrimage to Rome and died on the way back; Emma decided to devote her life to God. She gave liberally to the poor, founded several religious houses and a double monastery at Gurk, Austria, and may have become a nun there. Despite the above legend, scholars believe she was of the Friesach family rather than William and that her son was killed in a battle twenty years after the death of her husband, Count William of Sanngan, about 1015, and it was at this time that she began her foundations. Her cult was confirmed in 1938. June 29.

EMMELIA (4th century). *See* Basil (d. c. 370).

EMMERAMUS (d. c. 690). A missionary priest in the area around Poitiers, France, he left to preach the gospel in Bavaria at the request of Duke Theodo. After three years of successful convert work, Emmeramus went on pilgrimage to

Rome but on the way was attacked at Kleinhelfendorf, near Munich, by followers of Theodo (for reasons unknown), and died of his wounds at Feldkirchen. He is reputed to have been bishop of Poitiers and then of Regensburg, but these are probably not so. September 22.

EMYGDIUS (d. 304). According to legend, he was a pagan Teuton living in Trier who was converted to Christianity. He went to Rome and was forced to flee the wrath of the pagans when he destroyed an idol in a pagan temple. He was ordained and consecrated a bishop by Pope Marcellus I, who sent him to evangelize the region around Ascoli Piceno. His great success in making converts caused him to be arrested and beheaded during Diocletian's persecution of the Christians along with Eupolus, Germanus, and Valentius, three of his followers. He could not have been ordained by Marcellus, who was Pope 308–9, but could have been by Marcellinus, who reigned 296–304. Emygdius is the patron against earthquakes. August 9.

ENCRATIS (d. 304). Honored in a poem by the poet Prudentius, she was a native of Saragossa, Spain, who during Diocletian's persecution of Christians was subjected to terrible tortures by order of Governor Dacian but managed to survive them. April 16.

ENDA (d. c. 530). Legend has him an Irishman noted for his military feats who was convinced by his sister St. Fanchea to renounce his warring activities and marry. When he found his fiancée dead, he decided to become a monk and went on pilgrimage to Rome, where he was ordained. He returned to Ireland, built churches at Drogheda, and then secured from his brother-in-law King Oengus of Munster the island of Aran, where he built the monastery of Killeaney, from which ten other foundations on the island developed. With St. Finnian of Clonard, Enda is considered the founder of monasticism in Ireland. March 21.

ENECO. *See* Iñigo.

ENGELBERT (1187–1225). Son of the count of Berg, he was born at Berg and was made provost of several churches, including the Cologne cathedral while still a schoolboy studying at the cathedral school at Cologne. He was excommunicated for taking up arms against Emperor Otto IV, joined the crusade against the Albigensians, had the excommunication lifted, and was appointed archbishop of Cologne in 1217 when only thirty. He ruled the see well, restored clerical discipline, brought Franciscans and Dominicans into the diocese, held regular synods, encouraged monastic life, and was generous to the poor. He was also deeply involved in politics, supporting Emperor Frederick II (who appointed him regent during the minority of Henry's son in 1220 when the Emperor went to Sicily) and crowning Henry King of the Romans in 1222. He became embroiled in a dispute in 1225 with his cousin Count Frederick of Isenberg, whom he denounced for stealing the property of nuns in Essen for whom Frederick was acting as administrator. Frederick retaliated by waylaying Engelbert at Gevelsberg, Germany, and murdering him there on November 7. Although he has never been formally canonized, he is referred to in the Roman Martyrology as St. Engelbert, and his feast is observed in Cologne.

ENGELMUND (d. c. 720). Born and educated in Britain, he became a Benedictine monk in his youth, was ordained, and became abbot of his community, noted for his learning and holiness. He joined St. Willibrord in missionary work in the Netherlands and was most successful in making converts in the area around Haarlem. June 21.

ENNODIUS (473–521). Of a well-known Gallo-Roman family, Magnus Felix Ennodius was born at Arles, France, was educated at Milan, and was married. After several years together he and his wife parted—she to become a nun and he to be ordained deacon by St. Epiphanius of Ticinum (Pavia). Ennodius was a skilled rhetor, was secretary to the papal claimant Laurentius of Milan, and about 514 was appointed bishop of Ticinum. He went on two diplomatic missions to Emperor Anastasius II for Pope Honorius to admonish the Emperor over his leniency to the monophysites but was unsuccessful in his mission both times. He was noted for his help to the poor, his conversions, the churches he built, and his writings, among them biographies of St. Antonius of Lérins, an autobiography, a handbook of rhetoric, and poetry and letters. He died at Ticinum. July 17.

EOBAN (d. 755). Probably of Irish descent, he became a Benedictine, was ordained, and worked as a missionary with SS. Willibrord and Boniface in Germany. Eoban was put to death for his faith with Boniface at Dokkum, Holland. June 5.

EOGHAN. See Eugene (d. c. 618).

EPAPHRODITUS (1st century). Mentioned with great affection and esteem by St. Paul (Phil. 1:25), he is traditionally considered the first bishop of Philippi, Macedonia. Both Andriaci in Lycia and Terracina in Italy also list an Epaphroditus as their first bishop. March 22.

EPARCHIUS (d. 581). Also known as Cybard, he was the duke of Périgord, and despite the objections of his parents,

he became a monk at a monastery at Bordogne, France (later known as Saint-Cybard Monastery), and then to escape public attention, he lived as a hermit near Angoulême. He was compelled to accept ordination by his bishop and attracted numerous disciples, whom he governed. July 1.

EPHRAEM (c. 306–c. 373). Born at Nisibis, Mesopotamia, he was long thought to be the son of a pagan priest, but it is now believed his parents were Christians. He was baptized at eighteen, served under St. James of Nisibis, became head of his school, and probably accompanied him to the Council of Nicaea in 325. Syrian sources attribute the deliverance of Nisibis from the Persians in 350 to his prayers, but when Nisibis was ceded to the Persians by Emperor Jovian in 363, he took residence in a cave near Edessa in Roman territory, often preaching to the Christians, though he was probably only a deacon. It was here that he did most of his writing. Tradition says he visited St. Basil at Caesarea in 370 and on his return helped alleviate the rigors of the famine of winter 372–73 by distributing food and money to the stricken and helping the poor. He died at Edessa on June 9. Ephraem wrote voluminously in Syriac on exegetical, dogmatic, and ascetical themes, drawing heavily on scriptural sources. He wrote against the heretics—especially the Arians and the Gnostics—and on the Last Judgment, and was devoted to the Blessed Virgin (he is often invoked as a witness to the Immaculate Conception because of his absolute certainty of Mary's sinlessness). He was responsible in large measure for introducing hymns in public worship and used them effectively in religious instruction. His works were early translated into Greek, Armenian, and Latin. Particularly outstanding are his Nisibeian hymns and the canticles for the seasons. He was called "the Harp of the Holy Spirit," and in 1920 Pope Benedict XV declared him a Doctor of the Church, the only Syrian to be so honored. June 9.

EPIMACHUS (d. 250). A native of Alexandria, Egypt, he, with Alexander, was imprisoned, then tortured and burned to death for his faith at Alexandria during Decius' persecution of the Christians. At the same time and place four women were also tortured and executed for their faith: Ammonaria; the aged Mercuria; Dionisia, a mother; and a fourth, unknown woman, possibly also named Ammonaria. December 12.

EPIPHANIUS (439–96). Born at Pavia, Italy, he was elected bishop of Pavia in 467, rebuilt the city after it was destroyed by Odoacer, and was famous for his holiness. He converted many with his eloquence, gave aid to the famine-stricken, and made many missions to promote peace to such varied rulers as Emperor Anthemius, Visigoth King Euric, Ostrogoth King Theodoric, and the Burgundian Gondebald. His efforts won him the title of "Peacemaker." He died at Pavia on his return from a mission to secure the release of captives held by Gondebald and Godegisilus. January 21.

EPIPHANIUS OF SALAMIS (c. 315–403). Born at Besanduk, Palestine, he became an expert in the languages needed to understand Scripture. After a time as a monk in Palestine, he went to Egypt and stayed at several desert communities. He returned to Palestine about 333, was ordained, and became superior of a monastery at Eleutheropolis, which he had built. He achieved a widespread reputation for his scholarship, austerities, mortifications, spiritual wisdom, and advice. Called "the Oracle of Palestine," he became bishop of Constantia (Salamis), Cyprus, and met-

ropolitan of Cyprus in 367, although still continuing as superior of his monastery. His reputation was such that he was one of the few orthodox bishops not harassed by Arian Emperor Valens, though Epiphanius preached vigorously against Arianism. He supported Bishop Paulinus in 376 at Antioch against the claims of Metetius and the Eastern bishops, attended a council in Rome summoned by Pope Damasus in 382, and was embroiled in several unpleasant episodes with fellow prelates late in his life—denouncing his host, Bishop John of Jerusalem, in John's cathedral in 394 for John's softness to Origenism (he believed Origen responsible for many of the heresies of the times), ordaining a priest in another bishop's diocese, and in 402, at the behest of Theophilus of Alexandria, denouncing at Constantinople the four "Tall Brothers" and then admitting he knew nothing of their teachings. Epiphanius realized he was being used as a tool by Theophilus against John Chrysostom, who had given refuge to the monks who had been persecuted by Theophilus and were appealing to the Emperor, and started back to Salamis, only to die on the way home. He wrote numerous theological treatises, among them *Ancoratus,* on the Trinity and the Resurrection; *Panarion,* on some eighty heresies and their refutations; and *De mensuribus et ponderibus,* on ancient Jewish customs and measures. He was an authority on devotion to Mary and taught the primacy of Peter among the apostles. May 12.

EPIPODIUS (d. 178). *See* Alexander.

EPISTEME. *See* Galation.

EQUITIUS (d. c. 560). A native of the Abruzzi, Italy, he led a dissolute life as a youth but after a time as a hermit in Valeria became noted for his holiness and devotion to poverty. He founded his first monastery at Terni, and was its abbot, and then founded several other convents and monasteries throughout Italy. He was famous for his preaching but was denounced by a patrician named Felix for preaching without having been ordained. When some of the Roman clergy complained about him to the Pope, the Pope sent a priest named Julian to look into the matter. Before Julian could conduct his investigation, he received a message from the Pope telling him to desist, as he had had a vision about Equitius and he was not to be interfered with. Equitius died on March 7.

ERASMUS (d. c. 303). Also known as Elmo, he was the bishop of Formiae, Campagna, Italy, and suffered martyrdom during Diocletian's persecution of the Christians. His unreliable legend has him confused with a Syrian bishop who was martyred at Antioch, and according to it he became a hermit on Mount Lebanon to escape Diocletian's persecution. He was captured and brought before the Emperor, tortured, and emerged from being hurled into fiery pitch unhurt. He was then imprisoned, and released by an angel who brought him to Illyricum, where his success with converts brought him further tortures, whereupon the angel again saved him and brought him to Formiae, where he died of his wounds. He is one of the Fourteen Holy Helpers and is patron of sailors (a blue light seen before a ship's masthead before and after a storm were called St. Elmo's lights by Neapolitan sailors). June 2.

ERASTUS (1st century). One of St. Paul's companions, he was sent with Timothy from Ephesus to Macedonia by the apostle (Acts 19:22). Paul also mentions Erastus as the city treasurer of Corinth (Rom. 16:23), who is probably the same Erastus he mentions in II Timothy 4:20, though not the same as

the Erastus of Acts. Tradition says he became bishop of Philippi in Macedonia (of Philippi Paneas according to the Greeks) and suffered martyrdom. July 26.

ERBLON. See Hermenland.

ERCONGOTA (d. c. 660). Niece of St. Ethelburga and daughter of King Ercombert of Kent and St. Sexburga, she went to Gaul either as a nun or to be educated, and stayed for a time at Faremoutier Abbey. July 7.

ERCONWALD (d. c. 686). Son of Anna, King of the East Angles, he went to the kingdom of the East Saxons, and founded a monastery at Chertsey, Surrey, of which he was abbot, and a convent at Barking, Essex, of which his sister Ethelburga was abbess. About 675, he became bishop of London, which he ruled until his death. May 13.

EREMBERT (d. c. 672). A native of Waycourt, Seine-et-Oise, France, he became a Benedictine monk at Fontenelle about 640, and was appointed bishop of Toulouse by King Clotaire III about 656. Erembert resigned as bishop because of ill health in 668 and spent the rest of his life at Fontenelle, where he died. May 14.

ERENTRUDE (d. c. 718). Probably the niece of St. Rupert, though she may have been his sister, she was caring for lepers in Worms when he returned from Bavaria, where he was a missionary, and asked for nuns and monks to return with him. She was one of those who volunteered, and she became abbess of Nonnberg Convent, which he built at Salzburg. She remained there until her death on June 30.

ERHARD (d. c. 686). Unreliable sources say he may have been an Irishman who became auxiliary bishop of Ratisbon and may have been abbot of Ebersheim-münster Abbey. January 8.

ERIC IX OF SWEDEN (d. 1160). King of Sweden from 1150, he did much to aid Christianity in his realm and was responsible for codifying the laws of his kingdom, which became known as King Eric's Law (also the Code of Uppland). He led a victorious expedition against the marauding Finns and persuaded English Bishop Henry of Uppsala to remain in Finland to evangelize the Finns. Eric was killed and beheaded near Uppsala by rebelling Swedish nobles in the army of Magnus, son of the King of Denmark, who had invaded his territory, on May 18. Though never formally canonized, Eric was long considered the patron of Sweden.

ERIZZO (d. 1094). A native of Florence, Italy, he was St. John Gualbert's first follower and was later general of the Vallumbrosans. His cult was confirmed in 1600. February 9.

ERMENBURGA (d. c. 650). A Kentish princess also known as Domneva, she married Merewald, an Anglican chieftain, and the couple had three daughters: SS. Mildred, Milburga, and Mildgith. Ermenburga was founder-abbess of the convent of Minster-in-Thanet on land granted her by her uncle, King Egbert of Kent, in reparation for his murder of her two brothers. November 19.

ERMENGARD, BL. (c. 832–66). Daughter of King Louis the German and his wife, Emma, she was appointed abbess of Buchau Benedictine Convent by the King and later of the royal abbey of Chiensee in Bavaria, where she died on July 16. Her name is also spelled Irmengard. Her cult was confirmed in 1928.

ERMENGILD (d. 703). Daughter of King Ercombert of Kent and St. Sexburga, and also known as Ermengilda, she was married to King Wulfhere of the Mercians and helped spread Christianity in his realm. On the death of Wulfhere in 675, she became a nun at Milton under her mother until St. Sexburga went to Ely, when she became abbess of Minster on the Isle of Sheppey, of which her mother had been abbess. Ermengild later joined Sexburga at Ely. February 13.

ERMENGILDA. *See* Ermengild.

ERMINOLD (d. 1121). Unreliable sources have him brought to Hirschhau monastery as a child. He was later elected abbot of Lorsch, but when a dispute arose about his election, he resigned. He was appointed prior of Prüfening monastery in 1114 and abbott in 1117. He died on January 7 after being attacked by some of his monks for the strictness of his rule.

ERNEST (d. 1148). Abbot of the Benedictine abbey of Zwiefalten in Germany, he went on the Crusades, preached in Arabia and Persia, and was captured by the Moors and tortured to death in Mecca. November 7.

ERRINGTON, VEN. GEORGE (d. 1596). *See* Knight, Ven. William.

ESCRIVA, JOSEMARIA (1902–1975). The second of six children of a devout Spanish Catholic family, Josemaria Escriva de Balaguer was both a lawyer and a priest. In 1928 he founded the Opus Dei, an organization devoted to the promotion of sanctity through work and daily life. As the society developed into a "personal prelature"—a diocese without boundaries—it became controversial both inside and outside the

Church. Critics contend Opus Dei operates as a "church within a church" and that it requires undue loyalty and obedience from its members. Opus Dei leaders counter that the society brings laypersons closer to God in a manner in keeping with the teachings of the Second Vatican Council. Escriva's 2002 canonization was celebrated by millions around the world. Pope John Paul II said of him: "St. Josemaria was chosen by the Lord to proclaim the universal call to holiness and to indicate that everyday life, its customary activities, are a path towards holiness. It could be said that he was the saint of the ordinary." June 26.

ESKIL (d. c. 1080). An Englishman, he accompanied his relative St. Sigfrid on his missionary trip to Sweden, was consecrated a bishop at Strängnäs, and was most successful in his missionary work in Södermanland. When King Inge, an active supporter of the missionaries, was murdered, his successor, Sweyn the Bloody, revived pagan practices. When Eskil denounced a pagan festival at Strängnäs and a sacrificial altar was destroyed by lightning, he was accused of magic and stoned to death by Sweyn's order. June 12.

ESTERWINE (d. 686). A courtier at the Northumbrian court, he became a monk at Wearmouth under his relative St. Benedict Biscop, who appointed him acting abbot while Benedict was away from the abbey. Esterwine died at Wearmouth. March 7.

ETHBIN (6th century). Probably a Briton, he was educated under St. Samson, became a monk under St. Winwaloe in Brittany, and moved to Ireland when the monastery was destroyed by the Franks in 556. He became a recluse there but later became abbot of Kildare. October 19.

ETHELBERT (d. 616). He became King of Kent about 560, married Bertha, daughter of Frankish King Charibert and a Christian, and though defeated by the West Saxons in 568, strengthened his rule and kingdom. He permitted St. Augustine of Canterbury to preach in his realm and in 597 was baptized by Augustine, the first Christian English King, and brought thousands of his subjects to Christianity with him. He granted religious freedom to his subjects, believing conversion by conviction was the only true conversion, encouraged the Christian missionaries, helped convert King Sabert of the East Saxons and King Redwald of the East Angles, codified the laws of the kingdom, and ruled wisely for fifty-six years. His name is spelled Aedilberct in Bede's history of the English Church. February 25.

ETHELBERT (d. 794). Son of Ethelred, whom he succeeded as King of the East Angles, he visited King Offa of the Mercians at Sutton Walls to ask for his daughter Alfreda in marriage and was murdered there, reportedly at the instigation of Offra's wife, Cynethryth. May 20.

ETHELBURGA (d. c. 647). Daughter of King Ethelbert of Kent, who had been converted to Christianity by St. Augustine of Canterbury, and Bertha, and also called Tata, she was married to pagan King Edwin of Northumbria. She and her chaplain, Paulinus, helped persuade Edwin to become a Christian in 627. He encouraged the advance of Christianity in his kingdom, but on his death in 633, paganism returned, and Ethelburga and Paulinus were forced to return to Kent. She founded an abbey at Lyminge and was its abbess until her death. April 5.

ETHELBURGA (d. c. 664). Daughter of Anna, King of the East Angles, she accompanied her half sister, Sethrida, to Gaul and became a nun at Faremoutier under St. Burgundofara. Sethrida succeeded Burgundofara as abbess, and on the former's death about 660, Ethelburga succeeded her. Ethelburga died at Faremoutier and is known in France as Aubierge. July 7.

ETHELBURGA (d. c. 678). Sister of SS. Erconwald, Etheldreda, Sexburga, and Withburga, all of whom are saints, and daughter of Anna, King of the East Angles, she was born at Stallington, Lindsey, England, became a nun, and was appointed first abbess of a double monastery founded by Erconwald at Barking, where she died. October 12.

ETHELDREDA (d. 679). Also known as Audrey, she was the daughter of Anna, King of the East Angles, and Bertha, and the sister of Erconwald, Ethelburga, Sexburga, and Withburga, all saints. Etheldreda was born in Exning, Suffolk, England, was married at an early age to Tonbert, prince of the Gryvii, but convinced him to allow her to retain her virginity during their married life. He died three years after their wedding, and Etheldreda lived in seculsion on the island of Ely for the next five years. She then married Egfrid, son of King Oswy of Northumbria, who was only a boy at the time. When, after twelve years of marriage, he demanded his conjugal rights, she refused, saying she had dedicated herself to God. The case was referred to St. Wilfrid, who upheld her claim. With Egfrid's consent she then became a nun at Coldingham Convent. The following year she returned to Ely, built a double monastery there about 672, was abbess of the convent for the rest of her life, and died there. June 23.

ETHELNOTH (d. 1038). Dean of the cathedral church at Canterbury, he was appointed archbishop of Canterbury in

1020. Known as "the Good" because of his holiness, he was also noted for his learning and was responsible for King Canute's liberal contribution to the rebuilding of the cathedral of Chartres. October 30.

ETHELRED (d. 716). King of Mercia, England, he resigned his throne to become a monk at Bardsey and was later elected abbot there. May 4.

ETHELRED. *See* Aelred.

ETHELWALD (d. 699). Also known as Odilwald, he was a monk at Ripon, lived as a hermit for twelve years in St. Cuthbert's hermitage on Farnes Island, and died there. March 23.

ETHELWALD (d. c. 740). An assistant to St. Cuthbert, he became prior of Old Melrose in Scotland and later was made abbot. He was elected bishop of Lindisfarne to succeed Eadfrith on his death in 721 and was highly praised by Bede, the English historian. February 12.

ETHELWOLD (c. 908–84). Born at Winchester, England, he was ordained by St. Alphege the Bald and in 944 became a Benedictine monk at Glastonbury Abbey under St. Dunstan and was made dean there. Ethelwold was appointed abbot of Abingdon in Berkshire about 954 and with St. Dunstan and St. Oswald was mainly responsible for the restoration of monasticism in England after its virtual destruction by the Danes during their raids. He was consecrated bishop of Winchester in 963, restored discipline among the canons of his cathedral by expelling them and replacing them with monks, and did the same thing the following year with the seculars of Newminster Monastery. He restored ruined monasteries and convents in his diocese and became known as "the

Father of Monks." His reforms met with much opposition, but by the time of his death on August 1 he had rebuilt and reformed his see. He wrote several treatises and translated the rule of St. Benedict.

EUBULUS (d. 309). *See* Adrian.

EUCARPIUS (d. c. 304). He and Trophimus were soldiers stationed at Nicomedia during Diocletian's persecution of the Christians. They were assigned the task of rounding up Christians and in the process were themselves converted to Christianity. They were arrested when it was discovered they were Christians and burned to death for their faith. March 18.

EUCHERIUS (d. 449). A Gallo-Roman, he married Galla, had two sons (Salonius and Veranus, who both became bishops), and in 422 became a monk at Lérins; at the same time Galla became a nun. He left to become a hermit, was made bishop of Lyons about 434, and ruled the see wisely until his death. He wrote a book on the eremitical life dedicated to St. Hilary of Arles and wrote many letters, some of which are still extant. November 16.

EUCHERIUS (d. 743). Born at Orléans, France, he became a Benedictine monk at Jumièges about 714, and over his vehement objections was elected bishop of Orléans about 721. Though Charles Martel, mayor of the palace, had approved the election, Eucherius' opposition to his seizure of Church revenues to finance his war expenses caused Charles to exile him to Cologne. When he became extremely popular there, Charles put him under virtual arrest at Liège but then allowed him to retire to Saint-Trond Monastery near Maestricht, Flanders, where he spent the rest of his life and died. February 20.

EUDES, JOHN (1601–80). Born at Ri, Normandy, France, on November 14, the son of a farmer, he went to the Jesuit college at Caen when fourteen and despite his parents' wish that he marry, joined the Congregation of the Oratory of France in 1623. He studied at Paris and at Aubervilliers, was ordained in 1625, and worked as a volunteer, caring for the victims of the plagues that struck Normandy in 1625 and 1631, and spent the next decade giving missions, building a reputation as an outstanding preacher and confessor and for his opposition to Jansenism. He became interested in helping fallen women, and in 1641, with Madeleine Lamy, founded a refuge for them in Caen under the direction of the Visitandines. He resigned from the Oratorians in 1643 and founded the Congregation of Jesus and Mary (the Eudists) at Caen, composed of secular priests not bound by vows but dedicated to upgrading the clergy by establishing effective seminaries and to preaching missions. His foundation was opposed by the Oratorians and the Jansenists, and he was unable to obtain papal approval for it, but in 1650, the bishop of Coutances invited him to establish a seminary in that diocese. The same year the sisters at his refuge in Caen left the Visitandines and were recognized by the bishop of Bayeux as a new congregation under the name of Sisters of Our Lady of Charity of the Refuge. John founded seminaries at Lisieux in 1653 and Rouen in 1659 and was unsuccessful in another attempt to secure papal approval of his congregation, but in 1666 the Refuge sisters received Pope Alexander III's approval as an institute to reclaim and care for penitent wayward women. John continued giving missions and established new seminaries at Evreux in 1666 and Rennes in 1670. He shared with St. Mary Margaret Alacoque the honor of initiating devotion to the Sacred Heart of Jesus (he composed the Mass for the Sacred Heart in 1668) and the Holy Heart of Mary, popularizing the devotions with his *The Devotion to the Adorable Heart of Jesus* (1670) and *The Admirable Heart of the Most Holy Mother of God,* which he finished a month before his death at Caen on August 19. He was canonized in 1925.

EUDOCIA (2nd century). A Samaritan living in Heliopolis, she led an evil life until converted to Christianity by Bishop Theodotus. She was beheaded for her faith by Governor Vincent during the persecution of Christians during the reign of Emperor Trajan. March 1.

EUGENDUS (c. 449–c. 510). Also known as Oyend, he was a monk at Condat, France, near Geneva, who became abbot of Condat though never ordained a priest. He was a learned man, a Scripture scholar, and was noted for his austerity. January 1.

EUGENE (d. c. 618). Also known as Eoghan (Owen), unreliable sources have him born in Leinster, Ireland, and a relative of St. Kevin of Glendalough. Kidnaped into slavery while still a child and taken to Britain and then Brittany with two other boys, Tigernach and Coirpre, they were all released in time by their master and returned to Ireland. He spent fifteen years as a monk with St. Kevin at Kilnamanacg, helped Tigernach found Clones Monastery about 576 (Coirpre had meanwhile become bishop of Coleraine), and then settled with his disciples at Ardstraw, eventually being made its first bishop about 581. August 23.

EUGENE I (d. 657). A Roman priest who had held various positions in the Church and was known for his charity and sanctity, he was consecrated Pope on August 10, 654, while his predecessor, Pope St. Martin I, was still alive (he died on September 6), an exile and prisoner in the Crimea by order of Monothelite Emperor Constans II. Martin is reported to have approved the election, but many believed Eugene was a puppet of Constans. Eugene soon asserted his independence by refusing the Emperor's demands that he acknowledge Peter as Patriarch of Constantinople and allow toleration of the Monothelites. Constans was furious, and only the capture of Rhodes by the Moslems in 654 and their defeat of Constans at the naval battle of Phoenix in 655 saved Eugene from sharing the fate of his predecessor. Eugene died in Rome on June 2.

EUGENE III, BL. (d. 1153). Born at Montenagno, near Pisa, Italy, Pietro Paganelli became a canon at the Pisa cathedral and after meeting St. Bernard joined the Cistercians at Clairvaux in 1135, taking the name Bernard. He became abbot of St. Anastasius in Rome and was unexpectedly elected Pope on February 15, 1145, taking the name Eugene. Forced to flee the city when he refused to recognize the sovereignty of the Roman Senate and Arnold of Brescia, heading the opposition to his election, seized temporal power, he was secretly consecrated at Farfa Abbey on February 18. He moved to Viterbo and then returned to Rome under a truce, which the rebels immediately broke, pillaging churches and turning St. Peter's into an armory. At the invitation of King Louis VII, he went to France in 1147 and proclaimed the Second Crusade, which ended in failure, despite the efforts of St. Bernard, who preached it, when the armies of King Louis VII and Emperor Conrad II of Germany were defeated. Eugene held synods at Paris and Trier in 1147 and the following year at Rheims, where he condemned Gilbert de la Porrée, and at Cremona, where he excommunicated Arnold and threatened to use force against the Roman rebels. Terms were arranged and Eugene returned to Rome in 1149 but was again forced to leave the following year. He took up residence at Tivoli, concluded the Treaty of Constance in 1153 with Emperor Frederick I, guaranteeing the rights of the Church, and died at Tivoli on July 8. Eugene labored throughout a tumultuous pontificate to reunite the Eastern churches to Rome, to reform clerical conduct and discipline, removed unworthy clergymen (among them the archbishops of Mainz and York), fought the recurrence of Manichaeism, was known for his courage and simplicity, and lived according to the spiritual counsels of St. Bernard, who wrote *De consideratione* for his guidance. His cult was approved in 1872.

EUGENIA (d. c. 257). There definitely was a Roman martyr named Eugenia but the rest of her story is a romantic fictitious legend. According to it she was the daughter of Duke Philip of Alexandria, governor of Egypt during the reign of Emperor Valerian. She fled her father's house dressed in men's clothing and was baptized by Helenus, bishop of Heliopolis, who sent her to an abbey of which she later became abbot. Accused of adultery by a woman she had cured of a sickness and whose advances she had resisted, she was haled before a judge to answer the charges; the judge was her father. Exonerated when she revealed she was a woman and his daughter, she converted him to Christianity (he later became a bishop and was beheaded for his faith). Eugenia converted many others, including her mother, Claudia, and suffered martyrdom by sword for her faith in Rome, where she had gone with her mother. December 25.

EUGENIUS (d. 304). *See* Eustratius.

EUGENIUS II (d. 657). A Spanish Goth, he was born at Toledo, was a cleric in the cathedral there under St. Helladius, became a monk at Saragossa, and against his wishes was appointed bishop of Toledo in 647. He was a musician and a poet (some of his writings are still extant), and he ruled the see well. He died in Toledo on November 13.

EUGENIUS OF CARTHAGE (d. 505). A native of Carthage, he was noted for his learning, holiness, charity, and prudence. He was elected bishop of Carthage in 481 in an election permitted by King Huneric of the Vandals after the see had been vacant for fifty years. Huneric, who ruled the city and was an Arian, forbade him to occupy his episcopal chair, launched a persecution of Catholics, and forbade any Vandal to enter a Catholic church. He ordered a conference of bishops to be held, but when Eugenius learned it would be dominated by Arian bishops, he refused to attend. When the bishops assembled in 484 ostensibly to discuss relations between Catholics and Arians, Huneric seized the opportunity to plunder Catholic churches and banish many of the Catholic bishops, Eugenius among them. He was deported to the deserts of Tripoli and put in the custody of an Arian bishop, Anthony, who treated him with great cruelty. Huneric died in 484 and his nephew and successor, Gontamund, allowed Eugenius to return in 488 and later allowed the orthodox (Catholic) churches to be reopened. The next King, Thrasimund, renewed the persecution, sentenced Eugenius to death, but instead banished him to Languedoc, where he died at a monastery near Albi. July 13.

EUGRAPHIUS (4th century). *See* Mennas.

EUHTIS. *See* John of Nicomedia.

EULALIA OF BARCELONA (d. 304). Born at Barcelona, Spain, she was tortured and then put to death there for her faith during the persecution of Christians by Emperor Diocletian. She is known as Aulaire in French Catalonia and is probably the same as Eulalia of Mérida. February 12.

EULALIA OF MÉRIDA (d. c. 304). Though a Eulalia did live and suffer martyrdom in Mérida, Spain, all else about her is legendary. According to the legend, she was a twelve-year-old Spanish girl who despite her mother's efforts to prevent her from doing so, denounced Judge Dacian for attempting to get Christians to apostatize and was then tortured and put to death when she refused to sacrifice to the gods. She is mentioned by St. Augustine and had a hymn written in her honor by Prudentius. December 10.

EULAMPIA (d. c. 310). *See* Eulampius.

EULAMPIUS (d. c. 310). Unreliable sources state he was a Christian youth at Nicomedia who hid in caves outside the city to escape Emperor Galerius' persecution of the Christians. Apprehended while buying food in Nicomedia, he was brought before the magistrate, and when he refused to sacrifice to the gods, he was racked. When his sister Eulampia ran to him, she was arrested. They were both tortured and with two hundred other Christians were beheaded. October 10.

EULOGIUS (d. 259). *See* Fructuosus.

EULOGIUS (4th century). Born at Edessa, he became a priest there and was banished from his parish because of his firm opposition to Arianism. He returned on the death of Emperor Valens in 375 and was named bishop of Edessa. May 5.

EULOGIUS (d. c. 607). Born in Syria, he became a monk when a youth at Mother of God Monastery in Antioch and in time became its abbot. He was named patriarch of Alexandria, Egypt, in 579 and on a trip to Constantinople, met the papal delegate to the imperial court, who was to become Pope St. Gregory the Great; the two became friends and correspondents. Though Eulogius wrote against heresies, particularly monophysitism, little of his writing is still extant. September 13.

EULOGIUS OF CORDOVA (d. 859). Of a prominent Christian family in Moorish-occupied Cordova, Spain, he was educated by Abbot Sperando and was ordained. He became noted for his learning and knowledge of Scripture and for the rules he drew up for many of the monasteries of Navarre and Pamplona. He was imprisoned in 850 when the Moors unleashed a persecution of the Christians in Cordova, and while in prison he wrote his *Exhortation to Martyrdom* for two Christian girls, Flora and Mary, who had been threatened with slavery. They were both beheaded, but a few days later Eulogius and the other prisoners were released. During the continued persecution that followed, he was tireless in his encouragement of his fellow Christians and was elected archbishop of Toledo but never occupied the see. Before he was consecrated, he helped a Christian convert from Mohammedanism, Leocritia, to escape (the penalty for a Moor who became a Christian was death), but she was discovered, and all who aided her were arrested. Eulogius tried to convert the kadi before whom he was tried but was ordered executed. He was beheaded, as was Leocritia four days later. He wrote *Memorial of the Saints,* describing the sufferings of martyred saints to encourage the persecuted Christians, and an *Apologia,* defending martyrs who sought death by proclaiming their faith. March 11.

EUNAN. *See* Adamnan (c. 624–704).

EUNUS (d. 250). *See* Julian.

EUPHEMIA (d. c. 303). Though there was a martyr at Chalcedon named Euphemia who was early venerated (a church in her honor was built at Chalcedon early in the fifth century), all else that is known of her is from unreliable sources. According to them, she refused to attend a festival at Chalcedon honoring the pagan god of Ares, whereupon she was taken before a judge named Priscus, subjected to terrible tortures, and then mauled and bitten to death by a bear. September 16.

EUPHEMIANUS (d. 820). A native of Constantinople and christened Anne, she was forced to marry, but on the death of her husband, she left home, donned male attire, and became a recluse on Mount Olympus under the name of Euphemianus. October 29.

EUPHRASIA (d. c. 420). Daughter of Antigonus, she and her mother were taken in by Emperor Theodosius I when her father, a relative of the Emperor, died when she was a year old. Her mother became a nun in Egypt, and though Euphrasia had been betrothed to a senator when five, her mother took her with her. Euphrasia received a nuns' habit when seven and when she was twelve and now an orphan, the Emperor, now Arcadius, sent for her to marry the senator, but at her request, allowed her to give her inheritance to the poor, free her slaves, and continue as a nun. She spent the rest of her life in the convent, noted for her austerities and humility. Her name is also spelled Eupraxia. March 13.

EUPHRASIUS (1st century). *See* Torquatus.

EUPHROSYNE (5th century). A religious fiction makes her the daughter of wealthy Paphnutius, born after many years of his childless marriage. She was betrothed to a wealthy young man but began to give her possessions to the poor, and while her father was on retreat, she consulted with an old monk whose prayers had reputedly brought about her birth, and he gave her the veil. Fearful of her father's reaction, she donned men's clothing, became a monk at the monastery her father frequented, taking the name Smaragdus, and became famous for her holiness and spiritual wisdom. She was consulted by her father, who did not recognize her, and she did not reveal her identity to him until she was dying. After her death, her father became a monk and lived in her cell for ten years. January 1.

EUPHROSYNE OF POLOTSK (d. 1173). Daughter of Prince Svyatoslav of Polotsk, Russia, she became a nun there when twelve and then became a recluse at a cell in Holy Wisdom Cathedral, working as a copyist of manuscripts, the proceeds of which she gave to the poor. She founded a convent at Seltse and traveled quite a bit, including a trip to Constantinople and the Holy Land, where she died in Jerusalem. May 23.

EUPLIUS (d. 304). A deacon at Catania, Sicily, during Emperor Diocletian's persecution of the Christians, he was found guilty of possessing a copy of the gospels by the governor, Calvisian; when Euplius persisted in refusing to sacrifice to the gods, he was beheaded on April 29. August 12.

EUPRAXIA. *See* Euphrasia.

EUPREPIUS (d. 303). *See* Cosmas.

EUPSYCHIUS (d. 362). A young man of Caesarea in Cappadocia, he suffered martyrdom during the reign of Emperor Julian the Apostate as the leader of a band of Christians charged with destroying the Temple of Fortune there. April 9.

EUROSIA (8th century). According to a popular but probably fictitious tradition, she was a native of Bayonne, France, who was murdered by the Saracens at Jaca in the Pyrenees of Aragon near the French border when she refused to marry a Moorish leader. June 25.

EUSEBIA (d. c. 680). Daughter of St. Adalbald and St. Rictrudis, she was sent as a child to Hamage Abbey near Doudi, France, of which her great-grandmother St. Gertrude was abbess, by her mother after her father was murdered in 652. Though only twelve when Gertrude died, Eusebia was elected abbess, but Rictrudis, feeling she was too young and inexperienced for that position, merged the community of Hamage with that of Marchiennes, of which she was abbess. Some time later Rictrudis allowed Eusebia and her nuns to return to Hamage, and the young abbess ruled wisely and well until her death. March 16.

EUSEBIUS (d. 309). A Greek priest and the son of a physician, he was elected pope to succeed Pope St. Marcellus on April 18, 309 or 310. Eusebius inherited the *lapsi* controversy from his predecessor, whose policy of readmitting the *lapsi* after suitable penance he followed. His election was opposed by a group of *lapsi*, who elected Heraclius antipope and demanded immediate return to the sacraments without penance. They caused such disturbances that Emperor Maxentius banished both Heraclius and the Pope to Sicily, where Eusebius died after a reign of only four months. August 17.

EUSEBIUS (d. c. 357). A priest in Rome, he opposed the Arian Emperor Constantius, supported antipope Felix II, was forbidden to say Mass in any of the churches in Rome, but did so in his own home, and then was imprisoned in a small room of his house for seven months and died there. That he existed and founded a church in Rome are all the facts that are really known of him; all else is based on untrustworthy sources. August 14.

EUSEBIUS (d. c. 362). He and two brothers, Nestabus and Zeno, destroyed a pagan temple at Gaza, Palestine, during the reign of Emperor Julian the Apostate. They were scourged, imprisoned, and then carried off and beaten to death by a mob. The mob also dragged from the prison at the same time a young man named Nestor, who later died of the wounds inflicted on him by the mob at the house of another Zeno. September 8.

EUSEBIUS (c. 283–371). Born on Sardinia, son of a martyr, he was brought to Rome when an infant by his mother and raised there. He was ordained a lector and then went to Vercelli, where in 340 he was elected bishop of the city. He reformed his clergy, was the first Western bishop to unite the clerical and monastic life, and he lived in community with some of his clergy. He was sent by Pope Liberius in 354 with Bishop Lucifer of Cagliari to ask Emperor Constantius to call a council to settle the differences between Catholics and Arians, vehemently refused to sign the condemnation of St. Athanasius at the Council of Milan called by Constantius the following year, and demanded that all the bishops present sign the Nicene Creed before considering Athanasius' case. Eusebius was threatened with death by the Emperor and was banished to Scythopolis, Palestine, in the custody of Arian Bishop patrophilus, by the furious Constantius when, with Dionysius of Milan and Lucifer of Cagliari, Eusebius adamantly refused the Emperor's demand that he sign Athanasius' condemnation. There Eusebius was persecuted and subjected to numerous humiliations by the Arians. He was moved first to Cappadocia and then to Upper Thebaid, Egypt, where he continued his uncompromising opposition to Arianism. He returned from exile to attend a council at Alexandria in 362 after Constantius died and Julian the Apostate permitted the exiled bishops to return to their sees. Eusebius was delegated by the council to go to Antioch to heal the breach between the Eustathians, the followers of St. Eustathius, who had been exiled from that see by the Arians in 331, and the Meletians, the followers of Bishop Meletius, who had been elected bishop of Antioch in 361 mainly by Arians, by recognizing Meletius as bishop, only to find that Lucifer of Cagliari, who had also been a delegate to the council, had complicated the situation further by consecrating Paulinus, leader of the Eustathians, bishop of Carthage. Lucifer's refusal to obey the council's decree began the Luciferian schism. Unable to accomplish anything at Antioch in the face of this development, Eusebius traveled throughout Illyricum visiting various churches to bolster their orthodoxy and returned to Vercelli in 363. He spent the rest of his life fighting Arianism in the Western Church, with St. Hilary of Poitiers, and was one of the chief opponents of Arian Bishop Auxentius of Milan. Eusebius died at Vercelli on August 1. He was one of the authors of the Athanasian Creed, and a

manuscript copy of the Latin gospels he is reputed to have copied, the Codex Vercellensis, is the oldest such manuscript in existence. August 2.

EUSEBIUS (d. c. 379). A stanch defender of orthodoxy and bishop of Samosata, he was active at the synod of Antioch in 361, helping to elect Meletius bishop of Antioch. Most of those voting were Arians and expected Meletius to favor Arianism. When it became obvious that Meletius was orthodox, Emperor Constantius, an Arian, demanded that Eusebius surrender to him the election acts of the synod that were in his custody. When Eusebius refused, the Emperor threatened to cut off his right hand; when Eusebius still refused, Constantius, impressed by his courage, released him. Eusebius spent the next two years laboring to reconcile the orthodox (Catholics) and Arians but was unsuccessful. He helped elect St. Basil bishop of Caesarea in Cappadocia in 372, and the two became close friends. Eusebius traveled through Syria and Palestine encouraging the Catholics to resist Valens and his persecution, and in 374 was exiled to Thrace by Valens. Eusebius returned to Samosata when Valens died in 378 and died the following year at Dolikha, where he had gone to install a Catholic bishop, when struck on the head by a tile thrown from a rooftop by a woman who was an Arian. June 21.

EUSEBIUS (d. 884). An Irishman, he became a monk at Saint-Gall Monastery in Switzerland and was then permitted to live the eremitical life on Mount St. Victor near Röttris. After thirty years as a hermit, he was murdered with a scythe while berating a group of peasants for the godlessness of their lives. January 31.

EUSEBIUS OF CREMONA (d. c. 423). A native of Cremona, Italy, he met St.

Jerome while on a visit to Rome and accompanied him to the Holy Land. St. Paula and her daughter, St. Eustochium, met them at Antioch and after visiting the holy places, they all settled at Bethlehem. He returned to Italy to raise funds for a hostel for pilgrims Jerome wanted to build in Jerusalem and became involved in a dispute with Rufinus, a priest from Aquileia and formerly a friend of Jerome whom Jerome had denounced for false teachings. Rufinus accused Eusebius of being responsible for the theft of his translation of the writings of Origen. Eusebius supported the criticisms of Origen, and it is believed that Eusebius was instrumental in having Pope St. Anastasius condemn Origen's writings. Eusebius returned to Cremona in 400 and is believed to have remained in Italy the rest of his life. He was a lifelong friend of Jerome, who dedicated several commentaries to him; Eusebius contributed to the support of Jerome's work. Legend has Eusebius introducing the Hieronymites to Spain and funding Guadalupe monastery there, but these are doubtful. March 5.

EUSTACE (d. c. 118). According to his untrustworthy legend, he was a Roman general named Placida under Emperor Trajan who was converted to Christianity while hunting at Guadagnolo, Italy, when he saw a stag with the figure of Christ on the cross between its antlers. He changed his name to Eustace and sometime later he lost his fortune and was separated from his wife, Theopistis, and sons, Agapitus and Theopistus. Recalled to the army, he won a great victory, but when he refused to sacrifice to the gods during the victory celebration, he and his family, with whom he had been reunited, were roasted to death. It is not certain if he ever lived, and the whole story is proba-

bly a fictitious pious tale. He is also known as Eustathius. September 20.

EUSTACE (d. 1211). Born at Beauvais, France, he was ordained and served as a priest in his native diocese until he joined the Cistercians at Flay (St. Germer). He later was elected abbot, was apostolic legate to England for Pope Innocent III, and was later sent by Innocent as his legate to combat Albigensianism in southern France. September 7.

EUSTACE (d. 1342). See John.

EUSTATHIUS (c. 270–c. 340). Born at Side, Pamphylia, he was made bishop of Beroea, Syria, and then became Patriarch of Antioch about 323. In 325 he attended the General Council of Nicaea, where he was active in his opposition to Arianism; on his return to Antioch from the council, he banished any of his clergy he suspected of Arianism. His uncompromising orthodoxy led him into conflict with Eusebius of Caesarea, whom he denounced for favoring Arianism. About 330 Eusebius convinced Emperor Constantine to depose Eustathius, and he was exiled to Trajanopolis in Thrace, where he died. He was held in such regard by his people that they refused to accept not only his Arian successor but also St. Meletius, the compromise choice of the Catholic and Arian bishops, which led to the Meletian schism that was to endure for a century between his followers, the Eustathians, and those of Meletius, the Meletians. He wrote profusely, but little is still extant. July 16.

EUSTATHIUS. See Eustace.

EUSTATHIUS. See Eutychius (d. 741).

EUSTOCHIUM (d. c. 419). Daughter of St. Paula, Eustochium Julia joined her mother in choosing St. Jerome as a spiritual director when he came to Rome in 382, and soon took the veil of perpetual virginity—an event that caused Jerome to write his famous *Concerning the Keeping of Virginity* for her in 384. She accompanied her mother to the Holy Land with Jerome and then to Bethlehem, where she and her mother helped Jerome in his translation of the Bible when his sight failed. She assisted her mother in directing the three communities of women founded by Jerome and succeeded her as directress when Paula died in 404. She revitalized the monasteries but never recovered from the destruction of her monastery by a band of marauders. St. Jerome often wrote of her and provides all that we know of her. She died at Bethlehem. September 28.

EUSTOCHIUM, BL. (1432–68). Daughter of Countess Matilda of Calafato and called Smaragda of Calafato, she was born at Messina, Italy, and was betrothed by her father, but her fiancé died before the marriage took place. On the death of her father in 1446, she became a Poor Clare at Basico Convent, taking the name Eustochium, and devoted herself to penance and caring for the sick and the poor. Desirous of a stricter rule, she left Basico to go to Monte Vergine Convent, built by her mother and sister, and became abbess there in 1462. She died there, and her cult was approved in 1782. February 16.

EUSTOCHIUM OF PADUA, BL. (1443–69). The illegitimate child of a seduced nun, she was born at San Prosdocimo Convent in Padua, baptized Lucrezia, and raised and educated at the convent. When she grew older she wished to become a nun and despite the opposition of many in the community because of the circumstances of her birth, the bishop approved her noviceship and she was veiled, taking the name Eustochium. Though normally humble

and obedient, she soon began to display strange and curious spells of unusual behavior in which she acted like a madwoman. For a time she was tied up for days and when the abbess fell ill Eustochium was accused of poisoning her and was barely saved from a mob of townspeople who wanted her burned as a witch. Instead the bishop had her imprisoned in a cell; fortunately the abbess recovered, but Eustochium was shunned by the members of the community. Her spells continued, with such manifestations as self-inflicted wounds, walking on high roofs, and being found naked in her cell with marks on her throat; on her recovery from each of her attacks she was a model religious. At the insistence of her confessor she was allowed to become a nun and seems to have conquered what appeared to be diabolical attacks. In time she won the respect of her community by her patience and holiness. She died on February 13, at which time the name Jesus was found burned on her breast.

EUSTORGIUS (d. 518). Reportedly a Greek who lived in Rome, he was made bishop of Milan in 512, was respected for his ability and holiness, and spent all of his resources ransoming members of his flock who had been captured by the barbarians. June 6.

EUSTRATIUS (d. c. 304). Eustratius, an Armenian of a good family, was tortured during Diocletian's persecution by Lysias, then by Agricolaus, the governor at Sebastia, and then burned to death in a furnace. With him were martyred his servant Eugenius, two friends who had pleaded for his life, Mardarius and Auxentius, and Orestes, a soldier who was converted by Eustratius' courage and was roasted to death on a grill. December 13.

EUTHYMIUS (d. 840). A monk who was named bishop of Sardis, Lydia, he opposed the iconoclasm heresy so strenuously he was banished by Emperor Nicephorus. Euthymius was offered a pardon several times if he would become an iconoclast but refused each time. After twenty-nine years in exile, he was scourged to death during the reign of Emperor Theophilus. March 11.

EUTHYMIUS (d. 1028). Son of St. John the Iberian and a native of Iberia (Georgia, U.S.S.R.), he accompanied John to Mount Athos when his father brought him back from Constantinople, where he and other Iberian youths had been held as hostages by the Emperor. Euthymius helped his father build Iviron Monastery on Mount Athos for Iberian monks, and in about 1002 he succeeded his father as abbot. Euthymius translated the Bible from Greek into Iberian as well as the works of the Church Fathers, among them Basil, Gregory of Nyssa, St. Ephrem, Pope St. Gregory the Great, and John Cassian. Euthymius resigned as abbot after fourteen years to devote himself to his translations. Summoned to Constantinople by Emperor Constantine VIII to explain the disturbances that were taking place at Iviron between the Greek and the Iberian monks, he died on May 13 while on the way of injuries he sustained in a fall from his mule.

EUTHYMIUS THE GREAT (c. 378–473). Born of wealthy parents at Militene, Armenia, he studied under the bishop there and was ordained. He was appointed supervisor of the monasteries in the diocese but when twenty-nine he became a monk at the Pharan *laura* near Jerusalem. About 411, he left to live with a companion as a hermit in a cave near Jericho, attracted numerous disciples, left his companion, Theoctistus, as superior, and moved to a more remote spot. He still attracted many and converted so many, including a great many Arabs, that

Patriarch Juvenal of Jerusalem consecrated him bishop to minister to them. Juvenal built him a *laura* on the road from Jerusalem to Jericho, which Euthymius ruled by vicars. He attracted enormous crowds, among them Eudoxia, the widow of Emperor Theodosius II, who followed his advice to give up her allegiance to the Eutychians and return to orthodoxy in 459. He died on January 20 after sixty-six years in the desert.

EUTHYMIUS THE YOUNGER (c. 824–898). Born at Opso, near Ancrya, Galatia, he was baptized Nicetas and married early, having one daughter, Anastasia. In 842 he left his family and entered a *laura* on Mount Olympus in Bithynia, where he took the name Euthymius and then entered the monastery of the Pissidion. When Abbot Nicholas was removed as abbot for supporting Patriarch Ignatius of Constantinople, who was deposed in 858, Euthymius became a hermit on Mount Athos with an *in situ* hermit, Joseph. In 863, Euthymius visited the tomb of a fellow ascetic from Olympus, Theodore, at Salonika and lived for a time on a tower, preaching to crowds. He was ordained deacon there, returned to Mount Athos, but left to escape the crowds seeking him. After a time on a small island with two companions, he returned to Mount Athos and lived there with Joseph until Joseph's death. In response to a dream he had of Joseph, he took two disciples, Ignatius and Ephrem, to Mount Peristera in eastern Salonika, rebuilt ruined St. Andrew Monastery there, attracted numerous disciples, and served as their abbot for fourteen years. He built another double monastery, which he turned over to the metropolitan of Salonika, and then returned to Athos, where he remained until a few months before his death, when he went to Holy Island with

George, a fellow monk, and died there on October 15. He is called "the Younger" to distinguish him from St. Euthymius the Great.

EUTICIUS (d. c. 305). *See* Januarius.

EUTROPIA (d. c. 451). *See* Nicasius.

EUTROPIUS (3rd century). A Roman, he accompanied St. Denis to France to help evangelize the country and became the first bishop of Saintes. His efforts at conversion were resisted by the inhabitants of Saintes, who expelled him from the city. He lived in a cell in a rock just outside Saintes, preached, and made converts, among whom was Eustella, the daughter of the Roman governor. Enraged, he had the butchers of the town kill Eutropius by splitting his head open with an ax. April 30.

EUTROPIUS (d. 404). A lector at Constantinople and a supporter of St. John Chrysostom, he and a priest, Tigrius, were accused of setting fire to the cathedral church and the Senate building when Chrysostom was banished. Eutropius was tortured by the city prefect, Optatus, an enemy of Christianity, and then put to death. Tigrius too was tortured but escaped death and was later banished to Mesopotamia, where he died about 406. He was a former slave and a close friend of Chrysostom, whose banishment was supposedly the cause of the two men putting the cathedral to the torch. January 12.

EUTROPIUS (d. c. 476). A native of Marseilles, he led a dissolute life as a youth but reformed when he married. On the death of his wife, he became a priest, was named bishop of Orange, and helped rebuild the see, which had just been plundered by the Visigoths. May 27.

EUTYCHIAN (d. 283). Nothing is known of him except that he was born at Luni, Italy, succeeded Felix I as Pope on January 4, 275, died on December 7, and was buried in the catacomb of Callistus.

EUTYCHIUS (1st century). A native of Phrygia, he became a disciple of St. Paul and was raised from the dead by Paul when he fell out a window while listening to Paul preach (Acts 20:7–12). Eutychius is also believed to have been with St. John on Patmos while the evangelist wrote Revelation, preached the gospel in several countries, and was subjected to imprisonment and torture for his faith. August 24.

EUTYCHIUS (c. 512–82). Born in Phrygia, he became a monk and then was ordained at Amasea, Pontus. While on a mission in 552 to Constantinople for his bishop, Eutychius attracted the attention of Emperor Justinian I, who selected him to succeed Mennas as Patriarch of Constantinople. Eutychius was one of the patriarchs presiding at the General Council of Constantinople in 553 that condemned Origenism but did not stop the advances of the monophysites. He came into conflict with Justinian over the Emperor's approval of the teaching of a sect of monophysites that Christ's body was incorruptible and he suffered no pain while on earth, and Eutychius was exiled to an island in the Propontis in 565. He returned in 577 when Justinian died, but then came into conflict with Gregory the Great, then papal representative of the Holy See in Constantinople, when Eutychius denied the immortality of the body—a heresy he recanted on his deathbed. April 6.

EUTYCHIUS (d. 741). Also known as Eustathius, he was the son of a patrician. He was captured by the Arabs while fighting against them, and when the khalif who had captured them was defeated by Christian forces he had Eutychius and several companions tortured and then put to death at Carrhae, Mesopotamia, in retaliation when they refused to abjure their faith. March 14.

EVA OF LIÈGE, BL. (d. c. 1265). A recluse at Liège, Flanders, she joined Bl. Juliana of Cornillon in a joint effort to have the feast of Corpus Christi established; it was sanctioned by Pope Urban IV in 1264. May 26.

EVANGELIST, BL. (d. c. 1250). He and his lifelong friend Peregrine joined the Hermits of St. Augustine near Verona, Italy. Both experienced visions and had the gift of healing, attracting thousands to their services. They died a few hours apart, and their cult was confirmed in 1837. March 20.

EVANS, PHILIP (1645–79). Born in Monmouthshire, Wales, and educated at Saint-Omer, he joined the Jesuits when twenty and was ordained at Liège in 1675. He was then sent to minister to the Catholics of southern Wales and was arrested in 1678 at Sker in Glamorgan, and when he refused to take the Oath of Supremacy was imprisoned in Cardiff Castle, where soon after he had Bl. John Lloyd as a fellow prisoner. They had both been arrested in the hysteria of the Titus Oates plot, but when no evidence of their complicity could be produced, they were charged and convicted of being priests illegally in England. They were both executed at Cardiff on July 22. Evans was canonized by Pope Paul VI in 1970.

EVARISTUS (d. c. 105). The son of Juda, a Bethlehem Hellenic Jew, he was elected Pope succeeding St. Clement sometime between 97 and 100. He died sometime between 105 and 107 and was probably buried near St. Peter. October 26.

EVELLIUS (d. c. 60). Reportedly he was one of Emperor Nero's counselors and was so impressed by the constancy and patience of Christian martyrs that he became a Christian and suffered martyrdom for his faith. May 11.

EVENTIUS (d. 304). *See* Optatus.

EVENTIUS (d. c. 113). *See* Alexander.

EVERGISLUS (5th century). According to the legend repeated in the Roman Martyrology, he was presented to St. Severinus to be consecrated to God at Tongres, Belgium, and was raised and educated by Severinus, who in time made him his archdeacon. Evergislus succeeded Severinus as bishop of Cologne and was later beaten to death in a church at Tongres. Actually, he lived at a later time, probably died peacefully, and St. Gregory of Tours has him one of a group of bishops sent by Frankish King Childebert II (575–95) to reform a convent in Paris. October 24.

EVERILD (d. c. 700). Daughter of a noble family in Wessex, England, she became a Christian and then a nun at York. St. Wilfrid gave her a place named Bishop's Farm, where she became abbess of a large community of nuns. It was later named Everildsham and is now Everingham. July 9.

EVERMOD (d. 1178). Impressed by the preaching of St. Norbert at Cambrai in 1120, he joined the Premonstratensians under Norbert, accompanied him to Antwerp to undo the harm wrought there by the heretical teaching of Tanchelm, and in 1134 succeeded Norbert as superior of the Gottesgnaden monastery. Four years later he was made abbot of the abbey at Magdeburg, and in 1154 he was appointed first bishop of Ratzeburg in Schleswig-Holstein. He ruled the see so effectively he is called the apostle of the Wends. February 17.

EVILASIUS (d. 303). *See* Fausta.

EVODIUS (d. c. 64). One of the seventy disciples, tradition has him ordained and consecrated bishop of Antioch by one of the apostles, probably Peter. It is believed Evodius was the first person to use the word Christian. May 6.

EVROULT. *See* Ebrulf.

EWALD (d. c. 695). There were two Ewalds, brothers from Northumbria and educated in Ireland, who went as missionaries to Westphalia, Germany, about 694. Surnamed "the Dark" and "the Fair" to distinguish them, they were both murdered at Aplerbeke, Dortmund, by barbarians who feared that their friendship with a local chieftain would lead to the adoption of Christianity and the suppression of pagan rites. The chieftain put the murderers to death and destroyed their village. October 3.

EXMEW, BL. WILLIAM (d. 1535). *See* Middlemore, Bl. Humphrey.

EXPEDITUS (no date). Mentioned in the Roman Martyrology as one of a group of martyrs who were executed at Militene, Armenia, there is no proof he ever existed. The popular devotion to him may have mistakenly developed when a crate of holy relics from the Catacombs in Rome to a convent in Paris was mistakenly identified by the recipients as St. Expeditus by the word *expedito* written on the crate. They began to propagate devotion to the imagined saint as the saint to be invoked to expedite matters, and the cult soon spread. April 19.

EXSUPERANTIUS OF RAVENNA (d. 418). He became bishop of Ravenna,

Italy, in 398, persuaded Stilicho not to loot the cathedral when he occupied Ravenna, and built the town of Argenta. May 30.

EXSUPERIUS (d. c. 135). Also known as Hesperus, he and his wife, Zoë, both Christians, were slaves of Catulus at Pamphylia, Asia Minor, during the reign of Emperor Hadrian. When they refused to eat food offered to the gods by their master on the birth of his son, they and their two sons, Cyriacus and Theodulus, were tortured and then roasted to death in a furnace. May 2.

EXSUPERIUS (d. c. 412). Born at Arreau in the High Pyrenees, Gaul, he became bishop of Toulouse about 405. He was noted for his charity, and in response to his query, Pope Innocent I sent him a list of the authentic books of the Bible, a list still observed in the Church today. St. Jerome dedicated his commentary on Zacharias to him. He may have been exiled toward the end of his life. September 28.

EXUPERANTIUS (d. 303). *See* Sabinus.

EXUPERIA (d. 257). *See* Symphronius.

EXUPERIUS (d. c. 287). *See* Maurice.

EYMARD, PETER JULIAN (1811–68). Born on February 4 at La Mure d'Isère near Grenoble, France, son of a cutler (at which trade he worked for a time), he entered the Grenoble seminary in 1831 and was ordained there in 1835. He engaged in pastoral work for the next five years and then joined the Marists. He served as spiritual director of the junior seminary at Belley and in 1845 was named provincial at Lyons. Always devoted to the Blessed Sacrament, he began to plan a religious congregation dedicated to Jesus in the Blessed Sacrament, and in 1856 his proposal for an institute of Priests of the Blessed Sacrament devoted to perpetual adoration of the Blessed Sacrament exposed was approved by Archbishop de Sibour of Paris. At first progress was slow, but in time the institute attracted new members, and in 1858 Peter began the Servants of the Blessed Sacrament (established as a religious community in 1864), whose nuns devoted themselves to perpetual adoration of the Blessed Sacrament. His congregation of priests was approved by Pope Pius IX during his lifetime but did not receive final confirmation until 1895. He also founded the Priests' Eucharistic League (it was not canonically erected until 1887), organized the Confraternity of the Blessed Sacrament, and wrote several books on the Eucharist. He died at La Mure on August 1, and was canonized by Pope John XXIII in 1962.

EYNON, BL. JOHN (d. 1539). *See* Faringdon, Bl. Hugh.

EYSTEIN ERLANDSSON (d. 1188). Chaplain to King Inge of Norway, he was appointed second archbishop of Nidaros (Trondheim) in 1157 and then went on a pilgrimage to Rome from which he did not return until 1161, having been made papal *legate a latere.* He labored to free the Church in Norway from interference in its affairs by the nobles and to bring to the Norwegian Church the practices and customs of the churches of Europe at that time, though celibacy for the clergy was largely unobserved in his country. He crowned the child Magnus King of Norway at Bergen in 1164, and was closely associated with the boy's father, Jarl Erling Skakke, who approved Eystein's code of laws. He was forced to flee to England in 1181 when Sverre claimed the throne on the grounds that he was the illegitimate son of King Sigurd and the rightful heir; from there Eystein excommunicated Sverre. Eystein returned to Norway in 1183 and was aboard a ship in Bergen Harbor when Sverre's fleet defeated Magnus, causing the King to flee to Denmark. The following year Magnus was killed in battle, Sverre became King, and Eystein made peace with him. Eystein (Scandinavian for Austin or Augustine) died on January 26. Though proclaimed a saint by a thirteenth-century Norwegian synod, he has never formally been named a saint.

F

FABER, BL. PETER. *See* Favre, Bl. Peter.

FABIAN (d. 250). A Roman layman, he was elected Pope on January 10, 236, reportedly because a dove settled on his head during the election. Little is known of his pontificate. He condemned Bishop Privatus of Lambaesa, Africa, for heresy, had considerable restoration work done on the catacombs, and suffered martyrdom in the early stages of Decian's persecution of the Christians. January 20.

FABIOLA (d. 399). A wealthy Roman patrician of the famous Fabia family, she was for a time a member of St. Jerome's circle but fell away, divorced her husband for his dissolute life, and remarried. On the death of her second husband, she returned to the Church, devoted herself to charitable works and aiding churches, and built the first Christian public hospital in the West, where she personally tended the sick. She visited Jerome at Bethlehem in 395, supported him in his controversy with Patriarch John of Jerusalem, decided not to join Paula's community, and on her return to Rome, continued her charitable work, opening a hospice for poor pilgrims at Porto with St. Pammachius. Jerome wrote two treatises for her and is the source of most of our information about her. December 27.

FACHANAN (6th century). Born at Tulachteann, Ireland, he studied under St. Ita, founded Molana Monastery on an island in the Blackwater, and later the monastic school of Ross (Rosscarbery), Cork, which became one of the most famous monastic centers in Ireland. August 14.

FACTOR, BL. NICHOLAS (1520–83). Born at Valencia, Spain, son of a Sicilian tailor, he joined the Observant Friars there in 1537, worked to convert the Moors in Spain, and was known for his extreme mortifications, his visions, his ecstasies, and for the miracles he was reported to have performed. He transferred to the Capuchins at Barcelona in 1583 but a few months later returned to the Observants at Valencia, where he died on December 23. He was beatified in 1786. December 14.

FAITH (2nd century). *See* Charity.

FAITH (3rd century). Her unreliable legend is that she was haled before Dacian, procurator at Agen, France, for her Christianity during Diocletian's persecution of the Christians. She was then tortured to death for her Christianity on a red-hot brazier. Also executed with her was St. Alberta (March 11); when some of the spectators objected, Dacian had them beheaded. October 6.

FALBOURG. *See* Walburga.

FALCONIERI, ALEXIS (c. 1200–1310). Son of Bernard Falconieri, a wealthy Florentine merchant and a Guelph, he with six other young Florentines joined the Confraternity of the Blessed Virgin in Florence about 1225. On the feast of the Assumption in 1233, they experienced a vision of the Blessed Virgin in which Mary inspired them to a life of prayer and solitude as hermits. They founded a house at La Camarzia on the outskirts of Florence and then moved to nearby Monte Senario, and in 1240, as the result of another vision of Mary, founded the Servants of Mary (the Servites), with Buonfiglio Monaldo superior general. They were all ordained except Alexis, who felt he was not worthy enough to be a priest and devoted himself to the material needs of the community and helped build the Servite church at Cafaggio. He was the only one of the seven still alive when the order was approved by Pope Benedict XI in 1304 and died at Monte Senario on February 17, reputedly at the age of 110. He and his six companions were canonized in 1888 by Pope Leo XIII as the Seven Holy Founders. February 17.

FALCONIERI, JULIANA (1270–1341). Of a wealthy Florentine family, she was raised by her mother and Uncle Alexis, one of the founders of the Servites, on the death of her father when she was quite young. She rejected her family's plans for her to marry and when she was fifteen was vested with the Servite habit by St. Philip Benizi. She became a Servite tertiary when sixteen, continuing to live at home. When her mother died in 1304, she headed a group of women dedicated to prayer and charitable works, was named superior, drew up a rule (which was approved for Servite nuns 120 years later by Pope Martin V), and is considered the foundress of the Servite nuns. She died in Florence and was canonized in 1731. June 19.

FANCHEA (d. c. 530). A native of Clogher, Ireland, and sister of St. Enda,

whom she convinced to become a monk, she may have been founding abbess of a convent at Ross Oirthir or Rossory in Ireland. March 21.

FANGI, BL. AUGUSTINE (1430–93). Born at Biella, Italy, he became a Dominican there, served as prior, reformed several friaries of his order, and became famed for his preaching and miracles. He spent the last decade of his life at the Dominican house in Venice and died there on July 22. His cult was approved in 1872. July 24.

FANTI, BL. BARTHOLOMEW (1443–95). Born at Mantua, Italy, he joined the Carmelites when seventeen and was ordained. He became known for his preaching and his miracles of healing. He died on December 5, and his cult was confirmed in 1909.

FANTINUS (10th century). A Basilian monk and abbot of St. Mercury Greek Monastery in Calabria, he suddenly left the monastery and went about the countryside preaching and lamenting the destruction to come. The invading Saracens destroyed St. Mercury and he went to the Peloponnesus, moved to Corinth, then to Larissa, Thessaly, and finally to Salonika, where he died famed for the miracles he is reputed to have performed. August 30.

FANTOSAT, BL. ANTONY (1842–1900). Vicar apostolic of southern Hunan Province in China, he was martyred at Hangchow on July 7 during the Boxer Rebellion in China. July 4.

FANTOU, BL. THÉRÈSE (1747–94). *See* Fontaine, Bl. Madeleine.

FANTUCCI, BL. MARK (1405–79). Born at Bologna, Italy, he gave up the large fortune he had inherited to become an Observant Franciscan when twenty-two. He was named guardian of Monte Colombo, became a noted preacher, served as minister provincial twice, and was elected vicar general to succeed John Capistran in 1456. Bl. Mark put into effect numerous reforms, strictly enforced St. Francis' rule, and founded a Poor Clare convent at Bologna headed by St. Catherine of Bologna. He traveled all over Europe and the Near East visiting Observant foundations, refused a cardinalate from Pope Paul II, and was responsible for defeating Pope Sixtus IV's plan to reunite Conventuals and Observants without any reform of the Conventuals. Bl. Mark died at Piacenza while delivering a Lenten mission there. His cult was confirmed in 1868. April 10.

FARE. See Burgundofara.

FARINGDON, BL. HUGH (d. 1539). Born at Faringdon, Berkshire, England, he used the name of his birthplace as his surname rather than his real name, Cook. He became a monk at Reading Abbey and was elected abbot in 1520. He early supported Henry VIII (he signed the petition to Pope Clement VII requesting the nullification of Henry's marriage to Catherine of Aragon), but when Henry suppressed the abbeys in 1539, Hugh refused to surrender Reading, for which he was arrested and charged with treason. He was tried with John Eynon, the parish priest at St. Giles, Reading, and John Rugg, a retired prebendary living at the abbey, and was found guilty. All three were hanged at the gateway to Reading Abbey on November 15, and were beatified in 1895. December 1.

FARO (d. c. 672). Brother of St. Chainoaldus and St. Burgundofara, he was raised at the court of King Theodebert II of Austrasia, married Blidechild, and then served at the court of Clotaire II. When he was about thirty-five he and his wife, by agreement, separated, and in time he became a monk at Meaux and was ordained. About 628, he was named bishop of Meaux, became Dagobert I's chancellor, and was noted for his aid to the needy and for his conversions. October 28.

FASANI, BL. FRANCIS ANTONY (1681–1742). Son of a farmer, he was born at Lucera, Apulia, Italy, christened Donato Antony, and was educated by the Conventual Friars Minor at Lucera. He joined the Conventuals on Monte Gargano when fifteen and was ordained at Assisi in 1705. After getting his doctorate in theology, he taught at the Conventual college in Lucera and became known for his teaching and preaching abilities, his charity, his concern for prisoners, and his devotion to the Immaculate Conception. He died at Lucera on November 29, and was beatified in 1951. November 27.

FAUSTA (d. 303). A thirteen-year-old girl at Cyzicum, Pontus, she so impressed her judge, Evilasius, with her faith in the face of the torture he had ordered for her that he became a Christian and both were martyred. September 20.

FAUSTINUS (d. c. 121). He and his brother Jovita were born at Brescia, Italy, and were arrested there by one Julian for their Christian preaching. According to dubious sources, they converted thousands when taken to Milan, Rome, and Naples, and on their return to Brescia, when they refused to apostatize, they were beheaded by order of Emperor Hadrian, who was passing through the city. A court official named Calocerus (April 18) was so impressed by their constancy that he was converted and baptized by Bishop Apollonius. Taken into custody, Calocerus was tortured at Asti and other Italian towns and eventually beheaded at Albenga, Liguria. February 15.

FAUSTINUS (d. c. 304). *See* Simplicius.

FAUSTUS (d. c. 304). With Januarius and Martial, he was arrested for his Christianity during Diocletian's persecution of Christians at Cordova, Spain. All three were subjected to terrible tortures and then burned to death. They were called the "Three Crowns of Cordova" by Prudentius, the Christian Latin poet. October 13.

FAUSTUS (c. 403–c. 493). Born perhaps in Britain but probably in Brittany, he may have been a lawyer but then became a monk at Lérins, where he was ordained. He was elected abbot in 433, became noted for his preaching, and in 452 was named bishop of Riez. He was a determined opponent of Arianism and Pelagianism, and at the request of the bishops at Arles and Lyons in 475 he wrote two treatises on free will and grace, several passages of which caused him to be criticized for semi-Pelagianism; they were later condemned at the Council of Orange in 529. He incurred the enmity of Arian King Euric of the Visigoths for his attacks on Arianism and was driven into exile by Euric about 478. After Euric's death he returned to Riez, where he remained until his death. Several of his writings are still extant. September 28.

FAVRE, BL. PETER (1506–46). Born of a family of farmers at Vilardet, Savot, on April 13 and named Lefèvre, he was sent to St. Barbe College in Paris in 1525 and there roomed with Francis Xavier and met Ignatius Loyola; the three became close friends. Peter was ordained in 1534 and celebrated the Mass at Montmartre on August 15 when the Society of Jesus (the Jesuits) came into being. He went to Rome with Ignatius and Diego Laynez in 1537, was a professor at the university there, and was sent by Pope Paul III to diets at Worms in 1540 and at Ratisbon in 1541 convoked by Emperor Charles V in an unsuccessful attempt to reconcile religious differences in Germany. Peter was dismayed at the state of religion and of the clergy there and decided that the remedy was to reform the Church rather than by discussions with the Protestants. He then preached ceaselessly, giving retreats based on Ignatius Loyola's *Spiritual Exercises* to laypeople with tremendous success in Germany, France, Portugal, and Spain. Among the successful results of his preaching was attracting Peter Canisius and Francis Borgia to join the Jesuits. Peter Favre was selected by Pope Paul to be his theologian at the Council of Trent, but he died in Rome on August 1 while preparing for the council, and his cult was confirmed in 1872. His surname is sometimes spelled Faber. August 11.

FAZZIO (1190–1272). Born at Verona, Italy, he became a goldsmith there, made pilgrimages to Rome and Compostela, and founded the Order of the Holy Spirit for the care of pilgrims and the sick. January 18.

FEBRONIA (d. c. 304). Raised by her Aunt Bryene, abbess of a convent at Nisibis, she was arrested when eighteen by officers of the prefect, Selenus, at the outbreak of Diocletian's persecution of the Christians. Interrogated by Selanus' nephew, Lysimachus, she was offered her freedom by the prefect if she would marry Lysimachus. When she refused and remained constant in her Christian faith, she was scourged, roasted, had her teeth pulled out and her breasts and limbs cut off, and then was axed to death. Lysimachus recovered her relics and was later baptized and then became a monk. Though honored by the Ethiopian Church and in parts of Italy, the whole story is based on unverifiable legends and may be a purely fictional tale. June 25.

FECHIN (d. 665). Probably born at Luighne (Leyney), Ireland, he was trained by St. Nathy, was founding abbot of Fobhar, or Fore, in Westmeath, and died of the plague that devastated Ireland in 665. January 20.

FELICIAN (c. 159–254). A disciple of Pope St. Eleutherius, he worked as a missionary in Umbria, Italy, and was consecrated bishop of Foligno by Pope St. Victor I, who seems to have bestowed on him the pallium, the first recorded bishop to have received it. He was bishop for some fifty years when he was arrested during Decius' persecution of the Christians for refusing to sacrifice to the pagan gods. He was tortured, scourged, and died just outside Foligno while being conveyed to Rome for his execution. At the same time, Messalina (January 19), who had received the veil from him and ministered to him in prison, was clubbed to death when she too refused to sacrifice to the gods. January 24.

FELICIAN (d. c. 290). See Victor of Marseilles.

FELICIAN (d. c. 297). He and his eighty-year-old brother Primus were Roman patricians who had become Christians and devoted themselves to aiding the poor and visiting prisoners. About 297, during the persecution of Christians by Emperors Diocletian and Maximian, they were arrested, and when they refused to sacrifice to the pagan gods were imprisoned and scourged, again haled before a magistrate named

Promotus at Nomentum, near Rome, tortured, and when they persisted in their Christianity, both were executed. June 9.

FELICISSIMUS (d. 258). See Sixtus II.

FELICITY (d. c. 165). A woman named Felicity was a martyr in Rome and was buried in the cemetery of Maximus on the Salarian Way, but all else about her is derived from various dubious legends. According to them, she was a woman with seven children and devoted herself to charitable works. She was so effective in conversion work that the pagan priests lodged a complaint against her with Emperor Antonius Pius, who caused her to be arraigned before Publius, the prefect of Rome. He used various threats and pleas in an unsuccessful attempt to get her to worship the pagan gods, and was equally unsuccessful with her seven sons. He remanded the case to the Emperor, who ordered them all executed. Felicity was beheaded with Alexander, Vitalis, and Martial; Januarius was scourged to death; Felix and Philip were beaten to death with clubs; and Silvanus was drowned in the Tiber. Seven martyrs with these names, commemorated on July 10, were buried in Roman cemeteries, one of them, Silvanus, near Felicity's tomb. The proximity gave rise to the legend that they were brothers (the so-called Seven Brothers) and her sons, but there is no evidence that they were her sons nor even that they were brothers. July 10.

FELICITY (d. 203). See Perpetua.

FELICULA (d. c. 90). When Count Flaccus, who had been rejected by Petronilla, foster sister of Felicula, sought to marry Felicula after Petronilla's death, she refused him. He then denounced her to an official of the government as a Christian who refused to sacrifice to the gods. She was imprisoned and starved for a week, turned over to the vestal virgins, who were unable to shake her in her faith, tortured, and then suffocated to death in a city sewer. June 13.

FELIM (6th century). Son of four-times-married Dedivas, he became one of the followers of St. Columba and is traditionally regarded as the first bishop of Kilmore, Ireland, though more probably he was a regionary bishop. August 9.

FELIX (d. c. 165). *See* Felicity.

FELIX (d. 180). *See* Speratus.

FELIX (2nd century). *See* Andochius.

FELIX (d. c. 212). A priest, he was sent with Fortunatus and Achilleus by St. Irenaus, bishop of Lyons, to Valence, France, to preach the gospel. There all three suffered martyrdom during the reign of Emperor Caracalla when their preaching made many converts. April 23.

FELIX I (d. 274). Nothing is known of him except that he was a Roman, the son of one Constantius, was elected Pope to succeed Dionysius on January 5, 269, and ordered the celebration of Mass over the tombs of martyrs in the catacombs. He died on December 30 and was not martyred as the Roman Martyrology states. May 30.

FELIX (d. c. 296). He and his brother were natives of Vicenza, Italy, who, during the persecution of Christians by Emperors Diocletian and Maximian, were tortured and then beheaded for their faith at Aquileia. June 11.

FELIX (d. 303). Bishop of Thibiuca, Africa, he refused to surrender the sacred books in his custody to Magnilian, the magistrate of Thibiuca, and was sent

to the proconsul at Carthage. When Felix persisted in his refusal, he was beheaded, probably on July 15. A later fictional addendum to his story had him sent to Rome by the proconsul in chains, and when Felix would not reveal the whereabouts of the sacred books to the prefect at Venosa, Apulia, Italy, he was beheaded. October 24.

FELIX (d. 303). According to legend, he and Nabor were Moorish soldiers in the army of Maximian Herculeus at Milan who were beheaded for their Christianity at Lodi, Italy, during Diocletian's persecution of the Christians. July 12.

FELIX (d. c. 303). *See* Honoratus.

FELIX (d. 304). *See* Optatus.

FELIX (d. c. 304). A priest in Rome, he was tortured and put to death during Diocletian's persecution of the Christians. On the way to the execution site, he encountered a Christian who was so impressed by Felix's faith that he publicly proclaimed his own Christianity and was ordered put to death with Felix. Both were beheaded. Since the name of the Christian he met is unknown, he was called Adauctus, "the added one," because his martyrdom was added to that of Felix. August 30.

FELIX (d. c. 400). Consecrated bishop of Trier in 386 by St. Martin of Tours, he attended the synod there, and built a monastery to which he retired when he resigned his see in 398, probably because Pope Siricus refused to recognize his election because he was elected by those responsible for the death of Priscillian, the leader of the Priscillianists, who had been executed in his see by order of Emperor Maximus in 386. March 26.

FELIX (d. c. 484). *See* Cyprian.

FELIX, BL.

227

FELIX II (III) (d. 492). Of an old Roman senatorial family, he was married, and when his wife died, he became a priest. He was elected Pope to succeed Simplicius in 483 and at once became embroiled in a dispute with Emperor Zeno when Felix denounced the Emperor's interference in ecclesiastical affairs with the publication of the imperial *Henoticon* in 482, which attempted to settle the difference between the monophysites and orthodox but instead exacerbated the dispute and implicitly condoned monophysitism. He sent legates to summon Acacius, orthodox patriarch of Constantinople, to Rome, only to find that his legates had held communion with the heretics and Acacius; and the Emperor had not removed Peter Mongus, a monophysite, as Patriarch of Alexandria, as he had demanded. A synod at Rome in 484 excommunicated the legates and Acacius who, supported by the Emperor, disregarded the excommunication, thus beginning the Acacian schism. Felix aided the African churches during the persecution of the Catholics there by Arian Vandal King Huneric and helped restore them when the persecution ended. Felix died on March 1. He is sometimes referred to as Pope Felix III to distinguish him from antipope Felix II, but he is II in the order of legitimate Popes.

FELIX III (IV) (d. 530). A native of Samnium and a priest, he was the choice of Emperor Theodoric for the papacy and was elected Pope and consecrated on July 12, 526, succeeding Pope John I. He ruled well, denounced semi-Pelagianism at the Council of Orange in 529, converted two pagan temples in the Forum at Rome to the basilica of SS. Cosmas and Damian, and secured a decree reserving the trial of clerics solely to the Pope. He is often called Felix IV because of the disruption in papal numbers for Popes named Felix by antipope Felix II

but is III in the order of legitimate Popes. September 22.

FELIX (d. c. 580). Little is known of him beyond the fact that he was bishop of Bourges, France, where he has long been venerated, participated in the Council of Paris in 573, was highly praised for his charity by Gregory of Tours, and had a poem by Venantius Fortunatus addressed to him. January 1.

FELIX (c. 513–82). A nobleman of Aquitaine, he was married when named bishop of Nantes in 549; his wife entered a convent, and he was ordained and accepted the post. He was known for his charity to the poor and for the cathedral he built at Nantes. He died on January 6. July 7.

FELIX (7th century). He and Augebert were Englishmen who had been captured and then sold into slavery in France. Felix was ransomed by St. Gregory the Great, studied for the priesthood, and was ordained; Augebert was ordained deacon. They were on their way back to England as missionaries when they were murdered by pagans in Champagne. September 6.

FELIX (d. 853). *See* Anastasius.

FELIX, BL. (1715–87). Born at Nicosia, Sicily, son of a poor shoemaker, and baptized James, he became a Capuchin at Mistreta when twenty-seven, taking the name Felix, after having been refused admittance to the Order seven years earlier. After a year at Mistreta, he was sent back to Nicosia, where he was tireless in his efforts to aid the poor and the sick, acquired a reputation for his healing powers, and ministered to the stricken during the plague that struck Cerami in 1777, sent there at the request of the local superior. He died on May 31, and was beatified in 1888. June 1.

FELIX OF CANTALICE (c. 1515–87). Born of peasant parents at Cantalice, Apulia, Italy, he was a shepherd and farm laborer in his youth, became a Capuchin lay brother at nearby Città Ducale Monastery in Anticoli, and became noted for his austerities and piety. He was sent to Rome in 1549 and spent the next thirty-eight years in the monastery there as questor, aiding the sick and the poor and revered by all. He was a friend of St. Philip Neri and helped in St. Charles Borromeo's revision of the rule for his Oblates. Felix was canonized in 1709. May 18.

FELIX OF DUNWICH (d. 648). A bishop from Burgundy, he was sent to evangelize the East Angles at the request of their ruler, King Sigebert, whom he had converted in Burgundy. He made Dunwich, Suffolk, his episcopal see, was a successful missionary in the Norfolk, Suffolk, and Cambridge areas, and is called the "Apostle of the East Angles." He died at Dunwich. March 8.

FELIX OF NOLA (d. c. 260). The son of Hermias, a Syrian who had been a Roman soldier, he was born on his father's estate at Nola near Naples, Italy. On the death of his father, Felix distributed his inheritance to the poor, was ordained by Bishop St. Maximus of Nola, and became his assistant. When Maximus fled to the desert at the beginning of Decius' persecution of the Christians in 250, Felix was seized in his stead and imprisoned. He was reputedly released from prison by an angel, who directed him to the ailing Maximus, whom he brought back to Nola. Even after Decius' death in 251, Felix was a hunted man but kept well hidden until the persecution ended. When Maximus died, the people unanimously selected Felix as their bishop, but he declined the honor in favor of Quintus, a senior priest. Felix spent the rest of his life on a small piece of land sharing what he had with the poor, and died there on January 14. His tomb soon became famous for the miracles reported there, and when St. Paulinus became bishop of Nola almost a century later (410), he wrote about his predecessor, the source of our information about him, adding legendary material that had grown up about Felix in the intervening century.

FELIX OF VALOIS (1126–1212). A hermit at Cerfroid, France, he and his disciple, St. John of Matha, secured in 1198 the approval of the Holy See for the Order of the Most Holy Trinity (the Trinitarians) to ransom captives from the Moors. John worked in Spain and Barbary while Felix, now in his seventies, founded St. Mathurm Convent in Paris and administered the French province from Cerfroid, where he died on November 4. By 1240, the Order had some six hundred monasteries. The cult of the two men was approved by Pope Alexander VII in 1666, though members of the Order believe the two cofounders were canonized in 1262 by Pope Urban IV. November 20.

FELTON, BL. JOHN (d. 1570). Of a Norfolk family, he was born at Bermondsey, London, England, and lived in Southwark. When it was discovered that it was he who had posted Pope St. Pius V's bull excommunicating Queen Elizabeth on the door of the Anglican bishop of London's house, John was arrested and imprisoned for three months, during which time he was racked three times. When he affirmed his belief in the supremacy of the Pope, he was hanged, drawn, and quartered on August 8 in St. Paul's churchyard, opposite the house where he had posted the bull. He was beatified in 1886.

FELTON, BL. THOMAS (1568–88). Born at Bermondsey, London, England, the son of Bl. John Felton, who was executed for his faith when Thomas was two, he was educated at Rheims and became a Minim friar. He was sent back to England to recover from an illness, was captured while on the way back to his monastery, and was imprisoned for two years. Released, he was again arrested, tortured to reveal the names of priests he knew, and then was hanged when only twenty at Isleworth, London, during the persecution of Catholics under Queen Elizabeth I. He was beatified in 1929. August 28.

FENN, BL. JAMES (c. 1540–84). Born at Montacute, England, he attended Oxford, was elected a fellow, and then was expelled when he refused to take the Oath of Supremacy. He became a schoolteacher in Somerset, married, and had two children, and on the death of his wife went to Rheims, where he was ordained in 1580. He was sent on the English mission, worked in Somerset for a time, and then was arrested and imprisoned at Ilchester. He was transferred to London, and after two years in Marshalsea Prison there was charged, with Ven. George Haycock, whom he had never met, with a conspiracy in Rome, where he had never been, to assassinate Queen Elizabeth I. They were convicted of the charge, and when Fenn refused a pardon if he would accept the Queen's ecclesiastical supremacy, he was hanged, drawn, and quartered at Tyburn on February 12. He was beatified in 1929.

FENWICK, BL. JOHN (1629–79). Born at Durham, England, he was converted to Catholicism, studied at St. Omer, and in 1656 joined the Jesuits. He was sent to England in 1675 using the pseudonym Mr. Caldwell, was arrested, and was accused of participating in the alleged "Popish plot" fabricated by the notorious Titus Oates to kill King Charles II.

Found guilty, he was hanged, drawn, and quartered at Tyburn. He was beatified in 1929. June 20.

FERDINAND III OF CASTILE (c. 1199–1252). Son of King Alfonso IX of León and Berengaria, daughter of King Alfonso III of Castile, he was born near Salamanca and became King of Castile at eighteen when his mother relinquished her claim to the throne on the death of her brother Henry in 1217. Ferdinand married Beatrice, daughter of King Philip of Swabia, in 1219 and despite opposition from his two half sisters, also became King of León when his father died in 1230. He spent twenty years of his reign fighting the Moors, driving them from Ubeda, Cordova, Cadiz, and finally in 1249 from Seville. He ruled wisely, was an excellent administrator, and established internal peace in the two kingdoms. He had Archbishop Ximenes as his chancellor, founded the University of Salamanca in 1243, rebuilt the cathedral of Burgos, and converted the mosque in Seville to a church. He married Joan of Ponthieu on the death of Beatrice, and died in Seville on May 30. He was buried in the habit of a friar minor in the Seville cathedral, and was canonized in 1671.

FERDINAND OF PORTUGAL, BL. (1402–43). Son of King John I of Portugal and Philippa, daughter of John of Gaunt, he was born on September 29 at Santarem, Portugal. He led a life of piety unusual for a prince in those days, was appointed grand master of the Knights of Aviz (originally the New Militia to Fight the Moors), but refused a cardinalate from Pope Eugene IV. With his brother, Henry the Navigator, Ferdinand led an army against the Moors at Tangiers, Africa, an ill-conceived expedition approved by his brother, King Edward, and it ended in disaster with the Portuguese defeated. Henry escaped, but

Ferdinand was captured and maltreated by his captor when Edward refused to ransom him with the stronghold of Ceuta. After six years of captivity, he died in prison at Fez on June 5, and his body was hung from the prison walls. He is often surnamed "the Constant," as he is the hero of one of the most popular tragedies, *El Principe Constante,* of the famous Spanish dramatist Pedro Calderón. Ferdinand's cult was approved in 1470.

FERGUS (8th century). An Irish bishop, possibly of Downpatrick, and surnamed "the Pict," he went to Scotland as a missionary, settled at Strathearn, Perthshire, and founded several churches there. He may be the same as Fergustus, bishop of the Scots, who attended a synod in Rome in 721. November 27.

FERNANDEZ, BL. AMBROSE (1551–1620). Born at Sisto, Portugal, he became an adventurer, sailed to Japan in quest of riches, and became a Jesuit lay brother there in 1577. He was imprisoned for his faith at Omura and died in prison of apoplexy. He was beatified in 1867. March 14.

FERNANDEZ, BL. ISABEL (d. 1622). A Spanish widow at Nagasaki in Japan, she was accused of sheltering Bl. Charles Spinoza and the beheaded while her four-year-old son Ignatius watched; he was then beheaded. She was among the 205 persons, beatified in 1867 as the Martyrs of Japan, who suffered martyrdom in Japan between 1617 and 1632. September 10.

FERNANDEZ, JOHN (1526–67). Born at Cordova, Spain, he was a wealthy dilettante until he joined the Jesuits at Coimbra as a lay brother. He joined St. Francis Xavier in Goa and was his companion in his missionary work in Japan. John compiled the first Japanese gram-

mar and dictionary to help in his catechetical work and died in Japan. June 20.

FERNANDEZ, BL. JOSEPH (1774–1838). A Spaniard, he became a Dominican and was ordained. He was sent to Tonkin in Indochina as a missionary, was appointed provincial there, and was later beheaded for his faith. He was beatified in 1900. July 24.

FERREOLUS (d. c. 212). Possibly a Greek but more probably a Gaul educated in the East, he was ordained a priest by Bishop St. Irenaeus of Lyons with Ferrutio, who was ordained a deacon at the same time, and the two were sent by the bishop to evangelize the area around Besançon. After some thirty years of successful missionary activity, they were arrested for their Christianity during the reign of Emperor Caracalla, tortured, and then beheaded. June 16.

FERREOLUS (d. 304). A Christian tribune in the imperial army at Vienne, Gaul, he was arrested by the governor, Crispin, for not revealing that St. Julian of Brioude, who lived with him before his execution, was a Christian. When Ferreolus announced that he too was a Christian, he was scourged and imprisoned. Miraculously released from prison, he was captured near Vienne and beheaded. September 18.

FERREOLUS, BL. (d. c. 670). Little is known of him but he is reputed to have been bishop of Grenoble (though this is questionable) who was driven into exile and then executed by Ebroin, mayor of the palace, for refusing his demands. Ferreolus' cult was approved in 1907. January 16.

FERREOLUS OF LIMOGES (d. c. 591). He became bishop of Limoges in Gaul about 579 and was highly regarded by St. Gregory of Tours. September 18.

FERRETTI, BL. GABRIEL (1385–1456). Of the noble Ferretti family of Ancona, Italy, he joined the Franciscans when eighteen, served as a missionary in the Marches, and became guardian of the Observant house in Ancona, where he died on November 12. His cult was confirmed in 1753.

FERRINI, BL. CONTARDO (1859–1902). Born on April 4 at Milan, Italy, son of a mathematics and physics teacher, he studied law at Borromeo College at Pavia, received his doctorate in 1880, and studied for two years at the University of Berlin. He returned to Italy in 1883 to edit an edition of Justinian's *Institutes*. Bl. Contardo was acquainted with some dozen languages, became reader in Roman criminal law in Pavia and then professor of Roman law, and in 1887 was made professor of Roman law at Messina. In 1894 he returned to the University of Pavia, where he was soon recognized as one of the outstanding authorities on Roman law. He was active in social work, was associated with the Ambrosian library, was a member of the St. Vincent de Paul Society and a Franciscan tertiary, helped found the St. Severinus Boethius Society for university students, and in 1895 was elected to the Milan Municipal Council. He died of typhoid at Suna (Novara), Italy, on October 17. He wrote some two hundred monographs and throughout his lifetime was regarded by his students and colleagues as one who lived a life of holiness in the midst of academia and while engaging in intellectual pursuits. He was beatified in 1947 and is the patron of universities. October 20.

FERRUTIO (d. c. 212). *See* Ferreolus.

FESTUS (d. c. 305). *See* Januarius.

FETHERSTON, BL. RICHARD (d. 1540). A secular priest who earned his doctorate at Cambridge, he was appointed archdeacon of Brecon in 1523, became one of Queen Catherine's chaplains, and served as Latin tutor for Princess Mary for ten years. He supported the validity of the marriage of Queen Catherine to King Henry VIII at the Convocation of 1529, for which he was named in the bill of attainder that included Cardinal Fisher in 1534 and was imprisoned in the Tower of London. He was hanged, drawn, and quartered at Smithfield with Bl. Edward Powell and Bl. Thomas Abel on July 30. Bl. Richard and Bl. Edward were beatified in 1886.

FIACHRA. *See* Fiacre.

FIACRE (d. c. 670). Also known as Fiachra, he was a hermit at Kilfiachra, Ireland, left to go to France, and then lived as a solitary at Breuil. Brie, on land given him by St. Faro, bishop of Meaux. Fiacre built a hospice for travelers, attracted many disciples, was known for his charity and aid to the poor, and was consulted by many for his spiritual wisdom. His miracles of healing became legendary. He is the patron saint of gardeners and the cabdrivers of Paris, whose vehicles are called *fiacres*, since the first coach for hire in Paris was located near the Hotel Saint-Fiacre. September 1.

FIDELIS (d. c. 303). Legend says he was a Roman officer at Milan who during the persecution of Christians by Emperor Maximian helped five Christian prisoners escape. The prisoners and two fellow soldiers, Carpophorus and Exanthus, were captured near Como and executed. Fidelis escaped but was caught at Samolito on the other side of Lake Como, scourged, and beheaded. Another version has them three Christian soldiers who fled the persecution and were captured and then executed at Como. October 28.

FIDELIS OF SIGMARINGEN (1577–1622). Born at Sigmaringen, Prussia, Mark Rey was educated at the University of Freiburg-im-Breisgau, where he also taught philosophy and studied law. He was tutor, 1604–10, to a group of Swabian aristocrats and traveled all over Europe with them. He then earned his doctorate in law and became a lawyer in Alsace known as the "poor man's lawyer." He gave up law for the religious life, donated his wealth to the poor and to needy seminarians, was ordained, and became a Capuchin monk in 1612, taking the name Fidelis. He served as guardian at various Capuchin houses, became a successful preacher, and with eight other Capuchins converted many Protestants in the Grisons, Switzerland. He was appointed head of the Congregation for the Spreading of the Faith, and his continued success with the Grisons incurred bitter animosity against him. While preaching at Seewis on April 24, he was fired upon, but the assassin missed; however, on the way back to Grüsch, where he had preached earlier in the day, he was murdered by a group of his opponents. He was canonized by Pope Benedict XIV in 1746.

FIDOLUS (d. c. 540). Son of a Roman official at Auvergne, Gaul, he was taken prisoner by soldiers of King Clovis' army and sold into slavery. He was ransomed by Abbot Aventius of Aumont Abbey, near Troyes, became a monk there, and later was elected abbot. His name is Phal in French, and the abbey was renamed St. Phal after his death. May 16.

FILBY, BL. WILLIAM (1555–82). Born in Oxfordshire, England, he graduated from Oxford, became a convert to Catholicism, and went to Rheims to study for the priesthood. He was ordained there in 1581, was sent on the English mission, and was arrested later the same year with St. Edmund Campion. Convicted of conspiracy against the Queen because of his priesthood, he was hanged, drawn, and quartered at Tyburn on May 30. He was beatified in 1886.

FILIPPINI, LUCY (1672–1732). Born at Tarquinia, Tuscany, Italy, on January 13, she was orphaned when quite young. She was brought to Montefiascone by Marcantonio Cardinal Barbarigo to participate in Maestre Pie Institute for training teachers and was put in charge of a school for young girls founded by the cardinal. She devoted the rest of her life to Maestre Pie, dedicating herself to improving the status of women, founding schools and educational centers for girls and women all over Italy, including the first Maestre Pie school established in Rome at the invitation of Pope Clement XI in 1707. Stricken with cancer the last years of her life, she died on March 25 at Montefiascone, and was canonized in 1930.

FILLAN (8th century). Son of Feriach and St. Kentigerna and also known as Foelan, he became a monk in his youth and accompanied his mother from Ireland to Scotland, where he lived as a hermit near St. Andrew's Monastery for many years, and then was elected abbot. He later resigned and resumed his eremitical life at Glendochart, Perthshire, where he built a church and was renowned for his miracles. Various legends attribute the most extravagant miracles to him, such as the one in which his prayers caused a wolf that had killed the ox he was using to drag materials to the church he was building to take the ox's place. Fillan died on January 19.

FINA. See Seraphina.

FINAN (d. 661). An Irishman, he became a monk at Iona and then succeeded

St. Aidan as second bishop of Lindisfarne. Finan opposed the introduction of Roman liturgical practices to replace the Celtic usage, was a friend of King Oswy of Northumbria, and baptized Penda of the Middle Angles and later King Sigebert of the East Saxons, who had been converted by Oswy. February 17.

FINBAR (d. c. 633). Reportedly he was the illegitimate son of a master smith and a woman of royal background. Born in Connaught, Ireland, and baptized Lochan, he was educated at Kilmacahil, Kilkenny, where the monks named him Fionnbharr (white head); he is also known as Bairre and Barr. He went on pilgrimage to Rome with some of the monks, visiting St. David in Wales on the way back. Supposedly, on another visit to Rome the Pope wanted to consecrate him a bishop but was deterred by a vision, and Finbar was consecrated from heaven and then returned to Ireland. At any rate, he may have preached in Scotland, definitely did in southern Ireland, lived as a hermit on a small island at Lough Eiroe, and then, on the River Lee, founded a monastery that developed into the city of Cork, of which he was the first bishop. His monastery became famous in southern Ireland and attracted numerous disciples. Many extravagant miracles are attributed to him, and supposedly the sun did not set for two weeks after he died at Cloyne. September 25.

FINCH, BL. JOHN (d. 1584). A native of Lancashire, England, he was married and a farmer who had come back to the Catholic Church. He harbored priests working on the English mission and acted as a clerk and catechist for them. He was arrested, tried with Bl. James Bell, and then condemned for treason, and both were executed at Lancaster on April 20. They were beatified in 1929.

FINGLOW, VEN. JOHN (d. 1586). Born at Barnby, Yorkshire, England, he went to Rheims to study for the priesthood and was ordained in 1581. He was sent on the English mission, worked in the northern part of England until he was captured at York, and was hanged, drawn, and quartered for his priesthood. August 8.

FINNIAN (d. c. 579). Born near Strangford Lough, Ulster, Ireland, reportedly of a royal family, he studied at Dromore under St. Colman, at Mahee Island under St. Mochae, and at Whitern in Strathclyde, where he became a monk. Forced to leave Whitern because of a prank he played on a Pictish princess who was enamored of him, he went to Rome and was ordained there. He returned to Ulster, founded several monasteries (one of which, Moville, was outstanding), and had St. Columba as a disciple. He and Columba became engaged in a dispute when Columba made a copy of the first copy of Jerome's psalter in Ireland, which Finnian had brought from Rome. He demanded Columba's copy, and Columba refused to give it to him. The dispute was finally settled by King Diarmaid, who ruled in Finnian's favor, and Columba was obliged to turn over his copy to Finnian. Finnian is reputed to have performed numerous extravagant miracles—moving a river, for example—and preached and founded a monastery at Holywood, Dumfries, Scotland. September 10.

FINNIAN OF CLONARD (c. 470–c. 549). Unreliable legend has him born at Myshall, Carlow, Ireland, and spending several years in Wales at monasteries under St. Cadoc and St. Gildas. He became a monk in Wales, returned to Ireland, and founded several monasteries, most notable of which was Clonard in Meath, which became a great center of learning, especially of Bible studies

(Finnian was a great biblical scholar). He died at Clonard of yellow plague, which swept Ireland. Though called a bishop in Ireland, it is doubtful if he was ever consecrated. He is often called the "Teacher of Irish Saints" and at one time had as pupils at Clonard the so-called Twelve Apostles of Ireland, one of whom was St. Columba. December 12.

FINNIAN LOBHAR (d. c. 560). Born at Bregia, Leinster, Ireland, he may have been a disciple of St. Columba (or perhaps was trained at one of Columba's foundations), was ordained by Bishop Fathlad, and may have been consecrated by him. He built a church that is believed to have been at Innisfallen, and so is considered by some scholars to have been the founder of that monastery. Later he lived at Clonmore and then went to Swords near Dublin, where he was made abbot by Columba when he left. Another account has him abbot of Clonmore Monastery for the last thirty years of his life. Lobhar means "the Leper," a name he acquired when he reputedly assumed the disease of a leper to cure a young boy of an illness. As is evident, much of the information about him is uncertain and conflicting, and it is not even certain what century he lived in. March 16.

FINTAN (d. 603). Trained as a monk by St. Columba, he settled at Cloneenah, led an eremitical life of the most extreme austerities, and became abbot of the community that grew up about him. He became famous for his prophecies, clairvoyance, and for the numerous miracles attributed to him. February 17.

FINTAN (d. c. 635). Also known as Munnu, he was a monk under St. Seenell at Cluain Inis, Ireland, for eighteen years and then left to become a monk at Iona. On his arrival, he found that Columba had died (though one tra-

dition has him living at Iona for a time until Columba died in 597), whereupon he returned to Ireland, founded a monastery at Taghmon (Tech Munnu), Wexford, and became its abbot. He was a firm supporter of the Celtic liturgical practices at the synod of Magh Lene in 630, developed Taghmon into an outstanding monastery, and reportedly contracted leprosy in the late years of his life. October 21.

FINTAN (d. 879). Born in Leinster, Ireland, he was taken to the Orkneys as a slave by Norse raiders, escaped, stayed with a bishop in Scotland for two years, and then went on pilgrimage to Rome. He stopped off at Rheinau in the Black Forest on the way home, joined the hermits there, and spent the last twenty-two years of his life as a hermit there. November 15.

FIORETTI, PETER (1668–1750). Following the death of Peter's father, his mother took the five-year-old boy to the Shrine of Our Lady of the Oaks, near their hometown of Viterbo. She dedicated his life to the Virgin Mother, whom Peter referred to as "momma" or "my other mother." In 1693 Peter became a Franciscan brother and proceeded to take on a wide variety of jobs within the province. He was a cook, a gardener, and a "quester"—a beggar for the brothers. Through his work, he met many people of all ranks in society. Consequently word of his friendliness and piety spread. Known for miraculous cures, prophecies, and spiritual wisdom, he was canonized in 1982. May 23.

FIRMINUS (4th century). Untrustworthy sources say he was born at Pampeluna (Pamplona), Spanish Navarre, was baptized by St. Honestus, and was consecrated bishop by St. Honoratus. Firminus was probably a regionary bishop, though it has been claimed he was bishop of Toulouse. He went to Gaul as a missionary and built his church at Amiens, where he was tortured and beheaded for his faith during Diocletian's persecution of the Christians. September 25.

FISHER, JOHN (1469–1535). Born at Beverley, Yorkshire, England, son of a textiles dealer, he entered Cambridge at fourteen, became a fellow of Michaelhouse, and was ordained when twenty-two. He served in various offices at the university, becoming vice chancellor in 1501, but resigned in 1502 to be chaplain to Lady Margaret Beaufort, mother of King Henry VIII. She made numerous gifts to Cambridge, among them founding Christ's College and St. John's and providing chairs of divinity at Oxford and Cambridge, which Fisher administered and for which she is regarded as the outstanding benefactress in Cambridge history. Fisher helped raise the standard of scholarship at Cambridge and in 1504 was named chancellor, a post he occupied until his death. He was named bishop of Rochester the same year and became internationally known for his writings—against Luther, on prayer and the sacraments, on the identity of Mary Magdalen—and for his sermons. He was named one of Catherine of Aragon's counselors in 1529 and became her leading champion against King Henry VIII's attempt to divorce her, incurring Henry's enmity. Soon after the case was recalled to Rome, Fisher became a leading opponent of Henry's attempt to become supreme head of the Church in England and brilliantly defended the supremacy of the Pope. Fisher was twice imprisoned, and attempts were made on his life, but he persisted. In 1534 he refused to accept the Bill of Succession because the oath accompanying it was an oath of royal ecclesiastical supremacy; he was immediately arrested, imprisoned in

the Tower of London, and stripped of all his offices. While he was in prison, Pope Paul III named him a cardinal, further infuriating Henry. After ten months in prison and after a farce of a trial Fisher was convicted of treason on trumped-up charges and beheaded at Tyburn on June 22. Fisher was not only one of the great scholars of his times, a close friend of Thomas More and Erasmus, and possessor of one of the finest libraries in Europe, but he was also an outstanding bishop, devoted to the people of his diocese. He was canonized, with Thomas More, in 1935 by Pope Pius XI. June 22.

FLANNAN (7th century). Son of Turlough, a chieftain of Thomond, Ireland, he was educated by a monk, went on pilgrimage to Rome, where he was consecrated bishop by Pope John IV, and on his return settled at Killaloe, of which he is traditionally considered the first bishop. Supposedly his preaching caused his father to become a monk under St. Colman. December 18.

FLATHERS, VEN. MATTHEW (c. 1580–1607). Born at Weston, Yorkshire, England, he went to Douai to study for the priesthood, was ordained in 1606 at Arras, and was sent on the English mission. He was captured almost at once, was condemned to death as a priest educated abroad, but instead was banished from England. He returned to his native land again, was again arrested, and this time was hanged, drawn, and quartered for his priesthood at York on March 25.

FLAVIA DOMITILLA. *See* Domitilla.

FLAVIAN (d. 259). *See* Lucius.

FLAVIAN (4th century). *See* Bibiana.

FLAVIAN (d. 449). A priest and treasurer of the church at Constantinople, he succeeded St. Proclus as patriarch in

447. Flavian incurred the enmity of Chrysaphius, chancellor of Emperor Theodosius III, when Flavian refused to send an expensive gift to the Emperor on his coronation, declined to make the Emperor's sister, Pulcherius, a deaconess, and condemned Eutyches, abbot of a nearby monastery, for his errors, which denied that Christ had two natures after the Incarnation—the beginning of monophysitism. The condemnation was repeated by Eusebius of Dorylaeum at a synod called by Flavian in 448, and Eutychius was deposed and excommunicated. The decision was sustained by Pope Leo I in a letter to Flavian, Leo's famous "Tome." Chrysaphius persuaded Theodosius to convene a council at Ephesus in 449. Dioscorus of Alexandria presided, and in meetings characterized by violence and intimidation by the Eutychian faction and the Emperor's soldiers, who refused to allow the papal legates to read a letter from Pope Leo, both Flavian and Eusebius were ordered deposed, and Dioscorus was declared patriarch. The order was enforced by the Emperor's soldiers, who forced the bishops present to sign the deposition order. Flavian was beaten so severely during the meeting that he died of the injuries three days later when sent into exile near Sardis, Libya. The acts of this "robber synod," as Leo called it, was undone when Theodosius died in 450 and the Council of Chalcedon in 451 reinstated Eusebius and deposed and exiled Dioscorus; on his accession to the throne in 451, Emperor Marcian had Chrysaphius executed. February 18.

FLAVIAN (d. 512). A Syrian monk, he represented his patriarch at the imperial court in Constantinople and was made Patriarch of Antioch in 498. He had supported Emperor Zeno's attempt in 482 to reconcile Catholics and monophysites with the *Henotikon,* which was condemned by Rome for favoring monophysitism but remained loyal to orthodoxy. He was deposed, with Patriarch Elias of Jerusalem, by Emperor Anastasius I for supporting the decrees of the Council of Chalcedon and refusing to support Anastasius, a Monophysite, in his favoring of monophysitism, and was exiled to Petra, Arabia, where he died. July 20.

FLAVIUS CLEMENS (d. c. 96). Brother of Emperor Vespasian and uncle of Titus and Domitian, who were Vespasian's successors as Emperor, he married Flavia Domitilla, niece of Domitian, with whom he was consul in 95. When Domitian learned he was a Christian, he had him beheaded. June 22.

FLORA (d. 851). Daughter of a Mohammedan, she was born in Cordova, Spain, and secretly raised a Christian by her Christian mother. Flora was betrayed by her brother, scourged, and put into his custody that he might persuade her to apostatize. She escaped, but later while praying in St. Acislus Church she met Mary, sister of a deacon who had just been martyred, and they both decided to give themselves up as Christians. They were sent to a brothel, and when their ordeal there failed to shake their constancy, they were beheaded. November 24.

FLORA OF BEAULIEU (1309–47). Of a good family, she was born at Auvergne, France, and joined the nuns of the Order of St. John of Jerusalem (the Hospitalers) at Beaulieu in 1324 despite the attempts of her parents to have her marry. She experienced various supernatural phenomena, among them visions, ecstasies, and levitation, and sometimes went for weeks without any sustenance. October 5.

FLORENTIUS (d. c. 304). *See* Sisinius.

FLORENTIUS (d. c. 451). *See* Nicasius.

FLORENTIUS (5th century). A Bavarian, he was ordained by St. Martin of Tours and sent to work as a missionary at Poitou, Gaul. He later became a hermit on Mount Glonne, Anjou, and attracted numerous disciples, for whom he built St. Florent le Vieux Monastery, where he died. September 22.

FLORENTIUS (d. c. 693). An Irish priest, he went to Alsace and became a hermit at the foot of Mount Ringelburg in the wilds of Haselac. He reportedly cured the blind, mute daughter of King Dagobert, who in gratitude helped him found a monastery at nearby Haslach. He was made bishop of Strasbourg about 678, brought Irish monks into his see, and built a residence to house them, which developed into St. Thomas Monastery. November 7.

FLORES, BL. LOUIS (1570–1632). Born at Antwerp, Belgium, of Spanish parents, he accompanied his parents to Mexico, where he joined the Dominicans. He served as master of novices for a time and in 1602 was sent to the Philippines. In 1620, a ship he was on was captured by the Dutch, who turned him over to the Japanese, who tortured him, imprisoned him for two years, and then burned him to death at Nagasaki. He was beatified in 1867. August 19.

FLORIAN (d. 304). An officer of the Roman army in Noricum (Austria), he surrendered himself to Aquilinus, the governor, at Lorsch when Aquilinus' troops were hunting Christians during Diocletian's persecution, declaring he was a Christian. He was scourged and then thrown into the River Enns with a rock around his neck. He is a patron of Poland and Upper Austria. May 4.

FLORIBERT (d. 746). Son of St. Hubert and Floribane, who died in childbirth, he succeeded his father as bishop of Liège in 727 and governed the see for eighteen years. April 27.

FLORUS (2nd century). According to Greek legend, he and his brother Laurus were stonemasons working on a pagan temple in Illyria. When the temple was completed, they and the two owners, Maximus and Proculus, were converted to Christianity, whereupon they destroyed the idols and converted the temple into a Christian church. They were arrested by the governor, and all four were drowned for their Christianity. In all probability, their story is a pious fiction. August 18.

FLUË, BL. NICHOLAS VON. *See* Nicholas von Fluë, Bl.

FOELAN. *See* Fillan.

FOGOLLA, BL. FRANCIS (1839–1900). *See* Grassi, Bl. Gregory.

FOILLAN (d. c. 655). Born in Ireland, he and his brothers, St. Fursey and St. Ultan, went to England about 630, built a monastery at Burgh Castle near Yarmouth, and worked as missionaries among the East Angles. When their monastery was destroyed by the Mercians under Penda, Foillan and Ultan decided to follow Fursey, who had gone to Gaul sometime earlier. They were welcomed to Neustria by King Clovis II, and Foillan founded a monastery, of which he became abbot, at Fosses on land given him by Bl. Itta near Nivelles Abbey, which she had founded. He had great success converting the Brabanters but with three disci-

238 FONTAINE, BL. MADELEINE

ples was murdered by a band of out-
laws in the forest of Seneffe outside
Nivelles, where he had just said Mass.
October 31.

FONTAINE, BL. MADELEINE (1723–
94). Born at Etepagny, France, she became a Sister of Charity of St. Vincent de
Paul in 1748. She was superior of the
convent at Arras when she, Françoise
Lanel, Thérèse Fantou, and Joan Gerard,
all sisters at the convent, were arrested
by the French revolutionary authorities.
When they refused to take the
Constitutional Oath, they were accused
on trumped-up charges of counter-
revolutionary activities. Madeleine was
convicted of the charges by a tribunal at
Cambrai, and the other three of being
accomplices; all four were then guillotined. They were beatified in 1920.
June 27.

FONTANELLA, BL. MARY (1661–
1717). Daughter of John Donato
Fontanella, count of Santena, the ninth
of his eleven children, she was born at
Baldinero, near Turin, Italy, joined the
Cistercians at Saluzza when twelve, but
returned home on the death of her father. When she was sixteen, over the objections of her family, she joined the
Carmel at Santa Cristina in Turin, spent
the next three years experiencing a period of great spiritual aridity and subjected to diabolical attacks, and then
began to experience numerous mystical
experiences, which she described in
1690 in a letter to her spiritual adviser,
Fr. Lawrence. She practiced the most
rigorous mortifications, was appointed
novice mistress in 1691, and three years
later was named prioress—a position she
held four times. She founded a Carmel
at Moncaglieri and died at Santa Cristina
on December 16. She is also known as
St. Mary of the Angles and was beatified
in 1865.

FORANNAN (d. 982). Bishop of
Domhnach-Mòr, a diocese in Ireland
the whereabouts of which is unknown,
he went to Belgium with twelve companions, reportedly in response to a
dream, and settled at the abbey of
Waulsort on the Meuse River. He was
appointed abbot in 962 and reformed the
abbey according to the Benedictine rule.
April 30.

FORD, BL. THOMAS (d. 1582). Born in
Devonshire, England, he received his
M.A. from Oxford and became a fellow
at Trinity College there. He was converted to Catholicism, went to Douai to
study for the priesthood, and was ordained there in 1573. He was sent on the
English mission in 1576 and worked
successfully in Oxfordshire and
Berkshire until he was arrested with St.
Edmund Campion. Ford was convicted
of conspiring against the Queen but
really for his priesthood and was hanged,
drawn, and quartered at Tyburn on May
28 with BB. Robert Johnson and John
Shert, when Ford further denied the ecclesiastical supremacy of the Queen. He
was beatified in 1886.

FOREST, BL. JOHN (d. 1538). He
joined the Observant Franciscans when
seventeen at Greenwich, England, studied theology at Oxford, and acquired a
reputation for wisdom and learning. He
returned to Greenwich, where he was
Queen Catherine's confessor and knew
King Henry VIII. He thought he had
convinced Henry in 1529 not to suppress his Order for their opposition to
his divorce of Catherine, but when the
Pope denied the petition for divorce,
Henry suppressed the Order in 1534 and
John was imprisoned for a time in
London. Reportedly he gained his freedom by submitting, but in 1538 he was
at a Conventual house in Newgate
under what amounted to house arrest.

Accused of denouncing the Act of Supremacy, he was arrested, agreed to several propositions, but when asked to sign them refused, denying the King's ecclesiastical supremacy. He was then ordered burned at the stake, dragged on a hurdle to Smithfield, and burned to death. Also burned with him was a wooden statue of St. Derfel, of which centuries earlier it had been predicted would one day be used to set a forest afire. He was beatified in 1886. May 22.

FORGIONE, FRANCESCO (Padre Pio) (1887–1968). Born into a devout family of Southern Italy, Francesco gave little indication that he would go on to become one of the more celebrated and controversial church figures of the twentieth century. Ordained a Capuchin priest in 1910, he took the name "Pio." He became the first priest in Church history to receive the wounds of Christ—the Stigmata—first, temporarily in 1910, and then permanently in 1918. Working as priest at the friary of San Giovanni Rotondo, where he would live for more than fifty years, the legend of the stigmatized priest spread; people made pilgrimages to attend his masses or have him hear their confessions. It was said that he had the ability to "see into a person's heart" and would often prompt those who came to him for confession to reveal sins they thought they could keep hidden even in the confessional. His notoriety did not always serve him well as he was placed under Church scrutiny and accused by some of self-promotion and fakery during the 1920s and early 1930s. Despite the hostility Francesco's ministry generated, his popularity with the people continued, and Pope Pius XI restored his priestly function in 1934. He used money sent to him by his followers to build the House for the Relief of Suffering, a hospital. He was canonized in 2002. September 23.

FORTESCUE, BL. ADRIAN (1476–1539). Born at Punsbourne, England, of an old Devonshire family and a cousin of Anne Boleyn, he was twice married, first to Anne Stonor in 1499 and twelve years after her death to Anne Rede; he had two daughters by his first wife and three sons by Anne Rede. He became a Dominican tertiary at Oxford, was a knight of the Bath and in attendance at the royal court, served as a justice of the peace for Oxford County, fought in France in 1513 and 1523, was in Queen Catherine's retinue on her trip to Calais, and attended Anne Boleyn at her coronation. Deeply religious, he became caught up in the controversy over Henry VIII's divorce from Queen Catherine and his subsequent marriages. Fortescue was arrested late in August 1534 on grounds not now known but was released the following spring. He was again arrested and sent to the Tower of London in February 1539 for refusing to take the Oath of Supremacy. He was condemned by attainder in April for treason by Parliament; what the treason was was never stated, but it was probably for refusing to recognize royal supremacy in ecclesiatical matters over the Pope. He was permitted no trial and was beheaded with Ven. Thomas Dingley at Tower Hill, London, on July 8 or 9. Fortescue was beatified in 1895. July 11.

FORTUNATUS (1st century). *See* Hermagoras.

FORTUNATUS (d. c. 212). *See* Felix.

FORTUNATUS (d. c. 296). *See* Felix.

FORTUNATUS (d. c. 303). *See* Honoratus.

FOTHAD (8th century). A monk at Faham-Mura, Donegal, Ireland, he became adviser and bard to King Aedh

Oirnidh and accompanied him on a military expedition against Leinster in 804. For his services, he is reputed to have secured a dispensation from serving in the military for the clergy. He was often called Fothad na Canoine, since his request for this dispensation, the *Remonstrance,* was called a canon.

FOULQUE OF NEUILLY. *See* Fulco.

FOURIER, PETER (1565–1640). Born at Mirecourt, Lorraine, on November 30, he was sent to the Jesuit university at Pont à Mousson when fifteen and joined the Canons Regular of St. Augustine at Chaumousey when twenty. He was ordained in 1589, resumed his studies, received his doctorate, and was named vicar and procurator of the abbey parish of Chaumousey. In 1597, he was sent as parish priest to Mattaincourt, a run-down and neglected parish where he spent the next thirty years reforming the lives of the parishioners and combating Calvinism. He lived a simple, austere life, organized several confraternities, and supported education for poor children. He opened a free school with four women volunteers, with Alix Le Clerq as superior, and organized them into an institute in 1598. The institute received papal approval as the Canonesses Regular of St. Augustine of the Congregation of Our Lady in 1616 and soon spread all over France and later to other countries. In 1622, Bishop John de Maillane of Tours appointed him to reform and unite the houses of his order into one congregation, and the following year he headed the abbey of Lunéville. In 1629, the Observant canons regular of Lorraine were united into the Congregation of Our Savior, and Peter was elected superior in 1632. He was refused permission by the Holy See in 1627 to allow his congregation to teach boys in elementary schools, but it did become involved in some educational

work. He fled to Gray in Franche-Comté in 1636 when he refused to take an oath of allegiance to King Louis XIII and spent the last years of his life as a chaplain in a convent there. He died on December 9 and was canonized in 1897.

FOURNET, ANDREW HUBERT (1752–1834). Born on December 6 at Maillé, near Poitiers, France, he resisted his mother's desire in his youth for him to be a priest and studied philosophy and law at Poitiers. A visit to a holy uncle who was a priest in a desolate parish turned him to the religious life. He studied theology, was ordained, and became his uncle's assistant. He became a parish priest at Maillé and completely changed his comfortable style of living for one of great austerity and simplicity. When the French revolutionary government outlawed priests who would not swear allegiance to it, he went into hiding and in 1792 went to Spain. He returned in 1797 but was at once forced to live the life of a fugitive. He resumed his pastorate when a concordat between Napoleon and the Holy See was signed in 1807, and with St. Elizabeth Bichier founded the Daughters of the Cross, a congregation dedicated to the education of children, for whom he composed a rule. He retired to La Puye in 1820 and devoted the rest of his life to the Daughters of the Cross and as a confessor and spiritual adviser. He died at La Puye on May 13, and was canonized in 1933. May 16.

FRANCA VISALTA (1170–1218). Born at Piacenza, Italy, she was raised at St. Syrus Convent from the age of seven, was professed there when fourteen, and in time became abbess. She was ousted as abbess because of the strictness of her rule but after several years became abbess of a convent at Montelana built by the parents of one of her followers, Carentia, and installed the Cistercian rule. They later moved the foundation to

Pittoli, where she died. Her cult was approved for Piacenza by Pope Gregory X. April 26.

FRANCES OF ROME (1384–1440). Daughter of Paul Busso and Jacobella dei Roffredeschi, a wealthy noble couple, she was born in the Trastevere, Rome, was married when thirteen to Lorenzo Ponziani, and for forty years was a model wife in an ideal marriage. With her sister-in-law, Vannozza, she ministered to the poor of Rome and led a life of great holiness. After she recovered from a serious illness during which she reported a vision of St. Alexis, they devoted themselves to the sick of Santo Spiritu Hospital until her son John Baptist was born in 1404. Despite her objections she was obliged to assume the responsibilities as head of the household when her mother-in-law died; Frances had two more children: a boy, Evangelist, and a girl, Agnes. During a plague and famine that struck Rome, Frances worked to alleviate its effects and even sold her jewels to aid the plague victims. The family fortunes suffered during the occupation of Rome by the antipapal forces of Ladislaus of Naples in 1408 (Lorenzo was wounded in the fighting), and in 1410, when Ladislaus again seized the city, Lorenzo was forced to flee, though the women remained. The Ponziani castle was looted, and the family holdings in the Campagna were burned and looted. In 1401 another plague took the life of Evangelist, and Frances turned her home into a hospital; two years later Agnes died. By 1414, when peace was restored and the Ponziani were recalled from banishment and their property restored, Lorenzo's health was broken. Frances nursed her husband, continued her charitable activities, and organized the Oblates of Mary (later called the Oblates of Tor de' Specchi, after the building they moved into), a society of women living in the world, not bound by vows, but dedicated to helping the poor and affiliated with the Benedictines of Monte Oliveto. When Lorenzo died in 1436, she entered the foundation, was made superior, and spent the rest of her life practicing great austerities until her death in Rome on March 9. She experienced numerous visions and ecstasies, performed many miracles of healing, had the gift of prophecy (she is said to have prophesied the end of the Great Schism), and reportedly was guided the last twenty-three years of her life by an archangel visible only to herself. She was canonized in 1608 and is the patroness of motorists.

FRANCIS (d. 1597). *See* Miki, Paul.

FRANCIS OF ASSISI (c. 1181–1226). Son of Peter Bernadone, a wealthy silk merchant, he was born at Assisi, Italy, and christened John by his mother during his father's absence; on his return he insisted the child be renamed Francis. Francis spent his youth in extravagant living and pleasure-seeking, went gaily to war, and was taken prisoner in 1202. On his release he resumed his carefree ways, was seriously ill for a time, and returned to the wars in 1205. A vision of Christ he experienced at Spoleto, followed by another on his return to Assisi, caused him to change his whole lifestyle. He went on pilgrimage to Rome in 1206 and on his return devoted himself to a life of poverty and care of the sick and the poor. He was angrily denounced by his father as a madman and disinherited in one of the most dramatic scenes in religious history. After repairing several churches in Assisi, he retired to a little chapel, the Portiuncula, and devoted himself completely to his life's work of poverty and preaching. He soon attracted numerous disciples, among them several leading citizens, Bernard da Quintavalla, merchant, and Peter of

Cattaneo, a canon of the cathedral, whom he robed on April 16, 1209, thus founding the Franciscans. In 1210, he received verbal approval of a rule he had drawn up from Pope Innocent III. Two years later Francis was joined by St. Clare, who joined him over the violent objections of her family. Obsessed with the desire to preach to the Mohammedans, he set out for Syria in the fall of 1212, but was shipwrecked on the way; a second attempt, 1213–14, also failed when he fell ill in Spain while on the way to Morocco, and he was forced to return to Italy. He obtained the famous Portiuncula indulgence from Pope Innocent III in 1216 and the following year (when he probably met St. Dominic in Rome) Francis convened the first general chapter of his order at the Portiuncula to organize the huge number of followers he had attracted to his way of life. In 1219, he sent his first missionaries to Tunis and Morocco from another general chapter, attended by some five thousand friars. He himself went to Egypt to evangelize the Mohammedans in Palestine and Egypt with twelve friars, but though he met with Sultan Malek al-Kamil at Damietta, Egypt, which was being besieged by Crusaders, his mission was a failure. Obliged to hasten back to Italy to combat a movement in his Order to mitigate his original rule of simplicity, humility, and poverty led by Matthew of Narni and Gregory of Naples, he secured the appointment of Cardinal Ugolino as protector of the Order and presented a revised rule to a general chapter of the Order at the Portiuncula in 1221, which maintained his ideals. A movement in the Order toward mitigating his rule, led by Brother Elias, began to spread and was met by Francis with still another revision, but this time he secured for it the approval of Pope Honorius III in 1223. By this time Francis had retired from the practical activities of the Order, and its direction

was mainly in the hands of Brother Elias. At Christmas of 1223, Francis built a crèche at Grecchia, establishing the custom observed all over the Christian world to the present day. In 1224, while praying in his cell on Mount Alverna, he received on September 14 the stigmata, the climax of a series of supernatural events he had experienced throughout his lifetime. He died at Assisi on October 3, and was canonized in 1228. Though never ordained, Francis' impact on religious life since his times has been enormous. Probably no saint has affected so many in so many different ways as the gentle saint of Assisi who, born to wealth, devoted his life to poverty, concern for the poor and the sick, and so delighted in God's works as revealed in nature. October 4.

FRANCIS OF CALDEROLA, BL. (d. 1507). Born at Calderola, Camerino, Italy, he became a Franciscan and spent his life in missionary activities. He was noted as an outstanding confessor and for his peacemaking abilities and helped Bl. Bernardino in establishing *monti di pietà*, lending institutions to aid the poor. Francis died at Colfano, Italy, on September 12, and his cult was confirmed by Pope Gregory XVI. September 28.

FRANCIS OF FABRIANO, BL. (1251–c. 1322). Born at Fabriano, Italy, the son of Campagno Venimbeni, a physician, he joined the Franciscans when sixteen and became a successful preacher. He wrote a defense of the Portiuncula indulgence and is said to be the first of his order to build up a library. His cult was approved in 1775. April 22.

FRANCIS MARY OF CAMPOROSSO. *See* Croese, Francis Mary.

FRANCIS OF MIAKO. *See* Francis of Nagasaki.

FRANCIS OF NAGASAKI (d. 1597). A Japanese from Miako, he became a physician and later was converted to Catholicism by the Franciscan missionaries in Japan. He became a Franciscan tertiary, served as a catechist, and was one of the twenty-six Catholics crucified for their faith near Nagasaki on February 5 during the persecution of Christians by the *taikō,* Toyotomi Hideyoshi. They were all canonized as the Martyrs of Japan in 1862. He is also known as Francis of Miako. February 6.

FRANCIS OF PAOLA (c. 1416–1507). Born at Paola, Italy, he was educated at the Franciscan friary at San Marco there and when fifteen became a hermit near Paola. In 1436, he and two companions began a community that is considered the foundation of the Minim Friars. He built a monastery where he had led his eremitical life some fifteen years later and set a rule for his followers emphasizing penance, charity, and humility, and added to the three monastic vows one of fasting and abstinence from meat; he also wrote a rule for tertiaries and nuns. He was credited with many miracles and had the gifts of prophecy and insight into men's hearts. The order was approved by Pope Sixtus IV in 1474 with the name Hermits of St. Francis of Assisi (changed to Minim Friars in 1492). Francis established foundations in southern Italy and Sicily, and his fame was such that at the request of dying King Louis XI of France, Pope Sixtus II ordered him to France, as the King felt he could be cured by Francis. He was not but was so comforted that Louis' son Charles VIII became Francis' friend and endowed several monasteries for the Minims. Francis spent the rest of his life at the monastery of Plessis, France, which Charles built for him. Francis died there on April 2, and was canonized in 1519.

FRANCIS OF PESARO, BL. (c. 1300–c. 1350). Francis Ceoco was born at Pesaro, Italy, and became a Franciscan tertiary. He lived as a hermit on Monte San Bartolo near Pesaro for some fifty years, known for his holiness and miracles, and with Bl. Michelina Metelli, he founded the Confraternity of Mercy at Pesaro and built a hospice at Almetero. His cult was confirmed in 1859 by Pope Pius IX. October 1.

FRANCIS OF ST. MICHAEL (d. 1597). Born at Parilla, near Valladolid, Spain, he joined the Franciscans as a lay brother and was sent from the Philippines to Japan to engage in missionary activities. He was arrested with his companion, St. Peter Baptist, in 1596, and with Peter and twenty-four others, was crucified near Nagasaki on February 5 during a persecution of Christians by the *taikō,* Toyotomi Hideyoshi. The twenty-six were canonized as the Martyrs of Japan in 1862. February 6.

FRANCIS DE SALES (1567–1622). Born in the family castle at Thorens, Savoy, on August 21, he studied at Annecy and the Jesuit college of Clermont in Paris, 1580–88, and then studied law and theology at the University of Padua, receiving his doctorate in law when only twenty-four. Despite the opposition of his family and the offer of a senatorship, he abandoned his prospects for a brilliant secular career for the religious life and was ordained in 1593, when he was appointed provost of Geneva. He spent the next five years as a missionary in the Chablais, the residents of which were fiercely resisting the efforts of the duke of Savoy to impose Catholicism on them by military force. Despite repeated attacks on him by assassins and mobs of Calvinists, he was most successful in attracting thousands back to Catholicism and making new converts. He was named coadjutor to the bishop of Geneva in 1599 and succeeded to the see in 1602. He soon became one of the outstanding leaders of the Counter-Reformation, noted for his intellect and wisdom. An outstanding confessor (he was confessor of Bl. Marie Acarie in Paris for a time) and preacher, his theological knowledge and understanding impressed all. He founded schools, taught catechetics, and governed his diocese ably and well. In 1604, he met Frances de Chantal, became her spiritual adviser, and with her, in 1610, founded the Order of the Visitation (the Visitandines). He died in Lyons, France, on December 28. Two of his writings, *Introduction to the Devout Life* (1609) and *Treatise on the Love of God* (1616), stressing that sanctity is possible in everyday life, have become spiritual classics and are still widely read today. His beatification the year he died was the first formal beatification held in St. Peter's; he was canonized in 1665. He was declared a Doctor of the Church in 1877 and designated patron saint of the Catholic press in 1923. January 24.

FRANCIS XAVIER (1506–52). Born at the family castle of Xavier near Pamplona in the Basque area of Spanish Navarre on April 7, he studied at the University of Paris, received his licentiate in 1528, and while there met Ignatius Loyola. Despite initial opposition to Loyola's ideas, he was won over and was one of the first seven Jesuits who took their vows at Montmartre in 1534. He was ordained at Venice in 1537 with Ignatius and four other Jesuits, went to Rome in 1538, and in 1540 (the year the Pope formally approved the Society of Jesus), he and Fr. Simon Rodriguez were sent, as the first Jesuit missionaries, to the East Indies. They stopped off at Lisbon, where King John III made Rodriguez remain, and Francis lost eight months there before finally leaving for

the Orient on April 7, 1541, with a brief from the Pope appointing him apostolic nuncio to the Indies. He arrived at Goa thirteen months later and spent the next five months preaching, ministering to the sick and imprisoned, teaching children, and laboring to correct the immorality of the Portuguese there, especially denouncing the practice of concubinage so prevalent in the city among the Westerners. He then spent three years at Cape Comorin at the southern tip of India opposite Ceylon (Sri Lanka), ministering to the Paravas, baptizing them by the thousands. He visited Malacca, 1545; the Moluccas, near New Guinea, and Morotai, near the Philippines, 1546–47; and Japan, 1549–51. He became the first provincial of India and the East in 1551 when Ignatius established the area as a separate province. Francis set out for China which he had always dreamed of evangelizing, in 1552 but died alone except for one companion, a Chinese youth named Antony, on the island of Shangchwan (Sancian) on December 3 in sight of the goal he was never to reach. Francis, with the possible exception of St. Paul, was the greatest of all Christian missionaries. He traveled thousands of miles to the most inaccessible places under the most harrowing conditions. His converts are estimated to have been in the hundreds of thousands; and his missionary impact in the East endured for centuries. Working with inadequate funds, little co-operation, and often actively opposed, he lived as the natives and won them to Christianity by the fervor of his preaching, the example of his life, and his concern for them. His miracles are legion, and his conversions are all the more remarkable in view of the fact that, contrary to a belief long held, he did not have the gift of tongues but worked through interpreters. He was called the "Apostle of the Indies" and the

"Apostle of Japan," was canonized in 1622 by Pope Gregory XV, and was proclaimed patron of all foreign missions by Pope Pius X. December 3.

FRANCISCO, BL. ANTONY (d. 1583). *See* Aquaviva, Bl. Rudolf.

FRANCO, BL. APOLLINARIS (d. 1622). Born at Aguilar del Campo, Castile, he studied law at Salamanca and after receiving his doctorate became a Franciscan of the Observance. He was sent to the Philippines as a missionary in 1600 and was commissary general of the Franciscan missions, 1614–17. He went to Omura in 1617, was arrested and imprisoned there for five years, and on September 10 was burned to death there for his faith. He was among the 205 beatified as the Martyrs of Japan in 1867.

FRANCO LIPPI (1211–91). Born at Grotti, near Siena, Italy, he lived a depraved life as a youth, joined a group of bandits, and led a life of crime and violence until he lost his eyesight when fifty. He changed his lifestyle completely, went on pilgrimage to Compostela, where he recovered his sight, and then to Rome, and there had a vision of Mary in which she told him to make public reparation for his sinful life. He went about in a sackcloth scourging himself with a whip and when sixty-five was refused entrance to the Carmelites, who told him to return in five years. He returned five years later, was admitted to the Order as a lay brother, and lived an edifying life for the next ten years, revered for his austerities, holiness, visions, and miracles. He died on December 11 and his cult was confirmed in 1670.

FRASSINELLO, BENEDICTA CAMBIAGIO (1791–1858). At the behest of her family, twenty-four-year-old Benedicta married Giovannia Battista Frassinello.

After two years of married life, the couple agreed to live celibately and pursue religious vocations. Giovannia joined the Somaschan Order, and Benedicta became an Ursuline sister. She went on to found the Congregation of the Benedictine Sisters of Providence, a teaching Order. She was canonized in 2002.

FRASSINETTI, PAULA (1809–1882). Despite a lack of formal education, Paula, the only daughter in a family of five children raised in Genoa, founded the Sisters of Saint Dorothy, an Order devoted to teaching poor children. Upon the death of her mother and her aunt three years later, she cared for her father and brothers, all four of whom became priests. In her early twenties following a bout with respiratory problems, Paula started a school for girls in Quinto, Italy. Later she founded her congregation, establishing schools in Italy, Portugal, and Brazil. Paula was canonized in 1984. June 11.

FREDERICK (d. 838). Grandson of King Radbon of the Frisians, he became a priest at Utrecht and soon was known for his holiness and learning. He was in charge of conversion work at Utrecht when he was elected bishop about 825. He labored to put the see in order, sent missionaries to the pagan areas in the northern part of his diocese, and incurred the enmity of Empress Judith when he reproached her for her immorality. He was stabbed to death at Maastricht, Flanders, by assassins; one story had them hired by the Empress; more probably they were from Walcheren, whose inhabitants deeply resented his missionary activities in their area.

FREDERICK, BL. (d. 1329). Born at Regensburg, Bavaria, of poor parents, he joined the Augustinian Hermits there as a lay brother and spent his life with them as a carpenter and doing menial tasks assigned to him. He was credited with performing miracles, and he died on November 30. His cult was confirmed in 1909. November 29.

FREDIANO. *See* Frigidian.

FREEMAN, BL. WILLIAM (c. 1558–95). Born in East Riding, Yorkshire, England, he was educated at Oxford and in 1586 was so moved by the martyrdom of Bl. Edward Stransham at Tyburn that he returned to the Catholicism he had earlier abandoned. He went to Rheims, was ordained in 1587, was sent on the English mission in 1589, and ministered to the Catholics of Worcestershire and Warwickshire. He became a tutor to the son of a Mrs. Heath at Stratford-on-Avon and was arrested early in 1595 in her house. Convicted of being a Catholic priest seven months later, he was hanged, drawn, and quartered for his priesthood on August 13. He was canonized in 1929.

FREITAS, BL. LUCY DE (c. 1542–1622). A Japanese woman, the widow of Philip de Freitas, a Portuguese merchant, she became a Franciscan tertiary, aided the Franciscan missionaries, and was arrested for giving shelter to Bl. Richard of St. Anne, a Franciscan priest, in her home. She was convicted of this crime, for which she was burned to death at Nagasaki on September 10. She was beatified in 1867.

FRIDESWIDE (d. c. 735). According to legend, she was the daughter of Didan, King of a region around the upper Thames River in England, and was requested in marriage by Algar, a neighboring prince. She fled to escape his attentions, and when he was struck blind

(he later recovered his sight when he desisted from his attentions to her), she built a cell in Thornbury Wood (Binsey), where she lived until her death. Actually, she probably did resist a royal suitor and founded St. Mary Benedictine convent at Oxford. October 19.

FRIDOLIN (c. 650). Unreliable sources have him an Irish priest who preached all over Ireland and then went to Gaul. He settled at Poitiers, where he reportedly recovered the body of the founder of St. Hilary Monastery there through a vision, was elected abbot, and rebuilt the church that had been destroyed in a Vandal raid and housed the relics there. He left when the work was well under way and then settled on an island in the Rhine, Säckingham, near Coire, Switzerland. He built a monastery, of which he was abbot, and a convent on the island, and later a school for boys. He was surnamed "the Wanderer" for the many trips he made to preach the gospel. March 6.

FRIGIDIAN (d. c. 588). Also known as Frediano in Italy, he was born in Ireland, reputedly the son of a King, and was ordained there. On a pilgrimage to Italy, he became a hermit on Monte Pisano near Lucca and in time was made bishop of Lucca, accepting only when pressured to do so by Pope John II. Frigidian fled the Lombard invasion of Lucca and on his return rebuilt the destroyed cathedral and helped the needy and the sick. He was known for his holiness and desire for solitude, and it is believed he formed a community of his clergy and lived with them. More than nine hundred years later, in 1507, his canons were merged with those of St. John Lateran. March 18.

FROILAN (832–c. 905). Born at Lugo, Galicia, Spain, he became a hermit at eighteen and attracted numerous disciples, among them Attilanus, who joined him when he was fifteen. They organized their followers into a Benedictine community at Moreruela, Old Castile, with Froilan as abbot, and then founded several other monasteries. In 900, Froilan became bishop of León, and at the same time Attilanus (October 5) was named bishop of Zamora. They were both known for their great holiness and charity and are considered the restorers of Benedictine monasticism in western Spain. Froilan died at León. October 3.

FRONTO (1st century). An early missionary to Périgord, France, his untrustworthy legend has him born in Lycaonia, of the tribe of Juda. He became a follower of Christ, was baptized by Peter, and was one of the seventy-two disciples. He was with Peter in Antioch and Rome, whence he and a priest named George were sent to preach to the Gauls. Fronto made his center at Périgord, of which he is considered the first bishop, and was most successful in his missionary activities, as was George, who is considered the first bishop of Le Puy. Another legend has Fronto born at Leucuais in the Dordogne near Périgord. All kinds of extravagant miracles were attributed to him in these legends. October 25.

FRONTO (d. 304). *See* Optatus.

FRUCTUOSUS (d. 259). Bishop of Tarragona, Spain, he was arrested by Emilian, the governor, during the persecution of the Christians by Emperors Valerian and Gallienus in 259, with two of his deacons, Augurius and Eulogius. When they refused to sacrifice to the pagan gods, they were all burned to death in the amphitheater at Tarragona on January 21. St. Augustine wrote a panegyric on him.

FRUCTUOSUS (d. 665). The son of a Spanish general in the Visigoth armies, he resolved to follow a religious life when his parents died. He was educated at the school founded by Bishop Conantius of Palencia, freed his slaves, and gave his wealth to the poor and for the construction of a monastery, and built a monastery, Comlutum, on his estate near Vierzo. On its completion, he left to become a hermit, attracted numerous disciples, including whole families, and built a monastery and convent for them with a rule designed especially for families. Prevented by royal edict from going to Egypt to live as a hermit, he was named bishop of Dumium, and in 656, when he also attended the Council of Toledo, he became archbishop of Braga, Portugal. April 16.

FRUMENTIUS (d. c. 380). He and another young man named Aedesius, who may have been his brother were natives of Tyre, and while on a voyage with their teacher, Meropius, about 330, everyone on the ship except them were killed by natives when the ship stopped off at Ethiopia. Taken to the King at Aksum, they were made members of his court, Aedesius as his cup bearer and Frumentius as his secretary. Freed on the death of the King, they remained on at the request of the widowed Queen to help rule the country, introduced Christianity, and brought in traders from the West. When the King's sons, Abreha and Asbeha, came of age, they resigned their posts. Aedesius returned to Tyre and was ordained. Frumentius went to Alexandria to ask St. Athanasius to send a missionary to the country he had just left. Athanasius consecrated Frumentius bishop of the Ethiopians and sent him back. He returned to Aksum and made numerous converts, including the two royal brothers, despite the attempts of

Arian Emperor Constantius to discredit him because of his connection with Athanasius. Frumentius was called Abuna (our father) in Ethiopia, and to this day, the title of the dissident Ethiopian Church's primate is Abuna. October 27.

FULBERT (c. 952–1029). Born and raised in Italy, he studied at Rheims under Gerbert, went to Rome when his teacher was elected Pope Sylvester II, and returned to France when Sylvester died in 1003. Fulbert became chancellor of Chartres and head of the cathedral school there, which under his direction became one of the most famous educational centers in Europe. He later was elected bishop of Chartres, rebuilt the cathedral when it burned down, had great influence among the secular leaders of his day, fought simony, and opposed lay ecclesiastical endowments. Sermons, hymns, letters, and several of his treatises are still extant. April 10.

FULCO (d. 1201). A priest at Neuilly-sur-Marne, France, he acquired a widespread reputation as a preacher, traveled throughout northern France denouncing the immorality of the times, usury, and the sins of men, bringing thousands to repentance with his eloquence and fiery sermons. His fierce exhortations and denunciations caused him to be imprisoned repeatedly but he persisted, denouncing even Richard the Lion-hearted for his evil life. In 1198, at the request of Pope Innocent III, Fulco preached the Fourth Crusade in northern France with enormous success, reputedly causing some two hundred thousand men to take the Cross during the three years he preached. He was about to join the Crusade when he died on March 2 at Neuilly. He is also known as Foulque and Fulk.

FULGENTIUS (468–533). Of a noble senatorial family of Carthage, Fabius Claudius Gordianus Fulgentius helped manage the family estate when his mother was widowed, became well known for his ability, and was appointed procurator and tax receiver of Byzacena. When twenty-two, he entered a monastery there governed by an orthodox bishop, Faustus, who had been driven from his see by Arian King Huneric. Fulgentius' mother caused such an uproar with her violent objections to Faustus' accepting her son into the monastery that Faustus was obliged to leave, and Fulgentius also left, to enter a nearby monastery where the abbot, Felix, insisted he rule equally with him. The two ruled for six years until in 499 they were forced to flee invading Numidians and went to Sicca Veneria. There they were arrested on the demand of an Arian priest, scourged, and tortured, but refused to apostatize from their orthodoxy and were then released. Fulgentius set out to visit the monks in the Egyptian desert but instead went to Rome in 500 to visit the tombs of the apostles. He returned to Byzacena soon after, built a monastery of which he was abbot and lived as a hermit in a cell nearby. He was appointed bishop of Ruspee (Kudiat Rosfa, Tunisia) in 508 and began a monastery there to continue his austere lifestyle, but before he could finish it was banished with scores of orthodox bishops to Sardinia by King Thrasimund. Encouraged by supplies and money from Pope St. Symmachus, they persisted in their faith. Fulgentius founded a monastery at Cagliari, became spokesman for the exiled bishops, and wrote several treatises, including his *An Answer to Ten Objections,* a reply to objections raised to his orthodox position by King Thrasimund when he summoned him before him, and *Three Books to King Thrasimund,* a refutation of Arianism.

The King was so impressed that he allowed Fulgentius to return to Carthage, but complaints from the Arian bishops caused him in 520 to be again banished to Sardinia, where he built a new monastery near Cagliari. He was allowed to return from exile with the other bishops in 523 when Thrasimund died, and he set about reforming the abuses that had crept into his see during his absence. About 532, he retired to a monastery on an island named Circinia, but later in the year returned to Ruspe, where he died on January 1.

FULK (c. 600). A pilgrim on his way to Rome, he stopped off at Castrofutli, near Arpino, Italy, to help minister to the victims of a plague devastating the area and was himself stricken and died of the pestilence. He is the patron saint of that section of Italy. May 22.

FULK (c. 1155–1231). Born at Genoa, Italy, he became a minstrel there and then joined the Cistercians at Thoronnet, of which he was elected abbot in 1200. Six years later he was named bishop of Toulouse, France, becoming known as "the minstrel bishop." He aided St. Dominic during the time Dominic was trying to establish the Dominicans. December 25.

FULK OF NEUILLY. *See* Fulco.

FULRAD (d. 784). Born in Alsace, he became a Benedictine, founded monasteries at Lièvre, Saint-Hippolyte, and Salone, and in 750 was elected abbot of St. Denis near Paris. He served in high office under Pepin, Carloman, and Charlemagne, and in the year he was elected abbot, he, with St. Burchard, went to Rome and secured the approval of Pope St. Zachary of Pepin as King of the Franks. Fulrad acted for Pepin in 756 in turning over the exarchate of Ravenna

to the Holy See, the early seeds of the Papal States, and helped in setting up the Frankish Kings as supporters of the Holy See rather than the Byzantine Emperor, a move that was to have an incalculable impact on the future of Europe. Under his able guidance St. Denis flourished as one of the outstanding monasteries in Europe. July 16.

FULTHERING, VEN. JOHN (d. 1605). *See* Welbourn, Bl. Thomas.

FULTHROP, BL. EDWARD (d. 1597). A gentleman in Yorkshire, England, he was hanged, drawn, and quartered at York on July 4 when it was found he had been reconciled to the Catholic Church. He was beatified in 1929.

FURSEY (d. c. 648). Probably born on the island of Inisquin in Lough Corri, Ireland, of noble parents, he left home to build a monastery at Rathmat (probably Killursa), attracted throngs of disciples, and then after a time at home began preaching. After twelve years, about 630, he accompanied his brothers, St. Foillan and St. Ultan, to England, where he settled at East Anglia with them and built a monastery, probably at Burgh Castle near Yarmouth, on land donated by King Sigebert. Sometime about 542, he went to Gaul, settled in Neustria, built a monastery at Lagny, and died soon after. January 16.

FUSCIAN (date unknown). According to legend, he and Victoricus were Romans sent to convert the Morini in Gaul. Despite opposition from pagan Gauls and Romans, they were moderately successful. On the way to visit St. Quintinus, they learned from an old man named Gentian at Sains near Amiens that Quintinus had been executed six weeks earlier. Meanwhile Rictiovarus, the governor, had heard of their presence and arrived with a troop of soldiers to arrest Fuscian and Victoricus. When Gentian resisted Rictiovarus, Gentian was beheaded on the spot. Fuscian and Victoricus were taken to Amiens, tortured, and then beheaded at Saint-aux-Bois. December 11.

FUSCULUS (d. c. 484). *See* Donatian.

G

GABINUS (d. c. 295). Brother of Pope St. Caius and father of St. Susanna, he was ordained in his old age, was imprisoned for his faith during Diocletian's persecution of the Christians, and died in a prison in Rome. February 19.

GABRA MIKA'EL (1791–1855). Born in Ethiopia, he became a monk of the Church of Ethiopia and was known for his zeal and scholarship. He was fifty when named one of the party sent to Alexandria in 1841 to ask the Coptic patriarch to appoint one of his monks Abuna (primate) of the Ethiopian Church. Among the party was a Vincentian priest, Justin de Jacobis, whom he accompanied to Rome after their visit to Alexandria. As a result of Gabra's contact with Fr. Justin and his experience in Rome, he was converted to Catholicism in 1844 and helped Fr. Justin train Ethiopians for the priesthood, write a catechism, and found a college at Alitiena, with Gabra in charge. They were both banished to the island of Massawa as a result of the insistence of Abuna Salama, who had been named head of the Ethiopian Church during the visit to Alexandria in 1841. There Fr. Justin was consecrated bishop in 1846, returned to Ethiopia secretly and ordained Gabra, then sixty, in 1851. They worked together and were quite successful in making converts until Kedaref Kassa, supported by Abuna Salama, led a successful revolt and became King Theodore II in 1855. To redeem a promise to Salama the new King unleashed a persecution of Catholics. Gabra Mika'el, with four colleagues, was imprisoned, tortured for months, and condemned to death on May 31, 1855; the sentence was commuted to life imprisonment through the intercession of the British consul, Walter Plowden. However, for the next three months the King had Gabra dragged in chains wherever he went until finally, on August 28, he died of his ill treatment. He was beatified in 1926. September 1.

GABRIEL. The archangel who was God's messenger to Daniel to explain his vision (Dan. 8:16–26) and prophecy (Dan. 9:21–27), he also foretold the birth of John the Baptist to John's father, Zechariah (Luke 1:11–21) and proclaimed the birth of Christ to Mary (Luke 1:26–38). September 29.

GABRIEL (1578–97). *See* Miki, Paul.

GABRIEL, MARY, BL. *See* Nicolas, Bl. Gabriel Mary.

GABRIEL OF OUR LADY OF SORROWS. *See* Possenti, Gabriel.

GAETANO. *See* Cajetan.

GAIANA. *See* Rhipsime.

GAIUS (1st century). Baptized with St. Crispus at Corinth by St. Paul (1 Cor. 1:14), the only two baptized there by Paul, he was Paul's host (Rom. 16:23) and was the "dear friend Gaius, whom I love in truth" to whom the third Johannine epistle is addressed. According to tradition, Crispin, who was president of the Corinth synagogue (Acts 18:8), became bishop of the island of Aegina; Gaius became bishop of Thessalonika and suffered martyrdom there. October 4.

GALANTINI, BL. HIPPOLYTUS (1565–1619). The son of a silk weaver in Florence, Italy, where he was born on October 12, he became a silk weaver too and then tried to enter a monastery. When refused because of ill health, he followed an austere and penitential life at home. He founded the Institute of Christian Doctrine (the Vanchetoni) to teach religion, wrote its rule in 1602, and saw it become the model for similar groups all over Italy. He introduced the practice of nocturnal adoration but was accused of heresy and cruelty, of which he was exonerated by a papal investigation. He died at Florence on March 20, and was beatified in 1824.

GALATION (no date). There is a pious fiction according to which he was the son of Clitophon and Leucippe, married the pagan Episteme, and converted her to Christianity. They sold all their possessions, gave the proceeds to the poor, Galation became a hermit and Episteme joined a community of dedicated virgins. When Galation was arrested for his faith in Phoenicia during Decius' persecution of the Christians, Episteme hastened to his side; both were then tortured and beheaded for their faith at Emesa. November 5.

GALDINUS (1100–76). A member of the prominent Della Scala family in Milan, where he was born, he served as chancellor and archdeacon of that see and accompanied Archbishop Hubert into exile when he was forced to flee the wrath of Emperor Frederick when the Milanese supported the election of Pope Alexander III in 1159 over the Emperor's candidate. He was named a cardinal in 1165 and succeeded Hubert as archbishop of Milan the following year. Galdinus helped rebuild Milan after Frederick's occupation, ministered to the sick, restored discipline among his clergy, and fought the Catharist heresy so widespread in Lombardy. April 18.

GALFRIDO. *See* Walfrid.

GALGANI, GEMMA (1878–1903). Born at Camigliano, Tuscany, Italy, she experienced many supernatural manifestations—visions of Christ, diabolical assaults, and the stigmata—in her short lifetime. Ill with tuberculosis of the spine, she bore her illness and the scorn of her relatives and the townspeople who jeered at her visions with great fortitude and to a heroic degree. Many of her conversations while in ecstasy were recorded. After her death on April 11, a popular cult developed, which led to her canonization in 1940.

GALL (c. 486–551). Born at Clermont, Auvergne, France, of a distinguished family, he became a monk at Cournon Monastery, a deacon at Clermont, and then a cantor at the chapel of King Theodoric. He was appointed bishop of Clermont in 526 and ruled there the next quarter of a century noted for his charities and humility. July 1.

GALL (d. c. 635). Born in Ireland, he studied at Bangor under SS. Comgall and Columban, became versed in Scripture, and was ordained. Gall was one of the twelve who accompanied Columban to Gaul and was with him at Annegray and Luxeuil. He followed Columban into exile in 610 and then to Austrasia, where they preached with little success in the region around Lake Zurich, and for two years in the area near Bregenz. When Columban went to Italy in 612, Gall remained behind because of ill health and on his recovery became a hermit on the Steinach River, attracting numerous disciples. In time, St. Gall Monastery occupied this site and during the Middle Ages was a leading center of literature, the arts, and music. Reputedly he was twice offered bishoprics by King Sigebert, whose betrothed he had freed of a demon. He is also reported to have been offered the abbacy of Luxeuil on the death of St. Eustace but declined, to remain a hermit. He died sometime between 627 and 645 at Arbon, Switzerland, and is considered the apostle of that country. October 16.

GALLA (d. c. 550). The daughter of Quintus Aurelius Symmachus, who was consul in Rome in 485, she was widowed a year after her marriage and joined a community of consecreated women on Vatican Hill, where she lived until her death of cancer, devoted to the care of the sick and the needy. St. Gregory wrote of her in his *Dialogues,* and *Concerning the State of Widowhood* by Bishop St. Fulgentius of Ruspe is believed to have been written for her. October 5.

GALLICANUS (d. c. 352). A Roman patrician, he was probably joint consul with Symmachus in 330 and was known for his generosity to the Church. Beyond this, legend has him a famous general in the reign of Constantine who defeated the Persians and then the Scythians and during the latter campaign was converted to Christianity by his brother. Gallicanus retired to Ostia, became famous for his charity and good works, and was forced into exile by Emperor Julian the Apostate when he refused to sacrifice to the pagan gods. He joined a group of hermits in Egypt but eventually was beheaded there for his

faith, all of which is in all probability a later fabrication. June 25.

GALLO, MARY FRANCES (1715–91). Born at Naples, Italy, and baptized Mary Rose Nicolette, she resisted her father's demand that she marry and in 1731 became a Franciscan tertiary at Naples, taking the name Mary Frances of the Five Wounds. She remained at home living a life great piety and austerity, badly treated and scorned by her family until 1853, when she became housekeeper for a priest. She experienced visions, suffered the agony of Christ's Passion, received the stigmata, and several times was reported to have received the Host miraculously. She practiced extreme mortifications, was sought after for spiritual advice and direction, prophesied the coming disasters of the French Revolution, and died at Naples on October 6. She was canonized in 1867.

GALMIER. *See* Baldomerus.

GALVEZ, BL. FRANCIS (1567–1623). Born at Utiel, New Castile, Spain, he joined the Franciscans at Valencia in 1591, was sent to Manila in the Philippines in 1609, and then to Japan in 1612. Forced to leave Japan in 1614 because of persecution of the Christians, he went back to Manila but then returned to Japan via Macao in 1618. His effective preaching and subsequent conversions caused him to be hunted down, and when captured he was burned to death on December 4 at Yedo with Bl. Charles Spinoza and forty-eight other Christians. They were beatified in 1867.

GAMALIEL (1st century). One of the great teachers of the law, honored in rabbinical circles with the title Rabban, he was Paul's teacher in Jerusalem (Acts 22:3), and it was Gamaliel's counsel to the Sanhedrin that caused that body to release Peter and the apostles, who had been arrested for preaching, with only a flogging (Acts 5:34–41). According to an ancient tradition, Gamaliel later became a Christian, and the finding of his body in Jerusalem is celebrated on August 3 in the Roman Martyrology.

GAMBACORTA, BL. PETER (1355–1435). Born at Pisa, Italy, the son of the ruler of that city, he became a hermit on Monte Bello when twenty-five. He attracted followers (reputedly bandits he had converted) and organized them into a community in 1380 called the Hermits (or Poor Brothers) of St. Jerome, which was approved by Pope Martin V in 1421 and spread all over Italy. He died in Venice, and was beatified in 1693. June 17.

GAMBARA-COSTA, BL. PAULA (1473–1515). Born near Brescia, Italy, she was married when twelve, despite her desire to lead a religious life, to noble Ludovico Antonio Costa. She became a Franciscan tertiary, and her extreme generosity to the poor alienated her husband, who brought a mistress into their home. When she died, Paula, who had nursed her in her last illness, was accused of poisoning her. She cleared herself and won back her husband's affections and his support for her charitable works and austere practices. She died on January 24, and her cult was confirmed in 1845.

GANDULF, BL. (d. 1260). Born at Binasco, near Milan, Italy, he became a Franciscan at Palermo, and then with a companion, Bl. Pascal, lived as a solitary on Sicily for the rest of his life, venerated for his preaching and miracles. April 3.

GANGALA, JAMES (1394–1476). Born at Montebrandone, Ancona, he studied law and then joined the Franciscans at Assisi in 1416. He studied under St.

Bernardino of Siena at Fiesole, was ordained when he was twenty-nine, and became an effective and forceful preacher. He worked as a missionary with St. John Capistran in Italy and in Germany, Bohemia, Poland, and Hungary, and in 1426, with John, was named inquisitor against the Fraticelli by Pope St. Martin V. They destroyed some thirty-six Fraticelli houses, and their severity (some of the Fraticelli were burned at the stake) and their tactics resulted in great violence and caused many objections. James attended the Council of Basle-Florence, helped reconcile the Hussites, but was unsuccessful in attempts to reconcile the Observant and Conventual Franciscans. In 1456, he was sent to Austria and Hungary to combat the Hussites. He refused an offer of the see of Milan, and in 1462 became involved with the Inquisition because of a sermon he preached at Brescia. The case caused a sensation and was referred to Rome; silence was imposed on all parties, and no decision was ever rendered. He died in Naples, where he spent the last three years of his life, on November 28. He was canonized in 1726 as St. John of the Marches.

GARCIA, BL. ANNE (1549–1626). The daughter of peasants, she was born at Almendral, Spain, and was a shepherdess until at twenty she joined the Carmelites under St. Teresa of Ávila as a lay sister at Ávila. She was a constant companion and secretary of Teresa for six years and was with Teresa at her death. Anne was then sent with a group of nuns to Paris to establish the Carmelite Reform in France. She served as prioress at Pontoise and Tours and then founded a Carmelite convent in Antwerp, where she became revered for her holiness, prophecies, miracles, and religious verse. She died at Antwerp, and was beatified in 1917 as St. Anne of St. Bartholomew. June 7.

GARCIA, GONZALO (d. 1597). Born at Baceim, India, of Portuguese parents (or Indians who took a Portuguese name), he went into business in Japan, and in 1591 became a Jesuit lay brother in Manila in the Philippines. He accompanied St. Peter Baptist to Japan as an interpreter in 1593, was arrested with Peter at Verela in 1596, and with Peter and twenty-four others was crucified near Nagasaki on February 5 for his faith during the persecution of Christians by the *taikō,* Toyotomi Hideyoshi. Gonzalo was canonized in 1862 as one of the Martyrs of Japan.

GARDINER, BL. JERMYN (d. 1544). *See* Larke, Bl. John.

GARICOITTS, MICHAEL (1797–1863). Born of poor peasant parents at Ibarra, near Bayonne, France, on April 15, he was a shepherd as a boy, studied at St. Palais College there and at Aire and Dax, and was ordained at Bayonne in 1823. He engaged in pastoral work at Candos, became a professor of philosophy at diocesan Bétharram Seminary and then rector, and in 1838 drew up a constitution for priests devoted to missionary work, the Priests of the Sacred Heart of Bétharram. The congregation encountered difficulties when the bishop replacing Bishop d'Astros, who had ordained him and encouraged him, disapproved of his ideas. Michael persisted in his efforts, but papal approval was not forthcoming until fourteen years after his death on May 14. He was canonized in 1947.

GARNET, THOMAS (d. 1608). Of a distinguished English Catholic family and nephew of Jesuit Fr. Henry Garnet, he was born at Southwark, England, educated at St. Omer's in France, and then went to the English Jesuit college at Valladolid, Spain, where he arrived in 1596, and was ordained. He was sent on the English mission, with Bl. Mark Barkworth, in 1599, was admitted to the Jesuits by his uncle, who was superior of the Jesuits in England, and after ministering to the Catholics of Warwick for seven years was arrested in 1606, the year his uncle was arrested and executed in connection with the Gunpowder Plot. Thomas was tortured for information about the plot but after several months' imprisonment at Newgate was released and deported to Flanders with forty-six other priests. He made his Jesuit novitiate at Louvain and returned to England in the fall of 1607. He was arrested six weeks later, charged with treason for his priesthood and for being a Jesuit, and condemned to death. When he refused to take the Oath of Supremacy, he was hanged, drawn, and quartered at Tyburn on June 23. He was canonized in 1970 by Pope Paul VI as one of the English and Welsh Martyrs.

GARNIER, CHARLES (c. 1605–49). Son of the treasurer of Normandy, he was born at Paris, educated at Louis-le-Grand College there, and joined the Jesuits in Paris in 1624. He continued his studies at Clermont, taught at the Jesuit college at Eu for three years, and was ordained in 1635. The following year he was sent to Quebec, Canada, with Fr. Pierre Chastellain and two other priests as missionaries to the Huron Indians. Charles was murdered by a war party of Iroquois, the Hurons' traditional enemies, on December 7 at the Indian village of Etarita, where he was stationed. He was canonized in 1930 by Pope Pius XI as one of the North American Martyrs. October 19.

GATIAN (d. c. 301). One of the six bishops who accompanied St. Dionysius from Rome to Gaul, he preached in the area around Tours for fifty years and is considered the first bishop of that city. December 18.

GAUBERT. *See* Waldebert.

GAUCHERIUS (1060–1140). Born at Meulan-sur-Seine, France, he became a solitary in the forests of Limoges, with a friend, Germond, when he was eighteen, and attracted many disciples. He organized them into St. John's Monastery at Aureil, of which he was abbot, and founded a convent for women. He died in a fall from a horse while returning to Aureil from Limoges. He was canonized in 1194. April 9.

GAUDENTIUS (d. c. 359). A cleric from the East, he came to Rome in 332, was named bishop of Rimini in 346, was an ardent opponent of the Arians, whom he opposed at the Council of Rimini, and was murdered at Rimini by the Arians. October 14.

GAUDENTIUS (d. c. 410). A native of Brescia, Italy, he studied under St. Philastrius there, went on pilgrimage to Jerusalem, and then became a monk at Caesarea in Cappadocia. He was elected to succeed Philastrius as bishop of Brescia, despite his own objections, and was consecrated by St. Ambrose about 387. He was one of three bishops sent by Pope Innocent I and Emperor Honorius to Constantinople to defend St. John Chrysostom before Emperor Arcadius in 405. They were imprisoned in Thrace and offered bribes in an unsuccessful attempt to get them to denounce Chrysostom. Eventually, they were freed and returned to Italy, where Gaudentius died. October 25.

GAUDENTIUS (d. 997). *See* Adalbert of Prague.

GAUDIOSUS (d. c. 585). Son of Guntha, an officer at the court of King Theodoric the Visigoth, he became a monk at Asan, near Burgos, Spain, under St. Victorianus and about 565 was named bishop of Saragossa, Spain, where he reigned until his death on October 29. November 3.

GAUGERICUS (d. c. 625). Known as Géry in France, he was born at Yvoi, Ardennes, was ordained by St. Magnericus, bishop of Trier, and about 586 was appointed bishop of Cambrai. He founded St. Médard Monastery, built a chapel on an island in the Senne around which Brussels developed, and was active in combating paganism in his see during the thirty-nine years he was bishop. August 11.

GAVAN, BL. JOHN (c. 1640–79). Born in London, England, he joined the Jesuits in 1660 when he was twenty and studied at St. Omer, Liège, and Rome. He was sent to England about 1670 and was arrested and convicted of participating in the alleged "popish plot," fabricated by the notorious Titus Oates, to assassinate King Charles II. John was hanged, drawn, and quartered at Tyburn, and was beatified in 1929. June 20.

GEDROYE, BL. MICHAEL (d. 1485). Born of noble parents at Gedroye Castle near Vilna, Lithuania, he was a dwarf, crippled, and a sickly child. He joined the Augustinian canons regular at Our Lady of Metro Monastery at Cracow, was permitted to live as a hermit in a cell adjoining the monastery, and lived a life of extreme austerity and holiness the rest of his life. He is reputed to have been subjected to diabolical attacks but was given the gifts of prophecy and the power to work miracles. May 4.

GELASIUS I (d. 496). Born in Rome, the son of an African named Valerius, he was a member of the Roman clergy when he was elected Pope on March 1, 492, succeeding Pope Felix II. Known for his holiness, justice, charity, and learning, Gelasius soon ran into difficulties with Euphemius, patriarch of Constantinople, over the matter of the Acacian heresy when Euphemius refused to remove Acacius' name from the diptychs in the churches of his see. Gelasius also defended the rights of the patriarchates of Alexandria and Antioch against the encroachments of Constantinople and eloquently defended the rights of the Church against Emperor Anastasius in a famous letter to the Emperor. Gelasius caused the revived pagan festival of Lupercalia in Rome to be abandoned and is said to have ordered the reception of the Eucharist in both forms, thus opposing the Manichaeans, who preached that wine was impure and sinful. *Decretum de libris* . . . , listing the canonical books of the Bible, and the Gelesian *Sacramentary,* long attributed to him, are no longer considered of his authorship. He died at Rome on November 21.

GEMINIAN (d. 348). A deacon at Modena, Italy, he was named bishop of that see, opposed Jovianism, and gave St. John Chrysostom refuge when he was on his way to exile in Gaul. January 31.

GEMMA, BL. (d. 1429). Born at Solmona, Abruzzi, Italy, of peasant parents, she was a shepherdess in her childhood, and when she grew older followed her religious bent and became a recluse in a cell adjoining the church in her native town, and lived there for forty-two years, until her death in her cell. A tradition says she was kidnaped by a local count because of her great beauty but convinced him to free her and build her a hermitage. May 12.

GENEROSA (d. 180). *See* Speratus.

GENESIUS (3rd century). During a stage performance before Emperor

Diocletian in Rome, the actor Genesius portrayed a catechumen about to be baptized in a play satirizing the Christian sacrament. In the midst of the ceremony he was suddenly converted to Christianity. When presented to the Emperor, he declared his Christianity. Enraged, Diocletian had him turned over to Plautian, prefect of the praetorium, who tortured him in an effort to force him to sacrifice to the pagan gods. When Genesius persisted in his faith, he was beheaded. Though the legend is an ancient one, it is no more than that. Genesius is the patron of actors. August 25.

GENESIUS (d. c. 303). A catechumen who was a notary at Arles, Gaul, he refused to record the order of Emperors Diocletian and Maximian decreeing the persecution of Christians when it was read out in the court in which he was serving and denounced the decree to the judge. Genesius then fled, sought baptism (which was denied him because of his youth), and when captured was beheaded on the banks of the Rhone River. August 25.

GENESIUS (d. c. 660). Known in France as Genet and Genès, he was born at Clermont of an outstanding family and became a subdeacon there. Despite his protests he was named bishop of Clermont, served five years, and then went on pilgrimage to Rome, hoping to become a solitary, but was brought back at the insistence of the people of his diocese. He built a church, monastery, and hospice and was highly regarded for his holiness, learning, and wise rule. June 3.

GENESIUS (d. 888). *See* Ageranus.

GENET. *See* Genesius (d. c. 660).

GENEVIEVE (c. 422–500). Born at Nanterre, near Paris, and also known as

Genovefa, she dedicated herself to God when only seven after meeting St. Germanus of Auxerre. When her parents died, she moved to Paris and became a nun at fifteen. Her visions and prophecies evoked hostility from the inhabitants of Paris, and an attempt was made on her life, but the support of Germanus and the accuracy of her predictions changed this attitude. She helped mitigate the rigor of the occupation of Paris by Childeric and his Franks and brought in boatloads of food for the people. She pleaded successfully with Childeric and later with Clovis to secure the release of captive prisoners. In 451, she predicted that Attila II and his Huns would bypass Paris, and after she led a crusade of prayer with the citizens, the city was left unmolested. She helped get a church built in honor of St. Dionysius and also convinced Clovis to build SS. Peter and Paul Church, where she was later buried. Many miracles were reported at her tomb in the church, which was later renamed in her honor. She is credited with saving Paris from many catastrophes, and an epidemic that swept the city in 1129 was reputedly ended through her intercession. She died in Paris. January 3.

GENGOUL. *See* Gengulf.

GENGULF (d. 760). Also known as Gengoul, he was a knight from Burgundy in the service of Pepin the Short, who was then mayor of the palace. After discovering that his wife had been unfaithful, he returned to his castle at Avallon near Auxerre, where he lived as a hermit and devoted himself to doing penances and charitable enterprises. He is reported to have been killed by his wife's lover at her instigation. May 11.

GENNADIUS (d. 936). A monk at Argeo, Spain, he became abbot of San Pedro de Montes Abbey at Vierzo, which he restored, and about 895 was named bishop of Astorga. He built several religious houses, resigned his bishopric about 931, and lived as a monk (or perhaps as a hermit) the rest of his life. May 25.

GENNINGS, EDMUND (1567–91). Born at Lichfield, England, he was brought up a Protestant, but impressed by the example of a Catholic named Mr. Sherwood, for whom he was a page, he became a Catholic about 1583. He followed Sherwood to Rheims to study for the priesthood and was ordained in 1590 after recovering from a breakdown in his health. He was sent on the English mission but was arrested within a year while saying Mass at the home of St. Swithun Wells. Gennings was convicted of being a Catholic priest and hanged, drawn, and quartered with Wells at Gray's Inn Fields, London, on December 10. Arrested with him were St. Polydore Plasden, a priest; John Mason, a native of Kendal, Westmorland; and Sidney Hodgson, a layman. They too were hanged, drawn, and quartered on December 10, at Tyburn. Gennings and Plasden were canonized by Pope Paul VI in 1970 as two of the Martyrs of England and Wales; Mason and Hodgson were beatified in 1929.

GENTIAN (date unknown). *See* Fuscian.

GENTILIS, BL. (d. 1340). Born at Matelica, near Ancona, Italy, he joined the Friars Minor, was ordained, and was twice guardian at the Minors' convent on Mount Alvernia. He was sent as a missionary to Egypt, met a Venetian ambassador to the Persian court, and accompanied him across Arabia to Persia. Gentilis preached with great success but was executed at Toringa, Persia, for preaching Christianity. His cult was approved by Pope Pius V. September 5.

GENULF (d. c. 250). According to legend, he and his father, Genitus, were sent from Rome to preach the gospel in Gaul. After building a church, they became solitaries at Celles-sur-Nahon and attracted numerous disciples. Genulf, also known as Genou, was reputed to have been the first bishop of Cahors, but this is very doubtful. January 17.

GEORGE (1st century). *See* Fronto.

GEORGE (d. c. 303). Although he is the patron of England, Portugal, Germany, Aragon, Genoa, and Venice and is venerated in the East as one of the Fourteen Holy Helpers, all that is known of him with any certainty is that he suffered martyrdom at Lydda, Palestine, sometime before the reign of Emperor Constantine and that he may have been a soldier in the imperial army. All else is myth and legend that began to appear in the sixth century. The story of his slaying of the dragon does not appear until the twelfth century and became popular after its appearance in the *Golden Legend* in the thirteenth century. According to it he was a Christian knight who came to Sylene in Libya, where a dragon was terrorizing the city. The people were supplying the dragon with a victim at his demand; the latest victim was a princess. George sallied forth, attacked, and subdued the dragon; the princess led it back into the city, and George slew it after the inhabitants agreed to be baptized. A later accretion had him marry the princess. He was known in England as early as the eighth century and had tremendous appeal in the Middle Ages as the patron of knighthood and soldiers, particularly among the Crusaders. "St. George's arms," a red cross on a white background, became the basis of the uniforms of British soldiers and sailors; the red cross appears in the Union Jack; and the Order of the Garter, founded about 1347, is under his patronage. April 23.

GEORGE (d. 814). A monk who became bishop of Antioch, Pisidia, his attendance at the General Council of Nicaea in 787, which denounced iconoclasm, caused Emperor Leo V the Armenian to send him into exile, where he died. April 19.

GEORGE (d. c. 825). Born at Cromna near Amastris on the Black Sea, he was ordained and lived as an anchorite on Mount Sirik. He later became a monk at Bonyssa Monastery and then, despite his objections, he was elected bishop of Amastris. He reigned wisely and helped in the successful defense of the city against attacking Saracens. February 21.

GEORGE LIMNIOTES (c. 635–c. 730). A hermit on Mount Olympus in Greece, he was ninety-five when he suffered martyrdom for his opposition to iconoclasm during the reign of Emperor Leo the Isaurian. August 24.

GEORGE MTASMINDELI (1014–66). A disciple of the famed monk Hilarion Tvalei in his youth, he lived as a hermit in Syria, traveled extensively in the Holy Land, was for a time abbot of Iviron Monastery on Mount Athos in Greece, and then lived in Armenia on Black Mountain (hence his surname Mtasmindeli—of the Black Mountain). He is remembered mainly for his translations of several theological treatises into Iberian (Georgian) and his revision of St. Euthemius' (cofounder of Iviron) Iberian translation of the Bible. George died on June 27.

GEORGE THE YOUNGER (d. c. 816). A wealthy native of Lesbos, he donated his wealth to the poor, entered a monastery, and was named bishop of Mitylene, Lesbos. He was noted for his holiness and charity but was exiled to the Chersonese for his support of the Catholic position during the iconoclasm controversy under Emperor Leo the Armenian and died there. George was called "the Younger" to distinguish him from two of his predecessors as bishop of Mitylene named George. April 7.

GERALD (d. 732). Born in Northumbria, England, he became a monk at Lindisfarne, and when the Celtic liturgical practices were forbidden in Northumbria left England and entered a monastery on the island of Inishbofin off the coast of Ireland. When the English and Irish monks there quarreled, he built a monastery for the English monks on the mainland for them. He succeeded St. Colman as abbot of the English monastery (Colman had been abbot of both) and may have founded two other monasteries and a convent. March 13.

GERALD (855–909). Of noble birth, he suffered a lengthy illness in his youth, became count of Aurillac on the death of his father, and was noted for his piety and his charity to the poor. After a pilgrimage to Rome, he built a church and abbey at Aurillac. He was blind the last seven years of his life and died at Cézenac, Quercy. October 13.

GERALD (d. 1095). Born at Corbie, Picardy, he became a monk at the abbey there, accompanied his abbot to Rome, and was ordained there by Pope St. Leo IX after a severe illness. He was chosen abbot of St. Vincent Abbey at Laon on his return from a pilgrimage to Jerusalem and when unsuccessful in his attempts to reform the abbey, he resigned and with several companions in 1079 founded the abbey of Sauve Majeure (Silva Major) on land donated by Count William IV of Poitou near Bordeaux. Gerald served as abbot until his death, noted for his preaching and as a confessor. He was canonized in 1197. April 5.

GERALD, BL. (d. 1177). Born in Lombardy, he joined the Cistercians at Fossanuova, Italy, was later named abbot of the monastery there, and in 1170 became abbot of Clairvaux. He was killed by one of the monks at Igny while visiting there. October 16.

GERARD (date unknown). According to untrustworthy sources, he and three companions, Arduin, Bernard, and Fulk, were pilgrims from England to the Holy Land in the seventh (or eleventh) century who were martyred at Gallinaro in the Abruzzi in southern Italy. Another tradition has Gerard and two companions, Peter and Stephen, coming from Auvergne to the Abruzzi during the First Crusade. August 11.

GERARD (935–94). Born at Cologne, Germany, he was educated at the cathedral school there and after his mother was killed by lightning devoted himself to the religious life. He became a canon at the cathedral and in 963 was appointed bishop of Toul, which he ruled for thirty-one years. He was a noted preacher, made Toul a center of learning by bringing Irish and Greek monks into the diocese, rebuilt churches and monasteries, and founded the Hôtel-Dieu Hospital in Toul. He also obtained from Emperor II a confirmation of the privilege granted his predecessor by which Toul under the bishop had its independence recognized. Gerard died at Toul on April 23, and was canonized in 1050 by Pope St. Leo IX.

GERARD OF BROGNE (d. 959). Of the family of the dukes of Lower Austrasia, he was born at Staves, Namur, and gave up his military career for the religious life. He brought the relics of St. Eugenius to Brogne from Saint-Denis, is reported to have been a monk at Saint-Denis for eleven years, and founded an abbey on his estate at Brogne, Belgium, in 919. He lived for a time as a recluse there and then was sent to reform the abbey at Saint-Chislain near Mons, Hainault, by the archbishop of Cambrai. He was so successful that Count Arnulf of Flanders appointed him to a position in charge of all abbeys in Flanders, Lorraine, and Champagne. He spent the next twenty years reforming the monasteries and restoring monastic discipline despite some opposition. He died at Brogne on October 3.

GERARD OF CLAIRVAUX (d. 1138). Brother of St. Bernard, he was a soldier when Bernard entered Cîteaux but joined him after having been imprisoned after he was wounded at the siege of Grancy. He followed Bernard to Clairvaux, became cellarer there and Bernard's close confidant and assistant, noted for his fervor and holiness. June 13.

GERARD, BL. JOAN (1752–94). *See* Fontaine, Bl. Madeleine.

GERARD MAJELLA (1726–55). Born at Muro in southern Italy, son of a tailor, he was apprenticed to a tailor on the death of his father, was turned down by the local Capuchins when he tried to join (because of his youth), and became a servant in the household of the bishop of Lacedonga. On the death of the bishop in 1745, he returned home and opened a tailor shop. He joined the Congregation of the Most Holy Redeemer (the Redemptorists) as a lay brother in 1748 and was professed by its founder, St. Alphonsus Liguori, in 1752. He served as tailor and infirmarian and became known for his extraordinary supernatural gifts—bilocation, prophecy, ecstasies, visions, and infused knowledge. He served as spiritual adviser to several communities of nuns, was most successful in converting sinners, and was widely known for his holiness and charity. In 1754, he was accused of lechery by one Neria

Caggiano—a charge she later admitted was a lie. He was sent to Naples soon after but when the house there was inundated by visitors wanting to see him, he was sent to Caposele a few months later, served as the porter there, and ministered to the poor of the town. He spent the last months of his life raising funds for new buildings at Caposele, where he died of consumption on October 15. He was canonized in 1904 and is the patron of childbirth. October 16.

GERARD, BL. MILES (d. 1590). Born near Wigan, Lancashire, England, he taught for a time, studied for the priesthood at Douai College in Rheims, and was ordained in 1583. Using the alias William Richardson, he and Francis Dickenson were sent on the English mission in 1589, and when their ship was wrecked on the coast of Kent were arrested and imprisoned. They were convicted of treason for being Catholic priests and were hanged, drawn, and quartered at Rochester on April 30 (or April 13). They were beatified in 1929.

GERARD SAGREDO (d. 1046). Born in Venice, he joined the Benedictines at San Giorgio Maggiore Monastery there and while on pilgrimage to Jerusalem was made the tutor to the son of King St. Stephen while he was passing through Hungary. Gerard was appointed first bishop of Csanad by Stephen in 1035 and labored with some success to evangelize his see. Stephen's death in 1038 unleashed a pagan reaction, and a series of conflicts among claimants to the throne broke out. Gerard was murdered by one of the competing factions at Buda on September 24. He is considered the protomartyr of Venice and is called "the Apostle of Hungary," where he is known as Collert.

GERARD TINTORIO, BL. (d. 1207). Born at Monza, Lombardy, Italy, of a well-to-do family, he was orphaned in his youth, built a hospital for the poor with his inheritance, and ministered to the sick, especially lepers, and the poor the rest of his life. He died on June 6, and his cult was confirmed in 1582 through the effort of St. Charles Borromeo.

GERARD OF VILLEMAGNA, BL. (1174–1245). Born at Villemagna, Tuscany, Italy, he was orphaned at twelve, served in the household of a wealthy Florentine whom he accompanied on the Third Crusade, and was captured by the Saracens. Gerard was ransomed, returned to the Holy Land with another Crusader, and was made a knight of the Holy Sepulcher. On his return to Italy, he became a hermit in his native town and later is reported to have been made a Franciscan by St. Francis. Gerard's cult was confirmed in 1833. May 23.

GERASIMUS (d. 475). Born at Lycia, Asia Minor, he became a merchant and when he was in Palestine embraced for a time Eutychianism. He was brought back to orthodoxy by St. Euthymius, visited various communities of hermits in the Thebaïd, Egypt, and on his return to Palestine, founded a *laura* near Jericho for the disciples who gathered around him. He became famous for his mortifications, the austerity of his rule, and his miracles. March 5.

GEREBERNUS (d. c. 650). *See* Dymphna.

GEREMARUS (d. c. 658). A Frankish nobleman from Beauvais, France, and also known as Germer, he became a member of the court of Dagobert I and met there and married Domana. They had three children, and when Amalbert, their son, was grown (their two girls had died), they decided to embrace a reli-

gious life. Geremarus received the monastic habit at Pentale and became abbot but when an attempt was made on his life by some of his monks who objected to the strictness of his rule, he resigned and became a hermit on the banks of the Risle River. When Amalbert died in 655, Geremarus used his inheritance to build a monastery at Flay, of which he was abbot until his death. September 24.

GEREMIA, BL. PETER DE (d. 1452). Born at Palermo, Italy, son of an official serving King Alfonso I, he studied law at Bologna and was on the verge of taking his degree when a vision led him to change his life. He joined the Dominicans at Bologna despite his father's objections, which he overcame and became known for his preaching. He was a theologian at the Council of Florence, praised by Pope Eugene IV, who appointed him apostolic visitor to Sicily, and was successful in reforming the religious houses on the island. Peter lived a life of great austerity and died at Palermo, where he was prior. His cult was confirmed in 1784. March 10.

GEREON (d. c. 287). *See* Maurice.

GERIZO (d. c. 1087). Born at Cologne, Germany, he joined the Benedictines at Monte Cassino under St. Desiderius (who became Pope Victor III) and was sent to Croatia by Pope St. Gregory VII to crown King Zwoinimir. October 21.

GERLAC (d. c. 1170). A military man in his youth, he went to Rome on the death of his wife and spent seven years nursing the sick and doing penance for the sins of his youth. He then returned to his native Holland, gave his possessions to the poor, and became a hermit on his estate near Valkenburg. The last years of his life were embittered by a dispute with neighboring monks who wanted him to enter their monastery. He has never been canonized but is honored locally. January 5.

GERLAND (d. c. 1100). Born at Besançon, Burgundy, France, he was related to Robert Guiscard and Roger, two Norman knights who recaptured Sicily from the Arabs. They entrusted him with their ecclesiastical affairs, but disillusioned by the immorality of his colleagues, he returned to Burgundy to live the life of a hermit. Roger recalled him, appointed him bishop of Girgenti, and he spent the rest of his life rebuilding and revitalizing his see. February 25.

GERMAIN. *See* Germanus (d. 576); Germanus of Auxerre.

GERMANICUS (d. c. 155). All that is known of him is that he was condemned to death by wild beasts in the amphitheater at Smyrna and won the admiration of the crowd by provoking the animals to attack him when they hesitated. January 19.

GERMANUS (d. c. 484). *See* Donatian.

GERMANUS (d. c. 540). Bishop of Capua in southern Italy, he was a member of a delegation sent by Pope St. Hormisdas in 519 to negotiate with Emperor Justin about ending the Acacian schism—a mission that was successful. October 30.

GERMANUS (c. 496–576). Born near Autun, France, he was ordained by St. Agrippinus and later was made abbot of St. Symphorian Abbey in Autun. He was named bishop of Paris in 554 by King Childebert I, was known for his charity and convert-making, and is reported to have miraculously cured the King of a fatal illness. Germanus constantly opposed the immorality of the court and the nobles and did not hesitate to de-

nounce and excommunicate even King Charibert in 468 for his immoral behavior. Germanus endeavored but without success to put an end to the fratricidal wars between Childebert's nephews. Germanus died on May 28.

GERMANUS (d. c. 677). Born at Trier, Gaul, he was raised and educated by Bishop Modoard of Triers. When seventeen Germanus gave his possessions to the poor and lived for a time as a hermit with St. Arnulph. On his advice, Germanus and his younger brother, Numerian, entered the monastery at Romberg (Remiremont); Germanus later went to Luxeuil and then was appointed abbot of Granfel in the mountain pass of Val Moutier by Duke Gondo, who had just founded the monastery. Germanus later also headed two other monasteries, St. Ursitz and St. Paul Zu-Werd, in Moutier Valley. Gondo's successor, Cathic (or Boniface), constantly looted and robbed the poor of the area. On one occasion, when his soldiers were looting the houses of the poor, Germanus remonstrated with them and he and a companion, Randcald, were murdered by the soldiers. February 21.

GERMANUS (d. 732). Born at Constantinople, the son of a senator, he was ordained, served for a time in the metropolitan church, and then was named bishop of Cyzicus. He was appointed patriarch of Constantinople by Emperor Anastasius II in 715 and convoked a synod that denounced monothelitism. Germanus opposed Emperor Leo the Isaurian's support of iconoclasm so strenuously that he was forced from office by the Emperor in 730. Germanus retired to his family home and remained there until his death. May 12.

GERMANUS (14th century). All that is known of him is that he and St. Sergius were Greek monks who founded the Russian monastery of Valaam (Valamo) on an island in Lake Ladoga, southeastern Finland, and that they evangelized the Karelians in the area. An untrustworthy legend says that Germanus was a Karelian pagan named Munga who was converted to Christianity by Sergius. Even the date of the foundation of Valaam is uncertain, with some authorities believing it was founded in the tenth century, while others believe that 1329 is more likely. June 28.

GERMANUS OF AUXERRE (c. 378–448). Born at Auxerre, Gaul, of Christian parents and also known as Germain, he studied at Gallic schools and then law at Rome and became a lawyer. After his marriage to Eustochia, he was named governor of the Amorican border provinces of Gaul and in 418 was named bishop of Auxerre. He changed his lifestyle, embraced a life of poverty and austerity, built a monastery, and endowed various poor churches in the diocese. In 429, he and St. Lupus, bishop of Troyes, were sent to Britain to combat the Pelagian heresy so rife there and were most successful in restoring orthodoxy. It was on this trip that occurred the famous incident in which Germanus is reputed to have saved a force of Britons from destruction by a superior force of marauding Picts and Saxons. He led the Britons to a narrow ravine between two high mountains, and when the enemy approached had the Britons shout "Alleluia!" three times. The echoes magnified the shouts causing the invaders to believe they were confronted by a far superior force, and they fled. Also at this time Germanus baptized many of the Britons in the army. On his return to Gaul, he convinced Auxiliaris, prefect of Gaul, to reduce taxes (reputedly by healing Auxiliaris' sick wife), and in about 440 again returned to Britain to combat

Pelagianism. Again he was successful, eliminating the heresy, and founded numerous schools to teach true doctrine. When he returned to Gaul, he found that Aetius, a Roman general, had dispatched a barbarian army under Goar to put down a revolt in Amorica. Fearful of the savagery of the barbarian forces, Germanus persuaded Goar to desist and then went to Ravenna in an unsuccessful attempt to persuade Emperor Valentinian III to call off the attack. Germanus' effort came to naught when news of another Amorican uprising reached the Emperor. Germanus died on July 31 while he was still in Ravenna.

GERMER. *See* Geremarus.

GERMERIUS (c. 480–c. 560). Also known as Germier, he was born at Angoulême, Gaul, was educated at Toulouse, and when thirty is supposed to have become bishop of Toulouse and to have reigned for fifty years, though his name does not appear on the episcopal lists of Toulouse. He founded two churches and a monastery at Dux on land granted him by King Clovis and was active in aiding the poor. He died at Dux. May 16.

GERMIER. *See* Germerius.

GEROLD (d. 978). According to legend, he was a member of a noble Rhaetian family who gave his lands to Einsiedeln Monastery in Switzerland and then became a hermit in a forest near Mitternach in the Wallgau. April 19.

GERONTIUS (d. 501). Bishop of Cervia (Ficocle), Italy, near Ravenna, he was murdered by bandits near Ancona while returning from a synod in Rome. May 9.

GEROSA, VINCENTIA (1784–1847). Born at Lovere, Italy, and christened Catherine, she devoted herself to helping the poor when she was orphaned in her youth. About 1824, she and St. Bartholomea Capitanio organized an institute to help the sick and the poor and to educate children, the Sisters of Charity of Lovere (Suore della Carità). She carried on the work of the community after Bartholomea died in 1833, and after a long illness Vincentia died on June 29. She was canonized in 1950. July 4.

GERTRUDE (c. 1256–c. 1302). Of unknown parentage and often surnamed "the Great," she was placed in the care of the Benedictine nuns at Helfta in Saxony when five and became a pupil of and close friend of St. Mechtilde. When older Gertrude became a nun and when twenty-six had the first of many visions of Christ she was to experience during her lifetime. She became versed in the Bible and the writings of Augustine, Gregory, and Bernard and began to record her supernatural and mystical experiences, a record that eventually appeared in her *Book of Extraordinary Grace (Revelation of St. Gertrude),* together with Mechtilde's mystical experiences *Liber Specialis Gratiae,* which Gertrude recorded. She also wrote with St. Mechtilde a series of prayers that became very popular, and through her writing helped spread devotion to the Sacred Heart. She died on November 17 at Helfta and though never formally canonized, Pope Clement XII directed that her feast be observed throughout the Church in 1677. She is a patroness of the West Indies. November 16.

GERTRUDE OF ALTENBERG, BL. (1227–97). Daughter of Louis IV, landgrave of Thuringia, and St. Elizabeth of Hungary, she was born two weeks after the death of her father while he was on a crusade, and when two she was placed in the Praemonstratensian abbey at Altenberg. She was raised and became a nun there and when twenty-two was elected abbess. She built a church and an almshouse, which she directed, and introduced the feast of Corpus Christi to Germany in her monastery. Her cult was authorized by Pope Clement VI. August 13.

GERTRUDE OF DELFT, BL. (d. 1358). Born at Voorburch, Netherlands, she became a servant at Delft, was engaged to be married, but her suitor married another and she became a *béguine.* She received numerous supernatural gifts, including the stigmata, which appeared on her body in 1340 and attracted crowds from all over the Netherlands. She is also known as Gertrude van Oosten because of her constant use of an old Dutch hymn ending with these words. January 6.

GERTRUDE OF NIVELLES (626–59). The younger daughter of Bl. Pepin of Landen and Bl. Itta, she was born at Landen and early devoted herself to a religious life. On the death of Pepin in 639, Itta built a double monastery at Nivelles, and mother and daughter entered it, with Gertrude as abbess. She resigned in 656 and spent the rest of her life studying Scripture and doing penances, gifted with visions. She died on March 17 and is considered the patroness of travelers (for her hospitality to travelers) and of gardeners.

GERVASE (1st century). Untrustworthy tradition has Gervase and his twin brother, Protase, the sons of Vitalis and Valeria, who suffered martyrdom for their faith. Both children were also martyred for their faith; Gervase was beaten to death with a lead-tipped whip, and Protase was beheaded. They are considered the first martyrs of Milan ever since St. Ambrose, guided by a vision, supposedly unearthed their remains there. June 19.

GERVASE, BL. GEORGE (1569–1608). Born at Bosham, Sussex, England, he was raised a Protestant and in 1595 left Plymouth on St. Francis Drake's expedition to the Indies (he was probably "pressed" into service). He served in the Spanish army in Flanders for two years on his return, and in about 1599 entered the English college at Douai. He was ordained at Cambrai in 1603, was sent on the English mission, and within two months had been arrested and imprisoned. When he refused to take the Oath of Allegiance and admitted he was a Catholic priest, he was hanged at Tyburn on April 11. He was beatified in 1929.

GERVINUS (d. 1075). Born at Rheims, France, he studied at the episcopal school there, was ordained, and became a canon at Rheims. He then became a monk at Saint-Vanne Abbey at Verdun, was known for his learning, and in 1045 was appointed abbot of Saint-Riquier by King Henry I. Gervinus traveled widely on preaching tours, acquired an extensive collection of Greek and Latin manuscripts for his library (he was a scholar of Latin classics), and was a much-sought-after confessor. He visited England several times on abbey business, became a close friend of Edward the Confessor, and accompanied Pope St. Leo IX back to Rome after the Pontiff had consecrated St. Remigius Church in Rheims. Afflicted with leprosy the last four years of his life, Gervinus died on March 3.

GÉRY. *See* Desiderius (d. 655); Gaugericus.

GETULIUS (d. c. 120). The husband of St. Symphorosa, he resigned as an officer in the Roman army when converted to Christianity and retired to his estate near Tivoli in the Sabine Hills with a group of Christians. When he converted Cerealis, the imperial legate, who had been sent to arrest him, Consul Licinius, by order of Emperor Hadrian, arrested both of them and Getulius' brother Amantius (a tribune in the Roman army and a Christian). All three were executed for their faith at Tivoli, with one Primitivus, after torture and imprisonment. June 10.

GHÈBRE, MICHAEL. *See* Gabra Mika'el.

GHISLAIN. *See* Gislenus.

GIANELLI, ANTONY (1789–1846). Born at Cerreto, near Genoa, Italy, he studied there and was ordained in 1812 by special dispensation, since he was not of canonical age for ordination. He engaged in pastoral and educational work, gave numerous missions, and became known for his preaching and as a confessor. He founded a congregation of men, Missioners of St. Alphonsus Liguori, and one of women, Sisters of Mary dell' Orto, devoted to teaching poor children and caring for the sick, which spread to the United States and Asia. In 1838, he was appointed bishop of Bobbio, where he ruled wisely until his death. He was canonized in 1951. June 7.

GIBRIAN (d. c. 515). An Irish priest, he led his six brothers and three sisters to Brittany, and all ten of them became solitaries near the junction of the Marne and Coole rivers. They are all venerated as saints. May 8.

GIBSON, VEN. WILLIAM (d. 1596). *See* Knight, Ven. William.

GIL, BL. FRANCIS (1702–44). Born at Tortosa, Spain, he joined the Dominicans at Barcelona and was then sent as a missionary to Manila in the Philippines. After a time there he was sent to Tonkin (in northern Vietnam), where he worked at his missionary activities for years before being arrested. He was imprisoned for several years and then beheaded for his faith at Checo. He was beatified in 1906. January 22.

GILBERT (d. 1245). Born at Moray, Scotland, he was ordained and became archdeacon there. In 1176, at a council at Northampton, he is reputed to have spoken on behalf of the Scottish bishops opposing the suggestion that they should be suffragans of York, though this is doubtful, since he did not become bishop of Caithness until 1223. He served as high steward for several of the Scottish Kings, built several hospices and the cathedral at Dornoch, and was an eloquent preacher. April 1.

GILBERT OF SEMPRINGHAM (c. 1083–1189). Born at Sempringham, England, son of Jocelin, a wealthy Norman knight, he was sent to France to study and returned to England to receive the benefices of Sempringham and Tirington from his father. He became a clerk in the household of Bishop Robert Bloet of Lincoln and was ordained by Robert's successor, Alexander. He returned to Sempringham as lord on the death of his father in 1131. In the same year he began acting as adviser for a group of seven young women living in enclosure with lay sisters and brothers and decided the community should be incorporated into an established religious order. After several new foundations were established, Gilbert went to Cîteaux in 1148 to ask the Cistercians to take over the community. When the Cistercians declined to take on the governing of a group of women, Gilbert, with the approval of Pope Eugene III, continued the community with the addition of canons regular for its spiritual directors and Gilbert as master general. The community became known as the Gilbertine Order, the only English religious order originating in the medieval period; it eventually had twenty-six monasteries, which continued in existence until King Henry VIII suppressed monasteries in England. Gilbert imposed a strict rule on his Order and became noted for his own austerities and concern for the poor. He was imprisoned in 1165 on a false charge of aiding Thomas of Canterbury during the latter's exile but was exonerated of the charge. He was faced with a revolt of some of his lay brothers when he was ninety but was sustained by Pope Alexander III. Gilbert resigned his office late in life because of blindness and died at Sempringham. He was canonized in 1202. February 16.

GILDAS (c. 500–c. 570). Born in the lower Clyde River area in Scotland, he became an ascetic at Llanilltud, Wales, with St. Finnian as a disciple for a time and then visited Ireland. Gildas lived for a time on Flatholm Island in Bristow Channel and spent the last years of his life in Brittany, living for a while as a hermit on an island near Rhuys in Morbihan Bay. He was the author of *De excidio Britanniae,* decrying the moral evils rampant in Britain. January 29.

GILES (c. 712). A well-known legend of the Middle Ages has Giles, also known as Aegidius, an Athenian who, to escape the adulation showered on him for a miracle he performed, left Athens and went to Marseilles. He spent two years with St. Caesarius at Arles and then became a hermit at the mouth of the Rhone River. Supposedly he was fed by the milk of a deer that took refuge with him while being hunted by Gothic King Flavius. When one of the hunters shot into a thicket at the deer, he found Giles pierced with the arrow and holding the deer. Later King Flavius built a monastery with Giles as abbot. He attracted many disciples and his reputation reached Charlemagne, who sent for him for spiritual advice. In confessing to him, the King failed to mention a sin he had committed, which was revealed to Giles by an angel while he was saying Mass; he revealed this to the amazed King, who admitted the sin and repented. These are just two of the many fabled stories told of him, though it is probably true that he was a hermit of the sixth (or perhaps eighth) century who founded a monastery. He is also one of the Fourteen Holy Helpers, and his shrine was a great medieval pilgrimage center. He is the patron of cripples and beggars. September 1.

GILES, BL. (c. 1443–1518). Born at Lorenzano, Kingdom of Naples, of working-class parents, he became a hermit and attracted such crowds with his reported miracles that he left the area and became a farmhand. He later became a Franciscan lay brother, was made gardener of his community, and again attracted attention with his supernatural gifts—ecstasies, prophecies, levitation, and miracles. He died on January 10, and his cult was confirmed in 1880. January 14.

GILES OF ASSISI, BL. (d. 1262). A native of Assisi, Italy, he was one of the earliest followers of St. Francis, from whom he received the habit in 1208. He accompanied Francis on many of his missions around Assisi, made a pilgrimage to Compostela, visited Rome and the Holy Land, and then made an unsuccessful visit to Tunis to convert the Saracens. The Christians in Tunis, fearful of the repercussions of his religious fervor, forced him back on a boat as soon as he landed. He spent the rest of his life living in Italy, living from about 1243 at the Monte Rapido hermitage on the outskirts of Perugia, where he died. He experienced ecstasies, had a vision of Christ at Cetona, and is considered the most perfect example of the primitive Franciscan. He is spoken of at length in *The Little Flowers of St. Francis,* and Francis called him his "Knight of the Round Table." Known for his austerity and silence, his *The Golden Sayings of Brother Giles* is noted for its humor, deep understanding of human nature, and optimism. April 23.

GILES, BL. MARY OF ST. JOSEPH (1729–1812). Born at Taranto, Apulia, Italy, he became a ropemaker and when twenty-five joined the Discalced Friars Minor of St. Peter of Alcántara in Naples. He spent the rest of his life there as a porter, ministering to the sick and the leprous poor. He died on February 7 and was beatified in 1888.

GILES OF PORTUGAL (1185–1265). Born at Vaozela, Portugal, son of Rodrigues de Vagliaditos, governor of Coïmbra under King Sancho the Great, he studied at Coïmbra and started out for Paris to study medicine. On the advice of a stranger he met on the way, he went to Toledo instead and became a student of the black arts, reportedly signing a pact in blood with the Devil. After seven years, he went to Paris and became a successful physician. Troubled by nightmarish visions in which he was exhorted to amend his life, he repented, destroyed his magic books and potions, and started back to Portugal on foot. At Valencia, Spain, he joined the Dominicans, was troubled with diabolical attacks, but was finally set at peace by a vision of our Lady. He served at Santarem, Portugal, and Paris, and was elected prior general of the Dominicans in Portugal. He later resigned because of age, and spent his last years at Santarem, where he was gifted with ecstasies and the ability to prophesy. Many of the sensational episodes reported in his life are unverified. His cult was approved in 1748. May 14.

GILES OF SAUMUR, BL. (d. 1266). Chaplain of King St. Louis of France, he accompanied the King on the Seventh Crusade in 1248, was named bishop of Damietta, Egypt, by Louis in 1249, and later became archbishop of Tyre, Syria. He died at Dinant, Belgium, on April 23.

GIRLANI, BL. ARCHANGELA (1460–94). Born at Trino in northern Italy and baptized Eleanor, she convinced her father to let her become a nun at a Benedictine convent near her home. Reportedly, on the way her horse refused to budge and she returned home. Impressed by the stories of a Carmelite friar, she became a Carmelite at Parma, taking the name Archangela, and was professed in 1478. She was soon named prioress but then left to found a new convent at Mantua, where she died on January 25. She is reputed to have experienced ecstasies and levitation and to have performed miracles. Her cult was confirmed in 1864. February 13.

GISLENUS (d. c. 680). Also known as Ghislain, he was a Frank who became a hermit in Hainault and was founding abbot of a monastery there called The Cell (now Saint-Ghislain) near Mons. He encouraged St. Waldetrudis to found a convent at Castrilocus (Mons) and St. Aldegundis to found a convent at Mauberge. An apocryphal legend has him a native of Attica who became bishop of Athens, resigned his see, went to Rome, and was sent to Hainault, where he became a hermit. October 9.

GIULIANI, VERONICA (1660–1727). Born at Mercatello, Urbino, Italy, and christened Ursula, she was early attracted to things religious, refused her father's wish that she marry, and in 1677 joined the Capuchins at Città di Castello, taking the name Veronica. She began to experience Christ's Passion and received the stigmata in 1697; a personal

investigation by the bishop of Città di Castello resulted in a declaration that these manifestations were authentic. She combined her contemplative life with one of great activity, was novice mistress for thirty-four years, and in 1716 was elected abbess, a position she held until her death. She received many supernatural gifts, including levitation, and is considered one of the most extraordinary mystics of the eighteenth century. Afflicted with apoplexy in her later life, she died on July 9, leaving an account of her spiritual life and experiences, which she wrote at the order of her confessor. She was canonized in 1839. July 10.

GIUSTINIANI, LAURENCE (d. 1381–1455). Born at Venice of a noble family, his mother was widowed when he was a child and she devoted herself to raising her children. He refused his mother's wish for him to marry, and instead at nineteen, joined his Uncle Marino Querino, a canon regular of St. George's Chapter, in a community on the island of Alga near Venice. Laurence practiced the most severe austerities, went about the city begging, and was ordained in 1406. He was made provost of St. George's, preached widely, taught religion, and was appointed bishop of Castello (which then included Venice in its diocesan boundaries) in 1433. He became noted for his piety, charitable works, reforms, and peacemaking abilities. In 1451, Pope Nicholas suppressed the see of Castello and transferred the metropolitanship of Grado to Venice with Giustiniani as archbishop (and referred to by the honorary title of patriarch). He was venerated for his spiritual knowledge, his gifts of prophecy and miracles, and he wrote several mystical treatises, among them *The Degree of Perfection*. He died at Venice on January 8, and was canonized in 1670. September 4.

GLADYS. *See* Gundleus.

GLAPHYRA (d. c. 324). A slave of Emperor Licinius' wife, Constantia, she led the palace to protect her virginity, sought sanctuary with Bishop Basil of Amasea in Pontus but was captured and condemned to death. She died on her way to the place of execution. January 13.

GLEB (d. 1015). *See* Boris.

GLYCERIA (d. c. 177). That she was a Christian who suffered martyrdom at Propontis is probable. All else known of her is from untrustworthy legend that had her the daughter of a Roman senator living in Trajanopolis, Thrace. She was brought to the temple of Jupiter by Prefect Sabinus after declaring her Christianity, and when she broke a statue of Jupiter and refused to sacrifice, she was subjected to numerous tortures from which she was miraculously saved, and was finally thrown to the wild beasts; she died before they could reach her. May 13.

GOAR (d. c. 575). According to his legend, Goar was born in Aquitaine, was ordained, labored there for several years as a parish priest, and then became a solitary at Oberwesel on the Rhine River. Denounced as a faker to Bishop Rusticus of Trier, he was accused of hypocrisy and sorcery by the bishop. The furor caused by the bishop's charges reached King Sigebert I of Austrasia, who summoned Goar to Metz, found him innocent, and deposed Rusticus for his extravagant lifestyle. Goar asked for time to consider Sigebert's offer to appoint him bishop of Trier and returned to his cell, where he died before giving the King an answer. July 6.

GOBAN (d. c. 670). Born in Ireland, he was a disciple of St. Fursey, whom he accompanied to East Anglia. Later he went to Gaul with St. Ultan and then became a solitary in the forest near the Oise River and built a church and a hermitage near Prémontré. He was beheaded by a band of marauding bandits near what is now St. Gobain, France. June 20.

GODEBERTA (d. c. 700). Born at Amiens, France, and destined for marriage by her parents, she was allowed to follow a religious life through the intercession of Bishop St. Eligius of Noyon, who gave her the veil. King Clotaire III gave her a house in Noyon for a convent and she became known for her miracles, reportedly causing a plague to abate and a raging fire to subside by her prayers. April 11.

GODEFRIED OF MERVEL (d. 1572). *See* Pieck, Nicholas.

GODEHARD (962–1038). Also known as Gothard, he was born at Reichersdorf, Bavaria, was educated by the canons of Nieder-Altaich abbey there, and was taken to Rome by Archbishop Salzburg, who made him provost of canons when he was nineteen. He was ordained, became a monk at Nieder-Altaich in 990 when the Benedictine rule was restored there, and in time became abbot. His success as abbot caused Emperor Henry II to name him to reform several monasteries, and he was so successful that Henry named him bishop of Hildesheim in 1022. He built churches, schools, and a hospice, imposed strict discipline on the canons, encouraged education in his diocese, and ministered to the sick and the poor. St. Gothard Pass in the Alps takes its name from a chapel built on its summit named after him. He was canonized in 1131. May 4.

GODELEVA (c. 1049–70). Born at Hondeforte-lez-Boulogne, she was married to Bertulf of Ghistelles, a Flemish lord, when eighteen. She was deserted on her wedding day by her husband and left in the care of his mother, who treated her cruelly. Her parents brought the matter up before the count of Flanders and the bishop of Tournai when she fled home to them. Bertulf was ordered to take her back and treat her well. He took her back, pretended sorrow for her mistreatment, and then arranged to have his wife strangled by two of his servants, which was done at Ghistelles on July 6 while he was on a trip to Bruges. Miracles were reported at the place where she had been slain, and it became a place of pilgrimage. Among the miracles reported was the curing of Bertulf's daughter by a second marriage of blindness; after a pilgrimage to Rome and the Holy Land, Bertulf entered a monastery and spent the rest of his life doing penance for the crime he had committed.

GODFREY (1065–1115). Born at Soissons, France, he was placed in the care of the abbot of Mont-Saint-Quentin Abbey when he was five, was raised there, and became a monk. He was ordained, was named abbot of run-down Nogent Abbey in Champagne, restored discipline, and rebuilt it into a flourishing community. He refused the abbacy of Saint-Remi but in 1104 was appointed bishop of Amiens. There his strict discipline, insistence on clerical celibacy, and struggle against simony aroused much bitter opposition and even caused an attempt on his life. He died on the way to Soissons to visit his metropolitan see. November 8.

GODFREY OF KAPPENBERG, BL. (1097–1127). Count of Kappenberg, Westphalia, and a wealthy landowner, he married a noblewoman but after meeting St. Norbert, persuaded his wife to become a nun, with her two sisters, at a convent he founded for her near Kappenberg, and despite the objections of her father, turned his wealth over to the Premonstratensians and converted his castle into a monastery. He built several hospitals and other foundations and studied for the priesthood but died when only thirty on January 13 before he was ordained.

GODRIC (d. 1170). Born at Walpole, Norfolk, England, he was a peddler in his youth and then was a sailor for sixteen years. He became quite wealthy from his trading activities on his various voyages (one account says he was a pirate), but after a visit to Lindisfarne Monastery, he went on pilgrimage to Jerusalem, stopping off at Compostela on the way back. He became a steward to a landowner in Norfolk on his return, resigned after a time, and went on pilgrimage to St. Giles' shrine in Provence and to Rome. He was a hermit for two years with a recluse named Aelric, whom he met at Wolsingham, made another pilgrimage to Jerusalem, and on his return resumed his eremitical life near Durham. He spent the last sixty years of his life there, venerated for his austerity, gifts of prophecy, knowledge of distant events, and visions. He died at his hermitage at Finchdale on May 21.

GOERICUS (d. 647). Of the distinguished Ansbertina family of Aquitaine, and also known as Abbo, he was an officer at the court of Dagobert I when he suddenly went blind. While praying at St. Stephen Church in Metz, he recovered his sight and in thanksgiving became a priest. When his relative St. Arnulf resigned his see about 626, Goericus was named his successor. He founded a convent at Epinal. September 19.

GOHARD (d. 843). Bishop of Nantes, France, he was murdered with a large number of priests, monks, and laypeople while saying Mass in SS. Peter and Paul Church in Nantes by marauding Normans, who then pillaged and destroyed the entire city. June 25.

GOMIDAS KEUMURGIAN. See Keumurgian, Bl. Gomidas.

GOMMAIRE. See Gummarus.

GONSALO GUNDISALVUS OF AMARANTE, BL. (d. c. 1259). Of a distinguished Portuguese family, he was born at Vizella, near Braga; he became a priest but resigned his benefice to his nephew and spent fourteen years on pilgrimage to the Holy Land. On his return he was driven away by his nephew and joined the Dominicans, who allowed him to live as a hermit. He is reputed to have performed numerous extravagant miracles and to have built a bridge across the Tamega River. He died on January 10, and his cult was approved in 1560.

GONSON, BL. DAVID (d. 1541). Son of Vice Admiral Gonson (also spelled Genson or Gunstond) and a Knight of Malta, he was condemned by attainder and hanged, drawn, and quartered at Southmark, England, for refusing to acknowledge royal supremacy over the Pope in ecclesiastical matters. He was beatified in 1929. July 12.

GONTRAN. See Guntramnus.

GONZAGA, ALOYSIUS (1568–91). The oldest son of Marquis Ferrante of Castiglione, who was in the service of Philip II of Spain, he was born on March 9 at the family castle in Lombardy. He was destined for the military by his father, but early in his childhood decided on a religious life. He was sent to Florence to be educated in 1577, joined the court of the Duke of Mantua, who had appointed his father governor of Montserrat two years later, suffered a kidney attack that was to leave him with digestive trouble the rest of his life, and began to practice great austerities and to devote himself to religious practices and teaching catechism to the poor of Castiglione. While at the court of Prince Diego of the Asturias in Spain, he desired to enter the Jesuits, was refused permission by his father, and on their return to Italy in 1584 renewed his plea. He finally broke down his father, joined the Jesuits in Rome in 1585, and was sent to Milan to study. Because of his poor health he was recalled to Rome, made his vows in 1587, and when a plague struck the city in 1587, served in a hospital opened by the Jesuits. He caught the plague while ministering to its victims and died on June 21 after her received the last rites from St. Robert Bellarmine. Aloysius Gonzaga was canonized in 1726, was declared protector of young students by Pope Benedict XIII and patron of Catholic youth by Pope Pius XI. June 21.

GONZALEZ DE CASTRILLO, JOHN (1419–79). Born at Sahagún, Leon, Spain, he was educated by the Benedictine monks of San Fagondez Monastery there and when twenty, received a canonry from the bishop of Burgos, though he already had several benefices. He was ordained in 1445; concerned about the evil of pluralism, he resigned all his benefices except that of St. Agatha in Burgos. He spent the next four years studying at the University of Salamanca and then began to preach. In the next decade he achieved a great reputation as a preacher and spiritual director but after recovering from a serious operation became an Augustinian friar in 1463 and was professed the following year. He served as master of novices, definitor, prior at Salamanca, experienced visions, was famous for his miracles, and had the gift of reading men's souls. He denounced evil in high places, and several attempts were made on his life. He died at Sahagún on June 11, reportedly poisoned by the mistress of a man he had convinced to leave her. He was canonized in 1690 as St. John of Sahagún. June 12.

GONZALEZ, BL. ROQUE (1576–1628). Born of noble Spanish parents at Asunción, Paraguay, he was educated and ordained there when he was twenty-three. He began his priestly career working among the Indians, joined the Jesuits in 1609, and was active in the formation of the Paraguayan reductions devoted to improving the conditions of the Indians. With other Jesuits, he opposed Spanish imperialism, the imported Spanish Inquisition, and enslaving the Indians—for all of which he was bitterly opposed by the Spanish authorities. He worked among and for the Indians for two decades, heading the first Paraguayan reduction for three years and establishing another six in the Paraná and Uruguay rivers areas. In 1628, with two other Jesuits, Alonso Rodriguez and Juan de Castillo, he founded a new reduction near the Ijuhi River and then with Fr. Rodriguez established another reduction at Caaró in southern Brazil. He was opposed by the local medicine man, who instigated a raid by the Indians on the reduction during which both he and Fr. Rodriguez were tomahawked to death on November 15. Two days later, Ijuhi was attacked, and Fr. Castillo was stoned to death. The three Jesuits were beatified in 1934 as the Martyrs of Paraguay—the first martyrs in the Americas to be so honored. November 17.

GOODMAN, VEN. JOHN (1590–1642). Born at Bangor, Wales, he was educated at Oxford and became a minister. He was converted to Catholicism in Paris, studied for the priesthood at Douai, 1621–24, and was ordained. He was sent on the English mission and in the next few years was captured and imprisoned three times. The last time he was arrested, he was ordered executed, but his case was debated so violently in Parliament that he asked King Charles I to order the execution forthwith so the country would not be torn apart any farther. Goodman died in Newgate Prison, London, before the sentence of death could be carried out.

GORAZD (9th century). A follower of St. Methodius, who designated him his successor as archbishop of Moravia and Pannonia, he was driven into exile from Moravia by Svatopluk. An outstanding missionary, Gorazd is one of the Seven Apostles of Bulgaria. July 17.

GORDIAN (d. 362). The Roman Martyrology states he was scourged and beheaded in Rome for his faith and buried in the same tomb with the remains of St. Epimachus, which had just been brought to Rome from Alexandria. According to legend, he was the *vicarius* (minister) of Emperor Julian the Apostate, but Pope Damasus in his epitaph of Gordian describes him as a mere boy. May 10.

GORETTI, MARIA (1890–1902). Born at Corinaldo, near Ancona, Italy, on October 16, she was the daughter of a farmworker who moved the family to Ferriere di Conca, near Anzio. She was stabbed to death on July 6 by Alexander Serenelli, son of her father's partner, who lived in the same house with the Gorettis, while resisting his attempt to seduce her. She was canonized for her purity in 1950 by Pope Pius XII in the presence of her murderer, who completely reformed his life after he had a vision of Maria. July 6.

GORGONIA (d. c. 372). Daughter of St. Gregory Naziazen the Elder and St. Nonna and sister of St. Gregory Naziazen and St. Caesarius, she married and lived a life of great holiness, which her brother Gregory described in a panegyric at her funeral. December 9.

GORGONIUS (d. 303). *See* Peter.

GOTHARD. *See* Godehard.

GOTO, JOHN SOAN DE (1578–97). A native Japanese, he became a catechist at Osaka and a temporal coadjutor of the Jesuits. He was crucified with twenty-five other Christians on February 5 near Nagasaki, Japan, for his faith. They were canonized as the Martyrs of Japan in 1862.

GOTTSCHALK (d. 1066). A prince of the Wends and a Christian, he gave up his religion when his father was killed by a Christian Saxon. He served in the army of Canute of Denmark, accompanied Sweyn to England, married his daughter, and returned to his Christian religion. When he reconquered his realm, he was active in the conversion of his subjects to Christianity, brought in Saxon monks, and founded monasteries, but was killed at Lenzen on the Elbe by adherents of his brother-in-law, who was the leader of an anti-Christian uprising against him. Many scholars question his designation as either saint or martyr. June 7.

GOUPIL, RENÉ (1606–42). Born at Anjou, France, he joined the Jesuits, was forced to leave because of ill health, and became a successful surgeon. He went to Quebec to work among the Jesuits' missions there in 1638, was attached to the hospital in Quebec, and became a donné (a lay assistant) for the mission to the Huron Indians in 1640. While on a journey with Isaac Jogues in 1642, he was captured by a group of Iroquois Indians, implacable foes of the Hurons. He was subjected to torture and mutilations for two months and then tomahawked to death on September 29 before Jogues at Osserneon, near Albany, New York—the first of the North American Martyrs. He was canonized in 1930 by Pope Pius XI. October 19.

GRACIA (d. c. 1180). *See* Bernard.

GRAFATH. *See* Ratho, Bl.

GRANDE, BL. JOHN (1546–1600). Born at Carmona, Andalusia, Spain, he went to Seville when fifteen to work with a relative in the linen business and then returned to Carmona, where he established his own business. At twenty-two, he gave away his possessions to the poor and became a hermit near Marcena, using as a surname "the Sinner" to denote his feeling about himself. He abandoned his eremitical way of life to go to Xeres, where he ministered to prisoners for three years. He then worked in the badly run hospital there, incurring the enmity of the directors by his concern for the patients. He so impressed a wealthy couple with his care for the sick that they built a new hospital and put him in charge of it. He affiliated it with the Order of Hospitalers, which he joined at Granada. Meanwhile, he continued his interest in prisoners and extended his concern to orphans and all those in need. He was blessed with supernatural gifts, among them the gift of prophecy (he is reputed to have foretold the destruction of the Spanish Armada). He died of plague contacted while ministering to the plague-stricken in Xeres, and was beatified in 1853. June 3.

GRASSI, BL. ANTONY (1592–1671). Born at Fermo, Italy, he joined the Oratorians when he was seventeen, was ordained, and became a famous confessor noted for his ability to read consciences and in later life to see into the future. In 1635, he was elected superior of the Oratory at Fermo, a position to which he was regularly reelected each three years for the rest of his life, and often acted as spiritual adviser for high ecclesiastical officials. December 13.

GRASSI, BL. GREGORY (1833–1900). Born at Bologna, Italy, he became a Friar Minor, was sent to China in 1860, and was a missionary there for the next forty years. He was titular bishop of Orthosias and vicar apostolic to northern Shansi when the Boxer Rebellion broke out in China. With his coadjutor, Bl. Francis Fogolla, he was beheaded on July 9 by Yu Hsien, governor of Taiyüan, who was notorious for his hatred of Christians. At the same time and place were martyred a group of Franciscan Missionaries of Mary under Bl. Mary Hermina Grivot, and several priests, brothers, and laymen. Bl. Gregory was beatified in 1946. July 8.

GRATIA OF CATTARO, BL. (1437–1508). Born at Cattaro (Kotor), Dalmatia, he was a seagoing man until he was thirty, when he became an Augustinian lay brother at Monte Ortona, near Padua, Italy, where he served as gardener. He was transferred to St. Christopher friary in Venice, where many miracles of his were reported and where he died on November 9. His cult was confirmed in 1889. November 16.

GRAU, BL. BONAVENTURA (1620–84). Born at Riudoms, near Barcelona, Spain, he was a shepherd in his youth, married when he was seventeen, and when widowed two years later became a Franciscan lay brother at Escornalbou. He acquired fame for his visions and mystical experiences and was sent to

Rome, where despite his lowly position of doorkeeper at St. Isidore's, he was consulted for his spiritual wisdom by Popes and commoners. His cult was approved in 1906. September 11.

GREEN, BL. HUGH (c. 1584–1642). Born in London, he was educated at Cambridge and was converted to Catholicism. He went to Douai, studied for the priesthood, and was ordained there in 1612. He was sent back to England to serve the Catholics of Dorset, which he did until he was arrested and then hanged, drawn, and quartered on August 19 at Dorchester when convicted of being a Catholic priest. He was beatified as one of the Dorchester Martyrs in 1929. July 4.

GREEN, BL. THOMAS. *See* Reynolds, Bl. Thomas.

GREGORY (d. c. 603). Born near Girgenti (Agrigentum), Sicily, he spent four years studying in Byzantine monasteries in Palestine, was ordained deacon in Jerusalem, and won a reputation for holiness and wisdom. After visiting Antioch and Constantinople, he went to Rome and was appointed bishop of Girgenti. He was the victim of a plot to besmirch his reputation when a prostitute was found in his home but was cleared at a hearing in Rome. He wrote a Greek commentary on Ecclesiastes and may have died as late as 638. November 23.

GREGORY I THE GREAT (c. 540–604). Son of a wealthy patrician, Gordianus, he was born and educated at Rome. He was prefect of Rome when the Lombard invasion of Italy was threatening Rome in 571. Long attracted to the religious life, about 574 he converted his home in Rome into St. Andrew's Monastery under Valentius, became a monk there, and founded six monasteries on his estates in Sicily. After several years of seclusion at St. Andrew's, he was ordained by Pope Pelagius II and was made one of the seven papal deacons in 578. He served as papal nuncio to the Byzantine court, 579–85, was recalled in 586, resumed his monastic life, and became abbot of St. Andrew's. He set out to evangelize England but was brought back to Rome by Pope Pelagius when plague struck Rome, 589–90. Pelagius was stricken and died, and Gregory was elected Pope and consecrated on September 3, 590. He restored ecclesiastical discipline, removed unworthy clerics from office, abolished clerical fees for burials and ordinations, and was prodigious in his charities. He administered papal properties wisely and justly, ransomed captives from the Lombards, protected Jews from unjust coercion, and fed the victims of a famine. In 593, he persuaded the invading Lombards under Agilulf to spare Rome, and he negotiated a peace with the Lombard King—an unprecedented move that effectively set aside the authority of the Byzantine Emperor's representative, the exarch. This was the beginning of a series of actions by which Gregory resisted the arrogance, incompetence, and treachery of Byzantine authorities by which he appointed governors of the Italian cities, providing them with war materials and denouncing the heavy taxes levied on the Italians by Byzantine officials. He thus started on its course the acquisition and exercise of temporal power by the papacy. He was responsible for the conversion of England to Christianity by his interest in that country and his dispatch of St. Augustine of Canterbury and forty monks from St. Andrew's there (though the story in Bede's history of the English Church that he was motivated to do so by the sight of a group of blond, handsome Saxon slaves up for sale in the marketplace may be apocryphal). He was untiring in his efforts to ensure that the papacy was the supreme authority in the Church, and denouncing John, Patriarch of Constantinople, for his use of the title Ecumenical Patriarch (he himself preferred as his own title "Servant of the Servants of God," a title used by Popes to this day, fourteen centuries later). He was an eloquent preacher and was mainly responsible for the restoration of a Rome devastated by the invasions, pillages, and earthquakes of the century before his pontificate. He wrote treatises, notably his *Dialogues,* a collection of visions, prophecies, miracles, and lives of Italian saints, and *Liber regulae pastoralis* (on the duties of bishops), and hundreds of sermons and letters. Whether he was the compiler of the Antiphony on which the Roman *schola cantorum* was based and several hymns attributed to him is uncertain, but he did greatly influence the Roman liturgy. The custom of saying thirty successive Masses for a dead person goes back to him and bears his name, and to Gregory is due Gregorian Chant. He actively encouraged Benedictine monasticism, and his grants of privileges to monks often restricting episcopal jurisdictions was the beginning of later exemptions that were to bring religious orders directly under papal control. He is the last of the traditional Latin Doctors of the Church, is justly called "the Great," and is considered the founder of the medieval papacy. He died in Rome on March 12 and was canonized by acclamation immediately after his death. September 3.

GREGORY II (d. 731). Born at Rome, he became involved in ecclesiastical affairs in his youth, served as treasurer of the Church and librarian under four Popes, and became widely known for his learning and wisdom. He distinguished himself by his replies to Emperor Justinian when he accompanied Pope Constantine to Constantinople to oppose the Council of Trullo canon that had declared the patriarchate of Constantinople independent of Rome and helped to secure Justinian's acknowledgment of papal supremacy. He was elected Pope on May 19, 715, to succeed Constantine, put into effect a program to restore clerical discipline, fought heresies, began to rebuild the walls around Rome as a defense against the Saracens, and helped restore and rebuild churches, hospitals, and monasteries, including Monte Cassino, which had been destroyed by the Lombards a century and a half earlier. He sent missionaries to Germany, among them St. Corbinian and St. Boniface in 719, whom he consecrated bishop. The outstanding concern of his pontificate was his difficulties with Emperor Leo III the Isaurian. Gregory opposed his illegal taxation on the Italians, though Gregory counseled against the planned revolt of Italy against Byzantium and the election of an Emperor in opposition to Leo. He also demanded that Leo stop interfering with ecclesiastical matters, vigorously opposed iconoclasm supported by the Emperor, and severely rebuked him at a synod in Rome in 727; Gregory also supported Germanus, patriarch of Constantinople, against Leo. Gregory's relations with the Lombards who were intent on conquering Italy were friendly mainly due to his influence with their leader, Liutprand. February 11.

GREGORY III (d. 741). The son of a Syrian named John, he became a priest in Rome, and his reputation for learning and holiness was so great that he was acclaimed Pope while accompanying the funeral cortege of his predecessor, Gregory II, on February 11, 731. He continued Gregory II's opposition to iconoclasm and convoked two synods in Rome in 731, which condemned the heresy. In response, Emperor Leo the Iconoclast seized papal patrimonies in

Calabria and Sicily and transferred ecclesiastical jurisdiction of those two provinces and Illyrium to the patriarch of Constantinople. Gregory supported the missionary activities of St. Boniface in Germany and sent St. Willibald to assist him. Gregory completed rebuilding the walls around Rome begun by Gregory II and sought the assistance of Charles Martel against the attacks of Liutprand and his Lombards on the exarchate of Ravenna, the dukes of Spoleto and Benevento, and the duchy of Rome rather than from the Eastern Emperor, an appeal that was to have far-reaching historical implications. In the midst of this turmoil, Gregory died on November 28.

GREGORY VII (c. 1021–85). Born at Soana, Tuscany, Italy, and baptized Hildebrand, he was sent at an early age to St. Mary on the Aventine Monastery in Rome, where his uncle was superior. Hildebrand studied under John Gratian at the Lateran school and when Gratian was elected Pope as Pope Gregory VI, he appointed Hildebrand his secretary. According to tradition, Hildebrand became a monk at Cluny under St. Odilo when Gregory died in 1047. When Bishop Bruno of Toul was elected Pope as Pope Leo IX in 1049, he appointed Hildebrand his counselor and put him in charge of the treasury. He restored solvency to the Church's finances, was active in Leo's reforms, and was a most influential counselor for the next four Popes. He was made a cardinal-deacon, was legate to France during the controversy over the Eucharist between Lanfranc and Berengarius of Tours, and presided in 1054 at the Council at Sens, which condemned Berengarius. He was influential in securing the election of Bishop Gebhard of Eichstätt as Pope Victor II in 1055, was papal legate to Empress-regent Agnes of Germany's court in 1057 to get her to accept the

election of Pope Stephen, and helped secure the election of Bishop Gerhard of
Florence as Pope Nicholas II in 1059.
During the pontificate of Nicholas,
Hildebrand was instrumental in the
publication of the papal decree mandat-
ing that the election of Popes was to be
vested in the college of cardinals and was
responsible for negotiating a treaty of alliance with the Normans in the Treaty of
Melfi in 1059. By now he was the best-
known and most powerful prelate in the
Church. He was appointed chancellor of
the Apostolic See by Pope Alexander II,
and when Alexander died in 1073, he
was elected Pope by acclamation and
consecrated on June 30, taking the name
Gregory VII. He immediately set to
work to reform a very corrupt and deca-
dent Church. He deposed Archbishop
Godfrey of Milan for simony, enacted
decrees against simony and married
clergy at his first synod in Rome, in
1074, and ordered an end to lay investiture at his second synod, in 1075—decrees that aroused great opposition. He
appointed monks as papal legates to enforce the decrees. He was generally successful with his reforms in England
except in the matter of lay investiture,
which right William the Conqueror refused to surrender; gradually Gregory
succeeded in France by replacing practically the whole episcopate; but in
Germany he was resisted by Emperor IV
and by the clergy in Germany and northern Italy. Even the papal nobles in Rome
objected and kidnaped him while he was
celebrating Christmas Mass. Henry convened a diet at Worms in 1076 and sent
legates to Rome, informing the Pope that
the diet had decided he was deposed,
whereupon Gregory excommunicated
Henry—the first deposition of a King by
a Pope—and declared that his subjects
were free of allegiance to him. The
German nobles then stated that they
considered Henry to be dethroned if he
did not receive the Pope's absolution. In

January 1077, in a bitter winter, Henry's
famous submission to the Pope took
place at Canossa as barefoot and in penitential garb he stood in the snow and
begged the Pope's forgiveness. Though
suspicious of Henry's motives and the
validity of his repentance, Gregory lifted
the ban of excommunication. Later in
the year a group of German nobles
elected Rudolf of Swabia, Henry's
brother-in-law, King of Germany, and
civil war broke out. At first neutral,
Henry supported Rudolf when Henry
violated all his agreements with him, and
Gregory again excommunicated Henry,
in 1080. When Henry triumphed over
Rudolf, who was killed in battle in
October 1080, he arranged the election
of Archbishop Guibert of Ravenna as antipope Clement III, declared Gregory
deposed, invaded Italy, and laid siege to
Rome. He took the city in 1084, but
Gregory had taken refuge in Sant'
Angelo Castle. When he refused Henry's
demand that he crown him Emperor,
Henry had Guibert consecrated Pope,
and then Guibert crowned Henry
Emperor. Gregory remained in Sant'
Angelo until rescued by the Normans
under Robert Guiscard, duke of
Normandy, with whom Gregory had
signed an alliance. When the Normans
sacked the city, the Romans turned on
Gregory and he was forced to flee to
Monte Cassino and then to Salerno,
where he died on May 25, lifting all of
his excommunications except those on
Henry and Guibert. In large measure,
Gregory was successful in rejuvenating
the Church, and the reforms of his pontificate marked a turning point in the
history of the Church. It is now generally agreed among historians that his
struggles with the monarchs of Europe
were not a bid for great personal power,
as some historians in the past contended,
but a titanic defense of the freedom of
the Church against secular domination.
Though he did not clearly and unequiv-

ocally win the struggle, he did delineate the issues, particularly that of lay investiture, which thirty-seven years after his death was won by the Concordat of Worms in 1122, when Emperor Henry V guaranteed the free election of bishops and abbots and renounced the right to invest them with the ring and staff—the symbols of their spiritual authority. Gregory was unsuccessful in his efforts to reunite the Eastern churches to Rome, and his struggle with Henry prevented him from launching a crusade against the Turks and to drive the Saracens from Spain. He was canonized in 1606 by Pope Paul V, and despite French and Austrian objections, Pope Benedict XIII made his feast day of May 25 universal in the Church.

GREGORY X, BL. (1210–76). Of a distinguished family, Theobald Visconti was born at Piacenza, Italy, studied canon law at Paris and Liège, and became archdeacon of Liège. He accompanied Cardinal Ottoboni on a mission to England and was at Acre on pilgrimage to the Holy Land when he was informed that though he was not yet ordained, he had been selected as Pope by a committee of six cardinals who had been chosen to select a Pope when a candidate had not been elected by the cardinals at Viterbo to fill the pontifical throne, which has been vacant for three years. He returned to Rome, was ordained a priest on March 19, and then was consecrated Pope on March 27, 1272, taking the name Gregory X. He labored to end the warfare between the Guelphs and the Ghibellines, placed Florence under interdict for refusing efforts at reconciliation with its neighbors, and approved Rudolph of Hapsburg as German Emperor. Gregory convoked the fourteenth General Council at Lyons in 1274, which effected a short-lived reunion of the Eastern churches with Rome but was unsuccessful in launching

a crusade. He died at Rezzo, Italy, on his way back from the Council on January 10. His cult was approved in 1713.

GREGORY, BL. (d. 1300). *See* Dominic, Bl.

GREGORY DEI CELLI, BL. (1225–1343). Born at Verucchio, Italy, he was brought up by his mother when his father died when Gregory was four. He joined the Hermits of St. Gregory, lived for ten years in a monastery built by him and his mother, and was then driven from the monastery, apparently because of his strictness. He went to Reati, joined the Franciscans of Monte Carnerio there, and spent the rest of his life with them, reputedly living to 118. His cult was approved in 1769. May 4.

GREGORY THE ENLIGHTENER (d. c. 330). Also surnamed "the Illuminator," he is of unknown origins, but unreliable tradition has him the son of Anak, a Parthian who murdered King Khosrov I of Armenia when Gregory was a baby. The infant Gregory was smuggled to Caesarea to escape the dying Khosrov's order to murder the entire family, was baptized, married, and had two sons. When King Khosrov's son, Tiridates, regained his father's throne, Gregory was permitted to return, but he incurred the King's displeasure by his support of the Armenian Christians and his conversion activities. In time Tiridates was converted to Christianity by Gregory and proclaimed Christianity the official religion of Armenia. Gregory was consecrated bishop of Ashtishat, set about organizing the Church in Armenia and building a native clergy, and worked untiringly to evangelize the Armenians. Curiously enough, he set into motion the process that was to make his see a hereditary episcopate when he consecrated his son Aristakes to succeed him. He then retired to a hermitage on

Mount Manyea in Taron and remained there until his death. Many extravagant legends and miracles were attributed to him, many of which are celebrated as feasts by the Armenians. He is considered the apostle of Armenia. September 30.

GREGORY OF LANGRES (d. 539). Count of Autun, France, he ruled the area wisely and well for forty years until the death of his wife, Armentaria, when he devoted himself to a religious life. He was elected bishop of Langres and was known for his charities, austerities, and devotion to duty. He died at Langres, had his epitaph written by Venantius Fortunatus and his biography written by St. Gregory of Tours, his great-grandson. January 4.

GREGORY MAKAR (d. c. 1010). Born in Armenia, he became a monk at a monastery near Nicropolis, Little Armenia. He was ordained by the bishop of Nicropolis, was a successful preacher, and was chosen bishop of Nicropolis on the death of his predecessor. Desirous of living as a solitary, he went to Italy and then France, where he lived as a recluse at Pithiviers. His reputation for spiritual wisdom and as a miracle healer spread and attracted crowds of people. He spent the last seven years of his life at Pithiviers and died there. March 16.

GREGORY NAZIANZEN (c. 329–89). Son of St. Gregory Nazianzen the Elder, bishop of Nazianzus for forty-five years, and St. Nonna, he was born at Nazianzus, Cappadocia, studied at Caesarea, Cappadocia (where he met St. Basil), the rhetorical school at Caesarea, Palestine, and then for ten years at Athens (where both Basil and the future Emperor Julian the Apostate were also studying). When about thirty, Gregory returned to Nazianzus but soon joined Basil at Pontus on the Iris River to live the life of a solitary. After two years there, Gregory returned home to assist his father, now over eighty, in running his see, was ordained most unwillingly about 362 by his father, and in about 372 was named bishop of Sasima. The see was in Arian territory, was rent by civil strife, and had been created by his friend Basil, now metropolitan of Caesarea in Cappadocia, who had created it in an attempt to offset the jurisdictional claims of Bishop Anthimus of Tyana to the area. Gregory was consecrated but never went to Sesima, to the dismay of Basil, remaining instead as coadjutor to his father. When his father died in 374, he continued administering the see until a new bishop was chosen. He suffered a breakdown in 375 and spent the next five years at Seleucia, Isauria. On the death of Emperor Valens and the mitigation of his persecution of the orthodox, a group of bishops invited Gregory to Constantinople to help revitalize the Church in the East by restoring orthodoxy to the Arian-dominated city. There his eloquent preaching at the Church of Anastasia (a house he had converted to a church) brought floods of converts, and torrents of abuse and persecution from the Arians and the Apollinarists. He came into controversy with one Maximus, who tried to depose him while he was ill, but Gregory finally prevailed, and in 380 the newly baptized Emperor Theodosius decreed that his subjects must be orthodox, ordered the Arian leaders to submit or leave (they left), and named Gregory archbishop of Constantinople. A few months after his installation hostilities began anew, and the validity of his election was questioned at the Council of Constantinople in 381, at which he presided. He resigned the see in the hope of restoring peace now that he had restored orthodoxy to Constantinople. He retired to private life, lived a life of great austerity, and died at Nazianzus on January 25. A Doctor of the Church, Gregory is often surnamed "the Theologian" for his eloquent defense of orthodoxy and the decrees of the Council of Nicaea in his sermons and treatises, notably his celebrated sermons on the Trinity, *Five Theological Orations,* delivered at St. Anastasia in Constantinople. He also wrote a long poem, *De vita sua,* letters, and with St. Basil, compiled a selection of writings by Origen. January 2.

GREGORY NAZIANZEN THE ELDER (c. 276–374). A native of Nazianzus, Cappadocia, he was an official there when converted to Christianity by his wife, Nonna. They had three children, all saints: Gregory Nazianzen, Caesarius, and Gorgonia. Gregory the Elder became bishop of Nazianzus about 328, fell into heresy, but was brought back to orthodoxy in 361 by his son Gregory, who became his coadjutor in 372. Gregory the Elder continued as bishop until his death, having ruled for some forty-five years. January 1.

GREGORY OF NYSSA (c. 330–c. 395). Son of St. Basil and St. Emmilia, he was born at Caesarea, Cappadocia, and raised by his brother St. Basil and his sister Macrina. Gregory was well educated, became a rhetorician, and married Theosebeia. He became a professor of rhetoric and, depressed by his students, he was turned to the religious life by St. Gregory Nazianzen and was ordained a priest. He may have lived in seclusion at Iris in Pontus the first years of his priesthood and at the suggestion of his brother Basil, who was bishop of Caesarea, was named bishop of Nyssa, Lower Armenia, in 372. He found his see infested with Arianism, was falsely accused of stealing Church property by the governor of Pontus, Demosthenes, and was imprisoned. He escaped but was deposed by a synod of Galatian and Pontic bishops in

376 and remained in exile until 378, when Emperor Gratian restored him to his see. In 379 he attended the Council of Antioch, which denounced the Meletian heresy, and was sent by that council to Palestine and Arabia to combat heresy there. He was active in 381 in the General Council of Constantinople, which attacked Arianism and eloquently reaffirmed the decrees of the Council of Nicaea. By this time he was widely venerated as the great pillar of orthodoxy and the great opponent of Arianism. Greatly influenced by the writings of Origen and Plato, he wrote numerous theological treatises, which were considered the true exposition of the Catholic faith. Among them were his *Catechetical Discourse,* treatises against Eunomius and Appolinaris, a book on virginity, and commentaries on Scripture. The second General Council of Nicaea, 680–81, called him "Father of the Fathers." March 9.

GREGORY OF SPOLETO (d. c. 304). His apparently fictional story is that he was a priest at Spoleto, Italy, during the persecution of Emperor Maximian. On receipt of the imperial decree ordering punishment of Christians, Flaccus, governor of Umbria, gathered all the inhabitants of Spoleto in the forum and asked if they still worshiped the pagan gods. They assured him they did, but named Gregory as one who had destroyed images of the gods. Flaccus summoned Gregory, and when he refused to sacrifice to the gods, Flaccus had him beheaded. December 24.

GREGORY THAUMATURGUS (c. 213–68). Of a distinguished pagan family, he was born at Neocaesarea, Pontus, and studied law there. About 233, he and his brother, Athenodorus, accompanied his sister, who was joining her husband in Caesarea, Palestine, while they continued on to Beirut to continue their law studies. They met Origen and instead of going to Beirut, entered his school at Caesarea, studied theology, were converted to Christianity by Origen, and became his disciples. Gregory returned to Neocaesarea about 238, intending to practice law, but was elected bishop by the seventeen Christians of the city. It soon became apparent that he was gifted with remarkable powers. He preached eloquently, made so many converts he was able to build a church, and soon was so renowned for his miracles that he was surnamed Thaumaturgus (the wonder worker). He was a much-sought-after arbiter for his wisdom and legal knowledge and ability, advised his flock to go into hiding when Decius' persecution of the Christians broke out in 250, and fled to the desert with his deacon. On his return, he ministered to his flock when plague struck his see and when the Goths devastated Pontus, 252–54, which he described in his "Canonical Letter." He participated in the Synod of Antioch, 264–65, against Samosata, and fought Sabellianism and Tritheism. It is reported that at his death at Neocaesarea, only seventeen unbelievers were left in the city. He is invoked against floods and earthquakes (at one time he reportedly stopped the flooding Lycus, and at another, he moved a mountain). According to Gregory of Nyssa, Gregory Thaumaturgus experienced a vision of our Lady, the first such recorded vision. He wrote a panegyric to Origen, a treatise on the Creed, and a dissertation addressed to Theopompus; St. Gregory of Nyssa wrote a panegyric to Gregory Thaumaturgus. November 17.

GREGORY OF TOURS (538–94). Of a well-known Auvergne family, Gregorius Florentius was born at Clermont-Ferrand, Gaul, and later took the name Gregory. He was raised by his uncle, St. Gallus of Clermont, on the death of his father, studied Scripture under St. Avitus, a priest of Clermont, and in 573 was made bishop of Tours. He soon came into conflict with King Chilperic when Tours came under the King's control in 576, and Gregory supported Meroveus, the King's son, against the King. The differences culminated in a charge of treason against Gregory by Leudastis, whom Gregory had removed as count of Tours. The charges were proved false by a council appointed to investigate them, and Leudastis was punished for perjury. Things improved with subsequent monarchs after Chilperic's death in 584. Gregory rebuilt the cathedral and several churches, converted heretics, and was known for his ability, justice, charity, and religious fervor. He wrote books on the martyrs, saints, and Fathers, but is particularly remembered for his *History of the Franks,* one of the outstanding original sources of early French history. November 17.

GREGORY OF UTRECHT (c. 707–c. 775). Born at Trier, Gaul, he became a follower of St. Boniface after hearing him deliver a homily. He accompanied Boniface on his missionary travels and was named abbot of St. Martin Monastery at Utrecht, Flanders, by Boniface. Gregory administered the see of Utrecht after the martyrdom of St. Eoban (who had administered it since St. Willibrod's death in 739) in 755 for twenty years, although he was never consecrated bishop, until his death. Under his abbacy, St. Martin's became a noted missionary center. He was noted for his charity and spirit of forgiveness, so dramatically illustrated when the murderers of his two half brothers were sent to him for sentencing; he forgave and freed them. He suffered from paralysis the last three years of his life and died at Maastricht on August 25.

GREGORY THE WONDER WORKER.
See Gregory Thaumaturgus.

GRIGNION, LOUIS MARY (1673–1716). Born on January 31 of poor parents at Montford, France, he was educated at the Jesuit college in Rennes and was ordained there in 1700. He became a chaplain in a hospital at Poitiers, but his reorganization of the hospital staff there caused such resentment that he resigned. Before leaving, he organized a group of women into what became the congregation of the Daughters of Divine Wisdom. His missionary preaching to the poor caused his critics to complain to the bishop of Poitiers, who forbade him to preach in his diocese. He went to Rome, was named missionary apostolic by Pope Clement XI, and began preaching missions in Brittany, which he was to continue until his death. Though his sermons aroused much opposition for their emotionalism, he was tremendously successful, particularly in fostering devotion to Mary and the rosary; he wrote his *True Devotion to the Blessed Virgin* to foster this devotion, and it achieved great popularity. In 1715, he organized several priests into a group that developed into the Missionaries of the Company of Mary. He died at Saint-Laurent-sur-Sèvre, France, and was canonized in 1947. April 28.

GRIMALDI, BL. ANTONY. *See* Primaldi, Bl. Antony.

GRIMKELD (d. 870). *See* Theodore.

GRIMONIA (4th century). French legend has her the daughter of a pagan Irish chieftain who was converted to Christianity when she was twelve and dedicated her life to God. When she refused to marry, her father imprisoned her but she escaped and went to France, where she lived as a hermitess in Thiérache Forest in Picardy. Her father's emissaries traced her there, and when she refused to return and marry, they beheaded her. September 7.

GRIMWALD (d. 903). Born at Saint-Omer, Flanders, he became a monk at Saint-Bertin and later was prior, met King Alfred of England at Saint-Bertin, and at his invitation went to England in 885. He refused Alfred's offer of the archbishopric of Canterbury but was appointed abbot of the New Minster at Winchester by Alfred's son, King Edward, when he succeeded to the throne. July 8.

GRISSINGER, BL. JAMES (1407–91). Born at Ulm, Germany, on October 11, he went to Italy when twenty-five, served in the army in Naples, and then was secretary to a lawyer at Capua for five years. He left to go to Germany, again was a soldier for a time in Bologna, and then joined the Dominicans in 1441 as a lay brother. He became an outstanding painter on glass, was an exemplary religious, and was known for his ecstasies and miracles. He died on October 11, and was beatified in 1825.

GRISWOLD, VEN. ROBERT (d. 1604). Born at Rowington, Warwickshire, England, he became assistant to Ven. John Sugar and was arrested with him at Rowington in 1603. He was offered his freedom if he would apostatize; when he refused, he was hanged at Warwick on July 16.

GRIVOT, BL. MARY HERMINA (1866–1900). Born at Beaune, France, she joined the Franciscan Missionaries of Mary and was sent to China. She was superior of the convent at Taiyüan and had been in China only fifteen months when the Boxer Rebellion broke out. She and her six nuns were murdered at Taiyüan on July 9 with many others when the notorious Christian-hater Yu Hsien, governor of Taiyüan, unleashed a persecution of all Christians, Catholic and Protestant alike, in his domain. She was beatified in 1946.

GRODECZ, BL. MELCHIOR (d. 1619). *See* Körösy, Bl. Mark.

GROVE, BL. JOHN (d. 1679). *See* Ireland, Bl. William.

GUALA ROMANONI, BL. (c. 1177–1244). He and his brother Roger received the habit from St. Dominic at Bergamo in 1217, followed Dominic to Bologna, and Guala then became prior of the priory at Brescia. He had a presentiment of the death of Dominic in a vision that came true. An eloquent preacher, Guala was appointed bishop of Brescia about 1230 and reigned for twelve years until he was exiled during an uprising. He then retired to a Vallumbrosan monastery at Astino and remained there until he died. His cult was approved in 1868. September 3.

GUALFARDUS (d. 1127). Also known as Wolfhard, he was a leather-worker in Augsburg, Germany. He accompanied a group of German merchants to Verona in 1096, settled there, gave all his earnings to the poor, and to escape adulation for his holiness, became a hermit on the banks of the Adige River. Induced to return to Verona in 1117, he became a monk hermit at the Camaldese priory near there and was famed for the miracles attributed to him. April 30.

GUARINUS (d. 1150). A monk of Molesmes and also known as Guérin, he was appointed abbot of St. John of the Alps near Geneva and affiliated his community to Clairvaux. Later he became bishop of Sion, Switzerland. St. Bernard held him in great esteem. January 6.

GUARINUS (d. 1159). Born at Bologna, Italy, he was early attracted to the religious life and despite his father's objections was ordained. He joined the Augustinian canons of the Holy Cross at Mortaria, became known for his holiness, and when elected bishop of Mortaria, hid until someone else was elected. After forty years at Mortaria, he was appointed bishop of Praeneste (Palestria) by Pope Lucius II, who created him a cardinal at the same time. He donated many costly gifts the Pope gave him and the wealth of the see to the poor, lived a life of great austerity, and died at Praeneste. February 6.

GUDULA (d. c. 712). Daughter of Count Witger and Bl. Pepin of Landen's niece St. Amalberga, she was educated at Nivelles under her cousin St. Gertrude. Gudula returned to the family castle near Morzelles after Gertrude's death in 664 and led a most holy life dedicated to God until her death, noted for her aid to the poor of the area. She died on January 8, and is the patroness of Brussels.

GUDWAL (6th century). Probably a Welshman or a Briton, he was one of the early missionaries to Brittany, founded Plecit Monastery near Locoal and several other monasteries in Brittany, and died at one of them. He might have been a regionary bishop and is now considered to be the same as Gurval, who succeeded St. Malo at Aleth in Brittany. June 6.

GUÉRIN. *See* Guarinus (d. 1150).

GUÉNOLÉ. *See* Winealoe.

GUÉNOT, BL. THEODORE (1802–61). Born at Bessieux, France, he joined the Society of Foreign Missions and when ordained was sent as a missionary to Indochina. He became vicar apostolic of Cochin China, was imprisoned for his faith, and died of ill treatment in prison before his sentence of death could be carried out. November 4.

GUERRA, BL. HELEN (1835–1914). Born at Lucca, Italy, on June 23, she educated herself by reading her brother's books (he was studying for the priesthood), founded a school at the suggestion of Don Bosco, and then founded the Institute of the Oblates of the Holy Ghost (Sisters of St. Zita), with Helen as superior; the institute received diocesan approval in 1881. She wrote several devotional books, and it was in response to a suggestion from her that Pope Leo XIII issued the encyclical *Divinum illud munus,* on the Holy Spirit, doctrine, and devotion. She died at Lucca on April 11, and was beatified in 1959 by Pope John XXIII.

GUIBERT (892–962). Of a noble Latharingian family, he was a well-known military leader, but he abandoned his military career for the religious life. He became a hermit on his estate at Gembloux, Brabant, and with the help of his Grandmother Gisla, in 936 founded a Benedictine monastery on the estate with Herluin as abbot and donated the estate to the monastery. Guibert then became a monk at Gorze but was summoned before Emperor Otto I to defend his right to donate the estate (it was an imperial fief) to the monastery—which he did successfully. He was again obliged to defend the monastery when the count of Namur seized its revenues, claiming it belonged to his wife, and again successfully defended the monastery against the count, his brother-in-law. Guibert was active in missionary work among the Hungarian and Slav soldiers who remained in Brabant after an invasion in 954. He died on May 23, and was canonized in 1211.

GUMMARUS (717–c. 774). Son of the lord of Emblem in Brabant and also known as Gommaire, he served at the court of Pepin and married Guinimaria, a noblewoman, at Pepin's suggestion. The marriage was an unhappy one, and on his return from eight years of warfare under Pepin, Gummarus found that Guinimaria had alienated everyone connected with his estate and had mismanaged his affairs. He satisfied all those Guinimaria had offended, and though she was penitent for a time, she soon resumed her old ways; whereupon Gummarus obtained a separation and lived as a recluse. He is reported to have founded an abbey at Lierre with St. Rumold. October 11.

GUNDLEUS (6th century). According to legend, Gundleus (Latin for Gwynllyw) was a Welsh chieftain who desired to marry Gwladys, daughter of Brychan of Brecknow. When Brychan refused his daughter's hand, Gundleus kidnaped Gwladys (Gladys) and married her (one aspect of the legend has King Arthur helping to defeat the pursuing Brychan and being dissuaded from capturing Gwladys for himself by two of his knights). At any rate, Gundleus and Gwladys led a riotous life, engaging in violence and banditry until their first son, St. Cadoc, convinced them to adopt and follow a religious life together at Newport, Monmouthshire; later he had them separate and live as hermits, with Gwladys eventually living at Oencarnau, Bassaleg. The Anglicized version of Gundleus is Woolo. March 29.

GUNTER, BL. WILLIAM (d. 1588). Born at Raglan, Monmouthshire, England, he studied for the priesthood at Rheims and after his ordination in 1587 was sent on the English mission. He was soon arrested at Shoreditch and when convicted of being a Roman Catholic priest, was hanged there. He was beatified in 1929. August 28.

GUNTHER, BL. (c. 955–1045). A nobleman related to Emperor St. Henry, he led a worldly life until he was fifty when he was convinced by St. Gothard, then reforming Hersfeld Monastery, to make up for his sinful life by becoming a monk there. He gave most of his wealth to endow Hersfeld, went on pilgrimage to Rome, and then became a monk at Niederaltaich, Bavaria, of which Gothard was abbot. Meanwhile, at the time he had endowed Hersfeld, he also endowed and owned the abbey of Göllingen in Thuringia, and he now insisted on being its abbot. He was an unsuccessful abbot and incurred the enmity of the monks there. He was persuaded to resign and return to Niederaltaich by Gothard. In 1008, he became a hermit in Lalling Forest, attracted disciples, and then built a hermitage near Rinchnac, Bavaria, which developed into a monastery. He died at Hartmanice, Bohemia, on October 9, revered for his holiness and austerity, his eloquent preaching, and his gift of infused knowledge.

GUNTRAM. See Guntramnus.

GUNTRAMNUS (d. 592). What we know of him is from St. Gregory of Tours, who tells us he was King of Burgundy and part of Aquitaine from 561. He endowed churches and monasteries, was a just ruler, and supported three synods that sought to improve clerical discipline. His personal life was not of the most edifying (he divorced his wife and had the physician of another wife murdered), though he spent the later years of his life doing penance for his misdeeds. He is also known as Guntram or Gontran. March 28.

GURIAS (4th century). According to legend, Gurias and his friend Samonas were arrested during the persecution of Christians by Emperor Diocletian, and when they refused to offer sacrifice to the pagan gods were tortured and thrown into prison. Three days later they were subjected to further torture, and when they still refused to recant, were beheaded. Soon after, Abibus, a deacon at Edessa and a friend of Gurias and Samonas, was captured, refused an opportunity to escape, and was burned to death. His body survived the flames and the three friends were enshrine at Edessa, Syria. November 15

GURVAL. See Gudwal.

GUTHLAC (667–714). Of a noble family, he served in the army of Ethelred of Mercia, and when twenty-four became a monk at Repton. He left after two years to be a hermit on an island in the Fens, was ordained six years later, and from his hermitage developed Croyland Monastery. He experienced diabolical visitations, had visions, and was gifted with the ability to prophesy and to perform miracles. He died at Croyland, and his tomb became a pilgrimage shrine. April 11.

GUTIERREZ, BL. BARTHOLOMEW (c. 1580–1632). Born in Mexico of Spanish parents, he joined the Augustinians in 1596, was ordained at Puebla, and was sent to the Philippines in 1606. He was then sent to Japan, was prior at Ukusi in 1612, and worked among the Japanese until 1629, when he was arrested. After three years in prison at Omura, he was burned to death at Nagasaki. He was beatified in 1867. September 28.

GUY OF ANDERLECHT (d. c. 1012). Born of poor parents near Brussels, he had no education but was devoted to the poor and led an austere life. He became sacristan at Our Lady's Church at Laeken, lost what little he had in a commercial venture, and made a pilgrimage on foot to Rome and Jerusalem. On his return seven years later, he was taken ill, was hospitalized at Anderlecht, and died there. Miracles were soon reported at the grave of this "poor man of Anderlecht," as he was called, and a shrine was built in his honor. September 12.

GUY OF POMPOSA (d. 1046). Born at Ravenna, Italy, he donated all his possessions to the poor, went to Rome, and was tonsured there. He spent three years with Martin, a hermit, on an island in the Po River and then joined the community at Pomposa Abbey near Ferrara. He became abbot of St. Severus at Ravenna and then of Pomposa. He attracted so many disciples to his community by his sanctity and wisdom that he was obliged to build another monastery and was a much-sought-after spiritual adviser. For a time Archbishop Heribert of Ravenna threatened to do away with the monastery, but a personal meeting with Guy led to an understanding between the two men. Guy retired late in life to live as a hermit and died at Borgo San Donnino while on his way to Piacenza, where he had been summoned by Emperor Henry III, who wished to consult with him. March 31.

GUY VIGNOTELLI, BL. (c. 1185–1245). A resident of Cortona, Italy, known for his charities, he received the Franciscan habit from Francis at Cortona in 1211. Guy built a cell on a bridge near Cortona, was ordained, became famed for his holiness and miracles, and died in the Cortona convent of the Franciscans possibly in 1250. June 16.

GUYART, BL. MARIE. See Martin, Bl. Marie of the Incarnation.

GWENFREWI. See Winifred.

GWLADYS. See Gundleus.

GWYN, RICHARD (1537–84). Born at Llanidloes, Montgomeryshire, Wales, he was raised a Protestant, studied briefly at Oxford and then at St. John's College, Cambridge. He returned to Wales in 1562, opened a school at Overton, Flintshire, married, and had six children. He left Overton after becoming a Catholic, when his absence from Anglican services was noticed, but was arrested in 1579 at Wrexham, Wales. He escaped but was again arrested in 1580 and imprisoned at Ruthin. He was brought up before eight assizes, tortured, and fined, and four years later, in 1584, he was convicted of treason on charges by perjuring witnesses and sentenced to death. He was hanged, drawn, and quartered at Wrexham on October 15—the first Welsh martyr of Queen Elizabeth I's reign. He was canonized by Pope Paul VI in 1970 as one of the Forty Martyrs of England and Wales and is the protomartyr of Wales. October 17.

GWYNLLYW. See Gundleus.

H

HACKSHOT, VEN. THOMAS (d. 1601). *See* Tichborne, Ven. Nicholas.

HAILE, BL. JOHN (d. 1535). An aged parish priest at Islesworth, Middlesex, England, he was seized in the early days of Henry VIII's persecution of Catholics and executed at Tyburn with Bl. John Houghton and his companions on May 4. Haile was beatified in 1886. May 11.

HALLVARD (d. 1043). According to tradition, he was a Norwegian, son of Vebjörn of Husaby, and became a trader in the Baltic islands. While defending a woman who sought sanctuary on his ship from three men accusing her of theft (he offered to make restitution to them), he was killed, with the woman, by arrows from the men. Though they attached a stone to his body when they cast it into the sea, it came to the surface, and the whole story came out. He has long been revered as a martyr for his defense of an innocent person and is the patron of Oslo. May 15.

HANSE, BL. EVERARD (d. 1581). Born in Northamptonshire, England, of Protestant parents, he studied at Cambridge, became a popular Protestant minister, and in 1579 was converted to Catholicism. He went to the English college at Rheims, was ordained in 1581, and was sent on the English mission a month later. He used the alias Evans Duckett but was arrested three months after he landed while visiting Catholic prisoners in Marshalsea Prison. He was sentenced to die for his belief in the ecclesiastical supremacy of the Pope and was hanged, drawn, and quartered at Tyburn on July 31. He was beatified in 1886.

HARCOURT, BL. WILLIAM. *See* Barrow, Bl. William.

HARDING, STEPHEN. *See* Stephen Harding.

HARRINGTON, BL. WILLIAM (1566–94). Born at Mount St. John, North Riding, Yorkshire, England, he was so impressed on meeting St. Edmund Campion when he was fifteen that he went to Rheims and then Tournai to study for the priesthood. He was forced to return home by illness but after several years he returned to Rheims and was ordained in 1592. He was sent on the English mission later the same year, was arrested in London in 1593, and after some months in prison was hanged, drawn, and quartered for his priesthood at Tyburn on February 18. He was beatified in 1929.

HART, BL. WILLIAM (d. 1583). Born at Wells, Somerset, England, he was educated at Lincoln College, Oxford, and followed its rector, Dr. Bridgewater, to Douai. After teaching for a time at Rheims, he went to Rome, was ordained there in 1581, and was then sent on the English mission. He worked in Yorkshire, ministered to Catholic prisoners in York Prison, and on one visit to the prison became aware that he was suspected of being a Catholic priest and escaped by dropping down a wall into the moat around the prison. Betrayed soon after by an apostate at the house of St. Margaret Clitherow, he was hanged, drawn, and quartered for his priesthood at York. He was beatified in 1886. March 15.

HARTLEY, BL. WILLIAM (c. 1557–88). Born at Wilne, Derbyshire, England, he was educated at St. John's College, Oxford, and became an Anglican minister. He was converted to Catholicism, went to Rheims, and was ordained there in 1580. He was sent on the English mission later in 1580 and helped St. Edmund Campion and Fr. Robert Parsons in their clandestine publishing ventures. Hartley was arrested and imprisoned in 1582, spent three and a half years in prison, and was deported in 1585. He soon returned, was captured again at Holborn in 1588, and this time was convicted of being a Catholic priest and hanged at Shoreditch, London. He was beatified in 1929. October 5.

HARTMAN, BL. (d. 1164). Born at Polling, Austria, he was educated at St. Nicholas Augustinian Monastery at Passau and became a canon there. In 1122, he was appointed dean of the metropolitan chapter by Archbishop Conrad of Salzburg, reformed the clergy, and then was appointed provost of Herrenchiemsee Monastery by Conrad, with instructions to reform it. Margrave Leopold of Austria then summoned him to head a house of canons he had just founded at Klosterneuburg, and in 1140 Hartman was appointed bishop of Brixen (Bressanone, Italy), which he ruled for twenty-four years. He supported Pope Alexander III against Emperor Frederick I, founded Holy Cross Hospice for pilgrims at Brixen,

and died there on December 23. His cult was confirmed in 1784.

HARVEY. *See* Hervé.

HÉBERT, BL. FRANÇOIS (d. 1792). *See* Du Lau, Bl. John.

HEDDA (d. 705). A monk, probably at St. Hilda Monastery at Whitby, England, he was appointed bishop of the divided diocese of the West Saxons (Wessex) in 675 and located his see first at Dorchester, near Oxford, and then at Winchester. He assisted King Ine in drawing up his code of laws, endowed Malmesbury Abbey with land, and ruled his diocese for thirty years. July 7.

HEDDA (d. c. 870). Abbot of Medeshamstede (Petersborough, England), he and some eighty-four of his monks were murdered by Danes raiding the English coast. April 10.

HEDWIG (c. 1174–1243). Also known as Jadwiga, she was the daughter of Count Berthold IV of Andechs, Bavaria, where she was born. She was educated at Kitzingen Monastery in Franconia and when she was twelve, she was married to Duke Henry of Silesia. In 1202, on the death of his father, Henry succeeded to the dukedom and at Hedwig's request built a Cistercian monastery for nuns at Trebnitz, the first monastery for women in Silesia; the couple founded numerous other monasteries and hospitals. They had seven children, and two of them, Henry and Conrad, despite Hedwig's efforts, warred over the division of territories made by Duke Henry in 1112; and in 1227 Henry and Duke Ladislaus of Sandomir warred against Swatopluk of Pomerania. They were successful but when Ladislaus was killed, Henry went to war against Conrad of Masovia over Ladislaus' lands; Hedwig acted as peacemaker between the two and restored peace. On the death of Henry in 1238, Hedwig moved into the monastery at Trebnitz. Her son Henry was killed in 1240 in a battle against the Mongol Tartars near Wahlstadt, and she died at Trebnitz, Poland, on October 15. Many miracles were attributed to her, and she was canonized in 1267. She is the patroness of Silesia.

HEDWIG, BL. (1374–99). The youngest daughter of King Louis I of Hungary, nephew and successor in 1370 to King Casimir III of Poland as Louis the Great of Poland. She succeeded to the throne on Louis' death in 1382 and at thirteen was married to pagan Duke Jagiello of Lithuania—a marriage that began a four-hundred-year alliance between Poland and Lithuania when Jagiello by the marriage also became King Ladislaus II of Poland. As part of the marriage pact, Jagiello became a Christian, destroyed pagan temples, and forced baptism on his people. Hedwig became known for her charity, concern for the poor, and her asceticism. She died in childbirth. Venerated in Poland and honored on February 28 with a popular cult, Hedwig's cause for beatification was introduced but has never been approved.

HEGESIPPUS (d. c. 180). A Jewish convert to Christianity at Jerusalem, he spent twenty years in Rome, returned to Jerusalem in 177 after visiting most of the important Christian churches, and probably died at Jerusalem. He is considered the father of Church history for his five books on the history of the Church from the death of Christ up to the pontificate of St. Eleutherius (c. 174–c. 189); Eusebius drew on it heavily for his *Ecclesiastical History*. Unfortunately, only a few chapters of Hegesippus' work are extant. April 7.

HEIMRAD (d. 1019). Born in Swabia, the son of serfs, he was ordained, was a priest at Baden for a time, and then became chaplain to the lady of the estate on which his parents were serfs. He left his post as chaplain to go on pilgrimage to Rome and Jerusalem and then wandered throughout Germany as a pilgrim. After a time at Hersfeld Abbey, he went on the road again, to the relief of the abbot, who considered him a malingerer, and settled at an abandoned church given him by a parish priest in Westphalia. When his eccentricities drew the priest's parishioners to him and he refused a gift from the priest's wife denouncing her for immorality, the priest drove him from the town. He was denounced at place after place that he went—St. Cunegund had him flogged at Paderborn, as did Bishop St. Meinwek of Paderborn—but in other places he was venerated as a saint. He eventually settled down to an austere life in a forest near what is now Wolfhagen, Hesse-Nassau, and died there. Many miracles were recorded at his tomb, which attracted great numbers of pilgrims, and though a popular cult grew up around him it has never been officially approved. June 28.

HELDRAD (d. c. 842). Son of a feudal lord at Lambec, Provençal, he inherited a fortune in his youth, spent some of it building a church and a hospice, and gave the balance to the poor. He became a pilgrim, visiting holy places in France, Spain, and Italy, and finally settled at the Benedictine monastery of Novalese at the foot of the Alps and became a monk there. He was ordained, was put in charge of training novices, and in time was elected abbot. He devised methods for rescuing travelers stranded on Mount Cenis, built a hospice at the Lautaret Pass, and helped build up the monastery's library. His cult was approved in 1903. March 13.

HELEN DEI CAVALCANTI, BL. (1396–1458). Of the Valentini family of

Udine, Italy, she was married to Antony dei Cavalcanti when she was fifteen and had a happily married life for twenty-five years. On Antony's death, she became a tertiary of the Hermits of St. Augustine, took a vow of perpetual silence, and devoted herself to charitable works and an austere and penitential lifestyle. She was frequently beset by temptations but was gifted with spiritual visions and was known for her miracles of healing. She died on April 23, and her cult was confirmed in 1848.

HELEN ENSELMINI, BL. (c. 1208–42). Of a noble family, she was born at Padua, Italy, received the Poor Clare habit from St. Francis at Arcella in 1220, is reputed to have had visions of those in heaven and the souls in purgatory, and went for months with no other sustenance than the Eucharist. She had St. Anthony of Padua as her spiritual adviser in the last years of her life, when she became blind and mute. She died on November 4, and her cult was approved in 1695. November 7.

HELEN OF POLAND, BL. *See* Jolenta, Bl.

HELEN OF SKÖVDE (d. c. 1160). She was born at Västergotland, Sweden, of noble parents, and on the death of her husband gave her possessions to the poor and made a pilgrimage to Rome. On her return, she was accused of and executed for the death of her son-in-law, though it was later ascertained that he had been murdered by his servants. Miracles were reported at her tomb, and a cult developed that was authorized in 1164. July 31.

HELENA (c. 250–c. 330). Probably the daughter of an innkeeper, and born sometime between 248 and 255 at Drepanum, Bithynia (a legend that she was the daughter of an English prince

has long since been disproved), she met Roman General Constantius Chlorus about 270, and despite her lowly station, they were married. Sometime between 274 and 288, their son Constantine was born. When Constantius was named Caesar in 293 under Emperor Maximian, he divorced Helena for political reasons and married Maximian's stepdaughter, Theodora. When Maximian died at York, England, in 306, Constantine, who was with him, was declared Emperor by the troops there but did not win a clear title to the throne until his dramatic victory at the Milvian bridge in 312. He conferred the title Augusta on his mother, ordered all honor be paid to her as the mother of the sovereign, and had coins struck with her likeness on them. In 313, he and his fellow Emperor, Licinius, issued the Edict of Milan, permitting Christianity in the Empire and releasing all religious prisoners. About this time, Helena was converted to Christianity (she was then sixty-three, according to historian Eusebius). She zealously supported the Christian cause, built numerous churches, aided the poor, and ministered to the distressed. After several wars between them, Constantine defeated Licinius a final time, in 324; Licinius was executed, Constantine became sole Emperor of both East and West, and moved the capital to Constantinople. Helena went to Palestine, and while there, according to Rufinus, Sulpicius Severus, and a sermon of St. Ambrose, all dating from the late fourth century, she discovered the True Cross. She built basilicas on the Mount of Olives and at Bethlehem, traveled all over Palestine, and was known for her kindness to soldiers, the poor, and prisoners. She died somewhere in the East, probably at Nicomedia, and was buried at Constantinople. August 18.

HELGA. *See* Olga.

HELIER (6th century). Reportedly born at Tongres, Belgium, he was raised a Christian by a priest, Cunibert, who was murdered by Helier's pagan father. He spent some time with St. Marcou at Nanteuil and then became a hermit on the Isle of Jersey, where he has been venerated since he was murdered by a band of brigands. July 16.

HELIODORUS (c. 332–c. 390). Born at Altino, Italy, he was a soldier when he met St. Jerome in 372 and became one of his disciples. He followed Jerome to the East but would not join him in the Palestinian desert, evoking a famous letter from Jerome rebuking him for his decision. On his return to Italy, he was named bishop of Altino and helped finance Jerome's translation of the Bible. July 3.

HELLADIUS (d. 633). An official at the Visigothic court, he performed diplomatic functions and was one of the signatories of the Council of Toledo in 589. He was attracted to the religious life, became a monk at the monastery at Agali, Spain, and was later abbot. He was named bishop of Toledo in 615 and is reputed to have influenced King Sisebut to expel the Jews from Spain, though there is no certain evidence of this. February 18.

HEMERFORD, BL. THOMAS (d. 1584). Born in Dorsetshire, England, he received his bachelor's degree in law at Oxford in 1575, studied at Rheims and Rome, and was ordained in Rome in 1583. He was sent on the English mission, was arrested almost at once on his arrival in England, was convicted of treason for being a Catholic priest, and was hanged, drawn, and quartered at Tyburn on February 12. He was beatified in 1929.

HEMMA. *See* Emma.

HENARES, BL. DOMINIC (d. 1838). A Spanish Dominican, he was sent as a missionary to Tonkin, Indochina, where in 1803 he was named coadjutor to Bl. Ignatius Delgado, vicar apostolic of Tonkin. Bl. Dominic and a catechist, Bl. Francis Chien, were arrested during a persecution of Christians and beheaded for their faith. They were beatified in 1900. June 25.

HENRY II (972–1024). Son of Duke Henry II of Bavaria, and Gisela of Burgundy, he was born probably at Hildesheim, Bavaria, on May 6, succeeded his father as duke of Bavaria in 995, married Kunigunda about 998, and in 1002 was chosen Emperor on the death of his cousin Emperor Otto III. In the early years of Henry's reign he was involved in constant warfare as he strove to consolidate Germany into political unity. He defeated Arduin of Ivrea, leader of the opposition in Italy, in Lombardy when Arduin had himself crowned King of Italy in 1004. He drove Boleslaus I of Poland from Bohemia in 1004, though peace did not come until 1018, and in 1014 was crowned Holy Roman Emperor by Pope Benedict VIII. Henry founded and richly endowed the see of Bamberg in 1006 (in large measure to effect the Germanization of the Wends), restored the sees of Hildesheim, Magdeburg, Strasbourg, and Meersburg, made numerous foundations, and was benefactor of many churches. He often interfered in ecclesiastical matters, though he was usually supported by Rome. For example, the bishops of Würzburg and Eichstätt opposed his creation of the see of Bamberg, but Pope John XIX approved it. Henry quarreled with Aribo, his appointment as archbishop of Mainz, who had denounced appeals to Rome without episcopal approval and adamantly opposed the Cluniac reforms, both of which

Henry supported. Henry went to Italy in an unsuccessful expedition against the Greeks in Apulia in 1021, was taken ill at Monte Cassino, reportedly was miraculously cured by St. Benedict, but was lame thereafter. He was a monarch of great ability and outstanding piety and asceticism. An interesting story, perhaps apocryphal, had him desirous of becoming a monk at Saint-Vanne at Verdun. He pledged obedience to the abbot, whereupon the abbot commanded him under obedience to continue as Emperor. He died in his palace of Grona, near Göttingen, Germany, on July 13, and was canonized in 1146 by Pope Eugene III. July 15.

HENRY OF COCKET (d. 1127). A Dane, he was inclined to the religious life from his youth, went to England, and became a hermit on the island of Cocket off the coast of Northumberland. He died at his hermitage there on January 16.

HENRY OF TREVISO, BL. (d. 1315). Born at Bolzano, Italy, of poor parents, he devoted his life to aiding the poor and in religious devotions, practicing the greatest austerities and penances. Hundreds of miracles through the intercession of this poor, uneducated man were reported within a few days of his death on June 10, and his cult was confirmed by Pope Benedict XIV. Henry is called San Rigo in Italy.

HENRY OF UPPSALA (d. c. 1156). An Englishman living in Rome, he accompanied the papal legate, Nicholas Cardinal Breakspear (later Pope Adrian IV), to Scandinavia in 1151 and was consecrated bishop of Uppsala, Sweden, the next year by the cardinal. Henry was with King Eric of Sweden in the latter's invasion of Finland to punish Finnish pirates and remained behind when Eric returned to Sweden. Henry was murdered by a convert named Lalli, on whom he had imposed a penance for a murder he had committed. Henry is considered the patron saint of Finland, though he does not appear to have ever been formally canonized. January 19.

HENRY ZDIK, BL. (d. 1150). Born in Moravia, he was named bishop of Olomuc (Olmütz, Czechoslovakia) in 1126. He rebuilt the cathedral and in 1138 went on pilgrimage to Jerusalem, where he became a Premonstratensian. He supported Duke Ladislaus II of Bohemia when the princes of Moravia rebelled against him and was forced to flee to Prague when they were successful; he placed an interdict on the rebels but it was later removed by the papal legate. In 1141, he joined a group attempting to convert the Prussians and was St. Bernard's subdelegate for Bohemia and Moravia when Bernard was preaching the Second Crusade (1147–49). Henry founded Mount Sion Abbey at Strahov, restored Litomerice Monastery, labored to reform the clergy, and encountered great opposition in his efforts to impose clerical discipline. He was attacked and robbed by bandits near Boscowicz when he set out for Rome at the invitation of Pope Lucius II but escaped with his life. He is considered a beatus (blessed) in Czechoslovakia, though his cult has never been formally approved. June 25.

HERACLAS (c. 180–247). An Egyptian, he and his brother, St. Plutarch, were Origen's first pupils at his catechetical school at Alexandria and were converted to Christianity by him. Heraclas became Origen's assistant, was ordained, and succeeded Origen as head of the school when Bishop Demetrius of Alexandria condemned Origen in 231. Heraclas succeeded Demetrius as bishop of Alexandria the same year, and when Origen returned to Alexandria, Heraclas excommunicated him and drove him from the city. July 14.

HERBERT (d. 687). A disciple and close friend of St. Cuthbert, he was a priest and lived on an island in Lake Derwentwater, England, which was afterward named St. Herbert's Island in his honor. March 20.

HERCULANUS, BL. (d. 1451). Born at Piegaro, Emilia, Italy, he became an Observant Franciscan at Sarteano, was ordained, and became a popular preacher famed for his eloquence and zeal. He encouraged the inhabitants of Lucca to resist a Florentine siege, promising them relief if they did penance; the Florentines soon after lifted the siege. Known for his great austerities, he died at a convent in Castronovo, Tuscany, which he had founded. He was beatified in 1860. June 1.

HERCULANUS OF PERUGIA (d. c. 547). Bishop of Perugia, Italy, he was beheaded by order of King Totila of the Ostrogoths when they captured that city. He probably is the same Herculanus who was a Syrian sent from Rome to evangelize Perugia. November 7.

HERIBALD (d. c. 857). A monk at St. Germanus Abbey in Gaul, he became abbot and later was appointed bishop of Auxerre. April 25.

HERIBERT (d. 1021). Born at Worms, Germany, he studied at Gorze Abbey in Lorraine and on his return to Worms was given a canonry and ordained. He became chancellor for Emperor Otto III and in 998 was named archbishop of Cologne. He accompanied Otto on a trip to Italy and brought the Emperor's body back to Aachen when he died at Paterno in Italy in 1002. Heribert incurred the dislike of Duke Henry of Bavaria, who became Emperor Henry II through a misunderstanding, but the two men were later reconciled, and Heribert served as Henry's chancellor. Heribert built a monastery at Deutz on the Rhine (where he was buried on his death), was an active peacemaker, was devoted to the poor, maintained strict clerical discipline, and is reputed to have performed miracles, one of which caused a heavy rainfall ending a severe drought and that causes him to be invoked for rainfall. He died at Cologne on March 16, and was canonized by Pope Gregory VII sometime between 1073 and 1075.

HERLUIN, BL. (994–1078). A knight born at Brionne, Normandy, he gave up his knighthood to become a Benedictine monk. He was founding abbot of an abbey on his estate at Bonneville, which was moved to a site on the Bec River in Normandy in 1040, and he developed it into one of the most influential monastic centers of the Middle Ages. He died on August 26 and though often referred to as Blessed, he has never been beatified formally.

HERMAGORUS (1st century). According to tradition, he was chosen by St. Mark to tend his converts in Aquileia, Italy, of which he was consecrated first bishop by St. Peter. With his deacon Fortunatus, Hermagorus preached in the area until arrested by Sebastius, a representative of Emperor Nero, and then was tortured and beheaded with Fortunatus. Fortunatus' connection with Hermagorus, despite the tradition, has never been proven, but he did suffer martyrdom in Aquileia. July 12.

HERMAN CONTRACTUS. *See* Herman the Cripple.

HERMAN THE CRIPPLE, BL. (1013–54). Born a cripple on February 18 at Altshausen, Swabia, and so terribly deformed he was almost helpless, he was placed in Reichenau Abbey in Lake Constance, Switzerland, in 1020 when seven and spent all his life there. He was professed at twenty, became known to scholars all over Europe for his keen mind, wrote the hymns *Salve Regina* and *Alma Redemptoris mater* to our Lady, poetry, a universal chronicle, and a mathematical treatise. He died at Reichenau on September 21 and is sometimes called Herman Contractus. September 25.

HERMAN JOSEPH (1150–1241). Born at Cologne, Germany, he desired to join the Premonstratensians at Steinfeld when he was twelve but because of his youth was sent to study at a friary of the Order in Friesland. On his return he was professed at Steinfeld and was assigned to be a waiter in the refectory, became sacristan, and later was ordained. Throughout his life he experienced visions of Christ, Mary, and Joseph (a vision of Mary in which he was mystically betrothed to her gave him his second name), many of which were later used as subjects for great artists. He also wrote several hymns and treatises, though two books describing his visions attributed to him are not believed to be of his authorship. He died at a Cistercian convent at Hoven, and was canonized by Pope Pius XII in 1958. April 7.

HERMANNSÖN, BL. NICHOLAS (1331–91). Born at Skenings, Sweden, he was educated at Paris and Orleans, was ordained, and became tutor of the sons of St. Bridget of Sweden. He was appointed bishop of Lindköping, Sweden, in 1374, inaugurated many reforms, insisted on clerical celibacy and the rights of the clergy, and was known for his personal austerity and concern for the poor. He wrote poetry, including an office in St. Bridget's honor, and died on May 2. He was reputedly canonized in 1414, but no proof of the canonization has been found to exist. July 24.

HERMENEGILD (d. 585). Son of Leovigild, Arian Visigoth King of Spain, he was raised an Arian but was converted to orthodoxy by his wife, Indegundis, daughter of King Sigebert of Austrasia. When Leovigild disinherited him because of his conversion, Hermenegild led a revolt against his father. Unable to secure aid from the Eastern Emperor or the Romans, he was defeated by his father at Seville but was reconciled with him. Later Leovigild demanded he return to Arianism, and when he refused, Leovigild had him axed to death. April 13.

HERMENLAND (d. c. 720). Born near Noyon, France, and also known as Erblon, he was early attracted to the religious life. He became a courtier at the court of King Clotaire III and was destined for marriage when he convinced his father to allow him to become a monk at Fontenelle Monastery in Normandy. He headed a group of twelve monks sent to evangelize the region around Nantes with headquarters in a monastery on an island in the Loire estuary of which he was abbot. They were most successful in their conversion work, and Hermenland became famous for the miracles he was reputed to have performed and his gift of prophecy. He resigned his abbacy late in life and retired to the monastery at Aindreete, where he spent the last years of his life. March 25.

HERMES (d. c. 120). A resident of Rome, he was imprisoned there by a judge named Aurelian and then was executed for his faith. August 28.

HERMES (d. 304). *See* Philip.

HERMOGENES (date unknown). *See* Mennas.

HERMOGIUS (d. c. 942). Born at Tuy, Spain, he founded Benedictine Labrugia

Abbey in Galicia, Spain, in 915, and was made a bishop. He was captured by the Moors and imprisoned at Cordova but was released when his ten-year-old nephew, St. Pelagius, was accepted by the Moors as a hostage for him. He spent his last years at Ribas del Sil, where he died after resigning his see. June 26.

HERMOSILLA, BL. JEROME (d. 1861). Born at La Calzada, Old Castile, Spain, he joined the Dominicans and was sent to Manila in the Philippines, where he was ordained. He was sent to East Tonkin in Indochina in 1828, was named vicar apostolic to succeed Bl. Ignatius Delgado, and was consecrated bishop. He was captured by mandarin Nguyen, escaped, but was betrayed by a soldier and beheaded with Bl. Valentine Berrio-Ochoa, vicar apostolic of central Tonkin, and Bl. Peter Almató on November 1. Bl. Jerome was beatified in 1908. November 6.

HERON (d. 250). *See* Dioscorus.

HERST, BL. RICHARD (d. 1628). Born probably at Broughton, England, he was a well-to-do farmer known to be a recusant and probably a Catholic. While plowing his fields, he was approached by three pursuivants, who sought to arrest him. He resisted, and in the ensuing melee, the three were routed and fled. One of them, a man named Dewhurst, fell over a plow and broke his leg; an infection set in and he died of gangrene thirteen days later. Herst (also called Hurst and Hayhurst) was arrested, charged with murder, and was convicted. He was offered his freedom if he would take the Oath of Supremacy declaring the ecclesiastical supremacy of the English sovereign, and when he refused was hanged at Lancaster, England, on August 29. He was beatified in 1929.

HERUNDA (6th century). *See* Redempta.

HERVÉ (6th century). According to legend, he was the son of a British bard named Hyvarnion and was born blind in Brittany. He was raised by one Arthian and later his uncle at Plouvien, where he worked as a farmhand and as a teacher in his uncle's monastic school at Plouvien. On the death of his mother, who had lived as a hermitess since he was seven, he became head of his uncle's monastery and then moved to Lanhouarneau, where he founded a new monastery and remained until his death, venerated for his holiness and miracles. He is invoked against eye trouble. One of the most extravagant and most popular miracles ascribed to him is the story of the wolf that ate the donkey with which Hervé was plowing; at Hervé's prayers, the wolf put himself into the donkey's harness and finished the plowing. The Anglicized version of Hervé is Harvey. June 17.

HESPERUS. *See* Exsuperius.

HESYCHIUS (1st century). *See* Torquatus.

HESYCHIUS (d. c. 302). All that is known of him is that he consoled St. Julius as Julius was being led to his execution at Durostorum (Silestria, Bulgaria) during Diocletian's persecution of the Christians, and was himself executed soon after for his faith. June 15.

HESYCHIUS (4th century). A disciple of St. Hilarion at Majuma, near Gaza, Palestine, he accompanied Hilarion from Palestine to Egypt, and when Hilarion secretly left Egypt, searched for him for three years before finding him in Sicily. The two then went to Dalmatia and to Cyprus, whence Hilarion sent

Hesychius to report to his followers in Palestine and the monks at the Gaza monastery. Hesychius was in Palestine when he heard of Hilarion's death on Cyprus. He hastened back to Cyprus, lived there for ten months, and then secretly brought Hilarion's body back to the monastery at Majuma and died there several years later. October 3.

HEWETT, BL. JOHN (d. 1588). Born in Yorkshire, England, the son of a draper, he was educated at Cambridge and then went to Rheims to study for the priesthood. Ordained there in 1586, he was sent on the English mission (using the aliases Savell and Weldon) and was arrested in London in 1587. He was exiled but was falsely arrested in the Netherlands and returned to England. He was convicted of being a Catholic priest and was hanged at Mile End Green in London. He was beatified in 1929. October 5.

HEYNOERT, ANDREW WOUTERS VAN (d. 1572). *See* Hilvarenbeek, Adrian van.

HIBERNON, BL. ANDREW (c. 1534–1602). Of poor but noble parents, he was born at Alcantarilla, Spain, joined the Conventual Franciscans, but left to become an Alcantarine lay brother at Elche. His humility and the miracles he is reputed to have performed converted many. He was beatified in 1791. April 18.

HIDULF (d. c. 707). Born at Regensburg, Bavaria, he became a monk at the abbey of Maximus at Trier and sometime later was consecrated auxiliary bishop of Trier. He left to become a hermit in the Vosges Mountains and about 676 built Moyenmoutier Monastery, which became famed for the holiness of its monks. He was abbot of both Moyenmoutier and Bonmoutier (Galilaea, afterward called Saint-Dié), where he died. July 11.

HIERONYMUS OF WEERT (d. 1572). *See* Pieck, Nicholas.

HILARIA (date unknown). *See* Claudius.

HILARION (c. 291–c. 371). Born at Tabatha, south of Gaza, Palestine, of pagan parents, he was educated at Alexandria, where he was baptized when he was fifteen. He stayed for a time with St. Antony in the desert and then returned to Gaza, where he found that his parents had died. He gave his possessions to the poor, became a hermit near Majuma, Palestine, practiced the greatest austerities, and became known for his miracles. About 356, disturbed by the great numbers of people attacted to his hermitage by his holiness, he decided to leave, went to Egypt, visited St. Antony's hermitage, and lived for a time in Egypt, but when he found that his fame had spread there too he went to Sicily where, after three years of searching, his faithful disciple Hesychius found him. Again in quest of solitude, he left with Hesychius and went to Dalmatia, but word of his miracles attracted so much attention, they left and settled near Paphos on Cyprus. Soon after, when the inhabitants found out who he was, he moved farther inland, where he remained until his death a few years later. Miracles were attributed to Hilarion wherever he went. October 21.

HILARY (d. 468). Born on Sardinia, he was one of the papal legates to the Robber Council of Ephesus in 449 who barely escaped with their lives. He was an archdeacon when he was elected Pope and consecrated on November 19, 461. During his pontificate, he labored to improve ecclesiastical discipline and strengthen the church organization in Gaul and Spain. He adjudicated several disputes between contending bishops and held councils in Rome in 462 and 465 to settle the matters; the latter is the first council in Rome of which the original records are still extant. He rebuilt many Roman churches and built the chapel of St. John the Apostle in the baptistery of St. John Lateran in thanksgiving for his escape at Ephesus. He publicly rebuked Emperor Anthemius in St. Peter's for allowing one of his favorites, Philotheus, to promulgate the Macedonian heresy in Rome, and sent an encyclical letter to the East confirming the decisions of the General Councils of Nicaea, Ephesus, and Chalcedon, and the contents of Pope Leo I's letter to Flavian. Hilary died in Rome on February 28.

HILARY OF ARLES (c. 400–49). Of a noble family, he was born in Lorraine, was a pagan in high office in the local government when he gave up a promising secular career at the urging of his relative St. Honoratus, distributed his possessions to the poor, and joined Honoratus at his monastery at Lérins. When Honoratus was elected bishop of Arles; on his way back to Lérins, he learned of Honoratus' death (429) and was elected his successor. He continued his monastic austerities at Arles, maintained strict clerical discipline, built monasteries, ransomed captives, aided the poor, and was noted for his oratory. He became involved in controversy with Pope St. Leo the Great when Hilary deposed a Bishop Chelidonius for incapacity and was overruled by the Pope; and again when Hilary appointed a bishop to replace ill Bishop Projectus and supported his appointee when Projectus recovered. Leo reproved Hilary and transferred his metropolitanship to the bishop of Fréjus, but the two were reconciled by the time of Hilary's death on May 5.

HILARY OF GALATEA (c. 476–558). A native of Tuscany, he was first attracted to the religious life when only twelve. Soon after, he left home, built a hermitage, and was founding abbot of Galatea Monastery. He persuaded the invading Theodoric the Goth not to destroy his monastery and even convinced him to grant him land. May 15.

HILARY OF POITIERS (d. c. 368). Born at Poitiers, Gaul, of a noble family, he was converted from paganism to Christianity by his study of the Bible and was baptized when well on in years. He had been married before his conversion, and his wife was still alive when, despite his objections, he was elected bishop of Poitiers about 350. Almost at once he became involved in the Arian controversy. He refused to attend a synod at Milan called by Emperor Constantius in 355, at which the bishops present were required to sign a condemnation of St. Athanasius, and was condemned for his orthodoxy by the synod of Béziers in 356, presided over by Arian Bishop Saturninus of Arles and composed mainly of Arian bishops. Later in the year he was exiled by the Emperor to Phrygia. He was so successful in refuting Arianism at a council of Eastern bishops at Seleucia in 359 and in encouraging the clergy to resist the heresy that the Arians requested the Emperor to send him back to Gaul. The Emperor ended his banishment and ordered him back to Gaul in 360. A synod he was instrumental in convoking deposed and excommunicated Saturninus; in 361, the death of Constantius ended the Arian persecution of the Catholics. In 364, Hilary held a public dispute at Milan with Auxentius, the Arian usurper of that see, and was ordered from Milan by Auxentius' protector, Emperor Valentinian. Hilary died at Poitiers, probably on November 1. Hilary was one of the leading and most respected theologians of his times. He wrote numerous treatises, notable among which were his *De Trinitate* (written while he was in exile against the Arians), *De synodis,* and *Opus historicum.* He was declared a Doctor of the Church by Pope Pius IX in 1851. January 13.

HILDA (614–80). Daughter of the nephew of King Edwin of Northumbria, England, Hereric, she was baptized at the same time as Edwin by St. Paulinus in 627, when she was thirteen. She lived the life of a noblewoman of her times until she was thirty-three, when she proposed to go to Chelles Monastery in France, where her sister Hereswitha was a nun. Hilda returned to Northumbria at the request of St. Aidan, spent some time in a nunnery on the banks of the Wear River, and then became abbess of a double monastery at Hartlepool. She was transferred sometime later to the Streaneschalch (Whitby) double monastery as abbess. She became renowned for her spiritual wisdom, and her monastery for the caliber of its learning and of its nuns. She favored the Celtic liturgical customs at the Synod of Whitby, which she had convened in 664, but accepted the Roman usage when the synod and King Oswy's decree ordered them observed in the churches of Northumbria. She died on November 17.

HILDEBRAND. *See* Gregory VII.

HILDEGARD, BL. (c. 754–83). Probably of a noble family, she was seventeen when Charlemagne put Queen Hermengard aside and married her. She bore him nine children and died at Thionville (Diedenhofen), France. Said to have been the daughter of the duke of Swabia, she was known for her aid to nuns and monks and was greatly venerated at the time of her death. Her tomb is at Kempten Abbey, of which she is considered the foundress. April 30.

HILDEGARD (1098–1179). Born at Böckelheim, Germany, possibly of noble parents (her father may have been a soldier in the service of Count Meginhard of Spanheim), she was sickly as a child and when eight was placed in the care of Count Meginhard's sister Jutta, a recluse near Speyer. By the time Hildegard was old enough to become a nun, a community had grown up around Jutta. When she died in 1136, Hildegard became prioress of the community. About 1147, with eighteen nuns, she moved her community to Rupertsberg on the Rhine near Bingen and founded a convent; she founded another convent at Eibingen about 1165. From her childhood, Hildegard was favored with supernatural experiences—visions, prophecies, and revelations. When about forty, she began to relate these experiences to her spiritual adviser, a monk named Godfrey, who had them copied down by a monk named Volmar. They were approved as coming from God by Archbishop Henry of Mainz and were also approved by Bishop Albero of Chiny when he was appointed to investigate them by Pope Eugene II. Huge crowds from all over Germany and France flocked to see and consult with her. She was hailed as both a saint and as a fraud and sorceress. In the last year of her life she was involved in a dispute with ecclesiastical authorities when she permitted the burial of a young man who had been excommunicated in the cemetery adjoining her convent. Her defense that he had received the last rites was not accepted and the convent was put under interdict. The interdict was finally removed, and she died at Rupertsberg on September 17. She is called "the Sibyl of the Rhine" for her powers as seeress and prophetess. She wrote hundreds of letters to Popes, Emperors, bishops, abbots, clergy, and laity, many of which are still extant. Her best-known work is *Scrivias,* written between 1141 and 1151, which tells of twenty-six of her visions, written symbolically of the relationship between God and man as seen in the Creation, redemption, and the Church. She has long been venerated as a saint but has never been formally canonized. September 17.

HILDEGUND (d. 1183). Daughter of Count Herman of Lidtberg and Countess Hedwig, she followed her mother and her sister into the religious life. Hildegund made a pilgrimage to Rome and converted her castle of Mehre near Cologne into a convent. She became prioress and attracted so many followers she was obliged to enlarge the convent. February 6.

HILDEGUND (d. 1188). Daughter of a knight, she was born at Neuss, Germany, and after the death of her mother, accompanied her father when she was twelve on a pilgrimage to Jerusalem, dressed as a boy and named Joseph for her safety. When her father died, she made her way back to Europe, and on a pilgrimage to Rome became involved in several adventures (in one of them she was condemned to be hanged for robbery and escaped only when a comrade of the real robber cut her down from the gallows). She returned to Germany, received the Cistercian habit at Schönau, and concealed her sex until her death there. Her cult, popular in the Middle Ages, has faded and was never approved, though her story appears to be authentic. April 20.

HILDELID. See Hildelitha

HILDELITHA (d. c. 717). An Anglo-Saxon also known as Hildelid, she became a nun at Chelles or Farmoutier, France, returned at the request of St. Erconwald to train his sister Ethelburga in the duties of an abbess, and then became a nun at her convent at Barking, England. Hildelitha became abbess on the death of Ethelburga and held that office until her death. September 3.

HILLONIUS. See Tillo.

HILVARENBEEK, ADRIAN VAN (d. 1572). Born at Hilvarenbeek, Holland, he joined the Premonstratensians but left and became a parish priest at Monster, Holland. With Jacob Lacops and Andreas Wouters, parish priest of Heynoord, he was taken into custody and sent to Briel, where they were hanged with a group of Catholics for refusing to deny papal ecclesiastical supremacy and Catholic teaching on the Blessed Sacrament. They were all canonized in 1867 as the Martyrs of Gorkum. July 9.

HIMELIN (d. c. 750). An Irish priest who according to legend went on pilgrimage to Rome and was taken ill at Vissenaeken, Brabant, while on the way home. A maid of the parish priest gave him a drink of water from her pitcher, though forbidden to allow anyone to drink from the pitcher for fear of contamination from the plague ravishing the areas. When the parish priest tasted the water it was wine, whereupon he brought the sick man into his home and cared for him until he died. March 10.

HIPPARCHUS (d. 297 or c. 308). He and Philotheus were magistrates at Samosata on the Euphrates who had been converted to Christianity. On his return from a campaign against the Persians, Emperor Maximinus noticed that his magistrates were missing from the public celebration, which included sacrifices to the pagan gods, as he had ordered. When he found they had not made sacrifices for three years he had them and Abibus, James, Lollian, Paregrus, and Romanus, whom they had converted, brought before him. When they all refused to sacrifice to the gods, he had them all tortured and then imprisoned for two months. When they still persisted in their refusal, he had them all crucified at Samosata. They are known as the Martyrs of Samosata. December 9.

HIPPOLYTUS (d. c. 235). A priest at Rome known for his learning, he may have been a disciple of St. Irenaeus and became a major theological writer of the early Church. He denounced Pope St. Zephrinus for his leniency to the Christological heresies abroad in Rome, especially Modalism and Sabellianism. When Pope St. Callistus I was elected Pope in 217, Hippolytus allowed himself to be elected antipope by his small band of followers and opposed Callistus' successors, Popes Urban and Pontian as well. Hippolytus was banished to Sardinia during Emperor Maximinus' persecution of the Christians in 235 with Pope Pontian, who reconciled him and brought him back into the Church. He died on Sardinia, a martyr from the sufferings he endured. His most important work was *A Refutation of All Heresies;* he also wrote commentaries on Daniel and the Song of Songs and *The Apostolic Tradition.* He is often confused with the Hippolytus (mentioned in the Roman Martyrology on August 13) of St. Lawrence's unreliable *acta,* which names him the officer in charge of Lawrence's imprisonment who was baptized by Lawrence, was brought before the Emperor when he attended the saint's funeral, and was then scourged and torn apart by horses at the order of the Emperor. At the same time Hippolytus' nurse, Concordia, and nineteen other Christians of his household were beaten to death with leaden whips. August 3.

HIPPOLYTUS (3rd century). According to the Roman Martyrology, he was bishop of Porto, Italy, who was put to death either there or at Ostia for his faith during the reign of Emperor Alexander. He is often confused with antipope Hippolytus (d. 235). August 22.

HIRENARCHUS (d. c. 305). *See* Acacius.

HODGSON, BL. SIDNEY (d. 1591). *See* Gennings, Edmund.

HOFBAUER, CLEMENT MARY (1751–1820). Born at Tasswitz, Moravia, on December 26 and baptized John, he was the ninth child of a butcher who changed his Moravian name of Dvorak to the German Hofbauer. He was an apprentice baker in his youth, worked in the bakery of the Premonstratensian monastery at Bruck, and then became a hermit. When Emperor Joseph II abolished hermitages, he became a baker in Vienna but again became a hermit with a friend, Peter Kunzmann, with the permission of Bishop Chiaramonti of Tivoli (later Pope Pius VII). Clement studied at the University of Vienna and in Rome with a friend, Thaddeus Hubl, and both of them joined the Redemptorists (when Clement took the name Mary) in Rome and were ordained in 1785. They were sent to Vienna, but when unable to establish a Redemptorist foundation since Emperor Joseph II had banned many religious foundations in Austria-Hungary, they were sent to Courland. On the way, Clement's old friend Kunzmann joined them as a lay brother. At the request of the papal nuncio, they went to Warsaw, and using St. Benno Church as their center, engaged in missionary work. In the twenty years they were there they were highly successful with the Poles, Germans in Warsaw, Protestants, and Jews. Clement worked among the poor, built orphanages and schools, and sent Redemptorist missionaries to Germany and Switzerland. When Napoleon suppressed the religious orders in his territories, Clement and his fellow Redemptorists were arrested and imprisoned in 1808, and then each was expelled to his native country. Clement decided to settle in Vienna and worked in the Italian quarter there. When appointed chaplain of the Ursuline nuns and rector of the church attached to their convent, he began to attract attention by his sermons, the holiness of his life, and his wisdom and understanding as a confessor. He founded a Catholic college in Vienna and became enormously influential in revitalizing the religious life of the German nations, even defeating, with Prince Rupert of Bavaria, an effort at the Congress of Vienna to establish a national German church. Clement also fought vigorously the whole concept of Josephinism (secular domination of the Church and hierarchy by the secular ruler), a stand for which he was bitterly opposed; his expulsion was demanded by the Austrian chancellor but forbidden by Emperor Francis I. Clement died in Vienna on March 15 and was canonized in 1909.

HOLFORD, BL. THOMAS (d. 1588). Born at Aston, Cheshire, England, the son of a Protestant minister, he became a teacher in Herefordshire, a tutor in the household of Sir James Scudamore at Holme, Lacy, and was converted to Catholicism. He went to Rheims to study for the priesthood, was ordained there in 1583, and was sent on the English mission. He worked in Cheshire and London, using the aliases Acton and Bude, was arrested, convicted of being a Catholic priest, and then hanged at Clerkenwell, London, during the persecution of Catholics under Queen Elizabeth I. He was beatified in 1929. August 28.

HOLLAND, BL. THOMAS (1600–42). Born at Suffolk, Lancashire, England, he studied at St. Omer, France, and Valladolid in Spain, and joined the Jesuits in 1624. He was ordained, sent on the English mission in 1635, using the aliases Hammond and Sanderson, and ministered to the Catholics for seven years until he was arrested in London in 1642. Convicted of being a Catholic priest, he was hanged, drawn, and quartered at Tyburn. He was beatified in 1929. December 12.

HOMOBONUS (d. 1197). Son of a Cremona, Lombardy, Italy, merchant, he was taught the business by his father, married, and led a life of the utmost rectitude and integrity, known for his charity and concern for the poor. He died on November 13 while attending Mass at St. Giles Church in Cremona, was canonized in 1199, and is the patron of tailors and clothworkers. November 13.

HONORATUS (d. c. 303). He, Arontius, Fortunatus, Savinian, Felix, Januarius, Septimus, Repositus, Sator, Vitalis, Donatus, and another Felix were all natives of Hadrumetum, Africa, and are known as the Twelve Brothers, although they were probably not related. They were arrested at Hadrumetum during the reign of Emperor Maximian, tortured at Carthage, and then sent to Italy. The first four were beheaded at Potenza on August 27; Felix, Januarius, and Septimus suffered a similar fate at Venosa on August 28; Repositus, Sator, and Vitalis at Velleiano on August 29; and Donatus and the second Felix were beheaded on September 1 at Sentiana. September 1.

HONORATUS (c. 330–415). Born at Vercelli, Italy, he became a disciple of St. Eusebius, who had become bishop of Vercelli in 340. He followed Eusebius into exile in Scythopolis in 355 and accompanied the bishop on his travels. Honoratus returned to Vercelli in 362, was elected bishop of Vercelli in 396, gave St. Ambrose the last rites in 397, and reigned until his death. October 28.

HONORATUS (d. 429). Of a distinguished pagan Gallo-Roman family, he was converted to Christianity in his youth, converted his brother Venantius, and with him and St. Caprasius, over Honoratus and Venantius' father's objections, set out for Greece to live as a hermit. Venantius died at Modon, and when Honoratus was taken ill, he returned to Gaul, lived as a hermit near Fréjus, and then on one of the Lérins islands off Antibes, attracted disciples and in about 400 founded Lérins Monastery. He was named archbishop of Arles, against his wishes, in 426 and died there three years later. January 16.

HONORATUS (d. c. 600). Born at Port-le-Grand, near Amiens, Gaul, he became bishop of Amiens and governed the see until his death there. He had a widespread cult in France following reports of numerous miracles when his body was elevated in 1060. He is the patron of bakers and confectioners; the famous Rue Saint-Honoré in Paris is named after him. May 16.

HONORIUS (d. 653). Born at Rome, he became a Benedictine monk and was sent to England by Pope Gregory the Great at the request of St. Augustine of Canterbury. Honorius was named archbishop of Canterbury in 627 and governed that see for a quarter century. He was granted authority to consecrate bishops by Pope Honorius I, gave refuge to St. Paulinus when he fled Cadwallon of Wales, who had defeated and killed King Edwin, and named him bishop of Rochester. When Paulinus died in 644, Honorius appointed as his successor St. Ithmar, the first English-born bishop. Honorius died on September 30.

HOORNAER, JOHN VAN (d. 1572). A Dominican priest from the Dominican province of Cologne, he was parish priest at a town near Gorkum, Holland, when he heard that the Franciscan community there had been captured by a Calvinist mob. He hastened to the city to administer the sacraments to the Franciscans and was himself seized. After imprisonment at Gorkum they were all sent to Briel and summarily executed when they would not apostatize. They were canonized as the Martyrs of Gorkum in 1867. July 9.

HOPE (2nd century). *See* Charity.

HORMISDAS (d. c. 420). A Persian noble and son of a provincial governor, he was stripped of his rank and possessions and made a camel tender when he refused to denounce his Christianity at the demand of Bahram, King of Persia. When the King offered to restore his position if he would apostatize, Hormisdas again refused, was relegated again to his demeaning position, and eventually suffered martyrdom for his faith. August 8.

HORMISDAS (d. 523). Born at Frosinone, Compagna di Roma, Italy, he was married and then was widowered (his son became Pope Silverius). Hormisdas was a deacon in Rome when he was elected Pope, succeeding St. Symmachus, on July 21, 514. The outstanding event of his pontificate was the ending of the Acacian schism, which had divided East and West since 484. The Church in Constantinople was reunited to Rome in 519 as a result of the *Formula* of Hormisdas, which formally condemned Acacius and unequivocally stated the primacy and infallibility of the Roman see. It was signed by Patriarch John of Constantinople and in time by some 250 Eastern bishops. It is a landmark statement of the authority and primacy of the Pope and has been quoted down through the ages to substantiate that claim. Early in his pontificate, Hormisdas also received back into the Church the last group of Laurentian schismatics. He died at Rome on August 6.

HOUGHTON, JOHN (1487–1535). Born in Essex, England, he served as a parish priest for four years after his graduation from Cambridge and then joined the Carthusians. He was named prior of Beauvale Charterhouse in Northampton but a few months later became prior of the charterhouse in London. In 1534, he and his procurator, Bl. Humphrey Middlemore, were arrested for refusing to accept the Act of Succession, which proclaimed the legitimacy of Anne Boleyn's children by Henry VIII, but were soon released when they accepted the Act with the proviso "as far as the law of God allows." He was again arrested when he refused, the following year, to accept the Act of Supremacy of King Henry, the first man to so refuse, together with Bl. Robert Lawrence and Bl. Augustine Webster, while they were seeking an exemption from the Oath from Thomas Cromwell. They were dragged through the streets of London, treated with the utmost savagery, and then hanged, drawn, and quartered at Tyburn on May 4. After his death, John Houghton's body was chopped to pieces and hung in different parts of London. He was canonized by Pope Paul VI in 1970 as one of the Martyrs of Charterhouse.

HOWARD, PHILIP (1557–95). Eldest son of Thomas Howard, fourth duke of Norfolk, who had been beheaded under Queen Elizabeth I in 1572, he had Philip II of Spain as his godfather and was earl of Arundel and Surrey on his mother's side. Baptized a Catholic but raised a Protestant, he was married at twelve to Ann Dacres, studied at Cambridge for two years, and was a wastrel at Elizabeth's court. Deeply impressed by St. Edmund Campion when he debated at London, Philip reformed his life, was reconciled to his neglected wife, and returned to the Catholic Church in 1584. Imprisoned for a time in his own home for his religion, he wrote to the Queen and then tried to flee to Flanders with his family and brother William. He was captured at sea, returned to London, and accused of treason for working with Mary Queen of Scots. The charge was not provable, but he was fined ten thousand pounds. At the time of the Spanish Armada, he was again accused of treason (though he was in the Tower at the time) and ordered executed—a sentence that was never carried out. He was kept imprisoned in the Tower and died there six years later, on October 19, perhaps poisoned. He was canonized by Pope Paul VI in 1970 as one of the Forty Martyrs of England and Wales.

HOWARD, BL. WILLIAM (1616–80). Grandson of St. Philip Howard and fifth son of Thomas, earl of Arundel, who apostatized at the time of his son's birth, he was raised a Catholic. He was made a Knight of the Bath at the coronation of King Charles I in 1625 and secretly married Mary Stafford, a Catholic and sister of the late Baron Stafford, in 1637. He was made Baron Stafford by Charles in 1640, executed several missions for the King, collected art on a large scale, and was interested in the American colonies (Stafford County in Virginia is named after him). He was listed as paymaster general of the invading army in the infamous and fabricated "popish plot" of the notorious Titus Oates, and after two years in the Tower was condemned to be executed by the House of Lords. He was beheaded at Tyburn on December 29, and was beatified in 1929 as one of the martyrs of the Titus Oates plot.

HRODBERT. *See* Rupert.

HROZNATA, BL. (1160–1217). A nobleman of the court of Ottokar I of Bohemia, he left the court and vowed to go on crusade when his wife and son died about 1190. Released from his vow by Pope Celestine I to build a monastery, he built Tepl Premonstratensian Abbey in western Bavaria, where he became a canon, and two convents. Disagreement with his abbot caused him to leave for a time, but the two were reconciled after a time, and he returned. He died at Alt-Kinsberg near Eger, where he had been imprisoned, reputedly for defending ecclesiastical rights. His cult was approved in 1897. July 14.

HSÜ, BL. MARY CHENG (1828–1900). *See* Mangin, Bl. Leon.

HUBERT (d. 727). A married courtier serving Pepin of Heristal, he turned to the religious life after his wife died, reputedly after seeing a crucifix between the horns of a stag while he was hunting (for which he is the patron of hunters). He became a priest under St. Lambert, bishop of Maastricht, and when Lambert was murdered at Liège about 705, Hubert was elected to succeed him. He moved his see to Liège, where he had built a church to house Lambert's remains. He ended idol worship in his diocese, made numerous conversions, and became known for his miracles. He died on May 30 at Tervueren near Brussels while on a trip to consecrate a new church. November 3.

HUGH (1024–1109). Eldest son of the count of Semur, he entered the monastery at Cluny, France, when fifteen, was ordained five years later, was named prior shortly after, and in 1049 succeeded St. Odilo as abbot. Hugh attended the Council of Rheims and eloquently supported the reforms of Pope

St. Leo X, denouncing simony and the relaxation of clerical discipline. Hugh went back to Rome with Leo, attended a synod condemning Berengarius of Tours in 1050, and in 1057, as papal legate, effected peace between Emperor Henry IV and King Andrew of Hungary. Hugh assisted Pope Nicholas II in drawing up the decree on papal elections at a council in Rome in 1059 and continued his close relations with the Holy See when Hildebrand, who had been a monk at Cluny, was elected Pope as Gregory VII. Hugh worked closely with Gregory to reform the Church and revive spiritual life in it. He tried to mediate the bitter feud between Gregory and Emperor Henry IV and in 1068 settled the usage for the whole Cluniac order. He had Pope Urban II consecrate the high altar of the basilica at Cluny, then the largest church in Christendom, and in 1065 was a leader at the Council of Clermont in organizing the First Crusade. Hugh was abbot of Cluny for sixty years and under his abbacy the prestige of Cluny reached its highest point as new houses were opened all over Europe. He served nine Popes, was adviser of Emperors, Kings, bishops, and religious superiors. Universally admired for his intellectual and spiritual attainments and as a simple man of great prudence and justice, he exercised a dominant influence on the political and ecclesiastical affairs of his times. He died at Cluny, and was canonized by Pope Callistus III in 1120.

HUGH OF ANZY, BL. (d. c. 930). Born at Poitiers, France, and educated at Saint-Savin Abbey at Poitou, he became a monk there and was ordained. He helped reform St. Martin Monastery at Autun and with St. Berno did the same at Baume-les-Messieurs, near Besançon. Hugh joined Berno in establishing the community at Cluny when Duke William of Aquitaine gave Berno Cluny and toward the end of his life became prior of Anzy-le-Duc, where he built a hospital. April 20.

HUGH OF BONNEVAUX (d. 1194). Nephew of St. Hugh of Grenoble, he became a Cistercian novice at Mézières and was praised by St. Bernard, who ordered him to mitigate the penances he imposed on himself after he had a vision of Christ and Mary. He became abbot of Léoncel in 1163 and of Bonnevaux in 1169, revived the latter abbey, and became known for his clairvoyance and the ability to read men's minds. He was instrumental in negotiating a peace between Pope Alexander III and Emperor Frederick I at Venice in 1177. Hugh's cult was approved in 1907. April 1.

HUGH OF FOSSES, BL. (c. 1093–1164). Born at Fosses, near Namur, Belgium, he was orphaned in his youth and became a member of the staff of Bishop Burchard of Cambrai. When he met St. Norbert, he joined him in 1119 in his missionary work in Hainault and Brabant and drew up the constitutions for the Premonstratensians when Norbert founded that Order. In 1128, Hugh was elected superior general of the Order and abbot of the mother house. During the thirty-five years of his leadership, he built up the Premonstratensians and is considered the second founder of the Order. He died on February 10, and his cult was confirmed in 1927.

HUGH OF GRENOBLE (1052–1132). Born at Chateauneuf, France, he became a canon of the cathedral in nearby Valence though a layman. He became an aide of Bishop Hugh of Die, was active in the bishop's campaign against simony, and while attending a synod at Avignon in 1080 to discuss the problems besetting the vacant see of Grenoble, was elected bishop of that see. He was ordained by the papal legate and consecrated by the Pope in Rome. Hugh at once set in motion plans to reform the see, denounced simony and usury, restored clerical discipline and clerical celibacy, and rebuilt the empty diocesan treasury. Discouraged by his lack of progress, he became a Benedictine at Chaise-Dieu Abbey but was ordered back to his see by Pope Gregory VII. Hugh repeatedly tried to resign the see but each time the Pope in office turned down his request because of his outstanding ability. He welcomed St. Bruno and his companions, gave them the land on which the Grande Chartreuse was built, and encouraged the Order. He died on April 1 and was canonized two years later by Pope Innocent II.

HUGH OF LINCOLN (1140–1200). Son of William, lord of Avalon, he was born at Avalon Castle in Burgundy and was raised and educated at a convent at Villard-Benoît after his mother died when he was eight. He was professed at fifteen, ordained deacon at nineteen, and was made prior of a monastery at Saint-Maxim. While visiting the Grande Chartreuse with his prior in 1160, he decided to become a Carthusian there and was ordained. After ten years, he was named procurator and in 1175 became abbot of the first Carthusian monastery in England, built by King Henry II as part of his penance for the murder of Thomas Becket. On Hugh's arrival at the site of the monastery at Witham in Somersetshire, he found not a building started but soon built the monastery. His reputation for holiness and sanctity spread all over England and attracted many to the monastery. He chided Henry for keeping sees vacant to enrich the royal coffers (since income from vacant sees went to the royal treasury), and was then named bishop of the eighteen-year-old vacant see of Lincoln in 1186—

a post he accepted only when ordered to do so by the prior of the Grande Chartreuse. Hugh quickly restored clerical discipline, labored to restore religion to the diocese, and became known for his wisdom and justice. He was one of the leaders in denouncing the persecution of the Jews that swept England, 1190–91, repeatedly facing down armed mobs and making them release their victims. He had differences with Henry over the appointment of seculars to ecclesiastical positions and with King Richard I (flatly refusing to contribute to Richard's war chest to finance foreign wars in 1197, the first time a direct levy by an English King had been refused), but remained on good terms with both monarchs. He went on a diplomatic mission to France for King John in 1199, visiting the Grande Chartreuse, Cluny, and Citeaux, and returned from the trip in poor health. A few months later, while attending a national council in London, he was stricken and died two months later at the Old Temple in London on November 16. He was canonized twenty years later, in 1220, the first Carthusian to be so honored. November 17.

HUGH THE LITTLE (d. 1255). One of the most tragic stories of the Middle Ages had nine-year-old Hugh lured into the home of a Jew named Koppin, scourged, crowned with thorns, and crucified. His body was then thrown into a well. Koppin and ninety-two other Jews were arrested; Koppin confessed to the crime, denounced his fellow Jews, and said it was a Jewish custom to crucify a Christian child each year. He and eighteen others were executed at Lincoln; the others were imprisoned but eventually released when a group of Franciscans interceded for them and they paid heavy fines. Miracles were reported when Hugh's body was recovered from the well. That a Christian child may have been killed by a Jew or Jews may have taken place; but it was never proven nor is there any evidence of any ritual killing of the type described above. Hugh's story is told in Chaucer's *Prioresse's Tale*. August 27.

HUGH OF ROUEN (d. 730). Son of Duke Drogo of Burgundy and nephew of Charles Martel, he was the beneficiary of many sees (the practice of pluralism was rampant in those days). He became first *primicerius* of the church in Rouen, was named bishop of Rouen in 722, then of Paris and Bayeux, and was also made abbot of Fontenelles and Jumièges—all probably through the influence of his Uncle Charles. Hugh is reputed to have used the revenues from these benefices wisely, helped promote piety and learning, but in time resigned them all to become a simple monk at Jumièges, where he died. April 9.

HUGOLINO (d. 1227). *See* Daniel.

HUGOLINOS OF GUALDO, BL. (d. 1260). He joined the Order of the Hermits of St. Augustine and in about 1258 occupied a former Benedictine monastery at Gualdo, Umbria, Italy, of which he was prior. A local cult developed, which was confirmed in 1919. January 1.

HUMBELINE, BL. (1092–1135). Sister of St. Bernard, she was born at Dijon, France, married the noble Guy de Marcy, and lived the life of the nobility of the day. Reproved by Bernard for her ostentatious dress and lifestyle while she was visiting him one day, she took his reproof to heart and several years later, with her husband's permission, she became a nun at Benedictine Jully-les-Nonnais nunnery. She succeeded her sister-in-law, Elizabeth, as abbess, lived a life of great austerity, and died at Jully in

Bernard's arms. Her cult was approved in 1703. August 21.

HUMBERT OF ROMANS, BL. (1200–77). Born at Romans, near Valence, France, he studied at Paris, where he received his doctorate in law, joined the Dominicans in 1224, made a pilgrimage to the Holy Land, and on his return in 1240 was elected provincial of the Roman province of the Dominicans. He was elected provincial of France in 1244, and in 1254 became the fifth master general of the Dominicans. He approved a final revision of the Dominican liturgy, promoted education, and was active in clerical reformation. He resigned his generalate at a general chapter in London in 1263, retired to the priory at Valence, emerged briefly at the request of Pope Clement IV to settle a dispute among the Cistercians, and died at Valence on July 14 (or perhaps on January 15, 1274). He wrote several treatises, among them *Treatise on Preaching,* the fruit of his success as a preacher. Though called Blessed by some authorities, his cult has never been formally approved.

HUMBERT III OF SAVOY, BL. (1136–88). Son of Count Amadeus III of Savoy and Matilda of Vienna, he was born at Avigliana, educated by Bishop Amadeus of Lausanne, and became count of Savoy when quite young on the death of his father. Humbert ruled wisely and engaged in several wars to defend his principality. Late in life, he retired to the Cistercian abbey of Hautecombe, where he probably died, though legend says he emerged to lead his troops against invading German troops and died at Chambéry. His cult was approved in 1831. March 4.

HUMILITY (1226–1310). Born at Faenza, Italy, of a wealthy family, she was named Rosana and was married, when fifteen, to a nobleman named Ugoletto. They had two children who died in infancy and after a near-fatal illness of Ugoletto when she was twenty-four, they both entered St. Perpetua double monastery near Faenza, he as a lay brother and she as a nun with the name Humility. She lived as a recluse in a cell adjoining St. Apollinaris Church for twelve years, living a life of great austerity under the direction of the Vallombrosan abbey of St. Crispin. At the suggestion of the abbot general of the Vallumbrosans, she became founding abbess of Santa Maria Novella Convent at Malta, near Faenza (the first Vallombrosan convent for nuns), and later of a second house at Florence, Italy, where she died on May 22.

HUMPHREY (d. 871). Born in France, he became a monk at the Benedictine abbey of Prüm in the Ardennes. Elected bishop of Thérouanne in 856, he was forced to flee when the Norsemen sacked the city and set it afire, and then played a major role in rebuilding the city and Saint-Bertin Monastery at Saint-Omer. He was elected abbot of Saint-Bertin, retaining his bishopric, but was replaced as abbot in 868 by Hildwin, candidate of King Charles the Bold, though he continued governing as bishop until his death. He is also known as Hunfrid. March 8.

HUMPHREY, BL. LAURENCE (1572–91). A native of Hampshire, England, he was converted to Catholicism by a Jesuit priest, Fr. Stanney, after he had disputed with him. He was arrested when he was heard calling Queen Elizabeth I a heretic. Seriously ill at the time, he was convicted and hanged, drawn, and quartered at Winchester. He was beatified in 1929. July 7.

HUNFRID. *See* Humphrey.

HUNNA (d. c. 679). The daughter of an Alsatian duke, she was married to Huno of Hunnaweyer and devoted herself to the poor of Strasbourg, earning the title of "holy washerwoman" when she even washed for the poor. A local cult developed after her death, and she was canonized in 1520 by Pope Leo X. April 15.

HUNT, VEN. THOMAS (d. 1600). Born at Norfolk, England, he studied at the English college at Seville, Spain. After his ordination there, he was sent on the English mission. He was arrested and imprisoned at Wisbech but with several other prisoners escaped. He was recaptured at Lincoln with Ven. Thomas Sprott and was executed there on July 11.

HYACINTH (d. c. 120). A chamberlain of Emperor Trajan at Caesarea in Cappadocia, he was charged with being a Christian, scourged, and imprisoned. He died of starvation when he refused to eat the only food offered him—meat consecrated for sacrifice to the pagan gods. July 3.

HYACINTH (3rd century). Unquestionably a martyr whose relics were found in the cemetery of the basilica of St. Hermes on the Salernian Way in Rome in 1845, he and Protus (whose empty tomb was also unearthed nearby) were reputed to be brothers who were slaves of Eugenia, Christian daughter of the prefect of Egypt. They accompanied her when she fled from her father and were beheaded for their faith with Basilla, a Roman lady they had converted. Another tradition has them Romans and servants of Basilla in Rome. September 11.

HYACINTH (1185–1257). Born at Oppeln, Poland, he joined the Dominicans,

possibly in Rome in 1217 or 1218, and was sent to Silesia with a group of Dominicans to evangelize the area. He preached over a wide area including Scandinavia, Prussia, and Lithuania, is venerated as an apostle of Poland, and is credited with numerous miracles. He died on August 15 and was canonized in 1594. August 17.

HYGINUS (d. c. 142). Little is known of him or his pontificate beyond that he was a Greek and was Pope, probably 138–42, succeeding Pope Telesphorus. It is known that two Gnostics, Valentinus and Cerdo, were in Rome while he was Pope, but what action if any he took about them is unknown. January 11.

HYPATIUS (d. 273). *See* Lucillian.

HYPATIUS (c. 366–c. 446). Born in Phrygia, he was educated by his father, a scholar, left home when eighteen, after a quarrel with his father and reputedly at the instigation of a vision went to Thrace, where he became a solitary with a monk named Jonas. After a reconciliation with his father, he and Jonas went to Constantinople, where Jonas remained; Hypatius went to Bithynia with two comrades, Moschion and Timothy, and settled in the ruins of a deserted monastery near Chalcedon. Hypatius attracted many followers and became abbot of a flourishing *laura* and a leading opponent of Nestorianism. He gave shelter to St. Alexander Akimetes and his monks when they were driven from Constantinople and caused the defeat of a proposal to renew the Olympic games because of their pagan origins. He died at eighty sometime in the middle of the fifth century, venerated as "the scholar of Christ" for his miracles and prophecies. June 17.

IA (d. c. 360). Unreliable sources have her a Greek, perhaps a slave, who was so successful in converting Persian ladies to Christianity that she was arrested during the persecution of the Christians by King Sapor II of Persia. Tortured for months in an attempt to force her to apostatize, to no avail, she was eventually lashed to death and then beheaded. August 4.

IBAR (5th century). Perhaps a missionary to Ireland before Patrick but more probably one of his disciples, Ibar preached in Leinster and Meath and founded a monastic school on the island of Beg-Eire (Beggery). April 23.

IBARAKI, LOUIS (d. 1597). *See* Karasumaru, Leo.

IBARAKI, PAUL (d. 1597). *See* Karasumaru, Leo.

IBARCHI, LOUIS (1585–97). *See* Deynan, Antony.

IDA OF BOULOGNE, BL. (1040–1113). Descended from Charlemagne, she was the daughter of Duke Godfrey IV of Lorraine and his first wife, Doda. Married at seventeen to Count Eustace II of Boulogne, she had a happy married life and had St. Anselm as her spiritual adviser. When Eustace died, she spent much of her inheritance helping the poor and building and restoring monasteries. She spent the last years of her life as a Benedictine oblate at St. Vaast, Arras,

France. Two of her sons, Godfrey of Bouillon, the conqueror of Jerusalem, and Baldwin, became Kings of Jerusalem. April 13.

IDA OF HERZFELD (d. 825). Great-granddaughter of Charlemagne, in whose court she was raised, she was married to Egbert by the Emperor, was early widowed, and spent her time aiding the poor. She moved from her estate at Hofstadt, Westphalia, to Herzfeld when her son Warin became a monk at Corvey, built a convent, continued her good works, and died there. September 4.

IDA OF LOUVAIN, BL. (d. c. 1300). According to unreliable sources, she was born at Louvain, Belgium, of a well-to-do family and indulged in ascetic and devotional practices from her youth despite the objections of her family. She entered the Cistercian convent of Roosendael and became known for her ecstasies, visions, and miracles, and is reputed to have received the stigmata. The date of her death is uncertain. April 13.

IDA OF TOGGENBURG, BL. (1156–1226). There is a fictitious religious legend according to which Ida was the wife of the ill-tempered, heartily disliked Count Henry of Toggenburg. Attacked by a servant named Dominic, she was saved by another servant named Cuno, whom she swore to secrecy. Dominic suggested to Henry that she was having an affair with Cuno, and when Henry saw Cuno wearing a ring of Ida's he had found, he killed Cuno and threw Ida out a window. Saved by a thicket, Ida fled to the forest and lived there for seventeen years until found by one of Henry's woodsmen, who told Henry where she was. Henry begged her forgiveness, which she granted, but she refused to return to the castle and had him build her a cell so she could live as a hermitess. The crowds that came to see her forced her to retire to a nunnery at Fischingen, Switzerland, where she remained until her death. That a religious woman named Ida was venerated and buried at Fischingen and had a popular cult confirmed in 1724 are all that are really known of her. November 3.

IDESBALD (1100–67). A Flemish courtier, he became a canon at St. Walburga Church at Furnes and then a monk at Our Lady of the Dunes Monastery near Dunkirk, France. He was named cantor and in 1155 was elected abbot and was noted for his holiness. His cult was approved in 1894. April 18.

IGNATIUS OF ANTIOCH (d. c. 107). Probably a convert to Christianity and perhaps a disciple of St. John, legend has him appointed and consecrated bishop of Antioch by St. Peter after Peter left the deathbed of Evodius, previous bishop of the see. Ignatius governed for forty years but was arrested during the persecution of Emperor Trajan (untrustworthy legend has him questioned by the Emperor himself) and sent to Rome. The ship he was sent on traveled along the coast of Asia Minor, then Greece, and finally reached Rome. Ignatius was greeted by crowds of Christians wherever the ship touched port, but he received ill treatment from his captors. He arrived in Rome on December 20, the last day of the public games, was escorted to the amphitheater, and there was killed by lions in the arena. A detailed description

of the trip to Rome is provided by Agathopus and a deacon named Philo, who were with him, and who also wrote at his dictations seven letters of instruction on the Church, marriage, the Trinity, the Incarnation, Redemption, and the Eucharist, which are among the most important of the earliest Christian writings. He is often surnamed Theophorus (God bearer). October 17.

IGNATIUS OF CONSTANTINOPLE (c. 799–877). Son of Byzantine Emperor Michael I and the daughter of Emperor Nicephorus I and named Nicetas, he and his brother were mutilated and exiled to a monastery when their father was deposed by Leo the Armenian in 813. Ignatius later became a monk, was ordained, and in time was elected abbot of his monastery. He was named patriarch of Constantinople in 846, vigorously assailed evil in high places, and in 857, when he refused communion to Bardas because of alleged incestuous sexual relationships, he was deposed and exiled by Bardas' nephew, Emperor Michael III. Banished to the island of Terebinthos, Ignatius seems to have resigned his see, and Bardas secured the election of his secretary Photius, a layman, as patriarch. A long factional struggle ensued, and in 867 Michael was murdered and his successor, Basil the Macedonian, deposed Photius and recalled Ignatius, as much to secure the support of Ignatius' supporters as to secure justice. Ignatius then asked Pope Adrian II to convoke a council, and at the eighth General Council, 869–70, Photius and his supporters were condemned, and Photius was excommunicated. Ignatius later came into conflict with Rome when he claimed jurisdiction over the Bulgars and convinced their prince to expel Latin priests and replace them with the Greek priests he sent. Pope John VIII's legates, threatening Ignatius with excommunication, arrived in Constantinople to find he had died on October 23. Though he is recognized as personally holy, he was evidently deeply engaged in the politics of his times.

IGNATIUS OF LACONI. *See* Peis, Francis Ignatius Vincent.

IGNATIUS LOYOLA (1491–1556). Of a noble family and the son of Don Beltran Yáñez de Loyola and Maria Sáenz de Licona y Balda, he was born in the family castle in the Basque province of Gúipuzcoa, Spain, the youngest of thirteen children, and was christened Iñigo. He entered the military service of the Duke of Nagara, was wounded in the right leg during the siege of Pamplona in 1521, and while recuperating was so impressed by a life of Christ and biographies of the saints he read that he decided to devote himself to Christ. After he recovered he went on pilgrimage to Monserrat, where he hung up his sword at Our Lord's altar and then spent 1522–23 on retreat at Manresa, where he experienced visions and probably wrote the bulk of his *Spiritual Exercises* (which was not published until 1548). He spent the years 1524–35 studying at Barcelona, Alcalá, Salamanca (where he was accused and then exonerated of preaching heresy), and Paris. He received his master of arts degree in 1534, when he was forty-three, and in the same year founded the Society of Jesus (the Jesuits) with fellow students Francis Xavier, Peter Favre, Diego Laynez, Alfonso Salmeron, Simon Rodriguez, and Nicholas Bobadilla in Paris, though the formal title Society of Jesus was not adopted until 1537, when Ignatius and seven of his band were ordained in Venice after he had spent a year on pilgrimage in Spain. Unable to go on pilgrimage to Jerusalem, as they had vowed, they went to Rome and offered their services to the Pope. It was on the way to Rome that Ignatius had the famous vision of La Storta, in which Christ promised all would go well in Rome. The Society was approved by Pope Paul III in 1540, and the group took their final vows in 1541, with Ignatius named superior general. Jesuits were sent at once to missionary areas, soon Jesuit houses, schools, colleges, and seminaries were founded all over Europe, and the Jesuits became renowned for their prowess in the intellectual sphere and in the field of education. By the time Ignatius died in Rome on July 31, his three goals for the Church—reform of the Church (especially through education and more frequent use of the sacraments), widespread activity in the missionary field, and the fight against heresy—were well established as the bases of Jesuit activities. He was canonized in 1622 and was proclaimed patron of retreats and spiritual exercises by Pope Pius XI. July 31.

IGNATIUS OF ROSTOV (d. 1288). Archimandrite of the Theophany monastery at Rostov, he was named bishop of that city in 1262. He acted as peacemaker between quarreling nobles and helped defend his flock against the Tartars. He was removed from his bishopric because of charges made against him, but he was exonerated when they were proved false, and he returned to head his see. He attended a synod of the Russian Church at Vladimir in 1274, and died on May 28.

ILDEPHONSUS (607–67). Of distinguished parents and perhaps a pupil of St. Isidore of Seville, he was born at Toledo, became a monk at Agli (Agalia) near Toledo despite his parents' objections, was ordained, and in time was elected abbot. He attended councils in Toledo in 653 and 655, was named archbishop of Toledo about 657, and governed until his death on January 23. He had an intense devotion to Mary, wrote several theological treatises, notably *De virginitate perpetua sanctae Mariae* (according to a legend Mary appeared to him and presented him with a chasuble), and is honored as a Doctor of the Church in the Spanish Church.

ILLTUD. *See* Illtyd.

ILLTYD (450–535). Also known as Illtud, his life is derived mainly from legend and unreliable sources, though he is one of the most celebrated of the Welsh saints. According to them, he was the son of a Briton living in Letavia, Brittany (some scholars believe Letavia is an area in central Brednock, England, rather than in Brittany), who came to visit his cousin King Arthur of England about 470. Illtyd married Trynihid and then served in the army of a Glamorgan chieftain. When one of his friends was killed in a hunting accident, he and Trynihid lived as recluses in a hut by the Nadafan River. He left her to become a monk under St. Dubricius, but after a time resumed his eremitical life. He attracted many disciples and organized them into Llaniltud Fawr Monastery (Llanwit Major in Glamorgan), which soon developed into a great monastic foundation and a center of missionary activity in Wales. Another legend has him a disciple of St. Germanus of Auxerre, who ordained him, famed for his learning and wisdom, which caused him to be named head of the monastic school at Llanwit. Many extravagant miracles were attributed to him (he was fed by heaven when forced to flee the ire of a local chieftain and take refuge in a cave, his miraculous restoration of a collapsed seawall), and he is reputed to have sent grain to relieve a famine in Brittany. His death is variously reported at Dol, Brittany, where he had retired in his old age, Llanwit, and Defynock. One Welsh tradition has him one of the three knights put in charge of the Holy Grail

by Arthur, and another even has him Galahad. November 6.

IMBERT, BL. LAURENCE (d. 1839). A native of Aix-en-Provence, France, he joined the Paris Foreign Missionary Society and was sent to China in 1825. He worked there as a missionary for twelve years and was named titular bishop of Capsa. In 1837, he was sent to Korea and entered the country secretly, as Christianity was forbidden there. He was successful in his missionary activities, but in 1839 a wave of violent persecutions of the Christians swept the country. In the hope of ending the persecutions of native Christians, he, Fr. Philibert Maubant, and Fr. James Honoré Chasan, who had preceded him into Korea, surrendered to the authorities. They were bastinadoed and then beheaded at Seoul on September 21. During the same persecution, John Ri was bastinadoed and suffered martyrdom, and Agatha Kim was hanged from a cross by her arms and hair, driven over rough country in a cart, and then stripped and beheaded. In 1925, Bl. Laurence and his companions and many others, eighty-one in all, who had been executed for their faith, were beatified as the Martyrs of Korea. September 22.

INDALETIUS (1st century). *See* Torquatus.

INDRACTUS (c. 710). An old legend has him an Irishman, possibly the son of a chieftain, who was murdered either on his way to or from Rome with his sister Domenica (or Drusa) and several companions by Saxons, perhaps near Glastonbury, England. February 5.

INGENES (d. 250). *See* Ammon.

INGLEBY, VEN. FRANCIS (c. 1551–86). Born at Ripley, England, he studied at Oxford and the Inner Temple, and then went to the English college at Rheims to study for the priesthood in 1582. He was ordained there the following year and sent on the English mission in 1584. He worked in the area around York until he was captured, and when convicted of being a Catholic priest was hanged at York on June 3.

INGRAM, BL. JOHN (1565–94). Born at Stoke Edith, Hertfordshire, England, he was educated at Oxford and became a Catholic. He went to Rheims and then to Rome to study for the priesthood and was ordained at Rome in 1589. He was sent to Scotland to minister to the Catholics there in 1592, was arrested on the Tyneside at the end of 1593, and imprisoned in the Tower of London, where he was tortured. Convicted of being a Catholic priest, he was hanged, drawn, and quartered at Gateshead, opposite Newcastle, on July 26. He was beatified in 1929. July 24.

IÑIGO (d. 1057). Also known as Eneco, he is believed to have been a native of Calatayud, Bilbao, Spain. He became a hermit, then a monk at San Juan de Peña in Aragon, and after serving as prior, resumed his eremitical life in the Aragon Mountains. He was persuaded by King Sancho the Great about 1029 to be abbot of a group of monks the King had chosen to reform the monastery at Oña founded by the King's father-in-law in 1010. Iñigo was most successful in his reforms, became known for his peacemaking ability, and was reputed to have performed miracles. He died at Oña on June 1, and was probably canonized by Pope Alexander III.

INNOCENT (d. c. 350). Born at Tortona, Italy, of Christian parents, he was arrested for his Christianity but escaped and went to Rome. He became a deacon there, was appointed bishop of Tortona in 322, and was active in conversion work and in building churches during the twenty-eight years of his episcopate. April 17.

INNOCENT I (d. 417). Born at Albano, Italy, he became Pope, succeeding Pope St. Anastasius I, on December 22, 401. During Innocent's pontificate, he emphasized papal supremacy, commending the bishops of Africa for referring the decrees of their councils at Carthage and Milevis in 416, condemning Pelagianism, to the Pope for confirmation. It was his confirmation of these decrees that caused Augustine to make a remark that was to echo through the centuries: *"Roma locuta, causa finita est"* (Rome has spoken, the matter is ended). Earlier Innocent had stressed to Bishop St. Victrius and the Spanish bishops that matters of great importance were to be referred to Rome for settlement. Innocent strongly favored clerical celibacy and fought the unjust removal of St. John Chrysostom. He vainly sought help from Emperor Honorius at Ravenna when the Goths under Alaric captured and sacked Rome. Innocent died in Rome on March 12. July 28.

INNOCENT V (c. 1225–76). Born at Tarentaise-en-Forez, France, and known as Peter of Tarentaise, he became a Dominican under Bl. Jordan of Saxony when sixteen, received his master's degree in theology from the University of Paris in 1259, and then occupied a chair at the university. He soon became famous as a preacher and theologian, and in 1259, with a committee including his friend Thomas Aquinas, composed a plan of study that is still the basis of Dominican teaching. When thirty-seven, Innocent was appointed prior provincial of France, visited on foot all Dominican houses under him, and was then sent to Paris to replace Thomas Aquinas at the University of Paris. Pope Gregory V named Innocent archbishop of Lyons in

1272 and cardinal-bishop of Ostia the next year while still administering the see of Lyons. He was a prominent and active delegate to the General Council of Lyons in 1274 and was largely responsible for the short-lived healing of the Greek schism. After preaching the panegyric of St. Bonaventure, who died at the council, he returned to Italy with Pope Bl. Gregory X and was with Gregory when he died at Arezzo in 1276. He was unanimously elected his successor on January 21, 1276, the first Dominican Pope, and took the name Innocent V. During his short five-month pontificate, he struggled to reconcile Guelphs and Ghibellines, restored peace between Pisa and Lucca, and acted as mediator between Rudolph of Hapsburg and Charles of Anjou. Innocent attempted to consolidate the reunion with the Byzantines achieved at the General Council of Lyons but died suddenly on June 22. His cult was confirmed in 1898. He wrote several theological and philosophical treatises, chief of which was his *Commentary on the Sentences of Peter Lombard.*

INNOCENT XI, BL. (1611–89). Born at Como, Italy, on May 16, Benedetto Odescalchi studied under the Jesuits there, law at Rome and Naples, held numerous posts under Pope Urban VIII, among them administrator of Macerata and governor of Picena and was created a cardinal by Pope Innocent X in 1645. He served as legate to Ferrara, was appointed bishop of Novara in 1650, resigned in favor of his brother in 1656, and then returned to Rome. Known for his holiness and desire for reform, he was unanimously elected pope on September 21, 1676, and was consecrated on October 4. Throughout his entire pontificate he struggled against the absolutism of King Louis XIV of France, who had bitterly opposed his election, in Church matters. When an

assembly of French bishops called by Louis in 1682 passed *Declaration du clergy français* declaring the pope subject to a general council and the king subject to the pope only in spiritual matters, Innocent annulled the *Declaration* and refused to confirm any episcopal nomination made by those who had participated in the council. He disapproved Louis' Revocation of the Edict of Nantes in 1685 and sought milder treatment for the French Protestants. In 1687 Innocent's abolishment of diplomatic immunity to persons sought by papal courts sheltered in foreign consulates in Rome led to the occupation of the papal palace in Rome by French forces. The following year Innocent appointed Joseph Clement archbishop of Cologne against Louis' wishes; whereupon the French king imprisoned the papal nuncio, occupied papal Avignon and threatened to cut off the French Church's ties with Rome. Innocent supported James II in England but disapproved the Declaration of Indulgence in 1687 and feared the English king too was attracted by the concepts of Gallicanism. Innocent encouraged Christian resistance to the Turks in Austria and Hungary, put ecclesiastical reforms into effect and encouraged daily communion, and condemned quietism in 1687 with *Coelestis pastor.* He died in Rome on August 12, and was beatified in 1956 by Pope Pius XII.

IRELAND, BL. JOHN (d. 1544). *See* Larke, Bl. John.

IRELAND, BL. WILLIAM (1636–79). Born in Lincolnshire, England, he studied at St. Omer, France, joined the Jesuits there in 1655, and was professed in 1673. He was confessor to the Poor Clares at Gravelines for a time and then was sent to England, where he was known as William Ironmonger. He was arrested at a house in London where a group of Jesuits lived, with the house servant, John Grove, and charged in participating in the "popish plot" concocted by the infamous Titus Oates to assassinate King Charles II. They were both found guilty and executed at Tyburn on January 24. They were beatified in 1929.

IRENAEUS (c. 125–c. 203). Born in Asia Minor, probably at Smyrna, he was well educated and probably knew and was influenced by men who knew the apostles, especially St. Polycarp, who had been a pupil of St. John. According to Gregory of Tours, Polycarp sent him as a missionary to Gaul, where he was a priest under St. Pothinus at Lyons. Irenaeus was sent to Rome in 177 with a letter from his fellow Christians to Pope St. Eleutherius pleading for leniency to the Montanists in Phrygia. In Irenaeus' absence a violent persecution of Christians broke out at Lyons, claiming Pothinus as one of its martyrs, and Irenaeus returned to Lyons in 178 as bishop. He was active in evangelizing the area around Lyons and was the fierce opponent of Gnosticism in Gaul, which he refuted in a five-book treatise, *Adversus omnes haereses*. He was successful in 190 in reconciling the Quartodecimans, who had been excommunicated by Pope Victor III for refusing to celebrate Easter on the date of Western usage adopted by Rome. Irenaeus was the first great Catholic theologian. His treatise against the Gnostics is witness to the apostolic tradition and in it, at this early date, is a testimony to the primacy of the Pope. June 28.

IRENAEUS (d. 273). A deacon, he was arrested for burying the body of martyred Felix of Sutri and imprisoned at Chiusi, Italy, by Turcius, the local magistrate. When the noble and beautiful Mustiola attended him and other Christians in prison, Turcius attempted to force his attentions on her, and when she refused him, he tortured Irenaeus to death in her presence. When she still spurned his advances, he had her beaten to death with clubs. July 3.

IRENAEUS OF SIRMIUM (d. 304). Bishop of Sirmium (Mitrovica), Pannonia, near Belgrade, he was arraigned before Probus, governor of Pannonia during Emperor Diocletian's persecution of the Christians, accused of being a Christian, tortured, imprisoned, and then, when he refused to sacrifice to pagan gods, was beheaded. March 24.

IRENE (d. 304). *See* Agape.

IRMENGARD. *See* Ermengard.

IRMINA (d. c. 710). According to legend, she was the daughter of St. Dagobert II of the Franks and was betrothed to Count Herman. When a jealous suitor lured Herman to his death over a cliff outside Treves, Irmina became a nun at a monastery near Treves, which her father had either founded or restored. She aided St. Willibrord in his missionary work and in 698 gave him the building and grounds on which he founded the famous Echternach Monastery. She died in Alsace at Weissenburg Monastery, which her father had founded. December 24.

IRONMONGER, BL. WILLIAM. *See* Ireland, Bl. William.

ISAAC OF CONSTANTINOPLE (c. 318–c. 410). A hermit, he came to Constantinople to protest to Arian Emperor Valens about his persecution of Christians. Isaac prophesied disaster for the Emperor if he persisted in the persecution, escaped the Emperor's men, but when he repeated the prophecy was caught and imprisoned. He was released by Emperor Theodosius when Valens was killed at the Battle of Adrianople in 378 by the Visigoths, resumed his eremitical life, and attracted so many disciples that he was obliged to found a monastery for them at Constantinople, where he also attended the second General Council held there in 381. May 30.

ISAAC OF CORDOVA (c. 825–52). Born at Cordova, Spain, he was a Christian and so proficient in Arabic, he became a notary under the Moors. He resigned to become a monk at Tabanos near Cordova, emerged from the monastery to debate the chief magistrate, and in the course of the debate denounced Mohammed. He was arrested for his denunciation, tortured, and then executed. June 3.

ISAAC THE GREAT (d. 439). Son of Catholicos (Patriarch) St. Nerses I of Armenia, he studied at Constantinople, married, and on the early death of his wife became a monk. He was appointed Catholicos of Armenia in 390 and secured from Constantinople recognition of the metropolitan rights of the Armenian Church, thus terminating its long dependence on the Church of Caesarea in Cappodocia. He at once began to reform the Armenian Church. He ended the practice of married bishops, enforced Byzantine canon law, encouraged monasticism, built churches and schools, and fought Persian paganism. He supported St. Mesrop in his creation of an Armenian alphabet, helped to promote the translation of the Bible and the works of the Greek and Syrian doctors into Armenian, and was responsible for establishing a national liturgy and the beginnings of Armenian literatuc. He was driven into retirement in 428 when the Persians conquered part of his territory but returned at an advanced age to rule again from his see at Ashtishat, where he died. He was the founder of the Armenian Church and is sometimes called Sahak in Armenia. September 9.

ISAAC OF SPOLETO (d. c. 550). A Syrian, he left his native land to escape the Monophysite persecution and became a hermit on Monte Luco in Italy. In response to a vision of Mary, he trained disciples, organized them into a community resembling a *laura,* and became known for his miracles and gift of prophecy. April 11.

ISABEL OF FRANCE, BL. (d. 1270). Sister of St. Louis and daughter of King Louis VIII of France and Blanche of Castile, she refused offers of marriage from several noble suitors to continue her life of virginity consecrated to God. She ministered to the sick and the poor, and after the death of her mother founded the Franciscan Monastery of the Humility of the Blessed Virgin Mary at Longchamps in Paris. She lived there in austerity but never became a nun and refused to become abbess. She died there on February 23, and her cult was approved in 1521. February 26.

ISABELLA OF PORTUGAL. *See* Elizabeth of Portugal.

ISAIAH OF CRACOW, BL. (d. 1471). Born at Cracow, Poland, he studied at the academy there and received his doctor of divinity degree. He became an Augustinian at Kazimiertz and was known for his holiness, his knowledge and exposition of the Bible, and his ministering to the sick. He was subjected to diabolical visitations and experienced visions, in one of which his own death was foretold. February 8.

ISAIAS (d. 309). *See* Elias.

ISAIAS OF ROSTOV (d. 1090). Born at Kiev, Russia, he became a monk at the Monastery of the Caves there and in 1062 was named abbot of St. Demetrius in Kiev. He became bishop of Rostov in 1077, worked to convert the pagans of the area, and was known for his preaching ability and miracles. May 15.

ISAURI. *See* Ansurius.

ISCHYRION (d. 250). According to St. Dionysius, he was procurator for the magistrate of an Egyptian city, probably Alexandria, and was tortured and then impaled when he refused to sacrifice to the pagan gods during Emperor Decius' persecution of the Christians. December 22.

ISIDORE (d. 250). *See* Dioscorus.

ISIDORE (d. 856). *See* Elias.

ISIDORE OF ALEXANDRIA (319–404). A wealthy Egyptian, he distributed his possessions to the poor, became a hermit in the Nitrian desert, and then became a follower of St. Athanasius, who ordained him and whom he accompanied to Rome in 341. Isidore became director of the hospital in Constantinople, but the latter years of his life were troubled. Denounced by St. Jerome for his Origenist leanings, Isidore was excommunicated by his bishop, Theophilus, and returned to the Nitrian desert. Befriended by St. John Chrysostom, he spent the last years of his life with him at Constantinople and died there. January 15.

ISIDORE OF CHIOS (d. c. 251). Born at Alexandria, Egypt, he became an officer in the army of Emperor Decius and was with the fleet when it went to the Greek island of Chios. There he was denounced as a Christian to Numerius, commander of the fleet, tortured, and was then beheaded when he refused to apostatize. His body was thrown into a well, which became famous for its miracles of healing. May 15.

ISIDORE THE FARMER (1070–1130). Born at Madrid, Spain, of poor parents, he became a hired hand on the estate of wealthy John de Vergas just outside of Madrid. He lived a life of great devotion, is reputed to have performed numerous miracles, and despite his own poverty, shared what little he had with the poor. He died on May 15 at Madrid. His wife, Maria Torribia, who shared his devotion and poverty, is also honored as a saint under the name of Santa Maria de la Cabeza. Many miracles were reported at Isidore's shrine, and over the centuries his aid has been sought and granted to several Spanish monarchs. He was canonized in 1622 and is the patron of farmers and of the city of Madrid.

ISIDORE OF PELUSIUM (d. c. 450). Born at Alexandria, he left the city in his youth and became a monk at the monastery of Lychnos near Pelusium. He was ordained and in time became abbot. He was revered for his devotion to his religious duties and was famous for his voluminous correspondence; some two thousand letters of pious exhortation and theological instruction are still extant, though he is reported to have written ten thousand letters in his lifetime. He was a vigorous opponent of Nestorianism and Eutychianism and wrote *Adversus gentiles* and *De fato,* neither of which has survived. February 4.

ISIDORE OF SEVILLE (c. 560–636). Of a noble Hispanic-Roman family of Cartagena, Spain, and brother of SS. Leander, Fulgentius, and Florentina, he was born at Seville, was educated under the supervision of his elder brother, Leander, and succeeded him as bishop of Seville in about 600. Isidore became noted as one of the most learned men of his times, continued Leander's work of converting the Arian Visigoths, and presided over several important councils, including that of Seville in 619 and Toledo in 633. Greatly interested in education, he founded schools in each diocese similar to our present-day seminaries and broadened the curriculum to include liberal arts, medicine, and law as well as the conventional subjects. He compiled the *Etymologies,* an encyclopedia of the knowledge of his times, wrote treatises on theology, astronomy, and geography, histories (his history of the Goths is the principal source of information about them), biographies, and completed the Mozarabic liturgy begun by Leander. Isidore was known for his austerities and charities and is considered the last of the ancient Christian philosophers. He died on April 4, was canonized in 1598, and was declared a Doctor of the Church by Pope Benedict XIV in 1722.

ISNARDO, BL. (d. 1244). Born at Chiampa, Italy, he received the Dominican habit from St. Dominic in 1219. Isnardo was a forceful preacher, lived austerely, and founded and was first prior of the Dominican house at Pavia in 1240. He died there, and his cult was confirmed in 1919. March 22.

ISORÉ, BL. REMI (1852–1900). *See* Mangin, Bl. Leon.

ISRAEL, BL. (d. 1014). An Augustinian canon regular at Dorat, Limousin, France, he became precentor there and then an aid to Bishop Aldoin of Limoges, whom he accompanied to the French court. Israel was named provost in Haute-Vienne of St. Junian Monastery, which he reformed; he then returned to Dorat, where he died on December 31.

ISSERNINUS (5th century). *See* Auxilius.

ITA (d. c. 570). Reputedly of royal lineage, she was born at Decies, Waterford,

Ireland, refused to be married, and secured her father's permission to live a virginal life. She moved to Killeedy, Limerick, and founded a community of women dedicated to God. She also founded a school for boys, and one of her pupils was St. Brendan. Many extravagant miracles were attributed to her (in one of them she is reputed to have reunited the head and body of a man who had been beheaded; in another she lived entirely on food from heaven), and she is widely venerated in Ireland. She is also known as Deirdre and Mida. January 15.

ITHAMAR (d. c. 656). The famous English historian Bede says that Ithamar was born in Kent and was known for his learning. He succeeded St. Paulinus as bishop of Rochester in 644—the first Anglo-Saxon to become bishop of an English see. June 10.

IVETTA. *See* Jutta of Huy, Bl.

IVO (no date). According to a legend that developed when a skeleton was unearthed near Ramsey Abbey in 1001, he was a Persian bishop who left his native land with three companions and went to England to live as a recluse. He may be an imaginary figure. April 24.

IVO OF CHARTRES (c. 1040–1116). Born at Beauvais, France, he was a canon at Nesles and then became a canon regular of St. Augustine at Saint-Quentin. After teaching Scripture, theology, and canon law there, he became prior about 1078 and was elected bishop of Chartres in 1191. He was councilor of King Philip I, but when he denounced the King's plan to divorce his wife, Bertha, to marry Bertrada, third wife of Count Fulk of Anjou, Ivo was imprisoned in 1192 and had his revenues confiscated by the crown. He was freed through the intercession of the Pope and later reconciled Philip to the Holy See after Bertha died. Ivo acted as mediator in several investiture disputes and openly protested the simony of several members of the papal court. He wrote widely on canon law, and his *Decretum* had a great influence on its development; he was also a voluminous letter writer, and many of his letters reflecting the religious issues of his time are still extant. He died on December 23. May 23.

IVO HÉLORY OF KERMARTIN

(1253–1303). Son of the lord of the manor of Kermartin, Brittany, where he was born, he studied theology, canon law, and philosophy at Paris and civil law at Orléans. On his return to Brittany, he became a judge of the Rennes diocesan court and then of his own diocese, Tréguier, where he became known as "the poor man's advocate" for his defense of the poor and his refusal to accept fees from his poor clients. In 1284, he was ordained, resigned his legal position in 1287 to be parish priest at Trédrez, and later filled the same role at Lovannec. He built a hospital, tended the ill, ministered to the poor, and acquired a reputation for his preaching ability. He was much sought after as a mediator and was noted for the austerity and piety of his life. He died on May 19, was canonized in 1347, and is the patron of lawyers.

IXIDA, BL. ANTONY (1569–1632). A

Japanese, he joined the Jesuits, was ordained, and became famed for his learning and eloquent preaching. He was successful in conversion work in Arima Province until he was captured while on a sick call in Nagasaki and imprisoned for two years at Omura. He was then returned to Nagasaki with three Augustinians, BB. Bartholomew Guiterrez, a Mexican, Francis Ortega, and Vincent Carvalho, and two Franciscans, Bl. Jerome, a Japanese priest, and Bl. Gabriel of Fonseca, a lay brother. They were scalded for thirty-three days with boiling water to force them to apostatize, and when they persisted in their faith they were burned to death on September 3 at Nagasaki. They were beatified in 1867.

J

JACOBIS, JUSTIN DE (1800–60). Born at San Fele, Italy, on October 9, he was taken to Naples when a child by his parents, joined the Vincentians when eighteen, and was ordained. After helping found a Vincentian house at Monopoli, he served as superior at Lecce and in 1839 was sent as the first prefect and vicar apostolic to the new Catholic mission at Adua, Ethiopia. His efforts to evangelize met with great opposition, but in 1841 he was included in a delegation of Ethiopian prelates to Cairo to request the Coptic patriarch of Alexandria to appoint one of his monks Abuna (Patriarch) of the Ethiopian Church. In Cairo, the patriarch denounced the presence of Fr. de Jacobis on the delegation and intrigued to appoint one Salama as Abuna. Some of the delegation then accompanied Fr. de Jacobis to meet the Pope in Rome. On his return, Fr. de Jacobis founded a college and seminary at Guala, and in 1846 a vicariate apostolic of the Galla was established, with William Massaia its first bishop. These developments caused Salama to launch an anti-Catholic campaign. The college was closed, Catholicism was proscribed, and Bishop Massaia was forced to return to Aden. In 1848, he secretly consecrated Fr. de Jacobis, now a fugitive, bishop at Massawa, with authority to administer the sacraments in the Ethiopian rite. By 1853, the new bishop had ordained some twenty Ethiopians, was ministering to five thousand Catholics, and was able to reopen the college. In 1860, Kedaref Kassa became King as Theodore II and in return for the backing he had received from Abuna Salama launched a persecution of the Catholics. Bishop de Jacobis was arrested and after several months' imprisonment was released and managed to find his way to Halai in southern Eritrea. He spent the rest of his life in missionary work along the Red Sea coast and died in the valley of Alghedien on July 31 of fever he contracted while on a missionary trip. He was canonized by Pope Paul VI in 1975.

JACOBUS DE VORAGINE. *See* James of Voragine, Bl.

JACOPINO OF CANEPACI, BL. (1438–1508). Born of poor parents at Piasca, Italy, he became a Carmelite lay brother at Vercelli and was assigned the task of begging alms. He lived a life of great piety and had a great devotion to the Blessed Virgin. He was beatified in 1845. March 3.

JACOPO DE VORAGINE. *See* James of Voragine, Bl.

JACOPONE OF TODI, BL. (c. 1230–1306). Of the Benedetti family of Todi, Italy, he studied law at Bologna, where he probably received his doctorate, and returned to Todi to practice. He married Vanna di Guidone in 1267, and they lived a worldy life until the following year, when Vanna was tragically killed when a balcony on which she was standing collapsed. Blaming himself for her death, Jacopone completely changed his lifestyle, performed the most humiliating penances, and acquired a widespread notoriety for his eccentricities. In 1278, he became a Franciscan lay brother at San Fortunato friary in Todi and began to write religious hymns and poetry, some in Latin but chiefly in the Umbrian dialect, which became immensely popular. He was soon attracted to the Spiritual branch of the Franciscans (though San Fortunato was a Conventual house), and in 1294 he and some of his brethren were granted permission by Pope Celestine V to live in a separate community and follow the Franciscan rule in its original strictness. This permission was revoked by Pope Boniface VIII after his election to succeed Pope Celestine, who had resigned in 1294. With Cardinals Jacopo and Pietro Colonna, Jacopone issued a manifesto in 1297 declaring that Boniface, an opponent of the Spirituals, had been elected invalidly; when papal forces captured the Colonnas' stronghold, Palestrina, Jacopone was captured, excommunicated, and imprisoned for five years. While in prison, he wrote many of his best-known poems. He was freed in 1303 when Boniface died, lived as a hermit near Orvieto, and then moved to a Poor Clare convent at Collazzone, where he died on Christmas Day. He was one of the most important poets of the Middle Ages and is reputed to have written *Stabat Mater dolorosa* and *Stabat Mater speciosa,* though this is questioned by many authorities. Though referred to as Blessed, his cult has never been approved.

JADWIGA. *See* Hedwig.

JAMES (d. 259). A deacon, he and Marian, a lector, were arrested at Cirta (Constantine, Algeria) during the persecution of the Christians by Emperor Valerian and tortured. They were arraigned before the governor and then sent to Lambesa, Numidia, where they were beheaded in the arena with hundreds of other Christians, among them Agapius and Secindinus. April 30.

JAMES (d. 297). *See* Hipparchus.

JAMES THE ALMSGIVER, BL. (d. 1304). Born at Città delle Pieve, Lombardy, of well-to-do parents, he studied law, but gave it up to live an ascetic life and to become a priest. He restored a disused and ruined hospital and its chapel to care for the sick, especially the poor, to whom he gave spiritual and legal advice as well as medical treatment. In the course of researching the hospital's records, he uncovered proof of misappropriation of its revenues by former bishops of Chiusi. When he received no satisfaction from the current bishop for his claim to past revenues, he took the matter to court and secured a judgment against the diocese; whereupon the bishop invited him to dinner on January 15 and had him murdered. His body reputedly was discovered by a band of shepherds who came across a group of trees in full bloom in the middle of winter and a voice proclaimed to them who the body was.

JAMES OF BEVAGNA. *See* Bianconi, Bl. James.

JAMES OF BITETTO, BL. (d. c. 1485). Born at Sebenico, Dalmatia, and often called "the Illyrian" or "the Slav," he became a Franciscan lay brother at Bitetto, Italy. He served as a cook at the Franciscan house at Conversano for a time but returned to Bitetto, where he died. He was noted for his miracles, ecstasies, and visions, and had the gift of levitation. He was beatified by Pope Innocent XII. April 27.

JAMES OF CERQUETO, BL. (d. 1367). Born at Cerqueto, Italy, he joined the

Hermits of St. Augustine in his youth, was known for his preaching and miracles, and died at Perugia on April 17. According to legend, it was his prayers that secured permission for the Hermits to wear white habits in tribute to Mary. His cult was confirmed in 1895.

JAMES OF CERTALDO, BL. (d. 1292). Born at Certaldo, Italy, his parents moved to Volterra when their son Jacopo Guidi was young, and he joined the Camaldolese monks there in 1230. He was made pastor of a local parish, served as abbot (after having twice refused the honor), but resigned to resume his pastoral work, revered for his holiness and austerity. April 13.

JAMES, BL. EDWARD (d. 1588). Born at Breaston, Derbyshire, England, he was raised a Protestant, was educated at Oxford, and was converted to Catholicism. He went to Rheims to study for the priesthood, and after further study at Rome, was ordained there in 1583. He was sent on the English mission, was captured, and then spent four and a half years in prison with Bl. Ralph Crockett. Bl. Edward was accused of being a Catholic priest and when convicted was hanged, drawn, and quartered at Chichester. He was beatified in 1929. October 1.

JAMES INTERCISUS (d. c. 421). A favorite of King Yezdigerd I of Persia and a Christian, he abandoned his religion when Yezdigerd launched a persecution of the Christians. When the King died, James repented of his apostasy and declared himself a Christian to the new King, Bahram. When James refused to apostatize, he was executed by having his body cut apart piece by piece, beginning with his fingers (hence his surname Intercisus—cut to pieces), and then beheaded. November 27.

JAMES THE GREATER (d. 42). Son of Zebedee, he and his younger brother, John, were natives of Galilee and fishermen when called by Jesus to follow him as they were mending their nets with their father in a fishing boat on Lake Genesareth (Matt. 4:21–22; Mark 1:19–20; Luke 5:10). They were with Jesus when he cured Peter's mother-in-law at the house of Peter and Andrew (Mark 1:29–31), asked Christ if they could sit on either side of him in his glory and assured him they could drink his cup (Matt. 20:20–28; Mark 10:35–45), and were nicknamed Boanerges (Sons of Thunder) by Jesus (Mark 3:17), probably on the occasion when they asked Jesus if they should ask heaven to strike the inhospitable Samaritans with fire (Luke 9:54–56). James was with Peter and John at the raising of Jairus' daughter from the dead (Mark 5:37; Luke 8:51), and the three of them were the only apostles at the Transfiguration (Matt. 17:1–8; Mark 9:2–8) and the agony at Gethsemane (Matt. 26:37–46; Mark 14:33–42). James was the first of the apostles to be martyred when he was beheaded in Jerusalem by Herod Agrippa I (Acts 12:1–2). An old tradition, now largely discredited by scholars, says he preached in Spain before his martyrdom, and a Spanish tradition had his body translated to Santiago de Compostela in Spain, which was one of the great pilgrimage centers of the Middle Ages. He is the patron saint of Spain. July 25.

JAMES THE LESS (d. 62). James, the son of Alpheus, is named in the lists of the apostles in Matthew, Mark, and Luke and in Acts 1:13 is one of the eleven apostles in the upper room in Jerusalem after Christ's Ascension. James is mentioned as one of the brothers of the Lord (Matt. 13:55; Mark 6:3) with Joseph, Simon, and Jude, and is called the "brother of the Lord" (Galatians 1:19). It was to James that Peter wanted the news of his miraculous escape transmitted (Acts 12:17), and James seems to have been regarded as the head of the primitive Church in Jerusalem. It was he who suggested that only four Jewish practices be imposed on Gentiles wishing to be followers of Christ (Acts 15:13–21), beginning this statement with the words "I rule, then, that . . ." Paul reported to him and sought his approval several times. This James seems to be the James of the Epistle of James who opens the epistle by calling himself "servant of God and of the Lord Jesus Christ," which may indicate it was an official Church title; James uses the tone of authority of one well known in the Church and accustomed to wielding authority. Traditionally, biblical exegetes have considered James, the son of Alpheus, as the same James called "the brother of the Lord," the James who speaks with the voice of authority in the early Church; many modern scholars, however, hold that there may have been two Jameses, one the son of Alpheus and one of the Twelve, and the other "the brother of the Lord," the author of the Epistle of James, and an authoritative figure in the early Church. Among the reasons they cite for this belief is the fact that in his epistle, James speaks of the apostles in the past tense and does not identify himself as an apostle; the apparent distinction between this James and the apostle James in 1 Corinthians 15:7; and the elegant Greek literary style used by the author of the epistle, a style hardly likely to be used by a Galilean peasant. The name James the Less is usually applied to James, son of Alpheus, because of the reference in Mark 15:40, where he is called "James the Less" in the King James and Douay versions of the Bible; he is called James the Younger in the Jerusalem, Revised Standard Version, New English Bible, Living Bible, and the New International Version. According to Hegesippus, a second-century ecclesias-

tical historian, James was thrown from the pinnacle of the Temple in Jerusalem by the Pharisees and then stoned to death. May 3.

JAMES OF LODI, BL. (d. 1404). Born at Lodi, Italy, he led a carefree life as a youth, married an equally pleasure-addicted lady, but changed his lifestyle after he laughingly lay down on a reproduction of the Holy Sepulcher and compared his height to that of Christ. His wife, Catherine, also reformed and they both became Franciscan tertiaries. Later James was ordained and they turned their home into a church. He spent the last years of his life helping the sick and prisoners of the civil war that wracked Lodi. April 18.

JAMES OF MANTUA. See Benfatti, Bl. James.

JAMES OF THE MARCH. See Gangala, James.

JAMES OF MEVANIA. See Bianconi, Bl. James.

JAMES OF NAPLES, BL. (d. 1308). Born at Viterbo, Italy, James Capocci became an Augustinian when a youth, studied at the University of Paris, and after a short stay back in Italy, returned to Paris for his doctorate. He was known for his learning, taught at Paris and Naples, and in 1302 was appointed archbishop of Benevento. He was translated to Naples a few months later and ruled there until his death. His cult was confirmed in 1911. March 14.

JAMES OF NISIBIS (d. 338). A Syrian, he became a monk and in about 308 was named first bishop of Nisibis, Mesopotamia. He built a basilica there and founded the theological school of Nisibis, which became famous. A fierce opponent of Arianism at the Council of

Nicaea in 325 (according to the legend repeated in the Roman Martyrology, the prayers of James and Alexander of Constantinople were responsible for the death of Arius and his "bowels gushing out"), he was renowned for his great holiness, learning, and miracles. He died at Nisibis. July 15.

JAMES OF PADUA (d. 1321). *See* Thomas of Tolentino, Bl.

JAMES, BL. ROGER (d. 1539). *See* Whiting, Bl. Richard.

JAMES OF STREPAR, BL. (d. c. 1411). Of a noble Polish family in Galicia, he joined the Franciscans and in time was appointed guardian of the Franciscan friary at Lvov, Poland. He defended the mendicant friars against attacks from the secular clergy, worked among the Orthodox for a decade, and was vicar general of the Franciscans in western Russia. In 1392, he was appointed archbishop of Galich. He founded and built religious houses, schools, and hospitals, organized the areas of his see he had evangelized, and brought Polish priests into his diocese. He died at Lvov on June 1, and his cult was confirmed in 1791. October 20.

JAMES OF ULM. *See* Grissinger, Bl. James.

JAMES THE VENETIAN, BL. *See* Salomonius, Bl. James.

JAMES OF VORAGINE, BL. (c. 1230–1298). Born at Viraggio (Varazze) near Genoa, Italy, he became a Dominican when fourteen, taught theology and Scripture, was named prior at Genoa, and in 1267 was elected provincial of Lombard Province, a post he was to hold for nineteen years. He was famous for his eloquent and powerful preaching and was named archbishop of Genoa in 1286 but refused the appointment. In 1288, Pope Nicholas IV appointed him to raise the interdict placed on Genoa for aiding a revolt against the King of Naples. In 1292 James was again elected archbishop of Genoa and again refused; this time he was obliged to accept. The six years of his reign were spent in an unsuccessful attempt to reconcile the warring Guelphs and Ghibellines, in aiding the needy, building and repairing churches, monasteries, and hospitals, and maintaining clerical discipline. He is reputed to have translated the Bible into Italian (though no copy has ever been found), but he is probably best known today as the author of one of the most famous and most popular collections of legends and lives of the saints ever written, *The Golden Legend,* which has appeared in hundreds of editions over the centuries since it was first published in Latin in 1470. He died on July 13, and his cult was confirmed by Pope Pius VII in 1816.

JAMES THE YOUNGER. *See* James the Less.

JANE FRANCES DE CHANTAL. *See* Chantal, Bl. Jane Frances de.

JANE OF ORVIETO, BL. (d. 1306). Also known as Vanna, she was born of peasant parents at Carnaiola, Italy, was orphaned at five, refused marriage and joined the Third Order of St. Dominic at nearby Orvieto. She lived a life of great holiness, had visions and the gift of prophecy, and is reputed to have performed miracles. She died on July 23, and her cult was approved in 1754.

JANE OF REGGIO, BL. *See* Scopelli, Bl. Jane.

JANSSEN, BL. ARNOLD (1837–1909). Born at Goch, Germany, on November 5, he studied at Gaesdonck, Münster, and Bonn, and was ordained in 1861. He served as a parish priest, was chaplain of an Ursuline convent at Kempen in 1873, and two years later established the mission house of St. Michael at Steyl, Holland, which developed into the Society of the Divine Word, devoted to foreign missions, which received its formal approval in 1901. He founded the Servant Sisters of the Holy Ghost with the same purpose in 1889. He died at Steyl on January 15, and was beatified in 1975 by Pope Paul VI.

JANSSEN-POPPEL, NICHOLAS (d. 1572). *See* Vechel, Leonard.

JANUARIA (d. 180). *See* Speratus.

JANUARIUS (d. c. 165). *See* Felicity.

JANUARIUS (d. 258). *See* Sixtus II.

JANUARIUS (d. c. 303). *See* Honoratus.

JANUARIUS (d. c. 304). *See* Faustus.

JANUARIUS (d. c. 305). According to legend, he was born at Naples, or perhaps Benevento, Italy, and was bishop of Benevento when Emperor Diocletian launched his persecution of the Christians. On hearing that his friend, Sossus, a deacon of Miseno, had been imprisoned for his faith at Pozzuoli with Proclus, a deacon of Pozzuoli, and two laymen, Euticius and Acutius, Januarius went to visit them in prison. He was arrested with his deacon, Festus, and a lector, Desiderius, on order of the governor of Campania. They were all thrown to the wild beasts, and when the animals would not harm them, they were beheaded near Pozzuoli. Januarius' relics ended up in Naples, and for the past four centuries a vial containing a solid red substance reputed to be his blood liquefies and often bubbles and boils when exposed in the cathedral there. No satis-

factory scientific explanation has been adduced for this phenomenon, and devout Neapolitans accept it as a miracle. September 19.

JAPAN, MARTYRS OF (1633–1637). These seventeenth-century martyrs include one layman, ten Dominican priests, and thirteen Dominican laypeople. These martyrs were canonized in 1987.

JARLATH (d. c. 550). Born in the Galway district of Ireland, of the noble Conmaicne family, he was trained in his youth by a holy man and with his cousin Caillin was ordained. Jarlath founded a monastery at Cluain Fois near Tuam and was its abbot-bishop, renowned for his holiness and learning. He also began a monastery school that numbered among his students St. Brendan and Colman of Cloyne. He is considered the founder of the archdiocese of Tuam. June 6.

JASON (1st century). In Acts 17:5–9, it is recounted that St. Paul stayed at Jason's house while in Salonika during his second missionary journey. Jason was a prominent convert to Christianity and is probably the same Jason referred to in Romans 16:21 with Sosipater. Greek legend has Jason the bishop of Tarsus, Cilicia, who, with Sosipater, evangelized Corfu, where Jason died. Syrian legend has him evangelizing the area around Apamea and martyred there by being thrown to wild beasts. July 12.

JAVOUHEY, BL. ANNE (1798–1851). Daughter of a well-to-do farmer, she was born at Jallanges, France, on November 10 and early decided to devote her life to the poor and the education of children. After failing to adjust to life in several convents (it was in a convent at Besançon in 1800 that she had a vision of black children, which was to so influence her later life), she and eight companions were clothed by the bishop of Autun in 1807 and with their purchase of a friary at Cluny in 1812, the Congregation of St. Joseph of Cluny dedicated to the education of children was founded. The congregation became famous for its successful teaching methods, and Anne established houses in Africa and South America as well as in Europe. She was in French Guiana, 1828–32, and in 1834 was sent there by the French government to educate six hundred Guianan slaves who were to be set free. She left French Guiana in 1843 and spent her remaining years establishing new houses in Tahiti, Madagascar, and elsewhere. She died at Paris on July 15 and was beatified in 1950.

JEREMY (d. 309). *See* Elias.

JEROME (c. 342–420). Born at Strido, near Aquileia, Dalmatia, Eusebius Hieronymus Sophronius studied at Rome under Donatus, the famous pagan grammarian, acquired great skill and knowledge of the Latin, Greek, and great classical authors, and was baptized by Pope Liberius at Rome in 360. After further study at Treves and travel in Gaul, Jerome became an ascetic at Aquileia in 370, joining a group of scholars under Bishop Valerian, among whom was Rufinus. When a quarrel broke up the group, Jerome traveled in the East and in 374 settled at Antioch, where he heard Apollinarius of Laodicea lecture. A vision of Christ caused Jerome to go to Chalcis in the Syrian desert, after a serious illness, and he lived as a hermit for four years, praying and fasting, learning Hebrew, and writing a life of St. Paul of Thebes. On Jerome's return to Antioch, he was ordained by St. Paulinus and entered into the Meletian schism controversy, supporting Paulinus and denouncing the schism in a treatise, *Altercatio luciferiani et orthodoxi.* Jerome went to Constantinople to study

Scripture under St. Gregory Nazianzen, and in 382 Jerome went to Rome with Paulinus and St. Epiphanius to attend a council and remained there as secretary to Pope Damasus. While there, at the suggestion of Damasus, he revised the Latin version of the four gospels, St. Paul's epistles, and the Psalms, and wrote *Adversum Helvidium,* denouncing a book by Helvidius declaring that Mary had had several children besides Jesus. Jerome encouraged a group of noble ladies to study Scripture and made numerous enemies by his sermons to them on the virtues of celibacy and by his fiery attacks on pagan life and some influential Romans. On the death of Damasus, his protector and patron, in 384, his enemies and the vicious rumors that were circulated about him (including a scandalous rumor concerning his relations with St. Paula) decided him to return to the East, which he did in 385. He visited Antioch, Egypt, and Palestine. Paula, Eustochium, and others of the Roman group joined him in Antioch. In 386, they all settled at Bethlehem, where Paula built three convents for women and a monastery for men, which Jerome headed. Most of his time was devoted to his translation of the Bible into Latin from the original tongues, which had been suggested to him by Pope Damasus, but Jerome found time to become involved in numerous controversies. In 393, he wrote *Adversus Jovianianum* to refute Jovinian's belief that Mary had other children besides Jesus and attacking the desirability of virginity; and Jerome's *Contra Vigilantium* denounced Vigilantius' condemnation of celibacy and the veneration of relics. But Jerome's bitterest controversy was with Rufinus, his old friend from Aquileia, who supported Origen and translated many of his works into Latin, when Jerome attacked Origenism in *Apologetici adversus Rufinum* in 395. Soon after he even attacked St. Augustine, who had questioned

Jerome's exegesis of the second chapter of St. Paul's epistle to the Romans. Jerome's greatest achievement was his translation of the Old Testament from Hebrew and his revision of the Latin version of the New Testament in 390–405, a feat of scholarship unequaled in the early Church. This version, called the Vulgate, was declared the official Latin text of the Bible for Catholics by the Council of Trent, and it was from it that almost all English Catholic translations were made until the middle of the twentieth century, when scholars began to use original sources. It remained the official Latin text of the Bible for the Catholic Church until Pope John Paul II replaced it with the New Vulgate in 1979. From 405 until his death he produced a series of biblical commentaries notable for the range of linguistic and topographical material he brought to bear on his interpretations. In 415, his denunciation of Pelagianism in *Dialogi contra Pelagianos* caused a new furor, and in 416, groups of armed Pelagian monks burned the monasteries at Bethlehem, though he escaped unharmed, and left them poverty-stricken. He died at Bethlehem after a lingering illness on September 30. In addition to the works mentioned above, Jerome corresponded widely (some 120 of his letters, of great historical interest and importance, are still extant); he also compiled a bibliography of ecclesiastical writers, *De viris illustribus* and he translated and continued Eusebius' *Chronicle.* Jerome is venerated as a Doctor of the Church.

JOACHIM (1st century). Joachim is the name traditionally given to the father of Mary. According to the apocryphal and uncanonical *Protevangelium of St. James,* he was born at Nazareth, married St. Anne at a youthful age, and when publicly reproached for their childlessness, fasted forty days in the desert. An angel appeared to him and promised the cou-

ple a child. He died soon after witnessing the presentation of Jesus at the Temple. July 26.

JOACHIM OF SIENA, BL. *See* Piccolomini, Bl. Joachim.

JOAN OF ARC (1412–31). The daughter of Jacques d'Arc, a peasant farmer, she was the youngest of five children and was born on January 6 at Domrémy, France. A pious child, she was only thirteen when she experienced the first of her supernatural visions, which she described as a voice accompanied by a blaze of light. As time went on she identified the voices she heard as those of St. Michael, St. Catherine, St. Margaret, and others who she claimed revealed to her that her mission in life was to save France by aiding the Dauphin. Laughed at by Robert de Baudricourt, the French commander at Vaucouleurs, at first, his skepticism was overcome when her prophecies came true and the French were defeated in the Battle of Herrings outside Orléans in February 1429. He sent her to the Dauphin. Son of the insane King Charles VI, he had been kept from the French throne by the British in the Hundred Years' War and preferred the life of pleasure he had been pursuing since his father's death in 1422 to taking on the responsibilities of kingship if he mounted the throne. When she recognized him despite a disguise he had assumed and gave him a secret signal that he recognized, he was convinced of her mission. After an examination by theologians at Poitiers cleared her of all suspicion of heresy, she was allowed to lead an expedition to relieve besieged Orléans, and in a suit of white armor, she led her forces to victory. She followed this with a great victory over the British on June 18 and the capture of Troyes shortly after. Finally, on July 17, 1429, Charles was crowned as King Charles VII at Rheims, with Joan at his side. She failed in an attempt to capture Paris in August, and in the spring of 1430, she set out on a new campaign. She was captured on May 24 near Compiègne and sold to the British by John of Luxemburg on November 21. Charged with heresy and witchcraft before the court of Bishop Pierre Cauchon, her visions were declared to be of diabolical origin. She was tricked into signing a form of recantation on May 23, 1431, but when she again dressed in male attire, which she had agreed to abandon, she was condemned as a lapsed heretic and burned to death at the stake at Rouen on May 30, 1431, the victim of her enemies' determination to destroy her. A court appointed by Pope Callistus III found her innocent in 1456 and she was canonized in 1920. She is the second patron of France and is known as the Maid of Orléans.

JOAN OF AZA, BL. (d. c. 1190). Born in the castle of Aza, near Aranda, Old Castile, she was married to Felix de Guzman, warden of Calaruega in Burgos. They had four children, one of whom was St. Dominic. She was known for her physical and spiritual beauty, and on her death a cult developed, which was confirmed in 1828. Legend says she prayed for a son when her two eldest boys were grown and dreamed she bore a dog in her womb, while she was bearing Dominic, which would set the world afire with the torch in its mouth; the dog became the symbol of the Dominicans and gave rise to the expression *Domini canes* (watchdogs of the Lord) to describe the Dominicans. August 8.

JOAN OF FRANCE. *See* Joan of Valois.

JOAN OF PORTUGAL, BL. (1452–90). Daughter of King Alphonsus V of Portugal and Elizabeth of Coimbra, she was born at Lisbon and became heir to the throne because of the illness of her brother and the death of her mother. She

lived austerely from her early youth in the midst of the court and was refused permission by her father to enter the religious life. She was regent when her father and brother went to war against the Moors, and when they defeated the Moors in 1471, her father, in the first flush of victory, granted her request and she entered the Benedictine convent of Odivellas in 1472; later she transferred to the Dominican convent at Aveiro. Because of her family's objections, she was unable to take vows until 1485, when the succession to the throne was settled, repeatedly refusing offers of marriage from royal suitors in the meanwhile. At Aveiro, she lived as a simple nun and devoted her income to charity and to redeeming captives. She died there, and her cult was authorized in 1693. May 12.

JOAN OF SIGNA, BL. (c. 1245–1307). Born at Signa near Florence, Italy, of peasant parents, she was a sheep- and goatherder until she was twenty-three, when she became a solitary on the banks of the Arno near Signa. She lived there for forty years, acquired a great reputation for her spiritual wisdom, and was credited with numerous miracles. She died on November 9, and her cult was confirmed in 1798. November 17.

JOAN OF TOULOUSE (14th century). According to legend, she was a resident of Toulouse, France, and in 1265 received the Carmelite habit from St. Simon Stock, although she continued living at home and is thus considered to be the first Carmelite tertiary. Actually, she probably lived as a recluse at Toulouse toward the end of the fourteenth century. March 31.

JOAN OF VALOIS (1464–1505). Sometimes called Joan of France, she was the deformed daughter of King Louis XI and Charlotte of Savoy. She was married to the King's cousin, Duke Louis of Orléans, in 1476 and saved the duke's life when her brother King Charles VIII determined to execute him for rebellion. When the duke ascended the throne as King Louis XII, he had Pope Alexander VI declare his marriage to Joan void on the grounds that he had been forced to marry her by King Louis XI. Joan offered no objections and retired to the duchy of Berry given her by Louis and lived a secluded life of prayer at Bourges, where in 1501 she founded the Annonciades of Bourges, a contemplative order of nuns; she was professed in 1504. Joan suffered much throughout her life for her deformed body, which she accepted with great patience and equanimity. She was canonized in 1950. February 4.

JOANNA (1st century). Wife of Chuza, steward of King Herod Antipas, tetrarch of Galilee, she was one of the women who helped provide for Jesus and the apostles (Luke 8:3) and was one of the three women who discovered the empty tomb of Jesus on the first Easter morning (Luke 24:10). May 24.

JOANNICUS (c. 754–846). Born in Bithynia, he was a swineherd in his youth, lived a dissolute life, and was an ardent iconoclast. He was brought to a religious outlook on life by a monk, retired when forty from the military life he had embraced, and became a hermit on Mount Olympus in Bithynia and later a monk at Eraste. By now he was a vigorous defender of orthodoxy and fought iconoclasm, advised understanding in dealing with priests who had been ordained by iconoclast bishops, and defied Emperor Theophilus over the iconoclast issue. He was famed for his miracles and gift of prophecy (his prophecy that Theophilus would restore images to the churches was fulfilled by

the Emperor's wife, Theodora) and died on November 4.

JOAQUINA DE VEDRUNA. *See* Mas y Vedruna, Joaquina de.

JOGUES, ISAAC (1607–46). Born at Orléans, France, of well-to-do parents, he studied at the Jesuit school there and joined the Jesuits in 1624. After his ordination in 1636, he requested and was sent to Quebec. He worked with great success among the Hurons until 1642, when a war party of Iroquois, the traditional enemies of the Hurons, captured a group of Jesuits, among them Isaac and René Goupil, who was murdered. After a year of terrible torture and mutilation, Isaac escaped with the aid of the Dutch at Albany to New York and returned to France. At his request, he was sent back to Quebec in 1644. Two years later, he and Jean de Lalande set out for Iroquois country after a peace treaty with the Iroquois had been signed. They were captured by a Mohawk war party and he was tomahawked and beheaded at Ossernenon, near Albany, New York, on October 18; Jean de Lalande suffered martyrdom the next day. They were canonized with a group of other Jesuits in 1930 by Pope Pius XI as the Martyrs of North America. October 19.

JOHN (d. c. 303). *See* Cyrus.

JOHN (d. c. 304). *See* Abundius.

JOHN (d. c. 362). Beyond that he and his brother Paul were probably martyrs at Rome, all that is known of them is legend, according to which they were army officers assigned to the household of Emperor Constantine's daughter Constantia. While on an expedition to Thrace under Gallicanus, they told Gallicanus that a seemingly sure defeat by the Scythians could be turned into victory if he would turn Christian. He did, and a legion of angels put the enemy to flight. When Julian the Apostate became Emperor, they denounced his apostasy, and when they persisted in refusing to obey him, they were executed. Probably the whole story is fiction; the confusion about them may have arisen when the basilica in Rome erected over their "graves" was dedicated to John and Paul—but probably to the apostles rather than these two martyrs. June 26.

JOHN I (d. 526). Born in Tuscany, he became an archdeacon in Rome, and on August 13, 523, was elected Pope, succeeding St. Hormisdas. Despite his protests, he was sent by King Theodoric of the Ostrogoths, a champion of Arianism, to Constantinople to secure a moderation of Emperor Justin's decree of 523 against the Arians, compelling them to surrender to Catholics the churches they held. Theodoric also resented the increasing cordiality between the Latin and Greek churches, fearing it might lead to the restoration of imperial Byzantine authority in Italy, which he ruled. John was warmly received by Justin and huge crowds but returned to find that Theodoric had murdered the great philosopher Boethius and his father-in-law, Symmachus. Theodoric had John arrested as soon as he landed in Italy and had him imprisoned at Ravenna, where he died of ill treatment on May 18 or 19. May 18.

JOHN III (d. 577). Born near Antioch, he became a lawyer there and then was ordained. Called "the Scholastic" because of his learning, he acted as legate for his patriarch to Constantinople, edited a collection of canons of ecclesiastical law (the first to be made systematically), and in 565 was appointed Patriarch of Constantinople. His revision and enlargement of his collection of canons

developed into the *Nomokanon,* a compendium of Eastern Church law. August 28.

JOHN (d. c. 800). Grandson of an Armenian legionnaire, he was born in the Crimea, spent three years in Jerusalem, and in 761 was elected bishop of the Goths when the incumbent bishop was promoted to Heraclea. John defended the practice of veneration of relics and sacred images and attended the General Council of Nicaea in 787, which defined Catholic doctrine on the veneration of saints and relics. On his return he was captured by the invading Khazars but escaped to Amastris in Asia Minor, where he spent the last four years of his life. June 26.

JOHN I, BL. (d. 1146). Born at Lyons, France, he became a canon in the cathedral there. After a pilgrimage to Compostela, he joined the Benedictines at Cîteaux and was then sent to Bonnevaux, where he founded an abbey in 1117 and became its abbot. In 1141, he was chosen bishop of Valence, France, where he was revered for his spirituality and gentleness. His cult was approved in 1901. April 26.

JOHN XXIII, BL. (1881–1963). Born Angelo Giuseppe Roncalli. One of the twentieth century's most important figures, Roncalli came from humble roots as one of thirteen children in a farming family in northern Italy. While in the seminary he was drafted into the Italian army, in which he would also later serve as a chaplain during World War I. He studied theology for many years in Rome, eventually earning a doctorate in canon law. He made his way from being secretary to Bishop Radini-Tedeschi, to being director of the Italian organization for the support of foreign missions, to being Vatican diplomat. With the mission of protecting the interests of the Roman Catholic minority, he was appointed visitor to Bulgaria in 1925, apostolic delegate to Greece, and head of the diplomatic mission in Turkey. In 1944 he was named papal nuncio to France at a time of turmoil, with the goals of cooling the atmosphere, reestablishing the independence of the Church, and gaining the release of prisoners of war. As he was successful in all his assignments, he was named cardinal by Pius XII in 1953 and later patriarch of Venice at the age of seventy-one. Given his advanced age, he was surprised to be elected Pope in 1958 after twelve ballots of voting. He almost immediately summoned an ecumenical council, the first in almost a century, with the goal of updating the Church. Although some resisted, the Second Vatican Council commenced in the fall of 1962 and confronted, in a positive way, issues that had previously been avoided. He wrote several socially significant encyclicals, including *Pacem in Terris*. Expected by many to be at most an "interim" pope, he surpassed expectations with the historic changes of Vatican II, which were completed after his death by Pope Paul VI. Even years after his death he remains one of the most-loved Church figures of recent centuries.

JOHN (d. c. 1342). An official in the service of Duke Olgierd, ruler of Lithuania, he and his brother Antony and Eustace, fellow officials, were converted to Christianity. They were imprisoned, tortured, and then executed for their faith at Vilna, John on April 14; Antony on June 14; and Eustace on December 14. April 14.

JOHN THE ALMSGIVER (c. 550–c. 619). Of a noble family, he was born at Amathus, Cyprus, the son of Epiphanius, governor of the island. He married when quite young but when his wife and child died he entered the religious life, gave his income to the poor, and became widely known for his holiness and charity. He was named patriarch of Alexandria in 608, immediately distributed the wealth of his see to aid the poor, helped refugees from Syria and Jerusalem fleeing the marauding Persians in 614, visited the sick in hospitals, and built churches. He fought simony, ended corruption in his diocese, was generous to those in difficulty, and worked to alleviate the onerous new taxes levied by Nicetas, the governor. His concern for and financial aid to the poor were so well known he was surnamed "the Almsgiver." Throughout his patriarchate, he labored to end monophysitism and restore orthodoxy by peaceful means. He was forced to leave Alexandria when the Persians drew near to the city and was on the way to Constantinople with Nicetas to visit Emperor Heraclius when a vision of his own impending death caused him to return to his native Amathus, where he died on November 11. January 23.

JOHN THE ALMSGIVER (d. c. 1330). *See* Rainuzzi, Bl. John.

JOHN OF ALVERNIA (1259–1322). Born at Fermo, Italy, he joined the Friars Minor in 1272, was professed, and then spent several years as a hermit on Mount La Verna, where he experienced visions and ecstasies. He later preached with great effect in central and northern Italy, and with his ability to read men's minds, was a sought-after spiritual adviser. He died at La Verna on August 10, and his cult was confirmed in 1880. August 13.

JOHN OF ÁVILA (1499–1569). Born of wealthy parents at Almodóvar del Campo, New Castile, Spain, on January 6, he was sent to the University of Salamanca when fourteen to study law. He was attracted to the religious life instead and left to live a life of austerity.

Three years later he went to Alcalá to study philosophy under Dominic Soto and met Peter Guerrero and was ordained. Left wealthy when his parents died, he disposed of his wealth to aid the poor. He soon achieved fame as a powerful preacher and served as a missionary in Andalusia, drawing huge crowds to his missions. He made enemies by his fearless denunciation of evil even in high places, which led to his imprisonment by the Inquisition at Seville for his harshness and preaching that the rich could not reach heaven. When the charges were dismissed and he was released, his popularity reached new heights. He continued preaching all over Spain and was spiritual adviser to St. Teresa of Ávila, St. John of the Cross, St. Francis Borgia, and St. Peter of Alcantara, among others. John of Ávila died at Montilla on May 10, and was canonized by Pope Paul VI in 1970.

JOHN THE BAPTIST (1st century). Son of Zachary, a priest of the Temple in Jerusalem, and Elizabeth, a kinswoman of Mary who visited her, he was probably born at Ain-Karim southwest of Jerusalem after the angel Gabriel had told Zachary that his wife would bear a child even though she was an old woman. He lived as a hermit in the desert of Judea until about A.D. 27, when he was thirty, he began to preach on the banks of the Jordan against the evils of the times and called men to penance and baptism "for the kingdom of heaven is close at hand." He attracted large crowds, and when Christ came to him, John recognized him as the Messiah and baptized him, saying, "It is I who need baptism from you" (Matt. 3:14). When Christ left to preach in Galilee, John continued preaching in the Jordan Valley. Fearful of his great power with the people, Herod Antipas, tetrarch of Perea and Galilee, had him arrested and imprisoned at Machaerus Fortress on the

Dead Sea when John denounced his adulterous and incestuous marriage with Herodias, wife of his half brother Philip. John was beheaded at the request of Salome, daughter of Herodias, who asked for his head at the instigation of her mother. John inspired many of his followers to follow Christ when he designated him "the lamb of God," among them Andrew and John, who came to know Christ through John's preaching. John is presented in the New Testament as the last of the Old Testament prophets and the precursor of the Messiah. June 24 (August 29 for his beheading).

JOHN BAPTIST OF THE CONCEPTION (1561–1613). Born on July 7 at Almodóvar del Campo, Spain, John García was educated at Baeza and Toledo, where he joined the Trinitarians. Distressed that the decree of a general chapter of his order held in 1594 that several houses in each province should strictly observe the primitive rule was generally ignored, he founded a reform house at Valdepeñas in 1597. He received approval from Rome for his new reformed Trinitarian community in 1597, a step that aroused great opposition and caused him to be physically attacked by unreformed Trinitarians. By the time of his death at Cordova on February 14, some thirty-four Trinitarian monasteries had accepted the reforms of the Discalced Trinitarians. He was canonized by Pope Paul VI in 1975.

JOHN BAPTIST DE LA SALLE. *See* La Salle, John Baptist de.

JOHN OF BERGAMO (d. c. 690). Known for his learning and holiness, he was elected bishop of Bergamo, Italy, in about 656 and labored to eliminate all vestiges of Arianism in his diocese. Though reported slain by Arians in the Roman Martyrology, the report is not so, and he died of natural causes. July 11.

JOHN OF BEVERLY (d. 721). Born at Harpham, Yorkshire, England, he studied under Adrian at St. Theodore's School in Kent, and on his return to his native land became a monk at Whitby. He was named bishop of Hexham in 687 and then transferred to York as metropolitan in 705, succeeding St. Bosa. John was known for his holiness, his preference for the contemplative life, and his miracles, many of which are recounted in Bede's *Ecclesiastical History,* the author of which he had ordained. In ill health, John resigned the bishopric of York in 717 and retired to Beverly Abbey, which he had founded, and remained there until his death on May 7. His shrine was for centuries one of the most popular pilgrim centers in England. He was canonized by Pope Benedict IX in 1037.

JOHN BOSCO. *See* Bosco, John.

JOHN OF BRIDLINGTON. *See* Thwing, John.

JOHN CALYBITES (d. c. 450). According to legend he was born of a wealthy family in Constantinople, became a monk at Gomon on the Bosporus, and after six years returned home as a beggar. He lived, unrecognized, on his parents' charity in a shack (calybites) nearby, devoting himself to prayers and penances. Only when dying did he reveal his identity to his mother. January 15.

JOHN CANTIUS (1390–1473). Born on June 23 at Kanti, Poland, and also known as John of Kanti, he studied at the University of Cracow, was ordained, and then was appointed lecturer in Scripture at the university. He became famed for his preaching but was forced from his position by jealous associates and became parish priest at Olkusz. Fearful of the responsibility of the care of souls, he returned to Cracow as professor of Scripture, a position he held until his death at Cracow on December 24. He was noted for his scholarship, learning, austerities, and concern for the poor, was declared the patron of Poland and Lithuania by Pope Clement XII in 1737, and was canonized in 1767 by Pope Clement XIII. December 23.

JOHN OF CAPISTRANO (1386–1456). Born at Capistrano, Abruzzi, Italy, he studied law at Perugia, was appointed governor of that city in 1412, and married. Imprisonment during a war between Perugia and Malatesta caused him to change his life. He obtained a dispensation to enter a religious order, despite his marriage, and publicly repented of his sins. In 1416, he joined the Friars Minor, studied under Bernardino of Siena, and was ordained in 1420. He began preaching and met with immediate success, drawing thousands to his sermons and converting many more to a more religious way of life. He also labored with his friend Bernardino of Siena to heal the wounds among the Franciscans, drawing up the plans approved by the general chapter of the Franciscans held at Assisi in 1430 for a short-lived reunion of the various groups in the Order. The following year he was active at the Observant chapter at Bologna, and according to Gonzaga was appointed commissary general. In 1430, John had helped elect Bernardino vicar general of the Observants and soon after met St. Colette in France and joined her efforts to reform the Poor Clares. He was inquisitor in the proceedings against the Fraticelli and the charges made against the Gesuats and was frequently sent on papal diplomatic missions: In 1439 he was legate to Milan and Burgundy to oppose the claims of antipope Felix V; in 1446 he was sent on a mission to the King of France; and in 1451 he was selected by Pope Nicholas V, in response to an appeal from

Emperor Frederick, to go as commissary and inquisitor general with twelve Franciscans to combat the Hussites. He preached in Bavaria, Saxony, and Poland, bringing about great revivals of the faith, though some of the methods he employed against the heretics have been severely criticized. His campaign ended when the Turks captured Constantinople in 1453, and he devoted his energies to preaching a crusade against them. Unsuccessful in Bavaria and Austria, he joined Janos Hunyady in exhorting the Hungarians to resist the invading Turks and personally led the left wing of the Christian army at the Battle of Belgrade in 1456. The failure of the Turks to capture the city in the ensuing siege saved Europe from being overrun by the Turks. He died at Villach, Austria, on October 23 of the plague that followed, as had Hunyady a few weeks earlier. He was canonized in 1690.

JOHN CASSIAN (c. 360–c. 433). Probably born in Provence, though Gennadius, writing in the fifth century, says, probably erroneously, that he was born in Scythia, of wealthy parents, and about 380, went to Palestine with a friend, Germanus. They became monks at Bethlehem and then went to Egypt, where they lived as hermits under Archebius for a time and then went to Skete. In about 400 he became a follower of St. John Chrysostom at Constantinople and was ordained a deacon by him. When Chrysostom was deposed, he was one of the delegation that went to Rome in 405 to defend him before Pope Innocent I and may have been ordained a priest while there. Several years later he went to Marseilles and lived there until his death. He founded two monasteries about 415, importing to Gaul the plan and spirit of Egyptian asceticism and spirituality in them. He wrote two books of instructions for his monks, *Institutes of the Monastic Life,* set-

ting forth rules for the monastic life and listing eight chief hindrances to a monk's perfection, and *Conferences on the Egyptian Monks,* conversations with the leaders of Eastern monasticism. His *Institutes* greatly impressed St. Benedict and through him were to affect Western monasticism for centuries to come. John's *Conferences* was censured by Pope Pelagius for containing erroneous doctrine in some of its passages. His *De Incarnatione Domini,* against Nestorius, was written at the request of a Roman archdeacon who later became Pope Leo the Great, but it was evidently written in haste and does not compare with the other two works. In it he denounces Pelagianism but is considered the founder of semi-Pelagianism for his views on free will in several sections of the *Conferences,* for which he was condemned by St. Augustine. He died at Marseilles on July 23. He is considered a saint in the Eastern Church but has never been canonized in the West.

JOHN OF CHINON (6th century). A native of Brittany, he became a hermit near Chinon, Touraine, and was famed as a healer and as a prophet. He is reputed to have assured Queen Radegund of Neustria that her husband would not disturb her when she left him to become a nun after he had murdered her brother. John also served as her spiritual director. June 27.

JOHN CHRYSOSTOM (c. 347–407). Born at Antioch, Syria, the son of an imperial military officer, he studied rhetoric under the famous pagan rhetorician Libanius at Antioch and theology under Diodorus of Tarsus, leader of the Antiochene school. John was baptized by Bishop Meletius in about 369 and in about 374 became a hermit under St. Basil and Theodore of Mopsuestia. John returned home when his austere life in a cave undermined his health, became a deacon in 381, and was ordained in 386

336 JOHN CLIMACUS

by Bishop Flavian of Antioch, whom he served the next twelve years. He became famed for his preaching, which earned him the sobriquet Chrysostom (golden-mouthed) and had a tremendous effect on the spiritual life of the city. Beginning in 390, he preached a series of homilies on books of the New Testament (including eighty-eight on John, ninety on Matthew, and thirty-two on Romans), which established him as one of the great expositors of the Christian faith. In 398, against his wishes, he was named Patriarch of Constantinople and at once began to reform the Church there. He made extraordinary donations to the poor, abolished ecclesiastical pomp and luxury, sent missionaries to the East, and made friends but also many enemies by his honesty, his asceticism, and his firm opposition to idolatry, immoral entertainment, and aristocratic extravagances. Among the enemies he made were Empress Eudoxia, who resented his criticism of her vanity, lack of charity, and dress; Gainas, commander-in-chief of the army and leader of the Arians, when John curbed his exactions; the churchmen he antagonized by curtailing their power and restricting their extravagant lifestyle; and Archbishop Theophilus of Alexandria, who had aspired to be Patriarch of Constantinople when John was appointed. In 403, led by Theophilus, thirty-six hostile bishops at the Synod of the Oak condemned him on twenty-nine charges (among them an unjustified charge of Origenism and for an imagined attack on the Empress in a sermon in which he had denounced the luxury of women) and ordered him deposed and exiled. Civil war threatened and when an earthquake shook the city, Eudoxia revoked the banishment order. Soon after, though, when John denounced the excesses of the public games held to celebrate the erection of a silver statue of Eudoxia, she renewed her enmity. On June 24, 404, Emperor

Arcadius ordered John into exile at Cucusus, Armenia, despite the support of the people of Constantinople, Pope Innocent I, and the whole Western Church. From Cucusus, John wrote at least 238 letters that are still extant. Arcadius remained adamant about his banishment, and five bishops sent by the Pope and Emperor Honorius were imprisoned in Thrace by Theophilus' followers, who knew they had been sent to demand the restoration of John to his patriarchal see. Meanwhile, John was ordered exiled to a more distant location, Pityus, at the far end of the Black Sea, and died on the way at Comana, Pontus, on September 14 from exhaustion brought on by long forced marches on foot in the stifling heat and inclement weather. In addition to his sermons and letters, several of John's treatises are still extant, among them *The Priesthood,* which he wrote soon after his ordination in 386. He was declared a Doctor of the Universal Church at the Council of Chalcedon in 451 and was named patron of preachers by Pope Pius X. September 13.

JOHN CLIMACUS (c. 569–c. 649). Probably born in Syria, though perhaps in Palestine, he joined the monks on Mount Sinai when sixteen and was professed four years later. He lived as a hermit nearby, and later when he was thirty-five continued his eremitical life at Thole. He was learned in Scripture and the Church Fathers and became a sought-after spiritual adviser, noted for his ability to console distraught souls. When seventy years old, and over his objections, he was elected abbot of the monks on Mount Sinai and ruled until shortly before he died in the hermitage he had lived in for forty years. He is particularly known as the author of *Scala Paradisi (Ladder of Paradise,* sometimes called *Ladder of Perfection),* describing the thirty steps of the ladder required to attain religious perfection, which was enormously popular during the Middle Ages. He died on Mount Sinai on March 30. He is also known as John Scholasticus.

JOHN OF THE CROSS (1542–91). Born at Fontiveros, Old Castile, Spain, on June 24, Juan de Yepes y Alvarez was the youngest son of a silk weaver. John was educated at the catechism school at Medina del Campo, where his mother settled when his father died soon after his birth. When seventeen, he began working for the director of a hospital at Medina while at the same time studying at the Jesuit college there, 1559–63. He joined the Carmelites at Medina in 1563, taking the name Juan de Santo Matía, continued his studies at Salamanca, and was ordained in 1567. He met St. Teresa on a visit home to Medina and told her he was contemplating becoming a Carthusian to embrace a life of deeper solitude and prayer than that offered by the Carmelites, but she persuaded him to remain in the Carmelites and join her efforts to effect a reform in the Order. On November 28, 1568, John and four others, including the former prior of the Carmelite monastery in Medina, Antonio de Heredia, founded the first men's house of the reform at Duruelo, the beginning of the Discalced Carmelites, and John took the name John of the Cross. In 1570, he became rector of the newly established Discalced house of studies at Alcalá and in 1572 became spiritual director of Teresa's Convent of the Incarnation at Avila, where he spent the next five years. Meanwhile, dissension between the Calced and the Discalced Carmelites reached a climax, and in 1577 John was arrested by the Calced Carmelites and ordered to abandon the reform; when he refused to do so, he was imprisoned at Toledo. After being subjected to great hardships in prison and intense pressure

during the next nine months, he escaped. In 1579, the Discalced Carmelites were recognized and a separate province was established. He founded and became head of the Discalced college at Baeza, 1579–81; was elected prior of Granada in 1582; was appointed provincial of Andalusia in 1585; was elected prior at Segovia in 1587; and established several houses of his Order during these years. In 1590 controversy among the Discalceds broke out into the open, and the following year the Madrid general chapter deprived John of all his offices for his support of the moderates in the bitter dispute that had been raging in the Order for nine years and sent him as a simple monk to La Peñuela Monastery in Andalusia, though his enemies really wanted him expelled from the Order. Soon after he arrived at La Peñuela, he contracted a fever, went to the priory at Ubeda for medical attention, and died there on December 14. John of the Cross is now recognized as one of the great mystics of all time, and his writings are among the world's greatest spiritual classics. Among them are *Dark Night of the Soul,* which he wrote while in prison in Toledo, where he also wrote parts of his *Spiritual Canticle* and *Living Flame of Love,* which he probably finished at Granada. He was canonized in 1726, and was proclaimed a Doctor of the Church by Pope Pius XI in 1926.

JOHN DAMASCENE (c. 675–c. 749). Born of a wealthy Christian family at Damascus, he spent all his life under Mohammedan rule. He was educated by a brilliant monk named Cosmas, who had been captured in a Mohammedan raid on Sicily and was bought by John'a father, Mansur. John succeeded his father as chief revenue officer and counselor of Caliph Abdul Malek. In 726, when Emperor Leo the Isaurian issued his first edict prohibiting the veneration of images, John defended the practice and soon became a leading champion of the Catholic position, arousing the bitter enmity of the Byzantine Emperors, who could not molest him physically, since he was under the caliph's rule and protection. He resigned his position about 726, and with his adopted brother, another Cosmas, became a monk at St. Sabas' *laura* outside Jerusalem. He was denounced at a pseudosynod in Constantinople by iconoclast Emperor Constantine Copronymus, successor of Emperor Leo the Isaurian, but was ordained in Constantinople by Patriarch John V, who also appointed Cosmas bishop of Majuma. John soon after returned to the monastery and led the defenders of orthodoxy and expounders of the Catholic position in the iconoclasm controversy. Among his outstanding writings are the *Fount of Wisdom,* on philosophy, heresies, and the orthodox faith; *De Fide Orthodoxa,* a comprehensive presentation of the teachings of the Greek Fathers on the main Christian doctrines; and *Sacra Parallela,* a compilation of scriptural and patristic texts on Christian moral and ascetical works. His writings, especially his *De Fide Orthodoxa,* one of the most notable theological works of antiquity, has had great influence on theologians of both East and West. He also wrote poetry, and some of his poems are used in the Greek liturgy. The elegance of his Greek caused him to be called Chrysorrhoas (goldpouring). He died at Sabas, probably on December 5, the last of the Greek Fathers, and was made a Doctor of the Church by Pope Leo XIII in 1890. December 4.

JOHN THE DIVINE. *See* John the Evangelist.

JOHN OF DUKLA, BL. (1414–84). Born at Dukla, Poland, he became a Conventual Franciscan at Lamberg and then followed the rule of the Observants after hearing John of Capistrano preach. John of Dukla lived almost as a recluse for many years, was appointed guardian of the Lwow priory, became a successful preacher, and converted many Ruthenians and Hussites. He became blind in his old age and died on September 29. His cult was approved in 1739 and he is a patron of Poland and Lithuania. September 28.

JOHN THE DWARF (5th century). A native of Basta in Lower Egypt, he retired to the desert of Skete when a young man and became a disciple of St. Poemen. John lived a life of obedience, humility, and austerity the rest of his days. When he first arrived at Skete he is reputed to have watered a stick stuck in the ground unquestioningly when his spiritual director ordered him to do so; in the third year of his ministrations, it bore fruit. He left Skete to escape marauding Berbers and settled on Mount Quolzum, where he died. October 17.

JOHN OF EGYPT (c. 304–94). Born at Lycopolis (Asyut), Lower Egypt, he became a carpenter and when twenty-five a hermit under an old anchorite who directed him for more than a decade. On the death of his director, he spent several years visiting various monasteries and then built a hermitage on a hill near Lycopolis that was walled up except for a single small window. He taught from there on Saturdays and Sundays and soon drew huge crowds with his reported miracles, wisdom, and prophecies (he twice predicted victory for Emperor Theodosius I—first against Maximus in 388 and again in 392 against Eugenius). He had the ability to read men's minds and look into their souls and became one of the most famous of the desert hermits. He died in his cell, which was discovered in 1925. March 27.

JOHN THE EVANGELIST (c. 6–c. 104). Born in Galilee, the son of Zebede and Salome and younger brother of James the Greater, he was a fisherman on Lake Genesareth until with James he was called by Christ to follow him (Matt. 4:21–22; Mark 1:19–20). He was the youngest of the apostles. James the Greater and John were called "Sons of Thunder" by the Lord because of their volatile temperaments (Mark 3:17), and John became the beloved disciple (John 13:23; 19:26; 20:2ff.; 21:7; 21:24). That he was one of those closest to Christ was attested to by the fact that only he, Peter, and James were present at such events as the Transfiguration (Matt. 17:1; Mark 9:2; Luke 9:28), the healing of Peter's mother-in-law (Mark 1:29–31), the raising of Jairus' daughter from the dead (Mark 5:22–43; Luke 8:40–56), and the agony in the garden of Gethsemane (Matt. 26:37ff.; Mark 14:33ff.). He and Peter were sent to prepare the Passover (Luke 22:8ff.) and were the first apostles at the tomb of the risen Christ. He was the only apostle at the Crucifixion, where Jesus placed Mary in his care (John 19:25–27). He was imprisoned with Peter and appeared before the Sanhedrin (Acts 4:1–21), accompanied Peter to Samaria (Acts 8:14) to transmit the Holy Spirit to the new converts, and was at the Council of Jerusalem in 49. Soon after, he went to Asia Minor and in all probability was present at the passing away of Mary. He was named, with Peter and James, by Paul as "these leaders, these pillars" of the Church in Jerusalem (Gal. 2:9). According to tradition, he went to Rome during the reign of Emperor Domitian, miraculously escaped martyrdom (he emerged unscathed from a cauldron of boiling oil, according to Tertullian), and was exiled to the island of Patmos, where he wrote Revelation. He returned to Ephesus on the death of Domitian in 96, wrote the fourth gospel and three epistles, and died there, the only one of the apostles who did not suffer martyrdom. Although traditionally he has been considered the author of the fourth gospel, Revelation, and the three epistles, some modern scholars questioned his authorship; however, the preponderance of opinion among most contemporary biblical scholars now accepts the early tradition that he is the author of these New Testament books. John is often surnamed "the Divine" because of his theological brilliance and is represented in art as an eagle for the soaring majesty of his gospel. December 27.

JOHN THE GEORGIAN. *See* John the Iberian.

JOHN OF GOD (1495–1550). Born at Montemoro Novo, Portugal, on March 8, he served as a soldier in the wars between France and Spain and against the Turks in Hungary, as overseer of slaves in Morocco, and as a shepherd near Seville. At forty he decided to make amends for his dissolute life by going to Africa to rescue Christian slaves. Instead he accompanied a Portuguese family from Gibraltar to Ceuta, Barbary, and when he returned to Gibraltar, he became a peddler of holy pictures and religious books. He opened a shop in Granada in 1538, went berserk when a sermon by St. John of Avila filled him with remorse and guilt for his wastrel life, and was confined to a lunatic asylum. Helped by John, he found a new purpose in life and on his release in 1539 devoted himself to helping the sick and the poor and opened a house to serve the sick poor (the beginnings of the Order of the Brothers Hospitalers, also known as the Brothers of St. John of God). His holiness and dedication brought donations from the wealthy to carry on his work. He died in Granada, Spain, on March 8, and was canonized in 1690. He is the patron of the sick, nurses, and hospitals.

JOHN THE GOOD (d. 660). John Camillus Bonus became bishop of Milan, Italy, was surnamed "the Good" for his good works, was a fierce opponent of the Monothelites, and was an ardent defender of orthodoxy. He participated in the Lateran Council in 649 and probably died on January 3. January 10.

JOHN OF GORZE (d. 974). Born at Vandières, Lorraine, he was educated at Metz and St. Mihiel and on the death of his father inherited a wealthy estate, including several benefices from several churches in Fontenoy. He was attracted to the religious life, made a pilgrimage to Rome, and then visited several monasteries. He was about to go on pilgrimage to Rome again in 933 with Archdeacon Einhold of Toul when Bishop Adelborn of Metz sent them to the run-down abbey of Gorze, which they revitalized, with John as prior. He was head of a delegation sent to Caliph Abdur-Rahman of Cordova by Emperor Otto I, and on John's return in 960, he was elected abbot of Gorze. Always inclined toward austerity, he put into practice at the monastery many austere reforms that were later adopted by other Benedictine monasteries in the area. February 27.

JOHN OF THE GRATING (d. c. 1170). Born in Brittany of poor parents, he received a good education and was received into the Cistercians by St. Bernard. John founded religious houses at Bégard and Buzay, of which he became abbot, was named bishop of Aleth, and transferred the seat of the diocese to the island of Aaron in Brittany, which he renamed St. Malo. He became involved in a dispute with the Marmoutier monks at Tours when he replaced them in the cathedral with canons regular of St. Augustine, a dispute that went on for eighteen years before he won the case with his appeal to Rome. He also founded Sainte-Croix de Guingamp and Saint-Jacques de Montfort abbeys and reformed Saint-Méen de Gaël Monastery. His surname comes from the grating around his tomb. February 1.

JOHN GUALBERT (d. 1073). Of the noble Visdomini family, he was born at Florence, Italy, and had his life changed when, bent on revenge for the murder of his brother Hugh, he met the murderer, drew his sword to kill him, and then forgave him. He became a Benedictine monk at San Miniato del Monte Monastery, left to seek greater solitude when it seemed he might be made abbot, and while at the hermitage of Camaldoli decided to found a monastery of his own, which he did at Vallombrosa (Vallis Umbrosa), near Fiesole. Following the primitive rule of St. Benedict, the Vallumbrosans, as his followers came to be called, stressed charity and poverty and admitted lay brothers, an innovation for religious congregations of that time. John became known for his aid to the poor, his fierce opposition to simony, his miracles, gift of prophecy, and spiritual wisdom, which attracted great crowds seeking his advice. The Vallumbrosans soon spread all through Italy, particularly in Tuscany and Lombardy. He died at Passignano, near Florence, and was canonized in 1193.

JOHN THE IBERIAN (d. c. 1002). Of a noble Iberian (Georgian, U.S.S.R.) family and also known as John the Georgian, he was an outstanding military commander until middle age, when he resigned his position and with his wife's consent left her and their family to become a monk on Mount Olympus in Bithynia. He went to Constantinople for his son Euthymius, who with other young Iberian men was being held hostage by the Emperor, and brought him back to Olympus with him. Their reputation for holiness attracted so many disciples that they retired to St. Athanasius *laura* on Mount Athos in Macedonia in quest of greater solitude. With John's brother-in-law, retired General John Thornikios, who had become a monk, the father and son, about 980, founded a monastery for Iberians on Mount Athos, the beginning of the famous Iviron Monastery, with John as abbot. On the death of Thornikios, who had handled all the details of running the monastery, John and several of his disciples set out for Spain but were intercepted and brought to Constantinople, where Emperor Constantine VIII persuaded him to return to Athos. He was confined to bed the last years of his life and died at Iviron, after designating Euthymius as the new abbot. July 12.

JOHN JOSEPH OF THE CROSS. *See* Calosirto, John Joseph of the Cross.

JOHN OF KANTI. *See* John Cantius.

JOHN OF THE MARCHES. *See* Gangala, James.

JOHN OF MATERA (d. 1139). Born at Matera, Kingdom of Naples, he joined a monastery on an island off Taranto as a shepherd, left when his austerities and aloofness alienated the other monks, and then went to Calabria and later to Sicily. He next spent two and a half years as a hermit at Ginosa, rebuilt a church nearby, and then was sent to prison when it was reported he had found hidden treasure. He escaped to Capua, joined William of Vercelli's community on Monte Laceno, and when it was destroyed by fire moved to Bari. His preaching was very successful but caused him to be accused of heresy, whereupon he returned to Ginosa and the disciples he had left there. Shortly after he went to Monte Gargano, built a monastery at Pulsano, and became abbot. At the time of his death on June 20, he was widely venerated for his miracles and the gift of prophecy. He is also known as John of Pulsano.

JOHN OF MATHA (1160–1213). Born at Faucon, Provence, on June 23, he was educated at Aix, but on his return to Faucon lived as a hermit for a time. He then went to Paris where he received his doctorate in theology, was ordained there in 1197, and then joined St. Felix of Valois in his hermitage at Cerfroid. He confided to Felix his idea of founding a religious order to ransom Christian prisoners from the Moslems, and late in 1197, the two went to Rome and received the approval of Pope Innocent III for the Order of the Most Holy Trinity (the Trinitarians), with John as superior, in 1198; they also secured the approval of King Philip Augustus of France. The Order flourished, spread to France, Spain, Italy, and England, sent many of its members to North Africa, and redeemed many captives. John died at Rome on December 17, and his cult was approved in 1655 and again in 1694. February 8.

JOHN OF MATHA (1578–1618). Born at Prados, Spain, he joined the Franciscans, was ordained in 1606, and was sent as a missionary to Japan. He became fluent in the language and was quite successful in his missionary work until he was arrested at Maeco in 1615. After three years' imprisonment he was beheaded, and was beatified in 1867. August 16.

JOHN OF MEDA (d. c. 1159). A secular priest from Como, Italy, he joined the Humiliati, a penitential Order of laymen, who on the advice of St. Bernard, in 1134 withdrew from the world and established their first monastery at Milan. He adapted the rule of St. Benedict to their needs and had them recite the Little Office of Our Lady daily.

He was canonized by Pope Alexander III. September 26.

JOHN NEPOMUCEN (c. 1340–93). Born at Nepomuk, Bohemia, he used the name of his native town for his surname instead of his family name of Wölflein or Welflin. He studied at the University of Prague and was ordained. In time, he became vicar general of Archbishop John of Genzenstein at Prague and according to tradition incurred the enmity of dissolute King Wenceslaus IV when he refused to reveal what the Queen had told him in confession. He became involved in a dispute between Wenceslaus and the archbishop when the King, in 1393, sought to convert a Benedictine abbey into a cathedral for a new diocese he proposed to create for a favorite when the aged abbot died. The archbishop and John thwarted him by approving the election of a new abbot immediately on the death of the old abbot. At a meeting with John and other clerics, Wenceslaus flew into a rage, tortured them so that John was seriously injured, and then on March 20 had him murdered and thrown into the Moldau River at Prague. He was canonized in 1729 and is the principal patron of Bohemia. May 16.

JOHN OF NICOMEDIA (d. 303). An unnamed Christian at Nicomedia, he tore down Diocletian's decree against Christians when it was published in the forum there. He was tortured and burned to death for his act on February 24. He is known as Euhtis by the Syrians. September 7.

JOHN DELLA PACE, BL. (d. c. 1332). All that is known of him is that he was a hermit who later founded the Fraticelli della Penitenza at Pisa and had his cult confirmed in 1856. November 12.

JOHN OF PARMA, BL. (1209–89). Born at Parma, Italy, he became a teacher of logic there and when twenty-five, joined the Franciscans. He finished his studies at Paris, was ordained, and preached there and at Bologna, Naples, and Rome, attracting great crowds with his eloquence. He was chosen minister general of the Franciscans in 1247, labored to reform the laxness permitted by Brother Elias, and visited each of the Franciscan houses. He went on a papal diplomatic mission to the Eastern Emperor and on his return went to Paris to join in the successful defense of the mendicant Orders against the attacks of William of St. Armour. John's attempts to restore discipline in the Franciscans caused great opposition, and in 1257 he resigned as minister general, naming St. Bonaventure as his successor. John spent the last thirty years of his life in retirement at Greccio, Italy, but on hearing that the Greeks had lapsed into schism, received permission from the Pope to go to them in an attempt to reunite them to Rome. He died on the way at Camerino on March 19, and his cult was approved in 1777. March 20.

JOHN OF PENNA, BL. (c. 1193–1271). Born at Penna, Ancona, Italy, he joined the Franciscans at Recanati about 1213 and was sent to France, where he worked for a quarter century in Provence, founding several Franciscan houses there. About 1242 he returned to Italy, where he spent the last thirty years of his life, mainly in retirement, although he did serve as guardian several times. He experienced visions and had the gift of prophecy, but was also afflicted with extended periods of spiritual aridity. He died on April 3, and his cult was approved in 1806. His life is described in Chapters 4 and 5 of *The Little Flowers of St. Francis.*

JOHN OF PERUGIA, BL. (d. 1231). A Franciscan priest at Perugia, he and Peter, a Franciscan lay brother from

Sasso Ferrato, Piceno, Italy, were sent by St. Francis of Assisi to preach to the Moors in Spain in 1216. They lived for a time at Teruel, Aragon, and then went to Valencia, which was ruled by the Moors. As soon as they began to preach, they were arrested and arraigned before the emir. They admitted that their intention was to convert the Moors, and when they refused to apostatize, they were beheaded on August 29. Interestingly enough, the emir was converted to Christianity in 1238 and gave his house where the two had been executed to the Franciscans for a friary. They were beatified in 1783. September 1.

JOHN OF PINNA (6th century). A native of Syria and probably a refuge from the Monophysite persecution, he immigrated to Italy, built an abbey at Pinna, near Spoleto, became its abbot, and then founded another abbey near Pesaro. Legend has him arriving in December and immediately being recognized by a group of hunters as a man of God when they found him sitting under a tree that was in full bloom. He ruled for forty-four years and died in his monastery. March 19.

JOHN OF PRADO, BL. (1563–1631). Born at Morovejo, León, Spain, of a noble family, he studied at Salamanca University and in 1584 became an Observant Franciscan. He served as master of novices and guardian in several convents, was removed as guardian on charges that were later proved to be false, and in 1610 was made minister of the new province of San Diego. When his term expired in 1613, he was given permission to go to Morocco and was named missionary apostolic by Pope Urban VIII. When John began ministering to Christian slaves in Morocco and preaching, he was ordered to leave. When he persisted in his missionary activities, he was brought before Sultan Muley el-Walid at Marrakesh. When John asked the sultan to renounce Mohammed and embrace Christ, he stabbed the Franciscan to death on May 24. John was beatified in 1728.

JOHN OF PULSANO. *See* John of Matera.

JOHN OF REOMAY (c. 444–544). Born near Langres, France, he became a monk at Lérins and later returned to found an abbey, of which he became abbot, in his native town. In time, it was named Mount St. Jean in his honor. He was known for his holiness and miracles and was one of the early leaders of monasticism in Gaul. January 28.

JOHN OF RIETI, BL. (d. c. 1350). Born at Castel Porziano, near Rome, and brother of Bl. Lucy of Amelia, John Bufulari joined the Hermits of St. Augustine at Rieti and was known for his aid to the sick and his concern for his fellow man. Numerous miracles were reported at his tomb after his death, and his cult was confirmed in 1832. August 9.

JOHN OF SAHAGÚN. *See* Gonzalez de Castrillo, John.

JOHN OF SALERNO (c. 1190–1242). Born at Salerno, Italy, he studied at Bologna, where he met St. Dominic and joined the Dominicans. In 1219, he was the leader of a group of thirteen Dominicans sent to preach in Etruria. They went first to Ripoli near Florence and then to San Pancrazio adjoining the city walls and founded Santa Maria Novella Friary in 1221. He successfully preached to the Patarines, a sect resembling the Albigensians in their beliefs, and brought many of the Patarines back to the Church. He possessed the ability to read men's minds and souls. His cult was approved in 1783. August 9.

JOHN SCHOLASTICUS. *See* John Climacus.

JOHN THE SILENT (454–558). Born of a distinguished family at Nicropolis, Armenia, he built a monastery after his parents died when he was only eighteen and became its superior. He soon achieved a reputation for his austere life and great holiness, and when only twenty-eight, against his wishes, was named bishop of Colonia, Armenia. In 491, after nine years as bishop, he left to seek solitude and went to Jerusalem, where in a vision he was directed to St. Sabas' *laura* there. He served as guestmaster for a time and then lived as a hermit for three years, when he was made steward of the *laura*. In 503 controversy among the monks caused Sabas to leave, and John spent the next six years in the desert living as a hermit. He returned when Sabas was recalled and spent the rest of his years in his cell in silence, prayer, and contemplation, though dispensing spiritual wisdom to the many who were drawn to the *laura* by his sanctity. At the time of his death he had spent some seventy-five years of his life as a solitary. May 13.

JOHN THE SINNER, BL. *See* Grande, Bl. John.

JOHN THE SPANIARD (1123–60). Probably born at Almanza, León, Spain, he went to Arles for his education, was befriended by a wealthy man, lived as a hermit, and after two and a half years became a Carthusian at Montrieu. He served as sacristan, was elected prior, and at the end of his term went to Grande Chartreuse. He was selected by the abbot, St. Anthelm, to found a new Carthusian house on an estate donated by Haymo de Fulciano near Lake Geneva and was prior when Reposoir, as it was called, was built in 1151. He wrote a constitution for Carthusian nuns and died at Reposoir. His cult was approved in 1864. June 25.

JOHN OF TOSSIGNANO, BL. *See* Tavelli, Bl. John.

JOHN OF VALLOMBROSA, BL. (d. c. 1380). Born at Florence, Italy, he became a monk at Holy Trinity Monastery there, was caught practicing the black arts, and for penance was given a lengthy term in prison. On his release he was completely overwhelmed with remorse and was given permission by the abbot to live as a hermit. In time, he achieved a reputation for holiness and learning, particularly of Scripture, and was known as the "hermit of the cells." March 10.

JOHN OF VERCELLI (c. 1205–83). Born at Mosso Santa Maria, near Vercelli, Italy, he studied at Paris and taught law there and at Vercelli, where he joined the Dominicans. About 1245 he was elected prior at Vercelli and in 1264 was elected master general of the Dominicans. He was asked to act as peacemaker to the Italian states by Pope Gregory X and drew up a schema for the second General Council of Lyons in 1274. With Jerome of Ascoli (later Pope Nicholas IV), he mediated between Philip III of France and Alfonso X of Castile. He was the leader of devotion to the name of Jesus, decreeing that an altar of the Holy Name be established in every Dominican church. He maintained rigid discipline among the Dominicans, appointed Thomas Aquinas to the chair of theology at Paris, and died at Montpellier, France, on November 30. His cult was approved in 1903.

JOHN OF VINCENZA, BL. (d. 1183). Born at Cremona, Italy, of the Sordi (or Surdi) family, he took his stepfather's name, Cacciafronte, was made a canon when fifteen, and entered St. Laurence Benedictine Abbey the next year. He was appointed prior of St. Victor's when he was twenty-four and in 1155 of St. Laurence. His support of Pope Alexander III caused him to be expelled by Emperor Frederic Barbarossa, who was supporting antipope Victor IV. John then lived as a hermit at Mantua and in 1174 was named bishop of that see. He petitioned the Pope to reinstate his predecessor, Bishop Graziodorus, who had repented of his support of Victor and resigned when his request was granted. Soon after, John was appointed bishop of Vincenza and became very popular for his evident concern for the welfare of his people. He was stabbed to death by a tenant farmer of the diocese when John rebuked him for refusing to pay his rent. March 16.

JOHN OF WARNETON (d. 1130). Born at Warneton, French Flanders, he was taught in his youth by Lambert of Utrecht and St. Ivo of Chartres, became a monk at Mont St. Eloi near Arles, and then was archdeacon of Arles. He was named bishop of Thérouanne against his wishes and was so active in the reform of monastic discipline that an attempt was made on his life. He died on January 27.

JOHN ZEDAZNELI (d. c. 580). He was one of a group of thirteen Syrian monks who were sent as missionaries to evangelize the Caucasus area of Iberia (Georgia) in the middle of the sixth century. They introduced monastic life to that region, founded several flourishing monasteries, and they are known as the Fathers of the Iberian Church. November 4.

JOHNSON, BL. LAURENCE (d. 1582). Born at Great Crosby, Lancashire, England, he left Oxford when he became a Catholic and went to Douai to study for the priesthood. Ordained in 1577, he was sent on the English mission and was arrested early in 1581. Convicted of plotting against the Queen but in reality because of his priesthood, he was offered a pardon if he would apostatize, and when he refused, he was hanged, drawn, and quartered at Tyburn on May 30. Though his family name was Johnson, he was widely known as Richardson. He was beatified in 1886.

JOHNSON, BL. ROBERT (d. 1582). Born in Shropshire, England, he was a servant for a time and then studied at Rome and Douai for the priesthood and was ordained at Douai in 1576. He was sent on the English mission, worked in London for four years, and was arrested in 1580. He was accused of conspiring against the Queen, tortured, and then convicted. He was hanged, drawn, and quartered at Tyburn on November 21 with Bl. Thomas Ford and Bl. John Shert. Bl. Robert was beatified in 1886. May 28.

JOLENTA, BL. (d. 1299). Daughter of King Bela IV of Hungary, she was raised by her elder sister Bl. Cunegund, wife of Boleslaus V of Poland. Jolenta married Duke Boleslaus of Kalisz, and when he died in 1279, she, Cunegund (now widowed), and one of her daughters retired to the Poor Clare convent that Cunegund had founded at Sandeck. Later Jolenta became superior of the convent at Gnesen, which she had founded, and died there. Her cult was approved in 1827 and she is known as Helen of Poland in Poland. June 12.

JON HELGI OGMUNDARSON (d. 1121). A disciple of Isleifur, bishop of Skalholt, southern Iceland, he was named first bishop of Holar, an Icelandic see erected in 1106, and is venerated as one of the apostles of Iceland. He is sometimes called Ogmund. March 8.

JONAS (d. 327). *See* Barachisius.

JONES, BL. EDWARD (d. 1590). A native of Wales, he studied at Douai, was ordained, and in 1588 was sent on the English mission. Known for the fervor of his preaching, he was arrested and when convicted of being a Catholic priest, was hanged, with Bl. Antony Middleton, in front of the house on Fleet Street in London where they had been captured. May 6.

JONES, JOHN (d. 1598). Born of a Catholic family at Clynog Fawr, Carnarvonshire, Wales, he was ordained at Rheims and in 1587 was working among the Catholic prisoners in Marshalsea Prison in London. He was discovered, imprisoned at Wisbech Castle, but managed to escape to the Continent. He joined the Franciscans of the Observance, probably at Pontoise, France, and was professed at Ara Coeli Convent in Rome. He received permission to return to England in 1592, using the alias John Buckley, worked in London and other parts of England, and was arrested again in 1596. He was imprisoned for two years (he brought Bl. John Rigby back to the faith while in prison), and when convicted of being a Catholic priest guilty of treason for having been ordained abroad and returned to England, he was hanged, drawn, and quartered at Southwark in London on July 12. He was canonized by Pope Paul VI in 1970 as one of the Martyrs of England and Wales.

JORDAN OF PISA, BL. (d. 1311). He joined the Dominicans at Pisa in 1280, was sent to the University of Paris to finish his education, and was appointed lector at Santa Maria Novella in Florence in 1305. He became a famous preacher noted for his eloquence and learning, founded the Confraternity of the Holy Redeemer at Pisa, and in 1311 was appointed professor of theology at St. James Friary in Paris. He died at Piacenza, Italy, while on his way to Paris. He was one of the pioneers in the use of the vernacular in Italy, using the Tuscan dialect in his sermons, and with Dante and Petrarch is credited with being responsible for the development of the modern Italian language. Jordan's cult was approved in 1833. March 6.

JORDAN OF SAXONY, BL. (d. 1237). A Saxon named Gordanus or Giordanus, he received his bachelor of divinity degree at Paris, met St. Dominic, and in 1220 became a Dominican at Paris. Jordan was elected prior provincial of Lombardy the next year, and in 1222, on the death of Dominic, was elected second master general of the Dominicans. He expanded the Order, establishing many new foundations in Germany and Switzerland, sent missionaries to Denmark, and frequently preached at universities to young students. He was a powerful preacher, and St. Albert the Great became a Dominican after hearing one of his sermons. He was on his way to the Holy Land in 1237 when his ship was wrecked on the coast of Syria and all aboard perished. He is the author of a life of St. Dominic that is one of the main sources of information about the founder of the Dominicans. Jordan's cult was approved in 1825. February 15.

JORNET IBARS, TERESA OF JESUS (1843–97). Born on January 9 at Aytona (Lérida), Spain, the daughter of peasants, she joined the Poor Clares, was obliged to leave because of poor health, and with Fr. Saturnino López Novoa, founded a community to care for the aged at Barbastro (Huesca) and was its superior general. She moved the mother house to Liria (Valencia), where she died on

August 26. The community received
papal approval in 1887 and then spread
to other countries. She was canonized by
Pope Paul VI in 1974.

JOSAPHAT (no date). His story is a
pious fiction. It tells of Abenner, an
Indian King who persecuted Christians.
When it was prophesied that his son
Josaphat would become a Christian, he
had him confined. Despite his every pre-
caution, Josaphat was converted to
Christianity by Barlaam (the same saint
whose feast day is November 19), disguised as a merchant. Abenner tried by
every means to have Josaphat apostatize,
and when he failed he became a
Christian himself. He later resigned the
throne and became a hermit. Josaphat
ascended the throne but later he too resigned his crown and joined Barlaam at
Khutyn. Scholars are agreed that the
whole story is a Christian transposition
of the legend of Siddartha Buddha and
that Josaphat and Abenner never existed.
November 27.

JOSAPHAT (c. 1580–1623). Born at
Vladimir, Volhynia, Poland, John
Kunsevich in his youth became an apprentice to a merchant at Vilna.
Interested in pursuing a religious life, he
refused a partnership in the business
and marriage to his master's daughter
and in 1604 became a monk in the
Ukrainian Order of St. Basil a Holy
Trinity Monastery at Vilna with a friend,
Joseph Rutsky, taking the name
Josaphat. He was ordained a priest of
the Byzantine rite in 1609 and soon
achieved a reputation as a compelling
preacher and a leading advocate for the
union of the Ukrainian Church with
Rome. His friend Rutsky became abbot
of Holy Trinity, and Josaphat was sent
to found new houses in Poland, but returned in 1614 as abbot of the
monastery when Rutsky was named
metropolitan of Kiev. In 1617, Josaphat

was named bishop of Vitebsk, Russia,
with the right of succession to Polotsk,
and a few months later succeeded to
that see when Archbishop Brolnitsky
died. He found the diocese in a deplorable condition—widespread opposition to Rome, married clergy, lax
discipline, churches in a run-down
state—and called synods to put into effect his reforms, which by 1620 were
effective. At that time, one Metetius
Smotritsky was appointed archbishop of
Polotsk by a group of dissident bishops
and began to sow the seeds of dissension, claiming that Josaphat was really a
Latin priest and declaring that Roman
Catholicism was not for the Ruthenian
people. Riots broke out as people chose
sides, and Josaphat was falsely accused
of fomenting trouble and using force
against the dissidents by the chancellor
of Lithuania, Leo Sapiaha, a Catholic,
thus stirring up further dissent. Not
being given the support he should have
received from the Latin bishops of
Poland because of his insistence on
maintaining Byzantine rites and customs, he went to Vitebsk, the hotbed of
the opposition, in 1623 to meet it head
on despite threats of violence against
him. On November 12, a priest named
Elias who had harassed Josaphat several
times, was locked up by one of
Josaphat's deacons when Elias again
abused the archbishop. A mob assembled demanding Elias' release, and
though Josaphat released Elias, Josaphat
was beaten and shot to death on
November 12 by the mob and his body
thrown into the Divina River at Vitebsk,
Russia. He was canonized in 1867, the
first Eastern saint to be formally canonized.

JOSEPH (1st century). Our only reliable information about Joseph is to be
found in the Infancy narratives of
Matthew 1–2 and Luke 1–2. According
to them Joseph is of royal descent from

348 JOSEPH OF ARIMATHEA

David. Joseph's family came from Bethlehem in Judea but he had moved to Nazareth in Galilee, where he was a builder. He was betrothed to Mary, became alarmed when he found Mary was pregnant though she had not lived with him, and was dissuaded from divorcing her by the angel of the Lord who told him her pregnancy was "by the Holy Spirit." He was with Mary at the birth of Jesus and the visit by the Magi at Bethlehem. He took Mary and the child to Egypt to escape Herod's massacre of the infants, and after the death of Herod, brought them back to Nazareth. He and Mary had Jesus circumcised and presented to the Lord in the Temple in Jerusalem. When Jesus was twelve Joseph and Mary took him to Jerusalem, lost him, and found him discoursing with the doctors in the Temple. Thereafter the name of Joseph is absent from the New Testament except in Luke 4:22, where he is mentioned by name as the father of Jesus. Joseph was probably dead by the time of the Passion and death of Christ; the apocryphal *Photoevangelium of James* says he was an old man when he married Mary. Special veneration to Joseph began in the East, where the apocryphal *History of Joseph* enjoyed great popularity in the fourth to the seventh centuries. In the West the ninth-century Irish *Félire* of Oengus mentions a commemoration, but it was not until the fifteenth century that veneration of Joseph in the West became widespread, when his feast was introduced into the Roman calendar in 1479; his devotion was particularly popularized by St. Teresa and St. Francis de Sales. Joseph was declared Patron of the Universal Church by Pope Pius IX in 1870; a model for fathers of families by Pope Leo XIII, who confirmed that his preeminent sanctity places him next to the Blessed Virgin among the saints, in his encyclical *Quanquam pluries* in 1889; a protector of workingmen by Pope Benedict XV; the patron of social justice by Pope Pius XI; and in 1955, Pope Pius XII established the feast of St. Joseph the Worker on May 1. March 19.

JOSEPH OF ARIMATHEA (1st century). Mentioned in all four gospels, he was a secret follower of Jesus for fear of the Jewish authorities. He was present at the Crucifixion, and after the death of Jesus persuaded Pontius Pilate to let him have Jesus' body. He wrapped it in fine linen and herbs and laid it in a tomb carved from rock in the side of a hill. Beyond that all that is known of him is from medieval legend, according to which he accompanied Philip to Gaul to preach the gospel and was sent to England at the head of twelve missionaries. Supposedly inspired by the archangel Gabriel, they built a church made of wattles in honor of our Lady on an island given them by the King of England, which in time became Glastonbury Abbey; supposedly Joseph died there. Pious legend also had him catch the blood of Christ while he was dying on the cross; Joseph is also supposed to have inherited the chalice used at the Last Supper. March 17.

JOSEPH BARSASSAS (1st century). A follower of Christ and surnamed "the Just," he was probably one of the seventy-two disciples. In Acts 1:23–26 he was nominated with Matthias (who was chosen) to take Judas' place among the twelve apostles. July 20.

JOSEPH CALASANCTIUS. *See* Calasanctius, Joseph.

JOSEPH OF CUPERTINO (1603–63). Born of poor parents at Cupertino, Italy, on June 17, Joseph Desa was an apprentice shoemaker in his youth, was refused admittance by the Conventual Franciscans when he was seventeen, and then became a Capuchin lay brother. He was dismissed after eight months for clumsiness and low intelligence but was later accepted as a servant and Franciscan tertiary by the Conventual Franciscans at Grottela, where he was to remain for the next seventeen years. He was admitted as a novice in 1625 and though he was a poor scholar, was ordained in 1628. He became famous for his ecstasies, miracles, and supernatural gifts, particularly the gift of levitation, which he is reputed to have experienced some seventy times, all reported by numerous reputable eyewitnesses. He was accused of seeking publicity, and though even Pope Urban VIII was impressed by his holiness and sincerity, he was sent to Assisi in 1639. For a time he experienced the desolation of spiritual aridity and suffered great temptations but gradually he regained great spiritual joy and happiness. Despite the attempts to keep him secluded in Assisi, his fame spread all over Europe, and in 1653 the Inquisition of Perugia sent him to an isolated Capuchin friary in the hills of Pietrarossa, where he was cut off completely from communication with the outside world. But word he was there soon attracted pilgrims and he was again moved—this time to another Capuchin house, at Fossombrone. Finally, in 1657, he was allowed to return to his own order at Osimo and again kept in the strictest seclusion; he experienced daily supernatural manifestations until his death there on September 18. He was canonized in 1767 and is the patron of air travelers and pilots.

JOSEPH OF LEONESSA (1556–1612). Born at Leonessa, Umbria, Italy, and baptized Eufranio, he became a Capuchin there at eighteen, taking the name Joseph. He became noted for his preaching, was sent as a missionary to Pera, a suburb of Constantinople, in 1587, ministered to Christian galley slaves, and was arrested for preaching Christianity to the Mohammedans and making converts to Christianity. Released, he was again arrested, tortured, and banished. He returned to Leonessa, where he died of cancer on February 4, and was canonized in 1745.

JOSEPH OF PALESTINE (d. c. 356). Assistant to Rabbi Hillel, famous teacher of the Jews, he was very much impressed by the deathbed baptism of the rabbi and the Christian books he left. Joseph was appointed head of the synagogue at Tarsus, but when his congregation found him reading the gospels they beat him and threw him into the Cydnus River. He then became a Christian, was made a *comes* by Emperor Constantine, and built several churches in Galilee. He left Tiberias and took up residence at Scythopolis, where he gave shelter to refugees from Arian persecution, among them St. Eusebius of Vercelli and St. Epiphanus, who later wrote Joseph's biography. July 22.

JOSEPHA OF BENIGANIM, BL. See Albiniana, Bl. Iñes.

JOSSE. See Judoc.

JOVITA (d. c. 121). See Faustinus.

JUCUNDUS (d. 451). See Nicasius.

JUDAS QUIRIACUS. See Cyriacus.

JUDE (1st century). In the list of the Twelve in Luke 6:16 and Acts 1:13, he is called Jude; in the lists in Matthew and Mark appears the name Thaddeus, and scholars believe they are the same. In the Epistle of Jude, the author calls himself the brother of James, and in Matthew 13:55 and Mark 6:3, Jude is mentioned as among the brethren of the Lord. Some modern scholars believe that Jude of the Twelve and Jude the author of the Epistle of Jude are different individuals (in verse 17, the author refers to the apostles in the past tense, which seems unlikely if he was one of them). According to legend, he preached in Mesopotamia, and the apocryphal *Passion of Simon and Jude* describes the preaching and martyrdom of those two apostles in Persia. October 28.

JUDITH (9th century). *See* Salome.

JUDOC (d. c. 668). Also known as Josse, he was the son of King Juthaël of Amorica (Brittany) and occupied the throne for a few months when his brother Judicael abdicated. About 636, Judoc was ordained at Ponthieu and after a pilgrimage to Rome, became a hermit at Runiacum (later named Saint-Josse) and died there. December 13.

JUGAN, VEN. JEANNE (1792–1879). Born at Petites-Croix, Brittany, France, on October 25, she worked as a domestic and then in hospital work. In 1842, with two women who aided her, Virginia Tredaniel and Marie Jumet, she founded the Little Sisters of the Poor with Jeanne as superior. Reelected in early December in 1843, she was suddenly deposed two weeks later by Fr. Le Pailleur, the community's moderator. In 1845 she received an award from the French Academy for her work in aiding the poor. In 1852, she was sent to the mother house and spent the rest of her life in obscurity. She died at Pern, France, on August 29, and was declared Venerable by Pope John Paul II in 1979.

JULIA (d. 304). *See* Optatus.

JULIA OF CERTALDO, BL. (1319–67). Said to be related to the della Rena family, she was a servant in the Tinolfi household in Certaldo, and in 1337 she joined the third order of Augustinians at Florence. She returned to Certaldo to escape the turmoil of the city, and when her

rescue of a child from a burning building brought her great public attention, she had herself walled up in a cell adjoining SS. Michael and James Church at Certaldo and lived in it as a recluse the remaining thirty years of her life. She died there on January 9, and her cult was confirmed in 1819. February 15.

JULIA OF CORSICA (5th century). According to legend, she was of a noble Carthaginian family who was sold as a slave to a Syrian merchant named Eusebius when Genseric captured Carthage in 439. While on the way to Gaul, the ship on which she was a passenger with her master stopped off at Cape Corso, northern Corsica. When the governor of the island, Felix, learned she was a Christian when she did not debark with her master to participate in a pagan ceremony, he ordered her to sacrifice to the gods. When she refused to do so, he offered her her freedom if she would apostatize. When she still refused, he had her tortured and then crucified. Some scholars believe she may have lived a century or two later and was murdered by Saracen raiders. She is the patroness of Corsica. May 22.

JULIAN (d. 250). A resident of Alexandria and so crippled with gout he was unable to walk, he was scourged and then burned to death for his Christianity together with Cronion (surnamed Eunus), one of his litter bearers during Decius' persecution of the Christians. A soldier named Besas who defended them on their way to the place of execution was also beheaded for his Christianity; he is the same as Agatho commemorated in the Roman Martyrology on December 7. February 27.

JULIAN (d. 259). *See* Lucius.

JULIAN (d. c. 290). *See* Lucian of Beauvais.

JULIAN (d. c. 304). According to legend, he and his wife, Basilissa, devoted their possessions and energies to caring for the poor and the sick, using their home as a hospital. Years after Basilissa's death, Julian suffered martyrdom at Antioch with Antony, a priest, a child named Celsus, and his mother, Marcianilla, during Diocletian's persecution of the Christians. Julian, who is often confused with Julian the Hospitaler, and Basilissa may never have existed except as a pious fiction. January 9.

JULIAN (d. 309). A catechumen at Caesarea, Palestine, he was arrested for venerating the bodies of St. Elias and his four martyred comrades, and was burned to death for his faith by Firmilian, governor of Palestine. February 17.

JULIAN (date unknown). *See* Caesarius (date unknown).

JULIAN OF ANAZARBUS (d. c. 302). A native of Anazarbus, Cilicia, he was arrested for his faith during Diocletian's persecution of Christians and exhibited for a year in cities all over Cilicia. He was then sewn in a sack with scorpions and vipers and thrown into the sea. St. John Chrysostom preached a eulogy about him, which is the source of information about him. He is sometimes called Julian of Antioch, as that is where his body was brought eventually. March 16.

JULIAN OF BRIOUDE (d. c. 304). A native of Vienne in Gaul and a Christian officer in the Roman army there, he retired to Auvergne when Crispin, the governor of Vienne, launched a persecution of Christians. Julian later surrendered and was beheaded for his faith near Brioude. August 28.

JULIAN THE HOSPITALER (no date). According to a pious fiction that was very popular in the Middle Ages, Julian was of noble birth and while hunting one day was reproached by a hart for hunting him and told he would one day kill his mother and father. He was richly rewarded for his services by a King and married a wealthy widow. While he was away his mother and father arrived at his castle seeking him; when his wife realized who they were she put them up for the night in the master's bedroom. When Julian returned unexpectedly later that night and saw a man and a woman in his bed, he suspected the worst and killed them both. When his wife returned from church and he found he had killed his parents, he was overcome with remorse and fled the castle, resolved to do a fitting penance. He was joined by his wife and they built an inn for travelers near a wide river, and a hospital for the poor. He was forgiven for his crime when he gave succor to a leper in his own bed; the leper turned out to be a messenger from God who had been sent to test him. He is the patron of hotelkeepers, travelers, and boatmen. February 12.

JULIAN OF LE MANS (3rd century?). Unreliable sources have him a noble Roman who became first bishop of Le Mans and evangelized that area of France. His legend has him performing extravagant miracles, calls him one of our Lord's seventy-two disciples, and even has him Simon the Leper. Julian's legend is sometimes confused with that of Julian the Hospitaler. January 27.

JULIAN SABAS (d. 377). A hermit in Mesopotamia on the banks of the Euphrates River, he was noted for his austerities and asceticism. Reported by the Arians to have embraced Arianism when St. Meletius, bishop of Antioch, was driven from that see by the Arians, Julian went to Antioch in 372, refuted Arianism, and did much to offset its impact. He then returned to his cave, where he remained until his death. January 17.

JULIAN OF ST. AUGUSTINE. *See* Martinet, Bl. Julian.

JULIAN OF TOLEDO (d. 690). Of Christian parents and reputedly of Jewish descent, he studied under Archbishop Eugene II of Toledo, became abbot of the monastery of Agali, and in 680 was named archbishop of Toledo. He convened several synods, secured recognition of Toledo as primatial see of Spain and Portugal, and encouraged the Spanish Kings to revive the persecution of the Jews, though he had a reputation for kindness. He revised the Mozarabic liturgy then in use in Spain and wrote *Prognostics,* on death, a biography of Visigoth King Wamba, and several other works. March 8.

JULIANA OF CUMAE (d. c. 305). According to the Roman Martyrology, during Emperor Maximian's persecution of the Christians, she was scourged by her father for her Christianity and tortured by Evilasius, the prefect, whom she had refused to marry. She was then thrown into prison, where she fought an evil spirit. Condemned to death, she was beheaded when a furnace and boiling oil did no injury to her. She may have been martyred at Cumae near Naples, where her relics are reputed to be enshrined, although the Roman Martyrology states she suffered martyrdom at Nicomedia and her relics were later transferred to Cumae. February 16.

JULIANA OF MOUNT CORNILLON, BL. (1192–1258). Born at Retinnes near Liège, Flanders, she was orphaned when five and placed in the care of the nuns of Mount Cornillon. She experienced visions when she was young in which the Lord pointed out that there was no feast in honor of the Blessed Sacrament. She

became a nun at Mount Cornillon and in 1225 was elected prioress. She began to agitate for the establishment of the feast day of her vision, received support and opposition, and was driven from the monastery by the lay directors, who accused her of mismanaging the funds of a hospital under her control. An inquiry by the bishop of Liège exonerated her and resulted in her recall in 1246, when he introduced the feast of Corpus Christi to Liège. When he died, she was again driven from the monastery, in 1248, and found refuge at the Cistercian monastery of Salzinnes at Namur but was again homeless when the monastery was burned down during the siege of Namur by the troops of Henry II of Luxembourg. She then retired to Fosses and spent the rest of her days until her death on April 5 there. Her struggle for the establishment of the feast of Corpus Christi was carried on by her friend Bl. Eva of Liège and was sanctioned by Pope Urban IV in 1264 (the office for the feast was written by Thomas Aquinas). Juliana's cult was confirmed in 1869.

JULIANA OF NORWICH, BL. (c. 1342–1423). Of her early life before she became an anchorite outside the walls of St. Julian's Church in Norwich, England, nothing is known. In 1373, she experienced a series of sixteen revelations, while in a state of ecstasy, of Christ's passion and the Trinity, and spent the next twenty years meditating on them and the suffering she had endured just prior to the revelations. The result was her *Revelations of Divine Love,* on the love of God, the Incarnation, redemption, sin, penance, and divine consolation, one of the most important of English writings. At the time of her death she had a far-spread reputation for sanctity, which attracted visitors from all over Europe to her cell. Though she is often called Blessed, there has never been any formal confirmation of this title. May 13.

JULITTA (d. c. 304). A wealthy Christian widow of noble background, she fled from Iconium in Lycaonia with her three-year-old son Cyriacus (or Quiricus) to Seleucia and then to Tarsus to escape Diocletian's persecution of the Christians. She was arrested there, tried before the governor, Alexander, and then tortured. When her son tried to escape from the governor to his mother saying he was a Christian, Alexander threw him down a flight of stairs, killing him. When further torture to make Julitta apostatize proved futile, she was beheaded on July 15. The story was extremely popular in the Middle Ages but in all probability was a pious legend. An extensive cult developed in France when St. Amator, bishop of Auxerre, supposedly brought back the reputed relics of Cyriacus to France in the fourth century. Cyriacus is known in France as Cyr. June 16.

JULITTA OF CAESAREA (d. c. 303). A wealthy widow of Caesarea, Cappadocia, she was obliged to go to court to defend her estate from the claims of a neighbor. When his claims were rejected by the court, he denounced her as a Christian. When she refused to sacrifice to the pagan gods, her estates were handed over to her opponent and she was burned to death for her faith. July 30.

JULIUS (d. c. 302). A retired soldier of the Roman army, he was accused of being a Christian at Durostorum (Silistria, Bulgaria) before Maximus, governor of Lower Moesia. When Julius refused to recant, he was beheaded. On his way to be beheaded, on May 27, he was encouraged by a fellow Christian soldier, Hesychius, who was executed a few days later. On May 25 at the same place, Pasicrates and Valentino were also executed for their faith.

JULIUS (d. c. 304). He and Aaron, two Britons, were reportedly executed for their faith at Caerlon, Monmouthshire, England, during Diocletian's persecution of the Christians. Since Diocletian's decrees about the Christians were not enforced in Britain, some authorities have reservations about their martyrdom. July 3.

JULIUS I (d. 352). Son of a Roman named Rusticus, he was elected Pope to succeed Pope St. Mark on February 6, 337. Julius was soon involved in the Arian controversy when Eusebius of Nicomedia opposed the return of Athanasius to the see of Alexandria in 338. Eusebius and his followers elected George, whereupon the Arians elected Pistus. Julius convened a synod in Rome in 340 or 341 that neither group attended, and in a letter to the Eusebian bishops, Julian declared that Athanasius was the rightful bishop of Alexandria and reinstated him. The matter was not finally settled until the Council of Sardica (Sofia), summoned by Emperors Constans and Constantius in 342 or 343, declared Julius' action correct and that any deposed bishop had the right of appeal to the Pope in Rome. Julius built several basilicas and churches in Rome and died there on April 12.

JUSTA (d. c. 287). She and her sister Rufina earned their living by selling pottery in Seville, Spain, during Diocletian's persecution of the Christians. When they refused to sell their wares to be used in pagan ceremonies, their stock was destroyed. In retaliation, they destroyed the image of a pagan goddess, were denounced as Christians, and were tortured and executed, Justa on the rack and Rufina by strangling. July 19.

JUSTIN MARTYR (c. 100–c. 165). Born at Flavia Neapolis, of pagan Greco-Roman parents, he studied philosophy, rhetoric, history, and poetry, and was inspired by a meeting with an old man at Ephesus, where he taught for a time, to study Christian Scripture. When about thirty, Justin became a Christian and devoted himself to expounding his new faith to his fellow men. He traveled about debating with pagan philosophers and eventually he came to Rome, where he opened a school of philosophy. He incurred the enmity of a Cynic named Crescens for besting him in debate and was denounced, probably at the instigation of Crescens, to the authorities as a Christian. He was brought to trial with six companions, Charita, Chariton, Euelpistus, Hierax, Liberianus, and Paeon, before the Roman prefect, Rusticus. When they refused to sacrifice to the gods, they were scourged and beheaded. Justin is the first Christian apologist, and layman, to have written on Christianity at any length, and in his writings he sought to reconcile the claims of faith and reason. Two of his most important works are still extant: His *Apologies,* addressed to Emperor Antoninus and the first document addressed to the enemies of Christianity, defends the Christians, replies to charges of immorality leveled against them, explains how they are loyal subjects based on their beliefs in the teaching of Christ, and goes on to explain immortality, free will, and fasting; and *Dialogue with Trypho,* in which he debates the merits of Christianity over Judaism in a dialogue with Trypho, a Jew. June 1.

JUSTINA (no date). *See* Cyprian.

JUSTINA OF AREZZO. *See* Bizzoli, Francuccia.

JUSTINA OF PADUA (date unknown). All that is known of her is from an apparent twelfth-century forgery that says she was baptized by St. Prosdocimus, a disciple of St. Peter and reputed first

bishop of Padua, and was then martyred for her faith. October 7.

JUSTUS (d. c. 304). He and his brother Pastor, thirteen and nine, respectively, were scourged and then beheaded at Complutum (Alcalà, Spain) during Diocletian's persecution of the Christians by Dacian, governor of Spain, when they proclaimed their faith while he was interrogating suspected Christians. They are the patrons of Alcalà and Madrid. August 6.

JUSTUS OF BEAUVAIS (d. 297). According to his completely fictitious legend, nine-year-old Justus lived at Auxerre with his father, Justin, during Diocletian's persecution of the Christians. The two went to Amiens to ransom Justin's brother Justinian, who was a slave there. Justin was unable to pick out his brother from the other slaves, but Justus who had never seen his uncle, did. Justus was reported to the governor, Rictiovarus, as a Christian magician, and Rictiovarus sent four soldiers after them. They caught up with Justus at Sinomovicus (Saint Just-en-Chaussee) near Beauvais, but he was alone, and they demanded to know where his companions were (they were hiding in a nearby cave) and the names of the gods to whom they sacrificed. Justus replied that he was a Christian, whereupon one of the soldiers struck off his head. When the body stood upright with its head in its hands, the soldiers fled. October 18.

JUSTUS OF CANTERBURY (d. c. 627). Among the missionaries sent to Britain by Pope St. Gregory the Great to aid St. Augustine in 601 was a Benedictine named Justus. He was consecrated first bishop of Rochester by Augustine in 604, but when the death of King Ethelbert in 616 caused a revival of paganism in his Kingdom of Kent under his son and successor Eadbald, Justus returned to Gaul with Mellitus of London. Justus came back to Britain the following year and succeeded St. Laurence as fourth archbishop of Canterbury in 624. It was Justus who consecrated St. Paulinus when Paulinus accompanied Ethelburga of Kent to her marriage with King Edward of Northumbria. November 10.

JUSTUS OF LYONS (d. c. 390). Born in the Vivarais in southeastern France, he became a deacon at Vienne and in 350 was named bishop of Lyons. Distraught when a prisoner who had sought sanctuary in his church was put to death despite assurances to Justus that he would not be executed, Justus secretly left the Council of Aquileia he was attending in 381 and went to Alexandria with a deacon named Viator and joined a monastery in Egypt anonymously. Justus was discovered there by a visitor from Gaul but refused the request of Antiochus, a priest sent by the Lyonnais to convince him to return to his see, and died at the monastery. October 14.

JUSTUS OF URGEL (d. c. 550). First bishop of Urgel, Spain, he attended the Councils of Toledo in 527 and Lérida in 546 and wrote a commentary on the Canticle of Canticles. May 28.

JUTTA (d. 1260). Born at Sangerhausen, Thuringia, she was married at fifteen to a nobleman. After he died on a pilgrimage to the Holy Land and her children had grown up, she gave her wealth to the poor, lived in extreme poverty, and tended the sick. She moved to Prussia, where she became a recluse at Kulmsee and died there four years later. She experienced visions and was reputed to have performed miracles and to have experienced levitation. May 6.

JUTTA OF DIESSENBERG, BL. (d. 1136). Sister of Count Meginhard of

Spanheim, she became a recluse at a house in Diessenberg adjoining St. Disibod's Monastery and attracted numerous disciples, whom she formed into a community of which she was prioress. St. Hildegard was entrusted to her when a child, and Jutta raised and educated her. December 22.

JUTTA OF HUY, BL. (1158–1228). Born at Huy near Liège, Netherlands, she was married when a child and was widowed with three children at eighteen. She refused marriage to several suitors, spent ten years tending lepers, and from 1182 until her death lived as a recluse in a walled cell next to the leper house. She had a reputation for holiness and spiritual wisdom, had the ability to read men's minds, and had the gift of prophecy. She is also known as Ivetta. January 13.

JUVENAL (d. c. 376). A priest and physician from the East, he immigrated to Narni, Italy, and was named first bishop of that see by Pope Damasus. Juvenal is reported to have saved Narni from destruction by invading Ligurians and Sarmatians when thousands of the invaders were drowned in a downpour reputedly brought on by his prayers. He was noted for his eloquent preaching, which converted many, and is the patron of Narni. May 3.

JUVENTINUS (d. 363). He and Maximinus were officers in the guard of Julian the Apostate. During a campaign against the Persians, they were overheard decrying the Emperor's edicts against the veneration of relics. Haled before Julian, they were stripped of their estates, scourged, and beheaded at Antioch on January 25 when they refused to recant and sacrifice to the pagan gods. St. John Chrysostom wrote their eulogy.

K

KAGGWA, CHARLES. *See* Lwanga, Charles.

KALINOWSKI, RAPHAEL (1835–1907). As a twenty-eight-year-old Russian military officer, Kalinowski left the service and joined the Polish uprising, in which he took a leading role. He was captured by the Russian army and sentenced to a decade of hard labor in Siberia. Following his release, he pursued a long-delayed religious vocation and became a Carmelite priest. A noted confessor, he was canonized in 1991.

KARASUMARU, LEO (d. 1597). A native of Korea, he became a pagan priest and then was converted to Christianity and baptized by the Jesuits in Japan in 1589. He became the first Korean Franciscan tertiary and was the chief catechist for the Friars. During the persecution of the Christians in Japan by the *taikō*, Toyotomi Hideyoshi, he and twenty-five other Catholics were crucified near Nagasaki on February 5. With him was crucified his brother Paul Ibaraki and their twelve-year-old nephew Louis Ibaraki. They were all canonized as the Martyrs of Japan in 1862. February 6.

KATERI TEKAKWITHA, BL. *See* Tekakwitha, Bl. Kateri.

KATHERINE. *See* Catherine.

KEMBLE, JOHN (1599–1679). Born of Catholic parents at St. Weonard's, Herefordshire, England, he went to Douai to study for the priesthood and was ordained there in 1625. He was sent on the English mission and worked in Herefordshire and Monmouthshire for fifty-three years. He became a victim of the Titus Oates plot hysteria and was arrested in 1678 at Pembridge Castle, his brother's home, which he had used as his headquarters, and charged with complicity in the Titus Oates plot to assassinate King Charles II. When no evidence was found of his involvement in that notorious fraudulent "plot" when he was examined by the Privy Council in London, he was found guilty of being a Catholic priest. He was hanged, drawn, and quartered at Hereford on August 22 when he was eighty years old. He was canonized by Pope Paul VI in 1970 as one of the martyrs of England and Wales.

KENELM (d. c. 812). According to a popular legend of the Middle Ages, he was seven when his father, King Kenulf of Mercia, died, and he succeeded to the throne. His sister Quendreda bribed his teacher, Ascebert, to murder him so she could claim the throne. Ascebert did, but when the body was discovered and enshrined at Winchcombe in Gloucestershire, all kinds of marvels occurred at his grave. All three are actual figures, but Kenelm did not die at seven and may even have died before his father. July 17.

KENNETH. *See* Canice.

KENNOCH. *See* Mochoemoc.

KENTIGERN (c. 518–603). Also known as Mungo ("dear one" or "darling"), his mother was a British princess named Thenaw (or Thaney or Theneva). When it was discovered that she was pregnant of an unknown man, she was hurled from a cliff and, when discovered alive at the foot of the cliff, was set adrift in a boat on the Firth of Forth. She reached Culross, was given shelter by St. Serf, and gave birth to a child to whom Serf gave the name Mungo (darling). Raised by the saint, he became a hermit at Glasghu (Glasgow) and was so renowned for his holiness that he was consecrated bishop of Strathclyde about 540. Driven to flight because of the feuds among the neighboring chieftains, he went to Wales, met St. David at Menevia, and founded a monastery at Llanelwy. About 553, Kentigern returned to Scotland, settled at Hoddam, and then returned to Glasghu, where he spent his last days. He is considered the first bishop of Scotland and with Thenaw (July 18) is joint patron of Glasgow. January 14.

KENTIGERNA (d. 734). Daughter of Prince Cellach of Leinster, she left Ireland on the death of her husband and went, with her son Fillan, to Scotland, where she lived as a hermitess on the island of Inchebroida in Loch Lomond and died there on January 7.

KESSOG (d. c. 560). Son of the King of Cashel where he was born, he left Ireland to go to Scotland as a missionary and was consecrated a missionary bishop. Using Monks' Island in Loch Lomonad as his headquarters, he evangelized the surrounding area until he was martyred, though where is uncertain—some claim at Bandry, and others abroad. Many extravagant miracles were ascribed to him. March 10.

KEUMURGIAN, BL. GOMIDAS (c. 1656–1707). Born at Constantinople, the son of a dissident Armenian priest, he married when twenty, was ordained, and was assigned to St. George Armenian Church. He became known for his eloquence and religious fervor, and in 1696, when he was forty, with his wife, was reconciled to Rome. He stayed on at St. George's, and his success in reuniting five of the twelve priests there to Rome caused much opposition from the dissidents, who complained to the Turkish authorities. He then went to Jerusalem, where his activities at St. James Armenian Monastery incurred the opposition of a John of Smyrna. When Gomidas returned to Constantinople in 1702, John was vicar of Patriarch Avedik. Avedik was exiled for a time to Cyprus, and while there was kidnaped by the French ambassador. This angered the dissidents and they persuaded the Turkish authorities to move against the Catholics. Gomidas was arrested in 1707 and condemned to the galleys, but was ransomed by friends. He continued to preach reunion with Rome and was again arrested later in the same year at the instigation of dissident Armenian priests. By now John of Smyrna had become patriarch of the Armenians. Gomidas was accused of being a Frank (which meant being either a foreigner or a Latin Catholic), though he had been born in Constantinople, and of fomenting trouble among the Armenians in the city. Though the judge, Mustafa Kamal, the chief kadi, knew Gomidas was an Armenian priest, Kamal was unable to do anything in the case when a stream of perjured witnesses testified that Gomidas was a troublemaker, a Frank, and an agent of hostile Western powers, and Gomidas was found guilty. He was offered his freedom if he would apostatize to Islam, and was beheaded at Parmark-Kapu, on the outskirts of Constantinople, when he refused. He is sometimes mistakenly called Cosimo di Carbognano, but this was his son's name. Gomidas was beatified in 1929. November 5.

KEVIN (d. c. 618). Known in Ireland as Coemgen as well as Kevin, according to tradition he was born at the Fort of the White Fountain in Leinster, Ireland, of royal descent. He was baptized by St. Cronan and educated by St. Petroc, was ordained, and became a hermit at the Valley of the Two Lanes in Glendalough. After seven years there he was persuaded to give up his solitary life, went to Disert-Coemgen, where he founded a monastery for the disciples he attracted, and later moved to Glendalough. He made a pilgrimage to Rome, bringing back many relics for his permanent foundation at Glendalough, was a friend of St. Kieran of Clonmacnois, and was entrusted with the raising of the son of King Colman of Ui Faelain by the King. Many extravagant miracles were attributed to Kevin, and he was reputed to be 120 at his death. June 3.

KEVOCA. *See* Mochoemoc.

KEYNA (6th century). One of the twenty-four children of King Brychan of Brecknock, Wales, she refused several suitors' offers of marriage and became a hermitess on the banks of the Severn River in Somersetshire, England. After living there for several years, during which she traveled widely, she was persuaded by her nephew, St. Cadoc, to return to Wales, though exactly where she spent her last days is not known. During her travels, she founded numerous churches in South Wales, Cornwall, and perhaps Somerset. October 8.

KIERAN OF CLONMACNOIS (d. c. 556). Born in Connacht, Ireland, the son of Beoit, a carpenter, he studied at St.

Finnian's School at Clonard and taught the daughter of the King of Cuala, as he was considered the most learned monk at Clonard. Kieran spent seven years at Inishmore on Aran with St. Enda and then went to a monastery in the center of Ireland called Isel. Forced to leave by the monks because of what they considered his excessive charity, he spent some time on Inis Aingin (Hare island) and with eight companions migrated to a spot on the bank of the Shannon River in Offaly, where he built a monastery that became the famous Clonmacnois, renowned for centuries as the great center of Irish learning, and was its abbot. Many extravagant miracles and tales are told of Kieran, who is one of the Twelve Apostles of Ireland. He is often called St. Kieran the Younger to distinguish him from St. Kieran of Saighir. September 9.

KIERAN OF SAIGHIR (d. c. 530). Often called St. Kieran the Elder, to distinguish him from St. Kieran of Clonmacnois, and Cieran, the story of his life is based on conflicting and untrustworthy legends according to which he was born in Ossory (or Cork), went to Rome when he was thirty to learn more about his religion, and was consecrated bishop (some say in Rome; others that he was one of the twelve consecrated by St. Patrick when he arrived in Ireland). He lived for a time as a hermit, attracted numerous disciples, and built a monastery that developed into the town of Saighir; he is considered the first bishop of Ossory. His legend is replete with extravagant miracles and tall tales. March 5.

KILIAN (d. c. 689). An Irish monk, he was consecrated bishop, went to Rome with eleven companions in 686, and received permission from Pope Conon to evangelize Franconia (Baden and Bavaria). He was successful, with two followers—Colman, a priest, and

Totnan, a deacon—in his missionary endeavors until he converted Gosbert, duke of Würzburg, who had married Geilana, his brother's widow. According to legend, while Gosbert was away on a military expedition, Geilana is reputed to have had the three missionaries beheaded when she found that Gosbert was going to leave her after Kilian had told him the marriage was forbidden by the Church. July 8.

KILIAN (7th century). A relative of St. Fiacre, he was born in Ireland and became a missionary in Artois, Gaul. November 13.

KIM, BL. AGATHA (d. 1839). *See* Imbert, Bl. Laurence.

KIMURA, BL. LEONARD (1574–1619). A Japanese of noble birth, he was converted to Christianity, became a temporal coadjutor (lay brother) in the Jesuits, and was arrested for his Christianity. He was imprisoned for two and a half years and then, with four fellow Christians was burned to death for his faith at Nagasaki in a spectacle reportedly witnessed by 20,000 people on November 18.

KIMURA, SEBASTIAN (d. 1622). Reportedly a grandson of the first Japanese baptized by St. Francis Xavier, Sebastian joined the Jesuits when eighteen, was a catechist at Meaco, Japan, and was ordained—the first Japanese to become a priest. Imprisoned for two years at Omura for his Christianity with Bl. Charles Spinoza, Sebastian was brought to Nagasaki and both were burned to death there on September 10. Sebastian was beatified in 1867.

KINGA. *See* Cunegunda (d. 1292).

KINUYA, LEO (1569–97). *See* Miki, Paul.

KIRBY, LUKE (d. 1582). Born at Bedale, Yorkshire, England, he graduated from Cambridge, became a Catholic, and in 1576 went to Douai to study for the priesthood. After further study at Rome, he was ordained in 1577, was sent on the English mission in 1580, and was soon arrested and charged with conspiring against the Queen, though in reality because he was a Catholic priest. He was imprisoned in the Tower in London, subjected to the terrible torture known as "the scavenger's daughter," and then hanged, drawn, and quartered at Tyburn on May 30. He was canonized by Pope Paul VI in 1970 as one of the Forty Martyrs of England and Wales.

KIRKMAN, BL. RICHARD (d. 1582). Born at Addington, Yorkshire, England, he studied at Douai and was ordained at Rheims in 1579. He was sent on the English mission and became tutor to the three sons of Robert Dymoke, hereditary Champion of England, at Scrivelsby, Lincolnshire. When Dymoke was indicted for not attending Anglican services, Fr. Kirkman fled. He ministered to the Catholics of Yorkshire and Northumberland until he was arrested near Wakefield. He was sentenced to death for being a Catholic priest and for refusing to acknowledge the spiritual supremacy of Queen Elizabeth I and was hanged, drawn, and quartered, with Bl. William Lacey, at Knavesmire outside York on August 22. Bl. Richard was beatified in 1886.

KISAI, JAMES (1533–97). A native Japanese, he became a Jesuit catechist at Osaka, was secular coadjutor of the Jesuits in Japan, and was crucified for his faith on February 5 near Nagasaki with twenty-five other Catholics during the persecution of Christians by the *taikō*, Toyotomi Hideyoshi. They were all canonized in 1862.

KIZITO, BL. *See* Lwanga, Charles.

KNIGHT, VEN. WILLIAM (d. 1596). Born at South Duffield, England, he was imprisoned at York when he tried to collect his inheritance when he came of age and was denounced to the authorities as a Catholic by his uncle. A Protestant minister, a fellow prisoner, to whom he explained Catholicism, when released denounced Knight for proselytizing and also betrayed Henry Abbot of Howden, Yorkshire, who Knight had told him could direct him to a priest for further instruction. Abbot was arrested and both of them were hanged, drawn, and quartered at York on November 29, with George Errington of Herst and William Gibson of Ripon, who had been arrested with Knight.

KOA, BL. PETER (d. 1838). *See* Dumoulin-Borie, Bl. Peter.

KOLBE, MAXIMILIAN (1894–1941). Born at Zdunska-Wola, near Lodz, Poland, on January 7 and baptized Raymond, he joined the Conventual Franciscans, taking the name Maximilian. He pronounced his temporary vows in 1911 and in 1917 founded the Militia of Mary Immaculate in Rome to advance devotion to Mary. He was ordained in Rome in 1918, returned to Poland, and founded *Militia of the Immaculate Mary,* a monthly bulletin. In 1927, he founded Niepokalanów ("cities of the Immaculate Conception") about twenty-five miles from Warsaw to house some eight hundred religious and established similar foundations in Japan and India. He became superior of the Polish Niepokalanów in 1936, and in 1941 was arrested by the Gestapo when the Germans invaded Poland, and imprisoned in the notorious prison camp in Auschwitz in Poland. He took the place of a married man with a family who was one of ten men arbitrarily selected by the commandant to be executed in retaliation for a prisoner who had escaped. Fr. Kolbe was killed on August 14 by an injection of carbolic acid, and was beatified by Pope Paul VI in 1971.

KOREA, MARTYRS OF (1839–1867). During three waves of persecutions in the first two-thirds of the nineteenth century, hundreds of Christians were killed. The 103 Korean martyrs include fourteen catechists, two bishops, and seven priests. They were canonized in 1984. September 20.

KÖRÖSY, BL. MARK (d. 1619). Of a well-known Croat family, he studied at the Germanicum in Rome, was ordained, and returned to Esztergom, Hungary, where he became a canon. With two Jesuits—Stephen Pongracz, a Hungarian, and Melchior Grodecz, a Czech—he was assigned to missionary work near Kaschau (Kosice, Slovakia). In 1619, they were arrested by the invading Calvinist troops under George Racoczk, tortured, and executed. They were beatified in 1905. The Anglicized version of his name is Crisin. September 7.

KOSAKI, MICHAEL (d. 1597). A Japanese catechist and a hospital nurse working under the Franciscan missionaries in Japan, he was crucified for his faith on February 5 at Nagasaki with a group of Christians. Among them was his son, fifteen-year-old Thomas, an altar boy for the Franciscans in Nagasaki. They were all canonized as the Martyrs of Japan in 1862. His name is sometimes spelled Cozachi.

KOSAKI, THOMAS (d. 1597). *See* Kosaki, Michael.

KOSTKA, STANISLAUS (1550–68). Son of a Polish senator and born in Rostkovo Castle in Poland about October 28, he was educated by a private tutor and then sent to the Jesuit college in Vienna when he was fourteen. He was soon known for his studious ways, deep religious fervor, and mortifications. After he recovered from a serious illness during which he experienced several visions, he decided to join the Jesuits. Opposed by his father and refused admission by the Vienna provincial, who feared the father's reaction if he admitted the youth, Stanislaus walked 350 miles to Dillengen where Peter Canisius, provincial of Upper Germany, took him in and then sent him to Rome, where Francis Borgia, father general of the Society of Jesus, accepted him into the Jesuits in 1567, when he was seventeen. He practiced the most severe mortifications, experienced ecstasies at Mass, and lived a life of great sanctity. He died in Rome on August 15, only nine months after joining the Jesuits, and was canonized in 1726. He is one of the lesser patrons of Poland. November 13.

KUMMERNIS. *See* Wilgefortis.

L

LABOURÉ, CATHERINE (1806–76). Daughter of a farmer, she was born at Fain-les-Moutiers, France, on May 2 and named Zoé. She never went to school, as her mother died when she was eight, and she took care of the family. She joined the Sisters of Charity of St. Vincent de Paul at Chatillon in 1830, taking the name Catherine, and was sent to the Rue du Bac Convent in Paris. Almost at once she began to experience a series of visions of our Lady in the chapel of the convent, and in several of them was asked by the Lady in the vision to strike a medal showing the Lady and honoring the Immaculate Conception. Her confessor, Fr. Aladel, secured permission from Archbishop Quelen of Paris to have the medals struck, and in 1832 the first fifteen hundred of what were to be millions of medals were minted—the famous Miraculous Medal. The visions were approved as authentic in 1836 by a special commission appointed by the archbishop, and the popularity of the medal spread all over the world. Catherine spent the years from 1831 until her death performing menial tasks at the Hospice d'Enghien, revealing none of her visions to any but her confessor until a few months before her death on December 31 at Enghien. A widespread popular cult developed on her death, and she was canonized in 1947. November 28.

LABRE, BENEDICT JOSEPH (1748–83). Born at Amettes, France, on March 25, the eldest of eighteen children, he studied under his uncle, the parish priest at Erin, was unsuccessful in attempts to join the Trappists, Carthusians, and Cistercians, and in 1770 made pilgrimages to many of the major shrines in Europe. In 1774, he stayed in Rome, lived in the Colosseum, and became known as "the beggar of Rome" for his poverty and sanctity. He was noted for his attendance at and devotion to Forty Hours' devotion, died in Rome on April 16, and was canonized in 1883.

LACEY, BL. BRIAN (d. 1582). Born in Yorkshire, England, he was betrayed to the authorities by his brother, arrested, and when convicted of aiding a priest, was hanged at Tyburn on December 10.

LACEY, BL. WILLIAM (d. 1582). Born at Horton, West Riding, Yorkshire, England, he studied law, became a lawyer, and held an official position in the county. Suspected of being a Catholic because of the many visitors to his home, he was deprived of his position in 1565 and subjected to frequent prosecutions, fines, and imprisonment over the next fourteen months for his Catholicism. He finally fled, and when his second wife died in 1579, he went to Rheims the following year and then to Rome, where he was ordained. He was sent on the English mission in 1581, ministered to the Catholics of Yorkshire, but was captured the following year while assisting at a secret High Mass being celebrated by Fr. Thomas Bell while visiting Catholic prisoners in York Castle. After three weeks in prison he was condemned to death for refusing to acknowledge the ecclesiastical supremacy of the Queen and was hanged, drawn, and quartered on August 22 at the Knavesmire outside York. He was beatified in 1886.

LACOPS, JAMES (d. 1572). Born at Oudenaar, Holland, he became a Premonstratensian priest but led a frivolous life and neglected his religious duties. He later reformed and became a curate at Monster and was arrested with Adrian van Hilvarenbeek when the Calvinists captured Gorkum. James was sent with other Catholic prisoners to Brielle, where they were all summarily executed on July 9 when they refused to deny papal supremacy and Catholic teaching on the Blessed Sacrament. They were canonized as the Martyrs of Gorkum in 1867.

LADISLAUS OF GIELNIOW, BL. (1440–1505). Born at Gielniow, Poland, he was educated at the University of Warsaw and joined the Franciscans of the Observance there. He served as provincial several times, drew up a revised constitution for his Order, which was approved by a general chapter at Urbino in 1498, and was a successful missionary and an eloquent preacher. When the Tartars were threatening Warsaw in 1498, his prayers were credited with saving the city when a snowstorm, freezing weather, and floods decimated their forces; they were then put to rout by Prince Stephen. Ladislaus was credited with possessing supernatural gifts, among them the ability to levitate. He died at Warsaw on May 4, and was beatified in 1586. He is one of the patrons of Poland, Galicia, and Lithuania. May 11.

LADISLAUS OF HUNGARY (1040–95). Son of King Bela of Hungary, he was born at Neustra on July 29 and was elected King of Hungary by the nobles in 1077. He was at once faced with the claims of a relative and son of a former King, Solomon, to the throne, and defeated him on the battlefield in 1089. He supported Pope Gregory VII in his investiture struggle against Emperor Henry IV, and Rupert of Swabia, Henry's rival; Ladislaus married Adelaide, daughter of Duke Welf of Bavaria, one of Rupert's supporters. Ladislaus successfully repelled Cuman attempts to invade Hungary, encouraged Christian missionaries, and built many churches, but allowed religious freedom to the Jews and Mohammedans in his realms. In 1091, he marched to the aid of his sister Helen, Queen of Croatia, against the murderers of her husband, and when she died childless, annexed Croatia and Dalmatia despite objections from the Pope, the Emperor in Constantinople, and Venice. At the Synod of Szabolcs in 1092, he promulgated a series of laws on religious and civil matters. He was chosen to lead the armies of the First Crusade but before he could do so died at Nitra, Bohemia, on July 29. He is one of the great national heroes of Hungary and made Hungary a great state, extending its borders and defending it successfully against invasion. He was venerated from the time of his death for his zeal, piety, and moral life, and was canonized in 1192 by Pope Celestine III. Ladislaus is known in Hungary as Laszlo. June 27.

LAETANTIUS (d. 180). *See* Speratus.

LAETUS (d. c. 484). *See* Donatian.

LAISREN. *See* Laserian.

LALANDE, JOHN DE (d. 1646). Born at Dieppe, France, he went to Quebec, Canada, where he became a *donné* (lay assistant) to the Jesuit missionaries there.

In 1646, he accompanied Isaac Jogues on a trip to the territory of the Iroquois Indians after a peace treaty with them had just been signed. They were captured by a war party of Mohawks, and John was tomahawked and beheaded at Ossernenon near Albany, New York, on October 19, the day after Fr. Jogues had suffered a similar fate there. They were canonized by Pope Pius XI in 1930 as two of the Martyrs of North America.

LALEMENT, GABRIEL (1610–49). Born at Paris, France, he joined the Jesuits in 1630, taught at Moulins for three years, and after further study at Bourges, was ordained in 1638. After teaching at La Flèche and Moulins, he was sent to New France (Canada) at his request in 1646 as a missionary. He worked among the Hurons, became assistant to St. John de Brébeuf at St. Ignace in 1649, and was with him in the village when the Iroquois, traditional enemies of the Hurons, attacked and destroyed it on March 16, killing all the inhabitants except the two priests. After torturing them, the Iroquois tomahawked them to death the next day. They were canonized by Pope Pius XI in 1930 as two of the Martyrs of North America. October 19.

LAMBERT OF LYONS (d. 688). Raised from childhood at the court of King Clotaire III, he became a monk at Fontenelles under St. Wandregisilus and in 666 succeeded him as abbot. He founded the abbey of Donzère and about 679 was named archbishop of Lyons. April 14.

LAMBERT OF MAESTRICHT (c. 635–c. 705). Born of a noble family at Maestricht, Flanders, he was educated by St. Theodard and was chosen to succeed him as bishop of Tongres-Maestricht in 668 when Theodard was murdered. Lambert was expelled from

his see by Ebroin, mayor of the palace, for his support of Childeric II when the King was murdered in 674, and Lambert retired to Stavelot Monastery. When Ebroin was murdered in 681, his successor, Pepin of Herstal, reinstated Lambert, who devoted himself to building a convent at Munsterbilzen, converting pagans in the area, and tending his flock. He denounced Pepin for his adulterous affair with Alpais, sister of his wife, Plectrudis, and was murdered in Liège, allegedly by Alpais' brother, Dodo, and a group of his followers. Another version is that Lambert was killed with two relatives, Peter and Andolet, who had killed relatives of Dodo. September 17.

LAMBERT PÉLOGUIN OF VENCE (c. 1080–1154). Born at Bauduen near Riez, France, he was raised at Lérins Abbey and became a monk there. In 1114, against his will, he was named bishop of Vence in Provence and ruled there, noted for his learning and miracles, for the next forty years. May 26.

LAMBERTINI, BL. IMELDA (1322–33). Daughter of Count Egano Lambertini and Castora Galuzzi, she was born at Bologna, Italy, was exceptionally pious as a child, and was sent to the Dominican convent of Val di Pietra in Bologna when nine. She had great devotion to the Eucharist and reputedly, when eleven, unexpectedly received her first communion on the feast of the Assumption when after Mass one day a Host hovered over her head and was quickly given to her by the priest. Overcome with intense joy, she collapsed and died immediately. Her cult was confirmed in 1826. May 13.

LANDELINUS (c. 625–86). Born at Vaux, France, of Frankish parents, he was educated by St. Aubert, bishop of Cambrai. When eighteen, he joined a group of youths living a life of crime and violence but changed his lifestyle completely when one of his companions was killed, and he became a hermit at Lobbes. He soon attracted disciples by his holiness and in 654 formed them into a monastery with St. Ursmar its abbot. He left and went to Aulne and then Wallens, where disciples again gathered around him and finally, in search of solitude, he went to Crespin in 670, where he again organized the followers he attracted into an abbey, of which he served as abbot until his death. June 15.

LANDERICUS OF PARIS (d. c. 660). Also known as Landry, he became bishop of Paris in 650 and was known for his devotion to the poor, at one time selling church fixtures to provide food for them during a famine. He also founded St. Christopher's Hospital, which eventually grew into the world-famous Hôtel-Dieu. June 10.

LANDOALD (d. c. 668). According to untrustworthy sources, he was a Lombard, became a priest in Rome, and was selected by Pope St. Martin I to accompany St. Amand and a group of companions as missionaries to the Netherlands. He was very successful in the Maestricht area, built a church at Wintershoven, and was supported in his work by King Childeric II of Austrasia. March 19.

LANDRY. *See* Landericus of Paris.

LANEL, BL. FRANÇOISE (1745–94). *See* Fontaine, Bl. Madeleine.

LANFRANC, BL. (c. 1005–89). Born at Pavia, Italy, he studied law there, was a lawyer for a time, and in about 1035 went to France. He continued his studies at Avranches, Normandy, taught there, and in 1042 became a monk at Bec. He was made prior in 1045 and head of the monastery school, which

under him became famous for its scholarship. He became embroiled in the quarrel over the Eucharist with Berengar and was brought by Pope Leo IX to the Councils of Rome and Vercelli in 1050, where Berengar was condemned. Lanfranc's opposition to the proposed marriage of Duke William of Normandy to Matilda of Flanders in 1053 caused William to draw up a decree of exile, but the two were reconciled, and Lanfranc became a close adviser of the Duke and secured a papal dispensation for the marriage in 1059. Lanfranc was appointed abbot of St. Stephen's in Caen about 1063, accompanied William on his conquest of England, and was named archbishop of Canterbury in 1070. He brought Norman practices to the English Church, built churches, founded new sees, and in 1072 compelled the archbishop of York to accept the primacy of Canterbury when a council of bishops and abbots of Winchester so decreed. Lanfranc was regent for William in 1074 and put down a revolt against the Conqueror, fought any secular intrusion on ecclesiastical rights, and in 1076, at a synod at Winchester, ordered clerical celibacy for future ordinands. Though he persuaded William to name his son William Rufus his heir to the throne and crowned him on his father's death in 1087, he never had the influence over William Rufus that he had had over William. Lanfranc's *De Sacramento Corporis et Sanguinis Christi* became the classic statement of transubstantiation in the Middle Ages. He died at Canterbury on May 24, and though he has always been honored with the title Blessed, there does not seem to have ever been any public cult.

LANCFRANC BECCARIA OF PAVIA, BL. (d. 1194). Born at Grupello near Pavia, Italy, he became bishop of Pavia in 1179 and throughout his episcopate was involved in a dispute with the secular authorities over their attempts to seize part of the Church's properties and revenues. He had decided to resign and join the Vallumbrosans when he died. June 23.

LANG, BL. PAUL (d. 1900). *See* Mangin, Bl. Leon.

LANGHORNE, BL. RICHARD (d. 1679). Born in Bedfordshire, England, he read law at the Inner Temple, was admitted to the bar in 1654, and became a well-known lawyer. He was arrested in 1667 after the Great Fire of London and accused of helping Catholics who were blamed for the fire but was later released. He was again arrested in 1679 and accused of participating in the "popish plot," concocted by the notorious Titus Oates, to assassinate King Charles II, and held in solitary confinement for eight months. At his trial it was evident that Oates was perjuring himself, but despite this, Langhorne was convicted and was hanged at Tyburn on July 14. He was beatified in 1929.

LANGLEY, BL. RICHARD (d. 1586). Probably born at Grimthorpe, England, he inherited extensive estates there and at Ousethorpe, East Riding, which he used as hiding places for fugitive Catholic priests. When two priests were discovered at Grimthorpe, he was arrested at Ousethorpe, and when convicted of harboring Catholic priests was hanged, drawn, and quartered at York on December 1. He was beatified in 1929.

LANTRUA, BL. JOHN (1760–1816). Born at Triora, Italy, he joined the Franciscans in 1777 when he was seventeen and the following year was named guardian at Velletri near Rome. He volunteered for the foreign missions, was sent to China, and arrived there in 1798. He worked in Hupeh and Hunan provinces, was arrested for his Christian activities, and was imprisoned at

Changsha, capital of Hunan Province. Finally, he was strangled to death there on February 7. He was beatified in 1900.

LANVINUS, BL. (d. 1120). Born in Normandy, he joined the Carthusians at Grande Chartreuse about 1090 and accompanied St. Bruno to Calabria in 1101. He succeeded Bruno as superior of the two Calabrian Carthusian houses, attended a synod in Rome in 1102, and acted as papal legate in a dispute with a bishop in Calabria. He was appointed visitor of all monastic houses in Calabria in 1105 and instituted strict reforms. He died on April 11, and his cult was confirmed in 1893. April 14.

LARGUS (d. c. 304). *See* Cyriacus.

LARKE, BL. JOHN (d. 1544). Appointed rector of St. Ethelburga, Bishopsgate, England, in 1504 (a position he held almost until his death), he was also appointed rector of Woodford in Essex in 1526 but resigned to accept Thomas More's appointment as rector of Chelsea in 1530. John was arrested in 1544 and charged with treason, together with John Ireland, pastor of Eltham in Kent, and Jermyn Gardiner, secretary of Bishop Stephen Gardiner of Winchester and a layman who had been educated at Cambridge, for refusing to acknowledge the ecclesiastical supremacy of King Henry VIII. They were executed at Tyburn on March 7. John Larke and Jermyn Gardiner were beatified in 1886; John Ireland in 1929. March 11.

LA SALLE, JOHN BAPTIST DE (1651–1719). Born at Rheims, France, on April 30, the eldest of ten children of a wealthy and noble family, he was tonsured at eleven, became a canon at Rheims in 1667, studied at St. Sulpice Seminary in Paris, 1670–72, and was ordained in 1678. He was sent to Rheims, met Adrian Nyel, a layman who was opening a school for poor boys in 1679, and became involved in educational work. He resigned his canonry in 1683, distributed his fortune to the poor in 1684, and devoted himself to improving the caliber of teachers. He began to attract men desirous of receiving his training and formed twelve of his teachers into the Institute of the Brothers of the Christian Schools (which did not receive papal approval until 1725). He began to establish teachers' colleges (Rheims in 1687, Paris in 1699, Saint-Denis in 1709) and established a junior novitiate in 1685 for younger men. He steadily increased the number of schools for boys under his control. He decided to exclude priests from his institute and in about 1695 drew up in Paris a draft of his rule in which it was stated that no Christian Brother could become a priest and no priest could become a Christian Brother, and wrote his *Conduite des écoles Chrétiennes,* revolutionizing teaching methods by replacing individual instruction with classroom teaching; it also required teaching in the vernacular rather than in Latin. In 1698 he opened a college for the Irish followers of King James II of England who had followed him into exile in France. In later years he encountered opposition from secular teachers for his ideas and reported severity to novices, for which he was officially deposed in 1702. However, he remained in control of the Institute when the brothers all threatened to leave. Later, spurred by the Jansenists, an attack on teaching anything but manual education to poor students caused his schools in Paris to be closed, but the storm soon subsided, and they reopened. His schools spread to Italy and in time all over the world. He established a reformatory for boys at Dijon in 1705, and in 1717 a school for adult prisoners. He resigned in 1717 and died at St. Yon, Rouen, where he had retired to spend the last years of his life, on April 7. He

was canonized by Pope Leo XIII in 1900 and was named patron of teachers by Pope Pius XII in 1950.

LASERIAN (d. 639). Also known as Molaisse, he was at the monastery on Iona for several years and then went to Rome, where he was ordained by Pope St. Gregory the Great. He then went to the monastery at Leighlin in southern Ireland, firmly supported the Roman liturgical usages and date for Easter against the Celtic practices at a synod at nearby White Fields, and was sent to Rome in 635 with a group of monks when the synod reached an impasse, to have the matter resolved by Pope Honorius I. While there Laserian was consecrated bishop and named papal legate to Ireland, and on his return settled the matter in southern Ireland by decreeing in favor of the Roman practices. In 637, he succeeded his brother St. Goban as abbot of Leighlin, of which he also acted as bishop. April 18.

LASZLO. *See* Ladislaus of Hungary.

LATINI, BL. BERNARD (1605–67). A shoemaker at Corleone, Sicily, Philip Latini became an expert swordsman, was involved in several brushes with the law, and after seeking sanctuary in a church after having wounded a police officer in 1632, decided to mend his ways. He became a Capuchin lay brother, taking the name Bernard, practiced severe austerities and penances, and was known for his supernatural gifts—miracles, prophecies, ecstasies, and levitation. He died at Palermo on January 12, and was beatified in 1768.

LAUREL, BL. BARTHOLOMEW (d. 1627). Born at Mexico City, he joined the Franciscans as a lay brother and was sent to the Philippines in 1609. He studied medicine at Manila and in 1622 was sent to Japan, where he suffered martyrdom for his faith by being burned to death at Nagasaki. He was beatified in 1867. August 17.

LAURENTIUS (d. 251). According to legend, he and his brother, Pergentinus, were born of noble parents at Arezzo, Italy. They were arrested and charged with being Christians and making converts while still in school during Emperor Decius' persecution of the Christians. Released by Tiburtius, the magistrate, because of their family, they continued their proselytizing efforts, were again arrested, and when they refused to sacrifice to the pagan gods, were beheaded. June 3.

LAURUS (date unknown). *See* Florus.

LAVAL, MARTYRS OF (d. 1794). During the French Revolution a group of priests, nuns, and a laywoman were executed at Laval, the capital of Mayenne, in western France, for refusing to subscribe to the Civil Constitution of the Clergy which was condemned by Pope Pius VI in 1791. They were all beatified in 1955. They are: Françoise Mézière, a laywoman, who was guillotined at Laval on February 5, 1794, after having been found guilty of nursing wounded Vendean soldiers; two sisters of the Sisters of Charity de la Chapelle-au-Ribout, Françoise Trehet, executed March 13, and Jeanne Véron, executed March 20; Marie Lhullier (Sister Monica), an illiterate lay sister of the Hospital Sisters of the Mercy of Jesus; and fifteen priests: René Ambroise, Jacques André, Jacques Burin, François Duchesne, André Duliou, Jean Gallot, Louis Gastineau, François Migoret, Julien Morin de la Girardière, Julien Moulé, Joseph Pellé, Augustine Philipott, Pierre Thomas, Jean Baptiste Turpin du Cormier, all sec-

ular priests, and Jean Baptiste Triquerle, a Conventional Franciscan.

LAWRENCE (d. 258). One of the seven deacons of Rome, he was born, according to tradition, as Huesca, Spain, and suffered martyrdom in Rome during Emperor Valerian's persecution of the Christians. According to several early Christian writers, among them St. Ambrose and Prudentius, he was a deacon of Pope Sixtus II and was overwhelmed with grief when Sixtus was condemned to death in 258. Overjoyed when Sixtus predicted he would follow him in three days, he sold many of the Church's possessions and donated the money to the poor. When the prefect of Rome heard of his action, he had Lawrence brought before him and demanded all the Church's treasures for the Emperor. Lawrence said he would need three days to collect them and then presented the blind, the crippled, the poor, the orphans, and other unfortunates to the prefect and told him they were the Church's treasures. Furious, the prefect prepared a red-hot griddle and bound Lawrence to it; Lawrence bore the agony with unbelievable equanimity and in the midst of his torment instructed the executioner to turn him over, as he was broiled enough on the one side. According to Prudentius, his death and example led to the conversion of Rome and signaled the end of paganism in the city. There is no doubt that his death inspired a great devotion in Rome, which quickly spread throughout the entire Church. August 10.

LAWRENCE OF BRINDISI (1559–1619). Caesare de Rossi was born at Brindisi, Kingdom of Naples, on July 22, was educated by the Conventual Franciscans there and by his uncle at St. Mark's in Venice, and when sixteen joined the Capuchins at Verona, taking the name Lawrence. He pursued his higher studies in theology, philosophy, the Bible, Greek, Hebrew, and several other languages at the University of Padua, was ordained, and began to preach with great effect in northern Italy. He became definitor general of his order in Rome in 1596, a position he was to hold five times, was assigned to conversion work with Jews, and was sent to Germany, with Bl. Benedict of Urbino, to combat Lutheranism. They founded friaries at Prague, Vienna, and Gorizia, which were to develop into the provinces of Bohemia, Austria, and Styria. At the request of Emperor Rudolf II, Lawrence helped raise an army among the German rulers to fight against the Turks, who were threatening to conquer all of Hungary, became its chaplain, and was among the leaders in the Battle of Szekesfehevar in 1601; many attributed the ensuing victory to him. In 1602, he was elected vicar general of the Capuchins but refused re-election in 1605. He was sent to Spain by the Emperor to persuade Philip III to join the Catholic League, and while there founded a Capuchin house in Madrid. He was then sent as papal nuncio to the court of Maximilian of Bavaria, served as peacemaker in several royal disputes, and in 1618 retired from worldly affairs to the friary at Caeserta. He was recalled at the request of the rulers of Naples to go to Spain to intercede with King Philip for them against the duke of Osuna, Spanish envoy to Naples, and convinced the King to recall the duke to avert an uprising. The trip in the sweltering heat of summer exhausted him, and he died a few days after his meeting with the King of Lisbon on July 22. Lawrence wrote a commentary on Genesis and several treatises against Luther, but Lawrence's main writings are in the nine volumes of his sermons. He was canonized in 1881 and pro-

claimed a Doctor of the Church by Pope John XXIII in 1959. July 21.

LAWRENCE OF CANTERBURY (d. 619). One of the thirteen monks from St. Andrew's Monastery in Rome who accompanied St. Augustine of Canterbury to England in 597, he succeeded Augustine as archbishop of Canterbury in 604. Lawrence was unsuccessful in convincing the Britons to accept the Roman liturgical practices and was faced with great difficulties when Edbald succeeded his father, Ethelbert, as King of Kent in 616, married his father's wife, and allowed the country to lapse into pagan practices. Lawrence considered returning to Gaul but in a dream was rebuked by St. Peter for considering abandoning his flock and was lashed physically by the apostle for the thought. Lawrence decided to remain, and the day after his vision converted Edbald to Christianity when he displayed the stripes on his back to the King and told him their origin. Lawrence died on February 2. February 3.

LAWRENCE JUSTINIAN. *See* Giustiniani, Laurence.

LAWRENCE LORICATUS, BL. (d. 1243). Born at Fanello, Italy, he accidentally killed a young man while he was a youth in the army and made a pilgrimage to Compostela as penance. On his return, he became a Benedictine monk at Subiaco in 1209, was given permission to live as a hermit, and lived in seclusion for thirty-three years. He received the name Loricatus (the cuirassier) from the coat of mail with sharp points he wore against his skin. His cult was approved in 1778. August 16.

LAWRENCE O'TOOLE (1128–80). Son of Murtagh, chief of the Murrays, he was born near Castledermot, Kildare,

Ireland, was taken as hostage by the raiding King Dermot McMurrogh of Leinster, but was turned over to the bishop of Glendalough after two years. Lawrence became a monk at Glendalough, was named abbot in 1153, ruled well though there were some objections to his strict rule, and in 1611 was named archbishop of Dublin. He instituted reforms among the clergy, upgraded the caliber of new clerics, and imposed strict discipline on his canons. When a revolt drove Dermot McMurrogh from Ireland, the King sought the help of King Henry II of England, who dispatched an army of his nobles headed by Richard de Clare, earl of Pembroke. He landed in Ireland in 1170 and marched on Dublin. While Lawrence was negotiating with him, Dermot's men and allies raped and looted the city. When Dermot suddenly died, Pembroke declared himself King of Leinster as the husband of Dermot's daughter Eva (Lawrence's niece), but was recalled to England by Henry. Before Pembroke could return, the Irish united behind Rory O'Conor, and the earl barricaded himself in Dublin as the Irish forces attacked. While Lawrence was trying to effect a settlement, Pembroke suddenly attacked and won an unexpected victory. Henry himself then went to Ireland in 1171, received the submission of most of the Irish chieftains, and the great tragedy of Ireland, the beginning of the "troubles" with England that were to endure for eight centuries, had started. In 1172, a synod Lawrence convened at Cashel confirmed a bull of Pope Adrian IV imposing the English form of the liturgy on Ireland, and Lawrence accepted the decrees when Pope Alexander III confirmed them. In 1175, he went to England to negotiate a treaty between Henry and Rory O'Conor, and during his visit had an attack made on his life while he was visiting the shrine of Thomas Becket. He attended the General Lateran Council in Rome in 1179 and was appointed papal legate to Ireland. On his way home he stopped off in England to conduct further negotiations on behalf of Rory O'Conor and was forbidden to return to Ireland by Henry. He journeyed to Normandy where Henry was, received his permission to return, but died on the way back at Eu, near Rouen, on November 14. He was canonized in 1225.

LAWRENCE OF RIPAFRATTA, BL. (d. 1457). Born at Ripafratta, Tuscany, Italy, he joined the Dominicans at Pisa, preached for several years, became known for his biblical scholarship, and was appointed master of novices at Cortona, where Fra Angelico and St. Antoninus of Florence were among his students. He was named vicar general of the reformed Dominican friaries, and went to Pistoia, where he distinguished himself, ministering to those stricken by the plague that beset that city. His cult was approved in 1851. September 28.

LAWRENCE OF SPOLETO (d. 576). Forced to leave Syria in 514 because of the persecution of the orthodox (Catholics) by the Arians, he immigrated to Rome, where he was ordained by Pope St. Hormisdas. Lawrence preached with great success in Umbria, fought Arianism, and founded a monastery near Spoleto. Against his will, he was named bishop of Spoleto, was rejected by the people of the city, because he was a foreigner, but when the gates of the city were seemingly miraculously opened, they accepted him. He became famed for his charities and peacemaking abilities, settling a bitter dispute between rival factions at Bologna, resigned after twenty years as bishop, and was founding abbot of a monastery at Forfa, where he died. February 3.

LAWRENCE, ROBERT (d. 1535). Prior of the charterhouse at Beauvale, Nottinghamshire, England, he was on a visit to the London charterhouse when he and St. Augustine Webster accompanied its prior, St. John Houghton, to see Thomas Cromwell, who had them seized and imprisoned in the Tower. When they refused to accept the King's Act of Supremacy they were treated savagely and hanged at Tyburn on May 4. They were canonized by Pope Paul VI in 1970 as three of the Forty Martyrs of England and Wales.

LAZARUS (1st century). All that is really known of Lazarus is from John 11:1–44, which tells us he was a friend of Jesus, brother of Martha and Mary, and that he was raised from the dead by Jesus after being in the tomb for four days; and from John 12:1–11, where he is mentioned as among those present at a dinner in Bethany. According to tradition, Lazarus, Mary Magdalen, Martha, Maximus, and others were put into an oarless, rudderless boat and set adrift. It brought them to southwestern Gaul, where Lazarus made numerous converts, became the first bishop of Marseilles, and was martyred during the persecution of Christians by Emperor Domitian. In another tradition, Lazarus was put into a leaking boat with his sisters and others by the Jews at Jaffa and was conducted supernaturally in safety to Cyprus, where he became bishop of Kition (Larnaka), ruled for thirty years, and died there. Still another tradition has him following St. Peter to Syria. December 17.

LAZARUS (1st century). He is the poor man at the gate of the rich man in Christ's parable related in Luke 16:19–31. His name was perpetuated in the Middle Ages by such words as *lazaretto* (hospital), *lazarone* (a beggar in the streets), and the Order of St. Lazarus, which though a military order had as one of its objectives the care of lepers. June 21.

LAZARUS OF MILAN (d. c. 450). Named bishop of Milan about 439, he sustained his flock during the trying times of the Ostrogoth invasion of Italy and the occupation of Milan. He amplified the Ambrosian rite by introducing Rogationtide litanies, which later spread to France and England. He died on March 14. February 11.

LAZIOSI, PEREGRINE (1260–1345). Born at Forlì, Italy, of well-to-do parents, he was active in his youth in the antipapal party in Romagna but after an encounter with St. Philip Benizi changed his lifestyle. He joined the Servites at Siena, was ordained, and then went to Forlì and founded a new Servite house. He became famed for his preaching, austerities, holiness, and as a confessor, a fame that became widespread when an advanced cancer of his foot was seemingly miraculously cured overnight after he had experienced a vision. He was canonized in 1726 and is the patron against cancer. May 1.

LEANDER (c. 534–c. 600). Of a noble Hispanic-Roman family of Cartagena, Spain, and brother of SS. Fulgentius, Isidore, and Florentina, he was born at Cartagena and in 554 went to Seville when his family moved there. He became a monk there, fought Arianism in Spain, met St. Gregory the Great at Constantinople in 583 while on a diplomatic mission from King Leovigild to the Emperor, and on his return in about 584 was appointed bishop of Seville. He was banished by King Leovigild, who had executed his son Hermenegild for refusing communion from an Arian bishop. While in exile Leander wrote treatises against Arianism, was recalled by Leovigild who, on his deathbed, charged him with raising his son Reccared, who was his successor, in the Catholic faith. In the next few years Leander converted many of the Arian bishops and brought most of the Visigoths and Spanish Suevi to the Catholic faith. He presided at the third council of Toledo in 589 at which Visigothic Spain abjured Arianism and added the Nicene Creed to the Mass. In 590, he held a synod at Seville that solidified the work of conversion. He was responsible for the reform of the Spanish liturgy and wrote a rule for nuns that is still extant. It was at his suggestion that St. Gregory wrote his treatise on Job, *Moralia*. Leander died at Seville on March 13 and is considered a Doctor of the Church in the Spanish Church. February 27.

LEBUIN (d. c. 773). Called Liafwine in his native England, he became a monk at Ripon, was ordained, and sometime after 754 went to Germany to do missionary work. He was assigned, with St. Marchelm, to preach to the Frisians in the Overyssel area by St. Gregory, vicar of Utrecht, and built a church at Deventer. He was successful in his evangelization but encountered much opposition from the Westphalian Saxons, who burned down his church. He then went to their annual gathering at Marklo, preached of the true God, and denounced the pagan gods. Though some at the meeting wanted to put him to death, others admired his courage, and he was allowed to leave unharmed and permitted to travel and preach wherever he wished. He continued his activities from Deventer until his death. November 12.

LE CLERQ, BL. ALIX (1576–1622). Born at Remiremont, Lorraine, she became a nun when seventeen. When her family moved to Hymont she met Peter Fourier, who became her spiritual director, and in 1597 she and three other women formed a new foundation under his direction. At her father's insistence, she went to a convent at Ormes, was unimpressed by its secular atmosphere, and in 1598 the wealthy Judith d'Apremont gave Alix and her group a house on her estate, which they used as their mother house in the founding of a new congregation dedicated to the education of children. Despite opposition from Alix's father and others and the lack of formal ecclesiastical approval, they established several new foundations. In 1616 they received two papal bulls formally approving the Augustinian Canonesses of the Congregation of Our Lady from Rome. Differences about what the bulls granted and internal strife caused Fr. Fourier to replace Alix as superioress of the congregation, and the last years of her life were bitter, as even Fr. Fourier seemed to turn against her. She died in her convent at Nancy on January 9, and was beatified in 1947. October 22.

LEGER. *See* Leodegarius.

LEIGH, BL. RICHARD (c. 1561–88). Born at London, he studied for the priesthood at Rheims and Rome, where he was ordained in 1586. He was sent on the English mission, used the alias Bart, was arrested, and was banished. Soon after his return, he was again arrested, convicted of being a Catholic priest, and hanged, drawn, and quartered at Tyburn with five others, including Bl. Richard Martin. He was beatified in 1929. August 30.

LELIA (6th century). Though her feast is kept in the diocese of Limerick,

Ireland, little is known of her beyond that she seems to have been superior of a convent in Munster and was the great-granddaughter of Prince Cairthenn, who had been baptized by St. Patrick at Singland. August 11.

LELLIS, CAMILLUS DE (1550–1614). Born at Bocchianico, Italy, he fought for the Venetians against the Turks, was addicted to gambling, and by 1574 was penniless in Naples. He became a Capuchin novice, was unable to be professed because of a diseased leg he contracted while fighting the Turks, devoted himself to caring for the sick, and became director of St. Giacomo Hospital in Rome. He received permission from his confessor (St. Philip Neri) to be ordained and decided, with two companions, to found his own congregation, the Ministers of the Sick (the Camellians), dedicated to the care of the sick. They ministered to the sick of Holy Ghost Hospital in Rome, enlarged their facilities in 1585, founded a new house in Naples in 1588, and attended the plague-stricken aboard ships in Rome's harbor and in Rome. In 1591, the congregation was made into an order to serve the sick by Pope Gregory XIV, and in 1591 and 1605, Camillus sent members of his order to minister to wounded troops in Hungary and Croatia, the first field medical unit. Gravely ill for many years, he resigned as superior of the Order in 1607 and died in Rome on July 14, the year after he attended a general chapter there. He was canonized in 1746, was declared patron of the sick, with St. John of God, by Pope Leo XIII, and patron of nurses and nursing groups by Pope Pius XI. July 14.

LENARTZ, JOHN (d. 1572). Born at Oisterwijk, Holland, he joined the Augustinians at Briel and became spiritual director of a convent of Augustinian nuns at Gorkum. During a Calvinist persecution, he was taken by a mob of Calvinists who stormed the town and hanged at Briel, Holland, with a group of Catholics. They were all canonized in 1867 as the Martyrs of Gorkum. July 9.

LEO (d. c. 260). According to legend, he was a close friend of St. Paregorius (February 18), who suffered martyrdom at Patara, Lycia. On the way to visit his friend's grave, he desecrated the Temple of Fortune, where a pagan festival was in progress. He was arrested, brought before Lollian, the governor of Lycia, and when he refused to sacrifice to the gods, was scourged, tortured, and then executed. Their story may be a pious fiction. February 18.

LEO (d. c. 550). Also known as Lyé, he was born at Mantenay, near Troyes, Gaul, became a monk at the monastery there, and then succeeded St. Romanus, its founder, as abbot and died there. May 25.

LEO I THE GREAT (d. 461). Probably born in Rome of Tuscan parents, he served as deacon under Popes Celestine I and Sixtus III, acted as peacemaker between Aetius and Albinus, the imperial generals whose quarrels were leaving Gaul open to attacks by the barbarians, and was elected Pope to succeed Sixtus III while he was in Gaul. He was consecrated on September 29, 440, and at once began his pastoral duties with a series of ninety-six still extant sermons on faith and charity and strenuous opposition to Manichaeanism, Pelagianism, Priscillianism, and Nestorianism. In 448, he was faced with the Eutychian problem. Eutyches, an archimandrite in a monastery at Constantinople, had been deposed as abbot by Patriarch Flavian of Constantinople for denying the two natures of Christ. Supported by Emperor

Theodosius II, Eutyches appealed to Leo for reinstatement. The Emperor summoned a packed council at Ephesus in 449 (the notorious Robber Synod), which acquitted Eutyches and at which Flavian was physically assaulted (he later died from the attack), and refused to allow papal legates to read a letter from Leo; it also declared Flavian deposed. In 451, Leo called the General Council of Chalcedon at which his letter of 449 clarifying the doctrine of the Incarnation and vindicating Flavian was read; it excommunicated and deposed Dioscorus, Eutyches' friend, who had been intruded as patriarch of Constantinople in place of Flavian by Theodosius. It was Leo's famous *Tome* and was received with great acclamation. In 452, Attila and his Huns invaded Italy and were about to attack defenseless Rome when he was dissuaded by Leo in a face-to-face meeting with Leo at Peschiera. Three years later Leo was not so successful with the Vandal Genseric, who plundered Rome, though he agreed not to burn the city. Leo ministered to the stricken populace and worked to rebuild the city and the churches. He sent missionaries to Africa to minister to the captives Genseric took back with him. Leo died in Rome on November 10. Leo advanced the influence of the papacy to unprecedented heights with his authoritative approach to events, buttressed by his firm belief that the Holy See was the supreme authority in human affairs because of divine and scriptural mandate. In a time of great disorder, he forged an energetic central authority that stood for stability, authority, action, and wisdom; his pontificate was to affect the concept of the papacy for centuries to come. He was declared a Doctor of the Church in 1754. November 10.

LEO II (d. 683). Born in Sicily, he was elected Pope to succeed Pope St. Agatho on January 10, 681, though he was not consecrated until August 17, 682. He was an eloquent preacher, was interested in music, and was known for his concern for the poor. He confirmed the acts of the sixth General Council of Constantinople, 680–81 which condemned monothelitism and censured Pope Honorius I for not formally condemning that heresy. Leo died on June 28. July 3.

LEO III (d. 816). A Roman, son of Atypius and Elizabeth, he was chief of the pontifical treasury or wardrobe (*vestiarius*) and a cardinal-priest of Santa Susanna when he was elected Pope on the day his predecessor, Pope Hadrian (Adrian) I, was buried, December 26, 795. In 799 he was the victim of a plot by relatives of Hadrian to oust him from the papacy and was attacked by armed men who attempted to gouge out his eyes and cut out his tongue. He managed to escape to St. Erasmus Monastery, where he quickly recovered, a recovery many considered miraculous. He fled to Charlemagne's protection at Paderborn and was escorted back to Rome a few months later by a contingent of Charlemagne's men. In 800 Charlemagne came to Rome and at a synod completely exonerated Leo of charges brought against him by his enemies, though Leo insisted on taking an oath that he was innocent before the assembled bishops. On Christmas Day, Leo crowned Charlemagne in St. Peter's, an action that founded the Holy Roman Empire and was to have a profound effect on European history for centuries to come. In 804, Leo visited the Emperor and came to an agreement with him about the division of the Empire among Charlemagne's sons, which Leo formally agreed to two years later. With Charlemagne's help adoptionism was fought in Spain, but when Charlemagne wanted the expression *Filioque* (and the Son) added to the Nicene Creed, Leo refused, in part because he would not permit secular interference in ecclesiastical affairs, and in part because he did not wish to offend the Byzantine Church. Generally, the two acted in concert most of the time. They recovered his throne for Eardulf of Northumbria, settled the dispute between Canterbury and York, and in the quarrel between Archbishop Wulfred and King Cenulf of Mercia, Leo intervened, suspended the archbishop, and put the kingdom under interdict. He also created a fleet at the suggestion of Charlemagne to combat the Saracens, recovered some of the Church's patrimony in Gaeta with the Emperor's help, and was the beneficiary of much treasure from him. When Charlemagne died in 814 and Leo's protection was gone, his enemies again rose against him, but he crushed one conspiracy by executing the ringleader, and another revolt by the nobles of Campagna, who planned to march on Rome, was suppressed by the duke of Spoleto. Leo was a patron of the arts, using much of Charlemagne's gifts to help the poor and to rebuild and decorate churches in Rome and Ravenna, where the relationship between the two men is portrayed in magnificent mosaics. Leo died in Rome in June, and was canonized in 1673. June 12.

LEO IV (d. 855). Born in Rome, probably of Lombard ancestry, he studied at St. Martin's Monastery in Rome, was made subdeacon of the Lateran Basilica by Pope Gregory IV, and soon after was named cardinal by Pope Sergius II. Leo was unanimously elected Pope to succeed Sergius and was consecrated on April 10, 847. He immediately began to repair the fortifications of Rome in anticipation of another Saracen attack on the city, built a wall around St. Peter's and Vatican Hill, giving the area its name of the Leonine City, and also restored many churches in Rome. He tightened clerical discipline with a synod at Rome

in 853 and was confronted with numerous problems during his pontificate. A papal legate he sent to Archbishop John of Ravenna and his brother, the duke of Emilia, was murdered by the duke, and Leo went to Ravenna, tried him, and found him guilty. Duke Nomenoë deposed a number of bishops and erected a metropolitan see at Dol without papal permission, actions the Pope was unable to do anything about. Patriarch Ignatius of Constantinople had deposed Gregory Asbestas, the bishop of Syracuse, and Archbishop Hincmar of Rheims, and was forbidding clerics from appealing to Rome, actions that Leo refused to confirm. In 850, Leo crowned Louis, son of Lothair, Emperor, and in 853 King Ethelwulf of the West Saxons sent his son, Alfred, whom Leo adopted as his spiritual son, to be crowned. Just before his death on July 17, Leo was accused by a military officer (a *magister militum*) named Daniel of plotting with the Greek Emperor to overthrow Emperor Louis, a charge he easily disproved, though his death sentence on Daniel was remitted through the intercession of the Emperor.

LEO IX (1002–54). Born at Egisheim, Alsace, and named Bruno, on June 21, he was sent to study under his cousin Adalbert at Toul and received a canonry there in 1017. Although a deacon, he commanded troops under Emperor Conrad II when he invaded Italy in 1026 and made quite a reputation as a military man. He was elected bishop of Toul while in Italy and ruled for twenty years, instituting many reforms among the clergy and introducing the Cluny reform in the monasteries of his see. In 1048, with the support of his relative Emperor Henry III, he was elected Pope to succeed Pope Damasus II and was consecrated on February 12, 1049. He at once called a synod at Rome, which denounced simony and clerical incontinence, and he began a series of reforms, traveling all over Western Europe in his efforts to have them enforced, earning the title Peregrinus Apostolicus (the Apostolic Pilgrim). He condemned Berengarius of Tours for his denial of transubstantiation, acted as peacemaker in an attempt to reconcile the differences between the Emperor and King Andrew of Hungary in 1052, and succeeded in adding Benevento and territories in southern Italy to Peter's patrimony. Leo led an army against the Norman invaders in 1053 but was defeated and captured at Civitella and imprisoned, at Benevento. He was severely criticized by St. Peter Damian for this action—a Pope acting as a military commander and leading an army. Leo also became involved in 1053 in a dispute with Patriarch Michael Cerularius of Constantinople (a dispute that was the beginning of the complete separation of Rome and the Eastern churches) for increasing the ritual differences with the Latin Church. Leo's proposal that the Pope be elected only by cardinals was put into effect five years after his death and endures to the present day. He died in Rome on April 19. Many miracles were attributed to him, and he was canonized in 1087.

LEO (d. 1227). *See* Daniel.

LEO OF SAINT-BERTIN, BL. (d. 1163). Born at Furnes, Flanders, he was almoner at the court of the Count of Flanders when twenty but left to become a monk at the monastery at Auchin. He was appointed abbot of Lobbes Abbey, restored the abbey and discipline there, and in 1138 was named abbot of the famous Saint-Bertin Monastery. In 1146, he accompanied Thierry of Alsace, Count of Flanders, to Jerusalem during the Second Crusade, bringing back reputed drops of the blood of Christ supposedly collected by Joseph of Arimathea while he was washing the Savior's body. In 1152, his monastery was destroyed by fire but with the help of William of Ypres, he rebuilt it. He was blind the last two years of his life. February 26.

LEOBINUS (d. c. 558). Also known as Lubin, he was born near Poitiers, France, worked at the monastery at Noailles, spent some time as a hermit with St. Avitus, and then went to an abbey near Lyons. When raiders attacked the monastery, he was tortured to force him to reveal the hiding place of its treasure and was left for dead. He recovered, rejoined St. Avitus at Le Perche, and after Avitus' death continued living as a hermit. He was ordained and made abbot of Brou, resigned to become a monk at Lérins, but returned to Brou on the advice of St. Caesarius. Soon after, Leobinus was appointed bishop of Chartres, where he instituted reforms and participated in councils at Orléans and Paris. He died on March 14 after a lengthy illness.

LEOCADIA (d. c. 304). A member of the nobility at Toledo, Spain, during Emperor Diocletian's persecution of the Christians, she was tortured and imprisoned there for her faith by Dacian, the governor, and died in prison from the torture to which she had been subjected. She is the principal patroness of Toledo. December 9.

LEOCRITIA (d. 859). Also known as Lucretia, she was the daughter of wealthy Moorish parents in Cordova, Spain, which at that time was under Moorish rule. She was secretly converted to Christianity and was driven from her home when her parents learned of her conversion. With the help of St. Eulogius, she went into hiding and was sheltered by several Christian families. In time she was captured, with Eulogius, condemned for her

Christianity, scourged, and beheaded, as was Eulogius. March 15.

LEODEGARIUS (c. 616–79). Also known as Leger, he was raised at the court of King Clotaire II and by his uncle, Bishop Didon of Poitiers. Leodegarius was made archdeacon by Didon, was ordained, and in about 651 became abbot of Maxentius Abbey, where he introduced the rule of St. Benedict. He served Queen regent St. Bathildis and helped her govern when Clovis II died in 656, and was named bishop of Autun in 663. He reconciled the differing factions that had torn the see apart, introduced reforms, fortified the town, and was known for his concern for the poor. On the death of Clotaire III, he supported young Childeric II for King against his brother Thierry, who had been backed by Ebroin, mayor of the palace. Ebroin was exiled to Luxeuil and became a bitter enemy of Leodegarius, who became Childeric's adviser. When Leodegarius denounced the marriage of Childeric to his uncle's daughter, he also incurred the enmity of Childeric, and in 675 Leodegarius was arrested at Autun and banished to Luxeuil. When Childeric was murdered in 675, his successor, Theodoric III, restored Leodegarius to his see. Ebroin was also restored as mayor of the palace after he had the incumbent Leudesius murdered and persuaded the duke of Champagne and the bishops of Chalons and Valence to attack Autun. To save the town, Leodegarius surrendered. Ebroin had him blinded, his lips cut off, and his tongue pulled out. Not satisfied, several years later, he convinced the King that Childeric had been murdered by Leodegarius and his brother Gerinus. Gerinus was stoned to death, and Leodegarius was tortured and imprisoned at Fécamp monastery in Normandy. After two years Leodegarius was summoned to a court at Marly by Ebroin, deposed, and executed at Sarcing, Artois, protesting his innocence to the end. Though the Roman Martyrology calls him Blessed and a martyr, there is doubt among many scholars that he is entitled to those honors. October 2.

LEONARD (d. c. 559). According to unreliable sources, he was a Frank courtier who was converted by St. Remigius, refused the offer of a see from his godfather, King Clovis I, and became a monk at Micy. He lived as a hermit at Limoges and was rewarded by the King with all the land he could ride around on a donkey in a day for his prayers, which were believed to have brought the Queen through a difficult delivery safely. He founded Noblac monastery on the land so granted him, and it grew into the town of Saint-Leonard. He remained there evangelizing the surrounding area until his death. He is invoked by women in labor and by prisoners of war because of the legend that Clovis promised to release every captive Leonard visited. November 6.

LEONARD (d. c. 570). A hermit who settled at Vandoeuvre near Le Mans, France (now St. Leonard-aux-Bois), he attracted numerous disciples, and encouraged by Bishop Innocent of Le Mans, founded a monastery there and became its abbot. After an initial misunderstanding, King Clotaire I became his patron. October 15.

LEONARD OF PORT MAURICE. See Casanova, Leonard.

LEONARD I, JOHN (c. 1550–1609). Born at Diecimo, Italy, he became a pharmacist's assistant at Lucca, studied for the priesthood, and was ordained in 1572. He gathered a group of laymen about him to work in hospitals and prisons, became interested in the reforms proposed by the Council of Trent, and proposed a new congregation of secular priests. Great opposition to his proposal developed, but in 1583, his association (formally designated Clerks Regular of the Mother of God in 1621) was recognized by the bishop of Lucca with the approval of Pope Gregory XIII. John was aided by St. Philip Neri and St. Joseph Calasanctius, and in 1595 the congregation was confirmed by Pope Clement VIII, who appointed John to reform the monks of Vallombrosa and Monte Vergine. He died in Rome on October 9 of plague contracted while he was ministering to the stricken. He was venerated for his miracles and religious fervor and is considered one of the founders of the College for the Propagation of the Faith. He was canonized in 1938 by Pope Pius XI. October 9.

LEONIDES OF ALEXANDRIA (d. 202). Father of Origen and a noted scholar, he was imprisoned at Alexandria, Egypt, during the persecution of Christians in the reign of Emperor Septimus Severus by Laetus, governor of Egypt, had his property confiscated, and was beheaded for being a Christian. April 22.

LEONORIUS (d. c. 570). Son of King Hoel I of Brittany and also known as Lunaire, he was born in Wales, was educated there under St. Illtyd, and then went to Brittany, where under his brother King Hoel II, he founded Pontual Monastery. July 1.

LEONTIUS (c. 303). *See* Cosmas.

LEONTIUS (d. 1077). A Greek, he left Constantinople to become a monk at the Caves of Kiev, Russia, and in 1051 was named bishop of Rostov in Russia. He spent the rest of his life in missionary work in the area. May 23.

LEOPOLD (1073–1136). Born at Melk, Austria, he was educated by Bishop Altman of Passau and succeeded his father as margrave of Austria when he was twenty-three. He married the daughter of Emperor Henry IV, by whom he had eighteen children, in 1106, founded the monasteries of Heiligenkreuz in the Wienerwald, Klosterneuburg, near Vienna, and Mariazell in Styria, and was known for his piety and charity. He refused the imperial crown when his brother-in-law Henry V died in 1125. Leopold died after reigning as margrave for forty years at Klosterneuburg. He was surnamed "the Good" by his people and was canonized in 1486. November 15.

LEOPOLD OF GAICHE, BL. (1733–1815). Born at Gaiche near Perugia, Italy, and baptized John, he joined the Franciscans at Cibotola when he was eighteen, taking the name Leopold, and was ordained in 1757. He became known for his preaching and as a confessor and was papal missioner for the Papal States, 1768–78. He served as minister provincial and founded a retreat house for religious at Monte Luco near Spoleto, Italy. When Napoleon invaded Italy in 1808, he suppressed all religious houses, and Leopold became a parish priest and then pastor, though he was then seventy-five. He was imprisoned for a short time for refusing to take an oath to Napoleon, and when Napoleon was defeated he returned to Monte Luco, where he died a few months later, on April 15. He was beatified in 1893. April 2.

LÉSIN. *See* Licinius.

LESMES. *See* Adelelmus.

LESTONNAC, JOAN DE (1556–1640). Born at Bordeaux, France, she refused to follow the urging of her mother (Montaigne's sister) to become a Calvinist. When she was seventeen, she married Gaston de Montferrant, and the couple had a happily married life and four children. Gaston died in 1597 and when her children were old enough to take care of themselves, she, at the age of forty-seven and despite the objections of her son, joined the Cistercians at Toulouse. The harsh regimen caused her health to give way, and she was obliged to leave. Imbued with the idea of founding her own community, she gathered a group of women about her on her estate, La Mothe, ministered to the victims of a plague that struck Bordeaux, and with the help of two Jesuits, Frs. de Bordes and Raymond, formulated plans for a community of nuns devoted to teaching young girls. She and her followers received the habit from Cardinal de Sourdis, archbishop of Bordeaux, in 1608, and the religious of Notre Dame of Bordeaux were founded. She was elected superior in 1610, and the order spread and flourished but was shaken when one of the nuns, Blanche Hervé, circulated false rumors about Joan, caused her to be deposed as superior, and had herself elected superior. Eventually the two women were reconciled in Joan's old age, and a new superior was elected. Joan spent the last years of her life in retirement. Miracles were reported at her tomb at Bordeaux, and she was canonized in 1949. February 2.

LEU. See Lupus (d. 623).

LEUFROY. See Leutfridus.

LEUTFRIDUS (d. 738). Also known as Leufroy, he was born near Evreux, France, studied there and at Condat and Chartres, and then returned to Evreux and devoted himself to the education of boys. He next became a hermit at Cailly Monastery and was a monk for a time at Rouen under St. Sidonius, after which he returned to his native town, built a church and monastery nearby in about 690, and served as abbot until his death. June 21.

LEWINA (date unknown). All that is known of her is that she was a Briton who was believed to have been martyred by invading Saxons. Her story came to light in 1058 when her relics and those of St. Ideberga were translated from a church at Seaford, Sussex, to St. Winnoc's at Bergues, Flanders. July 24.

LEWIS. See Louis.

LEWIS, DAVID (1616–79). Born at Abergavenny, Monmouthshire, Wales, the son of a Protestant schoolteacher and a Catholic mother, he was the only one of their nine children raised a Protestant. He studied law at the Middle Temple in London, went to Europe as tutor for a nobleman's son, and while in Paris was converted to Catholicism. In 1638 he entered the English college in Rome, was ordained in 1642, and in 1644 joined the Jesuits. He was sent on the English mission but a short time later was brought back to Rome as spiritual director of the English college. In 1648, he was sent to Wales and made his headquarters at Cwm in Monnow Valley at a farmhouse that was the College of St. Francis Xavier, the center for Jesuit missionary activities in western England. He worked from there for thirty-one years until 1679, when the Titus Oates plot unleashed a wave of persecution of Catholics. He escaped from Cwm but was betrayed by a servant and captured at Llanfihangel Llantarnam. He was imprisoned at Monmouth jail and after two months was tried at Usk. When no evidence could be produced linking him with the Titus Oates plot, he was convicted of being a Catholic priest and hanged, drawn, and quartered at Usk on August 27. He was canonized by Pope Paul VI as one of the Forty Martyrs of England and Wales in 1970. August 27.

LEZINIANA, BL. MATTHEW ALONSO

(d. 1745). Born at Navas del Rey, Spain, he joined the Dominicans and after his ordination was sent to the Philippines as a missionary. He was later sent to Tonkin in Indochina, where he was beheaded for his faith. He was beatified in 1906. January 22.

L'HULIER, BL. MARIE (1766–94). See Mézière, Bl. Françoise.

LIAFWINE. See Lebuin.

LIBENTIUS (d. 1013). A native of southern Swabia, he was named bishop of Hamburg in 988 when he joined the Benedictines and is considered one of the apostles to the Slavs. January 4.

LIBERTA. See Wilgefortis.

LIBERATUS (d. 484). The abbot of a monastery near Capsa, Byzacene, in Africa, he was ordered to Carthage with his six monks—Boniface, a deacon; Rusticus and Serous, subdeacons; Rogatus and Septimus, monks; and Maximus, a child. There they were ordered to embrace Arianism to comply with a decree issued by Arian Vandal King Huneric, who had also ordered all Catholic monasteries closed. When they refused, they were tortured and set adrift in an old boat, which was set afire; when the fire did not spread, they were beaten to death with oars. August 17.

LIBERATUS OF LORO, BL. (d. c. 1258). Born at San Liberato, Italy, a member of the noble Brunforte family, he joined the Franciscans, led the life of a hermit, and worked for stricter obser-

vance of the rule in his Order. His cult was approved in 1868. September 6.

LIBERT (d. 1076). Also known as Lietbert or Liébert, he was born of a noble family in Brabant, was educated by his uncle, Bishop Gerard of Cambrai, served him as archdeacon and provost, and in 1051 was elected to succeed him as bishop; whereupon he was ordained and consecrated. In 1054 he led a pilgrimage to Jerusalem but never reached there when he learned the Saracens had closed the Holy Sepulcher to Christians. On his return, he built the monastery and church of the Holy Sepulcher in Cambrai. He lived in great austerity and fought the oppressive Hugh, castellan of Cambrai, who imprisoned the bishop in the castle of Oisy for excommunicating him. He was rescued by Count Arnulf of Flanders, and Hugh was driven out of Cambrai. Shortly before he died on June 23, though he was ill, Libert persuaded raiders to spare Cambrai.

LIBORIUS (d. 390). All that is known of him is that he was bishop of Le Mans, Gaul, for almost fifty years. July 23.

LICCIO, BL. JOHN (d. 1511). Born at Caccamo, Italy, he was raised by an aunt and joined the Dominicans when he was fifteen. He developed into a fine preacher, and in 1494 he founded a Dominican house at Caccamo of which he was prior. His cult was approved in 1753. November 14.

LICINIUS (c. 540–c. 616). Also known as Lésin, he was related to the French royal family and when twenty became a courtier at the court of King Clotaire I, his cousin. Licinius was made count of Anjou by King Chilperic, was engaged to be married, but when his intended bride was stricken with leprosy decided to become a religious. He was ordained and entered a monastery but was elected

bishop of Anjou in 586. He spent the rest of his life ministering to his diocese, venerated for his concern for the poor and for his miracles. February 13.

LIDANUS (1026–1118). Born at Antina, Abruzzi, Italy, he was founding abbot of the Benedictine abbey of Sezzar and was responsible for the draining of the Pontine marshes. He retired to Monte Cassino in his old age and died there. July 2.

LIDWINA. See Lydwina.

LIEBERT. See Libert.

LIEM, BL. VINCENT (d. 1773). See Casteñeda, Bl. Hyacinth.

LIETBERT. See Libert.

LIFARD. See Liphardus.

LIGUORI, BL. ALPHONSUS MARY DE (1696–1787). Born on September 21 at Marianelli near Naples, Italy, son of a captain of the royal galleys, he received his doctorate in both canon and civil law at the University of Naples when only sixteen and practiced law very successfully for the next eight years. He abandoned the practice of law when through an oversight he lost an important case, decided to become a priest, joined the Oratorians, and was ordained in 1726. He served as a missionary around Naples for two years, taught for a year, and in 1730, at the invitation of Bishop Thomas Falcoia, whom he had met while teaching, he went to Castellamare. During a nuns' retreat he was conducting at Scala, he met Sister Mary Celeste and became convinced that her vision of a new religious Order, which coincided with a vision Bishop Falcoia had experienced earlier in Rome, was genuine, and reorganized her convent according to the rule she had been given in the vi-

sion in 1731, thus founding the Redemptorines. He moved to Scala and in 1732 organized the Congregation of the Most Holy Redeemer (the Redemptorists), devoted to mission work, and using a hospice of the nuns at Scala for headquarters, with Bishop Falcoia as nominal superior. Dissension broke out almost immediately; Sister Mary Celeste left and founded a convent at Foggia, and in 1733 all the members of Alphonsus' group except one lay brother left to found their own congregation. New postulants were recruited, and in 1734 a second foundation was made at Villa degli Schiavi, and Alphonsus went there to live. In 1738 Scala had to be abandoned after Villa degli Schiavi had been closed the previous year. Despite all the difficulties, the congregation grew, and in 1743, on the death of Bishop Falcoia, a general council elected Alphonsus superior; Pope Benedict XIV approved the rule of the men in 1749 and of the women the following year. During this time Alphonsus was personally active in preaching missions in rural areas and small villages but was increasingly devoting himself to writing. He refused an appointment to the see of Palermo but in 1762 was obliged to accept appointment as bishop of Sant' Agata dei Goti. He inaugurated a program designed to reform the clergy, monasteries, and the entire diocese, and worked to alleviate the condition of the poor and the ignorant. Ill and inflicted with rheumatism that left him paralyzed until his death, he resigned his see in 1775 and retired to Nocera. Meanwhile, during this entire period, he had been engaged in running disputes with the anticlerical Marquis Bernard Tanucci, who governed Naples, 1734–76, as Prime Minister of Charles III of Spain, who had conquered Naples in 1734. Tanucci refused to grant royal approval for the Redemptorists and constantly threat-

ened to suppress Alphonsus' congregation as disguised Jesuits (the Jesuits
had been expelled from Spanish do-
mains in 1767). In 1780, with a new
governor in power, Alphonsus was
tricked into signing and submitting for
royal approval a new rule that completely altered his own rule, which had
been papally approved in 1750; when
this fraudulent rule was approved by the
King at Naples, a storm burst around
Alphonsus. Pope Pius VI refused to accept the new rule, recognized the
Redemptorists in the Papal States as the
true Redemptorists, and a new superior
was appointed to replace Alphonsus. For
the last few years of his life, in addition
to his ill health, he experienced deep
spiritual depression and he went
through a "dark night of the soul." But
this period was replaced by a time of
peace and light when he experienced visions, ecstasies, made prophecies that
were later fulfilled, and reportedly performed miracles. He died on August 1
at Nocera. Alphonsus wrote profusely
on moral, theological, and ascetical subjects (notably his *Moral Theology*), was
constantly engaged in combating anti-
clericalism and Jansenism, and was involved in several controversies over
probabilism. His devotional writings
were most successful, especially his
Glories of Mary. He was canonized in
1839 and was declared a Doctor of the
Church in 1871 by Pope Pius IX.

LILY OF QUITO, THE. *See* Paredesy y
Flores, Mariana de.

LIMNAEUS (d. c. 450). He became a
disciple of Thalassius at the latter's cave
near Tillima in Syria and learned about
being a hermit from that holy man.
Limnaeus then spent time with another
hermit, St. Maro, and on completion of
his training became a hermit himself. He
was soon widely known for his holiness
and healing prowess and built two

houses for the blind who came seeking
his help. February 22.

LINE, ANNE (d. 1601). Born at
Dunmow, Essex, England, the daughter
of William Heigham, who disowned her
when she became a Catholic, she married Roger Line, a Catholic. He was arrested for his religion but was permitted
to go to Flanders, where he died in 1594.
Anne spent the rest of her life aiding
fugitive priests at her home and later in a
house in London that had been set up to
provide shelter for Catholic priests by
Jesuit Fr. John Gerard. She was arrested
there and hanged for harboring Catholic
priests, with Fr. Roger Filcock, a Jesuit
priest who was her confessor, at Tyburn
on February 27. She was canonized by
Pope Paul VI in 1970 as one of the Forty
Martyrs of England and Wales.

LINUS (d. c. 76). A native of Tuscany, he
succeeded St. Peter as Pope about 67. St.
Irenaeus says he is the Linus mentioned
by St. Paul in 2 Timothy 4:21 and that he
was consecrated bishop by St. Paul.
September 23.

LIOBA (d. 780). Born in Wessex,
England, and baptized Truthgeba, she
was placed in Wimborne Monastery in
Dorsetshire under the care of St. Tetta
when quite young and became a nun
there, taking the name Liobgetha, of
which Lioba ("dear one") is a contrac-
tion. A relative of St. Boniface, she entered into correspondence with him
when he was made bishop and engaged
in missionary work in Germany. In 748,
he wrote St. Tetta asking for nuns to help
in his evangelical work. She sent him
thirty nuns, including Lioba, whom he
made abbess of Bischofsheim Monastery
at Mainz, which soon became famous as
a great center of Christianity in
Germany. Lioba became noted for her
wisdom, zeal, and holiness, and founded
numerous other houses in Germany.

LOMAN 383

After twenty-eight years as abbess, she resigned and retired to Schönersheim near Mainz, where she died soon after. September 28.

LIPHARD. *See* Liudhard.

LIPHARDUS (c. 477–550). Also known as Lifard, he became a successful lawyer and judge at Orléans in Gual. When forty, he became a monk at Micy, and after a time a hermit at a nearby ruined castle with a companion, Urbicius. They soon attracted numerous disciples, and Liphardus was ordained and founded the monastery of Meung-sur-Loire, of which he was abbot until he died when Urbicius succeeded him. June 3.

LIUDHARD (d. c. 602). Chaplain of Bertha, daughter of King Charibert of Paris, he accompanied her to England, when she married King Ethelbert of Kent. According to tradition, he helped prepare Ethelbert for baptism by St. Augustine and died at Canterbury. An unverifiable legend had Liphard archbishop of Canterbury and murdered at Cambrai while on the way back from a pilgrimage to Rome; however, there is no record of an archbishop of Canterbury named Liphard, as Liudhard is sometimes called. May 7.

LIVRADE. *See* Wilgefortis.

LIVINUS (no date). Son of a noble Scot and a royal Irish mother, he was baptized and ordained by St. Augustine of Canterbury and became a bishop. He and three companions went to Flanders as missionaries, preached in Brabant, and he was beheaded by pagans at Eschen in Belgium. Scholars believe he may be the same as St. Lebuin. November 12.

LLOYD, JOHN (d. 1679). A native of Breconshire, Wales, he was educated at

Ghent and Valladolid, where he was ordained in 1653. The following year he returned to Wales and ministered to the Catholics of his native land for the next twenty-four years. He was arrested at Penllyn, Glamorgan, in 1678 and was imprisoned in Cardiff Castle at the same time as St. Philip Evans and charged with complicity in the Titus Oates plot to assassinate King Charles II. Though no proof was produced to implicate them, they were both convicted of being Catholic priests unlawfully in the kingdom and were executed at Cardiff on July 22. They were canonized as among the Forty Martyrs of England and Wales by Pope Paul VI in 1970.

LOCKWOOD, BL. JOHN (1561–1642). Born at Sowerby, Yorkshire, England, he went to Rheims in 1579, studied at Douai and Rome, and was ordained in 1597. The following year he was sent on the English mission and served in England for forty-five years. He was arrested, imprisoned, and banished in 1610 but returned to his native land. Again arrested, he escaped and continued his work but was arrested once more, convicted of being a Catholic priest, and sentenced to death. He was hanged, drawn, and quartered when eighty-one with Bl. John Catherick at York. Bl. John Lockwood was beatified in 1929. April 13.

LOLLIAN (d. 297). *See* Hipparchus.

LOMAN (d. c. 450). Unreliable legend has him the son of St. Patrick's sister Tigris. He accompanied Patrick to Ireland and was left to navigate their boat up the Boyne while Patrick went to Tara. On the way, he met Fortchern, son of the chieftain of Trim, his mother, a Christian, and his father, Fedelmid, a pagan. In time, he converted Fedelmid and his whole household to Christianity. Fedelmid gave Patrick land at Trim for a church, and Loman became bishop of Trim. Some scholars believe that in reality Loman was a bishop of Trim in the seventh century and in no way related to Patrick. February 17.

LONGINUS (1st century). According to tradition, Longinus was the name of the centurion at the Crucifixion who acknowledged Christ as "the son of God" (Matt. 27:54; Mark 15:39; Luke 23:47). This centurion is also identified, with no evidence, with the soldier who "pierced his side with a lance" (John 19:34). Untrustworthy legend says he was converted, left the army, took instructions from the apostles, and then became a monk at Caesarea in Cappadocia. The legend further says he was arrested for his faith and tortured, destroyed idols in the presence of the governor who was trying him, and was beheaded; whereupon the governor was converted. March 15.

LONGINUS (d. c. 290). *See* Victor of Marseilles.

LOPEZ, GREGORY (1542–96). Born at Madrid of unknown parents, he was a page in the court of King Philip II in his youth but after a pilgrimage to the shrine of Our Lady of Guadalupe in Estremadura, he resolved to visit her shrine in Mexico. He went to Mexico, sold his possessions, gave the proceeds to the poor of Vera Cruz, lived for a time as a hermit and then on a plantation, and in 1571, he joined the Dominicans at Mexico City. He soon decided that the life of a Dominican was not the life for him and resumed his eremitical life. His unusual lifestyle caused him to be investigated by the archbishop of Mexico, who cleared him completely, calling him a man of holiness and virtue. To escape the publicity attendant upon the investigation, he served in a hospital, where he wrote a book on herbs, and in 1589, with a friend, he built a hermitage near Michoacan, where they spent the rest of their lives in prayer and Scripture studies. Gregory died on July 20. Many miracles were attributed to him after his death, and he is venerated locally. A popular cult spread over Mexico, but it has never been officially confirmed.

LOPEZ-NETO, BL. CASSIAN VAZ (1607–38). Born at Nantes, France, of Portuguese parents, he joined the Capuchins, was ordained, and was then sent to Cairo, Egypt, to work with Bl. Francis Noury (Agathangelus of Vendôme) in what proved a fruitless attempt to reconcile the Coptic Church with Rome. In 1638, they were sent to Abyssinia but were arrested on entering the country and hanged from the cords of their habits and then stoned to death on orders of King Fasilidas. They were beatified in 1904. August 7.

LOPEZ Y VICUÑA, VINCENTIA MARÍA (1847–96). Daughter of a lawyer, she was born at Cascante, Spain, on March 22 and was sent to school at Madrid. While living there with her Aunt Eulalia de Vicuña, Vincentia was so impressed with her aunt's work with serving girls that she took a vow of chastity and dedicated herself to helping working girls. With her aunt she gathered a group of followers who lived a communal life, 1871–76, drew up a constitution, and in 1878 pronounced her vows with three others, and the congregation of the Daughters of Mary Immaculate for Domestic Service was founded. The institute soon spread through Spain, then to other parts of Europe and to Latin America, and received the approval of the Holy See in 1888. Vincentia died in Madrid on December 26 and was canonized by Pope Paul VI in 1975.

LOUIS IX (1214–70). Born at Poissy, France, on April 25, son of King Louis VIII and Blanche of Castile, he was raised in a religious atmosphere by his mother. His father died in 1226 when he was twelve, and Blanche became regent. She defended his throne against Thibaut of Champagne and other ambitious nobles by alliances, and when necessary, by war. He married Margaret, daughter of Count Raymund Berenger of Provence, in 1234, and the couple had eleven children. On reaching his majority in the same year, he assumed the reins of ruler, though Blanche was his adviser until her death. He put down revolts in southern France, 1242–43, defeated King Henry III of England at Taillebourg in 1242, securing suzerainty over Guienne by his victory, and in the same year forced Poitou to submit to him; in 1243 he compelled Raymond VII of Toulouse to submit to him. He went on crusade in 1248 and captured Damietta in 1249 but suffered a disastrous defeat at the hands of the Saracens at El Mansura in 1250 and was taken prisoner. After he ransomed himself and his men, he went to the Holy Land and remained there until 1254, when Blanche died and he returned to France. He imposed peace on Flanders in 1256, and ceded Limoges, Cahors, and Perigueux to King Henry III of England in return for Henry's renunciation of any claims he had to Normandy, Anjou, Maine, Touraine, and Poitou with the Treaty of Paris ratified in 1259. He ended Aragon's claims to Provence and Languedoc by yielding French claims to Roussillon and Barcelona in the Treaty of Corbeil in 1258. He set forth on a new crusade in 1270 but contracted typhoid soon after landing in Tunisia and died there near Tunis on August 25. Noted for his justice, ability, charity, and personal piety, Louis founded numerous religious and educational institutions (he rebuilt the

Sainte-Chapelle in Paris, 1245–48, to house the Crown of Thorns given him by Emperor Baldwin II in 1239, and supported the founding of the Sorbonne in 1257) and forbade war among the feudal lords. He protected vassals from oppression by their lords and made the lords live up to their obligations. A man of his word, he was often sought out as an arbitrator and settled disputes about succession in Flanders, Navarre, and Hainaut and between King Henry III and his barons in 1263. Under his reign, France enjoyed unprecedented prosperity and peace as he followed a policy of peaceful coexistence with his European neighbors improved the tax system, simplified administration, extended the appellate jurisdiction of the crown to all cases, and encouraged the use of Roman law. Gothic architecture flowered during his regime, and he built the first French navy. He was one of the greatest of all French Kings and embodied the highest ideals of medieval kingship in the forty-four years of his rule. He was canonized in 1297 by Pope Boniface VII. August 25.

LOUIS OF ANJOU (1274–97). Son of King Charles II of Naples and Sicily and Mary, daughter of King Stephen V of Hungary, he was born at Brignolles, Provence. When his father was captured by the King of Aragon in 1284, he was sent to Barcelona with two of his brothers in 1288 as hostages of his father's release. He was freed after seven years there by a treaty in 1295 between his father and King James II of Aragon. Louis refused to marry James's sister, surrendered his rights to the throne, and after much opposition, was ordained when he was twenty-three, was named bishop of Toulouse, and joined the Friars Minor at Rome. He lived a life of great austerity despite his royal background, resigned his bishopric after a few months because he felt he was unequal to its demands, and died at Brignolles on August 19. He was canonized in 1317.

LOUIS OF MONTFORT. *See* Grignion, Louis Mary.

LOUIS OF THURINGIA, BL. (1200–27). Eldest son of Landgrave Herman I of Thuringia, he was betrothed to Elizabeth, daughter of King Andrew II of Hungary, when he was eleven and she was four. She was raised at the Thuringian court and the two were married in 1221, when Louis became landgrave. In 1225, he exacted retribution from the citizens of Lubitz in Poland for a robbery of Thuringian merchants who had been robbed and beaten nearby on Polish soil, and did the same thing soon after at Würzburg by exerting armed forces to make them comply with his demands. He supported Emperor Frederick II at the diet of Cremona in 1226, and in the following year accompanied Frederick on crusade as commander of a contingent of German troops. Louis died of malaria on the way at Otranto on September 11. Though never formally canonized, he is called St. Ludwig in Reinhardsbrunn, where he was buried.

LOUISA OF SAVOY, BL. (1461–1503). Daughter of Duke Amadeus IX of Savoy and niece of King Louis XI of France, she was raised by her mother when her father died when she was nine. She married Hugh de Châlons, lord of Nozeroy, when she was eighteen. When he died after nine years of married life, she became a Franciscan tertiary. After she distributed her fortune, she became a Poor Clare at Orbe, Switzerland, in 1490 and later was named abbess. Her cult was approved in 1839. July 24.

LOUISE DE MARILLAC. *See* Marillac, Louise.

LOYOLA, IGNATIUS. *See* Ignatius Loyola.

LUAN. *See* Moloc.

LUBIN. *See* Leobinus.

LUCHESIO (d. 1260). Born at Gaggiano, Umbria, Italy, he was forced to leave his birthplace because of his activities on behalf of the Guelphs and went to Poggibonsi, where he became a merchant and moneylender. When his children died, his interests changed from the making of money to concern for his fellow man, and he gave away his possessions, cared for the sick, and visited prisoners. When Francis of Assisi came to Poggibonsi, Luchesio and his wife, Bonadonna, became Franciscan tertiaries, perhaps the first husband and wife to do so. They both devoted the rest of their lives to charitable work. Luchesio was gifted with ecstasies and the ability to heal the afflicted. April 28.

LUCIAN (d. c. 250). He and his friend Marcian practiced black magic until they were converted to Christianity, when they publicly burned their magic paraphernalia and books in Nicomedia. They sold their possessions, gave the proceeds to the poor, and after a period as recluses began to preach. When Decius' edict against Christians was published in Bithynia, they were arrested and arraigned before Proconsul Sabinus. When they refused to worship pagan gods, they were tortured and burned to death. The whole story is probably a pious fiction. October 26.

LUCIAN OF ANTIOCH (d. 312). Born at Samosata, Syria, he studied Scripture under Macarius at Edessa and after he was ordained served as a priest in Antioch. He prepared an accurate version of the Old and New Testaments that was used by St. Jerome in preparing the Vulgate. Separated from the Church for a time (probably because he followed the teachings of Paul of Samosata), he was later reconciled. He was arrested at Nicomedia in 303 when Emperor Diocletian's persecution of the Christians began. After a long imprisonment, when he refused to sacrifice to pagan gods, he was convicted of being a Christian, racked, and sworded to death on January 7 at Nicomedia, Bithynia.

LUCIAN OF BEAUVIAS (d. c. 290). A missionary in Gaul, possibly a companion of St. Dionysius of Paris, he suffered martyrdom at Beauvais, where he may have been bishop. Two of his companions, Maximian (or Messien) and Julian, were executed shortly before him at the same place. The whole story is questioned by scholars. January 8.

LUCILLIAN (d. 273). A pagan priest in Nicomedia, he was converted to Christianity at an advanced age and was arrested during Emperor Aurelian's persecution of Christians, tortured, and imprisoned. While in prison, he encouraged Claudius, Dionysius, Hypatius, and Paul to remain constant in their faith. When Lucillian emerged unscathed from an oven, they were all sent to Byzantium, where Lucillian suffered death by crucifixion and the other four were beheaded. Also tortured and beheaded was Paula, a Christian who ministered to them in prison. Probably the whole story is a pious fiction. Another version has Lucillian and Paula married and the four boys their children; another has them Egyptians who were martyred for their faith in Egypt. June 3.

LUCIUS (d. c. 161). *See* Ptolomaeus.

LUCIUS (2nd century). According to the *Liber Pontificalis,* in a section collected

about 530, he was a British ruler who wrote to Pope Eleutherius (c. 174–c. 189) asking to be received as a Christian and asking the Pontiff to send missionaries to Britain. Although Bede, the English ecclesiastical historian, incorporated the incident in his book, scholars are dubious about the whole incident and even of the existence of Lucius. December 3.

LUCIUS I (d. 254). A Roman, he was elected Pope to succeed Pope St. Cornelius on June 25, 253, and ruled only eighteen months. He was exiled briefly during the persecution of Emperor Gallus but was allowed to return to Rome. A letter of St. Cyprian praises him for condemning the Novatians for their refusal of the sacraments to penitent *lapsi.* He did not suffer martyrdom, as erroneously stated in the *Liber Pontificalis,* but died probably on March 4 in Rome and was buried in St. Callistus' catacomb.

LUCIUS (d. 259). During Emperor Valerian's persecution of the Christians, a revolt broke out in 259 in Carthage that Solon, the procurator there, blamed on the Christians. He arrested Lucius and seven others, all followers of St. Cyprian, who had been executed for his faith the year before. Among the seven were Flavian, a deacon; Julian; Montanus; and Victorinus, a priest. All were tortured and then beheaded. February 24.

LUCIUS (d. 350). Named bishop of Adrianople, Macedonia, on the death of St. Eutropius, he too was driven into exile by the Arians. He was forced to flee again soon after his return and went to Rome to plead his case. He came back to Adrianople and was arrested with some of his followers when he refused to embrace Arianism. His followers were all beheaded and Lucius was condemned to prison and exile. He died in prison of the ill treatment he received. St. Athanasius, whom he met while in Rome, speaks admiringly of him in his writing. February 11.

LUCRETIA. See Leocritia.

LUCY (d. 304). According to unreliable tradition, she was born of noble parents at Syracuse, Sicily. When she refused marriage to a suitor during Emperor Diocletian's persecution of the Christians, he denounced her as a Christian. The governor sentenced her to a brothel, but when the guards tried to take her there they were unable to move her. She was then ordered burned to death, but the flames made no impression on her. Finally, she was stabbed through the throat. She is invoked by those with eye trouble, perhaps because of her name, which means light; one tradition has her eyes torn out by her judge, while another has her tearing them out to present to a suitor she disliked who admired them; in both cases they were miraculously restored. December 13.

LUCY OF AMELIA, BL. (d. 1350). Born at Castel Ponziano, Umbria, Italy, and sister of Bl. John of Rieti, Lucy Bufalari joined the Augustinians and was later made prioress of the Augustinian convent at Amelia. She was known for her austerities and the mortifications she practiced. Her cult was confirmed in 1832. July 27.

LUCY OF CALTAGIRONE (13th century). Born at Caltagirone, Sicily, she became a Poor Clare at Salerno, was novice of mistresses, promoted devotion to the Five Wounds, and was credited with numerous miracles. September 26.

LUCY OF NARNI. See Brocadelli, Lucy.

LUDAN (d. c. 1202). According to legend, he was the son of Scottish Prince Hiltebol and on the death of his father gave his inheritance to the poor and built a hospice for pilgrims and the ill. On the way back from a pilgrimage to Jerusalem, at a spot near Strasbourg, he dreamed of his death, was given communion by an angel when he awakened, and died; whereupon all the bells in the surrounding churches pealed his death. February 12.

LUDGER (d. 809). Born at Zuilen near Utrecht, Netherlands, he studied at Utrecht under St. Gregory, accompanied Aubert, a priest from York, to England, and continued his studies under Alcuin at York for three and a half years. On his return, he worked as a missionary, was ordained in 777 at Cologne, and spent seven years as a missionary in Friesland until the Saxons invaded the area and drove out all priests. He went on pilgrimage to Rome in 785, spent two years at Monte Cassino, where he probably met Charlemagne, and returned to Friesland in 787, charged with the spiritual direction of five provinces by Charlemagne. Ludger was highly successful in the Heligoland and Westphalia areas and built monasteries at Werden and Münster. He refused Charlemagne's offer of the bishopric of Trier in 793 but about 804 was consecrated first bishop of Münster. He died on March 26, after saying his last Mass, at Billerbeck, Westphalia, West Germany.

LUDMILA (c. 860–921). Daughter of a Slav prince, she married Duke Borivoy of Bohemia and was converted to Christianity with him. He attempted to force his people to accept Christianity but was unsuccessful. On the death of Borivoy, his sons, Ratislav and Spytihinev, succeeded him, and Ratislav put his son, Wenceslaus, in Ludmila's care. She raised him but when Ratislav died, his wife, Drahomira, was named regent and kept Wenceslaus from Ludmila, fearful she might stage a *coup* to put Wenceslaus on the throne early and restore Christianity, which was being attacked by the anti-Christian regency. Reportedly, Drahomira had Ludmila strangled to death at Tetin Castle near Podybrad on September 16.

LUDOLPH (d. 1250). A Premonstratensian, he became bishop of Ratzeburg, Schleswig-Holstein, in 1236, built a Benedictine convent at Rehna, and was imprisoned and then exiled for his opposition to Duke Albert of Sachsen-Lauenburg. He was taken in by Duke John the Theologian at Wismar, Mecklenburg, Germany, but died soon after of the ill treatment he had received in prison. He was canonized in the fourteenth century. March 29.

LUDWIG, BL. *See* Louis of Thuringia, Bl.

LUFTHILDIS (d. c. 850). Little is known of her beyond that she was mistreated by a stepmother for her charity to the poor, left home to become a hermitess near Cologne, and was credited with performing numerous miracles at her tomb. January 23.

LUGAIDH. *See* Moloc.

LUGHAIDH. *See* Molua.

LUKE (1st century). The author of the third gospel and the Acts of the Apostles is of unknown origin, though Eusebius and Jerome say he was probably a Greek and may have come from Antioch. He was a physician (Col. 4:14), accompanied Paul on his second missionary journey about 51, and then stayed at Philippi

as a leader of the Christian community there until 57, when he rejoined Paul on his third missionary journey. He was with Paul in Rome during Paul's imprisonment, 61–63, and also during his second imprisonment. After Paul's death in 66, he seems to have gone to Greece. An improbable legend has him the painter of several portraits of Mary, though he may very well have visited her in Jerusalem. Where and when he wrote his gospel are uncertain, though it was probably between 70 and 90 (Eusebius says before Paul's death, Jerome says after, and an early tradition says in Greece). It was unquestionably written by a Gentile Christian for Gentile Christians. His Acts, probably written in Rome (Eusebius and Jerome agree in saying during Paul's imprisonment, though Irenaeus says after Paul's death), is the story of the growth of the Church under the inspiration of the Holy Spirit from about 35 to 63. Legend has him one of the seventy disciples, and some scholars identify him with Lucius of Cyrene, a teacher and prophet at Antioch (Acts 13:1) and with Lucius, Paul's companion at Corinth (Rom. 16:21). He is believed to have died at Boetia when eighty-four. He is the patron of painters and physicians and is represented in art as an ox. October 18.

LUKE THE YOUNGER (d. c. 946). A Greek, he was brought to Thessaly by his family from the island of Aegina to escape Saracen attacks on the island. Inclined to the religious life, he left home on the death of his father but was arrested and imprisoned as a runaway slave. Freed, he returned to the joking and derision of his neighbors until two monks persuaded his mother to let him enter a monastery in Athens. He soon returned home but after a few months left again to become a hermit on Mount Joannitsa near Corinth, Greece, at the age of eighteen. He lived a life of great austerity and was venerated for his miracles, which earned him the surname Thaumaturgus (wonder worker). February 7.

LULL (d. 786). Probably a native of Britain, he was educated at Malmesbury Monastery, where he became a deacon, and when twenty went to Germany, where he labored as a missionary, noted for his learning, under St. Boniface, who ordained him. He was sent to Rome on a mission to Pope St. Zachary by Boniface, was consecrated his coadjutor when he returned, and succeeded to the see of Fulda on Boniface's death. He became involved in a jurisdictional dispute with St. Sturmi, abbot of Fulda, deposed him, but saw him restored and the abbey declared independent by King Pepin. Luke refounded the monastery of Hersfeld, where he retired late in life, and died there. October 16.

LUNAIRE. *See* Leonorius.

LUPERCUS (d. 304). *See* Optatus.

LUPICINUS (d. 480). *See* Romanus.

LUPUS (c. 383–478). Born at Toul, Gaul, he married the sister of St. Hilary of Arles, but after six years of marriage they parted by mutual agreement. He gave his wealth to the poor, entered Lérins Abbey under St. Honoratus, and about 426 was named bishop of Troyes. In 429, he accompanied St. Germanus of Auxerre to Britain to combat Pelagianism there, and on his return devoted himself to his episcopal duties. When Attila invaded Gaul, he persuaded him in 453 to spare Troyes, though he took Lupus with him as hostage. When Attila was defeated at Châlons, Lupus was accused of helping him escape and was forced to leave Troyes. He lived as a hermit for two years and then was al-

lowed to return to Troyes. Many scholars doubt the veracity of the account of the Attila incident. July 29.

LUPUS (d. 623). Also known as Leu, he was a monk at Lérins and in 609 succeeded St. Artemius as bishop of Sens. He supported Sigebert on the death of his father, King Thierry II. When Clotaire became King he dispatched Duke Farulf to Sens to care for his interests there; Farulf's unjust accusations of Lupus to the King caused Clotaire to banish Lupus to Ausène near Lyons in a pagan area. He converted the governor and several other prominent officials before being recalled by Clotaire, who realized he had been misled, especially by the lies of Medegislus, abbot of Saint-Remi, who thought to be appointed bishop of Sens when Lupus was banished (Medegislus was killed by the people of Sens for his false witness against Lupus). September 1.

LUTGARDIS (1182–1246). Born at Tongres, Brabant, she was sent to St. Catherine Benedictine Convent near Saint-Trond when she was twelve presumably because her dowry had been lost in a business venture. She had no particular vocation to the religious life until one day a vision of Christ caused a change in her outlook on life and she became a Benedictine nun when twenty. During the next twelve years she experienced numerous ecstasies, during which she had visions of our Lord, our Lady, and several of the saints, was levitated, and dripped blood when sharing in the Passion of Christ. Though the nuns of her convent wanted to make her abbess, she left in quest of a stricter rule and became a Cistercian at their convent at Aywières. She lived there the thirty remaining years of her life, famed for her spiritual wisdom, miracles, and prophecies. Blind the last eleven years of her life, she died on June 16 and is considered one of the leading mystics of the thirteenth century.

LUXORIUS (d. c. 303). A soldier in the imperial Roman army at Sardinia, he was converted to Christianity after reading Psalms. He was arrested during Emperor Diocletian's persecution of the Christians and brought before Delphius, the prefect. With him were two young boys, Cisellus and Camerinus, who had just been baptized and whom he encouraged in their faith. When Luxorius refused to deny Christ, he was scourged, and then all three were put to death by sword. August 21.

LWANGA, CHARLES (d. 1886). A master of pages at the court of King Mwanga of Uganda, he had succeeded Joseph Mkasa, a Catholic, whose censure of the King for his murder of a Protestant minister and his homosexuality and corruption of the young pages had intensified Mwanga's hatred of Catholics. Mwanga ordered Lwanga and fourteen of the pages who were Christians sent to Namugango. Three of them were murdered on the way; Lwanga and the others, with two soldiers, were burned to death. Among them were a thirteen-year-old, Kizito, and Mbanga, a boy who was killed by his uncle, who was the chief executioner, before being thrown on the pyre. Some one hundred people died in the persecution; among those martyred were a young catechist, Denis Sebuggawo, speared to death by Mwanga himself; Andrew Kaggwa, a native chief, beheaded; Pontain Ngondwe, a soldier; and Mathias Kalemba, a Membo judge, tortured to death. Also among those martyred in the same persecution were Matthias Murumba, an assistant judge to the provincial chief who was attracted to Christianity by Protestant missionaries and then was baptized a Catholic by Fr. Livinhac; also Andrew Kagwas, chief of Kigowa, who had been active in conversion work. In all, twenty-two martyrs were canonized in 1964 by Pope Paul VI as the Martyrs of Uganda. June 3.

LYDIA PURPURARIA (1st century). Born at Thyatira (Ak-Hissar), a town in Asia Minor famous for its dye works (hence her name, which means purple seller), she "was in the purple-dye trade" when she became Paul's first convert at Philippi. She was baptized with her household, and Paul stayed at her home there (Acts 16:12–15).

LYDWINA, BL. (1380–1433). Born at Schiedam, Holland, one of nine children of a workingman, she was injured in 1396 while ice skating and became a life-long invalid, suffering intensely, with each year bringing increasing pain. She bore the pain as reparation for the sins of others. Beginning in 1407, she began to experience supernatural gifts—ecstasies and visions in which she participated in the Passion of Christ, saw purgatory and heaven, and visited with saints. The last nineteen years of her life she took no sustenance but Communion, slept little if at all the last seven years of her life, and became almost completely blind. Her extraordinary suffering attracted widespread attention, and when a new parish priest accused her of hypocrisy, the people of the town threatened to drive him away. An ecclesiastical commission appointed to investigate declared her experiences to be valid. Thomas à Kempis wrote a biography of her, and her cult was approved in 1890. April 14.

LYÉ. See Leo (d. c. 550).

M

MACAIRE. *See* Macarius of Ghent.

MACANISIUS (d. 514). According to unreliable legends, Aengus MacNisse was baptized by St. Patrick, who years later consecrated him bishop. After a pilgrimage to the Holy Land and Rome, he founded a church and monastery at Kells, which developed into Connor, of which he is considered the first bishop. His story is filled with extravagant miracles, such as changing the course of a river for the convenience of his monks and rescuing a child about to be executed for his father's crime by causing him to be carried by the wind from the executioners to his arms. September 3.

MACARIUS (d. c. 335). Named bishop of Jerusalem in 314, he fought the Arian heresy and was one of the signers of the decrees of the Council of Nicaea. According to legend he was with Helena when she found three crosses and was the one who suggested that a seriously ill woman be touched with each of the crosses; when one of them instantly cured her it was proclaimed the True Cross. He was commissioned by Constantine to build a church over Christ's sepulcher and supervised the building of the basilica that was consecrated on September 13, 335. He died soon after. March 10.

MACARIUS (d. c. 350). Bishop of Petra, Palestine, he attended the Council of Sardica and was so active against the Arians that they had him banished to Africa. His name was originally Arius, but he was renamed Macarius to distinguish him from the founder of Arianism that he fought so vigorously. He died in exile. June 20.

MACARIUS OF ALEXANDRIA. *See* Macarius the Younger.

MACARIUS THE ELDER (c. 300–90). Born in Upper Egypt, he was a cattle-herder in his youth but early became a hermit, practicing the greatest austerities. He was accused of assaulting a woman but proved his innocence and became somewhat of a hero for his patience and humility during this trying ordeal. To escape the adulation, he retired to the desert of Skete when he was thirty, was ordained, and was much sought after for his spiritual wisdom. He was exiled for a time on a small island in the Nile with Macarius the Younger and other monks when Arian Lucius of Alexandria tried to drive out the desert monks, but was later allowed to return. He died after living in Skete for sixty years and is believed to be the first hermit to live there. January 15.

MACARIUS OF GHENT (d. 1012). Also known as Macaire, according to legend he was archbishop of Antioch, Pisidia, but left all his possessions to the poor and went on pilgrimage to Jerusalem. He was captured and tortured by the Saracens but managed to escape and traveled throughout Europe, performing numerous miracles. When he reached Ghent, Flanders, he was given food and shelter as a poor pilgrim by the monks of Saint-Bavon. He caught the plague ravaging the country and died; whereupon, as he had prophesied, the plague abated. He is the patron against epidemic diseases. April 10.

MACARIUS THE WONDER WORKER (d. c. 830). Born at Constantinople and baptized Christopher, he became a monk at Pelekete, taking the name Macarius. In time he was elected abbot and became known for the miracles he was reputed to have performed. He was ordained by Patriarch Tarasius of Constantinople, was imprisoned and tortured for his opposition to the iconoclasm proclaimed by Emperor Leo the Armenian, and was released by Leo's successor, Emperor Michael the Stammerer. When he refused Michael's demands that he support the iconoclastic heresy, he was exiled to the island of Aphusia off the coast of Bithynia and died there on August 18. April 1.

MACARIUS THE YOUNGER (d. c. 394). A successful businessman in Alexandria, Egypt, he gave up his business about 335 to become a monk in the Thebaid, Upper Egypt, and spent the remaining sixty years of his life as a hermit. In 373, he moved to Lower Egypt, where he built cells in the deserts of Skete and Nitria, but spent most of his time in the area called the Cells. He was ordained, lived a life of great austerity, and was known for his miracles. He was banished for a time with Macarius the Elder and other monks to an island in the Nile for his unswerving fidelity to orthodoxy by Lucius, the intruded Arian Patriarch of Jerusalem, but was later allowed to return. Macarius wrote a constitution for the monastery in Nitria named after him, and some of its rules were adopted by St. Jerome for his monastery. He is often surnamed "of Alexandria." January 2.

MACARTAN (d. c. 505). The little that is known of Aedh MacCairthinn from unreliable legends is that he may have been consecrated by St. Patrick, is considered the first bishop of Clogher, was probably abbot of Dairinis, and had many extravagant miracles attributed to him. March 26.

MACASSOLI, BL. CHRISTOPHER (d. 1485). Born at Milan, Italy, he joined the Franciscans in his youth, was ordained, and became a successful preacher. His holiness and wisdom drew thousands to his sermons and to the friary he had founded at Vigevano to receive his help and counsel. His cult was confirmed in 1890. March 11.

MACCABEES, THE HOLY (d. 160 B.C.). This is the name given to a group of Jews who were executed for resisting the attempts of King Antiochus IV Epiphanes to impose Greek paganism on the Jews and thus subvert their religion in his efforts to Hellenize them. Most prominent among the Maccabees are Eleazar, a prominent scribe who though ninety years old refused to succumb to the bribes and cajolery of the King's men, refused to violate the Jewish Torah by eating the flesh of swine, and was executed for his resistance; also tortured and executed were seven brothers who, encouraged by their mother, remained adamant in refusing to give up their Jewish faith. All seven and their mother were executed (2 Mac. 6–7), and their remains are believed to be enshrined in the Church of St. Peter in Chains in Rome. These are the only persons in the Old Testament liturgically venerated in the Western Church and are honored on August 1.

MACCALDUS. See Maughold.

MACCUL. *See* Maughold.

MACEDONIUS (c. 340–430). A Syrian anchoret who is reputed to have performed numerous miracles of healing, among them a miracle attributed to him by Theodoret by which his prayers caused Theodoret's mother, who had been childless for thirteen years of married life, to bear a child—Theodoret. Macedonius was surnamed "the Barley Eater," as he is said to have lived on barley for forty years. January 24.

MACHADO, BL. JOHN BAPTIST (1580–1617). Born at Terceira, Azores, he joined the Jesuits at Coimbra in Portugal and in 1609 was sent to Japan as a missionary. He worked for eight years at Nagasaki until he was arrested on the Gato Islands, brought back to Japan, and imprisoned at Omura with Bl. Peter of Cuerva. They were both beheaded, with Bl. John's server Leo, on May 22 at a place between Omura and Nagasaki. Bl. John was beatified in 1867.

MACHAR (6th century). An Irish missionary also known as Mochumna, he accompanied St. Columba to Scotland, evangelized the island of Mull, was consecrated bishop, and labored among the Picts in the Aberdeenshire area. He is believed to be the founder of Aberdeen. November 12.

MACHUTUS. *See* Malo.

MACIAS, JOHN. *See* Massias, John.

MACLOU. *See* Malo.

MACRINA THE ELDER (c. 270–340). Grandmother of St. Basil the Great and St. Gregory of Nyssa, both of whom she influenced with her religious fervor, she and her husband lived at Neocaesarea, Pontus, and suffered great hardships when they were forced to flee into hid-ing during Emperor Diocletian's persecution of the Christians. January 14.

MACRINA THE YOUNGER (c. 330–79). Granddaughter of Macrina the Elder and sister of St. Basil, St. Gregory of Nyssa, and St. Peter of Sebastea, she was well educated, especially in Scripture, was engaged to be married when twelve, but when her fiancé died, she decided to dedicate her life to God. On the death of her father, she and her mother retired to the family estate in Pontus and lived a life of prayer and contemplation in a community they formed there. Macrina became head of the group when her mother died and lived in Pontus until her death there. July 19.

MADELGAIRE. *See* Vincent Madelgarius.

MADELGISILUS (d. c. 655). Also known as Mauguille, he was an Irish monk, accompanied St. Fursey from Ireland to England and then to Gaul, and when Fursey died about 648, he became a monk at Saint-Riquier at Centula. To escape the adulation of his fellow monks, he became a hermit with St. Vulgan near Monstrelet, where Madelgisilus lived until his death. May 30.

MADERN (d. c. 545). A hermit of Cornish descent and in some way connected with Brittany, nothing is really known of him beyond that numerous churches in England were named after him, notably that of St. Madern's Well in Cornwall, which may have been the site of his hermitage. His name is also spelled Madron. May 17.

MADRON. *See* Madern.

MAEDOC. *See* Aidan.

MAELOR (d. c. 586). Born at Glamorgan, Wales, son of St. Umbrafel, he spent his

childhood under St. Illtyd at Llanityd
Fawr, became a monk and a disciple of
St. Samson, and accompanied him to
Brittany as a missionary. Maelor became
abbot of a monastery at Kerfunt and then
succeeded Samson as bishop of Dol. In
his old age, he resigned to live as a hermit
on Sark and when he miraculously cured
the chieftain of a skin disease, the chieftain gave him property on the island, and
Maelor founded a monastery there. He
helped organize resistance to Norsemen
raiding the island, visited Jersey, ministered to his people during famine and
plague, and reportedly performed numerous miracles. He is called Maglorius
in France. October 24.

MAELRUBHA. *See* Malrubius.

MAFALDA (1204–52). Daughter of King
Sancho I of Portugal, she was married
when eleven to King Henry I of Castile,
and when the marriage was annulled
because she was too closely related to
Henry, she became a Benedictine nun at
Arouca Convent. She was responsible
for the convent adopting the Cistercian
rule, devoted the sizable income from
her father to charitable works, built a
hostel for travelers and a home for widows, restored Oporto Cathedral, and
lived a life of great austerity. Her cult was
approved in 1793. May 2.

MAGALOTTI, BL. HUGOLINO (d.
1373). Born at Camerino, Italy, he was
orphaned in his youth, distributed his
inheritance to the poor, and became a
Franciscan tertiary living the life of a
hermit. He became known for his holiness and miracles of healing. He died on
December 11, and his cult was confirmed by Pope Pius IX in 1856.

MAGENULF (d. c. 857). Of a noble
Westphalian family and also known as
Méen and Meinulf, he was sent to the
cathedral school of Paderborn by

Charlemagne, who was his godfather,
received minor orders, was given a
canonry in Paderborn Cathedral, and became archdeacon there. He founded a
monastery for nuns on his estate at
Bödeken, for which he drew up a rule,
and his preaching caused him to be
called one of the apostles of Westphalia.
He died at Bödeken. October 5.

MAGGI, BL. SEBASTIAN (d. 1496).
Born at Brescia, Italy, of a noble family,
he joined the Dominicans at fifteen and
became known for his eloquent preaching, his large number of conversions,
and the reconciliations he effected. He
was Savonarola's confessor for a time
and appointed him master of novices at
Bologna, reformed those houses of his
order of which he served as superior, and
was twice vicar of Lombard Province.
He died at Santa Maria di Castello Priory
in Genoa on December 16 while on a
visitation of the province. His cult was
confirmed in 1760.

MAGI. *See* Balthasar.

MAGLORIUS. *See* Maelor.

MAGNERICUS (d. 596). Raised in the
household of Bishop Nicetius of Trier,
Gaul, who ordained him, he accompanied the bishop when King Clotaire I exiled Nicetius for excommunicating him
for his corruption and licentiousness.
Magnericus returned the following
year and six years later, about 566, was
named the first Frankish bishop of Trier.
He gave shelter to Bishop Theodore
of Marseilles when Guntramnus of
Burgundy banished him in 585 and
pleaded with King Childebert II on his
behalf. He had a great devotion to St.
Martin of Tours and built a monastery
and several churches dedicated to him.
July 25.

MAGNUS (d. 258). *See* Sixtus II.

MAGNUS (d. c. 670). *See* Agricolus.

MAGNUS OF ORKNEY (d. 1116). Son of Erling, cogovernor with his brother Paul of the Orkney Islands, he was taken on a raid on the Scottish and English coasts by King Magnus Barefoot of Norway, who had taken him prisoner when he conquered the Orkneys. Magnus refused to fight the Welsh at Anglesey, escaped, and took refuge at the court of King Malcolm III of Scotland. When his cousin Haakon, Paul's son, seized the government of the Orkneys, Magnus returned, and the two ruled jointly, as had their fathers. They later disagreed, and Magnus was tricked into a meeting with Haakon on the island of Egilsay to settle the dispute and was murdered there by Haakon. Magnus was considered a martyr, but the murder was evidently for strictly political reasons. April 16.

MAGUNDAT. *See* Anastasius the Persian.

MAHANES (d. 339). *See* Sapor.

MAHARSAPOR (d. 421). A Christian Persian of noble family, he was seized with Narses and Sabutaka when King Yezdigerd, angered at the destruction of a Mazdean temple, unleashed a persecution of Christians. They were tortured, and then Narses and Sabutaka were executed. Maharsapor was imprisoned for three years and was then thrown into a cistern to die of starvation and was found dead three days later. October 10.

MAILLÉ, BL. JOAN (1332–1414). Born at Roche-Saint-Quentin, Touraine, France, on April 14, the daughter of Baron Hardouin VI of Maillé, she was married to a neighbor, Baron Robert de Sillé, whom she is reputed to have saved from drowning when both were children; they agreed to live a life of celibacy.

Baron Hardouin was killed at Poitiers, and Baron Robert was captured but ransomed by Joan, who sold her jewelry to raise the large sum of money demanded. On his return, they lived a life of great austerity and devoted themselves to charitable work and to ransoming prisoners. When Robert died in 1362, his family drove Joan from the estate, blaming her for depleting the estate by encouraging Robert's charities, and she returned to her mother at Luynes. Joan refused numerous marriage offers, devoted herself to prayer, turned over all her possessions to the Carthusians of Liget, and thus alienated her own family, who disowned her. She became a Franciscan tertiary and was so impoverished she was obliged to beg for food and lodging. She then became a hermitess at Planche-de-Vaux, restored a chapel there, and then went to Tours in 1389, where she was known for her holiness, miracles of healing, gift of prophecy, and ministrations to prisoners. She died at Tours on March 28, and her cult was approved in 1871. November 6.

MAIMBOD (d. c. 880). An Irish missionary also known as Mainboeuf, he is believed to have been martyred by pagans while preaching near Kaltenbrunn, Alsace. January 23.

MAIN. *See* Méen.

MAINBOEUF. *See* Maimbod.

MAJOLUS (c. 906–94). Also known as Mayeul, he was born at Avignon, France, was forced to flee from his large estates near Rietz to relatives at Mâcon, Burgundy, to escape marauding Saracens. He received a canonry from his uncle, Bishop Berno, who sent him to Lyons to study under Abbot Antony of L'Isle Barbe, was named archdeacon on his return to Mâcon, and soon after was named bishop of Besançon. He became a monk at Cluny to escape this unwanted post and in 965 was elected abbot. The monasteries of Germany were entrusted to him by Emperor Otto the Great, and Majolus reformed many of them. He was noted for his scholarship and held in the greatest esteem by the rulers of his time, at one time settling a disagreement between Empress St. Adelaide and her son Emperor Otto II. Majolus appointed St. Odilo his coadjutor in 991 and devoted himself to prayer and penance. He died at Souvigny Abbey on May 11 on the way to reform St. Denis Abbey near Paris at the request of Hugh Capet.

MAJORICUS (d. 484). *See* Dionysia.

MALACHY (1095–1148). Malachy O'More (Mael Maedoc Ua Morgair) was the son of a schoolteacher and was born and raised in Armagh, Ireland. When his parents died, he became a disciple of Eimar, a hermit, and was ordained by St. Celsus when he was twenty-five. He continued his studies under Bishop St. Malchus of Lismore, was assigned the abbacy of run-down Bangor Abbey, and in 1125 was named bishop of Connor, using Bangor as his headquarters. He soon restored religious fervor to the people of his see. When marauding Norsemen overran Bangor in 1127, he and his monks fled to Lismore and then established a monastery at Iveragh, Kerry. St. Celsus named Malachy his successor as metropolitan of Armagh on his deathbed in 1129, but instead Celsus' family installed his cousin Murtagh, as the archbishopric had been hereditary for generations. Malachy refused to try to occupy the see but after three years was ordered to do so by the papal legate and others. He governed the see but would not enter the city until 1134, when Murtagh died, naming Celsus' brother Niall his successor. Armed conflict broke out between the followers of the two, but Malachy finally obtained possession of his cathedral. When Niall fled with two relics that were supposed to be in the possession of the true archbishop, a book (probably the Book of Armagh), and a crozier, both reputed to have been St. Patrick's, the division and conflict continued as many of the people turned to Niall as possessor of these all-important symbols. Malachy eventually recovered them, restored peace and discipline to the see, and became uncontested archbishop. He then resigned the archbishopric of Armagh and returned to Connor in 1137. He then divided Connor into two dioceses, Connor and Down, became bishop of the latter, and established a monastery on the ruins of Bangor. He went to Rome two years later, met St. Bernard on the way, and wanted to become a monk at Clairvaux but was refused permission to resign his see and do so by Pope Innocent II. Instead his actions in Ireland were approved and he was appointed papal legate to Ireland. He returned to his native land in 1142, founded Mellifont Abbey with four of his companions who had become Cistercian monks at Clairvaux on their return trip from Rome, and in 1148 was appointed by a synod on Inishpatrick to go to Rome to secure *pallia* for the two metropolitans from Pope Eugene III. Delayed in England by King Stephen for political reasons, Malachy set off for Rome, and when he found that the Pope had left France and returned to Rome, decided to stop off on the way to see Bernard at Clairvaux. Malachy was stricken there and died in Bernard's arms on November 2. Bernard proclaimed him a saint at his requiem Mass, an action formally confirmed by Pope Innocent III in 1190, the first papal canonization of an Irish saint. Malachy was one of the great saints of Irish history, being responsible for the unification of the Irish clergy, the restoration of discipline, the revival of religious fervor, and the restoration of morality by his determination, humility, and lack of any desire for self-aggrandizement. He is reputed to have performed many miracles, among them curing Henry, son of King David of Scotland, of a grave disease, but is probably best known for the so-called Prophecies of Malachy, a list of Popes from Celestine II (d. 1144) "to the end of the world." The Popes are not named but are described in general, symbolic terms, quite accurate to 1590 but extremely vague after that. One theory is that they were forgeries from the conclave of 1590 to support the aspirations of one of the papal candidates. Another theory is that Malachy wrote them while he was in Rome, showed them to Pope Innocent II, and then they were buried in the papal archives until found by a Don Arnold de Wyon, a Benedictine in 1597, 449 years after Malachy's death. Who wrote them is unknown but almost certainly it was not Malachy; they are considered spurious by scholars. November 3.

MALCHUS (d. 260). *See* Alexander.

MALCHUS (4th century). According to the story he told St. Jerome, he was born in Nisibia, fled to avoid the marriage his parents had planned for him, and became a monk with a group of recluses at Khalkis near Antioch. When his father died, he set out for home, despite the refusal of his abbot to grant him permission to do so. The caravan he was with was attacked by marauding Bedouins, and he and a young woman were carried off as slaves. When his master decided he should marry the girl, they lived as brother and sister after Malchus had told her he would rather die than marry. They decided to flee, he to return to the monastery and she to her husband, and were pursued by their master and an aide. Malchus and the girl hid near a cave, and the master, thinking they had taken refuge in the cave, went into it with his aide, and both were killed by a lioness. Malchus returned to Khalkis, and when she was unable to find her husband, she joined him as a hermitess. She died there and Malchus ended up in Maronia, where Jerome found him, old and venerated for his holiness. October 21.

MALLONUS (d. 314). Also known as Mellon and Melanius, he was the first bishop of Rouen. Legend had him a native of Cardiff, Wales, who was converted while in Rome and sent as a missionary to Gaul by Pope St. Stephen. October 22.

MALO (d. c. 621). Also known as Machutus and Maclou, he was born near Llancarfan, Wales, educated at a monastery there, and was ordained despite the opposition of his parents. He went to Brittany as a missionary, was successful for a time working in the area around Aleth from headquarters at what is now Saint-Malo, but pagan opposition forced him and his monks to move to Saintes. Several years later he was requested to return to Aleth, stayed there for a time, and then started back to Saintes. He died on the way. November 15.

MALRUBIUS (c. 642–722). Also known as Maelrubha, he was born in Ireland, became a monk at St. Comgall's Monastery at Bangor in Ireland, and after a stay at Iona went to Scotland in 671. He built a church and monastery of which he was abbot at Applecross, Ross, and from there labored as a missionary among the Picts for the next fifty-one years until his death. April 21.

MAMAS (d. c. 275). A shepherd at Caesarea, Cappadocia, he was noted for the fervor of his faith, for which he was executed. The Roman Martyrology says he was the son of SS. Theodotus and Rufina and was executed for his faith in his old age during the reign of Emperor Aurelian, but an Eastern tradition has him stoned to death when a boy. St. Basil and St. Gregory Nazianzen both write of him. August 17.

MAMERTIUS (d. c. 475). Known for his learning, he was named bishop of Vienne, Gaul, in 461, and in 463 was condemned by Rome for consecrating, without the authority to do so, a new bishop of Die, which had been transferred from his jurisdiction to Arles; but no papal action seems to have been taken in the matter. He is particularly remembered as the originator of the penitential practice of rogation days, which was marked by processions and psalm singing the three days before the feast of the Ascension. May 11.

MAMILIAN. *See* Maximilian (274–95).

MANCINI, BL., MARY (d. 1431). Of a distinguished Pisa family, she was born at Pisa, Italy, was married when twelve, widowed at sixteen with two children, and was married again. After eight years of marriage, she was again widowed, with five more children. She refused a third marriage and devoted herself to charitable work, using her home as a hospital. She became a Dominican tertiary, experienced ecstasies, and then became a Dominican nun, taking the name Mary. She left with Bl. Clare Gambacorta to seek a stricter rule, and Mary's father, who reputedly had been saved from death on the rack by Mary's prayers when she was five, built them a convent, where she died on December 22. Her cult was approved in 1855. January 28.

MANECHILDIS (6th century). Of a family of seven daughters, all of whom received the veil from Bishop St. Alpinus of Châlons, and also known as Ménéhoud, she was born at Perthois, Gaul, the daughter of Sigmarius, who was *comes* there. She dedicated herself to ministering to the poor, and on the death of her parents became a hermitess at Bienville, continued her care of the poor and the sick, and died there. October 14.

MANGIN, BL., LEON IGNACE (1857–1900). A French Jesuit priest in China, he suffered martyrdom for his faith during the Boxer uprising in 1900. It is estimated that more than thirty thousand Christians were killed from June to August, when the Boxers ran amok. In 1956, Pope Pius XII beatified fifty-six of the martyrs of this persecution. Among them were three French Jesuit priests: Paul Denn (b. 1847), executed at Chukiahoon on July 20; Remi Isoré (b. 1852), executed at Wuyi on July 20; and Modeste Andlayer (b. 1847), executed on July 19. Many of the martyrs were Chinese, among them: seven-year-old Paul Lang; nine-year-old Andrew Wang Tien-ching; eleven-year-old Anna Ann Hsin-shib; seventy-nine-year-old Paul Lieu Chinte; and Anna Wang. July 20.

MANNES, BL. (d. c. 1230). Son of Felix de Guzmán and Bl. Joan of Aza and brother of St. Dominic, he was born at Calaruega, Burgos, Spain, and was one of the original sixteen members of the Dominicans, making his profession at Prouille in 1217. He and six others were sent to Paris to make the first French Dominican foundation in the same year. He then became chaplain to the Dominican nuns at Prouille, in 1218 was sent to Madrid as chaplain to a convent of Dominican nuns there, and spent the rest of his life in Madrid. He died at St. Peter Monastery at Gumiel d'Izan near Caleruega, and Pope Gregory XVI, in 1834, approved his cult. There is a possibility he may not have died until 1235. July 30.

MANSUETUS (d. c. 484). *See* Donatian.

MANTOVANI, BL. MARIA DOMENICA (1862–1934). Cofounder of the Institute of the Little Sisters of the Holy Family, she worked together with Blessed Giuseppe Nascimbeni, her mentor. Her profound love for the Virgin Mary as her guide, she cared directly for the spiritual and apostolic formation of girls. Inspired by admiration for Mary Immaculate and a call to be consecrated by God, in 1886 she made a private vow of perpetual virginity. Her life work was guiding the women of Little Sisters in their service to the poor and underprivileged. Today this organization can be found in Italy, Switzerland, Albania, Africa, Argentina, Brazil, Uruguay, and Paraguay. She was beatified in 2003.

MAPPALICUS (d. c. 250). A resident of Carthage, he was tortured and then executed for his faith during the persecution of Christians under Emperor Decius when he refused to obey Decius' decree that all persons must sacrifice to the gods. Seventeen other Christians were put to death by various means at the same place and time. April 17.

MARAMALDI, BL. GUY (d. 1391). Born at Naples, Italy, he joined the Dominicans there and became known for his knowledge of theology and his preaching prowess. He taught at Naples, spent time at Ragusa, where he was a popular preacher, and on his return to Naples was appointed inquisitor general of the Kingdom of Naples. His cult was approved in 1612. June 25.

MARCELLA (d. c. 202). *See* Plutarch.

MARCELLA (d. 410). A Roman matron, she was widowed after nine months of marriage, refused to marry Cerealis, the consul, and formed a group of noble ladies to live a life of austerity and asceticism. She was tortured by the Goths looting Rome in 410 to force her to reveal the whereabouts of her wealth, which she had long since given to the poor, was released, but died shortly after, in August. She had a correspondence with St. Jerome in which he answered queries she put to him about spiritual matters. January 31.

MARCELLIAN (d. c. 287). According to tradition, he and his twin brother, Mark, were of a distinguished family, had been converted to Christianity, and were deacons living in Rome with their wives when Emperor Diocletian's persecution of the Christians broke out. They were arrested and refused to sacrifice to pagan gods despite the importunations of their wives, children, and parents. They were sentenced to be beheaded by Chromatius, the prefect's aide, who then sequestered them at the home of Nicostratus, the public registrar, so they could reconsider their decision. They converted Nicostratus, their pagan relatives, and then Chromatius, who set them free, and then resigned his office and retired. They were recaptured and executed by Chromatius' successor, Fabian. June 18.

MARCELLINA (d. c. 398). Daughter of the prefect of Gaul and sister of St. Ambrose, she was born at Trier, Gaul, went to Rome with her family when she was quite young, and was consecrated to a religious life by Pope Liberius in 353. She lived a life of great austerity, which St. Ambrose tried to persuade her to mitigate when she went to Milan to visit him. It was to Marcellina that he dedicated his treatise on virginity, *Libri III de virginibus ad Marcellinam.* July 17.

MARCELLINUS (d. 304). Born at Rome, the son of Projectus, he was elected Pope to succeed Pope St. Caius on June 30, 296, and witnessed the beginnings of Emperor Diocletian's persecution of the Christians. According to an ancient legend that may have been Donatist-inspired, he seems to have been apostatized and surrendered the sacred books and offered incense to pagan gods but later repented and died a martyr's death by being beheaded. He died in Rome on October 25, but whether he died a martyr or from natural causes is still very uncertain. April 26.

MARCELLINUS (d. 304). A priest at Rome, he and Peter, an exorcist, were arrested and imprisoned during the persecution of Christians launched by Emperor Diocletian. While in prison they made many converts, including the jailer, Arthemius, his wife, and his daughter. Marcellinus and Peter were sentenced to death by the magistrate, Serenus, and were beheaded. Pope Damasus wrote an epitaph for their tomb, and Constantine built a church in their honor. June 2.

MARCELLINUS (d. 320). See Argeus.

MARCELLINUS (d. c. 374). An African priest, he and two companions, Vincent and Domninus, went to Gaul and worked as missionaries in the Dauphiné area with headquarters at Embrun. He was appointed first bishop of Embrun by St. Eusebius of Vercelli, was persecuted by the Arians, and was forced to flee to the Auvergne Mountains where he spent the rest of his life in hiding. April 20.

MARCELLINUS (d. 413). Tribunal secretary to Emperor Honorius, he was sent to Carthage by the Emperor to chair a meeting between Catholic and Donatist bishops. At the end of the conference, Marcellinus ordered the Donatists to return to the Catholic faith and with

his brother Apringius enforced his decree with great severity. Angered, the Donatists accused them of being implicated in a rebellion led by Heraclion to Marinus, the general in charge of putting down the insurrection. Marinus had Marcellinus and Apringius peremptorily executed at Carthage, an action for which he was later reprimanded by the Emperor. St. Augustine dedicated his *City of God* to "My dear friend Marcellinus." April 6.

MARCELLINUS. See Marchelm (d. c. 762).

MARCELLUS (1st century). See Apuleius.

MARCELLUS (d. c. 178). Marcellus was a priest at Lyons, Gaul, when Marcus Aurelius' persecution of Christians was launched in 177. He was imprisoned but managed to escape, as did a fellow prisoner, Valerian. Marcellus was sheltered at Chalon-sur-saône by a pagan whom he converted to Christianity. After he left him, Marcellus encountered Priscus, the governor, who invited him to his home. When Priscus began preparing pagan rituals, Marcellus refused to participate. The governor demanded that he sacrifice to the gods, and when he refused to do so, Priscus had him buried to his waist near Chalon-sur-Saône, and he died three days later, on September 4, of exposure. Valerian was later recaptured and beheaded at Tournus near Autun. August 26.

MARCELLUS (d. c. 287). A tribune at Oxyrhynchus, Egyptian Thebäid, Marcellus and, his wife, Mammaea; their sons; Miletius, a bishop; and twelve other Christians, the whole Christian populace of the town, were summoned before the governor at Thmuis. They refused to sacrifice to pagan gods, and after a bear would not molest them nor a fire burn them, they were beheaded. August 27.

MARCELLUS (d. c. 303). *See* Sabinus.

MARCELLUS I (d. 309). After the death of Pope Marcellinus in 304, the intensity of Emperor Diocletian's persecution of the Christians prevented the election of a new Pope for years, and it was not until Diocletian abdicated in 305 and Maxentius became Emperor in 306 that a new election could be contemplated. Marcellus, a priest in Rome, was elected Pope in May or June 308. He reorganized the Church in Rome and was soon embroiled in the controversy concerning the *lapsi* when he insisted that they do penance before being readmitted to the sacraments. His decree caused widespread civil disorders, which caused Maxentius to exile Marcellus, who died shortly after leaving Rome on January 16 (although this may be the date of his burial) after a pontificate of about eighteen months.

MARCELLUS (d. c. 389). A judge on the island of Cyprus, he became bishop of Apamae, Syria, and was burned to death by a group of pagans while he was destroying their temple, probably at Aulona, in accordance with the edicts of Emperor Theodosius the Great that all pagan temples in the Empire were to be destroyed. August 14.

MARCELLUS (d. c. 430). Born at Paris, he was ordained a reader by Bishop Prudentius of Paris, who later made him his archdeacon. Marcellus succeeded Prudentius as bishop of the city, which he defended against the attacks of the barbarians. Marcellus was venerated for his reputed miracles and his holiness. November 1.

MARCELLUS AKIMETES (d. c. 485). Born at Agamea, Syria, he inherited a fortune on his parents' deaths, studied at Antioch and Ephesus, and then became a monk at Eirenaion Monastery across the Bosporus from Constantinople. He was named third abbot of the monastery and under his administration it was enlarged and flourished. He was active in the struggle against Eutyches at a synod called by St. Flavian in 448, attended the Council of Chalcedon, and his prayers were credited with saving Constantinople from a disastrous fire that destroyed half the city in 465. He died on December 29 after forty-five years as abbot. His surname is derived from the name of his monks, *Akoimetroi* (non-resters), because the divine office was chanted twenty-four hours a day in their monasteries.

MARCELLUS THE CENTURION (d. 298). A centurion in the Roman army at Tingis (Tangiers), he denounced the festivals held to celebrate the Emperor's birthday for their paganism and declared his Christianity. He was imprisoned and brought before Aurelius Agricolan, deputy for the praetorian prefects, after the festival was over. After an exchange between the two that is still preserved, Marcellus was condemned to death and was executed by sword. October 30.

MARCHAND, BL. JOSEPH (d. 1835). Born at Passavant near Besançon, France, he joined the Society of Foreign Missions in Paris, was ordained, and was sent as a missionary to Annam in Vietnam. Captured at Saigon, he was tortured to death during the persecution of Christians unleashed by Minh-Mang, ruler of Annam. Bl. Joseph was beatified in 1900. November 30.

MARCHELM (d. c. 762). Also known as Marculf and Marcellinus, he was one of the group of Anglo-Saxon monks who followed St. Willibrord to the Netherlands to evangelize the Frisians.

Marchelm worked among them for fifteen years and then joined St. Lebuin to help convert the Saxons. Marchelm built a church at Deventer that was burned down during an attack by pagans and died soon after at Oldenzaal, Frisia. July 14.

MARCHIONI, JOHN CHARLES (1616–70). Born at Sezze, Italy, on October 19, of humble parents, he became a shepherd and wanted to become a priest. When unable to do so because of his poor scholarship (he barely learned to read and write), he became a lay brother at Naziano, served in various menial positions—cook, porter, gardener—at different monasteries near Rome and became known for his holiness, simplicity, and charity. He wrote several mystical works, lived a life of great mortifications, and worked heroically to help the stricken in the plague of 1656. He died in Rome on January 6. His family name may have been Melchoir, and he is also known as Charles of Sezze. He was canonized by Pope John XXIII in 1959. January 5.

MARCIAN (d. c. 250). See Lucian.

MARCIAN (d. c. 304). See Abundius.

MARCIAN (4th century). See Nicander.

MARCIAN (d. c. 387). Born at Cyrrhus, Syria, of a patrician family, he became a hermit in Chalcis Desert near Antioch. In time he attracted numerous disciples, appointed Eusebius abbot over them, and was renowned for his holiness, spiritual wisdom, and miracles. November 2.

MARCIAN (d. 471). Born at Constantinople of a noble Roman family related to Emperor Theodosius, he was ordained in 455, practiced severe mortifications for which he was accused and

cleared of Novatianism, and ministered to the poor. He was named Oikonomos, second only to Patriarch Gennadius in the Church hierarchy in Constantinople, restored several churches, was reputed to have performed miracles, and may have written several hymns. January 10.

MARCIAN (d. c. 488). Also known as Marian, he fled Bourges in Gaul to escape the Visigoth occupation of the town and became a lay brother under St. Mamertinus at the monastery at Auxerre. Marcian was put in charge of the livestock, had a remarkable rapport with both wild and domestic animals, and became much admired for his humility. The monastery was named for him after his death. April 20.

MARCIANA (d. c. 303). Born at Rusuccur, Mauretania, she was persecuted for her faith during the persecution of Christians under Emperor Diocletian, had her virginity miraculously preserved when gladiators tried to rape her, and was then killed by a wild bull and a leopard in the amphitheater of Caesarea in Maurentania. She may be the same as the Marciana who is the patron of Tortosa, Spain, who is reported to have suffered martyrdom at Toledo. January 7.

MARCOLINI OF FORLI, BL. See Amanni, Bl. Marcolini.

MARCOUL. See Marculf.

MARCULF (d. c. 558). Also known as Marcoul, he was born at Bayeux, Gaul, of noble parents, was ordained when he was thirty, and did missionary work at Coutances. Desirous of living as a hermit, he was granted land by King Childebert at Nanteuil, attracted numerous disciples, and built a monastery, of which he was abbot. It became a great pilgrimage center after his death on May 1. He is considered the patron of skin diseases.

MARDARIUS (d. 304). *See* Eustratius.

MAREAS (d. c. 342). *See* Abdiesus.

MARELLO, GIUSEPPE (1844–95). Born on the day after Christmas in Turin, Italy in 1844, Giuseppe Marello entered seminary at the tender age of twelve. There he was known for his particular devotion to the Virgin Mother, to her husband Joseph, and to the needs of the poor. Ordained a priest in 1868, Giuseppe attended the First Vatican Council of 1869–70 as assistant to a bishop. At the Council, he came to the attention of Church leaders, and in 1878, while serving as secretary to his bishop, he founded the Oblates of Saint Joseph. This congregation of priests established schools and cared for the poor through the establishment of orphanages and homes for the elderly. The Oblates of Saint Joseph now serve the mission of the Church throughout the world, including the United States, India, Peru, Mexico, Brazil, Poland and Nigeria. Giuseppe was canonized in 2001.

MARERI, BL. PHILIPPA (d. 1236). Born at Cicoli, Abruzzi, Italy, of a wealthy landowner, she resisted the efforts of her family, especially of her brother Thomas, to have her marry, and when they persisted, she ran away and became a hermitess with a group of followers on Mount Marerio. Her brother relented, gave her a house for her community, and Bl. Roger Todi became their spiritual director. Philippa was elected abbess, was credited with numerous miracles and died on February 13. February 16.

MARGARET (No date). Nothing certain is known of her, but according to her untrustworthy legend, she was the daughter of a pagan priest at Antioch in Pisidia. Also known as Marina, she was converted to Christianity, whereupon she was driven from home by her father. She became a shepherdess and when she spurned the advances of Olybrius, the prefect, who was infatuated with her beauty, he charged her with being a Christian. He had her tortured and then imprisoned, and while she was in prison she had an encounter with the devil in the form of a dragon. According to the legend, he swallowed her, but the cross she carried in her hand so irritated his throat he was forced to disgorge her (she is patroness of childbirth). The next day attempts were made to execute her by fire and then by drowning, but she was miraculously saved and converted thousands of spectators witnessing her ordeal—all of whom were promptly executed. Finally she was beheaded. That she existed and was martyred are probably true; all else is probably fictitious embroidery added to her story, which was immensely popular in the Middle Ages, spreading from the East all over Western Europe. She is one of the Fourteen Holy Helpers, and hers was one of the voices heard by Joan of Arc. July 20.

MARGARET THE BAREFOOTED (d. c. 1395). Born of a poor family at San Severino, Anacona, Italy, she was married at fifteen, suffered the ill treatment of her husband for years patiently in prayer and penance and gained her name from her habit of begging for alms for poor beggars, barefooted as they were. August 27.

MARGARET OF CITTÀ-DI-CAS-TELLO, BL. (d. 1320). Blind and abandoned as a child, she was adopted by a group of women who found her in the church in Città-di-Castello, Umbria, Italy. She was later sent to a convent, but her austerities caused problems in the lax community there, which evicted her. She was taken in by one of the villagers, became a Dominican tertiary when she was fifteen, founded a school for the village children, and was reported to have performed miracles and to have experienced levitation. She died at Città-di-Castello, venerated for her holiness. Sometimes called Margaret of Metola, her cult was confirmed in 1609. April 13.

MARGARET COLONNA, BL. (c. 1254–80). Daughter of Prince Odo Colonna, she was born in Rome, was orphaned as a child, and was raised by her two brothers. She refused marriage and when unable to join the Poor Clares at Assisi because of illness, turned the family castle on the mountain above Palestrina into a convent of Poor Clares, for whom her brother, James Cardinal Colonna, provided a mitigated version of the Franciscan rule. She suffered from cancer the last seven years of her life and was reputed to have performed miracles. She died at Rome on December 30, and her cult was confirmed in 1847. November 7.

MARGARET OF CORTONA (1247–97). Daughter of a farmer, she was born at Laviano, Tuscany, Italy, and was raised by an unsympathetic stepmother after the death of her mother, when she was seven. She ran away to become the mistress of a young nobleman from Montepulciano, bore him a son, and lived ostentatiously in great luxury. Nine years after she went to live with him, he was murdered and she resolved to change her lifestyle. She made a public confession of her sins in the church at Cortona where she had gone to seek the aid of the Friars Minor, but her father refused to take her back into his home. She and her son were taken in by two ladies, Marinana and Raneria, living in Cortona. Margaret became a Fran-

ciscan tertiary and Frs. John da Castiglione and Giunta Bevegnati became her spiritual advisers and helped her through three years of spiritual despair and aridity, frequently admonishing her to moderate the severity of the penances and mortifications she imposed on herself. After a brief period as a recluse, she devoted herself to caring for the poor and the sick. She began to experience ecstasies and visions of Christ, acted as a peacemaker, often admonishing worldly prelates, and in 1286 received approval from Bishop William of Arezzo for her plan to form a community of women to care for the sick poor called the Poverelle. She founded a hospital at Cortona and the Confraternity of Our Lady of Mercy to support it. About 1289 false and vicious rumors about her relations to the friars began to circulate, and Fr. Giunta was transferred to Siena, but it was later proved that the rumors were the work of vicious gossips, and the holiness of her life became apparent to all. She converted great numbers of sinners and was sought after for spiritual advice and her miraculous healing powers by people from all over Italy, France, and Spain. She died at Cortona, acclaimed a saint at once, though she was not formally canonized until 1728. May 16.

MARGARET OF ENGLAND (d. 1192). According to tradition, she was an Englishwoman who went on pilgrimage to Jerusalem with her mother, lived a life of austerity and penance with her there and in Bethlehem, and on the death of her mother made pilgrimages to Monserrat, Spain, and Puy, France. She then settled at the Cistercian monastery at Seauve Bénite, and after her death there, her tomb became a pilgrimage shrine. Her father may have been Hungarian but her mother was either English or of English descent. February 3.

MARGARET OF HUNGARY (1242–70). Daughter of King Bela IV of Hungary, she was entrusted to the Dominican nuns at Veszprem when she was three and was professed when she was twelve by Bl. Humbert of Romans at a convent built by her parents near Buda. She refused an offer of marriage from King Ottokar of Bohemia to remain a nun and lived a life of such extreme austerity, penance, and fasting that she died on January 18 when only twenty-eight. She experienced visions, and numerous miracles were attributed to her. She was canonized in 1943. January 26.

MARGARET OF LORRAINE (1463–1521). Daughter of Duke Ferri of Lorraine and niece of Margaret of Anjou, she was born in Vaudément Castle, Lorraine, and married Duke René of Alençon when she was twenty-five. She was widowed with three children in 1492 and devoted herself to ably administering the ducal estate at Alençon and to works of charity. Influenced by St. Francis of Paula, she led a life of great austerity, and when her children were of age, she entered a convent at Mortagne, where she continued her care of the sick and the poor. She later left with some of the nuns to found a Poor Clare convent at Argentan, Brittany, where she became a nun but refused the position of abbess. She died there on November 2, and her cult was confirmed in 1921. November 6.

MARGARET OF LOUVAIN (c. 1207–25). Born at Louvain, Flanders, she was a serving maid at the inn of a relative named Aubert who, with his wife, decide to sell the inn and enter the religious life. The night before they were to become religious, they were attacked at home by a group of men and murdered for the money they had received from the sale of the inn. They kidnaped Margaret and when she refused to promise to keep silent about their identity, they murdered her too. Her body was found, reportedly through supernatural voices and an angelic light, and after her burial, miracles were reported at her tomb. Her cult was confirmed in 1905. September 2.

MARGARET MARY. *See* Alacoque, Margaret Mary.

MARGARET OF METOLA. *See* Margaret of Città-di-Castello.

MARGARET THE PENITENT. *See* Pelagia the Penitent.

MARGARET OF RAVENNA (1442–1505). Born at Russi near Ravenna, Italy, she lost her sight shortly after her birth and was maligned in her youth for her ascetical practices, but in time was venerated for her holiness. She was consulted for spiritual advice and formed a religious group of men and women living in the world, for which she drew up a rule, but it did not endure after her death on January 23. Her cult has never been formally confirmed.

MARGARET OF SAVOY, BL. (1382–1464). Daughter of Amadeus of Savoy, she was born at Pinerola, Italy, and married Theodore Palaeologus, marquis of Montferrat, in 1403. She was widowed in 1418, refused an offer of marriage from Philip, Visconti of Milan, and became a Franciscan tertiary, founding a community on her estate at Alba, Piedmont, in 1426. After twenty-five years she received permission from Pope Eugene IV for the women of her community to become nuns. She was gifted with ecstasies and reputedly performed miracles, but the last years of her life were saddened by charges that she was overly strict with her nuns, and the

rumor circulated by the rejected Philip
Visconti that her convent favored
Waldensianism—a charge later proved
false. She died at Alba on November 23,
and her cult was confirmed in 1669.

MARGARET OF SCOTLAND (1045–
93). Daughter of Prince Edward
d'Outremer (the Exile) and a German
princess, Agatha, who was probably the
niece of King St. Stephen of Hungary's
wife, Margaret was probably born in
Hungary and raised at Stephen's court,
where her father was an exile. When she
was twelve she was brought to the court
of King Edward the Confessor in
England, but was forced to flee England
with her mother, brother, and sister after
the Battle of Hastings in 1066. They
were given refuge at the court of King
Malcolm III of Scotland, and in 1070
she and Malcolm were married at
Dunfermline Castle. She became known
for her great personal piety expressed in
prayer, austerities, and fasting, her great
concern for the poor and the needy, and
for her royal benefactions. She supported synods that reformed abuses so
prevalent at the time, such as simony and
usury, regulated degrees of relationship
in marriage, and set regulations for the
Lenten fast and Easter Communion. She
encouraged arts and education, acted as
adviser in state matters, and with
Malcolm, founded Holy Trinity Church
at Dunfermline. She died at Edinburgh
Castle on November 16 soon after learning that her husband and son had been
killed by rebels attacking Alnwick Castle
and while rebel forces were attacking
Edinburgh. She was canonized in 1250
and declared patroness of Scotland in
1673. November 16.

MARI (d. c. 180). See Addai.

MARIA CROCIFISSA. See Di Rosa,
Mary.

MARIA DESOLATA. See Torres-Acosta,
Mary Soledad.

MARIA GORETTI. See Goretti, Maria.

MARIAN (d. 259). See James.

MARIAN. See Marcian (d. c. 488).

MARIANA OF QUITO. See Paredes y
Flores, Marian de.

MARIANI, BL. RAINERIUS (d. 1304).
Born at Arezzo, Italy, he became a
Franciscan lay brother and died at Borgo
San Sepolcro, venerated for his holiness
and miracles, which continued after his
death. His cult was confirmed in 1802.
November 12.

MARIANUS (d. 283). See Chrysanthus.

MARIANUS SCOTUS, BL. (d. 1088).
Born in Donegal, Ireland, Muiredach
mac Robartaigh was early destined for
the priesthood by his parents. In 1067,
he and a group of companions left
Ireland for Rome, stopped off at
Bamberg on the way, remained for a
year, and then became Benedictine
monks at Michelsburg. They again
set out for Rome, stopped off at
Regensburg, and stayed at the upper
monastery and then the lower
monastery, where Mirianus copied the
Bible and provided commentaries. He
decided to remain there, transcribed
many theological, spiritual, and liturgical
works, and many of his copies are
still extant. In 1078, a man named
Bezelin built St. Peter's Monastery at
Regensburg for Marianus and his companions, with Marianus as abbot, and its
fame spread, attracting disciples from all
over Ireland—the first of the Irish and
Scottish monasteries that were to come
into existence in southern Germany.
In addition to his fame as a scribe,

Marianus also wrote poetry and theological tracts of his own. February 9.

MARIE OF THE INCARNATION, BL. *See* Acarie, Bl. Marie; Martin, Bl. Marie of the Incarnation.

MARIE OF THE URSULINES. *See* Martin, Bl. Marie of the Incarnation.

MARILLAC, LOUISE DE (1591–1660). Born probably at Ferrières-en-Brie near Meux, France, on August 12, she was educated by the Dominican nuns at Poissy. She desired to become a nun but on the advice of her confessor, she married Antony Le Gras, an official in the Queen's service, in 1613. After his death in 1625, she met St. Vincent de Paul, who became her spiritual adviser, and she devoted the rest of her life to working with him. She helped direct his Ladies of Charity in their work of caring for the sick, the poor, and the neglected, and in 1633 she set up a training center, of which she was directess, in her own home for candidates seeking to help in the work. This was the beginning of the Sisters (or Daughters, as Vincent preferred) of Charity of St. Vincent de Paul (though it was not formally approved until 1655). She took her vows in 1634 and attracted great numbers of candidates, wrote a rule for the community, and in 1642, Vincent allowed four of the members to take vows. Formal approval placed the community under Vincent and his Congregation of the Mission, with Louise superior. She traveled all over France establishing her Sisters in hospitals, orphanages, and other institutions, and by the time of her death in Paris on March 15, the congregation had more than forty houses in France. Since then they have spread all over the world. She was canonized by Pope Pius XI in 1934 and was declared patroness of social workers by Pope John XXIII in 1960.

MARINA. The Latin form of the Greek Pelagia.

MARINA (no date). The daughter of Eugenius, a Bithynian who became a monk, she was brought into the monastery as a boy by her father. She dressed as a boy and lived the life of a monk until her father died when she was seventeen. She was accused of making the daughter of the local innkeeper pregnant but concealed her identity and was dismissed from the monastery. She became a beggar at the gates of the monastery and still maintained her silence about her sex when the innkeeper's daughter made her take custody of the child and was readmitted to the monastery with her "son" five years later. She was assigned the lowliest tasks and made to perform the most severe penances. Her sex was finally revealed at her death, when of course all concerned in the affair were filled with remorse. The whole story is typical of the pious fictions telling of women saints masquerading as men. February 12.

MARINA. *See* Margaret (no date).

MARINONI, BL. JOHN (1490–1562). The youngest son in a Bergamo, Italy, family, he was born at Venice and baptized Francis, was ordained, and became director of the hospital for incurables at Venice. Named a canon of St. Mark's, he resigned his benefice in 1528 and joined the Theatines, making his profession when he was forty, at which time he changed his name to John. He accompanied St. Cajetan to Naples to found a Theatine house there, served as superior of several houses and was a popular preacher and confessor. He was Cajetan's aide in establishing the *montes pietatis* (a type of pawnshop for the poor) in Naples in 1543, later refused the archbishopric of Naples, and died in Naples

MARK 409

on December 13. His cult was authorized in 1762.

MARINUS (d. c. 262). A soldier from a noble family in Caesarea, Palestine, he was denounced as a Christian by a rival for the position of centurion that he was about to receive. Given three hours by Achaeus, the governor, to give up his faith, he was exhorted by Theotecunus, bishop of Caesarea, to remain steadfast; when he did so, he was executed. A Roman senator, Astyrius, who was present at the execution, wrapped Marinus' body in his cloak and buried it; presumably he too suffered martyrdom. March 3.

MARINUS (4th century). Untrustworthy legend has him born in Dalmatia. He became a stonemason, went to Rimini with a fellow stonemason, St. Leo, and worked in the quarries there. They gave encouragement to the Christians sentenced to labor there, made new converts, and Leo became a priest and Marinus a deacon. Leo then went to Montefeltro, and Marinus spent the next twelve years working on an aqueduct. When a Dalmatian woman accused Marinus of being the husband who had deserted her, he fled into the mountains and spent the rest of his life living as a hermit. A monastery grew up around his hermitage, and later the town of San Marino, which was named after him, as was the tiny republic. September 4.

MARISCOTTI, HYACINTHA (1585–1640). Born of a noble family at Vignarello, Italy and named Clarice, she was educated at the Franciscan convent at Viterbo and against her will was forced by her family to enter the convent, taking the name Hyacintha. She had become unbearable after the Marquis Cassizucchi had passed over her when she was twenty to marry her younger sister. For ten years Hyacintha violated and flouted the rules of the convent, and though temporarily brought to a more religious life by a priest during an illness, she soon lapsed into her old ways when she recovered. A more serious illness again converted her, this time permanently, and she adopted a lifestyle characterized by great austerities, mortifications, and penances. She became mistress of novices, helped found two congregations to minister to the sick and the aged, and was widely known for her charity. She died on January 30, and was canonized in 1807.

MARIUS (c. 260). A Persian noble, he became a Christian and gave away his wealth to the poor in Jerusalem. With his wife, Martha, and two sons, Audifax and Abachum, he went on pilgrimage to Rome during a persecution of Christians by Emperor Claudius. Apprehended there while gathering the remains of Christians executed for their faith, they were all tortured and then put to death. Marius and his two sons were beheaded, and Martha was drowned at Santa Ninfa near Rome. January 19.

MARIUS (d. c. 555). Also called May (and erroneously Maurus), he was born at Orléans, Gaul, became a monk, was cured of a serious illness at the tomb of St. Denis in Paris, and was probably founding abbot of the abbey at Bodon later named after him. He is reputed to have prophesied the barbarian invasion of Italy and the destruction of his monastery. January 27.

MARK (d. c. 74). The son of Mary at whose house in Jerusalem the apostles stayed and a cousin of Barnabas, he was probably a Levite and perhaps a minor minister in the synagogue. He may have been the young man who attempted to follow Jesus after his arrest, was caught, but wiggled out of his cloak and fled naked (Mark 14:51–52), but this is uncertain. He accompanied Paul and Barnabas to Antioch in 44 (Acts 12:25), then to Cyprus, and with Barnabas was on Paul's first missionary journey (Acts 13:5), but left Paul at Pamphylia and returned to Jerusalem (Acts 13:13). Whatever the reason, he had evidently offended Paul, who did not take him on his second missionary journey, which was the occasion of the disagreement and separation of Paul and Barnabas (Acts 15:36–40). Mark accompanied Barnabas to Cyprus (Acts 15:39) and then, evidently back in Paul's good graces, was with him in Rome during his first imprisonment (Col. 4:10), where he was evidently a disciple of Peter, who affectionately called him "my son, Mark" (1 Pet. 5:13). An early uncertain tradition has him first bishop of Alexandria, and he is probably the same as the John Mark (Acts 12:25) mentioned several times in the New Testament. In the East this John Mark is believed to have been a separate person who became bishop of Biblos; his feast is celebrated on September 27. Mark was the author of the second gospel, written probably between 60 and 70 and based on the teaching of Peter. Papias, the bishop of Hierapolis in Asia Minor, called him the interpreter of Peter, in 130, and an ancient tradition had it written in Rome for Gentile Christians. Many modern scholars believe that Mark provided Matthew and Luke with a common source for their gospels. Mark is the patron of Venice, which claims his body is in St. Mark's Cathedral there, where it is reported to have been brought from Alexandria. In art he is represented as a lion. April 25.

MARK (d. c. 287). *See* Marcellian.

MARK (d. 336). Son of Priscus, he became a priest in Rome and was elected Pope to succeed Pope St. Sylvester on January 18, 336. Mark built two basilicas in Rome on land granted by Emperor Constantine and is believed to have decreed that the bishop of Ostia was to consecrate the bishop of Rome. Mark died in Rome on October 7 after a pontificate of only eight months.

MARK (d. c. 365). Bishop of Arethusa on Mount Lebanon in Lebanon, his destruction of a pagan temple caused much resentment among the pagan populace. When Julian the Apostate became Emperor in 361, he ordered all who had destroyed pagan temples to replace them. Mark was forced to flee when he refused, but surrendered when he heard that members of his flock had been arrested. He was dragged through the streets and tortured but bore his sufferings with such courage that many were converted and his tormentors set him free; he was pardoned by Julian at the request of the governor. March 29.

MARK. See Martin (d. c. 580).

MARK OF MODENA, BL. (d. 1498). Born at Modena, Italy, he joined the Dominicans, preached with great success in northern Italy, and for many years was prior of the friary at Pesaro, where he died on September 23, venerated for his miracles. His cult was approved in 1857.

MARK OF MONTEGALLO (1426–97). Born at Santa Maria di Montegallo near Ascoli, Italy, he studied at Perugia and Bologna, received his medical degree, and married. Soon he and his wife mutually agreed to separate, she to become a Poor Clare at Ascoli and he to become a Franciscan at Fabriano. He became an eloquent preacher and missionary, stressing love in his sermons, practiced great mortifications, and was active in the founding of *monti di pieta,* institutions to lend money to the poor unable to borrow except from usurers. He died at Vicenza after forty years of preaching throughout Italy. March 20.

MARO (d. 433). A disciple of St. Zebinus, he became a hermit near Cyrrhus, Syria, lived a life of prayer and mortifications, and drew great crowds by his spiritual wisdom. He trained many hermits and monks and founded three monasteries. It is believed the Maronites take their name from Bait-Marun Monastery near the source of the Orontes River, where a church was erected over his tomb. February 14.

MARS. See Martius.

MARSDEN, BL. WILLIAM (d. 1586). See Anderton, Bl. Robert.

MARTHA (1st century). Sister of Mary and Lazarus, with whom she lived in Bethany, she was evidently the eldest and in charge of the household. They were all friends of Jesus, who often stayed at their home, and she was most solicitous of his welfare. In the famous incident in Luke 10:38–42, she asked Christ to tell her sister Mary, who was listening to the Lord, to help her in the household preparations; whereupon he chided her for bustling about so, concluding, "it is Mary who has chosen the better part." She has thus become the prototype of the activist Christian and Mary the symbol of the contemplative life. It was Martha who went out to meet Jesus after the death of Lazarus, while Mary remained at home (John 11:20). According to a medieval legend, she, Mary, and Lazarus went to France after the death of Jesus and evangelized Provence. She is the patron of cooks. July 29.

MARTHA (d. c. 260). See Marius.

MARTIAL (d. c. 165). See Felicity.

MARTIAL (d. c. 250). According to tradition, he was one of the seven missionary bishops sent from Rome before 250 to preach the gospel in Gaul. He evangelized the Limousin area and founded Limoges, of which he was the first bishop. Later legends extravagantly (and erroneously) had him one of the followers of Christ, one of the seventy-two disciples, and the boy with the barley loaves when the Savior performed the miracle of the loaves and the fishes. June 30.

MARTIAL (d. c. 304). See Faustus.

MARTIAL (d. 304). See Optatus.

MARTIN (d. c. 580). Called Mark in the Roman Martyrology, he was probably a monk at Monte Cassino and then became a hermit on Mount Marsicus (Mondragone) in Campagnia, where according to St. Gregory, who called him Martin in his *Dialogues*, he performed many miracles. October 24.

MARTIN (d. 597). Though regarded as one of the outstanding scholars of his time, nothing is known of his early life. After a pilgrimage to Palestine, he went to Galicia, Spain, converted Arian King Theodomir, and won the inhabitants from Arianism to Catholicism. He built several monasteries, among them Dumium, which was his headquarters and of which he was first bishop, appointed by the Suevian rulers, who held him in the highest regard. He was later transferred to Braga as metropolitan of Galicia. He wrote several treatises, notably *Formula vitae honestae* and *De correctione rusticorum,* a collection of local superstitions. He died at Dumium (Mondonedo). March 20.

MARTIN I (d. c. 656). Born at Todi, Umbria, Italy, he came to Rome and was known for his great learning and piety. He was Pope Theodore I's nuncio to

Constantinople and succeeded him as Pope on July 21, 649. He called a council at the Lateran the same year, which condemned monothelitism and censured the imperial decrees of Heraclius, *Ekthesis,* and of Constans II, *Typos.* When Martin's condemnations were published in the East, Constans, who was a monothelite, was furious and sent Theodore Calliopas to Rome to bring Martin to Constantinople. Though Martin was ill and had taken refuge in the Lateran, Calliopas' soldiers broke in and forcibly took the Pope captive to Constantinople, where he arrived in the fall of 653. He was imprisoned for three months under terrible conditions and then tried and convicted, without being heard, by the Senate of treason and sent back to prison for another three months. His life was spared at the plea of the dying Patriarch Paul of Constantinople and he was exiled to Kherson in the Crimea, where he died on September 16 of neglect and ill treatment, the last of the Popes to die a martyr. November 12.

MARTIN, BL. MARIE OF THE INCARNATION (1599–1672). The daughter of a baker, Marie Guyard was born in Tours, France, on October 28 and married a silk manufacturer named Claude Martin when she was seventeen; the couple had one son. Claude died two years later and Marie became a bookkeeper for her brother-in-law. In 1629, she joined the Ursulines at Tours, taking the name Marie of the Incarnation. In 1639, she was sent to Canada where she laid the cornerstone of the first Ursuline convent in Quebec in 1641; she rebuilt it when it was destroyed by fire in 1650. She compiled dictionaries in Algonquin and Iroquois and taught the Indians the rest of her life until her death in Quebec on April 30. She experienced mystical visions and suffered periods of spiritual aridity about which she wrote and her *Letters* give a valuable account of life in

Quebec in 1639–71. Also known as Marie of the Ursulines, she was beatified in 1980 by Pope John Paul II.

MARTIN DE PORRES. *See* Porres, Martin de.

MARTIN, BL. RICHARD (d. 1588). Born in Shropshire, England, he was educated at Oxford and when convicted of hiding Catholic priests during the persecution of Queen Elizabeth I, was hanged, drawn, and quartered at Tyburn with Bl. Richard Leigh and four others. Bl. Richard Martin was beatified in 1929. August 30.

MARTIN, THÉRÈSE. *See* Thérèse of Lisieux.

MARTIN OF TOURS (c. 316–97). Born at Sabaria, Pannonia (Hungary), perhaps in 315, the son of a pagan army officer, he was taken to Pavia when his parents moved there, and when fifteen, against his will, was inducted into the army. About 337 occurred the famous incident at Amiens where he was stationed in which he cut his cloak in half and gave half of it to a poorly clad beggar in the freezing cold; that night he had a vision of Christ clad in his half cloak. He became a convert to Christianity, refused to fight, and was discharged soon after. He returned to Pannonia, converted his mother and others, and then went to Illyricum, where he was so active in opposing Arianism that he was scourged and forced to leave the country. He returned to Italy but was driven away by Bishop Auxentius of Milan, an Arian. After a time as a recluse on the island of Gallinaria in the Tyrrhenian Sea, he returned to Gaul in 360. When St. Hilary, bishop of Poitiers, was allowed to return to Poitiers from the exile imposed on him by Emperor Constantius, Martin joined him at Poitiers and became a hermit on land granted him by Hilary at

Ligugé. When other hermits joined Martin, a monastic community was organized—the first monastic community in Gaul. After ten years at Ligugé, despite his objections, Martin was named bishop of Tours in 371. He lived privately at Marmoutier as a monk, establishing the great monastic center of Marmoutier, while publicly devoting himself to his episcopal duties with great zeal. He worked ceaselessly to spread the faith and convert pagans, ruthlessly destroyed pagan temples, and was often saved from harm by seemingly miraculous means. He is reputed to have experienced visions and revelations and was gifted with the ability to prophesy. An opponent of Priscillianism, Martin interceded with Emperor Maximus at Trier in 384 to spare Priscillian's life when Bishop Ithacius of Ossanova demanded he be put to death for his heresy and was accused of the heresy himself. Priscillian was eventually beheaded by Prefect Evodius, to whom Maximus remanded the case—the first judicial death sentence for heresy and an infringement of the secular authority into ecclesiastical affairs that Martin vigorously opposed. Both Maximus and Ithacius were censured by Pope St. Siricius for their roles in the affair. Martin again returned to Trier to plead with the Emperor against the bloodbath about to be unleashed against the Priscillianists in Spain. Maximus agreed to do so only provided Martin became reconciled to Ithacius, which he did, though later bitterly reproaching himself for doing so. Martin made a visit to Rome and then went to Candes in Touraine, where he had established a religious center, and died there on November 8. Martin was one of the great saints of Gaul and the outstanding pioneer of Western monasticism before St. Benedict. Martin's shrine at Tours became one of the most popular pilgrim centers in Europe, and he is one of the patron saints of France. November 11.

MARTIN OF VERTOU (d. 601). Born at Nantes, Gaul, of a Frankish family, he was ordained deacon by St. Felix, preached at Poitou unsuccessfully, and became a hermit in the Dumen forest on the Sèvre River in Brittany. He attracted numerous disciples, and his hermitage developed into Vertou Abbey, of which he was abbot. Numerous extravagant miracles were ascribed to him before his death at Durieu convent, which he had founded. October 24.

MARTINA (d. c. 233). Early venerated at Rome, she was supposed to have been tortured and beheaded there under Emperor Severus. Many extravagant miracles were attributed to her, but scholars have doubts about her existence, believing she may have been confused with the legends of St. Tatiana. (January 12). January 30.

MARTINENGO, BL. MARY MAGDALEN (1687–1737). Born at Brescia, Italy, of the noble da Barco family, her mother died when she was an infant, and when she was eighteen, she joined the Capuchinesses of Santa Maria della Neva at Brescia. She served as novice mistress and portress and was elected prioress in 1732 and 1737. She practiced the most rigorous mortifications and was reported to have received supernatural gifts, including the ability to perform miracles. She was beatified in 1900. July 27.

MARTINET, BL. JULIAN (d. 1606). Born at Medinaceli near Segovia, Castile, he was apprenticed to a tailor in his youth, was admitted to the Franciscan monastery at Medinaceli but was later dismissed as not fitted for monastic life, and then moved to Santorcaz, where he was a tailor. Through the intercession of Fr. Francis de Torrez, he was accepted as a Franciscan lay brother at Our Lady of Salceda but was again dismissed as being mentally unbalanced and became a hermit. He returned to the monastery when his reputation for holiness became widespread, and he was noted for his extreme austerities and mortifications and for his ability in preaching missions. He died at St. Didacus Friary near Alcala Henares, and was beatified in 1825 as Julian of St. Augustine. April 8.

MARTINIAN (1st century). Although early venerated in Rome, the story of Martinian and Processes seems to be based on an unreliable sixth-century legend according to which they were the wardens of Peter and Paul when the two apostles were in Mammertine Prison in Rome. They were converted by the two (Peter is reputed to have baptized them from a spring that miraculously sprung into being in the prison), were tortured by their superior, Paulinus, when they would not sacrifice to Jupiter, and were then sworded to death. July 2.

MARTINIAN (d. 458). He, his brother Saturian, and their two brothers were slaves in Africa at the time of Arian King Genseric's persecution of Catholics and were converted to Christianity by another slave, Maxima. When their master insisted that Martinian marry Maxima, who had taken a vow of virginity, they fled to a monastery but were brought back and beaten for their attempt to escape. When their master died, his widow gave them to a Vandal, who freed Maxima (she later entered a monastery) and sold the men to a Berber chief. They converted many, petitioned the Pope to send them a priest, and were then tortured and dragged to their deaths by horses for their faith. October 16.

MARTINIAN THE HERMIT (4th century). According to untrustworthy legend, he was born at Caesarea, Palestine, became a hermit when he was eighteen, and lived a hermit's life for a quarter of a century on a mountain called the Place of the Ark near Caesarea. He resisted the blandishments of a wealthy woman of the city named Zoe by thrusting his feet in fire, converted her, and then sent her to Bethlehem, where she became a nun at St. Paulinus' convent. Later he rescued a girl from drowning from a shipwreck, left his provisions with her, and then swam from the island on which he had been staying to the mainland so he would not be tempted by her. She became a hermitess on his island and he then went to Athens, where he died. February 13.

MARTIUS (c. 440–530). Also known as Mars, he became a hermit in his youth, attracted disciples by his holiness, and organized them into a community of which he was abbot at Clermont, Auvergne. He was extolled by St. Gregory in his *Dialogues*. April 13.

MARTYRIUS (d. 397). *See* Sisinius.

MARUTHAS (d. c. 415). Bishop of Maiferkat, Mesopotomia, near the Persian border, he petitioned Emperor Arcadius at Constantinople in 399 to ask newly crowned King Yezdigerd of Persia to mitigate the deplorable conditions under which Christians in Persia were forced to live. While on a diplomatic mission to Yezdigerd for Emperor Theodosius, Maruthas gained the King's favor and despite the opposition of the Mazdeans, received permission from him to restore a Church organization in Persia and to build churches there wherever he pleased. Maruthas is considered the father of the Syrian Church, was known for his knowledge of medicine, compiled a record of Christians martyred in Persia during the persecution of Christians during the reign of King Sapor, and brought so many martyrs' relics to Maiferkat that it was renamed Martyropolis. He composed several hymns used in the Syriac liturgy and was the author of several theological treatises. December 4.

MARY (1st century). "Mary has by grace been exalted above all the angels and men to a place second only to her Son, as the most holy mother of God who was involved in the mysteries of Christ: She is rightly honored by a special cult in the Church. From the earliest times the Blessed Virgin is honored under the title Mother of God, [under] whose protection the faithful take refuge together in prayer in all their perils and needs." (Dogmatic Constitution on the Church, No. 66). Preeminent among the saints all the factual information we have about Mary is to be found in the New Testament, and it is from this source that the role of Mary in the Church has been developed. Aside from the Infancy narratives (Matt. 1–2; Luke 1–2), in which, of course, she plays a prominent role, there are only a few scattered references to her elsewhere in the New Testament. The Infancy narratives have been the subjects of prolonged and intensive study by biblical scholars, and they clearly and unequivocally declare her divine maternity, Jesus' messianic character, and Mary's virginity. Nothing is known of her childhood, though tradition has it that she was the daughter of Joachim and Anne, was born in Jerusalem, as a child was presented in the Temple, and took a vow of perpetual virginity. According to the evangelists, she was betrothed to Joseph when she was visited by the angel Gabriel, who announced to her that she was to be the mother of Jesus. She became pregnant of the Holy Spirit and then married Joseph after he was assured by an angel that "she has conceived what is in her by the Holy Spirit" (Matt. 1:20). Soon after she visited her Cousin Elizabeth, who was bearing John the Baptist; when Elizabeth acknowledged Mary as the mother of God, Mary replied with the Magnificat (Luke 1:5–25, 39–56). Shortly after the birth of Jesus, she and Joseph were forced to flee with Jesus to Egypt to escape the wrath of Herod, who feared the child as a rival to his throne. On the death of Herod, they returned and settled at Nazareth. Nothing is known of her life during the years she lived there except for Jesus' presentation in the Temple (Luke 2:22) and an incident recounted in Luke 2:41 on a trip back from Jerusalem when Jesus was twelve during which Mary and Joseph lost him; they finally found him in the Temple discoursing learnedly with the doctors there. Mary was instrumental in having Jesus perform his first miracle, changing water into wine at Cana (John 2:1–5), and then returned with him to Capernaum (John 2:12), which may mean they no longer lived at Bethlehem. There are references to her as the mother of Jesus in Matthew 13:55 and Mark 6:3, and she is again mentioned in Matthew 12:46–50, Mark 3:31–35, and Luke 8:19–21 when Jesus describes his "mothers and brothers" as "anyone who does the will of God." She was at the Crucifixion (but only in John 19:25–27), where she was given into John's care, which would seem to indicate that she had no relatives to care for her. She was present with the disciples at Jerusalem in the days before Pentecost (Acts 1:14), and it is believed that she was present at the Resurrection and Ascension, though this is not in Scripture; there is no further mention of her in the New Testament. According to tradition, she went to Ephesus, where she died; but another tradition has her living in Jerusalem until her death, which is believed to have occurred in 48. The belief her body was assumed into heaven is one of the oldest traditions in the Church and was declared dogma by Pope Pius XII in 1950; the feast of the Assumption is celebrated on August 15. Also declared dogma is that she is the Mother of God, the Second Person of the Holy Trinity, and hence free from original sin from the moment of her conception, the dogma of the Immaculate Conception proclaimed by Pope Pius IX in 1854 (celebrated on December 8), the only human being to be so honored. Catholics believe in the motherhood and perpetual virginity of Mary and that "the Blessed Virgin stands out in eminent and singular fashion as exemplar of virgin and mother" (ibid., No. 63). Her birthday has been celebrated since before the seventh century on September 8; among her other feast days are the Annunciation of the Blessed Virgin Mary, now called the Annunciation of the Lord (March 25), the Visitation (May 31), the Purification of the Blessed Virgin Mary, now called the Presentation of the Lord (also Candlemas, February 2), Our Lady of Sorrows (September 15), Our Lady of the Rosary (October 7), the Queenship of Mary (August 22), the Solemnity of Mary, Mother of God (January 1), and the Immaculate Heart of Mary (Saturday following the second Sunday of Pentecost), under which title Pope Pius XII dedicated the whole human race to Mary in 1944. One of the preeminent features of modern Catholicism has been the reported appearances of Mary in the last century and a half, notably at Lourdes, Fatima, and La Salette.

MARY (1st century). Mother of John Mark, her home in Jerusalem was a gathering place of the apostles and was the first place Peter went when released from Herod's imprisonment. (Acts 12:12ff.). June 29.

MARY (4th century). A slave of a Roman official named Tertullus, she was a Christian and refused to give up her faith when persecution of Christians broke out under Emperor Diocletian. Despite the attempts of Tertullus to pro-

tect her, he was obliged to deliver her to the prefect. She was tortured with such cruelty that the spectators demanded the prefect release her, which he did, into the custody of a soldier who helped her to escape. She died a natural death but is venerated as a martyr for the sufferings she endured. November 1.

MARY (d. 851). See Flora.

MARY (d. c. 1180). See Bernard.

MARY OF THE ANGELS, BL. See Fontanella, Bl. Mary.

MARY BERTILLA. See Boscardini, Bertilla.

MARY OF CEREVELLON (d. 1290). Born at Barcelona, Spain, daughter of a nobleman, she decided to devote herself to aiding Christian slaves of the Moors after hearing a sermon by Bernard Corbaria, a Mercedarian. Under his direction, she and a group of women formed a community that became the third Order regular of the Mercedarians (Order of Our Lady of Ranson), with Mary as first prioress. She was called Mary of Help for her prayers and work for the slaves. She died at Barcelona. She is considered the patroness of sailors in Spain, and her cult was confirmed in 1692. September 19.

MARY CLEOPHAS. See Mary Clopas.

MARY CLOPAS (1st century). Mother of James the Younger and Joseph (Matt. 27:56; Mark 15:40) and wife of Clopas and sister of Mary (John 19:25), she was present at the Crucifixion (Matt. 27:56; Mark 15:40; John 19:25) and accompanied Mary Magdalen to the tomb of Christ on the first Easter (Mark 16:1; Luke 24:10). Later legend had her going to Spain, where she died at Ciudad Rodrigo; another legend had her accompanying Lazarus, Mary Magdalen, and Martha to Provence. Mary Clopas' name is also spelled Cleophas. April 9.

MARY OF EGYPT (5th century). In Cyril of Scythopolis' life of St. Cyriacus, he tells of a woman named Mary found by Cyriacus and his companions living as a hermitess in the Jordanian desert. She told him she had been a famous singer and actress who had sinned and was doing penance in the desert; when they returned, she was dead. Around this story was built an elaborate legend that had tremendous popularity during the Middle Ages according to which she was an Egyptian who went to Alexandria when she was twelve and lived as an actress and courtesan for seventeen years. She was brought to the realization of her evil life before an icon of the Blessed Virgin, and at Mary's direction went to the desert east of Palestine, where she lived as a hermitess for forty-seven years, not seeing a single human being and beset by all kinds of temptations, which were mitigated by her prayers to the Blessed Virgin. She was discovered about 430 by a holy man named Zosimus, who was impressed by her spiritual knowledge and wisdom. He saw her the following Lent, but when he returned, he found her dead and buried her. When he returned to his monastery near the Jordan, he told the brethren what had happened and the story spread. April 2.

MARY FRANCES OF NAPLES. See Gallo, Mary Frances.

MARY OF THE INCARNATION, BL. (c. 1566–1618). See Acarie, Bl. Mary.

MARY OF THE INCARNATION, VEN. (1599–1672). See Martin, Ven. Mary.

MARY MAGDALEN (1st century). Probably from Magdala on the western shore of the Sea of Galilee near Tiberias,

she became a follower of Christ and has been the classic example of the repentant sinner from earliest times. She is identified with the unknown sinner who anointed Christ's feet in Simon's house (Luke 7:36ff.) and with Mary, the sister of Martha, but there are no real justifications for these indentifications in the Gospels, and modern scholars do not believe they are the same. She had seven devils cast out of her by the Lord (Mark 16:9; Luke 8:2), ministered to him in Galilee (Luke 8:2), was among the women at the Crucifixion (Matt. 27:56; Mark 15:40; John 19:25), and with Joanna and Mary, the mother of James and Salome, discovered the empty tomb and heard the angelic announcement of the resurrection of Christ (Matt. 28:1ff.; Mark 16:1–8; Luke 24:1–10). She was the first person to see Christ later the same day (Matt. 28:9; Mark 16:9; John 20:1–18). According to an ancient tradition, she accompanied John to Ephesus, where she died; a later unfounded pious legend in the West had her going to Provence, France, with Martha and Lazarus and dying there. July 22.

MARY OF OIGNIES, BL. (d. 1213). Born of wealthy parents at Nivelles, Brabant, she was married at fourteen despite her desire for the religious life. She persuaded her husband to live in continence and turned their home at Williambroux into a hospital for lepers, whom they personally nursed. She practiced the most rigorous austerities and soon achieved a reputation for holiness and spiritual wisdom that attracted numerous visitors seeking her counsel. Late in life she left Williambroux, with her husband's consent, and lived as a hermitess in a cell next to the Augustinian canons' monastery at Oignies, where she died on June 23. She experienced visions and ecstasies, had a great devotion to the Passion of Christ and to the Blessed Sacrament, had the gift of prophecy and the ability to look into the past and to know what was occurring in distant places; she was a mystic with great psychic powers as well.

MARY OF PISA, BL. See Mancini, Bl. Mary.

MARY SALOME (1st century). See Salome.

MARY SOLEDAD, BL. See Torres-Acosta, Bl. Mary Soledad.

MAS DE VEDRUNA, JOAQUINA DE (1783–1854). Born of a noble family at Barcelona, Spain, on April 16, she was refused admission to the Carmelites when she was twelve and in 1799 married Theodore de Mas, a lawyer. They were forced to flee with their children to Vich when Napoleon invaded Spain, and Theodore joined the Spanish forces. They returned to Barcelona in 1813, when Theodore resigned his commission. When he died in 1816, Joaquina brought her children to Vich, raised and educated them, and became a Franciscan tertiary, living a life of great austerity and ministering to the sick in the local hospital. In 1820 she met Capuchin Fr. Stephen Fabregas, who encouraged her in her desire to be a nun but counseled her not to join any existing Order but to found a new Order devoted to teaching the young and caring for the sick. She was clothed by Bishop Paul Corcuera in 1826 and he approved her new community, the Carmelites of Charity, which had six members, and a rule drawn up by Fr. Stephen. The spread of the Order throughout Catalonia was temporarily halted when civil war caused her to flee to France, but on her return in 1843, the community flourished. St. Antony Claret received final vows from Joaquina and her senior nuns in 1844. She suffered a stroke in 1850, relinquished direction of the congregation to Fr.

Stephen Sala the next year, and suffered creeping paralysis for the next four years, which culminated in her death from cholera at Barcelona on August 28. She had visions, ecstasies, and the gift of levitation during her lifetime, and she was canonized in 1959 by Pope John XXIII.

MASI, BL. FRANCIS (c. 1790–1860). He and his two brothers were Maronites living in Damascus when thousands of Christians were massacred in Syria in 1860. He was a wealthy businessman; his brother Muti lived with him, was a widower, and taught school at the Franciscan friary; and his other brother, Raphael, was his business associate and acted as sacristan at the friary. All three were murdered at the friary with eight Franciscans the night of July 9 when they refused to embrace Mohammedanism. They were all beatified in 1926. July 11.

MASCOLI, BL. LAURENCE (1476–1535). Born at Villamagna, Italy, on May 15, he joined the Franciscans at Ortona, was ordained, and became famous all over Italy for his preaching. He died at Ortona on June 6, and his cult was confirmed in 1923.

MASON, BL. JOHN (d. 1591). See Gennings, St. Edmund.

MASSIAS, JOHN (1585–1645). Born at Ribera del Fresno, Estramadura, Spain, on March 2, of an impoverished noble family, he was orphaned in his youth and worked as a shepherd. He went to Peru, worked on a cattle ranch for two years, and then went to Lima, where he became a Dominican lay brother and worked as a porter. He became known for his austerities, miracles, and visions, and attracted the poor and the sick of the city, ministering to them spiritually and physically. He died in Lima on September 16, and was canonized by

Pope Paul VI in 1975. His name is sometimes spelled Macias.

MATERNUS (d. c. 325). The first definitely known bishop of Cologne, Germany, he was one of the three bishops from Gaul asked by Emperor Constantine to hear the charges of the Donatist bishops of Africa against Bishop Caecilian in 313. They exonerated Caecilian but when the Donatists refused to accept their decision, Constantine referred the matter the next year to a council at Arles, which Maternus attended. Maternus may have been bishop of Trier at one time and died there. According to an apocryphal and totally worthless legend of the ninth century, he was the resurrected son of the widow at Nain (Luke 7:11–15) and was sent to Gaul by St. Peter with SS. Eucharius and Valerius; Maternus died at Ehl, Alsace, and when his companions told this to Peter on their return to Rome, Peter told them to place his staff on the dead man. When they did so, Maternus arose and resumed his preaching around Cologne and Trier. September 14.

MATHURIN. *See* Maturinus.

MATILDA (c. 895–968). Daughter of Count Dietrich of Westphalia and Reinhild of Denmark and also known as Mechtildis and Maud, she was raised by her grandmother, the abbess of Eufurt convent. Matilda married Henry the Fowler, son of Duke Otto of Saxony, in 909. He succeeded his father as duke in 912 and in 919 succeeded King Conrad I to the German throne. She was noted for her piety and charitable works, was widowed in 936, and supported her son Henry's claim to his father's throne. When her son Otto (the Great) was elected, she persuaded him to name Henry duke of Bavaria after he had led an unsuccessful revolt. She was severely criticized by both Otto and Henry for what they considered her extravagant charities, resigned her inheritance to her sons, and retired to her country home but was recalled to the court through the intercession of Otto's wife, Edith. When Henry again revolted, Otto put down the insurrection in 941 with great cruelty. Matilda censured Henry when he began another revolt against Otto in 953 and for his ruthlessness in suppressing a revolt by his own subjects; at that time she prophesied his imminent death. When he did die in 955, she devoted herself to building three convents and a monastery, was left in charge of the kingdom when Otto went to Rome in 962 to be crowned Emperor (often regarded as the beginning of the Holy Roman Empire), and spent most of the declining years of her life at the convent at Nordhausen she had built. She died at the monastery at Quedlinburg on March 14 and was buried there with Henry.

MATRONA (date unknown). According to the Roman Martyrology, she was the Christian maid of a Jewish mistress in Thessalonica. When her mistress discovered she was Christian, she subjected her to many tribulations; Matrona was later beaten to death at the instigation of her mistress. Another Matrona, a native of Barcelona, Spain, was taken to Rome and was executed there for ministering to Christian prisoners. And a third St. Matrona is reputed to have been a Portuguese of royal birth, was supernaturally instructed to go to Italy for a cure of her dysentery, and died there. She is venerated in Capua and is the patroness of those suffering from dysentery. March 15.

MATTHEW (1st century). Called Levi (though this may have been merely a tribal designation—that is, Matthew the Levite), he was probably born in Galilee, and was a publican tax collector (Matt.

9:9–13; 10:3) at Capharnaum when Christ called him to follow him (Mark 2:14; Luke 5:27–32), and he became one of the twelve apostles. He was the author of the first Gospel, written sometime between 60 and 90, perhaps originally in Aramaic (Papias in 130 records that Matthew wrote the Logia, presumably our Gospel, "in the Hebrew tongue"), though the Gospel we now have was in Greek and at the very least is a thorough and substantial revision of the original Aramaic, of which no traces have ever been found. It was without question written by a Jewish Christian of Palestinian origins for Jewish Christians. Some scholars believe it was written sometime after 70 and perhaps at Antioch, Syria. According to tradition, Matthew preached in Judea and then went to the East, where he suffered martyrdom in Ethiopia, according to the Roman Martyrology; in Persia, according to another legend. September 21.

MATTHEW, BL. (d. 1134). A canon at Rheims, France, he joined the Benedictines and in 1108 became a monk at St. Martin-des-Champs, of which he was named prior in 1117. He was an ardent supporter of the Cluniac reform and in 1125 was named cardinal-bishop of Albano; he served as papal legate to France and Germany in 1128. December 25.

MATTHEW OF BEAUVAIS (d. c. 1198). Born at Beauvais, France, he joined the crusaders after taking the cross from Bishop Roger of Beauvais, was taken prisoner by the Saracens and when he refused to renounce Christ, was beheaded. March 27.

MATTHEW OF GIRGENTI, BL. (d. 1450). Born at Girgenti, Sicily, he joined the Conventual Franciscans when he was eighteen but left to join the Observants under St. Bernardino of Siena. He traveled throughout Italy with Bernardino, became famed for his preaching, and on his return to Sicily, fought simony, spread devotion to the Holy Name, and restored religious fervor wherever he preached. Against his will, he was appointed bishop of Girgenti, restored clerical discipline, was forced to go to Rome to defend himself against the charges of those opposing his campaign against simony, and was exonerated but resigned as bishop because he felt his reforms were creating too great a disturbance in his see. Refused admittance to an Observant convent he had founded, he returned to the Conventuals but at the request of his minister general transferred back to the Observants. When he was stricken with an illness, he was taken to a Conventual convent because of its medical facilities and died there. His cult was confirmed in 1761. October 21.

MATTHEW OF MANTUA. *See* Carreri, Bl. Matthew

MATTHEW OF TERMINI. *See* Augustine Novello

MATTHIA OF MATELICA, BL. (c. 1233–1300). Born at Matelica, Ancona, Italy, the daughter of Count Gentile Nazzarei, she became a nun with her father's permission, though he would have preferred she marry, served as abbess at the Poor Clare convent of St. Mary Magdalen (later renamed St. Matthia) at Matelica for forty years, and died there on December 28. Many miracles were reported at her tomb, and her cult was confirmed in 1765. November 7.

MATTHIAS (1st century). Mentioned in the New Testament only in Acts 1:21–26, where he was selected by the apostles to replace Judas, unreliable legend had him preaching in Judea, Cappadocia, and on the shores of the

Caspian Sea, where he endured great persecutions; he suffered martyrdom at Colchis. May 14.

MATTHIAS (d. 1597). A Japanese born at Meaco, Japan, he was converted to Catholicism by the Franciscans and became a Franciscan tertiary. When the *taikō*, Toyotomi Hideyoshi, launched his persecution of Catholics, he listed some twenty-six Catholics who were to be executed for their faith. Among them was the Franciscans' cook, also named Matthias, who was away. Matthias took his place and was crucified with the twenty-five others near Nagasaki on February 5. They were all canonized as the Martyrs of Japan in 1862. February 6.

MATTHIAS, BL. MARY DE (1805–66). Born at Vallecorsa, Italy, she was named superior of a school at Acuto by Bishop Lais in 1834, determined to establish a religious community, and attracted several followers. Impressed by St. Caspar del Bufalo, whom she had met when she was seventeen, she founded a congregation in 1835 based on his Missioners of the Precious Blood with his successor, Ven. John Merlini, as director—the Sisters of the Adorers of the Sacred Heart—dedicated to the adoration of the Precious Blood and the education of children. The congregation expanded rapidly and by the time of her beatification in 1950 had some four hundred establishments. She died at Rome on August 20.

MATTIUSSI, BL. ODORIC (c. 1285–1331). Born at Villanova near Pordenone, Friuli, Italy, of Bohemian parentage, he joined the Franciscans at nearby Udine in 1300, became a hermit for a time, and then engaged in missionary work in the Udine area. He was tremendously successful, attracting huge crowds with his eloquence, and in 1316 set out for India as a missionary. He was at the court of the Great Khan Yisun Timur in Peking for three years. Bl. Orodic traveled throughout the East, spent 1322–28 in China, and was the first European to visit Tibet. On his return he dictated an account of his journeys that achieved great popularity. Reportedly he was most successful on his trip; one source attributed twenty thousand conversions to him and credited him with numerous miracles. After his return to Europe in 1330, he sought missionaries to accompany him back to China, but he died at Udine on January 14 before he could return. Also known as Odoric of Pordenone, his cult was approved in 1755.

MATURINUS (4th century). Also known as Mathurin, legend had him the son of pagan parents born at Larchant near Sens, Gaul. He was baptized at twelve, converted his parents, and was ordained by St. Polycarp when he was twenty-five. He became a successful missionary, achieved a reputation as an exorcist, and while in Rome ministering to a noble girl reputedly possessed, died there. November 1.

MATURUS (d. 177). *See* Pothinus.

MAUBANT, BL. PHILIBERT (d. 1839). *See* Imbert, Bl. Laurence.

MAUD. *See* Matilda.

MAUDEZ. *See* Mawes.

MAUGHOLD (d. c. 498). Also known as Maccaldus and Maccul, he was an outlaw in Ireland who was converted by St. Patrick who, as penance, ordered him to leave his native land. He set sail in an oarless, rudderless boat, landed on the Island of Man, was successful in missionary activities, was known for his austerities, and was elected bishop by the Manx people. April 27.

MAUGILLE. *See* Madelgisilus.

MAUNOIR, BL. JULIAN (1606–83). Born at Rennes, France, he joined the Jesuits in 1625, studied at Breton, and in 1640 was assigned to Brittany, which at the time was notorious for its indifference to religion and the low state of its clergy. He spent the next forty-three years preaching missions, converting thousands, and was in large part responsible for the resurgence of religion in that part of France. He died at Plevin, Cornouaille, on January 28 and was at once venerated for his holy life and the miracles he reportedly performed. He was beatified in 1951.

MAUR. *See* Maurus.

MAURA (d. c. 286). *See* Timothy.

MAURA (5th century). *See* Brigid.

MAURA OF LEUCADIA. *See* Anne (c. 840–c. 918).

MAURA OF TROYES (827–c. 850). Born at Troyes, Champagne, France, she devoted her life to prayer, fasting, and ministering to the poor, and was venerated for her holiness and the miracles attributed to her intercession. September 21.

MAURICE (d. c. 287). An officer of the Theban Legion of Emperor Maximian Herculius' army, which was composed of Christians from Upper Egypt, he and his fellow legionnaires refused to sacrifice to the gods as ordered by the Emperor to ensure victory over rebelling Bagaudae. When they refused to obey repeated orders to do so and withdrew from the army encamped at Octodurum (Martigny) near Lake Geneva to Agaunum (St. Maurice-en-Valais), Maximian had the entire legion of over six thousand men put to death. To the end they were encouraged in their constancy by Maurice and two fellow officers, Exuperius and Candidus. Also executed was Victor (October 10), who refused to accept any of the belongings of the dead soldiers. In a follow-up action, other Christians put to death were Ursus and another Victor at Solothurin (September 30); Alexander at Bergamo; Octavius, Innocent, Adventor, and Solutar at Turin; and Gereon (October 10) at Cologne. Their story was told by St. Eucherius, who became bishop of Lyons about 434, but scholars doubt that an entire legion was massacred; but there is no doubt that Maurice and some of his comrades did suffer martyrdom at Agaunum. September 22.

MAURICE OF CARNOËT, BL. (c. 1114–91). A native of Croixanvec, Loudéac, Brittany, he studied at Paris and became a Cistercian at Langonnet Abbey in 1144; three years after he was professed, he was elected abbot. He was an enthusiastic supporter of the Cistercian reform, and in 1176 became abbot of Carnoët, built by Duke Conan IV at his suggestion, which he governed until his death on October 9. His cult was approved by Pope Clement XI. October 13.

MAURICE OF HUNGARY, BL. (1281–1336). Son of the count of Csak, Hungary, Maurice Csaky was early attracted to the religious life, but when he was twenty, he was married to the daughter of Palatine Prince Amadeus. After a time, they mutually agreed to separate, she to enter a convent and he to join the Dominicans. The separation caused great controversy, and Maurice was imprisoned for five months by the governor of Budapest to test the genuineness of his vocation. When released, he was transferred to Bologna but later returned to his native Hungary as a peacemaker. He was noted for his dedication to helping the poor and his devotion to the Blessed Sacrament. He died at Raab, and though his cult is honored liturgically in Hungary, he has never been formally beatified. March 20.

MAURILIUS (d. 453). Born at Milan, Italy, he immigrated to Gaul and became a disciple of St. Martin, who ordained him. A successful missionary, he was named bishop of Angers in 423 and ruled the see for thirty years. He is credited with several extravagant miracles, in one of which he left Angers for Britain but was persuaded to return when one of his flock produced the key for the cathedral Maurilius had dropped overboard and that the member had recovered from the belly of a fish that had jumped into his boat on the way to Britain. September 13.

MAURUNTIUS (634–701). Eldest son of St. Adalbald and St. Rictrudis of Flanders, he was born in Flanders, served at the court of King Clovis II, and on the death of his father, planned to marry. Dissuaded by Bishop St. Amandus of Maestricht, Mauruntius entered the monastery of Marchionness, became a deacon, and was founding abbot of the abbey of Breuil, which he built on his estate of Merville near Thérouanne. He ruled for St. Amatus of Sens when that prelate was banished by King Thierry III, and on Amatus' death in 690, returned to Breuil. He was also superior of the double monastery of Marchiennes, where his sister was abbess, and died there. May 5.

MAURUS (6th century). Son of a Roman nobleman named Equitius who placed him in St. Benedict's care when he was twelve, he became Benedict's assistant and may have succeeded him as abbot of Subiaco when Benedict went to Monte Cassino in 525. Legend had him founding the abbey of Glenfeuil (later

Saint-Maur-sur-Loire) in Gaul, retiring at seventy, spending the last two years of his life as a hermit, and dying on January 15, 584, but this man is probably a different Maurus from St. Benedict's disciple. January 15.

MAWES (6th century). Also known as Maudez, he is believed to have been an Irish monk who after a time in Cornwall, England, as a hermit settled on the island of Modez off the coast of Brittany and preached throughout Amorica. He probably founded several churches and monasteries in Cornwall and Brittany, where he enjoyed great popularity. November 18.

MAXELLENDIS (d. c. 670). Born at Caudry near Cambrai, France, daughter of Humolin and Ameltrudis, according to legend, she fled into hiding when her father insisted she marry Harduin of Solesmes because she planned to become a nun. Discovered by Harduin and several of his friends, she fought to escape them, and in a rage he killed her with his sword—and was struck blind. About 673, her body was brought to Caudry, and Harduin's sight was restored when he begged her forgiveness before her coffin. November 13.

MAXENTIA OF BEAUVAIS (no date). Worthless legend has her an Irish princess who dedicated herself to God. She fled to Gaul with a man servant and a woman servant to escape marriage to a pagan chieftain, settled on the banks of the Oise River near Senlis, and was tracked down by the chieftain. When she spurned his pleas that she return with him to Ireland, he flew into a rage and beheaded her and the two servants. November 28.

MAXENTIUS (c. 445–c. 515). Born at Agde, Gaul, and baptized Adjutor, he was placed in the care of Abbot St.

Severus when a child, became a monk, and left the abbey for two years to escape the adulation of some of his fellow monks, only to be acclaimed a miracle worker when his return to Agde coincided with the end of a long drought. He again left the abbey, joined a community at Poitou under Abbot Agapitus, and changed his name to Maxentius. He became known for his austerities and holiness, was elected abbot about 500, and was credited with saving the monastery miraculously from marauding soldiers. He resigned in his later years and lived as a hermit near the monastery until his death there. June 26.

MAXFIELD, BL. THOMAS (c. 1590–1616). Born at The Mere, Enville, Stafford, England, when his father, William, was under a death sentence for harboring priests, Bl. Thomas studied for the priesthood at Douai, was ordained there, and was sent on the English mission in 1615. He was arrested in London three months later, failed in an escape attempt, and when he refused to take the Oath of Allegiance to King James, was hanged, drawn, and quartered at Tyburn on July 1 despite the plea of the Spanish ambassador. Bl. Thomas' name is sometimes Macclesfield.

MAXIMA. *See* Martinian (d. 458).

MAXIMIAN (d. c. 290). *See* Lucian of Beauvais.

MAXIMIAN (d. 363). *See* Bonosus.

MAXIMIAN (d. 404). Born in Africa, he became a Donatist but was converted to Catholicism and was named bishop of Bagae in Numidia but resigned when the people of the see objected. When he was almost killed when the Donatists threw him from the tower of the basilica of Calvianum, which he had recovered

from the Donatists, he went to Italy and received a decree from Emperor Honorius approving his activities and died there. October 3.

MAXIMIAN (d. 594). Born on Sicily, he became a monk at St. Andrew's Benedictine Abbey in Rome and served as *apocrisiarius* (delegate) at Constantinople for Popes Pelagius and Gregory the Great, who appointed him bishop of Syracuse and papal legate to Sicily, where he died. June 9.

MAXIMILIAN (274–95). Son of Fabius Victor and also known as Mamilian, he was beheaded at Theveste, Numidia (Tebessa, Algeria), on March 12 when he refused to be inducted into the army because of his Christianity.

MAXIMILIAN OF LORCH (d. c. 284). Born at Cilli (Steiermark), Styria, of wealthy parents, he gave his inheritance to charity, went on pilgrimage to Rome, and was sent as a missionary to Noricum by Pope Sixtus II. Maximilian became bishop of Lorch, made many converts, reigned for twenty years, and was then beheaded by order of Prefect Numerian outside Cilli when he refused to sacrifice to pagan gods. October 12.

MAXIMINUS (d. 363). *See* Juventinus.

MAXIMINUS OF AIX (5th century). According to legend, he was one of Christ's seventy-two disciples and accompanied Mary Magdalen, Martha, Lazarus, and Mary Clopas to Provence to evangelize the area. He made his headquarters at Aix, where he is considered its first bishop, and was reputed to have given communion to Mary Magdalen when she was miraculously transported to him from her cave at Sainte-Baume. In one legend, he is identified as "the man who had been blind from birth" in John 9:1–38. However, factual information about him is lacking, including even the century in which he lived, though he may have been a fifth-century bishop of Aix. June 8.

MAXIMINUS OF TRIER (d. c. 347). Probably born at Silly near Poitiers, Gaul, he studied at Trier and succeeded St. Agritius as bishop there in 332. Maximinus gave refuge to and defended the exiled St. Athanasius in 336, and St. Paul, patriarch of Constantinople, when he was exiled by Emperor Constantius. Maximinus called the Synod of Cologne, which condemned Euphratus, and was so ardent in his opposition to Arianism that he was named with Athanasius in the Arians' denunciation from Philippopolis. He died at Trier and was praised by Athanasius for his courage and miracles. Though he is known to have written several treatises, none have survived. May 29.

MAXIMUS (2nd century). See Florus.

MAXIMUS (d. 250). A merchant at Ephesus (or perhaps at Lampsacus), he was arrested for his Christianity during the persecution of Christians under Emperor Decius. He was tried before Optimus, the proconsul, and when he refused to sacrifice to Diana, he was tortured and then stoned to death, probably on May 14. April 30.

MAXIMUS (d. c. 350). Tortured during Emperor Diocletian's persecution of the Christians, he was crippled from the torture the rest of his life. He succeeded St. Macarius as bishop of Jerusalem on Macarius' death about 335 and opposed St. Athanasius at the instigation of his Arian friends, but later realized his error and was a firm supporter of the orthodox position. May 5.

MAXIMUS (d. c. 384). With his brother Victorinus, he was sent from Rome by

Pope Damasus to preach in Gaul. Both were murdered by pagans near Évreux. May 25.

MAXIMUS (d. 484). See Liberatus of Capua.

MAXIMUS (date unknown). See Cecilia.

MAXIMUS THE CONFESSOR (c. 580–662). Maximus Homologetes was born of a noble family at Constantinople and became secretary to Emperor Heraclius but resigned to become a monk at nearby Chrysopolis (Skutari), where he became abbot. He was one of the leaders in the struggle against monothelitism and Emperor Constans II, who favored the heresy. Maximus defended Pope Honorius against charges of monothelitism, was a supporter of papal authority, and in 645 refuted Pyrrhus in a public debate so decisively that Pyrrhus went to Rome to abjure the heresy. When Constans issued his decree *Typhos,* favoring monothelitism, Maximus was at the Lateran Council of 649, convened by Pope St. Martin I, which condemned the decree, a step that caused the Pope's exile and martyrdom from ill treatment at the Chersonese in 653. Maximus was seized at Rome, brought to Constantinople, and charged with conspiracy against the Empire. He was exiled to Bizya, Thrace, next to a monastery at Rhegium, and then spent the next six years at Perberis, with two of his supporters, both named Anastasius, subjected to great hardships. They were then brought back to Constantinople, tortured and mutilated (their tongues and right hands were cut off), and sentenced to life imprisonment. Maximus, after a terrible journey, died soon after his arrival at Skhemaris on the Black Sea; one Athanasius died before Maximus, and the other four years later. Maximus was a foremost exponent of Byzantine mysticism and wrote prolifically, theological, mystical, and ascetical treatises, biblical commentaries, a dialogue on the spiritual life between two monks, and *Mystagogia,* a treatise on liturgical symbolism. August 13.

MAXIMUS OF RIEZ (d. c. 460). Born near Digne, Provence, he became a monk at Lérins under St. Honoratus, and when Honoratus became bishop of Arles in 426, Maximus was named abbot. He attracted many to the monastery with his reputation for holiness, refused the see of Fréjus, but against his will was named bishop of Riez, which he ruled until his death. November 27.

MAXIMUS OF TURIN (c. 380–c. 467). Born probably at Vercelli, Rhaetia, Italy, he became a noted preacher, was an outstanding biblical scholar, and became bishop of Turin. He attended the synod of Milan in 451 and the Council of Rome in 465, but is mainly remembered for his writings, of which several hundred sermons, homilies, and other ascetical writing are still extant. June 25.

MAY. *See* Marius (d. 555).

MAYEUL. *See* Majolus.

MAYNE, CUTHBERT (1544–77). Born at Youlston, Devonshire, England, he was raised a Protestant by his uncle, a schismatic priest, and was ordained a minister when he was about nineteen. He studied at Oxford, where he received his M.A. and met Edmund Campion, at whose urging he became a Catholic in 1570. He was forced to flee England when letters from Campion were intercepted and went to Douai to study for the priesthood, was ordained in 1575, and was sent back to England the following year. He became estate steward of Francis Tregian at Golden, Cornwall, and was arrested the following year. He was found guilty of treason for being a Catholic priest and was hanged, drawn, and quartered at Launceton on November 25 when he refused to accept the supremacy of the Queen in ecclesiastical matters. He was the first Englishman trained for the priesthood at Douai to be martyred and is the protomartyr of England seminaries. He was canonized in 1970 by Pope Paul VI as one of the Forty Martyrs of England and Wales. November 30.

MAZENROD, BL. CHARLES JOSEPH EUGENE (1782–1861). Born at Aix-la-Chapelle, France, on August 1, he was forced to flee to Italy during the French Revolution but later returned and was ordained at Amiens in 1811. He was assigned to pastoral work at Aix, became interested in missionary work, and in 1816 founded an institute that became the Oblates of Mary Immaculate, approved by Pope Leo XII, and served as superior until his death. He was appointed titular bishop of Icosium in 1832, and five years later was named bishop of Marseilles, where he restored ecclesiastical discipline and became a leader in the defense of the papacy against the civil authorities and the Gallicanists. He died at Marseilles on May 21, and was beatified by Pope Paul VI in 1975.

MAZZARELLO, MARY (1837–81). Born at Mornese near Genoa, Italy, daughter of a peasant, she worked in the fields as a child, and when seventeen joined the sodality of Daughters of Mary Immaculate founded at the inspiration of St. John Bosco. Stricken by typhoid in 1860 and unable to work in the fields, she started a dressmaking business with a friend, Petronilla, and the two became interested in working with girls, as Don Bosco was doing with boys. In 1872 Don Bosco received permission from Pope Pius IX to found a congregation of nuns for that purpose and appointed Mary superioress of the Daughters of Our Lady Help of

Christians, popularly known as the Salesian Sisters, at Mornese. The congregation spread rapidly (by 1900 there were nearly eight hundred of its foundations in existence) and expanded its activities to charitable works as well as teaching. Mary died at Nizza Monferrato, where the mother house had been transferred in 1879, on April 27, and was canonized in 1951 by Pope Pius XII. May 14.

MAZZINGHI, BL. ANGELO AUGUSTINE (1377–1438). A noted preacher, he was born at Florence, Italy, of a noble family, joined the Carmelites, became prior of the Carmelite house at Le Selve, and later served in the same capacity at Frascati and Florence. He was elected provincial of Tuscany, and after his provincilate, he returned to Le Selve, worked to reform his order, and was known for his holiness and miracles. He died at Le Selve on August 16, and his cult was confirmed in 1761. August 18.

MCAULEY, CATHERINE (1778–1841). She founded the Sisters of Mercy in Dublin in 1831. The sisters were known as "the walking nuns" because they appeared outside the convent in the streets to assist the poor and needy. The Sisters of Mercy of the Americas is the largest congregation of women religious in the United States. Catherine was declared Venerable in 1990.

MCCARTHY, BL. THADDEUS (1455–97). Son of the lord of Muskerry and the daughter of the lord of Kerry, he was born in Munster, Ireland, was educated by the Franciscans at Kilcrea and on the Continent, and was appointed bishop of Ross by Pope Sixtus in 1482 while Thaddeus was in Rome. When he attempted to occupy the see, he was charged with intruding into the diocese by Hugh O'Driscoll, an auxiliary of the previous bishop, who claimed the bishopric. When Henry VII became King of England in 1485, the temporalities of the see were seized by the earl of Desmond, and Thaddeus was forced to flee and went to the Cistercian abbey near Parma, Italy. He was suspended by the Holy See in 1488 through the influence of his enemies and went to Rome to plead his case in person. In 1490, Pope Innocent VIII ruled in favor of Hugh O'Driscoll but appointed Thaddeus to the vacant see of Cork and Cloyne. He was refused admission to his cathedral again by his enemies, returned to Rome, and secured a papal condemnation of those resisting him from Pope Alexander VI but died at Ivrea, Italy, while on the way back to Ireland with the decree, on the night of October 24–25. He was buried there, and the cult that developed after miracles were reported at his tomb was confirmed in 1895. October 25.

MECHTILDIS (1125–60). Born in Bavaria, the daughter of Count Berthold of Andechs and his wife, Sophia, Mechtildis was placed by them in the double monastery they had founded on their estate at Diessen, Bavaria, when she was five, and she became a Benedictine nun there. She was subsequently elected abbess, became noted for the holiness of her life, and when twenty-eight, against her will, was appointed abbess of Edelstetten, charged by the bishop of Augsburg with the task of reforming that convent. She encountered much opposition but eventually was successful when the malcontents were expelled. She became famous for her miracles of healing, experienced ecstasies, and was regarded as the exemplar of religious life. She resigned her office shortly before her death to return to Diessen, where she died on May 31.

MECHTILDIS. See Matilda.

MECHTILDIS OF HELFTA (1241–98). Of the noble von Hackeborn family of

Helfta, Saxony, she was placed in the convent of Rossdorf, where her sister Gertrude was soon elected abbess, when she was seven, became a nun there, and moved with the nuns in 1258 to a monastery at Helfta, where in 1261 St. Gertrude the Great, then five, was placed in her care. They became close friends, and Mechtildis, who had mystical experiences of her own, helped Gertrude with her *Book of Special Graces* (also called *The Revelations of St. Mechtildis*), and the two saints collaborated on a series of prayers. Mechtildis died on November 19, and though never canonized, her feast is permitted in Benedictine convents. November 16.

MEDA, BL. FELICIA (1378–1444). Born at Milan, Italy, she was orphaned when a child, became a Poor Clare at St. Ursula Convent in her native city in 1400, and after twenty-five years was elected abbess. In 1439, she was sent to Pesaro to found a Poor Clare convent there, which was provided by the wife of Duke Galeazzo Malatesta, and served as abbess until her death on September 30. She was noted for her austerity, obedience, and miracles, and for the diabolical temptations to which she was subjected. Her cult was approved in 1812. July 24.

MEDARD (c. 470–c. 560). Born at Salency, Picardy, of a noble Frankish father and a Gallo-Roman mother, he was educated at Saint-Quentin and was ordained about 502. He became famed for his missionary activities and for his prowess as a preacher, and in 530 was named bishop of Vermandois. He is supposed to have moved his see from Saint-Quentin to Noyon to escape Vandal raids and also became bishop of Tournai. He consecrated St. Radegund a deaconess and gave her the veil after her husband, King Clotaire I, had murdered her brother. A local legend says that if it rains on his feast day it will be followed by forty days of rain, and forty days of sunshine will follow his feast day if it is clear. June 8.

MEDERICUS (d. c. 700). Also known as Merry, he was born at Autun, France, entered St. Martin's Monastery there when he was thirteen, and in time became abbot. When his holiness attracted much attention he resigned his abbacy and lived as a hermit a few miles from the monastery, but was obliged to return to the monastery when he became ill. In his old age he went on pilgrimage to the shrine of St. Germanus in Paris, resumed his eremitical life near the city, and died there. August 29.

MÉEN (6th century). Also known as Mewan and Main, he was born at Gwent, South Wales, became a monk at St. Samson's Monastery, and accompanied him to Cornwall and then to Brittany. He founded a monastery at Gaël that became a center for missionary work, and another that developed into Saint-Méen Abbey. His intercession is reputed to cure skin diseases, and a fountain at Gaël he is said to have caused to flow was believed to have curative powers by the thousands of pilgrims who visited there. June 21.

MÉEN. *See* Magenulf.

MEINGOLD (d. c. 892). According to untrustworthy legend, he was the son of English King Hugh (unknown in English history) and Emperor Arnulf's sister. He was adopted by Arnulf, became a member of Arnulf's court, and married Geyla, sister of Duke Albrecht, who refused to give to Meingold that portion of Geyla's dowry left from her first husband. The Emperor granted the property in question to Meingold, whereupon Albrecht and Duke Baldwin set fire to the buildings on the property. In the battle that ensued when

Meingold arrived on the scene and saw what was happening, he killed Baldwin. Seemingly Albrecht now accepted the Emperor's decision, but instead again attacked and was captured and imprisoned by Meingold; Albrecht disappeared from prison and was found dead later, murdered by two of Meingold's men. Meingold and Geyla then gave all their possessions to the poor and became wandering penitent pilgrims. After seven years they returned home, where Meingold was slain by some of his old enemies at Stierke on the Moselle River. The whole story sounds like a pious fiction, but a Count Meingaud of Wormsfeld was murdered in 892, and an ascetic named Meingold died near Huy, Belgium, shortly after. It seems that the stories of the two men may have been conflated by a later chronicler. February 8.

MEINRAD (d. 861). Related to the Hohenzollern family, he was ordained, became a Benedictine at Reichenau, taught for a time near Zurich, and then about 829, with his abbot's permission, became a hermit. Word of his holiness spread and attracted numerous visitors, and to escape them he sought solitude at Einsiedeln about 836. He lived in peace there for twenty-five years until he was clubbed to death by two thieves seeking his nonexistent treasure on January 21.

MEINULF. See Magenulf.

MEINWERK, BL. (d. 1036). Born in Saxony of a noble family, he studied at Halberstadt and the cathedral school of Hildesheim, where he formed a close friendship with the future Emperor Henry II, a relative, and was ordained. He became bishop of Paderborn in 1009, rebuilt the cathedral and city walls and fortifications, founded several monasteries, and developed the cathedral school of Paderborn into a center of learning famous all over Europe. He served as adviser to Henry, was a patron of the arts, was on equally friendly terms with Henry's successor, Conrad II, and built a replica of the Holy Sepulcher to house relics brought from Jerusalem. He has never been formally beatified but had a widespread cult in Germany. June 5.

MEL (d. c. 488). According to untrustworthy legend, he and his brother Melchu were sons of Conis and St. Patrick's sister, Darerca. They accompanied Patrick to Ireland, joined him in his missionary work, and became bishops. Patrick appointed Mel bishop of Armagh, and Melchu is reputed to have been bishop of Ardagh. Some scandal was circulated about Mel, who lived with his Aunt Lupait but both cleared themselves by miraculous means to Patrick, who ordered them to live apart. Two other brothers, Muinis and Rioch, also became missionary bishops. February 6.

MELAINE (d. c. 530). Born at Placet, Brittany, he became a monk, was elected bishop of Rennes, and in 511 was active at the Council of Rennes. He eliminated idolatry from his diocese and was highly regarded by King Clovis. He died at a monastery he had built at Placet. November 6.

MELANGELL (date unknown). Also known as Monacella, Welsh legend has her the daughter of an Irish (or Scots) King who fled to Powys in central Wales to escape marriage. Fifteen years later Brochwel Ysgythrog, prince of Powys, met her while hunting a hare that had sought refuge with Melangell, and after hearing her story, granted her land as a sanctuary. She attracted disciples, whom she organized into a community that she ruled as abbess for thirty-seven years. May 27.

MELANIA THE YOUNGER (383–439). Daughter of Publicola, a Roman senator who was the son of Melania the Elder, and Albina, the Christian daughter of a pagan priest, Melania the Younger was married against her will to Valerius Pinianus by her father when she was fourteen. After two children died soon after birth, Pinianus agreed to respect her desire to devote her life to God, and when her father died, leaving his enormous wealth to her, she, Pinianus, and her mother, Albina, left Rome and turned their country villa into a religious center. Melania sold some of her property for charitable purposes, encountered much family opposition, and finally appealed to Emperor Honorius, who granted her his protection. She became one of the great religious philanthropists of all time, endowing monasteries in Egypt, Syria, and Palestine, helping churches and monasteries in Europe, aiding the poor, sick, and captives, helping pilgrims, and freeing some eight thousand slaves in two years. In 406, she and her followers were forced to flee the invading Goths, went to Messina, and then decided to go to Carthage. They were shipwrecked on the island of Lipari, which she ransomed from pirates, and then settled at Tagaste in Numidia in about 410. She founded a monastery for men and another for women, where she lived in great austerity. In 417, with Pinianus and Albina, she made a pilgrimage to the Holy Land and visited the Egyptian desert monks. On their return they settled at Jerusalem, where Melania met her Cousin Paula, niece of St. Eustochium, who introduced her to the group in Bethlehem presided over by St. Jerome, whose friend she became. Albina died fourteen years after their arrival in Jerusalem, and Pinianus the following year. Melania built a cell near their tombs, and when she attracted numerous disciples, built a convent for them, of which she was superior for the rest of her life. She died at Jerusalem on December 31. Although she has been venerated in the Eastern Church for centuries, she has had no cult in the West, although Pope Pius X approved the observance of her feast in 1908 for the Somaschi, an observance followed by the Latin Catholics of Constantinople and Jerusalem.

MELANIUS. *See* Mallonus.

MELAR. *See* Mylor.

MELCHIADES. *See* Miltiades.

MELCHIOR (1st century). *See* Balthasar.

MELCHIOR, CHARLES. *See* Marchioni, John Charles.

MELCHU. *See* Mel.

MELETIUS OF ANTIOCH (d. 381). Born at Melitene, Lower Armenia, of a distinguished family, he was appointed bishop of Sebastea about 358 but fled to the desert and then to Beroea in Syria when the appointment caused great dissension. In 361 a group of Arians and Catholics elected him archbishop of Antioch as a compromise candidate between the two groups, and though confirmed by Emperor Constantius II, he was opposed by some Catholics because Arians had participated in his election. The Arians' hope that he would join them was dashed when he expounded the Catholic position before the pro-Arian Emperor, who was persuaded by Arian Bishop Eudoxus of Constantinople to exile Meletius to Lower Armenia only a month after he occupied his see and to appoint Arian Euzoius to his episcopal chair. On the death of the Emperor in 361, his successor, Emperor Julian, recalled Meletius, who found that in his absence, a faction of the Catholic bishops, led by Lucifer

MENNAS   431

Cagliari, had elected Paulinus archbishop—the beginning of the Meletian schism, which was to rend the Church of Antioch for years to come. The Council of Alexandria in 362 was unsuccessful in healing the breach, and an unfortunate rift between St. Athanasius and Meletius in 363 exacerbated the matter. During the next decade and a half, Meletius was exiled, 356–66 and 371–78, by Emperor Valens while the conflict between the Arian and the Catholic factions raged. Gradually, Meletius' influence in the East grew as more and more bishops supported him (by 379 the bishops backing him numbered 150, in contrast to his 26 supporters in 363), but the rift between the contending Catholic factions continued despite the untiring efforts of St. Basil, who was unswerving in his support of Meletius, to resolve the matter. In 374 the matter was further complicated when Pope Damasus recognized Paulinus as archbishop, appointed him papal legate in the East, and St. Jerome allowed himself to be ordained presbyter by Paulinus. In 378, the death of avidly pro-Arian Valens led to the restoration of the banished bishops by Emperor Gratian, and Meletius was reinstated. He was unable to reach an agreement with Paulinus before his death in Constantinople in May while presiding at the third General Council of Constantinople. February 12.

MELEUSIPPUS (d. c. 155). See Eleusippus.

MELITO (d. c. 180). Bishop of Sardis in Lydia, he wrote numerous theological treatises, including an *Apologia* for Christianity to Emperor Marcus Aurelius, for which Melito was highly praised by Eusebius and was reported to have had the gift of prophecy by Tertullian, who was unimpressed by his writings. April 1.

MELLITUS OF CANTERBURY (d. 624). Abbot of St. Andrew's Monastery in Rome, he headed the group of missionaries sent from Rome by Pope St. Gregory the Great in 661 to help St. Augustine in England. He worked in Kent for three years, was appointed first bishop of London (or of the East Saxons), and baptized Sabert, King of the East Saxons. After Sabert's death, he was exiled by the King's sons in 616 when he refused to give them communion, as they had not yet been baptized. After a time in France, he returned to England and was named archbishop of Canterbury in 619. He is reputed to have saved Canterbury from a devastating fire by his prayers. April 24.

MELLON. See Mallonus.

MELORUS. See Mylor.

MEMORIUS (d. 451). Also known as Mesmin, according to untrustworthy legend he was a deacon of Troyes, France, when Attila, King of the Huns, and his barbarians were approaching. St. Lupus, bishop of Trier, sent him and four others as a delegation to Attila to beg him to spare the town. Attila had them all beheaded. September 7.

MÉNÉHOUD. See Manechildis.

MENIGNUS (d. 251). A dyer at Parium, Mysia, Asia Minor, he tore down an anti-Christian edict of Emperor Decius and as punishment had his fingers cut off; he was later beheaded. March 15.

MENNAS (3rd century). According to legend, he was born in Egypt, became a soldier in the Roman army, and when Emperor Diocletian's persecution of the Christians began, fled to the mountains from his post at Cotyaeum in Phrygia. He lived as a recluse until he left his mountain hiding place to proclaim his Christianity during the games at the Cotyaeum amphitheater; he was at once tortured and then beheaded for his faith. When his remains were brought back to Egypt, miracles were reported at his tomb, and a cult to the warrior saint began, which spread all over the East, and the shrine built over his tomb near Alexandria became a great pilgrimage center. November 11.

MENNAS (4th century). His story is an extravagant fictional legend in which he is an Athenian sent to Alexandria by Emperor Galerius to end the troubles disturbing that city. Mennas successfully fulfilled that task and then announced his Christianity. With his assistant, Eugraphus, he made many converts and was haled before Judge Hermogenes for his Christianity. A great singer, he used his voice to defend himself in a four-hour song; despite the sensation his unique defense caused, his eyes and tongue were removed. The next morning, it was found they had been miraculously restored, whereupon Hermogenes was converted to Christianity. After all three recovered from further torture inflicted on them by order of Galerius, they were beheaded. December 10.

MENNAS (d. 552). Born at Alexandria, he became a priest at Constantinople and in 536 was consecrated patriarch of that city by Pope St. Agapitus, who had just deposed the former patriarch, Anthimus, for his monophysite leanings. An opponent of Origenism, Mennas signed Emperor Justinian's condemnation of the Three Chapters, three Nestorian documents by Theodore of Mopsuestia and Theodoret of Cyprus against the decrees of the Council of Cyprus and a letter of Ibas. Pope Vigilius excommunicated Mennas in 547 for supporting the condemnation (they were reconciled a few months later) and then vacillated in the matter, condemning the Three Chapters himself in 548 but in 551 excommunicating Mennas and those who had signed Justinian's condemnation. They were again reconciled, and at the General Council of Constantinople in 553 the Three Chapters were condemned, an action approved by Vigilius in 554. Meanwhile, Mennas had died on August 24, 552, before the council met. August 25.

MENNI, BENEDICT (1841–1914). An ordained priest in the Brothers of St. John of God, the Hospitallers Orders, Menni was sent to restore the Order in Spain and Portugal where Masonic laws had depleted them. Over three decades and often at personal risk, Menni attracted about a thousand Vocations, establishing twenty-two hospitals in Spain, Portugal, and Mexico. He also established a female branch of the order, the Hospitaller Sisters of the Sacred Heart of Jesus. He was canonized in 1999.

MENODORA (d. c. 304). According to a tenth-century story that is suspect, she, Metrodora, and Nymphodora were three orphan sisters living in Bithynia. When the persecution of Christians under Emperors Diocletian and Maximian broke out, they were denounced to Fronto, the governor, as Christians. When they refused to sacrifice to pagan gods, he had Menodora beaten to death before the other two. When they still refused, Metrodora was tortured, burned, and beheaded; Nymphodora was beaten to death. September 10.

MERCURIA (d. 250). *See* Epimachus.

MERCURIUS (d. c. 250). That he was a real martyr is all that is really known of him. All else is pious fiction, according to which he was the son of a Scythian officer in the Roman army, became a soldier himself, and led the army to a great victory with a sword an angel had given him in a battle against the barbarians attacking Rome. When Emperor Decius asked him why he did not participate in sacrifices to the gods after the victory, Mercurius proclaimed his Christianity, whereupon Decius sent him to Caesarea in Cappadocia, where he was tortured and beheaded for his faith. He was venerated as a warrior saint and is reputed to have appeared at various times in history to lend his sword to worthy causes, notably, with St. George and St. Demetrius, at Antioch during the First Crusade. November 25.

MERCURIUS (d. c. 300). One of a group of guards assigned to escort Christians to their place of execution at Lentini, Sicily, he and his comrades were so impressed by the Christians that they became converts to Christianity on the way. They were added to the Christian prisoners and all were beheaded. December 10.

MERIADOC (6th century). Also known as Meriasec, he was probably born in Wales, seems to have gone to Cornwall and then to Brittany, and probably became a regionary bishop in Brittany. His legend is told in the Cornish miracles play *Beunans Meriasec*. June 7.

MERIASEC. *See* Meriadoc.

MERICI, ANGELA (c. 1470–1540). Born at Desenzano, Lombardy, on March 21, she was orphaned at ten and raised by her uncle at Salo. She became a Franciscan tertiary when she was thirteen and began a life of great austerity. She returned to Desenzano and on the death of her uncle became interested in the education of poor children and began, with a group of friends, to teach young girls. She was invited to Brescia by a noble couple to open a school there,

temporarily lost her sight while on pilgrimage to the Holy Land, went to Rome during the 1525 Holy Year, and refused an offer of Pope Clement VII to head a congregation of nursing sisters. In 1533, she began training a group of women in Brescia, and on November 25, 1535, twenty-eight women dedicated themselves to the service of God under the protection of St. Ursula, and the Ursulines, devoted to the religious education of girls, especially poor children, were founded, with Angela as superior. The congregation was formally recognized by Pope Paul III four years after Angela's death at Brescia on January 27. Angela experienced many visions during her lifetime, one of which foretold that she would found the Ursulines. She was canonized in 1807.

MERRY. *See* Medericus.

MERRYN. *See* Modwenna.

MESMIN. *See* Memorius.

MESROP (d. 441). Born in Taron, Armenia, he became a government official in Armenia and then was a hermit and a disciple of St. Nerses the Great. Mesrop was ordained and devoted himself to the study of Greek, Syriac, and Persian (Armenia had recently been partitioned between Persia and the Empire). He joined St. Isaac the Great as a missionary to the Armenians, helped compose an Armenian alphabet, and translated the New Testament and Proverbs into Armenian. He organized schools in Armenia and Georgia, created a Georgian alphabet, founded his own school in Armenia, and continued preaching until his death at Valarshapat on February 19, when he was well past eighty. He was surnamed "the Teacher" for his educational activities and teaching ability.

MESSALINA (d. c. 254). *See* Felician.

METHODIUS. *See* Cyril.

METHODIUS I (d. 847). Born at Syracuse, Sicily, he was educated at Syracuse, went to Constantinople in quest of a position at the imperial court, but instead became a monk. He built a monastery on the island of Chios, returned to Constantinople under Patriarch Nicephorus, and opposed iconoclasm when Emperor Leo the Armenian launched his persecution of opponents of that heresy in 815. Methodius went to Rome when Nicephorus was exiled but returned in 821 when Emperor Michael the Stammerer was enthroned, bringing a letter from Pope Paschal asking the new Emperor to permit Nicephorus to return to his see. Instead the Emperor had Methodius scourged and exiled to prison. On his release from prison seven years later, he resumed his opposition to iconoclasm under Emperor Theophilus, but when the Emperor died in 842 his widow Theodora, the regent, repealed all decrees against images, and Methodius was named Patriarch of Constantinople to replace iconoclast supporter John the Grammarian. Methodius convoked a synod at Constantinople that endorsed the second Council of Nicaea's decrees regarding icons, became involved in a controversy with the monks under St. Theodore Studites, over some of Theodore's writings, and died of dropsy on June 14 at Constantinople. Though reputedly a prolific writer, few of his writings have survived, notable among those that have survived being a life of St. Theophanes.

METHODIUS OF OLYMPUS (d. c. 311). The Roman Martyrology and St. Jerome state that he was bishop of Olympus, Lycia, and then Tyre, while other sources declare that he was bishop of Patara in Lycia. He was famous for his preaching and scholarship, wrote several treatises, among them *On the Resurrection*, against Origen's teaching on the subject, and his *Symposium*, an ascetical treatise on virginity, which was marred by Millenarianism, and suffered martyrdom at Chalcis, Greece, for his faith. September 18.

METRAS (d. 249). *See* Apollomia.

METRODORA (d. c. 304). *See* Menodora.

METROPHANES (d. c. 325). According to unreliable sources, he was the son of Emperor Probus' brother Dometius. Dometius' father was converted to Christianity, went to Byzantium, and was ordained by Bishop Titus, whom he succeeded as bishop of Byzantium. He in turn was succeeded by his son Probus, who was succeeded by Metrophanes in 313. He was the first bishop of Byzantium after it was declared independent of the see of Heraclea, and reportedly it was his holiness that was one of the major factors in the decision of Emperor Constantine to make Byzantium the capital of the Empire. June 4.

MEURIS (d. 307). She and Thea, two women from Gaza, Palestine, were tortured during a persecution of Christians at Alexandria. Meuris died under torture, but Thea survived and died later. They are probably the same as the Thea and Valentina whose feast day is celebrated on July 25. December 19.

MEWAN. *See* Méen.

MEXICO, MARTYRS OF (1915–1937). In 1913 a Mexican decree closed all churches and ordered priests arrested. Religious congregations were expelled, convents and schools were closed and in 1917, an anticlerical constitution was promulgated. In 1926 after General

Plutarco Calles swore to destroy the Christian faith, open warfare erupted between the Catholic resistance, the "Cristeros," and the government. The twenty-five Mexican saints were martyred between 1915 and 1937. The three laymen and twenty-two priests were canonized in 2000.

MÉZIÉRE, BL. FRANÇOISE (1745–94). A teacher and known for her piety, she was guillotined on February 5 at Laval, Mayenne, France, for caring for wounded Vendean soldiers. She was beatified in 1925 as one of the nineteen Martyrs of Laval. Three other women were among those martyred at that time: Françoise Tréhet (b. 1756), guillotined at Ernée on March 13, and Jeanne Veron (b. 1766), guillotined at Ernée on March 20, both Sisters of Charity de la Chapelle-au-Riboul; and Marie L'Hulier (b. 1766), an illiterate lay sister of the Hospital Sisters of the Mercy of Jesus, who was guillotined on June 25, all for refusing to take the oath of the revolutionary government, which had been condemned by the Church. They were beatified in 1955.

MICHAEL. He is one of the three angels, with Gabriel and Raphael, liturgically venerated by the Church. He appears twice in the Old Testament (Dan. 10:13ff.; 12:1, as the helper of the Chosen People) and twice in the New Testament (Jude v. 9, where he disputes with the devil over Moses' body; and Rev. 12:7–9, where he and his angels fought the dragon and hurled him and his followers from heaven). He repeatedly appears in apocryphal literature and was early regarded in the Church as the captain of the heavenly host, the protector of the Christian against the devil, especially at the hour of death, when he conducts the soul to God, and as the helper of Christian armies against heathen armies. His cult apparently originated in Phrygia but soon spread to the West, where it received great impetus as a result of the legend that he appeared at Mount Garganus in northern Italy during the pontificate of Pope Gelasius (492–96) and indicated a spot at which a shrine in his honor was to be erected. Usually he is represented with a sword fighting with or standing over a conquered dragon. A feast day on September 29 (Michaelmas Day), celebrated since the sixth century to honor the dedication of a basilica in his honor on the Salerian Way in Rome, is no longer commemorated, and in 1970 his feast was joined with those of Gabriel and Raphael on that date.

MICHAEL (d. c. 820). A disciple of St. Tarasius, patriarch of Constantinople who consecrated him bishop of Synnada, Phrygia, he was sent to Rome to report to Pope St. Leo III by Tarasius on the situation in the East. Michael resolutely opposed iconoclasm, and his opposition caused him to be exiled to Galatia by iconoclast Emperor Leo the Armenian. May 23.

MICHAEL OF CHERNIGOV (d. 1246). Duke of Chernigov, he repented of his cowardice in abandoning Kiev to attacking Tartars, and surrendered to their leader, Bati, and pleaded for his people. When he refused to renounce his faith and worship idols, he was tortured and then beheaded with one of his nobles, Theodore. September 21.

MICHELINA OF PESARO, BL. (1300–56). Born of a wealthy noble family at Pesaro, Italy, Michelina Metelli was married at the age of twelve to Duke Malatesta of Rimini and was widowed at twenty with a son. When her son died soon after, she gave up her social life and became a disciple of a Franciscan tertiary named Syriaca, became a Franciscan tertiary herself, distributed her wealth, and lived on the alms she begged. She was considered insane by her family, who had her committed to an institution for a time, but she was soon released and devoted the rest of her life to charitable works and to caring for lepers. She made a pilgrimage to Rome, where she is reputed to have had an ecstasy in which she shared Christ's suffering during his Passion. She died at Pesaro and later the house she had lived in there was converted into a church. Her cult was approved in 1731. June 20.

MIDA. *See* Ita.

MIDDLEMORE, BL. HUMPHREY (d. 1535). With two other Carthusians, Bl. William Exmew, a Cambridge graduate and the subprior, and Bl. Sebastian Newdigate, he took over the direction of the London charterhouse on the execution of Bl. John Houghton in 1535. They were arrested a few weeks later, imprisoned at Marshalsea, and after being suspended in chains for two weeks, were executed on June 19 at Tyburn when they refused to accept the King's Act of Supremacy. They were beatified in 1886.

MIDDLETON, BL. ANTONY (d. 1590). A Yorkshireman, he studied for the priesthood at Douai College in Rheims, was ordained there, and in 1586 was sent to London on the English mission. He was arrested in Clerkenwell, London, for his Catholic priesthood and, with Fr. Edward Jones, was disemboweled while still alive, and hanged for his priesthood in front of the house where he had been arrested, on May 6. He was beatified in 1929.

MIGDONIUS. *See* Peter (d. 303).

MIKI, PAUL (1562–97). Son of a Japanese military leader, he was born at Tounucumada, Japan, was educated at the Jesuit college at Anziquiama, joined the Jesuits in 1580, and became known for his eloquent preaching. He was crucified on February 5 with twenty-five other Catholics during the persecution of Christians under the *taikō,* Toyotomi Hideyoshi, ruler of Japan in the name of the Emperor. Among the Japanese laymen who suffered the same fate were: Francis, a carpenter who was arrested while watching the executions and then crucified; Gabriel, the nineteen-year-old son of the Franciscans' porter; Leo Kinuya, a twenty-eight-year-old carpenter from Miyako; Diego Kisai (or Kizayemon), temporal coadjutor of the Jesuits; Joachim Sakakibara, cook for the Franciscans at Osaka; Peter Sukejiro, sent by a Jesuit priest to help the prisoners, who was then arrested; Cosmas Takeya from Owari, who had preached in Osaka; and Ventura from Miyako, who had been baptized by the Jesuits, gave up his Catholicism on the death of his father, became a bonze, and was brought back to the Church by the Franciscans. They were all canonized as the Martyrs of Japan in 1862. February 6.

MILBURGA (d. c. 700 or 722). Daughter of Merewald, an Anglican chieftain, and St. Ermenburga, a princess of Kent, and sister of SS. Mildred and Mildgytha, Milburga was founding abbess of Wenlock convent in Shropshire, built with funds from her father and King Wulfhere, her uncle. She was venerated for her humility, holiness, the miracles she is reputed to have performed, and for the gift of levitation she is said to have possessed. February 23.

MILDGYTHA (d. c. 676). Daughter of Anglican chieftain Merewald and St. Ermenburga, a Kentish princess, she was the sister of SS. Mildred and Milburga, became a nun at Minster on the Isle of

Thanet, of which her mother was founding abbess, and later was abbess of a convent in Northumbria. January 17.

MILDRED (d. c. 700 or 725). Daughter of Merewald, an Anglican chieftain, and St. Ermenburga, a Kentish princess, she was the sister of SS. Milburga and Mildgytha and was educated at a convent at Chelles near Paris. She rejected an ardent suitor and on her return from France entered the monastery of Minster on the Isle of Thanet, which had been founded by her mother, whom she succeeded as abbess. She attended a council in Kent, was known for the fervor of her religion and her aid to the poor and the afflicted, and was widely venerated in England after her death. July 13.

MILLAN DE LA COGOLLA. *See* Emilian Culcullatus.

MILLES (d. 342). *See* Abdiesus.

MILNER, BL. RALPH (d. 1591). An illiterate farmhand, he was born at Stacksteads, Hampshire, England, was converted to Catholicism, and was imprisoned the day he received his first communion. His imprisonment was quite lenient and he was frequently allowed out of prison. When allowed out, he sought aid for his fellow prisoners and helped refugee priests, among them Bl. Roger Dickenson at Winchester. When Dickenson was arrested, Milner was brought to trial with him, convicted of aiding a Catholic priest, and when he refused his freedom if he would visit a single Protestant church, was sentenced to death despite his age, wife, and eight children. He was hanged, drawn, and quartered at Winchester on July 7, and was beatified in 1929.

MILO OF SELINCOURT, BL. (d. 1158). A hermit with a group of disciples at Saint-Josse-au-Bois near Calais, France, they all joined the Premonstratensians of Donmartin Monastery, and in 1123 he was appointed abbot by St. Norbert. He was named bishop of Thérouanne in 1131 and was known for his learning, his enforcement of strict clerical discipline, and his insistence on ecclesiastical rights in his diocese. He supported his friend St. Bernard's attack on Gilbert de la Porrée's teachings on the Trinity and opposed Gilbert at the Council of Rheims, 1147–48. He was appointed mediator by Pope Adrian IV in 1157 to settle a dispute between the bishop of Amiens and the abbot of Corbie. Though never formally beatified, he is called Blessed because of the miracles at his tomb. July 16.

MILTIADES (d. 314). Also called Melchiades, he was probably an African and was elected Pope on July 2, 311, succeeding Pope St. Eusebius. Miltiades' reign saw the end of Christian persecutions with the victory of Constantine over Maxentius at the Milvian Bridge in 312, the granting of religious freedom throughout the Empire by Constantine in 313, and the beginnings of Donatism in Africa. He held a synod in 313 at the Lateran palace, given him by Constantine's wife, Fausta, which condemned Donatus. Miltiades died in Rome on January 10 or 11. December 10.

MIRIN (7th century). A disciple of St. Comgall, he was abbot of Bangor Monastery, County Down, Ireland, and became a missionary in Scotland. His tomb at Paisley became a pilgrimage center. September 15.

MKASA, JOSEPH (d. 1885). A Christian in charge of the pages at the court of King Mwanga of Uganda, he was beheaded on November 15 when he denounced the King's notorious immoralities and his murder of Joseph Harrington, a Protestant missionary, and his group. Joseph was canonized by Pope Paul VI as one of the Martyrs of Uganda in 1964. June 3.

MOCHOEMOC (d. c. 656). According to tradition, he was the son of Bevan and Nessa, sister of St. Ita (who reputedly had been miraculously raised from the dead), was born at Munster, Ireland, and was educated by Ita. He became a monk, was ordained by St. Comgall at his monastery at Bangor, and was sent out by Comgall to found another monastery, which he did, at Arderin on Slieve Bloom. He later moved to Liath, where he found Liath-mor (Leamokevoge, Tipperary) Church and Monastery, which developed into a noted monastic center. He founded numerous other monasteries before his death at an advanced age. It is believed by some scholars that he is the same as St. Kennoch, venerated around Glasgow, Scotland, whose name was transformed through a scribal error into a woman's name; her name often appears as Kevoca, which is a variation of Mochoemoc. March 13.

MOCHTA (c. 445–c. 535). Born in Britain, he was brought to Ireland as a child by his Christian parents, became a disciple of St. Patrick, and supposedly, while on a visit to Rome, was made a bishop by Pope St. Leo I. He collected a group of twelve disciples and returned to Ireland, where he eventually built a monastery at Louth, of which he was probably made bishop by Patrick. He died, reportedly at ninety, the last of Patrick's personal followers. August 19.

MOCHUDA. *See* Carthach.

MOCHUMNA. *See* Machar.

MOCIUS. *See* Mucius.

MODAN (d. c. 550). Legend has him a monk who was elected, against his will, abbot of his monastery in Scotland. He preached at Sterling and Falkirk and spent the end of his life living as a hermit. February 4.

MODESTUS (d. c. 300). *See* Vitus.

MODOALDUS (d. c. 640). Born in Aquitaine of a distinguished family and also known as Romoaldus, he was named bishop of Trier by King Dagobert, whose adviser he was, in 622, attended the Council of Rheims in 625, and founded several religious houses. His objections to the licentiousness of the King and his court caused Dagobert to reform his life. May 12.

MODOMNOC (6th century). Born in Ireland, reportedly a member of the O'Neil clan, he became a monk and went to Wales, where he studied under St. David. According to legend, Modomnoc introduced bees to Ireland when swarms of bees followed him when he returned there. He settled at Tipra-Fachtna (Tibraghny, Kilkenny) and is believed to have become bishop of Ossory. February 13.

MODWENNA (7th century). Believed to have been a hermitess on the island of Andresey in the Trent River in England and also known as Monenna, the facts of her life are hopelessly confused with those of other saints, among them the Irish Darerea (also known as Moninna and said to be the first abbess of Killeavy, who died about 517), Modwenna (St. Hilda's successor as abbess of Whitby, who died about 695), and Modwenna (abbess of Polesworth, Warwickshire, who died about 900). The name is also spelled Moninne and Merryn. July 6.

MOGROBEJO, TORIBIO ALFONSO DE (1538–1605). Born at Mayorga,

Spain, he studied law, became a lawyer and a professor of law at the University of Salamanca, and was named chief judge of the Inquisition court at Granada by King Philip II. He was named archbishop of Lima, Peru, in 1580 despite his objections and the fact that he was a layman, was ordained and consecrated, and arrived in Peru in 1581. He came into immediate conflict with the secular authorities over the treatment of the Indians whose rights he defended, restored ecclesiastical discipline in the see, fought for the poor, founded numerous churches, schools, and hospitals, and in 1591 he founded the first seminary in the New World. He learned to speak Indian dialects, was known for his charities, and despite great physical privations managed to visit every part of his dioceses, teaching and preaching with great effect. He died at Santa, Peru, on March 23 while on his way back to Peru from a visit, and was canonized in 1726. March 23.

MOLAISSE. *See* Laserian.

MOLING (d. 697). Probably born in Kinsellagh, Wexford, Ireland, of a family related to the Kings of Leinster, and also known as Daircheall (and Myllin in Wales), he became a monk at Glendalough and then founded an abbey at Achad Cainigb, which in time was named Tech Moling. He succeeded St. Aidan as bishop of Ferns, Leinster, lived a life of great austerity, resigned his see several years before his death, and was buried at Tech Moling. June 17.

MOLOC (d. c. 572). Probably born in Scotland of a noble family, Lugaidh was educated at Birr, Ireland, where he took the name Moloc or Moluanus, under St. Brendan the Elder. Moloc returned to Scotland to work as a missionary bishop near Lismore, the Hebrides, and Ross, where he spent most of his time. He died at Rossmarkie and is still venerated in Argyll and the Hebrides under the name of Luan; he is also known as Murlach. June 25.

MOLUA (d. 608). Also known as Lughaidh, he was the son of Carthach of Limerick, Ireland, was a cowherder in his youth, and then became a monk at Bangor under St. Comgall. He was ordained, founded many monasteries, notably one at Clonfertmulloe (Kyle), of which he was abbot, and on a pilgrimage to Rome presented his austere rule to Pope St. Gregory the Great, who praised him in accepting his rule for Celtic monasteries. August 4.

MOMMOLINUS (d. c. 686). A native of Coutances, France, he became a monk at Luxeuil and was sent to St. Omer, with SS. Bertram and Bertinus, as a missionary to the Morini in Artois. He was named superior of the Old Monastery (Saint-Momelin), moved to the New Monastery (St. Peter's) at Sithiu, and in 660 became bishop of Noyon. He built Saint-Quentin Monastery there, naming Bertram abbot, and ruled for twenty-six years until his death. October 16.

MONACELLA. *See* Melangell.

MONALDO, BUONFIGLIO (d. 1261). He and six fellow Florentine merchants, Bartholomes Amidei (Amadeus), Benedict Dell' Antell (Manettus), John Buonagiunta (Buonagiunta), Alexs Falconieri (Alexis), Gerardino Sostegni (Sostenes), and Ricovero Ugoccione (Hugh), all members of noble Florentine families, joined the Confraternity of the Blessed Virgin (the Laudesi—Praisers) in Florence about 1225, with James of Poggibonsi their spiritual director; the Confraternity was dedicated to Mary, especially in her Seven Sorrows. On the feast of the Assumption in 1233, they experienced a vision in which the Blessed

Virgin inspired them to live a life of prayer and solitude as hermits. They pursued an eremitical way of life at La Camarzia on the outskirts of Florence and then moved to nearby Monte Senario, where another vision of Mary in 1240 caused them to found a religious community—the Servants of Mary (the Servites)—and revealed to them the habit they were to wear. They were all ordained, except Alexis Falconieri, taking the names indicated above in parentheses after their real names, and Buonfiglio (Bonfilius) was elected their first superior general. He served until 1256 (he died on January 1) and was succeeded by John Buonagiunta, who died soon after his election. Their first foundation outside of Florence was a church at nearby Cafaggio, which was finished in 1252, and the Order soon spread to other Italian cities. In 1260, it was divided into two provinces: Tuscany, under Manettus, and Umbria, under Sostenes. At the invitation of King St. Louis, Manettus introduced the Order to France, and Sostenes brought it to Germany; in time it spread all over Europe, and when Manettus became fourth prior general, he sent missionaries to Asia. Though the Order was approved by the seven founders' superiors from the beginning and had the approval of Raniero Cardinal Capocci, papal legate to Tuscany, in 1249, it was not papally approved until 1304, by Pope Benedict XI, at which time only Alexis of the original seven founders was still alive. He reportedly was 110 when he died on February 17, 1310, at Monte Senario. The seven founders were cojointly canonized by Pope Leo XIII in 1888 as the "Seven Holy Founders." February 17.

MONAN (d. 874). A monk at St. Andrew's under St. Adrian, Monan worked as a missionary in the Firth of Forth area in Scotland until he and a large number of Christians were murdered by marauding Danes. March 1.

MONEGUNDIS (d. 570). Born at Chartres, France, she was married, and when her two children died, she became a recluse, with her husband's permission, in a cell at Chartres. Later she moved to Tours, built a cell near St. Martin's tomb, and attracted numerous disciples, who organized St. Pierre-le Puellier convent in Tours. After her death, many miracles were reported at her tomb. July 2.

MONICA (c. 331–87). Probably born at Tagaste, North Africa, of Christian parents, she was married to Patricius, a pagan, known for his dissolute habits and violent temper. They had three children: Augustine, Navigius, and Perpetua. Through her patience and prayers, she was able to convert Patricius and his mother in 370. She was widowed in 371 and for years prayed for the conversion of Augustine, who from the time he went to study at Carthage when he was seventeen lived a wayward life, embraced Manichaeism, dabbled in other philosophies, and had a mistress. She followed him to Rome in 383 and then to Milan where, in 386, he embraced Christianity and was baptized on Easter in 387. She lived with Augustine, his son Adeodatus, and his associates at Cassiciacum while Augustine was preparing for baptism, and she died at Ostia, Italy, soon after as they were awaiting a ship to take them back to Africa. Monica is the patroness of married women and is regarded as a model for Christian mothers. August 27.

MONINNE. *See* Modwenna.

MONTANUS (d. 259). *See* Lucius.

MORALES, BL. FRANCIS DE (d. 1622). Born at Madrid, Spain, he joined the Dominicans and was sent to Japan, where he worked as a missionary at Satzuma for two decades. He was sent to Fuximi in 1608 and six years later to Nagasaki, where he was burned to death for his faith with Bl. Charles Spinola and a group of fellow Christians. They were beatified in 1867. September 10.

MORAND (d. c. 1115). Born of noble parents near Worms, Germany, he was educated at the Worms cathedral school, was ordained, and after a pilgrimage to Compostela, became a Benedictine monk under St. Hugh at Cluny. He spent several years at Cluniac monasteries in Auvergne, but about 1100 he was sent as a missionary to lower Alsace at the request of Count Frederick Pferz, who had just restored St. Christopher Church at Altkirch. Morand became the confidant of the count and was highly regarded for his holiness, concern for the people, and miracles. He is regarded as the patron of wine growers because of the tradition that he once fasted throughout Lent eating nothing except a bunch of grapes. June 3.

MORBIOLI, BL. LOUIS (1433–85). Born at Bologna, Italy, he married and followed a carefree, pleasure-seeking life. After a serious illness in 1462, he reformed his lifestyle, became a Carmelite tertiary, separated from his wife, by mutual agreement, and spent the rest of his life doing penance, teaching religion to the young, and begging for the poor. He died at Bologna on November 8, and when miracles were reported at his grave, a cult developed, which was confirmed in 1843. November 16.

MORE, BL. HUGH (1563–88). Born at Grantham near Nottingham, England, he was raised a Protestant and studied at Oxford and law at Gray's Inn. He became a Catholic, studied for a time at Rheims, and on his return to England was arrested for having turned Catholic. When he refused to attend services of the Anglican Church, he was hanged at Lincoln's Inn Fields on August 28. He was beatified in 1929 as one of the Martyrs of London of 1588. September 1.

MORE, THOMAS (1478–1535). Born in London on February 6, the son of John More, a lawyer and a judge, he became a page in the household of Archbishop John Morton of Canterbury when he was about twelve. He went to Oxford, studied law at Lincoln's Inn, was admitted to the bar in 1501, and entered Parliament in 1504. He decided against becoming a Carthusian and married Jane Holt in 1505. Their home became a center of medieval and Renaissance culture in England, and he became one of the leading intellectual figures of his time, noted for his learning, intellect, and wit. He became England's leading humanist and one of the outstanding scholars of the age. He wrote poetry, history, treatises against Protestantism, devotional books and prayers, and translated Lucian from the Latin. His *Utopia* (1515–16), an account of an imaginary society ruled by reason, has become a classic, and his *Vindication of Henry Against Luther* (1523) was a spirited defense of King Henry VIII, whom he had tutored. He was undersheriff of London in 1510, and in 1511, a month after the death of his wife, Jane, he married Alice Middleton, a widow. When Henry became King he sent More on several diplomatic missions to France and Flanders, appointed him to the Royal Council in 1517, and knighted him in 1521. He was selected speaker of the House of Commons in 1523, was High Steward of Cambridge in 1525, and succeeded Cardinal Wolsey as Lord Chancellor in 1529 despite his grave misgivings about Henry's defiance of the Pope in divorcing Catherine of Aragon. More's silence about the matter disturbed Henry, who was angered when More refused to sign a petition to the Pope requesting permission for Henry to divorce Catherine. After opposing a series of measures against the Church, More resigned the chancellorship and retired, penniless, to his home in Chelsea in 1532 to write. When he refused to sign the oath in the Act of Succession recognizing the offspring of Henry and his second wife, Anne Boleyn, as heir to the throne, declaring that Henry's first marriage, to Catherine, was not a true marriage and repudiating the Pope, he was arrested in 1534 and imprisoned in the Tower of London. He remained there for fifteen months until July 1, 1535, and when asked by Cromwell to comment on the Act of Supremacy, he remained silent; whereupon he was accused of treason. Despite his refusal to break his silence, he was convicted of treason, and five days later, on July 6, was beheaded. As he mounted the scaffold, he proclaimed that he was "the King's good servant but God's first." He was canonized in 1935. He is a patron of lawyers. June 22.

MORSE, HENRY (1595–1645). Born at Broome, Suffolk, England, he was raised a Protestant, studied at Cambridge and law at Barnard's Inn, and in 1614 he became a Catholic at Douai. When he returned to England to settle an inheritance, he was arrested and spent the next four years in New Prison in Southwark for his faith. He was released in 1618 when a general amnesty was proclaimed by King James, returned to Douai to study for the priesthood, and continued his studies in Rome, where he was ordained in 1623. He was sent on the English mission the following year and was almost immediately arrested and imprisoned at York. While in prison, he became a Jesuit, and after three years in prison was exiled to Flanders, where he served as chaplain to English soldiers in the army of King Philip IV of Spain. He returned to England in 1633, worked in London under the pseudonym of Cuthbert Claxton, made many converts by his heroic labors in the plague of 1636–37, and was arrested for his priesthood. Released on bail through the intercession of Queen Marietta, he again left England in 1641 when a royal decree ordered all Catholic priests from the country, but returned again in 1643. He was arrested in Cumberland eighteen months later, escaped, but was captured and brought to trial. He was convicted of being a Catholic priest at the Old Bailey and was hanged, drawn, and quartered at Tyburn on February 1. His hanging was attended by the French, Spanish, and Portuguese ambassadors in protest. He was canonized by Pope Paul VI in 1970.

MORTON, BL. ROBERT (d. 1588). Born at Bawtry, Yorkshire, England, he studied for the priesthood at Rheims and Rome and was ordained in 1587. Sent on the English mission at once, he was soon captured and executed in London for being a Catholic priest during the persecution of Catholics under Queen Elizabeth I. He was beatified in 1929 as one of the Martyrs of London of 1588. August 28.

MOSCATI, GUISEPPE (1880–1927). Physician Moscati is one of twenty-five people associated with the sixteenth century-founded Incurabili Hospital in Naples to have been canonized, beatified, or named Venerable. Famed as a scientific researcher, university teacher, and diagnostician, Moscati called medicine the "sublime mission." He was canonized in 1987.

MOSES (d. 251). Probably of Jewish ancestry, he became a priest at Rome, opposed Novatian and his heresy, and was leader of a group of clergy that corresponded with St. Cyprian. He was arrested during the persecution of the Christians under Emperor Decius, and after almost a year in prison was executed in Rome on January 1 for his Christianity. November 26.

MOSES (d. c. 372). An Arab, he lived as a hermit in the desert between Syria and Egypt, ministering to wandering bands of Saracens. When a Roman expedition to end Saracen guerrilla attacks on Roman towns imposed a peace on the Saracens, their Queen, Mavia, agreed only if Moses was named their bishop. He refused consecration from Arian Archbishop Lucius of Alexandria but eventually was consecrated by an orthodox bishop. He maintained peace between the Saracens and Rome and was known as "the Apostle of the Saracens," the name given by the Romans to the nomadic tribes wandering the Syro-Egyptian desert. February 7.

MOSES THE BLACK (c. 330–c. 405). An Ethiopian born a slave, he was a servant in the household of an Egyptian official. Moses was dismissed from the official's service because of his viciousness, thievery, and evil propensities, and became the leader of a notorious band of outlaws who terrorized the area. How he was converted is not known, though it is believed by the hermits of the Skete Desert in Lower Egypt, where he was hiding out after some particularly vicious crime. He became a monk at Petra Monastery, was known for his extreme mortifications while living as a hermit, and was ordained by Archbishop Theophilus of Alexandria. Moses was murdered, with six other monks, by a band of marauding Berbers when he refused to defend himself by force. August 28.

MOSEUS (d. 250). *See* Ammonius.

MOYE, BL. JOHN (1730–93). Born at Cutting, Lorraine, he studied at Pont-à-Mousson, Strasbourg, and Metz Seminary, and was ordained in 1754. He became vicar of Metz, helped a group of women (which became the Sisters of Divine Providence in 1767) to establish schools for rural children, and then was appointed rector of the minor seminary of St. Dié. He joined the Society of Foreign Missions in Paris in 1769 and was sent to China in 1773. He founded the Christian Virgins to work as catechists and nurses in 1782, and in 1784 was forced to return to France because of ill health. He preached widely in Lorraine and Alsace, was forced into exile in 1791 to Trier when the French Revolution broke out, and died on May 4 of typhoid contracted while treating victims of the disease after the city was captured by the French. He was beatified in 1954. September 18.

MUCIUS (d. 304). Also known as Mocius, his untrustworthy legend has him a Christian priest noted for his eloquence who destroyed an altar to Bacchus during a pagan feast at Amphipolis, Macedonia. Sentenced to death, he miraculously escaped execution by fire there and by wild beasts at Heraclea before finally being beheaded at Constantinople. His cult goes back to the fourth century, and there is no doubt a Christian priest named Mucius suffered martyrdom at Constantinople during the persecution of the Christians under Emperor Diocletian. May 13.

MUINIS. *See* Mel.

MUNCHIN (7th century). Venerated as the patron of Limerick, Ireland, and called "the Wise," he may have come to Limerick from County Clare, and tradition has him a bishop, though scholars doubt this. He is also known as Maincin (Little Monk) in Ireland. January 2.

MUNDEN, BL. JOHN (d. 1584). Born at Coltley, Dorset, England, he studied at Winchester and New College, Oxford, where he became a fellow. In 1566, he lost his fellowship because he was a Catholic, taught school in Dorcestershire, and in 1580 was at Rheims. He then went to Rome, where he was ordained in 1582, and was sent on the English mission. He was arrested the following year at Staines, imprisoned in the Tower of London for a year and then, convicted of high treason for being a Catholic priest, he was hanged, drawn, and quartered at Tyburn on February 12 with four other priests. They were beatified in 1929.

MUNGO. *See* Kentigern.

MUNNU. *See* Fintan (d. c. 635).

MURUMBA, MATTHIAS. *See* Lwanga, Charles.

MUREDACH. *See* Murtagh.

MURIALDO, LEONARD (1828–1900). Born at Turin, Italy, on October 26, he studied at the university there and received his doctorate in 1850. He was ordained the following year, devoted himself to the education of poor boys, was named director of San Luigi Oratory by St. John Bosco, and after further study at San Sulpice in Paris, he headed Turin's Collegio Artigianelli, which became famed for its vocational training. In 1873, he founded the Pious Congregation of St. Joseph, was its first superior, began the first Catholic worker movement in Italy, and founded the

monthly periodical *La buona stampa*. He died at Turin on March 30, and was canonized by Pope Paul VI in 1970.

MURLACH. *See* Moloc.

MURTAGH (6th century). Also known as Muredach, he was of the royal family of King Laoghaire and was reputedly appointed first bishop of Killala by St. Patrick, though this seems improbable, since Murtagh is believed to have met with St. Columba at Ballysodare near Sligo in 575. Murtagh is said to have died while living as a hermit on the island of Inismurray. August 12.

MUSTIOLA (d. 273). *See* Irenaeus.

MYLLIN. *See* Moling.

MYLOR (date unknown). According to a pious medieval fable, Mylor, also known as Melar or Melorus, was the son of Duke Melianus of Cornouaille, Brittany. When he was seven, his Uncle Rivoldus murdered his father, maimed Mylor by cutting off his right hand and left foot, and had him confined to a monastery. After several years, it was reported that Mylor was performing miracles. Alarmed, Rivoldus bribed Cerialtanus, Mylor's guardian, to behead the boy, who was only fourteen. Miracles were reported at the tomb of the murdered boy, including the death of the murderers. An Anglicized version of the same fable had his father a duke in Cornwall, and a variation also appears in Celtic folklore. October 1.

MYROPE (d. 251). A native of the Greek island of Chios, she and Ammianus, a Roman soldier stationed there, recovered the body of St. Isidore when he was martyred on Chios. When she admitted doing so, she was scourged and imprisoned for hiding the body;

she died of mistreatment in prison. Ammianus too suffered martyrdom, at Cyzicus. July 13.

MZEC, BL. JOHN MARY (d. 1887). A native of Uganda, Africa, who had baptized many of his fellow Ugandans when they were waiting to be executed during the persecution launched by King Mwanga in 1885, he was arrested and then beheaded for his faith and his activities. He was canonized in 1964 as one of the twenty-two martyrs of Uganda by Pope Paul VI. June 3.

NABOR (d. c. 303). *See* Felix.

NAHUM (10th century). Converted by SS. Cyril and Methodius in Moravia, he helped them in their translations and succeeded to the see of Velitsa, probably on the death of St. Clement of Okrida in 916. He is one of the Seven Apostles of Bulgaria. July 17.

NAPPER, BL. GEORGE (1550–1610). Born at Holywell Manor, Oxford, England, he entered Corpus Christi College, Oxford, when he was fifteen but was expelled three years later because he was a Catholic. He was imprisoned in 1580 and was released nine years later when he accepted royal supremacy in ecclesiastical matters. He soon repented of his weakness, went to Douai to study for the priesthood, and was ordained in 1596. He was sent on the English mission in 1603 and worked in the Oxfordshire area until 1610, when he was arrested at Kirtlington. Convicted of being a Catholic priest, he was executed at Oxford on November 9 after he refused to sign the Oath of Supremacy. He was beatified in 1929. November 9.

NARCISSUS (1st century). *See* Ampliatus.

NARCISSUS (d. c. 215). A Greek, he was named bishop of Jerusalem in his old age, imposed strict discipline on his see, and was forced to flee his see when some of his opponents denounced him for his support of Roman customs at the Council of Jerusalem. He lived as a hermit for several years, then returned and was persuaded to resume his bishopric by the faithful of the city. He appointed St. Alexander his coadjutor, who stated that Narcissus was 116 years old in 212. October 29.

NARCISSUS (d. 320). *See* Argeus.

NARSES. Another form of Nerses.

NARSES (d. 421). *See* Maharsapor.

NARTZALUS (d. 180). *See* Speratus.

NATALIA (d. c. 304). *See* Adrian.

NATALIA (d. c. 852). *See* Aurelius.

NATHALAN (d. 678). Born at Tullicht near Aberdeen, Scotland, of a noble family, he abandoned the life of a noble to spend his life in farming and contemplation. He fed the people of the area during a famine, had seed restored miraculously, made a pilgrimage to Rome, and was made a bishop by the Pope. After years in Rome, he returned to Scotland, built churches at Tullicht, Bothelin, and Colle, and died at Tullicht on January 8. His cult was approved in 1898. January 19.

NATHANAEL. *See* Bartholomew.

NATHY (6th century). Surnamed Cruimthir (the Priest), he was born at Luighne, Sligo, Ireland, and became a disciple of St. Finnian of Clonard, who made him a bishop. He was founder-abbot of a monastery, which is questioned by some in view of his surname. His cult was confirmed in 1903. August 9.

NAVARETTE, BL. ALPHONSUS (d. 1617). Born at Vallodolid, Spain, he joined the Dominicans, was sent as a missionary to the Philippines and in 1611 was sent to Japan. He was named provincial vicar, was successful in conversion work at Nagasaki, founded confraternities to help the poor and rescue abandoned babies, and was known for the eloquence of his preaching. He was arrested at Omura while ministering to persecuted Christians there, with Bl. Ferdinand Ayalà, an Augustinian friar; they were beheaded on June 1 with a Japanese catechist. He was beatified in 1867.

NAVARRO, BL. PAUL (1560–1622). Born at Laino near Cassano, Italy, he joined the Jesuits in 1587, was sent to India while still a scholastic, and was ordained there. He was sent to Japan, became proficient in Japanese, served as rector of the Jesuit house at Amanguchi for two decades, and was successful in his missionary activities in and around Nagasaki. He was burned to death for his faith on November 1 at Shimabara, and was beatified in 1867.

NAZARIUS (c. 68). Unreliable legend has him born in Rome the son of a pagan Roman army officer and a Christian mother and taught by St. Peter. Nazarius was beheaded in Milan, with a young companion, Celsus, for preaching Christianity, during Emperor Nero's first persecution of the Christians. It is a fact that St. Ambrose discovered the bodies in Milan soon after 395 (reputedly Nazarius' blood was still liquid and red) and enshrined them there, but that is all that is really known of them factually. July 28.

NECTARAN (6th century). Also known as Nighton, all that is known of him is from untrustworthy legends, in one of which he is an Irish missionary who founded churches in Devon and Cornwall in England; in another he is the eldest of twenty-four children of King Brychan of Wales. Nectaran's shrine at Hartland, Devonshire, England, has been venerated since medieval times, and according to another legend he died by being beheaded by robbers. June 17.

NECTARIUS (d. 397). Son of a senator, he was born at Tarsus, Cilicia, became *praetor* at Constantinople, and in 381 succeeded Gregory Nazianzen on the latter's resignation as archbishop. Nectarius' appointment came about through a chance listing of his name on the list of candidates submitted to the Emperor, who chose him even though he was married and was not even baptized. He ruled for sixteen years, opposed the Arians, who burned down his house in 388, abolished public penance, and was considered by some to be too lenient with the Novatians. He died on September 27. October 11.

NELSON, BL. JOHN (d. 1578). Born at Skelton, Yorkshire, England, he went to Douai when he was forty and was ordained in 1576. Sent on the English mission later the same year, he became a Jesuit just before he was arrested and imprisoned in London. He was convicted of high treason for refusing to take Queen Elizabeth I's Oath of Supremacy and hanged, drawn, and quartered at Tyburn. February 3.

NEMESIAN (d. 257). A bishop of Numidia, he was imprisoned with eight other bishops and many of the clergy and laity at Alexandria for their Christianity. They were condemned to labor in the marble quarries of Signum in northern Africa, where he died. They were encouraged in their faith by a still extant letter of St. Cyprian from his exile at Curubis. Most of the prisoners were either executed or died of hardship and ill treatment. The eight other bishops were Davitus, Felix (two), Jader, Litteus, Lucius, Polyanus, and Victor. September 10.

NEMESIUS (d. 250). An Egyptian, he was arrested in Alexandria during the persecution of Christians under Emperor Decius. Nemesius was cleared of charges of thievery but was found guilty of being a Christian, scourged, and burned to death. December 19.

NENNIUS (6th century). All that is known of him is that he was Irish, became a disciple of St. Finnian of Clonard, and is one of the Twelve Apostles of Ireland. January 17.

NEON (d. c. 303). *See* Asterius.

NEOT (d. c. 880). Unreliable legend has him a monk at Glastonbury, England, who was ordained and became a hermit in Cornwall (at what is now St. Neot), where he was visited by his relative King Alfred seeking his advice. July 31.

NEREUS (1st century). Legend has him and Achilleus praetorian soldiers who were converted to Christianity and who refused to bear arms because of their new religion. They laid down their arms and left the army but were captured, exiled to the island of Terracina, and were beheaded there for their faith during the reign of Emperor Trajan. The burial place of the family vault in which they were buried later was named the cemetery of Domitilla; according to another legend they were eunuchs in the household of Flavia Domitilla, grandniece of Empress Domitian, and were exiled with Flavia to Terracina, where they all suffered martyrdom, she by being burned to death and they by beheading. May 12.

NERI, PHILIP (1515–95). Born at Florence, Italy, on July 22, he was the son of a notary and was educated by the Dominicans of San Marco in Florence. When he was eighteen, he was sent to San Germano to pursue a business career, but a mystical experience he had turned him to the religious life. He went to Rome in 1533, lived there almost as a recluse for two years while tutoring two sons of a wealthy Florentine, and then studied philosophy and theology at the Sapienza and Sant' Agostino for three years. He began to preach on the streets and in the markets to the Romans, whose religious practices had become lukewarm and were frequently neglected; the city was corrupt and the Church reflected the current malaise of the secular society. In 1548, with Fr. Persiano Rossa, his confessor, Philip founded the Confraternity of the Most Holy Trinity, composed of laypeople to minister to needy pilgrims (it developed into the famous Santa Trinità dei Pellegrini Hospital) and to spread the Forty Hours' devotion. He was ordained in 1551 and soon achieved fame as a confessor, attracting huge crowds of penitents to San Girolamo della Carità, where he lived in a community of priests. He had remarkable success in making converts and attracted many priests to aid him in ministering the informal conferences he devised for the throngs seeking spiritual advice and solace, and in time they became known as Oratorians because they summoned their groups to their oratory (room) for prayer. However, the actual founding of the Oratorians dates to 1564, when

Philip became rector of San Giovanni Church, and five of his disciples were ordained and installed there and followed the spiritual directions he established. The new society received formal approval in 1575, by which time Philip was the most popular person in Rome, from Pope St. Gregory XIII, who gave it the run-down Church of Sta Maria in Vallicela and named Philip superior. He demolished the old church and erected a new one on its site, naming it Chiesa Nuova, which became headquarters for the Oratorians in 1577, though Philip did not come to Vallicela from San Girolamo until 1583. By this time he was known as the "Apostle of Rome" and was venerated by popes, cardinals, rulers, and ordinary people. He was consulted by rich and poor, powerful and helpless for his spiritual wisdom and his ability to look into men's minds. He experienced ecstasies and visions, was credited with performing miracles, and had the gift of prophecy. He resigned as superior in 1593 because of ill health and in the same year prevented a serious conflict between France and the Holy See when he insisted on the absolution of Henry IV. He died in Rome on May 26, venerated as a saint, and was canonized in 1622 by Pope Gregory XV. May 26.

NERON, BL. PETER FRANCIS (1818–60). Born at Bornay, France, he joined the Society for Foreign Missions of Paris in 1846, was ordained two years later, and was sent to Hong Kong as a missionary. He was then sent to Indochina, where he became director of the seminary at West Tonkin and worked there until he was beheaded for his faith. He was beatified in 1919. November 3.

NERSES (263–343). Bishop of Sahgerd, Persia, he and a disciple, Joseph, were arrested during the persecutions of Christians under Sapor II and brought before the King. Nerses was offered his freedom if he would worship the sun, and when he refused, he and Joseph were beheaded. November 20.

NERSES I THE GREAT (d. c. 373). Born at Caesarea, Cappadocia, in 333 or 337, of royal descent, he married a princess, and when she died he became a chamberlain at the court of King Arshak of Armenia. Nerses was ordained, and in 353, against his will, was made Katholikos of the Armenians. He instituted reforms he had learned under St. Basil at Caesarea with the first national synod at Ashtishat in 365, founded hospitals, and encouraged monasticism. His vigorous new ecclesiastical program alienated Arshak, and when Nerses denounced the King for the murder of his wife, Nerses was banished to Edessa by Arshak, who intruded another bishop in his place. When Arshak was killed in battle with the Persians he was succeeded by Pap, and Nerses returned. However, his relationship with Pap was as strained as it had been with the previous King, and he refused to allow Pap into his church until he reformed his evil life. Seemingly repentant, Pap invited Nerses to a banquet and poisoned him at Khakh on the Euphrates.

NERSES KLAIETSI (d. 1173). Born at Hromkla, Cilicia, he was educated by his uncle Katholikos Gregory II, and Stephen Manuk, and was ordained by his brother, Katholikos Gregory III. Like his uncle, he favored the reunion of Rome and the Armenian Church, was himself reunited to Rome when he met Roman bishops with the crusaders, and when he succeeded his brother as Katholikos in 1166 remained in union with Rome, though formal reunion did not take place until 1198, when Leo II became King. He worked actively for the reunion of Rome and the Orthodox

Greeks and unsuccessfully for the union of the Greek and Armenian churches. He wrote poetry, prayers, hymns, and a history of Armenia, and is considered one of the outstanding figures of twelfth-century Armenian culture; he was surnamed "the Great" because of the quality of his writing. He died on August 13. August 3.

NERSES LAMPRONATS (1153–98). Born at Lampron, Cilicia, the son of the prince of Lampron, he was educated at Skeyra Monastery and became an outstanding scholar, theologian, and exegete, skilled in Greek, Latin, Syriac, and Coptic. When his father died, he was ordained in 1169, lived as a hermit for a time, and in 1176 was consecrated archbishop of Tarsus. He strongly supported the reunion of the Armenian Church with Rome at a council at Hromkla in 1179, but nothing came of it when the supporter of the move, Emperor Manuel Comnenus, died the next year. Nerses actively engaged in the negotiations that led to the reunion with Rome in 1198 and died six months after the reunion was confirmed by the crowning of Leo II as King of Lower Armenia by the papal legate with a crown sent by Pope Celestine III. Nerses wrote on the liturgy, scriptural commentaries, hymns, and lives of the desert saints, and translated St. Benedict's Rule and St. Gregory's *Dialogues* into Armenian. He died at Tarsus on July 14.

NERUCCI, BL. LAURENCE (d. 1420). He and his fellow Servites, Augustine Cennini, Bartholomew Donati, and John Baptist Petrucci, were sent to Bohemia to preach against the Hussites in a crusade called by Pope Martin V in 1420. Soon after their arrival, a mob of Hussites attacked the monastery at which they were staying in Prague, set it afire, and burned the four to death with sixty other resident friars. Their

cult was apparently confirmed in 1918, but the decree does not seem to have been published in *Acta Apostolicae Sedis,* which publishes all such decrees. August 31.

NESTABUS (d. c. 363). *See* Eusebius.

NESTOR (d. 251). Bishop of Magydus, Pamphylia, he was arrested for his faith during the persecution of Christians under Emperor Decius, sent to Pollio, governor of Pamphylia and Phrygia, at Perga, and when Nestor refused to sacrifice to pagan gods, he was tortured and then crucified. February 26.

NESTOR (d. c. 362). *See* Eusebius.

NETTER, BL. THOMAS (c. 1375–1430). Born at Saffron Walden, Essex, England, he joined the Carmelites in London, received his doctorate in theology from Oxford, and was ordained in 1400. He became a professor, attended the Council of Pisa in 1409, where he supported Pope Alexander V, and on his return to England, became one of the leading opponents of the disciples of John Wyclif, especially the Lollards. Bl. Thomas was elected prior provincial of England and became confessor of King Henry V. After attending the Council of Constance in 1415, which condemned the teachings of Wyclif and Hus, he went to Poland on a papal diplomatic mission. He established Carmelite friaries in Lithuania and Prussia, returned to England in 1420, and on the death of Henry, who died in his arms, he was appointed tutor of the infant Henry VI in 1422. Bl. Thomas died at Rouen on November 2 while on a visit to France with the young Henry. Bl. Thomas' writings earned him the title "the authoritative teacher," especially *Doctrinale fidei.* Though a Carmelite cult has developed around him, he has never been formally canonized.

NEUMANN, JOHN NEPOMUCENE (1811–60). Born at Prachatiz, Bohemia, on March 28, the third of six children of Agnes and Philip Neumann, he was early attracted to the religious life, entered the diocesan seminary of Budweis in 1831, and two years later the archiepiscopal seminary at Prague University. Unable to be ordained because of a surplus of priests in Bohemia, he went to the United States in 1836, was ordained in New York later the same year, and devoted the next four years to missionary work, especially among German-speaking Catholics, in upstate New York. In 1840, he joined the newly established branch of the Redemptorists at St. Philomena's in Pittsburgh and became the first Redemptorist to take his vows in the United States, in 1842. He continued his missionary activities in Maryland, Ohio, Pennsylvania, and Virginia, became rector of St. Philomena's in 1844, and was named vice regent and superior of the American Redemptorists in 1847. He was consecrated fourth bishop of Philadelphia in 1852 and reorganized the diocese, inaugurating a widespread program of new church and school building. He was an active proponent of Catholic education, and two catechisms he wrote were endorsed by the American bishops at their first Plenary Council in 1852 and were widely used in Catholic schools the next thirty-five years. At the time of his death in Philadelphia on January 5, he was renowned for his holiness, charity, pastoral work, and preaching. He was canonized in 1977 by Pope Paul VI, the first American male saint.

NEVOLO. *See* Novellone, Bl.

NEWDIGATE, BL. SEBASTIAN (d. 1535). Born at Harefield Place, Middlesex, England, he studied at Cambridge and became a member of King Henry VIII's court and privy councellor. On the death of Bl. Sebastian's wife in 1524, he became a Carthusian, and in 1535, on the execution of John Houghton, prior of the London charterhouse, he, Humphrey Middlemore, and William Exmew took over the management of the London house. All three were arrested three weeks after the death of Houghton, and when they refused to sign the Act of Supremacy stating that King Henry VIII was supreme head of the Church in England, they were executed on June 19. They were beatified in 1886.

NEWPORT, BL. RICHARD (d. 1612). Born at Harringworth, Northamptonshire, England, he studied for the priesthood in Rome, was ordained there, and then was sent on the English mission. He used the alias Smith, was arrested twice, and banished from the country, but he returned each time. The third time he was arrested, he was tried, with Bl. William Scott, and sentenced to death as a traitor because he was a Catholic priest. Both were hanged, drawn, and quartered at Tyburn on May 30, and beatified in 1929.

NEYROT, BL. ANTONY (d. 1460). Born at Rivoli, Italy, he joined the Dominicans at Florence, was professed, and was sent to Sicily. On the way, he was captured by pirates and sold as a slave in Tunis; by the time he was freed he had become a Moslem and married. Reportedly a vision of St. Antoninus brought him back to his Catholic faith; he left his wife, did penance, and then returned to Tunis, where he publicly denounced Mohammedanism and was stoned and cut to death by sword. His cult was approved in 1767. April 10.

NICANDER (d. c. 304). A doctor in Egypt, he was condemned to death for tending to Christian prisoners during the persecution of Christians under Emperor Diocletian. March 15.

NICANDER (4th century). He and Marcian were officers in the Roman army who resigned from the army when anti-Christian edicts were published. They were brought before the governor, Maximus, and when they refused to sacrifice to pagan gods were imprisoned to give them time to reconsider their decision. When they remained adamant, they were beheaded in the presence of their wives and Nicander's child. Sources of their story are untrustworthy, and the place of their martyrdom is unknown, but it is believed to have been at Durostorum, Bulgaria. June 17.

NICANOR (1st century). A resident of Jerusalem, he was one of the seven selected by the apostles to minister to the needs of the needy. Tradition says he later went to Cyprus, where he suffered martyrdom during the reign of Emperor Vespasian (69–79), though this is uncertain. January 10.

NICARETE (d. c. 410). Born of a good family in Nicomedia, she left home to live in Constantinople, where she devoted herself to good works. She ministered to St. John Chrysostom when he was ill, was his stanch defender, and was exiled, probably to Nicomedia, when John's foes forced St. Olympias and his other followers from the city. December 27.

NICASIUS (d. c. 451). Bishop of Rheims, he was beheaded by marauding barbarians while trying to save the lives of his faithful during a barbarian invasion he had prophesied. Murdered with him were St. Florentius, his deacon; St. Jucundus, his lector; and St. Eutropia, his sister, who was killed when she attacked her brother's murderers. December 14.

NICEPHORUS (d. 260). A resident of Antioch, he had a falling out with his priest friend Sapricius, who despite his every effort refused to forgive him. When Sapricius was arrested for being a Christian priest during the persecution of Christians under Emperors Valerian and Gallienus, he acknowledged his priesthood, refused to sacrifice to the gods despite torture, and was ordered beheaded. On the way to the place of execution, Nicephorus three times begged his forgiveness and was refused. At the last moment, when he was ordered to kneel down for the executioner's sword, Sapricius apostatized, and his life was spared when he agreed to sacrifice to the pagan gods. Nicephorus reproached him for his weakness, proclaimed his own Christianity, and was beheaded when he refused to sacrifice to the gods. The story is a pious fiction preaching a moral lesson. February 9.

NICEPHORUS (d. 284). *See* Victorinus.

NICEPHORUS (758–828). The son of the secretary of Emperor Constantine Copronymus who had been tortured and exiled when he refused to accept the Emperor's decrees banishing holy images, Nicephorus grew up a stanch opponent of iconoclasm. He became imperial commissioner known for his eloquence, scholarship, and statesmanship, and built a monastery near the Black Sea. Though he was a layman, he was named against his wishes Patriarch of Constantinople in 806, succeeding St. Tarasius. Nicephorus incurred the enmity of St. Theodore Studites for forgiving a priest who had illicitly married Emperor Constantine VI and Theodota while Constantine's wife, Mary, was still alive. The two were later reconciled and Nicephorus devoted himself to reforming his see, restoring monastic discipline, and reinvigorating the religion of his flock. He resisted the efforts of Emperor

Leo the Armenian who became Emperor in 813, to reimpose the heresy of iconoclasm, was deposed by a synod of iconoclastic bishops assembled by Leo, had several attempts made on his life, was exiled to the monastery he had built on the Black Sea, and spent the last fifteen years of his life there. He wrote several treatises against iconoclasm and two historical works, *Breviarum* and *Chronographia*. He died on June 2 at the monastery. March 13.

NICETAS (d. 824). A native of Caesarea, Bithynia, his father entered a monastery a few years after his mother died when he was a week old, and Nicetas was raised in the monastery. He became a monk at Medikion Monastery at the foot of Mount Olympus, Bithynia, was ordained in 790 by St. Tarasius, and in time became abbot. When he and a group of other abbots refused the demand of Emperor Leo the Armenian that they recognize the intruded Theodotus as Patriarch of Constantinople, whom Leo had appointed to replace the exiled Patriarch Nicephorus, Nicetas was exiled to Anatolia, where he was subjected to ill treatment. When he was brought back to Constantinople, he accepted Theodotus as patriarch and was returned to his monastery. He soon repented publicly, withdrew his allegiance to the patriarch, and denounced iconoclasm. He was exiled to the isle of Glyceria in 813, released when Michael the Stammerer became Emperor in 820, and lived as a hermit near Constantinople until his death there. April 3.

NICETAS (d. 1107). Born at Kiev, Russia, he became a monk in the Monastery of the Caves there and then became a hermit. Subjected to diabolic attacks, he abandoned his eremitical life and resumed his monastic state. He was named bishop of Novgorod, Russia, in 1095 and reigned for twelve years, during which he was venerated for the miracles he is reputed to have performed. January 31.

NICETAS OF CONSTANTINOPLE (d. c. 838). Of a Paphlagonian family related to Empress Irene, he was a courtier at her court and reportedly was one of her official representatives at the second General Council of Nicaea, in 787. He was appointed prefect of Sicily, a position he retained when Nicephorus' palace revolution put him on the throne in 802, but became a monk at Khrysonike Monastery in Constantinople when Nicephorus was killed in 811. Nicetas fled the monastery with an icon of Christ with some of the monks when Emperor Leo V began his attacks on icons, and was made a house prisoner at a country house when Leo's soldiers forcibly possessed the icon. Twelve years later Nicetas and three other monks were driven from the monastery when they refused to accept iconoclast Antony as Patriarch of Constantinople when Emperor Theophilus demanded they do so. They were driven from one place to another because of their refusal to accept iconoclasm until they finally found refuge on a farm at Katisia, Paphlagonia, where Nicetas lived the rest of his life. October 6.

NICETAS THE GOTH (d. 375). A Goth born near the Danube River, he was converted by Arian missionary Ulfilas, who ordained him. During a persecution of Christians by King Athanaric of the Eastern Goths, he was burned to death with other Christians when he refused to worship an idol sent through the towns and villages by the King. September 15.

NICETAS OF PEREASLAV (d. 1186). A tax collector at Pereaslav near Rostov, Russia, and notorious for his merciless enforcement of his duties, he suddenly reformed his life, left his wife and family to enter a monastery, and led a life of extreme penances and mortifications. Robbers, mistaking the metal links in a shirt he wore against his skin for silver, murdered him for the shirt. He was often called "the Wonder Worker" for the miracles he is reputed to have performed. May 24.

NICETAS OF REMESIANA (c. 335–c. 414). A close friend of St. Paulinus of Nola, he was bishop of Remesiana in Dacia (modern Romania and Yugoslavia) and was noted for his successful missionary activities, especially among the Bessi, which Paulinus commemorates in a poem. Nicetas wrote several dissertations on faith, the creed, the Trinity, and liturgical singing, and is believed by some scholars to be the author of *Te Deum*. June 22.

NICETIUS (d. 573). Also known as Nizier, he was early inclined to the religious life, was ordained, and became known for his preaching. His uncle, Bishop St. Sacerdos of Lyons, named him his successor, and Nicetius ruled the see of Lyons for twenty years. He revived ecclesiastical chant in the see, was known for his abilities as an exorcist, and was credited with miracles at his tomb after his death. April 2.

NICETIUS (d. c. 611). Also known as Nizier, he was elected bishop of Besançon, which he restored after it had been destroyed by the Huns, and was reputed to have been a friend of Pope St. Gregory the Great and St. Columban, to whom he gave shelter at Besançon when Columban fled from Queen Brunhilda and Thierry II. February 8.

NICETIUS OF TRIER (d. c. 566). Born at Auvergne, Gaul, he became a monk, probably at Limoges, and then abbot. He was named bishop of Trier (the last Gallo-Roman bishop of that see) by King Theodoric I, was exiled when he excommunicated King Clotaire I for his crimes, but was recalled by Sigebert on the death of Clotaire, Sigebert's father. Nicetius restored clerical discipline, rebuilt the city's fortifications and cathedral, and founded a school for clerics. A severe critic of evil wherever he found it, he wrote Emperor Justinian denouncing him for his semimonophysitism. He probably died on October 1, when his feast is kept at Trier. December 5.

NICHOLAS (d. c. 350). Probably born at Patara, Lycia, Asia Minor, of wealthy parents, he was named bishop of Myra, a run-down diocese, and became known for his holiness, zeal, and miracles. He was imprisoned for his faith during the persecution of Christians under Emperor Diocletian, was present at the Council of Nicaea, where he denounced Arianism and died at Myra. To these meager facts of his life were added colorful details from legends and untrustworthy biographies, according to which he was born at Patara and when his wealthy parents died, he devoted himself to the conversion of sinners and his wealth to the poor and to charitable works. One such is the story of three poverty-stricken girls whose father was about to turn them into prostitutes since he could not afford a dowry for them; Nicholas on three occasions threw bags of gold into their house, and all three were married. He destroyed pagan temples, forced a governor, Eustathius, to admit he had been bribed to condemn three innocent men to death (Nicholas saved them), and appeared in a dream to Emperor Constantine to tell the Emperor that three imperial officers condemned to death at Constantinople were innocent (Constantine freed them the next morning). His popularity, already great, increased enormously in the West when his relics were brought to Bari in 1087, and his shrine was one of the great pilgrimage centers of medieval Europe. He is the patron of storm-beset sailors (for miraculously saving doomed mariners off the coast of Lycia), of prisoners, of children (in some accounts the story of the three bags of gold and the three girls became the heads of three murdered children restored to life by the saint), which led to the practice of children giving presents at Christmas in his name and the metamorphosis of his name, St. Nicholas, into Sint Klaes into Santa Claus by the Dutch. It should be noted though that the figure of Santa Claus is really non-Christian and is based on the Germanic god Thor, who was associated with winter and the Yule log and rode on a chariot drawn by goats named Cracker and Gnasher. Nicholas is also the patron of Greece, Apulia, Sicily, Lorraine, and Russia. December 6.

NICHOLAS I (d. 867). Surnamed "the Great," he was born at Rome between 819 and 822 of a distinguished family, became a member of the Roman clergy, served in the Curia under Pope Sergius II, became a deacon under Pope Leo IV, and was a trusted adviser of Pope Benedict III. Nicholas was elected pope on April 22, 858, succeeding Benedict, and immediately exhibited the courage and energy for which he was famed. He insisted on the sanctity and indissolubility of marriage, despite the threat of an invasion of Rome, when he denounced the irregularity of the marriage of the Emperor's nephew, King Lothaire II of Lorraine, and insisted on the freedom to marry when he forced King Charles the Bald of Burgundy to accept the marriage of his daughter Judith to Baldwin of Flanders without the King's consent and compelled the Frankish bishops to withdraw the excommunication they had imposed on her for marrying without her father's consent. In 861 Nicholas compelled Archbishop Hincmar of Rheims

to accept papal appellate jurisdiction in important cases when he obliged Hincmar to restore Bishop Rothad of Soissons, whom he had deposed. Twice he excommunicated recalcitrant and powerful Archbishop John of Ravenna, who counted on imperial support, for infringing on the rights of the Holy See and for abuses of his office, and made him submit to papal authority. Nicholas was involved in controversy with Constantinople throughout his pontificate over the illegal deposition of Ignatius and the appointment of Photius as Patriarch of Constantinople by Emperor Michael III, and Nicholas excommunicated Michael in 863; the matter was not finally resolved until newly crowned Emperor Basil I expelled Photius, who had declared the Pope deposed, on the day Nicholas died. He encouraged missionary activities, sending St. Anskar as papal missionary to Scandinavia and bringing about the conversion of Bulgaria with missionaries he sent there. Nicholas is also known for his correspondence with King Boris, which led to Nicholas' famous *Responsa Nicolai ad consulta Bulgarum,* a classic summary of Christian faith and discipline. A champion of papal primacy and the ascendancy of the Church over Emperors, Kings, and other secular rulers in matters concerning the Church, he was responsible for restoring the papacy to the highest prestige. He was one of the most forceful of early medieval Popes, was famous for his concern for the poor, his justice, and for the reforms he instituted among the clergy and laity, was a patron of learning and the arts, and was a man of the highest personal integrity. He died at Rome on November 13.

NICHOLAS (d. 925). A member of the inner council of the Byzantine court, he was deposed as Patriarch of Constantinople by Emperor Leo the

Wise when Nicholas refused to sanction that monarch's fourth marriage. As a member of the secret council, he is often surnamed "the Mystic." May 15.

NICHOLAS (d. 1227). *See* Daniel.

NICHOLAS VON FLÜE (1417–87). Born on the Flüeli (hence his name), a fertile plain near Sachseln, Obwalden (Unterwalden) Canton, Switzerland, on March 21, he married Dorothea Wissling, and during their happily married life they had ten children. He fought in the forces of his canton in the war with Zurich in 1439, was a captain in the occupation of the Turgau in 1453, served as magistrate and councillor for Obwalden, and consistently refused the position of governor. In 1467, when he was fifty, with the consent and approval of his wife and children, he embraced the eremitical life in a cell at Ranft, near Sachseln, and spent the last nineteen years of his life there, subsisting solely on Holy Communion. He became famed for his holiness and wisdom and was consulted by a constant stream of leaders and common folk from all walks of life. He was responsible for the inclusion of Fribourg and Soleure in the Swiss Confederation in 1481 after independence had been won from Charles the Bold of Burgundy and Switzerland's leaders could not come to an agreement and civil war threatened. He was the outstanding religious figure in Swiss history, known affectionately as "Bruder Klaus." He died on March 21 in his cell at Ranft, and was canonized in 1947. March 22.

NICHOLAS OF FORCA PALENA (1349–1449). Born at Forca Palena, Abruzzi, Italy, he was ordained there, went to Rome, and then founded a society of eremitical priests, the Hermits of St. Jerome, at Naples. He established other foundations of his society at Florence and Rome and then joined it to a congregation of hermits founded by Bl. Peter of Pisa, the Hieronymites. His cult among the Hieronymites was confirmed in 1771, but he has never been solemnly beatified. October 1.

NICHOLAS OF LINDKÖPING, BL. *See* Hermannsön, Bl. Nicholas.

NICHOLAS PAGLIA, BL. (1197–1255). Of a noble family, he was born at Gio Vinazzo, near Bari, Apulia, Italy, and joined the Dominicans after hearing St. Dominic preach while he was a student at Bologna. Nicholas was prior provincial of the Roman province in 1230, founded a priory at Perugia in 1233 and another at Trani about 1254, and was again prior provincial in 1255. He is reputed to have experienced visions and other supernatural gifts, and died at Perugia on February 11. His cult was confirmed in 1828. February 14.

NICHOLAS THE PILGRIM (1075–94). A Greek, he immigrated to Italy, wandered from town to town in southern Italy bearing a cross and chanting *"Kyrie eleison,"* and eventually reached Trani, where he died. He attracted huge crowds and many considered him insane, but when miracles were reported at his grave, a cult developed, and he was canonized by Pope Urban II in 1098, only four years after his death. June 2.

NICHOLAS OF SIBENIK, BL. *See* Tavelic, Bl. Nicholas.

NICHOLAS STUDITES (793–863). Born at Sydonia (Canea), Crete, he was educated at Studius Monastery at Constantinople from the age of ten, and when he was eighteen he became a monk there. He aided those exiled by the iconoclast persecution until it ended in 842 on the death of Emperor Theophilus, and Nicholas was later elected abbot. When Emperor Michael III exiled St. Ignatius and made Photius Patriarch of Constantinople in 858, Nicholas refused to recognize Photius as Patriarch and went into voluntary exile; Michael then appointed a new abbot. After several years of exile, Nicholas was brought back to his monastery and imprisoned. He died at Studius on February 4.

NICHOLAS OF TOLENTINE (1245–1305). Born at Sant' Angelo, Ancona, Italy, he joined the Augustinians there and was professed in 1263, studied at San Ginesio, and was ordained at Cingoli about 1270. He served as master of novices at Sant' Elpidio for a time, and in 1274 was sent to Tolentino, where he became famous for the eloquence of his preaching and as a confessor, converting hardened sinners and ministering to the poor, the sick, criminals, and the needy. He died at Tolentino, where he had labored for thirty years, on September 10, venerated for the many miracles he is reported to have performed. He was canonized in 1446.

NICHOLS, VEN. GEORGE (c. 1550–89). Born at Oxford, England, he studied at Oxford, taught at St. Paul's in London, and then went to Rheims to study for the priesthood. After further study in Rome, he was ordained at Laon in 1584 and then sent on the English mission. He was arrested at Oxford with Fr. Richard Yaxley, Thomas Belson, and a Welshman named Prichard. All four were tortured and then executed for their faith at Oxford on July 5.

NICODEMUS (1st century). A leading Jew of Jerusalem and probably a member of the Sanhedrin, he visited Jesus secretly at night, acknowledged him as "a teacher who comes from God," and in response to his questions, the Lord discoursed on baptism (John 3:1ff.).

Nicodemus spoke on Jesus' behalf before the chief priests and the Pharisees, pointing out to them that the Law demanded the accused be given a hearing before judgment was passed (John 7:50–52). He brought large quantities of costly myrrh and aloes to Jesus' tomb, and with Joseph of Arimathea wrapped Christ's body "with spices in linen cloths" (John 19:39–42). It is believed that he became a disciple, though this is nowhere stated in the New Testament. August 1.

NICOLAS, BL. GABRIEL MARY (1463–1532). Born at Rion, France, and christened Gilbert, he was twice refused admission to the Franciscans but was finally accepted by the Observant Franciscans at La Rochelle. He became learned in philosophy and theology, was guardian of the friary at Amboise, and served as confessor of St. Joan of Valois. He helped her secure papal approval of her Order of the Annonciades in 1502, was visitor general of the Order for thirty years, and founded six convents of the Order in France and the Netherlands. In 1517, at a general chapter in Rome, he was elected commissary general of the Observants north of the Alps, a position he held until his death in the Annonciade convent at Rodez on August 27. He had his name changed to Gabriel Mary by Pope Leo X because of his devotion to the Annunciation. His cult was approved in 1647.

NICOMEDES (d. c. 90). Early venerated in Rome, where his body was buried in a catacomb on the Via Nomentana, he refused to sacrifice to pagan gods and was beaten to death with whips, according to the Roman Martyrology. The same untrustworthy source from which this account was derived says that he was a priest in Rome who buried the body of St. Felicula and was arrested and martyred as described above. September 15.

NICON (d. c. 250). A Roman soldier, he was converted to Christianity while traveling in the Near East and became a monk in Palestine. He attracted disciples and immigrated with them to Sicily, when persecution of Christians began. There they all suffered martyrdom during Emperor Decius' persecution. March 23.

NICOSTRATUS (d. 303). An apocryphal narrative names him a Roman tribune who was executed with Antiochus and a cohort of Christian soldiers under his command at Caesarea, Palestine, during the persecution of Christians under Emperor Diocletian. May 21.

NICOSTRATUS (d. c. 306). *See* Castorius.

NIKON "METANOEITE" (d. 998). Born at Pontus on the Black Sea in Asia Minor, he became a monk at Khrysopetro and after twelve years there was sent as a missionary to Crete, which had just been recaptured from the Saracens. He was most successful in his twenty years there in reconverting many of the inhabitants of the island from Islam, earning his surname from his practice of beginning every sermon with the word *metanoeite* (repent). He then preached in various parts of Greece, was known for his miracles, and died at a monastery in Peloponnesus. November 26.

NILUS (d. 310). *See* Peleus.

NILUS THE ELDER (d. c. 430). An imperial official, perhaps a prefect at Constantinople, he became a disciple of St. John Chrysostom. Though married with two children, Nilus became a monk on Mount Sinai, taking his son Theodulus, after Nilus and his wife mutually agreed to leave the secular world. During a raid on the monastery by Arabs, Theodulus was kidnaped and Nilus went looking for him, finally tracing him to Eleusa, where he had been given shelter by the local bishop, who ordained both of them. Nilus is reputed to have written theological and ascetical treatises and numerous letters (among them two to Emperor Arcadius rebuking the Emperor for his exile of St. John Chrysostom from Constantinople), but many authorities believe that Nilus the author was a monk called "the Wise" at Ancryna, Galatia (Ankara), and different from Nilus the elder. November 12.

NILUS THE YOUNGER (c. 910–1004). Born of Greek parents at Rossano, Calabria, Italy, he lived a rather dissolute life until the woman he lived with and their child died when he was thirty, when he joined the Byzantine Basilian monks of St. Adrian in Calabria. He was a hermit for a time, lived in several Basilian monasteries, and then became abbot of San Demetrio Corone. His reputation for holiness and spiritual wisdom spread far and wide, attracting many to the monastery for spiritual advice and consolation. He was forced to flee in 981 when the Saracens invaded southern Italy, was sheltered with many of his monks at Monte Cassino, and was given the monastery of Vallelucio by Abbot Aligern. After fifteen years there, they founded a monastery at Serpero. Nilus pleaded in vain with Emperor Otto III in 998 to show mercy to antipope John XVI, a fellow Calabrian whom he had tried to dissuade from his schism. While on a trip Nilus secured a grant of land from Count Gregory of Tusculum to found a monastery on Monte Cavo (Grotta Ferrata), but died at Frascati on December 27 before he could get it under way. September 26.

NINIAN (d. c. 432). According to the untrustworthy twelfth-century life of Ninian by St. Aelred, he was the son of a converted chieftain of the Cumbrian Britons, studied at Rome, was ordained, was consecrated a bishop, and returned to evangelize his native Britain. He had a stone church built by masons from St. Martin's Monastery in Tours, which became known as the White House (Whitern), and a monastery, which became known as the Great Monastery and was the center of his missionary activities. From it Ninian and his monks evangelized neighboring Britons and the Picts of Valentia. Ninian was known for his miracles, among them curing a chieftain of blindness, which cure led to many conversions. September 16.

NINO (4th century). A captive slave in Iberia (Georgia), variously reported as a native of Cappadocia, Asia Minor, Rome, Jerusalem, and Gaul, she impressed those around her with her prayers, virtue, and the miracles she wrought, which she proclaimed were performed through her by Christ. When she cured the Queen of an illness and aided the King on a hunting expedition, they took instructions from her and were converted to Christianity, and with them their people. The King requested Emperor Constantine to send bishops and priests to his realm, which the Emperor did, and Georgia became Christian. When this was accomplished, Nino is reputed to have become a hermitess on the slopes of a mountain at Bodbe in Kakheti, where she died and was buried; it eventually became an episcopal see, and Nino is entombed in the Cathedral of Mtzkheta. The story is first told by Rufinus who said that he had received it from Iberian Prince Bakur in Palestine late in the fourth century, and though embellished by later legend, is believed to be true and was translated into many Eastern languages. The girl's name is not given in the legend narrated by Rufinus, but she is called Nino by Georgians and

Christiana in the Roman Martyrology and was the apostle of Georgia in the U.S.S.R. Legend also has her the only one of St. Rhipsime's community at Valarshapat to escape slaughter by King Tiridate's soldiers. December 15.

NIZIER. *See* Nicetius.

NON (6th century). Also known as Nonnita, according to unreliable sources she was of noble birth and resided at a convent at Ty Gwyn near present-day St. Davids in Wales and was seduced by a local chieftain named Sant. The child born was St. David, and some sources say she was married to Sant either before or after the birth of the child. She was said to have gone later to Cornwall and then to Brittany. March 3.

NONIUS. *See* Pereira, Bl. Nonius Alvares de.

NONNA (d. 374). A Christian, she married Gregory, a magistrate at Nazianzus, Cappadocia, who was a member of the Hypsistarians, a Jewish-pagan group, and converted him to Christianity. He became a priest and then bishop and is St. Gregory Nanianzen the Elder. Their three children all became saints; St. Gregory Nazianzen, St. Caesarius of Nazianzen, and St. Gorgonia. August 5.

NONNITA. *See* Non.

NORBERT (c. 1080–1134). Born at Xanten, duchy of Cleves, Prussia, son of Count Heribert of Gennep and Hedwig of Guise, he received minor orders and several benefices but lived a life of pleasure at the court of Emperor Henry V, where he was almoner. Norbert avoided the priesthood and declined the bishopric of Cambrai in 1113, but when struck by lightning and hearing the words that Saul heard on the road to Damascus, Norbert reformed his life, was ordained in 1115, and took the monastic habit. His attempts to reform his brother canons at Xanten coupled with his extreme asceticism caused them to denounce him and his unauthorized preaching at the Council of Fritzlar in 1118. In response, he resigned his canonry, sold his possessions, and gave the proceeds to the poor, and on a visit of penance to Pope Gelasius II was given permission to preach where he wished. He became an itinerant preacher in northern France, was soon renowned for his preaching prowess, and was credited with performing miracles. Bl. Hugh of Fosses became his follower, close confidant, and eventually his successor. After unsuccessfully attempting to reform the canons regular of St. Martin's at Laon, Norbert received a grant of land from Bishop Bartholomes of Laon at Prémontré. In 1120, with thirteen followers, Norbert began the foundation, and in 1121, their number increased to forty, they made their profession, and the Canons Regular of Prémontré were founded. Eight abbeys and two convents were soon founded, and in 1125 Norbert's constitutions received papal approval from Pope Honorius II. When Count Theobald of Champagnes desired to enter the Order, Norbert counseled him to remain in the world, marry, and follow religious practices prescribed by Norbert—the first instance of a tertiary of a religious Order. Norbert was appointed archbishop of Magdeberg by Emperor Lothair II in 1126 and was the victim of several assassination plots as he put into effect stringent reforms in the see, especially in upholding ecclesiastical rights against local secular officials. He traveled throughout France, Belgium, and Germany preaching, and he successfully opposed the heresy of Tranchelm of Antwerp in 1124. He won the confidence and support of Lothair, supported Pope Innocent II against the claims of antipope Anacletus II, and persuaded Lothair to lead an army, which he accompanied, to Rome to place Innocent on the papal throne in 1133. The Emperor named him chancellor of Italy in 1133, and he died shortly after, on June 6, at Magdeburg, Saxony. He was canonized in 1582 by Pope Gregory XIII.

NOTBURGA (c. 1264–1313). Born at Rattenberg in the Tyrol, daughter of peasant parents, she became a kitchen maid in the household of Count Henry of Rattenberg when she was eighteen. She was dismissed by Henry's wife, Ottilia, because of her practice of giving leftover food to the poor, and became a servant to a farmer. When Count Henry remarried after Ottilia died, he rehired Notburga, attributing reversals he had suffered to her dismissal, and she spent the rest of her life as his housekeeper. She is reputed to have performed miracles, and her local cult was approved by Pope Pius IX in 1862. She is the patroness of poor peasants and servants in Tyrol. September 14.

NOTHELM (d. c. 740). A priest in London, he was named archbishop of Canterbury in 734. In his preface to his *Ecclesiastical History*, the historian Bede acknowledges that the chief authority for his work was Abbot Albinus, who passed along to him the recollections of Nothelm, including the research Nothelm had done in Roman archives on the history of Kent and adjacent areas. October 17.

NOTKER BALBULBUS, BL. (840–912). Born at Heiligau, Switzerland, in delicate health, which was to be with him all his life, as was the stammering that occasioned his surname, Balbulbus (the Stammerer), he was placed in St. Gall Abbey by his parents when he was a boy. He was taught music by an Irish monk, Marcellus, and with two friends, Tutilo and Radpert, developed St. Gall's

Music School. After they were professed, Notker became librarian and guestmaster at the abbey, often advised Emperor Charles the Fat, and was a sought-after spiritual adviser. He wrote a metrical life of St. Gall and martyrologies, composed hymns, and introduced sequences into Germany, composing several score of his own. His cult was confirmed in 1512. April 6.

NOURY, BL. AGATHANGELO (1598–1638). Born at Vendôme, France, and baptized Francis, he entered the Capuchin friary at Le Mans when he was twenty-one and was ordained in 1625, taking the name Agathangelo. After preaching in France for a time, he was sent as a missionary to Aleppo, Syria. An Arabic scholar, he published books on Catholicism in Arabic and was successful in ecumenical activities. In 1633, he was sent as superior to a Capuchin mission in Cairo and was soon joined by Fr. Cassian Lopez-Neto, who had been born in 1608 at Nantes, France, of Portuguese parents and who became his assistant and confidant. Agathangelo continued his ecumenical activities, concentrating on reconciling the Copts to the Holy See. A synod of Coptics in 1637 to discuss reunion failed because of the notoriously dissolute lives led by the Catholics in Egypt, from the French consul down through his staff to the others in the consulate. Agathangelo wrote to the prefect of propaganda in Rome for authority to excommunicate the worst of the offenders, but before receiving a reply set off with Fr. Cassian to establish a Capuchin mission in Ethiopia. In the summer of 1638, through the influence of one Peter Heyling, a Lutheran physician who was a bitter enemy of Catholicism, they were arrested at Dibarua, near Suakim, and taken in chains to Gondar. Brought before King Basilides, they were condemned to death when denounced by

Abuna Mark, the new Primate of the dissident Church of Ethiopia. They were hanged by the cords of their Franciscan habits; both were beatified in 1905. August 7.

NOVELLONE, BL. (d. 1280). Born at Faenza, Italy, and also known as Nevolo, he became a shoemaker there and lived a carefree life until he was twenty-five, when a serious illness made him decide to change his lifestyle and he became a Franciscan tertiary. He practiced great mortifications and made pilgrimages to Rome and Compostela. When his wife died, he became a hermit next to the cell of a Camaldolese hermit at San Maglorio Monastery at Faenza, though he does not seem to have joined the Camaldolese, and lived a life of prayer and penance there until his death. His cult was approved in 1817. August 13.

NUMIDICUS (d. 252). An African, he and a group of fellow African Christians were ordered burned to death for their faith at Carthage during the persecution of the Christians under Emperor Decius. He was dragged out of the ashes, found to be still alive, and survived the terrible ordeal. He was ordained by St. Cyprian sometime later. August 9.

NUÑES. See Pereira, Bl. Nonius Alvares de.

NUNILO (d. 851). See Alodia.

NUTTER, BL. JOHN (d. 1584). Born at Reedley Hallows, England, he received his bachelorate in divinity from Oxford, turned Catholic, and in 1577 entered the English college at Rheims and was ordained there in 1582. He was sent on the English mission later the same year, was arrested when he was shipwrecked on the coast of Suffolk, and was imprisoned in Marshalsea Prison in London for a year. He was then tried and when convicted of treason for being a Catholic priest was hanged, drawn, and quartered at Tyburn on February 12. He was beatified in 1929.

NYMPHA (no date). According to unreliable legend, she was a Panormitan who fled to Italy only to suffer martyrdom there for her Christianity at Porto in the fourth century. Another equally unreliable legend has her leaving Palermo for Tuscany when the Goths reconquered Sicily in the sixth century and dying of natural causes at Savona. November 10.

NYMPHODORA (d. 304). *See* Menodora.

OCTAVIUS (d. c. 287). *See* Maurice.

ODERISIUS, BL. (d. 1105). Born at Marsi, Italy, of a noble family, he became a Benedictine at Monte Cassino. In 1059, he was named cardinal-deacon of St. Agatha and soon after cardinal-priest of St. Cyriacus in Termis. He became abbot of Monte Cassino in 1087, was known for his encouragement of scholarship, wrote poetry, and acted as peacemaker between Greek Emperor Alexius and the crusaders. December 2.

ODHRAN. *See* Otteran.

ODILIA (d. c. 720). Also known as Ottilia and Adilia, according to legend she was born at Obernheim in the Vosges Mountains, the blind daughter of Adalric, an Alsatian lord. Dissuaded from putting her to death by his wife, Bereswindis, only on condition that the child be sent away to someone who was not to be told of her background, Bereswindis gave Odilia to a peasant woman. Bereswindis told the woman the story and sent her to Baume-les-Dames near Besançon. When she was twelve, Odilia was put in a convent at Baume, where she was baptized by Bishop St. Erhard of Regensburg and recovered her sight when the bishop touched her eyes with chrism during the baptism ceremony. The bishop told Adalric of the miracle but, angered at the prospect of her return, which had been arranged by his son Hugh, Adalric struck Hugh and killed him. He then changed his attitude toward his daughter and lavished affection on her, but she fled when he wanted her to marry a German duke. Miraculously saved from his murderous anger when he caught her, he was so struck by what had happened that he agreed to allow her to turn his castle at Hohenburg (Odilienberg, Alsace) into a convent, and she became its abbess. She founded another monastery, Niedermünster and lived there until her death, venerated for her visions and the miracles attributed to her. She died at Niedermünster on December 13, and her shrine became a great pilgrimage center. She is the patroness of the blind and of Alsace.

ODILO (962–1049). A monk at Cluny, he was named abbot in 994, practiced great austerities, and sold Church treasures to feed the poor during a famine in 1006. During his abbacy, he increased substantially the number of abbeys dependent on Cluny, and with Abbot Richard of Saint-Vanne was responsible for the acceptance in France of "the truce of God" and the rule guaranteeing sanctuary to those seeking refuge in a church. He was devoted to the Incarnation and the Blessed Virgin, inaugurated All Souls' Day with an annual commemoration of the departed faithful, and experienced ecstasies. Ill the last five years of his life, he died while on a visitation of his monasteries at a priory at Souvigny on January 1. He had been abbot for more than fifty years.

ODO (801–80). Born near Beauvais, France, he chose the military as a profession in his youth but abandoned this calling to become a Benedictine monk at Corbie. He taught Charles Martel's sons while he was a monk there and in 851 was elected abbot. He was named bishop of his native city in 861 and in the two decades of his bishopric helped reform the Church in northern France and mediated the differences between Pope Nicholas I and Archbishop Hincmar of Rheims over Hincmar's deposition of Rothadius of Soissons in 862 and Rothadius' restoration by the Pope in 865. His cult was approved by Pope Pius IX. January 28.

ODO (d. 1220). *See* Berard.

ODO OF CAMBRAI, BL. (1050–1113). Born at Orléans, France, he taught at Toul for a time and then was named director of the cathedral school at Tournai. A follower of Boethius, his scholarship and teaching made the school famous, and it attracted students from all over France and Italy. He completely changed his lifestyle after reading St. Augustine on free will about 1090, became interested in theology, restricted his teaching, gave his possessions to the poor, and devoted himself to prayer and mortifications. To keep him in Tournai, the bishop gave him the abandoned St. Martin Abbey in 1092, and he and some of his former pupils lived there as canons but after three years adopted the Benedictine rule. In 1105, Pope Paschal II appointed him bishop of Cambrai to replace Bishop Gaucher, who had been deposed and excommunicated by the Pope for simony and for permitting investiture by Emperor Henry IV. Odo was unable to take possession of the see until Henry died in 1108 but was driven into exile soon after, when he refused to be invested by Emperor Henry V. Odo was given refuge at the Abbey of Anchin,

France, and died there on June 19. One of the most learned men in the France of his time, he wrote treatises on original sin, the canon of the Mass, the coming of the Messiah, a harmony of the gospels, and a four-language psalter.

ODO OF CANTERBURY (d. 959). Born of Danish parents in East Anglia, he became a monk at Fleury-sur-Loire and was later named bishop of Ramsbury. He was with King Athelstan when the King defeated the Danes, Scots, and Northumbrians at the Battle of Brunanburh in 937, and in 942 became archbishop of Canterbury. He played an active role in secular as well as ecclesiastical affairs, established East Anglia as a separate diocese, and supported St. Dunstan's monastic reforms at Glastonbury. He was called Odo the Good and was reputed to have performed several miracles. July 4.

ODO OF CLUNY (c. 879–942). Born near Le Mans, France, he was raised in the households of Count Fulk II of Anjou and Duke William of Aquitaine, received the tonsure when he was nineteen, received a canonry at St. Martin's in Tours, and then spent several years studying at Paris, particularly music, under Remigius of Auxerre. Odo became a monk under Berno at Baume-les-Messieurs near Besançon in 909, was named director of the Baume Monastery school by Berno, who became abbot of the newly founded Cluny, and in 924 was named abbot of Baume. He succeeded Berno as second abbot of Cluny in 927, continued Berno's work of reforming abbeys from Cluny, and in 931 was authorized by Pope John XI to reform the monasteries of northern France and Italy. Odo was called to Rome by Pope Leo VII in 936 to arrange peace between Alberic of Rome and Hugh of Provence, who was besieging the city, and succeeded temporarily by negotiating a marriage between Alberic and Hugh's daughter; Odo returned to Rome twice in the next six years to reconcile Alberic and Hugh. Odo spread Cluny's influence to monasteries all over Europe, encountering and overcoming much opposition, and successfully persuaded secular rulers to relinquish control of monasteries they had been illegally controlling. He died at Tours on the way back to Rome on November 18. He wrote hymns, treatises on morality, an epic poem on the Redemption, and a life of St. Gerald of Aurillac.

ODO OF NOVARA, BL. (c. 1100–1200). A Carthusian monk, he became prior of Geyrach Monastery in Slavonia and was so harassed by the bishop of the diocese in which it was located that he asked for and was granted papal permission to resign. He became chaplain to the nuns of the convent at Tagliacozzo, where he was venerated for his holiness, spiritual wisdom, and miracles. He died on January 14, and his cult was confirmed in 1859.

ODORIC OF PORDENONE, BL. *See* Mattiussi, Bl. Odoric.

ODULF (d. c. 855). Born at Oorschot, North Brabant, he was ordained, did parish work at Oorschot, and then became a canon at Utrecht. He became known for his learning and eloquent preaching and was sent as a missionary to Friesland by Bishop St. Frederick of Utrecht. Odulf worked in Friesland with great success, built a church and a monastery at Stavoren, and in his old age returned to Utrecht, where he died. June 12.

OENGUS (d. c. 824). Born of a noble family in Ulster, Ireland, and also known as Aengus, he entered the monastery of Clonenagh in Leix and was in time regarded as one of the most learned men in Ireland. His desire for solitude led him

to retire to a cell at Dysartenos, a few miles from the monastery, but his asceticism and rigorous spiritual practices attracted so many visitors he was forced to leave. He eventually entered the monastery of Tallaght incognito as a servant. His true identity was discovered by the abbot, Maelruain, who insisted that he assume a rightful position of honor as a man of great learning. After the death of Maelruain in 787, Oengus returned to Clonenagh, became abbot there, and later was made a bishop. Toward the end of his life, he retired to Dysartbeagh, where he died on March 11, though the year is uncertain—either 819, 824, or 830. Often called "the Culdec" (God's Vassal) for his writings, he was particularly known for the *Félire*, a metrical hymn to the saints.

OGILVIE, JOHN (c. 1579–1615). Born in Banffshire, Scotland, son of the baron of Drum-na-Keith and Lady Douglas of Lochleven, he was raised a Calvinist and was sent to study at Louvain when he was thirteen. In 1596 he became a Catholic there, continued his studies at Ratisbon and Olmütz, and in 1600 joined the Jesuits at Brünn. He was ordained at Paris in 1610, worked in Austria and France, and in 1613 received permission to go to Scotland to minister to the persecuted Catholics there. Using the alias John Watson, purportedly a horse trader and/or a soldier back from the wars in Europe, he worked in Edinburgh and Glasgow and in time was most successful in winning back a number of converts to the Church. He was betrayed by one Adam Boyd, who trapped him by pretending to be interested in being converted. He was imprisoned, tortured for months, found guilty of high treason for refusing to acknowledge the spiritual supremacy of the King and for refusing to apostatize, and was hanged at Glasgow on March 10. He was canonized in 1976 by Pope Paul VI, the first Scottish saint since St. Mary of Scotland in 1250.

OGMUND. *See* Jon Helgi Ogmundarson.

OIDILWALD. *See* Ethelwald (d. 699).

OLAF (995–1030). The son of Harold Grenske, a lord in Norway, Olaf Haraldsson, often called "the Fat," spent his youth as a pirate, was baptized in Rouen, and in 1013 went to England to aid King Ethelred against the Danes. He returned to Norway in 1015, captured most of Norway back from the Danes and Swedes, defeated Earl Sweyn at the battle of Nesje in 1016, and became King. He set about unifying and Christianizing his realm, but the harshness of his rule precipitated a revolt of the nobles in 1029, and aided by Canute of Denmark, they defeated him and forced him to flee to Russia. He returned in 1031 and attempted to recover his kingdom but was slain at the Battle of Stiklestad in Norway on July 29. Though not too popular during his lifetime, miracles were reported at his shrine, and a chapel was built, which became the Cathedral of Trondheim; it became a great pilgrimage center for all Scandinavia. He is one of the great heroes of Norway for his efforts to unify and Christianize Norway, of which he is patron. He was canonized in 1164.

OLAF SKOTTKONUNG (d. 1024). A son of Eric the Conqueror, he was King of Sweden in 993–1024 and was converted by St. Sigfrid and established Christianity in Sweden. In a coalition with King Sweyn of Denmark and Eric, jarl of Lade, he defeated King Olaf I Tryggvesson of Norway at the battle of Svolder in 1000 and annexed part of his territory. He was murdered by rebellious followers at Stockholm when he refused to sacrifice to pagan gods. July 30.

OLAGUER. *See* Ollegarius.

OLDCORNE, BL. EDWARD (d. 1606). A native of York, England, he studied at Rheims and Rome and was ordained in Rome in 1587, when he also became a Jesuit. He was sent on the English mission in 1589, and using the pseudonym Hall, worked among the Catholics in Worcestershire for seventeen years, bringing many lapsed Catholics back to the faith as well as converting Protestants to Catholicism. Betrayed, with Fr. Garnet, superior of the English Jesuits, at Henlip by an informer named Littleton, he was taken to Worcester and then to the Tower of London and accused of complicity in the Gunpowder Plot. Unable to shake his protestations of innocence by five rackings, the authorities found him and his servant Robert Ashley, a Jesuit lay brother, guilty anyway, and they were hanged, drawn, and quartered at York. Littleton later recanted his false accusations and publicly asked pardon of Fr. Oldcorne; Littleton was put to death with the two martyrs. Oldcorne and Ashley were beatified in 1929. April 7.

OLDEGAR. *See* Ollegarius.

OLGA (c. 879–969). Also called Helga, she was born at Pskov, Russia, and in 903 married Igor, Varangarian prince of Kiev, Russia. After the assassination of Igor in 945, she punished the murderers of her husband by having them scalded to death and then had hundreds of their followers murdered. She ruled the country ably and well as regent for her son Svyastoslav until he came of age in 964. She became a Christian, was baptized at Constantinople about 957, and changed her lifestyle. She devoted herself to converting her people to Christianity, requesting missionaries from Emperor Otto I in 959, but was not too successful, unable to convert even

Svyastoslav; but her grandson Vladimir evangelized Russia. She died at Kiev on July 11.

OLIVE, BL. (9th century). According to a pious fictional legend, she was a beautiful girl of thirteen, of a noble Palermo, Italy, family who was carried off to Tunis by raiding Moslems. They allowed her to live in a nearby cave, but when they found that her miracles and cures had converted many Mohammedans, she was imprisoned, tortured, and after converting her executioners trying to burn her to death, was beheaded. June 10.

OLLEGARIUS (1060–1137). Also known as Olaguerand and Oldegar, he was the son of noble Visigoth parents in Barcelona, Spain. He was given a canon's benefice there, was appointed provost, was ordained, and became prior at St. Aidan's Monastery in Spain. A papal bull was required to make him accept the bishopric of Barcelona, which he had been administering, in 1115, and he was named archbishop when the see was transferred to Tarragona the next year. He attended the first General Council of the Lateran in 1123, where Pope Callistus II appointed him papal delegate to preach a crusade against the Moors in Spain; through his efforts Count Raymond mounted successful attacks on several Moorish strongholds. Ollegarius rebuilt Tarragona, which had been destroyed by the Moors, encouraged the Knights Templar in his see, and ministered to the sick poor, particularly the mentally ill. March 6.

OLYMPIAS (c. 361–c. 408). Of a wealthy noble Constantinople family, she was orphaned when a child and was given over to the care of Theodosia by her uncle, the prefect Procopius. She married Nebridius, also a prefect, was widowed soon after, refused several offers of marriage, and had her fortune put in trust until she was thirty by Emperor Theodosius when she also refused his choice for a husband. When he restored her estate in 391, she was consecrated deaconess and with several other ladies founded a community. She was so lavish in her almsgiving that her good friend St. John Chrysostom remonstrated with her and when he became Patriarch of Constantinople in 398, he took her under his direction. She established a hospital and an orphanage, gave shelter to the expelled monks of Nitria, and was a firm supporter of Chrysostom when he was expelled in 404 from Constantinople and refused to accept the usurper Arsacius as Patriarch. She was fined by the prefect, Optatus, for refusing to accept Arsacius, and Arsacius' successor, Atticus, disbanded her community and ended her charitable works. She spent the last years of her life beset by illness and persecution but comforted by Chrysostom from his place of exile. She died in exile in Nicomedia on July 25, less than a year after the death of Chrysostom. December 17.

OLYMPIUS (d. 257). *See* Symphronius.

OLYMPIUS (d. 343). Bishop of Enos, Rumelia, his fierce opposition to Arianism and his stanch support of St. Athanasius caused Emperor Constantius to banish him from his sec. June 12.

OMER (c. 595–c. 670). Also known as Audomarus, he was born near Coutances, France, and on the death of his mother he and his father became Benedictine monks at Luxeuil under St. Eustace. In 637, after twenty years at Luxeuil, Omer was named bishop of Thérouanne, a see that had become relaxed in religion and morals, and at once put into effect reforms. He ministered to the poor, the sick, and the needy, and with SS. Mommolinus,

Bertrand, and Bertinus, monks from Luxeuil, he founded Sithiu Monastery and developed it into one of the great spiritual centers in France. He was noted for the passion and eloquence of his preaching, was credited with performing miracles, and late in life became blind. September 9.

ONESIMUS (1st century). According to St. Paul's epistle to Philomena (10–18), Onesimus was a slave of Philemon in Colossae, Phrygia, who ran away. He met St. Paul while the apostle was in prison in Rome, was baptized, and became Paul's spiritual son. Paul sent him back to Philemon asking him to accept Onesimus "not as a slave . . . but . . . [as] a dear brother. . . ." Evidently Philemon did, as Paul mentions Onesimus again in Colossians (4:7–9), with Tychichus as the bearer of the epistle to the Colossians. According to St. Jerome, Onesimus became a preacher of the Word and later was a bishop, though probably not the bishop of Ephesus who succeeded St. Timothy and was stoned to death in Rome, as stated in the Roman Martyrology. February 16.

ONUPHRIUS (d. c. 400). While on a visit to the hermits of Thebaïd in Egypt to find out if the eremitical life was for him, Abbot Paphnutius met Onuphrius, who told him he had been a monk in a monastery but had left to follow the eremitical life, which he had done for seventy years. During the night the abbot stayed with the hermit; the next morning, after food had miraculously appeared the previous evening, Onuphrius told Paphnutius that the Lord had told him he, Onuphrius, was to die and that Paphnutius had been sent by the Lord to bury him. Onuphrius did die, Paphnutius buried him in a hole in the mountainside, and the site immediately disappeared, as if to tell the abbot that he was not to remain there. The story was

put into writing by one of his monks and was already popular in the sixth century. June 12.

OOSTERWYK, JOHN VAN (d. 1572). A native of Holland, he joined the canons regular of St. Augustine at Briel and became confessor of a convent of Augustinian nuns at Gorkum. When the Calvinists captured Gorkum, he was taken prisoner and sent to Briel, where he was executed with the other Catholics now known as the Martyrs of Gorkum, who were canonized in 1867. July 9.

OPPORTUNATA (d. c. 770). Born near Hyesmes, Normandy, she became a Benedictine nun early in her life at a convent near Almenèches and in time became abbess. She died of shock shortly after learning of the murder of her brother, Bishop Chrodegang of Séez, who had veiled her. April 22.

OPTATUS (d. 304). One of the eighteen martyrs of Saragossa, Spain, honored in a long poem by Prudentius, he and seventeen other Christians were executed for their faith at Saragossa under the governor, Dacian, during the persecution of Christians under Emperor Diocletian. Two other martyrs of the same persecution, Caius and Crementius, died later from the torture they had undergone. April 16.

OPTATUS (d. c. 387). A convert from paganism to Christianity, he became bishop of Milevis, Numidia, North Africa, was highly praised by St. Augustine, and was ranked with Ambrose and Augustine by St. Fulgentius. Optatus was a leading opponent of Donatism and wrote a famous treatise, *Against Parmenian the Donatist,* in about 370, refuting the teachings of Donatist Bishop Parmenian of Carthage; the treatise is still extant. It is a historically important document, since in it he speaks of the supremacy of the Pope, the validity of the sacraments, and refers to the veneration of relics. June 4.

ORESTES (d. 304). *See* Eustratius.

ORINGA, BL. (d. 1310). Also known as Christiana, according to her legend she was born at Castello di Croce, Italy, ran away from home to escape her brothers' demand that she marry, wandered about reputedly performing miracles, and eventually returned to her native town, where she formed a community of women living under the rule of St. Augustine, and died there. January 4.

ORIOL, JOSEPH (1650–1702). Born at Barcelona, Spain, he was early attracted to the religious life, studied at the university in Barcelona, received his doctorate in theology, and was ordained. He lived a life of great austerity, living solely on bread and water for twenty-six years, made a pilgrimage on foot to Rome in 1686, and on his return to Barcelona became a famous and sought-after confessor, though his facilities for hearing confession were suspended for a short time because of his severity to the penitents. Turned back from his desire to become a missionary by a vision he experienced at Marseilles on the way to Rome, he returned to Barcelona and spent the rest of his life there, venerated for his spiritual insights and prophecies, and he was credited with performing miracles. He died at Barcelona on March 23, and was canonized in 1909.

OROZCO, BL. ALPHONSUS DE, BL. (1500–91). Born at Oropesa, Spain, he early determined to be a priest, studied at Talavera, Toledo, and Salamanca, where he was a student under St. Thomas of Villanova, and became an Augustinian when he was twenty-two. He taught and preached, became famous as a confessor, served as prior at Seville, and in 1554 was appointed prior of the Augustinian priory at Valladolid. In 1556 he was appointed court preacher and in 1561 he accompanied King Philip II to the newly established court at Madrid, where Bl. Alphonsus lived a life of holiness and austerity amid the pomp and splendor of the court, exerting great influence on the spiritual lives of the royal family and the nobility. He wrote numerous mystical treatises and on our Lady, reputedly in response to a vision of Mary in which she told him to write on religious themes. He was beatified in 1881. September 19.

ORSIESIUS (d. c. 380). A disciple of St. Pachomius of Tabennisi in the Egyptian desert, with St. Theodore, Orsiesius' appointment as abbot of Khenoboski by Pachomius caused much discontent among the monks because of his youth. When Pachomius' successor, Petronius, died only two weeks after he was named abbot, Orsiesius was elected abbot of Tabennisi. His strict rule led to such opposition from some of the monks that he resigned in favor of Theodore. Though Theodore was officially abbot, they ruled jointly, since Theodore consulted him on every matter. When Theodore died in 368, Orsiesius again became abbot and ruled until his death. He wrote a collection of rules for the religious life, which St. Jerome translated into Latin. June 15.

ORSUCCI, BL. ANGELUS (1573–1622). Born at Lucca, Italy, he joined the Dominicans there, studied at Valencia, Spain, and was ordained. He was sent as a missionary to the Philippines and later to Japan, where he was imprisoned at Omura for four years for his religion and then was burned to death at Nagasaki. He was beatified in 1867 as one of the Martyrs of Japan. September 10.

ORTEGA, BL. FRANCIS OF JESUS (d. 1632). Born at Villamediana, Spain, he joined the Hermits of St. Augustine in 1614, was sent to Mexico as a missionary in 1622, and then with Bl. Vincent Carvalho to Manila. Bl. Francis was sent to Japan the following year and was burned to death at Nagasaki for his faith. He was beatified in 1867 as one of the Martyrs of Japan. September 3.

OSANNA OF CATARRO, BL. *See* Cosi, Bl. Osanna.

OSANNA OF MANTUA, BL. *See* Andreasi, Bl. Osanna.

OSBURGA (d. c. 1016). Though her shrine at Coventry, England, was a popular pilgrimage center noted for the many miracles reported there as early as the fourteenth century, nothing is known of her beyond that she was supposed to have been the first abbess of a convent founded by King Canute at Coventry. She may have lived at an earlier time. March 30.

OSMUND (d. 1099). Said to have been the son of Count Henry of Séez and Isabella, half sister of William the Conqueror, he accompanied the Normans to England, served as chancellor, and in 1078 was named bishop of Salisbury by William. Osmund finished the cathedral there, established a cathedral chapter of canons regular and a clergy school, helped prepare the Domesday survey, and was at Old Sarum when the Domesday Book was presented to William. Osmund supported King William II in an investiture dispute against Anselm at the Council of Rockingham, though Osmund later admitted his error and asked Anselm's pardon. Osmund drew up new liturgical books regulating the Mass, the Divine Office, and the administration of the sacraments that in the next century and a half were widely adopted in England, Ireland, and Wales. He assembled an ex-

tensive collection of manuscripts for the cathedral library, was an expert copyist and a skilled binder of books, and wrote a life of St. Aldhelm. Osmund died on December 4 and was canonized in 1457, the last English saint to be canonized until John More and John Fisher were canonized in 1935.

OSWALD OF NORTHUMBRIA (c. 605–42). Forced to flee from Northumbria to Scotland when his father, Aethelfrith, was defeated and killed by Raedwald in 617, Oswald was converted to Christianity at Iona while he was in Scotland. When his uncle, King St. Edwin of Northumbria, was killed in battle against pagan King Penda of Mercia and Welsh King Cadwallon in 633, Oswald assembled an army and in 634 defeated a superior force under Cadwallon, who was killed in a battle near Hexham, and Oswald became King of Northumbria. He attributed his victory to a vision he had had of St. Columba promising him victory and to a huge cross he had erected the night before the battle. He brought St. Aidan to his kingdom to preach Christianity, gave him the island of Lindisfarne for his see, and acted as his interpreter. He built churches and monasteries, brought in monks from Scotland to bring his people back to Christianity, and was known for his personal piety and charity. He married Cyneburga, daughter of Cynegils, first Christian king of Wessex, and died a few years later, on August 5, while fighting against the superior forces of Penda at Maserfield. He was only thirty-seven at his death. August 9.

OSWALD OF WORCESTER (d. 992). Of Danish descent, he was educated by an uncle, Archbishop Odo of Canterbury, was ordained, and became a priest and dean at Winchester. He then went to France, where he became a Benedictine at Fleury, returned, and joined another uncle, Archbishop Oskitall of York, until Oswald was appointed bishop of Worcester by King Edgar on the recommendation of St. Dunstan. Oswald founded a monastery at Westbury-on-Trym and in about 970 Ramsey Abbey in Huntingdonshire. He supported the efforts of St. Dunstan and St. Ethelwold to revive religion in England and encouraged the monastic life and learning and scholars. He was named bishop of York in 972 but retained the bishopric of Worcester as well. He died on February 29. February 28.

OSWIN (d. 651). When his father, King Osric of Deira, was killed by Welsh King Cadwallon in 633, he was taken to Wessex, was baptized, and was educated there. When St. Oswald was killed in battle against King Penda of Mercia in 642, Oswin became King of Deira, which Oswald had united to Bernicia, and Oswald's brother, Oswy, became King of Bernicia. Soon after, Oswy declared war on Oswin who, rather than precipitate a bloody battle, went into hiding at the estate of Earl Hunwald at Gilling near Richmond, York. Hunwald betrayed him and he was murdered there by Ethelwin on orders from Oswy. August 20.

OSYTH (d. c. 675). According to legend, she was the daughter of a Mercian chieftain named Frithwald, and Wilburga, daughter of King Penda of Mercia. Osyth was raised in a convent, probably Aylesbury, and against her will (since she wanted to be a nun), she was married to King Sighere of the East Saxons. She fled to escape his marital demands and he allowed her to become a nun. He gave her land at Chich, Essex, where she built a monastery and became abbess. She was beheaded there sometime later by raiding Danish pirates when she resisted them. October 7.

OTGER (8th century). *See* Wiro.

OTTERAN (d. 563). Also known as Odhran, he was said to be a Briton who became abbot of Meath and was one of the twelve who accompanied Columba to Iona. He died soon after their arrival, the first of the monks from Ireland to die at Iona. He may have founded the monastery at Leitrioch Odrain (Latteragh, Tipperary). October 27.

OTTILIA. *See* Odilia.

OTTO (d. 1139). Of a noble Swabian family, he was ordained while quite young, entered the service of Emperor Henry IV in 1090, and became his chancellor about 1101. He opposed Henry in the Emperor's struggle with the Holy See and when appointed bishop of Bamberg in 1103 by Henry refused to accept consecration until Pope Paschal II approved and consecrated him at Rome in 1106. He labored to heal the breach between the Pope and the Emperor under Emperor Henry V, and in 1124, at the invitation of Boleslaus III of Poland, headed a group of missionaries to eastern Pomerania, where they made thousands of converts. He returned in 1128 to reconvert the cities of Stettin and Julin and died at Bamberg on June 30, 1139. He was canonized in 1189. July 2.

OUDOCEUS (d. c. 600). Although he is one of the four saints to whom the cathedral at Llandaff, Wales, is dedicated, all that is known of him is that he is reported to have been the son of Budic, prince of Brittany, and the nephew of St. Teilo, who raised him in Wales and whom he succeeded as abbot of the monastery at Llandeilo Fawr, Carmarthenshire. He is also known as Eddocwy in Welsh. July 2.

OUEN (c. 610–84). Also known as Owen and Audoenus, he was the son of St. Authaire and was born at Sancy near Soissons, France. He was educated at St. Médard Abbey, served at the courts of King Clotaire II and his son Dagobert I, who made him his chancellor and in 636 built a monastery at Rebais. He was persuaded not to become a monk there by Dagobert, and despite the fact that Ouen was a layman, he was active in promoting religion and combating simony. He was continued as chancellor by King Clovis II, was ordained and in 641, was consecrated archbishop of Rouen. He encouraged learning and the founding of new monasteries, was known for his personal austerities and his charities, and supported missionary activities to pagan areas of his see. He supported Ebroin, mayor of the palace, against the nobles, and at the invitation of Thierry III negotiated a peace between Neustria and Austrasia in Cologne. He died at Clich near Paris on August 24 while returning from Cologne.

OUTRIL. *See* Austregisilus.

OWEN. *See* Eugene (d. c. 618).

OWEN, NICHOLAS (1606). Born at Oxford, England, he became a carpenter or builder and served Jesuit priests in England for two decades by constructing hiding places for them in mansions throughout the country. He became a Jesuit lay brother in 1580, was arrested in 1594 with Fr. John Gerard, and despite prolonged torture would not give the names of any of his Catholic colleagues; he was released on the payment of a ransom by a wealthy Catholic. Nicholas is believed responsible for Fr. Gerard's dramatic escape from the Tower of London in 1597. Nicholas was again arrested in 1606 with Fr. Henry Garnet, whom he had served eighteen years, Fr. Oldcorne, and Fr. Oldcorne's servant, Brother Ralph Ashley, and imprisoned in the Tower of London. Nicholas was subjected to such vicious torture that he died of it on March 2. He was known as Little John and Little Michael and used the aliases of Andrewes and Draper. He was canonized by Pope Paul VI in 1970 as one of the Forty Martyrs of England and Wales. March 22.

OWEN. *See* Ouen.

OYEND. *See* Eugendus.

P

PABU. *See* Tudwal.

PACHECHO, BL. ALFONSO (d. 1583). See Aquaviva, Bl. Rudolf.

PACHECHO, BL. FRANCIS (1566–1626). Born at Ponte da Lima, Portugal, he joined the Jesuits in 1584, was sent to Macao in 1592, and was ordained there. He engaged in missionary work in Macao and then was sent to Japan. He left after a short stay but returned with Bishop Louis Cerquiera as vicar general and diocesan administrator. When the bishop died in 1614, he again left Japan when all Christian priests were banished but slipped back in, disguised as a merchant. He was named episcopal administrator of the Church in Japan just before he was arrested for his faith and was burned to death at Nagasaki with eight others. They were beatified in 1867. June 20.

PACHOMIUS (c. 292–348). Born of heathen parents in the Upper Thebaïd, Egypt, he was drafted into the army against his will and was so impressed by the kindness of the Christians of Latopolis to the recruits that he became a Christian after he left the army. He became the disciple of a hermit named Palaemon, and in response to a vision bidding him to build a monastery at Tabennisi on the Nile, he built a cell there in about 320. He soon attracted numerous disciples, organized them into a community, and founded six other monasteries in the Thebaïd and a con-

vent for his sister across the Nile from Tabennisi. He opposed Arianism, was denounced to a council of bishops at Latopolis, but was completely exonerated, and by the time of his death on May 15, there were some three thousand monks and nuns in the nine monasteries and two convents he governed, though he was never ordained. He was really the founder of cenobitic monasticism, and St. Benedict made generous use of his rule in formulating the Rule of St. Benedict. May 9.

PACIAN (d. c. 390). Named bishop of Barcelona, Spain, in 365, little is known of him except that he wrote voluminously, though only a few of his writings, on penance, baptism, against Novatianism, and the supremacy of the Pope, are still extant. March 9.

PACIFICO OF CERANO, BL. *See* Ramota, Bl. Pacifico.

PACIFICO OF SAN SEVERINO. *See* Divini, Pacifico.

PADARN. *See* Paternus.

PAGE, VEN. ANTHONY (1571–93). Born at Harrow-on-the-Hill, Middlesex, England, he studied at Oxford and then at Rheims, where he was ordained in 1591. He was sent on the English mission and was soon arrested and hanged, drawn, and quartered for being a Catholic priest on April 20 or April 30.

474 PAGE, FRANCIS

PAGE, FRANCIS (d. 1602). Born at Antwerp, Flanders, of English parents, he was destined for a career in law, but when he was converted to Catholicism by a Catholic woman he met, he gave away his possessions, went to Douai to study for the priesthood, and was ordained there in 1600. He was sent on the English mission, was betrayed by a woman, and was convicted of being a Catholic priest, for which he was hanged, drawn, and quartered, with Bl. Robert Watkinson, at Tyburn on April 20. He was beatified in 1929.

PAINE, JOHN. *See* Payne, John.

PAIR. *See* Paternus (d. 564).

PALLADIUS (d. 432). A deacon at Rome, he was responsible for sending St. Germanus of Auxerre to Britain in 429 to combat Pelagianism and in 431 was consecrated by Pope Celestine I and sent as a missionary to Ireland—the first bishop of the Irish. He worked in Leinster, encountered much opposition, but made some converts and built three churches. Acknowledging his lack of success in Ireland, he went to Scotland to preach to the Picts, and died soon after he arrived at Fordun, near Aberdeen. July 7.

PALLOTTA, BL. MARIA ASSUNTA (1878–1905). Born at Force, Ancona, Italy, on August 20, she joined the Franciscan Missionaries of Mary at Rome in 1898, and worked in convents at Rome, Grottaferrata, and Florence until 1904, when she was sent to China. She worked in the orphanage at Tongeul-koo until stricken by typhus while ministering to victims of a plague and died there on April 7. She was beatified in 1954.

PALLOTTI, VINCENT (1795–1850). Born at Rome on April 21, the son of a

grocer, he was ordained when he was twenty-three, received his doctorate in theology, and taught theology at the Spaienza in Rome. He served in several parishes in his native city, suffering rebuffs from fellow curates for a decade, and then was involved in organizing a group of clergy and laity for conversion work and social justice on a worldwide scale. In 1835, he founded the Society of the Catholic Apostolate (called for a time the Pious Society of Missions), composed of priests, nuns, and laity, organized trade schools with evening classes for poor boys, worked among the poor, was a sought-after confessor and exorcist, and brought many back to the Church. He died in Rome on January 22, and was canonized in 1963 by Pope John XXIII. January 23.

PAMBO (d. c. 390). A disciple of St. Antony in his youth, he was one of the founders of the Nitrian Desert monasteries in Egypt and was noted for his austerities, mortifications, and wisdom. He was consulted by many, among them St. Athanius, St. Rufinus, and St. Melania the Elder, who was with him when he died. July 18.

PAMMACHIUS (d. 410). Of the Furii family, he was a Roman senator and a friend of St. Jerome. Pammachius married St. Paula's daughter Paulina in 385. His denunciation to Pope St. Siricius of Jovinian, who was later condemned at a synod at Rome, and by St. Ambrose at Milan, caused Jerome to write a treatise against Jovinian's teachings that Pammachius criticized, which led to two more letters from Jerome defending his treatise. Paulina died in 397, and Pammachius devoted the rest of his life to study and charitable works. With Fabiola he built a hospice at Porto for poor and sick pilgrims coming to Rome (the first such in the West) and had a church in his house (a site now occupied by the Passionists' SS. Peter and Paul Church). He often tried, unsuccessfully, to tone down the polemics of some of Jerome's controversial treatises and particularly the bitterness of Jerome's controversy with Rufinus. Pammachius urged Jerome to translate Origen's *De principiis*, and Pammachius' letter to tenants on his estate in Numidia in 401 to abandon Donatism evoked a letter of thanks from St. Augustine. Pammachius died in Rome. August 30.

PAMPHILUS (d. 309). Born of a wealthy family at Berytus (Beirut), Phoenicia, he studied there and at the catechetical school at Alexandria under Pierius, a follower of Origen. Pamphilus was ordained at Caesarea, Palestine, accumulated a large library, was noted for his learning, and was considered the leading biblical scholar of his time. He founded a Bible school at Caesarea (one of his students was the historian Eusebius), produced an accurate version of the Bible, lived an austere, hardworking life, and gave away his wealth to the poor. He was arrested in 308 for his Christianity by Urban, governor of Palestine, tortured, and imprisoned when he refused to sacrifice to pagan gods. After almost two years in prison, Firmilian, Urban's successor, found him, Paul of Jamnia, and Valens, an old deacon from Jerusalem, guilty of being Christians and sentenced them to death by beheading. At the same time he had one of his servants, Theodulus, crucified when he found he was a Christian; Porphyrius, a student of Pamphilus, was tortured and burned to death when Firmilian heard he had requested Pamphilus' body and was a Christian; and Seleucus, a Cappadocian, was decapitated when Firmilian heard him applauding Porphyrius' firmness under torture. Eusebius wrote a now lost biography of Pamphilus and praises him highly in his *Ecclesiastical History;* he col-

laborated with Pamphilus on *Apology for Origen* while Pamphilus was in prison and may have been a fellow prisoner. June 1.

PAMPHILUS (d. c. 700). Bishop of Sulmona and Corfinium, Abruzzi, Italy, he was venerated for his holiness and generosity to the poor but was denounced as an Arian to Pope Sergius for saying Mass at the then unheard-of hour of shortly after midnight on Sunday morning. He was completely vindicated by Sergius, who sent him a gift for his poor. April 28.

PAMPURI, RICCARDO (1897–1930). Pampuri, who lost his parents in childhood, had intended to become a missionary priest. Influenced by poor health and a physician uncle, he became a doctor instead. As a rural health officer and a Franciscan tertiary, he founded a group to care for the poor, offering treatment free of charge. Still called to the religious life, he became a member of the Hospitaller Order of St. John of God. He died of pleurisy, tuberculosis, and pneumonia at age thirty-two. He was canonized in 1989. May 1.

PANATTIERI, BL. MAGDALEN (1443–1503). Born at Trino-Vercellese, Italy, she became a Dominican tertiary in her own home when she was twenty and spent her life in prayer, living austerely and devoted to the poor and young children. She also gave conferences to women and children that were known for their fervor. She died at Trino on October 13, and her cult was confirmed by Pope Leo XII. October 13.

PANCRAS (d. c. 90). Untrustworthy legend has him a native of Antioch who was converted and baptized with his parents by St. Peter, who sent him as a missionary to Sicily and made him the first bishop of Taormina there. Pancras was quite successful, destroyed pagan idols, built a church, and was murdered by bandits. April 3.

PANCRAS (d. c. 304). According to unreliable sources, he was a native of Syria or Phrygia who when orphaned was brought by his uncle to Rome, where both were converted to Christianity. When only fourteen, Pancras was beheaded in Rome for his faith during the persecution of Christians under Emperor Diocletian and was buried in the cemetery of Calepodius, which was later named after him. May 12.

PANTAENUS (d. c. 200). A Stoic philosopher perhaps from Sicily, he became head of the catechetical school at Alexandria, Egypt, which he built into a leading center of learning. According to Eusebius, it was reported that Pantaenus had been a missionary in India (perhaps meaning Ethiopia) and there had met Christians who claimed to have received St. Matthew's Gospel in Hebrew from St. Bartholomew. July 7.

PANTALEON (c. 305). That he lived, was also known as Panteleimon, and was martyred are facts, but all else is dubious legend, according to which he was the son of a pagan father, Eustorgius of Nicomedia, and raised a Christian by his mother, Eubula. He became Emperor Maximian's physician and enjoyed the dissolute life of the court to such a degree that he lost his faith. He was brought back to Christian ways by Hermolaos, donated his medical skills to the poor free of charge, sold his possessions, and gave the proceeds to the poor. When the persecution of Christians under Emperor Diocletian broke out in Nicomedia in 303, he was denounced as a Christian by fellow physicians and was arrested with Hermolaos and two other Christians. They were condemned to death, and Pantaleon was finally exe-

cuted by beheading after being miraculously saved from execution by six other methods, including drowning, by fire, and by wild beasts. He is one of the Fourteen Holy Helpers and is called the Great Martyr and Wonder Worker in the East. His blood is reputed to liquefy on his feast day, as does that of St. Januarius in Naples. July 27.

PANTELEIMON. *See* Pantaleon.

PAPHNUTIUS (d. c. 350). Sometimes called "the Great," he was an Egyptian who served as a monk under St. Antony in the desert for several years and was then named bishop of Upper Thebaid. He was tortured and lost his right eye during Emperor Maximinus' persecution of Christians and was condemned to labor in the mines, as were so many other Christians at the time. On his release, he was an uncompromising opponent of Arianism, successfully convinced the Council of Nicaea in 325 to allow married men to be ordained and to be consecrated bishops, though opposing marriage after ordination, and at the Council of Tyre in 335 brought Bishop Maximus of Jerusalem back to orthodoxy from Arianism. September 11.

PAPIAS (d. 284). *See* Victorinus.

PAPYLUS (d. c. 170 or c. 250). *See* Carpus.

PARAGUAY, MARTYRS OF. These three Jesuits from Paraquay—Rocque Gonzalez, Alphonsus Rodriguez, and Juan de Castilo—met their deaths in Brazil. In 1628 they were slaughtered by indigenous people soon after opening the All Saints Mission in Caaro, Brazil. They were canonized in 1988.

PAREDES Y FLORES, MARIANA DE (1618–45). Born at Quito, Ecuador (then part of Peru), of noble Spanish parents, she was orphaned as a child and raised by her elder sister and her husband. Mariana early was attracted to things religious and became a solitary in her sister's home under the direction of Mariana's Jesuit confessor. Mariana practiced the greatest austerities, ate hardly anything, slept for only three hours a night for years, had the gift of prophecy, and reputedly performed miracles. When an earthquake followed by an epidemic shook Quito in 1645, she offered herself publicly as a victim for the sins of the people. When the epidemic began to abate, she was stricken and died on May 26. She is known as Mariana of Quito and is often called "the Lily of Quito." She was canonized in 1950. May 28.

PAREGORIUS (d. c. 260). *See* Leo.

PAREGRUS (d. 297). *See* Hipparchus.

PARISIO (1160–1267). Born either at Bologna or Treviso, Italy, he joined the Camaldolese when he was twelve, was ordained, and in 1190 was appointed chaplain of St. Christina convent at Treviso. He is reported to have held that position for seventy-seven years and to have been gifted with the ability to prophesy and to perform miracles. June 11.

PARMENAS (d. c. 98). He was one of the seven chosen by the apostles in Jerusalem to minister to the needs of the Hellenic Jewish converts to Christianity there (Acts 6:5). According to tradition, he preached for years in Asia Minor before being martyred at Philippi, Macedonia, during the persecution of the Christians under Emperor Trajan. January 23.

PARTHENIUS (3rd century). *See* Calocerus.

PASCHAL I (d. 824). Son of Bonosus, a Roman, he studied at the Lateran, was named head of St. Stephen's Monastery, which housed pilgrims to Rome, and was elected Pope to succeed Pope Stephen IV (V) on the day Stephen died, January 25, 817. Emperor Louis the Pious agreed to respect papal jurisdiction, but when Louis' son Lothair I came to Rome in 823 to be consecrated King, he broke the pact by presiding at a trial involving a group of nobles opposing the Pope. When two papal officials who had testified for the nobles were found blinded and murdered, Paschal was accused of the crime. He denied any complicity but refused to surrender the murderers, who were members of his household, declaring that the two dead officials were traitors and the secular authorities had no jurisdiction in the case. The result was the Constitution of Lothair, severely restricting papal judicial and police powers in Italy. Paschal was unsuccessful in attempts to end the iconoclast heresy of Emperor Leo V, encouraged SS. Nicephorus and Theodore Studites in Constantinople to resist iconoclasm, and gave refuge to the many Greek monks who fled to Rome to escape persecution from the iconoclasts. Paschal built and redecorated many relics from the catacombs to churches in the city. Although listed in the Roman Martyrology, he has never been formally canonized. February 11.

PASCHASIUS RADBERTUS (d. c. 860). Abandoned as an infant at the doorway of Notre Dame convent in Soissons, France, he was adopted by the nuns there, was educated by the monks of St. Peter's, Soissons, and became a monk at Corbie. In 822, he was one of the monks sent to found New Corbie in Westphalia, helped make the Corbie schools famous while he served as master of novices there, and was abbot of Corbie for seven years, though he never became a priest. After a time at Saint-Riquier Abbey, he returned to Corbie, where he died. He wrote numerous treatises, chief of which was *De Corpore et Sanguine Christe,* biblical commentaries, and biographies of two Corbie abbots, St. Adalhard and his brother Wala, whose friend and confidant Paschasius had been. April 26.

PASCUAL, BL. PETER (1227–1300). Born at Valencia, Spain, he was educated by a priest who had received his doctorate of divinity at Paris and had been ransomed from the Moors by Peter's parents. Peter received his doctorate from the University of Paris and was ordained at Valencia when he was twenty-four. He taught theology at the University of Barcelona, was named tutor to the son of James I of Aragon, Sancho, and when James named Sancho archbishop of Toledo, Peter administered the see, since Sancho was too young to be ordained. Peter was appointed titular bishop of Granada and in 1296 was named bishop of Jaén, both under Moorish rule. He ransomed captives, preached the gospel, and was imprisoned in Granada for bringing several apostates back to the Church. He used his ransom money to have others released and wrote a treatise against Islam that caused his jailers to order his execution. According to tradition he was beheaded, but he probably died of hardships he endured in prison. His cult was confirmed in 1673 by Pope Clement X. December 6.

PASSIONEI, BL. BENEDICT DE (1560–1625). Of a noble family and baptized Martin, he was orphaned at seven, studied philosophy at Perugia, and received his doctorate in law at Padua. Despite the opposition of relatives, he became a Capuchin in 1584, taking the name Benedict. He spent three years with the vicar general, St. Laurence of Brindisi, on his visitations to Austria, was a successful preacher of missions,

was stricken on the way to give a mission, and died at Fossombrone on April 30. He was beatified in 1867.

PASTOR (d. c. 304). *See* Justus.

PATENSON, BL. WILLIAM (d. 1592). Born at Durham, England, he studied at Rheims and was ordained there in 1587. He was sent on the English mission the next year, was arrested in London in 1591, converted six prisoners to Catholicism while he was in prison, and when convicted of being a Catholic priest, was hanged, drawn, and quartered at Tyburn on January 22. He was beatified in 1929.

PATERNUS (5th century). Also known as Padarn, confused legends have him born in Laetavia, Brittany, or perhaps Wales. He saw his father leave to become a hermit when he was a youth, and when he grew up he went to Wales and became a hermit there. He was founding abbot of a monastery at what became known as Llanbadarn Fawr (the great church of Paternus) at Ceredigion, Cardiganshire, Wales, and became bishop of that region. He preached widely, was known for his mortifications and charity, and ruled for some twenty-one years. Scholars believe his story is an amalgam of those of St. Paternus, an abbot-bishop of Wales, and St. Paternus, consecrated bishop of Vannes, Brittany, about 465. April 15.

PATERNUS (481–564). Born at Poitiers, Gaul, and also known as Pair, he became a monk at Ansion Monastery at Poitou and then left with a fellow monk, St. Scubilio, to become a hermit at Scissy near Granville, Normandy. They organized the disciples they attracted into an abbey (St. Pair), with Paternus as abbot. When he was seventy, Paternus was named bishop of Avranches and ruled that see until his death. April 16.

PATERNUS (d. 1058). Probably born in Ireland, he went to Westphalia and was one of the first to become a monk at Abdinghof monastery under St. Meinwerk. Paternus became a hermit in a cell adjoining the monastery, predicted the devastating fire that destroyed Abdinghof in 1058, including the monastery, and was burned to death when he refused to break his vow of enclosure and leave his cell when the fire was raging. April 10.

PATIENS (d. c. 480). Named bishop of Lyons, Gaul, about 450, he helped alleviate the horrors of famine brought about by the invasion of Burgundy by Goths by feeding thousands. He built and repaired many churches and was known for his asceticism, missionary success, and aid to the poor. He fought against Arianism, helped restore peace to the diocese of Chalon-sur-Saône at the invitation of St. Euphonius of Autun after the death of its bishop precipitated serious disagreements, and ordered Constantius, a priest in his see, to write his life of St. Germanus of Auxerre, which became so well known. September 11.

PATRICIA (d. c. 665). According to legend, she was of a noble and perhaps royal family in Constantinople who fled to Italy to escape marriage and became a virgin consecrated to God in Rome. She returned to Constantinople, distributed her wealth to the poor, and then went back to Italy, where she died soon after, at Naples. She is a patron of Naples, and like St. Januarius there, a vial believed to be filled with her blood reportedly liquefies thirteen hundred years after her death. August 25.

PATRICK (c. 389–c. 461). So much of the life of the apostle of Ireland is enshrouded in myth and legend that much of his biography must be conjecture. The son of a Romano-British official, Calpurnius, he was born somewhere in Roman Britain, perhaps in a village called Bannavem, but possibly in Gaul; or perhaps at Kilpatrick near Dunbarton, Scotland. He was captured by raiders when he was about sixteen and carried off in slavery to pagan Ireland. After sheepherding for six years, probably in Antrim or Mayo, he escaped, probably to Gaul. When about twenty-two, he returned to Britain and then seems to have studied at the monastery of Lérins, 412–15. He spent the next fifteen years at Auxerre and was probably ordained about 417. About 432 he was probably consecrated a bishop by St. Germanus and sent to Ireland to succeed St. Paulinus, who had died the previous year. Patrick traveled the length and breadth of the island meeting fierce opposition from hostile chieftains and Druids, whom he repeatedly overcame by miraculous means; eventually he converted most of the island to Christianity. He visited Rome in 442 and 444, founded the cathedral church of Armagh, and it soon became the center of the Church's activities in Ireland. During his three decades in Ireland, he raised the standards of scholarship, encouraged the study of Latin, brought Ireland into closer relations with the rest of the Western Church, and of course converted the Irish to the faith they have so fiercely defended through the centuries. He wrote *Confessio,* an apology against his detractors and the chief source of biographical information about him, and a *Letter to the Soldiers of Coroticus,* denouncing the slaughter of a group of Irish Christians by Coroticus' raiding Welshmen, who were also Christian. His cult began on his death, perhaps at Saul on Strangford Lough in Downpatrick, and has flourished ever since. March 17.

PATRIZZI, BL. FRANCIS (d. 1328). Of the noble Patrizzi family, Francis Arrigheto was born at Siena, joined the Order of Servants of Mary (the Servites) on the death of his blind mother, when he was twenty-one, became noted for his preaching, and was a tremendously popular confessor. He died at Siena, and his cult was approved in 1743. May 12.

PATROCCUS (d. c. 259). A Christian at Troyes, Gaul, he was arrested by Aurelian, the governor there (though it may have been Emperor Aurelian), and was sentenced to be executed for his faith. He escaped an attempt to drown him in the Seine but was captured and beheaded. January 21.

PAUL (d. c. 65). Born of Jewish parents of the tribe of Benjamin between 5 and 15 in Tarsus (which also made him a citizen of Rome), and named Saul, he studied under the famous Jewish rabbi, Gamaliel, in Jerusalem. A tentmaker by trade, Saul became a rigid Pharisee and a rabid persecutor of the Christians. He was present at the stoning of Stephen but only as a spectator. On the way to Damascus to arrest some Christians and bring them back to Jerusalem, he experienced his famous vision (sometime between 34 and 36), which led not only to his dramatic conversion but (in view of the tremendous impact he was to have on early Christianity) was to shape the whole Christian experience. He spent the next three years in Arabia (probably the Nabatean kingdom) and then returned to Damascus to preach. He immediately encountered resistance from the Jews, a resistance that was to continue throughout his life and travels. Forced to flee secretly from Aretas, the Nabatean King, he went, sometime between 36 and 39, to Jerusalem, where he met the apostles, and through the sponsorship of Barnabas was accepted by the Christian community. He returned to Tarsus for several years, then about 43 was brought to Antioch by Barnabas and was made a teacher in the church there. After accompanying Barnabas to Jerusalem in 44 with a donation from the church at Antioch to the church at Jerusalem, Saul was sent out, with Barnabas, to preach the gospel on the first of his three missionary journeys. During 45–49, it took them to Cyprus, Perga, Antioch in Pisidia, and the cities of Lycaonia; it was on this journey that Saul was changed to Paul. On his return he went to Jerusalem in 49 and was successful in convincing Peter, James, and the other apostles that Gentile Christians need not be circumcised and have Jewish law forced on them—a decision that ensured the universality of Christianity—and secured the approval of the Jerusalem Church for his mission to the Gentiles. Shortly after his return to Antioch, Paul and Barnabas set out on their second missionary journey (49–52). After revisiting the churches founded on the first journey, Paul crossed to Macedonia (as a result of a dream) and preached the gospel in Europe for the first time. He founded churches at Philippi (where he and Silas were imprisoned and miraculously escaped), Thessalonica, and Beroea; preached, with little effect, on the Unknown God in Athens; and then spent 50–52 at Corinth, where he founded a flourishing church. He then returned to Antioch but soon set out on a third journey (53–58). He spent two years at Ephesus teaching and working miracles there and in the surrounding areas but was driven out by rioting silversmiths, whose trade in statues and shrines of Diana was being adversely affected by Christianity; from there he went to Macedonia and then in 58 back to Jerusalem with contributions for the mother church. At Jerusalem, he was attacked by a mob for his missions to the Gentiles and put under protective arrest by the Roman soldiers. A plot against his life caused the Roman captain to send him to Governor Felix at Caesarea, where his trial was delayed two years (58–60) until Festus succeeded Felix, when Paul as a Roman citizen demanded and was granted a trial in Rome. On the way to Rome in 60–61, he was shipwrecked off the coast of Malta but eventually reached Rome, where he remained under house arrest in his own lodgings for two years, 61–62—the last time he is mentioned in the Acts of the Apostles, the major source of biographical material about him. According to Clement of Rome, writing only thirty years after Paul's death, Paul went to Spain after his imprisonment, and on his return, according to the pastoral epistles, revisited Ephesus, Macedonia, and Greece, 63–67. According to tradition he was again arrested, probably at Troas, and returned to Rome, where he was executed on the same day as St. Peter (in 67, according to Eusebius) during the persecution of Christians under Emperor Nero (by beheading, according to Tertullian). One of the most creative of Christian writers, Paul wrote epistles to the Romans (from Corinth, 57–58); 1 Corinthians (from Ephesus in 54); 2 Corinthians (probably from Philippi in 57); Galatians (from Ephesus about 54); Colossians, Philemon, Ephesians, and Philippians (probably from Rome in 61–63); 1 and 2 Thessalonians (from Corinth in 51–52); and two pastoral epistles to Timothy and one to Titus. The epistle to the Hebrews is now believed to have been written by another author of Alexandrian background; it was not accepted canonically in the West before 350 and was probably written sometime between 60 and 90. June 29.

PAUL (d. 251). *See* Peter (d. 251).

PAUL (d. 273). *See* Lucillian.

PAUL (d. 308). A Christian at Gaza, he was arrested during the persecution of the Christians under Emperor Maximin by Firmilian, governor of Palestine, and was beheaded for his faith. July 25.

PAUL I (d. c. 350). Born at Thessalonica, Greece, he became secretary to Alexander, Patriarch of Constantinople, was elected his successor about 336 by the orthodox bishops, and was immediately confronted by a rival, Macedonius, who had been elected patriarch by the Arians. Paul was deposed and banished by a council of Arian bishops called by Emperor Constans I, and the see was given to Eusebius of Nicomedia. Paul returned to Constantinople on the death of Eusebius only to find Macedonius again supported by the Arians. Civil war broke out between the two factions, and Constans' general, Hermogenes, who had been sent to restore order, was murdered when he ordered Paul from the city. When Constans arrived, he exiled Paul and refused to seat Macedonius. Constans accepted Paul in 344, but in 350 exiled him and installed Macedonius. Paul was sent to Mesopotamia, Syria, and finally to Cucusus, Armenia, where he was starved and then strangled to death. June 7.

PAUL (d. c. 362). *See* John.

PAUL I (d. 767). The brother of Pope Stephen III, he was educated at the Lateran school, ordained at Rome, and served on diplomatic missions for Stephen, including one to Lombard King Desiderius, who promised to return several papal cities to the Pope. Paul was elected to succeed his brother as Pope on April 26, 757. Paul maintained friendly relations with King Pepin throughout his pontificate, resisted Byzantine attempts to encroach on papal temporal power, and finally succeeded in 765 in coming to an agreement with

Desiderius about the boundaries of their respective territories. Paul rebuilt churches and monasteries in Rome, opposed the iconoclasm of Emperor Constantine Copronymus, and died at St. Paul's Outside the Walls in Rome on June 28.

PAUL IV (d. 784). Born at Salamis, he was named patriarch of Constantinople in 780 and requested the restoration of icons when Empress Irene became regent on the death of Emperor Leo IV in 780. He retired to Florus monastery in 784, whence he pleaded that a council be convoked to condemn iconoclasm; it was held, but not until three years after his death at Florus. August 28.

PAUL (d. 850). *See* Elias.

PAUL AURELIAN (d. c. 573). Son of Perphius, a Welsh chieftain, he was born in southern Wales (perhaps at Penychen), studied at Ynys Byr Monastic School under St. Illtyd, and when he was sixteen was given permission to live as a hermit. He was ordained, attracted twelve disciples, and with them was invited by a King Mark to evangelize his people. Paul refused an offer to make him a bishop, and after a time, he and his followers immigrated to Brittany. After making settlements at Porz-Pol on the island of Ushant and at Ploudalmézeau, Paul received a grant of land on the island of Batz from Withur, a local ruler, and built a monastery there. Despite his objections, he was made bishop with his see at Léon by King Childebert. Paul resigned his bishopric several years before his death and retired to Batz, where he died. Many miracles, many of them of the most extravagant nature, were ascribed to him. March 12.

PAUL OF THE CROSS (1694–1775). Born at Ovada, Italy, on January 3, Paul Francis Danei, the eldest son of impov-

erished noble parents, adopted a lifestyle of rigorous austerity and great mortifications at his home at Castellazzo, Lombardy, when he was fifteen. In 1714, he joined the Venetian army to fight against the Turks, and when discharged a year later resumed his life of prayer and penance. He refused marriage, spent several years in retreat at Castellazzo, and in 1720 had a vision of our Lady in a black habit with the name Jesus and a cross in white on the chest in which she told him to found a religious order devoted to preaching the Passion of Christ. He received permission to proceed from the bishop of Alessandria, who decided the visions were authentic, and Paul drew up a rule during a forty-day retreat that became the basic rule for the congregation he was to found. With his brother, John the Baptist, who became his inseparable companion and closest confidant, he went to Rome for papal approval, was refused at first, but on their return to Rome in 1725 were granted permission to accept novices from Pope Benedict XIII, who ordained them in 1727. They set up a house on Monte Argentaro, lost many of their first novices because of the severity of the rule, opened their first monastery in 1737, and in 1741 received approval of a modified rule from Pope Benedict XIV, and the Barefooted Clerks of the Holy Cross and Passion (the Passionists) began to spread throughout Italy, in great demand for their missions, which became famous. Paul was elected first superior general, against his will, at the first general chapter at Monte Argentaro and held that position the rest of his life. He preached all over the Papal States to tremendous crowds, raised them to a fever pitch as he scourged himself in public, and brought back to the faith the most hardened sinners and criminals. He was blessed with supernatural gifts— prophecy, miracles of healing, appearances to people in visions in distant

places—and was one of the most celebrated preachers of his time. People
fought to touch him and to get a piece of
his tunic as a relic. One of his particular
concerns was for the conversion of sinners, for which he prayed for fifty years.
The Passionists received final approbation from Pope Clement XIV in 1769,
and two years later, Paul's efforts to create an institute of nuns came into being
with the opening of the first house of the
Passionist nuns, at Corneto. Ill the last
three years of his life, he died in Rome
on October 18, and was canonized in
1867. October 19.

PAUL OF CYPRESS (d. c. 760). A resident of Cyprus, his opposition to the
iconoclasm of Emperor Constantine
Copronymus caused him to be arraigned
before the governor of the island. When
Paul refused to desecrate a crucifix, he
was tortured and then burned to death.
March 17.

PAUL THE HERMIT (c. 229–342).
Born in Lower Thebaïd, Egypt, he was
orphaned when he was fifteen, went
into hiding to escape the persecution of
Christians under Emperor Decius, and
then fled to the desert when he was
twenty-two when he learned that his
brother-in-law planned to report him as
a Christian to take over his estate. He
decided to stay a hermit when he found
that the eremitical life suited him.
Reportedly, St. Antony visited Paul in
his old age, found him an exemplar of
what a holy man should be, and buried
him when he died; Jerome also wrote a
life of Paul, who reputedly lived to be
113 years old, more than 90 of which
were spent as a hermit. He is sometimes
called Paul the First Hermit to distinguish him from other hermits named
Paul. January 15.

PAUL OF LATROS (d. 956). Son of an
officer in the imperial army who was
killed in battle, Paul was born at
Pergamos near Smyrna, Turkey, and
when his mother died was persuaded by
his brother Basil to become a monk at
Karia on Mount Olympus. When Paul's
abbot died, he became a hermit on
Mount Latros (Latmus) in Bithynia, and
when his holiness attracted followers, he
organized them into a *laura*. After twelve
years, he retired further into the mountain fastness in quest of greater solitude
and later retired to a cave on the island of
Samos; when he again attracted followers, he rebuilt three abandoned *lauras*
there. He then returned to Latros, spent
the rest of his life in prayer and spiritual
exercises, and died on December 6. He
is sometimes surnamed "the Younger."

PAUL OF NARBONNE (d. c. 290). With
a group of other missionaries, among
them SS. Sarturninus and Dionysius, he
was sent to Gaul from Rome to preach
the gospel. He founded several churches
and was closely associated with Narbonne in his missionary activities.
March 22.

PAUL THE SIMPLE (d. c. 339). A working man all his life, he left his unfaithful
wife when he was sixty and sought out
St. Antony in the Egyptian Thebaïd to
become one of his disciples. Antony at
first refused to accept him because of his
advanced age but was so impressed by
Paul's persistence that he took him in.
Antony subjected Paul to an arduous
training in an attempt to discourage him,
but was convinced by Paul's humility,
eagerness, and obedience, and assigned a
cell to him. There Paul performed miracles of healing, revealed his power to
read men's minds, and so impressed
Antony that he referred to him as the
ideal of what a monk should be. Paul was
surnamed "the Simple" because of his
childlike innocence. March 7.

PAULA (d. 273). *See* Lucillian.

PAULA (347–404). Born in Rome of a noble family on May 5, she married Toxotius, and the couple had five children—Toxotius, Blesilla, Paulina, Eustochium, and Rufina. They were regarded as an ideal married couple, and on his death in 379, she renounced the world, lived in the greatest austerity, and devoted herself to helping the poor. She met St. Jerome in 382 through St. Epiphanius and Paulinus of Antioch and was closely associated with Jerome in his work while he was in Rome. The death of her daughter Blesilla in 384 left her heartbroken, and in 385 she left Rome with Eustochium, traveled through the Holy Land with Jerome, and a year later settled in Bethlehem under his spiritual direction. She and Eustochium built a hospice, a monastery, and a convent, which Paula governed. She became Jerome's closest confidante and assistant, taking care of him and helping him in his biblical work, built numerous churches, which were to cause her financial difficulties in her old age, and died at Bethlehem on January 26. She is the patroness of widows.

PAULA OF MONTALDO (1443–1514). Born at Montaldo, Italy, she joined the Poor Clares at Santa Lucia in nearby Mantua when she was fifteen and served as abbess three times. She had many mystical experiences, and her cult was approved in 1906. August 18.

PAULINA (d. 302). *See* Artemius.

PAULINUS (d. 358). Born in Gascony, he was educated at the cathedral school at Poitiers, became a disciple of St. Maximinus, and succeeded him as bishop of Trier in 349. Paulinus met and became a firm supporter of St. Athanasius while Athanasius was in exile at Trier and defended him at the synod of Arles in 353. Paulinus denounced Arianism at the synod, and for his opposition to Emperor Constantius II's support of Arianism was exiled to Phrygia, where he died. August 31.

PAULINUS (c. 584–644). Sent as a missionary from Rome to England by Pope St. Gregory I, he worked in Kent and was consecrated bishop in 625. He accompanied Ethelburga, daughter of King Ethelbert of Kent, to Northumbria, when she married pagan King Edwin of Northumbria. Two years later he baptized Edwin on Easter at his see city of York, bringing Christianity to Northumbria; Paulinus and his assistants baptized thousands, who followed their King into Christianity. When Edwin was slain by the pagan Mercians at the Battle of Hatfield Chase in 633 and Northumbria reverted to paganism, Paulinus returned to Kent with Ethelburga, her two children, and Edwin's grandson Osfrid. Paulinus was named administrator of the vacant see of Rochester, administered it for ten years, and died there on October 10.

PAULINUS (c. 726–804). Born near Friuli, Italy, of a family of farmers, he was a farmer in his youth, became a priest, and was noted for his scholarship. About 776, against his will, he was named Patriarch of Aquileia. A favorite of Charlemagne, whom he represented at all Church councils, he held a synod at Friuli in 791 (or 796) to denounce Adoptionism and wrote a confutation of the heresy, which he sent to Charlemagne. Paulinus preached widely in Carinthia and Styria, sent missionaries to the Avars when they were conquered by Pepin, but opposed conversions to Christianity by force and wrote a treatise on the way to Christian perfection for the duke of Friuli. Paulinus died on January 11. January 28.

PAULINUS (d. 843). An Englishman, he went on pilgrimage to the Holy Land

and on his return in 835 stopped off at Capua, Italy, where he was made bishop by the people. After reigning for eighteen years, he was forced to leave by invading Saracens and fled to Sicopolis, where he died. October 10.

PAULINUS OF NOLA (c. 354–431). Born near Bordeaux, France, the son of the Roman prefect of Gaul, Pontius Meropius Anicius Paulinus studied rhetoric and poetry under the poet Ausonius and became a successful and prominent lawyer. He held several public offices, among them probably the prefecture of New Epirus, traveled extensively throughout Gaul, Italy, and Spain, and married a Spanish lady, Therasia. He resigned his public offices and retired to Aquitaine, where he met Bishop Delphinus of Bordeaux, who baptized him and his brother. In about 390 Paulinus moved to Therasia's estate in Spain and when their only child died a week after he was born they gave much of their property to the Church and to the poor and began living lives of great austerity. In about 393, the bishop of Barcelona, by popular demand of the populace, ordained him a priest. He then moved to an estate near the tomb of St. Felix at Nola near Naples, Italy, in about 395, and over the vehement objections of his relatives, sold his estate and belongings in Aquitaine and gave most of it to the poor. He became known for his charities, built a church at Fondi, an aqueduct at Nola, a basilica near the tomb of St. Felix, a hospice for travelers at Nola, and housed many of the poor and needy in his own home, where he lived a semimonastic life with several of his friends. In about 409, he was elected bishop of Nola, a position he held until his death there. Paulinus had a wide circle of friends, and a wide correspondence with, among others, St. Augustine and St. Jerome (Augustine's *On the Care of the Dead* was written in reply to an in-

quiry from Paulinus), and was a friend of SS. Ambrose and Martin of Tours. Of Paulinus' many writings some fifty-one letters, thirty-two poems, and a few prose pieces are still extant. His poetry, most of it written for the annual celebration in honor of St. Felix, has caused him to be ranked with Prudentius as the foremost Christian Latin poets of the patristic period. June 22.

PAVONI, ANTONY (1326–74). Born at Savigliani, Italy, he joined the Dominicans there and later was named inquisitor general of Piedmont and Liguria. He was murdered by a group of seven men at Bricherasio, presumably enemies he had made in the course of his official duties. His cult was approved in 1856. April 19.

PAVONI, BL. LUDOVIC (1784–1849). Born at Brescia, Italy, he studied under the Dominicans and was ordained in 1807. He engaged in pastoral work at Brescia and in 1818 became pastor of St. Barnabas there. He began a printing school for boys, spent twenty years overcoming secular objections to licensing it, and founded a school of design and a school of music. A cholera epidemic swept Brescia in 1836, and to care for children orphaned by it, he took over Mercy Orphanage and founded a school for deaf and mute children. In 1844, he received permission from the Holy See to found a congregation of priests and lay brothers but was unable to secure secular permission from Austrian authorities (required those days of Austrian rule) until 1847, and the Congregation of Sons of Mary Immaculate, with Ludovic as superior general, was founded. Two years later a revolt against Austrian domination of Brescia broke out, and when Austrian forces shelled the city, he gathered his boys together and in a driving storm escorted them to safety to his novitiate at Saiano, near Brescia; his institute in Brescia was destroyed by the Austrian guns. He died a few days later, on April 1 at Saiano, and was beatified in 1947 by Pope Pius XII.

PAYNE, JOHN (d. 1582). Born at Peterborough, England, he may have been a convert to Catholicism. He went to Douai in 1574, was ordained in 1576, and was sent at once on the English mission with St. Cuthbert Mayne. Payne was most successful in his work, bringing back many to the Church, until he was arrested a year after his arrival. He was released and left England but returned in 1579. He was again arrested in Warwickshire, where he was acting as steward for Lady Petre at Ingatestone Hall, which Lady Petre used as a hiding place for priests. He was accused of plotting to murder the Queen by one John Eliot, a seasoned criminal and murderer who denounced dozens of priests for money. Payne was imprisoned and tortured in the Tower for nine months before being condemned to death. He was hanged, drawn, and quartered at Chelmsford on April 2, and was canonized in 1970 by Pope Paul VI as one of the Forty Martyrs of England and Wales. His name is also spelled Paine.

PAZZI, MARY MAGDALEN DEI (1566– 1607). Born at Florence, Italy, of a distinguished Florentine family, and baptized Catherine, she was educated at St. John Convent at Florence, resisted attempts to have her marry, and joined the Carmelites at St. Mary of the Angels Convent in her native city in 1582, taking the name Mary Magdalen when professed the following year. She became seriously ill, during which she experienced numerous ecstasies, recovered, practiced great mortifications, and then spent five years in the depths of spiritual depression and aridity, from which she did not emerge until 1590.

She had the gifts of prophecy and the ability to read people's minds and to perform miracles of healing. Her utterances while in ecstasy and descriptions of her revelations were copied down by some of the sisters in the convent and were later published. Bedridden the last three years of her life, she died at the convent on May 25. She was canonized in 1669. May 25.

PEGA (d. c. 719). Sister of St. Guthlac, she lived a secluded life near his hermitage at Croyland in the Fens in England, was reputed to have cured a man of blindness, and after her brother's death went on pilgrimage to Rome, where she died. January 6.

PEIS, FRANCIS IGNATIUS VINCENT (1701–81). Born at Laconi, Sardinia, on December 17, the second of nine children of poor parents, he joined the Capuchins at Buoncammino when he was twenty, despite his father's objections, and was professed in 1722. He served at several friaries and then spent fifteen years as a weaver at the Capuchin friary at Cagliari. In 1741, he was sent out from St. Anthony's at Buoncammino to beg, and for the remaining forty years of his life spent his days seeking alms. He became famous for his holiness, concern for his fellow men, especially the sick and indigent, and as a peacemaker. Innumerable cures and miracles were reported of him before he died on May 11. He was canonized in 1951.

PELAGIA. The Greek form of the Latin Marina.

PELAGIA (d. c. 311). A fifteen-year-old girl of Antioch, she suffered martyrdom when she threw herself off a roof to protect her virginity when a squad of soldiers tried to arrest her for her Christianity. June 9.

PELAGIA THE PENITENT (no date). Often called Margaret, she was an actress at Antioch known for her great beauty and dissolute life. During a synod at Antioch, she passed Bishop St. Nonnus of Edessa, who was struck with her beauty; the next day she went to hear him preach and was so moved by his sermon that she asked him to baptize her, which he did. She gave her wealth to Nonnus to aid the poor and left Antioch dressed in men's clothing. She became a hermitess in a cave on Mount of Olivet in Jerusalem, where she lived in great austerity, performing penances and known as "the beardless monk" until her sex was discovered at her death. Though a young girl of fifteen did exist and suffer martyrdom at Antioch in the fourth century (see Pelagia, d. c. 311), the story here told is a pious fiction, which gave rise to a whole set of similar stories under different names. October 8.

PELAGIA OF TARSUS (d. c. 304). According to a pious fictional legend, her pagan parents wanted her to marry the son of Emperor Diocletian, though she did not wish to do so. To give her time to work out a plan to avoid the marriage, she went on a trip, and while away was baptized by a Bishop Clino. When, on her return, her fiancé found out she was a Christian, he committed suicide and she was denounced to the Emperor as a Christian by her mother. Diocletian, smitten by her beauty, wanted to marry her, but when she refused to marry him and would not renounce her faith, he had her roasted to death. May 4.

PELAGIUS (c. 912–25). Born at Asturias, Spain, he was left a hostage with the Moors for his uncle when he was a child of ten during the reign of Abd-ar-Rahman III at Cordova, Spain. When he was not ransomed after three years, Abd-ar-Rahman offered him his freedom if he would renounce his Christianity and become a Mohammedan. When he refused, he was tortured to death. His name is Pelayo in Spain. June 26.

PELAYO. See Pelagius.

PELEUS (d. 310). An Egyptian bishop, he, Nilus, another Egyptian bishop, Elias, a priest, and an Egyptian layman were burned to death at Phunon near Petra, Palestine, by Firmilian, governor of Palestine, when Emperor Galerius ordered the dispersal of a group of Christians condemned to the quarries of Palestine. September 19.

PELINGOTTO, BL. JOHN (1240–1304). A merchant of Urbino, Italy, he became a Franciscan tertiary, and when his wealthy parents opposed his plan to become a hermit, he lived a life of solitude and great austerity at home. After a time, he left to devote himself to caring for the sick and the poor, begging to obtain funds, food, and clothing for them, meanwhile living in the strictest poverty himself. He practiced the most rigorous mortifications, which at first caused him to be mocked and scorned, but as time went on, he became venerated by his fellow citizens for his holiness. He was reputed to have performed miracles and to have had the gift of prophecy. His cult was confirmed in 1918. June 1.

PELLETIER, MARY EUPHRASIA (1796–1868). Born on July 31 on the island of Noirmoutier off the Brittany coast and baptized Rose Virginia, she studied at Tours and in 1814 joined the Institute of Our Lady of Charity, founded by St. John Eudes in 1641 to help wayward women. She was professed in 1816, taking the names Mary Euphrasia, was elected superior in 1825, made a new foundation at Angers, and then decided that a new congregation under a central authority was needed rather than individual foundations under separate bishops. She founded the Institute of Our Lady of Charity of the Good Shepherd, dedicated to working with wayward girls, at Angers, and received papal approval in 1835. The Institute spread rapidly and by the time of Mother Euphrasia's death had almost three thousand nuns in foundations all over the world. She died at Angers, France, on April 24, and was canonized in 1940. April 24.

PEPIN OF LANDEN, BL. (d. c. 639). Duke of Brabant, husband of Bl. Itta, and often called Pippin, he served as mayor of the palace under Kings Clotaire II, Dagobert I, and Sigebert III. Pepin and Bishop Arnulf of Metz aided King Clotaire II of Neustria in overthrowing Queen Brunhilda of Austrasia in 613, and Clotaire appointed them mayors of the palace to rule Austrasia for Clotaire's son Dagobert I from 623. When Pepin rebuked Dagobert (who had succeeded his father about 629) for his licentious life, Dagobert discharged him and he retired to Aquitaine. Dagobert appointed him tutor of his three-year-old son Sigebert before his death in 638, and Pepin returned and ruled the kingdom until his own death the next year. He worked to spread the faith, defended Christian towns from Slavic invaders, and chose responsible men to fill vacant sees. The marriage of his daughter, St. Begga, and Arnulf's son, Segisilius, produced Pepin of Herstal, the first of the Carolingian dynasty in France. Pepin has never been canonized but is listed as a saint in some of the old martyrologies. February 21.

PERBOYRE, BL. JOHN (1802–40). Born at Puech, France, he joined the Lazarists (Vincentians) when he was fifteen and was ordained in 1826. He became professor of theology at Saint-Fleur seminary, served as rector of the minor seminary there for two years, and in 1832 became assistant director of the novitiate in Paris. In 1835 he was granted permission to go to China as a missionary. After four months at Macao, he was sent to the mission in Honan, was active in rescuing abandoned children, and after two years was sent to Hupeh. When persecution of Christians began, he was betrayed by a neophyte and brought before the governor of Wuchangfu. He was imprisoned, subjected to horrible torture for a year in an attempt to get him to reveal the names of his companions and their hiding places, and then on September 11, he was strangled to death. He was beatified in 1889, the first Christian in China to be beatified.

PERCY, BL. THOMAS (1528–72). Son of Sir Thomas Percy, who was hanged at Tyburn in 1537 as one of the leaders of the Pilgrimage of Grace, he became earl of Northumberland in 1557. He served Queen Mary during her reign and in 1558 married Anne Somerset, daughter of the earl of Worcester; they had four children. Though viewed with suspicion by Queen Elizabeth I's followers because of his Catholicism, Elizabeth bestowed the Order of the Garter on him in 1563. He supported Mary, Queen of Scots, when she took refuge at Carlisle in 1568. He and Charles Neville, earl of Westmorland, refused to appear before Elizabeth when ordered to do so in 1569 and became the leaders of what came to be known as the Rising of the North. They were defeated by Elizabeth's troops under the earl of Sussex, who destroyed towns and hanged hundreds to avenge the uprising. Percy fled to Scotland but was captured by the earl of Moray, the Scottish regent. Percy was held prisoner at Lochleven Castle for two and a half years until the earl of Mar became regent and sold him to Elizabeth for £2,000. He was brought to York, offered his freedom if he would apostatize, and when he refused, was beheaded there on August 22. He was beatified in 1896. August 26.

PEREGRINE (d. c. 261). Consecrated bishop by Pope Sixtus II in Rome, he was sent by Sixtus to Gaul to preach the gospel and is reported to have been successful in the area around Marseilles and Lyons and to have converted most of the inhabitants of Auxerre, of which he is considered the first bishop. When he went to nearby Intaranum (Entrains) to plead with the inhabitants to abandon their idolatry (they were dedicating a new temple to Jupiter), he was hauled before the governor, tortured, and beheaded. May 16.

PEREGRINE, BL. (d. 1240). He was born at Fallerone, Italy, and while a student at Bologna, he and his friend, Bl. Rizzerio were so impressed by a sermon preached there by St. Francis of Assisi in 1220 that they decided to become Franciscans. Francis accepted them but told Peregrine that he could be only a lay brother despite his learning. He made a pilgrimage to Palestine, lived as a lay brother at San Severino, and reportedly performed numerous miracles. September 6.

PEREGRINE, BL. (d. c. 1250). *See* Evangelist.

PEREGRINE LAZIOSI (1260–1345). *See* Laziosi, Peregrine.

PEREIRA, BL. NONIUS ALVARES DE (1360–1431). Also known as Nuñes and Nonius, he was born at Bomjardin near Lisbon, Portugal, married when he was seventeen, and was named commander of Portugal's armies in 1383, when he was only twenty-three, by the grand master of the knights of Aviz,

who became King John I. They revolted against Spanish domination and established Portugal as an independent state when they defeated the Castilian army at the battle of Aljubarrota in 1385, and John became King. After the death of his wife in 1422, Nuñes became a Carmelite lay brother in a friary he had founded in Lisbon and died there on November 1. Called the Great Constable, he is one of the great national heroes of Portugal, celebrated in the sixteenth-century epic *Chronica Condestavel;* his cult was approved for Portugal and the Carmelites in 1918. November 6.

PERGENTIUS (d. 251). *See* Laurentinus.

PERPETUA (d. 203). A matron of noble birth in Carthage with one child, an infant, Vivia (or Vibia), she was arrested during the persecution of Christians under Emperor Severus with fellow catechumens Revocatus and the pregnant Felicity, both slaves, Saturninus and Secundulus, and imprisoned in a private home. There they were all baptized, probably by Saturus, their instructor, who had joined them. Later they were moved to a prison, where Secundulus died and Felicity gave birth to a daughter. They were then examined by Hilarion, procurator of the province, and sentenced to death at the public games in the amphitheater. They were exposed to wild beasts, and when Perpetua and Felicity were unharmed, they were sworded to death. The descriptions of their passion written by Perpetua and Saturus and their death written by an unknown eyewitness (once thought by some to be Tertullian) are considered among the most remarkable of such acts and achieved such popularity that Augustine protested against their being read in African churches along with Scripture. March 7.

PERPETUUS (d. c. 494). Named bishop of Tours about 464, he enforced clerical discipline in his see, put into effect fasting and feast-day regulations, rebuilt the Basilica of St. Martin, and labored to inculcate his people with the tenets of the faith during the thirty years he was bishop. April 8.

PETER (d. c. 64). A native of Bethsaida, a village near Lake Tiberias, he was the son of John, was called Simon, and lived and worked as a fisherman on Lake Genesareth. His brother Andrew introduced him to Jesus, who gave him the name Cephas, the Aramaic equivalent of the Greek Peter (the Rock). He was present at Christ's first miracle at Cana and at his home at Capernaum when Jesus cured his mother-in-law, and his boat was always available to the Savior. When Peter acknowledged Jesus as "the Christ . . . the son of the living God" (Matt. 16:16), the Lord replied, "You are Peter and on this rock I will build my Church" (Matt. 16:18) and "I will give you the keys of the kingdom of heaven: Whatever you bind on earth will be considered bound in heaven; whatever you loose on earth shall be considered loosed in heaven," statements underlying Catholic teaching that Peter was the first Pope and the whole Catholic concept of the primacy of the papacy. Peter is mentioned more frequently in the gospels than any of the other apostles, was with Christ during many of his miracles, but denied him in the courtyard of Pontius Pilate's palace, where Christ was being held prisoner. He was the head of the Christians after the Ascension, designated Judas' successor, was the first of the apostles to preach to the Gentiles, was the first apostle to perform miracles, and converted many with his preaching. He was imprisoned by Herod Agrippa in about 43, but guided by an angel, escaped and firmly proclaimed that Christ wanted the Good News preached to all at the assembly at Jerusalem. After this episode, he is not mentioned in the New Testament again, but a very early tradition says he went to Rome, where he was Rome's first bishop and was crucified there at the foot of Vatican Hill in about 64 during the reign of Emperor Nero. Excavations under St. Peter's Basilica have unearthed what is believed to be his tomb, and bones found in the tomb are still under intensive study. June 29.

PETER (d. 251). A Christian living at Lampsacus, Mysia, he was arrested during the persecution of the Christians under Emperor Decius, haled before Proconsul Olympius, and when he refused to sacrifice to Venus and denounced the worship of Venus, he was tortured and then beheaded at Troas, Cyzigus. Also arrested at the same time were Andrew, Niomachus, and Paul. Andrew and Paul were tortured and stoned to death. Niomachus, under torture, apostatized. When sixteen-year-old Dionysia denounced his apostasy, she was arrested and then beheaded. May 15.

PETER (d. 303). A chamberlain in the household of Emperor Diocletian in Nicomedia, Asia Minor, he was subjected to terrible tortures when he refused to sacrifice to the gods. Two other officials objected to the torture, and when they proclaimed their own Christianity, Dorotheus and Gorgonius were tortured and then executed, as was Migdonius, a third Christian official. Peter was then roasted to death on a spit until he died. March 12.

PETER (d. 304). *See* Marcellinus.

PETER (d. 311). Born at Alexandria, Egypt, and known for his learning and knowledge of Scripture, he was named head of the catechetical school in Alexandria and in 300 was named Patriarch of that city. He fought

Arianism and Origenism and spent the last nine years of his episcopate, encouraging his flock to stand fast against the persecution of Christians launched by Emperor Diocletian. Peter eventually was forced into hiding, whereupon Bishop Meletius of Lycopolis began to usurp Peter's authority as metropolitan and accused Peter of treating the *lapsi* with too great leniency. When Peter excommunicated Meletius, a schism developed. Peter continued administering his see from hiding and returned to Alexandria when the persecutions were temporarily suspended. When Emperor Maximin renewed the persecution, Peter was arrested and then executed—the last Christian martyr put to death in Alexandria by the authorities. Peter's instructions on how *lapsi* were to be received back into the Church were later adopted throughout the East. November 26.

PETER (d. c. 350). Bishop of Braga, Portugal, in the fourth century, local unreliable legends have him a disciple of St. James the Greater, who consecrated him first bishop of Braga. He is reported to have suffered martyrdom after he baptized and cured the local ruler's daughter of leprosy. April 26.

PETER (d. 1220). *See* Berard.

PETER OF ALCÁNTARA (1499–1562). Son of the governor of Alcántara, Estremadura, Spain, where he was born, Peter Garavito studied law locally at Salamanca University, and when he was sixteen, joined the Observant Franciscans at Manjaretes. He practiced great austerities and penances, was sent to Badajoz to found a friary when he was twenty-two, and was ordained in 1524. He preached in Estremadura, served as superior at Robredillo, Plasencia, Lapa, and Estremadura, and had his request for solitude granted with an appointment to the friary at Lapa, though he was also named its superior. He served as a court chaplain for a time to King John III of Portugal and in 1538 was elected minister provincial of the Observants' province of St. Gabriel at Estremadura. He formulated a strict rule but when unable to convince the entire province to accept it at a provincial chapter at Placensia in 1540, he resigned as minister provincial. He lived as a hermit with Friar Martin of St. Mary on Arabida Mountain near Lisbon and was named superior of Palhaes community for novices when numerous friars were attracted to their way of life. Unable to secure approval for a stricter congregation of friars from his minister provincial, his idea was accepted by the bishop of Coria and he secured permission from Pope Julius III to build a friary under the Conventuals, but with his rule, in 1555—the beginnings of the Franciscans of the Observance of St. Peter of Alcántara (the Alcantarines), devoted to a life of penance and austerity. When other houses accepted his rule, St. Joseph Province was erected in 1561 and moved from Conventual to Observant jurisdiction despite much opposition from his former colleagues, the Conventuals. In 1560, he met St. Teresa of Ávila, who included much of what he told her about himself and his life in her autobiography, became her confessor and adviser, and encouraged her in her work of reforming the Carmelites. He wrote *Treatise on Prayer and Meditation,* which was later used by St. Francis de Sales, and was gifted with many supernatural experiences. He died in the convent at Estremadura on October 18, was canonized in 1669, and was declared patron of Brazil in 1862. October 22.

PETER ARMENGOL, BL. (c. 1238–1304). According to untrustworthy legend, he was of the family of the counts of Urgel in Catalonia, Spain, and in his youth ran away from home and joined a group of bandits. His father was in charge of an advance guard sent ahead of the main party of King James of Aragon, who was traveling through Catalonia in 1258 when they encountered the bandits. Father and son were about to engage in combat when Peter recognized his father and begged his forgiveness, which was granted. Peter joined the Mercedarians and made two trips to ransom captives of the Moors. On the second trip, he gave himself as hostage when he found he had insufficient funds to ransom eighteen young boys. When a messenger arrived with the balance of the payment, he found that Peter had been hanged for default in the payment of the ransom several days earlier. When he cut him down, he found that Peter was still alive. Peter returned to Guardia, where he lived another ten years until his death near Tarragona. His cult was approved in 1686. April 27.

PETER OF ASSCHE (d. 1572). *See* Pieck, Nicholas.

PETER OF THE ASSUMPTION, BL. *See* Peter of Cuerva, Bl.

PETER OF ATROA (773–837). Born near Ephesus, Asia Minor, and christened Theophylact, he became a monk when he was eighteen and joined St. Paul the Hesychast, who named him Peter, at Crypta, Phrygia. He was ordained several years later, set out with Paul on a pilgrimage to Jerusalem, but instead they went to Mount Olympus, where Paul founded St. Zachary Monastery near Atroa. When Paul died in 805, Peter succeeded him as abbot, but after ten years closed the monastery because of the iconoclastic persecution under Emperor Leo the Armenian. Peter went to Ephesus and Crete, and when he returned found he was a wanted man.

He escaped the imperial troops seeking him by miraculous means, and wandered from place to place, settling for several years at Kalonaros near the Hellespont. He was accused of practicing magic and using the devil because of the miracles he performed, but he was completely cleared by St. Theodore Studites. Peter again resumed his eremitical life near Atroa, restored St. Zachary Monastery, and reorganized several other monasteries, but when another outburst of iconoclastic persecution erupted, dispersed the monks and sent them into hiding. When the persecution became more violent, Peter retired to St. Porphyry Monastery on the Hellespont but eventually returned to his hermitage at St. Zachary and died there on January 1.

PETER OF ÁVILA (1562–1622). Born at Palomares, Castile, Spain, he joined the Franciscans, was sent to the Philippines as a missionary, and then was sent to Japan. He was arrested during a persecution of Christians and burned to death at Nagasaki. He was beatified in 1867 as one of the Martyrs of the Great Martyrdom of Japan. September 10.

PETER BALSAM (d. 311). Born in Eleutheropolis, Palestine, he was arrested during the persecution of Christians under Emperor Diocletian and brought before the governor, Severus. When he refused Severus' plea that he sacrifice to the gods, he was tortured; when he persisted, he was crucified on January 11, though Eusebius, who calls him Peter Absalamus, says he was burned to death. January 3.

PETER BAPTIST (1545–97). Born near Avila, Spain, he joined the Franciscans in 1567, worked as a missionary in Mexico, was sent to the Philippines in 1583, and then in 1593 was sent to Japan, where he served as commissary for the Franciscans. He was crucified with twenty-five other Christians on February 5 near Nagasaki during the persecution of Christians by the *taikō,* Toyotomi Hideyoshi. They were all canonized in 1862 as the Martyrs of Japan. February 6.

PETER OF CANTERBURY (d. 606). A Benedictine monk at St. Andrew's Monastery in Rome, he was one of the first group of missionaries under St. Augustine of Canterbury sent to England by Pope St. Gregory the Great in 596. Peter became first abbot of SS. Peter and Paul at Canterbury in 602. He was drowned at Ambleteuse near Boulogne while on a mission to Gaul. His cult was confirmed in 1915. January 6.

PETER OF CASTELNAU, BL. (d. 1208). Born near Montpellier, France, he became archdeacon of Maguelone in 1199 but resigned to become a Cistercian about 1202. He was appointed apostolic delegate and inquisitor against the Albigensians by Pope Innocent III in 1203 but was unsuccessful in his efforts to convert them. In the course of his duties he made many enemies, and on January 15 he was murdered at the instigation of Raymund VI of Toulouse near Saint-Gilles Abbey.

PETER OF CAVA (d. 1123). Born at Salerno, Italy, Peter Pappacarbone became a monk at Cava Monastery, founded by his uncle, St. Alferius, when quite young. In about 1062 Peter went to Cluny, spent six years there, and then returned to Italy and was appointed bishop of Policastro. He resigned his bishopric to return to Cava, was elected abbot, and when the monks protested his strict rule, he left for another monastery. At the request of the monks, he returned to Cava, attracted numerous novices and gifts for the monastery (the latter were used to aid the sick and the poor), imposed the strict Cluniac reform, and enlarged the monastery, which flourished under his leadership. Reportedly, he attracted some three thousand novices to the monastery while he was abbot. March 4.

PETER OF CHAVANON (1003–80). Born at Langeac, Haute-Loire, France, he was ordained and became a priest there. With land given him at Pébrac, Auvergne, he built a monastery for canons regular following the rule of St. Augustine and was its first provost. When the success of his monastery became known he was named to reform several cathedral chapters. He died on September 9. September 11.

PETER CHRYSOLOGUS (406–c. 450). Born at Imola, Emilia, Italy, he studied under the direction of Bishop Cornelius of Imola, who ordained him deacon. An unlikely legend has him named bishop of Ravenna in 433 by Pope St. Sixtus III, who reputedly selected him in place of another elected by the people because of a vision Sixtus had telling him to do so. At any rate, he at once set about the reform of his lax see and to eradicate paganism, was known for his charities, and preached with such effect that he was surnamed Chrysologus ("the golden-worded"). His first sermon impressed Empress Galla Placidia so much that thereafter she generously supported his ambitious building projects. He advised Eutyches to stop attempting to justify himself after his condemnation by the synod of Constantinople in 448 and officiated at the funeral of St. Germanus of Auxerre after his death at Ravenna in 448. Peter died at Imola on July 31, and his homilies, many still extant, caused Pope Benedict XIII to declare him a Doctor of the Church in 1729. July 30.

PETER CLAVER. See Claver, Peter.

PETER OF CLUNY, BL. See Peter the Venerable, Bl.

PETER OF CUERVA, BL. (d. 1617). Born at Cuerva near Toledo, Spain, he was sent to Japan in 1601 with fifty Franciscans and was named guardian of their friary at Nagasaki. He was arrested and imprisoned at Omura with Bl. John Machado for their faith, and on May 22 both were beheaded at a spot between Omura and Nagasaki; both were beatified in 1867. He is also known as Peter of the Assumption.

PETER DAMIAN (1001–72). Born of poor parents at Ravenna, Italy, he was orphaned when very young and raised by a brother for whom he tended swine in his youth. Another brother, a priest at Ravenna named Damian whose name he adopted as his surname, sent him to Faenza and then to Parma to be educated. Peter became a professor, began to practice great austerities, and in 1035 joined the Benedictines at Fonte Avellana, living as a hermit and devoting himself to intensive study of Scripture. About 1043 he was elected abbot by the monks, founded five other hermitages, and became famous for his uncompromising attitude toward worldliness and denunciations of simony. In 1057, he was named cardinal-bishop of Ostia by Pope Stephen IX but soon attempted to resign his see; refused by Pope Nicholas II, he finally persuaded Pope Alexander II to allow him to do so. He returned to the life of a monk but remained active in the work of ecclesiastical reform. He opposed the antipopes, especially Honorius II, and engaged in several papal diplomatic missions to France and Germany, notably to King Henry IV of Germany, whom he persuaded to abandon his plan to divorce his wife, Bertha. Peter died at Faenza while on the way back from Ravenna, which he had just reconciled with the Holy See. He wrote prolifically on purgatory, the Eucharist, in favor of the validity of sacraments administered by simoniacal priests, and clerical celibacy, and denounced immorality and simony. He was never formally canonized, but local cults developed on his death, and in 1828 Pope Leo XII extended his feast to the Universal Church and declared him a Doctor of the Church. February 21.

PETER GONZALEZ, BL. (1190–1246). Of a noble Castilian family, he was born at Astorga, Spain, and was educated by his uncle, the bishop of Astorga, who appointed him a canon of the cathedral. He resigned his canonry to join the Benedictines, became famed for his preaching, was appointed King Ferdinand III's chaplain, and labored to reform the court despite great opposition. He preached a crusade against the Moors and then persuaded the victors to be magnanimous to the defeated enemy after Cordova and Seville were captured. He then left the court to preach in Cilicia and along the coast and attracted huge crowds. He was particularly concerned with the welfare of sailors and is considered the patron of Spanish and Portuguese sailors with St. Erasmus; both are called Elmo or Telmo by them. Peter died at Tuy, Spain, and his cult was confirmed in 1741. April 14.

PETER OF GUBBIO (d. c. 1250). Born at Gubbio, Italy, of the Ghisengi family, he joined the Hermits of St. Augustine and is believed to have served as provincial. The miracles reported at his tomb at Gubbio made it a popular pilgrimage center. His cult was approved by Pope Pius IX. March 23.

PETER IGNEUS (d. 1089). A member of the distinguished Aldobrandini family of Florence, he joined the Vallombrosan monks under St. John Gualbert and soon after underwent the ordeal of fire at Florence to convict Bishop Peter of Pavia of simony. He emerged unscathed, earning the surname Igneus ("of the fire"). As a result, Pope Alexander deposed Peter as bishop of Florence. Peter Igneus was later appointed abbot of a monastery and then was made cardinal-bishop of Albano by Pope St. Gregory VII; he served as papal legate to France, Germany, and several of the Italian states. He died on February 8.

PETER OF JUILLY, BL. (d. 1136). Born and educated in England, he was early attracted to the religious life, studied theology, and when his parents died he went to France to continue his studies, probably at Paris. He met St. Stephen Harding, went on pilgrimage with him to Rome, and on the way back Stephen became a Cistercian at Molesme, but Peter continued on. He later returned, joined the Cistercians, and was ordained. He became known for his preaching and miracles and served as chaplain for a convent of nuns headed by St. Bernard's sister, Bl. Humbelina, at Juilly-les-Nonnains. June 23.

PETER OF LUXEMBURG, BL. (1369–87). Son of Guy of Luxemburg, count of Ligny, he was born in Lorraine, was orphaned when he was four, studied at Paris, where he became a canon at Notre Dame, and was held hostage for his brother by the English at Calais, 1380–81. Peter was named bishop of Metz in 1384 and cardinal shortly after by antipope Clement VII (who was recognized as Pope in France), though he was only fifteen and a deacon. He required the armed intervention of his brother Valerian against the followers of Pope Urban VI to enter his see. He introduced many reforms in his see but was driven from Metz by political unrest in 1386 and joined Clement at Avignon,

where Peter became known for his holiness, charities to the poor, and austerity. He died at the age of eighteen at a Carthusian monastery at Villeneuve, France, on July 2, and was beatified in 1527.

PETER MARTINEZ (d. c. 1000). Also known as Peter of Monzonzo, he was born in Spanish Galicia and joined the Benedictines at St. Mary Abbey at Monzonzo in about 950. He was named abbot of St. Martin of Antealares Abbey at Compostela, Spain, and in about 986 became archbishop of that see. He played a prominent role in the reconquest of Spain and is said to be the author of the hymn "Salve Regina." September 10.

PETER MARTYR (1205–52). Born at Verona, Italy, of parents who had embraced Catharism, he was educated at a Catholic school and at the University of Bologna and was accepted into the Dominicans by St. Dominic. He became well known in Lombardy for his preaching, was banished for a time when he was falsely accused of receiving women in his cell, but was cleared, and in about 1234 was appointed inquisitor of northern Italy, which was a hotbed of Catharists. He attracted huge crowds with his preaching but made enemies for his activities as inquisitor, and while returning from Como was attacked and murdered near Barassina on April 6 by a Catharist assassin named Carino. Peter was canonized by Pope Innocent IV as Peter of Verona. April 29.

PETER OF MOGLIANO, BL. (1442–90). Born at Mogliano, Ancona, Italy, he studied law at the University of Perugia and in 1467 joined the Observant Franciscans. He became known for his preaching, was adviser of the duke of Camerino, and served as vicar provincial of Rome and of the Marches three times.

In 1472, he went to Crete as commissary. He was tremendously popular as a spiritual director and was venerated for his holiness. He died on July 25, and his cult was confirmed in 1760. July 30.

PETER OF MONZONZO. *See* Peter Martinez.

PETER OF MOUNT ATHOS (8th century). According to an unreliable legend, he fought against the Saracens in his youth and was captured and imprisoned. Released through the intercession of St. Simeon, Peter went to Rome, where he received the monastic habit from the Pope. In response to a vision of our Lady, Peter became a hermit on Mount Athos—the first Christian hermit there. He lived the eremitical life for fifty years in great austerity ·and was subjected to numerous diabolical attacks, but was aided in times of extreme need by our Lady. June 12.

PETER OF NARBONNE (d. 1391). *See* Tavelic, Nicholas.

PETER NOLASCO (c. 1189–1258). Born at Mas-des-Saintes Puelles, France, of a noble family, he inherited a fortune when his father died when Peter was fifteen. He went to Barcelona and used his wealth to ransom Christian prisoners from the Moors, who ruled most of Spain at that time. In response to a vision (which according to legend was also experienced by St. Raymond of Peñafort and King James of Aragon), Peter decided to found a religious congregation dedicated to ransoming Christian slaves from the Moors. The Order of Our Lady of Ransom (the Mercedarians) developed from the decision, with the aid of St. Raymond, Peter's spiritual director, who is considered the cofounder of the Order; it was approved by Bishop Berengarius of Barcelona in 1223 (1218,

1222, 1228, and 1234 are also given as possible dates), with Peter as master general, and supported by King James of Aragon; papal approval came from Pope Gregory IX in 1235. In addition to the three traditional religious vows, the Mercedarians took a fourth—to give themselves if necessary in exchange for a slave. Peter traveled to Moorish-dominated Spain several times and to Algeria, where he was imprisoned for a time. He resigned his position as master general several years before his death on December 25 at Barcelona, and was canonized in 1628. January 28.

PETER ORSEOLO (928–87). Born of a distinguished family at Venice, Italy, he was named commander of the Venetian fleet when he was only twenty and waged successful campaigns against the Dalmatian pirates in the Adriatic Sea. He was chosen doge in 976 (St. Peter Damian accused him of culpability in the murder of his predecessor, Doge Peter Candiani IV), ruled successfully for two years, and then suddenly and secretly entered the Benedictine abbey at Cuxa, France. He led a life of great asceticism, and in time, on the advice of St. Romuald, became a hermit and followed the eremitical way of life until his death. January 10.

PETER OF POITIERS, BL. (1087–1115). Bishop of Poitiers, France, he was a leader in denouncing the marriage of King Philip I to Bertrada de Montfort while his wife Bertha was still alive, despite the threat against him and the others objecting to the marriage by Count William the Troubador of Poitou at a council that denounced the marriage and excommunicated the King. Peter encouraged Robert of Arbrissel in founding Fontevrault Abbey, getting approval for it from Rome in 1106, and was exiled to the Castle of Chauvigny in 1113 by Count William when Peter protested the count's transgressions. Peter died there two years later. Although venerated in Poitiers he has never been officially beatified. April 4.

PETER REGULATUS (1392–1456). Of a noble family, he was born at Valladolid, Spain, joined the Franciscans there when he was thirteen, and transferred to Peter Villacretios' monastery at Tribulos in quest of a more rigorous rule. Peter became known for his austerities, ecstasies, and levitations, and succeeded Villacretios as abbot of his reformed congregation. Peter died at Aguilar on March 30, surnamed Regulatus for his fervor in enforcing the rigorous rule of his community. May 13.

PETER OF RUFFIA, BL. *See* Cambian, Bl. Peter.

PETER OF SASSOFERRATO, BL. (d. 1231). *See* John of Perugia, Bl.

PETER OF SEBASTEA (c. 340–91). Son of St. Basil the Elder and St. Emmelia, brother of SS. Basil, Gregory of Nyssa, and Macrina, and the youngest of ten children, Peter was raised and educated by Macrina after their father died when he was an infant. He entered a monastery in Armenia on the Iris River founded by his mother and father and headed by Basil, and in time became abbot, in 362. Peter helped alleviate the distress of the famine that afflicted Pontus and Cappadocia, was ordained in 370, and was named bishop of Sebastea in 380. He labored to eliminate Arianism in his see and attended the General Council of Constantinople in 381. January 9.

PETER OF SIENA, BL. *See* Peter Tecelano, Bl.

PETER OF SIENA, BL. (d. 1321). *See* Thomas of Tolentino, Bl.

PETER OF TARENTAISE (1102–75). Born near Vienne, Dauphiné, France, he joined the Cistercians at Bonnevaux when he was twenty, and his father and two brothers joined him. He became superior of a new Cistercian house at Tamié in the Tarentaise Mountains overlooking the Alpine pass between Geneva and Savoy and built a hospice there. Against his wishes, he was named archbishop of Tarentaise in 1142, reformed the diocese, brought canons regular to the cathedral to replace the corrupt clergy there, helped the poor, encouraged education, restored clerical discipline, and was known for his miracles. In 1155, he abruptly left his see and anonymously became a lay brother at a Cistercian abbey in Switzerland, but after a year he was found out and made to return. He acted as peacemaker in several disputes, supported Pope Alexander III against antipope Victor IV and Emperor Barbarossa, whom he openly defied, and preached widely in Alsace, Lorraine, Burgundy, and Italy in support of Alexander. Peter was sent in 1174 by Alexander to reconcile King Louis VII of France and King Henry II of England, was unsuccessful, but on the way home was taken ill at Besançon and died at Bellevaux Abbey. He was canonized in 1191. May 8.

PETER OF TARENTAISE. *See* Innocent V, Bl.

PETER TECELANO, BL. (d. 1289). Born at Campi, Tuscany, Italy, he became a combmaker at Siena, married, and when his wife died, became a Franciscan tertiary. He lived in a cell next to the Franciscan infirmary, ministered to the sick in the hospital, became widely known for his holiness and as a mystic, and was widely consulted for his spiritual wisdom. Many miracles were reported at his tomb, and his cult was approved in

1802. He is often called Peter of Siena and is also surnamed Pettinaio (the combmaker). December 11.

PETER THOMAS (1305–66). Born at Salles, France, he joined the Carmelites at Condom and in 1342 was named procurator general, directing the Order from Avignon, where the Pope was then residing. He became known for his eloquent preaching, came to the attention of the papacy, and spent his life in the papal diplomatic service. He served on papal missions to Genoa, Milan, and Venice, was made bishop of Patti and Lipari, of Corona in 1359, archbishop of Candia in 1363, and titular patriarch of Constantinople in 1364. He went to Serbia, then to Hungary as peacemaker between Venice and Hungary, and then to Constantinople in an attempt to reunite the Byzantine Church and Rome. He led a military expedition to Constantinople in 1359 as papal legate and in 1365 headed an unsuccessful attack on Alexandria. He was severely wounded in the assault and died of the wounds three months later, on January 6 at Cyprus. He has never been formally canonized, but his feast was authorized among the Carmelites in 1608. January 28.

PETER OF TREIA, BL. (d. 1304). Born at Montecchio near Treia, Italy, of poor parents, he received the Franciscan habit when he was quite young from St. Francis and was ordained. He became a close friend of Bl. Conrad of Offida at Torano Convent, where they both spent several years, and they worked and preached together. He was reputed to have experienced ecstasies and visions and to have had the gift of levitation. He died at Sirolo Convent in the Marches, and his cult was approved in 1793. February 17.

PETER THE VENERABLE, BL. (1092–1156). Peter de Montboissier was born

of a noble Auvergne family, was educated at Sauxillanges, a Cluniac monastery, and when he was twenty was prior of Vézelay. He was elected abbot of Cluny in 1122 when he was thirty and in 1125 was faced with an armed force led by Pontius, the abbot he had succeeded, who took over Cluny while he was away. Both Peter and Pontius were summoned to Rome, where Pope Honorius II sentenced Pontius to prison. Peter then became involved in a controversy with St. Bernard, who accused Cluny of too relaxed a rule—a charge that led Peter to put into effect reforms in the Cluniac houses. He visited England in 1130 and Spain in 1139. He offered Peter Abelard shelter at Cluny in 1140, convinced the Pope to lighten Abelard's sentence, and reconciled Abelard and Bernard. He wrote against Petrobrusian heretics in southern France, defended the Jews, attended the synod of Rheims that denounced the teachings of Bishop Gilbert de la Porrée, and had a voluminous correspondence with his contemporaries. He ruled Cluny for thirty-four years, during which Cluny was the greatest and most influential abbey in Christendom. He died at Cluny on December 25, and though his cult has never been formally approved, he is venerated in the diocese of Arras on December 29.

PETER OF VERONA. *See* Peter Martyr.

PETRANTONI, LIVIA (1864–1913). Born the second of eleven children to a farming family in the tiny village of Pozzaglia Sabina, young Livia's life was typical of that of an older child in an agricultural community. Work dominated her days. Whether assisting in the care of her younger siblings or doing chores, she is said to have carried out her tasks cheerfully amidst a loving family. Livia was a beautiful girl and received much interest from young men of the area. Rather than pursue a family life, she decided at age twenty-three to join the Sisters of Charity. She was given the name Sister Agostina and began work in a Roman hospital staffed by the sisters. There she found the work perhaps less pleasant than that of the farm, for she would at different times contract typhus, malaria, and tuberculosis. She was murdered in 1913 by Giuseppe Romanelli, a tuberculosis patient. As she was dying, she reportedly prayed that Guiseppe be forgiven. She was canonized in 1999.

PETROC (6th century). Born in Wales, possibly the son of a Welsh King, he became a monk and with some of his friends went to Ireland to study. They immigrated to Cornwall in England and settled at Lanwethinoc (Padstow). After thirty years there, he made a pilgrimage to Rome and Jerusalem, at which time he is also reputed to have reached the Indian Ocean, where he lived for a time as a hermit on an island. He then returned to Cornwall, built a chapel at Little Petherick near Padstow, established a community of his followers, and then became a hermit at Bodmir Moor, where he again attracted followers and was known for his miracles. He died between Nanceventon and Lanwethinoc while visiting some of his disciples there. June 4.

PETRONAX (d. c. 747). A native of Brescia, Italy, he visited the tomb of St. Benedict at Monte Cassino while on a pilgrimage to Rome in 717, organized the group of hermits living there, and rebuilt the abbey, which had been destroyed by the Lombards in 581. He ruled for thirty years, attracted new disciples and was so successful in restoring Monte Cassino to its old vigor and influence that he is called the second founder of the abbey. May 6.

PETRONI, BL. PETER (1311–61). Born at Siena, Italy, of a leading family, he

joined the Carthusians at nearby Maggiano Monastery when he was seventeen, refused ordination (chopping off the index finger of his left hand to prevent it), was reputed to have been blessed with supernatural gifts, and persuaded Boccacio to reform his life. Peter died on May 29.

PETRONILLA (d. c. 251). A martyr in third-century Rome, she is erroneously called the daughter of St. Peter in legends and gnostic apocrypha and was executed when she refused to sacrifice her virginity by marrying a nobleman named Flaccus. May 31.

PETRONILLA, BL. (d. 1355). Of the family of the counts of Troyes, France, she was the first abbess of the Poor Clares' Le Moncel Convent at Oise, which had been founded by King Philip the Fair. May 14.

PETRONIUS (d. c. 445). Probably the son of Petronius, prefect of the praetorium in Gaul, and probably a Roman official himself, he became a cleric and after a trip to Palestine, became bishop of Bologna about 432. He rebuilt churches destroyed by the Goths and built a series of churches and buildings in imitation of churches in Jerusalem. October 4.

PETRUCCI, BL. JOHN BAPTIST (d. 1420). *See* Nerucci, Bl. Laurence.

PHAL. *See* Fidolus.

PHARAÏLDIS (d. c. 740). All that is known of her is that she was married against her will, was badly treated by her husband when she refused him his marital rights because of her secret vow of virginity, and is venerated in her native Flanders, where she is also known as Varelde, Veerle, and Verylde for the numerous miracles she is reported to have performed. January 4.

PHILADELPHUS (d. 251). *See* Alphius.

PHILASTRIUS (d. 387). A Spaniard, he traveled all over Italy disputing the Arians, suffering a scourging on one occasion for his zeal. He opposed the Arian Auxentius at Milan, and when Philastrius was named bishop of Brescia, he continued his opposition to the heresy. He wrote *Catalogue of Heresies* for his flock and was known for his gentleness, humility, and aid to the poor. July 18.

PHILEAS (d. 304). Born at Thmuis, Egypt, he became known for his learning, was converted to Christianity, and in time was named bishop of Thmuis. He was arrested during the persecution of Christians under Emperor Maximinus and imprisoned at Alexandria. When tried before Culcian, governor of Egypt, Phileas refused to sacrifice to the gods, despite the pleas of all engaged in the trial, and was sentenced to be executed. When Philoromus, tribune and imperial treasurer at Alexandria, whom he had converted, objected to the attempts to get Phileas to apostatize, he too was sentenced to death, and both were beheaded. February 4.

PHILEMON (1st century). A Christian of Colossae, Phrygia, he was converted by St. Paul, probably at Ephesus, and was the recipient of the Epistle to Philemon, a private personal letter in which Paul tells him that he is sending back to him his runaway slave Onesimus so that he could have him back "not as a slave anymore, but . . . [as] a dear brother." According to tradition, Philemon freed Onesimus and was later stoned to death with his wife, Apphia, at Colossae for their Christianity. November 22.

PHILEMON (d. 305). *See* Apollonius.

PHILIBERT (c. 608–c. 685). Son of Philiband who became bishop of Aire,

he was educated at the court of Dagobert I, where he was so impressed with St. Ouen that he became a monk at Rebais Abbey, founded by Ouen, when he was twenty. He was named abbot but left Rebais when he felt he was unable to deal with some of the recalcitrant monks there. He visited several monasteries and then founded a monastery at Jumièges in Neustria in 654 on ground granted him by King Clovis II, and a convent at Pavilly. When he denounced Ebroin, mayor of the palace, for his many injustices, he was imprisoned at Rouen and then obliged to leave Jumièges. He retired to the island of Herio off the coast of Poitou and founded Noirmoutier; he also founded Quinçay Abbey near Poitiers and had a monastery at Luçon put in his charge by Bishop Ansoald of Poitiers. August 20.

PHILIP (1st century). Born in Bethsaida, Galilee, he may have been a disciple of John the Baptist and is mentioned as one of the apostles in the lists of Matthew (10:3), Mark (3:18), Luke (6:14), and in Acts (1:13). Aside from the lists, he is mentioned only in John in the New Testament. He was called by Jesus himself (John 1:43–48) and brought Nathanael to Christ. Philip was present at the miracle of the loaves and fishes (John 6:1–15), when he engaged in a brief dialogue with the Lord (John 6:5–7), and was the apostle approached by the Hellenistic Jews from Bethsaida to introduce them to Jesus (John 12:21ff.). Just before the Passion, Jesus answered Philip's query to show them the Father (John 14:8ff.), but no further mention of Philip is made in the New Testament beyond his listing among the apostles awaiting the Holy Spirit in the upper room (Acts 1:13). According to tradition he preached in Greece and was crucified upside down at Hierapolis under Emperor Domitian. May 3.

PHILIP (d. c. 165). *See* Felicity.

PHILIP (d. 304). Bishop of Heraclea near Constantinople during the persecution of Christians under Emperor Diocletian, he was arrested with Hermes, formerly a magistrate of the city and now a deacon, when he persisted in saying Mass after the governor, Bassus, had ordered his church closed. Haled before the governor, Philip refused to surrender the sacred books of the church, as did Hermes, whereupon both were tortured. Bassus urged Philip to sacrifice to the gods to save himself, but Philip refused, as did Hermes. The governor ordered them returned to prison and soon after was succeeded by a new governor, Justin. At this time, Severus, a priest who had gone into hiding, surrendered and was subjected to the same treatment accorded the bishop. After seven months in prison, the three were brought before Justin at Adrianopolis, questioned further, tortured when they refused to sacrifice to the gods, and then burned to death at the stake. October 22.

PHILIP BENIZI (1233–85). Born of a noble family at Florence, Italy, on August 15, he studied medicine at Paris and Padua, where he received his doctorate in medicine and philosophy when he was nineteen and began practicing medicine at Florence. After a year in his practice, he joined the Servites at Monte Senario near Florence in 1254, was sent to the Servite house in Siena in 1258, and was ordained there. He became known for his preaching, served as master of novices at Siena in 1262, was superior of several friaries, and in 1267, despite his protests, he was elected prior general. He codified the rules of the Order, began to have miracles attributed to him, and in 1268, when Cardinal Ottobuoni proposed his name as a papal candidate on the death of Pope Clement

IV, Philip fled and hid in a cave until a new Pope was elected. He attended the General Council of Lyons in 1274, helped to reconcile the Guelphs and the Ghibellines in 1279, attracted many converts to the Church, and reconciled many others. He helped St. Juliana establish a Servite third Order in 1284 and sent the first Servite missionaries to the Far East. In declining health, he resigned the generalship at a general chapter in 1285, naming his close confidant and longtime friend, Lottaringo Stufa, his successor, and retired to an impoverished Servite house at Todi, where he died on August 22. He was canonized in 1671. August 23.

PHILIP THE DEACON (1st century). All that is known of him is what we are told in Acts. He was one of the seven chosen to assist the apostles (6:5) by ministering to the needy members of the Church so the apostles could be free to preach the gospel. He was the first to preach in Samaria (8:5–13), where he converted Simon Magus and then a eunuch who was chief treasurer of the Queen of Ethiopia on the road from Jerusalem to Gaza (8:26–40). Philip preached in the coastal cities on the way to his home at Caesarea, and twenty-four years later, St. Paul stayed at his home in Caesarea, where he still lived with his four unmarried daughters (21:8–9). A Greek tradition has him become bishop of Tralles, Lydia. He was so successful in his preaching that he was sometimes surnamed "the Evangelist," which has sometimes caused him to be confused with Philip the apostle. June 6.

PHILIP OF JESUS. *See* Casas, Philip de las.

PHILIP NERI. *See* Neri, Philip.

PHILIP OF ZELL (8th century). Born in England, he made a pilgrimage to

Rome, where he was ordained and became a hermit near Worms, Germany. He was highly regarded for his holiness and miracles and was consulted by many, including King Pepin. May 4.

PHILOGONIUS (d. 324). A layman at Antioch, he became a famous lawyer, and in 319, while a layman married with a daughter, he was named bishop of Antioch. He was one of the first to denounce Arianism and during the persecutions of Christians under Emperors Maximinus and Licinius, he was imprisoned for a time. He was eulogized by St. John Chrysostom in a still extant panegyric, which contains all that we know of him. December 20.

PHILOMENA. A cult began with the discovery of the bones of a young girl, a small vial containing what was believed to be blood, and a tablet nearby with an inscription that when translated read, "Peace be with you, Philomena" in St. Priscilla catacomb in Rome. When the remains were moved in 1805 to the church of Mugnano del Cardinale near Nola, miracles were reported at her tomb, and devotion to Philomena became widespread. Her cult was authorized by Pope Gregory XVI in 1837, with a feast day of August 11. However, her name was removed from the calendar of the saints in 1961, since nothing was known of her beyond the facts listed here to justify sainthood.

PHILOROMUS (d. 304). *See* Phileas.

PHILOTHEUS (d. 297). *See* Hipparchus.

PHOCAS OF ANTIOCH (date unknown). Though listed in the Roman Martyrology under March 5, he is probably the same as St. Phocas the Gardener (or of Sinope), whose relics are claimed by St. Michael's Church in Antioch. Reputedly anyone stung by a serpent is instantly cured by touching the door of his basilica. He is sometimes confused with Phocas, the bishop of Sinope on the Black Sea, who suffered martyrdom during the reign of Emperor Trajan. July 14.

PHOCAS THE GARDENER (date unknown). A gardener at Sinope, Paphlagonia, he lived as an anchorite pursuing an austere life of prayer and contemplation, offering shelter to travelers, and suffered martyrdom for his faith. According to legend, he was denounced as a Christian and sentenced to death. When a squad of soldiers arrived at his house, he gave them shelter; when they told him they were seeking one Phocas, he told them he would tell them where to find Phocas in the morning. After preparing his soul for death, he dug his grave and then told them who he was. Overcome by his courage and kindness, they hesitated, but at his urging they beheaded him. September 22.

PHOEBE (1st century). A deaconess of the church at Cenchreae, the port of Corinth, she was recommended to the Christian congregation at Rome by St. Paul, who praised her for her assistance to him and to many others (Rom. 16:1–2). She may have brought Paul's epistle to the Romans to Rome with her. September 3.

PHOTINA (no date). Untrustworthy legend has her the Samaritan woman of Sychar with whom Jesus talked at the well (John 4). She preached the gospel, was imprisoned for three years, and died for her faith at Carthage. She also reputedly converted Emperor Nero's daughter Domnina and one hundred of her servants to Christianity before suffering martyrdom in Rome. March 20.

PHOTINUS. *See* Pothinus.

PIBUSH, BL. JOHN (d. 1601). Born at Thirsk, North Riding, England, he studied at Rheims, was ordained there in 1587, and was sent on the English mission in 1589. He was arrested at Moreton-in-the-Marsh, Gloucestershire, in 1593 and imprisoned in London for a year without a trial. Brought to Gloucester for trial, he was convicted of being a Catholic priest and returned to prison. He escaped but was recaptured the next day, was returned to London in 1595, was again found guilty of being a Catholic priest, remained in prison for five years, and was then executed on February 18. He was beatified in 1929.

PICCOLOMINI, BL. JOACHIM (1258–1305). Born at Siena, Italy, he joined the Servites as a lay brother when he was fourteen, became so venerated for his holiness by the people of Siena that he asked to be transferred, and was sent to Arezzo. His transfer caused such an uproar in Siena that he was soon returned and remained there until his death. April 16.

PICENARDI, BL. ELIZABETH (d. 1468). Daughter of well-to-do parents at Mantua, Italy, she became a Servite tertiary. Her holiness attracted a group of followers who formed a community of Servite tertiaries under her direction. She was credited with possessing supernatural gifts, and numerous miracles were reported at her tomb. She was beatified in 1804. February 20.

PICKERING, BL. THOMAS (1621–79). Born in Westmorland, England, he became a Benedictine lay brother at St. Gregory's at Douai, took his vows in 1660, and then was sent to the community of Benedictine chaplains who served the chapel of Catherine of Braganza, wife of King Charles II, in London as procurators. He was arrested during the Titus Oates hysteria, falsely accused of

participating in the "popish plot" fabricated by Oates, and hanged at Tyburn. He was beatified in 1929. May 9.

PIECK, NICHOLAS (d. 1572). Guardian of the Observant Franciscan house at Gorkum, Holland, he was engaged in missionary activities among the Calvinists when he and four other priests were seized when Calvinist forces opposed to the Spanish rule seized the town in June. They were tortured, subjected to all kinds of indignities, and offered their freedom if they would abjure Catholic teaching on the Eucharist and the primacy of the Pope. When they refused, despite a letter from the prince of Orange ordering their release, he and eighteen other priests and religious were hanged at deserted Ruggen Monastery on the outskirts of Briel on July 9, and their bodies were callously thrown into a ditch. They were all canonized in 1867 as the Martyrs of Gorkum. Among those of the Franciscan community who were thus martyred were Jerome Weerden, vicar; Antony of Hoornaer; Antony of Weert; Theodore van der Eem of Amersfoort; Godefried of Mervel; Nicasius Jannsen, a native of Heeze, Brabant; Antony van Willehad of Denmark; and two lay brothers, Cornelius of Wyk near Utrecht, and Peter of Assche near Brussels.

PIERIUS (d. c. 310). Head of the catechetical school at Alexandria, Egypt, he was known for his learning and eloquent preaching and was sometimes called Origen the Younger for the errors of Origen manifest in some of his preachings and writings. He was praised by Eusebius and St. Jerome, managed to live through the persecution of Christians under Emperor Diocletian, and died in Rome. November 4.

PIEROZZI, ANTONY (1389–1459). Son of a notary, he was born at

Florence, Italy, on March 1, joined the Dominicans at Fiesole when he was sixteen, studied there and at Cortona, where Fra Angelico was a fellow student, and became noted for his scholarship. He served as superior of the Minerva convent in Rome, and was then successively prior at Naples, Gaeta, Cortona, Siena, Fiesole, and Florence. He served as superior of the Tuscan and Neapolitan congregations and was elected provincial of the Roman province. In 1436, he founded the famous San Marco Convent at Florence, attended the General Council of Florence, 1438–45, and became archbishop of Florence in 1446. He instituted many reforms in his see, abolished gambling, fought usury and sorcery, established aids for the poor, became known all over Europe for his knowledge of ecclesiastical affairs, and was called "the Counselor" for his expertise in canon law. Pope Pius II appointed him to a commission to reform the Roman court; Antony aided the victims of plagues, famines, and earthquakes, which wracked Florence in the 1450s, and was venerated as a saint for his holiness and miracles. He wrote several treatises, most notable of which was *Summa theologica moralis,* and, he died on May 2. He was canonized in 1523. May 10.

PIGNATELLI, JOSEPH (1737–1811). Born of a noble family at Saragossa, Spain, he joined the Jesuits at Tarragona when he was sixteen, was ordained in 1763, and was assigned to Saragossa. When Charles III banished the Jesuits from Spain in 1767, Fr. Pignatelli and his fellow Jesuits went to Corsica, where they were forced to leave when the French, who had also banished the Jesuits, occupied the island. They then settled at Ferrara, Italy. When Pope Clement XIV suppressed the Jesuits in 1773, Joseph and the members of the

Society of Jesus were secularized. He lived for the next twenty years at Bologna, aiding his less fortunate fellow Jesuit exiles. Meanwhile, Empress Catherine had refused to allow the bull of suppression to be published in Russia, and the Society continued in existence there. In 1792, the duke of Parma invited three Italian Jesuits in Russia to establish themselves in his realm, and after receiving permission from Pope Pius VI, Fr. Pignatelli became superior, thus bringing the Jesuits back to Italy. He began a quasinovitiate at Colorno in 1799 and saw Pope Pius VII give formal approval to the Jesuit province in Russia in 1801. Fr. Pignatelli worked to revive the Jesuits, and in 1804 the Society was reestablished in the Kingdom of Naples, with Fr. Pignatelli as provincial. The province was dispersed when the French invaded Naples later the same year, whereupon he went to Rome and was named provincial for Italy. He restored the Society in Sardinia and helped conserve it when the French occupied Rome. Though the Society of Jesus was not fully restored until 1814, three years after his death in Rome on November 11, Pope Pius XII called him the "restorer of the Jesuits" when he canonized him in 1954. November 28.

PIKE, VEN. WILLIAM (d. 1591). *See* Pilchard, Ven. Thomas.

PILCHARD, VEN. THOMAS (1557–87). Born at Battle, Sussex, England, he studied at Oxford and then went to Rheims to study for the priesthood. He was ordained at Laon in 1583 and was then sent on the English mission. He was arrested and banished but returned and was again arrested and imprisoned at Dorchester. While in prison he converted thirty of his fellow prisoners, among them William Pike, a native of Dorchester and a carpenter. Fr. Pilchard was tortured for his religious activities and then hanged, drawn, and quartered at Dorchester on March 21 for being a Catholic priest. Pike was executed on December 22, 1591.

PINOT, BL. NOEL (1747–94). Born at Angers, France, he was ordained, served as a parish priest in several parishes and at a hospital for incurables, and in 1788 became *curé* at Louroux-Béconnais. When the Constituent Assembly in 1790 reordered all priests to take an oath denounced by the Holy See, he refused and was arrested. Despite the order of an Angers court that he could not exercise his curateship for two years, he secretly continued his priestly functions, and when a revolt temporarily succeeded, he returned to his parish. He went into hiding when the revolt failed, was captured and imprisoned, and when he refused to take the oath, he was sentenced to death. He was guillotined on February 21, and was beatified in 1926. February 21.

PIONIUS (d. c. 250). A priest of Smyrna (Izmir, Turkey) who was known for his learning and the many conversions he had made, he was arrested during the persecution of Christians under Emperor Decius, tortured, and then burned to death when he forcibly resisted attempts to make him sacrifice to the gods. Also tortured and martyred with him were Sabinus and Ascelepiades. February 1.

PIPPIN. *See* Pepin.

PIRAN (6th century). A hermit near Padstow in Cornwall and sometimes called Perran, he is the patron saint of tin mines there and is often erroneously identified with St. Kyran (Kieran) of Saighir. March 5.

PIRMINUS (d. 753). A monk from southern Aragon, Spain, or southern Gaul, he fled the Moors and settled in the Rhineland, where he rebuilt Dissentis Abbey in the Grisons, which had been destroyed by the Avars in 724. He was founding abbot of Reichenau on an island in Lake Constance, reputedly the first Benedictine house in Germany. When he was forced into exile for political reasons, he went to Alsace, where he founded Murbach Monastery, and then founded Amorbach in Lower Franconis. He became a regionary bishop and wrote *Dicta Pirmini,* a popular catechism. November 3.

PIRROTTI, POMPILIO (1710–56). Born at Montecalvo, Campania, Italy, he joined the Piarists (also called Scolopini) and was professed in 1728, taking the name Mary of St. Nicholas. After his ordination, he taught in Apulia, was appointed missioner apostolic in Emilia and Venetia, and was so successful in his preaching in Naples that he aroused the resentment of those in high places and was banished; public indignation caused the King to recall him. He was later recalled to the Piarist house at Campo and died there. He was canonized in 1934. July 15.

PIUS I (d. c. 154). A native of Aquileia and son of Rufinus, he may have been the brother of Hermes, author of *The Shepherd,* and was perhaps a slave later freed. He succeeded Pope Hyginus as pope in about 140 and during his pontificate opposed the Valentinians and Gnostics under Marcion, whom he excommunicated. July 11.

PIUS V (1504–72). Born at Bosco near Alessandria, Italy, on January 17, of an impoverished noble family, Antonio Michael Ghislieri joined the Dominicans at Voghera when he was fourteen and was ordained in 1528. He taught theology and philosophy for sixteen years, served as master of novices and as prior of several Dominican houses, and was appointed bishop of Nepi and Butri by Pope Paul IV in 1556. Bishop Ghislieri was also named inquisitor of Milan and Lombardy and in 1557 was created a cardinal and inquisitor general of the entire Church. He was translated to Mondovi in 1559, restored wartorn Piedmont, opposed Pope Pius IV's attempt to make thirteen-year-old Ferdinand de' Medici a cardinal, and defeated the attempt of Emperor Maximilian II of Germany to abolish clerical celibacy. Cardinal Ghislieri was elected Pope to succeed Pope Pius IV on January 7, 1566, and at once set about putting into effect the decrees of the Council of Trent. He restored simplicity to the papal court, completed the new catechism (1566), reformed the breviary (1568) and the missal (1570), and ordered a complete new edition of the works of Thomas Aquinas, whom he proclaimed a Doctor of the Church in 1567. Pius gave large sums to the poor, lived a life of great austerity and piety, and personally visited the sick in hospitals. Throughout his entire pontificate, he fought Protestantism, and in 1570 he excommunicated Queen Elizabeth I of England and supported Mary Stuart. He reenergized the Inquisition and has been severely criticized for his harshness to heretics. He persistently sought to unite Christian monarchs against the Turks and ardently supported Don Juan of Austria and Marcantonio Colonna, rejoicing in their success in 1571 when they halted the Moslem tide at the Battle of Lepanto. He was attempting to form an alliance of the Italian cities, France, Poland, and other Christian nations of Europe to march against the Turks when he died in Rome on May 1. He was canonized in 1712. April 30.

PIUS X (1835–1914). The second of ten children of a cobbler and postman, Giuseppe Melchior Sarto was born on June 2 at Riese near Trevino, Italy, was educated there, and entered the seminary at Padua in 1850. He was ordained there in 1858, engaged in pastoral work at Tombolo and Salzano during the next seventeen years, and was diocesan chancellor at Treviso, 1875–84. He was appointed bishop of Mantua in 1884 and in the next nine years successfully revived that run-down diocese. He was named cardinal and patriarch of Venice but did not occupy his see for eighteen months until 1894 because of the claim of the Italian government that it had the right to nominate the patriarch of Venice. He was elected Pope to succeed Pope Leo XIII, when Austria vetoed the nomination of front-running Cardinal Rampolla, on August 4, 1903. He began a codification of canon law, set up a commission to revise the Vulgate, reorganized the papal court and ordered a revision of the psalter and the breviary. He urged frequent reception of Holy Communion, especially by children, told Italian Catholics to become more actively involved in politics, and in 1905 broke off diplomatic relations with France when the antireligious government of that country unilaterally denounced the Concordat of 1801, demanded control of ecclesiastical affairs, and confiscated Church property when Pius refused its demands. Throughout his pontificate, he was concerned with the heresy of modernism, which he denounced in his encyclicals *Lamentabilis sane exitu* (1907) and *Pascendi dominici gregis* (1907), and he demanded an oath against modernism by every priest. In 1910, he condemned the "Sillon," a French social movement that was attempting to spread an adapted concept of the French Revolution, and Action Française, which was advocating an intransigent nationalism. He died in Rome on August 20, and was canonized by Pope Pius XII in 1954, the first Pope to be so honored since the canonization of Pope Pius V in 1712. August 21.

PLACENTINI, BL. ARCHANGELO (c. 1390–1460). Born on Sicily, he early in his life became a hermit there, moved to Alcano when crowds of visitors disturbed his solitude, and reorganized a run-down hospice there. He joined the Observant Franciscans at Palermo when Pope Martin V decreed that all hermits in Sicily must join a religious Order, founded a Franciscan house at Alcano, and was named provincial of the Sicilian Observants. He died on April 10 and his cult was approved in 1836. July 30.

PLACID (6th century). Son of the patrician Tertulus, he was placed in the care of St. Benedict at Subiaco by his father when quite young. Reputedly he was miraculously saved from drowning in a lake through Benedict's intercession and became the close confidant of Benedict, who probably took him with him when he went to Monte Cassino, which reportedly was given to Benedict by Tertulus. According to a twelfth-century source that is now regarded as a forgery but was then believed to have been written by a companion of Placid's named Gordian, Placid was sent to Sicily, where he founded St. John the Baptist Monastery at Messina. A few years later he was put to death with his two brothers, a sister, and more than thirty companions by Saracen pirates when they would not worship the gods of King Abdallah (the veracity of this report may be judged by the fact that there were no Moors in Spain in the sixth century and no Saracen attack on Sicily until a century later). When bones were unearthed during the rebuilding of St. John's Monastery in 1585, they were believed to be those of Placid and his companions, and a widespread cult approved by Pope Sixtus V developed.

Placid was never in Sicily, though an earlier Placid was martyred at Messina. October 5.

PLACID (d. c. 650). A wealthy landowner in Switzerland, he donated a tract of land to St. Sigisbert to found the Benedictine abbey of Dissentis about 614 and later became a monk there under Sigisbert, who was abbot. Placid was murdered several years later for defending the rights of the abbey. October 4. Sigisbert died several years later, and his cult was approved in 1905. July 11.

PLASDEN, POLYDORE (d. 1591). Born at London, England, he studied for the priesthood at Rheims and Rome and was ordained in Rome in 1586. He was sent on the English mission, was captured with St. Edmund Gennings and convicted of being a Catholic priest, and was hanged, drawn, and quartered at Tyburn on December 10. He was canonized in 1970 by Pope Paul VI as one of the Forty Martyrs of England and Wales.

PLATO (c. 734–814). Orphaned in Constantinople when he was thirteen, he was raised by his uncle, the imperial treasurer. When Plato was twenty-four, he gave the proceeds from the sale of his possessions to his sisters and to the poor and became a monk at Symboleon Monastery on Mount Olympus in Bithynia. He was elected abbot in 770, visited Constantinople in 775, and refused ordination and the bishopric of Nicomedia, but later accepted the abbacy of Sakkudion, which had been founded by the children of his sister Theoctista near Constantinople. After twelve years as abbot, he resigned in favor of his nephew, St. Theodore Studites. The two of them were leaders in the denunciation of Emperor Constantine Porphyrogenitus' divorce from Mary and his marriage to

Theodota; Plato was imprisoned and exiled by the Emperor, but after a time returned and lived as a hermit under Studites. He was again exiled, this time to the islands of the Bosporus by Emperor Nicephorus, was released in 811 by Emperor Michael I after four years, and returned to Constantinople, where he was bedridden the rest of his life until his death there on April 4.

PLEASINGTON, BL. WILLIAM. *See* Plessington, Bl. John.

PLECHELM (d. c. 730). *See* Wiro.

PLEGMUND (d. 914). Born in Mercia, England, he became a hermit on an island near Chester and was noted for his holiness. He became a member of King Arthur's court and at Arthur's request was named archbishop of Canterbury in 890 and consecrated in Rome by Pope Formosus. Plegmund went to Rome in 908 probably to secure approval of his archbishopric by Pope Sergius III, since Formosus' consecrations were condemned in 897 and 905. Plegmund probably died at Canterbury on August 2.

PLESSINGTON, JOHN (d. 1679). Born at Dimples Hall, Lancashire, England, son of a Royalist Catholic, he was educated at St. Omer's in France, and the English college at Valladolid, Spain, and was ordained at Segovia in 1662. He returned to England the next year and worked in the Cheshire area, using the aliases Scarisbrick and William Pleasington, and in 1670 became tutor to the children of a Mr. Massey at Puddington Hall near Chester. Fr. Plessington was arrested and charged with participating in the "popish plot," fabricated by Titus Oates, to murder King Charles II. Despite the clear evidence of Oates' perjury, Fr. Plessington was found guilty and hanged at Barrowshill at Boughton outside Chester on July

19. He was canonized by Pope Paul VI in 1970 as one of the Forty Martyrs of England and Wales.

PLUMTREE, BL. THOMAS (d. 1570). Born in Lincolnshire, England, he was educated at Oxford, received his degree in 1546, became pastor at Stubton, but resigned when Elizabeth became Queen. He was a schoolmaster in Lincoln, was forced to leave his position because of his Catholic religion, and served as chaplain to the rebels in the Rising of the Two Earls (the Rising of the North). When the rebellion was suppressed, he was captured, and when he refused his freedom if he would apostatize, he was hanged at Durham Castle on January 4. He was beatified in 1886. February 4.

PLUNKET, OLIVER (1629–81). He was born on November 1 at Loughcrew, Meath, Ireland, of a noble family that supported King Charles I and the cause of Irish freedom. He studied at St. Mary's Benedictine Abbey in Dublin, went to the Irish college in Rome when he was sixteen, and was ordained in 1654. He spent the next fifteen years in Rome serving as professor of theology at the College of the Propagation of the Faith, was consultor of the Sacred Congregation of the Index, and was procurator for the Irish bishops. In 1669, he was named archbishop of Armagh and Primate of All Ireland and was consecrated at Ghent. He returned to Ireland in 1670 and spent the next four years reorganizing his diocese, reforming the abuses that had arisen during the absences of persecuted bishops, enforcing clerical discipline, and improving relations between secular and order clergy. In 1673 the renewed persecution of Catholics forced many bishops to flee, and he was forced into hiding. In 1678, in the aftermath of the Titus Oates plot, all Catholic priests and bishops were ordered expelled from Ireland,

and on December 6, 1679, he was imprisoned in Dublin Castle on charges of conspiring to bring about a rebellion against the British crown. The charges were obviously false but he was removed to Newgate Prison in London, where he was kept in solitary confinement for nine months. In a travesty of a trial, he was convicted of high treason, complicity in the Titus Oates plot, and hanged, drawn, and quartered on July 1 at Tyburn, the last Catholic to suffer martyrdom there. He was canonized by Pope Paul VI in 1975, the first Irish saint to be canonized since St. Laurence O'Toole in 1226. July 1.

PLUTARCH (d. c. 202). With his brother St. Heraclas, he attended Origen's catechetical school at Alexandria, Egypt, where both were converted to Christianity by Origen. Plutarch was arrested for his faith during the persecution of Christians under Emperor Septimus Severus and executed. Two women attending the school, Marcella and her daughter Potamiaena, were also arrested; Potamiaena was put to death with boiling pitch, and her mother was executed soon after. Also executed at that time was Basilides, who led Potamiaena to her death, was converted by a vision of her, was baptized in prison, and was then beheaded. June 28.

POEMEN (d. c. 450). With several brothers, he retired to Skete in the Egyptian desert to live as hermits. In 408, they were forced to flee Berber raids and set up a community in the ruins of a pagan temple at Terenuthis, with Poemen and his brother Anubis alternating as abbot. Poemen lived a life of great austerity, became sole abbot on Anubis' death, and was known for his insistence on frequent Communion, his holiness, and his short, pithy statements of spiritual wisdom and advice. August 27.

POLE, BL. MARGARET (1471–1541). Margaret Plantagenet, daughter of the duke of Clarence and niece of Kings Edward IV and Richard III of England, was born at Farley Castle near Bath, England, on August 14, and in about 1491 married Sir Richard Pole. When Henry VIII became King, she was widowed with five children and had her estates, which had been forefeited by attainder, returned by Henry, who made her countess of Salisbury. She was governess of the King's daughter Anne, but incurred his enmity by her disapproval of his marriage to Anne Boleyn, despite his remark that she was the holiest woman in England, and was forced to leave the court. When her son Reginald Cardinal Pole wrote against the Act of Supremacy, Henry swore to destroy the family. In 1538, two other sons were arrested and executed on a charge of treason, even though Cromwell wrote that their only crime was being brothers of the cardinal. Margaret was arrested ten days later and in May 1599 Parliament passed a bill of attainder against her for complicity in a revolt in the North, and she was imprisoned in the Tower. When another uprising occurred in Yorkshire in April 1541, she was summarily beheaded on May 28 at the Tower. She was never tried and no guilt was ever proven against her except her possession of a white silk tunic embroidered with the Five Wounds, which was supposed to connect her with the uprising in the North. She was beatified in 1886.

POLLIO (d. 304). A lector in the church at Cybalae, Lower Pannonia (Mikanovici, Yugoslavia), he became leader of the Christians there after Bishop Eusebius was martyred. When he defied the edicts of Emperor Diocletian and refused to sacrifice to the gods, he was condemned to death and burned at the stake. April 28.

POLYCARP (c. 69–c. 155). A disciple of St. John the apostle, he became bishop of Smyrna and was reputedly consecrated by John. Polycarp was a stanch defender of orthodoxy and an energetic opponent of heresy, especially Velentinianism and Marcionism. A letter to him from St. John has survived, as has his *Epistle to the Philippians*, in which he quotes from 1 John 4:3 and warns the Philippians against the false teachings of Marcion, whom he once called "the firstborn of Satan," and which was widely read in Asian churches. Toward the end of his life he visited Pope Anicetus in Rome, and when they could not agree on a date for Easter decided each should observe his own date. Soon after Polycarp's return to Smyrna, when he was eighty (according to Eusebius), he was arrested when the persecution of Christians under Emperor Marcus Aurelius broke out. When Polycarp refused to sacrifice to the gods and acknowledge the Emperor's divinity, he was ordered burned to death at the stake. When the flames failed to consume him, he was speared to death on February 23. Polycarp was probably the leading Christian in Roman Asia in the second century and an important link between the apostolic age and the great Christian writers of the late second century. The *Martyrium Polycarpi,* written in the name of the church of Smyrna and evidently from eyewitness accounts of his arrest, trial, and martyrdom, is the oldest authentic example of the *acta* of a martyr. February 23.

POLYEUCTUS (d. 259). A pagan Roman army officer of Greek parentage stationed at Melitene, Armenia, he was converted to Christianity by his friend Nearchus and was imprisoned and tortured when he proclaimed his Christianity; when he refused to apostatize, he was beheaded. A famous seventeenth-century French dramatist, Pierre Cor-

neille, made him the hero of his tragedy *Polyeucte.* February 13.

POLYXENA (1st century). *See* Xantippa.

PONGRACZ, BL. STEPHEN (1582–1619). A Croatian born at Alvinez, he became a Jesuit at Brünn (Brno, Moravia), taught theology at Graz, 1611–15, went to Slovakia as a missionary with Bl. Mark Körösy and Bl. Melchior Grodecz and was tortured and executed with them at Kaschau (Kosice, Slovakia) by Calvinists. They were beatified in 1905. September 7.

PONTIAN (d. c. 236). A Roman and son of Calpurnius, he was elected Pope to succeed Pope St. Urban I on July 21, 230. He held a synod at Rome in 232 that confirmed the condemnation of Origenism at Alexandria, 231–32. At the beginning of the persecution of Christians under Emperor Maximinus Pontian was exiled to Sardinia, probably to the mines there, where he met exiled antipope Hippolytus and reconciled him to the Church. Pontian resigned his office on September 28, 235, to allow the election of a nephew and probably died of ill treatment, though a tradition says he was beaten to death. August 13.

PONTICUS (d. 177). *See* Pothinus.

PONTIUS (d. c. 258). Supposedly the son of a Roman senator, he was instructed by Pope Pontian, gave his wealth to the poor on the death of his father, converted Emperor Philippus and his son, and when Philippus was murdered in 249, Pontius fled to Cimella (Cimiez, France). He lived there until he was arrested and beheaded for his Christianity. May 14.

PONTIUS (d. c. 260). Deacon of Cyprian, bishop of Carthage, he accompanied the bishop into exile in Curubia and later wrote a laudatory biography of him, *Vita et passio Cypriani,* which was praised by St. Jerome. March 8.

PONTIUS OF FAUCIGNY, BL. (d. 1178). Born of a noble family in Savoy, he became a canon regular at Abondance Abbey at Chablais when he was twenty, revised its constitutions, and in 1144 became the founding abbot of Sixt Monastery. After serving as abbot for twenty-eight years, he was named abbot of Abondance, resigned shortly after, and retired to Sixt (Switzerland), where he died on November 26. His cult was confirmed in 1896.

POPPO (978–1048). Born in Flanders, he served for a time in the army, refused an arranged marriage, and after a pilgrimage to Rome, became a Benedictine monk at St. Thierry's near Rheims, France, in 1006. He was transferred to St. Vanne at the request of Abbot Richard there in about 1008 and restored the monasteries at Beaulieu and Arras. He became abbot of Stavelot, acted as superior of a group of monasteries in Lotharingia, and was a counselor to Emperor St. Henry II. Poppo died at Marchiennes on January 25.

PORCARIUS (d. c. 732). Abbot of Lérins off the coast of Provence, he had a vision that the abbey was about to be attacked. He sent the younger members of the community to safety on the only available ship, and he and the rest of the religious at the abbey were slaughtered by marauding Moors except for four who were carried off as slaves to Spain or to northern Africa. August 12.

PORMORT, VEN. THOMAS (c. 1559–92). Born at Hull, England, he studied at Cambridge, went to Rheims to study for the priesthood, and was ordained in Rome. After serving as prefect of studies at the Swiss college in Milan in 1591, he

was sent on the English mission. He was captured twice in 1591 and released, but in 1592, he was again arrested and this time was tortured and then hanged at London on February 20 for being a Catholic priest.

PORPHYRY (d. 309). *See* Elias.

PORPHYRY (d. 362). A horse trader who was also an actor, he was in the middle of a performance, a burlesque on baptism that was attended by Emperor Julian the Apostate, when Porphyry suddenly broke off the performance and announced he was a Christian. He was executed on the spot. September 15.

PORPHYRY (353–420). Born at Thessalonica (Salonika), Macedonia, he became a monk in the desert of Skete, Egypt, when he was twenty-five. After five years in a monastery there, he spent the next five years living as a hermit on the Jordan in Palestine and then took up residence in Jerusalem. He had a friend, Mark, who became his disciple and confidant, sell his inheritance. Porphyry gave the proceeds to the poor, lived in great austerity as a shoemaker, and in 393, when he was forty, was ordained. He was named bishop of Gaza, Palestine, in 396, encountered much opposition from the pagans in his see, but was greatly aided by a decision of Emperor Arcadius that a temple to Marnas that had been the source of much difficulty for the Christians in Gaza be destroyed. The Emperor's emissary, Cynegius, also destroyed all other pagan temples and idols; rioting broke out, and Porphyry's life was threatened. He later built a church on the site of Marnas' temple, and by the time of his death in Gaza on February 26, he had eliminated paganism in his see.

PORRAS, RAPHAELA (1850–1925). Born at Pedro Abad near Cordova,

Spain, on March 1, she was the daughter of the mayor, who died when she was four. She and her sister Dolores joined the Sisters of Marie Reparatrice in 1873; when the bishop of the diocese, Ceferino Gonzalez, asked the community to leave his diocese, Raphaela and fifteen other novices remained behind to form a new community. When ready to take their vows in 1877, Bishop Gonzalez presented them with an entirely new rule; whereupon they left Cordova and settled at Madrid. After much initial confusion, Raphaela and Dolores took their vows later in 1877, and the Handmaids of the Sacred Heart, devoted to teaching children and helping at retreats, was founded. Approval from the Holy See was granted in the same year, with Raphaela as mother general. The new congregation was disturbed by differences between Raphaela and Dolores but despite this friction spread throughout Spain and abroad. Mother Raphaela resigned in 1893, lived the remaining thirty-two years of her life in obscurity in the Roman house of the congregation, and died there on January 6. She was canonized in 1977 by Pope Paul VI.

PORRES, MARTIN DE (1579–1639). Born at Lima, Peru, on November 9, he was the illegitimate son of John de Porres, a Spanish knight, and Anna, a freed Panamanian. He was apprenticed to a barber-surgeon when he was twelve and in 1594 became a Dominican lay brother at Rosary Convent in Lima. He served in various offices in the convent—barber, infirmarian, wardrobe keeper—and was active in caring for the sick throughout the city. He founded an orphanage and foundling hospital, was put in charge of the convent's food distribution to the poor, and ministered to African slaves brought to Peru. A close friend of St. Rose of Lima, his prodigious efforts to help the poor and his ho-

liness and penances caused him to be venerated by all. He is reputed to have been gifted with supernatural gifts, among them bilocation and aerial flights. He died at Rosary Convent on November 3, and was canonized in 1962 by Pope John XXIII. He is the patron of interracial justice.

PORRO, BL. JOHN ANGELO (d. 1506). Born at Milan, Italy, he joined the Servants of Mary (the Servites), was ordained, and was sent to Monte Senario to live as a contemplative. After a year there, he was appointed master of novices at Florence and served at various other houses, instructing the poor and the illiterate. He died at the Servite prior at Milan, and his cult was approved in 1737. October 24.

POSADAS, BL. FRANCIS DE (1644–1713). Born at Cordova, Spain, he was apprenticed in his youth but persisted in his desire to be a priest and joined the Dominicans in 1663 at Scala Caeli Convent in Cordova. He was ordained, became known for the eloquence of his preaching, and for forty years gave missions all over western Spain. He was much sought after as a confessor, was noted for his holiness and humility, and is reported to have had the gift of levitation. He wrote several books, among them a biography of St. Dominic and *The Triumph of Chastity*. He died at Scala Caeli on September 20, and was beatified in 1818.

POSSENTI, GABRIEL (1838–62). The eleventh of thirteen children of Sante Possenti, a lawyer in Assisi, Italy, he was christened Francis and was educated at the Jesuit college at Spoleto. He joined the Jesuits when he was seventeen after he had vowed to do so if cured of an almost fatal illness, but delayed entering the novitiate and finally in 1856 became a Passionist at Morroville with the name

Br. Gabriel of Our Lady of Sorrows. He led an exemplary life as a religious, filled with penances and self-effacement, was ordained but stricken with tuberculosis, and died at Isola di Gran Sasso in the Abruzzi on February 27 when he was only twenty-four. He was canonized in 1920.

POSSIDIUS (d. c. 440). Born in Africa, he studied under St. Augustine and was named bishop of Calama, Numidia, about 397. He was so active in his opposition to the Donatists that they attempted to assassinate him and he fought the Pelagians, especially at the Council of Milevum in 416. He took refuge with Augustine when the Vandals overran Numidia; Augustine died in his arms. Possidius died in exile, according to tradition at Mirandola, Italy. He wrote a life of Augustine that contained a bibliography of the saint's writings. May 16.

POSTEL, MARY MAGDALEN (1756–1846). Born at Barfleur, France, on November 28 and baptized Julia Frances Catherine, she was educated at the Benedictine convent at Valognes, and when eighteen she opened a school for girls at Barfleur. When the French Revolution broke out, the revolutionaries closed the school and she became a leader in Barfleur against the constitutional priests and sheltered fugitive priests in her home, where Mass was celebrated. When the concordat of 1801 between Napoleon and the Holy See brought peace to the French Church, she worked in the field of religious education, and in 1807, at Cherbourg, she and three other teachers took religious vows before Abbé Cabart, who had encouraged her in her work—the beginning of the Sisters of the Christian Schools of Mercy. She was named superior and took the name Mary Magdalen. During the next few years the community encountered great difficulties and was forced to move several times before settling at Tamersville in 1815. It was not until she obtained the abbey of St. Sauveur le Vicomte that the congregation finally began to expand and flourish. She died on July 16 at St. Sauveur, venerated for her holiness and miracles, and was canonized in 1925.

POSTGATE, VEN. NICHOLAS (c. 1596–1679). Born at Kirkdale House, Egton, Yorkshire, England, he studied for the priesthood at Douai and was ordained in 1628. He was sent on the English mission two years later, ministered to the Catholics of his native land for years until arrested near Whitby, and when convicted of being a Catholic priest, was executed at York on August 7.

POTAMIAENA (d. c. 202). *See* Plutarch.

POTAMON (d. c. 340). Bishop of Heraclea, Egypt, he was tortured so severely during the persecution of Christians under Emperor Maximinus that he lost an eye and was permanently crippled. He was active at the Council of Nicaea in 325, defended Athanasius at the Council of Tyre in 335, and was beaten to death for his orthodoxy and uncompromising opposition to Arianism during the reign of Arian Emperor Constantius II. May 18.

POTHINUS (d. 177). Bishop of Lyons and Vienne, Gaul, and also known as Photinus, he was ninety years old when, during the persecution of Christians under Emperor Marcus Aurelius, he and forty-seven other Christians were publicly humiliated, stoned, imprisoned, subjected to terrible tortures, and then executed for their faith. Among them were Alexander, a physician who had just been baptized; Maturus, a catechumen; fifteen-year-old Ponticus; Sanctus, a deacon of Vienne; Vettius Epagathus, their defense attorney; Attalus from

Perganos; Blanding, a slave; and Biblias. They are known as the Martyrs of Lyons and Vienne, and the description of their sufferings and martyrdoms, ascribed to St. Irenaeus and reproduced in the works of Eusebius, the historian, is the earliest and fullest authentic document of its kind. June 2.

POWELL, BL. EDWARD (c. 1478–1540). Born in Wales, he became a fellow at Oriel College, Oxford, received his doctorate in theology in 1506, and then became a fellow at Salisbury. In 1523, he published a book denouncing Luther, was one of the four canonists selected by Catherine of Aragon to defend her against Henry VIII's divorce suit, and incurred the enmity of Henry when he spoke against the divorce at the Convocation in 1529 and wrote a book setting forth his views. He made other enemies by his eloquent preaching defending the marriage and in 1534 was imprisoned at Dorchester, removed to the Tower in London, and kept in solitary confinement there for six years. All his property was confiscated for his denial of the supremacy of the Church of England over Rome, and in 1540 he was attainted for high treason for the same reason. He was hanged, drawn, and quartered at Smithfield on July 30 with Bl. Thomas Abel and Bl. Richard Fetherston. All three were beatified in 1886.

POWELL, BL. PHILIP (1594–1646). Born at Tralon, Brecknockshire, England, on February 2, he studied law at the Temple in London, joining the Benedictines at Douai, and was ordained in 1621. He was sent on the English mission the following year, assuming the alias Morgan, and spent the next two decades working among the Catholics of Devon, Somerset, and Cornwall, serving as an army chaplain during the Civil War. After the war, he was arrested while on the way to Wales, denounced for his priesthood, and imprisoned in London. He was tried, and when found guilty of being a Catholic priest, he was hanged, drawn, and quartered at Tyburn. He was beatified in 1929. June 30.

PRAEJECTUS (d. 676). Also known as Prix, Prest, and Preils, he was born in Auvergne, studied under Bishop Genesius of that city, and in about 666 was named bishop of Clermont. He founded monasteries, churches, and hospitals and was known for his learning and eloquence and for his aid to the poor. When Hector, patricius of Marseilles, was executed for an alleged conspiracy against King Childeric II of Austrasia, some of Hector's followers blamed Praejectus for his death, and he was assassinated by a group of men led by Agritius at Volvic near Clermont, with St. Amarin, abbot of a monastery in the Vosges, on January 25.

PRAESIDIUS (d. c. 484). See Donatian.

PRAETEXTATUS (d. 586). Also known as Prix, he was named bishop of Rouen in 549 and during the thirty-five years of his bishopric was drawn into the struggle between the sons of Clotaire I; Chilperic, who inherited Neustria, and Sigebert I, who inherited Austrasia, each of whom intrigued and warred against the other to gain the whole kingdom of their father. Praetextatus incurred the enmity of Fredegunde, Chilperic's mistress and later wife, who caused the murder of Sigebert and his sons (and probably Chilperic as well) to ensure the throne for her son Clotaire II, because of Praetextatus' constant censuring and denunciations of her actions. He was exiled after a trial of bishops in Paris after admitting he had helped Meroveus, Chilperic's son by his first marriage, in an uprising, although he denied the further charge that he had officiated at the marriage of Meroveus and his Stepaunt Brunhilda, Sigebert's widow. After the death of Chilperic in 584, King Gontram of Burgundy permitted Praetextatus to return, but he was stabbed to death in his church by an assassin sent by Fredegunde. February 24.

PRAXEDES (date unknown). According to untrustworthy legend, she was the daughter of Roman Senator Pudens and the sister of St. Pudentiana and helped care for and hide Christians during the persecution of Christians during the reign of Emperor Marcus Aurelius. She died on July 21, and though she was buried near Pudentiana in the catacombs of Priscilla, scholars doubt that they are sisters or that she was the daughter of a senator.

PRICHARD, VEN. HUMPHREY (d. 1589). *See* Nichols, Ven. George.

PRIMALDI (or GRIMALDI), BL. ANTONY (d. 1480). An elderly artisan of Otranto in southern Italy, he was beheaded during the massacre of some eight hundred men of the town by marauding Turks under Mohammed II when Bl. Antony encouraged and rallied them to refuse to denounce their Christianity and become Moslems. His cult was approved in 1771. August 14.

PRIMITIVUS (d. c. 120). *See* Getulius.

PRIMITIVUS (d. 304). *See* Optatus.

PRIMUS (d. c. 297). *See* Felician.

PRISCA (1st century). *See* Aquila; Priscilla.

PRISCA (d. c. 270). Also known as Priscilla, she had a very early cult in Rome, seems to have suffered martyrdom, and was buried in the catacomb of Priscilla there. Beyond that nothing is known of her. January 18.

PRISCILLA (d. c. 98). Wife of Mancius Aeilius Glabrio, who was executed by Domitian probably because he was a Christian, she is probably the mother of St. Pudens, the senator, and her home on Via Salaria was used by St. Peter as his headquarters in Rome. The catacomb of Priscilla under her home was named after her. She is also known as Prisca. January 16.

PRISCILLA (1st century). *See* Aquila.

PRISCILLA (d. c. 270). *See* Prisca.

PRISCUS (d. 260). *See* Alexander.

PRISCUS (d. c. 272). Also known as Prix, he and Cottus, a fellow citizen of Besançon, France, fled to escape the persecution of Christians under Emperor Aurelian but were captured with other Christians at Auxerre and put to death by sword. May 26.

PRIX. *See* Praejectus; Praetextatus; Priscus (d. c. 272).

PROBUS (d. 304). *See* Tarachus.

PROCESSUS (1st century). *See* Martinian.

PROCLUS (d. 446). Born at Constantinople, he was a disciple of St. John Chrysostom, became a lector, and then was secretary to John's opponent, Patriarch Atticus of Constantinople, who ordained him. He was named bishop of Cyzicus but the people there would not accept him. In 428 Nestorius was named Patriarch of Constantinople by Emperor Theodosius II, and Proclus, by now famed for his preaching, opposed his teachings. In 434, Maximian, who had succeeded Nestorius when he was deposed in 431, died, and Proclus was named Patriarch of Constantinople. He continued his opposition to Nestorianism, ministered to the people of the city when it was struck with a devastating earthquake, and was known for his dedication and tactful handling of those with whom he disagreed. He wrote several treatises, notably *Tome to the Armenians,* which opposed the Nestorian-flavored teaching of Theodore of Mopsuestia without mentioning him by name. Several of his letters and sermons have survived. He died on July 24. October 24.

PROCOPIUS (d. 303). Born at Jerusalem, he moved to Scythopolis (Bethsan) and became a lector, translator, and exorcist at the church there. During the persecution of Christians under Emperor Diocletian, he was arrested at Caesarea and brought before Flavian, who urged him to sacrifice to the gods and/or the Emperor. When he refused, he was beheaded. He is called "the Great" by Bishop Eusebius of Caesarea, who wrote the story of his martyrdom. July 8.

PROCULUS (2nd century). *See* Florus.

PROCULUS (d. c. 305). *See* Januarius.

PROCULUS (d. 542). Born at Bologna, Italy, he was named bishop of that city in 540 and two years later suffered martyrdom under Totila the Goth. It is believed he may be the same as St. Proculus, bishop of Terni. June 1.

PROCULUS THE SOLDIER (d. c. 304). Believed to have been an officer in the Roman army, he was beheaded for his faith at Bologna during the reign of Emperor Maximian, though St. Paulinus of Nola states he was crucified. He was long venerated as the patron of Bologna. June 1.

PROSPER (d. c. 466). Bishop of Reggio, Emilia, Italy, he was known for his char-

ities and ruled his see for twenty-two years until his death on June 25.

PROSPER OF AQUITAINE (c. 390–c. 465). Probably a layman who may have been married, he left Aquitaine for Provence and settled at Marseilles. He wrote to St. Augustine in 428, and in response, Augustine wrote his treatises on perseverance and predestination. Prosper opposed the semi-Pelagianism of St. John Cassian, accompanied his friend Hilary, who had asked him to write to Augustine, on a trip to visit Pope St. Celestine I in Rome, and is said to have become a secretary to Pope St. Leo the Great in Rome, where Prosper died. He wrote poetry and treatises, notably his *Chronicle,* a universal history from creation to the Vandal capture of Rome in 455. June 25.

PROTASE (1st century). *See* Gervase.

PROTERIUS (d. 457). Ordained by St. Cyril, Patriarch of Alexandria, he became the leader of the orthodox in Alexandria. Though appointed archpriest by Dioscorus, Cyril's successor, he opposed him when he supported Eutyches, and when Dioscorus was denounced and condemned at the Council of Chalcedon in 451, Proterius was elected Patriarch to replace him. The inhabitants of the city took sides, two opposing factions developed, and violence broke out. When Dioscorus died, his adherents elected Elurus his successor, and when Elurus was driven from the city by the imperial commander, his followers rioted and stabbed Proterius to death on February 28.

PROTUS. *See* Cantianella.

PROTUS (3rd century). *See* Hyacinth.

PRUDENCE, BL. *See* Casatori, Bl. Prudence.

PRUDENTIUS (d. 861). Born in Spain and baptized Galindo, he fled to Gaul to escape the Saracens' persecutions and studied at the Palatine school, where he changed his name to Prudentius. He was elected bishop of Troyes in 840 or 845 and was known for his learning and as a theologian. He was appointed by Bishop Hincmar of Rheims to judge the case of a monk named Gottschalk, whom Hincmar had tortured, imprisoned, and excommunicated for teaching that God would save only the elect and condemn most of humanity. Prudentius defended the theory of double predestination and that Christ died only for those who are saved—a theory that set off a widespread dispute. He wrote a still extant treatise against John Scotus Erigena in 851, *De praedistinatione contra Johannem Scotem,* a defense of his own theory, *Epistola tractoria ad Wenilonem,* in 856 and a history of the western Franks, *Annales Bertiani.* He died at Troyes on April 6, and though his feast is kept at Troyes, he is not otherwise recognized as a saint.

PTOLEMY (d. 250). *See* Ammon.

PTOLOMAEUS (d. c. 161). Denounced as a Christian by a man whose wife had been converted to Christianity by Ptolomaeus and left him, he was imprisoned and then sentenced to death by the magistrate, Urbicius. When Lucius, a bystander, protested the sentence, he too was sentenced to die with a third unnamed man when Urbicius found that they were Christians. October 19.

PUBLIA (d. c. 370). A widow in Antioch, Syria, she established a community of women there. Supposedly Julian the Apostate, on his way to fight the Persians in 362, passed their house and denounced their singing of the 115th Psalm as a personal insult; reportedly he planned to have them executed on his return from Persia— where he died in battle. October 9.

PUBLIUS (d. c. 112). Prefect of the island of Malta, he was host to Paul when the apostle was on his way to Rome as a prisoner; Paul cured his father of fever and dysentery (Acts 28:7–10). According to tradition, Publius later became the first bishop of Malta, though another tradition has him bishop of Athens and suffering martyrdom there during the reign of Emperor Trajan. January 21.

PUBLIUS (d. 303). *See* Optatus.

PUBLIUS (d. c. 380). Son of a senator at Zeugma, he sold his possessions, gave the proceeds to the poor, and became a hermit in the Euphrates area. He was later elected abbot of his community of hermits, imposed a strict rule, and lived in great austerity. He later founded two congregations, one of Greeks and the other of Syrians. January 25.

PUCCI, ANTONY (1819–92). Born at Poggiole, Italy, on April 16, and christened Eustace, his parents were peasants and opposed his religious vocation. He joined the Servites at Florence in 1837, taking the name Antony Mary, and was ordained in 1843. He became curate at Viareggio, was named pastor in 1847, and spent the rest of his life there engaged in pastoral activities. He was particularly active in the religious education of children and in helping the sick and the poor, especially during the virulent epidemics in 1854 and 1866, and was one of the pioneers of the Holy Childhood Society. He died at Viareggio on January 14, and was canonized by Pope John XXIII in 1962. January 12.

PUCCHI-FRANCESCHI, BL. BARTHOLOMEW (d. 1330). A wealthy resident of Montepulciano, he was married, but with the consent of his wife, who took a vow of chastity, he became a Franciscan priest, was known for his holiness and visions, and was reputed to have performed miracles. He died on May 6 at Montepulciano when quite old, and his cult was confirmed in 1880. May 23.

PUDENS. *See* Pudentiana.

PUDENTIANA (d. c. 160). A lady of Rome, the daughter of Pudens, whom some scholars believe is the same Pudens mentioned in 2 Timothy 4:21, she gave her wealth to the poor and helped bury martyred Christians. May 19.

PULCHERIA (399–453). Daughter of Emperor Arcadius and Empress Eudoxia, she was born on January 19 and lost her father in 408 when she was nine. Her younger brother Theodosius was proclaimed Emperor, and in 414 she was named *augusta* and regent of Theodosius by the Senate. She took a vow of virginity, devoted herself to the raising and education of her brother, changed the atmosphere of the court to an almost monastic environment, and in effect ran the Empire. In 421, Theodosius married Athenais, who was then baptized Eudocia, and two years later named her *augusta*. The clash between the two *augustae* was inevitable. Eudocia supported Nestorius, but Pulcheria was stanchly orthodox and eventually con-

vinced Theodosius to condemn Nestorius. Court intrigue, encouraged and abetted by Eudocia, caused Pulcheria to be banished from the court, but in 441, Eudocia was exiled to Jerusalem because of infidelity to the Emperor, and Pulcheria was recalled. When Theodosius supported Eutyches and his monophysitism and approved the decrees of the Robber Synod of Ephesus in 449, Pulcheria supported the plea of Pope St. Leo the Great for orthodoxy. In 450, Theodosius was killed in a fall from his horse while hunting, and Pulcheria was proclaimed Empress. She then married the aged General Marcian, with the condition he respect her virginity, and the two ruled the Empire. They sponsored the Council of Chalcedon in 451 (she attended the third session), which condemned monophysitism, and in a letter to her in 451, Pope Leo credited her with overcoming the Nestorian and Eutychian heresies and for the recall of the Catholic bishops who had been exiled by Theodosius. She built many churches, hospitals, and hospices and encouraged the building of a university in Constantinople, where she died in July. September 10.

PUSICIUS (d. 341). *See* Simeon Barsabae.

QUADRATUS (d. c. 129). Possibly a disciple of the apostles, he is believed to have been bishop of Athens and perhaps the author of a defense of Christianity addressed to Emperor Hadrian. May 26.

QUENTIN (d. 287). Also known as Quintinus, according to legend he was a Roman, went to Gaul as a missionary with St. Lucian of Beauvais, and settled at Amiens in Picardy. He was so successful in preaching that he was imprisoned by Prefect Rictiovarus, tortured, and then brought to Augusta Veromanduorum (Saint-Quentin), where he was again tortured and then was beheaded. October 31.

QUENTIN. *See* Quintius.

QUINTA (d. 249). *See* Apollonia.

QUINTILIAN (d. 304). *See* Optatus.

QUINTINUS. *See* Quentin.

QUINTIUS (d. c. 570). Born at Tours, Gaul, and also known as Quentin, he became an official at the Frankish court. When he rejected the attempts of the Queen, probably Fredegunde, to seduce him, she had him murdered at L'Indrois near Montresor. October 4.

QUINZANI, BL. STEPHANA (1457–1530). Born near Brescia, Italy, she became a Dominican tertiary at Soncino when she was fifteen, devoted herself to ministering to the poor and the sick, and founded a convent at Soncino. She experienced ecstasies, including participating in the various stages of the Passion, which was attested to by twenty-one witnesses in 1497 in an account that is still extant, and was credited with performing numerous miracles of healing. She died on January 2, and her cult was confirmed in 1740.

QUIRIACUS. *See* Cyriacus (d. c. 133).

QUIRICUS. *See* Julitta.

QUIRINUS (d. 308). Bishop of Siscia (Sisak, Croatia) during the persecution of Christians under Emperor Diocletian, he fled the city to escape arrest but was captured. Haled before Maximus, the magistrate, he refused to sacrifice to the gods and was brought to Amantius, the governor of Pannonia Prima. When he persisted in his refusal, he was drowned in the Raab River at Sabaria (Szombathely, Hungary). June 4.

QUITERIA (5th century). According to legend, she was the daughter of a Galician prince who fled to escape his demand that she marry and give up her Christianity. His followers found her at Aire, Gascony, and on his orders, beheaded her there. May 22.

R

RABANUS MAURUS, BL. (c. 784–856). Probably born at Mainz, Germany (though possibly in Ireland or Scotland), he was educated at the monastery school of Fulda under Abbot Bangulf and at Tours under Alcuin, whose favorite he became. He returned to Fulda as a monk, became known for his learning and knowledge of the early Church Fathers and the Bible, and in about 799 became master of Fulda's monastery school. He was ordained in 815, became abbot in 822, completed the monastery buildings, and founded several churches and monasteries. He resigned his abbacy to go into retirement, but in 847, at seventy-one, he was named archbishop of Mainz. He imposed strict discipline on his clergy (which led to an abortive conspiracy on his life), held two synods that condemned the heretical teaching of Gottschalk, a monk in his see, and helped alleviate a famine by feeding the poor at his house. He wrote a martyrology; poetry, including the hymn *Veni Creator Spiritus;* and some sixty-four of his homilies are still extant. He died at Winkel, near Mainz. February 4.

RABATA, BL. ALOYSIUS (c. 1430–90). He became a Carmelite at Trapani, Sicily, later was prior of the friary at Randazzo, and was known for his austerity, humility, and holiness. He was murdered by a fugitive from justice. May 11.

RADBOD (d. 918). Grandson of the last pagan king of Friesland, he was educated by his Uncle Gunther, bishop of Cologne, became a Benedictine monk, was named bishop of Utrecht in 900, and was known for his aid to the poor and as a poet. He died at Deventer, Flanders, where he had moved his see because of a Danish invasion. November 29.

RADEGUND (518–87). Daughter of Berthaire, pagan king of a portion of Thuringia, she was probably born at Erfurt, Thuringia, Germany. Her father was murdered by his brother Hermenefrid, who in 531 was defeated by King Theodoric of Austrasia and King Clotaire I of Neustria, and Clotaire took twelve-year-old Radegund captive; six years later he married her. She devoted herself to the poor, the sick, and captives, founded a leper hospital, and bore Clotaire's cruelties uncomplainingly until he murdered her brother Unstrut. She then left the court, received the deaconess habit from Bishop Médard at Noyon, and became a nun at Saix. About 557, she built the double monastery of the Holy Cross at Poitiers, to which she retired and which she developed into a great center of learning. She was active in peacemaking roles, lived in great austerity, and secured a relic of the True Cross for the church of her monastery. She lived the last years of her life in seclusion and died at the monastery on August 13. Venantius Fortunatus, a priest at Poitiers, wrote her biography.

RADULF. *See* Ralph (d. 866).

RAFAELA MARIA OF THE SACRED HEART. *See* Porras, Raphaela.

RAINERIUS (d. 1160). Born at Pisa, Italy, he led a dissolute life in his youth but was reformed by Alberto Leccapecore, a monk from San Vito Monastery. While on a business trip to Palestine, he had a religious experience that led him to become a penitential pilgrim. On his return home he lived at Santa Maria, then St. Andrew Abbey, and finally at St. Vitus Monastery, all in Pisa, leading the life of the cloister though he never did become a religious. He died at St. Vitus and had numerous miracles attributed to him after he died. He was sometimes called De Aqua for his use of holy water in his miracles of healing. June 17.

RAINERIUS INCLUSUS (d. 1237). A hermit at Osnabrück, Lower Saxony, Germany, he acquired his surname because he was enclosed in a cell next to the cathedral for twenty-two years. He was known for his great austerities, extreme mortifications, and practice of silence. April 11.

RAINUZZI, BL. JOHN (d. c. 1330). Bones discovered in a marble tomb in St. Margaret Church in Todi, Italy, are believed to be those of John Rainuzzi, a Benedictine monk known as John the Almsgiver for his charities. He died on June 8.

RALPH (d. 866). Also known as Raoul and Radulf, he was the son of Count Raoul of Cahors. He was educated under Abbot Bertrand of Solignac, served as abbot of several abbeys, though he does not seem to have been a monk, and in 840 was named bishop of Bourges. He attended numerous synods, among them the Synod of Meaux in 845, founded several monasteries and convents, was known for his learning, and compiled a summary of pastoral in-

structions for his clergy. He died on June 21.

RAMÓN LULL. *See* Raymond Lull.

RAMOTA, BL. PACIFICO (1424–82). Born at Novara, Piedmont, Italy, he was educated at the Benedictine abbey there, joined the Franciscans of the Strict Observance when he was twenty-one, and was ordained. He was a successful missionary in northern Italy for nineteen years, interrupted by a commission from Pope Sixtus IV to reform the Church in Sardinia, and founded a convent at Vigevano. He was ordered back to Sardinia by Sixtus in 1480 as visitor for the convents of the Strict Observance and as apostolic nuncio and to preach a crusade against Mohammed II. Bl. Pacifico was taken ill shortly after he arrived at Sardinia and died at Sassari on June 4. His treatise on moral theology, *Sommetta di Pacifica Coscienza* (1475), became a standard text on the subject. His cult was confirmed in 1745. June 9.

RANUZZI, BL. JEROME (d. 1455). Born at Sant' Angelo in Vado, Italy, he became a Servite there when he was twenty. He received his doctorate at the University of Bologna, was ordained, and taught at various Servite schools. He returned to the priory at Sant' Angelo, served as adviser to the duke of Urbino, and rebuilt the nuns' convent at Sant' Angelo. He died on December 11, revered for his holiness and learning. His cult was confirmed in 1775.

RAOUL. *See* Ralph (d. 866).

RAPHAEL. One of the seven archangels "who stand before the Lord" (Tob. 12:12, 15), he was sent by God to minister to Tobias and Sara and accompanied young Tobias into Media disguised as a man named Azarias. His name in Hebrew means "God heals," and he is identified as the angel who "healed" the earth when it was defiled by the sins of the fallen angels in the apochryphal Enoch (10:7) and who moved the waters of the healing sheep-pool (John 5:1–4). He is one of only three archangels identified by name, with Michael and Gabriel, in the Bible and has been venerated for ages in both the Jewish and the Christian traditions. September 29.

RASSO. See Ratho, Bl.

RATHO, BL. (d. 953). Also known as Grafath, Ratto, Rasso, Rago, and Rapoto, the Graf von Andechs was the son of the count of Diessen and Andechs in Bavaria. He became famous for his imposing stature and knightly feats of arms and was a leader of the Bavarians against the Hungarian invaders. In 948, he went on pilgrimage to Rome and the Holy Land and on his return built Wörth Monastery (now called Grafath) below Rassoburg Castle in 151. He donated to it relics he had brought back from the Holy Land, became a monk, and died there. May 17.

RAVASCO, BL. EUGENIA. (1845–1900). Founder of the Congregation of the Sisters of the Sacred Hearts of Jesus and Mary, or the Ravasco Institute, Eugenia, in the spirit of Pope Leo XIII's encyclical "Rerum Novarum," spent her life in the service of disadvantaged young women. Despite anticlerical persecution in her region, she persevered courageously to open a Christian school for girls and secular schools for the poor, and to devote herself to the dying and imprisoned. Bl. Eugenia traveled to Italy, France, and Switzerland to start new communities, and now the Ravasco Institute can be found in Albania, Italy, Switzerland, Argentina, Bolivia, Chile, Colombia, Mexico, Paraguay, Venezuela, Africa, and the Philippines. She was beatified in 2003.

RAWLINS, BL. ALEXANDER (d. 1595). Born in Worcestershire, England, he was imprisoned twice for his Catholic religion in 1585, went to Rheims in 1589, and was ordained there in 1590. He was sent on the English mission the following year, was arrested early in 1595, condemned to death for treason (which meant being a Catholic priest), and was hanged, drawn, and quartered with Bl. Henry Walpole on April 7 at York. He was beatified in 1929.

RAYMOND (d. 1242). See William Arnaud.

RAYMOND OF CAPUA, BL. (1330–99). Raymond delle Vigne was born at Capua, Italy, became a Dominican while studying at Bologna, was named prior of the Minerva in Rome, and then served as lector in Florence and Siena, where he met Catherine of Siena. He became her spiritual director in 1376 and was her close confidant. He helped care for the victims of a plague that had stricken Siena, was stricken himself, and was cured through Catherine's prayers. With Catherine he worked to launch a crusade, attempted to effect a peace between Florence and the Tuscan League and the Pope, who was then living at Avignon, and tried to persuade Pope Gregory XI to return to Rome. When Gregory died in 1378, they supported Pope Urban VI against antipope Clement VII, whose election began the Great Schism. Bl. Raymond was sent to France by Urban to win the support of King Charles V, an effort that was unsuccessful, and had his life threatened while on the trip by soldiers of Clement. After Catherine's death in 1380, he continued her efforts to end the schism, and in the same year he was elected master general of the Dominicans, remaining faithful to Urban. Bl. Raymond labored to reform the order and established several houses following a strict rule. He wrote biographies of Catherine and St. Agnes of Montepulciano and died at Nuremberg, Germany, on October 5. He was beatified in 1899.

RAYMOND OF FITERO (d. 1163). Born in Aragon, Spain, he became a canon at Tarazona Cathedral, joined the Cistercians at Scala Dei Monastery in France, founded Fitero Abbey in Navarre, and became its abbot. In 1158, when the Moors were threatening an attack on Calatrava, an outpost of Toledo, he persuaded King Sancho of Castile to give him and Diego Velasquez, a monk who had been a knight, the town, and with the help of the archbishop of Toledo, Raymond raised a large army and marched to the defense of Calatrava. When the attack failed to materialize, Raymond formed the military order of the Knights of Calatrava from the outstanding members of the army; they waged war against the infidels and observed the rule of St. Benedict. Raymond's cult was approved in 1719. February 6.

RAYMOND LULL, BL. (c. 1232–1316). Son of one of the military leaders who reconquered Majorca from the Moslems, he was born at Palma, Majorca, entered the service of King James I of Aragon, was appointed grand senechal by James, and in 1257 married Blanca Picany. Despite his marriage and two children, he led a dissolute life, but changed his lifestyle in 1263 when he had a vision of Christ while writing to a woman with whom he was having an affair, followed by five more visions. After pilgrimages to Compostela and Rocamadour, he became a Franciscan tertiary, provided for his family, gave the rest of his wealth to the poor, and determined to devote the rest of his life to converting the Mohammedans. He spent the next nine years learning all he could of Moslem philosophy, religion,

and culture, and learning Arabic. He founded the short-lived Trinity College on Majorca in 1276 to put into effect his idea of a missionary college, visited Rome in 1277 to enlist the Pope's support, went to Paris in 1286, and in 1290 joined the Friars Minor at Genoa. After a serious illness, he went to Tunis in 1292, began preaching, but was almost immediately forcibly deported by the Moors. Further appeals to Popes Boniface VIII and Clement V for aid in his mission to the Mohammedans were fruitless, as was a visit to Cyprus. After lecturing at Paris on Arabic metaphysics for a time, he was successful in getting to Bougie in Barbary in 1306 but was again imprisoned and deported. He continued his appeals for aid to the Pope and to the Council of Vienne in 1311 but with no success, resumed lecturing at Paris, and again returned to Bougie in 1315. This time he was stoned and left for dead but was rescued by Genoese sailors and died on board ship near Majorca on September 29. He wrote voluminously—more than three hundred treatises (many in Arabic) on philosophy, music, navigation, law, astronomy, mathematics, and theology, chief among his writings being *Arbre de philosophia de amor.* He also wrote mystical poetry of the highest order and is considered the forerunner of Teresa of Ávila and John of the Cross; his *Blanquera* is the first novel written in Catalan. His cult was confirmed in 1858 by Pope Pius IX. June 30.

RAYMOND NONNATUS (c. 1204–40). Born at Portella, Catalonia, Spain, he was delivered by caesarian operation when his mother died in childbirth, hence his name *non natus* (not born). He joined the Mercedarians under St. Peter Nolasco at Barcelona, succeeded Peter as chief ransomer, and went to Algeria to ransom slaves. He remained as hostage for several slaves when his ransom money ran out and was sentenced to be impaled when the governor learned that he had converted several Mohammedans. He escaped the death sentence because of the ransom he would bring, but was forced to run the gantlet. He was then tortured for continuing his evangelizing activities but was ransomed eight months later by Peter Nolasco. On his return to Barcelona in 1239, he was appointed cardinal by Pope Gregory IX but died at Cardona (Cerdagne) a short distance from Barcelona the next year while on the way to Rome. He was canonized in 1657 and is the patron saint of midwives. August 31.

RAYMOND OF PEÑAFORT (1175–1275). Born at Peñafort, Catalonia, Spain, he was teaching philosophy by the time he was twenty at Barcelona. He resigned his chair there in 1210 to study law at Bologna, where he received his doctorate in 1216. He was made archdeacon by Bishop Berengarius of Barcelona in 1219 and joined the Dominicans there in 1222. He became famed for his preaching and went all over Spain preaching to Moors and Christians returned from Moorish slavery. He preached the Spanish crusade that freed Spain from the Moors and is considered by many to be cofounder with St. Peter Nolasco of the Mercedarians, though the claim is disputed. In 1230, he was confessor to Pope Gregory IX in Rome and spent three years collecting and codifying papal decrees from 1150, which became the cornerstone of canon law until the revision of 1917. He was named archbishop of Tarragona, despite his protests, in 1235, and persuaded Pope Gregory to recall the appointment when he became seriously ill. He returned to Spain in 1236 to convalesce, resumed his work as a preacher and confessor, was tremendously successful in making conversions, and in 1238 was elected master

general of the Dominicans. He drew up a revision of the Dominican constitution, which was to remain in effect until 1924, but resigned his generalship, citing his age, sixty-five, as a factor. But he was to live another thirty-five years, active in the conversion work that was to bring thousands to the Church. He established friaries at Tunis and Murcia, helped to establish the Inquisition at Catalonia, introduced the study of Arabic and Hebrew into several Dominican houses, and was responsible for Thomas Aquinas writing *Summa contra Gentiles*. Raymond died at Barcelona on January 6 and was canonized by Pope Clement VIII in 1601. His *Summa de poenitentia* (also called *Summa casuum),* which he compiled between 1223 and 1238, had a profound influence on the development of the penitential system of the later Middle Ages. January 7.

RAYMOND OF TOULOUSE (d. 1118). Born at Toulouse, France, Raymond Gayrard married and on the death of his wife devoted himself to charitable works. He built a poorhouse for thirteen impoverished clerics and two bridges, became a canon at St. Sernin Church, and helped rebuild the church, which became a famous pilgrimage shrine. He died on July 3 and when numerous miracles were reported at his tomb, a cult developed, which was approved in 1652. July 8.

REALINO, BERNARDINO (1530–1616). Born at Carpi, Italy, he became a lawyer, and when he was thirty-four, he joined the Jesuits. He engaged in pastoral work at Naples for ten years and then went to the college at Lecce, of which in time he became rector. His reputation for holiness increased as he grew older. Just before his death, blood emerging from an unhealed leg wound he had sustained six years earlier was collected in vials, and reputable witnesses over the next 250 years testified that they had seen the blood in these vials, which remained in a red, liquid state, bubble and boil. He was canonized in 1947 by Pope Pius XII.

REDEMPTA (6th century). Raised and instructed in the life of a hermitess by St. Herundo in Palestine, Redempta went, in her old age, to live with St. Romula and another woman near St. Mary Major Church in Rome in about 575. Romula was stricken with paralysis and bedridden the last years of her life but bore her infirmities with great patience. St. Gregory praised them for their humility and piety. July 23.

REDEMPTUS OF THE CROSS, BL. (d. 1638). *See* Berthelot, Bl. Dionysius.

REDI, TERESA MARGARET (1747–70). Born at Arezzo, Italy, and christened Anne Mary, she was sent to St. Apollonia Convent in Florence, when she was ten, to be educated. She returned home after seven years there, and then, in 1765, joined the Discalced Carmelites at St. Teresa Convent at Florence, taking the name Teresa Margaret of the Sacred Heart. She lived a life of prayer and rigorous penance, was devoted to the Sacred Heart, and died at the convent when she was only twenty-three. She was canonized in 1934 by Pope Pius XI. March 11.

REGINA (2nd century). Also known as Reine, legend says she was the daughter of pagan Clement of Alise in Burgundy. She was raised by a Christian woman, when her mother died at her birth, as a Christian. When her father discovered she was a Christian, he put her out of his house and she went to live with the woman who had raised her, working as a shepherdess. When Regina refused to marry Olybrius, the prefect, she was imprisoned, tortured, and beheaded at Autun, Gaul. September 7.

REGINALD OF ORLÉANS, BL. (1183–1220). Born at St. Gilles, Languedoc, France, he taught canon law at Paris from 1206 to 1211 and was named dean at St. Aignan in Orléans in 1212. He joined the Dominicans when he met Dominic while on pilgrimage to Rome in 1218, founded Dominican houses at Bologna in 1218 and Paris in 1219, and attracted many to the new order. He died at Paris on February 1, and his cult was confirmed in 1875. February 17.

REGIS, JOHN (1597–1640). Born on January 31 at Fontcouverte, France, the son of a rich merchant, he studied at the Jesuit college of Béziers and joined the Jesuits in 1615. He pursued his studies, taught at Cahors and Toulouse, and was ordained in 1631. He was assigned to missionary work in southeastern France and became famed for his fervor, preaching ability, and as a confessor. He brought thousands back to their faith and his every appearance was marked by large crowds. He also ministered to the sick in hospitals and to prisoners, he organized groups to help the needy, and he founded a refuge for wayward women and girls. He is reputed to have performed numerous miracles, and his tomb at La Louvesc after his death there on December 31 became a popular pilgrimage center. He was canonized in 1737. June 16.

REGULUS (d. c. 250). Also known as Rieul, he is believed to have been of Greek origin, accompanied St. Dionysius to evangelize Gaul, and is honored as the first bishop of Senlis, of which he is the patron. March 30.

REINE. *See* Regina.

REINILDIS (d. c. 680). Daughter of Count Witger and St. Amalberga, she attempted to join her father at Lobbes Abbey when both parents became religious, and when refused entrance went on pilgrimage to the Holy Land. On her return seven years later, she devoted herself to charitable works at Saintes until she and her servant, Gundulf, and Grimoald, a subdeacon, were murdered by marauding barbarians, probably at Kontich in Antwerp Province. July 16.

REINOLD (d. c. 960). The youngest of the four sons in William Caxton's romantic poem *Aymon,* he became a monk at St. Pantaleon Monastery in Cologne, was put in charge of building, and was murdered by a group of stonemasons he had been overseeing who were annoyed because he worked harder and longer than they did. He is patron of stonemasons. January 7.

REMACLUS (d. c. 675). Born in Aquitaine, he studied under St. Sulpicius of Bourges and was ordained. St. Eligius appointed him first abbot of Solignac, and later he served as abbot at Cugnon, Luxemburg. He then joined the court of King Sigebert III, and in about 684 persuaded him to found the double monastery of Stavelot and Malmédy in Ardennes, of which Remaclus became abbot. He probably was a missionary bishop from 652 and was widely venerated for his austerities and holiness. September 3.

REMBERT (d. 888). Born near Bruges, Flanders, he became a monk at nearby Torhout Monastery, assisted St. Anskar in his missionary work, and succeeded him as archbishop of Hamburg and Bremen in 865. His jurisdiction extended to Sweden, Denmark, and Lower Germany, and he devoted himself to evangelizing the northern Slavs and ransoming Christian captives from the Slavs and Norsemen. He wrote a biography of Anskar and died on June 11. February 4.

REMI. The French form of Remigius.

REMIGIUS (c. 437–530). Also known as Remi, he was born at Laon, the son of Count Emilius of Laon and St. Celina. He became known for his preaching, and in 459, when he was only twenty-two, he was appointed bishop of Rheims. He was ordained and consecrated and reigned for more than seventy years, devoting himself to the evangelization of the Franks. In 496, Clovis, pagan King of northern Gaul, supposedly in response to a suggestion by his wife, Clotildis, a Christian, invoked the Christian God when the invading Alemanni were on the verge of defeating his forces, whereupon the tide of battle turned and Clovis was victorious. St. Remigius, aided by St. Vedast, instructed him and his chieftains in Christianity, and soon after baptized Clovis, his two sisters, and three thousand of his followers. Remigius was a zealous proponent of orthodoxy, opposed Arianism, and converted an Arian bishop at a synod of Arian bishops in 517. He was censured by a group of bishops for ordaining one Claudius, whom they felt was unworthy of the priesthood, but St. Remigius was generally held in great veneration for his holiness, learning, and miracles. He was the most influential prelate of Gaul and is considered the apostle of the Franks. He died at Rheims on January 13. October 1.

REPARATA (3rd century). Her untrustworthy legend has her a girl of twelve at Caesarea when she was denounced for being a Christian during the persecution of Christians under Emperor Decius. She was tortured, and when she persisted in her refusal to apostatize, she was hurled into a furnace. When she miraculously escaped unscathed, she still refused to sacrifice to the gods and was beheaded. October 8.

REPOSITUS (d. c. 303). *See* Honoratus.

RESTITUTA OF SORA (d. c. 271). A Roman who suffered martyrdom at Sora, Italy, during the persecution of Christians under Emperor Aurelian, her untrustworthy legend had her brought to Sora by an angel. She lived with a widow, cured her of leprosy, and converted her, her son, and thirty others. She was arrested by Proconsul Agathius, was scourged when she refused to sacrifice to the gods, and was bound in chains and cast into prison. An angel released her from the chains, whereupon she, Cyril (a priest she had converted), and two others were beheaded. May 27.

REVOCATUS (d. 203). *See* Perpetua.

REY, MARY. *See* Fidelis of Sigmaningen.

REYNOLDS, RICHARD (c. 1490–1535). Born in Devon, England, he studied at Cambridge, was elected a fellow of Corpus Christi College in 1510, and was appointed university preacher in 1513. He joined the Briggitine monks at Syon Abbey, Isleworth, the same year and became known for his sanctity and as one of the most learned monks of his time. He was imprisoned when he refused to subscribe to King Henry VIII's Act of Supremacy and was hanged on May 4 at Tyburn, one of the first group of martyrs there, after having been forced to witness the butchering of four other martyrs. He was canonized by Pope Paul VI in 1970 as one of the Forty Martyrs of England and Wales. May 11.

REYNOLDS, BL. THOMAS (c. 1560–1642). Born at Oxford, England, he was known as Reynolds, though his family name was Green. He studied at Rheims, Valladolid, and Seville, and was ordained when he was thirty. Sent on the English mission, he was one of the forty-seven Catholic priests banished from England in 1606. He returned and worked on the English mission until 1628, when he was arrested. He was sentenced to death for being a Catholic priest but spent the next fourteen years in prison. He was then hanged, drawn, and quartered at Tyburn when he was over eighty years old with Fr. Alban Roe, a Benedictine monk, on January 21. He was beatified in 1929.

RHIPSIME (d. c. 312). According to untrustworthy legend, she was a member of a community of dedicated virgins, headed by Gaiana, in Rome during the reign of Emperor Diocletian. Rhipsime was a great beauty, and when Emperor Diocletian saw her portrait, he desired her, but Rhipsime would have no part of him. To escape his wrath when Rhipsime refused him, Gaiana took her community from Rome to Alexandria, and eventually they settled at Valarshapat, Armenia. There Rhipsime's beauty caused such a stir that news of her whereabouts reached Diocletian in Rome, and he wrote about her to King Tiridates. He had her seized and brought to his palace, where she resisted him and then escaped. Enraged, he sent his troops to the community and they roasted Rhipsime to death and executed Gaiana and thirty-five of her companions; only one, Nino (called Christiana in the Roman Martyrology), escaped, and in time she became the apostle of Georgia. The cult is an ancient one in Armenia, and they probably were martyred under Tiridates, but all the other details seem to be a fictional embellishment of that fact. September 30.

RI, BL. JOHN (d. 1839). *See* Imbert, Bl. Laurence.

RIBERA, BL. JOHN DE (1532–1611). Son of Peter de Ribera, duke of Alcala who was viceroy of Naples for fourteen years, he was born at Seville, Spain, in December, studied at Salamanca, and was ordained in 1557. He taught theology at Salamanca, was named bishop of Badajoz in 1562, and in 1568 was appointed archbishop of Valencia, a position he held for forty-two years until his death on January 6 at the College of Corpus Christi in Valencia, which he had founded. He opposed the activities of the Moors and the Jews as economic enemies of the state and was one of those responsible for the edict of 1609, which ordered the deportation of the Moors from Valencia. He was canonized by Pope John XXIII in 1960.

RICCARDI, BL. PLACID (1844–1915). Born at Trevi, Italy, on June 24 and baptized Thomas, he studied at the Angelicum in Rome, joined the Benedictines in Rome at St. Paul Outside the Walls in 1867, taking the name Placid, and was imprisoned for not appearing for military service in 1870; he was soon released and was ordained in 1871. He was spiritual director of a convent of Benedictine nuns in Rome, master of novices at St. Paul's in 1885, spiritual director of the nuns at St. Magno d'Amelia, and then was rector of the basilic at Farfa. He was a much-sought-after confessor and widely venerated for his holiness. Illness made him return to Rome; he spent the last three years of his life there and died there on June 24. He was beatified in 1954.

RICCI, CATHERINE DEI. *See* Catherine dei Ricci.

RICHARD (d. 720). Father of SS. Willibald, Winnebald, and Walburga, he was on a pilgrimage to Rome from his native Wessex, England, with his two sons when he was stricken and died at Lucca, Italy. Miracles were reported at his tomb and he became greatly venerated by the citizens of Lucca, who embellished accounts of his life by calling him "King of the English." February 7.

RICHARD (12th century). An Englishman who became bishop of Andria, Italy, appointed perhaps by Pope Adrian IV, he attended the third General Council of the Lateran in 1179 and is the principal patron of Andria. An unsubstantiated legend had an Englishman named Richard appointed first bishop of Andria in 453 and was one of the three prelates appointed by Pope St. Gelasius I to dedicate the sanctuary on Monte Gargano erected in honor of the famous vision of the archangel there, but this story is most unlikely fact. June 9.

RICHARD DE WYCHE (c. 1197–1253). Born at Wyche (Droitwich), Worcestershire, England, he was orphaned when he was quite young, retrieved the fortunes of the mismanaged estate he inherited when he took it over, and then turned it over to his brother Robert. Richard refused marriage and went to Oxford, where he studied under Grosseteste and met and began a lifelong friendship with Edmund Rich. Richard pursued his studies at Paris, received his M.A. from Oxford, and then continued his studies at Bologna, where he received his doctorate in canon law. After seven years at Bologna, he returned to Oxford, was appointed chancellor of the university in 1235, and then became chancellor to Edmund Rich, now archbishop of Canterbury, whom he accompanied to the Cistercian monastery at Pontigny when the archbishop retired there. After Rich died at Pontigny, Richard taught at the Dominican house of studies at Orléans and was ordained there in 1243. After a time as a parish priest at Deal, he became chancellor of Boniface of Savoy, the new archbishop of Canterbury, and when King Henry III named

Ralph Neville bishop of Chichester in 1244, Boniface declared his selection invalid and named Richard to the see. Eventually, the matter was brought to Rome, and in 1245 Pope Innocent IV declared in Richard's favor and consecrated him. When he returned to England, he was still opposed by Henry and was refused admittance to the bishop's palace; eventually Henry gave in when threatened with excommunication by the Pope. The remaining eight years of Richard's life were spent in ministering to his flock. He denounced nepotism, insisted on strict clerical discipline, and was ever generous to the poor and the needy. He died at a house for poor priests in Dover, England, while preaching a crusade, and was canonized in 1262. April 3.

RICHARDIS (d. c. 895). Daughter of the count of Alsace, she was married to Charles the Fat, son of King Louis the German, when she was twenty. She and Charles were crowned Emperor and Empress of the Holy Roman Empire by Pope John VIII in Rome in 881, but several years later, Charles accused her of infidelity with his chancellor, Liutward, bishop of Vercelli. Both denied the charge, and Richardis successfully endured the ordeal by fire before the imperial assembly to prove her innocence. She left Charles (who was deposed in 887) to live as a nun at Hohenburg and then went to Andlau Abbey, which she had founded, and lived there until her death. September 18.

RICHARDSON, BL. LAURENCE (d. 1582). His real name was Johnson and he was born in Lancashire, studied at Brasenose College, Oxford, and left to become a Catholic. He went to Douai, was ordained there in 1576, and was sent on the English mission. He was arrested early in 1581, was tried for participating in an imaginary conspiracy against the

Queen known as the plot of Rome and Rheims, and tried with Edmund Campion, William Filby, Luke Kirby, and Thomas Cotten. Bl. Laurence was found guilty, and when he refused to acknowledge the ecclesiastical supremacy of the Queen, he was hanged, drawn, and quartered at Tyburn on May 30. He was beatified with six other priests as one of the Martyrs of London of 1582 in 1886. May 28.

RICHARDSON, BL. WILLIAM (d. 1603). Born in Wales, near Sheffield, England, he studied at Valladolid and Seville in Spain and was ordained at Seville in 1594. He was sent on the English mission, using the alias Anderson, and was arrested in London. Tried and convicted of being a Catholic priest, he was executed at Tyburn on February 17—the last Catholic martyr during the reign of Queen Elizabeth I. He was beatified in 1929.

RICHARIUS (d. c. 645). Also known as Riquier, he was born at Celles near Amiens, France, and became a priest after saving the lives of two Irish missionaries from the pagan inhabitants. After studying in England, he returned to his native land, preached with great success, and founded an abbey at Celles (the present town of Abbeville, named after his abbey), of which he became abbot. In his old age he resigned his abbacy and spent the rest of his life as a hermit on the spot where later Forest-Montiers Monastery was built. April 26.

RICHIMIR (d. c. 715). With the permission of Bishop Gilbert of Le Mans, France, he founded a monastery with some of his followers near the Loire River, though he was not yet ordained. He later left and founded another monastery at Saint-Rogomer-des-Bois, which he ruled as abbot until his death. January 17.

RICTRUDIS (c. 612–88). Of a distinguished Gascon family, she married St. Adalbald, a Frankish nobleman serving King Clovis II, despite some opposition from her family, and the couple had four children—Adalsind, Clotsind, Eusebia, and Mauront—all of whom became saints. After sixteen years of a happy married life at Ostrevant, Flanders, Adalbald was murdered by relatives of Rictrudis while visiting in Gascony. After several years, King Clovis ordered her to marry, but with the aid of her old friend and director, St. Amandus, Clovis relented and permitted her to become a nun at Marchiennes, Flanders, a double monastery she had founded. Adalsind and Clotsind joined her, and sometime later Mauront left the court and became a monk there. Rictrudis became abbess of Marchiennes and ruled for forty years. May 12.

RIEUL. See Regulus.

RIGBY, JOHN (c. 1570–1600). Born near Wigan, Lancashire, England, the son of an impoverished gentleman, he was a Catholic but was obliged to earn his living as a servant in a Protestant household. He attended Protestant services to conform with the law but repented of his actions and returned to his Catholic faith. While appearing to answer a summons for the daughter of his employer, he admitted he was a Catholic and was imprisoned at Newgate Prison. When he refused his freedom if he would attend Protestant services, he was sentenced to death and hanged, drawn, and quartered at Southwark on June 21. He was canonized by Pope Paul VI in 1970 as one of the Forty Martyrs of England and Wales.

RIGHI, BL. JOHN BAPTIST (1469–1539). Born at Fabriano, Italy, he became a Franciscan priest and was known for the austerity of his life, his rigorous penances, and his concern for the poor and the sick. A cult developed after his death at Massaccio because of the miracles reported at his grave; the cult was confirmed in 1903. March 11.

RIGO. See Henry of Treviso, Bl.

RIGOBERT (d. c. 745). Abbot of Orbais, France, he was named archbishop of Rheims but was banished to Gascony by Charles Martel when he refused to take sides in Charles' dispute with Raganfred, mayor of Neustria. Charles gave the see of Rheims to Milon, and when Rigobert's dispute with Charles Martel was settled, Rigobert returned to Rheims but persuaded Milon to remain as bishop, and he became a hermit. He was venerated for his holiness and patience and was credited with performing miracles. January 4.

RINIERI. See Rizzerio, Bl.

RIOCH. See Mel.

RIQUIER. See Richarius.

RITA OF CASCIA (1381–1457). Born at Roccaporena near Spoleto, Italy, of elderly parents, she was married against her will when twelve, had two sons, and after eighteen years of an unhappy marriage, her husband, who had treated her cruelly, was killed in a brawl. When her two sons died, she tried to enter the Augustinians at Cascia three times but was refused each time, as its rule permitted only virgins, but was finally allowed to become a nun there in 1413. She became known for her austerities, penances, and concern for others, and brought many back to their religion with her prayers. She experienced visions and in 1441 suffered a seemingly thorn-induced wound on her forehead after hearing a sermon on the crown of thorns. Several miracles were attributed to her after her death on May 22 at Cascia. She was canonized in 1900 and is venerated as the saint of desperate causes.

RIZZERIO (d. 1236). Of a wealthy family, he was born at Muccia in the Marches, became a student at the University of Bologna, and while there he and his friend Bl. Peregrine were so impressed by a sermon they heard Francis of Assisi preach at Bologna in 1222 that they joined the Franciscans. Rizzerio was ordained, became a close associate of Francis, and served as provincial of the Marches. He practiced great austerities and mortifications and was the recipient of a miracle from Francis that dissolved his despair of God's mercy. He died on March 26, and his cult was confirmed in 1836. He is called Rinieri in *The Little Flowers of St. Francis*. February 7.

ROBERT (d. 1159). Born at Gargrave, Yorkshire, England, he was ordained, served as rector at Gargrave, and then became a Benedictine at Whitby. He and a group of monks from St. Mary's Abbey in York settled in Skeldale to follow a strict Benedictine rule and founded Fountains Abbey in 1132. They affiliated with the Cistercians, and the abbey became famous for the holiness and austerity of its members. In 1138, Robert and twelve monks left Fountains to people Newminster Abbey, built by Ralph de Merly, lord of Morpeth, and Robert was named abbot. He founded houses at Pipewall, Sawley, and Roche, wrote a commentary on the Psalms, and ruled until his death on June 7. He was buried at Newminster, and his tomb became a pilgrimage center.

ROBERT OF ARBRISSEL, BL. (c. 1047–1117). Born at Arbrissel (Arbressec), Brittany, he studied at Paris, was ordained, and then became archpriest in Rennes in 1089 at the invitation of Bishop Sylvester de Gerche, who invited him to assist him in reforming that see. Robert was forced to flee the enemies he had made with his reforms when the bishop died, and he became a hermit in the Craon Forest in 1095. The following year he was founding abbot of La Roé monastery, which he established for the many disciples he had attracted with his holiness. He was appointed "preacher" by Pope Urban II the same year, attracted huge crowds, and in 1099 founded the double monastery of Fontvrault for the many postulants La Roé could not accommodate. He was at the Council of Poitiers in 1100, where he favored the excommunication of King Philip I of France, and attended the Council of Nantes in 1110. He called a chapter to set up a permanent organization of his monks in 1116, and died the next year at Orsan on February 25. Although called Blessed, he has never been formally beatified.

ROBERT OF CHAISE DIEU (d. 1067). Robert de Turlande was a native of Auvergne, was ordained, and became a canon at St. Julian's Church at Brioude, where he founded a hospice. He spent several years at Cluny under St. Odilo and then went on pilgrimage to Rome; on his return he became a hermit with a knight named Stephen near Brioude. Their holiness attracted numerous disciples, whom Robert organized into a community of three hundred monks, of which he was abbot. April 17.

ROBERT FLOWER, BL. *See* Robert of Knaresborough, Bl.

ROBERT OF KNARESBOROUGH, BL. (c. 1160–c. 1218). Born at York, England, Robert Flower was attracted to the priesthood but never advanced beyond subdeacon. He spent several months as a novice at Newminster Cistercian Abbey at Morpeth, decided the life was not for him, and became a hermit in a cave next to St. Giles' Chapel near Knaresborough. At the invitation of St. Hilda, he moved to Rudfarlington, then settled at Spofforth, where his hermitage was vandalized, and after a time at Hedley Priory, he returned to Rudfarlington. When the constable of Knaresborough suspected him of harboring criminals, he was forced to flee back to St. Giles. He built Holy Cross Chapel and became famed for his holiness, visions, miracles, and concern for the poor. Though he had a cult in medieval times known as the "Holy Hermit of Knaresborough," it was never formally recognized. September 24.

ROBERT OF MOLESMES (c. 1024–1110). Born of noble parents near Troyes, Champagne, France, he became a Benedictine at Moutier-la-Celle when he was fifteen, and when he finished his novitiate he was named prior. He was then named abbot of St. Michael of Tonnere, was unsuccessful in his attempts to reform that abbey, and after his recall to Moutier-la-Celle, Pope Alexander II named him superior of a group of hermits he had been instructing. He moved the community from Collan to Molesmes in 1075. The austerity and holiness of the members of the community led to a great influx of ill-qualified candidates, and when he was unsuccessful in raising the standards to their previous level, he, St. Stephen Harding, and St. Alberic with several others left and founded a new community, dedicated to strict observance of the rule of St. Benedict, at Cîteaux in 1098. It was designated an abbey with Walter as abbot by Bishop Walters of Chalon, and thus the Cistercians began. Robert was ordered back to Molesmes by Pope Urban II in 1099, was successful with his

reform, and lived there until his death on March 21. He was canonized in 1222. April 29.

ROBERTS, JOHN (1577–1610). Born near Trawsfynydd, Merionethshire, Wales, he was brought up a Protestant, studied at St. John's College, Oxford, and law at Furnivall's Inn. Though a Protestant, he had leanings toward the Catholic Church and left Oxford rather than take the Oath of Supremacy. He went to Paris in 1598, became a Catholic there, went to the English college at Valladolid, and joined the Benedictines. He was ordained in 1602, and within three weeks after the English monks at St. Martin's Monastery were granted permission to go on the English mission, he and Fr. Augustine Bradshaw returned to England, the first monks to return as missionaries since the suppression of the monasteries. They were soon arrested in London and expelled from the country; Fr. Roberts soon came back, ministered to the victims of the plague that killed 30,000 Londoners in the winter of 1603, and was again arrested, early in 1604. He was released when he was not recognized as a priest, but was arrested and imprisoned during the Gunpowder Plot, and was again released after eight months in prison through the intercession of the French ambassador. Fr. Roberts remained on the Continent for a year helping found a monastery for the English monks of Valladolid at Douai, and then returned to England. Arrested in 1607, he escaped, was rearrested in 1609, was banished through the intercession of the French ambassador, went to Spain and then went to Douai. He returned to England, was arrested once again with Bl. Thomas Somers, and this time he was convicted of being a Catholic priest. When he refused to take the Oath of Supremacy, he was hanged, drawn, and quartered at Tyburn with Fr.

Somers on December 10. Fr. Roberts was canonized by Pope Paul VI in 1970 as one of the Forty Martyrs of England and Wales.

ROBINSON, VEN. CHRISTOPHER (d. 1598). Born at Woodside, Cumberland, England, he studied for the priesthood at Rheims and was ordained in 1592. He was sent on the English mission, worked in Cumberland and Westmorland, and was arrested, convicted of being a Catholic priest, and hanged at Carlisle. He wrote an eyewitness account of the martyrdom of St. John Boste at Dryburn in 1594. August 19.

ROBINSON, BL. JOHN (d. 1588). Born at Ferrensby, Yorkshire, England, he went to Rheims to study for the priesthood when his wife died, and he was ordained in 1585. He was sent on the English mission, was arrested in London almost at once, and when convicted of being a Catholic priest, he was hanged, drawn, and quartered at Ipswich. He was beatified in 1929. October 1.

ROCCO. See Roch.

ROCH (1295–1378). Untrustworthy sources say he was probably born at Montpellier, France, son of the governor there. When he was orphaned when he was twenty, he went on pilgrimage to Rome and devoted himself to caring for the victims of a plague that was ravaging Italy. He became a victim himself at Piacenza but recovered and was reputed to have performed many miracles of healing. On his return to Montpellier, he was imprisoned for five years as a spy in pilgrim's disguise when his uncle, who was governor, ordered him imprisoned. (His uncle failed to recognize him, and Roch failed to identify himself.) Roch died in prison and was only then identified as the former governor's son by a

birthmark in the form of a cross on his chest. Another biographer says that he was arrested as a spy at Angers, Lombardy, and died in prison there. When miracles were reported at his intercession after his death, a popular cult developed, and he is invoked against pestilence and plague. He is known as Rocco in Italy and Roque in Spain. August 16.

ROCHE, BL. JOHN (d. 1588). See Ward, Margaret.

ROCHEFOUCAULD, FRANÇOIS JOSEPH DE LA (d. 1792). See Du Lau, Bl. John.

ROCHEFOUCAULD, PIERRE LOUIS (d. 1792). See Du Lau, Bl. John.

ROCHESTER, BL. JOHN (d. 1537). Born at Terling, Essex, England, he became a Carthusian at the London charterhouse. He was sent to Hull with a fellow Carthusian, Bl. William Walworth, when a monk from Sheen who had taken the Oath of Supremacy was made superior of the London house. When a letter from Walworth to the duke of Norfolk was intercepted, both were arrested, and when they refused to take the Oath of Supremacy were executed at York on May 11. Bl. John was beatified in 1886.

RODAT, EMILY DE (1787–1852). Born at Rodez, France, Marie Guillemette Emilie de Rodat was raised by her grandmother near Villefranche-de-Rouerge, attended school there at Maison Saint-Cyr, and when eighteen began to teach children there. With the approval of her spiritual adviser, Abbé Marty, she joined successively the Ladies of Nevers, the Picpus Sisters, and the Sisters of Mercy, but felt she did not fit in with any of these congregations. In 1815, she decided that teaching poor children was her vocation, and with three companions began teaching in her own room at Maison Saint-Cyr, and the Congregation of the Holy Family of Villefranche was founded. She started her own free school in 1816, and when the Saint-Cyr community broke up, she bought their property for her new congregation which, despite her constant ill health, she expanded to thirty-eight foundations in the next thirty-six years. In time, she extended the scope of the congregation to nursing sick poor, visiting prisoners, and caring for the aged, orphans, and wayward women; she also founded several cloistered convents. She died on September 19, and was canonized by Pope Pius XII in 1950.

RODERIC (d. 857). A priest at Cabra, Spain, during the persecution of Christians by the Moors, and also known as Ruderic, he was beaten into unconsciousness by his two brothers, one a Mohammedan and the other a fallen-away Catholic, when he tried to stop an argument between them. The Mohammedan brother then paraded him through the streets proclaiming that he wished to become a Mohammedan. He escaped but was denounced to the authorities by the same brother as an apostate from Mohammedanism and imprisoned though he denied he had ever given up his Christianity. While in prison, he met a man named Solomon, also charged with apostasy, and after a long imprisonment, they were both beheaded. March 13.

RODRIGUEZ, BL. ALONSO (d. 1628). See Gonzalez, Bl. Roque.

RODRIGUEZ, ALPHONSUS (1533–1617). Son of a wealthy merchant at Segovia, Spain, he was born there on July 25, was prepared for first communion by Bl. Peter Favre, a close friend of his father, and was sent to Alcala to study under the Jesuits. He returned to Segovia on the death of his father to oversee the family business, married, and when his wife died, sold the business. When his son died several years later, he applied to the Jesuits to join the Society of Jesus when he was almost fifty but was refused at Segovia. On the advice of a Jesuit friend, Fr. Louis Santander, he went back to grade school, abandoned an idea he had to become a hermit, and by a special ruling of the provincial was admitted to the Jesuits as a lay brother. He took his final vows when he was fifty-four and served in the lowly post of hall porter at Montesión College on Majorca for twenty-four years. He was soon known for his holiness, simplicity, obedience, and devotion to the Immaculate Conception, was consulted on matters spiritual by learned and simple alike (Peter Claver put himself under his spiritual guidance for three years while he was a student at Montesión), and suffered from ill health the last years of his life until his death at Montesión on November 1. He was canonized with Peter Claver in 1888 by Pope Leo XIII. October 31.

RODRON (d. 888). See Ageranus.

ROE, ALBAN BARTHOLOMEW (c. 1583–1642). Born probably at Bury St. Edmunds, England, he was a student at Cambridge when he met an imprisoned Catholic and was so impressed by his faith that he was converted to Catholicism. He studied at Douai but was dismissed for infraction of discipline and then became a Benedictine monk at Dieulouard, France, in 1612, taking the name Alban, was ordained, and was sent on the English mission. He was arrested in 1615, imprisoned, and then banished; he was back in England in four months and again was arrested, in 1618, and imprisoned in New Prison until 1623, when he was released through the intercession of the Spanish ambassador. Fr. Roe was banished but after a short stay at Douai, he returned to England and worked until his arrest in 1625. He spent the next seventeen years in prison until he was finally tried, and when convicted of being a Catholic priest was hanged, drawn, and quartered on January 21, two days after his sentencing, at Tyburn with Bl. Thomas Reynolds. Fr. Roe was canonized in 1970 by Pope Paul VI as one of the Forty Martyrs of England and Wales.

ROGATIAN (d. 289 or 304). *See* Donatian.

ROGATUS (d. 484). *See* Liberatus of Capua.

ROGER OF ELLANT, BL. (d. 1160). Born in England, he became a Cistercian at Lourroy Monastery at Berry, France, and then founded Ellant Monastery near Rheims. He was noted for his care of the sick, his austerity, and his strict adherence to the rule. He died on January 4.

ROGER LE FORT, BL. (c. 1277–1367). Born in the Limousin district of France, he was a subdeacon when elected bishop of Orléans in 1321. He was translated to Limoges in 1328 and in 1343 was named archbishop of Bourges. He popularized the feast of the Conception of Our Lady, which he established in his see, and was venerated for his holiness. His tomb became a pilgrimage center because of the miracles reported there, and he was honored on March 1, though he was never formally beatified.

ROGER OF TODI (d. 1237). Ruggiero da Todi received the habit from St. Francis of Assisi in 1236 and was appointed spiritual director of Bl. Philippa Mareri's community at Rieti by Francis. Roger died at Todi, shortly after Philippa's death, on January 5, and his cult was confirmed by Pope Benedict XIV.

ROJAS, BL. SIMON DE (1522–1624). Born at Valladolid, Spain, he became a Trinitarian friar, served as superior of the Order, and was known for his missionary activities. Late in life, he was appointed confessor to Isabella of Bourbon, wife of King Philip III of Spain, and tutor of the royal family. He was beatified in 1766. September 28.

ROLLE, BL. RICHARD (c. 1300–49). Born at Thornton, Yorkshire, England, he studied at Oxford, left when he was nineteen, was probably at the Sorbonne in Paris, 1320–26, probably received a doctorate in theology there, and may have been ordained. He returned to England in about 1326 and lived as a hermit on the estate of John Dalton, perhaps at Topcliffe, then at several other places before settling at Hampole in a cell near the priory of a community of Cistercian nuns who were under his spiritual guidance; he died there on September 29. He was one of the first religious writers to write in the vernacular as well as in Latin and is one of the best known of the mystical writers of his time. Among his numerous works are *De emendatione vitae,* which he wrote for another recluse he directed, Margaret Kirby of Ainderby; a translation of the Psalms; the ninety-six-hundred-line poem *Pricke of Conscience* (though some modern scholars dispute his authorship), denouncing contemporary abuses; and the mystical *De incendium amoris.* He had a popular cult, which was never formally approved, although the Cistercian nuns of Hampton wrote a service for a proposed feast day on January 20.

ROMAEUS, BL. (d. 1380). *See* Avertanus, Bl.

ROMANÇON, BENILDE (1805–62). Born at Thuret, France, on June 13 and christened Peter, he studied at the Christian Brothers school at Riom and joined them in 1820, taking the name Benilde, after he had been refused two years earlier. He headed the Brothers' school at Billom, and in 1841 he founded a school at Saugues, where he was to spend the rest of his life. Saugues became a model school, and Benilde was known for his dedication, his teaching ability and his sanctity. He died at Saugues on August 13, and was canonized by Pope Paul VI in 1967.

ROMANUS (d. 258). According to unreliable sources, he was a soldier in Rome, was instructed and baptized in prison by St. Lawrence, and when Romanus announced he had been converted, was beheaded the day before Lawrence suffered his martyrdom. August 9.

ROMANUS (d. 297). *See* Hipparchus.

ROMANUS (d. 304). Born in Palestine, he became a deacon at Caesarea and then at Antioch, where he was arrested when he exhorted Christian prisoners to resist the judge's orders that they sacrifice to pagan gods. He was saved from death by burning when rain extinguished the fire, was subjected to further torture, and then was strangled. Also beheaded, according to the Roman Martyrology, was seven-year-old Barula who, encouraged by Romanus, had professed his belief in one God. Modern scholars believe Barula was in reality a Syrian martyr named Baralaha or Barlaam whose name somehow became associated with Romanus and was included in the Roman Martyrology. November 18.

ROMANUS (d. c. 460). When thirty-five, he became a hermit in the Jura Mountains between Switzerland and France and was soon joined by his brother Lupicinus. In time they attracted disciples, including their sister and several other women, and built two monasteries, which they ruled jointly as abbots, at Condat and Leuconne, and a convent for women at La Beaume (now Saint-Romain de la Roche), with their sister as abbess. Romanus became renowned for his miraculous cure of two lepers while he was on a pilgrimage to Saint-Maurice, scene of the martyrdom of the Theban Legion. He died and was buried in the church at La Beaume. February 28. Lupicinus died twenty years later, revered too for his miracles, austerities, and holiness. March 21.

ROMANUS (d. c. 550). A monk at a monastery near Monte Subiaco, it was he who encouraged St. Benedict, brought him to the cave where Benedict lived as a hermit for three years, and supplied him with food during that time. According to legend, Romanus left Italy during the invasion of the Vandals, went to France, and founded Fontrouge abbey near Auxerre, where he died. May 22.

ROMANUS (d. c. 640). Of a Frankish family, he was raised at the court of King Clotaire II and in about 630 was named bishop of Rouen. He worked to extirpate idolatry in his see, destroyed a temple of Venus, ministered to criminals condemned to death, and was reputed to have performed many miracles. October 23.

ROMANUS. *See* Boris (d. 1015).

ROMANUS THE MELODIST (6th century). Born at Emesa, Syria, of Jewish descent, he became a deacon at the church at Beirut and during the reign of Emperor Anastasius I, a priest at Constantinople. Romanus was surnamed "the Melodist" for the thousand hymns he is reputed to have composed, eighty of which are still extant. Most famous is his "Kontakion," describing the first Christmas, which is still sung in the Byzantine Christmas office. October 1.

ROMARIC (d. 653). A Merovingian nobleman, he was converted by St. Amatus while he was at the court of King Clotaire II and became a monk at Luxeuil, Gaul. In 620 he and Amatus founded a monastery on Romaric's estate at Habendum, which became the famous Remiremont Abbey, with Amatus its first abbot. Romaric succeeded Amatus as abbot in 623 and ruled for thirty years. Romaric established the *laus perennis* at the monastery, welcomed St. Arnulf of Metz to a nearby hermitage in 629, and in the last days of his life journeyed to Metz to remonstrate with Grimoald, son of Pepin of Landen, and his supporters over the report that Grimoald planned to prevent young Prince Dagobert from ascending the throne of Austrasia. Romaric died at his monstery three days after his return from this mission. December 8.

ROMBAULT. *See* Rumold.

ROMOALDUS. *See* Modoaldus.

ROMUALD (c. 950–1027). Of the noble Onesti family of Ravenna, Italy, he retired when he was twenty to San Apollinare Monastery at Classe to expiate his father's killing of a relative in a duel and became a monk there. After three years at the monastery, he left in quest of a more austere life and became a disciple of a hermit named Marinus near Venice. About 978, the two of them with Abbot Guarinus of Cuxa in Catalonia persuaded Peter Orseolo, doge of Venice, to resign (he had become doge by acquiescing in the murder of his predecessor). Peter accompanied Marinus and Romuald back to Cuxa and became a Benedictine there, while Romuald and Marinus built a hermitage near the monastery and lived as hermits. Romuald returned to Italy ten years later to help his father, Sergius, who had become a monk after his duel, resolve his doubts about his vocation. Emperor Otto III appointed Romuald abbot of San Apollinare in Classe, but he left after two years to live as a hermit near Pereum. He then set out to evangelize the Magyars in Hungary but was forced to turn back because of illness and probably by his age. He spent the rest of his life founding monasteries and hermitages in northern and central Italy, notably at Vallombrosa in 1012, and in 1023 at Camaldoli near Arezzo. The five hermitages he built at Camaldoli developed into the mother house of the Camaldolese Order, which combined the cenobitic and eremitical life under a modified Benedictine rule that he drew up. He died at Valdi Castro near Fabiano on June 19. February 7.

ROMULA (6th century). *See* Redempta.

ROMULUS (d. c. 90). According to tradition, he was a Roman converted by St. Peter who became the first bishop of Fiesole, Italy, and suffered martyrdom there with Carissimus, Dulcissimus, and Crescentius during the reign of Emperor Domitian. A worthless eleventh-century fiction has him the illegitimate son of Lucerna and her father's slave Cyrus. Romulus was abandoned, suckled by a wolf, and captured by St. Peter when Emperor Nero was unable to do so. Romulus later performed all kinds of extravagant miracles after being instructed by Peter's companion Justin. After evangelizing much of central Italy, Romulus was put to death by the governor, Repertian. July 6.

RONAN. *See* Rumon.

ROQUE. *See* Roch.

ROQUE, PETER RENÉ, BL. (1758–96). Born at Vannes, France, he studied at the seminary there, was ordained in 1782, served as chaplain of the Dames de la Retraite for four years, and then joined the Lazarists in Paris. He became a professor of theology at Vannes, was forced into hiding at the outbreak of the French Revolution when he refused to take the Constitutional Oath of the revolutionary government, but was betrayed, captured, and sentenced to death. He was guillotined at Vannes on March 1, and was beatified in 1934 by Pope Pius XI.

ROSALIA (d. c. 1160). According to legend, she was born in Sicily, the daughter of Sinibald, lord of Quisquina and Rosae, and in her youth became a hermitess near Bivona, Sicily. She later moved to a cave on Monte Pellegrino near Palermo, where she died, probably on September 4. She is principal patron of Palermo, named as such in gratitude for her role in ending a plague there in 1640.

ROSCELLI, AGOSTINO (1818–1902). Agostino was literally a shepherd boy, an occupation which provided him plenty of time for contemplation and development of a prayer life. In 1835, with the assistance of some patrons, he went to Genoa to study. He was ordained in 1846 and lived a life of service thereafter. In Genoa he served as chaplain to the provinical orphanage, a prison chaplain to those condemned to death, and started a school for poor young women. He founded the Institute of Sisters of the Immaculata to administer the school. Agostino was canonized in 2001. May 7.

ROSE OF LIMA (d. 1586). Isabel de Santa Maria de Flores was born at Lima, Peru, of Spanish parents and took the name Rose at confirmation. Noted for her beauty, she resisted her parents' efforts to have her marry and practiced great austerities, taking St. Catherine of Siena as her model from her childhood days. She became a Dominican tertiary, lived as a recluse in a shack in the garden she had worked to help her parents, who had fallen on difficult times, and experienced mystical gifts and visions of such an extraordinary nature that a commission of priests and doctors was appointed to examine her. They decided they were of supernatural origin. Stories of her holiness spread, and her garden became the spiritual center of the city; when earthquakes struck nearby, her prayers were credited with sparing Lima. In ill health, she accepted the offer of Don Gonzalo de Massa and his wife to take care of her, and she spent the last three years of her life in their home in Lima and died there on August 24. She was canonized in 1671 by Pope Clement X, the first saint of the New World. She is patroness of South America. August 23.

ROSE OF VITERBO (1234–52). Born of poor parents at Viterbo, Romagna, Italy, she had a vision of Mary when she was eight and began preaching on the streets when she was twelve, supporting the Pope and exhorting the Guelphs to drive out the occupying Ghibelline garrison. She was banished by the *podestà* when adherents of Emperor Frederick II, whom she constantly denounced, sought her death, and she went to Soriano. In 1250 she prophesied Frederick's death, which took place a few days later. She was refused admittance to the convent of St. Mary of the Roses in Viterbo for lack of a dowry, had a house and a chapel she occupied near the convent closed down on the demand of the convent, returned to her parents' home in Viterbo, and died there on March 6 at the age of seventeen. She was canonized in 1457. September 4.

ROSELINE, BL. (d. 1329). Of a distinguished family, and the daughter of

Baron des Ares, Roseline de Villeneuve was educated by Poor Clare nuns and joined the Carthusians at Bertrand Convent when she was twenty-five. She became prioress of Celle Roubaud in Provence twelve years later, experienced visions and ecstasies, had the gift of reading men's souls, and practiced great mortifications. She died at Celle Roubaud on January 17, and her cult was confirmed in 1851.

ROSENDO. *See* Rudesind.

ROSSELLO, JOSEPHA (1811–80). Daughter of a potter, she was born at Albisola Marina, Liguria, Italy, and was baptized Benedetta. When she was sixteen, she became a Franciscan tertiary and was dissuaded from becoming a hermitess by her spiritual director, Capuchin Fr. Angelo of Savona. She took care of an invalid in Savona for nine years, and when her patient, Mr. Monteleone, died, she, Pauline Barla, and two cousins, Angela and Domenica Pescio, founded a community in Savona in 1837, the Daughters of Our Lady of Pity, devoted to the education of poor girls, the founding of hospitals, and doing charitable works. Angela was named superior, and Benedetta, now Josepha, mistress of novices; Josepha was elected superior in 1840 and held that position the rest of her life. The congregation received diocesan approval in 1846, and by the time of Josepha's death had some sixty-eight foundations—hospitals, schools, homes for wayward girls and even a House of Clerics to encourage vocations to the priesthood. Her last years were troubled by illness and spiritual aridity. She died on December 7, and was canonized in 1949 by Pope Pius XII.

ROSSI, JOHN BAPTIST (1698–1764). Born at Voltaggio near Genoa, Italy, he served in the household of a nobleman in Genoa for three years and when he

was thirteen entered Roman College. He left because of ill health but finished his training at the Minerva and was ordained in 1721. He spent the next forty years of his life ministering to the sick in hospitals and the needy—especially homeless women, for whom he founded a refuge. Assigned to St. Maria Church near the Aventine, he acquired a reputation as a confessor that drew crowds to the church, became canon there in 1736, but gave away the canonry's income and was a popular preacher, known for his supernatural gifts and reputed miracles. He died of apoplexy on May 23, and was canonized in 1881.

ROYE, FRANCIS DE (d. 1572). Born at Brussels, Belgium, he joined the Franciscans at Gorkum, Holland, and was stationed at their convent there. Soon after his ordination, a group of Calvinists seized the city and despite an order from the Prince of Orange to release them, he and eleven fellow Franciscans were taken to Briel and summarily executed. They were all canonized as the Martyrs of Gorkum by Pope Pius IX in 1867. July 9.

ROYO, BL. JOACHIM (1690–1747). *See* Sanz, Bl. Peter.

RUADAN (d. c. 584). Born in Leinster, Ireland, he became a disciple of St. Finian of Clonard, was founding abbot of Lothra Monastery in Tipperary, where he directed 150 monks, and is considered one of the 12 apostles of Ireland. April 15.

RUADAN. *See* Rumon.

RUAN. *See* Rumon.

RUDERIC. *See* Roderic.

RUDESIND (907–77). Of a noble Spanish Galician family and also known as Rosendo, he was named bishop of Dumium (Mondoñedo) against his wishes when he was only eighteen. He was put in charge of the see of Compostela when his wastrel cousin Bishop Sisnand was imprisoned by King Sancho for neglect of his ecclesiastical duties. During an absence of King Sancho, Rudesind headed an army that drove invading Norsemen from Galicia and then drove invading Moors from Portugal. When Sancho died in 967, Sisnand escaped from prison and threatened Rudesind with death if he did not relinquish the see of Compostela. Rudesind retired to St. John of Caveiro Monastery, which he had founded, built another monastery, Celanova, at Villar, and then founded several others. He became abbot of Celanova when Abbot Franquila died, was sought after for advice by ecclesiastics from all parts of Portugal, and was credited with many miracles of healing. He was canonized in 1195. March 1.

RUFINA (d. c. 257). According to legend, she and her sister Secunda were daughters of Asterius, a Roman senator. They were engaged to be married but when their fiancés apostatized during the persecution of Christians under Emperor Valerian, they refused to do so and were forced to flee from Rome to escape the persecution. They were captured, tortured, and then beheaded at the order of the prefect, Junius Donatus, for their Christianity. July 10.

RUFINA (d.c. 287). *See* Justa.

RUFINAS (d. c. 287). He and Valerius were Christians of Soissons, Gaul, who fled at the outbreak of Emperor Dioceltian's persecution of the Christians. They were captured, tortured, and then beheaded. Some scholars believe they were part of a group of missionaries sent from Rome to evangelize Gaul; others that they were Gallo-Romans who were keepers of the granaries of an imperial palace on the Vesle River. June 14.

RUFUS (d. c. 107). He and Zosimus were citizens of Antioch (or perhaps Philippi) who were brought to Rome with St. Ignatius of Antioch during the reign of Emperor Trajan. They were condemned to death for their Christianity and thrown to wild beasts in the arena two days before the martyrdom of Ignatius. December 18.

RUGG, BL. JOHN (d. 1539). *See* Faringdon, Bl. Hugh.

RUIZ, BL. EMMANUEL (1804–60). Born of humble parents in Santander, Spain, he became a Franciscan priest and in time was sent to Damascus, Syria, where he became superior of the Franciscan friary there. He was murdered on July 9 with seven other Franciscans and three Marionite laymen of the friary by having his head split open with an ax when he refused to become a Moslem during the anti-Christian Druse-inspired riots that shook Syria in 1860, during which thousands of Christians were massacred. He and his brother Franciscans together with the three Marionites were beatified in 1926 by Pope Pius XI. July 11.

RUMOLD (d. c. 775). Also known as Rombault, untrustworthy sources have him an Irish monk (though he may have been English) who went to Rome and was consecrated regionary bishop there. He joined St. Willibrord in missionary work in Brabant and Holland and preached with great success until he was murdered by two men he had denounced for their evil ways near Malines (Mechlin), Flanders. The Roman Martyrology commemorates him on

June 24 as bishop of Dublin and son of a Scottish King. July 3.

RUMON (6th century). Also known as Ruan, Ronan, and Ruadan, he was probably a brother of Bishop St. Tudwal of Trequier, but nothing else is known of him beyond that he was probably an Irish missionary and many churches in Devon and Cornwall in England were named after him. Some authorities believe he is the same as a St. Ronan (June 1) venerated in Brittany and believed consecrated bishop by St. Patrick, but others believe that he and St. Kea were British monks who founded a monastery at Street, Somerset. August 30.

RUMWALD (7th century). A farfetched legend has him the son of King Alehfrid of Northumbria and St. Cyneburga and born at King's Sutton, Northamptonshire, England. He declaimed his profession of faith at his baptism, preached to his parents, and died three days after his birth on November 3.

RUPERT (d. c. 710). A Frank (though he is said by some to have been the same as an Irishman named Robertach) and also known as Hrodbert, he became a bishop at Worms and in about 697 came to Regensburg, where he was encouraged by Duke Theodo, whom he converted along with many of his subjects. Rupert adapted heathen temples to churches, built churches, and converted most of Bavaria to Christianity. With the duke's help, he rebuilt an old town, Juvavum, renamed it Salzburg, and built a church, monastery, and school there. He brought in more missionaries, built a convent at Nonnberg, appointing a close relative, possibly his sister, first abbess, and developed the salt mines in the area. He died at Salzburg, of which he is considered the first bishop. March 29.

RUPERT (c. 795–c. 815). See Bertha (d. c. 840).

RUSTICUS (d. c. 258). See Dionysius.

RUSTICUS (d. c. 461). Born at Marseilles or Narbonnaise in Gaul, the son of Bishop Bonosus, he became a well-known preacher in Rome and then a monk at Lérins. He was ordained and was named bishop of Narbonne in 427. He asked permission of Pope Leo I to resign because of dissension among the orthodox of his see and the spread of Arianism in the wake of the Gothic siege of Narbonne, but was dissuaded by Leo. Rusticus attended the synod at Arles that approved St. Leo's *Epistola dogmatica* (his famous Tome) to Flavian of Constantinople denouncing Nestorianism. Rusticus also built a cathedral at Narbonne. October 26.

RUSTICUS (d. 484). See Liberatus of Capua.

RUYSBROECK, BL. JOHN (1293–1381). Born at Ruysbroeck near Brussels, Flanders, he was raised from the age of eleven and educated by his Uncle John Hinckaert, a canon at St. Gudule's in Brussels, and was ordained in 1317. For the next twenty-six years, he, his uncle, and another canon named Francis van Coudenberg lived a life of extreme austerity, retirement, and contemplation. During this time, John actively fought the heresies and false mysticism of the Brethren of the Free Spirit, writing several pamphlets attacking their teaching. In 1343, John, his uncle, and Francis retired to a hermitage at Groenendael near Brussels to live as hermits. They attracted so many disciples that in 1349 they formed a community of Canons Regular of St. Augustine, with John as prior. His fame as a contemplative, director of souls, and a man of God spread, bringing visitors from all over Europe. Groenendael became a school of sanctity, and John's *Devotio moderna* was to influence deeply the Brethren of the Common Life and the Canons Regular of Windesheim, notable among them Thomas à Kempis and Dionysius the Carthusian. John was the foremost Flemish mystic, and his treatises on mysticism and sanctity, all written in Flemish, had an enormous impact on his time. Among his works are *Spiritual Espousals, Spiritual Tabernacles,* and *The Kingdom of God's Lovers.* He died at Groenendael on December 2, and his cult was approved in 1908.

S

SABAS (439–532). Born at Mutalaska, Cappadocia, near Caesarea, he was the son of any army officers there who when assigned to Alexandria left him in the care of an uncle. Mistreated by his uncle's wife, Sabas ran away to another uncle, though he was only eight. When the two uncles became involved in a lawsuit over his estate, he again ran away, this time to a monastery near Mutalaska. In time the uncles were reconciled and wanted him to marry, but he remained in the monastery. In 456, he went to Jerusalem and there entered a monastery under St. Theoctistus. When he was thirty, he became a hermit under the guidance of St. Euthymius, and after Euthymius' death spent four years alone in the desert near Jericho. Despite his desire for solitude, he attracted disciples, organized them into a *laura* in 483, and when his 150 monks asked for a priest and despite his opposition to monks being ordained, he was obliged to accept ordination by Patriarch Sallust of Jerusalem in 491. He attracted disciples from Egypt and Armenia, allowed them a liturgy in their own tongue, and built several hospitals and another monastery near Jericho. He was appointed archimandrite of all hermits in Palestine who lived in separate cells, but his custom of going off by himself during Lent caused dissension in the monastery, and sixty of his monks left to revive a ruined monastery at Thecuna. He bore them no ill will and aided them with food and supplies. In 511, he was one of a delegation of abbots sent to Emperor Anastasius I, a supporter of Eutychianism, which Sabas opposed, to plead with the Emperor to mitigate his persecution of orthodox bishops and religious; they were unsuccessful. Sabas supported Elias of Jerusalem when the Emperor exiled him, was a strong supporter of theological orthodoxy, and persuaded many to return to orthodoxy. He was a vigorous opponent of Origenism and monophysitism. In 531, when he was ninety-one, he again went to Constantinople, this time to plead with Emperor Justinian to suppress a Samaritan revolt and protect the people of Jerusalem from further harassment by the Samaritans. He fell ill soon after his return to his *laura* from this trip and died on December 5 at Laura Mar Saba, after naming his successor. Sabas is one of the most notable figures of early monasticism and is considered one of the founders of Eastern monasticism. The *laura* he founded in the desolate, wild country between Jerusalem and the Dead Sea, named Mar Saba after him, was often called the Great Laura for its preeminence and produced many great saints; it is still inhabited by monks of the Eastern Orthodox Church and is one of the three or four oldest inhabited monasteries in the world.

SABAS. *See* Sava.

SABAS THE GOTH (d. 372). A Goth who had been converted to Christianity in his youth, he became lector to Sansala, a priest in Targoviste in Romania. Sabas denounced the practice of certain Christians of pretending to eat meat offered to pagan gods though in reality it had not been eaten and was forced out of the town but was later allowed to return. In another persecution of the Christians, he loudly proclaimed his Christianity but was allowed to go unharmed. During a third persecution a group of pagan Gothic soldiers under Atharidus arrested Sansala and Sabas. Despite the tortures to which he was subjected, he emerged from each of them unscathed. Finally Atharidus ordered him to be drowned, and though the leaders of the execution party offered to let him go free, he refused and was drowned in the Mussovo River near Targoviste. Another fifty Christians suffered martyrdom in the same persecution. April 12.

SABINA (d. c. 119). According to her untrustworthy legend, she was converted to Christianity by her Syrian servant, Serapia. Serapia suffered martyrdom for her faith during the reign of Emperor Hadrian on July 29, and Sabina suffered the same fate a month later. August 29.

SABINIAN (d. c. 275). Untrustworthy sources make him a native of the island of Samos who was converted to Christianity and with his sister St. Sabina went to Gaul. He was so successful in making converts that he was haled before Emperor Aurelian and condemned to death by beheading after fire and arrows had proved ineffective as means of execution. He was beheaded at Troyes, of which he is considered the apostle. January 29.

SABINUS (d. c. 303). According to legend he was an Italian bishop, but where is uncertain, since Assisi, Chiusi, Faenza, and Spoleto all claim him. He and several of his clergy were arrested during the persecution of Christians under Emperor Diocletian and brought before Venustian, governor of Etruria. When Sabinus smashed a statue of Jupiter to bits, Venustian ordered both his hands cut off and had two of Sabinus' deacons, Marcellus and Exuperantius, tortured to death. Sabinus was returned to prison and when he cured the blind son of Serena, a widow, he converted several of his fellow prisoners and then Venustian, who later suffered martyrdom. Sabinus was then beaten to death at Spoleto and buried a short distance from there. This last is all that is known factually of him—that a martyr named Sabinus was buried near Spoleto. December 30.

SABINUS (d. 420). Bishop of Piacenza, he was highly esteemed for his learning and attended the Council of Aquileia in 381, which condemned Jovinian. Sabinus probably was legate for Pope St. Damasus to Antioch during the Meletian schism, at which time he was a deacon at Milan. January 17.

SABINUS (5th century). According to untrustworthy legend, he was born at Barcelona, Spain, was also known as Savin, and was raised by his widowed mother. After a nephew he was tutoring became a monk at Ligugé, he too became a monk there. He left to become a hermit attached to a monastery at Palatium Aemilianum in the Pyrenees and became known for his austerities and miracles. He died in his cell near the village now called Saint-Savin de Tarbes. October 9.

SABINUS (d. c. 566). Born at Canosa, Apulia, Italy, he was most generous to the poor in his youth and in time was named bishop of his native town. He was legate for Pope St. Agapitus I to the court of Emperor Justinian to support Patriarch St. Mennas against the heretic Anthimus and attended Mennas' council in 536. Sabinus was blind the last years of his life. February 9.

SABUTAKA (d. 421). *See* Maharsapor.

SACERDOS (d. 551). Named bishop of Lyons, Gaul, in 544, he became an adviser to King Childebert and presided over the Council of Orléans in 549. Among the other names by which he is known are Sardot and Serdon. September 12.

SADOC, BL. (d. 1260). Probably a Hungarian, he became a Dominican and was sent with a group of Dominican missionaries under a Hungarian named Paul to evangelize Hungary. After working in Hungary for a time, Sadoc went to Sandomir, Poland, where he was founding superior of a Dominican friary. When the Tartars captured Sandomir in 1260 they murdered Sadoc and the forty-eight other members of his community. His cult and those of his comrades were confirmed by Pope Pius VII. June 2.

SADOTH (d. c. 342). Deacon to Bishop St. Simeon Barsabae of Seleucia-Ctesiphon, whom he represented at Nicaea in 325, Sadoth succeeded to the see when Simeon was martyred during the persecution of Christians by Persian King Sapor II. Sadoth was forced to go into hiding for a time, but when Sapor came to Seleucia, Sadoth and scores of the faithful were imprisoned. They were subjected to torture over the next five months, and Sadoth was then beheaded at Beit-Lapat, Persia, less than a year after he had become bishop. February 20.

SAHAK. *See* Isaac the Great.

SAIRE. *See* Salvius.

SAKAKIBARA, JOACHIM (1557–97). *See* Miki, Paul.

SALABERGA (d. c. 665). Cured of blindness by St. Eustace of Luxeuil when she was a child, she married a nobleman named Blandinus when her first husband died. They had five children and then by mutual consent they separated, he to become a hermit and she to enter a convent she had endowed at Poulangey. About 650, she founded the convent of St. John the Baptist at Laon and lived there until her death. September 22.

SALÈS, BL. JAMES (1556–93). Born at Auvergne, France, he was educated at the Jesuit college at Billom and joined the Jesuits there when he was seventeen. He continued his studies at the University of Pont-à-Mousson, was its first graduate, and then went to Paris for further study. He was refused permission to go to India as a missionary because of his talents as a teacher and preacher. In 1592, he was appointed to preach during Advent at Aubenas, a Huguenot stronghold, and was so successful in his preaching that the mayor of the town requested him to stay on and preach the Lenten sermons. He and a lay brother, William Saultemouche, a servant he had met at Billom, were attacked by a gang of Huguenots, brought before a kangaroo court of Calvinist ministers, and after a day of heated theological debate both were stabbed and shot to death on February 7. They were beatified in 1926.

SALMON, BL. PATRICK (d. 1594). *See* Cornelius, Bl. John.

SALOME (1st century). Wife of Zebedee and mother of the apostles James and John (Matt. 20:20; 27:56), she asked Christ to allow her sons to sit next to him in his kingdom (Matt. (20:20ff.). She was present at the crucifixion (Matt. 27:56; Mark 15:40) of Christ and was one of the women who discovered the empty tomb (Mark

16:1ff.). She is sometimes called Mary Salome. October 22.

SALOME (9th century). According to legend, she was an Anglo-Saxon princess who, on the way back from pilgrimage to Jerusalem, was temporarily blinded and lost all her possessions. When she arrived at Altaich, Bavaria, she became an anchoress in a cell attached to the monastery-church built by Walter the abbot, a reputed relative. Sometime later, Judith, an aunt or cousin sent by the English king to find Salome, arrived at Altaich, decided to become an anchoress and occupied a cell built for her adjoining that of Salome. She remained on after Salome's death, experienced diabolical attacks, and was buried with her niece when she died. Though a legend, some scholars believe Salome may have been Edburga, daughter of King Offa of Marcia. Beautiful but evil, she married King Beorhtric of the West Saxons and after murdering several of his nobles accidentally poisoned Beorhtric. She was banished from England, took refuge at the court of Charlemagne, was given a nunnery by the monarch, but was driven from it because of her disgraceful conduct. Poverty-stricken, she took to begging in the streets of Patavia (Passau) close to Altaich. She could then have become a recluse there, changing her name. June 29.

SALOME, BL. (c. 1202–68). Daughter of King Leszek the Fair of Poland, she was betrothed to Prince Coloman, son of King Andrew II of Hungary, and was taken to Andrew's court when she was three years old. Salome and Coloman were married ten years later. She became a Franciscan tertiary, reformed the court, and when Coloman was killed in battle about 1225, founded a Poor Clare convent at Zawichost; it was later transferred to Skala. She became a nun there in 1240 and later was abbess. She died on November 17, and her cult was approved by Pope Clement X. November 18.

SALOMONIUS, BL. JAMES (1231–1314). Born of a noble family at Venice, he distributed his inheritance to the poor when he was seventeen and joined the Dominicans. He served as prior at Forlì, Faenza, San Severino, and Ravenna and was known for his austerity, holiness, and devotion to the poor. He was gifted with ecstasies and visions, was reported to have performed numerous miracles, and was himself reported to have been cured of cancer shortly before his death at Forlì on May 31. His cult was approved for Forlì in 1526, for Venice by Pope Paul V, and for the Dominicans by Pope Gregory XV. He is also known as James the Venetian.

SALVATOR OF HORTA (d. 1567). Born at Santa Columba near Gerona, Spain, he was orphaned as a child, became a shoemaker in Barcelona, and joined the Observant Franciscans when he was twenty. He served as cook at friaries at Tortosa and Horta and then Barcelona and was venerated for his austerities and his miracles of healing. He died at Cagliari, Sardinia, and was canonized in 1938. March 18.

SALVIUS (6th century). Also known as Saire, all that is known of him is that he was a hermit in the forest of Bray in Normandy and is often confused with St. Salvius of Albi and St. Salvius of Amiens. October 28.

SALVIUS (d. 584). Born at Albi, Gaul, and also known as Salvy, he became a lawyer, served as a magistrate, and then became a monk. He was elected abbot but lived as a hermit until 574, when he was named bishop of Albi. He lived in great austerity, was known for his aid to the poor, and ransomed a number of prisoners taken by Mommolus, a patrician who had taken prisoners at Albi. Salvius, with his friend St. Gregory of Tours, helped King Chilperic correct his lapse from orthodoxy. Salvius died of plague contracted while ministering to plague victims on September 10.

SALVIUS (d. c. 625). Also known as Sauve, he succeeded Ado as bishop of Amiens, which is all that is known of Salvius. January 11.

SALVIUS (d. c. 768). Also known as Sauve, he was a regionary bishop who came to Valenciennes, France, in about 768 and was successful in evangelizing that area of France. He and his companion, called Superius (though his real name is not known), were murdered, reputedly by the son of an official of Valenciennes for his fine clothes. June 26.

SALVY. *See* Salvius.

SAMONAS (4th century). *See* Gurias.

SAMSON (c. 485–565). Born at Glamorgan, Wales, he was dedicated to God as a child and enrolled under St. Illtud at his monastery at Llanwit, Glamorgan. Samson was ordained, had an attempt made on his life by two of Illtud's nephews jealous of his ordination, and then lived for a time as a hermit under Piro on the island of Caldey (Ynys Byr) off the coast of Pembrokeshire. His father, Amon, and his Uncle Umbrafel joined him there after Amon recovered from a serious illness when he received the last rites from his son. When Piro died, Samson succeeded him as abbot but resigned after a trip to Ireland and resumed his eremitical life with Amon and two others. Samson was soon after appointed abbot of St. Dubricius Monastery and consecrated bishop. He then traveled through Cornwall where he worked as a missionary, founded

monasteries and churches at Southill and Golant, probably visited the Scilly Islands, and then went to Brittany to continue his missionary activities. He founded monasteries at Dol, of which he was abbot, and at Pental in Normandy, successfully supported Judual as ruler of Brittany against Conmor in 555, and is reported to have been named bishop of Dol by King Childebert. Samson died at Dol. July 28.

SAMSON (5th century). A wealthy physician at Constantinople, he became a priest, built a hospital for the sick there, and was known as "the father of the poor" for his charity and concern for the poor of the city. June 27.

SAMUEL (d. 309). *See* Elias.

SAMUEL (d. 1227). *See* Daniel.

SANCHIA (1182–1229). Daughter of King Sancho I of Portugal and sister of BB. Teresa and Mafalda, she retired to her father's estates at Alenquer when he died in 1211 and aided the first Franciscan and Dominican foundations in Portugal. She founded a convent at Celles with the Augustinian rule, which she later changed into a Cistercian abbey in 1223 and became a nun there. Her cult and that of her sister Teresa were approved in 1705. June 17.

SANCHO. *See* Sanctius.

SANCTIS, MICHAEL DE (1589–1625). Born at Vich, Spanish Catalonia, perhaps in 1591, he was early attracted to the religious life, was apprenticed to a merchant in his youth, and joined the Trinitarians at Barcelona in 1603, taking his vows at Saragossa in 1607. He transferred to the reformed Trinitarians, made his novitiate at Madrid, renewed his vows with the reformed at Alcalà, studied at Seville and Salamanca, and was ordained. He served as superior of the Valladolid convent twice, had a deep devotion to the Blessed Sacrament, and was reported to have experienced ecstasies, levitation, and to have performed miracles. He died on April 10, and was canonized in 1862.

SANCTIUS (d. 851). Also known as Sancho, he was born at Albi, France, was captured when a boy by the Moors, and was brought to Cordova, where he was trained as a janissary. When he declared his Christianity, he was condemned to death, was tortured, and was then impaled to death. June 5.

SANCTUS (d. 177). *See* Pothinus.

SANDYS, VEN. JOHN (d. 1586). Born at Chester, England, he studied for the priesthood at Rheims and was ordained there in 1584. He was sent on the English mission, was soon captured, and was executed at Gloucester on August 11.

SANSEDONI, BL. AMBROSE (1220–86). Son of a famous Sienese family, he was born in Siena with paralyzed arms and legs, which were reportedly cured instantly when he was taken to a church by his nurse. He joined the Dominicans when he was seventeen, studied at Cologne under St. Alber the Great, had Thomas Aquinas as a fellow student, and became noted for his teaching ability and knowledge. He taught at Paris for three years and was enormously successful as a preacher and also as a mediator between quarreling princes. He preached a crusade at the request of Pope Gregory X, halted a heresy in Bohemia, and twice convinced the Pope to lift interdicts he had placed on Siena. Throughout his lifetime, Ambrose remained a humble monk, performing the most menial tasks in the houses of his Order, leading a life

of great austerity and sanctity. He refused the offer of a bishopric. He was stricken while preaching and died soon after. His cult was confirmed in 1622, and he is also known as Ambrose of Siena.

SANTES OF MONTE FABRI (d. 1390). After killing a man in self-defense, he became a Franciscan lay brother, led a life of great holiness, and had numerous miracles attributed to him after his death. September 7.

SANTUCCIA TERREBOTTI, BL. (d. 1305). Born at Gubbio, Umbria, Italy, she married and when her daughter Julia died, the couple decided to enter the religious life. Santuccia became abbess of a community of Benedictine nuns in her native town and then moved it to Rome, where it became known as the Servants of Mary, the Santucci. Her cult has never been formally confirmed. March 22.

SANZ, BL. PETER (1680–1747). Born at Asco, Catalonia, Spain, he joined the Dominicans in 1697, in 1714 was sent as a missionary to the Philippines, and from there was sent to Fukien Province in China. In 1730, he was made bishop of Mauricastro and vicar apostolic of Fukien. A renewed persecution of Christians flared up in 1746 and he was accused of breaking the laws by converting thousands to Christianity by a man to whom he had refused to lend money. Imprisoned with him were fellow Spanish Dominicans Frs. Joachim Royo and John Alcober, and they were soon joined by Frs. Francis Serrano and Francis Diaz. After a year in prison at Foochow, Bl. Peter was beheaded; when word arrived that Fr. Serrano (October 20) had been appointed titular bishop of Tipsa and coadjutor to Bl. Peter, he and the other three were summarily executed at Fukien. They were all beatified by Pope Leo XIII in 1893. May 26.

SAPOR (d. 339). A bishop in Persia who was known for the conversions he made and for his church-building, he was arrested with another bishop named Isaac with Abraham, Mahanes, and Simeon during the persecution of Christians under King Sapor II. Bishop Sapor was arraigned before the King and beaten when he refused to subscribe to Mazdeism; he died several days later of his injuries. Isaac was stoned to death; Mahanes was flayed to death; Abraham had his eyes bored out with a red-hot iron; and Simeon was buried to his chest and then used for target practice and shot to death with arrows. November 30.

SARBELIUS (d. 101). Pagan high priest at Edessa, Mesopotamia, he was converted to Christianity with his sister Barbea and then tortured and martyred at Edessa during the persecution of Christians under Emperor Trajan. January 29.

SARDOT. *See* Sacerdos.

SARKANDER, JAN (1576–1620). Canonized 419 years after his birth in the Polish city of Skoczow, Jan Sarkander's life can be characterized in two ways. Pope John Paul II called Sarkander a martyr of the Church and a protector of the people of Moravia and their Catholic faith during the Thirty Years War. Protestants of the region—the majority of the population during Sarkander's life—view him as a persecutor and a traitor, accusing him of leading enemy troops into Morovia with the purpose of forcing the conversion of the non-Catholic population. Sarkander entered the priesthood after the death of his wife and served as a parish priest in Moravia. Charged with treason, he was put to death by Protestant officials in 1620. Said Pope John Paul II: "His can-

onization first of all gives honor to all those in this century, not only in Moravia and Bohemia but throughout Eastern Europe, who preferred the loss of property, marginalization and death, rather than submit to oppression and violence." He was canonized in 1995. March 17.

SASANDA, BL. LOUIS (d. 1624). Son of Michael Sasanda, who had been martyred at Yeddo, Japan, he joined the Franciscans in Mexico and was sent to the Philippines, where he was ordained in Manila in 1622. He accompanied Bl. Louis Sotelo back to Japan later the same year and was arrested and burned to death for his Christianity on August 25 with BB. Louis Sotelo and Louis Baba and two others. They were beatified in 1867.

SATOR (d. c. 303). *See* Honoratus.

SATURIAN (d. 458). *See* Martinian.

SATURNINUS (d. 203). *See* Perpetua.

SATURNINUS (3rd century). Also known as Sernin, he was sent as a missionary from Rome to the Pyrenees Mountains area and became first bishop of Toulouse. He was dragged to death by a bull after he was seized by the priests of a pagan temple and refused to sacrifice to pagan gods. November 29.

SATURNINUS (d 304). A priest at Abitina, Africa, he was arrested with forty-nine of his congregation while he was saying Mass and charged with possessing copies of the Bible, which Emperor Diocletian had forbidden. They were taken to Carthage, arraigned before the proconsul there, and then all were martyred, either from torture or from the rigors of prison. Among those martyred were Dativus and Felix, senators; Ampelius, Emeritus, Rogatian, and Thelica; also Saturninus, who were lectors, Mary, and Hilarion, a young child; and Victoria, a young noblewoman who had escaped the marriage arranged for her by her pagan parents by jumping out a window on her wedding day and had dedicated herself to God at a neighboring church. February 11.

SATURNINUS (d. 304). *See* Optatus.

SATURNINUS (d. c. 309). Said to be a priest who came to Rome from Carthage, he was arrested with Sisinius, a deacon, during the persecution of Christians under Emperor Maximian. They were tortured, burned, and then beheaded. November 29.

SATURUS (d. 203). *See* Perpetua.

SATURUS (d. c. 455). *See* Armogastes.

SATYRUS (d. c. 379). Brother of St. Ambrose and St. Marcellina, he was probably born at Trier, Gaul, moved to Rome with his family when his father, praetorium of the Gauls, died about 354, and became a lawyer. He was appointed prefect of one of the provinces, resigned to take care of the secular affairs of the see of Milan when Ambrose was appointed its bishop in 374, and after being shipwrecked on a voyage to Africa, was baptized. He died unexpectedly in Milan and was eulogized by Ambrose in his famous funeral sermon "On the Death of a Brother." September 17.

SAULI, ALEXANDER (1534–92). Born at Milan, Italy, of a well-known Genoese family, he became a Barnabite when he was seventeen, studied at the Barnabite college at Pavia, and was ordained in 1556. He taught at the university at Pavia and soon achieved a reputation as a fiery preacher. He became spiritual adviser to St. Charles Borromeo and Cardinal Sfondrati (later Pope Gregory XIV), was named provost general of his Order in 1567, resisted the efforts of Borromeo to incorporate a group of Humiliati friars with the Barnabites, and in 1570 was appointed bishop of Aleria, Corsica. During the next twenty years he put into effect numerous reforms with such success that he was called "the Apostle of Corsica." He refused translation to the see of Tortona and then Genoa, but in 1591 Gregory translated him to Pavia. He died on October 11 while on a visitation to Colozza the following year. He was reputed to have performed miracles during his lifetime and after his death, and was canonized in 1904 by Pope St. Pius X.

SAULTEMOUCHE, BL. WILLIAM (d. 1593). *See* Salès, Bl. James.

SAUVE. *See* Salvius.

SAVA (1174–1237). Son of Stephen I, founder of the Nemanydes dynasty, and also known as Sabas, he became a monk on Mount Athos in Greece when he was seventeen. With his father, who abdicated in 1196, he founded Khilandrai Monastery on Mount Athos for Serbian monks and became abbot. He returned home in 1207 when his brothers, Stephen II and Vulkan, began to quarrel, and civil war broke out. Sava brought many of his monks with him, and from the headquarters he established at Studenitsa Monastery, he founded several monasteries and began the reformation and education of the country, where religion had fallen to a low estate. He was named metropolitan of a new Serbian hierarchy by Emperor Theodore II Laskaris at Nicaea; was consecrated, though for political reasons unwillingly, by Patriarch Manual I in 1219; returned home bringing more monks from Mount Athos; and in 1222 crowned his brother Stephen II, King of Serbia.

Through his efforts, he finished the uniting of his people that had been begun by his father, translated religious works into Serbian, and gave his people a native clergy and hierarchy. He made a pilgrimage to the Holy Land, was later sent on a second visit there on an ecclesiastical mission, and died on the way back at Tirnovo, Bulgaria, on January 14. He is the patron of Serbia.

SAVIN. *See* Sabinus.

SAVINIAN (d. c. 303). *See* Honoratus.

SAVINUS (d. 870). *See* Theodore.

SAVIO, DOMINIC (1842–57). Born of peasant family at Riva, Italy, he became a student under St. John Bosco at St. Francis de Sales oratory in Turin when he was twelve. There he formed the Company of the Immaculate to help Don Bosco in his work. Though only a young boy, he was blessed with spiritual gifts far beyond his age—knowledge of people in need, knowledge of the spiritual needs of those around him, and the ability to prophesy. A vision of his is reported to have strongly influenced Pope Pius IX to restore a hierarchy to England in 1850. Dominic died at Mondonio, Italy, and was canonized by Pope Pius XII in 1954. He is the patron of choirboys. March 9.

SCAMMACA, BL. BERNARD (d. 1486). Born of a noble family at Catania, Italy, he lived a dissolute youth but after a brawl in which he was injured, he mended his ways, joined the Dominicans, and led a life of austerity and rigorous penances. He is reputed to have performed miracles and had the gifts of prophecy and levitation. He died on February 9, and his cult was approved in 1825. February 17.

SCHENURE. *See* Shenute.

SCHERVIER, MARY FRANCES (1819–76). Born at Aachen, Germany, on January 3, she began helping the sick and the poor early in her life and in 1840 joined a charitable group devoted to aiding the poor. In 1845, she and four other women founded the Sisters of the Poor of St. Francis, with Frances as superior. They set up an infirmary at Aachen during a smallpox plague, cared for cholera victims, and by 1850 had established a hospital for incurables, several relief kitchens, and home nursing centers. The foundation received papal approbation after the bishop of Cologne had approved, spread to other parts of Germany with the opening of new homes and hospitals, and in 1855 sent a group of six sisters to establish a hospital in the United States at Cincinnati, Ohio. Frances died at Aachen on December 14, and was beatified in 1974 by Pope Paul VI. December 15.

SCHÖFFLER, BL. AUGUSTUS (1822–51). Born at Mittelbronn, Lorraine, he joined the Society of Foreign Missionaries in Paris, was sent to Tonkin, Indochina, in 1848, was arrested three years later during a persecution of Christians, and was beheaded. He was beatified in 1900.

SCHOLASTICA (d. 543). The sister of St. Benedict (and perhaps his twin), she founded and was abbess, probably under Benedict's direction, of a convent at Plombariola near Monte Cassino. She died there days after a visit to her brother, which St. Gregory describes in detail. She is considered the first Benedictine nun. February 10.

SCOPELLI, BL. JANE (1428–910. Born at Reggio, Emilia, Italy, she was refused permission by her parents to become a nun and lived an austere life at home. On the death of her parents, she founded Our Lady of the People

Carmelite Monastery at Reggio, became its prioress, and practiced great mortifications. Her prayers were reported to have effected many miracles. Her cult was confirmed in 1771. July 9. She is also known as Jane of Reggio.

SCOTIVOLI, BENEVENUTO (d. 1282). Born at Ancona, Italy, he studied law at Bologna but abandoned his studies to become a Franciscan and was ordained. He was appointed archdeacon at Ancona, administered the see of Osimo, which had supported Emperor Frederick II against the papacy, and reconciled it to the Holy See. He was appointed bishop of Osimo in 1264 and governor of the Marches of Ancona. He died at Osimo, and was canonized four years later by Pope Martin IV. March 22.

SCOTT, VEN. MONTFORT (d. 1591). Born at Norfolk, England, he went to Douai in 1574, was ordained a deacon, and returned to England in 1576. He was captured but soon released and returned to Douai, where he was ordained a priest. He then went back to England and worked in different areas, including Kent and Yorkshire, until he was arrested in 1548. After seven years in prison, he was released but was arrested almost immediately and was executed in London on July 2.

SCOTT, BL. WILLIAM (d. 1612). Born at Chigwell, Essex, England, he studied law at Cambridge, was converted to Catholicism, and in 1604 went to Spain, where he became a Benedictine at St. Facundus at Sahagun, taking the name Maurus, and was ordained. He was sent on the English mission, was arrested in London and imprisoned for a year, and then banished from the country. He was arrested and exiled several more times but finally was tried at the Old Bailey in London, with Bl. Richard Newport, and with him was convicted of treason because they were Catholic priests and hanged, drawn, and quartered at Tyburn on May 30. Both men were beatified in 1929.

SCROSOPPI, LUIGI (1804–84). Following the example of his two older half-brothers, Luigi Scrosoppi was attracted to the priesthood as a child. At the age of twelve he entered seminary and was ordained in 1827 as a priest of the diocese of Udine in Northern Italy. Together with his older brother Carlo, Luigi worked to alleviate the suffering of Udine's many orphans—the victims of war, famine, and disease. Over time, several of the girls educated in the school administered by Fathers Luigi and Carlo set out to establish their own congregation. The Sisters of Providence were established by nine of these women in 1837. Father Luigi served as both their founder and spiritual director. While the sisters and Father Luigi went about their work aiding the poor of Udine, the reunification of Italy was under way. The sisters, Father Luigi, and the city itself were unscathed by the anti-clericalism that accompanied the creation of modern Italy. Friar Luigi was forced to abandon formal connections with the Oratory of St. Philip when it was suppressed by the new government. Father Luigi was able to save the "House of Orphans," but only by giving control to civil authorities. The work of the sisters flourished in Austrian territory and Father Luigi devoted his life to the Order and its mission. He was canonized in 2001. April 13.

SEACHNALL. *See* Secundinus.

SEBALD (d. c. 770). According to untrustworthy sources, he was a hermit near Vincenza, Italy, went to Rome, and then accompanied St. Willibald as a missionary to Germany. Sebald lived as a hermit in the Reichswald, was reported to have performed numerous miracles, including turning icicles into firewood while staying at the cottage of a poor peasant, and is patron of Nuremberg. August 19.

SEBASTIAN (d. c. 288). According to his untrustworthy legend, he was born at Narbonne, Gaul, became a soldier in the Roman army at Rome in about 283, and encouraged Marcellian and Marcus, under sentence of death, to remain firm in their faith. Sebastian made numerous converts, among them the master of the rolls, Nicostratus, who was in charge of prisoners, and his wife, Zoé, a deaf mute whom he cured, the jailer Claudius, Chromatius, prefect of Rome, whom he cured of gout, and his son Tiburtius. Chromatius set the prisoners free, freed his slaves, and resigned as prefect. Sebastian was named captain in the praetorian guards by Emperor Diocletian, as did Emperor Maximian when Diocletian went to the East, neither knowing that Sebastian was a Christian. When it was discovered during Maximian's persecution of the Christians that Sebastian was a Christian, he was ordered executed. He was shot with arrows and left for dead, but when the widow of St. Castulus went to recover his body, she found he was still alive and nursed him back to health. Soon after, Sebastian intercepted the Emperor, denounced him for his cruelty to Christians, and was beaten to death on the Emperor's orders. That Sebastian was a martyr and was venerated at Milan as early as the time of St. Ambrose and was buried on the Appian Way is fact; all else is pious fiction dating back no earlier than the fifth century. He is patron of archers, athletes, and soldiers, and is appealed to as protection against plague. January 20.

SEBBE (d. c. 694). He became coruler of the East Saxons with Sighere in 664 and remained Christian when Sighere returned to the pagan gods when a plague swept the realm the same year. Sebbe worked with Bishop Jaruman to bring his people back to the faith and ruled wisely and justly for thirty years. He then gave up the crown to become a monk in London, distributed his wealth to the poor, and died soon after, in London on September 1.

SECHNALL. *See* Secundinus.

SECUNDA (d. 180). *See* Speratus.

SECUNDA (d. c. 257). *See* Rufina.

SECUNCINUS (d. 259). *See* Agapius.

SECUNDINUS (c. 375–447). Also known as Sechnall and Seachnall, he was sent from Gaul in 439 to assist St. Patrick in Ireland, together with Auxilius and Iserninus, became the first bishop of Dunslaughlin in Meath, and then auxiliary bishop of Armagh. He wrote several hymns, notably *Audites, omnes amantes Deum* in honor of Patrick and the earliest Latin hymn written in Ireland, and, *Sancti, venite, Christi corpus sumite.* November 27.

SECUNDINUS (5th century). *See* Priscus.

SECUNDIUS (1st century). *See* Torquatus.

SECUNDULUS (d. 203). *See* Perpetua.

SEINE. *See* Sequanus.

SELEUCUS (d. 309). *See* Elias.

SENAN (d. 560). Born of Christian parents at Munster, Ireland, he was a soldier for a time and then became a monk under Abbot Cassidus, who sent him to Abbot St. Natalis at Kilmanagh in

Ossory. Senan became known for his holiness and miracles and attracted great crowds to his sermons. He made a journey to Rome, meeting St. David on the way back, built several churches and monasteries, and then settled on Scattery Island, where he built a monastery that soon became famous. He died at Killeochailli on the way back from a visit to St. Cassidus monastery. March 8.

SENATOR (d. 475). One of the delegates sent to Constantinople by Pope St. Leo the Great to request Emperor Theodosius II to call a council to define the doctrine of Christ's two natures, he found that Theodosius had died when he arrived. Emperor Marcian called the Council of Chalcedon in 451. When Senator returned he was named papal delegate to a synod at Milan and in 472 was appointed bishop of Milan. May 28.

SENERIDUS. *See* Serenus.

SENNEN (d. c. 303). *See* Abdon.

SENOCH (d. 576). Born at Poitous, Gaul, of pagan parents, he was converted to Christianity and then became a hermit in Touraine. He was known for his austerities and holiness, attracted disciples, and was praised highly by St. Gregory of Tours, though he was once reprimanded by Gregory for his vanity and withdrawals from his fellow monks who had made him abbot. He died in the arms of Gregory, who reported he had performed numerous miracles. October 24.

SEPTIMUS (d. c. 303). *See* Honoratus.

SEPTIMUS (d. 484). *See* Liberatus of Capua.

SEQUANUS (d. c. 580). Also known as Seine, he was born at Mesmont, Burgundy, lived for a time as a hermit at Verrey-sous-Drée, and was ordained. He studied Scripture at Réomé Monastery, built his own monastery in the forest of Segestre, which attracted many disciples because of the holiness of its founder, and was reported to have performed miracles. The village that developed around the monastery became Saint-Seine. September 19.

SERAPHINA (d. 1253). Also known as Fina, she was born of poor parents at San Gemininiano, Tuscany, Italy, and was stricken with paralysis when she was a girl soon after her father died. She passed her life in great pain, bearing her suffering with great patience for years until her death on March 12.

SERAPHINO (1540–1604). Born at Montegranaro, Italy, he was a shepherd in his youth, was harshly treated by his older brother when they were orphaned, and when Seraphino was sixteen, he became a Capuchin lay brother at Ascoli Piceno. He was noted for his holiness, devotion to the Blessed Sacrament and to the poor, and for his spiritual wisdom. He died at Ascoli Piceno on October 12, and was canonized in 1767.

SERAPIA (d. c. 119). *See* Sabina.

SERAPION (d. c. 211). Famed for his learning, he became bishop of Antioch in 190, opposed Montanism and docetism, and forbade the reading of the apocrypahl gospel of Peter in the church at Rhossos. October 30.

SERAPION (d. 249). *See* Apollonia.

SERAPION (d. 284). *See* Victorinus.

SERAPION (d. c. 370). Head of the catechetical school at Alexandria and called "the Scholastic" for his learning, he became a hermit in the desert, where he and St. Antony became friends. Serapion was called from the desert to be bishop of Thumis, Lower Egypt, actively supported St. Athanasius, and attended the Council of Sardis in 347. Serapion fought Arianism and Manichaeism and wrote a treatise against the Manichaeans, on the Psalms, and *Eucholocium*, a sacramentary. He was exiled by Emperor Constantius II for his opposition to Arianism and his support of St. Athanasius and probably died in exile. March 21.

SERAPION, BL. (d. 1240). Probably born in England, he served in the army of Alfonso IX of Castile against the Moors in Spain and then joined the Mercedarians. After an unsuccessful trip to England to get new members for the Order, he went to Murcia and Algiers to secure the release of Christian prisoners of the Moors. He was held hostage at Algiers for the balance of the ransom he was to pay, and when it was discovered he had converted several Mohammedans to Christianity, he was crucified. His cult was approved by Pope Benedict XIII in 1728. November 14.

SERDON. *See* Sacerdos.

SERENICUS (d. c. 669). Also known as Cerenicus, he and his brother Serenus were of a patrician family of Spoleto. They became Benedictines in Rome but after living in community for a time went to Charnie Forest near Saulges, Maine, Gaul, and lived as hermits. Their holiness soon attracted many visitors, and in quest of greater solitude, Serenicus established a hermitage near the Sarthe River. He soon again attracted numerous disciples and he organized them into a community, of which he was abbot, following the Benedictine rule. He died at his monastery. Serenus remained at Saulges, became renowned as a miracle worker, experienced ecstasies and visions, and was credited with end-

ing a plague and a devastating drought with his prayers. Also known as Seneridus, he died in 680. May 7.

SERENUS (d. 680). *See* Serenicus.

SERENUS THE GARDENER (d. c. 302). Also known as Cerneuf, according to his probably fictitious legend he was born in Greece, immigrated to Sirmium (Metrovica, Yugoslavia), and was known for his garden. He went into hiding for a time to escape a persecution of Christians that had just begun, and on his return rebuked a lady for walking in his garden at an unseemly time. She reported to her husband that he had insulted her, and the husband, a member of the imperial guards, reported the matter to Emperor Maximian. Upon orders from the Emperor, the governor investigated the matter, found Serenus innocent of insulting the woman, but while examining him found he was a Christian. When Serenus refused to sacrifice to pagan gods, he was beheaded. February 23.

SERF (6th century). Also known as Servanus, untrustworthy legend has him an Irishman who was consecrated bishop by St. Palladius, founded a monastery at Culross, Scotland, and died and was buried there. One particularly extravagant story has him the son of the King of Canaan who renounced the throne, became Patriarch of Jerusalem, then Pope, and resigned the papacy to preach to the Scots. He is the patron of the Orkney Islands, though it is doubtful if he ever preached there. July 1.

SERGIUS (d. 303). His legend has Sergius an officer in the Roman army and Bacchus an officer under him, and both were friends of Emperor Maximian. When they did not enter a temple of Jupiter with the Emperor, he ordered them to do so. When they further refused his order that they sacrifice to pagan gods, they were humiliated by being led through the streets of Arabissus in women's garb and then sent to Rosafa, Mesopotamia, where they were scourged so terribly that Bacchus died of the scourging; Sergius was then tortured further and beheaded. October 7.

SERGIUS I (d. 701). Son of an Antioch, Syria, merchant, he was born and brought up at Palermo, Italy, an educated at Rome, where he became a priest. He was elected Pope on December 15, 687, succeeding Pope Conon, despite the claims of Pascal and Theodosius, when he was supported by the exarch John. However, Sergius was forced to pay John the amount of the bribe that Pascal had promised John to support his (Pascal's) nomination. He became embroiled in a controversy with Emperor Justinian II in 693 when he refused to sign the decrees of the previous year's Council of Trullanun, called by Justinian, because the council, except for one bishop, was attended only by Eastern bishops but passed canons applicable to the whole Church. If Serfius accepted these decrees, it would have meant that Constantinople was on an ecclesiastical level with Rome. The Emperor sent Zachary, his bodyguard commander, to Rome to bring Sergius to Constantinople, but the people of Rome and Ravenna resisted Zachary, who was forced to seek the protection of the Pope; eventually, Zachary was forced to leave the city. The matter ended when Justinian was deposed in 695. Sergius baptized Caedwalla, King of the West Saxons, in 689, consecrated St. Willibrod in 695, and encouraged English missions in Germany and Friesland. Interested in music (he had attended the *schola cantorum* in Rome), Sergius encouraged liturgical music, decreeing that the *Agnus Dei* be sung at

Mass. He died on September 7 in Rome. September 8.

SERGIUS (c. 1315–92). Of a noble Russian family, he was born near Rostov and christened Bartholomew. When he was fifteen he was forced to flee with his family from the attack on Rostov by the rulers of Moscow. They lost all and became peasant farmers at Radonezh near Moscow. In 1335, after his parents died, he and his brother Stephen lived as hermits at Makovka until Stephen left to enter a monastery. Sergius received the tonsure from an abbot in the area, taking the name Sergius, and continued his eremitical way of life in the bitter cold and isololation of the Russian winter. But word of his holiness spread, and he soon attracted disciples, whom he organized into the famous Holy Trinity Monastery, of which he was named abbot, and he was ordained at Pereyaslav Zalesky. He thus reestablished community life in Russia, which had disappeared from the Russian scene because of the Tartar invasion. In 1354 Sergius' decision in favor of cenobitical life for the community caused disagreement when a faction led by Stephen, who had joined him, objected, whereupon Sergius left and became a hermit on the banks of the Herzhach River. When many of the monks followed him, the monastery went into decline until he returned four years later at the request of Metropolitan Alexis of Moscow. On the advice of Sergius, Prince Dmitry Donskoy of Moscow decided to do battle with the Tartars and defeated them in the momentous Battle of Kulikovo Polye in 1380, a victory that freed Russian from Tartar domination. Its attribution to Sergius' inspiration and prayers further enhanced his reputation. He then traveled widely, promoting peace among rival Russian princes and establishing some forty monasteries. He refused the metropolitan see in 1378, resigned his abbacy early in 1392, and died six months later, on September 25. Sergius is considered the greatest of Russian saints. Many miracles were attributed to him, and he experienced visions and ecstasies. He had great influence with all classes (he is reputed to have stopped four civil wars between Russian princes) and was sought by all for his spiritual wisdom and love of his people.

SERGIUS (14th century). According to legend, he was the head of a trading group at Novgorod, Russia (another legend says he was from Byzantium), and became a hermit at Vaage, engaging in stonemasonry to support himself. With St. Germanus, he founded and was abbot of a Russian monastery on Valaam (Valamo) Island in Lake Ladoga in southeastern Finland, whence they evangelized the pagan Karelians around the lake. When the monastery was founded is uncertain, but tradition says late in the tenth century; another more probable date is 1329. June 28.

SERLO, BL. (d. 1104). A Norman, he joined the Benedictines of Mont St. Michel, went to England, and in 1071 was named abbot of Gloucester by William the Conqueror. He ruled the abbey for thirty-three years and increased the community from eight to more than a hundred in that time. He is reported to have written to William II in 1100, telling the King that one of his monks had dreamed the ruler was about to be stricken for the evil of his life; the King laughed, went on a hunt, and was killed by a huntsman's arrow. Serlo has never been formally beatified but is called "Blessed" in several Benedictine martyrologies. March 3.

SERNIN. See Saturninus.

SERRA, JUNIPERO (1713–84). Born in Mallorca, one of Spain's Ballearic Islands,

Serra volunteered to serve in the New World after being ordained by the Franciscans in 1737. Instead he spent twelve years teaching philosophy and theology until at age thirty-seven he was sent to Mexico. In 1768 as Jesuits responsible for Baja and Alta California missions departed, Serra was designated to take over the missions. Over the next sixteen years, he founded nine missions in what is present-day California. Beatified in 1988, he died in 1784 and is buried at Mission San Carlos Borromeo in Carmel.

SERVAIS. See Servatius.

SERVANUS See Serf.

SERVATIUS (d. 384). Probably an Armenian and also known as Servais, he became bishop of Tongres, Belgium, was an ardent defender of St. Athanasius, defended him at the Council of Sardica, and gave him refuge when he was banished. Servatius was one of the two bishops sent by Magnentius to present his case to Emperor Constantius II and was active against Arianism at the Council of Rimini in 359. Servatius prophesied the Huns' invasion of Gaul, went on penitential pilgrimage to Rome to pray for the safety of his flock, and died of fever at Tongres (or perhaps Maestrich) on his return. May 13.

SERVULUS (d. c. 590). According to St. Gregory the Great, Servulus was a beggar in Rome, afflicted with palsy since infancy, who lived on alms he solicited from people passing St. Clement's Church. He spent his lifetime giving thanks to God for his goodness, despite the squalor and pain of life. December 23.

SERVUS (d. 484). See Liberatus of Capua.

SETHRIDA (d. c. 660). See Ethelburga (d. 664).

SETON, ELIZABETH ANN (1774–1821). Born at New York City on August 28, she was the daughter of Richard Bayley, professor of anatomy at King's College (now Columbia) in New York and the stepsister of Archbishop James Roosevelt Bayley of Baltimore. She was educated by her father, married William Magee Seton in 1794, and became involved in social work, helping to found the Society for the Relief of Poor Widows with Small Children in 1797. She was widowed with five children in 1803 when her husband died at Leghorn, Italy, where they had gone for his health. She returned to the United States and in 1805 became a Catholic—a step that led to her ostracization by her family and friends. She was invited to open a school in Baltimore by Dr. Dubourg, rector of St. Mary's Seminary there, and in 1809 with four companions founded a religious community, the Sisters of St. Joseph, and a school for poor children near Emmitsburg, Maryland, the beginning of the far-reaching Catholic parochial school system in the United States. The new community's rule was approved by Archbishop Carroll of Baltimore in 1812, she was elected superior, and with eighteen sisters she took vows on July 19, 1813, the founding of the Sisters of Charity, the first American religious society. The order spread throughout the United States and numbered some twenty communities by the time of her death at Emmitsburg on January 4. She was canonized by Pope Paul VI in 1975, the first American-born saint.

SEURIN. *See* Severinus.

SEVERIAN (d. c. 306). *See* Carpophorus.

SEVERIAN (d. 322). An Armenian senator in Sebaste, North Africa, he was so impressed by the heroic conduct of forty Christians executed there during the persecution of Christians under Emperor Licinius that he became a Christian. He too suffered martyrdom, by being torn to death by iron rakes. September 9.

SEVERIAN (d. 453). A stanch defender of orthodoxy and bishop of Scythopolis, he was seized during the persecution of Christians under Emperor Theodosius II and murdered by the Emperor's troop, who seized Jerusalem and persecuted those who adhered to the decrees of the General Council of Chalcedon in 451, which had denounced Eutyches and his imperially supported followers. February 21.

SEVERINUS (d. c. 420). Also known as Seurin, he was bishop of Trier, Gaul, and in about 405 was named to the see of Bordeaux, where he became known for his fervid opposition to Arianism and where he died. October 23.

SEVERINUS (d. c. 480). Believed to have been a Roman of good background (though perhaps from Africa, where he may have been a bishop), he spent his youth as a hermit in the deserts of the East and then went to Noricum (Austria) as a missionary. He became famous for his preaching and prophecies (he accurately foretold the destruction of Astura [Stockerau] when his missionary efforts met with no success there), made many conversions elsewhere, and was reported to have performed many miracles. He traveled constantly, founded several monasteries, helped ransom captives, and was consulted by ruler and and commoner for his spiritual wisdom. He died on January 5 sometime between 476 and 482.

SEVERINUS (d. 507). Born in Burgundy, he joined the monastery of Agaunum as a youth, cured King Clovis of a disease his doctors had been unable to cure in 504, and is reported to have performed miracles of healing before his death at Château-Landon. St. Séverin Church in Paris is named after him. February 11.

SEVERINUS (d. c. 550). Brother of St. Victorinus, he became bishop of Septempeda in the Marches of Ancona, Italy, which was later called San Severino after him. January 8.

SEVERINUS BOETHIUS (c. 480–524). Born in Rome of the famous Anicia family, the son of Flavius Manlius Boethius, who was a consul in 487, Ancius Manlius Severinus Boethius was orphaned as a child and was raised by Q. Aurelius Symmachus, whose daughter Rusticiana he married. He was known even in his youth for his learning, began to translate Plato and Aristotle into Latin, and made available translations of Pythagoras, Ptolemy, Nichomachus, Euclid, and Archimedes in Latin. He was knowledgeable in astronomy, music, logic, and theology, and wrote several theological treatises that are still extant, notably *De sancta Trinitate*. He was named consul by Ostrogoth Emperor Theodoric in 510 and then was named master of the offices. However, when he defended ex-Consul Albinus against charges of conspiring with Eastern Emperor Justin to overthrow the Ostrogoth rulers, he too was arrested. He was charged with treason and sacrilege for allegedly using astronomy for impious purposes and was imprisoned at Ticinum (Pavia). During the nine months he was in prison, he wrote *The Consolation of Philosophy*. He was then tortured and executed. Boethius is considered the first of the scholastics and had great influence in the Middle Ages. His *Consolation of Philosophy* was tremendously popular, and for long his translations of the Greek philosophers were the only translations avail-

able. He was canonized by Pope Leo XIII in 1883. October 23.

SEVERUS (d. 304). *See* Philip.

SEVERUS (d. c. 306). *See* Carpophorus.

SEVERUS (d. c. 455). Born in Gaul, he worked as a missionary with St. Germanus of Auxerre and Lupus of Troyes and went to England with them in 429 to combat Pelagianism there. He also worked along the lower Moselle River area in Germany and was named bishop of Treves in Gaul in 446, a position he held until his death. October 15.

SEXBURGA (d. c. 699). Daughter of King Anna of the East Angles and sister of SS. Etheldreda, Ethelburga, Erconwald, and Withburga, she married King Erconbert of Kent in 640 and on his death in 664 finished Minster Monastery, which she had founded on Sheppey Island, and joined the nuns there. She appointed her daughter St. Ermenilda, abbess and then went to Ely Abbey, where she succeeded her sister Etheldreda as abbess and where Sexburga died on July 6.

SFORZA, BL. SERAPHINA (c. 1432–c. 1478). Daughter of Guido, count of Urbino, and Catterina Colonna, and christened Sueva, she was born at Urbino, Italy, and raised in the household of her uncle, Prince Colonna, in Rome when she was orphaned as a child. She was married at sixteen to Alexander Sforza, duke of Pesaro, and they lived amicably until on his return from a military campaign under his brother the duke of Milan, he began an affair with the wife of a neighboring physician. After he was unsuccessful in an attempt to poison Sueva, he drove her from his home in 1457 and she joined the Poor Clares at Pesaro, taking the name Seraphina. There is some evidence that she may have plotted against her husband, but in the two decades she spent in the convent, she lived a life of great holiness and was elected abbess in 1475. Her cult was approved by Pope Benedict XIV in 1754. September 9.

SHENOUTE. *See* Shenute.

SHENUTE (d. c. 450). Born at Shenalolet, Akhym, Egypt, he became a monk in 370 at the double monastery at Dair-al-Abiad near Atripe in the Thebaid and in 385 succeeded his Uncle Bhôl, who had founded the abbey as abbot. Shenute's rigorous austerities, severe rule, rigid discipline, and severe punishment for slight infractions attracted many to the monastery (at one time it is estimated that some two thousand monks and eighteen hundred nuns lived there). He accompanied St. Cyril of Alexandria to the Council of Ephesus in 431, where Shenute was active in his opposition to Nestorius. He was a leader in the development of monastic communal life and in time was regarded as archimandrite of all the surrounding monasteries. He wrote extensively in Coptic, mainly letters of spiritual direction and sermons, is believed to have died when he was 118, and may have died as late as 466. His name is also spelled Schenute, Shenoute, and Sinuthius. July 1.

SHERT, BL. JOHN (d. 1582). Born at Shert Hall near Macclesfield, Cheshire, England, he was graduated from Oxford, taught in London, and was converted to Catholicism. After his conversion, he studied at Douai and Rome and was ordained in 1576. He was sent on the English mission in 1579, was arrested two years later, and was convicted of conspiring against the Queen but in reality for being a Catholic priest. He was hanged, drawn, and quartered at Tyburn, with Bl. Thomas Ford and Bl. Robert

Johnson, on May 28 after refusing his freedom if he would acknowledge the ecclesiastical supremacy of the Queen. He was beatified in 1886.

SHERWIN, RALPH (d. 1581). Born at Rodsley, Derbyshire, England, he was granted a fellowship at Oxford, studied at Exeter College there, and became a classical scholar of distinction, receiving his M.A. in 1574. He became a Catholic in 1575, went to Douai to study for the priesthood, and was ordained there in 1577. He continued his studies at the English college at Rome and was sent on the English mission in 1580. He arrived in England on August 1 and was arrested in London in November; he was imprisoned in the Tower, tortured, and was offered the bribe of bishopric if he would apostatize. Brought to trial the next year with Edmund Campion and others, he was convicted of attempting to foment a rebellion and condemned to death. He was hanged, drawn, and quartered at Tyburn on December 1 with Edmund Campion and Alexander Briant, and was canonized in 1970 by Pope Paul VI as one of the Forty Martyrs of England and Wales.

SHERWOOD, BL. THOMAS (1551–78). While a student in London, he had decided to become a priest but was arrested for attending Mass and on suspicion of being a Catholic. He was imprisoned in the Tower, racked in an unsuccessful attempt to force him to reveal the names of fellow Catholics, and then hanged, drawn, and quartered at Tyburn for refusing to take the Oath of Supremacy. He was beatified in 1886. February 7.

SIDONIUS APOLLINARIS (c. 430–c. 480). Caius Sollius Apollinaris Sidonius was born at Lyons, Gaul, on November 5 of a noble family, received a classical education at Arles, and was a student of

Claudianus Mamertus of Vienne. He married Papianilla, daughter of Avitus (who became Emperor in 455), in about 450 and lived at the imperial court at Rome for several years. He served under several Emperors, for whom he wrote panegyrics after Avitus was deposed in 456, retired for a time after Emperor Majorian's death in 461, but returned and was prefect of Rome in 468. He then retired to the life of a country gentleman in Auvergne, carrying on a large correspondence, much of it still extant, which gave valuable insights into the life of the times. Against his will, in 469, he was named bishop of Avernum (Clermont), partly because it was felt he was the only one able to defend crumbling Roman prestige against the Goths, abandoned his worldly lifestyle for a more humble mode, and was soon recognized as a leading ecclesiastical authority. He was a benefactor of monks, spent much of his wealth in charities, and provided food for thousands during a great famine. He led the populace against King Euric of the Goths, and when Clermont fell to the Goths in 474, he was exiled but returned in 476 and devoted the last few years before his death at Clermont to a collection of his letters. He was an outstanding orator, was famed as a poet (twenty-four of his poems have survived), and was one of the last representatives of the classical school. August 23.

SIFRARD (d. 888). *See* Ageranus.

SIGEBERT(d. 635). An exile in Gaul during the reign of his brother Eorpwald, King of the East Angles, he was converted to Christianity while in Gaul and became known for his learning. He succeeded his brother in 630 when Eorpwald was murdered by a pagan named Richbert in about 627. In the three years between Eorpwald's death and Sigebert's acsension to the throne, the kingdom had lapsed into paganism, and Sigebert worked successfully during his reign to bring his realm back to Christianity with the aid of Burgundian Bishop Felix of Dunwich. Sigebert later resigned the throne in favor of Ecgric, a relative, and became a monk in a monastery he had founded. When Penda of Mercia invaded East Anglia, Sigebert's subjects dragged him from the monastery against his will to lend morale to the East Angles opposing Penda. He refused to fight or bear arms and was killed, as was Ecgric, in a battle with Penda's army. September 27.

SIGEBERT III OF AUSTRASIA (631–56). Son of King Dagobert I, he was educated by Bl. Pepin of Landen and became King of Austrasia on the death of his father in 638 while his brother Clovis ruled the rest of France. Sigebert founded churches, hospitals, and monasteries, and was known for his aid to the poor and for his holiness. He died when only twenty-five. February 1.

SIGFRID (d. 690). A deacon at Wearmouth Abbey known for his knowledge of Scripture and for his frail health, he was elected coadjutor abbot in 688 on the death of St. Esterwine while Abbot St. Benedict Biscop was in Rome. Sigfrid died soon after Benedict. August 22.

SIGFRID (d. c. 1045). Untrustworthy sources say he was born in Northumbria, became a priest at York or perhaps Glastonbury, was consecrated missionary bishop, and with two other bishops, Grimkel and John, was sent to Norway at the request of King Olaf Tryggvason (who had just been converted to Christianity) for missionaries. Sigfrid went to Sweden in 1008, converted the King, also named Olaf, and was so successful he is called the Apostle of Sweden. He also labored in Denmark. He is reported to have been canonized by Pope Adrian IV, but there is no proof of such a canonization. February 15.

SIGISBERT. See Placid (d. c. 650).

SIGISMUND (d. 524). Son of Gundebald, Arian Vandal ruler of Burgundy, he was converted to Christianity the year before his father's death in 516, when he succeeded to the throne. He ruled for a year until one day in a rage he had his son Sigeric strangled for rebuking his stepmother. Stricken with remorse, he prayed to be punished and for atonement was most generous to the Church and to the poor. He was defeated in battle by the sons of Clovis in a war to avenge the murder of their grandfather, Chilperic, brother of Sigismund's father, Gundebald, who had murdered him to gain the throne. Sigismund escaped after the battle, lived as a hermit near St. Maurice, but was captured and executed by King Clodomir at Orléans. Sigismund restored the monastery of St. Maurice at Agaunum, endowed it, and brought in monks from other monasteries to celebrate the *laus perennis* (the constant chant) there. May 1.

SIGNORI, THEOPHILUS DE' (1676–1740). Born of noble parents at Corte, Corsica, on October 30 and baptized Blasius, he was refused admission to the Capuchins when he was fifteen but in 1693 joined the Franciscans at Corte, taking the name Theophilus. He studied at Rome and Naples, was ordained at Naples in 1700, and became lector in theology at the Franciscan retreat house at Civitella. He became famed for his missionary work and preaching, was named guardian at Civitella, and in 1730 was sent back to Corsica to found a retreat house at Luani. He founded another retreat house at Fucecchio near Florence in 1734 and died there on May 20. He was canonized in 1930. May 21.

SILAS (1st century). One of the leaders of the Church of Jerusalem, he was went with Paul and Barnabas to Antioch to communicate the decisions of the Council of Jerusalem to the Gentile community in Syria. When Paul and Barnabus quarreled over Paul Mark, Silas was chosen by Paul to accompany him on his second missionary journey to Syria, Cilicia, and Macedonia (Acts 15:38–40). Silas was beaten and imprisoned with Paul at Philippi (Acts 16:19ff.), was involved with Paul in the riot of the Jews at Thessalonica that drove Paul and Silas from the city to Beroea (Acts 17:5–10), remained at Beroea with Timothy when Paul left, but rejoined him at Corinth (Acts 18:5). The Silvanus mentioned with Timothy by Paul and who helped him preach at Corinth (2 Cor. 1:19) is believed to be the same as Silas, since Silvanus is a Greek variant of the Semitic Silas. Silvanus is also mentioned as the man through whom Peter communicated (1 Peter 5:12) and is considered by some scholars to be the author of that epistle. Tradition says he was the first bishop of Corinth and that he died in Macedonia. July 13.

SILVA MENESES, BEATRICE DA (1424–90). Daughter of the count of Viana and sister of St. Amadeus of Portugal, she was born at Ceuta, Portugal, where she is known as Brites. She was raised in the household of Princess Isabel and accompanied the princess to Spain when she married John II of Castile. Disenchanted with court life after being unjustly imprisoned by Isabel, she shortly after left the court and became a Cistercian nun at St. Dominic of Silos Convent at Toledo. In 1484, she founded the Congregation of the Immaculate Conception of the Blessed

Virgin Mary (the Conceptionists), head-quartered at the Castle of Galliana, donated by Queen Isabella. Beatrice died at Toledo on September 1, and was canonized by Pope Paul VI in 1976.

SILVANUS. *See* Silas (1st century).

SILVANUS (d. c. 165). *See* Felicity.

SILVANUS (d. c. 311). Bishop of Gaza, Palestine, he was arrested for his faith during the reign of Emperor Maximinus and sent to labor in the copper mines of Petras Arabia. When he and forty other aged Christians were judged unable to do heavy work in the mines because of their age and disabilities, they were beheaded. Eusebius wrote an account of the martyrdom of these martyrs from Egypt and Palestine. May 4.

SILVANUS (4th century). An actor, he became a monk at Tabennisi under St. Pachomius. After twenty years in the monastery, Silvanus was excommunicated by Pachomius because of his laxity and neglect of his religious duties. He repented, reformed his life, and became a model monk. May 15.

SILVERIUS (d. c. 537). Son of Pope Hormisdas, he was born at Frosinone, Campania, Italy. He became a subdeacon in Rome and on the death of Pope St. Agapitus I was named Pope in April 536 by Ostrogoth King Theodehad of Italy to forestall the election of a Byzantine nominee; on Silverius' consecration on June 1 or 8, he was accepted by the Roman clergy as Pope. He soon incurred the bitter enmity of Empress Theodora and the Byzantines when he refused to accept monophysites Antihimus and Severus as Patriarchs of Constantinople and Antioch, respectively, as she requested. In an attempt to save Rome from Ostrogoth General Vitiges, Silverius invited the imperial

General Belisarius into the city after Vitiges had overrun and devastated the suburbs of Rome. A forged letter accusing Silverius of being responsible for Vitiges' destruction proved unsuccessful in implicating Silverius, whereupon he was kidnaped and brought to Patara, Lycia, at the instigation of Theodora; as soon as he was kidnaped, Belisarius proclaimed Vigilius, a deacon, Pope in his stead. When Emperor Justinian learned what had happened, he ordered Silverius freed, and the Pope returned to Italy, where he was promptly captured by Vigilius; adherents and taken to the island of Palmarola off Naples, where he died of starvation or was murdered at the behest of Antonina, Belisarius' wife, who had engineered the whole plan to make Vigilius Pope. Silverius died on the island on December 2. June 20.

SILVESTER. *See* Sylvester.

SILVIN (d. c. 720). A member of the courts of Kings Childeric II and Thierry III, he decided against a proposed marriage, left the court, and was ordained in Rome. He was later consecrated a bishop, probably a regionary bishop (though some sources called him bishop of Toulouse, while others say of Thérouanne), and was successful in his missionary work in northern France. He spent his wealth in helping the needy, building churches, and ransoming slaves from the barbarians. He lived in great austerity, was credited with performing miracles of healing, and probably died at Auchy-les-Moines (now Arras), where he had become a Benedictine monk. February 17.

SIMEON (1st century). A resident of Jerusalem, he had his wish to see the Messiah before he died when he was privileged to hold the infant Jesus in his arms when Mary and Joseph brought the child to the Temple and uttered the words of praise to God that we know as the *Nunc dimittis* (Luke 2:25–35) and made his famous prophecy (Luke 2:34–35). October 8.

SIMEON (1st century). Surnamed the Zealot for his rigid adherence to the Jewish law in Luke 6:15 and Acts 1:13 and the Canaanite in Matthew 10:4 and Mark 3:18, he was one of the original followers of Christ. Western tradition is that he preached in Egypt and then went to Persia with St. Jude, where both suffered martyrdom; Eastern tradition says Simeon died peacefully at Edessa. October 28.

SIMEON (d. c. 107). Mentioned in Matthew 13:55 and Mark 6:3 as one of the brothers of the carpenter, he was, according to the Roman Martyrology, son of Cleophas, St. Joseph's brother, and hence first cousin of the Lord. He was elected successor to James as bishop of Jerusalem when James was martyred. According to tradition, Simeon was supernaturally warned of the destruction of Jerusalem by the Romans in 66 and led a group of Christians to the city of Pella, where they remained until it was safe for them to return to Jerusalem. He escaped the death ordered by Emperors Vespasian and Domitian when they decreed that all of Jewish origin were to be executed, but was arrested by the Roman Governor Atticus during the persecution fo Christians under Emperor Trajan, was tortured, and then crucified, reputedly when he was well over one hundred years old. He may be the same as the apostle Simeon the Zealot (Matt. 10:4; Mark 3:18; Luke 6:15; Acts 1:13). February 18.

SIMEON (d. 339). *See* Sapor.

SIMEON (d. 1016). Probably an Armenian, he went on pilgrimage to Jerusalem in 982 and then to Rome and was there accused of heresy. Exonerated by Pope Benedict VII, he visited shrines in France and Spain and then settled at the Benedictine monastery of Padrilirone near Padua, Italy, where he died, venerated for his holiness, charity, and miracles. His cult was permitted by Pope Benedict VIII. July 26.

SIMEON BARSABAE (d. 341). Bishop of Seleucia and Ctesiphon, he was arrested during the persecution of King Sapor II of Persia, and when he refused to worship the sun, was tortured and imprisoned. After being forced to witness the beheading of some one hundred of his followers, he was himself beheaded. Among those who suffered martyrdom were Usthazanes, the King's tutor, who had apostatized but was brought back to the faith by Simeon; Abdechalas and Ananias, two of Simeon's priests; and Pusicius, who had encouraged Ananias. April 21.

SIMEON THE LOGOTHETE. *See* Simeon Metaphrastes.

SIMEON METAPHRASTES (d. c. 1000). He was probably a Logothete (Secretary of State) to Emperor Constantine VII Porphyrogenitus, at whose order he compiled a *Menology* of legends and stories of the Byzantine saints under the name of Simeon the Logothete. It is the most famous of the medieval Greek collections, comparable to *The Golden Legend* of Bl. James Voragine in the West. Simeon also wrote a chronicle, prayers, letters, and collections of maxims of Basil and Macarius of Egypt. Simeon's feast is celebrated in the Orthodox Church on November 28 but has never been formally recognized in Rome.

SIMEON SALUS (d. c. 589). An Egyptian, he lived as a hermit for almost thirty years in the Sinai Desert by the

Red Sea and then at Emesa, Syria. He was nicknamed Salus (mad) for his extreme austerities and for his practice of allowing himself to be considered an idiot out of humility. July 1.

SIMEON STYLITES (c. 390–459). Son of a Cilician shepherd and born on the Syrian border of Cilicia, he was a shepherd in his childhood and when he was thirteen had a vision that he later interpreted as foretelling his later life on pillars. He spent two years in a nearby monastery and then became a monk at a stricter monastery at Heliodorus, where he practiced such severe mortifications that he was dismissed from the monastery. He then became a hermit at the foot of Mount Teleanissae near Antioch and after three years moved to the top of the mountain, where word of his holiness began to attact huge crowds. To escape them, in 423, he erected a ten-foot-high pillar and lived on top of it; he spent the rest of his life living on successfully higher pillars *(stylites* is from the Greek word *stylos,* meaning pillar), which were no wider than six feet in diameter at the top; his last pillar was sixty feet high. He practiced the greatest austerities, slept little if at all, was clad only in the skins of wild beasts, and fasted completely during Lent for forty years. He soon became greatly venerated as a holy man and had extraordinary influence. He preached daily exhorting his endless stream of listeners to greater holiness, converted many, and was listened to and consulted by all, from Emperors and prelates to commoners. He died on September 2 (or perhaps July 24), the first of the pillar ascetics.

SIMEON STYLITES THE YOUNGER (c. 517–92). Born at Antioch, his father died when he was five, and when he was seven, he became a stylite under the tutelage of the well-known St. John

Stylite, and lived on a pillar that was to be his home for the next sixty-eight years. By the time he was twenty, his reputation for holiness attracted such crowds that he retired to a more inaccessible spot in the mountains near Antioch, which was soon called the Hill of Wonders. When he was thirty, in response to a vision, he founded a monastery, and when he was thirty-three he was ordained on one of his pillars. Huge crowds were attracted to his pillars because of his preaching, and he as venerated for his holiness, spiritual wisdom and advice, prophecies, and the miracles reported of him. He was said to have gone for long periods of time with hardly any sleep or nourishment. September 3.

SIMEON OF SYRACUSE (d. 1035). Born at Syracuse, Sicily, he was educated at Constantinople, and after a pilgrimage to the Holy Land he became a hermit on the banks of the Jordan River. He then became a monk at Bethlehem, went to a monastery on Mount Sinai, spent two years as a hermit, and was then sent to Normandy to collect a tribute promised to the monastery by Duke Richard II. Simeon's ship was captured by pirates, and all on board were killed except Simeon, who escaped. He was arrested, with a monk named Cosmas, in Belgrade, and when set free proceeded to Rouen, where he found that Richard had died and his successor refused to pay the tribute. Simeon accompanied Archbishop Poppo of Trier on pilgrimage to Palestine, and on his return to Trier resumed his eremitical life. At one time he was accused of practicing black magic but was soon venerated for his holiness and ascetical practices. He was one of the first to be formally canonized in 1042. June 1.

SIMON. The Greek form of the Hebrew Simeon.

SIMON (d. 1082). Count of Crépy in Valois, France, he was raised at the court of William the Conqueror, fought against Philip I of France, desired to become a monk, but was restrained from doing so by William's desire that he marry his daughter, Adela. Simon went to Rome to ascertain if such a marriage would be legitimate, since he was related to William's wife, Matilda, and on the way became a monk at St. Claude Abbey at Condat. He served on several diplomatic missions, settled disputes between St. Hugh of Cluny and the King of France, between William and his sons, and negotiated successfully between Pope St. Gregory VII and Robert Guiscard, whereupon the Pope kept him in Rome, where he died. September 30.

SIMON BALLACHI OF RIMINI, BL. (1260–1319). Born at Sant' Arcangelo near Rimini, Italy, the son of Count Ballachi, he became a Dominican lay brother there when he was twenty-seven and was known for his humility, mortifications, and patience in the face of great suffering. He became blind in about 1307 and was bedridden the last years of his life. His cult was confirmed in 1821. November 3.

SIMON OF CASCIA, BL. (c. 1295–1348). Simon Fidati was born at Cascia, Umbria, Italy, was influenced in his youth by Angelo Clareno, joined the Augustinian Friars, and in about 1318 began to preach. He became famed for his preaching, was a much-sought-after confessor, and practiced severe mortifications and austerities. He was noted for his severe treatment of penitents, refused an episcopal appointment, had great influence in Perugia, Florence, and Siena, and founded a refuge for unmarried mothers. He is now considered by many scholars to be the author of several ascetical treatises formerly attributed to

Dominican Dominic Cavalca and was severely criticized for many of his theological positions. His *De gestis Domini Salvatoris* is now believed to have had great influence on the teaching of Martin Luther. Simon died on February 2 at Florence. February 3.

SIMON OF LIPNICZA, (d. 1482). Born at Lipnicza near Cracow, Poland, he was so touched by a mission preached by St. John Capistran that in 1453 he joined the Frairs Monks. He was ordained, began to preach in Lipnicza, and soon became famed for his eloquence. He served as master of novices, guardian, and provincial, and died at Cracow on July 18 of the plague he contracted while ministering to the stricken of the city. He was beatified in 1685. July 30.

SIMON RINALDUCCI OF TODI, BL. (d. 1322). Born at Todi, Italy, he joined the Hermits of St. Augustine in 1280, became known for his preaching, and served as prior of several Augustinian houses and as provincial of Umbria. He died at Bologna, and his cult was approved in 1833. April 20.

SIMON STOCK (c. 1165–1265). Born at Aylesford, Kent, England, he became a hermit and then went on pilgrimage to Jerusalem, where he joined the Carmelites. He returned to Kent when the Moslems drove the Carmelites out and in 1247 was elected superior general of the Carmelites. He greatly expanded the Order, established new foundations in England, Ireland, Scotland, France, and Italy, and revised the rule, which revision was approved by Pope Innocent IV in 1237. At about this time Simon experienced the controversial vision of Mary promising salvation to all Carmelites who wore the brown scapular she showed him—a vision that led to the widespread devotion to Mary over the next centuries of wearing this scapular in her honor. He died at Bordeaux on May 16. Though never formally canonized, he has long been venerated, and celebration of his feast was permitted to the Carmelites by the Holy See on May 16. The surname Stock may come from the legend that he lived inside a tree trunk in his youth.

SIMON OF TRENT (1472–75). According to reports of the time, Simon was a two-and-a-half-year-old Christian boy living in Trent, Italy, who was kidnaped by a Jewish doctor who allegedly crucified him out of hatred of Christ. Under intensive and terrible torture, those arrested for the crime admitted to it and were executed after further torture. Though the murder was blamed on the Jews of Trent, there never has been any proof that such a crime was committed for ritualistic purposes. Miracles were later reported at the child's tomb. March 24.

SIMPLICIAN (d. 400). A close friend of St. Ambrose, he was a confidant of St. Augustine and played a leading role in his conversion. Simplician was highly praised by Ambrose for his learning and zeal, and when an old man he succeeded Ambrose as bishop of Milan in 397. He ruled for only three years, until his death in May. August 13 (August 16 in Roman Martyrology).

SIMPLICIUS (d. c. 304). With his brother Faustinus, he was tortured and then beheaded (or drowned) for his Christianity at Rome during the persecution of Christians under Emperor Diocletian. Their sister Beatrice or Viatrix was able to recover their bodies from the Tiber River and bury them on the road to Porto. A few months later she was denounced as a Christian by a neighbor named Lucretius, and when she refused to sacrifice to the gods was strangled on May 11. July 29.

SIMPLICIUS (d. c. 306). *See* Castorius.

SIMPLICIUS (4th century). According to legend, he was of a leading Gallo-Roman family, married, and lived in continence with his wife. He was elected bishop of Autun in 390 and when denounced for still living with his wife after having been consecrated bishop, he and his wife successfully underwent the ordeal by fire to prove their celibacy. Their action led to many conversions, as did his miraculous destruction of a statue of the goddess Berecynthia. The details of his life are obscure, and some scholars believe he is the same Bishop Simplicius who signed the decrees of the Council of Sardica in 347. June 24.

SIMPLICIUS (d. 483). Born at Tivoli, Italy, he was elected Pope to succeed Pope St. Hilarus on March 3, 468. He defended the action of the Council of Chalcedon against the monophysite heresy, labored to help the people of Italy against the marauding raids of barbarian invaders, and saw the Heruli mercenaries in Roman service revolt and proclaim Odoacer King in 476 during his pontificate. Odoacer's deposition of the last Roman Emperor, Romulus Augustus, and his occupation of Rome in 476 marked the end of the Roman Empire. March 10.

SINUTHIUS. *See* Shenute.

SIRICIUS (d. 399). Son of Tiburtius, he was born in Rome, became a deacon, and was known for his learning and piety. He was elected Pope in December 384, succeeding Pope Damasus. Siricius' pontificate was marked by his denunciation of the monk Jovinian for denying the perpetual virginity of Mary and for a decretal Siricius sent to Bishop Himerius of Tarragona in Spain requiring married priests to desist from cohabitation with their wives; this is the earliest insistence on clerical celibacy and also the earliest papal decree that has survived in its entirety. He supported St. Martin of Tours, excommunicated Felix of Trier for his role in bringing about the execution of Priscillian by the Emperor, and died in Rome on November 26.

SISINIUS (d. c. 304). He, Diocletian, and Florentius were stoned to death at Osimo near Ancona, Italy, during the persecution of Christians under Emperor Diocletian. May 11.

SISINIUS (d. c. 309). *See* Saturninus.

SISINIUS (d. 397). He and his two brothers, Martyrius and Alexander, were natives of Cappadocia who immigrated to Milan, Italy. Sisinius was ordained deacon and Martyrius lector by Bishop Vigilius of Trent, who was looking for missionaries and sent to the Tyrol. Sisinius built a church at Methon and was so successful in his conversion work that pagans in the area attacked the church, beat Sisinius to death, dragged Martyrius to his death the next day, and burned Alexander to death several days later. May 29.

SISOES (d. c. 429). Born in Egypt, he became a hermit in the desert of Skete in his youth. He took St. Antony as example for his lifestyle, and soon his austerities and holiness attracted numerous disciples from among the neighboring hermits. In his old age, illness caused him to live for a time in Clysma near the Red Sea, but he soon returned to his eremitical life. He died on the mountain that had been Antony's abode after sixty-two years as a hermit. July 6.

SIXTUS I (d. c. 127). Born at Rome, he succeeded Pope St. Alexander I as Pope and reigned for about ten years. He is believed to have suffered martyrdom, but no details have survived. Two of his decrees directed that the people should join in saying the *Sanctus* at Mass and that only the clergy could touch the sacred vessels. April 3.

SIXTUS II (d. 258). Possibly a Greek and a philosopher, he was elected Pope on August 30, 257. His pontificate is known only for his correspondence with Dionysius of Alexandria and Firmilian of Antioch, in which Sixtus upheld the Roman position that heretical baptisms were invalid, though he did not break off relations with those African and Asian churches that held otherwise. During Emperor Valerian's persecution of the Christians, he was seized in the cemetery of Praetextatus outside Rome while saying Mass and executed on August 6. Also seized and executed were six deacons: Agapitus, Felicissimus, Januarius, Magnus, Stephen, and Vincent. August 7.

SIXTUS III (d. 440). A member of the Roman clergy, he was elected Pope to succeed Pope Celestine I on July 31, 432. He denounced Pelagianism and Nestorianism, but his kindness to the Pelagians and Nestorians caused some of his critics to accuse him of leanings toward these heresies. He restored St. Mary Major Basilica and dedicated St. Peter in Chains and several other churches. He died on August 19.

SLADE, BL. JOHN (d. 1583). Born at Manston, Dorchestershire, England, he studied at New College, Oxford, and then became a schoolteacher. He was arrested when he was heard denying royal supremacy in ecclesiastical matters, was tried with Bl. John Bodey, and was condemned at trials at Winchester and Andover. He was hanged, drawn, and quartered at Winchester on October 30, and was beatified in 1929.

SMARAGDUS (d. c. 304). *See* Cyriacus.

SNOW, VEN. PETER (d. 1598). Born near Ripon, England, he went to Rheims to study for the priesthood in 1589 and was ordained there two years later. He was sent on the English mission and ministered to English Catholics until his arrest near York in May 1598 with Ralph Grimston. Convicted of being a Catholic priest, Ven. Peter was executed at York on June 15.

SOCRATES (d. c. 304). He and Stephen were two Britons who, according to the Roman Martyrology, were followers of St. Amphibalus and suffered martyrdom in England, probably at Monmouth, during the persecution of Christians under Emperor Diocletian. Some authorities believe the entry was a copyist's error in which he misread Abretania (in Asia Minor or Bithynia) for Britannia and that they were not Britons. September 17.

SODERINI, BL. (1301–67). Born of a noble family at Florence, Italy, she resisted the efforts of her parents to have her marry and became a Servite tertiary under St. Juliana Falconieri in Florence. She became known for her gift of prophecies and austerities and for her care of the sick. She succeeded Juliana as prioress of her community. She died on September 1, and her cult was approved in 1828.

SOLA (d. 794). Born in England, he became a monk, went to Germany, and was a disciple of St. Boniface, who ordained him. He lived as a hermit at Fulda and then on the banks of the Altmuhl River

near Eichstätt, where the Abbey of Solnhofen developed on the grounds of his hermitage. He died on December 3.

SOLANGIA (d. 880). Born at Villemont near Bourges, France, the daughter of a vineyard worker, she was a shepherdess in her youth and early dedicated herself to God. Her beauty came to the attention of Bernard, son of the count of Poitiers, who attacked her while she was tending sheep and stabbed her to death when she resisted him. She is the patroness of the province of Berry. May 10.

SOLANO, FRANCIS (1549–1610). Born at Montilla, Spain, on March 10, of noble and pious parents, he joined the Observant Franciscans at Montilla in 1569 and was ordained in 1576. He served as master of novices at the convent of Arifazza and became known for his preaching and conversions. At his request he was sent as a missionary to Peru in 1589, and for the rest of his life he worked for the welfare of the Indians and the Spanish colonists in South America. He learned the dialects and customs of Indian tribes, served as custodian of Franciscan houses in Argentina, Paraguay, and finally in Lima, Peru, and had phenomenal success in his preaching and in making converts, earning the sobriquet the "Wonder Worker of the New World" for his extraordinary achievements. He died at Lima, and was canonized by Pope Benedict XIII in 1726. July 14.

SOLINA (d. c. 290). A native of Gascony, she fled to Chartres to avoid marrying a pagan, only to suffer martyrdom there by being beheaded. October 17.

SOLOMON (d. 857). *See* Roderic.

SOLUTAR (d. c. 287). *See* Maurice.

SOMERS, BL. THOMAS (d. 1610). Born at Skelmergh, Westmorland, England, he became a schoolmaster, later went to Douai, and was ordained. He was sent on the English mission, worked in London using the alias Wilson, was arrested, and when convicted of being a Catholic priest was hanged, drawn, and quartered at Tyburn with Bl. John Roberts. Bl. Thomas was beatified in 1929. December 10.

SOPATER (1st century). Son of Pyrrhus, a Christian of Beroea, he accompanied St. Paul on his journey from Greece to Jerusalem (Acts 20:4) and is considered by many scholars to be the same as the Sosipater whom Paul calls a compatriot and includes in his greetings to the Romans from Corinth (Rom. 16:21). According to tradition he later went to Corfu. June 25.

SOPHIA (2nd century). See Charity.

SOPHRONIUS (d. c. 638). Born at Damascus, Syria, he lived as a hermit, traveling throughout his native land, Asia Minor, and Egypt with another hermit named John Moschus. Sophronius became a monk in Egypt in about 580, lived for a time with Moschus at St. Sabas *laura* and then at St. Theorosius Monastery near Jerusalem. After visiting various Egyptian monasteries, he spent ten years at Alexandria under Patriarch St. John the Almsgiver, made a pilgrimage to Rome, where Moschus died in about 620, and then returned to Jerusalem, where he was elected patriarch. He called a synod that condemned monothelitism, became a leader of the orthodox, and sent Bishop Stephen of Dor to Rome to secure papal condemnation of monothelitism (which was finally condemned by the Lateran Council in 649). He was forced to flee Jerusalem when the Saracens captured the city in 638 and

probably died at Alexandria soon after. He wrote several biographies, doctrinal theses, homilies, and poems. March 11.

SOSIPATER. See Sopater.

SOSSUS (d. c. 305). See Januarius.

SOSTEGNI, GERARDINO (1204–76). See Monaldo, Buonfiglio.

SOSTHENES (d. 307). With St. Victor, he was ordered to torture St. Euphemia at Chalcedon during the persecution of Christians under Emperor Diocletian. Her courage converted both of them to Christianity, whereupon they both were martyred. September 10.

SOTELO, BL. LOUIS (d. 1624). Born of a noble family at Seville, Spain, he joined the Franciscans at Salamanca and after his ordination was sent to Manila in the Philippines in 1610; two years later he was sent to Japan and preached there with great success for a decade. He accompanied a delegation from the prince of Sendai, Date Musamune, to Pope Paul V and the King of Spain in 1613 and then traveled throughout Europe with its ambassador, Asakura Roku-yemon. He arrived back in Japan in 1622 at the outbreak of a new persecution of Christians and was arrested at Nagasaki. Two years later he was burned to death on August 25 at Simabura with Louis Baba, a native catechist who had been with him on his trip to Spain and who joined the Franciscans while imprisoned for his Christianity at Omura. Both were beatified in 1867.

SOTER (d. 175). Born at Fondi, Italy, nothing is known of his life beyond that he succeeded Pope St. Anicetus as Pope about 167, opposed the Montanist heresy, and according to a letter of Bishop St. Dionysius of Corinth, was know for his charity. April 22.

SOTERIS (d. 304). Of noble birth, she dedicated herself to God, lived austerely and with great simplicity, and was tortured (perhaps as early as Decius' [249–51] persecution of Christians) and then beheaded at Rome for her faith during Emperor Diocletian's persecution when she refused to sacrifice to pagan gods. February 10.

SOUBIRAN, BL. MARY TERESA DE (1835–89). Born at Castelnaudary near Carcassone, France, on May 16 and christened Sophia Teresa Augustina Mary, she was early attracted to the religious life. When she was nineteen, she joined a group of laywomen living in community and then became superior of a *Béguine* (laywomen living in community under temporary vows of obedience and chastity) house at Castelnaudary in 1854, taking the name Mary Teresa. Though her community flourished, she decided her real vocation in life was to found a new religious congregation, and in 1864 she founded the Society of Mary Auxiliatrix at Toulouse, devoted mainly to helping working girls but also orphans, teaching poor children, and to nocturnal adoration of the Blessed Sacrament. She received the approval of the archbishop of Toulouse in 1867 and of the Holy See in 1868. The society spread, especially in large cities, but was forced into exile in England during the Franco-Prussian War, 1869–70. In 1874 overexpansion, brought on in large measure by her assistant, the ambitious Mother Mary Frances, precipitated a financial crisis. Mother Mary Teresa was blamed for the situation, was persuaded to resign, and was dismissed from the Society in 1874. She was refused admission to the Visitation and Carmelite nuns but in 1877 joined the convent of Our Lady of Charity in Toulouse. Forbidden to have any contact with her former associates by the new superior,

Mother Mary Frances (who had dismissed Mary Teresa's sister, Mary Xavier, from the Society as too vivid a reminder of its foundress), she died in Paris on June 7, and was beatified in 1946. As a footnote to the sad story, it should be added that the arbitrary actions of Mother Mary Frances caused such protests within the Society that she was obliged to resign as superior and leave the Society in 1890; it was learned after her death in 1921 that she had been married and deserted her husband, so that canonically she had never been a nun. October 20.

SOUBIROUS, MARIE BERNARDE (1844–79). Born at Lourdes, France, on January 7, the oldest child of miller Francis Soubirous and his wife, Louise, she was called Bernadette as a child, lived in abject poverty with her parents, was uneducated, and suffered from asthma. On February 11, 1858, while collecting firewood on the banks of the Gave River near Lourdes, she saw a vision of the Virgin Mary in a cave above the riverbank. Her report provoked skepticism, but her daily visions of the Lady from February 18 through March 4 drew great crowds of people. Despite great hostility on the part of the civil authorities, she persisted in her claims, and on February 25 caused a spring to flow where none had been before. On March 25, the vision told her it was the Immaculate Conception and directed her to build a chapel on the site. In 1866, she became a Sister of Notre Dame at Nevers, and she remained there until she died at Nevers on April 16. Lourdes soon became one of the great pilgrimage centers of modern Christianity, attracting millions of visitors. Miracles were reported at the shrine and in the waters of the spring, and after painstaking investigation the apparitions were ecclesiastically approved. Bernadette was canonized in 1933 by Pope Pius XI.

SOUTHWELL, ROBERT (c. 1561–95). Born at Horsham Saint, Norfolk, England, the son of a favorite at the royal court (his father had conformed and married Queen Elizabeth's governess), he was sent abroad to study at Douai and then Paris. He joined the Jesuits at Rome in 1578, became prefect of studies at the English college at Rome, and was ordained in 1584. He was sent on the English mission, with Fr. Henry Garnet, in 1586, became chaplain to Countess Anne of Arundel in London in 1587, and ministered with great success to the Catholics, including Anne's husband imprisoned in the Tower, in and around London until 1592, when he was betrayed by Anne Bellamy, daughter of Richard Bellamy, whom he was visiting at Harrow. He was repeatedly tortured over the next three years before he was brought to trial, condemned to death for being a Catholic priest, and hanged, drawn, and quartered at Tyburn on February 21. He wrote a large number of moving poems, most of which were probably written in prison to encourage his fellow Catholics but which soon became very popular among both Catholics and Protestants. They were collected soon after his death as *St. Peter's Complaint and Other Poems* and *Maeoniae;* he also wrote prose treatises, among them *Mary Magdalen's Funeral Tears, Epistle of Comfort,* and *The Triumph over Death.* He was canonized in 1970 by Pope Paul VI as one of the Forty Martyrs of England and Wales.

SOUTHWORTH, JOHN (1592–1654). Born in Lancashire, England, he was sent to Douai to study for the priesthood in 1613, was ordained in 1618, lived as a Benedictine for a few months, and then decided to remain a secular priest. He was sent on the English mission in 1619,

worked around London for three years, and then returned to Belgium. He went back to England, was arrested in 1627, and was condemned to death for being a Catholic priest, but was released three years later with fifteen other priests through the intercession of Queen Henrietta Maria, the Catholic wife of King Charles I and sister of King Louis XIII of France. John apparently remained in England and was again in prison in 1632. He worked with St. Henry Morse to help victims of the London plague of 1635–36 but was required to stay in prison when complaints were made of his freedom to go in and out of prison as he wished. He was released again through the intercession of Henrietta Maria and then disappeared from view until he was arrested in 1654. Though there was no evidence against him, he insisted on proclaiming that he was a Catholic priest and was hanged, drawn, and quartered for his priesthood at Tyburn on June 28. His body was bought by the Spanish ambassador and sent to Douai; hidden during the French Revolution, it was discovered in 1927 and is now in Westminster Cathedral in London. He was canonized by Pope Paul VI in 1970 as one of the Forty Martyrs of England and Wales.

SOZON (date unknown). According to legend, he was a young Cilician named Tarasius (he became Sozon when he was baptized) who, while herding sheep, was summoned in a dream of Christ to Pompeiopolis, a nearby town. When he found a pagan festival in progress, he destroyed the golden idol in the temple there, was arrested, and after being tortured, was burned to death. September 7.

SPADAFORA, BL. DOMINIC (d. 1521). Born at Messina, Sicily, he became a Dominican at Palermo, was ordained, and then continued his studies at Padua. After a time at Palermo, he joined the staff of the master general of the Dominicans in Rome, was put in charge of a new shrine to our Lady near Monte Cerignone in 1493, and spent the rest of his life there and on missionary trips. He died at the shrine on December 21, and his cult was confirmed in 1921. October 3.

SPAIN (TURON), MARTYRS OF (1934). These Spanish Civil War martyrs were eight religious brothers who taught in the Astorias mining city of Turon along with a visiting Passionist priest, Inocencio (Manual Canoura Arnau). In October 1934, despite antigovernment and anticlerical opposition, the brothers kept their school open, defying the radicals' prohibition. When Friar Inocencio arrived on Thursday evening to celebrate the First Friday mass, all nine men were arrested and detained for the weekend. Then in the middle of the night, they were taken to the foot of a cemetery and shot. The oldest, Brother Cirilo Bertrán, (Jose San Tejedor) the director, was forty-six, the youngest, Brother Aniceto Adolfo (Manuel Seco Gutierrez), was twenty-two. These nine martyrs were canonized in 1999.

SPEED, BL. JOHN (d. 1594). A layman who used the alias Spence, he was convicted of aiding priests and was executed for this crime at Durham, England, on February 4 during the persecution of Catholics under Queen Elizabeth I. He was beatified in 1929 as one of the Durham Martyrs of 1594.

SPERATUS (d. 180). A resident of Scillium, Tunisia, he was arrested with Aquilinus, Cittinus, Donata, Felix, Generosa, Januaria, Laetantius, Nartzalus, Secunda, Vestia, and Veturius for their Christianity. Taken to Carthage and arraigned before Proconsul Saturninus, they were offered their freedom if they would worship pagan gods. With Speratus

as their main spokesman, they refused, and the seven men and five women were beheaded. They are known as the Sicilian Martyrs, and the account of their martyrdom is the earliest extant account of martyrdom in the African Church. July 17.

SPEUSIPPUS (d. c. 155). See Eleusippus.

SPINOLA, BL. CHARLES (d. 1622). Of the noble Italian Spinola family, he was born at Prague, Czechoslovakia, joined the Jesuits in 1584, was ordained, and was sent to Japan as a missionary in 1604. He spent the rest of his life evangelizing the Japanese and was known for his expertise as a mathematician and astronomer. He was arrested in 1618 during the persecution of Christians that had been unleashed by the decree of the *shogun* Ieyasu Tokugawa in 1614 that Christianity was to be eliminated. Bl. Charles was imprisoned at Omura with Bl. Sebastian Kimura for two years and then brought to Nagasaki, where they and a group of other Christians were slowly burned to death on September 10–11. They were among the 205 Martyrs of Japan who were beatified by Pope Pius IX in 1867 as Martyrs in the Great Martyrdom in Japan.

SPIRIDION (4th century). Also known as Spyridon, he was a native of Cyprus, became a shepherd, was married, and was named bishop of Tremithus near Salamis. He lost his right eye, had his left leg hamstrung, and was then sentenced to the mines for his faith during the persecution of Christians under Emperor Galerius Maximian. Spiridion was famed for his knowledge of the Bible though he was unschooled, was known for his simplicity and holiness, and was credited with many miracles. According to the Roman Martyrology, he attended the Council of Nicaea, where he converted a skeptical philosopher, and was a firm opponent of Arianism, but this is doubtful. December 14.

SPRATT, VEN. THOMAS. *See* Sprott, Ven. Thomas.

SPROTT, VEN. THOMAS (d. 1600). Born at Skelsmergh, Westmorland, England, he went to Douai to study for the priesthood and was ordained there in 1596. He was sent on the English mission, was arrested with Ven. Thomas Hunt at Lincoln, and was executed there on July 11 when found guilty of having a breviary in his possession. His name is also spelled Spratt.

SPYRIDON. *See* Spiridion.

STANISLAUS (1030–79). Born of noble parents on July 26 at Szczepanow near Cracow, Poland, he was educated at Gnesen and was ordained. He was given a canonry by Bishop Lampert Zula of Cracow, who made him his preacher, and soon he became noted for his preaching. He became a much sought after spiritual adviser, was successful in his reforming efforts, and in 1072 was named bishop of Cracow. He incurred the enmity of King Boleslaus the Bold when he denounced the King's cruelties and injustices and especially his kidnaping of the beautiful wife of a nobleman. When Stanislaus excommunicated the King and stopped services at the cathedral when Boleslaus entered, Boleslaus himself killed Stanislaus while the bishop was saying Mass in a chapel outside the city on April 11. Stanislaus has long been the symbol of Polish nationhood; he was canonized by Pope Innocent IV in 1253 and is the principal patron of Cracow. April 11.

STANISLAUS KOSKKA. *See* Kostka, Stanislaus.

STEEB, BL. KARL (1773–1856). Born in Tubingen, Germany, he was converted to Catholicism and ordained a priest, and founded the Sisters of Mercy of Verona. He died at Verona, Italy, on December 15, and was beatified by Pope Paul VI in 1975.

STEIN, EDITH (1891–1942). The youngest of seven children born to Orthodox Jewish parents in a region that was then part of Germany, her personal spiritual journey took place amidst the great horrors of the twentieth century— World War I and World War II—and the Nazi government's planned extermination of the Jewish population of Europe. As a young girl and into teenager, Edith was an exceptional student who developed an intense interest in philosophy. By age fifteen, however, she renounced her faith and declared herself an atheist. Although her studies were interrupted by World War I, after the war she received her doctorate in philosophy from the University of Freiburg. She was attracted to Catholicism during her studies; however it was not until she read the works of St. Teresa of Ávila, a sixteenth-century mystic, that her intellectual interest with leading Catholic philosophers blossomed into faith. Following her baptism in 1922, she went on to teach at a Dominican girls school, all the while continuing her studies and beginning what would become an extensive body of original work in Catholic philosophy. In 1933, she was forced to resign a position as lecturer at the Institute for Pedagogy at Munster because of Nazi laws banning Jews from holding such academic positions. She became a Carmelite nun, Sister Teresa Benedicta of the Cross, in 1934. Growing persecution of Jews in Germany forced her to flee to Holland in the late 1930s, though the Nazi invasion of that country again put her, and all Jews in Holland, at grave risk. In August 1942, she was taken by the Gestapo and was put to death in an Auschwitz gas chamber that same month. Her beatification in 1987 and her canonization in 1998 were controversial, with many Jewish leaders contending that her elevation to sainthood by the Church represented a diminution of Edith's Jewish roots. Pope John Paul II, however, said that Saint Teresa Benedicta's life and the way she died should help us "remember the Shoah, that cruel plan to exterminate a people, a plan to which millions of our Jewish brothers and sisters fell victim." John Paul II declared Edith Stein a "patron of Europe" in 1999. She was canonized in 1998. August 9.

STEPHEN (d. c. 35). A learned Greek-speaking Jew probably born in a foreign land but living in Jerusalem, he may have been educated at Alexandria, was converted to Christianity, and was one of the seven chosen by the Twelve to take care of the secular needs of the Hellenic Jewish Christian community in Jerusalem. They were ordained deacons by the Twelve and began to perform miracles. His success as a preacher caused some of the elders of some of the Jewish synagogues, unable to best him in debate, to charge him with blasphemy to the Sanhedrin; he was arrested and brought before that body. He spoke eloquently in his own defense, denounced his accusers, and then described a vision of Christ standing at the right hand of God after denouncing them for resisting the Holy Spirit, as had their fathers. At this those assembled seized him, dragged him to the outskirts of the city, and stoned him to death—the first Christian martyr. His story is told in Acts 6–7. December 26.

STEPHEN I (d. 257). Born in Rome, he became a priest there, succeeded Pope St. Lucius as Pope, and was consecrated on May 12, 254. He was subjected to much criticism, when he decreed that baptism by heretics was valid, by St.

Cyprian and other African bishops, and refused to see a delegation from an African council in 255 that had declared such baptisms invalid. It is now believed he did not die a martyr, as was once thought. August 2.

STEPHEN (d. 258). *See* Sixtus II.

STEPHEN (d. 304). *See* Socrates.

STEPHEN (d. c. 760). Born in Cappadocia, Asia Minor, he was named bishop of Surosh (Sudak) in the Crimea and was exiled for upholding the veneration of relics during the persecution of iconoclast Emperor Leo III. Stephen returned when Constantine became Emperor in 740, and devoted himself to missionary work among the Slavs, Khazars, and Varangians. December 15.

STEPHEN I (975–1038). Vaik, son of the Magyar *voivode* (duke) of Geza in Hungary, he was born at Asztergom and baptized in 985 when he was ten, at the same time as his father, and christened Stephen. He married Gisela, sister of Duke Henry III of Bavaria (who was to become Emperor Henry II in 1002) and became ruler of the Magyars on his father's death in 977. Through a series of wars against rival leaders who opposed his Christianization policies, he consolidated the country and in 1001 was crowned the first King of Hungary with a crown sent to him by Pope Sylvester II, the famous crown of St. Stephen captured in World War II by the American army and returned to Hungary by the United States in 1978. Stephen organized a hierarchy under St. Astrik (also known as Anastasius), who became Hungary's first archbishop and began establishing sees, building churches, and ordering tithes to be paid for their support. Stephen finished building St. Martin's Monastery (Pannonhalma), begun by his father, inaugurated widespread reforms, including a new legal code and a reorganization of the government in the kingdom, ruled wisely, and was very generous to the poor. He united the Magyars, made the nobles vassals to him, and was the founder of an independent Hungary. His later years were embittered by squabbles about the succession (his only son, Bl. Emeric, had died in a hunting accident in 1031). Stephen died at Szekesfehervar, Hungary, on August 15, and was canonized by Pope Gregory VII in 1083, when his relics were enshrined at the Church of Our Lady in Buda. August 16.

STEPHEN (d. 1396). A Russian, he became a monk at Rostov, Russia, and then engaged in missionary activities among the Zyriane southwest of the Urals. He translated the liturgy and part of the Bible into Zyriane, inventing an alphabet to do so, and founded several schools. In 1383, he was appointed first bishop of Perm, opposed the heretical teachings of the Strigolniks, a Hussite-type sect, and died in Moscow. April 26.

STEPHEN OF CUNEO (d. 1391). *See* Tavelic, Nicholas.

STEPHEN HARDING (d. 1134). Born at Sherborne, Dorsetshire, England, he was educated at Sherborne Abbey, traveled to Scotland, Paris, and Rome, and on his way back joined a group of hermits near Molesmes under Abbot St. Robert and Prior St. Alberic. In 1094, the abbot, the prior, Stephen, and four other monks obtained permission from Archbishop Hugh of Lyons, the papal delegate to France, to leave Molesmes to seek a more spiritual way of life. Robert, with twenty monks, then founded Cîteaux with Robert as abbot, Alberic as prior, and Stephen as subprior in 1098. Robert returned to Molesmes the following year, and Alberic became abbot and Stephen prior. When Alberic died in

1109, Stephen was elected abbot and immediately put into effect a series of austere regulations that cut off much of the abbey's income and discouraged new candidates. When a mysterious malady killed many of the monks, it seemed that the young community was doomed. Then dramatically one day in 1112, a troop of thirty horsemen led by a dashing young noble appeared requesting admission. His name was Bernard, and from then on the Cistercians flourished. By 1119, ten monasteries had been founded from Cîteaux, among them Clairvaux, with Bernard as abbot, though he was only twenty-four at the time; in that year Stephen drew up the rule for the Order, the Charter of Charity, which organized the Cistercians into an Order. He resigned in 1133 because of old age and blindness and died at Cîteaux. He was canonized in 1623. April 17 (July 16 among the Cistercians).

STEPHEN OF MURET (1046–1124). Son of a lord of Thiers, Auvergne, where he was born, he accompanied his father on a trip to Italy when he was twelve. He fell ill at Benevento, was left there, and was educated there. On his return he founded a monastery in the Muret Valley near Limoges, France, which he ruled for forty-six years; after his death the community moved to Grandmont and became the Grandmontines. He insisted on strict discipline, enclosure, and a most austere lifestyle that attracted disciples at first, but it soon declined and eventually disappeared. He died at his monastery, and was canonized by Pope Clement III in 1189. February 8.

STEPHEN OF NARBONNE (d. 1242). *See* William Arnaud.

STEPHEN OF OBAZINE (d. 1154). Born in the Limousin district of France, he was early attracted to the religious life, was ordained, and then became a hermit, with his friend Peter, in the Obazine Forest near Tulle after distributing his possessions to the poor. They soon attracted disciples and built a monastery of which Peter was abbot and imposed a strict unwritten rule of great austerity on the monks. Stephen later founded a convent of 150 nuns, and in 1142 he joined the Cistercians at Dalon, of which he was later named abbot. March 8.

STEPHEN OF PECHERSKY (d. 1094). A monk at the monastery of the Caves at Kiev, Russia, he was elected abbot to succeed St. Theodosius in 1074. Replaced four years later, Stephen founded the monastery of Blakhernae at Klov and in 1091 was named bishop of Vladimir, Volhynia, which he ruled until his death three years later. April 27.

STEPHEN OF RIETI (d. c. 560). Abbot of a monastery near Rieti, Italy, nothing is known of him except that St. Gregory the Great praised him in a homily. February 13.

STEPHEN OF SWEDEN (d. c. 1075). A monk at New Corbie in Saxony, he was ordained and then sent as a missionary bishop to Sweden, where he was most successful in making conversions. He was murdered by pagans either in Uppsala or Norrala, Sweden, for his efforts to suppress the worship of the pagan god Woden. June 2.

STEPHEN THE YOUNGER (714–64). Born at Constantinople, he was sent to St. Auxentius Monastery when he was fifteen. On the death of his father, Stephen distributed his share of the inheritance to the poor. He was elected abbot of his monastery when he was thirty but resigned several years later to seek greater solitude as a hermit in a tiny, inaccessible cell. He was seized by followers of Emperor Constantine

Copronymus when he refused to support the Emperor's iconoclasm, and when Stephen was tricked into illegally clothing a novice, the Emperor had the monastery burned and the monks dispersed. Stephen was tried by court bishops at a monastery at Chrysopolis and banished to the island of Proconnesus. After two years there he was brought before Copronymus and when he still insisted on venerating relics was scourged and then dragged through the streets and killed. November 28.

STILLA, BL. (d. c. 1140). Daughter of Count Wolfgang II of Abenberg, Bavaria, she was born at Abenberg, built St. Peter's Church near her home there in 1136, took a vow of virginity in it, and lived a life of prayer and meditation at her father's home. Her tomb at St. Peter's became a pilgrimage center, and her cult was confirmed in 1927. July 19.

STONE, JOHN (d. c. 1539). A native of Canterbury, England, he became an Augustinian friar of the Canterbury community was a Doctor of Divinity, and was highly regarded for his learning. He served as professor and prior at Droitwich for a time but was back at Canterbury when Henry VIII began his divorce proceedings. John denounced the claims of Henry to ecclesiastical supremacy from the pulpit, was arrested in December 1538, imprisoned at Westgate Prison, and when he reiterated his condemnation of the Act of Supremacy, was hanged, drawn and quartered at Canterbury sometime before December 1539. He was canonized by Pope Paul VI in 1970 as one of the Forty Martyrs of England and Wales. December 27.

STOREY, BL. JOHN (c. 1504–71). Born in northern England, he studied law at Oxford and became Oxford's first professor of civil law. He resigned in 1537 to practice law, married, and became a member of Parliament. Though he took the Oath of Supremacy during the reign of King Henry VIII, he attacked the Act of Uniformity and the liturgical changes of the advisers of child-King Edward VI, was imprisoned for three months for his opposition, and then retired with his family to Louvain. On the accession of Mary Tudor to the throne of England in 1553, he returned to England, was made chancellor of the dioceses of Oxford and London, and represented the Queen at the trial of Archbishop Cranmer of Canterbury on charges of treason in 1556, which led to his burning at the stake. Storey became a leading opponent in Parliament of Queen Elizabeth's Act of Supremacy and was arrested but escaped to Louvain, so impoverished that he became a pensioner of the King of Spain. He was kidnaped at Antwerp and brought back to England, where he was tried and executed at Tyburn. Despite some historians' claims that he was the most active of Mary's agents in bringing heretics to trial, it is now known that he helped save many of the victims. June 1.

STRAMBI, VINCENT (1745–1824). Son of a druggist, he was born on January 1 at Civitavecchia, Italy, resisted his parents' wish that he become a diocesan priest, and though he studied at the diocesan seminary and was ordained in 1767, he joined the Passionists in 1768 after attending a retreat given by St. Paul of the Cross. Vincent became a professor of theology, was made provincial in 1781, and in 1801 was appointed bishop of Macera and Tolentino. He was expelled from his see when he refused to take an oath of allegiance to Napoleon in 1808 but returned in 1813 with the downfall of Napoleon. When Napoleon escaped from Elba, Murat made Macerta his headquarters, and when his troops were defeated by the Austrians, Vincent dissuaded him from sacking and de-

stroying the town. He imposed reforms in his see that caused threats to his life, labored for his people during a typhus epidemic, and resigned his see on the death of Pope Pius VII to become one of the advisers of his old friend Pope Leo XII in Rome. Vincent died on January 1, and was canonized by Pope Pius XII in 1950. September 25.

STRANSHAM, BL. EDWARD (c. 1554–86). Born near Oxford, England, he received his bachelor of arts degree from St. John's College at Oxford, studied at Douai, 1577–78, returned home for a time because of ill health, but returned and was ordained at Soissons in 1580. He was sent on the English mission the following year with Nicholas Woodfen, another priest, used the alias Edmund Barber, was successful in converting students at Oxford to Catholicism, but was forced to return to France because of ill health. He returned to England in 1585, was arrested almost at once with Fr. Woodfen in London, and they were both hanged, drawn, and quartered on January 21 at Tyburn for their Catholic priesthood. He was beatified in 1929.

STRATA, BL. MARY VICTORIA (1562–1617). Born at Genoa, Italy, Mary Victoria Fornari married Angelo Strata when she was seventeen. When her husband died in 1587, she considered marrying again, but after a vision of our Lady, Mary Victoria decided to live in retirement, devoting herself to her six children, prayer, and aiding the poor. When her children were grown up, she and ten others were professed in 1605, and the Blue Nuns were founded with Mary Victoria as superior and dedicated to Mary in the Annunciation and her life at Nazareth. The congregation's second house was founded in 1612, and other houses were later founded in France. She died on December 15, and was beatified in 1828. September 12.

STREMOINE. *See* Austremonius.

STREPAR, BL. JAMES (d. 1409). Of a noble Polish family in Galicia, he was a senator and then joined the Franciscans at their friary at Lwow, where in time he became prior. He was a vigorous defender of the mendicant Orders against the attacks of the regular clergy, headed the Company of Christ's Itinerants, a group of Dominican and Franciscan preachers, was vicar general of Franciscan missions to the schismatics, and was highly successful in preaching to dissident Orthodox in western Russia. He was named archbishop of Galich in 1392 and during his bishopric built numerous churches, hospitals, and religious foundations. He died at Lwow, Galicia, on June 1 (perhaps in 1411). His cult was confirmed in 1791. October 21.

STURMI (d. 779). Born of Christian parents in Bavaria, he was placed in the custody of St. Boniface, who had him educated by St. Wigbert at Fritzlar Abbey. Sturmi was ordained, engaged in missionary work in Westphalia for three years, and then became a hermit at Hersfeld. Forced to leave by raiding Saxons, he founded Fulda Monastery in 744 and was appointed its first abbot by Boniface. He studied Benedictinism at Monte Cassino, was granted complete autonomy for Fulda by Pope St. Zachary, and under Sturmi's direction it became a great center of monastic learning and spirituality. He later became involved in a drawn-out dispute with Bishop St. Lull of Mainz, who claimed jurisdiction over the monastery, and in 763 Pepin banished Sturmi from Fulda. The monks rebelled at his banishment and persuaded Pepin to recall him after two years of exile. He was unsuccessful in attempts to convert the Saxons due in no small measure to the conquests and harsh treatment accorded them by Charlemagne and Pepin. When Charle-

magne led an expedition against the Moors of Spain, the Saxons rose up, drove out the monks, and threatened Fulda. On his return in 779, Charlemagne put down the uprising, but Sturmi was stricken at Fulda before he could reorganize his missions and died there on December 17. Known as "the Apostle of the Saxons," he was the first German to become a Benedictine and was canonized in 1139.

SUCCESSUS (d. 304). *See* Optatus.

SUGAR, VEN. JOHN (1558–1604). Born at Wombourne, Staffordshire, England, he studied at Oxford, where he evidently left before receiving his degree, may have been a minister at Cannven, and then went to Douai to study for the priesthood. He was ordained there in 1601 and sent on the English mission. Arrested at Rowington in 1603 with his assistant Ven. Robert Griswold, he was imprisoned for a year and then hanged at Warwick on July 16, with Robert, for his Catholic priesthood.

SUKEJIRŌ, PETER (d. 1597). *See* Miki, Paul.

SULIAU. *See* Tysilio.

SULPICE. *See* Sulpicius (d. 647).

SULPICIUS (d. 591). Appointed bishop of Bourges in 584, he attended the Council of Mâcon the following year and is mentioned in the writings of St. Gregory of Tours. January 29.

SULPICIUS (d. 647). Also called Sulpice and Pius, he was born of wealthy parents, aided the poor in his youth, and when he became bishop of Bourges in 624 fought for the rights of his people against King Dagobert's minister, Lullo. Sulpicius attended the Council of Clichy in 627, was known for his austerities and holiness, and is reported to have converted all the inhabitants of Bourges to Christianity with his holiness and charity. He resigned his bishopric late in life to devote himself to the poor. The famous St. Sulpice Seminary in Paris is named after him. January 17.

SUNNIVA (10th century). According to an old Norse legend, she was the daughter of an Irish King who fled by boat with her brother Alban and several women companions to escape marriage. They landed on the island of Selje off the coast of Norway, lived in a cave peacefully until a group of neighbors, missing cattle they had left to graze on the island, decided they were using them for their food, and sent an armed force against them. When the warriors arrived at the cave they found it had been sealed up by a landslide. King Olaf Tryggvason reportedly had the cave opened in 995, and when the body of Sunniva was found incorrupt, he built a church for it. July 8.

SUPERIUS (d. c. 768). See Salvius.

SURANUS (d. c. 580). Abbot of a monastery at Sora near Caserta, Italy, he was murdered by marauding Lombards infuriated when they found he had expended the treasure of the abbey they were expecting to loot to care for and feed refugees. His story is told by St. Gregory the Great. January 24.

SUSANNA (d. 295). The beautiful daughter of Gabinius, a priest, and niece of Pope Caius, she refused Emperor Diocletian's request that she marry his son-in-law Maximian and converted two of her uncles, Claudius and Maximus, who were court officers sent by Diocletian to persuade her to marry, to Christianity. Diocletian was so enraged by what she had done that he sent one of his favorites, Julian, to deal with the matter. Julian had Maximus, Claudius and his wife Praepedigna, and their two sons burned to death at Cumae, and then had Susanna and her father beheaded. There was a Susanna who lived in Rome, but the details of the story are fictitious. August 11.

SUSANNA. See Anne (d. c. 918).

SUSO, BL. HENRY (c. 1295–1365). Born at Bihlmeyer near Constance, Switzerland, he early began to use his mother's name, Suso, instead of his father's, von Berg. When he was thirteen, he entered the Dominicans at Constance, was professed, and went to Cologne for further study. He studied under Johann Eckhart, 1324–28, and defended him against charges of heresy in *Little Book of Truth*. His mystical life began when at eighteen he made himself "Servant of the Eternal Wisdom," to whom he devoted himself the rest of his life. For ten years he inflicted the most rigorous mortifications and penances on himself, endured arid periods of spirituality, and experienced visions of Christ, our Lady, and the saints. When he was forty, he began preaching and was tremendously successful in making converts and causing sinners to repent, and was a much sought after spiritual director in Dominican convents. He suffered innumerable slanders, was accused of theft, sacrilege, heresy, adultery, and even poisoning, but was completely exonerated of all charges. The climax came when his sister ran away from her convent; but he convinced her to return, and she lived an exemplary life thereafter. He was elected prior, probably of Diessenhofen, in 1343 and was at the Dominican house in Ulm, Germany, when he died on January 25. He wrote mystical treatises, notably *Book of Eternal Wisdom* (one of the most influential treatises in mystical literature), and an autobiography purportedly pieced together by Elizabet Stagel from material he gave her. His beatification was confirmed by Pope Gregory XVI in 1831. March 2.

SUSTINA (date unknown). *See* Aureus.

SUTTON, BL. ROBERT (d. 1588). Born at Kegwell, Leicestershire, England, he studied at Oxford and became Anglican rector at Lutterworth, Leicestershire, in 1571. He was converted to Catholicism by his brother William and in 1575 went to Douai with his brother Abraham. Robert returned to England, was a schoolteacher in London for a time, and then was arrested. Convicted of having been reconciled to the Catholic Church, he was hanged for this crime at Clerkenwell. He was beatified in 1925. October 5.

SUZUKI, PAUL (1563–97). A native of Owari, Japan, he was baptized by the Jesuits in 1584, became a Franciscan tertiary, and was an outstanding catechist until he was crucified for his faith with twenty-five other Catholics near Nagasaki on February 5. They were all canonized as the Martyrs of Japan in 1862. February 6.

SWALLOWELL, BL. GEORGE (d. 1594). Born near Durham, England, he became a Protestant minister and schoolmaster and was reconciled to the Catholic Church. He was arrested and charged with being a Catholic convert and when convicted, was executed at Darlington on July 26. He was beatified in 1929. July 24.

SWETHIN (d. 870). *See* Theodore.

SWITHBERT (647–713). Born in Northumbria, he became a monk at a monastery near the Scottish border, studied in Ireland under St. Egbert for a time, and was one of the missionaries who accompanied St. Willibrod to

Germany in 690 to convert the Frisians. Swithbert worked in southern Holland and northern Brabant with great success, converting many with his eloquence and zeal. He was consecrated regionary bishop by St. Wilfrid in England in 693 and on his return extended his missionary activities to the Rhine and converted many of the Boructuari. He was obliged to withdraw to Frankish territory when the Saxons invaded the area, built a monastery on an island in the Rhine near Düsseldorf given him by Pepin of Herstal (the town of Kaiserwerth grew up around the monastery), and died there. He is the patron saint invoked against angina. March 1.

SWITHIN. *See* Swithun.

SWITHUN (d. 862). Also spelled Swithin, he was born in Wessex, England, was educated at the Old Monastery, Winchester, and was ordained. He became chaplain to King Egbert of the West Saxons, who appointed him tutor of his son Ethelwulf, and was one of the King's counselors. Swithun was named bishop of Winchester in 852 when Ethelwulf succeeded his father as King. Swithun built several churches and was known for his humility and his aid to the poor and needy. He died on July 2. A long-held superstition declares it will rain for forty days if it rains on his feast day of July 15, but the reason for and origin of this belief are unknown.

SYAGRIUS (d. 600). A Gallo-Roman, he became bishop of Autun about 560, was unsuccessful in reconciling two dissident nuns with the abbess of Holy Cross convent, provided shelter to St. Augustine and his companions when they were on their way to England, and accompanied King Gontram to the baptism of Clotaire II at Nanterre in 591. August 27.

SYKES, VEN. EDMUND (d. 1587). Born in Leeds, England, he went to Rheims to study for the priesthood and was ordained there in 1581. He was sent on the English mission the following year and worked in Yorkshire until he was arrested in 1585. He was banished but returned to England the following year and continued his ministry for six months when he was betrayed to the authorities by his brother. Ven. Edmund was convicted and hanged for being a Catholic priest at York on March 23.

SYLVESTER I (d. 335). The son of Rufinus, a Roman, he was ordained and succeeded Pope Miltiades as Pope on January 31, 314. He had representatives at the Council of Arles and at the first General Council of Nicaea in 325, which condemned Donatism and Arianism, respectively. The tradition that he cured Emperor Constantine of leprosy when he baptized him and in return received great grants of territory (the Donation of Constantine) has no basis in fact. During his pontificate, many new churches were built, notably the basilicas of St. Peter and St. John Lateran. December 31.

SYLVESTER, BL. (1278–1348). Born near Florence, Italy, and baptized Ventura, he became a wool carder and bleacher and when he was forty became a Camaldolese lay brother at St. Mary's Monastery in Florence, taking the name Sylvester. Although illiterate and only a cook, he experienced visions and ecstasies, and his spiritual wisdom was soon recognized. He was consulted by scholars as well as the monks of the monastery for his spiritual advice. June 9.

SYLVESTER, GOZZOLINI (1177–1267). Born of a noble family of Osimo, Italy, he studied law at Bologna and Padua but then switched to the study of theology and Scripture. He was ordained and became a canon at Osimo until he berated his bishop for the dissolute life he was leading; Sylvester resigned his canonry in 1227, when he was fifty, and became a hermit near Osimo and then at Grotta Fucile. Directed by a vision of St. Benedict, he organized the disciples he had attracted into a monastery at Monte Fano near Fabriano in 1231, thus founding the Silvestrine Benedictines, known as the Blue Benedictines from the color of their habit. The congregation was approved by Pope Innocent IV in 1247, and Sylvester ruled it for thirty-six years until his death at Fabiano, by which time eleven monasteries were under his rule. He was equivalently canonized in 1598 by Pope Clement VIII. November 26.

SYMMACHUS (d. 514). Born on the island of Sardinia, the son of Fortunatus, he was baptized in Rome, where he became archdeacon of the Church under Pope Anastasius II and succeeded him as Pope on November 22, 498. The same day the archpriest of St. Praxedes, Laurence, was elected Pope by a dissenting faction with Byzantine leanings, which was supported by Emperor Anastasius, but Gothic King Theodoric ruled against him and in favor of Symmachus. In 501 the pro-Byzantine group, led by Senator Festus, accused Symmachus of various crimes, but the Pope refused to appear before the King to answer the charges, asserting that the secular ruler had no jurisdiction over him. A synod called by Theodoric exonerated Symmachus, whereupon Theodoric installed Laurence in the Lateran as Pope. The schism continued for four years when Theodoric ended it by withdrawing his support of Laurence. Symmachus helped the African bishops exiled to Sardinia by the Arian Thrasimund, founded three hospices, aided the victims of the barbarians' raids in northern Italy, helped ransom captives, and was known for his help to the poor. He died on July 19.

SYMPHORIAN (d. c. 180). A Christian of noble birth in Autun, Gaul, he was haled before the governor of the province, Heraclius, for his denunciation of the pagan goddess Cybele, and was beaten and imprisoned. When he persisted in his refusal to accept pagan gods, he was beheaded. August 22.

SYMPHORIAN (d. c. 306). See Castorius.

SYMPHOROSA (d. c. 135). According to her legend, she was the widow of the martyred St. Getulius, lived at Tivoli (Tibur) near Rome with her seven sons, and when she refused the order of Emperor Hadrian to sacrifice to pagan gods, was drowned in the Anio River. Her seven sons—Crescens, Eugenius, Julian, Justin, Nemesius, Primativus, and Staceteus—were all reputedly executed the next day. Though these men did suffer martyrdom, they were not her sons nor were they related to her. July 18.

SYMPHRONIUS (d. 257). A slave in Rome, he helped convert Olympius, the tribune, his wife, Exuperia, and their son Theodulus to Christianity. The four of them were burned to death for their faith on the Latin Way in Rome during the persecution of Christians under Emperor Valerian. July 26.

SYNCLETICA (c. 316–400). Born at Alexandria, Egypt, of wealthy Macedonian parents, she refused the numerous suitors her beauty attracted, and when her parents died she gave her inheritance to the poor and retired with her blind sister to the estate of a relative, where they lived as recluses. Syncletica consecrated herself to God, devoted herself to aiding the needy, and gave spiritual counsel to the women of the area. Stricken with cancer when she was eighty, she bore her affliction and suffering with great patience the rest of her life. January 5.

SYRUS OF GENOA (d. c. 380). A parish priest at St. Romulus (San Remo), he became bishop of Genoa and served in that position for fifty-six years. He is principal patron of Genoa. July 7.

T

TAIGI, BL. ANNE MARY (1769–1837). Daughter of an apothecary, Anne Mary Gesualda was born at Siena, Italy, on May 29, moved to Rome to take a domestic position to aid her impoverished family, and in 1790 married Dominic Taigi, a servant. The couple had seven children, and her confessor, Fr. Angelo, a Servite, testified that she led a life of heroic virtue, aided the poor, worked to help the sick, experienced visions and ecstasies, and had the gift of prophecy, though she also experienced periods of spiritual aridity and temptation. She died on June 9, and was beatified in 1920.

TAKEYA, COSMAS (d. 1597). *See* Miki, Paul.

TANCO (d. 808). Also known as Tatto, he was a monk from Ireland who immigrated to Amalbarich Abbey in Saxony and in time became abbot. He was a successful missionary in Cleves and Flanders, was named bishop of Verden, Saxony, and was stabbed to death by a mob for his denunciation of evildoing in his see, though another account had him murdered by pagans for destroying statues of pagan gods. February 15.

TAPARELLI, BL. AIME (1395–1495). Born at Savigliano, Piedmont, Italy, of a noble family, he married but later joined the Dominicans. He studied and taught at the University of Turin, was an effective preacher, winning many back to the faith, and was an adviser to Bl. Amadeus, duke of Savoy. He was named commissary of the Inquisition in 1466 and then inquisitor general for Upper Lombardy and Liguria, a position he held for the next thirty years until his death on August 15. His cult was confirmed in 1856. August 18.

TARACHUS (c. 239–304). A Roman born at Claudiopolis, Isauria, he became a soldier in the Roman army but left the army when he became a Christian. When he was sixty-five, he was arrested with Andronicus and Probus at Pompeiopolis in Cilicia during the persecution of Christians under Emperors Diocletian and Maximian. They were tried before Numerian Maximus, the governor, subjected to three interrogations (at Tarsus, Mopsuestia, and Anazarbus), and cruelly tortured. They remained steadfast in their faith and were ordered thrown to wild beasts in the arena near Anazarbus; when the beasts did not harm them, gladiators killed them by sword. Probus was a plebeian born at Side in Pamphylia of a Thracian father, and Andronicus was a patrician of Ephesus. October 11.

TARASIUS (d. 806). Of a noble family and also known as Thrasius, he was a layman serving as secretary to ten-year-old Emperor Constantine VI when he was named Patriarch of Constantinople by the regent, Empress Irene, and was consecrated in 784. Following the decrees of the General Council of Nicaea in 787, he restored statues and images to the churches of his see, worked to abolish simony, and lived a life of great austerity, known for his charity. He alienated Constantine when he refused to sanction his divorce from Empress Mary, whom Constantine had been forced to marry by his mother, so he could marry one of Mary's maids, Theodota, which he later did. Constantine was imprisoned and blinded by Irene, who in turn was exiled to Lesbos by Nicephorus when he seized the throne. Tarasius finished his twenty-one-year reign under Nicephorus. February 25.

TARSICIUS (3rd century). An acolyte or perhaps a deacon at Rome, he was accosted and beaten to death on the Appian Way by a mob while carrying the Eucharist to some Christians in prison. The incident is included in Cardinal Wiseman's novel *Fabiola,* and Pope Damasus wrote a poem about it. Tarsicius is the patron of first communicants. August 15.

TARSILLA. *See* Tharsilla under Emiliana.

TASSACH. *See* Asicus (d. 470).

TASSACH (d. c. 495). The first bishop of Raholp, Down, Ireland, and also known as Asicus, he was a skilled artisan and a disciple of St. Patrick, for whom he made croziers, patens, chalices, credences, and crosses for the many churches Patrick founded; Tassach gave the last rites to Patrick when Patrick was dying. April 14.

TATIAN DULAS (d. c. 310). A Christian at Zephyrium, Cilicia, he was arrested and brought before the prefect of the province, Maximinus. When Tatian refused to worship pagan gods and scorned Apollo, he was tortured; he died while being taken with other Christian prisoners to Tarsus. June 15.

TATIANA (d. c. 230). According to the Roman Martyrology, she was tortured and beheaded for her faith at Rome during the reign of Emperor Alexander Severus. January 12.

TATTO. *See* Tanco.

TAVELIC, NICHOLAS (d. 1391). Born at Sibenik, Dalmatia, he became a Friar Minor at Rivotorto near Assisi, Italy, and worked as a missionary in Bosnia for twenty years. He was then sent to Palestine, was arrested and imprisoned for preaching publicly on his faith to the Moslems, and with three other friars— Adeotus Aribert, Peter of Narbonne, and Stephen of Cuneo—was hacked to death in Jerusalem on November 14. They were canonized by Pope Paul VI in 1970. November 14.

TAVELLI, BL. JOHN (d. 1466). Born at Tossignano, Italy, and often called John of Tossignano, he studied at the University of Bologna and joined the Jesuits there. He was named bishop of Ferrara in 1431, hosted the General Council that met there in 1438, and built a hospital. He wrote a biography of Bl. John Colombini, translated parts of the Bible and works of Gregory and Bernard into Italian, and wrote several spiritual treatises. Bl. John Tavelli's cult was approved in 1748. July 24.

TEILO (6th century). Born near Penally, Pembrokeshire, Wales, where he is known as Eliud, he studied under St. Dubricius, reputedly accompanied St. David to Jerusalem, and then spent seven years with St. Samson at Dol in Brittany. Teilo returned to Wales in 554, preached with great success, and established several monasteries, notably at Llandeilo Fawr, Carmarthenshire, where he was abbot-bishop and where he died. February 9.

TEKAKWITHA, BL. KATERI (c. 1656–80). The daughter of a Christian Algonquin who was captured by Iroquois Indians and married to a pagan Mohawk chieftain, she was born at the Indian village of Osserneon (Auriesville), New York (where two Jesuit priests, St. Isaac Jogues and St. Jean de Lalande, had suffered martyrdom in 1646), and was orphaned as a child when her parents and brother died during an epidemic of smallpox, which left her with seriously impaired eyesight and a disfigured face. She was converted to Catholicism by Fr. Jacques de Lamberville, a Jesuit priest-missionary, in 1676 and was soon subjected to great abuse and ostracism by her relatives and the other Indians for her new religion. Fearful for her life, she fled her native village and trekked some 200 miles through the wilderness to the Christian Indian village of Sault Ste. Marie, near Montreal, Canada, in 1677. She made her First Communion on Christmas of that year, lived a life of great holiness and austerity, and in 1679 took a vow of chastity and dedicated herself to Christ. She died at Caughnawaga, Canada, on April 17, venerated for her holiness and concern for others. She was known as the Lily of the Mohawks, many miracles were attributed to her, and in 1943 she was declared Venerable by Pope Pius XII; she was beatified in 1980 by Pope John Paul II. She was canonized in 1991.

TELEMACHUS. See Almachius.

TELESPHORUS (d. c. 136). Born in Greece, he succeeded Pope St. Sixtus I as Pope, reigned for ten years, and according to tradition suffered martyrdom under Emperor Hadrian. January 5.

TERESA, BL. MOTHER, OF CALCUTTA (1910–97). Albanian-born Agnes Gonxha Bojaxhiu, Mother Teresa joined the Sisters of Loretto in 1928 and taught for seventeen years at the Order's school in Calcutta. She experienced her divine call to devote herself to caring for the sick and poor in 1946, moved into the slums, and founded the Order of the Missionaries of Charity, which would become a pontifical congregation in 1965. She also established Nirmal Hriday, a hospice where those poor and near death could die with dignity instead of on the streets of Calcutta, as so often happened. By 1971, though already well known in the Church, Mother Teresa and her Missionaries of Charity became familiar to the world at large, particularly through the publication of Malcolm Muggeridge's portrait of Teresa, *Something Beautiful for God*. She received many awards throughout her lifetime, including the 1979 Nobel Prize for Peace. Because of Mother Teresa's commitment, the Missionaries of Charity today has expanded throughout the world, running hospices, treatment centers, and hospitals, and caring for abandoned children, the aged, and the homeless. Her beatification took place October 19, 2003, and was televised worldwide. In history, no other person has ever been beatified so soon after death. The 1998 healing of a Bengali tribal woman, Monika Besra, diagnosed with tuberculosis and a cancerous tumor, was recognized as her first miracle.

TERESA OF ÁVILA (1515–82). Born at Ávila, Castile, Spain, on March 28, the daughter of Alonso Sanchez de Cepeda and his second wife, Beatrice Davila y Ahumada, she was educated by Augustinian nuns but was forced to leave their convent at Ávila in 1532 because of ill health. Long attracted to the religious life, she became a Carmelite at Ávila in

1536, was professed the next year, left in 1538 because of illness, but returned in 1540. She experienced visions and heard voices, 1555–56, which caused her great anguish until St. Peter of Alcántara became her spiritual adviser in 1557 and convinced her that they were authentic. Despite bitter opposition, she founded St. Joseph Convent at Ávila in 1562 for nuns who wished to live an enclosed spiritual life rather than the relaxed style so prevalent in convents of that time. In 1567, Fr. Rubeo, prior general of the Carmelites, gave her permission to establish other convents based on the strict rule followed at St. Joseph's; in time she was to found sixteen convents. While establishing her second convent, at Medino del Campo, she met a young friar named John Yepes (John of the Cross), founded her first monastery for men (the first reform Carmelite monastery) at Duruelo in 1568, and then turned the task of founding Carmelite reformed monasteries over to John. She traveled all over Spain, tireless in her struggle to reform the Carmelites, but violent opposition from the calced Carmelites developed, and at a general chapter of the Carmelites at Piacenza in 1575 Fr. Rubeo put strict restrictions on her reforming group. For the next five years a bitter struggle took place within the Carmelites until in 1580, Pope Gregory XIII, at the instigation of King Philip II, recognized the Discalced Reform as a separate province. During these turbulent years, while traveling all over Spain, Teresa wrote letters and books that are widely regarded as classics of spiritual literature, among them her *Autobiography* (1565), *The Way of Perfection* (1573), and *Interior Castle* (1577). One of the great mystics of all times, she was intelligent, hardheaded, charming, deeply spiritual, and successfully blended a highly active life with a life of deep contemplation. She died at Alba de Tormes,

Spain, on October 4 (October 14 by the Gregorian calendar, which went into effect the next day and advanced the calendar ten days), and was canonized in 1622 by Pope Gregory XV. She was declared a Doctor of the Church in 1970 by Pope Paul VI—the first woman to be so honored. October 15.

TERESA OF PORTUGAL (d. 1250). Eldest daughter of King Sancho I of Portugal and sister of SS. Mafalda and Sanchia, she married her cousin, King Alfonso IX of León. The couple had several children, but when the marriage was declared invalid because of consanguinity, she returned to Portugal and founded a Benedictine monastery on her estate at Lorvão. She replaced the monks with nuns following the Cistercian rule, expanded the monastery to accommodate three hundred nuns, and lived there. In about 1231, at the request of Alfonso's second wife and widow, Berengaria, she settled a dispute among their children over the succession to the throne of León, and on her return to Lorvão probably became a nun. Her cult, with that of her sister Sanchia, was approved by Pope Clement XI in 1705. June 17.

TERNAN (5th or 6th century). Conflicting traditions have him a monk at Culross Monastery in Scotland or a native of the province of Mearns in Scotland who was baptized by St. Paliadius, whose disciple he became and who may have consecrated him bishop in 432 (or he may have been named bishop of Rome). At any rate, he worked as a missionary among the Picts, had his headquarters at Abernethy, and was reputed to have founded the abbey of Culross in Fifeshire, where he died. June 12.

TERTULA (d. 259). *See* Agapius.

THADDEUS. *See* Jude.

THAIS (no date). According to legend, she was raised a Christian but became a famous courtesan in Alexandria, Egypt. She decided to mend her sinful ways when she was visited by the aged St. Paphnutius, destroyed her ill-gotten wealth, and entered a convent selected by Paphnutius, who sealed her up in a cell. After three years of penances, Paphnutius, on the advice of St. Antony and his monks, released her to live with the other women in the convent; she died fifteen days after her release. October 8.

THALASSIUS (5th century). See Limnaeus.

THALELAEUS (d. 284). The son of a Roman general, he was born in Lebanon, became a physician at Anazarbus, where he was called "the Merciful" for his services to the sick poor, and fled to escape the persecution of Christians under Emperor Numerian. Thalelaeus was captured, brought to Aegea, Cilicia (mistakenly called Edessa, Syria, in the Roman Martyrology), and then beheaded when an attempt to drown him failed. Also martyred with him were Alexander and Asterius, two bystanders who may have been the officers in charge of his execution, because of their compassion for him. May 20.

THALELAEUS (d. c. 450). Born in Cilicia, he lived as a hermit near Gala, where he converted to Christianity many of those who came to worship at a pagan shrine next to his shack. He was surnamed Epiklautos ("weeping much") because of his constant weeping during the sixty years he was a hermit. February 27.

THARASIUS. See Tarasius.

THARSILLA (d. c. 550). See Emiliana.

THEA (d. c. 307). See Meuris.

THEA (d. 308). Born at Gaza, Palestine, she was arrested with other Christians during the persecution of Christians under Emperor Maximian and brought before Firmilian, governor of Palestine, at Caesarea. When she denounced him for threatening to place her in a brothel, he had her scourged. When a Christian of Caesarea, Valentina, protested, Firmilian had her dragged to a pagan altar, and when she kicked over the fire and incense before the altar, he had her tortured. He then bound Thea and Valentina together and had them burned to death. Thea is sometimes referred to as Ennatha. July 25.

THEAU. See Tillo.

THECLA (1st century). According to a popular second-century tale, *Acts of Paul and Thecla,* she was a native of Iconomium who was so impressed by the preaching of St. Paul on virginity that she broke off her engagement to marry Thamyris to live a life of virginity. Paul was ordered scourged and banished from the city for his teaching, and Thecla was ordered burned to death. When a storm providentially extinguished the flames, she escaped with Paul and went with him to Antioch. There she was condemned to wild beasts in the arena when she violently resisted the attempt of Syriarch Alexander to kidnap her, but again escaped when the beasts did no harm to her. She rejoined Paul at Myra in Lycia, dressed as a boy, and was commissioned by him to preach the gospel. She did preach for a time in Iconium and then became a recluse in a cave at Meriamlik near Seleucia; she lived as a hermitess there for the next seventy-two years and died there (or in Rome, where she was miraculously transported when she found that Paul had died and was later buried near his tomb). The tale had tremendous popularity in the early Church but is undoubtedly a pious fiction and was labeled apocryphal by St. Jerome. September 23.

THECLA (d. 304). *See* Timothy.

THECLA OF KITZINGEN (d. c. 790). One of the nuns at Wimborne Abbey in England who was sent to Germany under St. Lioba to assist St. Boniface in his missionary work, she was at Bischofsheim Abbey for a time and was then made abbess of Ochsenfurt by Boniface and later was abbess of Kitzingen, where she was listed as Heilga. October 15.

THECUSA (d. c. 304). *See* Theodotus.

THENAW (6th century). *See* Kentigern.

THENEVA (6th century). *See* Kentigern.

THEOBALD (1017–66). Son of Count Arnoul of Champagne, he was born at Provins, Brie, France, was raised to be a soldier, but decided he wanted to lead an ascetic life. He left the military life, with his father's permission, and after a time at St. Remi Abbey in Rheims, he and another nobleman named Walter became hermits at Suxy, Ardennes, and in 1135 moved to Pettingen Forest in Luxemburg. They worked as masons and field hands during the day to earn their keep and spent the night in prayer. In quest of greater solitude, they went on pilgrimage to Compostela and Rome and then resumed their eremitical life at Salanigo near Vicenza, Italy; Walter died two years later. Theobald's sanctity attracted numerous disciples, and he was ordained and became a Camaldolese. His fame spread and reached his parents, who came to visit him, and his mother, Gisela, became a hermitess nearby. Theobald died at Salanigo on June 30, and was canonized by Pope Alexander II in 1073.

THEOBALD (d. 1150). Theobald Roggeri was born of well-to-do parents at Vico, Italy, left his comfortable home to become a shoemaker's apprentice at Alba, and on the death of his master went on pilgrimage to Compostela. On his return, he engaged in portering work, gave most of his earnings to the poor, and lived an austere life of great penances and mortifications. He is the patron of shoemakers and porters. June 1.

THEOBALD (d. 1247). Of the noble Montmorency family, he was born at the family castle at Marly, France, was trained in arms by his father, Bouchard de Montmorency, and spent some time at the court of King Philip Augustus II. Theobald left the court to become a Cistercian at Vaux-de-Cernay Abbey in 1220, was elected abbot in 1235, and died on December 8. July 27.

THEOCTISTA (no date). There is a pious religious fiction according to which she lived on the island of Lesbos in the Aegean Sea, was kidnaped by the Arabs, and was brought to the island of Paros but escaped her captors and lived as a hermitess for thirty years. She was discovered on Paros by a man named Simon while he was hunting, and in response to her plea, returned the following year with Holy Communion; she died soon after. The tale was reputedly told by an old priest to Nicetas, who visited Paros while he was on a military expedition against the Arabs on Crete with Admiral Himerius. November 10.

THEODARD (d. c. 670). A disciple of St. Remaclus at the Benedictine abbey of Malmédy-Stavelot, France, he succeeded Remaclus as abbot in 653 and as bishop of Tongres-Maastricht in 662. Theodard was murdered by a band of robbers in Bienwald Forest near Speyer, Germany, while on the way to protest to Childeric II of Austrasia against the confiscation of Church lands by a group of nobles. September 10.

THEODARD (d. 893). Born at Montauriol (Montauban, France) and also known as Audard, he studied at the Benedictine abbey there and law at Toulouse and became a lawyer. He attracted the attention of Archbishop Sigebold of Narbonne, who made him his secretary, ordained him, and made him archdeacon. He was named archbishop on Sigebold's death, worked to restore the faith of his flock and repair the ravages of Saracen incursions, rebuilt his cathedral, ransomed captives of the Saracens, and sold the church's treasure and gave his own income to alleviate the prolonged famine that afflicted the area. He returned to Montauriol in an attempt to recover his health, which had been undermined by his great austerities, but died there at St. Martin's Abbey (renamed St. Audard after his death). May 1.

THEODMARUS. *See* Thiemo.

THEODORA (d. c. 304). There is a pious fiction according to which Theodora, a beautiful Christian girl of Alexandria, was sentenced to a brothel during the persecution of Christians under Emperor Diocletian when she refused to sacrifice to the gods. She fell dead when she was rescued by Didymus; when Didymus' act was discovered, he was beheaded. April 28.

THEODORA (d. c. 305). A wealthy Roman of noble birth, she gave freely of her wealth to help Christian martyrs during the persecution of Christians under Emperor Diocletian and in time was martyred for her faith. September 17.

THEODORA OF ALEXANDRIA (no date). According to legend, she was the wife of Gregory, prefect of Egypt, but left him to do penance for a sin she had committed. She lived as a monk at a monastery in the Thebaid the rest of her life, and it was not until her death that her sex was discovered. September 11.

THEODORE (d. c. 310). Known for his skill in copying manuscripts, he became bishop of Cyrene in Libya, where he was executed when he refused to surrender copies of the Bible he had copied. July 4.

THEODORE (c. 775–c. 841). He and his brother Theophanes (b. c. 778) were born at Kerak, Moab (Transjordan), were brought to Jerusalem in their youth by their parents, and became monks at St. Sabas Monastery there. Theodore was ordained, was sent by the Patriarch of Jerusalem to protest to Emperor Leo the Armenian against the Emperor's persecution of those opposed to his iconoclasm, and was scourged and exiled with Theophanes to an island in the Black Sea. They returned to Constantinople on the death of Leo in 820 but were again banished by Emperor Theophilus in 829. Brought back to Constantinople by the Emperor in 831, they were tortured and had twelve lines of verses cut into their skins for their opposition to iconoclasm. They were then banished to Apamea, Bithynia, where Theodore died. Soon after the death of Theophilus, Theophanes was brought back and later was named bishop of Nicaea, where he was venerated for the suffering he had endured and where he died on October 11, 845. Theophanes wrote poetry, for which he is surnamed "the Poet," and both brothers are called Graptoi (the written-on) because of their branding. December 27.

THEODORE (d. 870). Abbot of the Benedictine abbey of Croyland, England, he was slain by invading Danes on a marauding raid. Among those murdered with him were Askega, the prior; Swethin, the subprior; Elfgete, a deacon; Savinus, a subdeacon; Eldred and Ulrick, acolytes; and two centenarians, Agamund and Grimkeld. April 9.

THEODORE (d. 1246). See Michael of Chernigov.

THEODORE (d. 1299). Duke of Yaroslav and Smolensk, Russia, and called "the Black," he ruled wisely, defended his people against the Tartars, aided the poor, built churches, and helped extend Christianity. Just before his death at Yaroslav on September 19, he became a monk at Transfiguration Monastery and was buried there. His two sons, David and Constantine, by his second wife, are also venerated and were buried next to him when they died in 1321.

THEODORE OF CANTERBURY (602–90). Born at Tarsus, Cilicia, he studied at Athens and became a Basilian monk at Rome. When he was sixty-six, he was named archbishop of Canterbury by Pope St. Vitalian in 668 and took possession of his see the following year. He made a visitation of all the churches in England, filled vacancies, restored clerical discipline, opened schools, instituted reforms, and introduced liturgical chant to the English churches. He settled the controversy between St. Wilfrid and St. Chad over the see of York, recognizing Wilfrid as bishop, and was famed for his learning and knowledge of Scripture. He held the first nationwide English Church council at Hertford in 673 where he introduced a new set of ten canons, which among other things set the date of Easter according to the Roman custom and established the diocesan system in England. Another council, at Hatfield in 680, condemned monophysitism while endorsing the decrees of the first five general councils of

the Church. In 678, a controversy erupted between Wilfrid of York and King Egfrid of Northumbria, whom Wilfrid had condemned for not allowing his wife to enter a convent, and over the division of the see of York into the dioceses of Hereford, Lindsey, and Worcester without Wilfrid's permission, and for which Egfrid appointed bishops. Wilfrid appealed to Rome, and Pope St. Agatho ruled that the see should remain divided but that Wilfrid should appoint the suffragans. When Egfrid refused to obey the Pope's order and exiled Wilfrid, Theodore evidently made no attempt to prevent Egfrid's action but was later reconciled to Wilfrid. In 679, Theodore acted as peacemaker between King Egfrid and King Ethelred, ending their war and establishing a peace between the two Kings for years. Theodore was the first metropolitan of all England. He changed the Church in England from a missionary body to an organized Church, with Canterbury as its metropolitan see. He died at Canterbury on September 19, universally mourned, after reigning for twenty-two years during which, according to the historian Bede, "the English Church made greater progress during his pontificate than they had ever done before." He is also known as Theodore of Tarsus.

THEODORE OF HERACLEA (no date). A resident of Heraclea in Pontus, he became a general in the army of Emperor Licinius and governor of Pontus and the surrounding area. When it was discovered that he was a Christian, he was tortured and then beheaded by order of Licinius. Theodore is often surnamed Stratelates (general) and is one of the four honored by the Greeks as "a great martyr." February 7.

THEODORE THE SANCTIFIED (c. 314–68). Born in the Upper Thebaid, Egypt, of wealthy parents, he joined St.

Pachomius at Tabenna, became his companion, and was ordained by him. He was named abbot of Tabenna about 347 soon after the death of Pachomius, restored order to the monastery, and ruled successfully for the rest of his life until he died on April 27, venerated for the many miracles he reportedly performed. He is also known as Theodore of Tabenna. December 28.

THEODORE STRATELATES (d. 319). *See* Theodore Tiro.

THEODORE STUDITES (759–826). Born at Constantinople and nephew of Abbot St. Plato of Symboleon on Mount Olympus in Bithynia, he became a novice at a monastery established by his father on his estate at Saccudium near Constantinople, where he was sent to study by Plato, who had become abbot of Saccudium. Theodore was ordained in 787 at Constantinople, returned to Saccudium, and in 794 succeeded Plato as abbot. He and Plato denounced the action of Emperor Constantine VI in leaving his wife and marrying Theodota, and in 796, Theodore and his monks were exiled to Thessalonica. He returned a few months later when Constantine's mother, Irene, seized power, dethroned, and then blinded her son. Theodore reopened Saccudium but moved to Constantinople to escape Saracen raids, was named abbot of the famous Studios Monastery, founded in 463 but now neglected and run-down, built it from a dozen monks to a thousand, and made it the center of Eastern monastic life. He encouraged learning and the arts, founded a school of calligraphy, and wrote a rule for the monastery that was adopted in Russia, Bulgaria, Serbia, and even on Mount Athos. When he opposed the appointment of a layman, Nicephorus, to succeed Tarasius, who had died in 806 as patriarch of Constantinople by Emperor Nice-

phorus, Theodore was imprisoned by the emperor. When in 809 Nicephorus, the Patriarch, and a synod of bishops reinstated the priest, Joseph, who had married Constantine and Theodota and declared the marriage valid, Theodore's denunciations of the decision caused him to be exiled to Princes' Island with Plato and Archbishop Joseph of Thessalonica, Theodore's brother, and the monks of Studios were dispersed. Theodore returned on the Emperor's death in 811 and was reconciled to Patriarch Nicephorus in a common fight against the iconoclasm of Emperor Leo V the Armenian. When Nicephorus was banished, Theodore became the leader of the orthodox and was himself banished in 813 to Mysia by Leo. When Theodore's correspondence (among it letters to Pope St. Pascal I emphasizing the primacy of the bishop of Rome) was discovered, he was removed to Bonita in Anatolia. He endured great hardships the three years he was in prison there and then was transferred to Smyrna and put in the custody of an iconoclast bishop who wanted him beheaded and treated him with great harshness. Released on the murder of Leo in 820, he was again faced with a renewed iconoclasm under Emperor Michael the Stammerer, who refused to restore him as abbot or to restore any of the orthodox bishops to their sees. Theodore left Constantinople and visited monasteries in Bithynia, founded a monastery on Akrita for many of his monks who had followed him, and died there on November 11. Many of his letters, treatises, sermons, and hymns are still extant.

THEODORE OF SYKEON (d. 613). Born at Sykeon, Galatia, Asia Minor, the son of a prostitute, he became a hermit at an early age and then, while on pilgrimage to Jerusalem, a monk. He was ordained, founded several monasteries (among them one at Sykeon, of which he was abbot), prophesied to Emperor Tiberius' general, Maurice, that he would become Emperor (which he did in 582), and was made bishop of Anastasiopolis against his will. He resigned after ten years as bishop and retired to Sykeon, where he died on April 22. He is credited with performing many miracles, among them curing the Emperor's son of leprosy.

THEODORE OF TABENNA. See Theodore the Sanctified.

THEODORE OF TARSUS. See Theodore of Canterbury.

THEODORE TIRO (d. c. 306). A recruit *(tiro)* in the Roman army at Pontus on the Black Sea, he was brought before his tribune and the governor of the province when he refused to participate in the pagan rites of his comrades in arms. Temporarily freed, he set fire to the pagan temple of Cybele near Amasea in Pontus, was brought before his judges again, and tortured. After a third examination he was condemned to be executed and was burned to death in a furnace. His cult was enormously popular in the East, and he was one of the best known of the "warrior saints," though the facts of his life, beyond that he was martyred, are from unreliable sources. He may have been the same as Theodore Stratelates who is also known as Theodore of Heraclea, a general in the army of Emperor Licinius. Theodore of Heraclea was reported to have been tortured and beheaded at Heraclea, Thrace, in 319; his feast day is February 7. November 9.

THEODORET (d. 362). A priest at Antioch, he refused to surrender sacred church vessels to Julian, prefect of the East and uncle of Emperor Julian the Apostate. The prefect charged him with destroying statues of pagan gods, whereupon Theodoret denounced Julian for his apostasy; Julian condemned him to death, and he was beheaded. Before his death, Theodoret prophesied that Julian would die painfully, and soon after, Julian died in agony. October 23.

THEODORIC (d. 533). Also known as Thierry, he was born near Rheims, Gaul, married against his will, and persuaded his wife to agree to a separation. He became a priest under St. Remigius, founded a religious community at Mont d'Or near Rheims, became known for his conversions (including that of his own father, a notorious sinner), and reportedly cured King Theodoric of ophthalmia. He died on July 1.

THEODOSIA (c. 288–c. 306). An eighteen-year-old Christian girl, a native of Tyre, she was on a visit to Caesarea, Palestine, during the persecution of Christians under Emperor Maximian and was tortured and thrown into the sea on Easter for speaking to a group of Christians waiting to be sentenced to death. April 2.

THEODOSIA (d. 745). Of a noble family, she was orphaned in her youth, became a nun at St. Anastasia Monastery in Constantinople, and led a band of nuns in resisting by force the soldiers sent to enforce the iconoclastic decrees of Emperor Leo the Isaurian by destroying the image of Christ over the main door of their monastery. She was imprisoned and died of the torture to which she was subjected with twelve other women. The whole story may be a pious fiction. May 29.

THEODOSIUS THE CENOBIARCH (423–529). Born at Garissus, Cappadocia, he went on a pilgrimage to Jerusalem, stopping off to see St. Simeon Stylites, and then entered a monastery under one Longinus. Theodosius was appointed head of a church near Bethlehem but left to become a hermit on a neighboring mountainside and soon attracted many disciples, whom he organized into a community of hermits and built a monastery for them at Cathismus near Bethlehem. He built three hospices for the sick, the aged, and the mentally disturbed, organized his community according to four language groups that predominated among his monks, and was appointed head of all cenobites living in Palestine by Patriarch Sallust of Jerusalem. With St. Sabas, Theodosius opposed the attempts of Emperor Anastasius to spread Eutychianism, and Theodosius' preaching against that heresy all over Palestine led to his exile by the Emperor. Theodosius was recalled by Emperor Justin soon after Anastasius' death and was ill the last years of his life. January 11.

THEODOSIUS PECHERSKY (d. 1074). The son of well-to-do parents, he abandoned their easy way of life, despite their opposition, labored in the fields with the serfs, apprenticed himself to a baker, and in about 1032 became a monk at the Caves of Kiev, founded by Antony Pechersky. Theodosius succeeded Barlaam as abbot and replaced the founding Antony's concept of monasticism based on the drastic austerities of the Egyptian hermits with the more moderate approach of the Palestinian monks, stressed the need for corporal work as well as prayer and mortifications, urged common sense rather than fanatical austerities and penances in their religious life, recommended that his monks participate in secular affairs, and emphasized a harmony between the active and the contemplative life. He expanded the number of buildings at the monastery, established a hospital and a hostel, and with his monks evangelized Kiev. He took part in secular affairs to help and defend the poor, and bitterly denounced Svyastoslav for driving his brother from the throne of Kiev, comparing him to Cain. During the four decades of his abbacy, Theodosius developed the Caves of Kiev into a great monastery, which marked the real beginning of Russian monasticism. His directions to the monks of the Caves of Kiev were to endure for generations. He died in one of the caves of the original monastery, and was canonized by the bishops of Kiev in 1108. With Antony Pechersky, he is the founder of Russian monasticism. July 10.

THEODOTA (d. c. 304). According to unreliable sources, she was of noble birth, lived at Nicaea during the persecution of Christians under Emperor Diocletian, and refused to marry Prefect Leucatius. He denounced her and her three children to Proconsul Nicetius in Bithynia as Christians, and when she and her three children refused to sacrifice to the pagan gods, they were all burned to death. August 2.

THEODOTA (d. c. 318). According to her extravagant and unreliable legend, she refused to obey the order of Prefect Agrippa that all the inhabitants of Philippopolis in Thrace join him in a festival in honor of Apollo, and some 750 other Christians followed her lead and refused to participate. She was imprisoned for twenty days, confessed that she had been a harlot, repented, became a Christian, and could not worship pagan gods. She was then tortured and stoned to death. September 29.

THEODOTUS (d. c. 304). There is a pious fiction according to which he was an innkeeper at Ancrya, Galatia, who had been raised by Thecusa. During the persecution of Christians under Emperor Diocletian, he aided imprisoned Christians and in a meeting with some freed Christians near the town of Malus, he promised them and the local priest, Fronto, relics of a martyr for a chapel they proposed to build there. Soon after, Thecusa and six Christian women were paraded naked in an open chariot during a feast to Artemis and Athene at the order of the governor, who threatened to drown them if they refused to wear the robes of pagan priestesses and join in the festival. When they refused, they were drowned. Theodotus recovered their bodies, was betrayed by an apostate, and was tortured and beheaded. That night Fronto came to the city, recovered Theodotus' body by tricking the guards, and sent it to Malus, where a chapel was built to enshrine it. May 18.

THEODULUS (d. c. 113). *See* Alexander.

THEODULUS (d. 257). *See* Symphronius.

THEODULUS (d. 303) *See* Agathopus.

THEODULUS (d. 309). An aged, high-ranking official in the household of Firmilian, governor of Palestine, at Caesarea and noted for his wisdom, he was crucified by Firmilian when the governor found that he had visited St. Elias and his Egyptian companions in prison. February 17.

THEONILLA (d. c. 303). *See* Asterius.

THEOPHANES (d. 817). Born at Constantinople and left a large fortune in his youth when his father died, he was raised at the court of Emperor Constantine V, married, but by mutual agreement he and his wife separated, she to become a nun and he to become a monk. He built monasteries on Mount Sigriana and on the island of Kalonymos; after six years at the latter, he became abbot of Mount Sigriana. He attended

the General Council of Nicaea in 787 and when he supported the decrees of the Council approving the veneration of sacred images, he came into conflict with Emperor Leo the Armenian, who supported iconoclasm. When Theophanes refused to accede to the Emperor's demands, he was scourged, imprisoned for two years, and then banished to Samothrace, where he died on March 12, soon after his arrival, of the ill treatment he had received in prison. He is called "the Chronicler" for his *Chronographia,* a history covering the years 284–813.

THEOPHANES (d. 845). *See* Theodore (d. c. 841).

THEOPHILUS (d. 250). *See* Ammon.

THEOPHILUS (d. 303). *See* Dorothy.

THEOPHILUS (d. 789). He was admiral of the Christian fleet at Cyprus when the Saracens invaded the island and captured him. After a year's imprisonment, he was tortured and then beheaded. July 22.

THEOPHILUS OF CORTE. *See* Signori, Theophilus de'.

THEOPHILUS THE PENITENT (no date). A tenth-century Latin play by Hrosvitha of Gandesheim depicts Theophilus as administrator of Adan, Cilicia, who declined a bishopric because of his humility. He was deposed of his office in the Church by the man who became bishop and was so furious that he made a pact with Satan, who had him restored to his position. He later repented, appealed to our Lady, found the pact he had signed with Satan on his chest when he awoke one morning, did penance for his deed, made a public confession of his sin, and had the bishop burn the pact before the congregation. Theophilus is a legendary figure often listed as a saint on February 4 and is the precursor of the Faust theme.

THEOPHYLACT (d. 845). Brought from Asia as a youngster to Constantinople, where he was educated, he became a monk with St. Michael the Confessor at a monastery founded by Tarasius, Patriarch of Constantinople, on the Bosporus. Theophylact was named bishop of Nicomedia by Tarasius and was a leader in proclaiming the Catholic position against iconoclasm at a council at Constantinople called by Tarasius' successor, Patriarch Nicephorus of Constantinople, and when Emperor Leo refused to be moved by the arguments against iconoclasm, denounced him and prophesied a tragic fate for him. Leo banished and imprisoned him in the fortress of Caria, Asia Minor, where he remained incarcerated for thirty years; he died there. Theophylact founded several hospices and was known for his aid to the poor, the orphans, and the afflicted. March 7.

THEOPISTIS (d. c. 118). *See* Eustace.

THEOTONIUS (1088–1166). Born at Ganfeo, Spain, he was early attracted to the religious life, was educated at Coimbra, Portugal, and was ordained. He engaged in pastoral work at Viseu, which he reformed, made a pilgrimage to the Holy Land, and refused to bishopric offered by the Queen, whom he later rebuked publicly for her affair with Count Ferdinand. On his return from a second visit to the Holy Land, he joined the Canons Regular of St. Augustine at Coimbra in 1136, became prior of their monastery there, and later was abbot. He died at Coimbra, venerated for his holiness and noted for his concern for the poor, his persuasion of King Alphonsus to release his Mozarabic captives, and his insistence on strict observance of liturgical practices. His cult was

approved by Pope Benedict XIV. February 18.

THÉRÈSE OF LISIEUX (1873–97). Marie Françoise Martin was born at Alençon, France, on January 2, the youngest of the nine children of Louis Martin, a watchmaker, and Zélie Guérin. Her mother died when she was five, and the family moved to Lisieux, where she was raised by her older sisters and an aunt. Two of her sisters became Carmelite nuns, and she resolved to emulate them. She was refused admission at first but a year later was admitted to the Carmel at Lisieux. She was professed in 1890, taking the name Thérèse of the Child Jesus. Afflicted with tuberculosis, she bore her illness with great patience and fortitude, devoting herself to prayer and meditation and serving for a time as mistress of novices. By order of the prioress, Mother Agnes (her sister Pauline), she began in 1894 to write the story of her childhood, and in 1897, after finishing it the previous year, she was ordered by the new prioress, Mother Marie de Gonzague, to tell of her life in the convent. Both were combined into *The Story of a Soul,* which became one of the most widely read modern spiritual autobiographies. She died of tuberculosis on September 30 at Lisieux, quickly attracted a tremendous following as "the Little Flower" and "the saint of the little way," and was canonized in 1925 by Pope Pius XI. She was declared copatron of the missions, with St. Francis Xavier, in 1927, and in 1944 was named copatroness of France with Joan of Arc. October 1.

THEUDERIUS (d. c. 575). Born at Arcisia (St. Chef d'Arcisse), Dauphiné, France, and known as Chef in France, he became a monk at Lérins, was ordained by St. Caesarius at Arles, and then returned to Dauphiné. A group of disciples gathered around him, and he founded a monastery near Vienne. He lived as a walled-up recluse at the Church of St. Laurence in Vienne the last twelve years of his life, venerated for his holiness and miracles. October 29.

THIBAUD. The French spelling of Theobald.

THIEMO (d. 1102). Of the family of the counts of Meglin in Bavaria, he joined the Benedictines at Niederaltaich and became famous as a painter, sculptor, and metalworker. He was elected abbot of St. Peter's Abbey in Salzburg, Austria, in 1077 and was named archbishop of that city in 1090. His support of Pope Gregory VII against Emperor Henry IV caused Thiemo to be imprisoned and then exiled. While in exile, he went on crusade, was captured by the Moslems, and imprisoned at Ascalon. When he refused to apostatize despite the tortures to which he was subjected, he was executed at Corozain. He is also known as Theodmarus. September 28.

THIERRY. *See* Theodoric.

THIRKELD, BL. RICHARD (d. 1583). Born at Durham, England, he studied at Oxford, and late in life, after studies at Douai and Rheims, he was ordained in 1579. He was sent on the English mission, worked in the area around York, and was arrested and imprisoned there. He was convicted of treason for being a Catholic priest and was hanged, drawn, and quartered at York on May 29. He was beatified in 1886.

THOMAIS (d. 476). The wife of a fisherman at Alexandria, she was murdered by her father-in-law when she repulsed his sexual advances. April 14.

THOMAS (1st century). Born probably in Galilee and surnamed Didymus (the twin), he became one of the twelve apostles, though where and when are uncertain. He was one of those with Jesus at the raising of Lazarus from the dead, but is best known for the incident in John 20:24–29 when he refused to believe that Christ had appeared to the apostles, saying he would do so only if he could "see the holes that the nails made in his hands and can put my finger into the holes they made, and . . . put my hand into his side . . . ," giving rise to the expression "doubting Thomas." When Christ appeared to him, he exclaimed, "My Lord and my God," thus becoming the first to acknowledge explicitly the divinity of Christ. He was also one of the group fishing to whom Jesus appeared in John 21. According to Eusebius, Thomas later preached in Parthia, and an ancient tradition has him bringing the gospel to India, where he was martyred and buried at Mylapore near Madras. He was declared the apostle of India by Pope Paul VI in 1972. July 3.

THOMAS, BL. (d. 1337). Born at Costacciaro near Gibbio, Italy, he joined the Camaldolese Hermits of St. Romuald at Sitria and after several years there became a recluse in a cave on Mount Cupo. He lived a life of extreme austerity and was reported to have performed many miracles. March 25.

THOMAS AQUINAS (c. 1225–74). Born at the family castle of Roccasecca near Aquino, Italy, the son of Count Landulf of Aquino, a relative of the Emperor and of the King of France, and Theodora, he was sent to nearby Benedictine Monte Cassino Monastery as an oblate when he was five years old to be educated. In about 1239 he went to the University of Naples to finish his education and joined the Dominicans there in 1244, a move so strongly opposed by his family that they kidnaped him and held him captive at Roccasecca Castle for fifteen months in an attempt to deter him from the Dominicans. He persisted, rejoined the Order in 1245, and studied at Paris, 1245–48. He accompanied Albertus Magnus to a new Dominican *studium generale* at Cologne in 1248, was ordained there sometime in 1250–51, and in 1252 returned to Paris as *sententarius,* lecturing on the *Sentences* of Peter Lombard. He was master of theology at Paris in 1256 and taught at Naples, Anagni, Orvieto, Rome, and Viterbo, 1259–68, finishing his *Summa contra Gentiles* and beginning his *Summa theologiae* during those years. He returned to Paris in 1269, became involved in the struggle between the Order priests and the seculars, and opposed the philosophical teachings of Siger of Brabant, John Peckham, and Bishop Stephen Tempier of Paris. When dissension racked the university in 1272, he was sent as regent to head a new Dominican house of studies at Naples. He was appointed to attend the General Council of Lyons, called to discuss the reunion of the Greek and Latin churches by Pope Gregory X in 1274, but died on the way to Lyons at the Cistercian abbey of Fossa Nuova near Terracina, Italy, on March 7. He was canonized by Pope John XXII in 1323, was declared a Doctor of the Church by Pope St. Pius V in 1567, and was named patron of all universities, colleges, and schools in 1880 by Pope Leo XIII, whose bull *Aeterni Patris* required all theological students to study his thought; the substance of his work became the official teaching of the Catholic Church. Aquinas was probably the greatest theological master of Christianity, and his thought dominated Catholic teaching for seven centuries after his death. His writings were voluminous, characterized by his sharp distinction between faith and reason, but emphasizing that the great fundamental Christian doctrines, though impossible to establish by reason, are not contrary to reason and reach us by revelation; never-

theless, he believed that such truths as the existence of God, his eternity, his creative power, and his providence can be discovered by natural reason. His *magnum opus,* the unfinished *Summa theologiae,* is probably the greatest exposition of theological thought ever written and became the accepted basis for modern Catholic theology. Among his other writings are *Quaestiones disputatae, Quaestiones quodlibetales, Summa contra Gentiles, De unitate intellectus contra Averroistas,* and his commentaries on the *Sentences* of Peter Lombard, on Boethius, on Dionysius, and on Aristotle. In addition to his towering intellect, Aquinas was a man of great humility and holiness. He experienced visions, ecstasies, and revelations (he left *Summa theologiae* unfinished because of a revelation he experienced while saying Mass in 1273), composed the office for the feast of Corpus Christi, and wrote hymns still used in Church services, notably *Pange lingua, Verbum supernum, Lauda Sion,* and *Adoro te devote.* He wrote commentaries on the Lord's Prayer, the Apostles' Creed, and parts of the Bible. In him the Middle Ages reached its full flowering and Christianity received its most towering and influential intellect. January 28.

THOMAS BECKET (1118–70). Son of Gilbert, sheriff of London, and Matilda, both of Norman descent, he was born on December 21 in London, studied at Merton Priory in Surrey and law in London, and continued his studies at the University of Paris. His father's death left him in straitened circumstances, and in about 1141 he joined the household of Archbishop Theobold of Canterbury, who sent him on several missions to Rome and in 1144 to Bologna and Auxerre to study common law. He was ordained deacon in 1154 and then became archdeacon of Canterbury when nominated by Theobold. Thomas became a favorite of Henry of Anjou when he convinced Pope Eugene III not to recognize the succession of King Stephen of Blois' son, Eustace, thus ensuring Henry's right to the English throne as Henry II. Thomas was appointed chancellor of England by Henry in 1155, soon became the most powerful man in England next to Henry, and was famed for the luxury and magnificence of his style of life. He accompanied Henry on his military expedition to Toulouse in 1159 at the head of his own troops. On the death of Theobold in 1161, Henry nominated Thomas as archbishop of Canterbury, and despite Becket's vigorous objections, he was elected in 1162. He resigned his chancellorship, was ordained a priest the day before his consecration, and became archbishop. He changed his life completely, lived a life of great austerity, and soon clashed with the King over clerical and Church rights. In 1164, Thomas refused to accept the Constitutions of Clarendon, which among other things denied clerics the right to be tried in ecclesiastical courts and to appeal to Rome, and he was forced to flee to France. He appealed to Pope Alexander III, then at Sens, but the Pope, not wishing to offend Henry, would not support Thomas. When Henry and Thomas both remained adamant, Thomas, at Alexander's suggestion, entered the Cistercian abbey at Pontigny. When Henry threatened to expel all Cistercians from his realm in 1166, Thomas moved to St. Columba Abbey near Sens, which was under the protection of King Louis VII of France. Through the efforts of Louis, Henry and Thomas patched up a peace in Normandy in 1170, and Thomas returned to England. But warfare between the two soon broke out again when Becket refused to lift the excommunication of the archbishop of York and those bishops who had participated at the coronation of Henry's son, a flagrant infringement of the rights of the

archbishop of Canterbury, unless they swore obedience to the Pope. Henry reacted violently and in a fit of rage said aloud in public that he wished he was rid of this troublesome prelate, though it is most doubtful that he really meant it. Four of his knights took him at his word and on December 29 murdered the archbishop in his cathedral. The act shocked all of Europe. Thomas was at once proclaimed a martyr, and in 1173 Pope Alexander III declared him a saint. The following year Henry did public penance, and the shrine of St. Thomas became one of the most popular pilgrimage centers in Europe. December 29.

THOMAS OF BIVILLE, BL. (c. 1187–1257). Thomas Hélye was born at Biville near Cherbourg, Normandy, became a schoolteacher there and in Cherbourg, was ordained a deacon by the bishop of Coutances, and after pilgrimages to Rome and Compostela went to Paris for further study. He was ordained a priest, became pastor at St. Maurice, and the engaged in missionary work in the surrounding area. He was most successful and ministered to the poor, the sick, and the needy until his death at Vauville Castle in La Manche on October 19. The miracles attributed to him after his death caused a cult to develop, which was confirmed in 1859.

THOMAS CANTELUPE (c. 1218–82). Of a distinguished Norman family, and son of Baron William of Cantelupe, steward of King Henry III's household, he was born at Hambleden, England, and was educated by his uncle, Bishop Walter of Worcester, at Oxford, and at Paris. Thomas was with his father at the General Council of Lyons in 1245 and was probably ordained then. After studying law at Orléans and Paris, he became a lecturer in canon law at Oxford and in 1262 was named chancellor. He supported the barons against

King Henry III, was one of three delegates to plead their cause to King St. Louis at Amiens in 1264, and when Henry was defeated at Lewes was named chancellor of England in 1265. He filled the office with great integrity and justice, but on the death of Simon de Montfort in 1265, he was dismissed and retired to Paris. He was again named chancellor of Oxford in 1274, and the following year became bishop of Hereford. He restored the fortunes of the see, recovered the rights that had been infringed on by the lords of the area, and ruled his see with great prudence and ability. Though the holder of many benefices (with the permission of Pope Innocent IV), he carefully supervised the administration of his benefices, a rare concern of those holding plural benefices in those times. The last years of his life were saddened by a jurisdictional dispute with Archbishop John Peckham of Canterbury. Thomas was the leader of the bishops opposing Peckham at the Council of Reading in 1279 and was excommunicated by the archbishop in 1282. He went to Orvieto to appeal his case personally to Pope Martin IV, but worn out by the trip, died at nearby Montefiascone on August 25 and was buried at Orvieto. When his body was returned to Hereford and enshrined in the cathedral, hundreds of miracles were reported, and it became a popular pilgrimage center. He was canonized by Pope John XXII in 1320. He is also known as Thomas of Hereford. October 3.

THOMAS OF CORI, BL. (1656–1729). Born at Cori, Italy, he was a shepherd in his youth, joined the Observant Franciscans at Cori in 1677, and was ordained six years later. He served as master of novices for a time and then at his request was transferred to the Franciscan friary at Civitella near Subiaco, where he spent the rest of his life in prayer and contemplation. He experienced ecstasies, was gifted with levitation, was known for his charity to the poor, and was reported to have performed miracles. He died on January 11 and was beatified in 1785. January 19.

THOMAS OF DOVER (d. 1295). Thomas of Hales, as he is also called, was a Benedictine monk at St. Martin Priory at Dover when French raiders attacked the priory on August 3. A feeble old man and the only one left in the priory, he was murdered by the raiders when he refused to divulge where the church treasure was hidden. Though a cult developed and he is honored locally on August 2, his canonization proceedings, requested by King Richard II and begun in 1382, have never been completed.

THOMAS OF HALES. *See* Thomas of Dover.

THOMAS OF HEREFORD. *See* Thomas Cantelupe.

THOMAS OF TOLENTINO, BL. (d. 1321). Born of a noble family at Piceno, Italy, he joined the Franciscans in his youth and was ordained. He and four fellow Franciscans were sent to Armenia as missionaries and labored there with great success. He returned to solicit aid from Pope Nicholas IV and the rulers of France and England when the Saracens threatened Armenia, and he returned with twelve more Franciscans. He went on to Perisa and then returned to Rome, where a hierarchy for the Far East was established with John of Monte Corvino, first archbishop of Cambelek (Peking). He was on his way to Ceylon and China when his ship was driven off course to the Salsette Islands near Bombay, where he and two Franciscans, Bl. James of Padua and Peter of Siena, and a layman, Bl. Demetrius of Tiflis, were taken captive by Mohammedans, tortured, and beheaded on April 9 at Tana. They were beatified by Pope Leo XIII in 1894.

THOMAS OF VILLANOVA (1488–1555). Son of Alonzo Tomás García and Lucía Martínez Castellanos, he was born at Fuentellana, Castile, Spain, near the birthplace of his parents, Villanueva de los Infantes (hence his surname), spent ten years at the University of Alcalá, where he received his masters in art and his licentiate in theology, and became a professor there when he was only twenty-six. He declined the chair of philosophy at Salamanca and joined the Augustinians there in 1516. He was ordained in 1518, served as prior of several houses, was named provincial of Andalusia and Castile in 1527, and was provincial of Castile in 1533, whence he sent the first Augustinian missionaries to America (to Mexico). He became chaplain to Emperor Charles V, refused the see of Granada, but in 1544 was appointed archbishop of Valencia by the Emperor. The see had been vacant for ninety years, but he soon reformed the diocese. He was noted for the austerity and poverty of his life, was known for his generosity to the poor and the needy, labored among the Moors, and gave funds for priests to be especially trained for this work, founding a college for the children of new converts and another for poor students. He did not attend the Council of Trent but was active in influencing the Spanish bishops to promote reform in the Church in Spain. He died at Valencia on September 8, and was canonized in 1658. September 22.

THOMAS OF WALDEN, BL. *See* Netter, Bl. Thomas.

THOMPSON, BL. JAMES (d. 1582). Born at York, England, he went to Rheims in 1580, was ordained, but was

forced to return to England because of ill health. Using the alias Mr. Hudson, he worked for a year in the underground, ministering to Catholics until he was arrested. Convicted of being a Catholic priest, he was hanged at York on November 28. He was beatified in 1895.

THORFINN (d. 1285). From Trondheim, Norway, he became a canon of the cathedral at Nidaros and in time bishop of Hamar. His support of Archbishop John of Nidaros against King Eric caused Thorfinn to be exiled. After being involved in a shipwreck, he reached the Cistercian abbey of Ter Doest near Bruges, Flanders, visited Rome, and died at Ter Doest on January 8. He may have become a Cistercian at Tautra Abbey near Nidaros before his exile. His life was commemorated in a poem written by Walter de Muda, one of his monks.

THORLAC THORHALLSSON (1133–93). Born in Iceland, he became a deacon when he was fifteen and was ordained when he was eighteen. He was sent abroad to study, reportedly visited London, and returned to Iceland in 1161. He founded a monastery at Thykkviboer, became its abbot, and in 1178 was named bishop of Skalholt, one of the two dioceses of Iceland. He reformed the see, insisted on clerical discipline and celibacy, abolished lay patronage, and fought simony. He planned to resign and retire to Thykkviboer, but he died on December 23 before he could do so. He was canonized by the Iceland Althing five years later, but his cult has never been formally approved by the Holy See.

THORNE, BL. JOHN (d. 1539). *See* Whiting, Bl. Richard.

THULIS, VEN. JOHN (c. 1568–c. 1616). Born at Upholland, Lancashire, England, he went to Rheims to study for the priesthood and was ordained at Rome in 1590. He was sent back to England in 1592, was arrested and imprisoned in Cambridgeshire, and then released. He then ministered to the Catholics of Lancashire, was again arrested, but escaped and was recaptured. He was executed at Lancaster on March 18 with a weaver named Roger Wrenno and three thieves he had converted to Catholicism.

THWING, JOHN (1319–79). Born at Thwing near Bridlington, Yorkshire, England, he went to Oxford when he was seventeen and two years later became a Canon Regular of St. Augustine in his native town. He filled various offices in the monastery there and in time was elected prior, a position he held for seventeen years until his death there on October 10. He was canonized by Pope Boniface IX as John of Bridlington in 1401 and is patron of women in difficult labor. October 21.

THWING, BL. THOMAS (1635–80). Born at Heworth, North Riding, Yorkshire, England, he studied at Douai, was ordained in 1664, and was sent to England. He worked in the Yorkshire area for the next fifteen years as chaplain for his cousin, Sir Miles Stapleton, as director of a school, and beginning in 1677 as chaplain to the nuns at the Institute of Mary at Dolebank, Thwing. With his uncle, Sir Thomas Gascoigne, he was arrested and charged with participating in Titus Oates' fabricated "popish plot" to assassinate King Charles II, and when convicted, was hanged, drawn, and quartered at York on October 23. He was beatified in 1929; his name is also spelled Thweng.

THYRSUS (2nd century). *See* Andochius.

TIBBA (7th century). *See* Cyneburga.

TIBURTIUS (date unknown). *See* Cecilia.

TIBURTIUS (d. c. 288). A subdeacon at Rome, he was betrayed by an apostate during the persecution of the Christians under Emperor Diocletian, haled before Prefect Flavian, reportedly walked barefooted over burning coals and emerged unharmed, and was then beheaded on the Via Lalicana three miles from Rome. August 11.

TICHBORNE, VEN. NICHOLAS (d. 1601). Born at Hartley Mauditt, Hampshire, England, he was arrested for his faith in 1597 but released when he gave evidence against his family. He secured his brother's release from the Gatehouse in London in 1598, was arrested again, and this time was executed at Tyburn on August 24 with Thomas Hackshot of Mursley, Buckinghamshire.

T'IEN CHING, BL. ANDREW WANG (d. 1900). *See* Mangin, Bl. Leon.

TIERNEY. *See* Tigernach.

TIERRY. *See* Tigernach.

TIGERNACH (d. 549). According to tradition he was born in Ireland of a family of royal descent and had St. Brigid as his godmother. He was captured by pirates in his youth and became the slave of an English King who later freed him. He joined Monennus at Rosnat Monastery in Scotland, made a pilgrimage to Rome, founded Clones Monastery in Monaghan, was its abbot on his return, and succeeded St. Macartan as bishop of Clogher. Tigernach was blind in his old age and devoted the last years of his life to prayer and meditation at Clones. He is also known as Tierney and Tierry. April 4.

TIGRIS (5th century). One of five sisters of St. Patrick, she married Gollit, and the two had five sons, all of whom became bishops. Where and when she died are uncertain.

TIGRIUS. See Eutropius.

TILBERT (d. 789). All that is known of him is that he was eighth bishop of Hexham, England, 781–89, and according to historian Simeon of Durham died on October 2. September 7.

TILLO (d. c. 702). Born in Saxony, he was taken as a captive to the Low Countries by raiders, was ransomed by St. Eligius, worked with him for a time as a goldsmith, and then became a monk at Solignac Abbey. He was ordained, worked as a missionary around Courtrai and in different sections of the Low Countries, and then returned to Solignac, where he spent the rest of his life as a recluse near the abbey. He is known as Theau in France, Tilman in Flanders, and Hillonius in Germany. January 7.

TILMAN. See Tillo.

TIMOTHY (d. c. 97). Born at Lystra, Lycaenia, he was the son of a Greek father and Eunice, a converted Jewess. He joined St. Paul when Paul preached at Lystra, replacing Barnabas, and became Paul's close friend and confidant. Paul allowed him to be circumcised to placate the Jews, since he was the son of a Jewess, and he then accompanied Paul on his second missionary journey. When Paul was forced to flee Berea because of the enmity of the Jews there, Timothy remained but after a time was sent to Thessalonica to report on the condition of the Christians there and to encourage them under persecution, a report that led to Paul's first letter to the Thessalonians when he rejoined Timothy at Corinth. Timothy and Erastus were sent to Macedonia in 58,

went to Corinth to remind the Corinthians of Paul's teaching, and then accompanied Paul into Macedonia and Achaia. Timothy was probably with Paul when the apostle was imprisoned at Caesarea and then Rome, and was himself imprisoned but then freed. According to tradition, he went to Ephesus, became its first bishop, and was stoned to death there when he opposed the pagan festival of Katagogian in honor of Diana. Paul wrote two letters to Timothy, one written about 65 from Macedonia and the second from Rome while he was in prison awaiting execution. January 25.

TIMOTHY (d. c. 286). A lector at Penapeis near Antinoë, Egypt, he was arrested by Arrian, prefect of the Thebaid, Upper Egypt, during the persecution of Christians under Emperor Diocletian and ordered to surrender the sacred books of his church. When torture failed to break him down and reveal their whereabouts, Maura, his bride of twenty days, was brought in to ask him to do as he was directed. Instead she encouraged him and was tortured, and then both were nailed to a wall until they died nine days later. May 3.

TIMOTHY (d. 290). See Apollinaris.

TIMOTHY (d. 304). Bishop of Gaza, Palestine, he was scourged and tortured and then burned to death at Gaza during the persecution of Christians under Emperor Diocletian. Also ordered to be executed by Urban, the governor of Palestine, were Agapius and Thecla. Thecla was killed by wild beasts in the amphitheater at Caesarea. Agapius was imprisoned for another two years and then put into the amphitheater at Caesarea with wild beasts. When he was not killed immediately, he was offered his freedom if he would sacrifice to the pagan gods, and when he refused, was returned to the arena. When a bear injured but did not kill him, he was taken back to prison and the next day was drowned. August 19.

TIMOTHY (d. 311). A priest from Antioch, Syria, he was arrested in Rome by Tarquin, the prefect of the city, during the persecution of the Christians under Emperor Diocletian, and when he refused to sacrifice to pagan gods, was imprisoned, tortured, and then beheaded. August 22.

TIMOTHY, BL. (1444–1504). Born at Montecchio near Aquila, Italy, he became an Observant Franciscan in his youth, was known for the austerity of his life and his visions of Christ, Mary, and St. Francis, and is reported to have performed many miracles. He died at St. Angelo Friary at Ocra, and his cult was confirmed by Pope Pius IX in 1870. August 26.

TITUS (1st century). Converted by St. Paul, he became his secretary and accompanied him to the Council of Jerusalem, where Paul refused to allow him to be circumcised. Paul sent him to Corinth to correct errors and settle dissensions that had arisen there and again later to collect alms for the poor Christians of Jerusalem. He was ordained bishop of Crete by Paul, to carry on Paul's work, met Paul at Nicopolis in Epirus, and was the recipient of a letter from Paul written from Macedonia in about 65 giving him instructions on spiritual matters, advising him on the qualities needed by a good bishop, the need to maintain strict discipline among the Cretans, and telling him to establish presbyters in all the cities of Crete. He visited Dalmatia and then returned to Crete, where he probably died at an advanced age. He is represented in the Acts of Titus, supposedly written by Zenas the lawyer (who is mentioned in Titus

3:13), as having been born of royal descent on Crete and went to Judea when he was twenty in response to a heavenly command and to have lived on Crete until he died there when in his nineties, but these Acts are considered a work of fiction by scholars. Other equally untrustworthy sources have him born at Iconium and at Corinth. January 26.

TOLOMEI, BL. BERNARD (1272–1348). Born at Siena, Italy, and baptized John, he studied at the university there, received his doctorate in law, and became an official in the local government. He resigned this post in 1312 to live as a solitary near the city with Ambrose Piccolomini and Patrick Patrizi. Falsely cited for unorthodox beliefs, they were exonerated before Pope John XXII, who ordered them to live under an approved monastic rule. They selected the Benedictine rule, and John was named their superior, taking the name Bernard. Their hermitage, founded in 1319 at Monte Oliveto, Chiusuri, became the Congregation of Our Lady of Monte Oliveto. It was successful, other foundations were established, and the Congregation received papal approval in 1344 from Pope Clement VI. Bernard and eighty of his monks were the victims of a plague ravaging Siena, contracted while they were ministering to its victims, and he died at Monte Oliveto on August 20. His cult was confirmed in 1644. August 21.

TOMASI, GUISEPPE MARIA (1649–1713). Son of a highly religious, noble family in Palermo (his parents both entered the religious life once their children were raised), Tomasi relinquished his noble title to his brother and was ordained a Theatine. A great linguist, writer, and confessor, Tomasi lived as a hermit and was chastised by church authorities for being over scrupulous. Persuaded by Tomasi that it would be a mortal sin to refuse to accept papal election, a reluctant Cardinal Alboni (Pope Clement XI) named Tomasi Cardinal. He was canonized in 1986. January 1.

TOMITANI, BL. BERNARDINO (1439–94). Born at Feltre near Venice, Italy, of the noble Tomitani family and baptized Martin, he studied at a local college and philosophy and law at the University of Padua. He joined the Franciscans at Padua in 1456, taking the name Bernard, and was ordained in 1463. He began preaching in Venice in 1469, and for the next quarter century was one of the most popular preachers in Italy, attracting thousands of people wherever he appeared. He denounced the evils of his time, especially gambling, usury, and sexual licentiousness, and successfully acted as peacemaker in quarrels among several cities, though he failed in three attempts at Perugia. He helped found the *monti di pietá* (lending institutions), thus incurring the enmity of the Lombards, who controlled the loan business in Italy, and was so forceful in some of his attacks on evildoers that his life was threatened several times. It is estimated that he delivered some 3,600 sermons, 120 of which are still extant. He died at Pavia on September 28, and his cult was approved in 1728.

TOMMASI, BL. JOSEPH (1649–1713). Born at Alicata, Sicily, on September 12, son of the duke of Palermo, he joined the Theatines at Palermo in 1664. He continued his studies at Messina, Rome, Ferrara, and Modena, was ordained, and then spent the next forty years in the study of Scripture and Hebrew and Greek philosophy, and writing the liturgical works at San Silvestro in Rome, for which he is known. Among his works are an edition of Augustine's *Speculum,* the *Codices Sacramentorum,* the *Psalterium,* and *Antiphonarium.* He was called to the Vatican by Pope Innocent XII in 1697,

was appointed theologian to the Congregation of Discipline of Regulars in 1704, and worked to reform religious orders. He became confessor to Cardinal Albani, ordered him to accept the papacy as Pope Clement XI when he was elected in 1700 under pain of mortal sin, and was made to accept a cardinalate from Clement for the same reason. Bl. Joseph continued his interest in the liturgy and Church music, ministered to the poor, experienced visions, and was reported to have performed miracles of healing. He died in Rome on January 1, and was beatified in 1803.

TORELLO, BL. (1201–82). Born at Poppi, Italy, he embarked on a dissolute life on the death of his father but decided to make amends when he received what he interpreted as a divine reporach. He distributed his possessions to the poor of Poppi, built a hermitage nearby, and spent the remaining fifty years of his life there as a recluse, doing penances and mortifications. His cult was approved by Pope Benedict XIV. March 16.

TORNIELLI, BL. BONAVENTURE (c. 1411–91). Born at Forlì, Italy, he joined the Servites in 1448, was ordained, and engaged in mission work. He became noted for his preaching in the Papal States, Tuscany, and Venice, and in 1488 was elected vicar general. He died while preaching a mission at Udine, and his cult was confirmed in 1911. March 31.

TORQUATUS (1st century). According to legend, he was one of the first seven missionaries sent out by Peter and Paul to evangelize Spain. The others were Caecilius at Granada, Ctesiphon at Verga, Euphrasius at Andujar, Hesychius at Gibraltas, Indaletius at Urci near Almeria, and Secundius at Ávila. Torquatus worked with great success at Guadix, Granada. Apparently all seven were martyrs, Torquatus at Cadiz. May 15.

TORRES-ACOSTA, MARY SOLEDAD (1826–87). Born on December 2 at Madrid, Spain, and christened Emanuela, she was unsuccessful in an attempt to join the Dominicans because of ill health, but in 1851 she joined a community formed by Fr. Michael Martinez y Sanz to minister to the poor sick, taking the names Mary Soledad (Maria Desolata in Spain). The community encountered early difficulties, and five years later divided, with half of its members going with Fr. Michael and the remainder staying with Mary Soledad under a new director, Fr. Gabino Sanchez, taking the name Handmaids of Mary Serving the Sick, and Mary was named superioress. It received diocesan approval in 1861, came to public attention through the work of Mary and her nuns in a cholera epidemic that struck Madrid in 1865, and though another division took place a few years later, the Handmaids of Mary spread throughout Europe and the Americas. Mary died at Madrid on October 11 after thirty-five years as superioress, and was canonized by Pope Paul VI in 1970.

TORTHRED (d. c. 870). A hermit near Thorney Abbey, Cambridgeshire, England, he and three fellow hermits were murdered by marauding Danes raiding the English coast. April 10.

TOTNAN (d. c. 689). *See* Kilian.

TOUSSAINT, PIERRE (1781–1853). Born a slave in Saint Domingue (now Haiti), Toussaint's cause for sainthood was opened in 1989. The young Toussaint was brought to the United States by his master, Jean Jacques Berard in 1797 and apprenticed as a hairdresser. Berard, Toussaints master, briefly returned to revolutionary Saint Domingue to retrieve his plantation, but soon died there. In New York the French-speaking slave became the sole support of his mistress, Marie Elisabeth Berard, her two sisters and three other slaves. Freed almost literally at his mistress's deathbed, the mature Toussaint risked his life caring for the sick and abandoned during yellow fever epidemics. While a successful society coiffeur and businessman, he was devoted, along with the support of his wife, Juliette, to aiding the poor, sick, and raising orphaned African American boys in his home. He attended mass daily at Old St. Peter's Church on Barclay Street for more than fifty years. He was declared Venerable by Pope John Paul II in 1996.

TRAVERSARI, BL. AMBROSE (1386–1439). Born at Portico, Italy, of a noble Tuscan family, he became a Camaldolese monk in Florence when he was fourteen. During the next thirty years he spent there, he became one of the leading intellectuals of the city, known for his scholarship and knowledge of classical languages, and he translated several Greek spiritual works. Cosimo de' Medici was his patron, and he taught many of the sons of nobility. In 1431, he was appointed abbot general of the Camaldolese, instituted widespread reforms in the Order, and then performed the same task for the Vallumbrosans. He became a confidant of Pope Eugene IV when the Pope sought refuge in Florence in 1434, was papal envoy to the Council of Basle in 1435, papal representative to Emperor John VII and his brother, Patriarch Joseph of Constantinople, and was active at the Council of Ferrara, which brought about a temporary reunion of Rome and the Eastern churches in 1439. He died at Florence on October 20. Though he was called Blessed when a cult grew up around him, he has never been officially beatified. November 20.

TRÉHET, BL. FRANÇOISE (1756–94). See Mézière, Bl. Françoise.

TRIPHINA (d. c. 306). See Agatho.

TRIPHYLLIUS (d. c. 370). A lawyer who was converted to Christianity, he was later named bishop of Nicosia, Cyprus, and was persecuted by the Arians for his opposition to Arianism and support of St. Athanasius. St. Jerome praised him as being the most eloquent ecclesiastic of his time. June 13.

TROND. See Trudo.

TROPHIMUS (1st century). A Gentile from Ephesus, he accompanied St. Paul on his third missionary journey (Acts 20:4) and to Jerusalem, where his presence in the Temple provoked violent protests against Paul that almost resulted in Paul's death (Acts 21:26–36). The only other mention of Trophimus is in 1 Timothy 4:20, in which Paul says he "left Trophimus ill at Miletus." He is often confused with Trophimus, the first bishop of Arles (see next entry). December 29.

TROPHIMUS (3rd century). According to St. Gregory of Tours, he was one of the six bishops sent from Rome with St. Dionysius in the middle of the third century to evangelize Gaul. He became the first bishop of Arles and is mentioned in a letter of Pope St. Zosimus to the bishops of Gaul in 417, which said he had been sent to Gaul by the Holy See and helped spread the Word at Arles. He is sometimes confused with Trophimus of the New Testament. December 29.

TROPHIMUS (d. 304). See Eucarpius.

TRUDO (d. c. 690). Also known as Trond, he was the son of Frankish parents and studied at the Metz Cathedral school, where he was ordained by St.

Clodulf. He returned to his native Hasbaye, Brabant, built a church and monastery on his estate (now St. Trond near Louvain) in about 660, founded a convent near Bruges, and worked to convert the pagans of Hasbaye, of which he is considered the apostle. November 23.

TRUMWIN (d. c. 690). An Englishman, he was named bishop of the southern Picts and established his see at Abercorn Monastery on the Firth of Forth. When King Egfrid of Northumbria was defeated and killed by the Picts in 685, the English in the area were forced to flee. Trumwin settled at Whitby Abbey in England with several of his followers and died there. February 10.

TRYPHO (3rd century). A native of Phrygia, he herded geese as a boy and suffered martyrdom at Nicaea during the persecution of Christians under Emperor Decius. Though popular in the early Greek Church, scholars believe his legend is a pious fiction. November 10.

TRYPHYLLIUS (d. c. 370). A native of Cyprus, he was educated at Beirut, Syria, planned to be a lawyer, and decided to pursue a religious life and became a disciple and confidant of St. Spiridion. They opposed Arianism at the Council of Sardica in 347, and later Tryphyllius was named bishop of Leucosia (Nicosia), Cyprus. He was an eloquent preacher, was known for his learning and writings, and wrote of Spiridion's miracles in poetry. June 13.

TSUGI, THOMAS (d. 1627). Of a noble Japanese family, he was educated by the Jesuits at Arima and became a Jesuit in 1587. He was known for his eloquent preaching, was exiled to Macao because of his religion, but returned to Japan in disguise. He was arrested, imprisoned for a year, and was then burned to death at Nagasaki on September 6 with Bl. Louis Maki after refusing to allow his family to buy his freedom. He was beatified in 1867.

TUDWAL (d. c. 564). A Briton, he, his mother, his sisters, and a group of monks from Wales went to Brittany, where his cousin Deroc was King of Dumnonia, and made several monastic foundations, among them one at Lan Pabu at Leon. While visiting King Childebert I in Paris to confirm his land grants, Tudwal was consecrated bishop and then settled at a monastery at Treher (Treguier, France, of which he is considered the first bishop) and died there. He is known as Pabu (Father) in Brittany and is also known as Tugdual. December 1.

TUGDUAL. *See* Tudwal.

TUNSTAL, BL. THOMAS (d. 1616). Born at Whinfell, England, he went to Douai to study for the priesthood in 1606, was ordained in 1608, and was sent on the English mission in 1610. He was arrested soon after, was imprisoned at Wisbech, managed to escape, but was recaptured and was imprisoned at Norwich. He became a Benedictine while he was in prison and was hanged, drawn, and quartered at Norwich when he refused to take the Oath of Supremacy. He was beatified in 1929. July 13.

TURIBIUS (d. c. 450). A forceful opponent of Priscillianism, he intensified his opposition to that heresy when he became bishop of Astorga, Spain, secured the support of Pope St. Leo the Great, and practically eliminated Priscillianism in Spain. He then devoted himself to reforming his see and enforcing strict clerical discipline. April 16.

TURIBIUS. *See* Mogrobejo, Toribio Alfonso de.

TURNER, BL. ANTONY (d. 1679). Son of a Protestant minister, he was born in Leicestershire, England, graduated from Cambridge, and was converted to Catholicism. He went to Rome to study, and when he was twenty-four joined the Jesuits at Watten Abbey in Flanders. He was ordained and in 1661 was sent on the English mission. He worked in the Worcester area for eighteen years until he was arrested and accused of participating in the "popish plot" to assassinate King Charles II, a fabrication of the notorious Titus Oates. Bl. Antony was convicted on perjured evidence (no defense witnesses who were Catholics were allowed to testify) and hanged, drawn, and quartered at Tyburn on June 20. He was beatified in 1929.

TUTILO (d. c. 915). Educated at St. Gall Benedictine Monastery in Switzerland, he became a monk there and later was head of its school. He was noted for his learning, was an outstanding orator, wrote poetry, was a painter, architect, and metalworker, was a proficient musician, and wrote music. March 28.

TYCHON (5th century). Son of a baker, he became bishop of Amathus (Limassol), Cyprus, and actively fought the worship of Aphrodite. He is venerated as patron of wine growers on Cyprus because of the legend that he caused a dead vine cutting to produce fruit. June 16.

TYRANNIO (d. 310). Bishop of Tyre, he had been present at and encouraged a group of Egyptian martyrs during their torture and execution at Tyre in 304. He was arrested for his Christianity in 310 and was taken with St. Zenobius, a priest and physician at Sidon, to Antioch, where Tyrannio was tortured and then drowned in the Orantes River when he refused to sacrifice to pagan gods.

Zenobius was racked and died during this torture. February 20.

TYSILIO (d. c. 640). According to legend he was the son of Brochwel Ysgythrog, a ruler in northern Wales, who ran away as a youth to become a monk at Meiford under Abbot Gwyddfarch. He fled to an island in the Menai Straits to escape his father's demand that he return home. He returned to Meiford seven years later and succeeded Gwyddfarch as abbot. Tysilio was again forced to leave Meiford when he refused to marry Haiarnwedd, wife of his deceased brother, who had succeeded their father as lord of Powys, and she drove him from the abbey. He went to Builth and when she still persisted in her efforts to force him to marry her, he left Wales with his monks and went to Armorica in about 617. They settled at a spot in Brittany now known as St. Suliac (by which name he is also known) and died and was buried there. November 8.

U

UBALD ADIMARI, BL. (1246–1315). Of a noble Florentine family, he led a dissipated life and was leader of a Ghibbeline gang in Florence until when thirty he was so impressed by a sermon of St. Philip Benizi that he became his disciple and joined the Servites. Ubald was ordained, became Philip's companion and confessor, and ministered to him on his deathbed. Ubald spent more than thirty years at Monte Senario Monastery and was noted for his preaching, penances, miracles, and gentleness. His cult was confirmed in 1821. He is also known as Ubald of Florence. April 9.

UBALD OF FLORENCE. *See* Ubald Adimari.

UBALD OF GUBBIO (c. 1100–60). Ubald Baldassini was born of a noble family in Gubbio, Italy, was orphaned in his youth, and was educated by his uncle, the bishop of Gubbio. Ubald was ordained, was named deacon of the cathedral, reformed the canons, and then left a few years later to become a hermit. Dissuaded from the eremitical life by Peter of Rimini, he returned to Gubbio and in 1126 was named bishop of Perugia but refused the honor. He became bishop of Gubbio in 1128 and persuaded Emperor Frederick II not to sack Gubbio, as he had Spoleto during one of his forays into Italy. Ill the last two years of his life, Ubald died at Gubbio on May 16, and was canonized in 1192.

UGOCCIONE, RICOVERO (1206–82). *See* Monaldo, Buonfiglio.

ULPHIA (d. c. 750). According to legend, she lived as a solitary under the direction of St. Domitius, a hermit, at St. Acheul near Amiens in northern France. When Domitius died, Ulphia attracted disciples, whom she organized into a community at Amiens. She later resumed her life as a recluse. January 31.

ULRIC (890–973). Born at Augsburg, Germany, he was educated at St. Gall Abbey in Switzerland and by his uncle, St. Adalbeo, bishop of Augsburg. Ulric succeeded to the see as bishop in 923, and when Augsburg was plundered and ravaged by the Magyars, he led its inhabitants in the task of rebuilding the city and its cathedral. In his old age, he retired to St. Gall, named his nephew as his successor, and was accused of nepotism for his action. His canonization by Pope John XV in 993 is the first recorded canonization by a Pope. July 4.

ULRIC (c. 1020–93). Born at Ratisbon, Germany, he became a page at the court of Empress Agnes but opted for the religious life. He was ordained a deacon by his uncle, Bishop Notker of Freising, and became archdeacon and provost of the cathedral. When he found that his position had been filled while he was on a pilgrimage to Rome and Jerusalem, he became a Benedictine monk at Cluny in 1052. He was ordained, was named chaplain to the nuns at Marcigny, but resigned when he lost the sight of an eye and then returned to Cluny. He served as prior at Peterlingen, was founding prior of Rüggersberg Priory, but returned to Cluny, when he opposed Bishop Burchard of Lausanne for his support of Emperor Henry IV against the Pope. He was founding abbot of a monastery at Zell in the Black Forest and of a convent at nearby Bollschweil. He became totally blind in 1091 and died two years later, on July 10, at Augsburg. He was the author of *Consuetudines cluniacences,* on the liturgy and the direction of monasteries and novices. July 14.

ULRICK (d. 870). *See* Theodore.

ULTAN (d. 657). Probably a bishop of Ardbraccan, Ireland, he was a successful evangelizer and was known for his learning, his aid to the sick and to orphans, and for helping in the education of poor students. Reputedly he collected the writings of St. Brigid and wrote her life and illuminated his own manuscripts. September 4.

ULTAN (d. 686). Brother of SS. Fursey and Foillan and like them an Irish monk, he went to East Anglia, founded Burgh Castle Monastery near Yarmouth but left and went to France to escape raiding Mercians. He built and became abbot of Fosses Monastery on land given him by St. Ita and St. Gertrude and then became abbot of a monastery at Péronne, where he died. May 2.

UNCUMBER. *See* Wilgefortis.

URBAN (1st century). *See* Ampliatus.

URBAN I (d. c. 230). Son of Pontianus, he was born at Rome and was elected Pope in about 222, succeeding Pope St. Callistus I, and ruled during a relatively peaceful period of the early Church. He died at Rome on May 23 and was buried there on May 25, which is celebrated as his feast day.

URBAN (d. 304). *See* Optatus.

URBAN II, BL. (c. 1042–99). Of a noble family, Odo of Lagery was born at Châtillons-sur-Marne, Champagne, France, studied under St. Bruno at Rheims, became archdeacon there, and in about 1070 became a Benedictine monk at Cluny. He was named prior by St. Hugh, was sent to Rome to assist Pope Gregory VII's reform of the Church, became his chief adviser, and was named cardinal-bishop of Ostia in 1078. He was legate to Germany, 1082–85, was briefly imprisoned there by Emperor Henry IV, and on March 12, 1088, he was elected Pope to succeed Pope Bl. Victor III and took the name Urban II. He was faced by antipope Clement III, who held Rome and whom he had anathematized at the Synod of Quedlinburg in Saxony he had held in 1085 and who was supported by Emperor Henry IV. Urban held a synod at Melfi in 1089 that decreed against lay investiture, simony, and clerical marriages, but it was not until 1094 that he was able to sit on the papal throne in Rome. In 1095, he summoned a council at Clermont-Ferrand, France, at which the Gregorian decrees requiring clerical celibacy and denouncing lay investiture and simony were reiterated and "the Truce of God" was proclaimed a law of the Church. It also anathematized King Philip I of France for putting aside his wife, Bertha, and marrying Bertrada, wife of the count of Anjou, and as the result of a request from Eastern Emperor Alexis I, Urban preached the First Crusade. His appeal was greeted with tremendous enthusiasm; launched in 1097, the crusade led to the capture of

Jerusalem in 1099. When Emperor Henry IV left Italy in 1097 and the party of antipope Clement III (Guibert) left Rome the following year, Urban was finally triumphant over his most persistent opponents. He called a council at Bari in 1098 that was unsuccessful in an attempt to effect a reconciliation between Rome and Constantinople. His entire pontificate was marked by conflicts with secular rulers, especially Emperor Henry IV; Urban excommunicated Henry, King Philip I of France, and would have excommunicated William Rufus of England except for the intercession of St. Anselm. Urban died at Rome on July 29, and was beatified by Pope Leo XIII in 1881.

URBAN, V, BL. (1310–70). Of a noble family, William de Grimoard was born at Grisac, Languedoc, France, became a Benedictine monk at Chirac, studied at Montpellier, Toulouse, Paris, and Avignon, and was ordained and received his doctorate. He taught canon law at Montpellier and Avignon and served as vicar general at Clermont and Uzès. He was appointed abbot of St. Germanus at Auxerre by Pope Clement VI in 1352 and served on several diplomatic missions to Italy. Pope Innocent VI appointed him abbot of St. Victor's in Marseilles in 1361 and legate to Queen Joanna of Naples. While there he was elected Pope to succeed Innocent VI on September 28, 1362, and took the name Urban V. He at once began to reform the Church, made peace with Barnabo Visconti in 1364, was unsuccessful in attempts to suppress the *condottieri* (marauding bands of soldiers) in France and Italy, and though Peter de Lusignan temporarily occupied Alexandria in 1365, his crusade against the Turks did not succeed. At the urging of Emperor Charles IV, he returned the papacy to Rome from Avignon (where it had been for half a century), despite the opposition of the French court and cardinals, when Cardinal Albornoz reconquered the Papal States in 1367. Urban worked to restore the run-down city, restore clerical discipline, and revive religion. In 1368, he crowned Emperor Charles IV's consort German Empress, and Charles agreed to respect Church rights in Germany. The following year Urban received Greek Emperor John V Palaeologus back into the Church, but the Emperor was unable to bring his people with him into the Church. When Perugia revolted and unrest beset Italy and war broke out between England and France in the same year, he decided to return to Avignon despite the prediction of St. Bridget that he would die an early death if he left Rome. He died at Avignon on December 19, three months after he left Rome. His cult was approved by Pope Piux IX in 1870.

URBICIUS (6th century). *See* Liphardus.

URSICINUS (d. c. 625). Probably from Ireland, he became a disciple of St. Columban, left Luxeuil to join the exiled Columbanus, founded a community of monks at what is now called St. Ursanne in Switzerland, and labored to convert the pagans of the area. December 20.

URSMAR (d. 713). Possibly a bishop, he became abbot of Lobbes Abbey in Flanders about 689, founded monasteries and churches at Aulne and Wallers, and was successful in missionary work in Flanders. April 19.

URSULA (date unknown). According to a legend that appeared in the tenth century, Ursula was the daughter of a Christian King in Britain and was granted a three-year postponement of a marriage she did not wish to a pagan prince. With ten ladies in waiting, each attended by a thousand maidens, she embarked on a voyage across the North Sea, sailed up the Rhine to Basle, Switzerland, and then went to Rome. On their way back they were all massacred by pagan Huns at Cologne in about 451 when Ursula refused to marry their chieftain. According to another legend, Amorica was settled by British colonizers and soldiers after Emperor Magnus Clemens Maximus conquered Britain and Gaul in 383. The ruler of the settlers, Cynan Meiriadog, called on King Dionotus of Cornwall for wives for the settlers, whereupon Dionotus sent his daughter Ursula, who was to marry Cynan, with eleven thousand noble maidens and sixty thousand common women. Their fleet was shipwrecked and all the women were enslaved or murdered. The legends are pious fictions, but what is true is that one Clematius, a senator, rebuilt a basilica in Cologne that had originally been built, probably at the beginning of the fourth century, to honor a group of virgins who had been martyred at Cologne. They were evidently venerated enough to have had a church built in their honor, but who they were and how many of them there were are unknown. From these meager facts, the legend of Ursula grew and developed. October 21.

URSULINA (1375–1410). Born at Parma, Italy, she experienced visions and ecstasies, and when fifteen, in response to a supernatural voice's direction, went to Avignon in an unsuccessful attempt to convince antipope Clement VII to give up his claim to the papal throne. She next went to Rome to ask Pope Boniface IX to resign and then returned to Avignon in another unsuccessful attempt to persuade Clement to resign. After a pilgrimage to Rome and the Holy Land, she returned to Parma, where she was expelled from the city during a civil war there. After a time at Bologna, she went to Verona, where she died. April 7.

URSUS (d. c. 287). *See* Maurice.

URSUS. *See* Alban of Mainz.

USTHAZANES (d. 341). *See* Simeon Barsabae.

V

VAAST. *See* Vedast.

VACLAV. *See* Wenceslaus.

VALENTINA (d. 308). *See* Thea.

VALENTINE (d. c. 269). A priest in Rome and a physician, he was beheaded there under Claudius the Goth on February 14 and buried on the Flaminian Way, where a basilica was erected in 350. On the same day in the Roman Martyrology is celebrated another Valentine who was bishop of Interamna (Terni) about sixty miles from Rome and who was scourged, imprisoned, and then beheaded there by order of Placidus, prefect of Interamna. Many scholars believe that the two are the same, and it is suggested that the bishop of Interamna had been a Roman priest who became bishop and was sentenced there and brought to Rome for his execution. The custom of sending Valentines on February 14 stems from a medieval belief that birds began to pair on that day.

VALENTINE (5th century). An abbot, he became a missionary bishop in Rhaetia and died at Mais in the Tyrol. January 7.

VALERIA (2nd century). *See* Vitalis.

VALERIAN (d. c. 178). *See* Marcellus.

VALERIAN (date unknown). *See* Cecilia.

VALERIAN (377–457). Bishop of Abbenza in Africa during the reign of Vandal King Genseric, Valerian was driven from his home at the age of eighty when he refused to surrender the sacred vessels of his church and died of exposure and neglect in the streets.

VALERIUS (date unknown). *See* Cecilia.

VALERIUS (d. c. 287). *See* Rufinus.

VALERIUS OF SARAGOSSA (d. 315). *See* Vincent of Saragossa.

VALÉRY. *See* Walaricus.

VALFRÉ, BL. SEBASTIAN (1629–1710). Born at Verduno, Piedmont, Italy, of a poor family, he joined the Oratorians in Turin in 1651, was ordained the following year, instructed a lay confraternity, and served as master of novices. He was elected prefect in 1661 and became famous as a confessor and spiritual director, attracting hordes of penitents, among them Duke Victor Amadeus II, later King of Sardinia, who unsuccessfully tried to make him archbishop of Turin in 1690. He preached numerous missions in the area around Turin, ministered to the poor of the city, and visited the sick in hospitals. He experienced periods of spiritual aridity but had the gifts of prophecy and great spiritual wisdom. He died on January 30, and was beatified in 1834.

VANENG. *See* Waningus.

VANNE. *See* Vitonus.

VARANI, BL. BAPTISTA (d. 1527). The daughter of the lord of Camerino and baptized Camille, she was given an unusually fine education for a woman of those times in anticipation of marriage. She decided she had a religious vocation, joined the Poor Clares in Urbino, taking the name Baptista, in 1481, and began to experience revelations on the Passion. Her father built a convent for Poor Clares at Camerino to which she was moved, and Bl. Peter of Mogliano became her spiritual director. During the next years she experienced extraordinary revelations and visitations, mainly concerned with the Passion and death of Christ, alternating with periods of great spiritual aridity and desolation. She established a convent at Ferms but after a year returned to Camerino, where she remained until her death. She wrote *The Sufferings of the Agonizing Heart of Jesus,* describing her revelations on the Passion, and a series of instructions on how to attain perfection. Her cult was approved in 1843. May 30.

VARELDE. *See* Pharaïdis.

VARUS (4th century). A Roman soldier in Upper Egypt during the reign of Emperor Maximinus, he was tortured and then martyred when he offered himself as a substitute for one of seven imprisoned monks he was guarding who had died. October 19.

VAUBOURG. *See* Walburga.

VAUDRU. Otherwise Waudru, q.v.

VECHEL, LEONARD (d. 1572). Born in Bois-le-Duc, Holland, he studied at Louvain, was ordained, became parish priest at Gorkum, and was active in his opposition to Calvinism. He and his assistant Nicholas Jannsen Poppel of Welde, Belgium, were among those seized by a Calvinist mob when the Calvinists captured Gorkum. Also arrested at the same time was Godefried Van Duynsen, who was a native of Gorkum and a priest there. They were sent to Briel, Holland, and then hanged with sixteen other Catholics. They were all canonized as the Martyrs of Gorkum in 1867. July 9.

VEDAST (d. 539). Also known as Vaast, he was born in western France, was ordained at Toul, accompanied King Clovis I to Rheims to instruct him for his baptism, and worked with St. Remigius in missionary work among the Franks. Vedast was named bishop of Rheims in 499 and by the time of his death forty years later had firmly established Christianity in his see. February 6.

VEERLE. *See* Pharaïldis.

VENANTIUS (d. c. 257). According to his legendary story, he was a seventeen-year-old resident of Camerino, Italy, who was tortured, miraculously saved from lions and from being thrown off a cliff, and then beheaded for his faith. May 18.

VENANTIUS FORTUNATUS (c. 535–c. 605). Venantius Honorius Clementianus Fortunatus was born near Treviso, Italy, was educated at Ravenna, and in 565 went to Germany. For some twenty years (567–87) he lived at Poitiers, where he was ordained and became adviser and secretary of King Clotaire I's wife, Radegund, and her adopted daughter at their convent there. In about 600 Venantius was appointed bishop of Poitiers, where he died. A fluent versifier, he wrote voluminously. Among his works were metrical lives of St. Martin de Tours, Hilary of Poitiers, Germanus of Paris, Radegund, and other religious figures; poems on a trip on the

Moselle, on church construction, and on the marriage of King Sigebert and Brunehilde in 566; elegies on the deaths of Brunehilde's sister, Queen Galeswintha, and Radegund's cousin, Amalafried; and several outstanding hymns, notably *Pange Lingua gloriosi* and *Vexilla Regis*. His poems revealed much valuable information about his times, Merovingian figures and customs, family life, descriptions of buildings, works of art, and the status of women. December 14.

VÉNARD, BL. THEOPHANE (1829–61). Born on November 21 at Poitiers, France, he studied at the college of Doué and the seminaries at Montmorillon and Poitiers, where he was ordained a subdeacon in 1850. He entered the Society of Foreign Missions in Paris the following year, was ordained in 1852, and was sent to Hong Kong later the same year. He remained there until he was sent as a missionary to West Tonkin (Vietnam) in 1854. He was captured during an outbreak of persecution of Christians in 1860, chained in a tiny cage for months, and on February 2 was beheaded at Ke Cho. He was beatified in 1900.

VENERINI, BL. ROSE (1656–1728). Daughter of Godfrey Venerini, a physician, she was born in Viterbo, Italy, and was engaged to be married, but when her fiancé died she entered a convent. She left to care for her widowed mother, and in 1685, with two companions under the direction of Fr. Ignatius Martinelli, opened a free school for girls in Viterbo. The success of the school caused Cardinal Barbarigo in 1692 to appoint her adviser in the educational system of his diocese of Montefiascone, where she met Lucy Filippini. Bl. Rose founded several more schools and in 1713 a school in Rome that was praised by Pope Clement XI. She died there on May 7.

Her foundation of lay teachers was organized into a religious community, the Venerini Sisters, after her death. She was beatified in 1952 by Pope Pius XII.

VENERIUS (d. 409). A deacon of St. Ambrose, he succeeded St. Simplician as bishop of Milan in 400, was known for his eloquence, was a supporter of St. John Chrysostom, and was evidently of such renown that he was appealed to by an assembly of African bishops at Carthage in 401 for his support together with Pope Anastasius. May 4.

VENTURA, BL. (d. c. 1278–1348). A wool carder at Valdiseve, Italy, where he was born, he joined the Camaldolese at Santa Maria degli Angeli in Florence when forty. Though uneducated, he became known for his spiritual wisdom and was widely consulted by those with spiritual difficulties. June 9.

VENTURA (d. 1597). *See* Miki, Paul.

VENUSTIAN (d. c. 303). *See* Sabinus.

VERDIANA, BL. (d. c. 1240). Of an impoverished noble family, she was born at Castelfiorentino, Tuscany, Italy, became housekeeper for a relative when twelve, went on a pilgrimage to Compostela, and on her return became a recluse in a hermitage near the Elba River. Here she lived a life of great austerity until her death thirty-four years later, venerated for her holiness and reported miracles. St. Francis of Assisi visited her in 1211, at which time she is said to have become a Franciscan tertiary. Her cult was approved by Pope Clement VII in 1533. February 16.

VEREMUND (d. 1092). Born in Navarre, Spain, he was sent to the Benedictine abbey of Hyrache, Navarre, when a boy, became a monk there, succeeded his Uncle Munius as abbot, and under his direction the abbey became one of the great spiritual centers of Spain. He was credited with numerous miracles, in one of which he miraculously provided food during a famine for three thousand supplicants at the abbey, and was a leading proponent of the Mozarabic rite. March 8.

VERENA (3rd century). According to legend she was a native of Thebaid, Egypt, was related to St. Victor (martyred in the Theban Legion), and came to Switzerland to search for his relics. She settled at Solothurn, ministered to the poor of the area and then became a recluse in a cave near Zurich. September 1.

VERON, BL. JEANNE (1766–94). *See* Mézière, Bl. Françoise.

VERONICA (1st century). According to legend, when Christ was carrying his cross to Calvary an unknown woman offered him a cloth to wipe his brow, and when he returned it to her it bore the imprint of his face. In time she came to be known as Veronica (Vera—true; icon—image). Her fate after this incident is told in several different legends. In one she came to Rome and cured Emperor Tiberius with her relic; on her death she bequeathed it to Pope St. Clement. In another she is the wife of Zacchaeus (the tax collector in the sycamore tree in Luke 19:1–10), accompanied him to France, where he was known as Amadour, and helped convert the inhabitants of southern France. And in the apocryphal *The Arts of Pilate,* she is identified with the woman Jesus cured of a hemorrhage she had suffered for twelve years (Matt. 9:20–22). In truth there is no factual information about her. July 12.

VERONICA OF BINASCO, BL. (1445–97). Born near Milan, Italy, of poor parents, she became an Augustinian nun at St. Martha's Convent there and was known for her miracles, visions, and ecstasies; an account of the life of Christ as she experienced it in her ecstasies is still extant. She was beatified by Pope Leo X in 1517. January 14.

VERYLDE. *See* Pharaïldis.

VERZERI, TERESA EUSTOCHIO (1801–1852). The oldest of six children, Teresa was drawn to the religious life at an early age. In 1831 she founded the Institute of the Daughters of the Sacred Heart, whose work included building and administering orphanages and schools for troubled children and caring for the sick. More than 3,500 letters Teresa wrote survive, providing ample evidence of the struggles and joys she experienced in building her order. Her order includes missions in Albania, Argentina, Bolivia, Brazil, the Central African Republic, India, and Italy. She was canonized in 2001. March 3.

VESTIA (d. 180). *See* Speratus.

VETURIUS (d. 180). *See* Speratus.

VEUSTER, VEN. JOSEPH DE (1840–89). Born at Tremeloo, Belgium, on January 3, he studied at the College of Braine-le-Comte, and in 1860 joined the Fathers of the Sacred Hearts of Jesus and Mary (the Picpus Fathers), taking the name Damien. At his request he was sent as a missionary to Hawaii in 1864, was ordained the same year in Honolulu, and spent the next nine years working to evangelize the peoples of Puno and Kohala. In 1873, again at his request, he was sent to the leper colony at Molokai and spent the rest of his life ministering to the lepers. He contracted the dread disease himself in 1885 but continued to live and work with and aid the lepers until his death on Molokai on

April 15. Though he was often slandered during his lifetime, his holiness and dedication were quickly recognized after his death (Robert Louis Stevenson wrote an impassioned defense of his character in 1905), and he was declared Venerable by Pope Paul VI in 1977.

VIALAR, EMILY DE (1797–1856). Daughter of Baron James de Vialar and Antoinette de Portal, she was born at Gaillac, Languedoc, France, studied at Paris, and became estranged from her father when, on the death of her mother when she was fifteen, she refused to marry. He was further antagonized when she began to teach abandoned and poor children and to treat and help the sick and the destitute at his house. When her grandmother died and left her a fortune in 1832, she bought a house at Gaillac and with the help of her spiritual director, Abbé Mercier, began with several companions, a congregation that was formally approved by Archbishop de Gauly of Albi as the Congregation of the Sisters of St. Joseph of the Apparition in 1835, dedicated to the care of the sick and needy and the education of young children in France and abroad. She traveled constantly, and the congregation soon spread all over the Near East— Algiers, Tunis, Malta, Jerusalem, and the Balkans. A jurisdictional dispute with Bishop Dupuch, bishop of Algiers, though decided in her favor, forced the closing of the house in Algiers. On her return to Gaillac in 1845 she found the organization in chaos and its existence threatened by lawsuits, quarrels among the nuns, and financial instability. She moved the mother house to Toulouse (and in 1854 to Marseilles), and by the time of Emily's death on August 14, there were some forty houses all over the world, from Europe to Burma to Australia. She was canonized in 1951. June 17.

VIANNEY, JOHN BAPTIST (1786–1859). Born at Dardilly, France, on May 8, he was a shepherd on his father's farm as a boy, was early attracted to the priesthood, and when twenty began his studies at Ecully, under Abbé Balley, encountering great difficulties with his studies, especially Latin. Though an ecclesiastical student, through an error he was drafted into the army in 1809 but deserted. He was able to return home when Napoleon granted amnesty to all deserters in 1810, and the following year was tonsured and went to the major seminary at Lyons in 1813. Beset by difficulties with his studies, he was finally ordained in 1815 through the intercession of Abbé Balley and the decision that his goodness was sufficient to offset his deficiencies in learning. He spent the next years as curate to Abbé Balley at Ecully until the abbé died in 1817; early in 1818 was appointed curé of Ars, where he spent the rest of his life. He labored to improve the indifferent religious attitude of his parishioners, and his war on immorality, indifference, and frivolities was unceasing, making him some enemies, but all charges against him were disproved. Eventually he was to reform the entire village. At his encouragement Catherine Lassagne and Benedicta Lardet in 1824 opened a free school for girls that three years later developed into La Providence, a shelter for orphans and deserted children. His reputation as a spiritual director and confessor (he often spent sixteen to eighteen hours a day in the confessional) spread, and a shrine he built to St. Philomena became a place of pilgrimage. Though he had the gift of insight into men's minds and souls, he was often referred to scornfully for his lack of learning and rejected for higher positions by his superiors. Even more trying were the continuing diabolical attacks he was subjected to over a thirty-year period.

Attracted all his life to the Carthusians, he left Ars three times in search of solitude but returned each time to aid the sinners who sought him in ever-increasing numbers. He refused all honors offered him late in life and died at Ars on August 4, venerated as the beloved "curé of Ars." He was canonized in 1925 by Pope Pius XI, who made him patron of parish priests in 1929.

VIATOR (d. 390). *See* Justus of Lyons.

VICELIN (c. 1086–1154). Born at Hemeln, Lower Saxony, Germany, he studied at the cathedral school at Paderborn and perhaps at Laon in France and became a canon at Bremen and head of the school there. He was ordained by St. Norbert at Magdeburg and in 1126 began his missionary work among the Wends with his headquarters at Lübeck, which he later moved to Wippenthorp near Bremen. He founded monasteries at Holstein (Neumünster), Högersdorf, and Segeberg, and was most successful in his missionary work until a group of marauding pirates attacked the area, plundering, burning, and killing. Though many of the priests were killed, most of those at Lübeck escaped. In 1149, Vicelin was named bishop of Staargard, though the opposition of Emperor Frederick Barbarossa probably prevented him from occupying the see. He was paralyzed the last three years of his life and died at Neumünster, Lorraine, on December 12.

VICI, BL. ANTONY (1381–1461). Of religious parents, he was born at Stroncone, Italy, became a Franciscan lay brother when twelve, and despite ill health remained a religious the rest of his life. He was deputy master of novices under Bl. Thomas of Florence at Fiesole when he was twenty-six, and in 1421 he accompanied Thomas on a papal mission to suppress the heretical Fraticelli in Siena and Sicily, a mission that lasted ten years. In 1431, Bl. Antony retired to the friary of the Carceri near Assisi and spent the next thirty years there living in great austerity. He was sent to St. Damian Friary in Assisi in 1460 and died there on February 8. Numerous miracles by him were recorded after his death, and his cult was confirmed in 1687. He is known as Bl. Antony of Stroncone. February 7.

VICTOR I (d. c. 199). A native of Africa, he succeeded Pope St. Eleutherius as Pope in about 189. During his pontificate Victor was embroiled in a dispute with a group of Christians from the province of Asia in Rome who celebrated Easter on a date of their choosing, and he was also faced with the arrival of Theodotus from Constantinople and his teaching that Christ was only a man endowed with supernatural powers by the Holy Spirit. July 28.

VICTOR (d. 284). *See* Victorinus.

VICTOR (d. 307). *See* Sosthenes.

VICTOR (d. c. 505). Born at Carthage, he became a member of the clergy there and was named bishop of Vita, Byzacena, Africa. His *Historia persecutionis Africanae provinciae* is an invaluable account of the Arian Vandals' persecution, under Huneric, of orthodox Christians in northern Africa. He was exiled to Sardinia, where he died. August 23.

VICTOR (6th century). Bishop of Capua, Italy, 541–54, he was known for his learning and wrote several important theological treatises, among them *De cyclo paschali* (550), *Capitula de resurectione Domini,* and commentaries on the Bible. He also edited the *Codex fuldensis,* one of the oldest manuscripts of the Vulgate, in which he substituted a harmony of the gospels in place of the four gospels in canonical order. October 17.

VICTOR III (c. 1027–87). Only son of Duke Dauferius Benevento, Daufar was born at Benevento, Italy, resisted his father's efforts to have him marry, and when his father was killed in battle in 1047, he became a hermit. He was forced to return home by his family bur escaped a year later, entered La Cava Monastery, and then, at the insistence of his family, transferred to St. Sophia Abbey at Benevento, where he was given the name Desiderius. He then spent several years wandering about—a time at an island monastery, a period studying medicine at Salerno, a time as a hermit in the Abruzzi—helped to negotiate a peace with the Normans for Pope Leo IX in 1053, and the following year joined the court of Victor II in Florence in 1054. Later the same year he joined the Benedictines at Monte Cassino, was elected abbot-designate in 1057, and was on his way to Constantinople as papal legate when Pope St. Stephen, who had retained the abbacy of Monte Cassino after he was elected Pope, died, and he was installed as abbot on Easter in 1058. He rebuilt Monte Cassino and developed it into one of the great centers of learning and culture in Europe, noted for the strict rule of its monks and the magnificence of its buildings and the art there. He became papal vicar for Campania, Apulia, Calabria, and Capua, served on diplomatic missions to the Normans for Pope St. Gregory VII, attempted to effect a reconciliation between Emperor Henry IV and Gregory in 1083, and was known as a firm upholder of papal rights. Despite his attempt to flee the honor, he was elected Pope to succeed Gregory and was forcibly vested on May 24, 1086, with the name Victor III. Four days later he was forced to flee to Monte Cassino from the imperial prefect and was not consecrated until May 9, 1087, at which time Guibert of Ravenna (antipope Clement III), who had been occupying the city, was temporarily driven out by Norman troops. Victor returned to Monte Cassino but came back to Rome a few weeks later, only to be forced to leave again when the forces of Countess Matilda of Tuscany attacked those of Guibert but were unsuccessful in their attempt to drive the antipope from the city. Stricken while presiding at a synod at Benevento, where he renewed the excommunication of Guibert, he returned, dying, to Monte Cassino, where he died on September 16 after a reign of only four months. His cult was approved by Pope Leo XIII in 1887.

VICTOR THE HERMIT (d. c. 610). Also known as Vittré, he was born near Troyes, France, was early attracted to the religious life, and was ordained. He became a hermit at Arcis-sur-Aube in Champagne and converted many with the example of his life. February 26.

VICTOR OF MARSEILLES (d. c. 290). According to legend, he was a soldier in the Roman army at Marseilles when he was haled before the prefects, Asterius and Eutychius, who sent him to Emperor Maximian for his exhortations to Christians to be firm in their faith in the face of an impending visit by the Emperor. He was dragged through the streets, racked, imprisoned (he converted three guards, Alexander, Felician, and Longinus while in prison), was again tortured after the guards were beheaded when it was discovered he had converted them to Christianity, and when he refused to offer incense to Jupiter, he was crushed in a millstone and beheaded. His tomb became one of the most popular pilgrimage centers in Gaul. July 21.

VICTOR MAURUS (d. c. 303). Born in Mauretania, he was converted to Christianity in his youth and served in the Praetorian guards. In his old age, he was arrested for his faith during the persecution of Christians under Emperor Maximian, was tortured, and then was decapitated. He is one of the patrons of Milan. May 8.

VICTORIA (d. c. 250). *See* Anatolia.

VICTORIA (4th century). *See* Acislus.

VICTORIA (d. 304). *See* Saturnius.

VICTORIAN (d. 484). A wealthy resident of Carthage, he was appointed proconsul by Huneric, Arian King of the Vandals. When Huneric launched a persecution of Catholics in 480, he tried to convert Victorian to Arianism; when Victorian refused, he was tortured to death. March 23.

VICTORIAN (d. 558). A native of Italy, he served in monasteries in France and Spain, was founding abbot of Asan (later renamed San Victorian in his honor) in Aragon, and ruled that community ably for many years. Venantius Fortunatus praised him highly. January 12.

VICTORICUS (date unknown). *See* Fuscian.

VICTORINUS (d. 259). *See* Lucius.

VICTORINUS (d. 284). He, Claudian, Doscorus, Nicephorus, Papias, Serapion, and Victor were Christian citizens of Corinth who were haled before the proconsul, Tertius, in 249 and tortured at the outbreak of the persecution of Christians under Emperor Decian. They were banished (or perhaps went of their own volition) to Egypt and were arrested at Diospolis in the Thebaid. Brought be-

fore the governor, Sabinus, during the reign of Numerian, they were all tortured and executed there on February 25 for their faith.

VICTORINUS (d. c. 303). A Greek, he became bishop of Pettau in Styria, Upper Pannonia. He wrote several biblical commentaries, fought several heresies, but for a time was believed favorably inclined to Millenarianism. He suffered martyrdom at Pettau during the persecution of Christians under Emperor Diocletian. November 2.

VICTORINUS (d. c. 306). *See* Carpophorus.

VICTORINUS (d. c. 384). *See* Maximus.

VICTRICIUS (c. 330–c. 407). Son of a Roman legionnaire and born near the Scheldt River, he became a soldier when he was seventeen, was converted to Christianity and was flogged and sentenced to death when he refused to bear arms any longer. Somehow, he escaped the death penalty and was discharged from the army. He became bishop of Rouen in about 386, brought a form of monasticism to Rouen, worked as a missionary in Flanders, Hainault, and Brabant, and established several parishes. He went to England in 396 to settle a dispute among several bishops, was accused of heresy later in his life, but was exonerated by Pope St. Innocent I when he went to Rome. He was the author of *The Praise of Saints*. August 7.

VIEL, BL. PLACIDA (1815–77). Born of a farming family at Val-Vacher, Normandy, and christened Victoria Eulalia, she joined the Sisters of the Christian Schools at Saint-Sauveur-le-Vicomte under Mother Mary Postel, the community's founder, when she was seventeen, taking the name Placida. She became novice mistress in 1837 and was named superior general in 1846 when Mother Mary died. She served in this position for thirty years and in that time expanded the institute, increasing the number of convents in France from 37 to 105, rebuilt the mother house church at Saint-Sauveur, built orphanages and nurseries, and opened some thirty-six schools for girls in Normandy. She died on March 4, and was beatified in 1951.

VIETNAM, MARTYRS OF (1745–1862). During fifty years of mid-nineteenth century persecution, between 100,000 and 300,000 Christians were slain or suffered for their religion. One-hundred-seventeen were declared martyrs of whom more than half were laypeople. The remainder included eight bishops and dozens of priests. These martyrs were canonized in 1988.

VIGILIUS (c. 353–405). Born at Trent, Italy, he was educated at Athens, returned to Trent, and in 385 was named bishop of that city. He fought usury, helped the poor, was active in conversion work, and by the time of his death, practically all of his see was Christian. He was stoned to death at Rendena, Italy, by pagans when he threw a statue of Saturn into the Sarka River. He is the patron of Trent and the Tyrol. June 26.

VIGOR (d. c. 537). Born at Artois, France, he was educated at Arras under St. Vedast and ran away to escape his father's opposition to his desire to become a priest. He preached at Raviere, was ordained, engaged in missionary work, and in 513 was named bishop of Bayeux. He destroyed a stone idol there, erected a church on its site, and founded a monastery at nearby St. Vigeur le Grand. November 1.

VIGRI, CATHERINE DE' (1413–63). Daughter of a lawyer and diplomat for Marquis Nicholas d'Este of Ferrara, she became Margaret d'Este's maid of honor and companion at eleven, left the court on the death of her father, and became a Franciscan tertiary at Ferrara with a group of women living a semimonastic life; they later became Poor Clares. She soon began to experience visions of Christ and Satan, and wrote of her experiences, one of which occurred one Christmas. It was a vision of Mary with the infant Jesus in her arms, a vision reproduced often in art since. Through her efforts the monastery in Ferrara received papal approval to be enclosed, but she left to become prioress of the new Poor Clares' Corpus Christi Convent in Bologna. The convent became famous for the sanctity and supernatural gifts of Catherine. She died there on March 9, was canonized in 1712, and is the patron of artists. She is also known as Catherine of Bologna. May 9.

VINCENT (d. 258). See Sixtus II.

VINCENT OF AGEN (d. c. 300). A deacon in Agen, Gascony, he was arrested for disrupting a pagan Druid ceremony, brought before the governor, tortured, and then beheaded at Agen. June 9.

VINCENT OF AQUILA, BL. (d. 1504). A native of Aquila, Italy, he joined the Friars Minor as a lay brother, lived a life of great holiness, and was famed for his gift of prophecy. He died at San Giuliano, and his cult was confirmed in 1785. August 13.

VINCENT OF CRACOW (c. 1150–1223). Born at Karnow, Poland, Vincent Kadlubeck studied in France and Italy, received his master's degree, and was provost of the cathedral chapter of Sandomir. He was elected bishop of Cracow in 1208. He worked to implement the reforms of Pope Innocent III in his see, encouraged the monastic orders, and was active throughout his diocese. He resigned his bishopric in 1128 to become a Cistercian monk at Jedrzejow Monastery, and while there wrote *Chronicles of the Kings and Princes of Poland,* the first Polish chronicle. He died at Jedrzejow on March 8, and his cult was confirmed in 1764.

VINCENT FERRER (1350–1419). Born at Valencia, Spain, on January 23, the son of William Ferrer and Constantia Miguel, both of noble families, he was educated at Valencia and joined the Dominicans in 1367. He was sent to Barcelona for further studies, taught philosophy at Lerida when twenty-one, and then returned to Barcelona in 1373. Three years later he continued his education at Toulouse, and in 1379 he became a member of Pedro Cardinal de Luna's court, the beginning of a long friendship that was to end in grief for both of them (De Luna had voted for Pope Urban VI in 1378, but convinced the election had been invalid, joined a group of cardinals who elected Robert of Geneva Pope as Clement VII later in the same year, thus creating a schism and the line of Avignon Popes). De Luna was elected to succeed antipope Clement VII in 1394 and became known in history as antipope Benedict XIII. Vincent was convinced of the legitimacy of the Avignon Popes and was their ardent champion. He taught at the cathedral in Valencia, 1385–90, was confessor to Queen Yolanda of Aragon, 1391–95, and was cited for heresy to the Inquisition for teaching that Judas had done penance. The charge was dismissed by the newly elected antipope Benedict XIII, who brought him to his papal court and made him his confessor and apostolic penitentiary. Vincent refused a cardinalate from the antipope and after recovering from a serious illness in 1398, during which he had a vision of Christ accompanied by SS. Dominic and

Francis directing him to preach penance, he devoted himself to preaching. Released by Benedict to do so, he began preaching in 1399, and in the next two decades he traveled all over Western Europe preaching penance for sin and preparation for the Last Judgment, attracting enormous crowds wherever he went and followed by thousands of disciples; among his converts were Bernadine of Siena and Margaret of Savoy. So successful was he in preaching in different countries, though he only knew his own language, that many believed he had the gift of tongues. In 1408, while ministering to the plague-stricken of Genoa, he tried and failed to persuade Benedict to withdraw his claims to the papacy so Christendom might be united under one Pope. Vincent then went to Spain, where his preaching was as phenomenally successful as it had been in other parts of Europe, making converts by the tens of thousands, including thousands of Jews and Moors. He was one of the judges of the Compromise of Caspe to resolve the royal succession and was instrumental in electing Ferdinand King of Castile. Still a friend of Benedict, he again begged him to resign after the Council of Constance had deposed a third claimant to the throne, antipope John XXIII, and demanded that the other two resign. When Benedict refused, he advised Ferdinand in 1416 to withdraw his allegiance to Avignon; when Ferdinand did so, Benedict was deposed, and the great Western Schism ended. Vincent spent the last three years of his life preaching in France and died at Vannes, Brittany, on April 5. He was canonized in 1455.

VINCENT OF LÉRINS (d. c. 445). Of a noble Gallic family and probably brother of St. Lupus of Troyes, he abandoned his military career to become a monk at Lérins Abbey off the coast of Cannes. He was ordained and in about 434 wrote his famous *Commonitorium* on orthodox Catholic teaching, which had a tremendous vogue. It commented on Catholic teaching and tradition and expounded the concept that only those doctrines are to be considered true that have been held "always, everywhere, and by all the faithful." May 24.

VINCENT MADELGARIUS (c. 615–77). Also known as Madelgaire, Mauger, and Vincent of Soignies, he was born at Strepy les Binche, Hainault, and in about 635 he married St. Waldetrudis; the couple had four children, all of whom were venerated as saints. He probably went to Ireland for King Dagobert I and brought back several missionary monks. In about 643 he became a Benedictine monk at an abbey he had founded in 642 at Hautmont (his wife was to become a nun), taking the name Vincent, and later became abbot. He also founded a monastery on his estate at Soignies, Belgium, where he died on July 14. September 20.

VINCENT DE PAUL (c. 1580–1660). Son of Jean de Paul and Bertrande de Moras, French peasants, the third of six children, he was born at Pouy, France, on April 24. He was educated at the college at Dax and the University of Toulouse and was ordained in 1600. While returning from Marseilles, where he had gone to claim a legacy left him, in 1605, he was captured by pirates and sold as a slave in Algeria. He eventually escaped in 1607 to Avignon, went to Rome for further studies, was sent back to France on a secret mission to Henry IV in 1609, and became chaplain to Queen Margaret of Valois in Paris. In the following years his work with the poor and his preaching attracted widespread attention. His meeting with St. Francis de Sales in Paris in 1618 made him a disciple of Francis, who had him appointed ecclesiastical superior of the Visitation. He was tutor in the household of Count de Gondi, general of the galleys, 1613–25, and began to minister to the galley slaves. In 1619 he became chaplain of galley slaves waiting to be shipped abroad, and in 1625 he founded the Congregation of the Mission (known as the Vicentians and Lazarists), devoted to missionary work among the peasants, and it soon spread all over France. He also began establishing parish confraternities to aid the poor, and in 1633, with Louise de Marillac, founded the Sisters of Charity. He established hospitals and orphanages, ransomed Christian slaves in northern Africa, helped better priest formation by founding new seminaries, sent his priests abroad to preach missions, organized far-flung relief among the victims of the wars of the Fronde, and wrote widely on spiritual topics. The friend of royalty and the nobility, his whole life was devoted to the alleviation of human suffering and misery. During his lifetime he vigorously opposed Jansenism and was active in securing its condemnation. He died in Paris on September 27, was canonized by Pope Clement XII in 1737, and was declared patron of all charitable groups by Pope Leo XIII in 1885. September 27.

VINCENT OF ST. JOSEPH, BL. (1596–1622). Born in Ayamonte, Seville, Spain, he went to Mexico, joined the Franciscans as a lay brother in 1615, and was sent to the Philippines three years later. He was sent to Japan in 1619, was arrested for his religion and exhibited in a cage for two years, and then burned to death at Nagasaki. He was beatified as one of the Martyrs of Japan in 1867. September 10.

VINCENT OF SARAGOSSA (d. 304). Born at Huesca, Spain, he was educated by Bishop St. Valerius of Saragossa, who ordained him and commissioned him to preach. They were both arrested by

Dacian, governor of Spain, at Saragossa during Emperor Maximian's persecution of the Christians and then imprisoned at Valencia. Valerius (January 28) was exiled (though later returned), but Vincent was subjected to frightful torture when he refused to sacrifice to pagan gods or surrender the sacred books of his church. He was then returned to prison, converted his warden, and died in prison of the effects of the tortures before he could be tortured further. January 22.

VINCENT OF SOIGNIES. *See* Vincent Madelgarius.

VINCENTIAN (d. c. 672). The untrustworthy biography of Vincentian by his supposed tutor Hermenbert states that he was orphaned as a child and was raised by Duke Berald of Aquitaine, who promised to aid him to become a priest. However, his son and successor, Berard, forced Vincentian to abandon his studies and put him in charge of the stables. He eventually ran away to escape the abuse to which he was constantly subjected and became a hermit in Limousin. He died on January 2, venerated for the many extravagant miracles attributed to him. It is doubtful if Vincentian ever lived, and scholars believe the whole story is a work of fiction.

VINCIOLI, BL. ALEXANDER (d. 1363). Born at Perugia, Italy, he joined the Franciscans, became Pope John XXII's confessor, was named bishop of Nocera, Umbria, by John, and died at Sassoferrato, Italy. May 3.

VINDICIAN (632–712). Born at Bullecourt, France, he was elected bishop of Cambrai about 669, made a visitation of all the parishes in his diocese, made numerous converts, and encouraged the establishment of monasteries in his see. When Bishop St.

Leodegarius of Autun was executed at the order of Ebroin, mayor of the palace, in 679, Vindician was delegated by a conference of bishops to reprove King Thierry for the heinous deed committed by his official. Thierry acknowledged Vindician's reproof and in reparation became a generous benefactor of Arras Monastery (St. Vaast), near the spot where Leodegarius had been slain. Vindician died while on a visit to Brussels. March 11.

VIRGIL (d. c. 610). Born in Gascony, he was educated at Lérins off the coast of Cannes, became a monk, and later was abbot there. He became abbot of St. Symphorien in Autun, was named archbishop of Arles and apostolic vicar to King Childebert II, and probably consecrated Augustine as bishop of Canterbury. He built several churches in Arles, was reproved by Pope St. Gregory I for his forcible conversion of Jews, and was credited with many miracles. March 5.

VIRGIL (d. 784). Also known as Feargal or Ferghil, he was an Irish monk, probably abbot of Aghaboe, and in about 743 went on pilgrimage to the Holy Land. He spent two years in France, then went to Bavaria, where he was appointed abbot of St. Peter's at Salzburg, Austria, and administrator of that see by Duke Odilo; Virgil was appointed its bishop in about 765. He was twice denounced by Rome by Archbishop St. Boniface of Mainz and each time was exonerated. He rebuilt the cathedral at Salzburg, sent missionaries to Carinthia, and on his return from a missionary trip to Carinthia died at Salzburg on November 27. He was canonized in 1233 by Pope Gregory IX and is venerated as the apostle of the Slovenes.

VITALIAN (d. 672). Born at Segni, Campania, he was elected Pope to succeed Pope Eugene I and was consecrated on July 30, 657. During his pontificate the conflict between English and Irish bishops over the date of Easter was resolved, and relations with the Church in England were strengthened when he sent SS. Adrian and Theodore of Tarsus there. However, the monothelite heresy in the East continued throughout his reign. He died on January 27.

VITALIS (2nd century). According to an account that is doubtlessly spurious, he was a wealthy citizen of Milan, and perhaps a soldier, was married to Valeria, and they were the parents of SS. Gervase and Protase (which they were not). When he encouraged St. Ursicinus to be steadfast at his execution, Vitalis was racked and then buried alive. Valeria died as the result of injuries she suffered when attacked by pagans. They were martyred near Milan probably under Emperor Marcus Aurelius, but all else is subject. April 28.

VITALIS (d. c. 165). *See* Felicity.

VITALIS (d. c. 303). *See* Honoratus.

VITALIS (d. c. 304). *See* Agricola.

VITALIS OF SAVIGNY, BL. (c. 1063–1122). According to untrustworthy sources, he was chaplain to William the Conqueror's half brother Count Robert of Mortain and then in 1095 became a hermit. He attracted numerous disciples, founded in 1112 and was abbot of Savigny Abbey on the border between Normandy and Brittany, became famed for his preaching, and visited England several times. He died on September 16 at Savigny.

VITONUS (d. c. 525). Also known as Vanne, he became bishop of Verdun in about 500, eradicated paganism in his

diocese, and is believed to have founded a college of clergy outside Verdun that developed into the Benedictine community of St. Vanne. November 9.

VITTRÉ. *See* Victor the Hermit.

VITUS (d. c. 300). Unreliable legend has Vitus, the only son of a senator in Sicily, become a Christian when he was twelve. When his conversions and miracles became widely known to the administrator of Sicily, Valerian, he had Vitus brought before him to shake his faith. He was unsuccessful, but Vitus with his tutor, Modestus, and servant, Crescentia, fled to Lucania and then to Rome, where he freed Emperor Diocletian's son of an evil spirit. When Vitus would not sacrifice to the gods his cure was attributed to sorcery. He, Modestus, and Crescentia were subjected to various tortures from which they emerged unscathed, and were freed when during a storm temples were destroyed and an angel guided them back to Lucania, where they eventually died. So much for the legend. What is fact is that their cult goes back centuries and that they were Christians who were martyred in Lucania. A great devotion to Vitus developed in Germany when his relics were translated to Saxony in 836. He is one of the Fourteen Holy Helpers and is the patron of epileptics, those afflicted with St. Vitus dance (named after him), dancers, and actors, and is a protector against storms. June 15.

VIVALDO, BL. (d. 1300). Born at San Gemignano, he became a Franciscan tertiary and a disciple of B. Bartolo, whom he took care of for twenty years when he contracted leprosy and then became a hermit at Montadone, Tuscany, where he died. His cult was confirmed in 1908 by Pope Piux X. May 11.

VIVIAN, VIVIANA. *See* Bibian.

VLADIMIR I OF KIEV (c. 975–1015). Illegitimate son of Grand Duke Sviastoslav and his mistress, Malushka, he was given Novgorod to rule by Sviastoslav. Forced to flee to Scandinavia in 977 when his half brother Yaropolk defeated and killed another half brother, Oleg, and captured Novgorod, he returned with an army, recaptured Nóvgorod, and captured and killed Yaropolk at Rodno in 980. Notorious for his cruelty and barbarity, he was now ruler of Russia. He conquered Kherson in the Crimea in 988, and impressed by the progress of Christianity, married Anne, daughter of Emperor Basil II, and became a Christian in about 989. His conversion marked the beginning of Christianity in Russia. He reformed his life (putting aside his five former wives), built schools and churches, destroyed idols, brought Greek missionaries to his realms, exchanged ambassadors with Rome, and aided St. Boniface in his mission to the Pechangs. In his later years he was troubled by rebellions led by the sons of his earlier marriages, but two of his sons by Anne, Romanus (Boris) and David (Gleb), became saints. He died at Beresyx, Russia, while leading an expedition against his rebellious son Yaroslav in Novgorod. Valdimir reportedly gave all his possessions to his friends and to the poor on his deathbed. He is the patron of Russian Catholics. July 15.

VODALUS (d. c. 720). Also known as Voel, he was from Ireland or Scotland, went to Gaul to preach, and became a recluse beside St. Mary's Convent at Soissons. He was known for his holiness and dedication to poverty and is reported to have performed miracles. February 5.

VOEL. *See* Vodalus.

VOLUSIAN (d. 496). A senator at Tours, he became bishop of that see in 488 but was driven from the city in 496 by the Arian Visigoths. He went to Spain and died there, martyred according to some accounts. January 18.

VULFLAGIUS (d. c. 643). Also known as Wulphy, legend has him born at Rue near Abbeville, France, married, and the father of three children when he was elected pastor. With his wife's consent, he was ordained, went on a penitential pilgrimage to the Holy Land to expiate his resumption of marital relations with his wife, and on his return, he lived as a hermit. He became famed as a spiritual adviser and for his miracles. He may be the same as St. Walfroy. June 7.

VULMAR (d. c. 700). Born at Boulogne, Picardy, he married, was forcefully separated from his wife, and became a Benedictine lay brother at Hautmont Abbey in Hainault, where he was put in charge of the abbey's cattle. He was ordained, lived as a hermit for a time near Mount Cassel, then was founding abbot of Samer Abbey near Calais, and also founded a convent at nearby Wierre-aux-Bois. July 20.

VULPHY. Otherwise Wulphy, q.v.

W

WALARICUS (d. c. 620). Also known as Valéry, he was born in Auvergne, was educated at Autumo Monastery, spent some time at St. Germanus abbey near Auxerre, and then with Bobo, a nobleman he had convinced to give away his wealth, he became a monk under St. Columban at Luxeuil. He left Luxeuil when Columban was expelled by King Theodoric, and with another monk, Waldolanus, became a missionary in Neustria. Walaricus was most successful in making converts, but attracted by the eremitical life, he became a hermit at the mouth of the Somme River. He attracted numerous disciples, organized them into Leuconans Abbey in about 614, and became abbot. He is reputed to have evangelized the Pas-de-Calais area and then the whole eastern shore of the English Channel. April 1.

WALBURGA (d. 779). Daughter of West Saxon chieftain Richard and sister of SS. Willibald and Winnebald, she was born in Devonshire, England, educated at Wimborne Monastery in Dorset, and became a nun there. She was one of the nuns under St. Lioba sent by St. Tatta in 748 to help St. Boniface in his missionary work in Germany. She spent two years at Bischofsheim, was appointed abbess of the convent of the double monastery at Heidenheim founded by her two brothers, and became abbess of both on the death of Winnebald, who was abbot, a position she held until her death. She may have studied medicine, and a fluid from the rocks on which her relics rest reputedly has produced many cures. She is known by many names, among them Walpurgis, Falbourg, Vaubourg, and Warpurg. February 25.

WALDEBERT (d. c. 665). A Frankish nobleman also known as Gaubert, he renounced his military career to become a monk at Luxeuil, France, and donated his wealth to the monastery. He was allowed to live as a hermit, but on the death of Abbot St. Eustace he was elected third abbot of Luxeuil in 628. He ruled for almost forty years, replaced the rule of St. Columban with that of St. Benedict, secured freedom from episcopal control for the monastery from Pope John IV, and helped build Luxeuil into one of the outstanding monasteries in France. He helped St. Salaberga found her convent at Laon and established many monasteries and convents from Luxeuil. May 2.

WALDETRUDIS (d. c. 688). Called Waltrude or Waudru in France, she was the daughter of SS. Walbert and Bertilia and sister of St. Aldegunus of Maubeuge. She married St. Vincent Madelgarius, a young nobleman, and two years after he became a monk about 643 at Hautmont, which he had founded, she became a recluse. In time she founded a convent at Chateaulieu (around which grew Mons) and was famed for her charity and miracles. The couple had four children, all of whom became saints—Aldetrudis, Dentelinus, Landericus, and Madelberta. September 20.

WALFRID (d. c. 765). Galfrido della Gherardesca was born in Pisa, Italy, married Thesia, and after they had six children, both decided to enter the religious life. Walfrid, Gunduald, a relative, and Fortis, a friend, built Palazzuolo Monastery near Volterra, of which Walfrid became abbot, and a convent several miles away, which their wives entered. Walfrid's cult was confirmed in 1861. February 15.

WALL, JOHN (1620–79). Born in Lancashire, England, he was sent to study at Douai in his youth, went to the Roman college in 1641, and was ordained there in 1645. He served as a missionary for a time, joined the Franciscans at St. Bonaventure Friary at Douai in 1651, taking the name Joachim of St. Anne, and in 1656 was sent on the English mission. Using the aliases Francis Johnson, Dormer, and Webb, he worked among the Catholics in Worcestershire for twenty-two years until December 1678, when he was arrested near Bromsgrove and charged with being a Catholic priest. After five months' imprisonment, he was exonerated of any complicity in the Titus Oates plot, but when he refused to renounce his Catholic faith, he was hanged, drawn, and quartered for his priesthood at Redhill, Worcester, on August 22. He was canonized by Pope Paul VI in 1970. June 12.

WALPOLE, HENRY (1558–95). Born in Docking, Norfolk, England, he studied at Cambridge and law at Gray's Inn, was reconciled to the Church when he witnessed the execution of Edmund Campion, gave up the study of law, and went to Rheims. He became a Jesuit in Rome in 1584 and was ordained there in 1588. He was sent on the missions to Lorraine, and in 1589, while acting as chaplain to the Spanish troops in the Netherlands, he was imprisoned by the Calvinists at Flushing for a year. When released he taught at Seville and Valladolid, engaged in missionary activities in Flanders, and in 1593 was sent on the English mission. Arrested almost on landing, he was imprisoned for a year in York and then the Tower, subjected to numerous tortures, and then convicted of treason for his priesthood at York. He was hanged, drawn, and quartered at York with Bl. Alexander Rawlins on April 7. He was canonized in 1970 by Pope Paul VI.

WALPURGIS. *See* Walburga.

WALSTAN (d. 1016). Born at Baber (Bawburgh) near Norwich, England, of a wealthy family, he early devoted himself to God, and in a spirit of humility, gave away his wealth and became a servant and a farmhand at nearby Taverham. He spent his life in prayer and penance, was known for his charity to the poor and miracles, and died on May 30.

WALTER OF L'ESTERP (d. 1070). Born of a noble family at Conflans Castle on the Vienne in Aquitaine, France, he was educated by the Augustinian canons of Dorat and became a monk there. After returning to Conflans for a time, he was elected abbot of L'Esterp Abbey, a position he held for thirty-eight years, famed for his holiness and as a confessor. May 11.

WALTER OF PONTOISE (d. 1095). Born in Picardy, France, he became known for his learning, was a professor of philosophy and rhetoric, and then joined the Benedictines at Rebais-en-Brie to escape worldly distractions and acclaim. Named first abbot of Pontoise by King Philip I, he fled the abbey and became a monk at Cluny; he was discovered and forced to return to Pontoise by his monks. Later he again fled to live as a hermit on the Loire, but again was forced to return. He later requested permission from Pope St. Gregory VII to resign but returned to rule his abbey for the rest of his life when ordered to do so by the Pope. Walter fought simony, denounced the lax lives of some of the secular clergy (for which he was once beaten up and imprisoned), and lived in great austerity himself. April 8.

WALTHEN. *See* Waltheof.

WALTHEOF (d. c. 1160). Son of Simon, Earl of Huntingdon, and also known as Walthen, he went with his mother, Maud, to Scotland when she married King St. David I after the death of her first husband. At David's court, he came under the influence of St. Aelred, master of the royal household. Of a religious bent from his boyhood, Waltheof left the court, became an Augustinian canon at Nostelle Monastery in Yorkshire, and then was named abbot of Kirkham when he experienced a vision of Christ and saw the Christ child in his hand instead of the Host while saying Mass. In quest of a stricter rule, he joined the Cistercians at Wardon, Bedfordshire, and four years later was named abbot of Melrose, just founded by King David. Waltheof became known for his austerity, his kindness to the poor, and was credited with performing miracles. In 1154 he was named archbishop of St. Andrews but refused the honor. He died on August 3.

WALTMAN, BL. (d. 1138). A disciple of St. Norbert, he, with Evermod, accompanied Norbert to Antwerp, Brabant, at the request of the archbishop of Cambrai, to combat Tanchelm, a layman, and his heretical teachings. Waltman became abbot of the new Premonstratensian St. Michael Abbey,

which the local clergy gave him in appreciation of his success in crushing the heresy. April 11.

WALWORTH, BL. WILLIAM (d. 1537). *See* Rochester, Bl. John.

WANDREGISILUS. *See* Wandrille.

WANDRILLE (d. 668). Also known as Wandregisilus, he was born near Verdun, France, of a noble family related to Bl. Pepin of Landen. When Wandrille came of age he was sent to the court of King Dagobert of Austrasia and married in deference to his parents' wishes but against his. In about 628, by mutual agreement, they separated, she to become a nun and he to become a Benedictine monk at Montfaucon Abbey in Champagne under St. Baudry. A few months later he left to become a hermit at St. Ursanne in the Jura. He remained there for about five years, then went to Bobbio and later to Romain-Moûtier Abbey on the Isère, where he spent the next decade and where he was ordained. He left to be founding abbot of Fontenelle Abbey in Normandy, which he developed into a missionary and spiritual center, founded a school there, and became involved in helping and preaching to the inhabitants of the surrounding area. July 22.

WANG, BL. ANNA (d. 1900). *See* Mangin, Bl. Leon.

WANINGUS (d. c. 683). Also known as Vaneng, he was the governor of Pays de Caux in Neustria when he decided to devote his life to God after he had a dream of St. Eulalia of Barcelona warning him of the difficulties in the way of a rich man entering heaven. He helped St. Wandrille found Fontenelle Abbey and Holy Trinity Church and Convent in Fécamp Valley. January 9.

WARCOP, BL. THOMAS (d. 1597). *See* Andleby, Bl. William.

WARD, MARGARET (d. 1588). Born in Congleton, Cheshire, England, she was a gentlewoman in service in London when arrested with her Irish servant, John Roche, alias Neale, for helping Fr. Richard Watson escape from Bridewell Prison. They were offered their freedom if they would ask the Queen's pardon but refused and were both hanged, drawn, and quartered at Tyburn on August 30 when they refused to divulge the priest's hiding place. She was canonized in 1970 by Pope Paul VI.

WARD, BL. WILLIAM. *See* Webster, Bl. William.

WARPURG. *See* Walburga.

WATERSON, BL. EDWARD (d. 1593). A native of London and a Protestant, he rejected an offer to marry a wealthy Turk's daughter if he would become a Mohammedan while on a trip to Turkey, but he was converted to Catholicism in Rome on the way back in 1588. He studied at Rheims, was ordained in 1592, and was sent on the English mission the following year. He was soon arrested and hanged, drawn, and quartered for his priesthood at Newcastle-upon-Tyne. He was beatified in 1929. January 7.

WATKINSON, BL. ROBERT (c. 1579–1602). Born at Hemingborough, Yorkshire, England, he studied at Douai and Rome, was ordained in 1602 at Arras, and was sent on the English mission using the alias John Wilson. He was arrested soon after in London, accused of being a Catholic priest, and hanged, drawn, and quartered at Tyburn with Bl. Francis Page on April 20. Bl. Robert was beatified in 1929.

WAUDRU. *See* Waldetrudis.

WAY, BL. WILLIAM (1561–88). Born at Exeter, England, he was educated at Rheims and ordained there in 1586. Sent on the English mission later the same year, using the alias Flower, he was arrested six months later, convicted of his Catholic priesthood, and sentenced to be executed. He was hanged, drawn, and quartered at Kingston-on-Thames on September 23, a victim of the persecution of Queen Elizabeth I. He was beatified in 1929.

WEBLEY, VEN. THOMAS (d. 1585). *See* Alfield, Bl. Thomas.

WEBSTER, AUGUSTINE (d. 1535). After studying at Cambridge, he became a Carthusian and then in 1531 prior of the charterhouse at Axholme, England. While on a visit to the London charterhouse, he accompanied St. John Houghton and St. Robert Lawrence to a meeting with Thomas Cromwell, who had the three arrested and imprisoned in the Tower. When they refused to accept the Act of Supremacy of Henry VIII, they were dragged through the streets of London, savagely treated, and executed at Tyburn on May 4. They were canonized in 1970.

WEBSTER, BL. WILLIAM (d. 1641). Born at Thornby, Westmorland, England, and also known as William Ward, he went to Douai in 1604, was ordained in 1608, and was sent on the English mission. Forced to land in Scotland because of bad weather, he was at once arrested and imprisoned for three years. On his release he went to England, where he was repeatedly arrested, spending some twenty years of the thirty-three he was on the English mission in prison. When he refused to leave London when Parliament on April

7, 1641, ordered all Catholic priests banished under pain of death, he was arrested and ten days later on July 26 was executed at Tyburn. He was beatified in 1929.

WEERDEN, JEROME (1522–72). Born at Weerden, Holland, he joined the Franciscans, was a missionary in Jerusalem for a time, and on his return, fought Calvinism. He was vicar of the Observant Franciscan friary at Gorkum under Nicholas Pieck when it was attacked by a Calvinist mob and the friars made prisoners. They were sent to Briel, where despite a letter from the Prince of Orange ordering their release, all were slain. They were canonized as the Martyrs of Gorkum in 1867. July 9.

WELBOURN, BL. THOMAS (d. 1605). Born in Kitenbushel (Hutton Bushel), Yorkshire, England, he became a schoolteacher and with a fellow Yorkshireman, John Fulthering, and William Brown of Northamptonshire were convicted of treason at York for their Catholicism and were hanged, drawn, and quartered there on August 1, and in Brown's case at Ripon on September 5. They were beatified in 1929.

WELLS, SWITHUN (1536–91). Born at Bambridge, Hampshire, England, he lived the life of a country gentleman, founded a boys' school in Wiltshire, and was converted to Catholicism in 1583. He moved to London with his wife in 1585 and the following year was charged with being involved in the Babington plot but released. He went to Rome on a mission for the Earl of Southampton but then returned to England to work in the English Catholic underground. Though he was not at home when St. Edmund Gennings was saying Mass in his home, Swithun was later arrested, convicted of harboring a Catholic priest, and hanged near his own home at Gray's Inn Fields, London, on December 10 with Fr. Gennings. Swithun was canonized by Pope Paul VI in 1970. His name is sometimes spelled Swithin.

WENCESLAUS (c. 903–29). Also known by the Czech form of his name, Vaclav, he was born near Prague and was the son of Duke Wratislaw (or Ratislav) of Bohemia and Drahomira, daughter of the chieftain of a northern Slav tribe called the Veletians. He was raised a Christian and educated by his grandmother, St. Ludmila, and her chaplain, Paul. When Ratislav was killed fighting the Magyars in about 920, Drahomira, with the anti-Christian faction who murdered Ludmila, took over the government and instituted anti-Christian policies. She was deposed by an uprising, and Wenceslaus became ruler in about 922. He encouraged Christianity, ruled strictly but justly, and ruthlessly suppressed disorders and oppression by the nobles. In about 926 his acknowledgment of King Henry the Fowler as his overlord, in keeping with his policy of friendship with Germany, as well as his religion, caused opposition among some of the nobles. When his wife bore him a son, his brother Boleslaus, no longer successor to the throne, joined the noble Czech dissenters. Boleslaus invited Wenceslaus to a religious festival at Boleslavvia, Bohemia, and while Wenceslaus was on his way to Mass on September 20, Boleslaus attacked him, and while they were struggling, a group of Boleslaus' followers joined the fray, and Wenceslaus was murdered. He was at once venerated as a martyr and is the patron of Bohemia. September 28.

WERBURGA (d. c. 700). Daughter of King Wulfhere of Mercia and St. Ermenilda, she was born in Staffordshire, refused offers of marriage, and became a nun at Ely under St. Etheldreda. She left Ely in 675 when her Uncle Ethelred became King, to supervise and reform the convents of the kingdom. She founded Hanbury Convent near Tutbury, Trentham, in Staffordshire, and Wedon in Northamptonshire. She is credited with many miracles and the ability to read men's minds. She died at Trentham on February 3.

WHITEBREAD, BL. THOMAS (d. 1679). Born in Essex, England, he was educated at St. Omer in France, and joined the Jesuits at Watten in 1635. He was ordained and sent to England, where he became provincial of the English mission. After the outbreak of persecution of Catholics in England occasioned by the notorious "popish plot" fabricated by Titus Oates, Bl. Thomas visited Liège and was arrested on his return to England. Charged with providing the headquarters for the alleged plotters against the life of King Charles II, he was convicted on perjured evidence and hanged, drawn, and quartered at Tyburn. He was beatified in 1929. June 20.

WHITE, EUSTACE (d. 1591). Born at Louth, Lincolnshire, England, he was converted to Catholicism and went to Rheims to study for the priesthood. He continued his studies at Rome and was ordained there in 1588. He was sent on the English mission later the same year, worked in western England, and was arrested three years later at Blandford. Tortured for six weeks, he was convicted of being a priest, then hanged, drawn, and quartered at Tyburn. He was canonized in 1970 by Pope Paul VI. December 10.

WHITING, BL. RICHARD (c. 1460–1539). Born at Wrington, Somerset, England, he was educated at Cambridge, receiving his M.A. in 1483 and his S.T.D. in 1505, by which time he was a monk. He was ordained in 1501, served as chamberlain of Glastonbury

Monastery and was named abbot in 1525. He and his monks took the Oath of Supremacy in 1534, but in 1539, when he refused to surrender the monastery, he was arrested, imprisoned in the Tower in London, convicted of treason without trial, and condemned to death. He was hanged, drawn, and quartered at Glastonbury on November 15. Executed with him were Bl. John Thorne, treasurer of the abbey church, and Bl. Roger James, sacristan, on charges of hiding church treasures from the King's men. They were beatified in 1895. December 1.

WIAUX, MUTIEN MARIE (Aloysius Joseph) (1841–1917). Born a Belgian blacksmith's son, Wiaux joined the Brothers of Christian Schools in 1852 at age eleven. He became an easygoing teacher who specialized in fine arts. Known as the "Praying Brother," his example led many young people to a life of prayer. In 1977 he was beatified by Pope Paul VI, who praised him for treating teaching not merely as a profession but also as a true religious vocation. He was canonized in 1989. January 30.

WIBORADA (d. 926). Born at Klingna, Aargau, Switzerland, of a noble Swabian family, she worked at St. Gall Monastery, accompanied her brother Hatto, a priest, when he became provost of St. Magnus Church, and turned their home into a hospital. After a pilgrimage to Rome, she became a Benedictine at St. Gall's, where she worked as a bookbinder. She lived as a recluse for a time and after reportedly undergoing the ordeal by fire at Constance to refute her critics she became a hermitess, first on a mountain near St. Gall's and then in a cell beside St. Magnus. She attracted many visitors with her mortifications, holiness, prophecies, and reputed miracles, and was murdered in her cell by marauding Hungarians, as she had prophesied. She was canonized in 1047. May 2.

WIDMERPOOL, BL. ROBERT (d. 1588). Born at Widmerpool, Nottinghamshire, England, he was educated at Oxford and became a teacher, tutoring for a time the sons of the earl of Northumberland. Arrested and convicted of sheltering a priest, Bl. Robert was hanged, drawn, and quartered, with Bl. Robert Wilcox, at Canterbury. Bl. Robert Widmerpool was beatified in 1929. October 1.

WIGBERT (d. c. 738). An English monk, he went as a missionary to Germany at the invitation of St. Boniface, who appointed him abbot of Fritzlar Monastery. He later was abbot of Ohrdruf in Thuringia but in time returned to Fritzlar, where he died, venerated for his austerities and holiness. August 13.

WILCOX, BL. ROBERT (1558–88). Born at Chester, England, he studied at Rheims and was ordained there in 1585. He was sent on the English mission the following year. He served in Kent, was arrested and imprisoned at Marshalsea the same year, was convicted of being a Catholic priest, and was hanged, drawn, and quartered, with Bl. Robert Widmerpool, at Canterbury. Bl. Robert Wilcox was beatified in 1929. October 1.

WILFRID (634–709). Perhaps born in Ripon, Northumbria, son of a thegn, he joined the court of King Oswy of Northumbria when thirteen, and became a favorite of Queen Eanfleda, who sent him to Lindisfarane for his education. After a stay at Canterbury, where he studied under St. Honorius and became an adherent of Roman liturgical practices, he left England for Rome in 654 in the company of St. Benet Bishop. After a

year at Lyons, where he refused an offer to marry Bishop St. Annemund's niece, he arrived in Rome, where he studied under Boniface, Pope St. Martin's secretary. He then spent three years at Lyons, where he received the tonsure, Roman instead of Celtic style, but escaped with his life when Annemund was murdered, because he was a foreigner. He returned to England in about 660, was asked by King Alcfrid of Deira to instruct his people in the Roman rite, and when the monks at Ripon decided to return to their native Melrose rather than abandon their Celtic customs, Wilfrid was appointed abbot. He introduced the Roman usage and the rule of St. Benedict to the monastery, was ordained, and was a leader in replacing Celtic practices with Roman in northern England. When the Roman party triumphed at the council held in 664 at St. Hilda Monastery at St. Streaneschalch (Whitby) largely through his efforts, Alcfrid named him bishop of York, but since Wilfrid regarded the northern bishops who had refused to accept the decrees of Whitby as schismatic, he went to France to be ordained. Delayed until 666 in his return, he found that St. Chad had been appointed bishop of York by King Oswy of Northumbria; rather than contest the election of Chad, Wilfrid returned to Ripon. But in 669 the new archbishop of Canterbury, St. Theodore, ruled Chad's election irregular, removed him, and restored Wilfrid as bishop of York. He made a visitation of his entire diocese, restored his cathedral, and instituted Roman liturgical chant in all his churches. At the insistence of Oswy's successor, King Egfrid, whom Wilfrid had alienated by encouraging Egfrid's wife, Etheldreda, in refusing the King's marital rights and becoming a nun at Coldingham, Theodore in 678 as metropolitan, and encouraged by Egfrid, divided the see of York into four dioceses despite the objections of Wilfrid, who was deposed. He went to Rome to appeal the decision in 677, the first known appeal of an English bishop to Rome. He spent the winter in Friesland making converts, and when he arrived in Rome in 679 he was restored to his see by Pope St. Agatho. When Wilfrid returned to England in 680, Egfrid refused to accept the Pope's order and imprisoned Wilfrid for nine months. When freed he went to Sussex, converted practically all the inhabitants, and built a monastery at Selsey on land donated by King Ethelwalh. On the death of Egfrid in battle in 685, Wilfrid met with Theodore, who asked his forgiveness for his actions in deposing him and ordaining the bishops of the newly formed dioceses in Wilfrid's cathedral at York. In 686 Egfrid's successor, King Aldfrid, at Theodore's request, recalled Wilfrid and restored him to Ripon, but in 691 Aldfrid quarreled with Wilfrid and exiled him. Wilfrid went to Mercia, where at the request of King Ethelred he administered the vacant see of Litchfield. In 703 Theodore's successor, St. Berhtwald, at Aldfrid's instigation, called a synod that ordered Wilfrid to resign his bishopric and retire to Ripon. When he still refused to accept the division of his see, he again went to Rome, where Pope John VI upheld him and ordered Berhtwald to call a synod clearing Wilfrid. Only when Aldfrid died in 705, repenting of his actions against Wilfrid, was a compromise worked out by which Wilfrid was appointed bishop of Hexham while St. John of Beverly remained as bishop of York. Wilfrid died at St. Andrew's Monastery in Oundle, Northamptonshire, while on a vistation of monasteries he had founded in Mercia. October 12.

WILFRID THE YOUNGER (d. c. 744). Educated at Whitby Abbey, England, he became a priest under Bishop St. John of York, whose chaplain and close aid he became. He was named bishop of the see on the death of John and ruled until he retired to a monastery, probably Ripon. April 29.

WILGEFORTIS (no date). Also known as Liberata, Kummernis in Germany, in England as Uncumber, and in France as Livrade, among other names, her story is a pious fiction, more folk tale than religious, according to which she was one of nine daughters of a pagan Portuguese King. When her father wanted her to marry King Wilgefortis of Sicily, despite her vow of virginity, she prayed for help in resisting the marriage, whereupon she grew a beard and mustache and the suit was withdrawn. Her father was so furious he had her crucified. July 20.

WILLEHAD (d. 789). Born in Northumbria, England, he was probably educated at York, became a friend of Alcuin, and was ordained. In about 766 he went to Friesland, preached at Dokkum and Overyssel, barely escaped with his life from Humsterland, where pagans wanted to put him to death, and then returned to the area around Utrecht, again escaping with his life when he and his comrades were attacked by a group of pagans whose pagan temples they had destroyed. In 780 Charlemagne sent him as a missionary to the Saxons, and in 782, when the Saxons rose against their Frankish conquerors, he fled to Friesland. After reporting on his missionary work to Pope Adrian I and spending two years at Echternach, where he reassembled his force of missionaries, he returned to the Weser-Elbe area, where Charlemagne had just finished ruthlessly suppressing the Saxons' revolt. In 787 Willehad was ordained bishop of the Saxons, with his see at newly founded Bremen. He founded numerous churches in his see, built a cathedral at Bremen, and died there on November 8.

WILLEHAD, ANTONY VAN (1483–1572). A native of Denmark, he joined the Franciscans there but was forced into exile when Lutheranism came into Denmark. He went to the Observant Franciscan monastery at Gorkum, Holland and was arrested with the members of the community when Calvinists captured the city. They were sent to Briel, Holland, summarily hanged for their religion, and then their bodies were mutilated. He was eighty-nine years old. The group was canonized in 1867 as the Martyrs of Gorkum. July 9.

WILLIAM ARNAUD (d. 1242). A Dominican, he and two other Dominicans were commissioned by Pope Gregory IX to combat Albigensianism in Languedoc. He and his companions were driven out of Toulouse, Narbonne, and several other towns by the Albigensians. After preaching a mission at Avignonet, William and his group were given shelter for the night at the castle of Count Raymond VII of Toulouse there; all were murdered by a military patrol let into the castle. There were eleven martyrs in addition to William, among them two Franciscans: Stephen of Narbonne and Raymond. Miracles were soon reported at their graves, but their cult was not approved until 1856, as the Martyrs of Toulouse. May 29.

WILLIAM OF BOURGES (d. 1209). William de Don Jeon was born at Nevers, France, was educated by his Uncle Peter, archdeacon of Soissons, became a canon of Soissons and of Paris, and then became a monk at Grandmont Abbey. He became a Cistercian at Pontigny, served as abbot at Fontaine-Jean in Sens, and in 1187 became abbot of Chalis near Senlis. He was named archbishop of Bourges in 1200, accepted on the order of Pope Innocent III and his Cistercian superior, lived a life of great austerity, was in great demand as a confessor, aided the poor of his see, defended ecclesiastical rights against seculars, even the King, and converted many Albigensians during his missions to them. He died at Bourges on January 10, and was canonized in 1218 by Pope Honorius III.

WILLIAM OF DIJON (962–1031). Also known as William of St. Benignus, he was the son of Count Robert of Volpiano. William was born in the family castle on San Giuglio Island in Lake Orta near Nocera while his father was defending the island against the attacking Emperor Otto, who became his sponsor when he captured the island. William was entered in the Benedictine abbey of Locadio when he was seven, became a monk there, and joined St. Majolus at Cluny in 987. He reorganized St. Sernin Abbey on the Rhone, was ordained in 990, named abbot of St. Benignus at Dijon, and built the abbey into a great center of spirituality, education, and culture, and the mother monastery of some forty monasteries in Burgundy, Lorraine, Normandy, and northern Italy. He traveled widely, spreading the Cluniac reform. He died at Fécamp Monastery in Normandy, which he had rebuilt, on January 1.

WILLIAM OF ESKILSOË (c. 1125–1203). Born at Saint-Germain, France, he became a canon at St. Genevieve in Paris, at St. Denis in 1148 under Suger, and in about 1170 was invited by the bishop of Roskilde, Denmark, to reform the monasteries in his see. William became abbot of Eskilsoë on Ise Fiord, was successful, after much opposition, in his reforms, and ruled there for the next three decades. He then devoted himself to reforming other monasteries, founded St. Thomas Monastery in Zeeland, briefly left Denmark, but returned and died at his abbey on April 6.

WILLIAM OF FENOLI, BL. (d. c. 1205). A Carthusian lay brother at the Casularum charterhouse in Lombardy, he was noted for his holiness and was credited with many miracles. His cult was confirmed by Pope Pius IX in 1860. December 19.

WILLIAM FIRMATUS (d. 1090). While still a young layman at Tours, he was appointed a canon of St. Venantius there, pursued a military career, studied medicine, and then in response to a vision became a recluse with his mother. When she died he became a hermit at Laval, Mayenne, made a pilgrimage to Jerusalem, and then resumed his eremitical life at Vitré, Savigny, and Mantilly. He made a second pilgrimage to Jerusalem and then spent the rest of his life at Mantilly, where he was held in high regard for his holiness and Franciscan-like rapport with animals. April 24.

WILLIAM OF GELLONE (d. 812). Son of Count Thierry of Toulouse, he attended the court of Charlemagne, who made him duke of Aquitaine and sent him to head an expedition against the Moslems, whom he defeated. He was regarded as the exemplar of all that the ideal Christian knight should be, but he abandoned this life for a life in religion. He founded a monastery and a convent at Gellone, received Charlemagne's permission and became a Benedictine monk at Gellone, where he died on May 18. He is the hero of several medieval romances, notably *Aliscans* and *La Prise d'Orange*. He was canonized in 1066.

WILLIAM OF HIRSCHAU, BL. (d. 1091). A monk at St. Emmeram Abbey at Ratisbon, Bavaria, he was appointed abbot of Benedictine Hirschau abbey in Würtemberg, against his wishes, to replace Bl. Frederick, who had been deposed. He installed Cluniac practices and reformed the abbey, reestablished its school, founded a large *scriptorium,* and established it as an exemplary monastic foundation. He took a lively interest in the well-being of the surrounding populace, helped develop the concept of lay brothers, founded seven abbeys, and encouraged learning among both the laity and clerics. He was knowledgeable in the learning and arts of his times—astronomy, mathematics, music, poetry—and wrote *De musica et tonis,* propounding his musical theories. July 4.

WILLIAM OF MALEVAL (d. 1157). Probably a Frenchman, he seems to have followed a military career, leading a dissolute life. He reformed and made a pilgrimage to Rome, where Pope Eugene III in 1145 sent him on a penitential pilgrimage to Jerusalem. After his return to Tuscany eight years later, he lived as a hermit, was named head of a monastery in Pisa, but left to resume his eremitical life on Monte Pruno, where he was unsuccessful in attempts to reform the monks. He left them in 1155 to become a monk in a desolate area near Siena and died there two years later, famed for his gifts of prophecy and miracles. A group of men who gathered around his disciple, Albert, and a doctor named Renaldo developed into the Hermits of St. William (the Guilielmites). February 10.

WILLIAM OF MONTE VERGINE. *See* William of Vercelli.

WILLIAM OF NORWICH (d. 1144). A twelve-year-boy, an apprentice to a tanner in Norwich, England, he allegedly was kidnaped by two Jews and ritually tortured and crucified. There is no doubt that the boy was murdered, and the murderers may have been Jews, but there is no evidence that the boy was killed by Jews out of hatred of Christians, as was alleged at the time. (See also Simon of Trent.) March 24.

WILLIAM PINCHON (d. 1234). Born in Brittany, he became a priest at Saint-Brieuc, France, was named its bishop in about 1220, and became known for his holiness and concern for the poor. He was banished from his see in 1228 for defending his ecclesiastical rights against Duke Peter Mauclerc of Brittany, went to Poitiers, and returned in 1230 to Saint-Brieuc, where he died. He is also known as William of Saint-Brieuc, and he was canonized in 1247. July 29.

WILLIAM OF POLIZZI, BL. (d. c. 1317). William Gnoffi was born at Polizzi, near Palermo, Italy, lived as a hermit for a time near Castelbuono, became a mendicant religious, and then resumed his eremitical life for the last eleven years of his life. He is the patron of Castelbuono. April 16.

WILLIAM OF ROCHESTER (d. 1201). A well-to-do burgher at Perth, Scotland, he went on pilgrimage to Jerusalem with his adopted son David, who murdered him near Rochester, England. Reportedly miracles occurred at his grave, and it is said that he was canonized by Pope Alexander IV in 1256, though there is no record of such a canonization. May 23.

WILLIAM OF ROSKILDE (d. 1070). An Anglo-Saxon priest, he became chaplain to King Canute, accompanied the King on a trip to Denmark, and remained to preach to the pagans there. He was named bishop of Roskilde on Zeeland Island, publicly rebuked King Sweyn Estridsen for his execution of several men without trial (Sweyn later publicly

repented his actions), and had several other run-ins with the ruler over Sweyn's lifestyle, but the two were friends and usually worked together. William died while participating in Sweyn's funeral procession, and both were buried in the cathedral at Roskilde. Though honored in Danish churches, William has never been formally canonized. September 2.

WILLIAM OF ST. BENIGNUS. See William of Dijon.

WILLIAM OF SAINT-BRIEUC. See William Pinchon.

WILLIAM OF SCICLI, BL. (1316–1411). Born at Noto, Sicily, William Cufitella became a Franciscan tertiary. He then moved to Scicli, Sicily, where he spent the remaining seventy years of his life as a hermit. He became known for his mortifications, holiness, help to the sick and poor, and spiritual wisdom, which led many to consult him on spiritual matters. His cult was approved in 1537. April 7.

WILLIAM TEMPIER, BL (d. 1197). Born at Poitiers, France, he became a canon regular at St. Helaire-de-la-Celle Monastery there and in time became abbot. He was named bishop of his native city in 1184, actively opposed simony, and was a sturdy defender of ecclesiastical rights against secular interference. March 27.

WILLIAM OF THWAYT. See William of York.

WILLIAM OF TOULOUSE, BL. (1297–1369). Born at Toulouse, France, William de Naurose joined the Hermits of St. Augustine there in his youth, was ordained, and was sent to Paris to continue his education. He began to preach missions and soon became known for his eloquence and zeal. He was a much-sought-after spiritual adviser, was a noted exorcist, and reportedly was often tempted himself by evil spirits. He died on May 18, and his cult was confirmed in 1893.

WILLIAM OF VERCELLI (1085–1142). Born at Vercelli, Italy, of noble parents, he was orphaned when an infant, was raised by relatives, and when fourteen went on a pilgrimage to Compostela. He was at Melfi in 1106 and then spent two years as a hermit on Monte Solicoli. After abandoning a pilgrimage to Jerusalem when attacked by robbers, he became a hermit on Monte Virgiliano (Vergine) and attracted so many disciples that he organized them into a community that by 1119 became known as the Hermits of Monte Vergine, and he built a monastery. When objections arose against the strictness of his rule, he and his friend St. John of Matera with five followers founded a community on Monte Laceno in Apulia. When fire destroyed their hermitages, William moved to Monte Cognato in the Basilicata. Again he left and founded monasteries at Conza, Guglietto, and Salerno opposite the palace where he became adviser to King Roger I of Naples. William died at Guglietto on June 25.

WILLIAM OF YORK (d. 1154). Also known as William of Thwayt, William Fitzherbert was the son of Count Herbert, treasurer to Henry I, and Emma, half sister of King Stephen. William became treasurer of the church of York when quite young and in 1140 was elected archbishop of York. Archdeacon Walter of York and several Cistercian abbots and Augustinian priors challenged his election, charging William with simony and unchastity, but eventually it was upheld by Rome and he was consecrated. When, through his procrastination, his pallium was sent back to Rome, he was obliged to go to Rome, where the new Pope, Eugene III, a Cistercian, suspended him. When his followers attacked Fountains Monastery in England where a colleague of Eugene's, Henry Murdac, was abbot, the Pope deposed William in 1147 and named Murdac archbishop of York. William retired to Winchester, led a penitential and austere life, and in 1153, when Eugene and Murdac died, was restored to his see by Pope Anastasius IV. William returned to York in 1154 but died there a month later on June 8, poisoned, some claim, by Osbert, the new archdeacon of York. William was canonized in 1227 by Pope Honorius III.

WILLIBALD (c. 700–86). Son of West Saxon Richard, often called the King, and brother of SS. Winebald and Walburga, he was born in Essex on October 21 and was educated at Waltham Monastery. He went on a pilgrimage to Rome with his father and brother in 721. When his father died on the way at Lucca, Italy, he continued on to Jerusalem in 724 after a time in Rome. He was captured and imprisoned by the Saracens as a spy at Emessa, but was released and continued his pilgrimage, visiting many monasteries, *lauras,* and hermitages. After spending some time in Constantinople, he returned to Italy in about 730 and spent the next ten years at Monte Cassino. While in Rome in 740 he met Pope St. Gregory III, who sent him as a missionary to aid his cousin, St. Boniface. Willibald went to Thuringia, where Boniface ordained him in 741, and was most successful in missionary work around Eichstätt in Franconia; Boniface then consecrated him bishop of Eichstätt. With his brother Winebald, he founded a double monastery at Heidenheim, appointing Winebald abbot and his sister Walburga abbess; Heidenheim became the center of Willibald's missionary activities. He ruled for some forty-five years before his death at Eichstätt on July 7. Willibald was the first known Englishman to visit the Holy Land, and the account of his wanderings, *Hodoeporicon,* is the earliest known English travel book. He was canonized in 938 by Pope Leo VII. June 6.

WILLIBRORD (c. 658–739). Born in Northumbria, England, he was sent to Ripon Monastery under St. Wilfrid when seven and spent twelve years studying at Irish monasteries with SS. Egbert and Wigbert, beginning about 678. Willibrord was ordained when thirty and in 690 he and eleven English monks went to Friesland as missionaries. He received permission from Pope Sergius I in Rome to preach in Friesland, and encourageed by Pepin of Herstal, who had just wrested Lower Friesland from the pagan leader Radbod, Willibrord began to preach there. In 695 he was ordained bishop of the Frisians by Sergius, who gave him the name Clement, and established his see at Utrecht. He founded Echternach Monastery in Luxemburg, extended his missionary activities to Upper Friesland and Denmark, and escaped with his life when attacked by a pagan priest at Walcheren for destroying an idol. Willibrord baptized Charles Martel's son Pepin the Short in 714 and then saw most of his missionary work in Friesland undone when in 715 Radbod regained the territory Pepin of Herstal had conquered earlier. Radbod's death in 719 set off a new wave of missionary activity, aided by St. Boniface, who worked in Friesland for three years before proceeding to Germany. Willibrord was so successful that he became known as "the Apostle of the Frisians." He died while on a retreat at Echternach, Luxemburg, on November 7.

WILLIGIS (d. 1011). Born at Schöningen, Germany, he studied for the priesthood, was ordained, and became a canon of Hildesheim. He became chaplain of Emperor Otto II, who appointed him chancellor of Germany in 971 and the archbishop of Mainz in about 973. Willigis crowned three-year-old Otto III at Aachen in 983, helped rule the country during his minority with his mother, Empress Theophano, and then Empress Adelaide, and on Otto's death in 1002 was instrumental in getting Henry of Bavaria named his successor. Willigis sent missionaries to Denmark and Sweden, rebuilt his cathedral at Mainz, founded many new churches, and placed able men in many of the German sees. A jurisdictional dispute with Bishop St. Bernward of Hildesheim over the convent and church of Gandersheim, instigated by one of the nuns, Sophia, sister of the Emperor, was resolved in favor of Bernward—a decision Willigis at once accepted. February 23.

WILTRUDIS (d. c. 986). Wife of Duke Berthold of Bavaria, she became a nun on the death of Berthold about 947, was noted for her piety, and in about 976 was founding abbess of a convent that became known as Bergen. January 6.

WINEBALD (d. 761). Son of a West Saxon, Richard, who died at Lucca while on pilgrimage to Rome with his two sons, Winebald and his brother, Willibald, proceeded to Rome, where Winebald remained because of illness, while Willibald went on to the Holy Land. After seven years of study in Rome Winebald went back to England but soon returned to Rome to devote himself to a religious life. In 739 he accompanied St. Boniface back to Germany as a missionary and worked in Thuringia, where he was ordained. He later labored in Bavaria, spent some time with Boniface at Rome, and then joined his brother, Willibald, now bishop of Eichstätt. With his sister, St. Walburga, he founded a double monastery at Heidenheim in Württemberg, fought the pagans who threatened his life, and developed the monastery into a leading spiritual and educational center. He died on December 18.

WINIFRED (d. c. 650). According to legend, she was the daughter of a wealthy resident of Tegeingl, Flintshire, Wales, and the sister of St. Beuno. She was most impressed by Beuno, was supposedly beheaded on June 22 by one Caradog when she refused to submit to him, had her head restored by Beuno, and sometime later became a nun of the convent of a double monastery at Gwytherin in Denbigshire. She succeeded an Abbess Tenoi as abbess and died there fifteen years after her miraculous restoration to life. A spring supposedly springing up where Winifred's head fell is called Holywell or St. Winifred's Well and became a great pilgrimage center where many cures have been reported over the centuries. She is also known as Gwenfrewi. November 3.

WINNOC (d. c. 717). Probably a Britain of royal blood, he was raised in Brittany and with three companions became a monk at St. Peter's Monastery at Sithiu (Saint-Omer) under St. Bertin. He and his three friends were sent to found a monastery among the Morini at Wormhont near Dunkirk, of which he was abbot, and made it the center of their missionary work. He built a church and a hospital and died on November 6, venerated for his holiness and credited with many miracles.

WINWALOE (6th century). Born in Ploufragan, Brittany, of Anglo-Saxon parents, when fifteen he entered a monastery on the island of Lauré under Abbot Budoc. After several years there Winwaloe and eleven monks founded a monastery in northern Brittany, which they abandoned three years later to found Landévennec Monastery near Brest on land donated by Prince Gallo. Winwaloe died there, venerated for his miracles, many of a most extravagant nature. March 3. There are many variant spellings of his name, among them Guénolé, Gwenno, Wannow, and Valois.

WIRO (d. c. 739). A native of Northumbria (although perhaps of Ireland or Scotland), he was ordained, and with another priest, Plechelm (a fellow Northumbrian) and a deacon, Otger, went to Rome, where Wiro and Plechelm were consecrated regionary bishops. After doing missionary work in Northumbria, they went to the Netherlands, evangelized the inhabitants of the lower Meuse Valley, and built a church and cells at Odilienberg on land granted them by Pepin of Herstal. May 8.

WISDOM. *See* Charity.

WISTAN (d. 849). The grandson of King Wiglaf of Mercia, legend had him killed by Bertulph, King of Mercia, his godfather, for opposing the King's marriage to his widowed mother because of the spiritual bond involved. Wistan was buried in Evesham Cathedral. June 1.

WITHBURGA (d. c. 743). Youngest daughter of King Anna of the East Angles, she lived as a solitary at Holkham, Norfolk, for several years and after her father's death in battle, moved to Dereham. When disciples gathered around her she began a convent and a church, which were unfinished at her death on March 17. Reputedly a fresh spring now called St. Withburga's Well sprang up in the churchyard at Dereham when she was first buried. July 8.

WITTIKUN, BL. (d. c. 804). Duke of Westphalia, he opposed Charlemagne and fought against him. According to legend, Wittikun saw a vision of the infant Jesus while Communion was being distributed to the soldiers of the Christian army on Christmas night; he took instructions, was converted, and was baptized in 785, with Charlemagne his sponsor. January 7.

WIVINA (d. c. 1170). Born in Oisy, Flanders, she refused marriage to several suitors and when twenty-three became a hermitess at Grand-Bigard near Brussels. She attracted disciples and built a convent there on ground given her by Count Godfrey of Brabant. As abbess she had some difficulties at first with her nuns over the strictness of her rule but ultimately prevailed and the convent prospered. December 18.

WOLFGANG (c. 930–94). Of a Swabian family, he was educated at Reichinan Abbey and Wurzburg, joined his friend Henry in a school at Wurzburg, and went with him as a teacher in the cathedral school of Trier when Henry became archbishop there in 956. After Henry died in 964, Wolfgang became a Benedictine at Einsiedeln, was appointed director of the monastery school there, and was ordained in 971. He then went as a missionary to the Magyars in Pannonia and in 972 was appointed bishop of Regensburg by Emperor Otto II. Wolfgang at once instituted a reform of the clergy and monasteries in his see, preached widely and vigorously, and was known for his concern for the poor. He attempted to leave his see and live as a hermit at one time but was brought back. He accompanied the Emperor on a trip to France, surrendered part of his see in Bohemia for a new diocese, and was tutor of Duke Henry of Bavaria's son, who later became Emperor. Wolfgang died at Puppingen near Linz, Austria, and was canonized in 1052 by Pope Leo IX. October 31.

WOLFHARD. *See* Gualfardus.

WOLFHELM, BL. (1020–91). A Rhinelander, he was educated at the Cologne cathedral school, became a Benedictine monk at St. Maximinus Abbey in Trier, was noted for his biblical knowledge, and then was a monk at St. Pantaleon's in Cologne. He served as abbot of Gladbach, then of Siegburg, but left to lead a more secluded life as abbot of Brauweiler Monastery, where he died. April 22.

WOODHOUSE, BL. THOMAS (d. 1573). Ordained during the reign of Queen Mary he became a parish priest in Lincolnshire but was forced to resign on Mary's death. He became a tutor in Wales but was arrested in 1561 for saying Mass. He was to spend the next twelve years in prison, and in 1572 was secretly admitted to the Jesuits. When he wrote to Lord Burleigh asking him to urge Queen Elizabeth to submit to Pope Pius V, who had excommunicated and deposed her with his bull *Regnans in excelsis* in 1570, Bl. Thomas was brought to trial, found guilty of high treason, and executed. He was beatified in 1886. June 19.

WOOLO. *See* Gundleus.

WRENNO, VEN. ROGER (d. c. 1616). *See* Thulis, Ven. John.

WRIGHT, BL. PETER (d. 1651). Born of poor parents at Slipton, Northampton, England, he became a servant when quite young. He lost his faith but was reconciled to the Church at Liège, where he joined the Jesuits in 1629. He ministered to English soldiers in Flanders and accompanied the commander, Sir Henry Gage, back to England. On Sir Henry's death he lived with the marquis of Winchester, at whose home he was arrested in 1650 during the persecution of

Oliver Cromwell and hanged, drawn, and quartered. May 19.

WULFRAM (d. c. 703). Son of Fuldert, a high court official of King Dagobert, he was born at Milly, France, joined the court of Theodoric III of Neustria, was ordained, and served at the court until appointed archbishop of Sens, though St. Amatus, its rightful archbishop, was still alive in exile. Plagued by doubts of the validity of his appointment and desirous of being a missionary to the Frisians, Wulfram resigned after two and a half years. Recruiting monks at Fontenelle, he went to Friesland, converted a son of King Radbod and many others, and fought to end human sacrifices. After years in missionary work he returned to Fontenelle, where he died. March 20.

WULFRIC (d. 1154). Born at Compton Martin, near Bristol, England, he was ordained and lived a life of ease and idleness until an encounter with a beggar caused him to change his lifestyle. He became a recluse in a cell next to the church at Haselbury, Somerset, and practiced great austerity and mortifications the rest of his life. He copied and bound books, was known for his prophecies, and was credited with miracles. He died on February 20, and it is doubtful if he was ever canonized, though his tomb was a popular pilgrimage center in the Middle Ages.

WULFSTAN (c. 1008–95). Also known as Wulstan, he was born at Long Itchington, Warwickshire, England, educated at Evesham and Peterborough monasteries, and then joined the staff of Bishop Brihtheah of Worcester, who ordained him. He entered the monastery at Worcester, became treasurer of the church and prior of the monastery, and in 1062 was named bishop of Worcester. A man of great simplicity, he was accused of being unfit to be a bishop at a synod at Westminster but eventually convinced all of his ability. He was the only bishop allowed to retain his see after Williams' conquest of England, and he tried to alleviate public unrest over the oppression of the Normans. He ended the practice in Bristol of kidnaping men into slavery, rebuilt his cathedral in about 1086, and ruled his see for more than thirty-two years. He was canonized in 1203. January 19.

WULMAR. Otherwise Vulmar, q.v.

WULPHY. *See* Vulflagius.

WULSTAN. *See* Wulfstan.

XAINCTONGE, VEN. ANNE DE (1567–1621). Born at Dijon, France, on November 21, she was the daughter of a councilor and planned to found an order of nuns devoted to educating women. Despite strong opposition, she, Claudine de Boisset, and several other women founded the Sisters of St. Ursula of the Blessed Virgin at Dole, Franche-Comte, then ruled by the Spanish, in 1606, and the Order spread throughout France and Switzerland. She died at Dole on June 8, and was declared Venerable in 1900.

XANTIPPA (1st century). Though described in the Roman Martyrology, with Polyxena, as "disciples of the apostles" who died in Spain, nothing else is known of them. September 23.

XAVIER. *See* Francis Xavier.

XYSTUS. The spelling used for Sixtus in old documents.

Y

YAXLEY, VEN. RICHARD (d. 1589). A native of Boston, Lincolnshire, England, he went to Rheims in 1582 to study for the priesthood and was ordained there three years later. He was sent on the English mission in 1586 and was captured at Oxford with Fr. George Nichols, Thomas Belson, and Humphrey Prichard. All four were tortured and then executed for their faith at Oxford on October 19.

YEMPO, BL. SIMON (d. 1623). A Japanese, he became a Buddhist monk but was converted to Christianity and became a lay catechist for the Jesuit missions. He was burned to death at Yeddo for his faith, and was beatified in 1867. December 4.

YOUVILLE, BL. MARGUERITE MARIE D' (1701–71). Born at Varennes, Quebec, on October 15, Marie Marguerite Dufrost de La Jemmerais studied under the Ursulines, married François D'Youville in 1722, and became a widow in 1730. She worked to support herself and her three children, devoted much of her time to the Confraternity of the Holy Family in charitable activities, and in 1737, with three companions, founded the Grey Nuns when they took their initial vows; a formal declaration took place in 1745. Two years later she was appointed directress of the General Hospital in Montreal, which was taken over by the Grey Nuns, and had the rule of the Grey Nuns, with Marguerite as superior, confirmed by Bishop Pontbriand of Quebec in 1755. She died in Montreal on December 23, and since her death the Grey Nuns have established schools, hospitals, and orphanages throughout Canada, the United States, Africa, and South America, and are especially known for their work among the Eskimos. She was beatified by Pope John XXIII in 1959.

ZACCARIA, ANTONY MARY (1502–39). Born in Cremona, Italy, he studied medicine at the University of Padua, practiced in his hometown after his graduation in 1524, but attracted by the religious life, began to study for the priesthood. He was ordained in 1528, moved to Metan, and in 1530, with Ven. Bartholomew Ferrari and Ven. James Morigia, founded the Clerks Regular of St. Paul (the Barnabites, named after St. Barnabas Church, which became their headquarters in Milan), dedicated to reviving spirituality in the Church. The congregation was approved by Pope Clement VI in 1533, with Antony its first provost general. He resigned in 1536, helped spread the community, and worked ceaselessly to reform the Church. He died at Cremona on July 15 when thirty-seven, and was canonized by Pope Leo XIII in 1897. July 5.

ZACHARY (1st century). A priest in the Temple in Jerusalem whose wife, Elizabeth, Mary's cousin, was beyond childbearing age, he was told by an angel in a vision that they would have a son and should name him John. When he doubted this he was struck dumb. Elizabeth was visited by Mary, at which time Mary spoke the hymn of praise now known as the Magnificat, and after John's birth Zachary's speech was restored. This is all that is known of Elizabeth and Zachary, and is found in Luke 1. An unverifiable tradition has Zachary murdered in the Temple when he refused to tell Herod where his son John was to be found. November 15.

ZACHARY (d. 752). Born at San Severino, Italy, of a Greek family, he became a deacon of the Church in Rome, was known for his learning and holiness, was elected Pope, succeeding St. Gregory III, and was consecrated on December 10, 741. He visited Liutprand, when Liutprand, King of the Lombards, was about to invade Roman lands at Terni, and made a treaty with him by which the King returned all prisoners of war and returned the Roman territory he had conquered; he then dissuaded Liutprand from attacking Ravenna. Zachary encouraged St. Boniface in his German mission and made him archbishop of Mainz, recognized Pepin the Short as King of the Franks in 751, and had Boniface, as papal legate, anoint Pepin King at Soissons. Zachary was known for his aid to the poor, provided shelter for nuns driven from Constantinople by the iconoclasts, ransomed slaves from the Venetians, and translated Gregory's *Dialogues*. He died in March. March 15.

ZACHEUS (d. 303). *See* Alphaeus.

ZDISLAV BERKA, BL. (d. 1552). Born near Letomerice, Bohemia, she was forced to marry a nobleman of her family's choice and persuaded him to allow her to minister to the poor and aid refugees of the Tartar invasion at their castle of Gabel. She so impressed him with her austerities and holiness that he agreed to allow her to become a Dominican tertiary and to found St. Laurence Priory for that Order. She experienced visions and ecstasies and died on January 1. Her cult was approved in 1907 by Pope Pius X.

ZEFFERINI, BL. HUGOLINO (d. c. 1470). All that is known of him is that he was an Augustinian hermit at Corona (or possibly Mantua), miracles were reported at his grave, and a cult developed that was approved by Pope Pius VII in 1804. March 22.

ZENAS (d. c. 304). *See* Zeno.

ZENO (d. 250). *See* Ainmon.

ZENO (d. c. 300). One of the more than ten thousand Christians condemned to work on the baths of Diocletian in Rome by that Emperor, Zeno was evidently their spokesman. All of them were slaughtered by Diocletian's orders. July 9.

ZENO (d. c. 304). A wealthy landowner at Philadelphia near the Black Sea, he freed all his slaves and gave his wealth to the poor. With his servant Zenas, a slave who stayed with him, he was arrested during Diocletian's persecution and both were beheaded for their faith. June 23.

ZENO (d. c. 362). *See* Eusebius.

ZENO OF VERONA (d. 371). Born in Africa, he received an excellent classical education and in 362 was named bishop of Verona, Italy. He was active in missionary work, converted many, and fought Arianism. He built a basilica at Verona, founded a convent that he directed, encouraged charities in his

people, and wrote widely on eccesiastical subjects, particularly the virgin birth of Christ, in which are revealed many of the customs and practices of the times.

ZENOBIA (d. 310). *See* Zenobius.

ZENOBIUS (d. 310). A priest and physician in Sidon Phoenicia, he was arrested at Tyre during Dicoletian's persecution, and there suffered martyrdom. He is probably the same as the Zenobius who is honored on October 30 as bishop-physician at Aegae (Alexandretta), martyred there with his sister Zenobia. October 29.

ZENOBIUS (c. 310–90). Of the famous Florentine Geronimo family, he was ordained by Bishop Theodore, who made him his archdeacon. Zenobius became a friend of St. Ambrose, at whose recommendation he was brought to Rome to serve Pope St. Damasus, who sent him on a diplomatic mission to Constantinople. On his return he was named bishop of Florence, was credited with many miracles, including raising five people from the dead, and was venerated for his holiness and eloquence. May 25.

ZEPHYRINUS (d. c. 217). A Roman of humble origins, he was elected Pope to succeed Pope St. Victor I in 199 and named Callistus his deacon and adviser. Though Zephyrinus excommunicated the two Theodati for their Monarchianism, he was denounced by Hippolytus, a severe critic who later became a schismatic, for failure to act decisively and authoritatively in repressing prevalent heresies and as a tool of Callistus in his *Philosophoumena*. Zephyrinus died on December 20, and though listed in the Roman Martyrology as a martyr, it is most doubtful that he suffered martrydom. August 26.

ZITA (1218–78). Born at Monte Sagrati, Italy, she became a servant in the household of a wool dealer at nearby Lucca when she was twelve, was initially disliked by the other servants for her diligence, holiness, and austerities, but in time won them over. She was credited with many miracles, worked to alleviate the misery of the poor and criminals in prison, and died on April 27 after having been a servant in the Fatinelli family for some forty-eight years. She was canonized in 1696 and is the patroness of servants.

ZOË (d. c. 135). *See* Exsuperius.

ZOILUS (d. c. 304). A patrician youth at Cordova, Spain, he and nineteen others suffered martyrdom at Cordova for their Christianity during Diocletian's persecution. Zoilus is commemorated with St. Acislus in a poem by Prudentius. June 27.

ZOLA, BL. JOHN BAPTIST (1576–1626). Born at Brescia, Italy, he joined the Jesuits in 1595, and was sent as a missionary to India in 1602. Four years later he was sent to Japan, settled at Tàcacu, and worked there until he was banished to China in 1614. He returned to Japan, was again arrested, and was then burned to death at Nagasaki with John Kimsako, a Japanese who had become a Jesuit. Bl. John Baptist Zola was beatified as one of the Martyrs of Japan in 1867. June 20.

ZOSIMUS (d. c. 107). *See* Rufus.

ZOSIMUS (d. 418). Son of Abram, a presbyter, and a Greek, he was consecrated Pope on March 18, 417, succeeding Pope Innocent I. His pontificate was marred by two disputes that were not settled until after his death. The first involved his recognition of Bishop Patrocus as metropolitan of his area, which neighboring bishops opposed. In the other case he seems to have acted too hastily in accepting the appeal of Apiarius of Sicca from a condemnation by African bishops who objected to Zosimus' interference. He also formally and strongly denounced Pelagianism in *Epistola Tractoria* after being misled for a time by Pelagius and his supporter Caelestius. Zosimus died on December 27. December 26.

ZOSIMUS (5th century). *See* Mary of Egypt.

ZOSIMUS (c. 570–c. 660). Born near Syracuse, Sicily, he was entered in nearby St. Lucy Monastery when he was seven, became a monk there, and years later was appointed abbot and ordained. Against his wishes he was appointed bishop of Syracuse in 649 when he was almost eighty. His episcopate was noted for his concern for the poor and his encouragement of teaching. March 30.

ZUÑIGA, BL. PETER (1585–1622). Born at Seville, Spain, he went to Mexico, where his father was viceroy, as a youth and on his return to Spain joined the Augustinians at Seville. He was ordained, asked to be sent to Japan, and arrived at Manila in the Philippines in 1610. He finally reached Japan in 1618 but was forced to leave the following year. He was captured by a British ship on the way back to Japan in 1620 and turned over to the Dutch, who imprisoned him for two years and then turned him over to the Japanese. He was burned to death at Nagasaki with Bl. Luis Flores, and they were beatified in 1867 with the Martyrs of Japan. August 19.

THE SAINTS

AS PATRONS AND INTERCESSORS

AS PATRONS OF COUNTRIES AND PLACES

THEIR SYMBOLS IN ART

THE SAINTS AS PATRONS
AND INTERCESSORS

Abandoned Children: Jerome Emiliani
Academics: Thomas Aquinas
Accommodations: Gertrude of Nivellas
Accountants: Matthew
Actors: Genesius; Vitus
Adopted children: Clotilde; Thomas More
Advertising: Bernardine of Siena
Air travelers: Joseph of Cupertino
Alcoholics: John of God; Monica
Altar servers: John Berchmans
Anesthetists: René Goupil
Angina sufferers: Swithbert
Animals: Francis of Asissi
Archaeologists: Damascus
Archers: Sebastian
Architects: Barbara; Thomas the Apostle
Art: Catherine of Bologna
Artists: Luke; Catherine of Bologna
Astronauts: Joseph of Cupertino
Astronomers: Dominic
Athletes: Sebastian
Authors: Francis de Sales
Aviators: Joseph of Cupertino; Thérèse of
  Lisieux
Bakers: Elizabeth of Hungary; Honoratus;
  Nicholas
Bankers: Matthew
Barbers: Cosmas and Damian; Louis
Barren women: Anthony of Padua; Felicity
Basket-makers: Anthony; Abbot
Beggars: Alexius; Giles; Martin of Tours
Birth: Margaret
Blacksmiths: Dunstan
Blind: Odilia; Raphael
Blood banks: Januarius
Boatmen: Julian the Hospitaler
Bookbinders: Peter Celestine
Bookkeepers: Matthew
Booksellers: John of God
Boy Scouts: George
Brewers: Augustine; Luke; Nicholas of
  Myra
Bricklayers: Stephen
Brides: Nicholas of Myra

Bridges: John of Nepomucene
Broadcasaters: Gabriel
Brushmakers: Anthony; Abbot
Builders: Barbara; Vincent Ferrer
Bus drivers: Christopher
Butchers: Antony; Hadrian; Luke
Butchers: Adeleimus
Cab drivers: Fiacre
Cabinetmakers: Anne
Cancer patients: Peregrine Laziosi
Candlemakers: Ambroise; Bernard of
  Clairvaux
Canonists: Raymond of Peñafort
Carpenters: Joseph
Catechists: Charles Borromeo; Robert
  Bellarmine; Viator
Catholic action: Francis of Assisi
Catholic press: Francis de Sales
Chandlers: Ambrose; Bernard of
  Clairvaux
Chaplains: John of Capistrano
Charitable societies: Vincent de Paul
Chastity: Thomas Aquinas
Childbirth: Gerard Majella; Raymond
  Nonnatus
Children: Nicholas of Myra
Choirboys: Dominic Savio
Church, the: Joseph
Circus people: Julian the Hospitaller
Clerics: Gabriel
Colleges: Thomas Aquinas
Comedians: Vitus
Communications personnel: Bernardine
Confessors: Alphonsus Liguori; John
  Nepomucene
Converts: Helena; Vladimir
Convulsive children: Scholastica
Cooks: Lawrence; Martha
Coopers: Nicholas of Myra
Coppersmiths: Maura
Dairy workers: Brigid
Dancers: Vitus
Deaf: Francis de Sales
Dentists: Apollonia

652 THE SAINTS

Desperate situations: Gregory of Neo-
Caesarea; Jude; Rita of Cascia
Dietitians (in hospitals): Martha
Diplomats: Gabriel
Divorce: Helena
Drug addiction: Maximilian Kolbe
Domestic animals: Antony
Druggists: Cosmas and Damian; James
the Less
Dyers: Maurice and Lydia
Dying: Barbara; Joseph
Dysentery sufferers: Matrona
Earthquakes: Emygdius
Ecologists: Francis of Assisi
Ecumenists: Cyril; Methodius
Editors: John Bosco
Emigrants: Frances Xavier Cabrini
Endurance: Pantaleon
Engineers: Ferdinand III
Epilepsy, Motor diseases: Dymphna;
Vitus
Eucharistic Congresses and Societies:
Paschal Baylon
Expectant mothers: Gerard Majella;
Raymond Nonnatus
Eye disease: Hervé; Lucy
Falsely accused: Raymond Nonnatus
Farmers: George; Isidore the Farmer
Farriers: John the Baptist
Fathers of families: Joseph
Firemen: Florian
Fire prevention: Barbara; Catherine of
Siena
First communicants: Tarcisus
Fishermen: Andrew
Florists: Thérèse of Lisieux
Forest workers: John Gualbert
Founders: Barbara
Foundlings: Holy Innocents
Friendship: John the Divine
Fullers: Anastasius the Fuller; James the
Less
Funeral directors: Joseph of Arimathea;
Dismas
Gardeners: Adelard; Dorothy; Fiarce;
Gertrude of Nivelles; Phocas; Tryplon
Girls: Agnes
Glassworkers: Luke
Goldsmiths: Dunstan; Anastasius
Gravediggers: Antony
Greetings: Valentine
Grocers: Michael
Grooms: King Louis IX of France
Hairdressers: Martin de Porres
Happy meetings: Raphael

Hatters: James the Less; Severus of
Ravenna
Haymakers: Gervase and Protase
Headache sufferers: Teresa of Avila
Heart patients: John of God
Homeless: Margaret of Cortona; Benedict
Joseph Labre
Horses: Giles; Hippolytus
Hospital administrators: Basil the Great;
Frances Xavier Cabrini
Hospitals: Camillus de Lellis; John of God;
Jude Thaddeus
Housewives: Anne
Hunters: Eustachius; Hubert
Infantrymen: Maurice
Innkeepers: Amand; Julian the Hospitaler
Innocence: Hallvard
Interracial justice: Martin de Porres
Invalids: Roch
Janitors: Theobald
Jewelers: Eligius; Dunstan
Journalists: Francis de Sales
Jurists: John Capistran
Laborers: Isidore; James; John Bosco
Lawyers: Genesius; Ivo; Thomas More
Learning: Ambrose
Leather workers: Crispin and Crispinian
Librarians: Jerome
Lighthouse keepers: Dunstan; Venerius
Linguists: Gottschalk
Locksmiths: Dunstan
Lost articles: Anthony of Padua
Lost souls: Nicholas of Tolentino
Lovers: Raphael; Valentine
Maidens: Catherine of Alexandria
Maids: Zita
Marble workers: Clement I
Mariners: Michael; Nicholas of Tolentine
Married women: Monica
Medical record librarians: Raymond of
Penafort
Medical social workers: John Regis
Medical technicians: Albert the Great
Mentally ill: Christina; Dymphna
Merchants: Francis of Assisi; Nicholas of
Myra
Messengers: Gabriel
Metal workers: Eligius
Military chaplains: John Capistran
Midwives: Raymond Nonnatus
Millers: Arnulph; Victor
Missions: Francis Xavier; Thérèse of
Lisieux; Leonard of Port Maurice
(parish)
Monks: Benedict of Nursia

Mothers: Monica

Motorcyclists: Our Lady of Grace

Motorists: Christopher; Frances of Rome

Mountaineers: Bernard of Montjoux

Musicians: Cecilia; Dunstan; Gregory the Great

Mystics: John of the Cross

Notaries: Luke; Mark

Nuns: Bridget

Nurses: Agatha; Camillus de Lellis; John of God; Raphael

Nursing service: Catherine of Siena; Elizabeth of Hungary

Orators: John Chrysostom

Organ builders: Cecilia

Orphans: Jerome Emiliani

Painters: Luke

Paratroopers: Michael

Parish priests: John Baptist Vianney

Pawnbrokers: Nicholas of Myra

Pharmacists: Cosmas and Damian; James the Greater

Pharmacists (in hospitals): Gemma Galgani

Philosophers: Catherine of Alexandria; Justin; Thomas Aquinas

Physicians: Cosmas and Damian; Luke; Pantaleon; Raphael

Pilgrims: James

Pilots: Joseph of Cupertino

Plague: Roch

Plasterers: Bartholomew

Plumbers: Vincent Ferrer

Poets: Cecilia; David

Poisoning: Benedict

Politicians: Thomas More

Policemen: Michael

Poor: Anthony of Padua; Lawrence

Poor souls: Nicholas of Tolentino

Popes: Gregory I the Great

Porters: Christopher

Possessed: Bruno; Denis

Postal employees: Gabriel

Preachers: Catherine of Alexandria; John Chrysostom

Pregnant women: Gerard Majella; Margaret; Raymond Nonnatus

Priests: John-Baptiste Vianney

Printers: Augustine; Genesius; John of God

Prisoners: Barbara; Dismas

Prisoners of war: Leonard

Prisons: Joseph Cafasso

Protector of crops: Ansovinus

Public relations: Bernardine of Siena

Public relations (for hospitals): Paul

Race relations: Martin de Porres

Radiologists: Michael

Radio workers: Gabriel

Refugees: Alban

Retreats: Ignatius Loyola

Rheumatism: James the Greater

Saddlers: Crispin and Crispinian

Sailors: Brendan; Christopher; Cuthbert; Elmo; Erasmus; Eulalia; Peter Gonzales; Nicholas

Scholars: Brigid; Bede the Venerable

Schools, Catholic: Thomas Aquinas; Joseph Calasanz

Scientists: Albert the Great

Sculptors: Claude

Sailors: Francis of Paola

Searchers of lost articles: Anthony of Padua

Secretaries: Genesius

Secular Franciscans: Louis of France; Elizabeth of Hungary

Seminarians: Charles Borromeo

Servants: Martha; Zita

Shepherds: Drogo

Shoemakers: Crispin and Crispinian

Sick: John of God; Camillus de Lellis; Michael

Silversmiths: Andronicus; Dunstan

Singers: Cecilia; Gregory

Single mothers: Margaret of Cortona

Skaters: Lidwina

Skiers: Bernard

Skin diseases: Marculf

Social justice: Joseph

Social workers: Louise de Marillac

Soldiers: George; Hadrian; Ignatius Loyola; Joan of Arc; Martin of Tours; Sebastian

Speleologists: Benedict

Stamp collectors: Gabriel

Stenographers: Cassian; Genesius

Stonecutters: Clement

Stonemasons: Barbara; Reinhold; Stephen

Stress: Walter of Portnoise

Students: Catherine of Alexandria; Thomas Aquinas

Surgeons: Cosmas and Damian; Luke

Swimmers: Adjutor

Swordsmiths: Maurice

Tailors: Homobonus

Tanners: Crispin and Crispinian; Simon

Tax collectors: Matthew

Teachers: Gregory the Great; John Baptist de la Salle

Telecommunications workers: Gabriel

Television: Clare of Assisi

Television workers: Gabriel

Tertiaries: Elizabeth of Hungary; Louis

Theologians: Alphonsus Liguori; Augustine
Thieves: Dismas
Throat ailments: Blaise
Torture victims: Alban; Eustachius; Regina; Vincent; Victor of Marseilles
Toy makers: Claude
Travelers: Anthony of Padua; Christopher; Nicholas of Myra; Raphael; Three Magi (Caspar, Melchior, and Balthasar)
Flight attendants: Bona
Truck drivers: Christopher
Universities: Bl. Contardo Ferrini
Veterinarians: Blaise
Vocations: Alphonsus

Watchmen: Peter of Alcantara
Weavers: Anastasia; Anastasius; Paul the Hermit
Whales: Brendan the Voyager
Widows: Paula
Wine merchants: Amand
Wineries: Morand; Vincent
Women in labor: Anne
Workingmen: Joseph
Writers: Francis de Sales; Lucy
Yachtsmen: Adjutor
Youth: Aloysius Gonzaga; Gabriel Possenti; John Berchmans

AS PATRONS OF COUNTRIES AND PLACES

Albany: Our Lady of Good Counsel
Alsace: Odila
Americas: Rose of Lima, Our Lady of Guadalope
Angela: Immaculate of Copacabana
Aragon: George
Argentina: Our Lady of Lujan
Armenia: Gregory the Illuminator; Bartholomew
Asia Minor: John the Evangelist
Australia: Our Lady Help of Christians
Austria: Severino
Bavaria: Kilian
Belgium: Joseph
Bohemia: Ludmilla; Wenceslaus
Bolivia: Our Lady of Copacabana
Borneo: Francis Xavier
Brazil: Immaculate Conception; Peter of Alcántara; Our Lady of Aparecida
Canada: Anne, Joseph
Chile: Our Lady of Mount Carmel; James
China: Joseph
Colombia: Louis Bertrand; Peter Claver
Corsica: Immaculate Conception; Alexander Sauli; Julia of Corsica
Crete: Titus
Cuba: Our Lady of Charity
Cyprus: Barnabas
Czech Republic: John Nepomucene; Procopius; Wenceslaus
Denmark: Ansgar; Canute
Dominican Republic: Our Lady of High Grace; Dominic

East Indies: Francis Xavier; Thomas
Ecuador: Sacred Heart
El Salvador: Our Lady of Peace
England: Augustine of Canterbury; George; Gregory the Great
Equatorial Guinea: Immaculate Conception
Ethiopia: Frumentius
Europe: Benedict III; Cyril and Methodius; St. Catherine of Siena; St. Bridget of Sweden; Edith
Finland: Henry of Uppsala
France: Our Lady of the Assumption; Denis; Joan of Arc; Martin of Tours; Remigius; Thérèse of Lisieux
Genoa: George
Georgia (in U.S.S.R.): Nino
Gibraltar: Blessed Virgin Mary
Germany: Boniface; Michael; Peter Canisius; Suitbert
Greece: Andrew; Nicholas of Myra
Holland: Plechelm; Willibrord
Hungary: Bl. Astricus; Gerard; Stephen
Iceland: Thorlac
India: Our Lady of the Assumption
Ireland: Brigid; Columba; Patrick
Italy: Bernardine of Siena; Catherine of Siena; Francis of Assisi
Japan: Francis Xavier; Peter Baptist
Korea: Joseph and Mary, Mother of the Church
Lesotha: Immaculate Heart of Mary
Lithuania: Casimir; Bl. Cunegunda; John Cantius

Luxembourg: Willibrord
Malta: Paul; Our Lady of Assumption
Madrid: Isidore the Farmer
Mexico: Our Lady of Guadalupe
Monaco: Devota
Moravia: Cyril and Methodius
New Zealand: Our Lady Help of
Christians
North America: Isaac Jogues and
companions
Norway: Olaf
Papua New Guinea: Michael the Archangel
Paraguay: Our Lady of the Assumption
Paris: Genevieve
Persia: Maruthas
Peru: Joseph
Philippines: Sacred Heart of Mary
Poland: Casimir; Cunegunda; Hyacinth;
John Cantius; Our Lady of
Czestochowa; Stanislaus
Portugal: Francis Borgia; George;
Immaculate Conception; Vincent;
Anthony of Padua
Prussia: Adalbert; Bruno of Querfurt
Romania: Nicetas

Rome: Philip Neri
Russia: Andrew; Nicholas of Myra;
Thérèse of Lisieux; Vladimir I of Kiev
Ruthenia: Bruno
Saxony: Willihad
Scandinavia: Ansgar
Scotland: Andrew; Columba; Margaret of
Scotland; Palladius
Silesia: Hedwig
Slovakia: Our Lady of the Assumption
Solomon Islands: BVM, Most Holy Name
of Mary
South Africa: Our Lady of the Assumption
South America: Rose of Lima
Spain: Euphrasius; Felix; James; John of
Ávila; Teresa of Ávila
Sri Lanka (Ceylon): Lawrence
Sweden: Ansgar; Bridget; Eric; Gall; Sigfrid
Switzerland: Gall
Tanzania: Immaculate Conception
United States: Immaculate Conception
Uruguay: Our Lady of Lujan
West Indies: Gertrude
Wales: David
West Indies: Gertrude

THEIR SYMBOLS IN ART

Agatha: tongs, veil
Agnes: lamb
Ambrose: bees, dove, ox, pen
Andrew: transverse cross
Angela Merici: ladder, cloak
Anne: door
Anthony of Padua: Christ Child, book,
bread, lily
Antony: bell, hog
Augustine: child, dove, pen, shell
Barbara: cannon, chalice, palm, tower
Barnabas: ax, lance, stones
Bartholomew: flayed skin, knife
Benedict: bell, broken cup, bush, crozier,
raven
Bernard: bees, pen, instrument of passion
Bernardine of Siena: chrism, sun inscribed
with IHS, tablet
Blaise: iron comb, wax candle
Bonaventure: cardinal's hat, ciborium,
communion
Boniface: ax, book, fox, fountain, oak,
raven, scourge, sword
Bridget of Sweden: book, pilgrim's staff
Brigid: candle, cross, flame over her head

Bruno: chalice
Catherine of Alexandria: lamb, sword,
wheel
Catherine di Ricci: crown, crucifix, ring
Catherine of Siena: cross, lily, ring, stigmata
Cecilia: organ
Charles Borromeo: Eucharist
Christopher: Christ Child, giant, torrent,
tree
Clare: monstrance
Colette: birds, lamb
Cosmas and Damian: box of ointment, vial
Cyril of Alexandria: pen
Cyril of Jerusalem: book, purse
Dominic: rosary, star
Dorothy: flowers, fruit
Edmund: arrow, sword
Elizabeth of Hungary: bread, flowers,
pitcher
Francis of Assisi: birds, deer, fish, skull,
stigmata, wolf
Francis Xavier: bell, crucifix, ship
Genevieve: bread, candle, herd, keys
George: dragon
Gertrude: crown, lily, taper

Gervaise and Protase: club, scourge, sword
Giles: crozier, hermitage, hind
Gregory the Great: crozier, dove, tiara
Helena: cross
Hilary: child, pen, stick
Ignatius Loyola: book, chasuble, Eucharist
Isidore: bees, pen
James the Greater: key, pilgrim's staff, shell, sword
James the Less: club, halberd, square rule
Jerome: lion
John the Baptist: head on platter, lamb, skin of animal
John Berchmans: cross, rosary
John Chrysostom: bees, dove, pen
John Climacus: ladder
John the Evangelist: armor, chalice, eagle, kettle
John of God: alms, crown of thorns, heart
Josaphat: chalice, crown, winged deacon
Joseph: carpenter's square, infant Jesus, lily, plane, rod
Jude: club, square rule, sword
Justin Martyr: ax, sword
Lawrence: book of Gospels, cross, gridiron
Leander: pen
Liborius: pebbles, peacock
Longinus: lance
Louis: crown of thorns, nails
Lucy: cord, eyes on a dish
Luke: book, bush, ox, palette
Margaret: dragon
Mark: book, lion
Martha: dragon, holy water sprinkler
Mary Magdalen: alabaster box of ointment

Matilda: alms, purse
Matthew: lance, purse, winged man
Matthias: lance
Maurus: crutch, scales, spade
Meinrad: two ravens
Michael: banner, dragon, scales, sword
Monica: girdle, tears
Nicholas: anchor, boat, boy in boat, three purses
Patrick: baptismal font, cross, harp, serpent, shamrock
Paul: book, scroll, sword
Peter: boat, cock, keys
Philip: column
Philip Neri: altar, chasuble, vial
Rita: crucifix, rose, thorn
Roch: angel, bread, dog
Rose of Lima: anchor, city, crown of thorns
Sebastian: arrows, crown
Sergius and Bacchus: military uniform, palm
Simon: cross, saw
Simon Stock: scapular
Teresa of Ávila: arrow, book, heart
Thérèse of Lisieux: roses entwining a crucifix
Thomas: ax, lance
Thomas Aquinas: chalice, dove, monstrance, ox
Ursula: arrow, clock, ship
Vincent: boat, gridiron
Vincent de Paul: children
Vincent Ferrer: captives, cardinal's hat, pulpit, trumpet

CHRONOLOGICAL
CHART OF
POPES AND
WORLD RULERS

CENTURY	THE PAPACY	ROMAN EMPIRE
1st	St. Peter, ?–67	Augustus, 27 B.C.–A.D. 14
		Tiberius, 14–37
		Caliguis, 37–41
		Claudius, 41–54
		Nero, 54–68
	St. Linus, 67–76	Galba, 68–69
		Otho, 69
		Vitellius, 69
	St. Cletus (Anacletus), 76–88	Vespasian, 69–79
	St. Clement, 88–97	Titus, 79–81
		Domitian, 81–96
2nd	St. Evaristus, 97–105	Nerva, 96–98
	St. Alexander I, 105–115	Trajan, 98–117
	St. Sixtus I, 115–125	Hadrian, 117–138
	St. Telesphorus, 125–136	
	St. Hyginus, 136–140	Antoninus Pius, 138–161
	St. Pius I, 140–155	
	St. Anicetus, 155–166	
	St. Soter, 166–175	Marcus Aurelius, 161–180
	St. Eleutherius, 175–189	Lucius Aurelius Verus, 161–169
	St. Victor I, 189–199	
		Commodus, 180–192
		Pertinax, 193
		Didius Julian, 193
3rd	St. Zephyrinus, 199–217	Septimus Severus, 193–211
	St. Callistus I, 217–222	Caracalla, 211–217
	[St. Hippolytus, antipope,	Geta, 211–212
	217–235]	Macrina, 217–218
		Heliogabalus, 218–222
	St. Urban I, 222–230	Alexander Severus, 222–235
	St. Pontian, 230–235	Maximin, 235–238
	St. Anterus, 235–236	Gordian I, 237–238
	St. Fabian, 236–250	Popienus, 238
		Balbinus, 238
		Gordian III, 238–244
		Philippus, 244–249
		Decius, 249–251
	St. Cornelius, 251–253	Gallus, 251–253
	[Novatian, antipope, 251]	Aemelian, 252–253
	St. Lucius I, 253–254	Valerian, 253–259
	St. Stephen I, 254–257	Gallienus, 259–268
	St. Sixtus II, 257–258	Claudius II, 268–270
	St. Dionysius, 259–268	Aurelian, 270–275
	St. Felix I, 269–274	Tacitus, 275–276
	St. Eutychianus, 275–283	Probus, 276–282
		Carus, 281–283

CENTURY	THE PAPACY	EAST	WEST
4th	St. Caius, 283–296	Diocletian, 284–305	Maximin-Maximian (Maximianus
	St. Marcellinus, 296–304		Herculius), 286–305
	Marcellus I, 308–309	Galerius, 305–311	Constantius, 305–306
	St. Eusebius, 309	Licinius, 311–324	Severus, 306–307
	St. Miltiades, 311–314	Constantine I, 311–324	Maxentius, 311–324
	St. Sylvester I, 314–335		Constantine I, 324–337
	St. Mark, 336		(emperor of East and West)
	St. Julius I, 337–352	Constantius II, 337–350	Constantine II, 337–340
			Constans I, 337–350
			Constantius II, 350–361
	Liberius, 352–366		Julian the Apostate, 361–363
	[Felix II, antipope, 355–365]		Jovian, 363–364
	St. Damasus I, 366–384		(emperors of East and West)
	[Ursinus, antipope, 366–367]	Valens, 364–378	Valentinian I, 364–372
		Theodosius the Great, 379–392	Gratian, 375–383
	St. Siricius, 384–399	Maximus, 383–388	Valentinian II, 375–392
			Theodosius the Great, 392–395
			(emperor of East and West)
5th	St. Anastasius I, 399–401	Theodosius the Great, 392–395	Theodosius the Great, 379–395
	St. Innocent I, 401–417		Eugenius, 392–394
	St. Zosimus, 417–418	Arcadius, 395–408	Honorius, 395–423
	St. Boniface I, 418–422	Theodosius II, 408–450	Valentinian III, 425–454
	[Eulalius, antipope, 418–419]		Petronius, 455
	St. Celestine I, 422–432		Avitus, 455–457
	St. Sixtus III, 432–440	Marcian, 450–457	Majorian, 457–461
	St. Leo I, 440–461	Leo I, 457–474	Severus, 461–465

CENTURY	THE PAPACY	ROMAN EMPIRE		FRANCE
		EAST	WEST	
	St. Hilary, 461–468		Anthemius, 467–472	
	St. Simplicius, 468–483		Olybrius, 472	
		Leo II, 473–474	Glycerius, 473–474	
		Zeno, 474–491	Julius Nepos, 473–475	
	St. Felix III (II), 483–492		Romulus Augustulus,	
	St. Gelasius I, 492–496		475–476	
	Anastasius II, 496–498	Anastasius I, 491–518		
6th	St. Symmachus, 498–514			
	[Lawrence, antipope, 498;			
	501–505]			
	St. Hormisdas, 514–523	Justin I, 518–527		
	St. John I, 523–526			
	St. Felix IV (III), 526–530	Justinian, 527–565		
	Boniface II, 530–532			
	[Dioscorus, antipope, 530]			
	John II, 533–535			
	St. Agapetus I, 535–536			
	St. Silverius, 536–537			
	Vigilius, 537–555			
	Pelagius I, 556–561			
	John III, 561–574	Justin II, 565–578		
	Benedict I, 575–579	Tiberius, 578–582		
	Pelagius II, 579–590	Maurice, 582–602		
7th	St. Gregory I, 590–604	Phocas, 602–610		
	Sabinianus, 604–606			
	Boniface III, 607	Heraclius I, 610–641		
	St. Boniface IV, 608–615			
	St. Deusdedit (or Adeodatus I),			
	615–618			
	Boniface V, 619–625			
	Honorius I, 625–638			
	Severinus, 640			
	John IV, 640–642	Constantine III, 641		
		Heracleonas, 641		
	Theodore I, 642–649	Constans II, 641–668		
	St. Martin I, 649–655			
	St. Eugene I, 654–657			
	St. Vitalian, 657–672	Constantine IV, 668–685		
	Adeodatus II, 672–676			Pepin of Herstal,
	Donus, 676–678			676–714
	St. Agatho, 678–681			
	St. Leo II, 682–683			
	St. Benedict II, 684–685			
	John V, 685–686	Justinian II, 685–695;		
	Conon, 686–687	705–711		
	[Theodore, antipope, 687]			
	[Paschal, antipope, 687]			
	St. Sergius I, 687–701	Leontius, 695–698		
8th	John VI, 701–705	Tiberius III, 698–705		
	John VII, 705–707	Philippicus, 711–713		Charles Martel,
	Sisinnius, 708			714–741
	Constantine, 708–715			
		Anastasius II, 713–715		
	St. Gregory II, 715–731	Theodosius III, 715–717		Pepin, 751–768
	St. Gregory III, 731–741	Leo III the Isaurian,		
		717–741		
	St. Zachary, 741–752	Constantine V, 741–775		Charlemagne,
	Stephen II, 752			768–814
	Stephen III (II), 752–757			
	St. Paul I, 757–767			
	[Constantine, antipope,			
	767–769]			
	767–769] [Philip, antipope,			
	768]			
	Stephen IV (III), 768–772			
	Adrian I, 772–795	Leo IV the Khazar,		
		775–780		
		Constantine VI,		
		780–797		

| CENTURY | THE PAPACY | ROMAN EMPIRE | | FRANCE |
		EAST	WEST	

9th	St. Leo III, 795–816	Irene, 797–802
		Nicephorus I,
		  802–811
		Michael I, 811–813
			Charlemagne
			  (Charles the
			  Great), 800–814	

	Stephen V (IV), 816–817
	St. Paschal I, 817–824
	Eugene II, 824–827
	Valentine, 827
	Gregory IV, 827–844
	  [John, antipope, 844]
		Leo V, 813–820
		Michael II, 820–829
		
		Theophilus,
		  829–842
		Michael III, 842–867
			Louis I the Pious,
			  814–840
			
			Lothair, 840–855
			
			Louis II the German,
			  855–875
				Louis I, the Pious,
				  814–840
				
				Lothaire, 840–855
				Louis II, 855–875
				Charles the Bald,
				  843–877
				Charles the Fat,
				  844–887

	Sergius II, 844–847
	
	St. Leo IV, 847–855
	Benedict III, 855–858
	  [Anastasius,
	    antipope, 855]
	St. Nicholas I, 858–867
	
	Adrian II, 867–872
	John VIII, 872–882
	Marinus I, 882–884
	
	St. Adrian III, 884–885
		Basil I the Mace-
		  donian, 867–886
			Charles II the Bald,
			  875–877
			
			Charles III the Fat,
			  881–887
				Louis II, 877–879
				Louis III, 879–882
				Carloman, 879–884
				Eudes, 888–898

10th	Stephen VI (V), 885–891
	Formosus, 891–896
	Boniface VI, 896
	Stephen VII (VI), 896–897
	Romanus, 897
	Theodore II, 897
	John IX, 898–900
	Benedict IV, 900–903
	Leo V, 903
	  [Christopher, antipope,
	  903–904]
	Sergius III, 904–911
	Anastasius III, 911–913
	
	Lando, 913–914
	
	John X, 914–928
	Leo VI, 928
	Stephen VIII (VII),
	  928–931
	John XI, 931–935
	Leo VII, 936–939
	Stephen IX (VIII), 939–942
	Marinus II, 942–946
	Agapetus II, 946–955
	John XII, 955–964
	Leo VIII, 963–965
	Benedict V, 964–966
	  964–966
	John XIII, 965–972
	Benedict VI,
	  973–974
	  [Boniface VII,
	    antipope,
	    974; 984–985]
	Benedict VII, 974–983
		Leo VI, 896–912
		  [Alexander, 912–913]
		
		Constantine VII,
		  912–959
		  [Romanus I,
		  919–944]
		
		Romanus II, 959–963
		
		Basil II, 963–1025
		{Constantine VIII,
		  963–1028
		[Nicephorus II
		  Phocas,
		  963–969]
		[John I Tzi-
		  misces,
		  987–996]
			Guy of Spoleto,
			  891–894
			Lambert of Spoleto,
			  894–898
			Arnulf of Carinthia,
			  896–899
			Louis of Provence, 901
			
			Berenger (of Friuli),
			  915
			Henry I, the Fowler,
			  919–936
			
			Otto I, 936–937
			
			Otto II, 973–983
				Robert I, 922–923
				Charles the Simple,
				  893–923
				Louis IV, L'Outre-
				  mer, 936–954
				
				Lothaire, 954–986
				
				Louis V, 986–987
				Hugh Capet,
				  987–996

ENGLAND	POLAND	HUNGARY	SCOTLAND
Egbert, 828–839			
Ethelwuff, 839–858			Kenneth MacAlpine, 834–860
Ethelbald, 858–860 Ethelbert, 860–866			
			Grig, 860–863 Constantine I, 863–879
Ethelred I, 866–871 Alfred, 871–899			
			Aedh, 879–900
Edward the Elder, 899–924			Constantine II, 900–943
Athelstan, 924–940			
Edmund I, 940–946			Malcolm I, 943–954
Edred, 946–955	Mieszko I, 962–992		
Edwy, 955–959 Edgar, 959–975		Duke Géza, 970–997	Culren, 967–971? Kenneth II, 971–995
Edward the Martyr, 975–979			

CENTURY	THE PAPACY	EASTERN ROMAN EMPIRE	HOLY ROMAN EMPIRE	FRANCE
	John XIV, 983–984		Otto III, 983–1002	Robert I, 996–1031
	John XV, 985–996			
	Gregory V, 996–999			
	[John XVI, antipope, 997–998]			
11th	Sylvester II, 999–1003		St. Henry II, 1002–1024	
	John XVII, 1003			
	John XVIII, 1004–1009			
	Sergius IV, 1009–1012			
	Benedict VIII, 1012–1024			
	[Gregory, antipope, 1012]			
	John XIX, 1024–1032		Conrad II, 1024–1039	
		Zoe, 1028–1042		Henry I, 1031–1060
	Benedict IX, 1032–1044	[Romanus III, 1028–1034]		
	(also 1045; 1047–1048)	[Michael IV, 1034–1041]	Henry III, 1039–1056	
	Sylvester III, 1045	[Michael V, 1041–1042]		
	Gregory VI, 1045–1046			
	Clement II, 1046–1047			
	Benedict IX, 1047–1048	⎧Zoe, 1042–1050		
	Damasus II, 1048	⎩Theodora, 1042–1056		
	St. Leo IX, 1049–1054	[Constantine IX, 1042–1055]		
	Victor II, 1055–1057		Henry IV, 1056–1106	
	Stephen X (IX), 1057–1058	Michael VI Stratioticus, 1056–1057		
	[Benedict X, antipope, 1058–1059]	Isaac I Comnenus, 1057–1059		
	Nicholas II, 1059–1061	Constantine X Ducas, 1059–1067		Philip I, 1060–1108
	Alexander II, 1061–1073			
	[Honorius II, antipope, 1061–1072]	Michael VII Ducas, 1067–1078		
	St. Gregory VII, 1073–1085	[Romanus IV, 1067–1071]		
	[Clement III, antipope, 1080–1100]	Nicephorus III Botaniates, 1078–1081		
	Bl. Victor III, 1086–1087			
	Bl. Urban II, 1088–1099			
12th	Paschal II, 1099–1118	Alexius I, 1081–1118	Henry V, 1106–1125	Louis VI, 1108–1137
	[Theodoric, antipope, 1100]	John II, 1118–1143		
	[Albert, antipope, 1102]			
	[Sylvester IV, antipope, 1105–1111]			
	Gelasius II, 1118–1119			
	[Gregory VIII, antipope, 1118–1121]			

ENGLAND	SPAIN	POLAND	HUNGARY	SCOTLAND
Ethelred the Unready, 979–1016		Boleslav I, 992–1025	St. Stephen I, 997–1038	Kenneth III, 997–1005?
	Sancho the Great, Castile & Navarre, 1000–1035	Miezko II, 1025–1034		Malcolm II, 1005–1034
Edmund Ironside, 1016 Canute, 1016–1035			Peter, 1038–1046 [Aba Samú, 1038–1046]	
Harold I, 1035–1040 Hardicanute, 1040–1042	Ramiro I, Aragon, 1035–1065 Ferdinand I, Castile & León, 1035–1065 García Navarre, 1035–1054	Casimir I, 1040–1058		Duncan, 1034–1040 Macbeth, 1040–1057
Edward the Confessor, 1042–1066			Andrew I, 1047–1060	
	Sancho Ramirez, Aragon, 1063–1094; Navarre, 1076–1094 Alfonso VI, Castile, 1072–1109; León, 1065–1109 Sancho V, Navarre, 1054–1076	Boleslav II, 1058–1079	Béla I, 1060–1063 Solomon, 1063–1074	Malcolm III, 1058–1093
Harold II, 1066				
William I, 1066–1087 1066–1087		Ladislas I, 1081–1102	Géza I, 1074–1077 St. Ladislaus I, 1077–1095	
William II, 1087–1100 Henry I, 1100–1135	Pedro I, Aragon & Navarre, 1094–1104		Coloman, 1095–1114	Donald Bane, 1094–1097 Edgar, 1097–1107 Alexander I, 1107–1124
	Alfonso I, Aragon & Navarre, 1104–1134 Ramiro II, Aragon, 1134–1137 Urraca, Castile & León,1109–1126	Boleslav III, 1102–1138		
			Stephen II, 1114–1131	

CENTURY	THE PAPACY	EAST ROMAN EMPIRE	HOLY ROMAN EMPIRE	FRANCE	ENGLAND
	Callistus II, 1119–1124				
	Honorius II, 1124–1130		Lothair II, 1125–1137		
	[Celestine II, antipope, 1124]				
	Innocent II, 1130–1143	Manuel I, 1143–1180			Stephen, 1135–1154
	[Anacletus II, antipope, 1130–1138]		Conrad III, 1137–1152	Louis VII, 1137–1180	
	[Victor IV, antipope, 1138]				
	Celestine II, 1143–1144				
	Lucius II, 1144–1145				
	Bl. Eugene III, 1145–1153		Frederick I Barbarossa, 1152–1190		
	Anastasius IV, 1153–1154				Henry II, 1154–1189
	Adrian IV, 1154–1159				
	Alexander III, 1159–1181				
	[Victor IV, antipope, 1159–1164]				
	[Paschal III, antipope, 1164–1168]				
	[Callistus III, antipope, 1168–1178]				
	[Innocent III, antipope, 1179–1180]	Alexius II, 1180–1183		Philip II Augustus, 1180–1223	
	Lucius III, 1181–1185	Andronicus, 1183–1185			
	Urban III, 1185–1187	Isaac II, 1185–1195			
	Gregory VIII, 1187				
	Clement III, 1187–1191		Henry VI, 1190–1197		Richard I, 1189–1199
	Celestine III, 1191–1198		Philip of Swabia, 1197–1208		
13th	Innocent III, 1198–1216	Alexius III, 1195–1203	Otto IV, 1198–1212		
	Honorius III, 1216–1227	Isaac II, 1203–1204 Alexius IV, 1203–1204	Frederick II, 1212–1250	Louis VIII, 1223–1226	John, 1199–1216 Henry III, 1216–1272
	Gregory IX, 1227–1241	Alexius V Ducas, 1204		St. Louis IX, 1226–1270	
	Celestine IV, 1241				
	Innocent IV, 1243–1254		Conrad IV, 1250–1254		
	Alexander IV, 1254–1261				
	Urban IV, 1261–1264				
	Clement IV, 1265–1268				
	Bl. Gregory X, 1271–1276		Rudolf I, 1273–1291		
	Bl. Innocent V, 1276			Philip III, 1270–1285	Edward I, 1272–1307
	Adrian V, 1276				
	John XXI, 1276–1277				
	Nicholas III, 1277–1280				
	Martin IV, 1281–1285				
	Honorius IV, 1285–1287				
	Nicholas IV, 1288–1292		Adolf, 1292–1298	Philip IV, the Fair, 1285–1314	

SPAIN	POLAND	HUNGARY	SCOTLAND	PORTUGAL
		Béla II, 1131–1141	David I, 1124–1153	
Petronila, Aragon, 1137–1162 Alfonso VII, Castile & León, 1126–1157 Sancho III, Castile, 1157–1158 García Ramírez, Navarre, 1134–1150	Ladislas II, 1139–1146 Boleslav IV, 1146–1173	Géza II, 1141–1161	Malcolm IV, 1153–1165	Alfonso Henriques, 1139–1185
Alfonso II, Aragon, 1162–1196 Alfonso VIII, Castile, 1158–1214 Ferdinand II, León, 1157–1188 Sancho VII, Navarre, 1150–1194	Miezko III, 1173–1177; 1194–1202 Casimir II, 1177–1194	Stephen III, 1162–1172 Béla III, 1173–1196	William, 1165–1214	Sancho I, 1185–1211
Pedro II, Aragon, 1196–1213 Alfonso IX, León, 1188–1230 Sancho VIII, Navarre, 1194–1234 James I, Aragon, 1213–1276 Henry I, Castile, 1214–1217 Ferdinand III, Castile, 1217–1252; León, 1230–1252 Teobaldo I, Navarre, 1234–1253 Pedro III, Aragon, 1276–1285; Sicily, 1282–1285 Alfonso X, Castile & León, 1252–1284 Teobaldo II, Navarre, 1253–1270 Henry I, Navarre, 1270–1274 Alfonso III, Aragon, 1285–1291 Sancho IV, Castile & León, 1284–1295 Juana, Navarre, 1274–1305	Ladislas III, 1202–1206 Leszek I, 1206–1227 Boleslav V, 1227–1279 Leszek II, 1279–1288 Henry Probus, 1288–1290 Przemyslav, 1290–1296	Emeric, 1196–1204 Ladislaus III, 1204–1205 Andrew II, 1205–1235 Béla IV, 1235–1270 Stephen V, 1270–1272 Ladislaus IV, 1272–1290 Andrew III, 1290–1301	Alexander II, 1214–1249 Alexander III, 1249–1286 Margaret of Norway 1286–1290 John Baliol, 1292–1296	Alfonso I, 1211–1223 Sancho II, 1223–1245 Alfonso III, 1245–1279 Diniz, 1279–1325

CENTURY	THE PAPACY	HOLY ROMAN EMPIRE	FRANCE	ENGLAND	SPAIN
	St. Celestine V, 1294–1296				James II, Aragon & Sicily, 1291–1327
14th	Boniface VIII, 1294–1303	Albert I, 1298–1308			Ferdinand IV, Castile, 1295–1312
	Bl. Benedict XI, 1303–1304	Henry VII, 1308–1314	Louis X, 1314–1316		
	Clement V, 1305–1314		John I, 1316	Edward II, 1307–1327	
	John XXII, 1316–1334	Louis of Bavaria, 1314–1347	Philip V, 1316–1322	Edward III, 1327–1377	
	[Nicholas V, antipope, 1328–1330]		Charles IV, 1322–1328		Alfonso IV, Aragon, 1327–1336
	Benedict XII, 1334–1342		Philip VI, 1328–1350		Alfonso XI, Castile, 1312–1350
	Clement VI, 1342–1352				Pedro IV, Aragon, 1336–1387
	Innocent VI, 1352–1362	Charles IV, 1347–1378			Pedro the Cruel, Castile, 1350–1369
	Bl. Urban V, 1362–1370		John II, 1350–1364		
	Gregory XI, 1370–1378		Charles V, 1364–1380	Richard II, 1377–1399	Henry II, Castile, 1369–1379
	Urban VI, 1378–1389	Wenceslaus, 1378–1400	Charles VI, 1380–1422	Henry IV, 1399–1413	John I, Aragon, 1387–1395
15th	Boniface IX, 1389–1404				John I, Castile, 1379–1390
	Innocent VII, 1404–1406	Rupert, 1400–1410			
	Gregory XII, 1406–1415				Martin, Aragon & Sicily 1395–1410
	[Clement VII, antipope, 1378–1394]	Sigismund, 1410–1437			Henry III, Castile, 1390–1406
	[Benedict XIII, antipope, 1394–1423]				
	[Alexander V, antipope, 1409–1410]				Ferdinand I, Aragon & Sicily, 1412–1416
	[John XXIII, antipope, 1410–1415]			Henry V, 1413–1422	Alfonso V, Aragon, Sicily, & Naples, 1416–1458
	Martin V, 1417–1431		Charles VII, 1422–1461	Henry VI, 1422–1461	John II, Castile, 1406–1454
	Eugene IV, 1431–1447	Albert II, 1438–1439			John II, Aragon & Sicily, 1458–1479
	[Felix V, antipope, 1439–1449]	Frederick III, 1440–1493			Henry IV, Castile 1454–1474
	Nicholas V, 1447–1455				
	Callistus III, 1455–1458			Edward IV, 1461–1483	
	Pius II, 1458–1464		Louis XI, 1461–1483	Edward V, 1483	
	Paul II, 1464–1471		Charles VIII, 1483–1498	Richard III, 1483–1485	{ Ferdinand II, Aragon, 1479–1516
	Sixtus IV, 1471–1484				{ Isabella, Castile, 1474–1504
	Innocent VIII, 1484–1492	Maximillian I, 1493–1519		Henry VII, 1485–1509	
16th	Alexander VI, 1492–1505		Louis XII, 1498–1515	Henry VIII, 1509–1547	Charles I, (Emperor Charles V) 1516–1556
	Pius III, 1503		Francis I, 1515–1547		
	Julius II, 1503–1513	Charles V, 1519–1556			
	Leo X, 1513–1521				
	Adrian VI, 1522–1523				
	Clement VII, 1523–1534				
	Paul III, 1534–1549				
	Julius III, 1550–1555			Edward VI, 1547–1553	
	Marcellus II, 1555		Henry II, 1547–1559	Mary I, 1553–1558	

POLAND	HUNGARY	SCOTLAND	PORTUGAL
Wenceslas, 1300–1305 Ladislas IV 1305–1333	Charles I (Robert of Anjou) 1308–1342 [Wenceslaus] [Otto of Bavaria]	Robert I, 1306–1329	
Casimir III, 1333–1370	Louis I the Great, 1342–1382	David Bruce, 1329–1370	Alfonso IV, 1325–1357
			Pedro I, 1357–1367 Ferdinand I, 1367–1383
Louis I of Hungary, 1370–1382 Sigismund, 1382–1384 Hedwig (Jadwiga), 1384–1399 Ladislas V (Jagello), 1386–1434	Maria of Anjou, 1382–1385 Charles II, 1385–1386; of Naples, 1381–1385 Sigismund, 1387–1437	Robert II, 1370–1390 Robert III, 1390–1406 James I, 1406–1437	John I, 1385–1433
Ladislas VI, 1434–1444 Casimir IV, 1447–1492	Albert, 1438–1439 Wladislaw I, 1442–1444; as Ladislas VI of Poland, 1434–1444 [John Hunyady (regent), 1444–1453] Ladislaus V, 1444–1457; of Bohemia, 1453–1457 Matthias I Corvinus, 1458–1490 Wladislaw II, 1490–1516	James II, 1437–1460 James III, 1460–1488 James IV, 1488–1513	Edward, 1433–1438 Alfonso V, 1438–1481 John II, 1481–1495 Emanuel, 1495–1521
John Albert, 1492–1501 Alexander, 1501–1506 Sigismund I, 1506–1548 Sigismund II, 1548–1572	Louis II, 1516–1526; of Bohemia, 1509–1526 After 1526 the throne of Hungary was claimed by the Hapsburgs.	James V, 1513–1542 Mary Stuart, 1542–1567 James VI, 1567–1625	John III, 1521–1557 Sebastian, 1557–1578

CENTURY	THE PAPACY	HOLY ROMAN EMPIRE	FRANCE	ENGLAND	SPAIN
	Paul IV, 1555–1559	Ferdinand I, 1558–1564	Francis II, 1559–1560	Elizabeth I, 1558–1603	Philip II, 1556–1598
	Pius IV, 1559–1565	Maximillian II, 1564–1576	Charles IX, 1560–1574		
	St. Pius V, 1566–1572	Rudolf II, 1576–1612	Henry III, 1574–1589		
	Gregory XIII, 1572–1585		Henry IV, 1589–1610		
	Sixtus V, 1585–1590				
	Urban VII, 1590				
	Gregory XIV, 1590–1591				
	Innocent IX, 1591				
17th	Clement VIII, 1592–1605			James I, 1603–1625	Philip III, 1598–1621
	Leo XI, 1605	Matthias, 1612–1619	Louis XIII, 1610–1643	Charles I, 1625–1649	Philip IV, 1621–1665
	Paul V, 1605–1621	Ferdinand II, 1619–1637			
	Gregory XV, 1621–1623	Ferdinand III, 1637–1657			
	Urban VIII, 1623–1644	Leopold I, 1658–1705	Louis XIV, 1643–1715		
	Innocent X, 1644–1655			Oliver Cromwell, 1653–1658	
	Alexander VII, 1655–1667			Richard Cromwell, 1658–1659	Charles II, 1665–1700
	Clement IX, 1667–1669			Charles II, 1660–1685	
	Clement X, 1670–1676			James II, 1685–1688	
	Bl. Innocent XI, 1676–1689			Mary II, 1689–1694	
	Alexander VIII, 1689–1691			William III, 1689–1702	
18th	Innocent XII, 1691–1700			Anne, 1702–1714	
	Clement XI, 1700–1721	Joseph I, 1705–1711	Louis XV, 1715–1774	George I, 1714–1727	Philip V of Anjou, 1700–1724;
	Innocent XIII, 1721–1724	Charles VI, 1711–1740		George II, 1727–1760	1724–1746
	Benedict XIII, 1724–1730	Charles VII of Bavaria, 1740–1745			Louis I, 1724
	Clement XII, 1730–1740	Francis I, 1745–1765			
	Benedict XIV, 1740–1758			George III, 1760–1820	Ferdinand VI, 1746–1759
	Clement XIII, 1758–1769	Joseph II, 1765–1790			Charles III, 1759–1788
	Clement XIV, 1769–1774				
	Pius VI, 1775–1799	Leopold II, 1790–1792	Louis XVI, 1774–1793		Charles IV, 1788–1807
19th	Pius VII, 1800–1823	Francis II, 1792–1806	Louis XVII, 1793–1795		Joseph Napoleon, 1807–1814
	Leo XII, 1823–1829		Napoleon, 1799–1814	George IV, 1820–1830	Ferdinand VII, 1814–1833
	Pius VIII, 1829–1830		Louis XVIII, 1814–1824	William IV, 1830–1837	
			Charles X, 1824–1830		Isabella II, 1833–1868
				Victoria, 1837–1901	Amadeo, 1871–1873
	Gregory XVI, 1831–1846		Louis Philippe, 1830–1848	(William E. Gladstone, prime minister, 1868–1874, 1880–1885, 1886, 1892–1894)	Alfonso XII, 1874–1885
			Napoleon III, 1848–1870		
			Adolphe Thiers, 1871–1873		
	Pius IX, 1846–1878		Patrice M. MacMahon, 1873–1879	(Benjamin Disraeli, prime minister, 1868, 1874–1880)	

POLAND	AUSTRIA	PORTUGAL	UNITED STATES OF OF AMERICA
Stephen Bathory, 1576–1586 Sigismund III, 1587–1632	Ferdinand I, 1558–1564 Maximillian II, 1564–1576 Rudolph II, 1572–1608; of Bohemia, 1575–1611	Henry, 1578–1580 Philip I, 1580–1598	
		Philip II, 1598–1621 Philip III, 1621–1640	
	Matthias II, 1608–1619; of Bohemia, 1611–1619 Ferdinand II, 1619–1635	John IV, 1640–1656	
Ladislas IV (VII), 1632–1648 John II Casimir, 1648–1668 Michael Wisniowiecki, 1669–1673 John III Sobieski, 1674–1696	Ferdinand III, 1635–1657 Leopold I, 1658–1705	Alfonso VI, 1656–1667	
		Pedro II, 1683–1706	
		John V, 1706–1750	
Augustus II of Saxony, 1697–1733 Stanislas Lesczynski, 1704–1709; 1733–1736 Augustus III, 1734–1763	Joseph I, 1705–1711 Charles III (Emperor Charles VI), 1711–1740 Maria Theresa, 1740–1780		
		Joseph I, 1750–1777 Maria I, 1777–1816	
Stanislas II Poniatowski, 1764–1795	Joseph II, 1780–1790 Leopold II, 1790–1792 Francis I, 1792–1835	Pedro III, 1777–1786	George Washington, 1789–1797 John Adams, 1797–1801 Thomas Jefferson, 1801–1809 James Madison, 1809–1817
		John VI, 1816–1826 Pedro IV, 1826–1828 Miguel, 1828–1834	James Monroe, 1817–1825 John Quincy Adams, 1825–1829 Andrew Jackson, 1829–1837
	Francis Joseph, 1867–1916		Martin Van Buren, 1837–1841
	Charles I, 1916–1918		William Henry Harrison, 1841 John Tyler, 1841–1845
	Michael Hzmisch, 1920–1928	Maria II, 1834–1853 Pedrov, 1853–1861	James K. Polk, 1845–1849 Zachary Taylor, 1849–1850 Millard Fillmore, 1850–1853
	William Minles, 1928–1938	Louis I, 1861–1889	Franklin Pierce, 1853–1857
		ITALY	James Buchanan, 1857–1861
	Wilhelm I, 1861–1888	Victor Emmanual II, 1861–1878	Abraham Lincoln, 1861–1865

CENTURY	THE PAPACY	FRANCE	ENGLAND	SPAIN
20th	Leo XIII, 1878–1903	Jules Grévy, 1879–1887 Marie François Sadi-Carnot, 1887–1894 Jean Casimir-Périer, 1894–1895 Félix Faure, 1895–1899 Émile Loubet, 1899–1906 Armand Fallières, 1903–1913	Edward VII, 1901–1910	Alfonso XIII, 1886–1931
	St. Pius X, 1903–1914	Raymond Poincaré, 1913–1920 Paul Deschanel, 1920 Alexandre Millerand, 1920–1924	George V, 1910–1936	
	Benedict XV, 1914–1922 Pius XI, 1922–1939	Gaston Doumergue, 1924–1931 Paul Doumer, 1931–1932 Albert Lebrun, 1932–1940 Henri Philippe Pétain, 1940–1944	Edward VIII, 1936	Alcalá Zamora, 1931–1936
	Pius XII, 1939–1958	Charles de Gaulle, 1945–1946 Georges Bidault, 1946–1947 Félix Gouin, 1946 Vincent Auriol, 1947–1954 René Coty, 1954–1959	George VI, 1936–1952 (Winston Churchill, prime minister, 1940–1945, 1951–1955) Elizabeth II, 1952–	Manual Azafia, 1936 Francisco Franco, 1938–1975
	John XXIII, 1958–1963 Paul VI, 1963–1978	Charles de Gaulle, 1959–1969 George J.R. Pompidou, 1969–1974 Valéry Giscard d'Estaing, 1974–1981		King Juan Carlos, 1975–
21st	John Paul I, 1978 John Paul II, 1978–	Francois Mitterand 1981–1995 Jacques Chirac 1995–		

POLAND	GERMANY	ITALY	UNITED STATES OF AMERICA
			Andrew Johnson, 1865–1869
			Ulysses S. Grant, 1869–1877
			Rutherford B. Hayes, 1877–1881
	Frederick III, 1888–1928	Umberto I, 1878–1900	James A. Garfield, 1881
			Chester A. Arthur, 1881–1885
			Grover Cleveland, 1885–1889; 1893–1897
			Benjamin Harrison, 1889–1893
		Victor Emmanuel III, 1900–1946	William McKinley, 1897–1901
			Theodore Roosevelt, 1901–1909
			William Howard Taft, 1909–1913
Ignace Paderewski, 1919–1921			Woodrow Wilson, 1913–1921
Gabriel Narutowicz, 1922			
Stanislas Wojchiechowski, 1922–1926	Frederich Ebert, 1919–1925	(Benito Mussolini, prime minister, 1922–1943)	Warren Gamaliel Harding, 1921–1923
Ignace Moscicki, 1926–1939			Calvin Coolidge, 1923–1929
Wladyslaw Raczkiewicaz, 1939–1947	Paul von Hindenburg, 1925–1934		Herbert Hoover, 1929–1933
August Zaleski, 1947–1972	Adolf Hitler, 1934–1945		Franklin Delano Roosevelt, 1933–1945
Stanislaw Ostrowski, 1972–1979			Harry S. Truman, 1945–1953
Edward Raczynski, 1979–1986			
Kazimieri Sabbat, 1986–1989			
Ryszard Kaczorowski, 1989–1990			
Lech Walesa, 1990–1995			
Aleksander Kwasniewski, 1995–			
	WEST GERMANY		
	Theodor Hess, 1949–1959	Umberto II, 1946	
	Heinrich Lübke, 1959–1969	Enrico de Micola, 1946–1948	Dwight David Eisenhower, 1953–1961
	Gustav Heinemann, 1969–1974	Luigi Einaudi, 1948–1955	
	Walter Scheel, 1974–1979	Giovanni Gronchi, 1955–1962	John Fitzgerald Kennedy, 1961–1963
	Karl Carstens, 1979–1984	Antonio Segni, 1962–1964	Lyndon Baines Johnson, 1963–1969
	Richard von Weizsacker, 1984–1994	Giuseppe Saragat, 1964–1971	Richard Milhous Nixon, 1969–1974
	Roman Herzog 1994–1999	Giovanni Leone, 1971–1978	Gerald Rudolph Ford, 1974–1977
	Johannes Rau 1999–	Sandro Pertini, 1978–1985	Jimmy Carter, 1977–1981
			Ronald Reagan, 1981–1989
		Francesco Cossiga, 1985–1992	George H. W. Bush, 1989–1993
		Oscar Luigi Scalfaro, 1992–1999	William J. Clinton, 1993–2001
		Carlo Azeglio Ciampi, 1999–	George W. Bush, 2001–

THE ROMAN CALENDAR

The calendar of the Roman Rite of the Catholic Church was thoroughly revised after the Second Vatican Council. Pope Paul VI announced his approval of the reorganization of the liturgical year and calendar in 1969, declaring that the purpose was "no other . . . than to permit the faithful to communicate in a more intense way, through faith, hope and love, in the whole mystery of Christ."

In the ecclesiastical year presented here, all the revisions pertaining to the universal Church, have been incorporated. Included also are the saints who are traditionally honored on certain days, either locally or universally, but who are not in the liturgical calendar for the universal Church.

The names of saints who are celebrated liturgically in the universal Church are in capital letters. The names of saints celebrated liturgically but only in certain areas are in lower-case letters and are italicized. The saints who are traditionally honored on certain days but are not liturgically celebrated are in lower-case letters. Names appearing with an asterisk (*) are those of saints from the United States.

KEY

RANKS:
Solemnity	SOL
Feast	FEAST
Memorial	MEM
Optional Memorial	OPT MEM

ABBREVIATIONS:

abt.	abbot(s)		m.	martyr(s)
abs.	abbess(es)		mat.	matron(s)
bp.	bishop(s)		pat.	patriarch
cnf.	confessor(s)		p.	pope
dea.	deacon(s)		pr.	priest(s)
dr.	doctor(s)		rel.	religious
evang.	evangelist		v.	virgin(s)
her.	hermit		wd.	widow
k.	king			

JANUARY

1 SOLEMNITY OF MARY, MOTHER OF GOD   SOL
   Concordius, m.; Felix of Bourger; Almachius or Telemachus, m.; Euphrosyne, v.; Eugendus or Oyend, abt.; William of Saint Benignus, abt.; Fulgentius, bp.; Clarus, abt.; Peter of Atroa, abt.; Odilo, abt.; Franchea, v. Guiseppe Maria Tomasi

2 BASIL THE GREAT and GREGORY NAZIANZEN, bps., drs.   MEM
   Macarius of Alexandria; Munchin, bp.; Vincentian; Adalhard or Adelard, abt.; Caspar del Bufalo.

3 Antherus, p. m.; Peter Balsam, m.; Geneviève, v.; Bertilia of Mereuil, wd.
4 *Elizabeth Ann Seton*★
   Gregory of Langres, bp.; Pharaïldis, v.; Rigobert of Rheims, bp.
5 *John Neumann,* bp.★
   Apollinaris Syncletica, v.; Syncletica, v.; Simeon Stylites; Convoyon, abt.; Dorotheus the Younger, abt.; Gerlac.
6 EPIPHANY   SOL
   John of Ribera, bp.; Charles Melchior from Sezze, rel.; Raphaela Maria Porras of the Sacred Heart of Jesus, v.; Wiltrudis, wd.; Erminold, abt.; Guarinus or Guérin, bp.
7 Raymond of Peñafort   OPT MEM
   Lucian of Antioch, m.; Valentine, bp.; Tillo; Aldric, bp.; Reinold; Canute Lavard; Kentigerna, wd.
8 Apollinaris of Hierapolis, bp.; Lucian of Beauvais, m.; Severinus of Noricum; Severinus of Septempeda, bp.; Erhard, bp.; Gudula, v.; Pega, v.; Wulsin, bp.; Thorfinn, bp.
9 Marciana, v., m.; Julian, Basilissa and Companions, m.; Peter of Sebaste, bp.; Waningus or Vaneng; Adrian of Canterbury, abt.; Berhtwald of Canterbury, abt.
10 Marcian; John the Good, bp.; Agatho, p.; Peter Orseolo; William, bp.
11 Theodosius the Cenobiarch; Salvius or Sauve, bp.
12 Arcadius, m.; Tigirius and Eutropius, m.; Caesaria, v.; Victorian, abt.; Benedict or Benet Biscop, bp.; Antony Pucci, pr.
13 HILARY, bp., dr.   OPT MEM
   Agrecius or Agritius, bp.; Berno, abt.
14 *Felix Nola,* cnf.
   Macrina the Elder, wd.; Barbasymas and Companions, m.; Datius, bp.; Kentigern or Mungo, bp.; Sava, bp.
15 *Paul the First Hermit,* cnf.; *Maur,* abt.; Macarius the Elder; Isidore of Alexandria; John Calybites; Ita, v.; Bonet or Bonitus, bp.; Ceowulf.
16 *Marcellus I,* p.
   Priscilla, mat.; Honoratus, bp.; Fursey, abt.; Henry of Cocket; Berard and Companions, m.
17 ANTHONY, abt.   MEM
   Speusippus, Eleusippus and Meleusippus, m.; Genulf or Genou, bp.; Julian Sabas, her.; Sabinus of Piacenza, bp.; Richimir, abt.; Sulpicius II or Sulpice.
18 *Prisca,* v., m.
   Volusian, bp.; Deicolus or Desle, abt.
19 *Canute or Knute,* k., m.
   Germanicus, m.; Nathalan, bp.; Albert of Cashel, bp.; Fillan or Foelan, abt.; Wulstan, bp.; Henry of Uppsala, bp., m.
20 FABIAN, p., m.   OPT MEM
   SEBASTIAN, m.   OPT MEM
   Euthymius the Great, abt.; Fechin, abt. Eustochia Calafato
21 AGNES, v., m.   MEM
   Fructuosus of Tarragona, bp., m.; Patroclus, m.; Epiphanius of Pavia, bp.; Meinrad, m.; Alban Roe, pr., m.
22 VINCENT, dea., m.   OPT MEM
   Anastasius, m.
   Blesilla, wd.; Dominic of Sora, abt.; Berhtwald, bp.; Valerius of Saragossa; Vincent Pallotti, pr.
23 *Emerentiana,* v., m.
   Asclas, m.; Agathangelus and Clement, m.; John the Almsgiver, pat.; Ildephonsus, bp.; Bernard or Barnard, bp.; Lufthildis, v.; Maimbod, m.
24 FRANCIS DE SALES, bp., dr.   MEM
   Babylas, bp., m.; Felician, bp., m., and Messalina, m.; Macedonius.
25 CONVERSION OF PAUL, APOSTLE   FEAST
   Artemas, m.; Juventinus and Maximinus, m.; Publius, abt.; Apollo, abt.; Praejectus or Prix, bp., m.; Poppo, abt.

26 TIMOTHY AND TITUS, bp.   MEM
    Paula, wd.; Conan, bp.; Alberic, abt.; Eystein, bp.; Margaret of Hungary, v.
27 ANGELA MERICI, v.   OPT MEM
    Julian of Le Mans, bp.; Marius or May, abt.; Vitalian, p.
28 THOMAS AQUINAS, pr., dr.   MEM
    Peter Nolasco, cnf.
    John of Reomay, abt.; Paulinus of Aquileia, bp.; Charlemagne; Amadeus, bp.; Peter
    Thomas, bp.
29 Sabinian, m.; Gildas the Wise, abt.; Sulpicius "Severus," bp.
30 *Martina,* v., m.
    Barsimaeus, bp.; Bathildis, wd.; Aldegundis, v.; Adelelmus or Aleaume, abt.; Hyacintha
    Mariscotti, v. Mutien Marie Wiaux
31 JOHN BOSCO, pr.   MEM
    Cyrus and John, m.; Marcella, wd.; Aidan or Maedoc of Ferns, bp.; Adamnan of
    Coldingham; Ulphia, v.; Eusebius, m.; Nicetas of Novgorod, bp.; Francis Xavier Bianchi.
Sunday after Jan. 6: BAPTISM OF THE LORD   FEAST
Sunday within the octave of Christmas: HOLY FAMILY   FEAST

FEBRUARY

 1 Pionius, m.; Brigid or Bride, v.; Sigebert III of Austrasia; John "of the Grating," bp.;
    Henry Morse, pr., m.
 2 PRESENTATION OF THE LORD   FEAST
    Adalbald of Ostrevant, m.; Joan of Lestonnac, wd.
 3 BLASE, bp., m.   OPT MEM
    ANSGAR, bp.   OPT MEM
    Laurence of Spoleto, bp.; Ia, v.; Laurence of Canterbury, bp.; Werburga, v.; Anskar, bp.;
    Margaret "of England," v.; Aelred of Rievaulx, abt.
 4 *Andrew Corsini,* bp., cnf.
    Theopilus the Penitent; Phileas, bp., m.; Isidore of Pelusium, abt.; Modan, abt.; Nicholas
    Studites, abt.; Rembert, bp.; Joan of Valois, mat.; Joseph of Leonessa; John de Britto, m.
 5 AGATHA, v., m.   MEM
    Avitus of Vienne, bp.; Bertoul or Bertulf; Indractus and Dominica, m.; Vodalus or Voel;
    Adelaide of Bellich, v.; The Martyrs of Japan: Peter Baptist, Martin de Aguirre, Francis
    Blanco, Francis-of-St.-Michael, Philip de las Casas, Gonsalo Garcia, Paul Miki, John
    Goto, James Kisai, Caius Francis, Francis of Miako, Leo Karasuma, Louis Ibarki, Antony
    Deynan, and Thomas Kasaki.
 6 PAUL MIKI AND COMPANION MARTYRS   MEM
    Mel and Melchu, bp.; Vedast or Vaast, bp.; Amand, bp.; Guarinus, bp.; Hildegund, wd.
 7 Adaucus, m.; Theodore of Heraclea, m.; Moses, bp.; Richard, "King"; Luke the Younger.
 8 JEROME EMILIANI   OPT MEM
    John of Matha, cnf.
    Nicetius or Nizier of Besançon, bp.; Elfleda, v.; Meingold, m.; Cuthman; Stephen of
    Muret, abt.
 9 *Apollonia,* v., m.
    Nicephorus, m.; Sabinus of Canosa, bp.; Teilo, bp.; Ansbert, bp.; Alto, abt.
10 SCHOLASTICA, v.   MEM
    Soteris, v., m.; Trumwin, bp.; Austreberta, v.; William of Maleval.
11 OUR LADY OF LOURDES   OPT MEM
    Saturninus, Dativus and Companions, m.; Lucius, bp., m.; Lazarus, bp.; Severinus, abt.;
    Caedmon; Gregory II, p.; Benedict of Aniane, abt.; Paschal I, p.
12 Marina, v.; Julian the Hospitaler; Meletius, bp.; Ethelwald, bp.; Antony Kauleas, bp.;
    Ludan.
13 Polyeuctus, m.; Martinian the Hermit; Stephen of Rieti, abt.; Modomnoc; Licinius or
    Lesin, bp.; Ermengild or Ermenilda, wd.; Catherine dei Ricci, v.

14 CYRIL, MONK AND METHODIUS, bp.   MEM
    John Baptist of the Conception (John García), pr.
    Valentine, pr., m.
    Abraham, bp.; Maro, abt.; Auxentius; Conran, bp.; Antonius of Sorrento, abt.; Adolf, bp.
15 Agpae, v., m.; Walfrid, abt.; Tanco or Tatto, bp., m.; Sigfrid, bp.
16 Onesimus, m.; Juliana, v., m.; Elias, Jeremy and Companions, m.; Gilbert of
    Sempringham.
17 SEVEN FOUNDERS OF THE ORDER OF SERVITES   OPT MEM
    Theodulus and Julian, m.; Loman, bp.; Fintan of Cloneenagh, abt.; Finan, bp.; Evermod,
    bp.; Silvin, bp.
18 *Simeon,* bp., m.
    Leo and Paregorius, m.; Flavian, bp., m.; Helladius, bp.; Colman of Lindisfarne, bp.;
    Angilbert, abt.; Theotonius, abt.
19 Mesrop, bp.; Barbatus, bp.; Beatus of Liebana; Boniface of Lausanne, bp.; Conrad of
    Piacenza.
20 Tyrannio, Zenobius and Companions, m.; Sadoth, bp., m.; Eleutherius of Tournai, bp.;
    Eucherius of Orléans, bp.; Wulfric.
21 PETER DAMIAN, bp., dr.   OPT MEM
    Severian, bp., m.; Germanus of Granfel, m.; George of Amastris, bp.; Robert Southwell,
    pr., m.
22 CHAIR OF PETER, APOSTLE   FEAST
    Thalassius and Limnaeus; Baradates; Margaret of Cortona.
23 POLYCARP, bp., m.   MEM
    Serenus the Gardener or Cerneuf of Billom, m.; Alexander Akimetes; Dositheus; Boisil
    or Boswell, abt.; Milburga and Mildgytha, v.; Willigis, bp.
24 Montanus, Lucius and Companions, m.; Praetextatus or Prix, bp., m.
25 Victorinus and Companions, m.; Caesarius Nazianzen; Ethelbert of Kent; Walburga, v.;
    Tarasius, bp.; Gerland, bp.
26 Nestor, bp., m.; Alexander of Alexandria, bp.; Porphyry, bp.; Victor or Vittre the Hermit.
27 *Gabriel of Our Lady of Sorrows,* cnf.
    Besas, Cronion and Julian, m.; Thalelaeus the Hermit; Leander, bp.; Baldomerus or
    Galmier; Alnoth; John of Gorze, abt.; Ann Line, m.
28 Proterius, bp., m.; Romanus and Lupicinus, abt.; Hilarus, p.; Oswald of Worcester, bp.

                                   MARCH

1   David or Dewi, bp.; Felix II(III), p.; Albinus or Aubin of Angers, bp.; Swithbert, bp.;
    Rudesind or Rosendo, bp.
2   Chad or Ceadda, bp.
3   Marinus and Astyrius, m.; Chelidonius and Emeterius, m.; Arthelais, v.; Non or
    Nonnita; Winwaloe or Guénolé, abt.; Anselm of Nonantola, abt.; Cunegund, wd.;
    Gervinus, abt.; Aelred of Rievaulx, abt. Teresa Eustochio Verzeri.
4   CASIMIR, cnf.   OPT MEM
    Adrian and Companions; Peter of Cava, bp.
5   Adrian and Eubulus, m.; Phocas of Antioch, m.; Eusebius of Cremona; Gerasimus, abt.;
    Ciaran or Kieran of Saighir, bp.; Piran, abt.; Virgil of Arles, bp.; John Joseph of the Cross.
6   Fridolin, abt.; Cyneburga, Cyneswide and Tibba; Chrodegang, bp.; Balred and Bilfred;
    Cadroe or Cadroel, abt.; Ollegarius or Oldegar, bp.; Cyril of Constantinople; Colette, v.
    Agnes of Bohemia.
7   PERPETUA AND FELICITY, m.   MEM
    Paul the Simple; Drausius or Drausin, bp.; Esterwine, abt.; Ardo; Theophylact, bp.
8   JOHN OF GOD, rel.   OPT MEM
    Pontius; Philemon and Apollonius, m.; Senan, bp.; Felix of Dunwich, bp.; Julian of
    Toledo, bp.; Humphrey or Hunfrid, bp.; Duthac, bp.; Veremund, abt.; Stephen of
    Obazine, abt.

9 FRANCES OF ROME, rel.   OPT MEM
   Pacian, bp.; Gregory of Nyssa, bp.; Bosa, bp.; Catherine of Bologna, v.; Dominic
   Savio.
10 Codratus and Companions, m.; Marcarius of Jerusalem, bp.; Simplicius, p.; Kessog, bp.,
   m.; Anastasia Patricia, v.; Droctoveus or Drotté, abt.; Attalas, abt.; Himelin; John Ogilvie,
   pr., m.
11 Constantine, m.; Sophronius, bp.; Vindician, bp.; Benedict Crispus, bp.; Oengus or
   Aengus, abt.-bp.; Eulogius of Cordova, m.; Aurea, v.; Teresa Margaret Redi, v.
12 Maximilian of Theveste, m.; Peter, Gorgonius and Dorotheus, m.; Paul Aurelian, bp.;
   Theophanes the Chronicler, abt.; Alphege of Winchester, bp.; Bernard of Capua, bp.;
   Fina or Seraphina, v.
13 Euphrasia or Euphraxia, v.; Mochoemoc, abt.; Gerald of Mayo, abt.; Nicephorus of
   Constantinople, bp.; Ansovinus, bp.; Heldrad, abt.; Roderic and Solomon, m.
14 Leobinus or Lubin, bp.; Eutychius or Eustathius, m.; Matilda, wd.
15 Longinus, m.; Matrona, v., m.; Zachary, p.; Leocritia or Lucretia, v., m.; Louise de
   Marillac, wd.; Clement Mary Hofbauer.
16 Julian of Antioch, m.; Abraham Kidunia; Finnian Lobhar, abt.; Eusebia, abs.; Gregory
   Makar, bp.; Heribert, bp.
17 PATRICK, bp.   OPT MEM
   Joseph of Arimathea; Agricola, bp.; Gertrude of Nivelles, v.; Paul of Cyprus; The Martyrs
   of the Serapeum. Jan Sarkander.
18 CYRIL OF JERUSALEM, bp., dr.   OPT MEM
   Alexander of Jerusalem, bp., m.; Frigidian or Frediano, bp.; Edward the Martyr; Anselm
   of Lucca, bp.; Salvator of Horta.
19 JOSEPH, HUSBAND OF MARY   SOL
   John of Panaca; Landoald and Companions; Alcmund, m.
20 Photina and Companions, m.; Martin of Braga, bp.; Cuthbert, bp.; Herbert; Wulfram,
   bp.; The Martyrs of Mar Saba.
21 Serapion, bp.; Enda, abt.
22 Paul of Narbonne and Companions; Basil of Ancyra, m.; Deogratias, bp.; Benvenuto of
   Osimo, bp.; Nicholas of Flue; Nicholas Owen, m.
23 TURIBIUS DE MONGROVEJO, bp.   OPT MEM
   Victorian and Companions, m.; Benedict the Hermit; Ethelwald or Oidilwald the
   Hermit; Joseph Oriol.
24 Irenaeus of Sirmium, bp., m.; Aldemar, abt.; Catherine of Vadstena, v.; Simon of Trent
   and William of Norwich.
25 ANNUNCIATION OF THE LORD   SOL
   Dismas; Barontius; Hermenland, abt.; Alfwold, bp.; Lucy Filippini, v.; Margaret
   Clitherow, m.
26 Castulus, m.; Félix of Trier, bp.; Macartan, bp.; Braulio, bp.; Ludger, bp.; Basil the
   Younger.
27 John of Egypt.
28 Guntramnus; Tutilo.
29 Barachisius and Jonas, m.; Cyril of Heliopolis, m., and Mark, bp.; Armogastes,
   Archinimus and Saturus, m.; Gundleus and Gwaladys or Gladys; Rupert, bp.; Berthold;
   Ludolf, bp.
30 Regulus or Rieul, bp.; John Climacus, abt.; Zosimus, bp.; Osburga, v.; Leonardo
   Murialdo, pr.
31 Balbina, v.; Acacius or Achatius, bp.; Benjamin, m.; Guy of Pomposa, abt.

APRIL

1 Melito, bp.; Walaricus or Valery, abt.; Macarius the Wonder-Worker; Hugh of Grenoble,
   bp.; Hugh of Bonnevaux, abt.; Gilbert of Caithness, bp.; Catherine of Palma, v.
2 FRANCIS OF PAOLA, h.   OPT MEM

Apphian and Theodosia, m.; Mary of Egypt; Nicetius or Nizier of Lyons, bp.; Ebba the Younger, v.; John Paine, pr., m.

3   Pancras of Taormina, bp., m.; Sixtus or Xystus I, p., m.; Agape, Chionia and Irene, v., m.; Burgundofara or Fare, v.; Nicetas, abt.; Richard Wyche or Richard of Chichester, bp.; Luigi Scrosoppi.

4   ISIDORE, bp., dr.   OPT MEM
Agathopus and Theodulus, m.; Tigernach, bp.; Plato, abt.; Benedict the Black.

5   VINCENT FERRER, pr.   OPT MEM
Derfel Gadarn; Ethelburga of Lyminge, mat.; Gerald of Sauve-Majeure, abt.; Albert of Montecorvino, bp.

6   The Martyrs in Persia; Marcellinus, m.; Celestine I, p.; Eutychius, bp.; Prudentius of Troyes, bp.; William of Eskhill, abt.

7   JOHN BAPTISTE DE LA SALLE, pr.   MEM
Hegesippus Aphraates; George the Younger, bp.; Celsus or Ceallach, bp.; Aybert; Henry Walpole, pr., m.

8   Dionysius of Corinth, bp.; Perpetuus, bp.; Walter of Pontoise, abt.; Julie Billiart, v.

9   Mary of Cleophas, mat.; Waldetrudis or Waudru, wd.; Hugh of Rouen, bp.; Gaucherius, abt.

10 Bademus, abt.; The Martyrs under the Danes; Macarius or Macaire of Ghent; Fulbert, bp.; Paternus of Abdinghof; Michael de Sanctis.

11 STANISLAUS, bp., m.   MEM
Barsanuphius; Isaac of Spoleto; Godeberta, v.; Guthlac; Gemma Galgani, v.

12 Julius I, p.; Zeno of Verona, bp.; Sabas the Goth, m.; Alferius, abt.

13 MARTIN I, p., m.   OPT MEM
Hermenegild, m.
Agathonica, Papylus and Carpus, m.; Martius or Mars, abt.

14 *Tiburtius, Valerius and Maximus*, m.
Ardalion, m.; Lambert of Lyons, bp.; Bernard of Tiron, abt.; Caradoc; Bénezet; Antony, Eustace and John, m.; Lidwina of Schiedam, v.

15 Basilissa and Anastasia, m.; Padarn or Patern, bp.; Ruadan of Lothra, abt.; Hunna or Huva, mat.

16 Optatus and Companions and Encratis, v., m.; Turibius of Astorga, bp.; Paternus or Pair, bp.; Fructuosus of Braga, bp.; Magnus, m.; Drogo or Druon; Contardo; Joseph Benedict Labre; Bernadette Soubirous, v.

17 Mappalicus and Companions, m.; Innocent of Tortona, bp.; Donnan and Companions, m.; Robert of Chaise-Dieu, abt.; Stephen Harding, abt.

18 Apolonius the Apologist, m.; Laserian, Laisren or Molaisse, bp.; Idesbald, abt.; Galdinus, bp.

19 Leo IX, p.; Expeditus; Ursmar, abt., bp.; Geroldus; Alphege, bp., m.

20 Marcellinus of Embrun, bp.; Marcian or Marian; Caedwalla; Hildegund, v.; Agnes of Montepulciano, v.

21 ANSELM, bp., dr.   OPT MEM
Simeon Barsabae, bp., and Companions, m.; Anastasius I of Antioch, bp.; Bueno, abt.; Malrubius or Maelrubba, abt.; Conrad of Parzham.

22 Epipodius and Alexander, m.; Leonides, m.; Agapitus I, p.; Theodore of Sykeon, bp.; Opportuna, v., abs.

23 GEORGE, m.   OPT MEM
Felix, Fortunatus and Achilleus, m.; Ibar, bp.; Gerard of Toul, bp.; Adalbert of Prague, bp., m.

24 FIDELIS OF SIGMARINGEN, pr., m.   OPT MEM
Mellitus, bp.; Ivo, bp.; Egbert; William Firmatus; Mary Euphrasia Pelletier, v.

25 MARK, EVANGELIST   FEAST
Anianus, bp.; Heribald, bp.

26 Peter of Braga, bp.; Richarius or Riquier, abt.; Paschasius Radbertus, abt.; Franca of Piacenza, v., abs.; Stephen of Perm, bp.

27 Anthimus, bp.; Asicus or Tassach, bp.; Maughold or Maccul, bp.; Floribert, bp.; Stephen Pechersky, bp.; Zita, v.; Turibius of Lima, bp.; Theodore the Sanctified, abt.
28 PETER CHANEL, pr., m.   OPT MEM
    Vitalis, m.
29 CATHERINE OF SIENA, v.   MEM
    Peter of Verona
    Wilfrid the Younger, bp.; The Abbots of Cluny: Berno, Odo, Mayeul, Odilo, Hugh, Aymard, and Peter the Venerable; Robert of Molesome, abt.; Joseph Cottolengo.
30 PIUS V, p.   OPT MEM
    Maximus, m.; Eutropius of Saintes, bp., m.; James and Marian, m.; Forannan, abt.; Gualfardus or Wolfhard.

MAY

1   JOSEPH THE WORKER   OPT MEM
    Amator or Amatre, bp.; Brioc or Brieuc, abt.; Sigismund of Burgundy; Marculf or Marcoul, abt.; Theodard of Narbonne, bp.; Peregrine Laziosi. Riccardo Pampuri.
2   ATHANASIUS, bp., dr.   MEM
    Exsuperius or Hesperus and Zoë, m.; Waldebert, abt.; Ultan, abt.; Wiborada, v., m.; Mafalda or Matilda.
3   PHILIP AND JAMES, APOSTLES   FEAST
    Alexander, Eventius and Theodulus, m.
    Juvenal, bp.
    Timothy and Maura, m.; Philip of Zell.
4   Cyriacus or Judas Quiricus, bp.; Pelagia of Tarsus, v., m.; John Houghton, Robert Lawrence, Augustine Webster, Richard Reynolds, pr., m.; Venerius, bp.; Godehard or Gothard, bp.; Florian, m.
5   Hilary of Aries, bp.; Maurantius, abt.; Mauruntius, abt.; Avertinus; Angelo, m.; Jutta, wd.
6   Evodius, bp.; Edbert, bp.; Petronax, abt.
7   Domitian, bp.; Liuhard, bp.; Serenicus and Serenus; John of Beverly, bp.
8   Victor Maurus, m.; Acacius or Agathus, m.; Gibrian; Desideratus, bp.; Boniface IV, p.; Benedict II, p.; Wiro, Plechlem and Oteger; Peter of Tarentaise, bp.
9   Beatus; Pachomius, abt.; Gerontius, bp.
10 *Antoninus of Florence,* bp., cnf.
    Gordian and Epimachus, m.
    Calepodius, m.; Alphius, Cyrinus and Philadelphus, m.; Catald and Conleth, bp.; Solangia, v., m.; John of Ávila, pr.
11 Mamertus, bp.; Comgall, abt.; Asaph, bp.; Gengulf or Gengoul; Majolus or Mayeule, abt.; Ansfrid, bp.; Walter of L'Esterp, abt.; Francis di Girolamo; Ignatius of Laconi.
12 NEREUS AND ACHILLES, m.   OPT MEM
    PANCRAS, m.   OPT MEM
    Epiphanius of Salamis, bp.; Modoaldus, bp.; Rictrudis, wd.; Germanus of Constantinople, bp.; Dominic of the Causeway.
13 Glyceris, v., m.; Mucius or Mocius, m.; Servatius or Servais, bp.; John the Silent; Erconwald, bp.; Euthymius the Illuminator, abt.; Peter Regalatus.
14 MATTHIAS, APOSTLE   FEAST
    Pontius, m.; Carthage, Carthach or Mochuda, abt.; Erembert, bp.; Michael Garicoïts; Mary Mazzarello, v.
15 *Isidore the Farmer*
    Torquatus and Companions, m.; Isidore of Chios; Hilary of Galeata, abt.; Dympna and Gerebernus, m.; Bertha and Rupert; Hallvard, m.; Isaias of Rostov, bp.; Peter of Lampsacus and Companions, m.
16 *Ubaldus,* bp., cnf.
    Peregrine of Auxerre, bp., m.; Possidius, bp.; Germerius, bp.; Brendan, abt.; Domnolus,

bp.; Carantoc or Carannog, abt.; Honoratus of Amiens, bp.; Simon Stock; John Nepomucen, m.; Andrew Hubert Fournet.

17 *Paschal Baylon,* cnf.
Madron or Madern; Bruno of Würzburg, bp.

18 JOHN I, p., m.   OPT MEM
Venantius, m.
Theodotus, Thecusa and Companions, m.; Potamon, bp., m.; Eric of Sweden, m.; Felix of Cantalice.

19 *Peter Morrone or Peter Celestine V,* her., p.
Pudentiana and Pudens, m.
Calocerus and Parthenius, m.; Dunstan, bp.; Ivo of Kermartin.

20 BERNARDINO OF SIENA, pr.   OPT MEM
Thalelaeus, m.; Basilla or Basilissa, v., m.; Baudelius, m.; Austregisilus or Outril, bp.; Ethelbert, m.

21 Godric; Andrew Bobola, m.; Theophilus of Corte. Eugene de Mazenod.

22 Aemilius and Castus, m.; Quiteria, v., m.; Romanus; Julia, m.; Aigulf or Ayoul, bp.; Humility, wd.; Rita, wd.

23 Desiderius or Didier, bp., m.; Guibert; Leonitus of Rostov, bp., m.; Ivo of Chartres, bp.; Euphrosyne of Polotsk, v.; William of Rochester, m.; John Baptist Rossi; Peter Fioretti.

24 Donatian and Rogatian, m.; Vincent of Lérins; David I, King of Scotland; Nicetas of Pereaslav, m.

25 BEDE, pr., dr.   OPT MEM
   GREGORY VII, p.   OPT MEM
   MARY MAGDALEN DE PAZZI, v.   OPT MEM
   Dionysius of Milan, bp.; Zenobius, bp.; Leo or Lyé, abt.; Aldhelm, bp.; Gennandius, bp.; Madeleine Sophie Barat, v.

26 PHILIP NERI, pr.   MEM
   Quadratus, bp.; Priscus or Prix and Companions, m.; Lambert of Vence, bp.; Marian of Quito, v.

27 AUGUSTINE OF CANTERBURY, bp.   OPT MEM
   Restituta of Sora, v., m.; Julius and Companions, m.; Eutropius of Orange, bp.; Melangell or Monacella, v.

28 Senator, bp.; Justus of Urgel, bp.; Germanus or Germain, bp.; William of Gellone; Bernard of Menthon or Montjoux; Ignatius of Rostov, bp.

29 Cyril of Caesarea, m.; Maximinus, bp.; Sisinnius, Martyrius and Alexander, m.; Theodosia, v., m.; William, Stephen, Raymund and Companions, m.

30 Isaac of Constantinople, abt.; Exsuperantius, bp.; Madelgisilus or Mauguille; Walstan; Ferdinand III, King of Castile; Joan of Arc, v.; Eleutherius, p.; Luke Kirby, pr., m.

31 VISITATION   FEAST
   Petronilla, v., m.
   Cantius, Cantianius and Cantianella, m.; Mechtildis of Edelstetten, v.

First Sunday after Pentecost: HOLY TRINITY   SOL
Thursday after Holy Trinity: CORPUS CHRISTI   SOL
Friday after Second Sunday after Pentecost: SACRED HEART   SOL
Saturday after Second Sunday after Pentecost: IMMACULATE HEART OF MARY

JUNE

1 JUSTIN, m.   MEM
Pamphilus and Companions, m.; Proculus, "the soldier," and Proculus of Bologna, bp.; Caprasius or Caprais; Wistan; Simeon of Syracuse; Eneco or Iñigo, abt.; Theobald of Alba.

2 MARCELLINUS AND PETER, m.   OPT MEM

Erasmus, bp., m.

Pothinus and Companions, m.; Eugenius I, p.; Stephen of Sweden, bp. m.; Nicholas the Pilgrim; Blandina, m.

3 CHARLES LWANGA AND COMPANIONS, m.   MEM
Cecilius; Pergentinus and Laurentinus, m.; Lucillian and Companions, m.; Clotilda, wd.; Liphardus and Urbicius, abt.; Kevin or Coegmen, abt.; Genesius of Clermont, bp.; Isaac of Córdova, m.; Morand.

4 *Francis Caracciolo,* cnf.
Quirinus, bp., m.; Metrophanes, bp.; Optatus of Milevis, bp.; Petroc, abt.; Vincentia Gerosa, v.

5 BONIFACE, bp., m.   MEM
Dorotheus of Tyre, m.; Sanctius or Sancho, m.

6 NORBERT, bp.   OPT MEM
Philip the Deacon; Ceratius or Céras, bp.; Eustorgius of Milan, bp.; Jarlath, bp.; Gudwal or Gurval; Claud, bp.

7 Paul of Constantinople, bp.; Meriadoc, bp.; Colman of Dromore, bp.; Vulflagius or Wulphy; Willibald, bp.; Gottschalk, m.; Robert of Newminster, abt.; Antony Gianelli, bp. Agostino Roscelli

8 Maximinus of Aix; Médard, bp.; Clodulf or Cloud, bp.; William of York, bp.

9 EPHREM, dea., dr.   OPT MEM
Primus and Felician, m.
Columba or Columcille, abt.; Vincent of Agen, m.; Pelagia of Antioch, v., m.; Richard of Andria, bp.

10 Getulius and Companions, m.; Ithamar, bp.; Landericus or Landry, bp.; Bogumilus, bp.

11 BARNABAS, APOSTLE   MEM
Felix and Fortunatus, m.; Parisio. Paula Frassinetti

12 *John of Sahagun,* cnf.
Antonina, m.; Onuphrius; Ternan, bp.; Peter of Mount Athos; Leo III, p.; Odulf; Eskil, bp., m.

13 ANTHONY OF PADUA, dr., pr.   MEM
Felicula, m.; Aquilina, m.; Triphyllius, bp.

14 Valerius and Rufinus, m.; Dogmael; Methodius I of Constantinople, bp.

15 *Vitus,* m.
Hesychius, m.; Tatian Dulas, m.; Orsieslus, abt.; Landelinus, abt.; Edburga of Winchester, v.; Bardo, bp.; Aleydis or Alice, v.; Germaine of Pibrac, v.

16 Ferreolus and Ferrutio, m.; Cyricus and Julitta, m.; Tychon, bp.; Aurelian, bp.; Benno, bp.; Lutgardis, v.; John Francis Regis.

17 Nicander and Marcian, m.; Bessarion; Hypatius, abt.; Avitus, abt.; Nectan; Hervé or Harvey, abt.; Botulf or Botolph, abt.; Adulf, bp.; Moling, bp.; Rainerius of Pisa; Teresa and Sanchia of Portugal; Emily de Vialar, v.; Albert.

18 *Mark and Marcellian,* m.
Gregory Barbarigo, bp.; Amandus, bp.; Elizabeth of Schönau, v.

19 ROMUALD, abt.   OPT MEM
Juliana of Falconieri, v.
Gervase and Protase, m.
Deodatus or Dié, bp.; Bruno or Boniface of Querfurt, bp., m.

20 *Silverius,* p.
Goban or Gobain, m.; Bagnus or Bain, bp.; Adalbert of Magdeburg, bp.; John of Maters, abt.

21 ALOYSIUS GONZAGA, rel.   MEM
Eusebius of Samosata, bp.; Alban or Albinus of Mainz, m.; Méen or Mewan, abt.; Engelmund; Leutfridus or Leufroy, abt.; Ralph or Raoul, bp.; John Rigby, m.

22 PAULINUS OF NOLA, bp.   OPT MEM
JOHN FISHER, bp., m. and THOMAS MORE, m.   OPT MEM

Alban, m.; Nicetas of Remesiana, bp.; Eberhard, bp.

23 Agrippina, v., m.; Etheldreda or Audrey, wd.; Lietbertus or Libert, bp.; Joseph Cafasso; Thomas Garnet, pr., m.

24 THE BIRTH OF JOHN THE BAPTIST   SOL
The martyrs under Nero; Simplicius, bp.; Bartholomew of Farne.

25 *William of Vercelli,* abt.
Febronia, v., m.; Gallicanus; Prosper of Aquitaine; Prosper of Reggio, bp.; Maximus of Turin, bp.; Moloc or Luan, bp.; Adalbert of Egmond; Eurosia, v., m.; Gohard, bp., and Companions, m.

26 *John and Paul.*
Vigilius, bp., m.; Maxentius, abt.; Salvius or Sauve and Superius; John of the Goths; Pelagius or Pelayo, m.; Anthelm, bp. Josemarie Escriva.

27 CYRIL OF ALEXANDRIA, bp., dr.   OPT MEM
Zoilus and Companions, m.; Samson of Constantinople; John of Chinon; George Mtasmindeli of the Black Mountains, abt.; Ladislaus of Hungary; Benvenuto of Gubbio.

28 IRENAEUS, bp., m.   MEM
Plutarch, Potamiaena and Companions, m.; Paul I, p.; Heimrad; Sergius and Germanus of Valaam, abt.; John Southworth, pr., m.

29 PETER AND PAUL, Apostles.   SOL
Cassius, bp.; Salome and Judith; Emma, wd.

30 FIRST MARTYRS OF THE CHURCH OF ROME   OPT MEM
The Commemoration of Paul, Apostle.
Martial, bp.; Bertrand of Le Mans, bp.; Erentrude, v.; Theobald or Thibaud of Provins.

JULY

1 Shenute, abt.; Theodoric or Thierry, abt.; Carilefus or Calais, abt.; Gall of Clermont, bp.; Eparchius or Cybard; Simeon Salus; Serf or Servanus, bp.; Oliver Plunkett, bp., m.

2 *Processus and Martinian,* m.
Monegundis, wd.; Otto of Bamberg, bp.

3 THOMAS, Apostle.   FEAST
Leo II, p., cnf.
Anatolius, bp.; Irenaeus and Mustiola, m.; Julius and Aaron, m.; Heliodorus, bp.; Anatolius of Constantinople, bp.; Rumold or Rombaut, m.; Bernardino Realino.

4 ELIZABETH OF PORTUGAL   OPT MEM
Bertha, wd.; Andrew of Crete, bp.; Odo of Canterbury, bp.; Ulric of Augsburg, bp.

5 ANTHONY ZACCARIA, pr.   OPT MEM
Athanasius the Athonite, abt.

6 MARIA GORETTI, v., m.   OPT MEM
Romulus of Fiesole, bp., m.; Dominica, v., m.; Sisoes; Goar; Sexburga, wd.; Modwenna, v.; Godelva, m.

7 Pantaenus; Palladius, bp.; Félix of Nantes, bp.; Ethelburga, Ercongota and Sethrida, v.; Hedda, bp.

8 Aquila and Prisca; Procopius, m.; Kilian and Companions, m.; Withburga, v.; Adrian III, p.; Grimbald; Sunniva and Companions; Raymund of Toulouse.

9 Everild, v.; The Martyrs of Gorkum: Nicholas Pieck, Jerome Weerden, Leonard Vechel, Nicholas Janssen, Godfrey van Duynen, John van Oosterwyk, John van Hoornaer, Adrian van Hilvarenbeek, James Lacops, Andrew Wouters, Antony van Willehad, and Nicasius van Heeze; Veronica Giuliani, v.

10 *Rufina and Secunda,* v., m.
Amalburga, wd.; Amalburga, v.; Antony and Theodosius of Pechersk, abt.

11 BENEDICT, abt.   MEM
Drostan, abt.; John of Bergamo, bp.; Hidulf, bp.; Olga, wd.

12 *John Gualbert,* abt.

Nabor and Felix, m.

Veronica; Jason, m.; Hermagoras and Fortunatus, m.; John the Iberian, abt.; John Jones, pr., m.

13 HENRY THE EMPEROR   OPT MEM
Silas or Silvanus; Maura and Brigid; Eugenius of Carthage, bp.; Mildred, v.; James of Voragine, bp.; Francis Solano.

14 CAMILLUS DE LELLIS, pr.   OPT MEM
Deusdedit, bp.; Marchelm; Ulric of Zell, abt.

15 BONAVENTURE, bp., dr.   MEM
James of Nisibis, bp.; Barhadbesaba, m.; Donald; Swithun, bp.; Athanasius of Naples, bp.; Edith of Polesworth; Vladimir of Kiev; David of Munktorp, bp.; Pompilio Pirrotti.

16 OUR LADY OF MOUNT CARMEL   OPT MEM
Athenogenes, bp., m.; Eustathius of Antioch, bp.; Helier, m.; Reineldis, v., m.; Fulrad, abt.

17 Speratus and Companions, the Scillitan Martyrs; Marcellina, v.; Ennodius, bp.; Kenelm; Leo IV, p.; Clement of Okhrida and Companions, the Seven Apostles of Bulgaria; Nerses Lampronazi, bp.; Mary Magdalen Postel.

18 Pambo; Philastrius, bp.; Arnulf or Arnoul of Metz, bp.; Frederick of Utrecht, bp., m.; Bruno of Segni, bp.

19 Justa and Rufina, v., m.; Arsenius; Symmachus, p.; Ambrose Autpert; Macrina the Younger, v.; William John Plessington, pr., m.

20 Wilgefortis or Liberta; Joseph Barsabas; Aurelius, bp.; Flavian and Elias, bp.; Vulmar or Wulmar, abt.; Ansegisus, abt.

21 LAWRENCE OF BRINDISI, pr., dr.   OPT MEM
Praxedes, v.
Victor of Marseilles, m.; Arbogast, bp.

22 MARY MAGDALEN   MEM
Joseph of Palestine; Wandregisilus or Wandrille, abt.; Philip Evans and John Lloyd, pr., m.

23 BRIDGET, rel.   OPT MEM
Apollinaris of Ravenna, bp., m.
Liborius, bp.
The Three Wise Men; John Cassian, abt.; Romula and her Companions, v.; Anne or Susanna, v.

24 *Christina,* v., m.
Lewina, v., m.; Declan, bp.; Boris and Gleb, m.; Christina the Astonishing, v.; Christina of Tyre, v., m.; John Boste, pr., m.

25 JAMES THE APOSTLE   FEAST
Christopher, m.
Thea, Valentina and Paul, m.; Magnericus, bp.

26 JOACHIM AND ANN, PARENTS OF MARY   MEM
Simeon the Armenian; Bartholomea Capitanio, v.

27 *Pantaleon,* m.
The Seven Sleepers of Ephesus; Aurelius, Natalia, Felix and Companions, m.; Theobald of Marly, abt.

28 *Nazarius and Celsus,* m.
Samson, bp.; Botvid.

29 MARTHA, v.   MEM
Felix II, p.
Simplicius, Faustinus and Beatrice, m.
Lupus or Loup, bp.; Olaf, m.; William Pinchon, bp.

30 PETER CHRYSOLOGUS, bp., dr.   OPT MEM
Abdon and Sennen, m.
Julitta, wd., m.

31 IGNATIUS OF LOYOLA, pr.   MEM
    Neot; Helen of Skövde, wd.; Germanus of Auxerre, bp.; Justin de Jacobis, bp.

AUGUST

1   ALPHONSUS LIGUORI, bp., dr.   MEM
    The Holy Machabees, m.
    Faith, Hope, Charity, and their mother, Wisdom, m.; Aled, Almedha, or Eiluned, v., m.;
    Ethelwold, bp.; Peter Julian Eymard, pr.
2   EUSEBIUS OF VERCELLI, bp.   OPT MEM
    Stephen I, p., m.
    Theodota, m.; Thomas of Dover.
3   *The Finding of the Body of Stephen,* protomartyr.
    Waltheof of Walthen, abt.; Nicodemus.
4   JOHN VIANNEY, pr.   MEM
    Ia and Companions, m.; Molua or Lughaidh, abt.
5   DEDICATION OF ST. MARY MAJOR   OPT MEM
    Addai and Mari, bp.; Afra, m.; Nonna, mat.
6   THE TRANSFIGURATION OF OUR LORD   FEAST
    Justus and Pastor, m.; Hormisdas, p.
7   SIXTUS II, p., m., AND COMPANIONS, m.   OPT MEM
    CAJETAN, pr.   OPT MEM
    Donatus, bp., m.
    Claudia, mat.; Dometius the Persian, m.; Victricius, bp.; Albert of Trapani; Donatus of
    Besançon, bp.
8   DOMINIC, pr.   MEM
    Cyriacus, Largus and Smaragdus, m.
    The Fourteen Holy Helpers; Hormisdas, m.; Altman, bp. Edith Stein.
9   *Romanus,* m.
    Emygdius, m.; Nathy and Felim, bp.; Oswald of Northumbria, m.
10 LAWRENCE, dea., m.   FEAST
    Philomnea or Philumena.
11 CLARE, v.   MEM
    Tiburtius
    Susanna
    Alexander the Charcoal-Burner, bp., m.; Equitius, abt.; Blane, bp.; Attracta or Araght, v.;
    Lelia, v.; Gaugericus or Géry, bp.; Gerard of Gallinaro and Companions.
12 Euplus, m.; Murtagh or Muredach, bp.; Porcarius and Companions, m.
13 PONTIAN, p., m., and HIPPOLYTUS, pr., m.   OPT MEM
    Cassian, m.
    Simplician, bp.; Radegund, mat.; Maximus the Confessor, abt.; Benildi (Peter
    Romançon), rel.; Wigbert, abt.; Nerses Klaiëtsi, bp.
14 *Eusebius of Rome,* cnf.
    Marcellus of Apamea, bp., m.; Fachanan, bp.; Athanasia, mat.
15 ASSUMPTION OF MARY   SOL
    Tarsicius, m.; Arnulf or Arnoul of Soissons, bp.
16 STEPHEN OF HUNGARY, KING   OPT MEM
    Arsacius; Armel, abt.; Roch.
17 *Hyacinth,* cnf.
    Mamas, m.; Eusebius, p.; Liberatus and Companions, m.; Clare of Montefalco, v.
18 *Agapitus,* m.
    Florus and Laurus, m.; Helena, wd.; Alipius, bp.
19 JOHN EUDES, pr.   OPT MEM
    Andrew the Tribune, m.; Timothy, Agapius and Thecla, m.; Sixtus or Xystus III, p.;
    Mochta, abt.; Bertulf, abt.; Sebald; Louis of Anjou, bp.

20 BERNARD, abt., dr.   MEM
    Amadour; Oswin, m.; Philibert, abt.
21 PIUS X, p.   MEM
    Luxorius, Cisellus and Camerinus, m.; Bonosus and Maximian, m.; Sidonius
    Apollinaris, bp.; Abraham of Smolensk, abt.
22 QUEENSHIP OF MARY   MEM
    Timothy and Symphorianus, m.
    Sigfrid, abt.; Andrew of Fiesole; John Kemble and John Wall, pr., m.
23 ROSE OF LIMA, v.   OPT MEM
    Philip Benizi, cnf.
    Claudius, Asterius, Neon, Domnina and Theonilla, m.; Eugene or Eoghan, bp.
24 BARTHOLOMEW, Apostle.   FEAST
    The Martyrs of Utica; Audoenus or Ouen, bp.
25 LOUIS IX, KING, cnf.   OPT MEM
    JOSEPH CALASANZ, pr.   OPT MEM
    Genesius the Comedian, m.; Genesius of Arles; Patricia, v.; Mennas of Constantinople,
    bp.; Ebba the Elder, v.; Gregory of Utrecht, abt.; Joan Antide-Thouret, v.; Mary Michaela
    Desmaisières, v.
26 Joan Elizabeth Bichier des Ages, v.; Teresa of Jesus Jornet Ibars, v.
27 MONICA   MEM
    Marcellus and Companions, m.; Poemen, abt.; Caesarius of Arles, bp.; Syagrius, bp.;
    Hugh or Little Hugh of Lincoln; Margaret the Barefooted, wd.; David Lewis, pr., m.
28 AUGUSTINE, bp., dr.   MEM
    Hermes
    Julian of Brioude, m.; Alexander, John III, and Paul IV, bp.; Moses the Black; Edmund
    Arrowsmith, pr., m.; Joachim of Vedruña, rel.
29 BEHEADING OF JOHN THE BAPTIST, m.   MEM
    Sabina, m.
    Medericus or Merry, abt.
30 *Felix and Adauctus,* m.
    Pammachius; Rumon or Ruan; Fantinus, abt.; Margaret Ward, m.
31 *Raymond Nonnatus,* cnf.
    Paulinas of Trier, bp.; Aidan of Lindisfarne, bp.

                            SEPTEMBER

 1 *Giles,* abt.
    Verena, v.; Lupus or Leu, bp.; Fiacre; Sebbe; Drithelm; Beatrice de Silva Meneses, v.
 2 Antoninus of Apamea, m.; Castor, bp.; Agricolus, bp.; William of Roskilde, bp.; Brocard.
 3 GREGORY THE GREAT, p., dr.   MEM
    Phoebe; Macanisius, bp.; Simeon Stylites the Younger; Remaclus, bp.; Aigulf, m.;
    Hildelitha, v.; Cuthburga, wd.
 4 Marcellus and Valerian, m.; Marinus; Boniface I, p.; Ultan of Ardbraccan, bp.; Ida of
    Herzfeld, wd.; Rosalia, v.; Rose of Viterbo, v.
 5 *Lawrence of Justinian,* bp., cnf.
    Bertinus, abt.
 6 Donatian, Laetus and Companions, bp., m.; Eleutherius, abt.; Chainoaldes or Cagnoald,
    bp.; Bega or Bee, v.
 7 Regina or Reine, v., m.; Sozon, m.; Grimonia, v., m.; John of Nicomedia, m.; Anastasius
    the Fuller, m.; Cloud or Clodoald; Alcmund and Tilbert, bp.
 8 BIRTH OF MARY   FEAST
    Hadrian, Natalia, m.
    Eusebius, Nestabus, Zeno, and Nestor, m.; Disibod; Sergius I, p.; Corbinian, bp.
 9 *Peter Claver,* pr.*
    Gorgonius

Isaac or Sahak I, bp.; Ciaraa or Kieran, abt.; Audomarus or Omer, bp.; Bettelin.
10 *Nicholas of Tolentino,* cnf.
Nemesian and Companions, m.; Menodora, Metrodora, and Nymphodora, v., m.; Pulcheria, v.; Finnian of Moville, bp.; Salvius of Albi, bp.; Theodard, bp.; Aubert, bp.; Ambrose Barlow, pr., m.
11 *Protus and Hyacinth,* m.
Theodora of Alexandria; Paphnutius the Great, bp.; Patiens of Lyons, bp.; Deiniol, bp.; Peter of Chavanon; Bodo, bp.
12 Ailbhe, bp.; Eanswida, v.; Guy of Anderlecht.
13 JOHN CHRYSOSTOM, bp., dr.   MEM
Maurilius, bp.; Eulogius of Alexandria, bp.; Amatus, abt.; Amatus, bp.
14 TRIUMPH OF THE HOLY CROSS   FEAST
Maternus, bp.; Notburga, v.
15 OUR LADY OF SORROWS   MEM
Nicomedes, m.
Nicetas the Goth, m.; Aichardus or Archard, abt.; Mirin; Catherine of Genoa, wd.
16 CORNELIUS, p., m., and CYPRIAN, bp., m.   MEM
Euphemia, Lucy and Geminianus, m.
Abundius, Abundantius, and Companions, m.; Ninian, bp.; Ludmila, m.; Edith of Wilton, v.; John Macias, rel.
17 ROBERT BELLARMINE, bp., dr.   OPT MEM
Stigmata of Francis
Socrates and Stephen, m.; Satyrus; Lambert of Maestricht, bp., m.; Columba, v., m.; Hildegard, v.; Peter Arbues, m.; Francis of Camporosso.
18 *Joseph of Cupertino,* cnf.
Ferreolus, m.; Methodius of Olympus, bp., m.; Richardis, wd.; Ferreolus of Limoges, bp.
19 JANUARIUS, bp., m.   OPT MEM
Peleus and Companions, m.; Sequanus or Seine, abt.; Goericus or Abbo, bp.; Theodore of Tarsus, bp.; Mary of Cerevellon, v.; Theodore, David, and Constantine; Emily de Rodat, v. Alonso de Orozco
20 Vincent Madelgarius, abt. Martyrs of Korea
21 MATTHEW, Apostle and Evang.   FEAST
Maura of Troyes, v.; Michael of Chernigov and Theodore, m.
22 *Thomas of Villanova,* bp.
Maurice and Companions, m.
Phocas the Gardener, m.; Felix III (IV), p.; Salaberga, wd.; Emmeramus, bp.
23 Adamnan, abt.; Martha of Persia, v., m.
24 *Our Lady of Ransom*
Geremarus or Germer, abt.; Gerard of Csanad, bp., m.; Pacifico of San Severino.
25 Firminus, bp., m.; Cadoc, abt.; Aunacharius or Aunaire, bp., Finbar, bp.; Coelfrid, abt.; Albert of Jerusalem, bp.; Sergius of Radonezh, abt.; Vincent Strambi, bp.
26 COSMOS AND DAMIAN, m.   OPT MEM
Colman of Lann Elo, abt.; John of Meda; Nilus of Rossano, abt.; Therese Couderc (Marie Victoire Couderc), v.
27 VINCENT DE PAUL, pr.   MEM
Elzear.
28 WENCESLAUS, m.   OPT MEM
Exsuperius, bp.; Eustochium, v.; Faustus of Riez, bp.; Annemund, bp.; Lioba, v.
29 MICHAEL, GABRIEL, AND RAPHAEL, Archangels.   FEAST
Rhipsime, Gaiana, and Companions, v., m.; Theodota of Philippolis, m.
30 JEROME, pr., dr.   MEM
Gregory the Illuminator, bp.; Honorius of Canterbury, bp.; Simon of Crepy.

OCTOBER

1 THERESA OF THE CHILD JESUS, v.   MEM
   Remigius, bp., cnf.
   Romanus the Melodist; Melorus Melar or Mylor, m.; Bavo or Allowin.
2 GUARDIAN ANGELS   MEM
   Eleutherius, m.; Leodegarius or Leger, bp., m.
3 Hesychius; The Two Ewalds, m.; Gerard of Brogne, abt.; Froilan and Attilanus, bp.;
   Thomas of Hereford, bp.
4 FRANCIS OF ASSISI, cnf.   MEM
   Ammon; Petronius, bp.
5 Apollinaris of Valence, bp.; Galla, wd.; Magenulf or Meinulf; Flora of Beaulieu, v.;
   Aymard of Cluny, abt.
6 BRUNO, pr.   OPT MEM
   Faith, v., m.; Nicetas of Constantinople; Mary Frances of Naples, v.
7 OUR LADY OF THE ROSARY   MEM
   Mark, p.
   Justina, v., m.; Osyth, v., m.; Artaldus or Arthaud, bp.
8 *Marcellus*, m.
   Simeon; Pelagia the Penitent; Thaïs; Reparata, v., m.; Demetrius, m.; Keyne, v.
9 DENIS, bp., m., RUSTICUS and ELEUTHERIUS, m.   OPT MEM
   JOHN LEONARDI, pr.   OPT MEM
   Demetrius of Alexandria, bp.; Publia, wd.; Andronicus and Athanasia; Savin; Gislenus or
   Ghislain, abt.; Gunther; Louis Bertrand.
10 *Francis Borgia*, cnf.
   Gereon and Companions, m.; Eulampius and Eulampia, m.; Maharsapor, m.; Cerbonius,
   bp.; Paulinus of York, bp.; Daniel and Companions, m.
11 Andronicus, Tarachus and Probus, m.; Nectarius, bp.; Canice or Kenneth, abt.; Agilbert,
   bp.; Gummarus or Gommaire; Bruno the Great of Cologne, bp.; Alexander Sauli, bp.;
   Maria Desolata (Emmanuela Torres Acosta), v.
12 Maximilian, bp., m.; Felix and Cyprian and Companions; Edwin, m.; Ethelburga of
   Barking, v.; Wilfrid, bp.
13 *Edward the Confessor.*
   Faustus, Januarius, and Martial, m.; Comgan, abt.; Gerald of Aurillac; Coloman, m.;
   Maurice of Carnoët, abt.
14 CALLISTUS I, p., m.   OPT MEM
   Justus of Lyons, bp.; Manechildis, v.; Angadrisma or Angadrême, v.; Burchard, bp.;
   Dominic Lauricatus.
15 THERESA OF ÁVILA, v., dr.   MEM
   Leonard of Vandoeuvre, abt.; Thecla of Kitzingen, v.; Euthymius the Younger, abt.
16 HEDWIG, rel.   OPT MEM
   MARGARET MARY ALACOQUE, v.   OPT MEM
   Martinian and Companions and Maxima; Gall; Mommolinus, bp.; Bercharius, abt.; Lull,
   bp.; Anastasius of Cluny; Bertrand of Comminges, bp.; Gerard Majella.
17 IGNATIUS OF ANTIOCH, bp., m.   MEM
   John the Dwarf; Anstrudis or Anstrude, v.; Nothelm, bp.; Seraphino, cnf.; Richard
   Gwyn, m.
18 LUKE THE EVANGELIST   FEAST
   Justus of Beauvais, m.
19 ISAAC JOGUES, pr., m., and COMPANIONS, m.*   OPT MEM
   PAUL OF THE CROSS, pr.   OPT MEM
   Peter of Aicántara, cnf.
   Ptolemaeus and Lucius, m.; Cleopatra, wd., and Varus, n.; Ethbin; Aquilinus. bp.;
   Frideswide, v.; Philip Howard, m.

20 Caprasius, m.; Artemius, m.; Acca, bp.; Andrew of Crete, m.; Maria Bertilla (Ann Francis Boscardin), v.
21 *Hilarion,* abt.
   Malchus; Fintan or Munnu of Taghmon, abt.; Condedus; John of Bridlington.
22 Abercius, bp.; Philip of Heraclea, bp.; and Companions, m.; Mallonius or Mellon, bp.; Nunilo and Alodia, v., m.; Donatus of Fiesole, bp.
23 JOHN OF CAPISTRANO, pr.   OPT MEM
   Theodoret, m.; Severinus or Seurin, m.; Severinus Boethius, m.; Romanus of Rouen, bp.; Ignatius of Constantinople, bp.; Allucio.
24 ANTHONY CLARET, bp.   OPT MEM
   Felix of Thibiuca, bp., m.; Proclus, bp.; Aretas and the martyrs of Najran and Elesbaan; Senoch, abt.; Martin or Mark; Maglorius or Maelor, bp.; Martin of Vertou, abt.; Ebregislus or Evergislus, bp.
25 *Chrysanthus and Daria,* m.
   Crispin and Crispinian, m.; Fronto and George, bp.; Gaudentius, bp.
26 Lucian and Marcian, m.; Rusticus of Narbonne, bp.; Cedd, bp.; Eata, bp.; Bean, bp.
27 Frumentius, bp.; Otteran or Odhran, abt.
28 SIMON AND JUDE, Apostles.   FEAST
   Anastasia and Cyril, m.; Fidelis of Como, m.; Salvius or Saire, Faro, bp.
29 Narcissus of Jerusalem, bp.; Theuderius or Chef, abt.; Colman of Kilmacduagh, bp.; Abraham of Rostov, abt.
30 Serapion of Antioch, bp.; Marcellus, m.; Asterius, bp.; Germanus of Capua, bp.; Ethelnoth, bp.; Alphonsus Rodriguez.
31 Quentin or Quintinius, m.; Foillan, abt.; Wolfgang, bp.

NOVEMBER

1 ALL SAINTS   SOL
   Caesarius and Julian, m.; Benignus of Dijon, m.; Austremonius or Stremoine, bp.; Mary, v., m.; Maturinus or Mathurin; Marcellus of Paris, bp.; Vigor, bp.; Cadfan, abt.
2 ALL SOULS   OPT MEM
   Victorinus, bp., m.; Marcian.
3 MARTIN DE PORRES, rel.   OPT MEM
   Winifrid, v., m.; Rumwald; Hubert, bp.; Pirminus, bp.; Amicus; Malachy, bp.
4 CHARLES BORROMEO, bp.   MEM
   Vitalis and Agricola, m.
   Pierius; John Zedazneli and Companions; Clarus, m.; Joannicus.
5 Elizabeth and Zachary; Galation and Episteme; Bertilla, v.
6 Leonard of Noblac; Melaine, bp.; Illtud or Illtyd, abt.; Winnoc, abt.; Demetrian, bp.; Barlaam of Khutyn, abt.
7 Herculanus, bp., m.; Florentius of Strasbourg, bp.; Willibrord, bp.; Engelbert, bp., m.
8 *The Four Crowned Martyrs*
   Cybi or Cuby, abt.; Deusdedit, p.; Tysilio or Suliau, abt., Willehad, bp.; Godfrey of Amiens, bp.
9 DEDICATION OF ST. JOHN LATERAN   FEAST
   Theodore Tiro
   Benignus or Benen, bp.; Vitonus or Vanne, bp.
10 LEO THE GREAT, p., dr.   MEM
   Andrew Avellino, cnf.
   Theoctista, v.; Aedh Mac Bricc, bp.; Justus of Canterbury, bp.
11 MARTIN OF TOURS, bp.   MEM
   Menna, m.
   Theodore the Studite, abt.; Bartholomew of Grottaferrata, abt.
12 JOSAPHAT, bp., m.   MEM
   Nilus the Elder; Emilian Cucullatus, abt.; Machar, bp.; Cunibert, bp.; Cumian, abt.;

Livinus, bp., m.; Lebuin or Liafwine or Livinius; Benedict of Benevento and Companions, m.; Astrik or Anastasius, bp.; Cadwallader.

13 *Francis Xavier Cabrini,* v.*
    Didacus or Diego, cnf.
    Arcadius and Companions, m.; Brice or Britius, bp.; Eugenius of Toledo, bp.; Maxellendis, v., m.; Kilian; Nicholas I, p.; Abbo of Fleury, abt.; Homobonus; Stanislaus Kostka; Nicholas Tavelic, Adeodatus Aribert, Stephen of Cueno and Peter of Narbonne, p., m.

14 Dyfrig, bp.; Laurence O'Toole, bp.

15 ALBERT THE GREAT, bp., dr.										OPT MEM
    Abibus, Gurias, and Samonas, m.; Desiderius or Didier, bp.; Malo, bp.; Fintan of Rheinau; Leopold of Austria.

16 MARGARET OF SCOTLAND										OPT MEM
    GERTRUDE THE GREAT, v.										OPT MEM
    Mechtilde, v.; Eucherius of Lyons, bp.; Afan, bp.; Edmund of Abingdon, bp.; Agnes of Assisi, v.

17 ELIZABETH OF HUNGARY, rel.									MEM
    Gregory the Wonderworker, bp., cnf.
    Dionysius of Alexandria, bp.; Alphaeus and Zachaeus, m.; Acislus and Victoria, m.; Anianus or Aignan of Orleans, bp.; Gregory of Tours, bp.; Hilda, v.; Hugh of Lincoln, bp.

18 DEDICATION OF THE CHURCHES OF PETER AND PAUL					OPT MEM
    Romanus of Antioch, m.; Mawes or Maudez, abt.; Odo of Cluny, abt.

19 Nerses, bp., m.; Barlaam, m.

20 *Félix of Valois,* cnf.
    Dasius, m.; Nerses of Sahgerd, bp.; and Companions, m.; Maxentia, v., m.; Edmund the Martyr; Bernward, bp.

21 PRESENTATION OF MARY											MEM
    Gelasius I, p.; Albert of Louvain, bp., m.

22 CECILIA, v., m.												MEM
    Philemon and Apphia, m.

23 CLEMENT I, p., m.											OPT MEM
    COLUMBANUS, abt.												OPT MEM
    Felicity, m.
    Amphilochius, bp.; Gregory, bp.; Trudo or Trond. Francesco Forgione

24 *Chrysogonus,* m.
    Colman of Cloyne, bp.; Flora and Mary, v., m.

25 Mercurius, m.; Moses, m.

26 *Silvester,* abt.
    Peter of Alexandria, bp., m.
    Siricius, p.; Basolus or Basle; Conrad of Constance, bp.; Nikon "Metanoeite"; John Berchmans; Leonard of Port Maurice.

27 Barlaam and Josaphat; James, Intercisus, m.; Secundinus or Sechnall, bp.; Maximus of Riez, bp.; Cungar, abt.; Fergus, bp.; Virgil or Fergal, bp.

28 Stephen the Younger, m.; Simeon Metaphrastes; James of the March; Joseph Pignatelli; Catherine Labouré, v.

29 *Saturninus,* m.
    Saturninus or Sernin, bp., m.; Radbod, bp.

30 ANDREW THE APOSTLE											FEAST
    Sapor and Isaac, bp., m.; Cuthbert Mayne, pr., m.

Last Sunday of the liturgical year: CHRIST THE KING						SOL

DECEMBER

1 Ansanus, m.; Agericus or Airy, bp.; Tudwal, bp.; Eligius or Eloi, bp.; Edmund Campion, Alexander Briant, and Ralph Sherwin, pr., m.

2 *Viviana* or Bibiana, v., m.
   Chromatius, bp.
3 FRANCES XAVIER, pr.   MEM
   Lucius; Claudius, Hilaria and Companions, m.; Cassian, m.; Sola.
4 JOHN DAMASCENE, pr., dr.   OPT MEM
   Maruthas, bp.; Anno, bp.; Osmund, bp.; Bernard of Parma, bp.
5 SABAS, abt.
   Crispina, m.; Nicetius of Trier, bp.; Birinus, bp.; Sigramnus or Cyran, abt.; John
   Almond, pr., m.
6 NICHOLAS, bp.   OPT MEM
   Dionysia, Majoricus, and Companions, m.; Abraham of Kratia, bp.
7 AMBROSE, bp., dr.   MEM
   Eutychian, p.; Josepha Rosello, v.
8 IMMACULATE CONCEPTION   SOL
   Romaric, abt.
9 Hipparchus and Companions, m.; the Seven Martyrs of Samosata; Leocadia, v., m.;
   Gorgonia, wd.; Budoc or Beuzec, abt.; Peter Fourier.
10 *Melchiades,* p.
   Mennas, Hermogenes, and Eugraphus, m.; Eulalia of Merida, v., m.; Gregory III, p.;
   Edmund Gennings, Eustace White, Polydore Plasden, pr., m., and Swithun Wells, m.;
   John Roberts, pr., m.
11 DAMASUS I, p.   OPT MEM
   Barsabas, m.; Fuscian, Victoricus, and Gentian, m.; Daniel the Stylite.
12 JANE FRANCES DE CHANTAL, rel.   OPT MEM
   *Our Lady of Guadalupe**
   Epimachus Alexander and Companions, m.; Finnian of Clonard, bp.; Corentin or Cury,
   bp.; Edburga, v.; Vicelin, bp.
13 LUCY, v., m.   MEM
   Eustratius and Companions, m.; Judoc or Josse; Aubert of Cambrai, bp.; Odilia or
   Ottilia, v.
14 JOHN OF THE CROSS, pr., dr.   MEM
   Spiridion, bp.; Nicasius, bp., and Companions, m.; Venantius Fortunatus, bp.; Dioscorus
   and others, m.
15 Nino, v.; Valerian and other martyrs in Africa; Stephen of Surosh, bp.; Paul of Latros;
   Mary di Rosa, v.
16 Adelaide, wd.
17 Lazarus; Olympias, wd.; Begga, wd.; Sturmi, abt.; Wivina, v.
18 Rufus and Zosimus, m.; Gatian, bp.; Flannan, bp.; Winebald, abt.
19 Nemesius, m.; Anastasius I, p.
20 Ammon and Companions, m.; Philogonius, bp.; Ursicinus, abt.; Dominic of Silos, abt.
21 PETER CANISIUS, pr., dr.   OPT MEM
   Anastasius II of Antioch, bp., m.
22 Chaeremon, Ischyion, and other martyrs.
23 JOHN OF KANTY, pr.   OPT MEM
   The Ten Martyrs of Crete; Victoria and Anatolia, v., m.; Servulus; Dagobert II of
   Austrasia; Thoriac, bp. Marie Marguerite d'Youville.
24 VIGIL OF CHRISTMAS
   Gregory of Spoleto, m.; Delphinus, bp.; Tharsilla and Emiliana, v.; Irmina, v., and
   Adela, wd.
25 CHRISTMAS   SOL
   Anastasia of Sirmium, m.
   Eugenia, v., m.; The Martyrs of Nicomedia.
26 STEPHEN, THE FIRST MARTYR   FEAST
   Archelaus, bp.; Dionysius, p.; Zosimus, p.

27 JOHN, Apostle and Evang.   FEAST
    Fabiola, wd.; Nicarete, v.; Theodore and Theophanes; John Stone, pr., m.
28 HOLY INNOCENTS, m.   FEAST
    Antony of Lérins.
29 THOMAS À BECKET, bp., m.   OPT MEM
    Trophimus, bp.; Marcellus Akimetes, abt.; Ebrulf or Evroult, abt.; Peter the Venerable,
    abt.
30 Sabinus and Companions, m.; Anysia, m.; Anysius, bp.; Egwin, bp.
31 SYLVESTER I, p.   OPT MEM
    Columba of Sens, v., m.; Melania the Younger, wd.
Sunday within the octave of Christmas or if there is no Sunday within the octave, Dec. 30:
HOLY FAMILY   FEAST

THE BYZANTINE CALENDAR

The most widely used calendar, after that of the Roman Rite, is the Byzantine. There are some variants, especially in Slavic countries. But substantially it corresponds to the calendar and martyrology for the Byzantine Rite—Slavonic Usage—which are here given.

SEPTEMBER

1   The Beginning of the "Indiction," i.e., of the Church Year; Simeon, the Elder, the Stylite, and his mother Martha; Synaxis of the Most Holy Mother of God in Missina; Sts. Aithelas, 40 Women of Macedonia and Ammon, Martyrs; Sts. Callistus, Evodius, and Hermogenes, Martyrs; Venerable Josue son of Nave.
2   St. Mammas, Martyr; John of the Fast, Patriarch of Constantinople.
3   St. Anthimus, Priest-Martyr; Theoktistus, Co-Faster of Euthymius the Great.
4   St. Babilas, Priest-Martyr; Three Youths; St. Moses, Prophet and Patriarch; St. Babilas, Priest-Martyr; 84 Youths; Sts. Hermione and Eutychia, Martyrs.
5   St. Zachary, Prophet.
6   Commemoration of the miracle by St. Michael the Archangel at Colossa in Chonia; Sts. Eudoxius and with him 1104, Martyrs; Archippus.
7   St. Sozon, Martyr.
8   Nativity of Our Most Holy Mother of God and Ever-Virgin Mary.
9   Sts. and Venerable, Joachim and Anna; St. Severianus, Martyr.
10 Sts. Menodora, Metrodora and Nymphodora, Martyrs.
11 Theodora, of Alexandria, Penitent.
12 St. Autonomus, Priest-Martyr.
13 Commemorating the Restoration of the Church of the Resurrection of Our Lord Jesus Christ; St. Cornelius, Priest-Martyr.
14 Exaltation of the Holy and Vivifying Cross.
15 St. Nicetas, the Great-Martyr.
16 St. Euphemia, the Great, Virgin-Martyr.
17 Sts. Sophia and her Three Daughters, Faith, Hope, and Charity.
18 Eumenius, Bishop of Gortyna.
19 Sts. Trophimus, Sabbatius, and Dorymedont, Martyrs.
20 Sts. Eustace (Placidus), the Great Soldier-Martyr, and his wife, Theopista, and their sons, Agapius and Theopistus, Martyrs.
21 St. Quadratus.
22 St. Phocas, Priest-Martyr; St. Jonas, Prophet; Venerable Jonas, father of St. Theophanes.
23 Conception of St. John the Baptist, the glorious Prophet and Precursor of Our Lord, Jesus Christ.
24 St. Thecla, First Virgin-Martyr.
25 Venerable Euphrosyna.
26 The Death of St. John the Theologian, Apostle and Evangelist.

27   St. Callistratus, Soldier-Martyr.
28   Chariton, Confessor-Martyr.
29   Cyriacus, Hermit.
30   St. Gregory, Priest-Martyr and the Illuminator of Greater Armenia.

OCTOBER

1   Patronage of the Most Holy Queen, Mother of Our God and Ever-Virgin Mary; St. Ananias, Apostle; Roman, the sweet-singer.
2   St. Cyprian, Priest-Martyr; St. Justina, Virgin-Martyr; St. Andreas.
3   St. Dionysius, the Aeropagite, Priest-Martyr; Rusticus and Eleutherius, Athenian converts.
4   St. Hierotheus, Priest-Martyr.
5   St. Charitina, Martyr.
6   St. Thomas, the glorious Apostle.
7   Sts. Sergius and Bacchus, Martyrs.
8   Pelagia and Taisia.
9   St. James, son of Alpheus, Apostle and Brother of St. Matthew, the Apostle and Evangelist; Andronicus and his wife, Athanasia.
10   Sts. Eulampius and his sister, Eulampia, Martyrs.
11   St. Philip, one of Seven Deacons; Theophan, Confessor.
12   Sts. Probus, Tarachus and Andronicus, Martyrs; Cosmas, Bishop of Majuma.
13   Sts. Carpus, Bishop and Papylus, his Deacon, and with them Agathonica, sister of Papylus, and Agathodorus, their servant.
14   Paraskevas; Sts. Nazarius, Gervase, Protase and Celsus, Martyrs; St. Vitalis, Martyr.
15   Euthymius, the New; St. Lucian, Venerable-Martyr.
16   St. Longinus, the Centurion.
17   St. Osee, Prophet; St. Andrew of Crete, Venerable-Martyr.
18   St. Luke, Apostle and Evangelist.
19   St. Joel, Prophet; St. Varus, Martyr; St. Sadoth, Priest-Martyr.
20   St. Artemius, Great Martyr.
21   Hilarion the Great, Hegumen-Abbot.
22   St. Abercius, Bishop of Hieropolis; Sts. Seven Youths of Ephesus.
23   St. James the Less, Apostle, brother of the Lord, the first Bishop of Jerusalem; Ignatius, Confessor.
24   Sts. Arethas and other Martyrs.
25   Sts. Marcian and Martyrius, Martyrs.
26   St. and Glorious Demetrius, the Great Martyr.
27   St. Nestor, Martyr; Sts. Capitolina, a Cappadocian lady, with her handmaid; Erotheides, Martyrs.
28   St. Parasceva, Martyr, surnamed "Friday"; Sts. Terentius and Neonila and their Children: Photius, Anicetas, Theodulus, Hierarchus and Eunicius; Stephen of Sabbas.
29   St. Anastasia, Venerable-Martyr; Sts. Abram, Hermit of Edessa and Mary, his niece.
30   Sts. Zenobius and Zenobia, his sister, Martyrs; Venerable Peter, Bishop of Syracuse; Sts. Asterius, Claudius, Neon, Theonilla, Martyrs; Sts. Terentius, Mark, Justus, and Artem, Apostles.
31   Sts. Stachis, Ampliatus, Urban and Narcissus, Apostles; St. Epimachus, Martyr; Maura.

NOVEMBER

1   Sts. Cosmas and Damian, Martyrs; Leontius, Anthimus and Euthropius; Venerable Theodotia.
2   Sts. Acindynus, Pegasius, Aphdonius, Elpidephorus and Anempodistus, Martyrs.
3   Sts. Acepsimas, Bishop; Joseph, Presbyter, and Aithalus, Deacon; Renovation of the Church of St. George the Great-Martyr, in Lydia.

4   Joannicius the Great; Sts. Nicander, Bishop of Myra, and Hermas, Presbyter.
5   Sts. Galacteon and Epistemis; Sts. Patrobas, Hermias, Linus, Gaius and Philologus.
6   Paul, Archbishop of Constantinople.
7   Sts. Hieron and Others with him; Lazarus, wonderworker.
8   Synaxis of St. Michael the Archangel and the Angelic Hosts.
9   Sts. Onesiphorus and Porphyrius, Martyrs; Venerable Theoktista.
10 Sts. Erastus, Olympus, Rodeon, Sosipater, Tertius and Quartus, Apostles.
11 Sts. Mennas, Victor and Vincent, Martyrs; St. Stephenida, Martyr; Theodore Studite,
    Confessor, Hegumen-Abbot.
12 St. Josaphat, Priest-Martyr; John the "Almoner"; Nilus.
13 St. John the Chrysostom, Archbishop of Constantinople.
14 St. Philip, one of the Twelve.
15 Sts. Gurias, Samonis and Aviva, Martyrs at Edessa.
16 St. Matthew, Apostle and Evangelist.
17 Gregory, Thaumaturgus, i.e., wonderworker.
18 Sts. Plato and Romanus, Martyrs.
19 St. Abdias, Prophet; St. Barlam, Martyr.
20 Gregory of Decapolis; Proclus, Archbishop of Constantinople.
21 Presentation in the Temple of Our Most Holy Queen, Mother of God and Ever-Virgin
    Mary.
22 Sts. Philemon and Others with him, Apostles; St. Caecilia, Virgin-Martyr.
23 Amphilochius, Bishop of Iconium, and Gregory, Bishop of Agrigentum.
24 St. Catharine, Great Virgin-Martyr; St. Mercurius, Great Martyr.
25 Clement, Pope of Rome; Peter, Bishop of Alexandria.
26 Alypius, Stylite.
27 St. James the Persian, Great-Martyr; Palladius.
28 St. Stephen "the Younger" Venerable Martyr; St. Irenarchus, and Seven Women, Martyrs.
29 Sts. Paramon and Philemonus, Martyrs; Bessarion; Venerable Acacius.
30 St. Andrew, the "First-called" Apostle.

DECEMBER

1   St. Nahum, Prophet; St. Filaret, the "Almsgiver" and St. Ananias, Martyr.
2   St. Habacuc, one of the Twelve Lesser Prophets.
3   St. Sophonias, Prophet; Theodulus.
4   St. Barbara, Great Virgin-Martyr; St. John Damascene, Doctor of the Church.
5   St. Sabbas, Hegumen-Abbot.
6   Nicholas, Archbishop of Myra.
7   Ambrose, Bishop of Milan.
8   The Immaculate Conception of Our Most Holy Queen, Mother of God and Ever-Virgin
    Mary; "The Conception of St. Ann," i.e., when she conceived the Most Holy Mother of
    God.
9   Patapius, of Thebes.
10 Sts. Mennas, Hermogenes and Eugraphus, Martyrs.
11 Daniel, Stylite.
12 Spiridion, wonderworker.
13 Sts. Eustratius, Auxentius, Eugene, Mardarius and Orestes, Martyrs; St. Lucy, Virgin-
    Martyr.
14 Sts. Thyrsus, Leucius, Philemon, Appollonius, Arianus, and Callinicus, Martyrs.
15 St. Eleutherius, Priest-Martyr; Paul of Latra.
16 St. Aggeus, Prophet.
17 St. Daniel, and Sts. Three Youths, Ananias, Azarias, and Misael.
18 St. Sebastian and Companion.
19 St. Boniface, Martyr.
20 St. Ignatius, "Theophorus" Priest-Martyr Bishop at Antioch.

21 St. Juliana, Virgin-Martyr.
22 St. Anastasia, Great-Martyr.
23 Sts. Ten Martyrs at Crete.
24 Sts. Eugenia, Venerable Martyr and her two slaves, Protus and Hyacinth.
25 The Nativity of Our Lord, God and Savior, Jesus Christ, or "Christmas Day."
26 Synaxis of the Most Holy Mother of God and St. Joseph, her Spouse; St. Euthymius, Priest-Martyr.
27 St. Stephen, Protomartyr, Apostle and Archdeacon; Theodore, brother of St. Theophanes.
28 Sts. 20,000 Martyrs in Nicomedia; St. Domna, Martyr.
29 The Holy Innocents; Marcellus, Hegumen-Abbot.
30 St. Anysia; Venerable Zoticus.
31 Venerable Melania.

JANUARY

1 Feast of Circumcision of Our Lord and Savior, Jesus Christ; The Feast of St. Basil the Great, Archbishop of Caesarea.
2 Silvester, Pope of Rome.
3 St. Malachias, Prophet; St. Gordius, Martyr.
4 Synaxis of 70 Apostles; Theoktistus, Hegumen-Abbot.
5 Sts. Theopemptus and Theonas, Martyrs; Syncletica, Venerable; St. Micheas, Prophet.
6 Epiphany, or Holy Manifestation of the Divinity of Our Lord and Savior, Jesus Christ.
7 Synaxis of St. John, the glorious Prophet.
8 George, the Chozebite and Emilian, Confessor; Dominika, of Carthage; Sts. Juliana and Basilissa, Martyrs.
9 St. Polyeucte, Martyr; Eustratius, Venerable.
10 Gregory, Bishop of Nyssa; Dometian, Venerable, Bishop of Melite; Marcian, Presbyter.
11 Theodosius, Hegumen-Abbot.
12 St. Tatiana, Martyr; Eupraxis, Venerable.
13 Sts. Hermylas and Stratonicus, Martyrs.
14 Fathers of Sinai and Raitha.
15 Paul of Thebes and John the "Tent-dweller."
16 Veneration of the venerable Chains of St. Peter.
17 Anthony, the Great.
18 Athanasius and Cyril, Archbishops of Alexandria.
19 Macarius of Egypt, and Macarius of Alexandria, Monks; St. Euphrosinia, Virgin.
20 Euthymius the Great, Hegumen-Abbot.
21 Maximus, Confessor; St. Neophitus, Martyr; Sts. Eugene, Canidius, Valerian and Aquilas, Martyrs.
22 St. Timothy, Apostle; St. Anastiasius, Venerable-Martyr of Persia.
23 St. Clems, Priest-Martyr; St. Agathangel, Martyr.
24 Xenia.
25 Gregory, the Theologian.
26 Xenophon, his wife, Mary and sons, Arcadius and John; Theodore, Hegumen-Abbot of Monks of Studites, and his brother, Joseph.
27 Translation of the Relics of St. John Chrysostom.
28 Ephraem, "Prophet of Syrians and cithara of Holy Spirit."
29 Translation of the Relics of St. Ignatius, the "Theoforos," Priest-Martyr, Bishop of Antioch; Sts. Roman, James, Philotheus, and St. Aphraates, Martyrs.
     ⁀ of the Three Holy Bishops, i.e., Three Cappadocian Fathers; namely, St. Basil the
     ⁀t. Gregory, the Theologian, and St. John, the Chrysostom; St. Hippolytus, Priest-

     ⁀d John, Wonderworkers and Unmercenaries.

FEBRUARY

1 St. Tryphon, Martyr.
2 Presentation of Our Lord Jesus Christ in the Temple (Feast of the Purification of the Blessed Virgin Mary or Candlemas Day).
3 St. Simeon, the Venerable-Senex and Theofer.
4 Isidore of Pelusium; St. Jador, Martyr.
5 St. Agatha, Martyr.
6 Bukolus, Bishop of Smyrna.
7 Parthenius, Bishop of Lampsachia; Luke.
8 St. Theodore, the great Martyr; St. Zacharias, the Prophet.
9 St. Nicephorus, Martyr.
10 St. Charalampias, Martyr.
11 St. Blase, Priest-Martyr.
12 Meletius, Archbishop of Great Antioch; St. Marina, Virgin.
13 Martinian, Hegumen; St. Zoe and St. Photina, Venerable Women.
14 Auxentius, Hegumen; Cyril, Bishop of Catania.
15 St. Onesimus, Apostle; Paphnutius, Venerable-Hermit in Egypt and his daughter, Euphrosyne.
16 Sts. Pamphilius, Valentine, Paul, Seleucus, Porphyrus, Julian, Theodulus, and the five Martyrs of Egypt, Elias, Jeremias, Isaias, Samuel and Daniel; Flavianus, Archbishop of Constantinople.
17 St. Theodore of Tyre, the Great Martyr; Memory of St. Mariamna, sister of Philip, the Apostle.
18 Leo the Great, Pope of Rome.
19 St. Archippus, Apostle, a co-worker with St. Paul; Sts. Maxim, Theodot, Isychus and Asklepiodotus, Martyrs.
20 Leo, Bishop of Catania; St. Sadok, Priest-Martyr; St. Agatho, Venerable, Pope of Rome.
21 Timothy, Hermit; Eustacius, Archbishop of Antioch.
22 Finding of the venerable Relics of Sts. Martyrs at Eugenia; Venerable Peter, Monk, and Athanasius, Martyrs.
23 St. Polycarp, Priest-Martyr.
24 First and Second Finding of the Venerable Head of St. John, the Precursor.
25 St. Tharasius, Archbishop of Constantinople.
26 Porphyrius, Archbishop of Gaza; St. Sebastian, Martyr; St. Photina, of Samaria, Martyr.
27 Procopius, venerable confessor and monk.
28 Basil, confessor and co-faster of St. Procopius; Marina, Cyra and Domnicia, Venerable Women.

MARCH

1 St. Eudoxia, Venerable-Martyr.
2 St. Theodotus, Priest-Martyr.
3 St. Eutropius and his bodyguards, Sts. Cleonicus and Basiliscus, Martyrs.
4 Gerasimus, a Hermit; Sts. Paul and his sister Juliana, Martyrs.
5 St. Conon, Martyr.
6 Forty-two Martyrs at Ammorius: Theodore, Constantin, Callistus, Theophil and others with them.
7 Sts. Priest-Martyrs at Chersonia; Basil, Ephrem, Capito, Eugene, Everius, Missionary Bishops; Venerable Paul, the Simple, in Egypt, a Solitary.
8 Theophylact, Bishop of Nicomedia.
9 Sts. Forty Martyrs at Sebaste in Armenia.
10 Sts. Codratus and companions: Cyprian, Anectus, and Criscent.
11 Sophronius, Patriarch of Jerusalem.
12 Theophan of Syngria; Gregory the Great, Dialogue, Pope of Rome.

13 Translation of Relics of our father, Nicephor, Patriarch of Constantinople.
14 Benedict, Abbot; St. Alexander of Pidna, Priest-Martyr.
15 St. Agapius, Martyr and with him six others: Timolaus, two Alexanders, Romel, two Dionisii.
16 Sts. Sabinus and Papas, Martyrs; St. Julian, Martyr; St. Alexander, Priest-Martyr, Pope of Rome.
17 Venerable father Alexis.
18 Cyril, Archbishop of Jerusalem; Sts. Alexandra, Claudia, Euphrasia and other Martyrs.
19 Sts. Chrysantus and Darias, Martyrs; Thomas, Patriarch of Constantinople.
20 Martyrs of the Monastery of St. Sabbas.
21 Jacob, Bishop and Confessor.
22 St. Basil, Priest-Martyr, Presbyter of the Church in Ancyra; Venerable Isaak, Monk.
23 St. Nicon, Venerable-Martyr and two hundred companions.
24 Zachary, and James, Confessor; Artemius, Bishop of Thessalonica; St. Artemon, Martyr-presbyter of Laodicea.
25 Annunciation of our Most Holy Queen, the Mother of God and Ever-Virgin Mary.
26 Synaxis of the Archangel Gabriel.
27 Matrona of Seluna, Martyr.
28 Hilary, Monk and St. Stephen, wonderworker; St. Jonas and his brother, St. Barachisius of Bethasa, Martyrs.
29 Mark, Bishop of Arethusa and Cyril, a Palestinian Deacon.
30 John Climacus, Hegumen-Abbot; Venerable John the Silent, Bishop of Colonia in Armenia.
31 Hypatius, Bishop of Gangra.

APRIL

1 Mary of Egypt.
2 Titus, wonderworker; Sts. Amphianus and Edesius, Martyrs.
3 Nicetas, Confessor and Hegumen-Abbot; St. Theodosia, Virgin-Martyr.
4 Venerable fathers Joseph and George; St. Platon, Hegumen-Abbot, Studite.
5 Sts. Theodulus and Agathopodus, "The Cretan Martyrs."
6 Eutyches, Archbishop of Constantinople.
7 George, Bishop of Melete; Serapion, an Egyptian Monk and later Bishop of Thumuis.
8 Sts. Herodion, Agavus, Ruphus, Asyncritus, Phlegon, Hermas, et al., Bishop-Martyrs; Celestine, Pope of Rome.
9 St. Eupsychius, Martyr.
10 Sts. Terence, Africanus, Maximus, Pompilius, and a band of Thirty-six Martyrs.
11 St. Antipas, Bishop-Martyr, of Pergamus; Pharmuthius.
12 Basil, Bishop of Pharia.
13 St. Artemon, Priest-Martyr, of Laodicea.
14 Martin, Pope of Rome; Sts. Anthony, John, and Eustathius, Martyrs.
15 Sts. Aristarchus, Pudus, and Trophimus, Apostles; St. Sabbas Gothinus, Martyr; Sts. Basilissa and Anastasia, Martyrs.
16 Sts. Agapia, Irene, and Chionia, Martyrs.
17 Simeon of Persia, Martyr; Acacius, Bishop of Melite; St. Agapitus, Pope of Rome.
18 John, a disciple of St. Gregory, Decapolites; Cosmas, Bishop of Chalcedonia; John, Archbishop of Antiochia.
    John, the ancient Hermit; St. Paphnutius, Martyr.
    ʾeodore, surnamed "Trichinas."
        ʾuarius, Bishop-Martyr, and Sts. Proculus, Sosius and Faustus, Deacons; St.
        ʾs, Lector; St. Eutyches and Akutionus; St. Theodore from Pergia, Priest-

    ʾykeon; Sts. Nathanael, Luke and Clement, Apostles.

23 Feast of St. George, the glorious Great-Martyr and wonderworker; St. Alexandra, Martyr.
24 St. Sabbas, Martyr.
25 St. Mark, Apostle and Evangelist.
26 St. Basil, Priest-Martyr; Virgin Glaphyra.
27 St. Simeon, Priest-Martyr.
28 Sts. Jason and Sosipater, Apostles; Sts. Masimus, Dadas, Quinctillianus, Martyrs.
29 Sts. Nine Martyrs at Cyzice; Memnon, wonderworker.
30 St. James the Greater, Apostle.

MAY

1   St. Jeremias, Prophet.
2   Athanasius the Great, Patriarch of Alexandria.
3   Theodosius of the Cave, Hegumen-Abbot; Sts. Timothy and Maurus, Martyrs.
4   St. Pelagia, Venerable-Martyr; Venerable-Mother Pelagia.
5   St. Irene, Glorious Martyr.
6   St. and Venerable, Job, the "Patient."
7   Commemoration of the appearance of the Sign of the Cross; St. Acacius, Martyr.
8   St. John, the Apostle and Evangelist; Arsenius the Great.
9   Translation of the Venerable Relics of our holy father, Nicholas, Wonderworker, from Myra to Bari (Italy); St. Christopher, Martyr; St. Isaias, Prophet.
10 St. Simon Zelotes, Apostle.
11 The Holy and equal to the Apostles, Doctors of the Slava, our holy father, Cyril and Methodius.
12 Epiphanius, Bishop in Cyprus, and Germanus, Patriarch of Constantinople.
13 St. Glyceria, Martyr; St. Alexander, Martyr.
14 St. Isidore, Martyr.
15 Pachomius the Great.
16 Theodore, disciple of St. Pachomius; Sts. Vitus, Modestus and Crescentia, Martyrs.
17 St. Andronicus, Apostle and others with him; St. Junia.
18 St. Theodotus of Ancyra in Galatia; Sts. Petrus, Dennis, Andreas, Paul, Christina, Heracleus, Paulinus and Venedimus Martyrs; Sts. Seven Virgins: Alexandra, Thekusa, Claudia, Falina, Evphrasia, Matrona and Julia.
19 St. Patritius, Bishop-Martyr of Prusa in Bithynia and his companions, Menander and Acatius.
20 St. Thalaleus, Martyr and others.
21 Sts. Constantine the Great, King and Co-Apostle and Helen, his mother.
22 St. Basiliscus, Martyr; Commemorating the Second Ecumenical Council Fathers at Constantinople A.D. 381.
23 Michael, Bishop of Synnada at Phrygia.
24 Simeon of the Wonderful Montain, Stylite.
25 The Third Finding of the Venerable Head of St. John, the Glorious Prophet, Baptist and Precursor of our Lord.
26 St. Carpus, Apostle.
27 St. Therapontus, Priest-Martyr.
28 Nicetas, Bishop of Chalcedon; St. Helladius, Priest-Martyr; St. Eutyches, Martyr in Miletus.
29 St. Theodosia, Venerable-Virgin-Martyr of Tyre.
30 Isaac, Monk in Dalmatia.
31 St. Hermas, Apostle, Bishop of Philippi; St. Hermeas, Martyr.

JUNE

1 St. Justin, Martyr; Another St. Justin, Martyr and Co-Martyrs.
2 Nicephorus, Patriarch of Constantinople; Alexander, Archbishop of Constantinople.
3 St. Lucillian, Martyr and with him: Claudius, Hypatius, Paul, and Dionysius; St. Paula, Martyr.
4 Metrophanes, Patriarch of Constantinople.
5 St. Dorotheus, Priest-Martyr, Bishop of Tyre.
6 Bessarion, wonderworker; Venerable Hilarion, the "Newer."
7 St. Theodotus, Priest-Martyr, Bishop of Ancyra.
8 Translation of the Relics of St. Theodore the Great Martyr; Ephrem; Patriarch of Antiochia.
9 Cyril, Archbishop of Alexandria; Sts. Thecia, Martha, and Mary, Martyrs.
10 St. Timothy, Priest-Martyr, Bishop of Prusia; Sts. Alexander and Antonina, Martyrs.
11 Sts. Bartholomew and Barnabas, Apostles.
12 Onufrius the Great, Hermit; Peter of Athon.
13 St. Aquilina, Martyr; St. Trephillus, Bishop of Levkusia in Cyprus.
14 St. Elisseus, Prophet; Methodius, Patriarch of Constantinople.
15 St. Amos, Prophet; Venerable Jerome; Translation of the Relics of our father, Theodore of Sykeon.
16 St. Tychon, wonderworker, Bishop of Amathunsa.
17 Sts. Manuel, Sabel and Izmael, Persian Martyrs; Sts. Isaurus, Basil, Innocent, Jeremias, and others.
18 St. Leontius, Martyr.
19 St. Jude, Apostle, brother of St. James the Less; St. Zosimus, Martyr.
20 St. Methodius, Priest-Martyr, Bishop of Patara.
21 St. Julian of Tarsus, Martyr.
22 St. Eusebius, Priest-Martyr, Bishop of Samos; Sts. Galacteon and Juliana, Martyrs.
23 St. Agrippina, Virgin-Martyr.
24 Feast of the Nativity of St. John, the Glorious Prophet, Precursor and the Baptist.
25 St. Febronia, Virgin-Martyr.
26 Venerable David, Hermit.
27 Venerable Sampson, "Father of the Poor."
28 Translation of the Relics of Sts. Cyrus and John, wonderworkers and unmercenary physicians.
29 Feast of Sts. Peter and Paul, prime Apostles.
30 Synaxis of the holy and most praiseworthy Twelve Apostles.

JULY

1 Sts. Cosmas and Damian, Martyrs.
2 Deposition of the Venerable Vestment of our most holy Queen, Mother of God in the church of Blachernae; Juvenal, Patriarch of Jerusalem.
3 St. Hyacinthus, Martyr; Anatolius, Patriarch of Constantinople.
4 Andreas, Archbishop of Crete; Martha, mother of St. Simeon of the "Wondermount."
5 Athanasius, Hegumen-Abbot of Mt. Athos; Lampadus, wonderworker of Irenepolis; Martha, mother of the Holy Simeon of the wonderful Mountain.
6 Sisoes the Great, Hermit and Anchoret.
 Thomas of Malea and Acacius; St. Cyriaca, Martyr.
 Procopius, Great-Martyr.
 ratius, Priest-Martyr, Bishop of Taormina; St. Theodore, Bishop of Edessa; and
 Ten Thousand Saints.
 e "Kiev-Cave"; Forty-five Martyrs at Nicepolis in Arminia, Mauricius,
 ius, and others.

11 St. Euphemia, Martyr; The death of Blessed Olga, Grand Duchess of Kiev.
12 Sts. Proclus and Hilarion, Martyrs; Michael of Malea; St. Mary, Martyr.
13 Synaxis of St. Gabriel, the Archangel; Stephen of Sabbas.
14 St. Aquila, Apostle; Onesimus, Venerable.
15 St. Vladimir the Great, of Apostolic zeal; Sts. Kirykos and his mother, Julitta, Martyrs.
16 St. Athenogenes, Priest-Martyr, with ten of his flock.
17 St. Marina, the Great Martyr.
18 Sts. Hyacinth and Aemilian, Martyrs.
19 Venerable Macrina, sister of St. Basil.
20 St. Elias of Thesbite, Glorious Prophet.
21 Venerable Simeon, surnamed Salus (fool) and John, his co-faster, Hermits; St. Ezechiel.
22 St. Mary, Magdalene, myrrh-bearer and of Apostolic zeal; Translation of the Relics of St. Phocas, Priest-Martyr, a Bishop of Sinope.
23 Sts. Trophimus, Theophilus, and others; St. Apollynaris, Priest-Martyr.
24 Sts. Boris and Gleb, Martyrs; St. Christina, Martyr.
25 Dormition of St. Anna, Mother of the Blessed Virgin Mary, Mother of God.
26 Sts. Hermolaus, Priest-Martyr, and two brothers Hermippas and Thermocrates, Martyrs; St. Parasceva, Venerable-Martyr.
27 Pantaleon or Panteleimon, the Great Martyr; Venerable Anthusa, mother of St. John Chrysostom.
28 Sts. Prochorus, Nicanor, Timon, and Parmenas, Apostles and Deacons; Innocentius, Pope of Rome.
29 St. Callincus, Martyr at Gangrae; Sts. Seraphina, Virgin-Martyr, Theodotia, and her Children.
30 Sts. Silas, Silvanus, Criscentus, Hepenctus, and Andronicus, Apostles; St. John, Soldier-Martyr; St. Julitta, Martyr.
31 St. Eudocimus, Venerable.

AUGUST

1 Procession of the Venerable and Life-giving Cross; Commemoration of the Sts. Seven Machabee Brothers, Martyrs, and their Mother, Solomonia, and their Master, Eleazar.
2 Translation of the Holy Relics of St. Stephen, the First Martyr and Archdeacon, from Jerusalem to Constantinople; St. Stephen, Priest-Martyr, Pope of Rome, and others.
3 Isaacius, Dalmatius, and Faustus.
4 Sts. Seven Youths of Ephesus, Martyrs; Maximilian, Dionisius, Amblichus, Martin, Antonin, John, and Marcell; St. Eudokia, Venerable-Martyr.
5 St. Eusignius, Martyr.
6 The Transfiguration of Our Lord God and Savior, Jesus Christ.
7 St. Domitius, Venerable-Martyr; St. Pulcheria.
8 St. Aemilian, Confessor, Bishop of Cyzicus; Sts. Eleutherius and Leonidas, Martyrs.
9 St. Matthias, Apostle.
10 St. Lawrence, Archdeacon-Martyr.
11 St. Euplus, Archdeacon-Martyr.
12 Sts. Photius and Anicetus, Martyrs.
13 Maximus, Confessor.
14 St. Michaeas, Prophet; Translation of the Relics of Our Venerable Father, Theodosius, Hegumen-Abbot of Cave.
15 Dormition (Assumption) of our Most Holy and Glorious Queen, Mother of God and Ever-Virgin Mary.
16 Translation of the miraculously formed Icon of Our Lord Jesus Christ, from Edessa to Constantinople, called "Veronica's Veil"; St. Diomidius, Martyr.
17 St. Myron, Priest-Martyr; Sts. Paul and Juliana, his sister, Martyrs.

18 Sts. Florus and Laurus, Martyrs.
19 St. Andrew, a Tribune in the Greek army and with his 2,593 soldiers, Martyrs; Sts. Timothy, Agapius, and Thecla, Martyrs.
20 St. Samuel, Prophet; St. Stephen the First, Ap. King of Hungary.
21 St. Thaddeus, Apostle; Sts. Bassa and her children, Theogonius, Agapius, and Pista (Fidelis), Martyrs.
22 St. Agathonicus and with him Zoticus, Theoprepius, Acindynus, and Severianus, Martyrs.
23 St. Lupus, Martyr; St. Iraeneus, Priest-Martyr, Bishop of Lugdun in Gallia, Martyr; Callinicus, Patriarch of Constantinople.
24 St. Eutyches, Priest-Martyr.
25 Return of the Relics of Bartholomew, Apostle; St. Titus, Apostle.
26 Sts. Adrian and Natalia, Martyrs.
27 Poemen, an Egyptian.
28 Moses, an African Negro of Abyssinia styled the "Ethiopian Hermit"; Augustine, Confessor and Bishop of Hippo; St. Anna, Daughter of Phanuel.
29 The Beheading of St. John, Glorious Prophet, Precursor and Baptist.
30 Alexander, John, and Paul the New, Patriarchs of Constantinople.
31 Deposition of the Venerable Girdle of the Blessed Virgin Mary, Mother of God.